EVANSTON PUBLIC LIBRARY
3 1192 00759 1835

D1557766

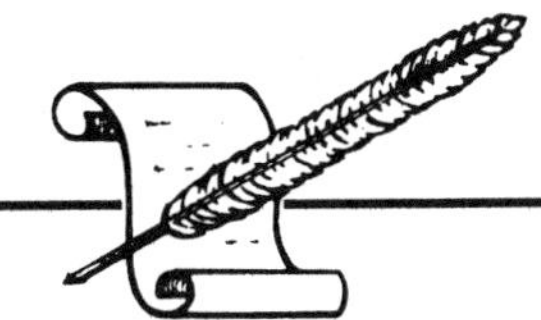

HISTORIC DOCUMENTS OF 1993

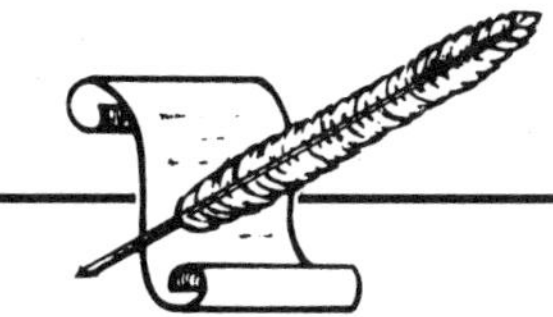

HISTORIC DOCUMENTS OF 1993

Cumulative Index, 1989-1993
Congressional Quarterly Inc.

Historic Documents of 1993

Editor: John Moore
Production and Assistant Editor: Laura M. Carter
Main Contributors: Hoyt Gimlin, Margaret C. Thompson
Contributors: Laura M. Carter, Nadine Cohodas, Carolyn Goldinger, Marty Gottron, James R. Ingram, Bruce Maxwell, Susanna Spencer, Michael D. Wormser
Indexer: Rhonda Holland

Printed in the United States of America

Congressional Quarterly Inc.
1414 22nd St. N.W., Washington, D.C. 20037

The Library of Congress cataloged the first issue of this title as follows:

Historic documents. 1972—
Washington. Congressional Quarterly Inc.

1. United States — Politics and government — 1945— — Yearbooks. 2. World politics — 1945— —Yearbooks. I. Congressional Quarterly Inc.

E839.5H57 917.3'03'9205 72-97888
ISBN 0-87187-799-6
ISSN 0892-080X

PREFACE

Domestic and international issues shared the spotlight in 1993 as the first Democratic president since 1976 took office. Bill Clinton had promised change during his campaign, and in the new year he set about trying to accomplish that by finding a home for his ideas on health care, the economy, and the military. Some changes on the domestic front were unanticipated, however, with several familiar Washington faces disappearing from the scene during the year. After the president was plagued for months with problems in appointing several cabinet nominees, Washington seemed to settle down only to then witness the resignation of several public figures. Clinton was called on in 1993 to appoint a new FBI director and a new secretary of defense, and he placed the second-ever female justice on the Supreme Court.

Two nonpolitical faces also gained household recognition in 1993. Both caused anguish in the hearts of the nation. In July the adoption case of two-year-old Jessica DeBoer captured the attention of the media; millions followed her journey on television as her biological parents, who had given her up for adoption at birth, fought for custody in a bitter court battle and won. Months before, cult leader David Koresh had made the nation witness to a different kind of pain when he led his followers to a mass suicide in Waco, Texas, after a fifty-one-day standoff with Alcohol, Tobacco, and Firearms (ATF) and FBI officials. In the months following the disaster, the government was battered by harsh criticism suggesting that the end result would have been different had officials handled the situation more appropriately.

Another government institution, the U.S. military, found itself in the public eye during the year as it undertook controversial measures for change. Normally a bastion of tradition, the armed forces demonstrated an unprecedented flexibility in 1993. In January the president announced a "don't ask, don't tell" policy for homosexuals in the military, and

How to Use This Book

The documents are arranged in chronological order. If you know the approximate date of the report, speech, statement, court decision, or other document you are looking for, glance through the titles for that month in the table of contents.

If the table of contents does not lead you directly to the document you want, turn to the index at the end of the book. There you may find references not only to the particular document you seek but also to other entries on the same or a related subject. The index in this volume is a five-year cumulative index of *Historic Documents* covering the years 1989-1993. There is a separate volume, *Historic Documents Index, 1972-1989,* which may also be useful.

The introduction to each document is printed in italic type. The document itself, printed in roman type, follows the spelling, capitalization, and punctuation of the original or official copy. Where the full text is not given, omissions of material are indicated by the customary ellipsis points.

eventually made it illegal for military personnel to be dismissed because of their sexual preferences as long as they remained discreet. In late April Secretary of Defense Les Aspin announced that women would be allowed to fly combat aircraft. However great these changes were for the military establishment, they represented only a fraction of what was expected by gay rights and women's rights advocates.

The attitude of the military toward women had been publicly explored during 1992 and 1993 as the Defense Department investigated the controversial behavior that had occurred at the Tailhook convention. The final report on Tailhook, released at the end of April 1993, revealed a record of sexual assault and harassment by thousands of Navy and Marine Corps personnel. Many senior-level officials were implicated, and several were discharged.

The military establishment was further scrutinized when Aspin announced in late 1993 the results of the "Bottom-Up Review," which reevaluated the military's structure and programs and made recommendations for improvements. The initiative was intended to shape the reorganization of the military in light of the breakup of the Soviet Union in 1991. In the post-cold war era, the capacity for the production of nuclear weapons had spread to smaller countries, many with extremely volatile leadership and unstable governments. The review recommended a shift in focus from the former Soviet Union to the dangers posed by regional conflicts with the potential for escalation into full-scale wars.

In this new world order the United States took an active role in 1993. The year began with the signing of the second Strategic Arms Reduction Treaty (START II), calling for sweeping arms reductions between Russia and the United States. It ended with the conclusion of the Uruguay Round of negotiations for the General Agreement on Tarriffs and Trade (GATT), opening the door to the possibility of the largest expansion of international trading rules ever implemented.

Between these bookends fell two other significant treaties. The United States signed a landmark international chemical weapons agreement that banned the production, assimilation, and use of chemical weapons throughout the world, the first time that an entire class of weapons had been eliminated. By August 147 nations had signed the treaty, which was scheduled to be implemented in January 1995. In November Congress approved passage of the North American Free Trade Agreement (NAFTA), which took effect January 1, 1994, and eliminated trade barriers between the United States, Mexico, and Canada. The debate over NAFTA divided the country: environmental groups allied themselves with organized labor; Ross Perot, Pat Buchanan, and consumer advocate Ralph Nader joined forces in opposition; Democrats and Republicans fell on both sides. The public was equally split between protectionists who feared a loss of American jobs and those who saw benefits from the competition created by an expanded economy.

Outside the United States, the year brought a mix of developments. Most striking was the international triumph in the negotiations between Israel and the Palestine Liberation Organization (PLO), which resulted in the signing on U.S. soil of a "Declaration of Principles" and a resolution to settle differences peacefully. In contrast was the attempted coup in Russia in late September and early October that shocked the world with its violence and bloodshed. When Russian president Boris Yeltsin dissolved the Congress of People's Deputies in the face of continued opposition from antireform conservatives, the legislature voted to depose him. Setting up barricades outside the legislative building, the rebels set off a chain of events that led Yeltsin to declare a state of emergency and place a temporary ban on free speech and expression. After several days, pro-Yeltsin forces subdued the insurrection, and two months later, in December, Russia held the first open elections in its history and adopted a new constitution.

These are but some of the topics of national and international interest chosen by the editors for *Historic Documents of 1993.* This edition marks the twenty-second year of a Congressional Quarterly project that began with *Historic Documents of 1972.* The purpose of this continuing series is to give students, librarians, journalists, scholars, and others convenient access to important documents on a range of world issues. In our judgment, the official statements, news conferences, speeches, special studies, and court decisions presented here will be of lasting interest.

Each document is preceded by an introduction that provides background information and, when relevant, an account of continuing developments during the year. We believe that these introductions will become increasingly useful as memories of current times fade.

Laura M. Carter
Production and Assistant Editor

CONTENTS

January

February

March

April

May

June

July

August

September

October

December

[illegible]

January

HOUSE TASK FORCE REPORT ON THE "OCTOBER SURPRISE"

January 3, 1993

Throughout the 1980s investigative journalists, foreign businessmen, conspiracy theorists, and others produced a variety of allegations that the 1980 presidential campaign of Ronald Reagan struck a deal with Iran to delay the release, until after the November elections, of the fifty-two Americans held hostage at the U.S. Embassy in Tehran. The Reagan campaign team, it was alleged, was so anxious to defeat President Jimmy Carter that it was willing to do just about anything—including helping prolong the imprisonment of the American hostages.

These allegations came to be known as the "October Surprise" theory. Supposedly, the Reagan campaign's effort to influence timing of the hostages' release stemmed from a concern that Carter himself would reach a deal with Iran to gain release of the hostages just before the 1980 elections and win a second term on a wave of patriotic fervor.

Connection to Iran-Contra Affair

The October Surprise theories gained a certain degree of credibility as a result of the Iran-contra affair. In 1986 press reports revealed (and subsequent investigations confirmed) that the Reagan administration secretly provided weapons to Iran in 1985 and 1986 in return for the release of American hostages held in Lebanon. President Reagan's willingness to ship Hawk missile batteries and other military equipment to Iran, the reasoning went, could be seen as a belated reward for Iran's cooperation in delaying release of the embassy hostages.

The special congressional Iran-contra committee conducted a brief investigation into the October Surprise question in 1987 but found no credible evidence that the Reagan campaign team had made the alleged 1980 deal with Iran.

Then in 1991, Gary Sick, who had been Carter's chief National Security Council aide on the Iranian hostage question, published a column in the

New York Times *saying he had concluded the October Surprise allegations were true. In particular, Sick said he had found information substantiating reports that in 1980 William J. Casey, Reagan's campaign director and later head of the CIA, had met secretly in Madrid and Paris with representatives of the Iranian government.*

Sick's column stimulated new interest in the issue and prompted calls, mostly from Democrats, for a congressional investigation. The Senate debated the matter in November 1991, but a filibuster prevented passage of a resolution (S Res 198) authorizing a formal investigation. Instead, the Foreign Relations Subcommittee on Near Eastern and South Asian Affairs conducted a scaled-back investigation and issued a report shortly after the November 1992 elections. That report found "no credible evidence" that Reagan campaign officials struck a secret deal with the Iranians to delay release of the hostages.

House Investigation and Findings

The House of Representatives in February 1992 launched a more formal and comprehensive investigation, passing a resolution (H Res 258) establishing a bipartisan October Surprise Task Force, chaired by Lee Hamilton, D-Ind., and Henry J. Hyde, R-Ill.

With the aide of a professional investigative staff, the House task force interviewed more than 230 people in the United States and ten foreign countries. Among those interviewed were former senior officials of the Carter administration and senior Reagan campaign aides, several of whom later served in the Reagan administration. The task force also had access to tens of thousands of documents, including many classified items from executive branch agencies and private records of some individuals alleged to have been involved in October Surprise events. The investigation cost $1.35 million.

The task force submitted its report to the House January 3, 1993. All major conclusions in the 967-page report were supported by both Democratic and Republican members of the task force. However, there were partisan disagreements about several minor points.

The task force echoed the Senate panel in finding no credible evidence that Reagan's campaign team sought to, or was able to, delay Iran's release of the embassy hostages until after the November 1980 elections. The task force said it was unable to provide satisfactory answers to every question or rumor that had been raised in connection with the October Surprise theory. But in its report, the task force said it could provide definitive answers to the five major issues cited in House Resolution 258.

Those issues were:

1. *The task force said it found "wholly insufficient credible evidence" that any officials of the 1980 Reagan president campaign communicated with the Iranian government, or those holding the hostages,*

between the time the hostages were taken in November 1979 and released in January 1981.

In particular, the task force said it could find no credible evidence supporting numerous allegations that Casey met with Iranian representatives at the Plaza Hotel in Madrid in July 1980 or that other Reagan aides met with Iranian representatives in New York, London, and Washington.

The report noted that rumors of these meetings were initiated by several persons, among then Middle Eastern arms dealers and businessmen, who were unable to corroborate their statements or whose word otherwise proved unreliable.

2. *In its central finding, the task force said it found "no credible evidence" supporting the claim that the Reagan campaign, or persons associated with the campaign, tried to delay release of the hostages in Iran.*

   The core of this claim was that Casey and other Reagan aides held several secret meetings with Iranian representatives in Paris in October 1980, just a few weeks before the elections. The task force said it interviewed several of the people who claimed to have been present at the Paris meetings, or at least to have knowledge of them. Among those interviewed were Israeli businessman Ari Ben-Menashe, Iranian-born businessman Jamshid Hashemi, and American businessman Richard Brenneke. Their claims, the task force said, were false or could not be backed up with credible evidence. For example, the task force said it determined that neither Ben-Menashe nor Brenneke were in Paris at the time of the alleged meetings, as they had claimed they were.

3. *The task force said the Reagan campaign did obtain and disseminate information about the Carter administration's efforts to win release of the hostages in Iran. This finding partially supported claims by some observers that Reagan's aides mounted a major effort to keep track of the hostage issue prior to the election. But the task force said it found no credible evidence to support the more important allegation that Reagan's aides illegally used classified information as part of that effort.*

   The task force documented reports that the Reagan campaign asked retired military officers to monitor activities at U.S. military bases to determine whether the Carter administration was trying to stage a hostage rescue mission or was shipping military supplies to Iran in return for the hostages. Reagan's aides also succeeded in obtaining some secret information about the hostage issue.

   But the task force said it found no credible evidence that any of the Reagan campaign's information-gathering activities were illegal.

   Democrats on the task force said there were "legitimate questions" about the Reagan campaign's use of some of the information it received, particularly the leaking of information to selected media outlets. However, the task force said these actions did not jeopardize the conduct of U.S. foreign policy or the release of the hostages.

4. *The task force said it found "no credible evidence" that the Reagan administration, once in office, provided arms or spare parts to Iran as a quid pro quo for delaying release of the embassy hostages until after the 1980 elections.*

   Witnesses who had alleged a link between the arms sales and the delay of the hostage release proved to be "unworthy of belief" and were contradicted by independent documentary evidence, the task force said.

5. *The task force said it found "no credible evidence" that Reagan aides, in 1980 and later during the Reagan administration, tried to cover up their October Surprise activities.*

   This finding covered several allegations, among them that Reagan aides in 1980 deliberately failed to pass on to the Carter administration information that might have been useful to the hostage-release negotiations, and that the Reagan administration later took actions to silence those who were privy to its October Surprise dealings.

   In a partisan dispute, task force Democrats said Reagan campaign aides should have told the Carter administration about information they received at a meeting with Iranian representatives in Washington. Republicans, however, said the Reagan aides were under no obligation to pass on the information they received.

Following is the executive summary of the "Joint Report of the Task Force to Investigate Certain Allegations Concerning the Holding of American Hostages by Iran in 1980" ("October Surprise Task Force"), committed to the Whole House, January 3, 1993:

Findings and Conclusions

1. Conduct of Investigation

The House October Surprise Task Force with an authorized budget of $1.35 million was fully staffed to investigate thoroughly the October Surprise allegations. Ten attorneys and six professional investigators on loan from various law enforcement agencies were employed by the Task Force throughout the duration of the investigation.

With a few exceptions the Task Force located and interviewed nearly all the individuals around the world who claimed either to have participated in, or have knowledge of, the alleged events. The Task Force interviewed and/or deposed more than 230 people. Interviews were conducted across the United States as well as in Algeria, Belgium, France, Germany, Italy, Portugal, South Africa, Spain, Switzerland and the United Kingdom.

The Task Force also had direct access to voluminous documents which had heretofore been unavailable to the scores of investigative reporters and authors who have examined these allegations. The Task Force received and reviewed tens of thousands of documents from the Department of State; the Department of Defense, the Central Intelligence Agency, the National Security Council, and from other executive branch agencies. The Task Force staff was particularly fortunate to have had access to the FBI's electronic surveillance tapes of Cyrus Hashemi and others in the September 1980-February 1981 time period, as well as critical telephone toll records for the summer of 1980 from Cyrus Hashemi's residence and the residence and office of his lawyer, Stanley Pottinger. The Hashemi electronic surveillance included over 21,000 recorded conversations on 548 tapes. With coverage that comprehensive, what did not appear was often as important as what did appear. Further, the Task Force had access to a significant collection of intelligence community material which often filled in holes in the factual record and corroborated testimony. This intelligence material included thousands of raw, unredacted documents from the CIA, NSC, and National Security Agency (NSA). The Task Force also obtained access to documents and evidence gathered during previous congressional investigations such as the Iran-Contra and Debategate inquiries. Likewise, the Task Force obtained access to the privately held documents of many of the individuals involved in the October Surprise allegations. This material included hundreds of pages of documents from foreign private citizens, former government officials of Iran, foreign journalists, former Reagan-Bush campaign officials, the families of deceased individuals (including William Casey) and many others. The Task Force also obtained public service documents available from various electronic information networks, the Foreign Broadcast Information Service, and the Library of Congress. In the final analysis, the Task Force staff expended thousands of hours reviewing and analyzing these materials.

While these documents and materials did not establish to a certainty each person's whereabouts or activities on every single day during the relevant period, or conclusively resolve all of the October Surprise questions, when combined with certain sworn testimonial evidence and related government documents they made it possible for the Task Force to reach with confidence the conclusions in this report. In fact, they dictated the conclusions that follow.

The Task Force believes that it has conducted the most thorough and complete investigation and analysis of the October Surprise allegations to date. This report does not and could not analyze or report every single lead that was investigated, every single phone call that was made or received, every single contact that was initiated. Similarly, the Task Force did not resolve every single one of the scores of curiosities, coincidences, sub-allegations or unanswered questions that have been raised over the years and become part of the October Surprise literature. The Task Force concluded that attempting to "prove a negative"—or in this case many of them—would indeed be a fool's errand that would satisfy no one and serve no useful purpose. Given the time available to it, the Task Force fully investigated all of the principal allegations and most of the less significant ones before it reached the conclusions contained in this report.

It is worth noting that the work of the Task Force simultaneously benefited from and was handicapped by the passage of twelve years since the period during which the October Surprise events were said to have occurred. The Task Force benefited from the fact that it could, when investigating the complicated world of Iranian politics during the 1979-1981 period, draw upon years of historical analysis and the clarity of hindsight. For example, the Task Force was able to evaluate the stops and starts of the formal U.S.-Iranian hostage negotiations without having to guess blindly as to the underlying political reasons for these interruptions. In this respect, the Task Force benefited from the insight of several Iran scholars who were periodically consulted by the Task Force on discreet areas of inquiry.

The passage of time also sometimes prevented the Task Force from acquiring records that could have confirmed the whereabouts of several alleged participants in the October Surprise scenario. This was principally because many of the records generated by businesses—such as credit card receipts and telephone bills, tickets and expense vouchers—are routinely destroyed after several years. As a consequence, the Task Force was unable to determine conclusively all the movements of several of the principal protagonists with irrefutable documentary evidence. This inability to obtain certain records did not affect the quality or content of the conclusions ultimately reached by the Task Force.

Before summarizing its conclusions, the Task Force believes it necessary to describe the standard which guided its evaluation of the evidence it reviewed.

2. Standard of Review

The principal allegations that were the focus of this investigation are extraordinarily serious and strike at the heart of the constitutional government of this country. The suggestion, in essence, that leaders of one of our two principal political parties would attempt to "steal" a presidential election by seeking to prolong the incarceration of fellow American citizens by foreign terrorists is little short of treachery. If true, it would not only call into question the legitimacy of an entire presidency, but expose a series of heinous acts unparalleled in the history of the American political system. While such conduct might be expected in certain dark corners of the world, it would be wholly beyond the wildest excesses in our constitutional history. But if these allegations are not true, the cloud that has settled over the reputations of those alleged to have been involved must be lifted.

Accordingly, in evaluating the testimonial and documentary evidence gathered to determine whether there was any credible evidence tending to support these allegations, the Task Force was very careful to determine:

1. Whether the evidence was from a credible source;
2. Whether the evidence was independently corroborated;
3. Whether the evidence was handicapped by internal inconsistencies;
4. Whether the evidence was inconsistent with other more credible evidence; and
5. Whether the evidence had probative value.

Furthermore, the Task Force particularly focused on certain contemporaneous documentary evidence, the creation and contents of which were clearly independent of and relevant to the events alleged. The Task Force benefited from the extensive law enforcement experience of its professional staff in evaluating the testimony, motives, and conduct of witnesses who had made significant allegations after they had either been indicted, tried, or incarcerated in the American criminal justice system. The Task Force also was sensitive to the fact that witnesses to the same event often describe that event differently due to variances in recollection, perception and personal biases. Indeed, often the most difficult witness to evaluate is the one who is telling the truth, but for a variety of reasons, may be mistaken as to the facts he is describing.

Because this was not a criminal investigation, the Task Force did not apply to these allegations strict evidentiary standards of admissibility or a burden of proof beyond a reasonable doubt. Rather, it focused on collecting and evaluating whatever evidence it could obtain relating to these allegations in an effort to determine if there was any credible evidence tending to support these allegations, and if so, how much. The Task Force only reached a conclusion or made a finding after determining that there was substantial credible evidence to support it.

3. Conclusions

The following are the bipartisan conclusions the Task Force reached regarding the five inquiries mandated by its authorizing legislation, House Resolution 258:

(1) There is wholly insufficient credible evidence of any communications by or on behalf of the 1980 Reagan Presidential campaign with any persons representing or connected with the Iranian government or with those holding Americans as hostages during the 1979-1981 period.

The Resolution directed the Task Force to determine whether there was any credible evidence of communications by or on behalf of the 1980 Reagan Presidential Campaign, or individuals representing or associated with that campaign, with any person or persons representing, or associated with, the Iranian government, or with those persons in Iran holding American hostages during the 1979-1981 period. This directive primarily concerns certain alleged meetings in 1980 between Reagan campaign officials and Iranian government representatives in Madrid and Washington. In each case, the Task Force met with the living alleged participants in, or proponents of, these allegations including: Jamshid Hashemi; Ahmed Madani; Arif Durrani; Heinrich Rupp; Ari Ben-Menashe; and Richard Babayan. In addition, the Task Force was able to obtain invaluable documentary evidence relating to the whereabouts of the participants (living and dead) alleged to have been at these meetings, including the original records from the Plaza Hotel in Madrid, calendars of some alleged participants, telephone toll records, as well as certain credit card bills and receipts. Based upon these interviews, and a thorough review of the documents, the Task Force has concluded that there is wholly insufficient credible evidence of any communications by or on behalf of the Reagan Presidential campaign with any persons representing or connected with the Iranian government or with those holding American hostages during 1979-1981.

Specifically, with respect to the alleged meetings in Madrid, the Task Force found that the evidence allegedly supporting each of these meetings was neither from credible sources nor corroborated. That is, of the five individuals, in addition to Jamshid Hashemi, who were alleged to have independent knowledge of the Madrid meetings, three (Madani, Durrani, and Rupp) testified under oath that they had no knowledge of the meetings. The Task Force found the testimony of Babayan and Ben-Menashe to be wholly lacking of any credibility. In addition, the Task Force found that other evidence said to support the Madrid meetings was either of limited probative value or inconsistent with credible evidence which indicated that the meetings had not occurred. For example, the hotel records, which could be said to corroborate the presence of Jamshid Hashemi in Madrid are not by themselves proof of any other individual's presence when balanced against other evidence. Telephone toll records from Cyrus Hashemi and his attorney, as well as his attorney's notes, renders unlikely Cyrus Hashemi's presence in Madrid. Similarly, the Task Force found no evidence establishing that Reagan campaign manager William J. Casey was in Madrid rather than in London attending a conference. Furthermore, overwhelming evidence indicates that the preceding weekend (July 25 to July 27, 1980) Casey attended the Bohemian Grove encampment and then flew to London; arriving on July 28 and remaining in London until he returned to the United States on July 29, 1980.

With respect to the allegation that the L'Enfant Plaza meeting was for the purpose of discussing an October Surprise deal, the Task Force concluded that those allegations by Houshang Lavi and Ari Ben-Menashe, concerning their participation in and description of the meeting, are internally inconsistent and not credible. The testimony of Lavi's attorney, Mitchell Rogovin, as well as Rogovin's contemporaneous notes, further undercut Lavi's assertion that he participated in this meeting. Furthermore, the testimony of Lavi and Ben-Menashe is inconsistent with the more credible testimony of Richard Allen, Laurence Silberman and Robert McFarlane as to who was present and what actually happened in the meeting.

With regard to three additional meetings alleged to have occurred in 1980 and 1981 between certain Reagan campaign officials and Iranians at different hotels in New York, Washington, and London, the Task Force found no credible evidence as to the Washington and New York meetings and insufficient credible evidence as to the London meeting. The Task Force found the uncorroborated testimony as to each of the meetings to be the product of a non-credible source. The testimony was wholly inconsistent with the more credible testimony of those alleged to have been there and the circumstantial evidence strongly suggested that the alleged participants were elsewhere. In one of these instances, in fact, the source denied ever alleging the meeting took place.

Finally, in certain limited instances, the Task Force encountered evidence relating to possible communications between Republicans and Iranians in 1980 from sources that were either credible or whose credibility could not be assessed. In those instances, the probative value of the evidence was so limited that it did not tend to either support or undermine the occurrence of the possible communication. For example, it is worth noting that with regard to the meeting alleged to have taken place in Paris, discussed in this Report, the Task Force reviewed evidence of possible contacts between Republicans and Iranians offered in the public statements and writings of Sadegh Ghotbzadeh. It also spoke to those individuals with whom Ghotbzadeh himself had spoken about these alleged contacts. While the Task Force could not directly assess Ghotbzadeh's credibility, the Task Force determined that the basis for his beliefs may well be irrelevant to the October Surprise allegations. That is, as discussed fully in Section VII of the Report, Ghotbzadeh most probably was referring to earlier non-hostage related contacts made by Henry Kissinger and/or David Rockefeller on behalf of the Shah, and not by William Casey on behalf of the Reagan Presidential campaign when he spoke of Republican contacts. Thus, while Ghotbzadeh's statements may well be credible, they remain subject to interpretation. What is certain, is that he never offered corroborative evidence to those with whom he spoke and the Task Force found none. Accordingly, the Task Force concludes that there is wholly insufficient credible evidence to support the allegations of contacts between Republicans and Iranians.

(2) There is no credible evidence supporting any attempt or proposal to attempt, by the Reagan Presidential Campaign—or persons representing or associated with the campaign—to delay the release of the American hostages in Iran.

Several individuals have alleged that William Casey and other Reagan campaign officials engaged in discussions with Iranians calculated to delay the release of the American hostages until after the 1980 election. These discussions are said to have occurred primarily in a series of meetings in Paris in October 1980.

The Task Force questioned under oath the witnesses who claimed to have relevant knowledge of these alleged meetings and reviewed any documentary evidence purporting to support the existence of these meetings. The Task Force found no credible evidence that the meetings took place as alleged. Particularly, the Task Force has found the testimony of those individuals claiming personal knowledge of the meetings to lack credibility.

The Task Force identified and investigated various allegations of an October meeting in Paris between representatives of the Reagan campaign and of the Iranian government. One of the most prominent accounts is attributed by numerous reporters and journalists to Ari Ben-Menashe. Another account has been given by Richard Brenneke. Variations have also been by Jamshid Hashemi, Houshang Lavi and others.

Ari Ben-Menashe made several allegations that proved to be factually incorrect. Documentary evidence showed that Ben-Menashe was not in Paris during the time period he had alleged. Brenneke's accounts of the meetings also were disproved by forensically examined documentary evidence that showed that he too was not in Paris during the period alleged. When deposed under oath by the Task Force, Jamshid Hashemi denied that he had any knowledge of a Paris meeting, that he had ever been told about a meeting, and that he had ever meant to say that he had such knowledge, even though numerous reputable journalists had attributed the story to him. Lavi's assertion that he and Cyrus Hashemi were in Paris is refuted by authorized wiretaps and the diary of Mitchell Rogovin, Lavi's lawyer. The testimony of others claiming personal knowledge of these events was impeached either by documentary evidence or, in the case of one, by an admission that he had fabricated his story. In addition to the absence of corroborative evidence to support them, their accounts are riddled with internal inconsistencies and are contradicted by a considerable amount of credible documentary evidence. The Task Force also found credible, consistent and corroborated Secret Service evidence demonstrating that Vice Presidential candidate George Bush was in Washington on the weekend in question, not in Paris, as has been alleged. Similarly, the presence of Donald Gregg in the United States rather than in Paris, as has been alleged, was verified during the investigation.

Finally, the Task Force concludes that to the extent there was any supporting evidence provided by parties claiming to have heard statements from others about such meetings, the information was either of limited probative value or far less compelling than the more credible evidence which suggested that the meetings had not occurred. Accordingly, the Task Force has concluded that there is no credible evidence supporting these delay allegations.

(3) There is substantial credible evidence that individuals associated with the 1980 Reagan Presidential campaign did acquire and or disseminate information relating to actions being taken or considered by the United States government to obtain the release of the Americans being held as hostages in Iran.

The Task Force has found that a number of Reagan Presidential Campaign staff members had obtained and/or disseminated information relating to actions being taken or considered by the United States government to obtain the release of the Americans being held as hostages in Iran. But the Task Force found no credible evidence that these campaign aides illegally sought or disseminated classified information.

The record further demonstrates that the Reagan campaign was very concerned with the impact a release of the hostages before the November election would have on the American electorate. Thus, they established both formal and informal working groups that concentrated on hostage related issues. Additionally, the Reagan campaign perceived that President Carter had manipulated the timing of a press statement on the hostage situation for political gain during the April 1980 Wisconsin primary. To insure that the hostage issue would not upset their campaign strategy, the Reagan campaign undertook a series of activities to remain abreast of the Carter administration's hostage-related activities. Included among the Reagan campaign activities was the purposeful monitoring of public source information concerning the hostage crisis. Reagan-Bush campaign foreign policy advisors often spoke with their counterparts in the executive branch to learn what information they could. In addition to monitoring information of developments concerning the hostage crisis, the campaign staff additionally conducted visual monitoring of certain military locations to determine whether it could detect any activities suggesting either a possible rescue mission, staging for the hostages' return, or shipment of military equipment in exchange for the hostages' release. The Reagan campaign staff also obtained non-public information regarding a variety of issues including the Iran-Iraq war, a possible second rescue mission, and the location of the hostages. The Task Force has found no credible evidence that these activities were illegal.

The Majority believes that legitimate questions can be raised about the campaign staffs failure to notify U.S. government officials about the receipt of certain "over the transom" conveyances of information, and about the transmission of this information to selected media outlets to influence reporting on activities of the Carter administration. But, the Task Force found that none of the information received or disseminated was acquired or passed on for the purpose of undermining the Carter administration's efforts to gain the release of the hostages. Although the Majority believes that an argument can be made that some materials that were disseminated had an unintended impact on the hostage negotiations, the Task Force found insufficient credible evidence suggesting that

Reagan campaign officials willfully received, obtained or disseminated classified information, the release of which might have jeopardized either the conducting of American foreign policy or the release of the hostages.

(4) There is no credible evidence of any link between any sales or transmittals of U.S. arms, spare parts or other assistance to Iran with the release of American hostages in Iran.

The central, and unifying allegation, among those the Task Force investigated was that the Iranians received arms from, or through, the Reagan Administration as a *quid pro quo* for delaying the release of the hostages. The Task Force investigated the specific transactions cited by the accusers, as well as the records of the various government agencies involved in maintaining and participating in all other arms transactions involving Iran in the pertinent time period. Based on this extensive review, the Task Force has concluded that there is no credible evidence linking the release of the hostages to any arms transactions with Iran.

First, as to the credibility of those alleging a link between the two, these witnesses were found to be unworthy of belief as to their allegations regarding arms sales. Further, in some cases, these accusers were contradicted by independent documentary evidence.

With respect to those arms transactions supposedly linked to the hostages, the Task Force interviewed and deposed most of the principles involved in those transactions. These individuals specifically denied any knowledge linking their sale with the hostages, and described the events surrounding each transaction in such a way as to obviate the possibility of linkage. That is, all of the participants in the October 23, 1980 sale of F-4 tires by Israel to Iran testified that this sale was a small part of a series of private arms deals the purpose of which was to make money for the arms brokers. They had no hostage-related ulterior motive for the sale. The Task Force found their testimony credible.

Moreover, the Task Force through its documentary evidence gathering process was able to review the United States government agency records relating to Iranian arms transactions during relevant periods. Interviews relating thereto clearly demonstrate that the myriad intelligence, defense, and foreign service personnel monitoring such transactions found no evidence of the *quid pro quo* alleged.

Indeed, in the one instance in October 1980 where the Iranians had the opportunity to obtain military spare parts, among the other assets which President Carter would unfreeze upon the release of the hostages, they refused to pursue the opportunity despite the pressures of the Iraqi war. In the absence of credible evidence of a better deal by the Republicans, Iran's refusal to deal with the United States strongly suggests that the release of the hostages was a political decision inextricably linked to an array of complex internal factors.

Finally, the Task Force reviewed extensive cable traffic between the State Department and the U.S. Embassy in Israel, as well as the Embassy's contacts with the Israeli government, in an effort to determine whether the Reagan Administration might have secretly authorized Israel to facilitate post-release arms deals with Iran as a *quid pro quo*. This documentary review, combined with the sworn testimony of key Reagan and Carter administration officials, including career senior State Department officials and intelligence officers, conclusively established that the Reagan Administration upheld the arms embargo with Iran and encouraged its allies to do the same. An internal Israeli investigation conducted for the Task Force, corroborated the Task Force's findings. The Task Force concluded that arms transactions of the kind suggested by the allegations could not have occurred without many career intelligence and foreign affairs officers learning about them. Accordingly, the Task Force finds no credible evidence to support this allegation.

(5) There is no credible evidence of any actions being taken by Reagan campaign officials to keep any communications or actions from being revealed to the Government of the United States, other than in one instance about which the Majority and Minority disagree.

Allegations that Reagan campaign officials covered up certain communications or actions have been less central to the key allegations which prompted this investigation. A number of discrete events could be included under the umbrella of this mandate. As to those, the Task Force has concluded that these acts, in and of themselves, cannot convincingly be said to have been performed for the ulterior motive of concealing information of a supposed October Surprise deal or denying the U.S. government of information to which it was objectively entitled.

For example, it has been alleged that certain Reagan Administration law enforcement decisions (i.e., the termination in 1981 of the FBI's electronic surveillance of the Hashemi brothers, and the dismissing of the indictment against Jamshid Hashemi), were intended to cover up an October Surprise deal. Interviews with the principals involved, as well as a thorough review of the relevant documents, led the Task Force to conclude that these decisions were made for legitimate law enforcement reasons.

It has also been alleged that the sudden death of Cyrus Hashemi in 1986 was actually an assassination by an American Customs agent to prevent Cyrus from revealing the Reagan Campaign's 1980 arms for hostages deal. Again, as with the other law enforcement issues, there is no credible evidence to support this allegation and there is overwhelming evidence indicating that Cyrus Hashemi's death was, in fact, caused by natural causes.

In one instance, the Majority Members of the Task Force believe that Reagan campaign officials received information at the L'Enfant Plaza Hotel which should have been brought to the attention of the U.S. government, and that their failure to do so constitutes some credible evidence of "an action being taken ... to keep [that information] from being revealed." On the other hand, given the nature and contents of this conversation, the Minority Members of the Task Force neither believe that these individuals were required by any objective standard to bring that information to the attention of the U.S. government, nor that their failure to do so constituted an "action" to conceal that information from the U.S. government. Regardless, both the Majority and Minority agree that contrary to what has been alleged, the purpose of the L'Enfant Plaza meeting was not connected to any attempt to affect the release of the American hostages.

Otherwise, both the Majority and Minority agree that there is no credible evidence indicating Reagan campaign officials kept communications of the kind described in the mandate from U.S. government officials.

U.S.-RUSSIAN START II ARMS PACT

January 3, 1993

Less than three weeks before he left office, President George Bush capped his foreign policy agenda by signing what could be the most sweeping arms reduction agreement ever reached between the two major possessors of strategic nuclear weapons. After last-minute personal negotiations with Russian president Boris N. Yeltsin, Bush arrived in Moscow on January 3 to initial the second Strategic Arms Reduction Treaty (START II), of which president-elect Bill Clinton said he was "fully supportive."

The signing ceremony, which took place in the ornate St. Vladimir Hall of the Grand Kremlin Palace, was noted with nostalgia by some, because it was probably the last time the two former superpowers would negotiate on their weapons of mass (and mutual) destruction.

Sweeping Terms of Treaty

The treaty would ban all long-range land-based nuclear warheads held by both the United States and the Russian Federation (formerly the Soviet Union). Under the terms of the treaty, Russia agreed to give up its entire arsenal of more than 300 heavy land-based SS-18 missiles, each equipped with ten warheads capable of hitting targets in the United States. The pact would allow Russia to retain ninety SS-18 silos to house the smaller SS-25 missiles, but it required that the silos be partially filled with concrete, so that the SS-18s, which were to be destroyed, could not be reinserted. Russia also was permitted to convert more than half of its 170 six-warhead SS-19 missiles to single-warhead weapons.

For its part, the United States would have to destroy or modify its fifty MX missiles, with ten warheads each, and modify its Minuteman III missiles to carry one warhead instead of three. In what some observers considered to be a U.S. advantage, the United States was permitted to retain about half of its nuclear warheads on submarines and its

Trident II missiles, equipped with multiple warheads. "The United States has a tangible superiority in anti-submarine warfare," noted Vladimir Belous, a Russian strategic analyst, in an article for the newspaper Nezavisimaya Gazeta. *The United States was also allowed to convert some of its B-1 strategic bombers to non-nuclear status. For the first time, Russians would be allowed to inspect the bomb bays of the top-secret U.S. B-2 "Stealth" bomber and other long-range bombers, as would the United States vis-à-vis Russia.*

Background: From START I to START II

The first START agreement was signed by Bush and Soviet president Mikhail Gorbachev in Moscow in July 1991, after negotiations lasting almost ten years. That treaty would require reductions of between 25 percent and 35 percent in the number of long-range nuclear warheads on both sides, for a combined total of about 16,000. The second START treaty would reduce the total number of warheads to between 3,000 and 3,500 on each side in two stages spread over seven to ten years. (START I treaty, Historic Documents of 1991, p. 475) *However, it could not come into force until the first treaty was ratified and carried out. Although the United States and Russia had signed START I, its implementation depended in large part on ratification by Ukraine, Belarus, and Kazakhstan—three states of the former Soviet Union that had strategic nuclear weapons on their territory—and on their agreement to be nonnuclear nations under the terms of the Non-Proliferation Treaty. As of the end of the year, Ukraine continued to balk at signing the pact, and, given the October upheaval in Russia, it was uncertain whether either of the two nuclear arms treaties could be ratified by Russia.* (Attempted revolt in Russia, p. 769)

Last-Minute Negotiations, New Treaty

The second START agreement was worked out in record time. Bush and Yeltsin announced agreement on a major nuclear arms reduction at a June 17 summit meeting in Washington, but negotiations led by acting Secretary of State Lawrence S. Eagleburger and Russian foreign minister Andrei Kozyrev became mired in technical issues raised by the Russians intended to reduce the cost of their compliance. In addition, the Russians modified their June agreement to destroy all 150 of their complete SS-18 missiles and silos by countering that they should be allowed to retain at least some of the SS-18 silos to house single-warhead missiles.

Beginning in December, with less than two months remaining in his presidency, Bush initiated personal negotiations with Yeltsin by telephone and letter. On December 18 Yeltsin announced that he was ready to sign a nuclear arms pact. "Preliminarily, I can say that an agreement is prepared on START II in global cuts in strategic weapons by two-thirds between America and Russia and can be signed by January next year," he told an audience of 300 intellectuals in Beijing.

Late in the month, the two leaders agreed to hold a summit meeting in Russia. On December 29, after a ninety-minute meeting in Geneva, Eagleburger and Kozyrev announced that the two nations had reached agreement on the final text of the treaty. Bush left Washington December 30 to visit U.S. troops in Somalia, after which he met with Yeltsin in Moscow.

In a news conference following signing ceremonies, Yeltsin said that the treaty was "the core of the system of global security guarantees.... From the very outset, the new democratic Russian state has been pursuing a policy of building equal partnership with the United States. Today we have every right to say that relations between the two major powers have undergone a genuine revolution."

Bush's remarks focused more on Russia's internal difficulties in its attempts to navigate the road to democracy from communism. "Today, the cold war is over," he said. "Today ... I want to assure the Russian people on behalf of all Americans, we understand that Russia faces a difficult passage. We are with you in your struggle to strengthen and secure democratic rights, to reform your economy."

Despite Hope, Outlook Uncertain

For Yeltsin, one advantage of signing the treaty was to strengthen his image as international peacemaker and to encourage the Clinton administration and Congress to provide increased funding for Russia's economic reforms. "On balance, this treaty is likely to help Yeltsin," said political analyst Igor Klyamkin. "It will be opposed by the national patriots, but these people are already critical of every step that Yeltsin takes. But the political and military elite seems ready to go along with it. On the popular level, Yeltsin can make the argument that less weapons means more bread."

Nonetheless, Yeltsin faced considerable opposition from communist and nationalist members of the Supreme Soviet (Russian parliament). "The Americans are simply wiping their feet over the sovereignty of Russia with this agreement," said Iona Andronov, an influential member of the parliament's international relations committee. However, Yeltsin insisted that, "As president and commander-in-chief, I can state with complete certainty that the document we have just signed will strengthen—not weaken—the security of Russia."

One of the largest stumbling blocks to ratification of the treaty by the Russian parliament was the position of Ukraine, whose parliament had not yet ratified the initial START I treaty, despite the government's pledge to do so. After arduous negotiations, Russia and Ukraine had hammered out an agreement whereby Ukraine would dismantle and transfer to Russia all 176 missiles on its territory. In a statement issued January 3, Ukrainian President Leonid Kravchuk restated his country's pledge to become a nonnuclear state and ratify START I. However, Ukraine continued to seek a formal security guarantee from the West as *well as additional financial aid. (On October 19, speaking with reporters after a closed session of parliament, Kravchuk said that destruction of the country's 130 aging SS-19 missiles would begin after parliament ratified START I, but he indicated that Ukraine would retain control of its more modern SS-24s. Secretary of State Warren Christopher pledged $175 million in economic aid to help Ukraine dismantle the weapons. Christopher also promised $155 million in economic aid. These promises were subject to approval by Congress, and it was still uncertain whether Ukraine would comply.)*

Even if the problem with Ukraine could be solved, observers pointed to major economic and environmental problems involved in implementing the treaty. One problem would be created by the displacement of an estimated one million or more U.S. and Russian workers in nuclear arsenal facilities; another problem results from the need to dispose of huge amounts of liquid rocket propellent that explodes on contact with air. And there remained the continuing existence of nuclear capability or potential on the part of other nations, whose numbers were likely to increase.

Following are the letter of transmittal from President George Bush to the Senate; Acting Secretary of State Lawrence S. Eagleburger's letter of submittal to the Senate and his Article-by-Article analyses of the treaty; and excerpts from the January 3, 1993, news conference by President Boris N. Yelstin and President Bush after signing the treaty:

LETTER OF TRANSMITTAL

THE WHITE HOUSE, *January 15, 1993.*

To the Senate of the United States:

I am transmitting herewith, for the advice and consent of the Senate to ratification, the Treaty Between the United States of America and the Russian Federation on Further Reduction and Limitation of Strategic Offensive Arms (the START II Treaty) signed at Moscow on January 3, 1993. The Treaty includes the following documents, which are integral parts thereof:

The Protocol on Procedures Governing Elimination of Heavy ICBMs and on Procedures Governing Conversion of Silo Launchers of Heavy ICBMs Relating to the Treaty Between the United States of America and the Russian Federation on Further Reduction and Limitation Of Strategic Offensive Arms (the Elimination and Conversion Protocol);

The Protocol on Exhibitions and Inspections of Heavy Bombers Relating to the Treaty Between the United States of America and the Russian Federation on Further Reduction and Limitation of Strategic Offensive Arms (the Exhibitions and Inspections Protocol); and

> The Memorandum of Understanding on Warhead Attribution and Heavy Bomber Data Relating to the Treaty Between the United States of America and the Russian Federation on Further Reduction and Limitation of Strategic Offensive Arms (the Memorandum on Attribution).

In addition, I transmit herewith, for the information of the Senate, the report of the Department of State and letters exchanged by representatives of the Parties. The letters are associated with, but not integral parts of, the START II Treaty. Although not submitted for the advice and consent of the Senate to ratification, these letters are provided because they are relevant to the consideration of the Treaty by the Senate.

The START II Treaty is a milestone in the continuing effort by the United States and the Russian Federation to address the threat posed by strategic offensive nuclear weapons, especially multiple warhead ICBMs. It builds upon and relies on the Treaty Between the United States of America and the Union of Soviet Socialist Republics on the Reduction and Limitation of Strategic Offensive Arms (the START Treaty) signed at Moscow on July 31, 1991. At the same time, the START II Treaty goes even further than the START Treaty.

The START Treaty was the first treaty actually to reduce strategic offensive arms of both countries, with overall reductions of 30–40 percent and reductions of up to 50 percent in the most threatening systems. It enhances stability in times of crisis. It not only limits strategic arms but also reduces them significantly below current levels. In addition, the START Treaty allows equality of forces and is effectively verifiable. Finally, commitments associated with the START Treaty will result in the elimination of nuclear weapons and deployed strategic offensive arms from the territories of Belarus, Kazakhstan, and Ukraine within 7 years after entry into force, and accession of these three states to the Treaty on the Non-Proliferation of Nuclear Weapons (NPT) as non-nuclear-weapon State Parties. As a result, after 7 years, only Russia and the United States will retain any deployed strategic offensive arms under the START Treaty.

The START II Treaty builds upon and surpasses the accomplishments of the START Treaty by further reducing strategic offensive arms in such a way that further increases the stability of the strategic nuclear balance. It bans deployment of the most destabilizing type of nuclear weapons system—land-based intercontinental ballistic missiles with multiple independently targetable nuclear warheads. At the same time, the START II Treaty permits the United States to maintain a stabilizing sea-based force.

The central limits of the START II Treaty require reductions by January 1, 2003, to 3000-3500 warheads. Within this, there are sub-limits of between 1700-1750 warheads on deployed SLBMs for each Party, or such lower number as each Party shall decide for itself; zero for warheads on deployed multiple-warhead ICBMs; and zero for warheads on deployed heavy ICBMs. Thus, the Treaty reduces the current overall deployments of strategic nuclear weapons on each side by more than two-thirds from current levels. These limits will be reached by the end of the year 2000 if both Parties reach agreement on a program of assistance to the Russian Federation with regard to dismantling strategic offensive arms within a year after entry into force of the Treaty. Acceptance of these reductions serves as a clear indication of the ending of the Cold War.

In a major accomplishment, START II will result in the complete elimination of heavy ICBMs (the SS-18s) and the elimination or conversion of their launchers. All heavy ICBMs and launch canisters will be destroyed. All but 90 heavy ICBM silos will likewise be destroyed and these 90 silos will be modified to be incapable of launching SS-18s. To address the Russians' stated concern over the cost of implementing the transition to a single-warhead ICBM force, the START II Treaty provides for the conversion of up to 90 of the 154 Russian SS-18 heavy ICBM silos that will remain after the START Treaty reductions. The Russians have unilaterally undertaken to use the converted silos only for the smaller, SS-25 type single-warhead ICBMs. When implemented, the Treaty's conversion provisions, which include extensive on-site inspection rights, will preclude the use of these silos to launch heavy ICBMs. Together with the elimination of SS-18 missiles, these provisions are intended to ensure that the strategic capability of the SS-18 system is eliminated.

START II allows some reductions to be taken by downloading, i.e., reducing the number of warheads attributed to existing missiles. This will allow the United States to achieve the reductions required by the Treaty in a cost-effective way by downloading some or all of our sea-based Trident SLBMs and land-based Minuteman III ICBMs. The Treaty also allows downloading, in Russia, of 105 of the 170 SS-19 multiple-warhead missiles in existing silos to a single-warhead missile. All other Russian launchers of multiple warhead ICBMs—including the remaining 65 SS-19s—must be converted for single-warhead ICBMs or eliminated in accordance with START procedures.

START II can be implemented in a fashion that is fully consistent with U.S. national security. To ensure that we have the ability to respond to worldwide conventional contingencies, it allows for the reorientation, without any conversion procedures, of 100 START-accountable heavy bombers to a conventional role. These heavy bombers will not count against START II warhead limits.

The START Treaty and the START II Treaty remain in force concurrently and have the same duration. Except as explicitly modified by the START II Treaty, the provisions of the START Treaty will be used to implement START II.

The START II Treaty provides for inspections in addition to those of the START Treaty. These additional inspections will be carried out according to the provisions of the START Treaty unless otherwise specified in the Elimination and Conversion Protocol or in the Exhibitions and Inspections Protocol. As I was convinced that the START Treaty is effectively verifiable, I am equally confident that the START II Treaty is effectively verifiable.

The START Treaty was an historic achievement in our long-term effort to enhance the stability of the strategic balance through arms control. The START II Treaty represents the capstone of that effort. Elimination of heavy ICBMs and the effective elimination of all other multiple-warhead ICBMs will put an end to the most dangerous weapons of the Cold War.

In sum, the START II Treaty is clearly in the interest of the United States and represents a watershed in our efforts to stabilize the nuclear balance and further reduce strategic offensive arms. I therefore urge the Senate to give prompt and favorable consideration to the Treaty, including its Protocols and Memorandum on Attribution, and to give its advice and consent to ratification.

GEORGE BUSH.

LETTER OF SUBMITTAL

DEPARTMENT OF STATE,
Washington, January 12, 1993.

THE PRESIDENT,
The White House.

THE PRESIDENT: I have the honor to submit to you the Treaty Between the United States of America and the Russian Federation on Further Reduction and Limitation of Strategic Offensive Arms (START II Treaty) signed at Moscow on January 3, 1993.

In addition to the main body of the text, the START II Treaty includes the following documents, which are integral parts thereof:

> The Protocol on Procedures Governing Elimination of Heavy ICBMs and on Procedures Governing Conversion of Silo Launchers of Heavy ICBMs Relating to the Treaty Between the United States of America and the Russian Federation on Further Reduction and Limitation of Strategic Offensive Arms (the Elimination and Conversion Protocol);
>
> The Protocol on Exhibitions and Inspections of Heavy Bombers Relating to the Treaty Between the United States of America and the Russian Federation on Further Reduction and Limitation of Strategic Offensive Arms (the Exhibitions and Inspections Protocol); and
>
> The Memorandum of Understanding on Warhead Attribution and Heavy Bomber Data Relating to the Treaty Between the United States of America and the Russian Federation on Further Reduction and Limitation of Strategic Offensive Arms (the Memorandum on Attribution).

Also attached, for the information of the Senate, are documents that are associated with, but not integral parts of, the START II Treaty. These include three exchanges of letters by the sides addressing SS-18 missiles on the territory of Kazakhstan, heavy bomber armaments, and heavy ICBM silo conversion. Although not submitted for the advice and consent of the Senate to ratification, these documents are relevant to the consideration of the START II Treaty by the Senate.

Introduction

The START II Treaty builds upon the reductions that will be implemented pursuant to the Treaty Between the United States of America and the Union of Soviet Socialist Republics on the Reduction and Limitation of Strategic Offensive Arms signed at Moscow on July 31, 1991 (the START Treaty), and yet goes even further than the START Treaty. The START Treaty was negotiated over a nine-year period; it requires a reduction of 30 to 40 percent in the overall number of long-range nuclear warheads deployed by both Parties, with a 50-percent reduction in the most threatening systems. The START II Treaty will further substantially reduce those numbers and enhance stability.

The START II Treaty's central limits require the Parties to reduce their strategic offensive arms so that specified limits are reached by the year 2003, with the possibility of those limits being reached by the end of the year 2000 if both Parties agree on a program of U.S. assistance within a year after entry into force. The START II Treaty, together with the START Treaty, will reduce both nations' deployed strategic offensive arms by more than two-thirds, and will completely eliminate land-based intercontinental ballistic missiles (ICBMs) deployed with multiple warheads. Strict, lower limits will be imposed on all deployed strategic offensive arms, including warheads carried on ICBMs, submarine-launched ballistic missiles (SLBMs), and heavy bombers. Stabilizing sea-based forces will be retained but will carry significantly lower numbers of warheads. In contrast to the START Treaty, all heavy bombers will be attributed with warheads based on the number of nuclear weapons for which they are actually equipped.

There are five Parties to the START Treaty: the United States and, as START Treaty successors to the Soviet Union, the Republic of Belarus, the Republic of Kazakhstan, and Ukraine, as well as the Russian Federation. In contrast, the START II Treaty is bilateral: the United States and the Russian Federation are its only Parties since, in association with the Lisbon Protocol, the other three Parties to the START Treaty have pledged to eliminate strategic offensive arms located on their territories. Accordingly, no nuclear warheads or deployed strategic offensive arms will be located on their territories at the time the first phase of the reductions in this Treaty are required to be completed. Nevertheless, the START II Treaty draws upon the START Treaty for definitions, counting rules, prohibitions, and verification provisions and only modifies those as necessary to meet unique requirements of the START II Treaty. The START II Treaty is therefore built upon the START Treaty and will not enter into force without the prior entry into force of the START Treaty.

Background

The terms of the START II Treaty are based on the Joint Understanding signed between the United States of America and the Russian

Federation on June 17, 1992. Its impetus was the desire to strengthen stability by eliminating the most destabilizing systems remaining under the START Treaty. The Joint Understanding established the START II Treaty guidelines.

Central Limits

At the core of the START II Treaty is the obligation to reduce and limit ICBMs, ICBM launchers, SLBMs, SLBM launchers, heavy bombers, ICBM warheads, SLBM warheads, and heavy bomber nuclear armaments in two phases. Seven years after entry into force of the START Treaty, the aggregate number for each Party shall not exceed 4250 deployed strategic warheads. By the same date the following sublimits are to be reached as well:

2160, for warheads on deployed SLBMs;
1200, for warheads on deployed multiple-warhead ICBMs; and
650, for warheads on deployed heavy ICBMs.

Upon the completion of the above reductions, the Parties shall further reduce their strategic offensive arms so that no later than January 1, 2003, and thereafter, the aggregate number for each Party shall not exceed 3,500 deployed strategic warheads. By the same date the following sublimits would also apply:

1750, for warheads on deployed SLBMs;
Zero, for warheads on deployed multiple-warhead ICBMs; and
Zero, for warheads on deployed heavy ICBMs.

Under the terms of the START II Treaty, the final numerical limits shall be fulfilled by the end of the year 2000, rather than by January 1, 2003, provided that the Parties conclude, within one year after entry into force of the START II Treaty, an agreement on a program of assistance to promote the reduction and conversion obligations of the START II Treaty.

Multiple-Warhead ICBMs and SLBMs

The START II Treaty provides that after January 1, 2003 (or after the end of the year 2000, if accelerated), neither Party may deploy land-based missiles with more than one warhead and all heavy ICBMs must be destroyed. Specifically, all launchers of ICBMs to which more than one warhead is attributed under Article III of this Treaty, including test and training launchers, must either be destroyed or be converted to launchers of ICBMs to which no more than one warhead is attributed. This will require, for the United States, the elimination or conversion of launchers of Peacekeeper ICBMs and, for the Russian Federation, the elimination or conversion of launchers of SS-24 ICBMs and the elimination or conversion of those launchers of SS-19 ICBMs, excepting those that contain the permitted number of SS-19s downloaded to a single-warhead configuration. Also excepted from this provision are launchers of non-heavy ICBMs located at space launch facilities that are permitted under the START

Treaty. For the United States, this means the Peacekeeper can be used as a vehicle for space launch. All launchers of SS-18 ICBMs, including all those at space launch facilities, must be physically destroyed. There is one exception—90 deployed launchers may be converted, under agreed provisions, to launchers of single-warhead SS-25 type ICBMs with canisters of no more than 2.5 meters in diameter, such that rapid reconversion is effectively precluded.

All Minuteman III ICBMs, for the United States, and 105 of the 170 SS-19 ICBMs, for the Russian Federation, may be retained and downloaded to one warhead pursuant to Article III of this Treaty. Any number of SLBMs with multiple warheads may also be downloaded by up to four warheads per missile. Thus, the United States will be able to meet the numerical constraints of the START II Treaty on SLBM warheads by downloading and retaining 18 Trident submarines with missile warhead loads reduced from eight warheads to four.

Heavy ICBMs

The START Treaty requires that 154 of the 308 former Soviet heavy ICBM launchers must be destroyed by the end of the seven-year reduction period. The START II Treaty goes further and requires the elimination or physical conversion of all heavy ICBM launchers. Under the START II Treaty, the Russian Federation will be allowed to convert, under agreed constraints and subject to inspection, 90 of these deployed missile launchers within which, thereafter, only single-warhead missiles of the SS-25 type ICBM may be deployed. The remaining 64 heavy ICBM launchers must be destroyed by the end of the second phase of reductions in accordance with START Treaty procedures. The constraints on SS-18 silo conversion require that the Russians pour concrete to a height of five meters above the silo base and mount in the upper portion of the silo a restrictive ring that is smaller in diameter than the diameter of the SS-18. These modifications preclude an SS-18 from being launched from these silos, and would be extremely difficult and time-consuming to reverse. The constraints also require the destruction of all deployed and non-deployed SS-18 missiles and their launch canisters.

Bombers

In the START II Treaty, all deployed heavy bomber nuclear armaments will be counted according to how the bombers are actually equipped. Each deployed heavy bomber (except for 100 bombers reoriented to a conventional role) will be attributed with the aggregate number of long-range nuclear air-launched cruise missiles, nuclear-armed air-to-surface missiles with ranges of less than 600 kilometers, and nuclear gravity bombs for which it is actually equipped. Under this Agreement, heavy bombers will be attributed with a realistic number of warheads that reflects operational considerations; in many cases, this number may be lower than the maximum number of weapons that could be physically loaded on the aircraft using all available attachment points. In addition, each Party may reorient to a conventional role up to 100 of its heavy bombers that were never accountable under the START Treaty as heavy bombers equipped for long-range nuclear ALCMs. Such bombers would not count toward START II warhead ceilings, but would continue to count against the START Treaty limits.

Each Party may, on a one-time basis, return such bombers back to a nuclear role, if it wishes. If some, but not all, bombers within a specific type or variant, in the START Treaty sense, are reoriented to a conventional role, they must be given a difference observable by national technical means from the bombers within that type or variant that remain in a nuclear role. Likewise, if a bomber that has been reoriented to a conventional role is subsequently returned to a nuclear role, it must receive an observable difference from other heavy bombers of the same type and variant.

Verification

The START Treaty provisions will be used to verify the START II Treaty's limits except as otherwise provided. The START II Treaty provides for additional inspections to confirm the elimination of heavy ICBMs and their launch canisters, as well as additional inspections to confirm the conversions of heavy ICBM silo launchers. In addition, the START II Treaty provides for exhibitions and inspections to observe the number of nuclear weapons for which heavy bombers are actually equipped and their relevant observable differences.

Collateral Constraints

The START II Treaty requires the elimination or conversion of launchers of deploy ICBMs with multiple warheads. To reinforce this limitation, it prohibits the acquisition, after the second phase of reductions, of such weapons from another state. After that date, the START II Treaty also prohibits the production, flight-testing (except from space launch facilities), or deployment of ICBMs to which more than one warhead is attributed. The Parties are obligated under the Treaty not to produce, flight-test, or deploy an ICBM or SLBM with more warheads than it has been attributed with under the START II Treaty. Also, the Parties are obligated not to transfer heavy ICBMs to any other state, including any other Party to the START Treaty. The START II Treaty provides that this last prohibition is to be applied provisionally from the date of signature of the START II Treaty. It has no effect on the United States since there are no U.S heavy ICBMs.

Implementation and Entry into Force

To provide a forum for discussion of implementation of the START II Treaty, the Treaty establishes the Bilateral Implementation Commission (BIC). Through the BIC, the Parties can resolve questions of compliance and agree upon additional measures to improve the viability and effectiveness of the Treaty.

The START II Treaty will enter into force upon the exchange of instruments of ratification by the Parties. However, since the START II Treaty is built upon the START Treaty, it cannot enter into force prior to the START Treaty's entry into force. It will remain in force as long as the START Treaty remains in force.

Conclusion

Accompanying this report is an analysis of the START II Treaty. This Treaty is truly an historic achievement. By significantly reducing strategic offensive arms, and by eliminating those that pose the greatest threat to stability, the START II Treaty will enhance the national security of the United States. It is in the best interest of the United States of America, the Russian Federation, and, indeed, the entire world that this Treaty enter into force promptly. I strongly recommend its transmission to the Senate for advice and consent to ratification.

Respectfully submitted,

LAWRENCE S. EAGLEBURGER.

Attachments: As stated.

ARTICLE-BY-ARTICLE ANALYSIS OF THE TREATY TEXT

The Treaty Between the United States of America and the Russian Federation on Further Reduction and Limitation of Strategic Offensive Arms (the START II Treaty) consists of the main Treaty text and three documents which are integral parts thereof:

> The Protocol on Procedures Governing Elimination of Heavy ICBMs and on Procedures Governing Conversion of Silo Launchers Of Heavy ICBMs Relating to the Treaty Between the United States of America and the Russian Federation on Further Reduction and Limitation of Strategic Offensive Arms (the Elimination and Conversion Protocol);
>
> The Protocol on Exhibitions and Inspections of Heavy Bombers Relating to the Treaty Between the United States of America and the Russian Federation on Further Reduction and Limitation of Strategic Offensive Arms (the Exhibitions and Inspections Protocol); and
>
> The Memorandum of Understanding on Warhead Attribution and Heavy Bomber Data Relating to the Treaty Between the United States of America and the Russian Federation on Further Reduction and Limitation of Strategic Offensive Arms (the Memorandum on Attribution).

The START II Treaty shall enter into force upon the exchange of instruments of ratification between the United States and the Russian Federation, but Article VI of the START II Treaty specifically provides that it shall not enter into force prior to entry into force of the START Treaty.

In addition to the documents that are integral parts of the START II Treaty, there are three exchanges of letters associated with START II. The first exchange of letters relates to the ongoing negotiations of an agreement between Russia and Kazakhstan regarding SS-18 missiles and launchers now on the territory of Kazakhstan. In his December 29, 1992, response to Russian Foreign Minister Kozyrev's commitment of December 29, 1992, to spare no effort to conclude such an agreement, Secretary of State Eagleburger confirmed that the START II Treaty would be submitted to the United States Senate for its advice and consent on the understanding that the agreement referred to by Minister Kozyrev (providing for the movement to Russia and elimination of heavy ICBMs from Kazakhstan) would be signed and implemented, and that, not later than seven years after entry into force of the START Treaty, all deployed and non-deployed heavy ICBMs now located on the territory of Kazakhstan will have been moved to Russia where they and their launch canisters will have been destroyed.

The second exchange of letters of December 29, 1992, and December 31, 1992, between Secretary of State Eagleburger and Russian Foreign Minister Kozyrev, relates, to heavy bombers, and constitutes the assurance of the United States of America, during the duration of the START II Treaty, never to have more nuclear weapons deployed on any heavy bomber than the number specified in the Memorandum on Attribution for that type or variant. This letter creates no new legal obligation for the United States but merely reiterates the obligation already assumed under paragraph 3 of Article IV of the START II Treaty.

The third exchange of letters of December 29, 1992, and January 3, 1993, between Russian Minister of Defense Grachev and Secretary of Defense Cheney, sets forth a number of assurances on Russian intent regarding the conversion and retention of 90 silo launchers of RS-20 (referred to by the U.S. as SS-18) heavy ICBMs. In his letter, which is politically binding on Russia, Minister Grachev reaffirms the steps that Russia will take to convert these silos and assures the Secretary of Defense that missiles of the SS-25 type will be deployed in these converted silos.

Title and Preamble

The title of the START II Treaty is the "Treaty Between the United States of America and the Russian Federation on the Further Reduction and Limitation of Strategic Offensive Arms."

Of primary importance is the word "further," which establishes from the outset the integral relationship between the START Treaty and the START II Treaty. As will become evident as this analysis progresses, without entry into force of the START Treaty there can be no entry into force or implementation of the START II Treaty. This is true not only with respect to the formalities of the entry into force of the two Treaties, but also with respect to every aspect of implementation of the START II Treaty. Indeed, paragraph 1 of Article V states that except as otherwise specifically provided for, "the provisions of the START Treaty, including the verification provisions, shall be used for implemention of this Treaty." Thus, whenever a question arises, reference must be made to the START Treaty. It is on this basis that the terms used throughout the START II Treaty have their meaning, beginning with Article I. This means that terms such as "reduction and limitation" and "strategic offensive arms" are to be understood in precisely the same manner as in the START Treaty.

As in the START Treaty, the term "reduction and limitation" highlights the fact that START II also calls for elimination of arms, not merely the imposition of ceilings. The arms subject to "further" reductions beyond those of the START Treaty are "strategic," in the same sense that the term is used in the START Treaty. There, it should be noted, in term itself is undefined, but as explained in the Article-by-Article Analysis of the START Treaty, the term refers to ICBMs and their associated launchers, SLBMs and their associated launchers, and heavy bombers. These strategic offensive arms covered by the Treaty are systems of intercontinental range, in contrast to shorter-range and intermediate-range systems covered by the 1987 Treaty Between the United States of America and the Union of Soviet Socialist Republics on the Elimination of Their Intermediate-Range and Shorter-Range Missiles. Similarly, the term "offensive" is used in contrast to "defensive" arms, such as anti-ballistic missile systems covered by the 1972 Treaty Between the United States of America and the Union of Soviet Socialist Republics on the Limitation of Anti-Ballistic Missile Systems and under discussion in the talks on a Global Protection System.

The Preamble commences with the designation of the United States of America and the Russian Federation as "the Parties," to obviate the use of their full names throughout the Treaty. The Parties to the START II Treaty are different from the Parties to the START Treaty. While the Republic of Belarus, the Republic of Kazakhstan, and Ukraine are Parties to the START Treaty, they are not Parties to the START II Treaty. It was not necessary to involve these three states because, within seven years after entry into force of the START Treaty, all nuclear weapons and deployed strategic offensive arms are to be eliminated from their territories. The second and third paragraphs of the Preamble contain a reaffirmation of commitment to the START Treaty and the Treaty on the Non-Proliferation of Nuclear Weapons (NPT). The fourth paragraph calls attention to the commitment of Belarus, Kazakhstan, and Ukraine, as set forth in the Lisbon Protocol, to accede to the NPT as non-nuclear-weapon States Parties. The fifth paragraph of the Preamble is similar to the fifth paragraph of the Preamble to the START Treaty, but adds to the list of undertakings of which the Parties are mindful two documents signed since the conclusion of the START Treaty: the Joint Understanding on Further Reductions in Strategic Offensive Arms and the Joint Statement on a Global Protection System signed by President Bush and President Yeltsin on June 17, 1992, in Washington, that relate to START II and the creation of a global system against ballistic missile attack. The sixth through tenth paragraphs parallel paragraphs two through four of the Preamble to the START Treaty. There is also a reference to UN General Assembly resolution 47/52K of December 9, 1992, which specifically welcomes the Joint Understanding on Further Reductions in Strategic Offensive Arms Between the United States of America and the Russian Federation of June 17, 1992, and urges the early conversion of this Joint Understanding into a formal treaty.

Article I

Paragraph 1 of Article I obligates the United States and Russia each to reduce its ICBMs and ICBM launchers, SLBMs and SLBM launchers, and heavy bombers, along with ICBM and SLBM warheads and heavy bomber nuclear armaments, so that by seven years after entry into force of the START Treaty neither Party has more than a total of 4250 warheads attributable to deployed ICBMs, deployed SLBMs, and deployed heavy bombers, as counted pursuant to Articles III and IV of this Treaty (importantly, *not* the START Treaty, whose counting rules differ in some respect from those of the START II Treaty). The paragraph underscores through repetition that the aggregate number must never exceed 4250, and adds that a Party may establish a lesser aggregate number for itself. The reference to the number 3800 implies no legal constraint but rather represents the lower end of a range of deployments contemplated by the Parties.

Paragraph 2 sets forth the sublimits within the overall 4250 limit that each Party must observe. It does so by reference to the numbers of warheads that are attributed to deployed SLBMs, deployed ICBMs of types of ICBMs to which more than one warhead is attributed, and deployed heavy ICBMs in the Memorandum on Attribution or, if the data are not present in the categories contained in the Memorandum on Attribution, in the Memorandum of Understanding to the START Treaty. In order to understand precisely what is meant by, *inter alia,* "warhead," "deployed SLBM," "deployed," "heavy ICBMs" etc., reference must be made to the START Treaty, its counting rules, and its Annex on Terms and Their Definitions. The discussion of such terms and their application, set forth in the Article-by-Article Analysis of the START Treaty, will not be repeated here. But it is worth calling special attention to the fact that, for the purposes of the START Treaty and therefore START II, a "warhead" is not a physical object, but a unit of account. The sublimits set forth in paragraph 2, described in terms of the total number of warheads attributed to certain missiles, are: (a) 2160 for deployed SLBMs, (b) 1200 for those types of ICBMs to which more than one warhead is attributed, and (c) 650 for deployed heavy ICBMs.

Paragraph 3 provides that, once a Party has fulfilled its obligations pursuant to paragraph 1, it shall continue the reductions process so that by

January 1, 2003, it does not have more than a total of 3500 warheads attributable to its deployed ICBMs, deployed SLBMs, and deployed heavy bombers. As in the case of the first phase of further reductions set forth in paragraph 1, a Party is free to establish a lower aggregate number for itself. Also, as in the first phase of further reductions, there is mention made of a number, in this case 3000, that implies no legal constraint, but which represents the lower end of a range of deployments contemplated by the Parties.

Paragraph 4 establishes the sublimits applicable to the aggregate of 3500 or less as follows: (a) 1750 for warheads attributed to deployed SLBMs; (b) zero for warheads attributed to deployed ICBMs of types to which more than one warhead is attributed; and (c) zero for warheads attributed to deployed heavy ICBMs.

The effect of these reductions is that by January 1, 2003, the aggregate number for deployed warheads must not exceed 3500 (no more than 1750 of which can be attributed to deployed SLBMs) and neither Party may have a deployed launcher of an ICBM to which more than one warhead is attributed nor a deployed launcher of heavy ICBMs or any heavy ICBMs. Note that, in a sense, subparagraph 4(c) is redundant. The only deployed heavy ICBM (the SS-18) is in fact a deployed ICBM of a type to which more than one warhead is attributed, and under the terms of both the START and the START II Treaties, the number of warheads attributed to heavy ICBMs may not be reduced through downloading. However, in light of the separate reference to heavy ICBMs that is maintained throughout the START Treaty and in the START II Treaty for other purposes, the separate treatment in subparagraph 4(c) leaves no room for doubt that the complete elimination of heavy ICBMs is necessary and recognizes that their elimination has great military and political significance. Also, under START rules for eliminations, launchers may either be destroyed or converted and, in most cases, the missiles need not be destroyed. The START II Treaty, like the START Treaty, is more severe on heavy ICBMs than on other strategic offensive arms. Under START II, all heavy ICBM silo launchers must be destroyed (except for 90 that may be converted under stringent procedures) and all heavy ICBMs must also be destroyed.

Paragraph 5 establishes that the Parties have committed to a sustained rate of reductions throughout the entire period of reductions. It makes it clear that the Parties may not delay commencing their reductions, and repeats the obligation set forth in paragraph 3 that, upon the completion of the first phase of further reductions, the second phase of reductions must be commenced.

The effect of this provision is to provide significant additional reductions, as compared to the phased reductions provided in the START Treaty. For example, in the seven-year reduction period set forth in the START Treaty, Russia and Kazakhstan are required to destroy deployed heavy ICBM launchers at the rate of no fewer than 22 a year, in order to reach the requisite reduction of 154 no later than at the end of seven years.

Under this Treaty, Russia is to reach the level of 65 deployed heavy ICBM launchers at the end of the seven-year START reduction period (650 attributed warheads, 10 warheads per missile). Thus, to reach this level at a "sustained" rate, Russia will have to destroy or convert (conversion being permitted under the START II Treaty up to a level of 90 heavy ICBM silo launchers) at a rate significantly greater than that to which it is obligated under the START Treaty.

Whereas the START Treaty rate of 22 per year is a specific obligation to a minimum rate of reductions, the requirement of paragraph 5 of Article I for sustained reductions throughout the reductions period is a more generalized commitment and not a specific legal obligation to reduce at a given rate. Thus, Russia is not obligated to eliminate or convert exactly 35 SS-18 silo launchers a year, but eliminating or converting substantially fewer over a sustained period could cause concern with regard to compliance with the commitment contained in paragraph 5 of Article I.

It is important to note that, while the Parties agreed to sustained reductions, they did not agree to "straight-line" or annual reduction rates. The Parties understood that sustained reductions refer to the continual decline of the strategic offensive arms associated with the aggregate number of warheads and are not necessarily related to specific systems. Straight-line reductions, or the reduction of warheads at a constant annual rate, are not practical due to the "step" nature of many reductions. For example, a Party cannot take credit for ICBM downloading until all ICBMs at a base have been downloaded. Similarly, SLBM downloading is not credited until all the SLBMs on submarines based adjacent to one ocean have been downloaded. On the other hand, partial steps in the conversion or elimination process, such as the notification that a single launcher was being converted or that a few heavy bombers were being eliminated, will provide confidence that the reductions are being sustained.

Paragraph 6 sets forth the agreement of the Parties, that if they reach a separate agreement within one year after entry into force on a program of assistance to promote the implementation of these reductions, then the time frame for accomplishment of the second phase of further reductions, as well as meeting additional constraints contained in Article II, will not extend beyond December 31, 2000. Bearing in mind that seven years after entry into force of the START II Treaty will probably closely approach the end of the year 2000, it becomes apparent that the Parties must be prepared to complete their reductions in less time than the periods in which they are originally obligated to complete such reductions. The qualification of this obligation that agreement on such a program of assistance must be achieved by one year after entry into force was added at Russian request. The Parties wanted to make it clear that such an agreement must be reached long before the accelerated completion date for the second phase of reductions, in order to give Russia the requisite time to meet this revised obligation.

Article II

Article II consists of nine paragraphs.

Paragraph 1 contains several different undertakings that are at the heart of the START II Treaty. Foremost is the requirement that each Party, no later than January 1, 2003, will have either eliminated all of its deployed and non-deployed launchers of ICBMs to which more than one warhead is attributed under Article III of this Treaty (including test launchers and training launchers), or else will have converted them to launchers of ICBMs to which one warhead is attributed, and will not thereafter have launchers of ICBMs to which more than one warhead is attributed. An exception to this requirement is made for those launchers, other than launchers of heavy ICBMs, that are allowed under the START Treaty at space launch facilities. Paragraph 1 goes on to state the agreement of the Parties that ICBM launchers that have been converted to launch an ICBM of a different type shall not be capable of launching an ICBM of the former type. Thus, for example, converted SS-18 silos must not be capable of launching SS-18s. The Parties also agree to carry out such elimination or conversion using the procedures provided for in the START Treaty, except as otherwise provided in paragraph 3 of this Article.

Paragraph 2 excepts from the obligations of paragraph 1 silo launchers of ICBMs on which the number of warheads has been reduced to one pursuant to paragraph 2 of Article III of the START II Treaty. Thus, for example, the launchers of all Minuteman III ICBMs and the 105 launchers of SS-19 ICBMs that have been downloaded to one warhead pursuant to Article III of the START II Treaty need not be eliminated, even though under the START Treaty they would be attributed with more than one warhead at entry into force.

Paragraph 3 sets forth the means by which silo launchers of heavy ICBMs, including test launchers and training launchers, are to be eliminated or converted. Eliminations are to be carried out in accordance with the procedures provided for in Section II of the Conversion or Elimination Protocol to the START Treaty. Not more than 90 silo launchers of heavy ICBMs may be converted in accordance with the procedures provided for in the Elimination and Conversion Protocol to the START II Treaty; the remainder must be physically destroyed.

Paragraph 4 sets forth the undertaking of the Parties not to emplace an ICBM launch canister which has a diameter greater than 2.5 meters in any silo launcher of heavy ICBMs that has been converted in accordance with subparagraph (b) of paragraph 3 of Article II. This is one of the constraints placed on the 90 SS-18 heavy ICBM silo launchers that may be converted rather than eliminated pursuant to paragraph 3. Although this paragraph, standing alone, would not preclude the subsequent installation of a new type of single-warhead ICBM different from the SS-25, its purpose is to reinforce the assurance from Defense Minister Grachev, during the negotiations, that only ICBMs of the SS-25 type will be installed in converted heavy ICBM launchers. The U.S. interpretation of this Russian political commitment would preclude such subsequent installation.

The political commitment is contained in a letter, dated December 29, 1992, from Defense Minister Grachev to Secretary of Defense Cheney, which offers five assurances with respect to the conversion of 90 silo launchers of RS-20 (SS-18) heavy ICBMs under the Elimination and Conversion Protocol in order to install single-warhead missiles other than heavy ICBMs into such silo launchers.

The first assurance is the Russian commitment to install in the upper portion of each converted SS-18 silo launcher a restrictive ring with a diameter of not more than 2.9 meters, so as to preclude loading of a heavy ICBM in the silo launcher.

The second assurance is that each such converted silo launcher will be filled with concrete to a depth of five meters, thereby making the usable depth of the silo too short to contain a heavy ICBM.

The third assurance is that Russia will not install in a converted silo launcher a missile launch canister with a diameter exceeding 2.5 meters.

The fourth assurance is that a single-warhead ICBM of the RS12M (SS-25) type missile will be installed in such converted silo launcher. The word "type" is understood to refer to an ICBM in the sense that the term is described in the START Treaty. During the negotiations the Defense Minister stated that "only single-warhead ICBMs of the RS-12M (SS-25) type would be installed in such a converted launcher of heavy ICBMs." The United States, therefore, understands the political commitment contained in the letter to be a permanent commitment not to install any missile other than an SS-25 type in these converted silos.

The fifth assurance is that such a conversion of silo launchers of heavy ICBMs (including filling with concrete) will be verified in accordance with the agreement reached between the Parties.

Except for the fourth assurance, all of the assurances in the letter are obligations included in either the main body of the START II Treaty or its Elimination and Conversion Protocol. Thus, the 90 converted heavy ICBM silos must never again contain heavy ICBMs or ICBMs equipped with MIRVs and may contain only an SS-25 type missile.

Paragraph 5 requires that elimination of launchers of heavy ICBMs at space launch facilities be carried out only in accordance with subparagraph 3(a) of Article II. Thus, such launchers may not be converted but must be destroyed. There are no such launchers in Russia at the present time and, during the negotiations, the Russians said they had no plans for such launchers. Should, however, Russian plans change such that any be designated as part of a space launch facility, they must be destroyed by January 1, 2003, pursuant to this paragraph and paragraph 1 of this Article (which does not exempt such launchers used at space launch facilities).

Paragraph 6 addresses the elimination of deployed and non-deployed heavy ICBMs and their launch canisters. All such missiles must be eliminated no later than January 1, 2003, either in accordance with the procedures provided for in the Elimination and Conversion Protocol, or by using such missiles for delivering objects into the upper atmosphere or space. The Parties also agree not to have such missiles or launch canisters thereafter. The heavy ICBMs must be removed from their canisters before they are eliminated. The United States has the right to observe these eliminations. The provisions of this Article were not meant to exclude elimination through test flights during the period of reductions.

In this context the exchange of letters on Kazakhstan is important. Russia pledges its best efforts to reach agreement with Kazakhstan, as contemplated by the Lisbon Protocol, on the movement of the SS-18 heavy ICBMs and their launch canisters, which are now located in Kazakhstan, to Russia, where they will be destroyed. The United States asserts for its part that it is entering into the START II Treaty regime on the understanding that this agreement will be signed and implemented, and all the SS-18 missiles in Kazakhstan will be returned to Russia and destroyed along with their launch canisters.

Paragraph 7 gives each Party the right to conduct inspections in connection with the elimination of heavy ICBMs and their launch canisters, as well as inspections in connection with the conversion of silo launchers of heavy ICBMs. Except as otherwise provided in the Elimination and Conversion Protocol, such inspections must be conducted subject to the applicable provisions of the START Treaty.

Paragraph 8 sets forth the commitment of each Party not to transfer heavy ICBMs to any recipient whatsoever, including any other Party to the START Treaty. Pursuant to paragraph 2 of Article VI, this obligation is to be applied provisionally from the date of signature of the Treaty. This provides a useful collateral constraint since there are SS-18 silo launchers located outside Russia, and such transfers by Russia to the other Parties to the START Treaty—Belarus, Kazakhstan, and Ukraine—are not prohibited by the START Treaty.

Paragraph 9 requires that, beginning on January 1, 2003, and thereafter, neither Party will produce, acquire, flight-test (except for flight tests from space launch facilities conducted in accordance with the provisions of the START Treaty), or deploy an ICBM to which more than one warhead is attributed under Article III of the START II Treaty. This provision adds to the START Treaty prohibition "not to produce, flight-test, or deploy," an explicit ban on acquisition of such systems from a third state—a relevant concern since other countries (particularly Ukraine) presently have sophisticated ballistic missile production facilities. The practical impact of paragraph 9 is that, after the specified date, Peacekeeper and the SS-24 ICBMs can be launched only from space launch facilities to deliver objects into the upper atmosphere or space.

Article III

Article III sets forth the specific Treaty provisions regarding the attribution of warheads to deployed ICBMs and SLBMs. Paragraph 1 of

Article III specifies that the number of nuclear warheads attributed to an ICBM or SLBM will be determined in accordance with START procedures, except as otherwise provided for in paragraph 2 of Article III. Since paragraph 2 covers only downloading, this means that the warhead attribution of existing ICBMs and SLBMs is that listed in Section I of the START Memorandum of Understanding, unless they are downloaded in accordance with the START Treaty or in accordance with paragraph 2 of this Article, and that the provisions for determining the warhead attribution of new types of ICBMs and SLBMs set forth in paragraph 4 of Article III of the START Treaty apply with equal force to the START II Treaty.

Paragraph 2 of Article III sets forth rules for reducing the warhead attribution (downloading) of existing types of ICBMs and SLBMs other than heavy ICBMs. The actual number of reentry vehicles on any given ballistic missile may be less than the attributed number of warheads, but that missile still counts at the attributed number. Like the START Treaty, the START II Treaty bans downloading of heavy ICBMs and of new types of ICBMs or SLBMs. Downloading under this Treaty follows the same rules as downloading under the START Treaty, except that the following provisions apply only to downloading for the purposes of the START II Treaty:

Subparagraphs 2(a) and 2(b) allow a Party to exceed the 1250 START Treaty total warhead downloading limit and the 500 START Treaty warhead limit on downloading ICBMs and SLBMs other than the U.S. Minuteman III ICBM and the Russian SS-N-18 SLBM. This provision would allow the United States to maintain the viability of the sea-based component of the Triad while meeting the limit of 1750 SLBM warheads found in subparagraph 4(a) of Article I of the Treaty by, for example, downloading each of the 432 Trident SLBMs on 18 Trident ballistic missile submarines from eight to four warheads.

Subparagraph 2(c) allows downloading no more than 105 ICBMs of one type of existing ICBM by more than four, but not more than five, warheads. (Downloading otherwise is limited to no more than four warheads per missile by subparagraph 5(c)(iii) of Article III of the START Treaty.) The ICBM so downloaded must be one of the two types of ICBM or SLBM whose downloading is permitted by subparagraph 5(c)(ii) of Article III of the START Treaty. This provision has the practical effect of allowing Russia to download 105 SS-19 ICBMs from six warheads to one warhead, and thus to retain them past January 1, 2003, when all MIRVed ICBMs are banned. The 105 downloaded SS-19 ICBMs must be deployed only in silos in which an SS-19 ICBM was deployed on July 31, 1991, the date of signature of the START Treaty.

Subparagraph 2(d) allows downloading of a ballistic missile type by more than two warheads without destroying the reentry vehicle platform and replacing it with a new reentry vehicle platform. Such destruction and replacement would otherwise be required by subparagraphs 5(b)(iii) and 5(c)(vi) of Article III of the START Treaty, in order to take advantage of that Treaty's downloading provisions. Not requiring reentry vehicle platform destruction will allow the Parties to restructure their forces under START II to meet the START II Treaty's lower limits in a more economical manner.

All other downloading provisions of the START Treaty apply to this Treaty as well. In particular, downloading of ICBMs must be accomplished base-by-base, while downloading of SLBMs must include all SLBMs at bases adjacent to the same ocean. Neither Party may download more than two existing types of ballistic missiles, either ICBMs or SLBMs, in addition to the Minuteman III and the SS-N-18.

As a result of the differences in the provisions of the two Treaties, the warhead attribution of a given ICBM or SLBM may differ under START and under the START II Treaty. For example, if the United States were to elect to download the Trident II (D-5) SLBM from eight to four warheads, without replacing the reentry vehicle platform, it could be attributed with four warheads under this Treaty, while it could continue to be attributed with eight warheads under START (or a number of seven or six consistent with START Treaty downloading rules). The United States would not be in violation of the 1250 or 500 warhead downloading limit in START. As noted above, there are no numerical limits on the aggregate number of reentry vehicles that may be downloaded under this Treaty, except as implied by other constraints, e.g., the limits on the number of existing types of missiles and the number of warheads per missile that can be downloaded.

In a similar fashion, the United States could elect to download the Minuteman III to one warhead for purposes of the START II Treaty without destroying the reentry vehicle platform. Since this Treaty cannot amend the START Treaty, in this case the Minuteman III would continue to be attributed with three warheads for purposes of the START Treaty.

Paragraph 3 of Article III of the START II Treaty contains two requirements that parallel similar requirements in paragraph 12 of Article V of the START Treaty. Subparagraph 3(a) translates the warhead attribution rule into a physical prohibition by banning production, flight-testing, or deployment of an ICBM or SLBM with more reentry vehicles than the number of warheads attributed to it. Subparagraph 3(b) bans uploading of ICBMs or SLBMs that have been downloaded.

The provisions of subparagraph 3(a) do not preclude production of Trident SLBMs for transfer to the United Kingdom, regardless of the number of reentry vehicles with which the United Kingdom subsequently equips them. As the Article-by-Article Analysis of the First Agreed Statement in the Agreed Statements Annex to the START Treaty makes clear: ". . . as a sovereign nation, the United Kingdom has the right to test and deploy the Trident II missile with any warhead configuration the UK deems appropriate."

Paragraph 3 is necessary, even though similar provisions exist in the START Treaty, since the warhead attribution under START and under the START II Treaty may differ. For example, if all Trident II (D-5) SLBMs were downloaded to four warheads under this Treaty, while continuing to be attributed with eight warheads under START, there would, absent this paragraph, be no legal bar to continuing to test and deploy them with eight reentry vehicles. Similarly, without the provisions of paragraph 3 of this Treaty, there would be no bar to uploading. For example, START provisions against uploading would not preclude returning the Trident II (D-5) SLBMs to an attribution of eight warheads under the START II Treaty, since, in terms of START accountability, its accountability would always have been eight.

Article IV

Article IV establishes the constraints on heavy bombers. Paragraphs 1 through 6 deal with attributing warheads to heavy bombers; paragraphs 7 through 14 regulate nuclear-armed heavy bombers reoriented to a conventional role. Article IV is complemented by the Exhibitions and Inspections Protocol.

Paragraphs 1, 2, and 3 of Article IV provide the basic counting rules for heavy bomber nuclear armaments. Paragraph 1 specifies that the number of nuclear warheads attributed to a deployed heavy bomber (other than heavy bombers reoriented to a conventional role) shall be equal to the number of nuclear weapons (including long-range nuclear ALCMs, nuclear gravity bombs, and short-range nuclear missiles) with which any bomber of that type or variant is actually equipped. This is a significant departure from the START Treaty, under which 150 U.S. and 180 Soviet ALCM-equipped heavy bombers were discounted up to 50 percent and heavy bombers equipped for nuclear weapons other than long-range nuclear ALCMs were attributed with only one warhead. Paragraph 2 provides that the number of nuclear weapons for which a heavy bomber is actually equipped shall be the number listed in the Memorandum on Attribution, while paragraph 3 prohibits heavy bombers from being equipped with more nuclear weapons than are attributed to it.

One of the most difficult issues during the START II negotiations was what was meant by the number of nuclear weapons for which a heavy bomber is actually equipped. The Russian delegation initially asserted that any approach other than one based on counting attachment points (i.e., the physical devices used to attach weapons to heavy bombers or weapons racks), and the subsequent calculation of the maximum number of weapons that could physically be loaded on the aircraft given those attachment points, would not result in a "real" counting rule. The design of U.S. heavy bombers makes counting attachment points an inappropriate and misleading measure that could greatly overstate the realistic operational load that a U.S. heavy bomber could carry on a strategic mission. The United States successfully rejected this approach, arguing in favor of an approach that would count all bombers of any type or variant with the largest number of nuclear weapons for which any bomber of that type or variant would be actually deployed.

In support of the U.S. position, the December 29, 1992 letter from Secretary of State Eagleburger to Russian Foreign Minister Kozyrev provided assurances that the United States has an "absolute legal and political requirement" to have no more nuclear weapons deployed on a heavy bomber than the number specified in the Memorandum on Attribution. The letter does not create a new U.S. obligation, but simply notes a series of provisions set forth in the Treaty. The word "type," as used in the letter, as in the Treaty, to refer to heavy bombers, is used in the same sense as the term is used in the START Treaty.

Russian Foreign Minister Kozyrev, in his response to Secretary of State Eagleburger's letter of December 29, 1992, agreed that, on the basis of the U.S. letter, "all questions associated with heavy bombers have been resolved for the purposes of [the START II] Treaty to our mutual satisfaction." This provides formal assurance that Russia no longer insisted on counting attachment points to determine the number of nuclear weapons for which a heavy bomber is actually equipped or on eliminating "excess" attachment points that would allow the aircraft to carry a larger number of nuclear weapons than listed. Instead, the Parties agreed that the number of warheads attributed to a heavy bomber of a given type or variant of a type would be the number listed in the Memorandum on Attribution. This agreement paved the way for agreement on the heavy bomber portions of the Treaty.

Paragraph 4 of Article IV requires a one-time exhibition of one heavy bomber of each type and variant specified in the Memorandum on Attribution for the purpose of demonstrating the number of nuclear weapons for which such bombers are actually equipped. No distinction is made between heavy bombers equipped for long-range nuclear ALCMs and those that are not so equipped. In a significant departure from the procedures of the START Treaty, these exhibitions will include the U.S. B-2 heavy bomber. The exhibitions are to be conducted no later than 180 days after entry into force of the START II Treaty. This date was selected for two reasons: to allow adequate time to prepare for the exhibitions, especially for shrouding of the B-2 (and, if necessary, shrouding other heavy bombers) permitted by paragraph 2 of Section II of the Exhibition and Inspection Protocol, and to avoid conflict with START Treaty baseline inspections in the event that the START and START II Treaties enter into force at approximately the same time.

The START II Treaty allows each Party to increase or decrease the number of warheads for which a heavy bomber is actually equipped. Paragraph 5 of Article IV requires exhibitions similar to those required by paragraph 4 in the event the number of nuclear weapons for which a heavy bomber is actually equipped is changed. This paragraph also provides for the timing of any change in attribution. Both the exhibition and the accountability change are triggered by a notification of intent. Ninety days after such notification both the change in accountability and the exhibition occur. While the Parties may, by agreement, delay the exhibition, this does not delay the change in accountability.

In practical terms, the application of paragraph 5 will vary according to circumstances:

If a Party intends to decrease the number of nuclear weapons for which a heavy bomber of a given type and variant is actually equipped, but without the intent to create a new variant, the last heavy bomber would have to be modified before one is exhibited. This is necessary since otherwise a Party would still have one or more heavy bombers equipped for more nuclear weapons than the number listed in the Memorandum on Attribution, which would be in violation of paragraph 3 of Article IV.

If a Party intends to increase the number of nuclear weapons for which a heavy bomber of a given type and variant is actually equipped, but without the intent to create a new variant, the *first* heavy bomber to be modified would have to be exhibited. Once again, this is necessary to avoid having any heavy bomber equipped for more nuclear weapons than the number listed in the Memorandum on Attribution for heavy bombers of that type and variant.

If a Party intends to increase or decrease the number of nuclear weapons for which a heavy bomber is actually equipped through creation of a new variant (for example, by removing external ALCM carriage from some, but not all, of a particular type of heavy bomber), the first aircraft of that variant would have to be exhibited. The new variant would, under the START Treaty, need to be made distinguishable (as that term is used in the START Treaty) and to be exhibited in accordance with paragraph 12 of Article XI of the START Treaty. The exhibitions required under START and those required under paragraph 5 of Article IV of the START II Treaty may be combined, but there is no legal requirement to do so. Additional aircraft would count at the changed number of weapons as they were modified to become bombers of the newly declared variant.

If a Party intends to increase or decrease the number of nuclear weapons for which a heavy bomber is actually equipped, incident to converting heavy bombers from heavy bombers equipped for long-range nuclear ALCMs to heavy bombers equipped for nuclear armaments other than long-range nuclear ALCMs or to heavy bombers equipped for non-nuclear armaments, the procedures set forth in Section VI of the Conversion or Elimination Protocol to the START Treaty would be followed, including the inspections provisions associated therewith. Once again, the conversion inspection required under the START Treaty and the exhibition required under paragraph 5 of Article IV of the START II Treaty may be combined, but there is no legal requirement to do so.

In any of these cases, a 90-day advance notification would be required.

Paragraph 6 of Article IV specifies that exhibitions and inspections referred to in paragraphs 4 and 5 of Article IV will be conducted in accordance with the provisions of the Exhibitions and Inspections Protocol and, to the extent not modified by that Protocol, with the provisions of the START Treaty, as provided for in paragraph 1 of Article V of the START II Treaty.

Under the START Treaty, older U.S. heavy bombers awaiting elimination at the Davis-Monthan conversion or elimination facility are included in the Memorandum of Understanding, since such bombers count against the START Treaty delivery vehicle and warhead totals. Since these older bombers will be eliminated before the expiration of the seven-year reductions period, when the first limits under START II must be reached, it was agreed that the number of nuclear weapons for which they are actually equipped would not be included in the START II Memorandum on Attribution and, in such case, they will not be exhibited.

The United States declared two different categories of the B-52G heavy bomber under the START Treaty: a B-52G equipped for long-range nuclear ALCMs and a B-52G equipped for nuclear armaments other than long-range nuclear ALCMs. At the time of signature of the START II Treaty, all B-52Gs equipped for long-range nuclear ALCMs had been removed from operational service and were awaiting elimination at the Davis-Monthan Air Force Base elimination facility. Therefore, the United States listed only one category of B-52G in the Memorandum on Attribution.

The United States informed Russia during the negotiations that, since the only deployed B-52G heavy bombers Russian inspectors will actually encounter at operational air bases will be B-52Gs that are not equipped for long-range nuclear ALCMs, that is the configuration of the heavy bomber that the United States will exhibit. The United States further noted that, if U.S. plans were to change and the United States were to return any B-52Gs equipped for long-range nuclear ALCMs to operational status, we would conduct an additional exhibition of the ALCM-configured B-52G in order to avoid any confusion during subsequent data update inspections.

Paragraph 7 of Article IV gives each Party the right to reorient to a conventional role—without undergoing any conversion procedures—heavy bombers that have never been accountable under the START Treaty as heavy bombers equipped for long-range nuclear ALCMs. This provision is applied on an airplane-by-airplane basis; for example, the fact that B-1 test heavy bombers have been tested with long-range nuclear ALCMs is not a bar to reorienting heavy bombers of that type to a conventional role. Note that the right to reorient without any physical conversion is modified by the requirement in subparagraph 8(d) of this Article that such reoriented bombers have differences, observable to national technical means of verification (NTM) and visible during inspection, from other heavy bombers that have not been reoriented, so that they can be differentiated from other heavy bombers of the same type and variant with a nuclear role (if any).

The right to reorient heavy bombers to a conventional role is *in addition* to the right under START to convert, using specified procedures, no more than 76 heavy bombers to heavy bombers equipped for non-nuclear armaments. A Party could, if it chose, have both 75 converted non-nuclear heavy bombers and 100 heavy bombers reoriented to a conventional role that did not require conversion procedures. Heavy bombers reoriented to a conventional role will not count against the START II warhead limits. However, since heavy bombers reoriented to a conventional role need not undergo any conversion, they remain fully accountable under the START Treaty as heavy bombers equipped for nuclear armaments other than long-range nuclear ALCMs (i.e., each counts as one delivery vehicle and as one warhead towards the START Treaty's ceilings).

Paragraph 8 of Article IV sets forth specific restrictions on heavy bombers reoriented to a conventional role. Subparagraph 8(a) limits the number of reoriented bombers to 100 at any one time, while subparagraph 8(b) mandates segregated basing for such bombers. Subparagraph 8(c) bans use of reoriented heavy bombers for nuclear missions or in nuclear exercises and bars their crews from training or exercising for nuclear missions. This prohibition does not ban such training or exercising by crews of bombers of the same type and variant that have not been reoriented.

Subparagraph 8(d) requires that heavy bombers reoriented to a conventional role have differences observable to national technical means (NTM) from heavy bombers of that type and variant that have not been reoriented. This provision aids in confirming adherence to the requirements of subparagraph 8(b) for segregated basing. The specific differences are listed in the Memorandum of Attribution. While these observable differences are primarily an aid to NTM, they are also required to be visible during on-site inspections. Alternately, if all heavy bombers of a type have been reoriented to a conventional role, the requirement to have differences observable to NTM is unnecessary since these aircraft are observably different from other types or variants and it would be clear in which category they fell. In addition, there would be no need or purpose in exhibiting an aircraft if all heavy bombers of that type and variant fell into the same category.

The observable differences referred to in subparagraph 8(d) need not be functional. As a result, they need not necessarily make heavy bombers reoriented to a conventional role "distinguishable" (as that term is defined in the START Treaty) from other heavy bombers.

Paragraph 9 of Article IV provides each Party the right, following 90-day advance notification to the other Party, to return to a nuclear role heavy bombers that have been reoriented to a conventional role. This right is important to the United States. We currently plan to reorient B-1 heavy bombers to a conventional role, but need to preserve the option to return these bombers to a nuclear role if and when B-52H heavy bombers are retired. Once returned to a nuclear role, such heavy bombers will count "as actually equipped" and may not subsequently be reoriented to a conventional role a second time.

Paragraph 9 also requires observable differences if only some, but not all, reoriented heavy bombers of a given type or variant of a type are returned to a nuclear role. These differences aid in enforcing the prohibition on a subsequent reorientation to a conventional role. As a result of the combination of paragraphs 8 and 9, a Party may be obligated to allow the other Party to identify, both through its NTM and through inspections, three separate groups of heavy bombers within a given variant: those that have never been reoriented to a conventional role, those that are currently reoriented to a conventional role, and those that were once reoriented to a conventional role but have subsequently been returned to a nuclear role.

Paragraph 10 of Article IV requires at least 100 kilometers separation between air bases for heavy bombers reoriented to a conventional role and storage areas for heavy bomber nuclear armaments. This restriction is based on a similar restriction in subparagraph 11(e) of Article IV of the START Treaty. Note that this restriction would not preclude nuclear weapons for other strategic or tactical systems (e.g., ICBM reentry vehicles or weapons for tactical aircraft) from being stored within the 100 kilometers specified, nor would it preclude deployment of nuclear warheads on ICBMs at ICBM bases co-located with air bases for heavy bombers reoriented to a conventional role. There are no specific verification provisions specified in the START II Treaty for this restriction.

Paragraph 11 provides that reoriented heavy bombers remain subject to the provisions of the START Treaty, including the inspection provisions. Such heavy bombers are accountable under the START Treaty as heavy bombers equipped for nuclear armaments other than long-range nuclear ALCMs.

Paragraphs 12 and 13 of Article IV provide for exhibitions related to observable differences. In the case where only some bombers of a given type and variant have been reoriented to a conventional role, while others of the same type and variant continue to have a nuclear role, there is a requirement for the former to have a difference observable to NTM from the latter. This obligation is provided for in subparagraph 8(d) of Article IV. Similarly, if only some bombers of a given type and variant are returned to a nuclear role after having been reoriented to a conventional role, and there are other bombers of the same type and variant that have a conventional role, or have a nuclear role but that have never been reoriented to a conventional role, then the bombers in the first "category" (the word "category" is not used in this Analysis in the sense of the term as used in the START Treaty) must be observably different to NTM from bombers in the latter two categories. This obligation is recorded in paragraph 9 of the START II Treaty.

The purpose of these obligations is to allow the other Party to determine into which category a particular aircraft falls (i.e., original nuclear, reoriented to a conventional role, or nuclear that had once been reoriented to a conventional role). This is required not only for the purposes of warhead counting (heavy bombers reoriented to a conventional role are not attributed with warheads; other deployed heavy bombers count as actually equipped), but also to confirm adherence to the ban on reorienting a heavy bomber to a conventional role for a second time. Of course, such observable differences are not necessary in the case in which all the aircraft of a given type or variant are reoriented to a conventional role, or are returned to a nuclear role from a conventional role. Since these aircraft are already observably different from aircraft of other types or variants, it would already be clear into which category they fell.

Paragraphs 12 and 13 of Article IV of the START II Treaty record the obligations for an exhibition of an aircraft for the purpose of demonstrating, and allowing the inspection of, the observable difference identified. As noted above, there would be no need or purpose in exhibiting an aircraft if all aircraft of that type and variant fell into the same category. However, if a Party has two different types or variants that have changed categories, e.g., B-1s and B-52s, and only one of them falls into more than one category (and has been given a difference observable to NTM), the use of the phrase "each type" in these paragraphs does not mean that a requirement exists to exhibit an aircraft of the second type or variant whose status could not be confused since all aircraft of that type or variant fall into the same category. This was clearly not the intent of the Parties, since there would be no purpose in exhibiting an aircraft of the second type or variant, because all of them had been reoriented.

Paragraph 14 of Article IV specifies that exhibitions and inspections referred to in the preceding two paragraphs will be conducted in accordance with the provisions of the Exhibitions and Inspections Protocol.

Article V

Article V sets forth provisions for the implementation of the Treaty. Paragraph 1 of Article V specifies that, except as provided for in the START II Treaty, the provisions of the START Treaty, including its verification provisions, shall be used for implementing START II. As noted above, this includes, for example, the counting rules, the definitions in the Definitions Annex and elsewhere in the START Treaty, as well as the various inspection procedures and related notification requirements and agreed statements.

Paragraph 2 of Article V establishes the bilateral Implementation Commission (BIC). The BIC will meet at the request of either Party and will serve as the framework within which the Parties will seek to resolve any questions related to compliance with the START II Treaty and agree on any additional measures that might be necessary to improve the viability and effectiveness of the START II Treaty. The language establishing the BIC is identical to that establishing the START Treaty's Joint Compliance and Inspection Commission. Both Parties envision that the two Commissions would work together closely.

Article VI

Article VI consists of four paragraphs covering ratification, entry into force, provisional application, duration, and withdrawal.

Paragraph 1 of Article VI provides that the two Protocols and the Memorandum on Attribution are integral parts of the Treaty. Paragraph 1 also specifies that the Treaty is subject to ratification prior to entering into force, and will not enter into force prior to entry into force of the START Treaty.

Paragraph 2 of Article VI specifies that paragraph 8 of Article II, the ban on the transfer of heavy ICBMs to a third state or states, shall be provisionally applied as of the date of signature of the START II Treaty.

Paragraph 3 of Article VI provides that the START II Treaty shall remain in force for the duration of the START Treaty.

Paragraph 4 of Article VI, identical in content to paragraph 3 of Article XVII of the START Treaty, provides each Party the right to withdraw from the Treaty on six months notice if extraordinary events related to the subject matter of this Treaty have jeopardized its supreme interests.

Article VII

Article VII, identical in content to Article XVIII of the START Treaty, provides for amendments to the START II Treaty. Such amendments would be subject to ratification as specified in Article VI of the Treaty.

Article VIII

Article VIII, identical in content to Article XIX of the START Treaty, provides for registration with the United Nations in accordance with Article 102 of the Charter of the United Nations. The entire Treaty, including the two Protocols and the Memorandum on Attribution, are to be so registered.

Final Provision

The final paragraph of the START II Treaty records that the Treaty was done at Moscow on January 3, 1993, in two copies, each in the English and Russian languages, and each being equally authentic.

ARTICLE-BY-ARTICLE ANALYSIS OF THE ELIMINATION AND CONVERSION PROTOCOL

Structure and Overview of the Protocol

The Elimination and Conversion Protocol consists of two Sections. The first Section sets forth procedures for the elimination of heavy ICBMs and their launch canisters. The second Section establishes procedures for the conversion and confirmation of conversion of silo launchers, silo training launchers, and silo test launchers of heavy ICBMs. Although written as general procedures, these procedures were designed for Russian SS-18 silo launchers.

Section I—Procedures for Elimination of Heavy ICBMs and Their Launch Canisters

Paragraph 1 of Section I provides two alternatives for eliminating heavy ICBMs. A Party may either use the procedures set forth in Section I, which are to take place at elimination facilities for ICBMs specified in the START Treaty, or it may eliminate heavy ICBMs by using them for delivering objects into the upper atmosphere or outer space. For the former, notice of elimination must be provided to the other Party, via the Nuclear Risk Reduction Centers (NRRCs), 30 days in advance of the initiation of the elimination process at the particular facility involved. If, however, the elimination of a heavy ICBM is to be accomplished by the "space launch" alternative, notification thereof shall be governed by the provisions of the Agreement Between the United States of America and the Union of Soviet Socialist Republics on Notifications of Launches of Intercontinental Ballistic Missiles and Submarine-Launched Ballistic Missiles of May 31, 1988, which requires notification 24 hours in advance through the NRRCs.

Paragraph 2 lists several steps that either shall or may be taken, in any order, by the inspected Party before the confirmatory inspection provided for in paragraph 3 of Section I. The inspected party shall remove the missile's reentry vehicles; may remove the electronic and electro-mechanical devices of the missiles' guidance and control system from the missile and its launch canister, as well as other elements that are not ("shall not be" in the text is used in the sense of "are not") subject to elimination pursuant to paragraph 4 of Section I (which addresses the elimination process for heavy ICBMs); shall remove the missile from its launch canister and disassemble the missile into stages; shall remove liquid propellant from the missile; may remove or actuate auxiliary pyrotechnic devices installed on the missile and its launch canister; may remove penetration aids, including devices for their attachment and release; and may remove propulsion units from the self-contained dispensing mechanism.

Paragraph 3 describes the confirmatory inspection, which is to take place after arrival of the inspection team and prior to the initiation of the actual destruction. During the confirmatory inspection, the inspectors are to confirm the type and number of missiles to be eliminated. Inspectors have the right to both visually observe and measure items (including missiles outside of their launch canisters) presented for elimination to confirm that they are SS-18 missiles and missile canisters. The elimination process for the missiles and the launch canisters may begin once the above procedures have been carried out.

Paragraph 3 requires that inspectors observe the elimination process. On-site observation is necessary since NTM cannot confirm that the objects presented for destruction are real. Other provisions governing the inspection team and the inspection are found in the START Treaty.

Paragraph 4 specifies the elimination process to be followed for destruction of heavy ICBMs. Missile stages, nozzles, and missile interstage skirts are to be cut into two pieces of approximately equal size; and the self-contained dispensing mechanism (as well as the front section), including the reentry vehicle platform and the front section shroud, is to be cut into two pieces of approximately equal size and crushed. In the negotiations, the Russian side assured the U.S. side that this process would ensure the destruction of all of the critical elements of the missile system—stages, including propellant tanks; engines (since the nozzle, which is destroyed, is the most critical engine element); interstage skirts; and self-contained dispensing mechanisms and their elements.

Paragraph 5 states that during the process of destruction of launch canisters of heavy ICBMs, the launch canister shall be cut into two pieces of approximately equal size or, alternatively, into three pieces such that pieces no less than 1.5 meters long are cut from the ends of the body of the launch canister. These procedures apply to launch canisters eliminated with their heavy ICBMs, as well as to launch canisters for missiles eliminated through flight-testing, or through launching into the upper atmosphere or space. They also apply to empty launch canisters existing at the time of entry into force of the Treaty.

Paragraph 6 requires that the inspection team leader and a member of the in-country escort confirm that the inspection team has completed its inspection. Such confirmation shall be included in a factual written report by them that contains the results of the inspection team's observation of the elimination process. Such confirmation shall be made upon completion of the requirements set forth in Section I.

Paragraph 7 states that heavy ICBMs will no longer be subject to the limitations of this Treaty upon completion of the procedures set forth in Section I. Notification thereof shall be provided in accordance with paragraph 3 of Section I of the Notification Protocol to the START Treaty.

Section II—Procedures for Conversion of Silo Launchers, Silo Training Launchers, and Silo Test Launchers of Heavy ICBMs

Paragraph 1 requires that conversion of silo launchers of heavy ICBMs (including silo training launchers of heavy ICBMs and silo test launchers of heavy ICBMs) be carried out *in situ* and be subject to inspection. Pursuant to paragraph 5 of Article II of the Treaty, launchers of heavy ICBMs at space launch facilities may not be converted, but must be destroyed. Silo elimination, as opposed to conversion, follows START Treaty rules.

Paragraph 2 provides that, prior to the initiation of the conversion process for any of the silo launchers described in paragraph 1, the missile and launch canister must be removed from the silo launcher.

Paragraph 3 states that a Party shall be considered to have initiated the conversion process for silo launchers of heavy ICBMs (including silo training launchers of heavy ICBMs and silo test launchers of heavy ICBMs) as soon as the silo door has been opened and a missile and its canister have been removed from the silo launcher. Notification thereof is to be provided in accordance with paragraphs 1 and 2 of Section IV of the Notification Protocol to the START Treaty.

Paragraph 4 sets forth steps to be included in the conversion process for silo launchers of heavy ICBMs (including silo training launchers of heavy ICBMs and silo test launchers of heavy ICBMs). They are: opening of the silo door and removal of the missile and the launch canister from the silo launcher; pouring of concrete into the base of the silo launcher up to the height of five meters from the bottom of the silo launcher; and installing a restrictive ring with a diameter of no more than 2.9 meters into the upper portion of the silo launcher in a manner that precludes removal without destruction of the ring and its attachment to the silo wall.

Paragraph 5 provides each Party the right to confirm that the procedures specified in paragraph 4 of Section II have been carried out. For purposes of confirming that such procedures have been carried out, the Party doing the conversion is required to notify the other Party (through the NRRCs) (a) no later than 30 days in advance of the date when the process of pouring concrete will commence, and (b) upon completion of all of the procedures specified in paragraph 4 of Section II. Once it receives the first notification, the inspecting Party has two options for confirming compliance with the conversion procedures. These are set forth in paragraph 6 and paragraph 7 of Section II. The primary difference between paragraphs 6 and 7 is whether a Party chooses to observe the concrete being poured into the silo (paragraph 6) or not (paragraph 7).

Paragraph 6 confers upon the Parties the right to observe the entire process of pouring concrete into each heavy ICBM silo launcher that is to be converted and to measure the diameter of the restrictive ring.

Subparagraph 6(a) requires the other Party to inform the Party converting the heavy ICBM silo no later than seven days in advance of the commencement of the pouring that it will observe the filling of the silo in question.

Subparagraph 6(b) requires the Party converting a silo to take such steps as are necessary to ensure that the base of the silo launcher is visible to the inspecting Party and that the depth of the silo can be measured by the inspecting Party. This must be done immediately prior to the commencement of the process of pouring concrete. The purpose of these requirements is to ensure that the inspecting Party can view the bottom of the silo and accurately measure its depth prior to the concrete being poured.

Subparagraph 6(c) states that the inspecting Party shall have the right to observe the entire process of concrete pouring from a location providing an unobstructed view of the silo interior, and to confirm by measurement that concrete has been poured into the base of the launcher to a depth of five meters. Measurements are to be taken from the level of the lower edge of the closed silo door to the base of the silo launcher, prior to the pouring of the concrete, and from the level of the lower edge of the closed silo door to the top of the concrete fill, after the concrete has hardened.

Subparagraph 6(d) states that following notification of completion of the procedures specified in paragraph 4 of Section II, the inspecting Party may measure the diameter of the restrictive ring, that during such inspection the ring shall not be shrouded, and that the Parties shall agree on the date for such inspections.

Subparagraph 6(e) requires that the results of the measurements conducted to subparagraphs 6(c) and 6(d) above be recorded in written, factual inspection reports and signed by the inspection team leader and a member of the in-country escort.

Subparagraph 6(f) states that inspection teams are to consist of no more than ten inspectors, all of whom are to be drawn from the list of inspectors under the START Treaty. The list referred to is that specified by Section II of the Inspection Protocol to the START Treaty, which also sets forth the legal status of such inspections.

Subparagraph 6(g) states that such inspections shall not count against any inspection quotas established by the START Treaty. In addition, heavy ICBM elimination inspections do not count against START Treaty quotas.

Subparagraph 7 provides an alternative method for confirming conversion. It provides for the right to measure the depth of each heavy ICBM silo launcher that is to be converted before the concrete has been poured, and to return and remeasure the silo depth after the concrete has hardened. This alternative was suggested by the Russian side as a cost-reduction measure since the on-site presence required by it could be considerably lower than that required by the first method. The U.S. indicated an interest if appropriate equipment to confirm the integrity of the concrete fill could be identified. In addition, paragraph 7 provides for the right to measure the diameter of the restrictive ring.

Subparagraph 7(a) requires the other Party to inform the Party converting the heavy ICBM silo no later than seven days in advance of the commencement of the pouring that it will measure the depth of the silo in question both before and after the concrete has been poured.

Subparagraph 7(b) requires the Party converting a silo to take such steps as are necessary to ensure that the base of the silo launcher is visible and that the depth of the silo can be measured. This must be done immediately prior to the commencement of the process of pouring concrete. The purpose of these requirements is to ensure that the inspecting Party can view the bottom of the silo and accurately measure its depth.

Subparagraph 7(c) states that the inspecting Party shall measure the depth of the silo launcher prior to the commencement of the process of pouring concrete.

Subparagraph 7(d) states that, following notification of completion of the procedures specified in paragraph 4 of Section II, the inspecting Party may measure the diameter of the restrictive ring, and remeasure the depth of the silo launcher, and that the Parties shall agree on the date for such inspections. The restrictive ring may not be shrouded during such inspections.

Subparagraph 7(e) states that, for purposes of measuring the depth of the concrete in the silo, measurements are to be taken from the level of the lower edge of the closed silo door to the base of the silo launcher, prior to the pouring of the concrete, and from the level of the lower edge of the closed silo door to the top of the concrete fill, after the concrete has hardened.

Subparagraph 7(f) requires that the results of the measurements conducted to subparagraphs 7(c), 7(d), and 7(e) above the recorded in written, factual inspection reports and signed by the inspection team leader and a member of the in-country escort.

Subparagraph 7(g) states that inspections teams are to consist of no more than ten inspectors, all of whom are to be drawn from the list of inspectors under the START Treaty.

Subparagraph 7(h) states that such inspections shall not count against any inspection quotas established by the START Treaty.

Paragraph 8 gives the Party converting a silo the right to carry out further conversion measures after the completion of the procedures specified in paragraph 6 or 7 of Section II or, if such procedures are not conducted, upon expiration of 30 days after notification of completion of the procedures specified in paragraph 4 of Section II.

In addition to the reentry vehicle inspections provided for in the START Treaty, paragraph 9 authorizes four additional reentry vehicle inspections each year of ICBMs deployed in silo launchers of ICBMs that have been converted pursuant to Section II. Procedures set forth in the Inspection Protocol to the START Treaty will be used during these inspections. In addition to confirming that the missile installed in the converted silo has only one reentry vehicle, these inspections permit the inspecting Party visually to confirm the continued presence of the restrictive ring and of the launch canister (and missile) that the inspected Party has placed in the silo. Towards this end, the inspectors have the right visually to confirm both the presence of the ring and that the observable portions of the launch canister of the deployed ICBM do not differ externally from that of the launch canister that was exhibited pursuant to paragraph 11 of Article XI of the START Treaty. While the sides agreed that launch-related equipment and instrumentation could be placed on the ring and could be shrouded, they further agreed that any shrouding of the upper portion of the silo launcher shall not obstruct observation of the upper portion of the launch canister and the restrictive ring. To further ensure that the necessary observations could be made, the Parties also agreed that, if requested by the inspecting Party, the inspected Party must partially remove any shrouding of the restrictive ring, except for shrouding of instruments installed thereon, to confirm its presence. In discussions of this provision, the Russian side assured the U.S. that there would be places on the ring where equipment or instruments would not be emplaced and inspectors could see the integrity of the ring and that the ring was permanently attached to the sides of the launcher. These additional rights apply only to the four extra inspections authorized by this paragraph and do not apply to reentry vehicle inspections which are conducted solely pursuant to the START Treaty.

Paragraph 10 states that, upon completion of the procedures specified in paragraphs 6 or 7 of Section II (or, if such procedures are not conducted, upon expiration of 30 days after notification of completion of the procedures specified in paragraph 4 of Section 11), the silo launcher of heavy ICBMs being converted shall, for purposes of this Treaty, be considered to contain a deployed ICBM to which one warhead is attributed. Without this provision, the silo would continue to be considered to contain a heavy ICBM until the installation of a new missile or a new training model of a missile (which will remain the case with respect to accountability under the START Treaty). This provision was included at the Russian's request to avoid exceeding START II Treaty limits in the event of delay in the installation of the replacement single-warhead ICBM.

Section III—Equipment; Costs

Paragraph 1 provides the right to use agreed equipment to support the inspection activities of the Protocol and requires the Parties to agree in the Bilateral Implementation Commission on such equipment, including but not limited to equipment for the measurement of the concrete fill in silo launchers of heavy ICBMs.

Paragraph 2 addresses costs for inspections conducted pursuant to Section II of this Protocol. Such costs shall be handled in accordance with paragraph 19 of Section V of the Inspection Protocol to the START Treaty. For practical purposes, this means that the United States will bear almost all of the costs of inspections under this protocol, since there are no U.S. heavy ICBMs to inspect. The United States accepted this provision because of the great importance we place on verification of heavy ICBM silo conversion.

This Protocol concludes with a statement that it is an integral part of the Treaty, shall enter into force on the date of entry into force of the Treaty, and shall remain in force as long as the Treaty remains in force. The Parties agree that they may agree upon such additional measures as may be necessary to improve the viability and effectiveness of the Treaty. They agree that, if it becomes necessary to make changes in this Protocol that do not affect substantive rights or obligations under the Treaty, they shall use the Bilateral Implementation Commission to reach agreement on such changes, without resorting to the procedure for making amendments set forth in Article VIII of the Treaty.

ARTICLE-BY-ARTICLE ANALYSIS OF THE EXHIBITIONS AND INSPECTIONS

Protocol

The Protocol on Exhibitions and Inspections (the Protocol) consists of a Preamble and two Sections and sets forth detailed procedures for the conduct of exhibitions of heavy bombers, as well as for the conduct of inspections conducted incident to those exhibitions.

Preamble

The Preamble links the Protocol to the basic rights and obligations with respect to heavy bomber exhibitions and inspections set forth in Article IV.

Section I—Exhibitions of Heavy Bombers

Section I provides for heavy bomber exhibitions that are different from the heavy bomber exhibitions required under the START Treaty. Paragraph 1 repeats the requirements of Article IV for three types of exhibitions:

> Exhibitions of heavy bombers equipped for nuclear armaments. Paragraph 4 of Article IV specifies that the purpose of such exhibitions is to demonstrate to the other Party the number of nuclear weapons for which a heavy bomber is actually equipped. Paragraph 5 of Article IV requires a similar exhibition if the number of nuclear weapons for which a heavy bomber is actually equipped is changed. (See the analysis accompanying Article IV for a discussion of the meaning of the phrase "number of nuclear weapons for which a heavy bomber is actually equipped.")
>
> Exhibitions of heavy bombers reoriented to a conventional role. Paragraph 12 of Article IV specifies that the purpose of such exhibitions is to demonstrate to the other Party the specified differences between such reoriented bombers and other heavy bombers of the same type or variant of a type with a nuclear role. Paragraph 8(d) of Article IV mandates that such differences be both observable by national technical means of verification and visible during on-site inspection.
>
> Exhibitions of heavy bombers reoriented to a conventional role and subsequently returned to a nuclear role. Such exhibitions serve both to demonstrate the number of nuclear weapons for which the heavy bomber being returned to a nuclear role is actually equipped and also to demonstrate the differences between the heavy bombers being returned and heavy bombers of the same type and variant that are either (a) still in a conventional role or (b) were never reoriented to such a role. Providing observable differences between heavy bombers returned to a nuclear role and those of the same type and variant that were never reoriented to a conventional role helps enforce the prohibition of paragraph 9 of Article IV against subsequently reorienting to a conventional role any heavy bomber returned to a nuclear role.

Paragraph 2 of Section I provides identical basic rules on location, date, duration, and inspection team composition for each of the three types of exhibitions. Pursuant to paragraph 1 of Article V, the procedures of the START Treaty apply to these exhibitions, except as modified by the Protocol.

Subparagraph 2(c) limits the time that each heavy bomber shall be subject to inspection to no more than two hours.

Subparagraph 2(d) requires that inspectors for these exhibitions be drawn from the list of START Treaty inspectors. The list referred to is that specified by Section II of the Inspection Protocol to the START Treaty, which also sets forth the legal status of such inspectors.

Subparagraph 2(e) requires the provision of certain photographs of observable differences. The number of such photographs is determined by the inspected Party, but the photograph or photographs provided must be sufficient to show all relevant differences.

Subparagraph 2(f) ensures that these exhibitions do not count against any START Treaty inspection quotas.

Section II—Inspections of Heavy Bombers

Section II provides rules for the inspections of heavy bombers during the exhibitions provided for in Section I. In addition, Section II provides additional procedures for data update inspections and new facility inspections conducted pursuant to the START Treaty beginning 180 days after the entry into force of the START II Treaty. New facility inspections are included since, under the provisions of Section VII of the Inspection Protocol to the START Treaty, such inspections include inspection of applicable heavy bombers at new air bases.

The delay of 180 days is to allow the initial exhibitions required by paragraph 4 of Article IV of the START II Treaty to be conducted. These exhibitions provide an initial demonstration of the number of nuclear weapons for which heavy bombers of a given type and variant are actually equipped. The additional inspection procedures for data update and new facility inspections allow periodic reconfirmation of this number.

The Protocol does not specify whether or not actual, simulated, or no weapons are to be used during these initial demonstrations. During the negotiations, U.S. negotiators told their Russian counterparts that U.S. heavy bombers would have either weapons or training shapes loaded on launchers, pylons, and bomb racks during the exhibitions in a way that demonstrated an operational load. The Russian negotiators were also told, however, that during data update and new facility inspections their inspectors would normally see heavy bombers without weapons. Since the United States has discontinued the practice of maintaining U.S. heavy bombers on peacetime alert, it is normal that these bombers not be loaded with weapons on a routine basis. The purpose of the additional inspection rights provided under this Protocol for data update and new facility inspections is fully satisfied by access to weapons bays and external weapons stations with no weapons loaded. The Parties understood during the negotiations that weapons bays are normally empty and that no requirement exists to load armaments for inspections.

Members of inspection teams conducting data update and new facility inspections pursuant to the START Treaty could be citizens of Belarus, Kazakhstan, or Ukraine, as well as of Russia. Although the START II Treaty is only between the United States and Russia, the United States intends to grant access to all members of such inspection teams without regard to nationality.

Subparagraph 1(a) covers inspections to confirm the number of nuclear weapons for which a specific heavy bomber is actually equipped does not exceed the number specified in the Memorandum on Attribution. The access inspectors are given is, therefore, limited to that necessary to accomplish the stated purpose. Provided that this requirement is met, the extent of access is at the discretion of the inspected Party. There is, for example, no requirement to give direct access to the underside of the wings of the B-2 heavy bomber in order to "prove" that no weapons are located there. The Parties agreed there would be no access to the interior of heavy bombers (except for weapons bays) because it is not required to fulfill the purpose of the inspection.

Subparagraph 1(b) covers inspections of heavy bombers reoriented to a conventional role in order to confirm the observable differences required by subparagraph 8(d) of Article IV. Once again, access is limited to those areas required to fulfill the purpose of the inspection.

Subparagraph 1(c) covers inspections of heavy bombers reoriented to a conventional role and subsequently returned to a nuclear role. In essence, inspections conducted pursuant to this subparagraph are a combination of those conducted pursuant to subparagraphs 1(a) and 1(b).

Paragraph 2 of Section II provides a right to shroud portions of a heavy bomber that are not subject to inspection. This right applies to any heavy bomber, but is primarily intended to protect the B-2 heavy bomber, as well as future advanced technology bombers. Shrouding time shall not count against the period of inspection. The "period allocated for inspection" refers both to the two hours allocated by subparagraph 2(c) of Section I of this Protocol for inspections during exhibitions, and to the maximum 32-hour period allowed by paragraph 31 of Section VI of the Inspection Protocol to the START Treaty for the conduct of data update or new facility inspections.

Since the Inspection Protocol to the START Treaty requires that inspectors return to the point of entry immediately following the allowed 32-hour period, there is a possible conflict between the two Treaties. In order to provide for the situation where a longer time would be required than allocated by the START Treaty, the United States will, if necessary, seek, in the Joint Compliance and Inspection Commission established by the START Treaty, the right to extend the period of inspection to allow for the completion of START II inspection procedures.

Paragraph 3 of Section II requires the in-country escort to provide explanations to the inspection team, for inspections conducted pursuant to subparagraph 1(a) or 1(c) of this Section, of the number of nuclear weapons for which the heavy bomber is actually equipped. Paragraph 3 of Section II also requires the in-country escort to provide explanations, for inspections conducted pursuant to subparagraph 1(b) or 1(c) of this Section, of the differences that are observable by NTM and visible during inspection.

A final provision provides that, pursuant to subparagraph 2(b) of Article V, additional measures may be agreed upon by the Parties with respect to the Protocol to improve the viability and effectiveness of the START II Treaty. The Parties agree that if changes need to be made to the Protocol that do not affect substantive rights or obligations under the START II Treaty, then such changes as are agreed upon shall be made within the framework of the Bilateral Implementation Commission (BIC), without resorting to the amendment procedures set forth in Article VII of the Treaty.

Pursuant to Article VI, the Protocol is deemed to be an integral part of the START II Treaty.

ARTICLE-BY-ARTICLE ANALYSIS OF THE MEMORANDUM ON ATTRIBUTION

The Memorandum on Attribution (MOA) consists of a Preamble and four Sections.

The MOA establishes the data base needed to record the following data:

> The number of nuclear weapons for which each heavy bomber of a type and a variant of a type equipped for nuclear weapons is actually equipped;
>
> The aggregate number of bomber weapons counted against the limits established in Article I of the Treaty;
>
> The numbers and locations for heavy bombers reoriented to a conventional role and for heavy bombers subsequently returned to a nuclear role;
>
> The differences observable to national technical means of verification for heavy bombers reoriented to a conventional role, and for heavy bombers reoriented to a conventional role that are subsequently returned to a nuclear role, which differentiate these two groups from each other and from heavy bombers of the same type and variant with nuclear roles that have never been reoriented;
>
> The number and location of ICBMs and SLBMs downloaded by amounts greater than allowed by the START Treaty, or ICBMs and SLBMs downloaded without destruction of the reentry vehicle platform;
>
> The number and location of heavy ICBM silos converted to carry single-RV ICBMs; and
>
> The number of heavy ICBMs eliminated and remaining to be eliminated.

Only Treaty-related data that differ from the data in the START Memorandum of Understanding are included in this Memorandum on Attribution; the Parties chose this approach to avoid duplication.

Unlike past arms control treaties, such as the START Treaty and the INF Treaty, the START II Treaty included almost no preliminary data at the time of signing. Instead, the Parties agreed to exchange data 30 days after entry into force, with the data effective as of the date of entry into force. This was done for four reasons. First, there was no immediate need for the data since the limits of the START II Treaty will not take effect for seven years. Second, because many data categories were not agreed until a few days before signature, exchange of preliminary data at signature would have been impractical. Third, much of the data will not exist until specific Treaty actions are taken. Finally, the data exchange associated with the START Treaty provides much of the baseline information necessary to implement the START II Treaty.

The one exception to the foregoing is the number of nuclear weapons for which heavy bombers are actually equipped. This data was exchanged effective as of the date of signature, both because it could not be derived from the START Treaty data and because of the central political importance of these data to the overall agreement.

Section I—Number of Warheads Attributed to Deployed Heavy Bombers Other Than Heavy Bombers Reoriented to a Conventional Role

Section I sets forth the number of warheads for which deployed heavy bombers (other than those reoriented to a conventional role) are actually equipped. Note that the number of warheads for which deployed heavy bombers are actually equipped is not an "agreed" or negotiated number, and the accuracy of the data provided is the responsibility of the Party owning the given heavy bomber. (See the analysis of Article IV of the Treaty for a discussion of the proper interpretation of the term "the number of warheads for which a heavy bomber is actually equipped.")

In addition, this Section provides a record of the aggregate number of warheads attributed to such heavy bombers. This aggregate number is derived by multiplying the number of deployed heavy bombers of a given type and variant (data found in the Memorandum of Understanding to the START Treaty) by the number of warheads for which such bombers are actually equipped.

As a legal matter, the inclusion of a summary of the provisions of Article IV on heavy bomber warhead attribution is redundant and therefore adds no new obligations. The provisions were included in the MOA at the request of Russia.

Under the START Treaty, older U.S. heavy bombers awaiting elimination at the Davis-Monthan conversion or elimination facility are included in the Memorandum of Understanding, since such bombers count against the START Treaty delivery vehicle and warhead totals. Since these older bombers will be eliminated before the expiration of the seven-year reductions period, when the first limits under START II must be reached, the number of nuclear weapons for which they are actually equipped was not included in the START II MOA.

The United States declared two different categories of B-52G heavy bombers under the START Treaty: a B-52G equipped for long-range nuclear ALCMs and a B-52G equipped for nuclear armaments other than long-range nuclear ALCMs. At the time of signature of the START II Treaty, all B-52Gs equipped for long-range nuclear ALCMs had been removed from operational service and were awaiting elimination at the Davis-Monthan Air Force Base elimination facility. Therefore, the United States listed only one variant—the B-52G—in the MOA. The United States stated that it would include the nuclear weapons attributed to all B-52Gs in the aggregate number of warheads attributed to heavy bombers to be provided 30 days after entry into force. The non-operational B52Gs at Davis-Monthan will only count at the START II attributed number of 12 only until those heavy bombers are actually eliminated.

Section II—Data on Heavy Bombers Reoriented to a Conventional Role and Heavy Bombers Reoriented to a Conventional Role That Have Subsequently Been Returned to a Nuclear Role

Section II provides a location for recording the aggregate number of heavy bombers reoriented to a conventional role and the bases at which they are located. These data are required in support of paragraph 8 of Article IV of the Treaty, which limits the aggregate number of heavy bombers reoriented to a conventional role to 100 and requires that they be based separately from heavy bombers with a nuclear role.

In addition, this Section allows the recording of observable differences—those between heavy bombers reoriented to a conventional role and other heavy bombers of the same type or variant with a nuclear role, and those between heavy bombers reoriented to a conventional role that have subsequently been returned to a nuclear role and heavy bombers which remain reoriented to a conventional role. In each case, each type or variant of a type of heavy bomber need have only one difference. These distinctions are required by paragraphs 8 and 9 of Article IV of the Treaty, respectively.

Since no heavy bombers have yet been reoriented to a conventional role, this Section is unlikely to contain any data when the first data exchange occurs 30 days after entry into force of the START II Treaty.

Section III—Data on Deployed ICBMs and Deployed SLBMs to Which a Reduced Number of Warheads is Attributed

Section III provides data on the numbers and locations of ICBMs and SLBMs downloaded under the provisions of Article III of the Treaty. The format is identical to that of Section III to the START Treaty Memorandum of Understanding; a separate listing in the Memorandum on Attribution is required since the downloading rules under the Treaty differ from those under the START Treaty.

Section IV—Data on Eliminated Heavy ICBMs and Converted Silo Launchers of Heavy ICBMs

Section IV provides data on the numbers and locations of heavy ICBM silos (in practice, silo launchers for Russian SS-18 ICBMs) which have been converted pursuant to the Elimination and Conversion Protocol. These data are required because of the limit of 90 such converted silos established in subparagraph 3(b) of Article II. Since the START Treaty requires that geographic coordinates not be released to the public, the locations referred to in this Section will be given by use of the silo designators found in the Memorandum of Understanding to the START Treaty that correspond to coordinate data in the Agreement on the Exchange of Geographic Coordinates and Site Diagrams Relating to the Treaty.

Section IV also provides data on the number of heavy ICBMs (in practice, Russian SS-18 ICBMs) which remain deployed in Russia, remain non-deployed in Russia, or have been eliminated. Such data are needed to measure progress toward the elimination of all heavy ICBMs mandated by paragraph 6 of Article II. See the Article-by-Article Analysis of the Treaty text for further discussion of heavy ICBMs located in Kazakhstan.

Although paragraph 6 of Article II of the Treaty requires the elimination of all launch canisters for heavy ICBMs (including empty launch canisters), the Parties elected not to include a separate listing for such canisters in the MOA. Launch canisters for heavy ICBMs will be eliminated as will the heavy ICBMs that they contained.

Since the United States has no heavy ICBMs, all U.S. data in this Section will be zero. The United States was included in this Section to meet the Russian request that the Treaty (and thus the MOA) be phrased in a neutral fashion with respect to the rights and obligations of the two Parties.

Section V—Changes

Section V requires each Party to notify the other of changes in the attribution and data contained in this Memorandum. Unlike the START Treaty, the START II Treaty does not prescribe in detail the specific content of notifications. Should the Parties wish to agree on specific content, they can do so within the framework of the Bilateral Implementation Commission.

The concluding paragraphs note that, in signing the Memorandum, the Parties accept the categories of data contained in the Memorandum. These paragraphs also provide that each Party is responsible for the accuracy only of its own data.

A final provision, like that in each Protocol, provides that, pursuant to subparagraph 2(b) of Article V of the Treaty, additional measures can be agreed upon by the Parties with respect to the Memorandum to improve the viability and effectiveness of the Treaty. The Parties agree that, if changes need to be made in the Memorandum that do not affect substantive rights or obligations under the Treaty, then such changes as are agreed upon shall be made within the framework of the Bilateral Implementation Commission (BIC), without resorting to the amendment procedures set forth in Article VII.

Pursuant to Article VI, the Memorandum on Attribution is deemed to be an integral part of the Treaty.

YELTSIN'S STATEMENT

Today the Presidents of the two great powers, the United States and Russia, have signed a treaty on further radical cuts in strategic offensive arms of Russia and the United States, . . .

In its scale and importance, the treaty goes further than all other treaties ever signed in the field of disarmament. This treaty is the triumph for politicians and diplomats of Russia and the United States. It is also an achievement for all mankind and benefits all peoples of the earth. The Start II treaty becomes the core of the system of global security guarantees....

From the very outset, the new democratic Russian state has been pursuing a policy of building equal partnership with the United States. Today we have every right to say that relations between the two major powers have undergone a genuine revolution....

We open up real prospects for cooperation based on trust between people in military uniform, between people with military discipline and military thinking. Thus the Start II treaty will change and gradually replace the very psychology of confrontation.

At the same time as President and Supreme Commander in Chief, I can say with absolute certainty the signed treaty strengthens the security of Russia rather than weakens it.... President Bush can make a similar statement concerning the security of the United States.

The implementation of the new treaty will not be economically destructive for Russia. We have made our ... calculations and they show that the proposed reductions would cost us much less than the mere maintenance of the nuclear weapons systems in a safe condition....

I would like to pay tribute to my colleague and friend, George. His remarkable personal and political qualities and competence have contributed to a successful transition from the cold war to a new world order.

I am grateful to him for all he has done to establish new relations between Russia and the United States, for his solidarity and support during the push for the Freedom Support Act, for the Start II treaty. Thank you, George.

I consider it of fundamental importance that the future President of the United States, Mr. Clinton, fully supported the conclusion of the Start II treaty. We can without delay proceed to the direct implementation of this instrument and consider further steps to strengthen global stability, the system of global protection and international security.

President Bush and I have maintained regular contacts with President-elect Clinton. Today's signing ceremony would not have taken place had there been the slightest reason to doubt his solidarity with our endeavors.

BUSH'S STATEMENT

Today, the cold war is over....

Mr. President, I salute you for your unwavering commitment to democratic reform and for the history you've written since the heroic day in August '91 when you climbed atop that tank to democratic destiny. And I also want to salute the heroism of the Russian people themselves, for it is they who will determine that Russia's democratic course is irreversible.

Today, we meet on Russian soil, home to 1,000 years of heritage and history, to a people rich in scientific and creative talent, I want to assure the Russian people on behalf of all Americans, we understand that Russia faces a difficult passage. We are with you in your struggle to strengthen and secure democratic rights, to reform your economy, to bring to every Russian city and village a new sense of hope and the prospect of a future forever free.

Let me say clearly, we seek no special advantage from Russia's transformation. Yes, deep arms reductions, broader and deeper economic ties, expanded trade with Russia, all are in the interest of my country. But they're equally in the interest of the Russian people....

EPA REPORT ON THE EFFECTS OF SECONDHAND SMOKE

January 7, 1993

Secondhand tobacco smoke is a potent carcinogen that kills at least 3,000 Americans annually, according to a report released January 7 by the U.S. Environmental Protection Agency. Secondhand smoke also causes a wide range of respiratory problems for up to 1 million children, the agency said.

The report, "Respiratory Health Effects of Passive Smoking: Lung Cancer and Other Disorders," was the latest in a string of scientific studies documenting the harm that smokers cause to nonsmokers. Between 1986 and 1992 the U.S. Surgeon General, the National Research Council of the National Academy of Sciences, the World Health Organization, and the National Institute of Occupational Safety and Health all concluded that secondhand smoke causes lung cancer and other respiratory problems in nonsmokers. The EPA's report, however, was the first to estimate how many people are harmed by secondhand smoke.

The report classified secondhand smoke as a Group A human carcinogen. This classification is reserved for those substances for which the evidence is strongest that they cause cancer in humans. Other Group A carcinogens include radon, asbestos, and benzene.

The EPA lacks the authority to impose regulations based on its report. However, the Occupational Safety and Health Administration, states, localities, and businesses were expected to use the study to support new restrictions on smoking in the workplace, restaurants, airports, and other public facilities. A growing number of such restrictions have been imposed in recent years.

The Tobacco Institute, the industry trade group, strongly criticized the report. The institute, which still disputes the overwhelming evidence that smoking causes lung cancer, said the EPA used a flawed statistical analysis and ignored evidence that the threat from secondhand smoke is small. Shortly after the report was released, the institute filed a federal suit challenging its findings.

The EPA report was not based on original research. Instead, it examined evidence from more than thirty studies of secondhand smoke conducted in eight countries.

In testimony before a House subcommittee on July 21, William Farland, director of EPA's Office of Health and Environmental Assessment, divided the 3,000 deaths per year from secondhand smoke by source. About 800 deaths occur among people exposed to smoke by their spouses, Farland said, while the other 2,200 occur among people exposed at work and in other public places.

"A Higher Level of Risk"

Secondhand smoke is one of the nation's most dangerous environmental hazards, Farland said. The increased risk of dying from lung cancer is about 1 in 10,000 from exposure to secondhand smoke outside the home, he said. That is a much higher level of risk than the EPA allows when it sets standards or regulations for other environmental hazards. "The increased lung cancer risks associated with exposure to environmental tobacco smoke are at least an order of magnitude greater than the cancer risks for virtually any other chemical or agent that EPA regulates," Farland said.

Virtually all Americans are exposed to secondhand tobacco smoke. Only two weeks after the EPA issued its report, the federal Centers for Disease Control and Prevention reported that the first 800 people examined in a huge federal study all had signs of nicotine in their bodies. "We really weren't expecting that," said James Pirkle of the CDC. The study included both people who had smoked and those who had not. Eventually, CDC researchers will examine 23,000 people over age four for signs of exposure to secondhand smoke.

On July 27 an article in the Journal of the American Medical Association *reported that workers in restaurants and bars face significantly increased risks for lung cancer because of patrons' cigarette smoke. The article, by Dr. Michael Siegel of the University of California at Berkeley, said that levels of secondhand smoke are 1.6 to 2.0 times higher in restaurants and 3.9 to 6.1 times higher in bars than in offices. "The epidemiological evidence suggested that there may be a 50 percent increase in lung cancer risk among food service workers that is in part attributable to tobacco smoke exposure in the workplace," Siegel wrote. To protect workers' health, Siegel said, smoking should be prohibited in bars and restaurants.*

Further EPA Recommendations

In her recommendations to Congress, EPA head Carol M. Browner did not go that far. While not advocating a smoking ban in public places, Browner told a House subcommittee on July 21 that businesses and other public places should take effective measures to ensure that nonsmokers are not exposed to tobacco smoke. "Simply separating smokers and non-smokers within the same area, such as a cafeteria, may reduce exposure, but non-smokers will still be exposed to recirculated smoke or smoke drifting into non-smoking areas," she said. Browner also recommended that people not smoke in their homes, especially if children are present.

In a related development, the CDC reported August 27 that the proportion of Americans who smoked rose slightly from 25.5 percent in 1990 to 25.7 percent in 1991. The unexpected increase was the first since the mid-1960s. Michael Eriksen, director of the CDC's Office on Smoking and Health, attributed the increase to the introduction of discount-brand cigarettes.

The encouraging news in the CDC's report was that the number of Americans who died from cigarette smoking fell from 434,000 in 1988 to 419,000 in 1990. It was the first decline in smoking deaths since the CDC started keeping records in 1985. Nonetheless, smoking continued to be responsible for one of every five deaths in the United States.

Following is an excerpt from "Respiratory Health Effects of Passive Smoking: Lung Cancer and Other Disorders," released January 7, 1993, by the U.S. Environmental Protection Agency:

[1. Summary and Conclusions]

1.2. Background

Tobacco smoking has long been recognized (e.g., U.S. Department of Health, Education, and Welfare [U.S. DHEW], 1964) as a major cause of mortality and morbidity, responsible for an estimated 434,000 deaths per year in the United States (Centers for Disease Control [CDC], 1991a). Tobacco use is known to cause cancer at various sites, in particular the lungs (U.S. Department of Health and Human Services [U.S. DHHS], 1982; International Agency for Research on Cancer [IARC], 1986). Smoking can also cause respiratory diseases (U.S. DHHS, 1984, 1989) and is a major risk factor for heart disease (U.S. DHHS, 1983). In recent years, there has been concern that nonsmokers may also be at risk for some of these health effects as a result of their exposure ("passive smoking") to the tobacco smoke that occurs in various environments occupied by smokers. Although this ETS [environmental tobacco smoke] is dilute compared with the mainstream smoke (MS) inhaled by active smokers, it is chemically similar, containing many of the same carcinogenic and toxic agents.

In 1986, the National Research Council (NRC) and the Surgeon General of the U.S. Public Health Service independently assessed the health effects of exposure to ETS (NRC, 1986; U.S. DHHS, 1986). Both of the 1986 reports conclude that ETS can cause lung cancer in adult nonsmokers and that children of parents who smoke have increased frequency of respiratory symptoms and acute lower respiratory tract infections, as well as evidence of reduced lung function.

More recent epidemiologic studies of the potential associations between ETS and lung cancer in nonsmoking adults and between ETS and noncancer respiratory effects more than double the size of the database available for analysis from that of the 1986 reports. This EPA report critically reviews the current database on the respiratory health effects of passive smoking; these data are utilized to develop a hazard identification for ETS and to make quantitative estimates of the public health impacts of ETS for lung cancer and various other respiratory diseases.

The weight-of-evidence analysis for the lung cancer hazard identification is developed in accordance with U.S. EPA's *Guidelines for Carcinogen Risk Assessment* (U.S. EPA, 1986a) and established principles for evaluating epidemiologic studies. The analysis considers animal bioassays and genotoxicity studies, as well as biological measurements of human uptake of tobacco smoke components and epidemiologic data on active and passive smoking. The availability of abundant and consistent human data, especially human data at actual environmental levels of exposure to the specific agent (mixture) of concern, allows a hazard identification to be made with a high degree of certainty. The conclusive evidence of the dose-related lung carcinogenicity of MS in active smokers (Chapter 4), coupled with information on the chemical similarities of MS and ETS and evidence of ETS uptake in nonsmokers (Chapter 3), is sufficient by itself to establish ETS as a known human lung carcinogen, or "Group A" carcinogen under U.S. EPA's carcinogen classification system. In addition, this document concludes that the overall results of 30 epidemiologic studies on lung cancer and passive smoking (Chapter 5), using spousal smoking as a surrogate of ETS exposure for female never-smokers, similarly justify a Group A classification.

The weight-of-evidence analyses for the noncancer respiratory effects are based primarily on a review of epidemiologic studies (Chapter 7). Most of the endpoints examined are respiratory disorders in children, where parental smoking is used as a surrogate of ETS exposure. For the noncancer respiratory effects in nonsmoking adults, most studies used spousal smoking as an exposure surrogate. A causal association was concluded to exist for a number of respiratory disorders where there was sufficient consistent evidence for a biologically plausible association with ETS that could not be explained by bias, confounding, or chance. The fact that the database consists of human evidence from actual environmental exposure levels gives a high degree of confidence in this conclusion. Where there was suggestive but inconclusive evidence of causality, as was the case for asthma induction in children, ETS was concluded to be a risk factor for that endpoint. Where data were inconsistent or inadequate for evaluation of an association, as for acute upper respiratory tract infections and acute middle ear infections in children, no conclusions were drawn.

This report also has attempted to provide estimates of the extent of the public health impact, where appropriate, in terms of numbers of ETS-attributable cases in nonsmoking subpopulations. Unlike for qualitative hazard identification assessments, where information from many sources adds to the confidence in a weight-of-evidence conclusion, for quantitative risk assessments, the usefulness of studies usually depends on how closely the study population resembles nonsmoking segments of the general population. For lung cancer estimates among U.S. nonsmokers, the substantial epidemiology database of ETS and lung cancer among U.S. female never-smokers was considered to provide the most appropriate information. From these U.S. epidemiology studies, a pooled relative risk estimate was calculated and used in the derivation of the population risk estimates. The large number of studies available, the generally consistent results, and the condition of actual environmental levels of exposure increase the confidence in these estimates. Even under these circumstances, however, uncertainties remain, such as in the use of questionnaires and current biomarker measurements to estimate past exposure, assumptions of exposure-response linearity, and extrapolation to male never-smokers and to ex-smokers. Still, given the strength of the evidence for the lung carcinogenicity of tobacco smoke and the extensive human database from actual environmental exposure levels, fewer assumptions are necessary than is usual in EPA quantitative risk assessments, and confidence in these estimates is rated medium to high.

Population estimates of ETS health impacts are also made for certain noncancer respiratory endpoints in children, specifically lower respiratory tract infections (i.e., pneumonia, bronchitis, and bronchiolitis) and episodes and severity of attacks of asthma. Estimates of ETS-attributable cases of LRI in infants and young children are thought to have a high degree of confidence because of the consistent study findings and the appropriateness of parental smoking as a surrogate measure of exposure in very young children. Estimates of the number of asthmatic children whose condition is aggravated by exposure to ETS are less certain than those for LRIs because of different measures of outcome in various studies and because of increased extraparental exposure to ETS in older children. Estimates of the number of new cases of asthma in previously asymptomatic children also have less confidence because at this time the weight of evidence for asthma induction . . . is not conclusive.

Most of the ETS population impact estimates are presented in terms of ranges, which are thought to reflect reasonable assumptions about the estimates of parameters and variables required for the extrapolation models. The validity of the ranges is also dependent on the appropriateness of the extrapolation models themselves.

While this report focuses only on the respiratory health effects of passive smoking, there also may be other health effects of concern. Recent analyses of more than a dozen epidemiology and toxicology studies (e.g., Steenland, 1992; National Institute for Occupational Safety and Health [NIOSH], 1991) suggest that ETS exposure may be a risk factor for cardiovascular disease. In addition, a few studies in the literature link ETS exposure to cancers of other sites; at this time, that database appears inadequate for any conclusion. This report does not develop an analysis of either the nonrespiratory cancer or the heart disease data and takes no position on whether ETS is a risk factor for these diseases. If it is, the total public health impact from ETS will be greater than that discussed here.

1.3. Primary Findings

A. Lung Cancer in Nonsmoking Adults

1. Passive smoking is causally associated with lung cancer in adults, and ETS, by the total weight of evidence, belongs in the category of compounds classified by EPA as Group A (known human) carcinogens.
2. Approximately 3,000 lung cancer deaths per year among nonsmokers (never-smokers and former smokers) of both sexes are estimated to be attributable to ETS in the United States. While there are statistical and modeling uncertainties in this estimate, and the true number may be higher or lower, the assumptions used in this analysis would tend to underestimate the actual population risk. The overall confidence in this estimate is medium to high.

B. Noncancer Respiratory Diseases and Disorders

1. Exposure of children to ETS from parental smoking is causally associated with:
   a. increased prevalence of respiratory symptoms of irritation (cough, sputum, and wheeze),
   b. increased prevalence of middle ear effusion (a sign of middle ear disease), and
   c. a small but statistically significant reduction in lung function as tested by objective measures of lung capacity.
2. ETS exposure of young children and particularly infants from parental (and especially mother's) smoking is causally associated with an increased risk of LRIs (pneumonia, bronchitis, and bronchiolitis). This report estimates that exposure to ETS contributes 150,000 to 300,000 LRIs annually in infants and children less than 18 months of age, resulting in 7,500 to 15,000 hospitalizations. The confidence in the estimates of LRIs is high. Increased risks for LRIs continue, but are lower in magnitude, for children until about age 3; however, no estimates are derived for children over 18 months.
3. a. Exposure to ETS is causally associated with additional episodes and increased severity of asthma in children who already have the disease. This report estimates that ETS exposure exacerbates symptoms in approximately 20% of this country's

2 million to 5 million asthmatic children and is a major aggravating factor in approximately 10%.

b. In addition, the epidemiologic evidence is suggestive but not conclusive that ETS exposure increases the number of new cases of asthma in children who have not previously exhibited symptoms. Based on this evidence and the known ETS effects on both the immune system and lungs (e.g., atopy and airway hyperresponsiveness), this report concludes that ETS is a risk factor for the induction of asthma in previously asymptomatic children. Data suggest that relatively high levels of exposure are required to induce new cases of asthma in children. This report calculates that previously asymptomatic children exposed to ETS from mothers who smoke at least 10 cigarettes per day will exhibit an estimated 8,000 to 26,000 new cases of asthma annually. The confidence in this range is medium and is dependent on the conclusion that ETS is a risk factor for asthma induction.

4. Passive smoking has subtle but significant effects on the respiratory health of nonsmoking adults, including coughing, phlegm production, chest discomfort, and reduced lung function.

This report also has reviewed data on the relationship of maternal smoking and sudden infant death syndrome (SIDS), which is thought to involve some unknown respiratory pathogenesis. The report concludes that while there is strong evidence that infants whose mothers smoke are at an increased risk of dying from SIDS, available studies do not allow us to differentiate whether and to what extent this increase is related to in utero versus postnatal exposure to tobacco smoke products. Consequently, this report is unable to assert whether or not ETS exposure by itself is a risk factor for SIDS independent of smoking during pregnancy.

Regarding an association of parental smoking with either upper respiratory tract infections (colds and sore throats) or acute middle ear infections in children, this report finds the evidence inconclusive.

CHEMICAL WEAPONS TREATY
January 13, 1993

Culminating a twenty-year effort, delegates from more than 120 nations in January began initialing a treaty banning the production, stockpiling, and use of chemical weapons over a ten-year period. The landmark agreement marked the first time an entire class of weapons of mass destruction was banned. In addition to mustard gas and nerve gas, the treaty prohibited the use of herbicides and riot-control agents during warfare. The treaty—entitled the Convention on the Prohibition of the Development, Production, Stockpiling and Use of Chemical Weapons and on Their Destruction—would go into effect 180 days after sixty-five nations ratified it, but not before January 1995. The signing ceremonies occurred over a several-day period, beginning January 13, at the Paris headquarters of the United Nations Educational, Scientific and Cultural Organization, with the U.S. and Russian delegations among the first to sign. By August 1993, 147 nations had signed the pact.

The United States has about 60,000 tons of the weapons, and Russia about 40,000 tons—by far the largest arsenals. Both were given a five-year extension to destroy the stockpiles, a process that was expected to cost the United States more than $8 billion. Western nations agreed to provide Russia with technical and financial assistance to dispose of its weapons. It was estimated that their destruction could cost $10 billion and take more than ten years.

Previous Use of Chemical Weapons

The first use of a chemical weapon, mustard gas, on a massive scale occurred during World War I. It killed an estimated 100,000 persons and maimed another million. Responding to these atrocities, a number of nations negotiated the 1925 Geneva Protocol that banned the use of chemical weapons; however, the pact was not global and did not contain sanctions or verification procedures.

Although negotiations on the chemical weapons convention began in 1968, they took on a sense of urgency in 1988 after poison gas was used to kill about 5,000 Kurds in northern Iraq. It was uncertain whether Iraq or Iran, which were at war with one another, was responsible for the attack. After Iraq threatened to use chemical weapons against Israel, the UN Security Council adopted resolutions requiring the government to begin destroying its arsenal, subject to international supervision.

Despite Accord, Signing Not Unanimous

Applauding the convention as a "decisive advance in history for which the entire international community can take credit," UN Secretary General Boutros Boutros-Ghali characterized chemical weapons as one of the most gruesome methods of inflicting "terror, pain, and suffering." The secretary general said, "We are here to say that we will no longer accept such atrocities. This treaty bans weapons that are not only extremely dangerous but less expensive than others ... which has allowed them to spread easily throughout the world." The weapons were also relatively easy to produce. Intelligence agencies had estimated that between fourteen and twenty nations had stockpiles of the deadly toxins. Among those nations were China, India, Pakistan, Iran, and Israel, all of which agreed to abide by the treaty.

Syria and North Korea, nations that were generally believed to have chemical weapons stockpiles, refused to sign the accord. So, too, did Iraq, the only nation besides the United States and Russia to acknowledge producing the weapons. Shortly before the signing ceremonies, the twenty-two-member Arab League called for a boycott of the treaty on the grounds that Israel possessed a nuclear arsenal. However, a number of nations broke ranks and said they would abide by the terms of the convention. Among those signing the pact were Algeria, Mauritania, Morocco, and Tunisia. Kuwait, Jordan, Lebanon, Oman, Yemen, and—surprisingly—Libya (which was thought to possess the capability to manufacture the weapons) were expected to follow suit. Egypt and Saudi Arabia upheld the boycott, despite an appeal by U.S. Secretary of State Lawrence S. Eagleburger to "seize this opportunity" as one stage in "making the Middle East a zone free of all weapons of mass destruction." Israeli Foreign Minister Shimon Peres echoed Eagleburger in calling on all Arab nations to construct "a mutually verifiable zone, free of surface-to-surface missiles and of chemical, biological, and nuclear weapons." However, he stopped short of agreeing to Arab demands that Israel allow international inspection of its nuclear plants.

French President François Mitterrand said action on the chemical ban should be replicated with regard to nuclear disarmament. He restated his government's pledge to ban nuclear testing so long as the United States and Russia did likewise. Other observers suggested that a similar pact be negotiated on biological weapons; although a 1972 convention banned their use, it lacked a system of verification and sanctions.

Tough Sanctions, On-Site Inspection

The chemical convention prescribed a uniquely rigorous inspection and verification process that covered twenty-nine toxic chemicals in four categories—blister, nerve, choking, and blood agents. A new body, the Organization for the Prohibition of Chemical Weapons, would be established in The Hague to conduct routine checks on compliance, including inspecting chemical weapons destruction sites and civilian chemical plants. A signatory could demand spot inspections of a participating country believed to be in violation. A country found in violation would be subject to sanctions. International inspectors would have the power to quarantine an area within forty-eight hours to prevent the possibility of smuggling out chemical weapons. Britain had sought even more stringent policing measures but gave up on its lobbying because, according to a number of observers, the Bush administration wanted to have the accord ready for signature before the president left office.

Some negotiators said a major test of the treaty's effectiveness would be whether nonsignatories, who would face stringent international sanctions against their procurement of chemicals or technology that could advance their production of chemical weapons, could be persuaded to join.

Following are excerpts from the Convention on the Prohibition of the Development, Production, Stockpiling and Use of Chemical Weapons and on Their Destruction, signed beginning January 13, 1993:

Preamble

The States Parties to this Convention,

Determined to act with a view to achieving effective progress towards general and complete disarmament under strict and effective international control, including the prohibition and elimination of all types of weapons of mass destruction,

Desiring to contribute to the realization of the purposes and principles of the Charter of the United Nations,

Recalling that the General Assembly of the United Nations has repeatedly condemned all actions contrary to the principles and objectives of the Protocol for the Prohibition of the Use in War of Asphyxiating, Poisonous or Other Gases, and of Bacteriological Methods of Warfare, signed at Geneva on 17 June 1925 (the Geneva Protocol of 1925),

Recognizing that this Convention reaffirms principles and objectives of and obligations assumed under the Geneva Protocol of 1925, and the Convention on the Prohibition of the Development, Production and Stockpiling of Bacteriological (Biological) and Toxin Weapons and on their Destruction signed at London, Moscow and Washington on 10 April 1972,

Bearing in mind the objective contained in Article IX of the Convention on the Prohibition of the Development, Production and Stockpiling of Bacteriological (Biological) and Toxin Weapons and on their Destruction,

Determined for the sake of all mankind, to exclude completely the possibility of the use of chemical weapons, through the implementation of the provisions of this Convention, thereby complementing the obligations assumed under the Geneva Protocol of 1925,

Recognizing the prohibition, embodied in the pertinent agreements and relevant principles of international law, of the use of herbicides as a method of warfare,

Considering that achievements in the field of chemistry should be used exclusively for the benefit of mankind,

Desiring to promote free trade in chemicals as well as international cooperation and exchange of scientific and technical information in the field of chemical activities for purposes not prohibited under this Convention in order to enhance the economic and technological development of all States Parties,

Convinced that the complete and effective prohibition of the development, production, acquisition, stockpiling, retention, transfer and use of chemical weapons, and their destruction, represent a necessary step towards the achievement of these common objectives,

Have agreed as follows: . . .

Article I

General Obligations

1. Each State Party to this Convention undertakes never under any circumstances:
   (a) To develop, produce, otherwise acquire, stockpile or retain chemical weapons, or transfer, directly or indirectly, chemical weapons to anyone;
   (b) To use chemical weapons;
   (c) To engage in any military preparations to use chemical weapons;
   (d) To assist, encourage or induce, in any way, anyone to engage any activity prohibited to a State Party under this Convention.
2. Each State Party undertakes to destroy chemical weapons it owns or possesses, or that are located in any place under its jurisdiction or control, in accordance with the provisions of this Convention.
3. Each State Party undertakes to destroy all chemical weapons it abandoned on the territory of another State Party, in accordance with the provisions of this Convention.
4. Each State Party undertakes to destroy any chemical weapons production facilities it owns or possesses, or that are located in any place under its jurisdiction or control, in accordance with the provisions of this Convention.

5. Each State Party undertakes not to use riot control agents as a method of warfare. . . .

[Article II omitted]

Article III

Declarations

1. Each State Party shall submit to the Organization, not later than 30 days after this Convention enters into force for it, the following declarations, in which it shall:
   (a) With respect to chemical weapons:
      (i) Declare whether it owns or possesses any chemical weapons, or whether there are any chemical weapons located in any place under its jurisdiction or control;
      (ii) Specify the precise location, aggregate quantity and detailed inventory of chemical weapons it owns or possesses, or that are located in any place under its jurisdiction or control. . . ;
      (iii) Report any chemical weapons on its territory that are owned and possessed by another State and located in any place under the jurisdiction or control of another State. . . ;
      (iv) Declare whether it has transferred or received, directly or indirectly, any chemical weapons since 1 January 1946 and specify the transfer or receipt of such weapons. . . ;
      (v) Provide its general plan for destruction of chemical weapons that it owns or possesses, or that are located in any place under its jurisdiction or control. . . .

[Articles IV-VII omitted]

Article VIII

The Organization

A. General Provisions

1. The States Parties to this Convention hereby establish the Organization for the Prohibition of Chemical Weapons to achieve the object and purpose of this Convention, to ensure the implementation of its provisions, including those for international verification of compliance with it, and to provide a forum for consultation and cooperation among States Parties.
2. All States Parties to this Convention shall be members of the Organization. A State Party shall not be deprived of its membership in the Organization.
3. The seat of the Headquarters of the Organization shall be The Hague, Kingdom of the Netherlands.
4. There are hereby established as the organs of the Organization: the

Conference of the States Parties, the Executive Council, and the Technical Secretariat.

5. The Organization shall conduct its verification activities provided for under this Convention in the least intrusive manner possible consistent with the timely and efficient accomplishment of their objectives. It shall request only the information and data necessary to fulfill its responsibilities under this Convention. It shall take every precaution to protect the confidentiality of information on civil and military activities and facilities coming to its knowledge in the implementation of this Convention and, in particular, shall abide by the provisions set forth in the Confidentiality Annex.
6. In undertaking its verification activities the Organization shall consider measures to make use of advances in science and technology.
7. The costs of the Organization's activities shall be paid by States Parties in accordance with the United Nations scale of assessment adjusted to take into account differences in membership between the United Nations and this Organization....

[IX]

Procedures for challenge inspections

8. Each State Party has the right to request an on-site challenge inspection of any facility or location in the territory or in any other place under the jurisdiction or control of any other State Party for the sole purpose of clarifying and resolving any questions concerning possible non-compliance with the provisions of this Convention, and to have this inspection conducted anywhere without delay by an inspection team designated by the Director-General and in accordance with the Verification Annex.
9. Each State Party is under the obligation to keep the inspection request within the scope of this Convention and to provide in the inspection request all appropriate information on the basis of which a concern has arisen regarding possible non-compliance with this Convention as specified in the Verification Annex. Each State Party shall refrain from unfounded inspection requests, care being taken to avoid abuse. The challenge inspection shall be carried out for the sole purpose of determining facts relating to the possible non-compliance.
10. For the purpose of verifying compliance with the provisions of this Convention, each State Party shall permit the Technical Secretariat to conduct the on-site challenge inspection pursuant to paragraph 8.
11. Pursuant to a request for a challenge inspection of a facility or location, and in accordance with the procedures provided for in the Verification Annex, the inspected State Party shall have:

(a) The right and the obligation to make every reasonable effort to demonstrate its compliance with this Convention and, to this end, to enable the inspection team to fulfill its mandate;
(b) The obligation to provide access within the requested site for the sole purpose of establishing facts relevant to the concern regarding possible non-compliance; and
(c) The right to take measures to protect sensitive installations, and to prevent disclosure of confidential information and data, not related to this Convention.

12. With regard to an observer, the following shall apply:
    (a) The requesting State Party may, subject to the agreement of the inspected State Party, send a representative who may be a national either of the requesting State Party or of a third State Party, to observe the conduct of the challenge inspection.
    (b) The inspected State Party shall then grant access to the observer in accordance with the Verification Annex.
    (c) The inspected State Party shall, as a rule, accept the proposed observer, but if the inspected State Party exercises a refusal, that fact shall be recorded in the final report.
13. The requesting State Party shall present an inspection request for an on-site challenge inspection to the Executive Council and at the same time to the Director-General for immediate processing.
14. The Director-General shall immediately ascertain that the inspection request meets the requirements specified in Part X, paragraph 4, of the Verification Annex, and, if necessary, assist the requesting State Party in filing the inspection request accordingly. When the inspection request fulfills the requirements, preparations for the challenge inspection shall begin.
15. The Director-General shall transmit the inspection request to the inspected State Party not less than 12 hours before the planned arrival of the inspection team at the point of entry.
16. After having received the inspection request, the Executive Council shall take cognizance of the Director-General's actions on the request and shall keep the case under its consideration throughout the inspection procedure. However, its deliberations shall not delay the inspection process.
17. The Executive Council may, not later than 12 hours after having received the inspection request, decide by a three-quarter majority of all its members against carrying out the challenge inspection, if it considers the inspection request to be frivolous, abusive or clearly beyond the scope of this Convention as described in paragraph 8. Neither the requesting nor the inspected State Party shall participate in such a decision. If the Executive Council decides against the challenge inspection, preparations shall be stopped, no further action on the inspection request shall be taken, and the States Parties concerned shall be informed accordingly. . . .

[Articles X-XIX omitted]

Article XX

Accession

Any State which does not sign this Convention before its entry into force may accede to it at any time thereafter.

Article XXI

Entry into Force

1. This Convention shall enter into force 180 days after the date of the deposit of the 65th instrument of ratification, but in no case earlier than two years after its opening for signature.
2. For States whose instruments of ratification or accession are deposited subsequent to the entry into force of this Convention, it shall enter into force on the 30th day following the date of deposit of their instrument of ratification or accession....

[Annex]

Inspections and visits

44. The particular storage facility to be inspected shall be chosen by the Technical Secretariat in such a way as to preclude the prediction of precisely when the facility is to be inspected. The guidelines for determining the frequency of systematic on-site inspections shall be elaborated by the Technical Secretariat, taking into account the recommendations to be considered and approved by the Conference....
45. The Technical Secretariat shall notify the inspected State Party of its decision to inspect or visit the storage facility 48 hours before the planned arrival of the inspection team at the facility for systematic inspections or visits. In cases of inspections or visits to resolve urgent problems, this period may be shortened. The Technical Secretariat shall specify the purpose of the inspection or visit.
46. The inspected State Party shall make any necessary preparations for arrival of the inspectors and shall ensure their expeditious transportation from their point of entry to the storage facility. The facility agreement will specify administrative arrangements for inspectors.
47. The inspected State Party shall provide the inspection team upon its arrival at the chemical weapons storage facility to carry out an inspection, with the following data on the facility:
    (a) The number of storage buildings and storage locations;
    (b) For each storage building and storage location, the type and the identification number or designation, shown on the site diagram; and

(c) For each storage building and storage location at the facility, the number of items of each specific type of chemical weapon, and, for containers that are not part of binary munitions, the actual quantity of chemical fill in each container. . . .

70. Inspectors shall, in accordance with facility agreements:

(a) Have unimpeded access to all parts of the chemical weapons destruction facilities and the chemical weapons storage facilities located at such facilities, including any munitions, devices, bulk containers, or other containers, therein. The items to be inspected shall be chosen by the inspectors in accordance with the verification plan that has been agreed to by the inspected State Party and approved by the Executive Council. . . .

SUPREME COURT ON SENATE IMPEACHMENT POWERS

January 13, 1993

In a landmark ruling on congressional impeachment powers, the Supreme Court on January 13 upheld the Senate's authority to carry out impeachment trials as it saw fit. The unanimous decision effectively upheld the removal in 1989 of U.S. District Judge Walter L. Nixon, Jr., who had been convicted of perjury by a criminal court. Nixon challenged his subsequent impeachment conviction because the Senate had used a twelve-member panel, rather than the full body, to gather evidence for the trial.

The Supreme Court held that courts had no standing to review impeachment proceedings because the Constitution granted the Senate the "sole power" to try those cases. The ruling in Nixon v. United States *was the first time the Court had ruled directly on Congress's impeachment powers. In concluding that congressional impeachment proceedings were off-limits to judicial review, the Court relinquished an opportunity to enlarge the judiciary's powers to oversee the legislative branch of government.*

Background and Ruling

Nixon's case centered on a 1935 Senate rule that allowed the chamber to use a twelve-member committee to gather evidence in impeachment trials and report the results, but not recommendations, to the full Senate. The rule was first used during the 1986 impeachment trial of U.S. District Judge Harry E. Claiborne, who was convicted and removed after unsuccessfully challenging the procedure in the lower courts. At that time, several other judicial impeachment cases were working their way to the Senate, and a number of members feared that other, more pressing Senate business would be put on hold if the entire body had to spend weeks engulfed in a fact-finding process.

David O. Stewart, Nixon's lawyer, had argued that the committee rule violated the constitutional directive that the Senate "try" impeachment cases. Stewart said a fair trial required that all the "jurors" hear the evidence. A federal district court and, subsequently, an appeals court had refused to address the merits of the challenge, ruling that the case presented a "political question" that should not be resolved by the courts. But the Supreme Court agreed to examine two aspects of the case: first, whether the courts had a right to review impeachment proceedings and, second, whether the use of an evidence panel represented an unconstitutional shortcut.

Writing the majority opinion, Chief Justice William H. Rehnquist said that the Constitution's directive that the Senate try impeachment cases did not carry with it specific requirements for such proceedings. Judicial review of impeachment trials would upset the system of checks and balances among the branches of government, he argued. "Judicial involvement in impeachment proceedings, even if only for purposes of judicial review, is counterintuitive because it would eviscerate the 'important constitutional check' placed on the Judiciary by the Framers" of the Constitution.

Rehnquist also noted practical obstacles to allowing court review of impeachment proceedings, saying it could create political disorder by throwing impeachment convictions into question indefinitely. Five of the justices, John Paul Stevens, Sandra Day O'Connor, Antonin Scalia, Anthony M. Kennedy, and Clarence Thomas, joined Rehnquist's opinion.

Justices Harry A. Blackmun, Byron R. White, and David H. Souter argued that courts should have an oversight role in impeachment trials, but they nonetheless upheld Nixon's conviction. In a separate opinion, White and Blackmun said that the judiciary did have a role in ensuring the fairness of Senate impeachment proceedings. "In a truly balanced system, Senate impeachment trials would serve as a check on the judicial branch even as judicial review would ensure that the Senate adhered to a minimal set of procedural standards," White wrote. However, the two justices rejected the substance of Nixon's appeal, holding that the Senate was within its rights to use a special panel to gather evidence. "Textual and historical evidence reveals that the impeachment trial clause was not meant to bind the hands of the Senate beyond establishing a set of minimal procedures," White wrote.

Souter offered a more limited qualification to the majority opinion, agreeing that the courts had no grounds to review Nixon's impeachment trial but arguing that judicial scrutiny might be warranted in extreme cases—for example, if the Senate resorted to a "coin toss" to decide an impeachment charge.

Impact on Other Cases and Reaction

The Court's ruling on Nixon might have a bearing on the case of Rep. Alcee L. Hastings, D-Fla., who was impeached and convicted by

Congress in 1989, when he was a judge, under the same procedures. Hastings had been charged with accepting a bribe from a lawyer but was acquitted after a jury trial. U.S. District Judge Stanley Sporkin overturned Hastings's impeachment conviction because the full Senate did not gather the evidence. But Sporkin stayed his own ruling pending appeal, predicting that the matter would be settled by the Supreme Court. With the Nixon ruling in hand, it appeared that the appeals court would have justification to reverse Sporkin's decision.

Terence J. Anderson, Hastings's lawyer, said his client, who was acquitted in criminal court, still deserved to have his impeachment conviction reversed. However, Hastings predicted that the appeals court would reinstate his conviction. The ruling was not expected to affect Hastings's status as a new member of Congress. On January 4, a federal judge rejected a lawsuit claiming that Hastings's conviction disqualified him from holding office.

Historically, the Senate has held separate votes to convict an impeached official and to disqualify him from holding another office. In Hastings's case, the Senate took no vote on the disqualification. "I don't think anyone in the world now has jurisdiction" to challenge Hastings's status, said Anderson, a professor at the University of Miami's law school. "Congressman Hastings is Congressman Hastings."

Michael Davidson, the Senate's legal counsel, said he was pleased that the majority opinion affirmed the Senate's independence on impeachment proceedings, while White and Blackmun endorsed its specific methods. Two other federal judges had recently been convicted of crimes, and the Nixon decision removed the specter of seeing the entire Senate tied up in lengthy impeachment proceedings.

Moreover, some observers pointed out that the use of an evidence-gathering committee might improve fairness because panel members would feel strong individual responsibility about and commitment to their task. Davidson observed that when the full Senate was charged with taking evidence, information was sometimes presented to a near-empty chamber.

Lawmakers are also concerned with the system as it functions now. Senator Howell Heflin of Alabama, a Democrat who sits on the Judiciary Committee, is among those who have agreed in favor of creating a new system to remove federal judges. In 1990, after watching the Hastings and Nixon trials, Heflin wrote that the many demands on senators' time "preclude them from thoughtfully considering the evidence presented at an impeachment trial."

Following are excerpts from the majority opinion on Senate impeachment powers in the case of Nixon v. United States, *written by Chief Justice William H. Rehnquist; a separate concurring opinion by Justices Byron R. White and Harry A. Blackmun; and a separate concurring opinion by Justice David H. Souter:*

No. 91-740

Walter L. Nixon, Petitioner *v.* United States et al.	On writ of certiorari to the United States Court of Appeals for the District of Columbia Circuit

[January 13, 1993]

CHIEF JUSTICE REHNQUIST delivered the opinion of the Court.

Petitioner Walter L. Nixon, Jr., asks this court to decide whether Senate Rule XI, which allows a committee of Senators to hear evidence against an individual who has been impeached and to report that evidence to the full Senate, violates the Impeachment Trial Clause, Art. I, § 3, cl 6. That Clause provides that the "Senate shall have the sole Power to try all Impeachments." But before we reach the merits of such a claim, we must decide whether it is "justiciable," that is, whether it is a claim that may be resolved by the courts. We conclude that it is not.

Nixon, a former Chief Judge of the United States District Court for the Southern District of Mississippi, was convicted by a jury of two counts of making false statements before a federal grand jury and sentenced to prison. See *United States* v. *Nixon* (CA5 1987). The grand jury investigation stemmed from reports that Nixon had accepted a gratuity from a Mississippi businessman in exchange for asking a local district attorney to halt the prosecution of the businessman's son. Because Nixon refused to resign from his office as a United States District Judge, he continued to collect his judicial salary while serving out his prison sentence.

On May 10, 1989, the House of Representatives adopted three articles of impeachment for high crimes and misdemeanors. The first two articles charged Nixon with giving false testimony before the grand jury and the third article charged him with bringing disrepute on the Federal Judiciary.

After the House presented the articles to the Senate, the Senate voted to invoke its own Impeachment Rule XI, under which the presiding officer appoints a committee of Senators to "receive evidence and take testimony." The Senate committee held four days of hearings, during which 10 witnesses, including Nixon, testified. Pursuant to Rule XI, the committee presented the full Senate with a complete transcript of the proceeding and a report stating the uncontested facts and summarizing the evidence on the contested facts. Nixon and the House impeachment managers submitted extensive final briefs to the full Senate and delivered arguments from the Senate floor during the three hours set aside for oral argument in front of that body. Nixon himself gave a personal appeal, and several Senators posed questions directly to both parties. The Senate voted by more than the constitutionally required two-thirds majority to convict Nixon on the first two articles. The presiding officer then entered judgment removing Nixon from his office as United States District Judge.

Nixon thereafter commenced the present suit, arguing that Senate Rule XI violates the constitutional grant of authority to the Senate to "try" all impeachments because it prohibits the whole Senate from taking part in the evidentiary hearings. Nixon sought a declaratory judgment that his impeachment conviction was void and that his judicial salary and privileges should be reinstated. The District Court held that his claim was nonjusticiable, and the Court of Appeals for the District of Columbia Circuit agreed.

A controversy is nonjusticiable—*i.e.*, involves a political question—where there is "a textually demonstrable constitutional commitment of the issue to a coordinate political department; or a lack of judicially discoverable and manageable standards for resolving it. . . ." *Baker* v. *Carr* (1962). But the courts must, in the first instance, interpret the text in question and determine whether and to what extent the issue is textually committed. . . . As the discussion that follows makes clear, the concept of a textual commitment to a coordinate political department is not completely separate from the concept of a lack of judicially discoverable and manageable standards for resolving it; the lack of judicially manageable standards may strengthen the conclusion that there is a textually demonstrable commitment to a coordinate branch.

In this case, we must examine Art. I, § 3, cl. 6, to determine the scope of authority conferred upon the Senate by the Framers regarding impeachment. It provides:

> "The Senate shall have the sole Power to try all Impeachments. When sitting for that Purpose, they shall be on Oath or Affirmation. When the President of the United States is tried, the Chief Justice shall preside: And no Person shall be convicted without the Concurrence of two thirds of the Members present."

The language and structure of this Clause are revealing. The first sentence is a grant of authority to the Senate, and the word "sole" indicates that this authority is reposed in the Senate and nowhere else. The next two sentences specify requirements to which the Senate proceedings shall conform: the Senate shall be on oath or affirmation, a two-thirds vote is required to convict, and when the President is tried the Chief Justice shall preside.

Petitioner argues that the word "try" in the first sentence imposes by implication an additional requirement on the Senate in that the proceedings must be in the nature of a judicial trial. From there petitioner goes on to argue that this limitation precludes the Senate from delegating to a select committee the task of hearing the testimony of witnesses, as was done pursuant to Senate Rule XI. " '[T]ry' means more than simply 'vote on' or 'review' or 'judge.' In 1787 and today, trying a case means hearing the evidence, not scanning a cold record." Petitioner concludes from this that courts may review whether or not the Senate "tried" him before convicting him.

There are several difficulties with this position which lead us ultimately to reject it. The word "try," both in 1787 and later, has considerably broader meanings than those to which petitioner would limit it. Older dictionaries define try as "[t]o examine" or "[t]o examine as a judge." In more modern usage the term has various meanings. For example, try can mean "to examine or investigate judicially," "to conduct the trial of," or "to put to the test by experiment, investigation, or trial." Petitioner submits that "try," as contained in T. Sheridan, Dictionary of the English Language (1796), means "to examine as a judge; to bring before a judicial tribunal." Based on the variety of definitions, however, we cannot say that the Framers used the word "try" as an implied limitation on the method by which the Senate might proceed in trying impeachments. "As a rule the Constitution speaks in general terms, leaving Congress to deal with subsidiary matters of detail as the public interests and changing conditions may require...."...

Petitioner devotes only two pages in his brief to negating the significance of the word "sole" in the first sentence of Clause 6. As noted above, that sentence provides that "[t]he Senate shall have the sole Power to try all Impeachments." We think that the word "sole" is of considerable significance. Indeed, the word "sole" appears only one other time in the Constitution—with respect to the House of Representatives' "*sole* Power of Impeachment." The common sense meaning of the word "sole" is that the Senate alone shall have authority to determine whether an individual should be acquitted or convicted. The dictionary definition bears this out. "Sole" is defined as "having no companion," "solitary," "being the only one," and "functioning ... independently and without assistance or interference." If the courts may review the actions of the Senate in order to determine whether that body "tried" an impeached official, it is difficult to see how the Senate would be "functioning ... independently and without assistance or interference."...

The history and contemporary understanding of the impeachment provisions support our reading of the constitutional language. The parties do not offer evidence of a single word in the history of the Constitutional Convention or in contemporary commentary that even alludes to the possibility of judicial review in the context of the impeachment powers....

There are two additional reasons why the Judiciary, and the Supreme Court in particular, were not chosen to have any role in impeachments. First, the Framers recognized that most likely there would be two sets of proceedings for individuals who commit impeachable offenses—the impeachment trial and a separate criminal trial. In fact, the Constitution explicitly provides for two separate proceedings. The Framers deliberately separated the two forums to avoid raising the specter of bias and to ensure independent judgments....

Second, judicial review would be inconsistent with the Framers' insistence that our system be one of checks and balances. In our constitutional system, impeachment was designed to be the *only* check on the Judicial Branch by the Legislature....

Judicial involvement in impeachment proceedings, even if only for purposes of judicial review, is counterintuitive because it would eviscerate the "important constitutional check" placed on the Judiciary by the Framers. Nixon's argument would place final reviewing authority with respect to impeachments in the hands of the same body that the impeachment process is meant to regulate.

Nevertheless, Nixon argues that judicial review is necessary in order to place a check on the Legislature. Nixon fears that if the Senate is given unreviewable authority to interpret the Impeachment Trial Clause, there is a grave risk that the Senate will usurp judicial power. The Framers anticipated this objection and created two constitutional safeguards to keep the Senate in check. The first safeguard is that the whole of the impeachment power is divided between the two legislative bodies, with the House given the right to accuse and the Senate given the right to judge. This split of authority "avoids the inconvenience of making the same persons both accusers and judges; and guards against the danger of persecution from the prevalency of a factious spirit in either of those branches." The second safeguard is the two-thirds supermajority vote requirement....

In addition to the textual commitment argument, we are persuaded that the lack of finality and the difficulty of fashioning relief counsel against justiciability. We agree with the Court of Appeals that opening the door of judicial review to the procedures used by the Senate in trying impeachments would "expose the political life of the country to months, or perhaps years, of chaos."...

In the case before us, there is no separate provision of the Constitution which could be defeated by allowing the Senate final authority to determine the meaning of the word "try" in the Impeachment Trial Clause. We agree with Nixon that courts possess power to review either legislative or executive action that transgresses identifiable textual limits. As we have made clear, "whether the action of [either the Legislative or Executive Branch] exceeds whatever authority has been committed, is itself a delicate exercise in constitutional interpretation, and is a responsibility of this Court as ultimate interpreter of the Constitution." But we conclude, after exercising that delicate responsibility, that the word "try" in the Impeachment Clause does not provide an identifiable textual limit on the authority which is committed to the Senate.

For the foregoing reasons, the judgment of the Court of Appeals is

Affirmed.

JUSTICE WHITE, with whom JUSTICE BLACKMUN joins, concurring in the judgment.

Petitioner contends that the method by which the Senate convicted him on two articles of impeachment violates Art. I, § 3, cl. 6 of the Constitution, which mandates that the Senate "try" impeachments. The Court is of the view that the Constitution forbids us even to consider his contention. I find no such prohibition and would therefore reach the merits of the claim. I concur in the judgment because the Senate fulfilled its constitutional obligation to "try" petitioner. . . .

[I omitted]

II

The majority states that the question raised in this case meets two of the criteria for political questions set out in *Baker* v. *Carr* (1962). It concludes first that there is " 'a textually demonstrable constitutional commitment of the issue to a coordinate political department.' " It also finds that the question cannot be resolved for " 'a lack of judicially discoverable and manageable standards.' "

Of course the issue in the political question doctrine is *not* whether the Constitutional text commits exclusive responsibility for a particular governmental function to one of the political branches. There are numerous instances of this sort of textual commitment, and it is not thought that disputes implicating these provisions are nonjusticiable. Rather, the issue is whether the Constitution has given one of the political branches final responsibility for interpreting the scope and nature of such a power. . . .

A

The majority finds a clear textual commitment in the Constitution's use of the word "sole" in the phrase "the Senate shall have the sole Power to try all impeachments." It attributes "considerable significance" to the fact that this term appears in only one other passage in the Constitution. The Framers' sparing use of "sole" is thought to indicate that its employment in the Impeachment Trial Clause demonstrates a concern to give the Senate exclusive interpretive authority over the Clause.

In disagreeing with the Court, I note that the Solicitor General stated at oral argument that "[w]e don't rest our submission on sole power to try." The Government was well advised in this respect. The significance of the Constitution's use of the term "sole" lies not in the infrequency with which the term appears, but in the fact that it appears exactly twice, in parallel provisions concerning impeachment. That the word "sole" is found only in the House and Senate Impeachment Clauses demonstrates that its purpose is to emphasize the distinct role of each in the impeachment process. As the majority notes, the Framers, following English practice, were very much concerned to separate the prosecutorial from the adjudicative aspects of impeachment. Giving each House "sole" power with respect to its role in impeachments effected this division of labor. While the majority is thus right to interpret the term "sole" to indicate that the Senate ought to " 'functio[n] independently and without assistance or interference,' " it wrongly identifies the judiciary, rather than the House, as the source of potential interference with which the Framers were concerned when they employed the term "sole." . . .

The majority's review of the historical record thus explains why the power to try impeachments properly resides with the Senate. It does not explain, however, the sweeping statement that the judiciary was "not chosen to have any role in impeachments." Not a single word in the historical materials cited by the majority addresses judicial review of the Impeachment Trial Clause. And a glance at the arguments surrounding the Impeachment Clauses negates the majority's attempt to infer nonjusticiability from the Framers' arguments in support of the Senate's power to try impeachments.

What the relevant history mainly reveals is deep ambivalence among many of the Framers over the very institution of impeachment, which, by its nature, is not easily reconciled with our system of checks and balances. As they clearly recognized, the branch of the Federal Government which is possessed of the authority to try impeachments, by having final say over the membership of each branch, holds a potentially unanswerable power over the others. In addition, that branch, insofar as it is called upon to try not only members of other branches, but also its own, will have the advantage of being the judge of its own members' causes. . . .

The historical evidence reveals above all else that the Framers were deeply concerned about placing in any branch the "awful discretion, which a court of impeachments must necessarily have." Viewed against this history, the discord between the majority's position and the basic principles of checks and balances underlying the Constitution's separation of powers is clear. In essence, the majority suggests that the Framers' [*sic*] conferred upon Congress a potential tool of legislative dominance yet at the same time rendered Congress' exercise of that power one of the very few areas of legislative authority immune from any judicial review. While the majority rejects petitioner's justiciability argument as espousing a view "inconsistent with the Framers' insistence that our system be one of checks and balances," it is the Court's finding of nonjusticiability that truly upsets the Framers' careful design. In a truly balanced system, impeachments tried by the Senate would serve as a means of controlling the largely unaccountable judiciary, even as judicial review would ensure that the Senate adhered to a minimal set of procedural standards in conducting impeachment trials.

B

The majority also contends that the term "try" does not present a judicially manageable standard. It notes that in 1787, as today, the word "try" may refer to an inquiry in the nature of a judicial proceeding, or, more generally, to experimentation or investigation. In light of the term's multiple senses, the Court finds itself unable to conclude that the Framers used the word "try" as "an implied limitation on the method by which the Senate might proceed in trying impeachments." Also according to the majority, comparison to the other more specific requirements listed in the Impeachment Trial Clause—that the senators must proceed under oath and vote by two-thirds to convict, and that the Chief Justice must preside over an impeachment trial of the President—indicates that the word "try" was not meant by the Framers to constitute a limitation on the Senate's conduct and further reveals the term's unmanageability. . . .

III

The majority's conclusion that "try" is incapable of meaningful judicial construction is not without irony. One might think that if any class of concepts would fall within the definitional abilities of the judiciary, it would be that class having to do with procedural justice. Examination of the remaining question—whether proceedings in accordance with Senate Rule XI are compatible with the Impeachment Trial Clause—confirms this intuition. . . .

Petitioner argues . . . that because committees were not used in state impeachment trials prior to the [Constitutional] Convention, the word "try" cannot be interpreted to permit their use. It is, however, a substantial leap to infer from the absence of a particular device of parliamentary procedure that its use has been forever barred by the Constitution. And there is textual and historical evidence that undermines the inference sought to be drawn in this case.

The fact that Art. III, § 2, cl. 3 specifically exempts impeachment trials from the jury requirement provides some evidence that the Framers were anxious not to have additional specific procedural requirements read into the term "try." Contemporaneous commentary further supports this view. Hamilton, for example, stressed that a trial by so large a body as the Senate (which at the time promised to boast 26 members) necessitated that the proceedings not "be tied down to . . . strict rules, either in the delineation of the offence by the prosecutors, or in the construction of it by the Judges . . . ." The Federalist No. 65, p. 441 (J. Cooke ed. 1961). . . .

In short, textual and historical evidence reveals that the Impeachment Trial Clause was not meant to bind the hands of the Senate beyond establishing a set of minimal procedures. Without identifying the exact contours of these procedures, it is sufficient to say that the Senate's use of a factfinding committee under Rule XI is entirely compatible with the Constitution's command that the Senate "try all impeachments." Petitioner's challenge to his conviction must therefore fail.

IV

Petitioner has not asked the Court to conduct his impeachment trial; he has asked instead that it determine whether his impeachment was tried by the Senate. The majority refuses to reach this determination out of a laudable desire to respect the authority of the legislature. Regrettably, this concern is manifested in a manner that does needless violence to the Constitution. The deference that is owed can be found in the Constitution itself, which provides the Senate ample discretion to determine how best to try impeachments.

JUSTICE SOUTER, concurring in the judgment.

I agree with the Court that this case presents a nonjusticiable political question. Because my analysis differs somewhat from the Court's, however, I concur in its judgment by this separate opinion.

As we cautioned in *Baker* v. *Carr* (1962), "the 'political question' label" tends "to obscure the need for case-by-case inquiry." The need for such close examination is nevertheless clear from our precedents, which demonstrate that the functional nature of the political question doctrine requires analysis of "the precise facts and posture of the particular case," and precludes "resolution by any semantic cataloguing." . . .

Whatever considerations feature most prominently in a particular case, the political question doctrine is "essentially a function of the separation of powers," existing to restrain courts "from inappropriate interference in the business of the other branches of Government," *United States* v. *Munoz-Flores* (1990), and deriving in large part from prudential concerns about the respect we owe the political departments. . . . Not all interference is inappropriate or disrespectful, however, and application of the doctrine ultimately turns, as Learned Hand put it, on "how importunately the occasion demands an answer." L. Hand, The Bill of Rights 15 (1958).

This occasion does not demand an answer. The Impeachment Trial Clause commits to the Senate "the sole Power to try all Impeachments," subject to three procedural requirements: the Senate shall be on oath or affirmation; the Chief Justice shall preside when the President is tried; and conviction shall be upon the concurrence of two-thirds of the Members present. It seems fair to conclude that the Clause contemplates that the Senate may determine, within broad boundaries, such subsidiary issues as the procedures for receipt and consideration of evidence necessary to satisfy its duty to "try" impeachments. . . . As the Court observes, see *ante*, at 11-12, judicial review of an impeachment trial would under the best of circumstances entail significant disruption of government.

One can, nevertheless, envision different and unusual circumstances that might justify a more searching review of impeachment proceedings. If the Senate were to act in a manner seriously threatening the integrity of its results, convicting, say, upon a coin-toss, or upon a summary determination that an officer of the United States was simply " 'a bad guy,' " judicial interference might well be appropriate. In such circumstances, the Senate's action might be so far beyond the scope of its constitutional authority, and the consequent impact on the Republic so great, as to merit a judicial response despite the prudential concerns that would ordinarily counsel silence. . . .

COURT ON CLINIC BLOCKADES

January 13, 1993

A federal civil rights law cannot be used to halt massive human blockades at abortion clinics, the Supreme Court ruled 6 to 3 January 13. The blockades were a tactic commonly used by Operation Rescue, an antiabortion group, to stop both patients and workers from entering abortion clinics. Frequently, members of Operation Rescue chained themselves in clinic doorways.

Before the Court's ruling in Bray v. Alexandria Women's Health Clinic, *some clinics responded to blockades by seeking federal court injunctions to stop them. They sought relief under an 1871 statute commonly known as the "Ku Klux Klan law," which was designed to protect blacks from mob violence. To invoke the law, they had to prove that Operation Rescue members conspired to deprive clinic patients of equal protection under the law. They also had to prove that Operation Rescue members had a "class-based" animosity toward clinic patients. In court, attorneys for the abortion clinics said the "class" targeted by Operation Rescue included all women, since only women can have abortions.*

The Supreme Court rejected that argument. In the majority opinion, Justice Antonin Scalia, joined by Chief Justice William H. Rehnquist and Justices Byron R. White, Anthony M. Kennedy, and Clarence Thomas, wrote that Operation Rescue targeted both women and men involved in abortions. Scalia also rejected a contention that the protesters had illegally interfered with women's rights to interstate travel. Scalia said the protesters did not care whether the women had crossed state lines to get abortions.

The ruling's net result was that abortion clinics had to rely on various state and local laws to halt the protests. It also meant that local police, frequently overwhelmed by the huge blockades, were responsible for enforcing the laws. However, Justice Kennedy, who wrote a concurring opinion, said state and local officials could ask the U.S. attorney general to send in federal marshals if they could not control the protests.

In an unusual move, the Court heard the abortion protest case twice. It had heard oral arguments during the prior term, when there were only eight justices. It asked to hear the case again after Justice Thomas joined the Court, leading some to speculate that the justices were evenly divided.

The decision came seven months after the Court narrowly upheld the constitutional right to abortion but gave states great latitude in restricting it. On June 29, 1992, the Court upheld provisions in a Pennsylvania law that required doctors to tell women who sought abortions about risks and alternatives to the procedure, mandated a twenty-four-hour waiting period, required women under age eighteen to obtain the consent of one parent or a judge, barred abortions after twenty-four weeks of pregnancy except when needed to protect the woman's life or prevent permanent physical harm, and required doctors to keep detailed records of abortions and the reasons for performing late-term abortions.

In the Pennsylvania case, four justices argued for overturning Roe v. Wade, *the 1973 Supreme Court decision that established the right to abortion. However, the majority disagreed. The majority said states could not bar abortion, but could adopt restrictions as long as they did not impose an "undue burden" on women seeking abortions. The majority did not precisely define what constituted an "undue burden." Activists on both sides of the abortion battle predicted the ruling would lead to more state laws restricting abortion, more legal challenges to those laws, and ultimately more Supreme Court rulings.* (Supreme Court on Abortion Rights, Historic Documents of 1992, p. 589)

In the two decades after the Roe *decision, more than 22 million legal abortions were performed in the United States. An estimated 1.6 million abortions were performed in 1993. While abortion was undoubtedly the most divisive issue in the nation, a* Washington Post-*ABC poll found that 65 percent of Americans supported* Roe v. Wade *and thus the right to abortion.*

Actions by the New President

One week after the Court's abortion protest decision, President Bill Clinton took office and moved almost immediately to lift abortion restrictions imposed by presidents Ronald Reagan and George Bush. Two days after taking office, Clinton fulfilled campaign pledges by:

- *Overturning the so-called "gag rule" that barred abortion counseling nationwide at the 4,000 family planning clinics that received federal funds.*
- *Lifting restrictions on federally funded research about the medical use of fetal tissue.*
- *Ending a ban on the use of U.S. funds by the United Nations to provide information or counseling about abortion.*

- *Overturning a ban on performing abortions at overseas U.S. military hospitals.*
- *Ordering a review of the ban on the private importation of the French abortion pill RU-486, and an end to the ban unless a sound medical reason existed to keep it.*

Clinton carefully portrayed his actions as efforts to give women back the right to make their own medical decisions. The president said his actions did not indicate he supported abortion. "Our vision should be of an America where abortion is safe and legal but rare," Clinton said in a televised Oval Office ceremony.

Increasing Violence Outside Clinics

Abortion protests continued across the country, and some turned deadly. In March Dr. David Gunn, who performed abortions at the Pensacola Women's Health Services Clinic in Florida, was shot to death during a protest at the clinic. Michael Griffin, a thirty-one-year-old chemical plant worker, was charged with first-degree murder in the attack. At his first court appearance, Griffin said he wanted to defend himself and to use the Bible as a defense document.

In August, Dr. George Tiller was shot in both arms as he tried to drive away from an abortion clinic he owned in Wichita, Kansas. Rachelle Shannon, an antiabortion activist from Oregon, was arrested in the attack. She was charged with one count of attempted first-degree murder and two counts of aggravated assault. In light of the attacks, doctors at some abortion clinics started hiring bodyguards, wearing bulletproof vests, and carrying guns for protection.

Following are excerpts from the Supreme Court's opinion of January 13, 1993, in the case of Bray v. Alexandria Women's Health Clinic:

No. 90-985

Jayne Bray, et al., Petitioners *v.* Alexandria Women's Health Clinic et al.	On Writ of Certiorari to the United States Court of Appeals for the Fourth Circuit

[January 13, 1993]

JUSTICE SCALIA delivered the opinion of the Court.

This case presents the question whether the first clause of Rev. Stat. § 1980, 42 U.S.C. § 1985(3)—the surviving version of § 2 of the Civil Rights

Act of 1871—provides a federal cause of action against persons obstructing access to abortion clinics. Respondents are clinics that perform abortions, and organizations that support legalized abortion and that have members who may wish to use abortion clinics. Petitioners are Operation Rescue, an unincorporated association whose members oppose abortion, and six individuals. Among its activities, Operation Rescue organizes antiabortion demonstrations in which participants trespass on, and obstruct general access to, the premises of abortion clinics. The individual petitioners organize and coordinate these demonstrations.

Respondents sued to enjoin petitioners from conducting demonstrations at abortion clinics in the Washington, D.C., metropolitan area. Following an expedited trial, the District Court ruled that petitioners had violated § 1985(3) by conspiring to deprive women seeking abortions of their right to interstate travel. The court also ruled for respondents on their pendent state-law claims of trespass and public nuisance. As relief on these three claims, the court enjoined petitioners from trespassing on, or obstructing access to, abortion clinics in specified Virginia counties and cities in the Washington, D.C., metropolitan area....

The Court of Appeals for the Fourth Circuit affirmed, *National Organization for Women* v. *Operation Rescue* (CA4 1990), and we granted certiorari (1991). The case was argued in the October 1991 Term, and pursuant to our direction was reargued in the current Term.

I

Our precedents establish that in order to prove a private conspiracy in violation of the first clause of § 1985(3), a plaintiff must show, *inter alia,* (1) that "some racial, or perhaps otherwise class-based, invidiously discriminatory animus [lay] behind the conspirators' action," *Griffin* v. *Breckenridge* (1971), and (2) that the conspiracy "aimed at interfering with rights" that are "protected against private, as well as official, encroachment," *Carpenters* v. *Scott* (1983). We think neither showing has been made in the present case.

A

In *Griffin* this Court held, reversing a 20-year-old precedent, see *Collins* v. *Hardyman* (1951), that § 1985(3) reaches not only conspiracies under color of state law, but also purely private conspiracies. In finding that the text required that expanded scope, however, we recognized the "constitutional shoals that would lie in the path of interpreting § 1985(3) as a general federal tort law." *Griffin.* That was to be avoided, we said, "by requiring, as an element of the cause of action, the kind of invidiously discriminatory motivation stressed by the sponsors of the limiting amendment." ... We said that "[t]he language [of § 1985(3)] requiring intent to deprive of *equal* protection, or *equal* privileges and immunities, means that there must be some racial, or perhaps otherwise class-based, invidiously discriminatory animus behind the conspirators' action."

We have not yet had occasion to resolve the "perhaps"; only in *Griffin* itself have we addressed and upheld a claim under § 1985(3), and that case involved race discrimination. Respondents assert that there qualifies alongside race discrimination, as an "otherwise class-based, invidiously discriminatory animus" covered by the 1871 law, opposition to abortion. Neither common sense nor our precedents support this.

To begin with, we reject the apparent conclusion of the District Court (which respondents make no effort to defend) that opposition to abortion constitutes discrimination against the "class" of "women seeking abortion." Whatever may be the precise meaning of a "class" for purposes of *Griffin*'s speculative extension of § 1985(3) beyond race, the term unquestionably connotes something more than a group of individuals who share a desire to engage in conduct that the § 1985(3) defendant disfavors. Otherwise, innumerable tort plaintiffs would be able to assert causes of action under § 1985(3) by simply defining the aggrieved class as those seeking to engage in the activity the defendant has interfered with. This definitional ploy would convert the statute into the "general federal tort law" it was the very purpose of the animus requirement to avoid....

Respondents' contention, however, is that the alleged class-based discrimination is directed not at "women seeking abortion" but at women in general. We find it unnecessary to decide whether *that* is a qualifying class under § 1985(3), since the claim that petitioners' opposition to abortion reflects an animus against women in general must be rejected. We do not think that the "animus" requirement can be met only by maliciously motivated, as opposed to assertedly benign (though objectively invidious), discrimination against women. It does demand, however, at least a purpose that focuses upon women *by reason of their sex*—for example (to use an illustration of assertedly benign discrimination), the purpose of "saving" women *because they are women* from a combative, aggressive profession such as the practice of law. The record in this case does not indicate that petitioners' demonstrations are motivated by a purpose (malevolent *or* benign) directed specifically at women as a class; to the contrary, the District Court found that petitioners define their "rescues" not with reference to women, but as physical intervention "between abortionists and the innocent victims," and that "all [petitioners] share a deep commitment to the goals of stopping the practice of abortion and reversing its legalization." Given this record, respondents' contention that a class-based animus has been established can be true only if one of two suggested propositions is true: (1) that opposition to abortion can reasonably be presumed to reflect a sex-based intent, or (2) that intent is irrelevant, and a class-based animus can be determined solely by effect. Neither proposition is supportable.

As to the first: Some activities may be such an irrational object of disfavor that, if they are targeted, and if they also happen to be engaged in exclusively or predominantly by a particular class of people, an intent to disfavor that class can readily be presumed. A tax on wearing yarmulkes is a tax on Jews. But opposition to voluntary abortion cannot possibly be considered such an irrational surrogate for opposition to (or paternalism towards) women. Whatever one thinks of abortion, it cannot be denied that there are common and respectable reasons for opposing it, other than hatred of or condescension toward (or indeed any view at all concerning) women as a class—as is evident from the fact that men and women are on both sides of the issue, just as men and women are on both sides of petitioners' unlawful demonstrations....

Respondents' case comes down, then, to the proposition that intent is legally irrelevant; that since voluntary abortion is an activity engaged in only by women, to disfavor it is *ipso facto* to discriminate invidiously against women as a class. Our cases do not support that proposition.... Moreover, two of our cases deal specifically with the disfavoring of abortion, and establish conclusively that it is not *ipso facto* sex discrimination. In *Maher* v. *Roe* (1977) and *Harris* v. *McRae* (1980), we held that the constitutional test applicable to government abortion-funding restrictions is not the heightened-scrutiny standard that our cases demand for sex-based discrimination, see *Craig* v. *Boren* (1976), but the ordinary rationality standard.

The nature of the "invidiously discriminatory animus" *Griffin* had in mind is suggested both by the language used in that phrase ("invidious ... [t]ending to excite odium, ill will, or envy; likely to give offense; esp., unjustly and irritatingly discriminating," Webster's Second International Dictionary 1306 (1954)) and by the company in which the phrase is found ("there must be *some racial, or perhaps otherwise class-based,* invidiously discriminatory animus," *Griffin* (emphasis added)). Whether one agrees or disagrees with the goal of preventing abortion, that goal in itself (apart from the use of unlawful means to achieve it, which is not relevant to our discussion of animus) does not remotely qualify for such harsh description, and for such derogatory association with racism. To the contrary, we have said that "a value judgment favoring childbirth over abortion" is proper and reasonable enough to be implemented by the allocation of public funds, and Congress itself has, with our approval, discriminated against abortion in its provision of financial support for medical procedures. This is not the stuff out of which a § 1985(3) "invidiously discriminatory animus" is created.

B

Respondents' federal claim fails for a second, independent reason: A § 1985(3) private conspiracy "for the purpose of depriving ... any person or class of persons of the equal protection of the laws, or of equal privileges and immunities under the laws," requires an intent to deprive persons of a right guaranteed against private impairment.... No intent to deprive of such a right was established here.

Respondents, like the courts below, rely upon the right to interstate travel—which we have held to be, in at least some contexts, a right constitutionally protected against private interference.... But all that respondents can point to by way of connecting petitioners' actions with that particular right is the District Court's finding that "[s]ubstantial numbers of women seeking the services of [abortion] clinics in the Washington Metropolitan area travel interstate to reach the clinics."... That is not enough....

Our discussion in *Carpenters* makes clear that it does not suffice for application of § 1985(3) that a protected right be incidentally affected. A conspiracy is not "for the purpose" of denying equal protection simply because it has an effect upon a protected right. The right must be *"aimed at"*; its impairment must be a conscious objective of the enterprise. Just as the "invidiously discriminatory animus" requirement, discussed above, requires that the defendant have taken his action "at least in part 'because of,' not merely 'in spite of,' its adverse effects upon an identifiable group," so also the "intent to deprive of a right" requirement demands that the defendant do more than merely be aware of a deprivation of right that he causes, and more than merely accept it; he must act at least in part for the very purpose of producing it. That was not shown to be the case here, and is on its face implausible. Petitioners oppose abortion, and it is irrelevant to their opposition whether the abortion is performed after interstate travel.

Respondents have failed to show a conspiracy to violate the right of interstate travel for yet another reason: petitioners' proposed demonstrations would not implicate that right. The federal guarantee of interstate travel does not transform state-law torts into federal offenses when they are intentionally committed against interstate travelers. Rather, it protects interstate travelers against two sets of burdens: "the erection of actual barriers to interstate movement" and "being treated differently" from intrastate travelers. *Zobel* v. *Williams* (1982).... As far as appears from this record, the only "actual barriers to movement" that would have resulted from Petitioners' proposed demonstrations would have been in the immediate vicinity of the abortion clinics, restricting movement from one portion of the Commonwealth of Virginia to another. Such a purely intrastate restriction does not implicate the right of interstate travel, even if it is applied intentionally against travelers from other States, unless it is applied *discriminatorily* against them. That would not be the case here, as respondents conceded at oral argument.

The other right alleged by respondents to have been intentionally infringed is the right to abortion. The District Court declined to rule on this contention, relying exclusively upon the right-of-interstate-travel theory; in our view it also is an inadequate basis for respondents' § 1985(3) claim. Whereas, unlike the right of interstate travel, the asserted right to abortion was assuredly "aimed at" by the petitioners, deprivation of that federal right (whatever its contours) cannot be the object of a purely private conspiracy. In *Carpenters,* we rejected a claim that an alleged private conspiracy to infringe First Amendment rights violated § 1985(3).

The statute does not apply, we said, to private conspiracies that are "aimed at a right that is by definition a right only against state interference," but applies only to such conspiracies as are "aimed at interfering with rights . . . protected against private, as well as official, encroachment." There are few such rights (we have hitherto recognized only the Thirteenth Amendment right to be free from involuntary servitude, *United States* v. *Kozminski* (1988), and, in the same Thirteenth Amendment context, the right of interstate travel). . . . The right to abortion is not among them. It would be most peculiar to accord it that preferred position, since it is much less explicitly protected by the Constitution than, for example, the right of free speech rejected for such status in *Carpenters*. Moreover, the right to abortion has been described in our opinions as one element of a more general right of privacy, see *Roe* v. *Wade* (1973), or of Fourteenth Amendment liberty, see *Planned Parenthood of Southeastern Pennsylvania* (1992), and the other elements of those more general rights are obviously *not* protected against private infringement. (A burglar does not violate the Fourth Amendment, for example, nor does a mugger violate the Fourteenth.) Respondents' § 1985(3) "deprivation" claim must fail, then, because they have identified no right protected against private action that has been the object of the alleged conspiracy. . . .

[II Omitted]

III

Because respondents were not entitled to relief under § 1985(3), they were also not entitled to attorney's fees and costs under 42 U.S.C. § 1988. We therefore vacate that award.

Petitioners seek even more. They contend that respondents' § 1985(3) claims were so insubstantial that the District Court lacked subject-matter jurisdiction over the action, including the pendent state claims; and that the injunction should therefore be vacated and the entire action dismissed. We do not agree. While respondents' § 1985(3) causes of action fail, they were not, prior to our deciding of this case, "wholly insubstantial and frivolous," *Bell* v. *Hood* (1946), so as to deprive the District Court of jurisdiction.

It may be, of course, that even though the District Court had jurisdiction over the state-law claims, judgment on those claims alone cannot support the injunction that was entered. We leave that question for consideration on remand.

* * *

JUSTICE STEVENS' dissent observes that this is "a case about the exercise of federal power to control an interstate conspiracy to commit illegal acts" and involves "no ordinary trespass," or "picketing of a local retailer," but "the kind of zealous, politically motivated, lawless conduct that led to the enactment of the Ku Klux Act in 1871 and gave it its name." Those are certainly evocative assertions, but as far as the point of law we have been asked to decide is concerned, they are irrelevant. We construe the statute, not the views of "most members of the citizenry." By its terms, § 1985(3) covers concerted action by as few as two persons, and does not require even interstate (much less nationwide) scope. It applies no more and no less to completely local action by two part-time protesters than to nationwide action by a full-time force of thousands. And under our precedents it simply does not apply to the sort of action at issue here.

Trespassing upon private property is unlawful in all States, as is, in many States and localities, intentionally obstructing the entrance to private premises. These offenses may be prosecuted criminally under state law, and may also be the basis for state civil damages. They do not, however, give rise to a federal cause of action simply because their objective is to prevent the performance of abortions, any more than they do so (as we have held) when their objective is to stifle free speech.

The judgment of the Court of Appeals is reversed in part and vacated in part, and the case is remanded for further proceedings consistent with this opinion.

It is so ordered.

JUSTICE KENNEDY, concurring.

In joining the opinion of the Court, I make these added observations.

The three separate dissenting opinions in this case offer differing interpretations of the statute in question, 42 U.S.C. § 1985(3). Given the difficulty of the question, this is understandable, but the dissenters' inability to agree on a single rationale confirms, in my view, the correctness of the Court's opinion. . . .

Of course, the wholesale commission of common state-law crimes creates dangers that are far from ordinary. Even in the context of political protest, persistent, organized, premeditated lawlessness menaces in a unique way the capacity of a State to maintain order and preserve the rights of its citizens. . . . For this reason, it is important to note that another federal statute offers the possibility of powerful federal assistance for persons who are injured or threatened by organized lawless conduct that falls within the primary jurisdiction of the States and their local governments.

Should state officials deem it necessary, law enforcement assistance is authorized upon request by the State to the Attorney General of the United States, pursuant to 42 U.S.C. § 10501. In the event of a law enforcement emergency as to which "State and local resources are inadequate to protect the lives and property of citizens or to enforce the criminal law," § 10502(3), the Attorney General is empowered to put the full range of federal law enforcement resources at the disposal of the State, including the resources of the United States Marshals Service, which was presumably the principal practical advantage to respondents of seeking a federal injunction under § 1985(3). . . .

. . . Thus, even if, after proceedings on remand, the ultimate result is dismissal of the action, local authorities retain the right and the ability to request federal assistance, should they deem it warranted.

JUSTICE SOUTER, concurring in the judgment in part and dissenting in part.

I

This case turns on the meaning of two clauses of 42 U.S.C. § 1985(3) which render certain conspiracies civilly actionable. The first clause (the deprivation clause) covers conspiracies

> "for the purpose of depriving, either directly or indirectly, any person or class of persons of the equal protection of the laws, or of equal privileges and immunities under the laws";

the second (the prevention clause), conspiracies

> "for the purpose of preventing or hindering the constituted authorities of any State or Territory from giving or securing to all persons within such State or Territory the equal protection of the laws...."

For liability in either instance the statute requires an "act in furtherance of the... conspiracy, whereby [a person] is injured in his person or property, or deprived of... any right or privilege of a citizen of the United States...."

Prior cases giving the words "equal protection of the laws" in the deprivation clause an authoritative construction have limited liability under that clause by imposing two conditions not found in the terms of the text. An actionable conspiracy must have some racial or perhaps other class-based motivation, *Griffin* v. *Breckenridge* (1971), and, if it is "aimed at" the deprivation of a constitutional right, the right must be one secured not only against official infringement, but against private action as well. *Carpenters* v. *Scott* (1983). The Court follows these cases in applying the deprivation clause today, and to this extent I take no exception to its conclusion....

[II and III Omitted]

[IV]

... I conclude that the prevention clause may be applied to a conspiracy intended to hobble or overwhelm the capacity of duly constituted state police authorities to secure equal protection of the laws, even when the conspirators' animus is not based on race or a like class characteristic, and even when the ultimate object of the conspiracy is to violate a constitutional guarantee that applies solely against state action....

[V Omitted]

JUSTICE STEVENS, with whom JUSTICE BLACKMUN joins, dissenting.

After the Civil War, Congress enacted legislation imposing on the

Federal Judiciary the responsibility to remedy both abuses of power by persons acting under color of state law and lawless conduct that state courts are neither fully competent, nor always certain, to prevent. The Ku Klux Act of 1871 was a response to the massive, organized lawlessness that infected our Southern States during the post-Civil War era. When a question concerning this statute's coverage arises, it is appropriate to consider whether the controversy has a purely local character or the kind of federal dimension that gave rise to the legislation.

Based on detailed, undisputed findings of fact, the District Court concluded that the portion of § 2 of the Ku Klux Act now codified at 42 U.S.C. § 1985(3) provides a federal remedy for petitioners' violent concerted activities on the public streets and private property of law-abiding citizens. *National Organization for Women* v. *Operation Rescue* (ED Va. 1989). The Court of Appeals affirmed. *National Organization for Women* v. *Operation Rescue* (CA4 1990). The holdings of the courts below are supported by the text and the legislative history of the statute and are fully consistent with this Court's precedents. Admittedly, important questions concerning the meaning of § 1985(3) have been left open in our prior cases, including whether the statute covers gender-based discrimination and whether it provides a remedy for the kind of interference with a woman's right to travel to another State to obtain an abortion revealed by this record. Like the overwhelming majority of federal judges who have spoken to the issue, I am persuaded that traditional principles of statutory construction readily provide affirmative answers to these questions.

It is unfortunate that the Court has analyzed this case as though it presented an abstract question of logical deduction rather than a question concerning the exercise and allocation of power in our federal system of government. The Court ignores the obvious (and entirely constitutional) congressional intent behind § 1985(3) to protect this Nation's citizens from what amounts to the theft of their constitutional rights by organized and violent mobs across the country. . . .

I

Petitioners are dedicated to a cause that they profoundly believe is far more important than mere obedience to the laws of the Commonwealth of Virginia or the police power of its cities. To achieve their goals, the individual petitioners "have agreed and combined with one another and with defendant Operation Rescue to organize, coordinate and participate in 'rescue' demonstrations at abortion clinics in various parts of the country, including the Washington Metropolitan area. The purpose of these 'rescue' demonstrations is to disrupt operations at the target clinic and indeed ultimately to cause the clinic to cease operations entirely."

The scope of petitioners' conspiracy is nationwide; it far exceeds the bounds or jurisdiction of any one State. They have blockaded clinics across the country, and their activities have been enjoined in New York, Pennsylvania, Washington, Connecticut, California, Kansas, and Nevada, as well as the District of Columbia metropolitan area. They have carried out their "rescue" operations in the District of Columbia and Maryland in defiance of federal injunctions.

Pursuant to their overall conspiracy, petitioners have repeatedly engaged in "rescue" operations that violate local law and harm innocent women. Petitioners trespass on clinic property and physically block access to the clinic, preventing patients, as well as physicians and medical staff, from entering the clinic to render or receive medical or counseling services. Uncontradicted trial testimony demonstrates that petitioners' conduct created a "substantial risk that existing or prospective patients may suffer physical or mental harm." Petitioners make no claim that their conduct is a legitimate form of protected expression.

Petitioners' intent to engage in repeated violations of law is not contested. They trespass on private property, interfere with the ability of patients to obtain medical and counseling services, and incite others to engage in similar unlawful activity. They also engage in malicious conduct, such as defacing clinic signs, damaging clinic property, and strewing nails in clinic parking lots and on nearby public streets. This unlawful conduct is "vital to [petitioners'] avowed purposes and goals." They show no signs of abandoning their chosen method for advancing their goals.

Rescue operations effectively hinder and prevent the constituted authorities of the targeted community from providing local citizens with adequate protection. The lack of advance warning of petitioners' activities, combined with limited police department resources, makes it difficult for the police to prevent petitioners' ambush by "rescue" from closing a clinic for many hours at a time. The trial record is replete with examples of petitioners overwhelming local law enforcement officials by sheer force of numbers. In one "rescue" in Falls Church, Virginia, the demonstrators vastly outnumbered the police department's complement of 30 deputized officers. The police arrested 240 rescuers, but were unable to prevent the blockade from closing the clinic for more than six hours. Because of the large-scale, highly organized nature of petitioners' activities, the local authorities are unable to protect the victims of petitioners' conspiracy.

Petitioners' conspiracy had both the purpose and effect of interfering with interstate travel. The number of patients who cross state lines to obtain an abortion obviously depends, to some extent, on the location of the clinic and the quality of its services. In the Washington Metropolitan area, where interstate travel is routine, 20 to 30 percent of the patients at some clinics were from out of State, while at least one clinic obtained over half its patients from other States. The District Court's conclusions in this regard bear repetition:

> "[Petitioners] engaged in this conspiracy for the purpose, either directly or indirectly, of depriving women seeking abortions and related medical and counselling services, of the right to travel. The right to travel includes the right to unobstructed interstate travel to obtain an abortion and other medical services.... Testimony at trial establishes that clinics in Northern Virginia

provide medical services to plaintiffs' members and patients who travel from out of state. Defendants' activities interfere with these persons' right to unimpeded interstate travel by blocking their access to abortion clinics. And, the Court is not persuaded that clinic closings affect only intra-state travel, from the street to the doors of the clinics. Were the Court to hold otherwise, interference with the right to travel could occur only at state borders. This conspiracy, therefore, effectively deprives organizational plaintiffs' non-Virginia members of their right to interstate travel."

To summarize briefly, the evidence establishes that petitioners engaged in a nationwide conspiracy; to achieve their goal they repeatedly occupied public streets and trespassed on the premises of private citizens in order to prevent or hinder the constituted authorities from protecting access to abortion clinics by women, a substantial number of whom traveled in interstate commerce to reach the destinations blockaded by petitioners. The case involves no ordinary trespass, nor anything remotely resembling the peaceful picketing of a local retailer. It presents a striking contemporary example of the kind of zealous, politically motivated, lawless conduct that led to the enactment of the Ku Klux Act in 1871 and gave it its name.

II

The text of the statute makes plain the reasons Congress considered a federal remedy for such conspiracies both necessary and appropriate. In relevant part the statute contains two independent clauses which I separately identify in the following quotation:

> "If two or more persons in any State or Territory conspire or go in disguise on the highway or on the premises of another, [*first*] for the purpose of depriving, either directly or indirectly, any person or class of persons of the equal protection of the laws, or of equal privileges and immunities under the laws; or [*second*] for the purpose of preventing or hindering the constituted authorities of any State or Territory from giving or securing to all persons within such State or Territory the equal protection of the laws; ... in any case of conspiracy set forth in this section, if one or more persons engaged therein do, or cause to be done, any act in furtherance of the object of such conspiracy, whereby another is injured in his person or property, or deprived of having and exercising any right or privilege of a citizen of the United States, the party so injured or deprived may have an action for the recovery of damages occasioned by such injury or deprivation, against any one or more of the conspirators." 42 U.S.C. § 1985(3).

The plain language of the statute is surely broad enough to cover petitioners' conspiracy. Their concerted activities took place on both the public "highway" and the private "premises of another." The women targeted by their blockade fit comfortably within the statutory category described as "any person or class of persons." Petitioners' interference with police protection of women seeking access to abortion clinics "directly or indirectly" deprived them of equal protection of the laws and of their privilege of engaging in lawful travel. Moreover, a literal reading of the second clause of the statute describes petitioners' proven "purpose of preventing or hindering the constituted authorities of any State or

Territory" from securing "to all persons within such State or Territory the equal protection of the laws."

No one has suggested that there would be any constitutional objection to the application of this statute to petitioners' nationwide conspiracy; it is obvious that any such constitutional claim would be frivolous. Accordingly, if, as it sometimes does, the Court limited its analysis to the statutory text, it would certainly affirm the judgment of the Court of Appeals. For both the first clause and the second clause of § 1985(3) plainly describe petitioners' conspiracy.

III

The Court bypasses the statute's history, intent, and plain language in its misplaced reliance on prior precedent. Of course, the Court has never before had occasion to construe the second clause of § 1985(3). The first clause, however, has been narrowly construed in *Collins* v. *Hardyman* (1951), *Griffin* v. *Breckenridge* (1971), and *Carpenters* v. *Scott* (1983). In the first of these decisions, the Court held that § 1985(3) did not apply to wholly private conspiracies. In *Griffin* the Court rejected that view but limited the application of the statute's first clause to conspiracies motivated by discriminatory intent to deprive plaintiffs of rights constitutionally protected against private (and not just governmental) deprivation. Finally, *Carpenters* re-emphasized that the first clause of § 1985(3) offers no relief from the violation of rights protected against only state interference. To date, the Court has recognized as rights protected against private encroachment (and, hence, by § 1985(3)) only the constitutional right of interstate travel and rights granted by the Thirteenth Amendment.

For present purposes, it is important to note that in each of these cases the Court narrowly construed § 1985(3) to avoid what it perceived as serious constitutional problems with the statute itself. Because those problems are not at issue here, it is even more important to note a larger point about our precedent. In the course of applying Civil War era legislation to civil rights issues unforeseeable in 1871, the Court has adopted a flexible approach, interpreting the statute to reach current concerns without exceeding the bounds of its intended purposes or the constitutional powers of Congress. We need not exceed those bounds to apply the statute to these facts.

The facts and decision in *Griffin* are especially instructive here. In overruling an important part of *Collins,* the Court found that the conduct the plaintiffs alleged—a Mississippi highway attack on a white man suspected of being a civil rights worker and the two black men who were passengers in his car—was emblematic of the antiabolitionist violence that § 1985(3) was intended to prevent. A review of the legislative history demonstrated, on the one hand, that Congress intended the coverage of § 1985(3) to reach purely private conspiracies, but on the other hand, that it wanted to avoid the "constitutional shoals" that would lie in the path of a general federal tort law punishing an ordinary assault and battery committed by two or more persons. The racial motivation for the battery committed by the defendants in the case before the Court placed their conduct "close to the core of the coverage intended by Congress." It therefore satisfied the limiting construction that the Court placed on the reference to a deprivation of "equal" privileges and immunities in the first clause of the Act. The Court explained that construction:

> "The constitutional shoals that would lie in the path of interpreting § 1985(3) as a general federal tort law can be avoided by giving full effect to the congressional purpose—by requiring, as an element of the cause of action, the kind of invidiously discriminatory motivation stressed by the sponsors of the limiting amendment. The language requiring intent to deprive of *equal* protection, or *equal* privileges and immunities, means that there must be some racial, or perhaps otherwise class-based, invidiously discriminatory animus behind the conspirators' action."

A footnote carefully left open the question "whether a conspiracy motivated by invidiously discriminatory intent other than racial bias would be actionable *under the portion of § 1985(3) before us.*" ([E]mphasis added.) Neither of our two more recent opinions construing § 1985 (3) has answered the question left open in *Griffin* or has involved the second clause of the statute.

After holding that the statute did apply to such facts, and that requiring a discriminatory intent would prevent its over-application, the *Griffin* Court held that § 1985(3) would be within the constitutional power of Congress if its coverage were limited to constitutional rights secured against private action. The facts in that case identified two such grounds.

One ground was § 2 of the Thirteenth Amendment. The other was the right to travel. The Court explained how the petitioners could show a violation of the latter. As with the class-based animus requirement, the Court was less concerned with the specifics of that showing than with the constitutionality of § 1985(3); it emphasized that whatever evidence they presented had to "make it clear that the petitioners had suffered from conduct that Congress may reach under its power to protect the right of interstate travel."

The concerns that persuaded the Court to adopt a narrow reading of the text of § 1985(3) in *Griffin* are not presented in this case. Giving effect to the plain language of § 1985(3) to provide a remedy against the violent interference with women exercising their privilege—indeed, their right—to engage in interstate travel to obtain an abortion presents no danger of turning the statute into a general tort law. Nor does anyone suggest that such relief calls into question the constitutional powers of Congress. When the *Griffin* Court rejected its earlier holding in *Collins,* it provided both an "authoritative construction" of § 1985(3) and a sufficient reason for rejecting the doctrine of *stare decisis* whenever it would result in an unnecessarily narrow construction of the statute's plain language. The Court wrote:

> "Whether or not *Collins* v. *Hardyman* was correctly decided on its own facts is a question with which we need not here be concerned. But it is clear, in the

> light of the evolution of decisional law in the years that have passed since that case was decided, that many of the constitutional problems there perceived simply do not exist. Little reason remains, therefore, not to accord to the words of the statute their apparent meaning."

Once concerns about the constitutionality of § 1985(3) are properly put aside, we can focus more appropriately on giving the statute its intended effect. On the facts disclosed by this record, I am convinced that both the text of the statute and its underlying purpose support the conclusion that petitioners' conspiracy was motivated by a discriminatory animus and violated respondents' protected right to engage in interstate travel.

IV

The question left open in *Griffin*—whether the coverage of § 1985(3) is limited to cases involving racial bias—is easily answered. The text of the statute provides no basis for excluding from its coverage any cognizable class of persons who are entitled to the equal protection of the laws....

The legislative history of the Act confirms the conclusion that even though it was primarily motivated by the lawless conduct directed at the recently emancipated citizens, its protection extended to "all the thirty-eight millions of the citizens of this nation." Cong. Globe, 42d Cong., 1st Sess. 484 (1871). Given then prevailing attitudes about the respective roles of males and females in society, it is possible that the enacting legislators did not anticipate protection of women against class-based discrimination. That, however, is not a sufficient reason for refusing to construe the statutory text in accord with its plain meaning, particularly when that construction fulfills the central purpose of the legislation....

The gloss that Justice Stewart placed on the statute in *Griffin,* then, did not exclude gender-based discrimination from its coverage. But it does require us to resolve the question whether a conspiracy animated by the desire to deprive women of their right to obtain an abortion is "class-based."

V

The terms "animus" and "invidious" are susceptible to different interpretations. The Court today announces that it could find class-based animus in petitioners' mob violence "only if one of two suggested propositions is true: (1) that opposition to abortion can reasonably be presumed to reflect a sex-based intent, or (2) that intent is irrelevant, and a class-based animus can be determined solely by effect."...

Both forms of class-based animus that the Court proposes are present in this case.

Sex-Based Discrimination

... To satisfy the class-based animus requirement of § 1985(3), the conspirators' conduct need not be motivated by hostility toward individual women. As women are unquestionably a protected class, that requirement—as well as the central purpose of the statute—is satisfied if the conspiracy is aimed at conduct that only members of the protected class have the capacity to perform. It is not necessary that the intended effect upon women be the sole purpose of the conspiracy. It is enough that the conspiracy be motivated "at least in part" by its adverse effects upon women.... The immediate and intended effect of this conspiracy was to prevent women from obtaining abortions. Even assuming that the ultimate and indirect consequence of petitioners' blockade was the legitimate and nondiscriminatory goal of saving potential life, it is undeniable that the conspirators' immediate purpose was to affect the conduct of women. Moreover, petitioners target women *because of* their sex, specifically, because of their capacity to become pregnant and to have an abortion.

It is also obvious that petitioners' conduct was motivated "at least in part" by the invidious belief that individual women are not capable of deciding whether to terminate a pregnancy, or that they should not be allowed to act on such a decision. Petitioners' blanket refusal to allow any women access to an abortion clinic overrides the individual class member's choice, no matter whether she is the victim of rape or incest, whether the abortion may be necessary to save her life, or even whether she is merely seeking advice or information about her options. Petitioners' conduct is designed to deny *every* woman the opportunity to exercise a constitutional right that *only* women possess. Petitioners' conspiracy, which combines massive defiance of the law with violent obstruction of the constitutional rights of their fellow citizens, represents a paradigm of the kind of conduct that the statute was intended to cover....

Statutory Relief from Discriminatory Effects

As for the second definition of class-based animus, disdainfully proposed by the Court, there is no reason to insist that a statutory claim under § 1985(3) must satisfy the restrictions we impose on constitutional claims under the Fourteenth Amendment. A congressional statute may offer relief from discriminatory effects even if the Fourteenth Amendment prevents only discriminatory intent....

VI

Respondents' right to engage in interstate travel is inseparable from the right they seek to exercise. That right, unduly burdened and frustrated by petitioners' conspiracy, is protected by the Federal Constitution....

The District Court's conclusion that petitioners intended to interfere with the right to engage in interstate travel is well-supported by the record. Interference with a woman's ability to visit another State to obtain an abortion is essential to petitioners' achievement of their ultimate goal—the complete elimination of abortion services throughout the United States....

VII

Respondents have unquestionably established a claim under the second clause of § 1985(3), the state hindrance provision. The record amply demonstrates petitioners' successful efforts to overpower local law enforcement officers. During the "rescue" operations, the duly constituted authorities are rendered ineffective, and mob violence prevails. A conspiracy that seeks by force of numbers to prevent local officials from protecting the victims' constitutional rights presents exactly the kind of pernicious combination that the second clause of § 1985(3) was designed to counteract. As we recognized in *Griffin,* the second clause of § 1985(3) explicitly concerns such interference with state officials and for that reason does not duplicate the coverage of the first clause. *Griffin.*

Petitioners' conspiracy hinders the lawful authorities from protecting women's constitutionally protected right to choose whether to end their pregnancies. Though this may be a right that is protected only against state infringement, it is clear that by preventing government officials from safeguarding the exercise of that right, petitioners' conspiracy effects a deprivation redressable under § 1985(3). See *Carpenters* v. *Scott* (1983); see also *Great American Federal Savings & Loan Assn.* v. *Novotny* (1979). A conspiracy that seeks to interfere with law enforcement officers' performance of their duties entails sufficient involvement with the State to implicate the federally protected right to choose an abortion and to give rise to a cause of action under § 1985(3).

We have not previously considered whether class-based animus is an element of a claim under the second clause of § 1985(3). We have, however, confronted the question whether the class-based animus requirement developed in *Griffin* should extend to another part of the Ku Klux Act, the portion now codified at § 1985(2). That provision, which generally proscribes conspiracies to interfere with federal proceedings, was enacted as part of the same paragraph of the Ku Klux Act that also contained what is now § 1985(3). For that reason, in *Kush* v. *Rutledge* (1983), the defendants contended that the plaintiffs had the burden of proving that the alleged conspiracy to intimidate witnesses had been motivated by the kind of class-based animus described in *Griffin.* The Court of Appeals rejected this contention. Its reasoning, which we briefly summarized in *Kush,* is highly relevant here: "Noting the Federal Government's unquestioned constitutional authority to protect the processes of its own courts, and the absence of any need to limit the first part of § 1985(2) to avoid creating a general federal tort law, the Court of Appeals declined to impose the limitation set forth in *Griffin* v. *Breckenridge.*"

Kush suggests that Griffin's strictly construed class-based animus requirement, developed for the first clause of § 1985(3), should not limit the very different second clause. We explained:

> "Although *Griffin* itself arose under the first clause of § 1985(3), petitioners argue that its reasoning should be applied to the remaining portions of § 1985

> as well. We cannot accept that argument for three reasons. First, the scope of the *Griffin* opinion is carefully confined to 'the portion of § 1985(3) now before us.' There is no suggestion in the opinion that its reasoning applies to any other portion of § 1985. Second, the analysis in the *Griffin* opinion relied heavily on the fact that the sponsors of the 1871 bill added the 'equal protection' language in response to objections that the 'enormous sweep of the original language' vastly extended federal authority and displaced state control over private conduct. That legislative background does not apply to the portions of the statute that prohibit interference with federal officers, federal courts, or federal elections. Third, and of greatest importance, the statutory language that provides the textual basis for the 'class-based, invidiously discriminatory animus' requirement simply does not appear in the portion of the statute that applies to this case."

It is true, of course, that the reference to "equal protection" appears in both the first and the second clauses of § 1985(3), but the potentially unlimited scope of the former is avoided by the language in the latter that confines its reach to conspiracies directed at the "constituted authorities of any State or Territory." The deliberate decision in *Griffin* that "carefully confined" its holding to "the portion of § 1985(3) now before us," coupled with the inapplicability of *Griffin*'s rationale to the second clause, makes it entirely appropriate to give that clause a different and more natural construction. Limited to conspiracies that are sufficiently massive to supplant local law enforcement authorities, the second clause requires no further restriction to honor the congressional purpose of creating an effective civil rights remedy without federalizing all tort law. The justification for a narrow reading of *Griffin*'s judicially crafted requirement of class-based animus simply does not apply to the state hindrance clause. An action under that clause entails both a violation of the victims' constitutional rights and state involvement. This situation is so far removed from the question whether facially neutral legislation constitutes a violation of the Equal Protection Clause that the strict intent standards developed in that area can have no application.

In the context of a conspiracy that hinders state officials and violates respondents' constitutional rights, class-based animus can be inferred if the conspirators' conduct burdens an activity engaged in predominantly by members of the class. Indeed, it would be faithful both to *Griffin* and to the text of the state hindrance clause to hold that the clause proscribes conspiracies to prevent local law enforcement authorities from protecting activities that are performed exclusively by members of a protected class, even if the conspirators' animus were directed at the activity rather than at the class members. Thus, even if yarmulkes, rather than Jews, were the object of the conspirators' animus, the statute would prohibit a conspiracy to hinder the constituted authorities from protecting access to a synagogue or other place of worship for persons wearing yarmulkes. Like other civil rights legislation, this statute should be broadly construed to provide federal protection against the kind of disorder and anarchy that the States are unable to control effectively.

With class-based animus understood as I have suggested, the conduct covered by the state hindrance clause would be as follows: a large-scale conspiracy that violates the victims' constitutional rights by overwhelming the local authorities and that, by its nature, victimizes predominantly members of a particular class. I doubt whether it would be possible to describe conduct closer to the core of § 1985(3)'s coverage. This account would perfectly describe the conduct of the Ku Klux Klan, the group whose activities prompted the enactment of the statute. This description also applies to petitioners, who have conspired to deprive women of their constitutional right to choose an abortion by overwhelming the local police and by blockading clinics with the intended effect of preventing women from exercising a right only they possess. The state hindrance clause thus provides an independent ground for affirmance....

JUSTICE O'CONNOR, with whom JUSTICE BLACKMUN joins, dissenting.

Petitioners act in organized groups to overwhelm local police forces and physically blockade the entrances to respondents' clinics with the purpose of preventing women from exercising their legal rights. Title 42 U.S.C. § 1985(3) provides a federal remedy against private conspiracies aimed at depriving any person or class of persons of the "equal protection of the laws," or of "equal privileges and immunities under the laws." In my view, respondents' injuries and petitioners' activities fall squarely within the ambit of this statute....

SENATE REPORT ON VIETNAM POWS

January 13, 1993

There is no "compelling evidence" that American servicemen listed as missing during the Vietnam War are still alive and being held prisoner, a special Senate committee concluded in a 1,223-page report released January 13. Nearly all of the 2,264 men still missing died before the United States pulled its troops out of Vietnam in 1973, the committee said.

The Senate Select Committee on POW/MIA Affairs said it cannot prove that no American POW remains alive in Vietnam or Laos, and that some reports remain to be investigated. "But neither live-sighting reports nor other sources of intelligence have provided grounds for encouragement, particularly over the last decade," the committee said. "The live-sighting reports that have been resolved have not checked out; alleged pictures of POWs have proven false; purported leads have come up empty; and photographic intelligence has been inconclusive, at best."

However, the committee said that President Richard Nixon and Henry Kissinger, his national security adviser and chief negotiator at talks to end the war, had good reason to suspect that some POWs were not released when the war ended. Recently declassified documents from the State Department, Defense Department, and White House supported that contention. During hearings before the committee, senior Nixon administration officials testified that Nixon and Kissinger felt compelled to end the war even though they knew some POWs remained behind. The officials, including two former defense secretaries under Nixon, said administration officials felt that neither Congress nor the American public would support a resumption of the war over the POW issue. Any prisoners left behind were probably held in Laos, although some also may have been held in Vietnam. Some officials said any remaining POWs were probably killed after American troops left Vietnam.

In testimony before the committee, Kissinger strongly denied that either he or the former president knew American POWs were left behind. He called the charge "a flat-out lie." In the weeks before the committee issued its report, both Kissinger and Nixon lobbied to get the allegations against them toned down in the final document.

While 2,264 men were still officially listed as missing in action, the report said the actual number whose fate remained unknown was very small. "The bottom line is that there remain only a few cases where we know an unreturned POW was alive in captivity and we do not have evidence that the individual also died while in captivity," it said.

Criticism of Pentagon

The committee was sharply critical of Pentagon intelligence efforts to find out what happened to the missing men. For years, the POW issue had a low priority, it said. Yet the committee did not find any proof that government agencies conspired to withhold information about POWs.

The committee's study was the most comprehensive examination of the POW issue ever undertaken. It involved review of more than 1 million pages of classified documents, nearly two dozen public hearings, interviews with nearly 200 witnesses, and several trips to Vietnam and Laos by committee members and their staff.

The committee was appointed only months after Col. Millard Peck, director of the Defense Intelligence Agency's Special Office for POW/MIA Affairs, resigned. In his resignation letter, Peck said government officials had a "mindset to debunk" information that U.S. POWs might still be alive, and suggested that a "cover-up may be in progress."

Lingering Doubts and the Embargo

The committee's report was unlikely to satisfy those who believed that the U.S. government continued withholding information about POWs. More questions arose only months after the committee released its report, when previously secret documents were found in archives in the former Soviet Union. In April historian Stephen J. Morris of Harvard University found a Russian document indicating that North Vietnam withheld more than 600 American POWs at the end of the war. Some experts said the discrepancy arose because North Vietnam held hundreds of Asian civilians who it classified as American POWs. Morris disagreed, saying he believed that several hundred American POWs were killed after the war. Zbigniew Brzezinski, President Carter's national security adviser, told the Washington Post *that he tentatively agreed with Morris's conclusion. In September a second Russian document surfaced that contained some of the same numbers as the first document. Pentagon officials said both documents were authentic, but their numbers could not possibly be right. Earlier in the year, Oleg Kalugin, a former senior KGB official, testified that KGB officers questioned U.S. POWs in Vietnam in 1975 or later, well after all POWs were supposed to have returned home.*

The report was also unlikely to satisfy American businesses that were clamoring to lift the economic embargo imposed against Vietnam in 1975. Resolution of the POW issue was the last major barrier to restoring relations between the United States and Vietnam. In July President Bill Clinton sent a high-level delegation to Vietnam to discuss improving relations. In that same month, he also let Vietnam become eligible for loans from the World Bank. In September Clinton relaxed the trade embargo to allow U.S. firms to bid on projects in Vietnam financed by the World Bank and similar international organizations. Clinton's actions followed a move by his predecessor, George Bush, that allowed U.S. firms to open offices in Vietnam and to sign contracts that would take effect when the embargo ended. All three presidential actions were seen both as rewards for Vietnam's cooperation on the POW issue and as reminders that the nation still had to do more before the embargo would end.

The U.S. and Vietnamese governments seemed eager to resolve the POW issue. American officials praised Vietnam's new cooperation in trying to determine what happened to the missing soldiers. That cooperation allowed U.S. experts to search the Vietnamese countryside for the remains of missing Americans and to study POW-related documents held in Vietnamese government archives, efforts that reportedly cost the United States more than $100 million annually.

Following is an excerpt from "POW/MIA's: Report of the Select Committee on POW/MIA Affairs," released by the Senate Select Committee on POW/MIA Affairs on January 13, 1993:

Summary of Findings and Recommendations

Americans "last known alive" in Southeast Asia

Information available to our negotiators and government officials responsible for the repatriation of prisoners indicated that a group of approximately 100 American civilians and servicemen expected to return at Operation Homecoming did not. Some of these men were known to have been taken captive; some were known only to have survived their incidents; others were thought likely to have survived. The White House expected that these individuals would be accounted for by our adversaries, either as alive or dead, when the war came to an end. Because they were not accounted for then, despite our protests, nor in the period immediately following when the trail was freshest and the evidence strongest, twenty years of agony over this issue began. This was the moment when the POW/MIA controversy was born.

The failure of our Vietnam war adversaries to account for these "last known alive" Americans meant that families who had had good reason to expect the return of their loved ones instead had cause for renewed grief.

Amidst their sorrow, the nation hailed the war's end; the President said that all our POWs are "on the way home"; and the Defense Department, following standard procedures, began declaring missing men dead. Still, the governments in Southeast Asia did not cooperate, and the answers that these families deserved did not come. In 1976, the Montgomery Committee concluded that because there was no evidence that missing Americans had survived, they must be dead. In 1977, a Defense Department official said that the distinction between Americans still listed as "POW" and those listed as "missing" had become "academic." Nixon, Ford and Carter Administration officials all dismissed the possibility that American POWs had survived in Southeast Asia after Operation Homecoming.

This Committee has uncovered evidence that precludes it from taking the same view. We acknowledge that there is no proof that U.S. POWs survived, but neither is there proof that all of those who did not return had died. There is evidence, moreover, that indicates the possibility of survival, at least for a small number, after Operation Homecoming:

> First, there are the Americans known or thought possibly to have been alive in captivity who did not come back; we dismiss the chance that some of these known prisoners remained captive past Operation Homecoming.
>
> Second, leaders of the Pathet Lao claimed throughout the war that they were holding American prisoners in Laos. Those claims were believed—and, up to a point, validated—at the time; they cannot be dismissed summarily today.
>
> Third, U.S. defense and intelligence officials hoped that forty or forty-one prisoners captured in Laos would be released at Operation Homecoming, instead of the twelve who were actually repatriated. These reports were taken seriously enough at the time to prompt recommendations by some officials for military action aimed at gaining the release of the additional prisoners thought to be held.
>
> Fourth, information collected by U.S. intelligence agencies during the last 19 years, in the form of live-sighting, hearsay, and other intelligence reports, raises questions about the possibility that a small number of unidentified U.S. POWs who did not return may have survived in captivity.
>
> Finally, even after Operation Homecoming and returnee debriefs, more than 70 Americans were officially listed as POWs based on information gathered prior to the signing of the peace agreement; while the remains of many of these Americans have been repatriated, the fates of some continue unknown to this day.

Given the Committee's findings, the question arises as to whether it is fair to say that American POWs were knowingly abandoned in Southeast Asia after the war. The answer to that question is clearly no. American officials did not have certain knowledge that any specific prisoner or prisoners were being left behind. But there remains the troubling question of whether the Americans who were expected to return but did not were, as a group, shunted aside and discounted by government and population alike. The answer to that question is essentially yes.

Inevitably the question will be asked: who is responsible for that? The answer goes beyond any one agency, Administration or faction. By the time the peace agreement was signed, a decade of division, demonstrations and debate had left our entire nation weary of killing and tired of involvement in an inconclusive and morally complex war. The psychology of the times, from rural kitchens to the Halls of Congress to the Oval Office, was to move on; to put the war out of mind; and to focus again on other things. The President said, and our nation wanted to believe, that all of our American POWs were on the way home. Watergate loomed; other crises seized our attention. Amidst it all, the question of POW/MIA accountability faded. In a sense, it, too, became a casualty of war.

The record does indicate that efforts to gain accountability were made. Dr. Henry Kissinger personally raised the issue and lodged protests with Le Duc Tho and leaders of the Pathet Lao. Defense and State Department spokesmen told Congress of their continuing dissatisfaction with the accounting process; stressed their view that the POW/MIA lists received were not complete, and referred to the cases of Americans last known alive as the "most agonizing and frustrating of all."

However, compared to the high-level, high-visibility protests about prisoners made public during the war, post-Homecoming Administration efforts and efforts to inform the American public were primarily low-level and low-key.

Before the peace agreement was signed, those "last known alive," were referred to as "POWs"; afterward, they were publicly, although not technically, lumped together with all of the others called "missing."

Before the agreement, Secretary of Defense Melvin Laird and other Administration officials had berated the North Vietnamese for their failure to disclose the status of these "last known alive" cases, while citing their dramatic case histories and distributing photographs to the press. After Homecoming, Administration criticisms were less vociferous and names and case histories cited only rarely and, even then, not publicly by cabinet officials, but by their assistants and their assistants' assistants.

When the war shut down, so, too, did much of the POW/MIA related intelligence operations. Bureaucratic priorities shifted rapidly and, before long, the POW/MIA accounting operation had become more of a bureaucratic backwater than an operations center for matters of life and death.

From the fall of Saigon in 1975 through the early 1980's, efforts to gain answers from the Government of Vietnam and the other communist governments of Southeast Asia bore little fruit. In 1982, President Reagan wisely raised the issue of accounting for our missing to a "matter of highest national priority." In 1987, a Special Presidential Emissary to Vietnam was named and serious discussions resumed. More recently, the disintegration of the Soviet empire has opened new doors and created compelling new incentives for foreign cooperation—almost 20 years after the last American soldier was withdrawn. Today, the U.S. spends at least $100 million each year on POW/MIA efforts.

Still, the families wait for answers and, still, the question haunts, is there anyone left alive? The search for a definitive answer to that question prompted the creation of this Committee.

As much as we would hope that no American has had to endure twenty years of captivity, if one or more were in fact doing so, there is nothing the Members of the Committee would have liked more than to be able to prove this fact. We would have recommended the use of all available resources to respond to such evidence if it had been found, for nothing would have been more rewarding than to have been able to re-unite a long-captive American with family and country.

Unfortunately, our hopes have not been realized. This disappointment does not reflect a failure of the investigation, but rather a confrontation with reality. While the Committee has some evidence suggesting the possibility a POW may have survived to the present, and while some information remains yet to be investigated, there is, at this time, no compelling evidence that proves that any American remains alive in captivity in Southeast Asia.

The Committee cannot prove a negative, nor have we entirely given up hope that one or more U.S. POWs may have survived. As mentioned above, some reports remain to be investigated and new information could be forthcoming. But neither live-sighting reports nor other sources of intelligence have provided grounds for encouragement, particularly over the past decade. The live-sighting reports that have been resolved have not checked out; alleged pictures of POWs have proven false; purported leads have come up empty; and photographic intelligence has been inconclusive, at best.

In addition to the lack of compelling evidence proving that Americans are alive, the majority of Committee Members believes there is also the question of motive. These Members assert that it is one thing to believe that the Pathet Lao or North Vietnamese might have seen reason to hold back American prisoners in 1973 or for a short period thereafter; it is quite another to discern a motive for holding prisoners alive in captivity for another 19 years. The Vietnamese and Lao have been given a multitude of opportunities to demand money in exchange for the prisoners some allege they hold but our investigation has uncovered no credible evidence that they have ever done so.

Yes, it is possible even as these countries become more and more open that a prisoner or prisoners could be held deep within a jungle or behind some locked door under conditions of the greatest security. That possibility argues for a live-sighting follow up capability that is alert, aggressive and predicated on the assumption that a U.S. prisoner or prisoners continue to be held. But, sadly, the Committee cannot provide compelling evidence to support that possibility today.

Finally, there is the question of numbers. Part of the pain caused by this issue has resulted from rumors about hundreds or thousands of Americans languishing in camps or bamboo cages. The circumstances surrounding the losses of missing Americans render these reports arithmetically impossible.

In order for Americans to judge for themselves, we will append to this report a summary of the facts surrounding each known discrepancy case. An analysis of these incidents will show that:

> Only in a few cases did the U.S. Government know for certain that someone was captured;
>
> In many of the cases, there is only an indication of the potential of capture; and
>
> In a large number of the cases, there is a strong indication that the individual was killed.

The Committee emphasizes that simply because someone was listed as missing in action does not mean that there was any evidence, such as a radio contact, an open parachute or a sighting on the ground, of survival. We may make a presumption that an individual could have survived, and that is the right basis upon which to operate. But a presumption is very different from knowledge or fact, and cannot lead us—in the absence of evidence—to conclude that someone is alive. Even some of the cases about which we know the most and which show the strongest indication that someone was a prisoner of war leave us with certain doubts as to what the circumstances were. The bottom line is that there remain only a few cases where we know an unreturned POW was alive in captivity and we do not have evidence that the individual also died while in captivity.

There is at least one aspect of the POW/MIA controversy that should be laid to rest conclusively with this investigation and that is the issue of conspiracy. Allegations have been made in the past that our government has had a "mindset to debunk" reports that American prisoners have been sighted in Southeast Asia. Our Committee found reason to take those allegations seriously. But we also found in some quarters a "mindset to accuse" that has given birth to vast and implausible theories of conspiracy and conscious betrayal. Those theories are without foundation.

Yes, there have been failures of policy, priority and process. Over the years, until this investigation, the Executive branch's penchant for secrecy and classification contributed greatly to perceptions of conspiracy. In retrospect, a more open policy would have been better. But America's government too closely reflects America's people to have permitted the knowing and willful abandonment of U.S. POWs and a subsequent coverup spanning almost 20 years and involving literally thousands of people.

The POW/MIA issue is too important and too personal for us to allow it to be driven by theory; it must be driven by fact. Witness after witness was asked by our Committee if they believed in, or had evidence of, a conspiracy either to leave POWs behind or to conceal knowledge of their fate—and no evidence was produced. The isolated bits of information out of which some have constructed whole labyrinths of intrigue and deception have not withstood the tests of objective investigation; and the vast archives of secret U.S. documents that some felt contained incriminating evidence have been thoroughly examined by the Committee only to find that the conspiracy cupboard is bare.

The quest for the fullest possible accounting of our Vietnam-era POW/MIAs must continue, but if our efforts are to be effective and fair to families, they must go forward within the context of reality, not fiction.

Investigation of issues related to Paris Peace Accords

Most of the questions and controversies that still surround the POW/MIA issue can be traced back to the Paris Peace Accords and their immediate aftermath. If that agreement had been implemented in good faith by North Vietnam and with necessary cooperation from Cambodia and Laos, the fullest possible accounting of missing Americans would have been achieved long ago.

During negotiations, the American team, headed by Dr. Henry Kissinger, had sought an agreement that would provide explicitly for the release of American prisoners and an accounting for missing American servicemen throughout Indochina. The U.S. negotiators said, when the agreement was signed, that they had "unconditional guarantees" that these goals would be achieved.

The great accomplishment of the peace agreement was that it resulted in the release of 591 American POWs, of whom 566 were military and 25 civilian. It also established a framework for cooperation in resolving POW/MIA related questions that remains of value today. Unfortunately, efforts to implement the agreement failed, for a number of reasons, to resolve the POW/MIA issue.

Obstacles faced by U.S. negotiators

During its investigation, the Committee identified several factors that handicapped U.S. officials during the negotiation of the peace agreement, and during the critical first months of implementation.

The first and most obvious obstacle to a fully effective agreement was the approach taken to the POW/MIA issue by North Vietnam (DRV) and its allies. During the war, the DRV violated its obligations under the Geneva Convention by refusing to provide complete lists of prisoners, and by prohibiting or severely restricting the right of prisoners to exchange mail or receive visits from international humanitarian agencies.

During negotiations, the DRV insisted that the release of prisoners could not be completed prior to the withdrawal of all U.S. forces, and consistently linked cooperation on the POW/MIA issue to other issues, including a demand for reconstruction aid from the United States. Once the agreement was signed, the DRV was slow to provide a list of prisoners captured in Laos. Following Operation Homecoming, the North Vietnamese refused to cooperate in providing an accounting for missing Americans, including some who were known to have been held captive at one time within the DRV prison system. Perhaps most important of all, the DRV's continued pursuit of a military conquest of South Vietnam dissipated prospects for cooperation on POW/MIA issues.

A second factor inhibiting the achievement of U.S. objectives was the limited leverage enjoyed by U.S. negotiators. It was U.S. policy, fully known to the North Vietnamese, that the U.S. sought to disengage from the war. President Nixon was elected on a platform calling for an end to U.S. involvement; support was building rapidly within the Congress for measures that would have mandated a withdrawal conditioned on the return of prisoners; and the American public had become increasingly divided and war-weary as the conflict continued. These same factors, along with the debilitating effects of the Watergate scandal on the Nixon Presidency, weakened the U.S. hand in responding to DRV violations after the peace agreement was signed.

A third factor limiting the success of the agreement was the absence of Lao and Cambodian representatives from the peace table. Although the U.S. negotiators pressed the DRV for commitments concerning the release of prisoners and an accounting for the missing throughout Indochina, the peace accords technically apply only to Vietnam. Although the DRV, in a side understanding, assured Dr. Kissinger that it would cooperate in obtaining the release of U.S. prisoners in Laos, the fact is that the prisoners captured in Laos who were actually released had long since been transferred to Hanoi. No Americans held captive in Laos for a significant period of time have ever been returned. Neither the peace agreement, nor the assurances provided by North Vietnam to Dr. Kissinger, established procedures to account for missing Americans in Cambodia or Laos.

American protests

The Paris Peace Accords provided for the exchange of prisoner lists on the day the agreement was signed and for the return of all prisoners of war within 60 days. It also required the parties to assist each other in obtaining information about those missing in action and to determine the location of graves for the purpose of recovering and repatriating remains.

U.S. officials, especially in the Department of Defense, were disappointed that more live American prisoners were not included on the lists exchanged when the peace agreement was signed or—with respect to prisoners captured in Laos—four days after the agreement was signed. The record uncovered by the Committee's investigation indicates that high level Defense Department and Defense Intelligence Agency officials were especially concerned about the incompleteness of the list of prisoners captured in Laos.

This concern was based on intelligence that some Americans had been held captive by the Pathet Lao, on repeated Pathet Lao claims that prisoners were being held, and on the large number of American pilots who were listed as missing in action in Laos compared to the number being proposed for return. Top military and intelligence officials expressed the hope, at the time the peace agreement was signed, that as many as 41 servicemen lost in Laos would be returned. However, only ten men (7 U.S. military, 2 U.S. civilian and a Canadian) were on the list of prisoners captured in Laos that was turned over by the DRV.

During the first 60 days, while the American troop withdrawal was underway, the Nixon Administration contacted North Vietnamese officials repeatedly to express concern about the incomplete nature of the prisoner lists that had been received. In early February, President Nixon sent a message to the DRV Prime Minister saying, with respect to the list of only ten POWs from Laos, that:

> U.S. records show there are 317 American military men unaccounted for in Laos and it is inconceivable that only ten of these men would be held prisoner in Laos.

Soon thereafter, Dr. Kissinger presented DRV officials with 19 case folders of Americans who should have been accounted for, but who were not. The U.S. protests continued and in mid-March, the U.S. threatened briefly to halt the withdrawal of American troops if information about the nine American prisoners on the DRV/Laos list *and* about prisoners actually held by the Pathet Lao were not provided. By the end of the month, top Defense Department officials were recommending a series of diplomatic and military options aimed at achieving an accounting for U.S. prisoners thought to be held in Laos.

Ultimately, the Nixon Administration proceeded with the withdrawal of troops in return for the release of prisoners on the lists provided by the North Vietnamese and Viet Cong.

Post-homecoming

The public statements made by President Nixon and by high Defense Department officials following the end of Operation Homecoming did not fully reflect the Administration's prior concern that live U.S. prisoners may have been kept behind. Administration officials did, however, continue to stress publicly the need for Vietnam to meet its obligations under the peace agreement, and U.S. diplomats pressed both the North Vietnamese and the Pathet Lao for information concerning missing Americans. Unfortunately, due to the intransigence of our adversaries, those efforts were largely unavailing.

During the Committee's hearings, it was contended by Dr. Kissinger and some Members of the Committee that Congressional attitudes would have precluded any Administration effort to respond forcefully to the DRV's failure to provide an accounting for missing American servicemen. These Members of the Committee contend that their view is supported by the Senate's rejection on May 31, 1973 of an amendment offered by U.S. Sen. Robert Dole that would have permitted the continued bombing of Laos and Cambodia if the President certified that North Vietnam "is not making an accounting, to the best of its ability, of all missing in action personnel in Southeast Asia."

Conclusions

The Committee believes that its investigation contributed significantly to the public record of the negotiating history of the POW/ MIA provisions of the Paris Peace Accords, and of the complications that arose during efforts to implement those provisions both before and after the completion of Operation Homecoming. That record indicates that there existed a higher degree of concern within the Administration about the possibility that prisoners were being left behind in Laos than had been known previously, and that various options for responding to that concern were discussed at the highest levels of government.

The Committee notes that some Administration statements at the time the agreement was signed expressed greater certainty about the completeness of the POW return than they should have and that other statements may have understated the problems that would arise during implementation and that, taken together, these statements may have raised public and family expectations too high. The Committee further notes that statements made after the agreement was signed may have understated U.S. concerns about the possibility that live prisoners remained, thereby contributing in subsequent years to public suspicion and distrust. However, the Committee concludes that the phrasing of these statements was designed to avoid raising what were believed to be false hopes among POW/MIA families, rather than to mislead the American people.

Investigation of the accounting process

The Committee investigation included a comprehensive review of the procedures used by the U.S. Government to account for American prisoners and missing from the beginning of the war in Southeast Asia until the present day. The purposes were:

> To determine accurately the number of Americans who served in Southeast Asia during the war who did not return, either alive or dead;
>
> To evaluate the accuracy of the U.S. Government's own past and current process for determining the like status and fate of missing Americans;
>
> To learn what the casualty data and intelligence information have to tell us about the number of Americans whose fates are truly "unaccounted for" from the war in Vietnam; and
>
> To consider whether efforts to obtain the fullest possible accounting of our POW/MIAs was treated, as claimed, as a matter of "highest national priority" by the Executive branch;
>
> To assess the extent to which Defense Department and DIA accounting policies and practices contributed to the confusion, suspicion and distrust that has characterized the POW/MIA issue for the past 20 years; and
>
> To determine what changes need to be made to policies and procedures in order to instill public confidence in the government's POW/MIA accounting process with respect to past and future conflicts.

Although 2,264 Americans currently are listed as "unaccounted for" from the war in Indochina, the number of Americans whose fate is truly unknown is far smaller. Even during the war, the U.S. Government knew and the families involved knew that, in many of these cases, there was certainty that the soldier or airman was killed at the time of the incident. These are generally cases involving individuals who were killed when their airplanes crashed into the sea and no parachutes were sighted, or where others witnessed the death of a serviceman in combat but were unable to recover the body.

Of the 2,264 Americans now listed as unaccounted for, 1,095 fall into this category. These individuals were listed as "killed in action/body not recovered" (KIA/BNR) and were not included on the lists of POW/MIAs that were released publicly by the Defense and State Departments during the war or for several years thereafter. It was not until the late 1970's that KIA/BNRs were added to the official lists of "missing" Americans.

The next largest group of Americans now on the list of 2,264 originally was listed by the military services or by DIA as "missing in action." These are individuals who became missing either in combat or in non-combat circumstances, but who were not known for certain either to have been killed or to have been taken into captivity. In most, but not all, of these cases, the circumstances of disappearance coupled with the lack of evidence of survival make it highly probable that the individual died at the time the incident occurred. Approximately 1,172 of the still unaccounted for Americans were originally listed either as MIA or as POW. Of these, 333 were lost in Laos, 348 in North Vietnam, 450 in South Vietnam, 37 in Cambodia and 4 in China. Since before the war ended, the POW/MIA accounting effort has focused, for good reason, on a relatively small number of these 1,172 Americans, that is, those who were either known to have been taken captive, or who were lost in circumstances under which survival was deemed likely or at least reasonably possible. These cases, in addition to others in which intelligence indicates a Southeast Asian Government may have known the fate of the missing men, are currently referred to as "discrepancy cases."

In 1987, Gen. John W. Vessey, Jr. (USA-Ret.) was appointed Presidential Emissary to Vietnam on POW/MIA matters. Gen. Vessey subsequently persuaded Vietnam to allow in-country investigations by the U.S. Government of high-priority discrepancy cases. The DIA and DOD's Joint Task Force-Full Accounting (JTF-FA) have identified a total of 305 discrepancy cases, of which 196 are in Vietnam, 90 are in Laos, and 19 are in Cambodia.

In 61 of the cases in Vietnam, the fate of the individual has been determined through investigation, and the Committee finds that Gen. Vessey correctly states that the evidence JTF-FA has gathered in each of these cases indicates that the individuals had died prior to Operation Homecoming. The first round of investigation of the 135 remaining cases in Vietnam is expected to be completed by January 18, 1993. A second round of investigation, which will proceed geographically on a district by district basis, will commence in February, 1993.

None of the discrepancy cases in Laos and Cambodia has been resolved. Because many of the Americans lost in those countries disappeared in areas that were under the control of North Vietnamese forces at the time, resolution of the majority of Laos/Cambodia cases will depend on a process of tripartite cooperation that has barely begun. The Committee further finds that, in addition to the past reluctance of the Vietnamese and Lao to agree to a series of tripartite talks with the United States, both the Department of State and the Department of Defense have been slow to push such a process forward.

As mentioned above, the Committee will append a case-by-case description of the circumstances of loss of each unresolved discrepancy case to this report. Those descriptions demonstrate that the U.S. Government has knowledge in only a small number of cases that the individuals involved were held captive and strong indications in only a small number more.

However, that is not to say that the Governments of Vietnam and Laos do not have knowledge pertaining to these or other MIA cases which may indicate survival. Answers to these troublesome questions will best be obtained through an accounting process that enjoys full cooperation from those governments.

The findings of this phase of the Committee's investigation include:

> By far the greatest obstacle to a successful accounting effort over the past twenty years has been the refusal of the foreign governments involved, until recently, to allow the U.S. access to key files or to carry out in-country, on-site investigations.
>
> The U.S. Government's process for accounting for Americans missing in Southeast Asia has been flawed by a lack of resources, organizational clarity, coordination and consistency. These problems had their roots during the war and worsened after the war as frustration about the ability to gain access and answers from Southeast Asian Governments increased. Through the mid-1980's, accounting for our POW/MIAs was viewed officially more as a bureaucratic exercise than as a matter of "highest national priority."
>
> The accounting process has improved dramatically in recent years as a result of the high priority attached to it by Presidents Reagan and Bush; because of the success of Gen. Vessey and the JTF-FA in gaining permission for the U.S. to conduct investigations on the ground in Southeast Asia; because of an increase in resources; and because of the Committee's own efforts, in association with the Executive branch, to gain greater cooperation from the Governments of Vietnam, Laos and Cambodia.
>
> After an exhaustive review of official and unofficial lists of captive and missing Americans from wartime years to the present, the Committee uncovered numerous errors in data entry and numerous discrepancies between DIA records and those of other military offices. The errors that have been identified, however, have since been corrected. As a result, the Committee finds no grounds to question the accuracy of the current, official list of those unaccounted for from the war in Southeast Asia. This list includes 2,222 missing servicemen except deserters and 42 missing civilians who were lost while performing services for the United States Government. The Committee has found no evidence to support the existence of rumored "secret lists" of additional missing Americans.
>
> The decision by the U.S. Government to falsify "location of loss" data for American casualties in Cambodia and Laos during much of the war contributed significantly both to public distrust and to the difficulties experienced by the DIA and others in trying to establish what happened to the individuals involved.
>
> The failure of the Executive branch to establish and maintain a consistent, sustainable set of categories and criteria governing the status of missing

Americans during and after the war in Southeast Asia contributed substantially to public confusion and mistrust. During the war, a number of individuals listed as "prisoner" by DIA were listed as "missing in action" by the military services. After the war, the legal process for settling status determinations was plagued by interference from the Secretary of Defense, undermined by financial and other considerations affecting some POW/MIA families and challenged in court. Later, the question of how many Americans remain truly "unaccounted for" was muddied by the Defense Department's decision to include KIA/BNR's—those known to have been killed, but with bodies not recovered—in their listings. This created the anomalous situation of having more Americans considered unaccounted for today than we had immediately after the war.

The Committee's recommendations for this phase of its investigation include:

Accounting for missing Americans from the war in Southeast Asia should continue to be treated as a "matter of highest national priority" by our diplomats, by those participating in the accounting process, by all elements of our intelligence community and by the nation, as a whole.

Continued, best efforts should be made to investigate the remaining unresolved discrepancy cases in Vietnam, Laos and Cambodia.

The United States should make a continuing effort, at a high level, to arrange regular tripartite meetings with the Governments of Laos and Vietnam to seek information on the possible control and movement of unaccounted for U.S. personnel by Pathet Lao and North Vietnamese forces in Laos during the Southeast Asia War.

The President and Secretary of Defense should order regular, independent reviews of the efficiency and professionalism of the DOD's POW/MIA accounting process for Americans still listed as missing from the war in Southeast Asia.

A clear hierarchy of responsibility for handling POW/MIA related issues that may regretably arise as a result of future conflicts must be established. This requires full and rapid coordination between and among the intelligence agencies involved and the military services. It requires the integration of missing civilians and suspected deserters into the overall accounting process. It requires a clear liaison between those responsible for the accounting (and related intelligence) and those responsible for negotiating with our adversaries about the terms for peace. It requires procedures for the full, honest and prompt disclosure of information to next of kin, at the time of incident and as other information becomes available. And it requires, above all, the designation within the Executive branch of an individual who is clearly responsible and fully accountable for making certain that the process works as it should.

In the future, clear categories should be established and consistently maintained in accounting for Americans missing during time of war. At one end of the listings should be Americans known with certainty to have been taken prisoner; at the other should be Americans known dead with bodies not recovered. The categories should be carefully separated in official summaries and discussions of the accounting process and should be applied consistently and uniformly.

Present law needs to be reviewed to minimize distortions in the status determination process that may result from the financial considerations of the families involved.

Wartime search and rescue (SAR) missions have an urgent operational value, but they are also crucial for the purposes of accounting for POW/MIAs. The records concerning many Vietnam era SAR missions have been lost or destroyed. In the future, all information obtained during any unsuccessful or partially successful military search and rescue mission should be shared with the agency responsible for accounting for POW/MIAs from that conflict and should be retained by that agency.

Investigation of POW/MIA-related intelligence activities

The Committee undertook an investigation of U.S. intelligence agency activities in relation to POW/MIA issues. This included a review of the DIA's primary role in investigating and evaluating reports that Americans missing from the Vietnam war were or are being held against their will since the end of the war in Southeast Asia. The investigation also included a review of signals intelligence (SIGINT) obtained by the National Security Agency (NSA), a review of imagery intelligence (IMINT) obtained by aerial photography and a review of covert U.S. Government activities associated with POW/MIA concerns.

In the area of intelligence, more than any other, the Committee and the Executive branch had to balance concerns about the public's right to know with a legitimate national need to maintain secrecy about intelligence sources and methods. The Committee insisted, however, that the fullest possible accounting of government activities in the intelligence field be made public and that no substantive information bearing directly on the question of whether there are live American POWs in Southeast Asia be withheld.

As a result of Executive branch cooperation, especially from CIA Director Robert Gates and National Security Adviser Brent Scowcroft, the Committee gained unprecedented access to closely-held government documents, including access to relevant operational files, the President's Daily briefs, the Executive Registry and the debriefs of returning POWs. Unfortunately, the limited number of individuals affiliated with the Committee who were given access to these materials prevented as thorough a review as the Committee would have preferred.

At the Committee's insistence, and despite the reservations of the Executive branch, public hearings were held for the first time on the products of satellite imagery related to the POW/MIA issue. Two former employees of the National Security Agency testified in public about information they gathered while working as specialists in the field of signal intelligence. And two days of hearings culminated an exhaustive Committee investigation of reports that American captives had been seen in Southeast Asia during the postwar period. In addition, thousands of pages of live-sighting reports have been declassified and made available to the public.

The Committee understands that the process of analyzing intelligence information is complicated and subjective. In most instances, the quality and source of information is such that it can be interpreted in more than one way and isolated bits of information may easily be misinterpreted. As a result, the Committee believes in the importance of taking all sources of information and intelligence into account when judging the validity of a report or category of data.

PRESIDENT CLINTON'S INAUGURAL ADDRESS

January 20, 1993

William Jefferson Clinton took office January 20 as the nation's forty-second president, declaring that "a new season of American renewal has begun." Pledging "an end to the era of deadlock and drift," the new president's inaugural address echoed the dominant theme of his election campaign, that the nation was in dire need of economic and political change. The fourteen-minute address, brief by Clinton's standards of speechmaking, urged sacrifice to "renew America" and, in turn, received positive reviews. Applause repeatedly rippled through the crowd of 250,000 onlookers assembled before the West Front of the Capitol in clear, crisp weather.

The speech followed the formal oath-taking at noon—actually administered at 11:58 a.m. by Chief Justice William H. Rehnquist—at which Clinton, with his wife, Hillary Rodham Clinton, at his side, placed his hand on a Bible and swore to uphold the laws of the land. Only moments before, Albert Gore, Jr., was sworn in as vice president. Sitting opposite the Clintons on a dignitary-filled platform were the outgoing president, George Bush, and Barbara Bush.

Clinton's Praise of Defeated Foe

As is traditional, the outgoing and incoming president and first lady rode together from the White House to the Capitol for the transfer of power. While it launched a new administration, the inaugural also marked the end of Bush's thirty-year political career, which only eighteen months earlier seemed secure. As the U.S. economy sagged, Bush's popularity tumbled from a pinnacle it reached after the U.S.-led military victory in Kuwait. (Bush on War Victory and Middle East Peace Plans, Historic Documents of 1991, p. 121)

Throughout the hour-long ceremony, Bush seemed subdued but appeared mildly surprised and pleased to hear Clinton praise his long public service. In an obvious appeal for national healing—and undoubtedly for Republican support—Clinton chose to overlook harsh words that Bush had directed at him and Gore in the election campaign's closing weeks.

In his defeat for a second term, Bush drew a lower percentage of the vote in all fifty states and the District of Columbia in 1992 than he had in 1988 as Ronald Reagan's heir apparent. Bush had emphasized foreign policy issues over economic concerns, and he paid a heavy price with the voters whose priorities were the reverse. Many Republicans accused him of running a poor campaign, although some analysts attributed his defeat partly to the strong showing of outspoken critic Ross Perot, who won 19 percent of the popular vote, the highest percentage by an independent candidate since 1912.

Broad but Tenuous Election Victory

Clinton had persuaded a plurality of American voters that he, better than Bush or Perot, could revive a sluggish economy, scale back a soaring fiscal deficit, and address a host of social concerns. His triumph brought to office the first Democratic president in twelve years and placed control of the White House and Congress in the same party after twelve years of divided government—Republican presidents and a Congress controlled by Democrats.

But the victory was notable for its tenuousness as well as for its scope. A record number of Americans, some 104.4 million, cast their ballots, giving Clinton 44.9 million votes, the most a Democratic candidate had ever received. Moreover, he captured the electoral votes of thirty-two states and the District of Columbia. But in the three-way race, he won only 43 percent of the popular vote. Only three other presidents—John Quincy Adams in 1824, Abraham Lincoln in 1860, and Woodrow Wilson in 1912—had won with smaller percentages.

Inaugural Symbolism and Revelry

Clinton's lack of a popular majority did not dampen the enthusiasm of the president or of thousands of Democratic partisans who flocked to Washington to take part in a week of festivities. Inaugural week began with Clinton taking a tour of Monticello, President Thomas Jefferson's home near Charlottesville, Virginia. With Gore, he proceeded by bus to Washington generally along the route that Jefferson took, by horseback and carriage, for his inauguration in 1801.

Offering a message of inclusion—"We must go forward together or not at all"—Clinton led a march across the Arlington Memorial Bridge to ring the "bells for hope" at Lady Bird Johnson Park along the Potomac River. The next day, Monday, January 18, Clinton attended ceremonies at Georgetown and Howard universities in observance of Martin Luther King Day. Tuesday, he visited the grave of John F. Kennedy at Arlington National Cemetery and had lunch with the nation's governors, promising that as a former governor (of Arkansas) he would be especially receptive to their concerns.

Inauguration Day was filled with the usual festivities—a long post-inaugural parade along Pennsylvania Avenue, followed that evening by eleven balls—but it also included specific Clinton touches. At the Arkansas ball, the new president played his saxophone, a trademark of his election campaign. The following day, perhaps in imitation of President Andrew Jackson, he held an open house at the White House, receiving thousands of visitors. Another Clinton trademark, his difficulty keeping to schedules, was on display shortly after he became president. He emerged thirty minutes late from the customary lunch with congressional leaders at the Capitol to lead the parade. On the way to the White House, the new president and his wife left their limousine to walk the last few blocks, as had the last Democratic predecessor, President Jimmy Carter, in 1977.

At the oath-taking ceremony, writer Maya Angelou read a poem she had composed for the occasion. Titled "On the Pulse of Morning," it ended with the words "With hope, good morning." Hope for the future had been a refrain in Clinton's campaign; he pointedly recalled, again and again, that he came from a town in Arkansas named Hope. Angelou's appearance on the platform recalled Kennedy's presidential inauguration in 1961 when poet Robert Frost read a poem he had written for the ceremony.

Following is the Reuter transcript of President Bill Clinton's inaugural address, delivered on the West Front of the Capitol, January 20, 1993:

My fellow citizens, today we celebrate the mystery of American renewal. This ceremony is held in the depth of winter, but by the words we speak and the faces we show the world, we force the spring, a spring reborn in the world's oldest democracy that brings forth the vision and courage to reinvent America. When our Founders boldly declared America's independence to the world and our purposes to the Almighty, they knew that America, to endure, would have to change; not change for change's sake but change to preserve America's ideals: life, liberty, the pursuit of happiness. Though we marched to the music of our time, our mission is timeless. Each generation of Americans must define what it means to be an American.

On behalf of our Nation, I salute my predecessor, President Bush, for his half-century of service to America. And I thank the millions of men and women whose steadfastness and sacrifice triumphed over depression, fascism, and communism.

Today, a generation raised in the shadows of the cold war assumes new responsibilities in a world warmed by the sunshine of freedom but threatened still by ancient hatreds and new plagues. Raised in unrivaled prosperity, we inherit an economy that is still the world's strongest but is weakened by business failures, stagnant wages, increasing inequality, and deep divisions among our own people.

When George Washington first took the oath I have just sworn to uphold, news traveled slowly across the land by horseback and across the ocean by boat. Now, the sights and sounds of this ceremony are broadcast instantaneously to billions around the world. Communications and commerce are global. Investment is mobile. Technology is almost magical. And ambition for a better life is now universal.

We earn our livelihood in America today in peaceful competition with people all across the Earth. Profound and powerful forces are shaking and remaking our world. And the urgent question of our time is whether we can make change our friend and not our enemy. This new world has already enriched the lives of millions of Americans who are able to compete and win in it. But when most people are working harder for less; when others cannot work at all; when the cost of health care devastates families and threatens to bankrupt our enterprises, great and small; when the fear of crime robs law-abiding citizens of their freedom; and when millions of poor children cannot even imagine the lives we are calling them to lead, we have not made change our friend.

We know we have to face hard truths and take strong steps, but we have not done so; instead, we have drifted. And that drifting has eroded our resources, fractured our economy, and shaken our confidence. Though our challenges are fearsome, so are our strengths. Americans have ever been a restless, questing, hopeful people. And we must bring to our task today the vision and will of those who came before us. From our Revolution to the Civil War, to the Great Depression, to the civil rights movement, our people have always mustered the determination to construct from these crises the pillars of our history. Thomas Jefferson believed that to preserve the very foundations of our Nation, we would need dramatic change from time to time. Well, my fellow Americans, this is our time. Let us embrace it.

Our democracy must be not only the envy of the world but the engine of our own renewal. There is nothing wrong with America that cannot be cured by what is right with America. And so today we pledge an end to the era of deadlock and drift, and a new season of American renewal has begun.

To renew America, we must be bold. We must do what no generation has had to do before. We must invest more in our own people, in their jobs, and in their future, and at the same time cut our massive debt. And we must do so in a world in which we must compete for every opportunity. It will not be easy. It will require sacrifice, but it can be done and done fairly, not choosing sacrifice for its own sake but for our own sake. We must provide for our Nation the way a family provides for its children.

Our Founders saw themselves in the light of posterity. We can do no less. Anyone who has ever watched a child's eyes wander into sleep knows what posterity is. Posterity is the world to come: the world for whom we hold our ideals, from whom we have borrowed our planet, and to whom we bear sacred responsibility. We must do what America does best: offer more opportunity to all and demand more responsibility from all. It is time to break the bad habit of expecting something for nothing from our Government or from each other. Let us all take more responsibility not only for ourselves and our families but for our communities and our country.

To renew America, we must revitalize our democracy. This beautiful Capital, like every capital since the dawn of civilization, is often a place of intrigue and calculation. Powerful people maneuver for position and worry endlessly about who is in and who is out, who is up and who is down, forgetting those people whose toil and sweat sends us here and pays our way. Americans deserve better. And in this city today there are people who want to do better. And so I say to all of you here: Let us resolve to reform our politics so that power and privilege no longer shout down the voice of the people. Let us put aside personal advantage so that we can feel the pain and see the promise of America. Let us resolve to make our Government a place for what Franklin Roosevelt called bold, persistent experimentation, a Government for our tomorrows, not our yesterdays. Let us give this Capital back to the people to whom it belongs.

To renew America, we must meet challenges abroad as well as at home. There is no longer a clear division between what is foreign and what is domestic. The world economy, the world environment, the world AIDS crisis, the world arms race: they affect us all. Today, as an older order passes, the new world is more free but less stable. Communism's collapse has called forth old animosities and new dangers. Clearly, America must continue to lead the world we did so much to make.

While America rebuilds at home, we will not shrink from the challenges nor fail to seize the opportunities of this new world. Together with our friends and allies, we will work to shape change, lest it engulf us. When our vital interests are challenged or the will and conscience of the international community is defied, we will act, with peaceful diplomacy whenever possible, with force when necessary. The brave Americans serving our Nation today in the Persian Gulf, in Somalia, and wherever else they stand are testament to our resolve. But our greatest strength is the power of our ideas, which are still new in many lands. Across the world we see them embraced, and we rejoice. Our hopes, our hearts, our hands are with those on every continent who are building democracy and freedom. Their cause is America's cause.

The American people have summoned the change we celebrate today. You have raised your voices in an unmistakable chorus. You have cast your votes in historic numbers. And you have changed the face of Congress, the Presidency, and the political process itself. Yes, you, my fellow Americans, have forced the spring. Now we must do the work the season demands. To that work I now turn with all the authority of my office. I ask the Congress to join with me. But no President, no Congress, no Government can undertake this mission alone.

My fellow Americans, you, too, must play your part in our renewal. I challenge a new generation of young Americans to a season of service: to act on your idealism by helping troubled children, keeping company with those in need, reconnecting our torn communities. There is so much to be done; enough, indeed, for millions of others who are still young in spirit to give of themselves in service, too. In serving, we recognize a simple but powerful truth: We need each other, and we must care for one another.

Today we do more than celebrate America. We rededicate ourselves to the very idea of America, an idea born in revolution and renewed through two centuries of challenge; an idea tempered by the knowledge that, but for fate, we, the fortunate and the unfortunate, might have been each other; an idea ennobled by the faith that our Nation can summon from its myriad diversity the deepest measure of unity; an idea infused with the conviction that America's long, heroic journey must go forever upward.

And so, my fellow Americans, as we stand at the edge of the 21st century, let us begin anew with energy and hope, with faith and discipline. And let us work until our work is done. The Scripture says, "And let us not be weary in well doing: for in due season we shall reap, if we faint not." From this joyful mountaintop of celebration we hear a call to service in the valley. We have heard the trumpets. We have changed the guard. And now, each in our own way and with God's help, we must answer the call.

Thank you, and God bless you all.

CLINTON ON BAIRD AND RENO

January 22 and March 12, 1993

President Bill Clinton began having personnel problems even before he took the oath of office. Revelations about the domestic help employed by Zoë Baird, Clinton's first choice for attorney general, embarrassed the president and scuttled the nomination. After Baird dropped out, it took Clinton two more tries to appoint someone to head the Justice Department.

On January 14 the New York Times *reported that Baird and her husband, Paul Gewirtz, had hired illegal immigrants to work in their home and had failed to pay Social Security payroll taxes for them. Eight days later, amidst a barrage of public criticism, Clinton withdrew Baird's nomination at her request.*

The withdrawal, which came only two days after Clinton's inauguration, dealt a sharp blow to his administration. Senior administration officials—including Clinton—knew about Baird's illegal workers before she was nominated, but thought they would not be a major problem. They could not have been more wrong.

Public Reaction

When news about the illegal workers and unpaid taxes became public, the American people responded angrily. They flooded Senate offices with demands that Baird be rejected. The public might not have understood scandals involving savings and loans or BCCI, but it clearly understood that the woman nominated to be the nation's chief law enforcement officer had broken two laws by hiring illegal workers and not paying taxes. The public also understood that as attorney general Baird was to oversee the Immigration and Naturalization Service, the agency that enforces the law barring the hiring of illegal workers. The intensity of the public's response surprised many senators.

Baird's questionable activities began in 1990, shortly after she ran a newspaper ad seeking a nanny for her son and received no response from legal U.S. residents. Baird and Gewirtz then hired a South American couple who were in the country illegally; the woman served as nanny, and the man as Baird's driver. Baird did not pay Social Security payroll taxes for the couple. However, just before Baird's nomination as attorney general in December 1992, she and her husband paid the back taxes on the advice of Clinton transition officials.

After the controversy over her actions erupted, Baird repeatedly apologized. Her chief defense was that she acted on the advice of a Connecticut immigration attorney. That explanation did not go over well with the American people, since both Baird and Gewirtz were attorneys. She made more than $500,000 annually as senior vice president and general counsel for Aetna Life & Casualty Company, and her husband was a professor at Yale Law School.

Some of Baird's supporters said she was being held to a higher standard than other people in similar circumstances. They said that thousands of Americans employed illegal nannies, paid no taxes for them, and were seldom prosecuted. The public did not buy that defense either, especially because most of the people violating the law could have easily afforded to comply with the law.

"Nannygate," as Baird's problem came to be called, overshadowed questions about her qualifications to be attorney general. There was no question that she was a gifted corporate attorney, but critics said she had never been a prosecuting attorney and had little or no experience with the criminal justice system. Her only prior work in government had been a two-year stint in Governor Clinton's administration more than a decade earlier. Some liberal interest groups questioned whether her extensive corporate background meant she would take the side of big business in disputes with the federal government. Despite these concerns, however, Baird's confirmation seemed assured until her nanny problem surfaced.

With support for Baird eroding, the Clinton administration did little to save her nomination. Nor did women's groups do much to help her, even though they had demanded a female attorney general. As Baird's confirmation hearing began before the Senate Judiciary Committee, it soon became clear her nomination would be defeated if the committee proceeded to a vote. After two days of hearings, Baird faxed a letter to Clinton asking him to withdraw her nomination. The Washington Post *called the time between Baird's nomination and withdrawal "eight swift, cruel days of public humiliation for the corporate lawyer with the perfect resume."*

Clinton's Insistence on a Woman

Baird was not Clinton's first choice to be attorney general. He had selected federal appeals court judge Patricia M. Wald, who told transition officials she did not want the job. Clinton was intent on naming a woman as attorney general, largely to fulfill a campaign promise to make his cabinet "look like America." He had appointed white men to three of the four biggest jobs in the cabinet—the Departments of State, Treasury, and Defense—leaving only the Justice job open for a woman.

After Baird asked him to withdraw her nomination, Clinton set his sights on U.S. district court judge Kimba M. Wood. However, it was soon revealed that Wood also had employed an illegal alien as a nanny for one year. Although, unlike Baird, Wood had paid all Social Security and other taxes for her baby sitter, the issue remained a problem. Once Wood was asked to withdraw from consideration, Clinton was again criticized, this time for not standing up for a nominee whose error was less serious than Baird's.

Clinton then chose Janet Reno, the state attorney in Dade County, Florida. Reno, a graduate of Cornell University and Harvard Law School, had extensive experience as a prosecutor and was particularly noted for her prosecution of child abuse and sexual assault cases. Perhaps just as important at that point in the selection process, she was a single woman who had never had children and thus had no nanny problem. The Senate quickly confirmed her, and Reno was sworn in March 12. She became the last Clinton cabinet secretary to take office and the first female attorney general in the nation's history.

> *Following are the text of a statement by President Bill Clinton on January 22, 1993, announcing the withdrawal of Zoë Baird's nomination to be attorney general, and a statement by Clinton on March 12, 1993, at the swearing in of Janet Reno as attorney general:*

CLINTON'S STATEMENT ON BAIRD

Tonight, I received a letter from my Attorney-General-designate, Ms. Zoë Baird, asking that I withdraw her nomination to lead the United States Department of Justice from further consideration by the Senate.

Ms. Baird is a gifted attorney, and a woman of decency and integrity. She responded to the call to public service with energy and a firm dedication to the mission of the Justice Department. Her candid disclosure of the child care matter to officials of my transition, and to the Senate Judiciary Committee, led to the circumstances we face today.

Clearly, our review process prior to her selection failed to evaluate this issue completely. For that, I take full responsibility. I hold Zoë Baird in the highest regard, and I believe she has much to give to her profession and to our country. I hope to continue to seek her advice and counsel. With sadness, I have accepted her request that the nomination be withdrawn, and have so informed the Senate Majority Leader, George Mitchell.

CLINTON'S STATEMENT ON RENO

THE PRESIDENT: Thank you very much. Please be seated. We are honored here in the White House to be joined today by distinguished members of the Senate and the House: Senator Biden, Senator Hatch, Senator Kennedy, Senator Sarbanes—one of Janet Reno's senators, Senator Connie Mack. Senator Graham called me last night. He's in Florida today with the First Lady at a health care hearing. And he said he had an excused absence from the Attorney General. (Laughter.)

The Speaker and Congressman Edwards are here, and we're delighted to see all of them. I also would say we're delighted to be joined by Mr. Justice White and Mrs. White. Thank you very much for coming. Let me say that it is a great honor for me to be able to be here at this ceremony today with Janet Reno, her family and a few of her many friends.

I'd like to say a special word of thanks to Stuart Gerson, who has served ably and honorably as Acting Attorney General since the Inauguration. I think we owe him a round of applause. (Applause.)

Somehow I don't think any of my other proposals will pass the Senate with the same vote margin—(laughter)—that Janet's confirmation did. I especially want to thank Senator Biden and Senator Hatch, and the members of the Judiciary Committee for waiving the normal waiting period between hearings and the confirmation vote, making this event possible today and making it possible for us to proceed immediately with the urgent tasks at hand.

But more than anything else, I think it is clear that Janet Reno made her own swift confirmation possible, showing the Senate and all who followed the hearings the qualities of leadership and integrity, intelligence and humanity that those gathered in this room have recognized for a very long time.

You shared with us the life-shaping stories of your family and career that formed your deep sense of fairness and your unwavering drive to help others to do better. You showed us your career in public service, working on the front lines in your community, fighting crime, understanding the impact on victims and on neighborhoods. Mending the gritty social fabric of a vibrant but troubled urban area is excellent preparation for carrying forward the banner of justice for all the American people.

You'll help to guide the federal government to assist state and local law enforcement in ways that really count. You've demonstrated that you will be a formidable advocate for the vulnerable people in our society and especially for our children.

Most of all, you have proved to the nation that you are a strong and an independent person who will give me your best legal judgment whether or not it's what I want to hear. (Laughter.) It's an experience I've already had, I'm glad to say. (Laughter.) That is the condition upon which you accepted my nomination and the only kind of attorney general that I would want serving in this Cabinet.

As Janet Reno begins her work at the Justice Department, she will enter a building that symbolizes our nation's commitment to justice, to equality, to the enforcement of our laws. On the side of that building, carved above one of the portals is the inscription: "The halls of justice are a hallowed place." With Janet Reno serving as our nation's Attorney General, those words will have great meaning for all Americans. (Applause.)

MS. RENO: I'd like you all to meet little Janet Reno. (Laughter.)

(Justice White administers the oath to Janet Reno.)

ATTORNEY GENERAL RENO: Mr. President, Mr. Vice President, Mr. Justice White, Mr. Speaker, Senators, this is an extraordinary moment. I just think of the history that is here today when I think of Mr. Justice White and the administration that he was involved in and the Department of Justice, probably the most historic attorney generalship in the history of this country and one—an example which I would like to follow.

Mr. President, you have done me a great honor. And, Senators, you have done something very special. I have sensed for the last three days that there will be a new spirit in America where people will want to become involved in public service because it is the greatest undertaking you can commit for your nation. They will want to become involved in public service because it will be a time where people can address issues that we're all concerned about: crime and drugs and giving our children an opportunity to grow as strong and healthy human beings. And that we can address them together in a spirit of free discussion with great respect for each other, with sometime disagreement, but with a common commitment to do what's right for America.

And the spirit of these confirmation hearings, the grand words that people were very gracious to say about me yesterday give me such encouragement and they make me think that this is such an extraordinary challenging time.

I say to all Americans, particularly young Americans—and Mr. President you see my major commitment to children by the one standing next to you and the youngest one of the family back there—(laughter)—that public service is a great undertaking and that this is a new and wonderful time in American history where we want to make government reflective of its people, make its people come first and give all Americans an opportunity to be attorney general, senators and serve the people.

Thank you ever so much, Mr. President. (Applause.)

COURT ON NEW EVIDENCE CLAIM AS BASIS OF DEATH-ROW APPEAL

January 25, 1993

The Supreme Court, continuing a trend of recent years, again in 1993 narrowed the leeway of prisoners to appeal their convictions. In the case of Herrera v. Collins, *the Court on January 25 refused a death-row appeal by a Texas prison inmate who claimed new evidence to prove his innocence. Leonel Torres Herrera was convicted and sentenced to death in 1982 for murdering a police officer in Los Fresnos, Texas. He lost a round of appeals in Texas courts and later was unable to move the case to federal court.*

In 1992, however, he returned to federal court seeking a hearing so that he could present what he described as new evidence. Herrera said he had learned that his brother, shortly before dying in 1984, had confessed to the killing. A federal district court stayed Herrera's impending execution to ensure he could pursue his claims. But the Court of Appeals for the Fifth Circuit vacated the stay of execution, saying that there was no basis for the claims. That decision was then upheld by the Supreme Court.

As described by Chief Justice William H. Rehnquist, writing for the majority, Herrera had already pursued an array of challenges to his conviction. The prosecution's evidence at trial was strong, including eyewitness identification, blood stains on Herrera's belongings, and a letter he wrote implying that he shot the officer because of a dispute over drug dealing. Herrera later pleaded guilty to killing a second officer in the incident.

Whatever weight his new evidence carried, Herrera faced two legal hurdles. First, Texas rules of criminal procedure required that it be presented within thirty days of sentencing. Second, federal courts in habeas corpus proceedings—as this was—normally do not consider questions of guilt or innocence, but only violations of constitutional rights in state courts.

Rehnquist denied Herrera's assertion that the Eighth Amendment's ban on cruel and unusual punishment entitled him to a new hearing, and declared that the thirty-day limit on new evidence did not violate due process of law under the Fourteenth Amendment. The Court made clear that few convicts in state prisons, with the aid of new evidence, could expect to obtain federal hearings long after the trial was held. The chief justice said a convict relying on posttrial evidence had to meet an "extraordinarily high standard" to persuasively demonstrate "actual innocence."

Divided Court on Prisoner Rights

As in several other decisions limiting prisoner rights, the Court was badly divided. Rehnquist spoke for a six-member majority that, in addition to himself, included Justices Byron R. White, Anthony M. Kennedy, Sandra Day O'Connor, Antonin Scalia, and Clarence Thomas. White, O'Connor, and Scalia filed concurring opinions. Justice Harry A. Blackmun issued a strongly worded dissent in which he argued that an individual's constitutional rights did not end with his conviction of a crime. Moreover, Blackmun said the majority never spelled out the high standard it applied, thus leaving lower courts without guidance. Blackmun left his sharpest comment for last. "The execution of a person who can show he is innocent comes perilously close to simple murder," Blackmun concluded. Justices David Souter and John Paul Stevens concurred with most of Blackmun's arguments but did not endorse his final statement. Justice O'Connor responded by saying Hererra "is not innocent, in any sense of the word."

Other Rulings Against Prisoners

The Court ruled that same day in two other capital punishment cases. By 5-4 it upheld the death sentence of Gary Graham, a Texas man convicted of murder. Justice White, writing for the majority, said Graham's conviction was left undisturbed by a 1989 Supreme Court decision that overturned certain provisions of the Texas death penalty law. O'Connor joined Blackmun, Stevens, and Souter in dissent. The Court also reversed, by a 7-2 vote, an appeals court decision staying the execution of Bobby Ray Fretwell, who awaited execution for murder in Arkansas. Fretwell argued that he was deprived of due process because his lawyer failed to make a legal argument that would have allowed him to escape the death sentence. Blackmun and Stevens dissented.

Before announcing the death sentence decisions, Rehnquist read a statement paying respects to former justice Thurgood Marshall, who had died one day earlier. Marshall, a strong opponent of the death penalty, retired from the Court in 1991, expressing frustration with its expanding conservative ideology.

In his last dissent, in Payne v. Tennessee, *Marshall accused the majority of conducting a "far-reaching assault upon this Court's prece-*

dents." He said the Court was ignoring previous decisions in order to uphold the the use of evidence at a murder sentencing about the effects of the crime on the victim's family. (Resignation of Justice Marshall from the Supreme Court, Court on Murder Case Sentencing, Historic Documents of 1991, p. 377 and p. 381) *Earlier that year, the Court ruled that an outright ban on the use of coerced confessions in criminal trials no longer applied to all cases.* (Supreme Court on Coerced Confessions, Historic Documents of 1991, p. 175)

Following are excerpts from the majority, concurring, and dissenting opinions in the Supreme Court's decision in Herrera v. Collins, *decided January 25, 1993, requiring a convict who introduces posttrial evidence to meet a very high standard of proof to demonstrate innocence:*

No. 91-7328

Leonel Torres Herrera, Petitioner *v.* James A. Collins, Director, Texas Department of Criminal Justice, Institutional Division	On writ of certiorari to the United States Court of Appeals for the Fifth Circuit

[January 25, 1993]

CHIEF JUSTICE REHNQUIST delivered the opinion of the Court.

Petitioner Leonel Torres Herrera was convicted of capital murder and sentenced to death in January 1982. He unsuccessfully challenged the conviction on direct appeal and state collateral proceedings in the Texas state courts, and in a federal habeas petition. In February 1992—10 years after his conviction—he urged in a second federal habeas petition that he was "actually innocent" of the murder for which he was sentenced to death, and that the Eighth Amendment's prohibition against cruel and unusual punishment and the Fourteenth Amendment's guarantee of due process of law therefore forbid his execution. He supported this claim with affidavits tending to show that his now-dead brother, rather than he, had been the perpetrator of the crime. Petitioner urges us to hold that this showing of innocence entitles him to relief in this federal habeas proceeding. We hold that it does not.

Shortly before 11 p.m. on an evening in late September 1981, the body of Texas Department of Public Safety Officer David Rucker was found by a passerby on a stretch of highway about six miles east of Los Fresnos, Texas, a few miles north of Brownsville in the Rio Grande Valley. Rucker's body was lying beside his patrol car. He had been shot in the head.

At about the same time, Los Fresnos Police Officer Enrique Carrisalez observed a speeding vehicle traveling west towards Los Fresnos, away from the place where Rucker's body had been found, along the same road. Carrisalez, who was accompanied in his patrol car by Enrique Hernandez, turned on his flashing red lights and pursued the speeding vehicle. After the car had stopped briefly at a red light, it signaled that it would pull over and did so. The patrol car pulled up behind it. Carrisalez took a flashlight and walked toward the car of the speeder. The driver opened his door and exchanged a few words with Carrisalez before firing at least one shot at Carrisalez' chest. The officer died nine days later.

Petitioner Herrera was arrested a few days after the shootings and charged with the capital murder of both Carrisalez and Rucker. He was tried and found guilty of the capital murder of Carrisalez in January 1982, and sentenced to death. In July 1982, petitioner pleaded guilty to the murder of Rucker.

At petitioner's trial for the murder of Carrisalez, Hernandez, who had witnessed Carrisalez' slaying from the officer's patrol car, identified petitioner as the person who had wielded the gun. A declaration by Officer Carrisalez to the same effect, made while he was in the hospital, was also admitted. Through a license plate check, it was shown that the speeding car involved in Carrisalez' murder was registered to petitioner's "live-in" girlfriend. Petitioner was known to drive this car, and he had a set of keys to the car in his pants pocket when he was arrested. Hernandez identified the car as the vehicle from which the murderer had emerged to fire the fatal shot. He also testified that there had been only one person in the car that night.

The evidence showed that Herrera's Social Security card had been found alongside Rucker's patrol car on the night he was killed. Splatters of blood on the car identified as the vehicle involved in the shootings, and on petitioner's blue jeans and wallet were identified as type A blood—the same type which Rucker had. (Herrera has type O blood.) Similar evidence with respect to strands of hair found in the car indicated that the hair was Rucker's and not Herrera's. A handwritten letter was also found on the person of petitioner when he was arrested, which strongly implied that he had killed Rucker.

Petitioner appealed his conviction and sentence, arguing, among other things, that Hernandez' and Carrisalez' identifications were unreliable and improperly admitted. The Texas Court of Criminal Appeals affirmed, and we denied certiorari.... Petitioner's application for state habeas relief was denied. Petitioner then filed a federal habeas petition, again challenging the identifications offered against him at trial. This petition was denied, and we again denied certiorari.

Petitioner next returned to state court and filed a second habeas petition, raising, among other things, a claim of "actual innocence" based on newly discovered evidence. In support of this claim petitioner presented the affidavits of Hector Villarreal, an attorney who had represented petitioner's brother, Raul Herrera, Sr., and of Juan Franco Palacious, one of Raul Sr.'s former cellmates. Both individuals claimed that Raul Sr., who died in 1984, had told them that he—and not petitioner—had killed Officers Rucker and Carrisalez. The State District Court denied this application, finding that "no evidence at trial remotely suggest[ed] that anyone other than [petitioner] committed the offense." ... The Texas Court of Criminal Appeals affirmed, ... and we denied certiorari....

In February 1992, petitioner lodged the instant habeas petition—his second—in federal court, alleging, among other things, that he is innocent of the murders of Rucker and Carrisalez, and that his execution would thus violate the Eighth and Fourteenth Amendments. In addition to proffering the above affidavits, petitioner presented the affidavits of Raul Herrera, Jr., Raul Sr.'s son, and Jose Ybarra, Jr., a schoolmate of the Herrera brothers. Raul Jr. averred that he had witnessed his father shoot Officers Rucker and Carrisalez and petitioner was not present. Raul Jr. was nine years old at the time of the killings. Ybarra alleged that Raul Sr. told him one summer night in 1983 that he had shot the two police officers. Petitioner alleged that law enforcement officials were aware of this evidence, and had withheld it....

The District Court dismissed most of petitioner's claims as an abuse of the writ. However, "in order to ensure that Petitioner can assert his constitutional claims and out of a sense of fairness and due process," the District Court granted petitioner's request for a stay of execution so that he could present his claim of actual innocence, along with the Raul Jr. and Ybarra affidavits, in state court....

... Absent an accompanying constitutional violation, the Court of Appeals held that petitioner's claim of actual innocence was not cognizable because, under *Townsend v. Sain* (1963), "the existence merely of newly discovered evidence relevant to the guilt of a state prisoner is not a ground for relief on federal habeas corpus." We granted certiorari (1992), and the Texas Court of Criminal Appeals stayed petitioner's execution. We now affirm.

[T]he evidence upon which petitioner's claim of innocence rests was not produced at his trial, but rather eight years later. In any system of criminal justice, "innocence" or "guilt" must be determined in some sort of a judicial proceeding. Petitioner's showing of innocence, and indeed his constitutional claim for relief based upon that showing, must be evaluated in the light of the previous proceedings in this case, which have stretched over a span of 10 years.

A person when first charged with a crime is entitled to a presumption of innocence, and may insist that his guilt be established beyond a reasonable doubt....

Once a defendant has been afforded a fair trial and convicted of the offense for which he was charged, the presumption of innocence disappears.... Here, it is not disputed that the State met its burden of proving at trial that petitioner was guilty of the capital murder of Officer

Carrisalez beyond a reasonable doubt. Thus, in the eyes of the law, petitioner does not come before the Court as one who is "innocent," but on the contrary as one who has been convicted by due process of law of two brutal murders.

Based on affidavits here filed, petitioner claims that evidence never presented to the trial court proves him innocent notwithstanding the verdict reached at his trial. Such a claim is not cognizable in the state courts of Texas. For to obtain a new trial based on newly discovered evidence, a defendant must file a motion within 30 days after imposition or suspension of sentence. The Texas courts have construed this 30-day time limit as jurisdictional....

Claims of actual innocence based on newly discovered evidence have never been held to state a ground for federal habeas relief absent an independent constitutional violation occurring in the underlying state criminal proceeding.... This rule is grounded in the principle that federal habeas courts sit to ensure that individuals are not imprisoned in violation of the Constitution—not to correct errors of fact....

... Few rulings would be more disruptive of our federal system than to provide for federal habeas review of free-standing claims of actual innocence....

The dissent would place the burden on petitioner to show that he is "probably" innocent....

The dissent fails to articulate the relief that would be available if petitioner were to meets its "probable innocence" standard. Would it be commutation of petitioner's death sentence, new trial, or unconditional release from imprisonment? The typical relief granted in federal habeas corpus is a conditional order of release unless the State elects to retry the successful habeas petitioner, or in a capital case a similar conditional order vacating the death sentence. Were petitioner to satisfy the dissent's "probable innocence" standard, therefore, the District Court would presumably be required to grant a conditional order of relief, which would in effect require the State to retry petitioner 10 years after his first trial, not because of any constitutional violation which had occurred at the first trial, but simply because of a belief that in light of petitioner's new-found evidence a jury might find him not guilty at a second trial.

Yet there is no guarantee that the guilt or innocence determination would be any more exact. To the contrary, the passage of time only diminishes the reliability of criminal adjudications....

This is not to say that our habeas jurisprudence casts a blind eye towards innocence. In a series of cases culminating with *Sawyer v. Whitley* (1992), decided last Term, we have held that a petitioner otherwise subject to defenses of abusive or successive use of the writ may have his federal constitutional claim considered on the merits if he makes a proper showing of actual innocence.... But this body of our habeas jurisprudence makes clear that a claim of "actual innocence" is not itself a constitutional claim, but instead a gateway through which a habeas petitioner must pass to have his otherwise barred constitutional claim considered on the merits....

... This is not to say, however, that petitioner is left without a forum to raise his actual innocence claim. For under Texas law, petitioner may file a request for executive clemency.... Clemency is deeply rooted in our Anglo-American tradition of law, and is the historic remedy for preventing miscarriages of justice where judicial process has been exhausted....

... Today, all 36 States that authorize capital punishment have constitutional or statutory provisions for clemency.

Executive clemency has provided the "fail safe" in our criminal justice system.... It is an unalterable fact that our judicial system, like the human beings who administer it, is fallible. But history is replete with examples of wrongfully convicted persons who have been pardoned in the wake of after-discovered evidence establishing their innocence.... Recent authority confirms that over the past century clemency has been exercised frequently in capital cases in which demonstrations of "actual innocence" have been made....

In Texas, the Governor has the power, upon the recommendation of a majority of the Board of Pardons and Paroles, to grant clemency....

... History shows that the traditional remedy for claims of innocence based on new evidence, discovered too late in the day to file a new trial motion, has been executive clemency.

We may assume, for the sake of argument in deciding this case, that in a capital case a truly persuasive demonstration of "actual innocence" made after trial would render the execution of a defendant unconstitutional, and warrant federal habeas relief if there were no state avenue open to process such a claim. But because of the very disruptive effect that entertaining claims of actual innocence would have on the need for finality in capital cases, and the enormous burden that having to retry cases based on often stale evidence would place on the States, the threshold showing for such an assumed right would necessarily be extraordinarily high. The showing made by petitioner in this case falls far short of any such threshold....

The judgment of the Court of Appeals is

Affirmed.

JUSTICE O'CONNOR, with whom JUSTICE KENNEDY joins, concurring.

I cannot disagree with the fundamental legal principle that executing the innocent is inconsistent with the Constitution.... [T]he execution of a legally and factually innocent person would be a constitutionally intolerable event. Dispositive to this case, however, is an equally fundamental fact: Petitioner is not innocent, in any sense of the word....

Ultimately, two things about this case are clear. First is what the Court does *not* hold. Nowhere does the Court state that the Constitution permits the execution of an actually innocent person. Instead, the Court assumes for the sake of argument that a truly persuasive demonstration of actual innocence would render any such execution unconstitutional and that federal habeas relief would be warranted if no state avenue were open to process the claim. Second is what petitioner has not demonstrated. Petitioner has failed to make a persuasive showing of actual innocence. Not one judge—no state court judge, not the District Court Judge, none of the three Judges of the Court of Appeals, and none of the Justices of this Court—has expressed doubt about petitioner's guilt. Accordingly, the Court has no reason to pass on, and appropriately reserves, the question whether federal courts may entertain convincing claims of actual innocence. That difficult question remains open. If the Constitution's guarantees of fair procedure and the safeguards of clemency and pardon fulfill their historical mission, it may never require resolution at all.

JUSTICE SCALIA, with whom JUSTICE THOMAS joins, concurring.

We granted certiorari on the question whether it violates due process or constitutes cruel and unusual punishment for a State to execute a person who, having been convicted of murder after a full and fair trial, later alleges that newly discovered evidence shows him to be "actually innocent." I would have preferred to decide that question, particularly since, as the Court's discussion shows, it is perfectly clear what the answer is: There is no basis in text, tradition, or even in contemporary practice (if that were enough), for finding in the Constitution a right to demand judicial consideration of newly discovered evidence of innocence brought forward after conviction. In saying that such a right exists, the dissenters apply nothing but their personal opinions to invalidate the rules of more than two thirds of the States, and a Federal Rule of Criminal Procedure for which this Court itself is responsible. If the system that has been in place for 200 years (and remains widely approved) "shocks" the dissenters' consciences, perhaps they should doubt the calibration of their consciences, or, better still, the usefulness of "conscience-shocking" as a legal test.

I nonetheless join the entirety of the Court's opinion, including the final portion because there is no legal error in deciding a case by assuming *arguendo* that an asserted constitutional right exists....

JUSTICE WHITE, concurring in the judgment.

In voting to affirm, I assume that a persuasive showing of "actual innocence" made after trial, even though made after the expiration of the time provided by law for the presentation of newly discovered evidence, would render unconstitutional the execution of petitioner in this case. To be entitled to relief, however, petitioner would at the very least be required to show that based on proffered newly discovered evidence and the entire record before the jury that convicted him, "no rational trier of fact could [find] proof of guilt beyond a reasonable doubt." *Jackson v. Virginia* (1979). For the reasons stated in the Court's opinion, petitioner's showing falls far short of satisfying even that standard, and I therefore concur in the judgment.

JUSTICE BLACKMUN, with whom JUSTICE STEVENS and JUSTICE SOUTER join with respect to Parts I-IV, dissenting.

Nothing could be more contrary to contemporary standards of decency, see *Ford v. Wainwright* (1986), or more shocking to the conscience, see *Rochin v. California* (1952), than to execute a person who is actually innocent.

I therefore must disagree with the long and general discussion that precedes the Court's disposition of this case. That discussion, of course, is dictum because the Court assumes, "for the sake of argument in deciding this case, that in a capital case a truly persuasive demonstration of 'actual innocence' made after trial would render the execution of a defendant unconstitutional." Without articulating the standard it is applying, however, the Court then decides that this petitioner has not made a sufficiently persuasive case. Because I believe that in the first instance the District Court should decide whether petitioner is entitled to a hearing and whether he is entitled to relief on the merits of his claim, I would reverse the order of the Court of Appeals and remand this case for further proceedings in the District Court.

I

The Court's enumeration of the constitutional rights of criminal defendants surely is entirely beside the point. These protections sometimes fail. We really are being asked to decide whether the Constitution forbids the execution of a person who has been validly convicted and sentenced but who, nonetheless, can prove his innocence with newly discovered evidence. Despite the State of Texas' astonishing protestation to the contrary, I do not see how the answer can be anything but "yes."

A

...The protection of the Eighth Amendment does not end once a defendant has been validly convicted and sentenced. In *Johnson v. Mississippi* (1988), the petitioner had been convicted of murder and sentenced to death on the basis of three aggravating circumstances. One of those circumstances was that he previously had been convicted of a violent felony in the State of New York. After Johnson had been sentenced to death, the New York Court of Appeals reversed his prior conviction. Although there was no question that the prior conviction was valid at the time of Johnson's sentencing, this Court held that the Eighth Amendment required review of the sentence because "the jury was allowed to consider evidence that has been revealed to be materially inaccurate." In *Ford v. Wainwright*, the petitioner had been convicted of murder and sentenced to death. There was no suggestion that he was incompetent at the time of his offense, at trial, or at sentencing, but subsequently he exhibited changes in behavior that raised doubts about his sanity. This Court held that Florida was required under the Eighth Amendment to provide an additional hearing to determine whether Ford was mentally competent, and that he could not be executed if he were incompetent. Both *Johnson* and *Ford* recognize that capital defendants may be entitled to further proceedings because of an intervening development even though they have been validly convicted and sentenced to death.

Respondent and the United States as *amicus curiae* argue that the Eighth Amendment does not apply to petitioner because he is challenging his guilt, not his punishment. The majority attempts to distinguish *Ford* on that basis. Such reasoning, however, not only contradicts our decision in *Beck v. Alabama* (1980), but also fundamentally misconceives the nature of petitioner's argument. Whether petitioner is viewed as challenging simply his death sentence or also his continued detention, he still is challenging the State's right to punish him....

The Court also suggests that allowing petitioner to raise his claim of innocence would not serve society's interest in the reliable imposition of the death penalty because it might require a new trial that would be less accurate than the first. This suggestion misses the point entirely. The question is not whether a second trial would be more reliable than the first but whether, in light of new evidence, the result of the first trial is sufficiently reliable for the State to carry out a death sentence. Furthermore, it is far from clear that a State will seek to retry the rare prisoner who prevails on a claim of actual innocence. ... I believe a prisoner must show not just that there was probably a reasonable doubt about his guilt but that he is probably actually innocent. I find it difficult to believe that any State would chose to retry a person who meets this standard....

[B and C Omitted]

II

The majority's discussion of petitioner's constitutional claims is even more perverse when viewed in the light of this Court's recent habeas jurisprudence. Beginning with a trio of decisions in 1986, this Court shifted the focus of federal habeas review of successive, abusive, or defaulted claims away from the preservation of constitutional rights to a fact-based inquiry into the habeas petitioner's guilt or innocence....

Having adopted an "actual innocence" requirement for review of abusive, successive, or defaulted claims, however, the majority would now take the position that "the claim of 'actual innocence' is not itself a constitutional claim, but instead a gateway through which a habeas petitioner must pass to have his otherwise barred constitutional claim considered on the merits." In other words, having held that a prisoner who is incarcerated in violation of the Constitution must show he is actually innocent to obtain relief, the majority would now hold that a prisoner who is actually innocent must show a constitutional violation to obtain relief. The only principle that would appear to reconcile these two positions is the principle that habeas relief should be denied whenever possible.

III

The Eighth and Fourteenth Amendments, of course, are binding on the States, and one would normally expect the States to adopt procedures to consider claims of actual innocence based on newly discovered evidence.... The majority's disposition of this case, however, leaves the States uncertain of their constitutional obligations.

A

Whatever procedures a State might adopt to hear actual innocence claims, one thing is certain: The possibility of executive clemency is not sufficient to satisfy the requirements of the Eighth and Fourteenth Amendments. The majority correctly points out: "A pardon is an act of grace." The vindication of rights guaranteed by the Constitution has never been made to turn on the unreviewable discretion of an executive official or administrative tribunal. Indeed, in *Ford v. Wainwright,* we explicitly rejected the argument that executive clemency was adequate to vindicate the Eighth Amendment right not to be executed if one is insane....

[B Omitted]

C

The question that remains is what showing should be required to obtain relief on the merits of an Eighth or Fourteenth Amendment claim of actual innocence....

In articulating the "actual-innocence" exception in our habeas jurisprudence, this Court has adopted a standard requiring the petitioner to show a " 'fair probability that, in light of all the evidence ..., the trier of facts would have entertained a reasonable doubt of his guilt.' " ... In other words, the habeas petitioner must show that there probably would be a reasonable doubt....

I think the standard for relief on the merits of an actual-innocence claim must be higher than the threshold standard for merely reaching that claim or any other claim that has been procedurally defaulted or is successive or abusive. I would hold that, to obtain relief on a claim of actual innocence, the petitioner must show that he probably is innocent....

In considering whether a prisoner is entitled to relief on an actual-innocence claim, a court should take all the evidence into account, giving due regard to its reliability.... Because placing the burden on the prisoner to prove innocence creates a presumption that the conviction is valid, it is not necessary or appropriate to make further presumptions about the reliability of newly discovered evidence generally. Rather, the court charged with deciding such a claim should make a case-by-case determination about the reliability of the newly discovered evidence under the circumstances.... Obviously, the stronger the evidence of the prisoner's guilt, the more persuasive the newly discovered evidence of innocence must be. A prisoner raising an actual-innocence claim in a federal habeas petition is not entitled to discovery as a matter of right.... The district court retains discretion to order discovery, however, when it would help the court make a reliable determination with respect to the prisoner's claim....

It should be clear that the standard I would adopt would not convert the federal courts into " 'forums in which to relitigate state trials.' " It would not "require the habeas court to hear testimony from the witnesses who testified at the trial," though, if the petition warrants a hearing, it may require the habeas court to hear the testimony of "those who made the statements in the affidavits which petitioner has presented." I believe that if a prisoner can show that he is probably actually innocent, in light of all the evidence, then he has made "a truly persuasive demonstration," and his execution would violate the Constitution. I would so hold.

IV

In this case, the District Court determined that petitioner's newly discovered evidence warranted further consideration. Because the District Court doubted its own authority to consider the new evidence, it thought that petitioner's claim of actual innocence should be brought in state court, but it clearly did not think that petitioner's evidence was so insubstantial that it could be dismissed without any hearing at all. I would reverse the order of the Court of Appeals and remand the case to the District Court to consider whether petitioner has shown, in light of all the evidence, that he is probably actually innocent....

V

I have voiced disappointment over this Court's obvious eagerness to do away with any restriction on the States' power to execute whomever and however they please.... I have also expressed doubts about whether, in the absence of such restrictions, capital punishment remains constitutional at all.... Of one thing, however, I am certain. Just as an execution without adequate safeguards is unacceptable, so too is an execution when the condemned prisoner can prove that he is innocent. The execution of a person who can show that he is innocent comes perilously close to simple murder.

CLINTON PLAN TO REMOVE MILITARY HOMOSEXUAL BAN

January 29 and July 19, 1993

Candidate Bill Clinton's pledge to let homosexuals serve openly in the armed forces received only minor attention during the 1992 presidential election campaign, but as the time for him to take office drew near, military leaders and major congressional figures voiced strong objections. During Clinton's first weeks as president, the issue threatened to sidetrack economic concerns, which had been foremost in the election campaign and on the new administration's agenda.

After several days of delay, Clinton announced an interim policy at his first White House news conference, January 29, that made some concessions to the opponents, led by the Joint Chiefs of Staff and their chairman, Gen. Colin L. Powell, and by Sen. Sam Nunn, D-Ga., chairman of the Senate Armed Services Committee. After several days of negotiations between Nunn and Senate Majority Leader George Mitchell, D-Maine, a compromise was worked out.

Under the plan, homosexuals could be removed from active duty during a six-month period while a permanent policy was being formulated, but, instead of being discharged as in the past, they would be placed on standby reserve status without pay. They could petition to be returned to active service if the ban was lifted permanently. The armed services, in turn, would no longer ask recruits about their sexual orientation nor investigate allegations that individuals were homosexual, unless there was evidence of misconduct. That feature became known as "don't ask, don't tell."

Clinton conceded that he had been forced to bargain. "This compromise is not everything that I would have hoped for, or everything I would have stood for, but it is plainly a substantial step in the right direction," he said at the news conference. He added, "The issue is whether men and women who can and have served with distinction should be excluded from military service solely on the basis of their status. And I believe they should not."

The president said that he had asked Secretary of Defense Les Aspin, "after full consultation with military and congressional leaders and concerned individuals outside the government," to propose an executive order by July 15 to lift the homosexual ban.

Reaction to Clinton's Interim Plan

Rep. Barney Frank, D-Mass., an openly homosexual member of Congress, said the compromise plan "stinks," but he did not blame Clinton, who "gets sandbagged by Sam Nunn and Colin Powell." According to numerous press commentaries, the president had been hurt politically by the furor. Some right-wing religious groups claimed it had boosted their fund-raising and organizing activities. "Clinton's decision to press this forward is a godsend to us," said Randall Terry, an anti-abortion activist.

At hearings Nunn's committee conducted March 29-31, several high-ranking military officers, a military psychiatrist, and a military affairs author testified that homosexuals were detrimental to troop morale and impeded necessary small-unit cohesion in combat. However, Lawrence Korb, a former assistant defense secretary in the Reagan administration who in 1982 had helped write the Defense Department regulation Clinton sought to erase—that "homosexuality is incompatible with military service"—said he had changed his mind and now found "no convincing evidence that changing the current policy would undermine unit cohesion any more than the other social changes that society has asked the armed forces to make over the past fifty years." Other witnesses testified that morale in the Canadian and Australian armed forces was not hurt after their homosexual bans were lifted in 1992.

At a new round of hearings in May, Col. Fred Peck of the Marine Corps said that he favored the ban even though he had just learned that his son was homosexual. "I have spent twenty-seven years in the military," Peck told the committee, "and I know what it would be like for him if he went in. And it would be hell. . . . I would be very fearful that his life would be in jeopardy from his own troops."

Making "Don't Ask, Don't Tell" Permanent

At the outset of the hearings, Nunn suggested that the "don't ask, don't tell" policy be made permanent. He had previously rejected Representative Frank's proposal that off-base conduct be exempt from military control. Clinton, appearing May 27 on the CBS-TV program "This Morning," appeared to support some version of the policy. "Most people believe if you don't ask and you don't say and you're not forced to confront it, [homosexual] people should be able to serve," Clinton said. "We are trying to work this out so that our country . . . does not appear to be endorsing a gay lifestyle, but we accept people as people and give them a chance to serve if they play by the rules."

Gay-rights groups, which had strongly supported Clinton in the election, seemed upset that he had endorsed a compromise strategy. Thomas

B. Stoddard, director of the gay-rights coalition Campaign for Military Service, said the "don't ask, don't tell" plan did not eliminate discrimination. (Gay/Lesbian March on Washington, p. 327)

That plan remained the foundation of the permanent policy the president announced in a speech to military officers July 19 at Fort McNair National Defense University in Washington, D.C. He called the policy an "honorable compromise" between those who wanted to keep the ban and those who wanted to remove it. "It provides a sensible balance between the rights of the individual and the needs of our military to remain the world's number one fighting force." Whether the policy succeeds or not, he said, "will depend in large measure on the commitment it receives from the leaders of the military services." At the same time, Aspin issued a set of guidelines for enforcement of the new policy due to take effect October 1.

Before that date, it became subject to congressional and court action. In September the House and Senate passed identical bills calling homosexuality "unacceptable" in the military services. The White House, which supported the legislation in order to defeat a Republican-led measure in Congress to codify the earlier ban, said it would not change the workings of the president's plan.

Situation Unsettled by Court Order

But all of this was rendered moot, at least temporarily, by a federal judge. On January 29, U.S. District Judge Terry J. Hatter, Jr., in Los Angeles, had declared the existing ban unconstitutional. He ruled in a case filed by Keith Meinhold, a sailor who had been discharged for homosexuality. The ruling was credited with giving Clinton some political leverage in his efforts to lift the ban. On October 7 Judge Hatter issued a sweeping order barring all military services from discriminating against homosexuals "in the absence of proven sexual conduct—if such conduct is proven to interfere with the military mission of the armed forces."

The government said the next day it was compelled by the ruling to permit gay service members to serve openly without fear of punishment. Consequently, it said it would shelve the "don't ask, don't tell" policy unless the ruling was reversed on appeal. It was appealed to the U.S. Court of Appeals for the Ninth District, in San Francisco. That court twice had refused to narrow the judge's ruling pending the appeal. At the end of September, however, the U.S. Supreme Court lifted the lower court's order. The Supreme Court action cleared the way for Clinton's "don't ask, don't tell" policy to take effect and allowed the military to continue discharging openly gay personnel.

Following are excerpts from President Bill Clinton's White House news conference, January 29, 1993, announcing an interim plan for homosexuals to serve in the armed forces;

excerpts from the final plan he announced July 19, 1993; and enforcement guidelines issued the same day by Defense Secretary Les Aspin:

CLINTON NEWS CONFERENCE

P: ... Today, as you know, I have reached an agreement, at least with [Sen. Sam] Nunn [D-Ga.] and [Sen. George J.] Mitchell [D-Maine] about how we will proceed in the next few days. But first I'd like to explain what I believe about this issue and why, and what I have decided to do, after a long conversation, and a very good one with the Joint Chiefs of Staff, and discussions with several members of Congress.

The issue is not whether there should be homosexuals in the military. Everyone concedes that there are. The issue is whether men and women who can and have served with real distinction should be excluded from military service solely on the basis of their status. And I believe they should not. The principle on which I base this position is this: I believe that American citizens who want to serve their country should be able to do so unless their conduct disqualifies them from doing so.

Military life is fundamentally different from civilian society. It necessarily has a different and stricter code of conduct, even a different code of justice.

Nonetheless, individuals who are prepared to accept all necessary restrictions on their behavior, many of which would be intolerable in civilian society, should be able to serve their country honorably and well.

I have asked the secretary of Defense to submit by July the 15th a draft executive order, after full consultation with military and congressional leaders and concerned individuals outside of the government, which would end the present policy of exclusion from military service solely on the basis of sexual orientation, and at the same time establish rigorous standards regarding sexual conduct to be applied to all military personnel.

This draft order will be accompanied by a study conducted during the next six months on the real practical problems that would be involved in this revision of policy so that we will have a practical, realistic approach consistent with the high standards of combat effectiveness and unit cohesion that our armed services must maintain.

I agree with the Joint Chiefs that the highest standards of conduct must be required. The change cannot and should not be accomplished overnight. It does require extensive consultation with the Joint Chiefs, experts in the Congress and in the legal community, joined by my administration and others. We've consulted closely to date and will do so in the future. During that process, interim measures will be placed into effect, which I hope again sharpen the focus of this debate.

The Joint Chiefs of Staff have agreed to remove the question regarding one's sexual orientation from future versions of the enlistment application, and it will not be asked in the interim.

We also all agree that a very high standard of conduct can and must be applied. So the single area of disagreement is this: Should someone be able to serve their country in uniform if they say they are homosexual but they do nothing which violates the code of conduct, undermines unit cohesion or morale apart from that statement?

That is what the furor of the last few days has been about. And the practical and not insignificant issues raised by that issue are what will be studied in the next six months.

Through this period ending July 15, the Department of Justice will seek continuances in pending court cases involving reinstatement, and administrative separation under current Department of Defense policies based on status alone will be stayed, pending completion of this review.

The final discharge in cases based only on status will be suspended until the president has an opportunity to review and act upon the final recommendations of the secretary of Defense with respect to the current policy. In the meantime, a member whose discharge has been suspended by the attorney general will be separated from active duty and placed in standby reserve until the final report of the secretary of Defense and the final action of the president.

This is the agreement that I have reached with Sen. Nunn and Sen. Mitchell. During this review process, I will work with the Congress, and I believe the compromise announced today by the senators and by me shows that we can work together to end the gridlock that has plagued our city for too long. This compromise is not everything I would have hoped for, or everything that I have stood for, but it is plainly a substantial step in the right direction. And it will allow us to move forward on other terribly important issues affecting far more Americans. My administration came to this city with a mission—to bring critical issues of reform and renewal, and economic revitalization to the public debate—issues that are central to the lives of all Americans. . . .

I applaud the work that has been done in the last two or three days by Sen. Nunn, Sen. Mitchell and others, to enable us to move forward on a principle that is important to me, without shutting the government down and running the risk of not even addressing the family and medical leave issue which is so important to America's families, before Congress goes into its recess. I am looking forward to getting on with this issue over the next six months, and with these other issues which were so central to the campaign, and far more importantly, are so important to the lives of all the American people.

Q: Yesterday a federal court in California said that the military ban on homosexuals was unconstitutional. Will you direct the Navy and the Justice Department not to appeal that decision, and how does that ruling strengthen your hand in this case?

P: Well, it makes one point—I think it strengthens my hand, if you will, in two ways. One, I agree with the principle embodied in the case. As I understand—I've not read the opinion—but as I understand, the opinion draws the distinction that I seek to draw between conduct and status.

And secondly, it makes the practical point I have been making all along, which is that there is a not insignificant chance that this matter would ultimately be resolved in the courts in a way that would open admission into the military, without the opportunity to deal with this whole range of practical issues which everyone who's ever thought about it, or talked it through, concedes are there....

Q: Obviously you didn't intend the first week of your administration—[given] your promise to have the laser focus on the economy—to be seen around the country as military gay rights week. I wonder if, in retrospect, you think you could have done things differently to avoid that happening?

P: I don't know how I could have done that. The Joint Chiefs asked for a meeting about a number of issues of which this was only one. We spent a lot of time talking about other things. This issue was not put forward in this context by me, it was put forward by those in the United States Senate who sought to make it an issue early on....

Q: [On] July 15, this happens, period, regardless of what comes out at these hearings, is that correct? The ban will be issued—or will be lifted, rather?

P: That is my position. My position is that I still embrace the principle, and I think it should be done. The position of those who are opposed to me is that they think the problems will be so overwhelming everybody with good sense will change their position. I don't expect to do that.

Q: You definitely expect to do it.

P: I don't expect to change my position....

FORT McNAIR SPEECH

... I have come here today to discuss a difficult challenge and one which has received an enormous amount of publicity and public and private debate over the last several months—our nation's policy toward homosexuals in the military.

I believe the policy I am announcing today represents a real step forward. But I know it will raise concerns in some of your minds. So I wanted you to hear my thinking and my decision directly and in person, because I respect you and because you are among the elite who will lead our Armed Forces into the next century, and because you will have to put this policy into effect and I expect your help in doing it.

The policy I am announcing today is, in my judgment, the right thing to do and the best way to do it. It is right because it provides greater protection to those who happen to be homosexual and want to serve their country honorably in uniform, obeying all the military's rules against sexual misconduct.

It is the best way to proceed because it provides a sensible balance between the rights of the individual and the needs of our military to remain the world's number one fighting force. As President of all the American people, I am pledged to protect and to promote individual rights. As Commander in Chief, I am pledged to protect and advance our security. In this policy, I believe we have come close to meeting both objectives. . . .

Let me review the events which bring us here today. Before I ran for President, this issue was already upon us. Some of the members of the military returning from the Gulf War announced their homosexuality in order to protest the ban. The military's policy has been questioned in college ROTC programs. Legal challenges have been filed in court, including one that has since succeeded. In 1991, the Secretary of Defense Dick Cheney was asked about reports that the Defense Department spent an alleged $500 million to separate and replace about 17,000 homosexuals from the military service during the 1980s, in spite of the findings of a government report saying there was no reason to believe that they could not serve effectively and with distinction.

Shortly thereafter, while giving a speech at the Kennedy School of Government at Harvard, I was asked by one of the students what I thought of this report and what I thought of lifting the ban. This question had never before been presented to me, and I had never had the opportunity to discuss it with anyone. I stated then what I still believe: that I thought there ought to be a presumption that people who wish to do so should be able to serve their country if they are willing to conform to the high standards of the military, and that the emphasis should be always on people's conduct, not their status.

For me, and this is very important, this issue has never been one of group rights, but rather of individual ones—of the individual opportunity to serve and the individual responsibility to conform to the highest standards of military conduct. For people who are willing to play by the rules, able to serve, and make a contribution, I believed then and I believe now we should give them the chance to do so.

The central facts of this issue are not much in dispute. First, notwithstanding the ban, there have been and are homosexuals in the military service who serve with distinction. I have had the privilege of meeting some of these men and women, and I have been deeply impressed by their devotion to duty and to country.

Second, there is no study showing them to be less capable or more prone to misconduct than heterosexual soldiers. Indeed, all the information we have indicates that they are not less capable or more prone to misbehavior.

Third, misconduct is already covered by the laws and rules which also cover activities that are improper by heterosexual members of the military.

Fourth, the ban has been lifted in other nations and in police and fire departments in our country with no discernible negative impact on unit cohesion or capacity to do the job, though there is, admittedly, no absolute analogy to the situation we face and no study bearing on this specific issue.

Fifth, even if the ban were lifted entirely, the experience of other nations and police and fire departments in the United States indicates that most homosexuals would probably not declare their sexual orientation openly, thereby making an already hard life even more difficult in some circumstances.

But as the sociologist, Charles Moskos, noted after spending many years studying the American military, the issue may be tougher to resolve here in the United States than in Canada, Australia, and in some other nations because of the presence in our country of both vocal gay rights groups and equally vocal antigay rights groups, including some religious groups who believe that lifting the ban amounts to endorsing a lifestyle they strongly disapprove of.

Clearly, the American people are deeply divided on this issue, with most military people opposed to lifting the ban because of the feared impact on unit cohesion, rooted in disapproval of homosexual lifestyles, and the fear of invasion of privacy of heterosexual soldiers who must live and work in close quarters with homosexual military people.

However, those who have studied this issue extensively have discovered an interesting fact. People in this country who are aware of having known homosexuals are far more likely to support lifting the ban. In other words, they are likely to see this issue in terms of individual conduct and individual capacity instead of the claims of a group with which they do not agree; and also to be able to imagine how this ban could be lifted without a destructive impact on group cohesion and morale.

Shortly after I took office and reaffirmed my position, the foes of lifting the ban in the Congress moved to enshrine the ban in law. I asked that congressional action be delayed for six months while the Secretary of Defense worked with the Joint Chiefs to come up with a proposal for changing our current policy. I then met with the Joint Chiefs to hear their concerns and asked them to try to work through the issue with Secretary Aspin. I wanted to handle the matter in this way on grounds of both principle and practicality....

For months now, the Secretary of Defense and the service chiefs have worked through this issue in a highly charged, deeply emotional environment, struggling to come to terms with the competing consideration and pressures and, frankly, to work through their own ideas and deep feelings.

During this time many dedicated Americans have come forward to state their own views on this issue. Most, but not all, of the military testimony has been against lifting the ban. But support for changing the policy has come from distinguished combat veterans including Senators Bob Kerrey, Chuck Robb, and John Kerry in the United States Congress. It has come from Lawrence Korb, who enforced the gay ban during the Reagan administration, and from former Senator Barry Goldwater, a distinguished veteran, former Chairman of the Senate Armed Services Committee, founder of the Arizona National Guard, and patron saint of the conservative wing of the Republican Party.

Senator Goldwater's statement, published in The Washington Post recently, made it crystal clear that when this matter is viewed as an issue of individual opportunity and responsibility rather than one of alleged group rights, this is not a call for cultural license, but rather a reaffirmation of the American value of extending opportunity to responsible individuals and of limiting the role of government over citizens' private lives.

On the other hand, those who oppose lifting the ban are clearly focused not on the conduct of individual gay service members, but on how nongay service members feel about gays in general and, in particular, those in the military service.

These past few days I have been in contact with the Secretary of Defense as he has worked through the final stages of this policy with the Joint Chiefs. We now have a policy that is a substantial advance over the one in place when I took office. I have ordered Secretary Aspin to issue a directive consisting of these essential elements:

One, servicemen and women will be judged based on their conduct, not their sexual orientation.

Two, therefore, the practice, now six months old, of not asking about sexual orientation in the enlistment procedure will continue.

Three, an open statement by a service member that he or she is a homosexual will create a rebuttable presumption that he or she intends to engage [in] prohibited conduct, but the service member will be given an opportunity to refute that presumption, in other words, to demonstrate that he or she intends to live by the rules of conduct that apply in the military service.

And four, all provisions of the Uniform [Code of] Military Justice will be enforced in an even-handed manner as regards both heterosexuals and homosexuals. And, thanks to the policy provisions agreed by the Joint Chiefs, there will be a decent regard to the legitimate privacy and associational rights of all service members.

Just as is the case under current policy, unacceptable conduct, either heterosexual or homosexual, will be unacceptable 24 hours a day, seven days a week, from the time a recruit joins the service until the day he or she is discharged. Now, as in the past, every member of our military will be required to comply with the Uniform Code of Military Justice, which is federal law and military regulations, at all times and in all places.

Let me say a few words about this policy. It is not a perfect solution. It is not identical with some of my own goals. And it certainly will not please everyone, perhaps not anyone, and clearly not those who hold the most adamant opinions on either side of this issue.

But those who wish to ignore the issue must understand that it is already tearing at the cohesion of the military, and it is today being considered by the federal courts in ways that may not be to the liking of those who oppose any change. And those who want the ban to be lifted completely on both status and conduct must understand that such action would have faced certain and decisive reversal by the Congress and the cause for which many have fought for years would be delayed probably for years.

Thus, on grounds of both principle and practicality, this is a major step forward. It is, in my judgment, consistent with my responsibilities as President and Commander in Chief to meet the need to change current policy. It is an honorable compromise that advances the cause of people who are called to serve our country by their patriotism, the cause of our national security and our national interest in resolving an issue that has divided our military and our nation and diverted our attention from other matters for too long.

The time has come for us to move forward. As your Commander in Chief, I charge all of you to carry out this policy with fairness, with balance and with due regard for the privacy of individuals. We must and will protect unit cohesion and troop morale. We must and will continue to have the best fighting force in the world. But this is an end to witch hunts that spend millions of taxpayer dollars to ferret out individuals who have served their country well. Improper conduct, on or off base, should remain grounds for discharge. But we will proceed with an even hand against everyone regardless of sexual orientation.

Such controversies as this have divided us before. But our nation and our military have always risen to the challenge before. That was true of racial integration of the military and changes in the role of women in the military. Each of these was an issue because it was an issue for society, as well as for the military. And in each case our military was a leader in figuring out how to respond most effectively....

I must now look to General Powell, to the Joint Chiefs, to all the other leaders in our military to carry out this policy through effective training and leadership. Every officer will be expected to exert the necessary effort to make this policy work. That has been the key every time the military has successfully addressed a new challenge, and it will be key in this effort, too....

I strongly believe that our military, like our society, needs the talents of every person who wants to make a contribution and who is ready to live by the rules. That is the heart of the policy that I have announced today. I hope in your heart you will find the will and the desire to support it and to lead our military in incorporating it into our nation's great asset and the world's best fighting force.

ASPIN GUIDELINES

On January 29, 1993, the President directed me to review DoD [Department of Defense] policy on homosexuals in the military. The President further directed that the DoD policy be "practical, realistic, and consistent with the high standards of combat effectiveness and unit cohesion our armed forces must maintain."

An extensive review was conducted. I have paid careful attention to the hearings that have been held by both the House and Senate Armed Services Committees, conferred with the Joint Chiefs and acting Secretaries of the Military Departments and considered recommendations of a working group of senior officers in the Department of Defense and those of the Rand Corporation.

The Department of Defense has long held that, as a general rule, homosexuality is incompatible with military service because it interferes with the factors critical to combat effectiveness, including unit morale, unit cohesion and individual privacy. Nevertheless, the Department of Defense also recognizes that individuals with a homosexual orientation have served with distinction in the armed services of the United States.

Therefore, it is the policy of the Department of Defense to judge the suitability of persons to serve in the armed forces on the basis of their conduct. Homosexual conduct will be grounds for separation from the military services. Sexual orientation is considered a personal and private matter, and homosexual orientation is not a bar to service entry or continued service unless manifested by homosexual conduct.

I direct the following:

Applicants for military service will not be asked or required to reveal their sexual orientation. Applicants will be informed of accession and separation policy.

Servicemembers will be separated for homosexual conduct.

Commanders and investigating agencies will not initiate inquiries or investigations solely to determine a member's sexual orientation. Servicemembers will not be asked or required to reveal their sexual orientation. However, commanders will continue to initiate inquiries or investigations, as appropriate, when there is credible information that a basis for discharge or disciplinary action exists. Authority to initiate inquiries and investigations involving homosexual conduct shall be limited to commanders. Commanders will consider, in allocating scarce investigative resources, that sexual orientation is a personal and private matter. They will investigate allegations of violations of the Uniform Code of Military Justice in an evenhanded manner without regard to whether the conduct alleged is heterosexual or homosexual or whether it occurs on-base or off-base. Commanders remain responsible for ensuring that investigations are conducted properly and that any abuse of authority is addressed.

The constraints of military service require servicemembers to keep certain aspects of their personal lives private for the benefit of the group. Our personnel policies will be clearly stated and implemented in accordance with due process of law.

Commanders remain responsible for maintaining good order and discipline. Harassment or violence against other servicemembers will not be tolerated.

Homosexual conduct is a homosexual act, a statement by the servicemember that demonstrates a propensity or intent to engage in homosexual acts, or a homosexual marriage or attempted marriage.

A statement by a servicemember that he or she is homosexual or bisexual creates a rebuttable presumption that the servicemember is engaging in homosexual acts or has a propensity or intent to do so. The servicemember has the opportunity to present evidence that he does not engage in homosexual acts and does not have a propensity or intent to do so. The evidence will be assessed by the relevant separation authority.

A homosexual act includes any bodily contact, actively undertaken or passively permitted, between members of the same sex for the purpose of satisfying sexual desires or any bodily contact which a reasonable person would understand to demonstrate a propensity or intent to engage in homosexual acts. Sexual orientation is a sexual attraction to individuals of a particular sex.

The interim policy and administrative separation procedures that I established on February 3, 1993, will remain in effect until October 1, 1993. Secretaries of the Military Departments and responsible officials within the Office of the Secretary of Defense shall, by October 1, 1993, take such actions as may be necessary to carry out the purposes of this directive. Secretaries of the Military Departments will ensure that all members of the armed forces are aware of their specific responsibilities in carrying out this new policy. This memorandum creates no substantive or procedural rights. Any changes to existing policies shall be prospective only.

February

SCHOTT SUSPENSION FOR RACIST REMARKS

February 3, 1993

A club owner's "racially and ethnically offensive" language embarrassed professional baseball, the major league's ruling Executive Council announced February 3. It fined the offender, Marge Schott of the Cincinnati Reds, $25,000 and barred her from operating the club for up to one year.

The decision was announced in Chicago by Bud Selig, president of the Milwaukee Brewers and chairman of the ten-member council representing all twenty-eight major league owners. Schott became the first owner ever to be punished for use of offensive language—and only the fifth ever to be removed, temporarily or permanently, for any reason.

Her suspension and fine, imposed in "the best interest of baseball," resulted from the council's three-month investigation of racial and ethnic slurs attributed to her in press reports and court records. In a lawsuit brought against Schott by Tim Sabo, the ball club's former controller—or treasurer—he contended that she had referred to highly paid players as "million-dollar niggers" and had spoken of "Japs" and "moneygrubbing" Jews.

The New York Times *reported that Schott had said "Hitler was all right in the beginning but went too far" and kept a swastika arm band in her home, although she later explained that it was a battlefield souvenir given her by a World War II veteran. Sharon Jones, a former employee of the Oakland Athletics, quoted Schott as saying she would "rather have a trained monkey working for me than a nigger."*

Schott denied some of the accusations but admitted to others, issuing public apologies for what she called her occasional "insensitive" behavior. In its statement February 23, the Executive Council acknowledged her apologies, and said she "has been meeting with diverse members of the Cincinnati community on these issues." But the council added that "Mrs. Schott's practice of using language that is racially and ethnically offensive has brought substantial disrepute and embarrassment to the game—and is not in the best interest of baseball."

Related Issue of Minority Hiring

Civil rights leader Jesse Jackson called the punishment "an adequate response to the indignities that Marge Schott heaped upon some people." But he contended that it did not absolve professional baseball's "neglect" in promoting black players to management positions. "[T]he other 27 owners' record of behavior is as abhorrent as were her words despicable," he said. Jackson had threatened to lead a boycott of opening day games in April to protest the hiring pactices but later relented.

Jackson was joined at a news conference in Washington by Rep. Kweisi Mfume, D-Md., chairman of the Congressional Black Caucus, and Rep. Jose E. Serrano, D-N.Y., chairman of the Hispanic Caucus. "The real issue is not Marge Schott," Mfume said. "The real issue is fairness, equity, and inclusion in major league sports. The issue is ending the system of major league apartheid that for too long has been part of our national athletic makeup."

Selig rejected an argument that the baseball team owners made Schott a scapegoat for their shortcomings. He said her remarks "reflect the most base and demeaning type of racial and ethnic stereotyping, indicating an insensitivity that cannot be accepted or tolerated by anyone in baseball."

Question of a Court Challenge

Baseball writer Thomas Boswell of the Washington Post *contended that Schott's punishment was light because the Executive Council feared that she might challenge its authority in court. The council, composed of eight owners and presidents of the American and National leagues, assumed interim control in the absence of a new baseball commissioner to replace Fay Vincent, whom the owners forced to resign in 1992.* (Vincent's resignation, Historic Documents of 1992, p. 855)

Attorney Robert Bennett represented Schott during the council's deliberations and said at their conclusion that he had obtained some concessions in exchange for her pledge not to contest her punishment. She was permitted to remain as a managing general partner of the Cincinnati Reds, retain her ownership interest, continue to earn revenue, and engage in major policy decisions, although not in day-to-day management.

Removal of Other Baseball Owners

Four other club owners had been relieved of their duties for improper activity during the past half-century. William Cox of the Philadelphia Phillies drew a suspension in 1943 for betting on his team. Ten years later, Fred Saigh was forced to sell his St. Louis Cardinals after he pleaded no contest to tax evasion. George Steinbrenner was temporarily banned twice—in 1974 after pleading guilty to conspiring to make illegal contributions to Richard Nixon's presidential campaign and in 1990 for paying a gambler to gather information to discredit Dave Winfield, a disgruntled Yankees player. Steinbrenner returned to the Yankees in March 1993. Ted Turner of the Atlanta Braves was suspended in 1977 for tampering in trade negotiations for Gary Matthews, then a player with the San Francisco Giants.

Following is the text of a statement made public February 3, 1993, by Milwaukee Brewers president Bud Selig, chairman of major league baseball's Executive Council, which suspended Cincinnati Reds owner Marge Schott:

An investigation was begun Dec. 1, 1992, by a subcommittee of the Executive Council of Major League Baseball into allegations involving Marge Schott, the principal owner and general partner of the Cincinnati Reds baseball club.

Witnesses were interviewed, depositions were received, memoranda of conversations were reviewed and voluminous newspaper, magazine and television reports were studied.

Proper and adequate notice of these proceedings was given to Mrs. Schott and her attorney and they were both kept apprised and informed of evidentiary material and our lengthy subcommittee report.

The final report of the subcommittee contains substantial and convincing evidence that, while serving as the principal owner of the Reds baseball club, Mrs. Schott commonly used language that is racially and ethnically insensitive, offensive and intolerable.

For purposes of this press conference, we do not feel it necessary to repeat examples of the racial and ethnic slurs that were used by Mrs. Schott.

We do want to say that Mrs. Schott's remarks reflect the most base and demeaning type of racial and ethnic stereotyping . . . indicating an insensitivity that cannot be accepted or tolerated by anyone in baseball.

It should be noted that Mrs. Schott, in her submission to the subcommittee of the Executive Council, has apologized and has recognized that this type of language is insensitive and offensive and that Mrs. Schott has been meeting with diverse members of the Cincinnati community on these issues. We are also mindful that Mrs. Schott and the Cincinnati Reds ballclub have done substantial community service for the city of Cincinnati.

Nevertheless, we find, based on considerable evidence that Mrs. Schott's practice of using language that is racially and ethnically offensive has brought substantial disrepute and embarrassment to the game — and it is not in the best interest of baseball.

There should be no question that the type of language commonly used by Mrs. Schott is offensive and unacceptable. There is simply no place for this in major league baseball.

Accordingly, and pursuant to the authority granted the Executive Council under the Major League Agreement and Major League Rules, we unanimously impose the following sanctions on Mrs. Schott:

1. Commencing on March 1, 1993, and for a period of one year, Mrs. Schott shall be suspended from baseball. In the event Mrs. Schott complies with the terms of this decision and the order of implementation, she will be entitled to reinstatement on Nov. 1, 1993, after which date, if reinstatement is granted, until Feb. 28, 1994, she shall be on probation.
2. Mrs. Schott is fined $25,000, the maximum fine permitted of an individual under the Major League Agreement.
3. During 1993, Mrs. Schott is directed to attend and complete multicultural training programs.
4. Mrs. Schott is reprimanded and censured in the strongest terms for her use of racially and ethnically insensitive language and sternly warned not to engage in such conduct in the future.

COMMISSION REPORT ON RESTRUCTURING COLLEGE AID

February 3, 1993

"Making College Affordable Again" was the painfully self-explanatory title of a report issued February 3 by the National Commission on Responsibilities for Financing Postsecondary Education. After studying the plight facing American families seeking to send their children to college, the nine-member bipartisan panel, composed of business, education, and civic leaders, concluded that a major restructuring of the confusing and complicated postsecondary aid system was required. "To make college affordable again, we must make changes at virtually all levels and involve all of the major participants in the postsecondary financing system," the panel concluded. "Only by making college affordable can our students succeed and our nation prosper during the next decade—and into the 21st century."

To buttress its argument for reform, the panel cited statistics showing that during the 1980s the cost of attending college rose by 146 percent—a higher rate than that registered by medical, home, food, and car expenses. Moreover, the cost burden had shifted since 1975, when the federal government paid 24 percent and families paid 39 percent. In 1990 the federal contribution had dropped to 11 percent, and the families' responsibility had risen to 49 percent.

Created by Congress in 1990, the commission held two years of hearings and seminars throughout the country as well as a national symposium. It also sponsored research at the University of Vermont and the University of California at Los Angeles. A principal theme of its eighty-page report was to urge the government to overhaul its financial aid program to guarantee all college-bound students a fixed amount of aid, as well as to recommend support for community service as a way for them to repay their debts after graduation. The idea of community service had been warmly embraced by Bill Clinton during his campaign for the presidency; Congress responded by enacting a limited, pilot program. The commis-

sion's version would be considerably smaller than even the president's scaled-back proposal.

The report's recommendations focused principally on the need for the federal government to do more to help finance postsecondary education, although its mandate also had included examining the role of states, families, businesses, and philanthropic institutions in defraying the soaring costs of college expenses.

"Our thrust is to get the federal government back to its level of responsibility, on the one hand, and to help families plan for the future," said panel member William Cotter, president of Colby College in Maine. "We know there are very good reasons that costs have risen in different sectors. Each state and institution has to work these issues out for themselves. And we agreed that the marketplace works."

Among its proposals, the commission recommended direct federal student loans with income-contingent repayment and aid to families to plan for college expenses while their children were still young. The panel also suggested that the Pell Grant program of federal aid to needy students should be reconfigured. (The program came under intense scrutiny by a Senate committee in October when multimillion-dollar abuses on the part of schools not eligible to receive the grants were revealed.)

STEP and Other Reform Proposals

The centerpiece of the panel's proposal was what it called the Student's Total Education Package (STEP), whereby full-time undergraduates would receive grants, loans, and work-study aid. The amount could be as large as $14,000, which the panel estimated was the average per-student cost at public and private institutions for 1993. The amount would be altered according to annual adjustments for estimated college costs.

The types of aid available would vary according to family income. Students from families with annual incomes of $40,000 or less would receive primarily grants and work-study jobs, while students from families with incomes of up to $100,000 could receive subsidized loans (those on which the government paid interest while the student was in school). For example, students from a family of four earning $30,000 a year would be eligible for a $2,000 grant and another $12,000 divided among subsidized loans, work-study, and unsubsidized loans. Grant aid would end as family income exceeded $50,000, and work-study aid would be terminated as income reached $70,000. When family income reached $100,000, assistance would take the form of unsubsidized loans only.

Supporters of the STEP concept pointed to the fact that, under the existing system, the amount of grants and loans students received from the government varied according to the cost of tuition and the amount appropriated by Congress. The STEP program "adds one heck of a lot more certainty to the system," said Robert Atwell, president of the

American Council on Education, which represents most of the nation's colleges. "Students would now know how much aid to expect."

"Right now there is so much confusion and complexity," said Jamie Merisotis, executive director of the commission. "If every student knows they [sic] are going to get a fixed amount of aid, we think that students will begin to shop around for colleges that they could afford."

Further Recommendations

The panel's other recommendations to make postsecondary education more affordable were: (1) federal tax incentives to encourage families to save for their children's college early on by allowing penalty-free withdrawals from Individual Retirement Accounts; (2) using U.S. savings bonds to shelter college savings from taxation; (3) ending taxation of scholarships; and (4) restoring income tax deductions for college loans.

"This final report of the commission represents a bold and compelling document that could help to shape federal policy on financing higher education," said Sen. James M. Jeffords, R-Vt., who had sponsored the bill establishing the panel. Jeffords, who spoke at a news conference announcing release of the report, said it was in the "national interest" to make college more affordable. He was joined by seven other members of the House and Senate from both political parties, who endorsed the commission's findings.

Secretary of Education Richard W. Riley said he welcomed the fact that the "bipartisan commission agrees with many of the Clinton administration proposals." He added, "We are interested in the views of the commission and will study its recommendations carefully in formulating our policies on postsecondary education."

Following is the text of the executive summary of the final report of the National Commission on Responsibilities for Financing Postsecondary Education, entitled "Making College Affordable Again," released February 3, 1993:

With the end of the Cold War, Americans are turning their attention to a more subtle yet equally complex issue—economic security. To compete effectively in this global economy, the nation needs a top-flight, cost-effective higher education system with quality programs and access for all interested and able individuals.

For decades, America has offered college and university programs that rank among the best in the world. But their escalating cost now threatens to set up new, impenetrable barriers for many Americans.

For example:

- Paying for college now ranks as one of the most costly investments for American families, second only to buying a home;

- During the 1980s, the cost of attending college increased 126 percent, twice the rate of inflation for the decade;
- State budget cuts are causing sizable tuition increases at public institutions, increases that have outpaced those in the traditionally higher-priced private institutions.

For the 21st century, America needs a well-educated, well-trained workforce capable of competing with our international neighbors. Yet at this very critical juncture, we believe there is a crisis in the nation's postsecondary education finance system—one that poses a major risk to the very fabric of higher education.

At the federal level, fiscal pressures have cut or limited the growth of many important financial aid programs, leaving students and their parents unsure about the future. Among the hardest hit are low- and middle-income students. Since 1980, the purchasing power of federal grants has steadily eroded as grant levels have failed to keep pace with tuition increases. Mounting costs have forced many of these students to take out costly loans that carry heavy repayment burdens.

These financial pressures also affect the outlook of families as they plan to pay for college. Recent public opinion polls show that the dream of sending a child to college—once so important for many parents—is growing more elusive every year. This is largely because families have increasingly shouldered more of the burden for financing higher education as the federal commitment has eroded.

In addition, the complexity and paperwork of the available student aid programs often undermines their worthy goals. Many students and parents are confused by a system with a multitude of loan and grant programs—each with its own complex eligibility and application requirements.

Yet even as a college education appears to slip out of reach for some American families, the need to maintain and improve access to higher education grows in importance. The Commission realizes that the country cannot afford to subsidize individuals who drop out of school, who are unemployed, underemployed, or who fail to understand the basic principles of our democratic institutions and political system. We must make every effort to reach all citizens and include every individual as an essential part of the nation's future—or risk the consequences of having to support those who fall behind.

Nationwide, higher rates of child poverty and single-parent families also will require a new level of commitment from government, education, and the private sector. Getting a college education is an essential opportunity for those left behind. In short, America must be prepared to work with children from low- and middle-income families from their early years through high school and postsecondary education.

Since February 1991, the nine members of this Commission have examined many options to improve the affordability of American higher education. Based on our discussions, we believe that the partnership among governments, institutions, and individuals in the financing of postsecondary education is an essential concept that must represent the foundation of future financing policy. Such a partnership requires each participant to contribute to the system's success. Given its historical role in helping to guide national policy, the federal government is in the best position to encourage this partnership. It can do this by promoting a greater sense of shared responsibility for financing postsecondary education among the system's various participants.

The most productive step the federal government can take in strengthening the postsecondary education financing partnership is to lead by example. We believe the federal government bears a rudimentary responsibility to lay the groundwork for a new national compact that will improve the affordability of higher education for all Americans. By leading the way in this new partnership, the federal government will recapture the national leadership it once held in this area.

To help make college affordable again, we recommend that the following integrated package of policies and programs be implemented:

> **Make federal student aid a reliable and comprehensible source of college assistance for all Americans by developing a new concept called the Student's Total Education Package (STEP), which links to a national norm the total amount of federal aid any full-time undergraduate college student may receive annually.**

Currently, students receive varying amounts of aid based on many different programs, their particular rules and their complex need-based formulas. This intricate system leaves many students and families confused about their eligibility—and intimidated by the potential cost of college.

Under STEP, all full-time undergraduate college students would be eligible to receive the same amount of federal aid—but the type of aid they receive would vary widely depending on their own financial needs and the cost of attendance.

In general, the poorest student would receive an aid package based primarily on grants, work-study, and subsidized loans. The student from the middle-income family would receive a mix of subsidized and unsubsidized loans, work-study, and grants. The student from the affluent family would not be eligible for subsidized aid but still could receive an unsubsidized loan.

The federal government would set the STEP based on the weighted national average per-student expenditure at all four-year institutions. In current dollars the STEP would be approximately $14,000; this amount would be adjusted annually. Less than full-time students would receive a pro-rated amount.

The government, higher education institutions, and the general media could distribute and publicize this information to prospective students, cutting away much of the confusion about their prospects for receiving assistance.

It is important to emphasize that the STEP concept reflects the *federal* commitment to student assistance. In many cases states and institutions will offer their own financial aid resources to students independent of the federal contribution.

Remove uncertainty from the Pell Grant program by ensuring that all eligible students receive grants at levels authorized by federal law and by tying future maximum grant levels to what students pay for college.

In the 1992 Higher Education Act reauthorization, both Congress and the President acknowledged the critical need to increase grants for low- and middle-income students to meet national education goals. In that law, Congress authorized a maximum Pell Grant of $3,700 for the 1993-94 school year. But later, under budget pressures, Congress actually appropriated only enough for a $2,300 maximum grant—a cut of $100 from the previous year.

This widening gap between authorized and actual funding of the Pell Grant causes uncertainty in the system and limits access to postsecondary education for needy students. Further, current actual grant levels represent a major erosion in the federal commitment to access....

We urge Congress and the President to ensure that students receive grants at amounts fully authorized by law. The federal government should view this grant level as an unbreakable promise that promotes greater opportunities for postsecondary education in our nation.

Equally as important, we believe that future maximum Pell Grant award levels should be set at an amount equal to 75 percent of the national median cost of attendance (tuition, fees, room and board) at public four-year colleges. This would create a rational basis for future maximum awards and restore the purchasing power of Pell Grants that has been lost in the last decade.

To further improve access and simplify the federal aid system, we also recommend the following steps:

- Consolidate the Federal Supplemental Educational Opportunity Grant Program (SEOG) with the Pell Grant program, providing that our recommendation for removing uncertainty from the Pell program is implemented.
- Convert the Federal Perkins Loan Program to a grant program by depositing all loan collections into an institutional endowment fund that could be invested and used to provide grants for low- and middle-income students.

Simplify the complex student loan system by offering a single program that makes direct loans to students and parents and provides "user friendly" repayment options.

The current federal loan system contains five components—all with different names, requirements and financial limits. We are calling for a much more streamlined program with only three components: a subsidized student loan program (where interest does not accrue during the time the student is in school); an unsubsidized student loan program (where interest accrues throughout the life of the loan); and an unsubsidized parent loan program.

Students could pay back loans under two options: income-contingent repayment, with payments based on a percentage of the borrower's income, and conventional repayment, with payments spread out at regular intervals over a fixed number of years. Those who fall behind on conventional repayments would move automatically to an income-contingent system—thereby offering students a "second chance" to fulfill their obligations and, hopefully, avoid default.

Each component program would receive capital through Treasury borrowing, eliminating the current system with its heavy government subsidies for banks and guarantee agencies. The Internal Revenue Service also could act as a loan servicing and collection agency for income-contingent loans, thereby permitting borrowers to remit payments through regular income tax withholding.

Create a Community Service Incentive Program to promote student service in exchange for loan forgiveness, thereby fostering the dual goals of scholarship and citizenship.

The government has a responsibility to foster a sense of community values and partnership among individuals, states, communities and the private sector. To this end, both undergraduate and graduate students should have the option to work and serve their communities in exchange for financial aid benefits.

Students could participate in this incentive program for up to three years, with 20 percent of the loan principal forgiven for every year of service. In limited instances, the program also could offer complete loan forgiveness for those performing five years of service in certain designated "critical need" areas. In addition, students would accrue no interest costs during their time of service. Eligible programs would be determined by guidelines established by the federal Commission on National and Community Service.

This program also will work well in a system where income-contingent repayment is an option for borrowers. Under an income-contingent repayment system, borrowers choosing lower paying, public service-type jobs would not be unduly burdened by fixed student loan payments, since these payments would be based on income and not on the amount borrowed. We believe this will be a powerful incentive for borrowers to choose careers in teaching, law enforcement, or any of numerous other areas where the need for skilled college graduates is essential. Thus the Community Service Incentive Program would complement the public service incentives provided through an income-contingent repayment option.

Create new tax-related incentives to encourage college savings and increase postsecondary education opportunities, such as allowing penalty-free withdrawals from Individual Retirement Accounts to pay for college expenses and removing the income eligibility ceiling on the use of Series EE U.S. Savings Bonds for education.

We call for allowing penalty-free withdrawals from IRAs to pay for higher education expenses, a plan similar to one proposed by Senators Lloyd Bentsen (D-TX) and William Roth (R-DE) in 1992. Under that proposal, qualified higher education expenses—tuition, fees, books, supplies, and equipment—could be paid for via early withdrawal from an IRA. Such funds could pay for the college education of the taxpayer, his or her spouse, the taxpayer's child, or the taxpayer's grandchild.

The Commission also supports expanding the use of U.S. Savings Bonds for college to all family income levels, promoting increased savings through a national advertising campaign, and implementing Tax Code provisions that: 1) allow students and parents to deduct interest on loans used for education; 2) allow deductions for employer-provided educational assistance; and 3) encourage charitable giving of gifts of appreciated property to higher education institutions.

In addition to these recommendations, the Commission also endorses a variety of other new ideas to improve the student financial aid system and make college more affordable. Specifically, we call on the federal government to:

- Focus greater resources on graduate and professional study by repealing the taxation of scholarships and fellowships, offering graduate students greater flexibility under federal student loan programs, and funding programs under Title IX of the Higher Education Act.
- Eliminate fraud and abuse by strengthening accountability measures, repairing structural problems in student aid programs and providing the necessary resources to implement existing accountability policies.
- Establish a federal interagency council to coordinate student aid and other human resource benefits, so that government can reduce paperwork and promote more consistent eligibility requirements among programs.
- Create and distribute computer software that estimates the components of a student's total financial aid package, thereby improving the flow of information about eligibility. Students and their families could gain easy access to these programs through wide distribution to schools or school guidance counselors.
- Implement the National Early Intervention Scholarship and Partnership Program, which was established in the 1992 Higher Education Amendments to provide matching funds to the states for creating and expanding initiatives for at-risk students.

We also view agencies and individuals outside Washington, DC, as key partners in the drive to improve opportunities in postsecondary education. State governments, the private sector, philanthropic organizations, and individual colleges and universities all must increase their vigilance in support of higher education and affordability.

For their part, states should institute a collaborative accountability process with centralized planning to help promote the quality and affordability of higher education. Higher education institutions need to undertake comprehensive strategic planning as well, mindful of their educational mission and their duty to control cost increases.

The Commission also recommends that states conduct their own independent studies of "high tuition, high aid" policies, one of the hottest topics in higher education finance. Under this concept, states would withdraw some of their funding for public colleges and instead focus on student aid subsidies for lower income students. If tuition would increase, so would financial aid—possibly making college more affordable for needy students.

We believe that a headlong rush into "high tuition, high aid" as a national strategy would be a mistake, particularly in the current economic climate. During the past two years, at least 10 states have raised tuitions but reduced student aid. Despite states' best intentions, we believe the potential for damaging consequences—such as "high tuition, low aid"—could jeopardize access to higher education.

Whatever their decision, states should have the freedom to evaluate this issue free from federal involvement. We recommend, however, that all states—regardless of their decision—increase their own financial aid programs to match any increases in attendance costs. We also believe states and institutions bear a fundamental responsibility to set tuitions at levels that reflect a college's mission and the type of student it serves.

Elsewhere in the finance system, we believe that philanthropy should play an important role by continuing to support higher education as an important national resource. We also believe that corporate philanthropy should expand efforts to promote access, particularly for low- and middle-income students. Another key player, the private sector, must promote postsecondary education and training that strengthens the nation's competitiveness and furthers democratic principles.

The economic, environmental, and social challenges ahead will require cooperation among all sectors of American society—from government and industry to individuals and families. We need both the courage to dream and the will to change.

Amid global uncertainty, the nation must stand firm behind its goal of offering educational opportunity to all interested and able Americans. Only by making college affordable can our students succeed and our nation prosper during the next decade—and into the 21st century.

CLINTON'S FIVE-YEAR ECONOMIC PLAN

February 17, 1993

In an address to a joint session of Congress February 17, 1993, President Bill Clinton presented the main features of a massive five-year economic plan for the country. Less than six months later, he signed into law a bill that encompassed most of his plan. The measure, the Omnibus Budget Reconciliation Act, was designed to reduce federal budget deficits from projected levels by $496 billion. No Republican members of Congress voted for the bill, and its passage was by the narrowest of margins in both the Senate and the House.

In his address, the president said, "Our country needs a new direction." He told the senators and representatives, and the audience watching on television, that it had been too long "since a president has come and challenged Americans to join him on a great national journey, not merely to consume the bounty of today but to invest for a much greater one tomorrow."

So important did approval of the plan by Congress become for the Clinton administration that many observers believed the effectiveness of the administration was at stake as the Senate cleared the legislation for Clinton's signature August 6. Only a vote by Vice President Al Gore, breaking a 50-50 tie, sent the measure to the White House. The previous day the House had passed the legislation by a similar cliffhanger vote, 218-216.

During debate in the Senate, Sen. Robert Dole, R-Kan., the minority leader, charged that the plan included "the largest tax increase in the history of the world." Congressional historians said that record actually belonged to a tax bill enacted in 1982, and Clinton's bill provided for the second-largest tax increase. Historians also said it was the first time a major piece of legislation had received the approval of Congress without the support of a single vote from the minority party.

The impact of the increased taxes fell largely on corporations and well-

off Americans. Indeed, the thrust of the new taxes was widely viewed as a repudiation of the Reagan and Bush administrations' judgment that tax cuts for corporations and the affluent would stimulate economic growth.

Congress made substantial changes in the Omnibus Budget Reconciliation Act, especially in the Senate-House conference in the final days before passage. Still, when the bill arrived on Clinton's desk, it broadly expressed his view of the economic course the federal government should take over the next five years.

However, another part of Clinton's overall plan—a $22.8 billion package designed to support the country's recovery from the deep 1990-1991 economic recession—was withdrawn by Democrats on April 21, 1993, after it was confronted by unified Republican opposition in the Senate. After passage of the Omnibus Budget Reconciliation Act, the Baltimore Sun *said in an editorial August 8, "One budget victory does not a presidency make, but it is far better to win it than to lose it."*

Address to Joint Session

Excited over having a Democratic president for the first time in twelve years, Democrats in Congress repeatedly jumped to their feet during Clinton's address February 17. Some Republican members openly heckled the president, foreshadowing the struggle over the next five-and-a-half months to pass the deficit-reduction plan.

Two days earlier, in a ten-minute televised address from the Oval Office at the White House, Clinton acknowledged that his five-year budget bill would increase taxes on middle-class Americans. Early in his campaign for the presidency, he had said he would reduce taxes middle-class Americans were paying. Months later, in a debate with President George Bush, Clinton said he would not increase taxes on that group. In fact, as enacted, the Omnibus Budget Reconciliation Act largely spared the middle class a greater tax burden. Under that law, Americans with incomes of less than $100,000 a year would see their overall tax burden increase by less than 1.5 percent. And the burden on those with incomes under $30,000 was reduced.

Deficit Reduction

While the Omnibus Budget Reconciliation Act provided for some spending increases and reductions in specific taxes, the great thrust of the measure was toward reducing the deficit. Deficit reductions over the five years of the legislation were projected by the House Budget Committee as follows: 1994—$47 billion; 1995—$75 billion; 1996—$98 billion; 1997—$127 billion; and 1998—$148 billion. Total deficits in the same years were projected as follows: 1994—$255 billion; 1995—$227 billion; 1996—$204 billion; 1997—$201 billion; and 1998—$213 billion. But projections showed the deficit climbing steeply again after 1996-1997.

Writing in the April 19 Congressional Quarterly Weekly Report, *George*

Hager quoted Barry Bosworth, an economist at the Brookings Institution, as saying that Clinton's program "should be looked at as a one-shot deficit reduction." Something more would have to be done to reverse the long-term trend, Bosworth said.

Provisions of the Act

The Omnibus Budget Reconciliation Act provided for almost equal amounts of spending cuts and new taxes: $255 billion of the former and $241 billion of the latter. After the measure had been enacted, Democratic leaders conceded that Republicans in Congress had, as Newsweek *in its August 16 issue put it, "convinced the nation that most of the burden would fall on the middle class." The magazine also said that the Democrats actually were "playing old-fashioned redistributive politics, sticking it to the rich."*

The legislation raised the income tax on incomes above $115,000 for individuals and $140,00 for couples to 36 percent from 31 percent. It raised the tax on incomes above $250,000 a year to 39.6 percent. Most of the increased burden on taxpayers with incomes of less than $100,000 came from a higher tax on gasoline and diesel fuel.

The deficit-reduction goal was reached in a number of ways in addition to increases in the income tax. Prominent among them were a larger share of Social Security benefits made subject to taxes, a substantial cut in the federal Medicare program for the elderly, and the additional tax on gasoline, which amounted to 4.3 cents a gallon.

The legislation raised the portion of Social Security benefits subject to income tax to 85 percent from 50 percent for individuals earning more than $34,000 a year and couples earning more than $44,000 a year. Medicare was slated to grow $55.8 billion less over the following five years than it would have without the cut. The Medicare reduction was seen as deep enough to have an impact on patients. For example, some physicians might refuse to take Medicare patients at all.

The increased tax on gasoline, diesel fuel, and other transport fuels was expected to raise about $23 million over the five-year period. President Clinton had proposed a broad-based energy tax, based on the heat content of fuels, which was designed to raise $72.8 billion over the period, but that idea became the victim of opposition by senators from oil-producing states.

Working Families

Many observers were astonished that the Omnibus Budget Reconciliation Act, which focused so intensely on deficit-reduction, included among its provisions a $20.8 billion increase in a program for the poor. The increase, in the earned-income tax credit (EITC), was believed to be the broadest antipoverty initiative by the federal government in twenty years.

The EITC program offered an income tax credit to any adult who *worked, had a child at home, and made less than $23,050. Under the Omnibus Budget Reconciliation Act, the amount of the top bonus doubled to $3,370, and, for the first time, families without children became eligible. The August 16 issue of* U.S. News & World Report *quoted Sen. Bill Bradley, D-N.J., as saying that the larger tax credit would "help millions escape the clutches of poverty of working full-time yet never being able to make ends meet."*

Stimulus Package

The only major part of the president's economic plan to fail was his $22.8 billion economic stimulus package. It was withdrawn April 21 by Senate majority leader George J. Mitchell, D-Maine, after four failed attempts to end a Republican filibuster in the Senate.

The package was introduced separately as an appropriations bill for fiscal 1993 and would have provided financing for dozens of public works projects, social services, summer jobs, and business programs. Political observers said the Republicans' opposition to the bill in part grew out of their desire to stake out a role for themselves in a Washington now dominated by Democrats.

Following is the text of President Bill Clinton's February 17, 1993, address before a joint session of Congress:

Mr. President, Mr. Speaker, Members of the House and the Senate, distinguished Americans here as visitors in this Chamber, as am I. It is nice to have a fresh excuse for giving a long speech. [*Laughter*]

When Presidents speak to Congress and the Nation from this podium, typically they comment on the full range [of] challenges and opportunities that face the United States. But this is not an ordinary time, and for all the many tasks that require our attention, I believe tonight one calls on us to focus, to unite, and to act. And that is our economy. For more than anything else, our task tonight as Americans is to make our economy thrive again.

Let me begin by saying that it has been too long, at least three decades, since a President has come and challenged Americans to join him on a great national journey, not merely to consume the bounty of today but to invest for a much greater one tomorrow.

Like individuals, nations must ultimately decide how they wish to conduct themselves, how they wish to be thought of by those with whom they live, and later, how they wish to be judged by history. Like every individual, man and woman, nations must decide whether they are prepared to rise to the occasions history presents them.

We have always been a people of youthful energy and daring spirit. And at this historic moment, as communism has fallen, as freedom is spreading around the world, as a global economy is taking shape before our eyes,

Americans have called for change. And now it is up to those of us in this room to deliver for them.

Our Nation needs a new direction. Tonight I present to you a comprehensive plan to set our Nation on that new course. I believe we will find our new direction in the basic old values that brought us here over the last two centuries: a commitment to opportunity, to individual responsibility, to community, to work, to family, and to faith. We must now break the habits of both political parties and say there can be no more something for nothing and admit frankly that we are all in this together.

The conditions which brought us as a Nation to this point are well-known: two decades of low productivity, growth, and stagnant wages; persistent unemployment and underemployment; years of huge Government deficits and declining investment in our future; exploding health care costs and lack of coverage for millions of Americans; legions of poor children; education and job training opportunities inadequate to the demands of this tough, global economy. For too long we have drifted without a strong sense of purpose or responsibility or community.

And our political system so often has seemed paralyzed by special interest groups, by partisan bickering, and by the sheer complexity of our problems. I believe we can do better because we remain the greatest nation on Earth, the world's strongest economy, the world's only military superpower. If we have the vision, the will, and the heart to make the changes we must, we can still enter the 21st century with possibilities our parents could not even have imagined and enter it having secured the American dream for ourselves and for future generations.

I well remember 12 years ago President Reagan stood at this very podium and told you and the American people that if our national debt were stacked in thousand-dollar bills, the stack would reach 67 miles into space. Well, today that stack would reach 267 miles. I tell you this not to assign blame for this problem. There is plenty of blame to go around in both branches of the Government and both parties. The time has come for the blame to end. I did not seek this office to place blame. I come here tonight to accept responsibility, and I want you to accept responsibility with me. And if we do right by this country, I do not care who gets the credit for it.

The plan I offer you has four fundamental components. First, it shifts our emphasis in public and private spending from consumption to investment, initially by jump-starting the economy in the short term and investing in our people, their jobs, and their incomes over the long run. Second, it changes the rhetoric of the past into the actions of the present by honoring work and families in every part of our public decisionmaking. Third, it substantially reduces the Federal deficit honestly and credibly by using in the beginning the most conservative estimates of Government revenues, not, as the executive branch has done so often in the past, using the most optimistic ones. And finally, it seeks to earn the trust of the American people by paying for these plans first with cuts in Government waste and efficiency; second, with cuts, not gimmicks, in Government spending; and by fairness, for a change, in the way additional burdens are borne.

Tonight I want to talk with you about what Government can do because I believe Government must do more. But let me say first that the real engine of economic growth in this country is the private sector, and second, that each of us must be an engine of growth and change. The truth is that as Government creates more opportunity in this new and different time, we must also demand more responsibility in turn.

Our immediate priority must be to create jobs, create jobs now. Some people say, "Well, we're in a recovery, and we don't have to do that." Well, we all hope we're in a recovery, but we're sure not creating new jobs. And there's no recovery worth its salt that doesn't put the American people back to work.

To create jobs and guarantee a strong recovery, I call on Congress to enact an immediate package of jobs investments of over $30 billion to put people to work now, to create a half a million jobs: jobs to rebuild our highways and airports, to renovate housing, to bring new life to rural communities, and spread hope and opportunity among our Nation's youth. Especially I want to emphasize, after the events of last year in Los Angeles and the countless stories of despair in our cities and in our poor rural communities, this proposal will create almost 700,000 new summer jobs for displaced, unemployed young people alone this summer. And tonight I invite America's business leaders to join us in this effort so that together we can provide over one million summer jobs in cities and poor rural areas for our young people.

Second, our plan looks beyond today's business cycle because our aspirations extend into the next century. The heart of this plan deals with the long term. It is an investment program designed to increase public and private investment in areas critical to our economic future. And it has a deficit reduction program that will increase the savings available for the private sector to invest, will lower interest rates, will decrease the percentage the Federal budget claimed by interest payments, and decrease the risk of financial market disruptions that could adversely affect our economy.

Over the long run, all this will bring us a higher rate of economic growth, improved productivity, more high-quality jobs, and an improved economic competitive position in the world. In order to accomplish both increased investment and deficit reduction, something no American Government has ever been called upon to do at the same time before, spending must be cut, and taxes must be raised.

The spending cuts I recommend were carefully thought through in a way to minimize any adverse economic impact, to capture the peace dividend for investment purposes, and to switch the balance in the budget from consumption to more investment. The tax increases and the spending cuts were both designed to assure that the cost of this historic program to face and deal with our problems will be borne by those who could readily afford it the most. Our plan is designed, furthermore, and perhaps in some ways most importantly, to improve the health of American business through lower interest rates, more incentives to invest, and better trained workers.

Because small business has created such a high percentage of all the new jobs in our Nation over the last 10 or 15 years, our plan includes the boldest targeted incentives for small business in history. We propose a permanent investment tax credit for the smallest firms in this country, with revenues of under $5 million. That's about 90 percent of the firms in America, employing about 40 percent of the work force but creating a big majority of the net new jobs for more than a decade. And we propose new rewards for entrepreneurs who take new risks. We propose to give small business access to all the new technologies of our time. And we propose to attack this credit crunch which has denied small business the credit they need to flourish and prosper.

With a new network of community development banks and $1 billion to make the dream of enterprise zones real, we propose to bring new hope and new jobs to storefronts and factories from south Boston to south Texas to south central Los Angeles. This plan invests in our roads, our bridges, our transit systems, in high-speed railways, and high-tech information systems. And it provides the most ambitious environmental cleanup in partnership with State and local government of our time, to put people to work and to preserve the environment for our future.

Standing as we are on the edge of a new century, we know that economic growth depends as never before on opening up new markets overseas and expanding the volume of world trade. And so, we will insist on fair trade rules in international markets as a part of a national economic strategy to expand trade, including the successful completion of the latest round of world trade talks and the successful completion of a North American Free Trade Agreement, with appropriate safeguards for our workers and for the environment.

At the same time—and I say this to you in both parties and across America tonight, all the people who are listening—it is not enough to pass a budget or even to have a trade agreement. This world is changing so fast that we must have aggressive, targeted attempts to create the high-wage jobs of the future. That's what all our competitors are doing. We must give special attention to those critical industries that are going to explode in the 21st century but that are in trouble in America today, like aerospace. We must provide special assistance to areas and to workers displaced by cuts in the defense budget and by other unavoidable economic dislocations.

And again I will say we must do this together. I pledge to you that I will do my best to see that business and labor and Government work together for a change.

But all of our efforts to strengthen the economy will fail—let me say this again; I feel so strongly about this—all of our efforts to strengthen the economy will fail unless we also take this year, not next year, not 5 years from now but this year, bold steps to reform our health care system.

In 1992, we spent 14 percent of our income on health care, more than 30 percent more than any other country in the world, and yet we were the only advanced nation that did not provide a basic package of health care benefits to all of its citizens. Unless we change the present pattern, 50 percent of the growth in the deficit between now and the year 2000 will be in health care costs. By the year 2000 almost 20 percent of our income will be in health care. Our families will never be secure, our businesses will never be strong, and our Government will never again be fully solvent until we tackle the health care crisis. We must do it this year.

The combination of the rising cost of care and the lack of care and the fear of losing care are endangering the security and the very lives of millions of our people. And they are weakening our economy every day. Reducing health care costs can liberate literally hundreds of billions of dollars for new investment in growth and jobs. Bringing health costs in line with inflation would do more for the private sector in this country than any tax cut we could give and any spending program we could promote. Reforming health care over the long run is critically essential to reducing not only our deficit but to expanding investment in America.

Later this spring, after the First Lady and the many good people who are helping her all across the country complete their work, I will deliver to Congress a comprehensive plan for health care reform that finally will bring costs under control and provide security to all of our families, so that no one will be denied the coverage they need but so that our economic future will not be compromised either. We'll have to root out fraud and overcharges and make sure that paperwork no longer chokes your doctor. We'll have to maintain the highest American standards and the right to choose in a system that is the world's finest for all those who can access it. But first we must make choices. We must choose to give the American people the quality they demand and deserve with a system that will not bankrupt the country or further drive more Americans into agony.

Let me further say that I want to work with all of you on this. I realize this is a complicated issue. But we must address it. And I believe if there is any chance that Republicans and Democrats who disagree on taxes and spending or anything else could agree on one thing, surely we can all look at these numbers and go home and tell our people the truth. We cannot continue these spending patterns in public or private dollars for health care for less and less and less every year. We can do better. And I will work to do better.

Perhaps the most fundamental change the new direction I propose offers is its focus on the future and its investment which I seek in our children. Each day we delay really making a commitment to our children carries a dear cost. Half of the 2-year-olds in this country today don't receive the immunizations they need against deadly diseases. Our plan will provide them for every eligible child. And we know now that we will save $10 later for every $1 we spend by eliminating preventable childhood diseases. That's a good investment no matter how you measure it.

I recommend that the women, infants, and children's nutrition program be expanded so that every expectant mother who needs the help gets it. We all know that Head Start, a program that prepares children for school, is a success story. We all know that it saves money, but today it just reaches barely over one-third of all the eligible children. Under this plan, every eligible child will be able to get a head start. This is not just the right thing to do; it is the smart thing to do. For every dollar we invest today we'll save $3 tomorrow. We have to start thinking about tomorrow. I've heard that somewhere before. [*Laughter*]

We have to ask more in our schools of our students, our teachers, our principals, our parents. Yes, we must give them the resources they need to meet high standards, but we must also use the authority and the influence and the funding of the Education Department to promote strategies that really work in learning. Money alone is not enough. We have to do what really works to increase learning in our schools.

We have to recognize that all of our high school graduates need some further education in order to be competitive in this global economy. So we have to establish a partnership between businesses and education and the Government for apprenticeship programs in every State in this country to give our people the skills they need. Lifelong learning must benefit not just young high school graduates but workers too, throughout their career. The average 18-year-old today will change jobs seven times in a lifetime. We have done a lot in this country on worker training in the last few years, but the system is too fractured. We must develop a unified, simplified, sensible, streamlined worker training program so that workers receive the training they need regardless of why they lost their jobs or whether they simply need to learn something new to keep them. We have got to do better on this.

And finally, I propose a program that got a great response from the American people all across this country last year: a program of national service to make college loans available to all Americans and to challenge them at the same time to give something back to their country as teachers or police officers or community service workers; to give them the option to pay the loans back, but at tax time so they can't beat the bill, but to encourage them instead to pay it back by making their country stronger and making their country better and giving us the benefit of their knowledge.

A generation ago when President Kennedy proposed and the United States Congress embraced the Peace Corps, it defined the character of a whole generation of Americans committed to serving people around the world. In this national service program, we will provide more than twice as many slots for people before they go to college to be in national service than ever served in the Peace Corps. This program could do for this generation of Members of Congress what the land grant college act did and what the GI bill did for former Congressmen. In the future, historians who got their education through the national service loan will look back on you and thank you for giving America a new lease on life, if you meet this challenge.

If we believe in jobs and we believe in learning, we must believe in rewarding work. If we believe in restoring the values that make America special, we must believe that there is dignity in all work, and there must be dignity for all workers. To those who care for our sick, who tend our children, who do our most difficult and tiring jobs, the new direction I propose will make this solemn, simple commitment: By expanding the refundable earned income tax credit, we will make history. We will reward the work of millions of working poor Americans by realizing the principle that if you work 40 hours a week and you've got a child in the house, you will no longer be in poverty.

Later this year, we will offer a plan to end welfare as we know it. I have worked on this issue for the better part of a decade. And I know from personal conversations with many people that no one, no one wants to change the welfare system as badly as those who are trapped in it. I want to offer the people on welfare the education, the training, the child care, the health care they need to get back on their feet, but say after 2 years they must get back to work, too, in private business if possible, in public service if necessary. We have to end welfare as a way of life and make it a path to independence and dignity.

Our next great goal should be to strengthen our families. I compliment the Congress for passing the Family and Medical Leave Act as a good first step, but it is time to do more. This plan will give this country the toughest child support enforcement system it has ever had. It is time to demand that people take responsibility for the children they bring in this world

And I ask you to help to protect our families against the violent crime which terrorizes our people and which tears our communities apart. We must pass a tough crime bill. I support not only the bill which didn't quite make it to the President's desk last year but also an initiative to put 100,000 more police officers on the street, to provide bootcamps for first-time nonviolent offenders for more space for the hardened criminals in jail, and I support an initiative to do what we can to keep guns out of the hands of criminals. Let me say this. I will make you this bargain: If you will pass the Brady bill, I'll sure sign it.

Let me say now, we should move to the harder parts.

I think it is clear to every American, including every Member of Congress of both parties, that the confidence of the people who pay our bills in our institutions in Washington is not high. We must restore it. We must begin again to make Government work for ordinary taxpayers, not simply for organized interest groups. And that beginning must start with real political reform. I am asking the United States Congress to pass a real campaign finance reform bill this year. I ask you to increase the participation of the American people by passing the motor voter bill promptly. I ask you to deal with the undue influence of special interest by passing a bill to end the tax deduction for lobbying and to act quickly to require all the people who lobby you to register as lobbyists by passing the lobbying registration bill.

Believe me, they were cheering that last section at home. I believe lobby reform and campaign finance reform are a sure path to increased popularity for Republicans and Democrats alike because it says to the voters back home, "This is your House. This is your Senate. We're your hired hands, and every penny we draw is your money."

Next, to revolutionize Government we have to ensure that we live within our means, and that should start at the top and with the White House. In the last few days I have announced a cut in the White House staff of 25 percent, saving approximately $10 million. I have ordered administrative cuts in budgets of Agencies and Departments. I have cut the Federal bureaucracy, or will over the next 4 years, by approximately 100,000 positions, for a combined savings of $9 billion. It is time for Government to demonstrate, in the condition we're in, that we can be as frugal as any household in America.

And that's why I also want to congratulate the Congress. I noticed the announcement of the leadership today that Congress is taking similar steps to cut its costs. I think that is important. I think it will send a very clear signal to the American people.

But if we really want to cut spending, we're going to have to do more, and some of it will be difficult. Tonight I call for an across-the-board freeze in Federal Government salaries for one year. And thereafter, during this 4-year period, I recommend that salaries rise at one point lower than the cost of living allowance normally involved in Federal pay increases.

Next, I recommend that we make 150 specific budget cuts, as you know, and that all those who say we should cut more be as specific as I have been.

Finally, let me say to my friends on both sides of the aisle, it is not enough simply to cut Government; we have to rethink the whole way it works. When I became President I was amazed at just the way the White House worked, in ways that added lots of money to what taxpayers had to pay, outmoded ways that didn't take maximum advantage of technology and didn't do things that any business would have done years ago to save taxpayers' money.

So I want to bring a new spirit of innovation into every Government Department. I want to push education reform, as I said, not just to spend more money but to really improve learning. Some things work, and some things don't. We ought to be subsidizing the things that work and discouraging the things that don't. I'd like to use that Superfund to clean up pollution for a change and not just pay lawyers.

In the aftermath of all the difficulties with the savings and loans, we must use Federal bank regulators to protect the security and safety of our financial institutions, but they should not be used to continue the credit crunch and to stop people from making sensible loans.

I'd like for us to not only have welfare reform but to reexamine the whole focus of all of our programs that help people, to shift them from entitlement programs to empowerment programs. In the end we want people not to need us anymore. I think that's important.

But in the end we have to get back to the deficit. For years there's been a lot of talk about it but very few credible efforts to deal with it. And now I understand why, having dealt with the real numbers for 4 weeks. But I believe this plan does; it tackles the budget deficit seriously and over the long term. It puts in place one of the biggest deficit reductions and one of the biggest changes in Federal priorities, from consumption to investment, in the history of this country at the same time over the next 4 years.

Let me say to all the people watching us tonight who will ask me these questions beginning tomorrow as I go around the country and who've asked it in the past: We're not cutting the deficit just because experts say it's the thing to do or because it has some intrinsic merit. We have to cut the deficit because the more we spend paying off the debt, the less tax dollars we have to invest in jobs and education and the future of this country. And the more money we take out of the pool of available savings, the harder it is for people in the private sector to borrow money at affordable interest rates for a college loan for their children, for a home mortgage, or to start a new business.

That's why we've got to reduce the debt, because it is crowding out other activities that we ought to be engaged in and that the American people ought to be engaged in. We cut the deficit so that our children will be able to buy a home, so that our companies can invest in the future and in retraining their workers, so that our Government can make the kinds of investments we need to be a stronger and smarter and safer nation.

If we don't act now, you and I might not even recognize this Government 10 years from now. If we just stay with the same trends of the last 4 years, by the end of the decade the deficit will be $635 billion a year, almost 80 percent of our gross domestic product. And paying interest on that debt will be the costliest Government program of all. We'll still be the world's largest debtor. And when Members of Congress come here, they'll be devoting over 20 cents on the dollar to interest payments, more than half of the budget to health care and to other entitlements. And you'll come here and deliberate and argue over 6 or 7 cents on the dollar, no matter what America's problems are. We will not be able to have the independence we need to chart the future that we must. And we'll be terribly dependent on foreign funds for a large portion of our investment.

This budget plan, by contrast, will by 1997 cut $140 billion in that year alone from the deficit, a real spending cut, a real revenue increase, a real deficit reduction, using the independent numbers of the Congressional Budget Office. [*Laughter*] Well, you can laugh, my fellow Republicans, but I'll point out that the Congressional Budget Office was normally more conservative in what was going to happen and closer to right than previous Presidents have been.

I did this so that we could argue about priorities with the same set of numbers. I did this so that no one could say I was estimating my way out of this difficulty. I did this because if we can agree together on the most prudent revenues we're likely to get if the recovery stays and we do right things economically, then it will turn out better for the American people than we say. In the last 12 years, because there were differences over the revenue estimates, you and I know that both parties were given greater elbow room for irresponsibility. This is tightening the rein on the Democrats as well as the Republicans. Let's at least argue about the same set of numbers so the American people will think we're shooting straight with them.

As I said earlier, my recommendation makes more than 150 difficult reductions to cut the Federal spending by a total of $246 billion. We are eliminating programs that are no longer needed, such as nuclear power research and development. We're slashing subsidies and canceling wasteful projects. But many of these programs were justified in their time, and a lot of them are difficult for me to recommend reductions in, some really tough ones for me personally. I recommend that we reduce interest subsidies to the Rural Electronic Administration. That's a difficult thing for me to recommend. But I think that I cannot exempt the things that exist in my State or in my experience, if I ask you to deal with things that are difficult for you to deal with. We're going to have to have no sacred cows except the fundamental abiding interest of the American people.

I have to say that we all know our Government has been just great at building programs. The time has come to show the American people that we can limit them too; that we can not only start things, that we can actually stop things.

About the defense budget, I raise a hope and a caution. As we restructure our military forces to meet the new threats of the post-cold-war world, it is true that we can responsibly reduce our defense budget. And we may all doubt what that range of reductions is, but let me say that as long as I am President, I will do everything I can to make sure that the men and women who serve under the American flag will remain the best trained, the best prepared, the best equipped fighting force in the world. And every one of you should make that solemn pledge. We still have responsibilities around the world. We are the world's only superpower. This is still a dangerous and uncertain time, and we owe it to the people in uniform to make sure that we adequately provide for the national defense and for their interests and needs. Backed by an effective national defense and a stronger economy, our Nation will be prepared to lead a world challenged as it is everywhere by ethnic conflict, by the proliferation of weapons of mass destruction, by the global democratic revolution, and by challenges to the health of our global environment.

I know this economic plan is ambitious, but I honestly believe it is necessary for the continued greatness of the United States. And I think it is paid for fairly, first by cutting Government, then by asking the most of those who benefited the most in the past, and by asking more Americans to contribute today so that all of us can prosper tomorrow.

For the wealthiest, those earning more than $180,000 per year, I ask you all who are listening tonight to support a raise in the top rate for Federal income taxes from 31 to 36 percent. We recommend a 10-percent surtax on incomes over $250,000 a year, and we recommend closing some loopholes that let some people get away without paying any tax at all.

For businesses with taxable incomes in excess of $10 million we recommend a raise in the corporate tax rate, also to 36 percent, as well as a cut in the deduction for business entertainment expenses. Our plan seeks to attack tax subsidies that actually reward companies more for shutting their operations down here and moving them overseas than for staying here and reinvesting in America. I say that as someone who believes that American companies should be free to invest around the world and as a former Governor who actively sought investment of foreign companies in my State. But the Tax Code should not express a preference to American companies for moving somewhere else, and it does in particular cases today.

We will seek to ensure that, through effective tax enforcement, foreign corporations who do make money in America simply pay the same taxes that American companies make on the same income.

To middle class Americans who have paid a great deal for the last 12 years and from whom I ask a contribution tonight, I will say again as I did on Monday night: You're not going alone any more, you're certainly not going first, and you're not going to pay more for less as you have too often in the past. I want to emphasize the facts about this plan: 98.8 percent of America's families will have no increase in their income tax rates, only 1.2 percent at the top.

Let me be clear: There will also be no new cuts in benefits for Medicare. As we move toward the 4th year, with the explosion in health care costs, as I said, projected to account for 50 percent of the growth of the deficit between now and the year 2000, there must be planned cuts in payments to providers, to doctors, to hospitals, to labs, as a way of controlling health care costs. But I see these only as a stopgap until we can reform the entire health care system. If you'll help me do that, we can be fair to the providers and to the consumers of health care. Let me repeat this, because I know it matters to a lot of you on both sides of the aisle. This plan does not make a recommendation for new cuts in Medicare benefits for any beneficiary.

Secondly, the only change we are making in Social Security is one that has already been publicized. The plan does ask older Americans with higher incomes, who do not rely solely on Social Security to get by, to contribute more. This plan will not affect the 80 percent of Social Security recipients who do not pay taxes on Social Security now. Those who do not pay tax on Social Security now will not be affected by this plan.

Our plan does include a broad-based tax on energy, and I want to tell you why I selected this and why I think it's a good idea. I recommend that we adopt a BTU tax on the heat content of energy as the best way to provide us with revenue to lower the deficit because it also combats pollution, promotes energy efficiency, promotes the independence, economically, of this country as well as helping to reduce the debt, and because it does not discriminate against any area. Unlike a carbon tax, that's not too hard on the coal States; unlike a gas tax, that's not too tough on people who drive a long way to work; unlike an ad valorem tax, it doesn't increase just when the price of an energy source goes up. And it is environmentally responsible. It will help us in the future as well as in the present with the deficit.

Taken together these measures will cost an American family with an income of about $40,000 a year less than $17 a month. It will cost American families with incomes under $30,000 nothing because of other programs we propose, principally those raising the earned income tax credit.

Because of our publicly stated determination to reduce the deficit, if we do these things, we will see the continuation of what's happened just since the election. Just since the election, since the Secretary of the Treasury, the Director of the Office of Management and Budget, and others who have begun to speak out publicly in favor of a tough deficit reduction plan, interest rates have continued to fall long-term. That means that for the middle class, who will pay something more each month, if they had any credit needs or demands, their increased energy costs will be more than offset by lower interest costs for mortgages. consumer loans, credit cards. This can be a wise investment for them and their country now.

I would also point out what the American people already know, and that is because we're a big, vast country where we drive long distances, we have maintained far lower burdens on energy than any other advanced country. We will still have far lower burdens on energy than any other advanced country. And these will be spread fairly, with real attempts to make sure that no cost is imposed on families with incomes under $30,000 and that the costs are very modest until you get into the higher income groups where the income taxes trigger in.

Now, I ask all of you to consider this: Whatever you think of the tax program, whatever you think of the spending cuts, consider the cost of not changing. Remember the numbers that you all know. If we just keep on doing what we're doing, by the end of the decade we'll have a $650-billion-a-year deficit. If we just keep on doing what we're doing, by the end of the decade 20 percent of our national income will go to health care every year, twice as much as any other country on the face of the globe. If we just keep on doing what we're doing, over 20 cents on the dollar will have to go to service the debt.

Unless we have the courage now to start building our future and stop borrowing from it, we're condemning ourselves to years of stagnation interrupted by occasional recessions, to slow growth in jobs, to no more growth in income, to more debt, to more disappointment. Worse, unless we change, unless we increase investment and reduce the debt to raise productivity so that we can generate both jobs and incomes, we will be condemning our children and our children's children to a lesser life than we enjoyed. Once Americans looked forward to doubling their living standards every 25 years. At present productivity rates, it will take 100 years to double living standards, until our grandchildren's grandchildren are born. I say that is too long to wait.

Tonight the American people know we have to change. But they're also likely to ask me tomorrow and all of you for the weeks and months ahead whether we have the fortitude to make the changes happen in the right way. They know that as soon as I leave this Chamber and you go home, various interest groups will be out in force lobbying against this or that piece of this plan, and that the forces of conventional wisdom will offer a thousand reasons why we well ought to do this but we just can't do it.

Our people will be watching and wondering, not to see whether you disagree with me on a particular issue but just to see whether this is going to be business as usual or a real new day, whether we're all going to conduct ourselves as if we know we're working for them. We must scale the walls of the people's skepticisms, not with our words but with our deeds. After so many years of gridlock and indecision, after so many hopeful beginnings and so few promising results, the American people are going to be harsh in their judgments of all of us if we fail to seize this moment.

This economic plan can't please everybody. If the package is picked apart, there will be something that will anger each of us, won't please anybody. But if it is taken as a whole, it will help all of us. So I ask you all to begin by resisting the temptation to focus only on a particular spending cut you don't like or some particular investment that wasn't made. And nobody likes the tax increases, but let's just face facts. For 20 years, through administrations of both parties, incomes have stalled and debt has exploded and productivity has not grown as it should. We cannot deny the reality of our condition. We have got to play the hand we were dealt and play it as best we can.

My fellow Americans, the test of this plan cannot be what is in it for me. It has got to be what is in it for us. If we work hard and if we work together, if we rededicate ourselves to creating jobs, to rewarding work, to strengthening our families, to reinventing our Government, we can lift our country's fortunes again.

Tonight, I ask everyone in this Chamber and every American to look simply into your heart, to spark your own hopes, to fire your own imagination. There is so much good, so much possibility, so much excitement in this country now that if we act boldly and honestly, as leaders should, our legacy will be one of prosperity and progress. This must be America's new direction. Let us summon the courage to seize it.

Thank you. God bless America.

OTA REPORT ON PRESCRIPTION DRUG PRICES

February 24, 1993

The soaring prices of prescription drugs, market imperfections, and the high cost of research and development (R&D), as well as hefty outlays for advertising were the topics of a critical study of the drug industry by the congressional Office of Technology Assessment (OTA). The February 24 report, one of many investigations of the pharmaceutical industry released during the 1990s and the most comprehensive analysis to date, concluded that smaller drug R&D expenditures and marketing budgets could go a long way toward keeping a more reasonable cap on what consumers had to pay for prescriptions.

Between 1980 and 1992, prices for prescription drugs rose by 128 percent—six times the overall rate of inflation. Moreover, drug prices increased even faster than other health care services, forcing millions of Americans, particularly the low-income and elderly population, to stop taking the medicines they needed or to cut back on their prescribed doses, according to industry critics.

By 1992 the "shameful and unrelenting price increases" had reached "crisis" proportions, according to Sen. David Pryor, D-Ark., one of the most outspoken congressional critics of the drug industry. "For the 12th year in a row, prescription drug price inflation has been the leader of the pack in pushing up the cost of medical care in our country.... Over five million people over 55 now say they are having to make choices between food and their prescription drugs—between fuel for their homes for heat or paying for prescription drugs. If that is the case, what kind of a country have we become?"

Congressional Regulation, Pricing Controversy

The federal government's formal involvement with the drug industry began in 1906 with the passage of the Pure Food and Drug Act. Among other things, the new law called for government analysis of patent medicines and prohibited false and misleading claims. But as time passed, it became apparent that the law was insufficient and that a firmer federal hand was required. In response, Congress in 1938 passed the Food, Drug and Cosmetic Act (FDCA), which remains the basis of modern drug regulation. Among other things, the act required that prescription drugs be proven safe before they could be offered for sale.

Congress also made frequent—although seldom successful—attempts to regulate prescription drug prices. In 1959 Sen. Estes Kefauver, D-Tenn., chairman of the Senate Judiciary Subcommittee on Antitrust and Monopoly, initiated hearings on the drug industry's pricing, patent, and business policies. The panel concluded that drug prices were "unreasonable" and that some companies had an unfair competitive advantage because of the seventeen-year period of patent exclusivity. Kefauver subsequently introduced a drug safety and price regulation bill, but the price regulation provisions were dropped.

It was not until 1984 that Congress squarely addressed the drug-price question with passage of the Drug Price Compensation and Patent Term Restoration Act. The law made it easier to market generic copies of drugs whose patents had expired, while giving drug manufacturers patent extensions to make up for time lost in going through the lengthy Food and Drug Administration (FDA) review process.

The pricing issue intensified in the 1990s, as the cost of drugs continued its upward spiral and several members of Congress reacted by introducing various regulatory measures. (The United States was the only Western nation that did not control the costs of prescription drugs, according to the OTA report.) High drug prices had produced "excessive and unconscionable profits" for the pharmaceutical companies, stated a staff report issued in September 1991 by the Senate Special Committee on Aging, chaired by Pryor. "At a time when Americans are scrimping and saving to afford their medications, the drug industry's annual average 15.5 percent profit margin more than triples the 4.6 percent profit margin of the average Fortune 500 company," Pryor wrote in the introduction to the panel's study.

Debate over R&D Funding

A principal concern among some legislators who were interested in the pharmaceutical industry was whether spending on R&D was excessive and pushing drug prices higher. To find out, Rep. Henry A. Waxman, D-Calif., chairman of the House Energy and Commerce Subcommittee on Health and the Environment, commissioned the OTA study "Pharmaceutical R&D: Costs, Risks and Rewards."

Pharmaceutical companies argued that the need for hefty R&D budgets to develop new products justified the prices they set for drugs. According to a May 1992 press briefing by the Pharmaceutical Manufacturers Association (PMA), drug manufacturers spent an average of $231 million to bring each new drug to market. That covered a process of *testing for safety and effectiveness and obtaining approval from the FDA that averaged twelve years. But OTA researchers found that most of the new drugs appearing in the United States between 1975 and 1989 "offered little therapeutic advantage over preexisting competitors." Moreover, each new drug introduced between 1981 and 1983 had an after-tax return of "at least $36 million more to its investors than was needed to pay off the R&D investment," according to the report.*

Lower R&D costs should result in less costly prescription drugs, said Waxman on release of the report. "Put another way," he said, "58 percent of industry research was invested in so-called 'me too' drugs, drugs that are designed to make a profit but which add nothing in terms of therapeutic benefits to patients." Waxman said that capping R&D might also lead to a significant reduction in high marketing budgets to sell competing drugs. In recent years, more than 22 cents of each dollar spent on prescription drugs went for advertising, marketing, and promotion, according to the OTA report. Pryor's 1991 subcommittee staff report had projected advertising and marketing expenditures for the average drug company at 25 percent of sales, compared with 22.5 percent for R&D.

Market Issues

One frequently cited reason for the high price of drugs was marketplace imperfections: many patients who used pharmaceutical products and services did not pay for them and therefore had less incentive to shop around for comparable, lower-priced drugs. Insurance companies had assumed more responsibility for paying for prescription drugs. The result was a lack of price competition among manufacturers during the 1980s. "It's the market, not the industry, that's the problem," said Judith Wagner, who directed the OTA study. "The market for drugs doesn't work, and the industry responds to those inappropriate market signals."

On the other hand, although prescription insurance coverage for consumers with insurance rose to 30 percent in 1989 from 9 percent in 1977, prescription drugs remained one of the largest out-of-pocket medical expenses for individuals. For many people, the need for even inexpensive medications could cause hardship. According to the nonpartisan Washington-based Employee Benefit Research Institute (EBRI), nearly three-quarters of all prescriptions were paid for directly by the patient. Elderly Americans—who consumed about 30 percent of all drugs sold in the United States annually—were hardest hit because they were the group least likely to have insurance coverage for prescriptions. A principal reason was that Medicare, the federal health care program for the elderly and disabled, did not cover most outpatient prescription medications.

Industry Response

The drug industry contended that the OTA report overestimated the industry's revenue but underestimated its costs. The report focused on drugs introduced in the early 1980s and therefore "comes to some inaccurate conclusions that simply do not pertain to the marketplace today," said a spokesman for the PMA. He added that the report did not take account of recent pledges by drug manufacturers to hold price increases to the level of inflation.

One of the pharmaceutical industry's chief defenses against accusations of overcharging was that their products actually lowered the nation's total health bill by reducing or eliminating hospital stays and avoiding costly surgery. They cited vaccines to prevent childhood diseases as a prime example. In an effort to bolster that claim, Schering-Plough, one of the nation's top ten drug companies, commissioned a study, released in March 1991, showing that over the next twenty-five years drugs were expected to prevent 9 million cases of heart disease and save 5 million lives. During that same period, drug intervention would reduce deaths from lung cancer by 662,000 and lower new arthritis cases by 2.1 million.

"Other things being equal, it is likely that policies that restrict prescription drug prices will reduce drug industry profitability," according to a January 1992 report by EBRI. "Whether such policies would lead to reduced investment in future products is an unanswered question."

The OTA researchers put it another way: "If price competition among therapeutically similar compounds became more common, the directions of R&D would change and the total amount of R&D would probably decline. Whether a decrease in R&D would be good or bad for the public is hard to judge. It is impossible to know whether today's level of pharmaceutical R&D is unquestionably worth its costs to society."

Following are excerpts from the summary report, "Pharmaceutical R&D: Costs, Risks and Rewards," released February 24, 1993, by the congressional Office of Technology Assessment:

Summary of Findings

- Pharmaceutical R&D is a costly and risky business, but in recent years the financial rewards from R&D have more than offset its costs and risks.
- The average aftertax R&D cash outlay for each new drug that reached the market in the 1980s was about $65 million (in 1990 dollars). The R&D process took 12 years on average. The full aftertax cost of these outlays, compounded to their value on the day of market approval, was roughly $194 million (1990 dollars).
- The cost of bringing a new drug to market is very sensitive to changes in science and technology, shifts in the kinds of drugs under development and changes in the regulatory environment. All of these changes

are occurring fast. Consequently, it is impossible to predict the cost of bringing a new drug to market today from estimated costs for drugs whose development began more than a decade ago.

- Each new drug introduced to the U.S. market between 1981 and 1983 returned, net of taxes, at least $36 million more to its investors than was needed to pay off the R&D investment. This surplus return amounts to about 4.3 percent of the price of each drug over its product life.
- Dollar returns on R&D are highly volatile over time. Changes in R&D costs, tax rates, and revenues from new drugs are the most important factors influencing net returns. Drugs approved for marketing in 1984-88 had much higher sales revenues (in constant dollars) in the early years after approval than did drugs approved in 1981-83. On the other hand, R&D costs may be increasing and generic competition could be much stiffer for these drugs after they lose patent protection.
- Over a longer span of time, economic returns to the pharmaceutical industry as a whole exceeded returns to corporations in other industries by about 2 to 3 percentage points per year from 1976 to 1987, after adjusting for differences in risk among industries. A risk-adjusted difference of this magnitude is sufficient to induce substantial new investment in the pharmaceutical industry.
- The rapid increase in revenues for new drugs throughout the 1980s sent signals that more investment would be rewarded handsomely. The pharmaceutical industry responded as expected, by increasing its investment in R&D. Industrywide investment in R&D accelerated in the 1980s, rising at a rate of 10 percent per year (in constant dollars).
- The rapid increase in new drug revenues was made possible in part by expanding health insurance coverage for prescription drugs in the United States through most of the 1980s. Health insurance makes patients and their prescribing physicians relatively insensitive to the price of a drug. The number of people with prescription drug coverage increased, and the quality of coverage improved.
- Almost all private health insurance plans covering prescription drugs are obligated to pay their share of the price of virtually any FDA-approved use of a prescription drug. FDA approval acts as a de facto coverage guideline for prescription drugs. Most health insurers have almost no power to influence prescribing behavior or to control the prices they pay for patented drugs.
- Manufacturers of drugs that are therapeutically similar to one another compete for business primarily on quality factors, such as ease of use, side-effect profiles and therapeutic effect. With price-conscious buyers such as health maintenance organizations (HMOs) and hospitals, however, they have engaged in more vigorous price competition.
- If price competition among therapeutically similar compounds became more common, the directions of R&D would change and the total amount of R&D would probably decline. Whether a decrease in R&D

would be good or bad for the public interest is hard to judge. It is impossible to know whether today's level of pharmaceutical R&D is unquestionably worth its costs to society.

- The National Institutes of Health (NIH) and other Public Health Service laboratories have no mechanism to protect the public's investment in drug discovery, development and evaluation. These agencies lack the expertise and sufficient legal authority to negotiate limits on prices to be charged for drugs discovered or developed with Federal funds.

Introduction

Pharmaceutical R&D is the process of discovering, developing, and bringing to market new ethical drug products. [Ethical drugs are biological and medicinal chemicals advertised and promoted primarily to the medical, pharmacy, and allied professions. Ethical drugs include products available only by prescription as well as some over-the-counter drugs. Strictly speaking, ethical drugs include diagnostic as well as therapeutic products, but this report concentrates on R&D for therapeutic ethical drugs.] Most pharmaceutical R&D is undertaken by private industrial firms, and this report is about how and why industrial pharmaceutical companies make decisions to undertake R&D, what they stand to gain from such investments, and how they are helped or hindered by public policies that influence the process.

Industrial R&D is a scientific and an economic process. R&D decisions are always made with both considerations in mind. Science defines the opportunities and constraints, but economics determines which opportunities and scientific challenges will be addressed through industrial research.

This report focuses mainly, but not entirely, on the economic side of the R&D process. In this perspective, pharmaceutical R&D is an investment. The principal characteristic of an investment is that money is spent today in the hope that even more money will be returned to the investors sometime in the future. If investors (or the corporate R&D managers who act on their behalf) believe that the potential profits from R&D are worth the investment's cost and risks, then they will invest in it. Otherwise, they will not. . . .

Origins and Scope of OTA's Study

. . . By itself, the average cost of pharmaceutical R&D tells little about whether drug prices are too high or are increasing too fast. A more important question is whether the dollar returns on R&D investments are higher or lower than what is needed to induce investors to make these investments. The long-run persistence of higher dollar returns in the industry as a whole than the amount needed to justify the cost and risk of R&D is evidence of unnecessary pricing power for ethical pharmaceuticals (45). OTA examined the economic returns to investors in pharmaceutical R&D.

The U.S. Federal Government is anything but a passive observer of the industrial pharmaceutical R&D process. The Federal Government subsidizes private R&D, regulates the introduction and marketing of new drugs, and pays for many drugs through Federal health care programs. Federal tax policies also alter R&D costs and returns. OTA assessed how Federal policies affect R&D costs and returns and how well Federal agencies protect the direct and indirect Federal investment in pharmaceutical R&D....

...Before any new therapeutic ethical pharmaceutical product can be introduced to the market in the United States and most other industrialized countries, some R&D must be undertaken, but the specific activities and required R&D expenditures vary enormously with the kind of product under development. New therapeutic ethical pharmaceutical products fall into four broad categories:

- **New chemical entities** (NCEs)—new therapeutic molecular compounds that have never before been used or tested in humans.
- **Drug delivery mechanisms**—new approaches to delivering therapeutic agents at the desired dose to the desired site in the body.
- **Follow-on products**—new combinations, formulations, dosing forms, or dosing strengths of existing compounds that must be tested in humans before market introduction.
- **Generic products**—copies of drugs that are not protected by patents or other exclusive marketing rights.

R&D is needed to bring all of these products to the market. National regulatory policies determine some of the required R&D, but some R&D would be undertaken even if there were no new drug regulation.

NCEs are discovered either through screening existing compounds or designing new molecules; once synthesized, they must undergo rigorous preclinical testing in laboratories and animals and clinical testing in humans to establish safety and effectiveness. The same is true for novel drug delivery mechanisms, such as monoclonal antibodies or implantable drug infusion pumps. Follow-on products also must undergo preclinical and clinical testing before they can be marketed, but the amount of R&D required to prove safety and effectiveness is usually less than for the original compound.

Even after a new drug has been approved and introduced to the market, clinical R&D may continue. Some of this postapproval clinical evaluation is required by regulatory agencies as a condition of approval, but other clinical research projects are designed to expand the market for the drug. For example, much clinical research is done to test new therapeutic uses for a drug already on the market or to compare its effectiveness with that of a competing product.

The research required on a generic product is typically much less than on the original compound it copies. In the United States, the makers of generic products must show the U.S. Food and Drug Administration

(FDA) that the drug is therapeutically equivalent to the original compound, not that the compound itself is effective against the disease. This involves much less R&D than is necessary to introduce either NCEs or follow-on products.

The discovery and development of NCEs is the heart of pharmaceutical R&D, because the developers of follow-on or generic products build on the knowledge produced in the course of developing them. The market for the compound and all its follow-on products or generic copies in future years rests on the R&D that led to its initial introduction to the market. Most of the money spent on pharmaceutical R&D goes to the discovery and development of NCEs. Companies responding to the Pharmaceutical Manufacturers Association's (PMA) annual survey estimated that 83 percent of total U.S. R&D dollars in 1989 were spent in "the advancement of scientific knowledge and development of new products" versus "significant improvements and/or modifications of existing products."

A patent on an NCE gives its owner the right to invest in further R&D to test new therapeutic uses or produce follow-on products. This continuing R&D may extend the compound's life in the market or increase its market size. Therefore, a complete analysis of returns on R&D for NCEs should encompass the costs of and returns on these subsequent investments as well.

NCEs comprise two poorly-defined subcategories: pioneer drugs and "me-too" drugs. Pioneer NCEs have molecular structures or mechanisms of action that are very different from all previously existing drugs in a therapeutic area. The first compound to inhibit the action of a specific enzyme, for example, is a pioneer drug. Me-too drugs are introduced after the pioneer and are similar but not identical to pioneer compounds in molecular structure and mechanism of action. Many me-too drugs are developed through deliberate imitation of the pioneer compound and have a shorter and more certain discovery period. But, the R&D cost advantage gained by imitation is typically met by a reduction in potential dollar returns from being a late entrant to the market....

Postpatent Revenues

Net Return on Investment

[N]et postapproval cash flows must be compared with the present value of the investment in R&D required to discover and develop the compounds. An upper bound on the fully capitalized R&D costs of drugs introduced in the early 1980s is about $359 million before tax savings, or $194 million after tax savings are considered. **Thus, OTA concluded that the average NCE introduced to the U.S. market in the period 1981-83 can be expected to produce dollar returns whose present value is about $36 million more (after taxes) than would be required to bring forth the investment in the R&D.**

Some of the revenue and cost assumptions underlying this analysis were very uncertain, so OTA analyzed the sensitivity of the estimated returns to changes in critical assumptions. The results are somewhat sensitive to the ratio of global sales (about which we know relatively little) to U.S. sales (about which we know much more). If the ratio of global sales to U.S. sales is much greater than 2, as we have reason to believe it may be, the present value of the cash flows would be even more (after taxes) than is necessary to repay the R&D investment.

The results were not very sensitive to changes in the speed with which originator brand sales decline after patent expiration. If the average sales per compound were to decline by 20 percent per year after patent expiration, the present value of the cash flows would be $311 million before taxes and $209 million after taxes, still above the full after-tax cost of R&D. Fully 6 years after the passage of the Drug Price Competition and Patent Term Restoration Act there is no evidence that the rate of sales decline for originator compounds after patent expiration is approaching this rate.

What does it mean to have the average revenue per compound deliver $36 million more in present value than was needed to bring forth the research on the drugs in the cohort? **OTA estimated that excess returns over R&D costs would be eliminated if the annual revenue per compound was reduced by 4.3 percent over the product's life....**

Payment Policy and Returns on R&D

Future returns to the research-intensive pharmaceutical industry depend not only on the opportunities created by scientific research, but also on the regulatory and market conditions that will govern the sale of pioneer and me-too products. OTA examined recent trends in payment policies that affect the market for new pharmaceuticals.

Sales of new ethical drugs depend on physicians' decisions to prescribe them and on patients' decisions to buy them. Physicians and patients base these decisions on judgments about a drug's quality and price compared with the quality and price of existing alternatives. The tradeoff between perceived quality and price depends on many factors, including the severity of the disease or condition for which a drug is intended, evidence of its effectiveness compared with alternative courses of action, the availability of close substitutes, and the effectiveness of advertising and promotion in convincing doctors the drug is the right choice for the patient.

Importance of Health Insurance in Determining Demand

When a patient's health insurance plan covers prescription drugs, the balance between perceived quality and price tips in favor of quality. While it protects consumers from uncontrollable and catastrophic expenses, health insurance also reduces the effective price of health care services and products. By reducing patients' out-of-pocket cost, health insurance makes them less sensitive to price than they would otherwise be.

Insurance coverage for prescription drugs in the United States changed during the 1980s in two ways that made the demand for prescription drugs even less sensitive to price than it was before. First, the percent of Americans with outpatient prescription drug benefits increased, albeit modestly, over the 1980s, from 67-69 percent in 1979 to 70-74 percent in 1987, the latest year for which good data are available. Although few Americans had insurance plans that covered outpatient drugs in full, the mere existence of insurance coverage makes patients less sensitive to price than they would be without such coverage.

Second, the structure of outpatient prescription drug benefits changed markedly over the period. In the past, almost all nonelderly people with outpatient drug benefits had "major medical" plans with an overall annual deductible that had to be met before insurance would help pay for any services or drugs. By 1989, 30 percent of these people had policies that required fixed copayments for prescription drugs instead of including them in the overall deductible. The vast majority of people with fixed copayments per prescription in 1989 paid $5 or less per prescription. The insurance company picked up the rest of the bill regardless of its amount.

The switch from overall deductibles to fixed copayments for prescription drugs means a richer insurance benefit structure for prescription drugs. For people whose annual medical expenses lie below their plan's annual deductible (commonly $200 or $250 per year), a flat copayment for prescription drugs means lower out-of-pocket prescription drug costs than do major medical restrictions. Even when patients do meet the deductible in a year, many would have higher out-of-pocket prescription drug costs under a major medical plan than under a fixed copayment.

The impact of these improvements in prescription drug insurance benefits shows up in insurance reimbursements. The percent of total outpatient prescription drug spending in the United States paid for by insurance increased substantially, from 28 to 44 percent, between 1977 and 1987. The same trend holds among elderly Americans, for whom private insurance paid for about 36 percent of outpatient prescription drug expenses in 1987 compared with only 23 percent in 1977.

Most private and public health insurers have little power to restrict physicians' prescribing decisions. Private insurers generally cover all prescription drugs the FDA has licensed for sale in the United States. Thus, FDA approval is a *de facto* insurance coverage guideline. If the physician orders a specific compound, the insurer routinely pays its share of the costs.

Despite the fact that many compounds, though protected from generic competition by patents or other market exclusivity provisions, compete for market share with similar compounds, that competition tends to focus on product characteristics, such as ease of use, favorable side-effect profiles, or therapeutic effects, and not on price. Companies spend a great deal on this product competition. One major U.S. pharmaceutical company reported recently that about 28 percent of its sales went for marketing (advertising and promotion) expenses.

Emphasizing product competition over price competition is a rational strategy for companies operating in a market that is not very sensitive to price differentials among similar compounds. If prescribing physicians will not be swayed by lower prices, it would be foolhardy for firms to set prices for their products much lower than those of competitors. Unless or until the demand for prescription drugs becomes more price sensitive, the benefits of the competitive R&D on prices will not be felt. . . .

Different Buyers Pay Different Prices

Price-Sensitive Buyers Gain from Price Competition

The success of some HMOs and hospitals in getting price concessions from manufacturers of single-source drugs (i.e., those with patent protection) attests to the potential for price competition to lower the cost of drugs to patients or their insurers. For price competition among close therapeutic alternatives to be effective in a market with price-sensitive buyers, enough similar competing products must exist to allow providers to choose among alternatives on the basis of price as well as quality. Me-too products, often derided as not contributing to health care, are therefore necessary to obtain the benefits of price competition in segments of the market that are price sensitive.

Most of the new drugs entering the world market in recent years have offered little therapeutic advantage over pre-existing competitors. A 1990 European study of the therapeutic value of new drugs first introduced in at least one of seven industrialized countries between 1975 and 1980 found that only 30 percent of all NCEs were classified by a group of experts as "adding something to therapy" compared with compounds already on the market. The rest fell into categories that could be called me-toos. About 42 percent of those NCEs originated in the United States were judged to offer therapeutic benefits, so well over one-half of all drugs introduced in the United States were judged to offer no therapeutic benefit. Over the entire study period, the majority of drugs in almost every therapeutic category did not "add something to therapy." These results suggest the supply of therapeutic competitors is large and the potential for price competition in those segments of the market with price-sensitive buyers is potentially vast.

The problem with me-too drugs is not that they are sometimes imitative or of modest therapeutic benefit. Imitation is an important dimension of competition, and the more choices consumers have, the more intense will be the competition. The personal computer industry provides a clear illustration of how rapid improvements in quality can coincide with steep price reductions. The problem with me-too drugs is that a large part of the market in the United States is very insensitive to price and does not get the full benefits of price competition that would be expected from the availability of an array of similar products.

Generic Competition Gives Insurers More Control Over Drug Prices

Once a drug loses patent protection, it is vulnerable to competition from copies whose therapeutic equivalence is verified by the FDA. These generic competitors compete largely on the basis of price, since they can claim no quality advantage over the brand-name drug.

Private and public health insurers have initiated programs to encourage dispensing of cheaper versions of multisource compounds (those with generic equivalents on the market). These strategies include using mail-order pharmacies, waiving beneficiaries' cost-sharing requirements when prescriptions are filled with generic versions, or refusing to pay more than a certain amount for a drug with a generic competitor. Medicaid, the health insurance program for the poor, mandates substitution with cheaper generic drugs unless the prescribing physician specifically prohibits it in writing on the prescription form.

These programs have substantially reduced brand-name compounds' unit sales and revenues, but it takes several years after the compound's patent expires for the full brunt of generic competition to be felt. **Indeed, OTA found that 6 years after patent expiration, brand-name drugs still held over 50 percent of the market in physical units.**

Pricing Systems Differ Across Countries

Not only is the market for prescription drugs segmented among different classes of buyers in the United States, but it is also segmented internationally. Pharmaceutical companies charge different prices for the same drug in different countries.

Most other industrialized countries have universal health insurance that includes prescription drugs, so patients' demand for drugs is not very sensitive to the price charged. Nevertheless, the prices paid tend to be more strictly controlled by the third-party payers in these countries than in the United States. Drug payment policy in each of these other countries is governed by two potentially conflicting objectives: minimization of health insurance prescription drug costs and encouragement of the domestic pharmaceutical industry. National prescription drug payment policies represent a blend between these objectives. In other industrialized countries, drug payment policy is generally developed with explicit recognition of the two policy objectives.

Virtually all of the five countries whose pharmaceutical reimbursement systems OTA reviewed—Australia, Canada, France, Japan, and the United Kingdom—use some mechanism for con-

trolling the price of single-source as well as multiple-source drugs. Four of the five countries do so directly by setting payment rates for new drugs based on the cost of existing therapeutic alternatives. The pricing policies in these countries reward pioneer, or "breakthrough," drugs with higher prices than me-too drugs, although they accomplish this objective through different mechanisms, and the prices of breakthrough drugs may still be low in comparison with those obtained in the United States. . . .

EISENHOWER FOUNDATION REPORT ON INNER CITIES

February 28, 1993

Twenty-five years after a presidential commission found that the United States was becoming "two societies, one black, one white—separate and unequal," a new study, released February 28, found that little had changed. The earlier panel, known as the Kerner Commission, was appointed by former president Lyndon B. Johnson after devastating riots shook some of the nation's largest cities. The commission made numerous recommendations aimed at improving the lives of low-income Americans and avoiding future riots.

The new study was prepared by the Milton S. Eisenhower Foundation, which runs anticrime programs in several cities. The foundation, named for former president Dwight D. Eisenhower's youngest brother, was formed by people who worked on the Kerner Commission and two other presidential panels in the 1960s.

Federal Policies That Failed

The urban poor had made some gains since the late 1960s, according to the Eisenhower study. However, those gains were overwhelmed by problems that had not been properly addressed by the federal government, the emergence of multiracial disparities, and growing income segregation.

As evidence that federal policies had largely failed the urban poor, the report cited several statistics from the 1980s:

1. *The number of children living in poverty nationwide increased by 22 percent.*
2. *Average hourly wages fell by more than 9 percent.*
3. *Infants in Detroit and Washington, D.C., had higher mortality rates than those in Cuba and Bulgaria.*
4. *The number of prison cells doubled, while housing for the poor was cut by 80 percent.*

5. *One out of four African-American males was in prison, on probation, or on parole at any one time.*
6. *The United States had the highest rate of incarceration in the industrialized world, yet it also had the highest rates of violent crime.*

The nation had enough experience with urban aid programs to know which work and which do not, according to the report. It cited Head Start, a federally funded program for preschool children, as a strong example of a program that worked. Evaluations of Head Start found it was "perhaps the most cost-effective ... inner-city prevention strategy ever developed," the report said. It advocated increasing funding for Head Start so that all eligible children could participate. President Bill Clinton also had endorsed more funding for Head Start. The report said many of the best programs were community-based nonprofit ventures. These efforts should get additional funding and be expanded nationwide, it said.

The report also made numerous other recommendations. It called for strengthening gun control laws, letting tenants manage public housing, creating job training and placement programs for urban youths, and providing health care coverage for the working poor, among other measures. It also advocated shifting the emphasis in federal drug control efforts. Some 70 percent of the $12 billion spent annually on antidrug efforts went toward law enforcement and interdiction, while 30 percent was spent on prevention and treatment. The report said those percentages should be reversed.

Managing the Cost of the Solution

Solving urban ills would carry a heavy price tag: $30 billion annually for ten years, according to the report. It suggested the money could come from savings from decreased military spending, cuts in funding for the Agency for International Development, higher tax rates on the very rich, increased taxes on tobacco and alcohol, and a higher gasoline tax that would include tax credits for the poor. Lynn Curtis, the foundation's president and author of the report, also said some improvements would cost little or nothing. For example, Curtis said the Job Training Partnership Act could be restructured so that it emphasized training disadvantaged youths.

The report also recommended dropping programs that do not work. It said enterprise zones had failed, especially in employing sufficient numbers of high-risk youths. Enterprise zones would be effective, the report said, only if they were one small part of a much larger package. Businesses that locate in enterprise zones, which are created in blighted urban areas, typically receive tax breaks and regulatory relief.

While criticizing enterprise zones, however, the report also blasted former president George Bush for vetoing a bill that embraced them. The bill, passed by Congress in October 1992 in response to the Los Angeles riots, promoted urban enterprise zones and "weed and seed" initiatives aimed at removing drug dealers from targeted neighborhoods and then providing educational and employment opportunities for the people who remained. Bush vetoed the bill the day after the 1992 election, claiming it would result in new taxes.

"The contents of the vetoed bill and the motivations of Congress and the White House over the spring, summer and fall of 1992 raised grave doubts about whether the gridlocked American federal political process would or could ever enact informed solutions to the problems of the inner cities and the persons who live in them," the report said. It noted, however, that Congress passed and the president signed into law a $1.3 billion aid package that included small business loans for Los Angeles and a $500 million program to create summer jobs for youths nationwide.

The 350-page report and its recommendations for increasing spending on the inner cities drew favorable responses on newspaper editorial pages around the country. "If America can find hundreds of billions of dollars to bail out the savings and loan industry, it should be able to find the money for a long-term strategy of youth investment and community reconstruction," said the Star Tribune *of Minnesota.*

Following is the executive summary from the prepublication copy of "Investing in Children and Youth, Reconstructing Our Cities: Doing What Works to Reverse the Betrayal of American Democracy," released February 28, 1993, by the Milton S. Eisenhower Foundation:

With the memory of the 1965 Watts riots in Los Angeles still vivid, the summer of 1967 again brought racial disorders to American cities, and with them shock, fear and bewilderment.

The worst came during a two-week period in July, first in Newark and then in Detroit. Each set off a chain reaction in neighboring communities.

On July 28, 1967, President Johnson established the National Advisory Commission on Civil Disorders—which came to be known as the Kerner Commission, after its Chairman, Governor Otto Kerner of Illinois.

Led by Washington, D.C. lawyer David Ginsburg, the staff recommended a policy based on three principles, which the Commission accepted in its final report to the President on March 1, 1968:

- To mount programs on a scale equal to the dimension of the problems;
- To aim these programs for high impact in the immediate future in order to close the gap between promise and performance;
- To undertake new initiatives that can change the system of failure and frustration that now dominates the ghetto and weakens our society.

The now classic conclusion of the Commission was that, "Our Nation is moving toward two societies, one black, one white—separate and unequal."

One of the witnesses invited to appear before the Commission was Dr. Kenneth B. Clark. Referring to the reports of earlier riot commissions, he said:

> I read that report . . . of the 1919 riot in Chicago, and it is as if I were reading the report of the investigating committee on the Harlem riot of '35, the report of the investigating committee on the Harlem riot of '43, the report of the McCone Commission on the Watts riot.
>
> I must again in candor say to you members of this Commission—it is a kind of Alice in Wonderland—with the same moving picture reshown over and over again, the same analysis, the same recommendations, and the same inaction.

The 1992 Los Angeles Riots and the Federal Response

It is the twenty-fifth anniversary of the Kerner Report. We can reflect, again, on the same moving picture—now the April, 1992 riots in south central Los Angeles after the verdicts in the trial of the police officers accused of beating motorist Rodney King.

After the Los Angeles rioting, Congress enacted and the President signed a \$1.3B aid package that included small business loans for Los Angeles and a \$500M program to create summer jobs for youth nationwide.

This was accompanied by talk in Congress and the White House of a longer run plan. Central to the plan were urban enterprise zones and "weed and seed" initiatives. The enterprise zones were to provide tax breaks and regulatory relief to businesses and corporations if they located in blighted areas, like south central Los Angeles. "Weed and seed" programs were to use tough law enforcement to get dealers and drugs out of targeted neighborhoods and then to provide educational and employment opportunities plus related services to the people in those places.

Congress passed this so called long run package in October, 1992. The day after the 1992 election, the President vetoed the bill. So ended the federal response to the riot, at least for the 102nd Congress.

The contents of the vetoed bill and the motivations of Congress and the White House over the spring, summer and fall of 1992 raised grave doubts about whether the gridlocked American federal political process would or could ever enact informed solutions to the problems of the inner cities and the persons who live in them.

Enterprise Zones and Weed and Seed

The long-term bill reflected an emerging consensus within both parties in Congress that enterprise zones were key to reform. This view was more than shared by the White House. It was the Secretary of Housing and Urban Development (HUD), after all, who had originally and tenaciously pressed for the zones from the beginning of the Administration. Yet almost all evaluations of the many enterprise zones that have been tried to date at the state and local levels showed them to fail, especially in employing sufficient numbers of high risk young people in the devastated areas—like members of the Crips and Bloods, the south central Los Angeles gangs. The evaluations were done by such respected institutions as the U.S. General Accounting Office and the Urban Institute in Washington, D.C. Their conclusions were echoed in warnings by such conservative and business-oriented publications as the *Economist* and *Business Week* that enterprise zones, alone, and in the form proposed in 1992, were not the answer.

There appeared to be little recognition by Congressional Democrats, Congressional Republicans and the White House that, based on existing evidence of what works in the inner city, enterprise zones could only become one part, eventually, of a long run solution.

Members of Congress in both parties and the Executive Branch for the most part appeared to take little note of the fact that "weed and seed" was mostly "weed." The initiative was heavy on law enforcement—something that, indeed, appeared necessary to help stabilize neighborhoods for economic development. But the "seed" part of the initiative was barren. There were almost no new funds. Just reallocations from existing programs. The "seed" plan was never thought out, and never came close to integrating all the "multiple solutions" that inner city evaluations since the Kerner Commission had indicated were necessary.

The Byzantine Ways of Congress

Because the Congress and the White House saw enterprise zones as the legislative centerpiece, and because such zones involve tax breaks to businesses, the urban legislation became incorporated into a much larger package of tax changes. The tax bill cost $27B over five years, only $7B of which was targeted on cities. The bill also repealed the luxury tax on furs and yachts, granted corporations automatic tax writeoffs for purchases of intangible assets like lists of potential customers, subsidized retirement savings for high-income families, and provided many other benefits for the advantaged.

To people outside the Washington, D.C. Beltway, this might have appeared as just another example of the outmoded procedures and rules of Congress. Not only were most of the tax breaks included in the package irrelevant to the inner city, but they deprived the federal government of revenues to fund devastated neighborhoods.

By choosing enterprise zones as the key solution, Congress needed to process the legislation primarily through committees that dealt with taxation, revenues and finance. Because encrusted Congressional rules say little about keeping focused—here on the inner city—it was easy for all of the other provisions, irrelevant to the city, to be added. This meant that the many contributors to the package had many motivations other than what to do in the wake of the Los Angeles riots. For example, one Congressional player wanted to help shipbuilder constituents. Another was concerned about wealthy constituents who were saving for retirement.

There appeared to be little reflection in Congress that, based on inner city programs that already had seemed to work best—like, as we shall see, Head Start, Job Corps and non-profit community development corporations—other committees should have had the lead much more—especially those committees with expertise in human resources, education, employment and economic development.

No New Taxes?

Why did the President veto the bill? Because enterprise zones were an unworthy centerpiece? No, the President was enthusiastic about them. Because of the deficiencies of "weed and seed?" No, the President said the opposite—the bill fell short on his weed and seed proposals. Because the bill failed to include programs that had worked? No—the veto message said nothing about that.

Rather, the President vetoed the bill primarily because it included some tax increases. The President never again wanted to violate his pledge of "no new taxes." In the election campaign, he defined an extraordinary range of revenue measures as "tax increases," and some of those measures were in the $27B tax bill. The bill therefore was not politically viable, given the way the President had backed himself into a corner with his definitions. This was so even though the bill included tax decreases that offset tax increases. Critics also claimed that the President followed a double standard, because he *did* sign an energy bill with tax increases in it.

So the President vetoed the wrong bill for the wrong reasons, leaving the people of south central Los Angeles and other inner cities with nothing more than the original $1.3B emergency aid—which was called a "quick fix" by advocates for the cities and the poor.

Alice in Wonderland All Over Again

It all was Dr. Clark's Alice in Wonderland written large, Yogi Berra's "deja vu all over again." Congress and the White House misunderstood the problem. They then constructed a solution that flew in the face of what really did work. The status quo gridlock was guaranteed even more because Byzantine Congressional procedures packaged the misperceived solution as part of a plan of tax changes, some of which heightened the President's political fear of tax increases. The question was not seriously raised of whether or not, from a substantive and economic point of view, tax increases on the rich might logically have been part of the financing, after years of favored federal government treatment of the well off and the deepening crisis of the inner city.

Keeping the Kerner Prophesy Alive and Well

Over the last twelve years, the pursuit of folly became the conventional wisdom. As a result of trickle down economics, the rich got richer and the poor got poorer. During the 1980s, children living in poverty nationwide increased twenty-two percent and average hourly wages fell by more than nine percent. In the shadow of some of the most sophisticated medical centers anywhere, infants in Washington and Detroit had higher rates of mortality than in Cuba and Bulgaria. The number of prison cells doubled while housing for the poor was cut by eighty percent. One of four African American males was in prison, on probation or on parole at any one time. The ratio was one to three in California, which usually leads the rest of the nation. Yet violent crime increased by thirty five percent. America had the highest rates of incarceration in the industrialized world—but also the highest rates of violent crime. The "war on drugs" became a domestic Vietnam. The English spoken by inner city African Americans became more and more different from the English spoken by whites.

Overall, in spite of some gains since the 1960s but especially because of the federal disinvestments of the 1980s, we conclude that the famous prophesy of the Kerner Commission, of two societies, one black, one white—separate and unequal—is more relevant today than in 1968, and more complex, with the emergence of multiracial disparities and growing income segregation.

The Goal of This Report

The goal of this twenty-fifth anniversary report is to suggest a policy that works. It is not our intention to provide detailed comparisons between recommendations in the voluminous Kerner report and policy today. Instead, we will concentrate on new policy for the rest of the twentieth century that is in keeping with the principles of the Kerner Commission and the spirit of the new Administration in Washington. Our focus is on the hard core poor in the cities, the roughly ten percent of the population who live in urban areas of concentrated long-term poverty, and whose violence and suffering has a disproportionate effect on American life, class tension and race tension.

We Know of Much That Works

Those with vision need not despair about the experiment in democracy that Alexis de Tocqueville described so eloquently in *Democracy in America* in 1835. The fact is that we already know quite a bit about which investments work in the American inner city. They are cheaper and more productive, economically and in terms of human capital, than trickle down economics, prison building and drug interdiction.

Based on scientific evaluations over the last two decades, the policies that work can be summarized as investing in people—especially children and youth—and using those investments as much as possible for reconstructing our cities, as part of what now have become new national economic priorities.

Investing in Children

Head Start is not perfect. But it has been evaluated as perhaps the most cost-effective, across-the-board inner-city prevention strategy ever developed. Yet, today, whereas more than fifty percent of the nation's higher income families ($35,000 and above) enroll their three-year-olds in preschool, the enrollment rate is only seventeen percent for lower income families. It is noteworthy, if frustrating, that the Kerner Commission called for "building on the successes of Head Start" more than twenty-five years ago. It is time to extend Head Start to all eligible children, even though it is clear from programs like Project Beethoven in Chicago public housing that preschool needs to be complemented by multiple youth, employment, economic and community policing innovations in the most deteriorated neighborhoods.

Investing in Youth

Over the last twenty years, despite pessimistic rhetoric that "nothing works," and in the face of twelve years of federal government disinvestment, many community-based, non-profit ventures have shown encouraging successes in tackling the problems of violence and drug abuse among urban youth. Illustrations include the Argus Community in the Bronx, Centro Sister Isolina Ferre in Puerto Rico, Delancey Street in San Francisco and Project Redirection nationwide. Many of them have been judged successful in careful scientific evaluations. Most have "bubbled up" from the grassroots, thus providing "ownership" for the disadvantaged. Often, they have evolved because the more traditional service delivery mechanisms for the youth of the inner city—including the schools—have failed.

When we look at the successes for high risk youth in the inner city that have built up a reasonable amount of scientific evaluation, as well as the initiatives that seem on the right track but need more rigorous evaluation, several lessons seem clear:

- There is value in organizing and implementing non-profit youth organizations at the grassroots level.
- Multiple solutions are needed for multiple problems—the "butterfly effect" applies.
- Solutions need to be flexible and staff need to be caring and tenacious.
- Sound management must be put in place.
- A way must be found to secure at least minimal resources year after year.

The Butterfly Effect

For example, Vaclav Havel, President of the Czech Republic, has written of the "butterfly effect":

> It is a belief that everything in the world is so mysteriously and comprehensively interconnected that a slight, seemingly insignificant wave of a butterfly's wing in a single spot on this planet can unleash a typhoon thousands of miles away.

We are not certain about typhoons far away, but, in the inner city, interconnectedness is not at all mysterious in successful programs for children and youth.

Most of the successful programs begin with some form of "sanctuary" (a place to go) off the street. It may be residential, as Delancey, non-residential, as Centro or both, as Argus. Paid and volunteer mentors function as "big brothers" and "big sisters"—offering *both* social support and discipline in what amounts to an "extended family."

Often youth who need such social investments are teen parents who receive counseling in parenting skills, as in Project Redirection. In some successes, where feasible, mentoring and counseling also involve the parents of the youth who receive the mentoring.

Not uncommonly, a goal of the mentoring process is to keep youth in high school or to help them receive high school equivalency degrees, sometimes in alternative, community-based organizational settings, as Argus. Here, too, there are many variations among successful programs. They include day care for the infants of teen parents. Remedial education in community-based settings often can be pursued with the help of computer-based programs, like those developed by Robert Taggert with US Basics, which allow a youth to advance an entire school year through two or three months of one-on-one work with a computer. There are vocational incentives to stay in school, like the Hyatt hotel management and food preparation course being run by Youth Guidance, at Roberto Clemente Community Academy in Chicago, which assures a job with Hyatt upon graduation.

Some successful community non-profit programs also link high school education either to job training or to college. When job training is undertaken, social support and discipline continue, frequently in community-based settings, as is the case with Argus, and there is a link between job training and job placement. *The training-placement link is crucial because the present American national job training program for high risk youth—the Job Training Partnership Act—does not adequately place such youth in jobs.* In successful programs, sometimes job placement is in the immediate neighborhood of a sponsoring community-based organization—as in initiatives which train young workers to rehabilitate houses, like YouthBuild. This can help in the social and economic development of the neighborhood.

There are some promising ventures where this combination of youth, social and economic development is assisted by community-based and problem-oriented policing, as is the case with the Centro San Juan residential police mini-station and the residential police mini-station being planned by Argus. Such community policing does not usually reduce crime in inner-city neighborhoods, based on careful evaluations—but it can reduce fear. The fear reduction can help encourage businesses and the public sector to stay or build in the inner city. If this economic development is planned correctly, it can provide jobs for high-risk youth. The youth can qualify for the jobs if they have adequate job training, and if they stay in school. Staying in school is made easier by "big brother/big sister" mentoring and "extended family sanctuaries off the street." Children can survive long enough to get into these sanctuary initiatives if they have Head Start.

What works, then, for youth at risk of getting into trouble seems to embrace a "multiple-solutions" formula including: sanctuary, extended family, mentoring, positive peer pressure, social support, discipline, educational innovation that motivates a youth to obtain a high school degree, job training (which continues social support) linked to job placement, feasible options for continuing on to college, employment linked to economic development, and problem-oriented policing, which is supportive of the process for youth social, community and economic development.

Not all youth successes have all of these components, but multiple solutions always are evident in the formula.

Similarly, the program successes tend to have multiple good outcomes. Not uncommonly, in successfully evaluated programs, these outcomes include some combination of less crime, less gang-related behavior, less drug abuse, less welfare dependency, fewer adolescent pregnancies, more school completion, more successful school-to-work transitions and more employability among targeted high-risk youths. The communities where young people live can experience business, housing, job and economic development.

As with the multiple solutions in the program formula, not all model programs and replications achieve all of these good outcomes. But the point is that multiple good outcomes are the rule, not the exception.

Replication is Possible But Not Easy

In a speech before the nation's governors, President Clinton has talked about "the need to make exceptions to the rule." In the private sector, he said, exceptions do become the rule quickly, if they are successful. Everyone else in the market needs to adapt or be driven out. But, in the public sector, he said, it is much more difficult to make exceptions the rule.

These are important insights. It is true that the "social technology" of how to replicate inner-city community-based non-profit programs is rather primitive. However, the difficulties that must be overcome are, in the words of Lisbeth Schorr, "not insurmountable." David Hamburg, President of the Carnegie Corporation, believes that, "we know enough to act and can't afford not to act." And Joy Dryfoos, in *Adolescents at Risk* concludes:

> Enough is known about the lives of disadvantaged high-risk youth to mount an intensive campaign to alter the trajectories of these children. Enough has been documented about the inability of fragmented programs to produce the necessary changes to proceed toward more comprehensive and holistic approaches.

In many important ways, then, we need to stop thinking in terms of experiments and demonstration programs alone. We need to start implementing and replicating what already works.

It is time for a new, dynamic, creative implementing agency. We propose a national non-profit Corporation for Youth Investment, funded by the federal government and the private sector. The Corporation needs to replicate the shared components that seem to underlie success of community-based, non-profit development programs for high risk youth at a sufficient scale to begin to create a national impact.

National Education Policy for the Inner City

Unlike Japan and many European nations, the U.S. makes its decisions about education locally, without mandates from a government ministry. The U.S. Department of Education does not build schools, hire teachers, write textbooks, dictate curricula, administer exams or manage colleges and universities.

But the federal Department of Education' s mission is to expand educational opportunity, set standards, innovate new ideas which, if successful, can be replicated locally, undertake careful evaluations and disseminate information.

We recommend that the Department of Education implement the recently proposed reforms of the Elementary and Secondary Education Act of 1965, carry out the National Urban Schools Program proposed by the Carnegie Foundation and the middle school reform proposed by the Carnegie Council, replicate the School Development Plan of Yale Professor, James Comer, replicate the Eugene Lang "I Have A Dream" Program and the Cities in Schools Program *if* comprehensive evaluations show their worth, experiment with still unproven vocational and apprenticeship training, replicate already successful vocational and apprenticeship training (like Project Prepare in Chicago), push for more school integration based on plans that have worked (like the one in St. Louis), and begin a demonstration that allows inner-city students to pay off college loans through community service. Department of Education monies should be leveraged at the rate of one new federal dollar for each eight state and local dollars, as recommended by the Carnegie Foundation for the Advancement of Teaching.

Job Training and Placement

We need a new federal job training and placement system focused on high-risk youth that builds on Job Corps, JobStart, YouthBuild, Comprehensive Competencies, and appropriate American variations on German vocational training. As part of the policy, the minimum wage should be fully restored to its 1981 purchasing power.

Next to Head Start, the Job Corps appears to be the second most successful, across-the-board American prevention program ever created for high-risk kids. Job Corps is an *intensive* program with multiple solutions over one year that takes seriously the need to provide a supportive, structured environment for the youth it seeks to assist. Job Corps features classroom courses, which can lead to high school equivalency degrees, counseling and hands-on job training for very high-risk youths. Hence, as in individual community-based non-profit programs, like Argus, Job Corps carefully links education, training, placement and support services.

As with Head Start, Job Corps surely is not perfect, but its results have been consistently positive and its performance highly cost-effective. A 1991 analysis by the Congressional Budget Office calculated that for each $10,000 invested in the average participant in the mid-1980s, society received roughly $15,000 in returns—including about $8,000 in "increased output of participants" and another $6,000 in the "reductions in the cost of crime-related activities."

Evaluations conducted during the Reagan Administration (which year after year tried to eliminate Job Corps) found that seventy-five percent of Job Corps enrollees move on to a job or to full-time study. Graduates retain jobs longer and earn about fifteen percent more than if they had not participated in the program. Along the same lines, a U.S. General Accounting Office study concluded that Job Corps members are far more likely to receive a high school diploma or equivalency degree than comparison group members and that the positive impact on their earnings continues after training.

In comparison to Job Corps, the present major federal job training system, the Job Training Partnership Act (JTPA) begun in the early 1980s, has failed high-risk youth and needs to be scrapped, not just modestly reformed. Evaluations have shown that, while the results were marginally positive for disadvantaged adults, high-risk youth in the JTPA program actually did worse than comparable youth not in the program. For example, young men under age twenty-two who participated in the program had earnings $854 lower than their comparison group, with significantly greater deficits for those who took on-the-job training.

Part of the JTPA reform should be based on *Thinking for a Living,* the new book by Ray Marshall, Secretary of Labor in the late 1970s, and Marc Tucker, head of the National Center on Education and the Economy. They call for a national employment and training board. It would be composed of government officials and business, labor, and education leaders. The goal is to coordinate and streamline present job training programs. However, we believe that at least one-third of the members of the national board and of local boards should be representatives of community-based non-profit organizations. The local boards should replace Private Industry Councils (PICs) as the grassroots public-private implementing agencies.

The comprehensive new federal program needed should return job training and placement to pre-1980 levels. The entire focus should be on the truly disadvantaged. Training and placement should be through private, non-profit community development corporations, for the most part. Public works employment, public service employment and expansion of Job Corps by at least fifty new centers should be part of the plan.

Welfare Reform

Real welfare reform will not be easy, considering all the many previous unsuccessful legislative attempts. Accordingly, we recommend a process whereby the reform in Head Start, education in the inner city, job training and placement and housing recommended in the report takes the lead. When these programs are reorganized to be more cost effective, including a more community-oriented approach to service delivery and implementation, and when existing levels of funding are supplemented by the funding increases proposed here, then welfare reform can proceed more quickly.

Because we must wait and see how the other reforms proceed, we do not speculate in this report on the additional costs of welfare reform. Without the other multiple solution reforms, we do not believe that efforts to reduce welfare rolls will be successful. Instead, the result would only be increased stress and deprivation for low income women—and their children.

The same Congressional committees to which most welfare reform proposals would be referred are the ones that must deal with health care reform, expansion of Head Start, reform of job training and placement and economic recovery. It is best to take first things first, and to then reform welfare when both Congress and the Administration are able to give it the attention it deserves.

Drug Prevention and Treatment

We should reverse the current federal spending formula—in which seventy percent of our $12B-plus annual anti-drug budget is spent on law enforcement and "interdiction," and just thirty percent on prevention and treatment.

The expansion of Head Start, creation of a Corporation for Youth Investment and replacement of JTPA with a new comprehensive Job Corps/JobStart/YouthBuild-type federal job training and placement program forms perhaps the most effective drug prevention strategy for the inner city. These multiple solutions tend to simultaneously produce multiple good outcomes, including reduction in the use of drugs. The demand-side drug initiatives that have been evaluated as successful view social ills as interwoven, requiring a more comprehensive solution than has been attempted over the last twelve years.

Something close to a consensus has emerged that significantly more funding is required to close the gap between treatment need and availability among the disadvantaged. Without it, hard drugs will continue to ravage families and communities in the inner city; drug-related violence will continue at levels that place many neighborhoods in a state of siege. Unless we begin to reverse that situation, it will undermine all of our other efforts to develop the inner city economically and socially.

We need not only *more* treatment, however, but also *better* treatment. Too often, conventional drug treatment is little more than a revolving door, through which addicts return to essentially unchanged communities with few new skills for legitimate life—and predictably return again. Many addicts, too, are alienated by most existing treatment models and do their best to avoid them.

To overcome these limitations, expanded drug abuse treatment, intensive outreach and aftercare need to be linked closely with youth enterprise development, family supports, intensive remedial education and other services. As a high official at the National Institute of Drug Abuse has observed, "For many addicts, it's not rehabilitation; it's habilitation. They don't know how to read or look for work, let alone beat their addictions."

If we do not address these issues in addicts' lives, we insure that much drug treatment will remain both ineffective and expensive.

Health Care Reform

From the perspective of the minority poor in the inner city, the goals of associated health care reform should be to supply Medicaid to all those eligible; provide solid coverage for the working poor; produce health quality-of-life outcomes (like infant mortality rates) on a par with Japan, Western Europe and Canada; and link improved physical and mental health to improved education and job opportunity.

As with welfare, we do not speculate here on the costs of health care reform for the truly disadvantaged. More time is needed for debate.

However, from a Kerner perspective, the right question is not, ... "How can we design a health care reform strategy that preserves the power of the insurance industry?" Rather, the right question is, "How can we guarantee high-quality coverage for all Americans while holding down costs?"

The answer to the latter question may be to follow the Canadian-style or German-style national health plans—which are working well in supplying universal insurance coverage, allowing patients to choose their doctors and providing high quality prevention and treatment in ways that are reasonably popular with the public. In addition, the Canadian system, financed by taxation, provides such quality health care *for about one fourth the cost per capita as the current American system.*

Better Evaluation is Needed

In the absence of sound evaluation criteria, national, state and local programs will continue to be supported more because they fit the political fashion of the moment or because they are able to capture media attention than because of their demonstrated effectiveness. In a time of limited resources, we can't afford that.

Experience has suggested the need for evaluations of inner city nonprofit programs to include qualitative, journalistic "process" measures as well as quantitative "impact" outcome measures for up to five years with "test" and "comparison" groups. These should be measures both of change among high risk children and youth and change in the community. This means that we need to "triangulate" measures from multiple imperfect sources and studies of any one program—so that judgments of success are based on accumulated wisdom.

To begin a process of reform, we recommend hard-hitting Congressional hearings and critiques by Office of Management and Budget, the U.S. General Accounting Office and the Office of Technology Assessment to expose the inadequacy of most federal evaluations of community-based, high risk child and youth initiatives, and to devise strategies to reverse the politicalization of evaluations, which has occurred especially during the last twelve years. Non-profit organizations in the private sector must advocate tenaciously until this is done.

Linking Investment in Children and Youth with Investment in Housing and Infrastructure

America needs a conscious federal policy to link investment in children and youth with urban repair and economic revitalization. Again, we have many examples of what already works, based on years of experience. We need to expand them to scale, so that there is significant change across the entire nation in the lives of the disadvantaged, the physical structure of the neighborhood where they live and the national economy which impacts on the poor and their communities.

The first priority for a new policy should be a federal program in which HUD funds national, private non-profit sector intermediaries like the Local Initiatives Support Corporation (LISC) and the Enterprise Foundation. In turn, these intermediaries should fund local, private non-profit community development corporations. The private sector non-profit intermediaries must retain their efficient and successful rehabilitation of housing, without being burdened by the infamous red tape of HUD. The federal government will need to provide oversight, of course, because the monies are from the public sector. Yet HUD bureaucrats should not meddle in what has become a small miracle over the last decade in revitalizing urban neighborhoods.

Moving Beyond the Kerner Commission

LISC, the Enterprise Foundation and our proposed Corporation for Youth Investment move considerably beyond the vision of the Kerner Commission. In passing, the Commission referred to "the great potential in private community development corporations. . . ." But the Commission was not particularly prescient in forecasting the roles of national non-profit intermediaries which work directly with local non-profits.

Non-Profit/For-Profit Integration

We need to create a variety of options for how non-profit and for-profit activity can be interrelated. For example, although we believe that a priority for housing rehabilitation should be on non-profit community development corporations, we recommend that HUD also build on the model of the TELESIS Corporation, which is a for-profit economic development organization with great cost-effectiveness but also social development wisdom.

A National Community Development Bank

We recommend that, directly and through national private sector intermediaries, a network of community development banks be capitalized. The banks should be owned by inner city community partners and should reinforce the creation of local for-profit/non-profit linkages.

We believe that the model for this initiative should be the South Shore Bank in Chicago. Over the last twenty years, South Shore has proven that a determined lender can reverse the process of urban decay and simultaneously make a profit.

The capitalization of community development banks should be linked to tougher enforcement by HUD of the Community Reinvestment Act of 1977, which requires banks to invest in their communities.

We believe that a traditional federal agency might impose too much bureaucracy on a new community development banking system. A new institution probably is needed—a National Community Development Bank. One partial model is the National Cooperative Bank (though without the power struggles that revolved around its creation).

Public Housing and Tenant Management

Public housing should not be scrapped. There are many horror stories. However, when public housing is well managed, as it is by the New York City Housing Authority, for example, it should remain as one of several options for housing the poor. The key to making public housing work better is resident management of public housing properties. Where tenants are well organized and exercise real power, conditions improve, based on demonstration programs to date. Tenant managed developments appear to save money in the long run because tenants have a greater stake in their homes and therefore are less tolerant of destructive and costly behavior.

However, over the 1980s while there was much talk about tenant management and "empowerment," there was little action. A few exemplary programs were touted, but these experiments had little national impact. Accordingly, the Administration and Congress should provide adequate funds delivered by HUD to public housing authorities and then to tenants, so that tenants can be properly trained in managing their own housing projects. This can be a first step to tenant-owned developments.

Innovative Policing as Community Development

Innovative policing can play an important supportive role to economic and social development in low income neighborhoods, whether they be public housing communities or other locales. We emphasize the word supportive. *In a departure from traditional policy, we view innovative policing not as a criminal justice end but as a means to secure the community for economic development.*

Innovations include problem-oriented policing, community-based policing, police mini-stations that become neighborhood security anchors to facilitate economic and youth development, police mentoring of high risk youth and more sensitive training of police.

These are all activities in which the 100,000 more community police officers called for in the last Presidential campaign can be employed. We urge the implementation of this recommendation—*but it only will have an impact if the new police work in innovative problem-oriented and community-based policing.* As the experience in Washington, D.C.—with the highest police-to-citizen ratios *and* homicide rates in the nation—shows, more police per se will not change a thing. As many high-risk youth from inner-city neighborhoods as possible should be trained for such police employment.

Handgun Control and Congressional Inaction

Such improvement in public safety, reduction in fear and enhancement of neighborhood stability can be further accelerated by strong legislation to control handguns, as advocated by the police, who have lobbied through their national organizations for a decade against the National Rifle Association (NRA). More teenage inner city males die from gunshots than from all natural causes combined. Yet, this malignancy of handguns in urban America, which contributes greatly to inner-city neighborhood breakdown, is likely to continue unabated.

We believe that the litany of unpopular issues which the NRA has come to defend—like "cop killer" bullets, plastic "terrorist special" handguns and assault weapons—make the NRA increasingly out of touch with American opinion polls and the police.

As with tobacco, we believe that firearms should be considered a broad based public health problem. It should be attacked as such by, among many other officials, the Surgeon General of the U.S.—just as former Surgeon General Everett Koop launched the successful attack against smoking in the eighties. The new public health campaign must focus on the widespread and virtually unregulated distribution of a hazardous consumer product—which must therefore be taken off the market. Handguns and other firearms enjoy a unique role in the American consumer marketplace. Almost all products sold in America come under the regulatory power of a specific federal agency—to assure safety to Americans. Guns are one of the notable exceptions.

It is past time for a strong, coordinated federal gun control policy. We support passage of the Brady bill requiring a five-day waiting period between purchase and delivery of a handgun, and also support the recent Torricelli bill proposing a federal "one gun a month" limit on gun purchases. But we also believe more is needed. We need to build on the tough policy proposed by Josh Sugermann in his new book, *NRA: Money-*

Firepower-Fear, as we move beyond the twenty-fifth anniversaries of the firearms assassinations of Reverend Martin Luther King and Senator Robert F. Kennedy.

Reducing the Investment Gap and Employing Youth in Infrastructure Repair

Reducing the investment gap that exists between the United States and its major competitors has become perhaps one of the defining metaphors of the 1990s.

Above and beyond targeted economic development and housing policy that employs high-risk youth in the inner city, we must incorporate the employment of high-risk young people into the process that reduces the investment gap and increases productivity.

Estimates of the infrastructure bill vary from the $30B to $40B that will be needed simply to refurbish the most deteriorating bridges and roads to the $500B investment over the next decade proposed by New York City investment banker Felix Rohatyn.

We endorse public sector jobs for both public works and public service. We believe that the jobs can be administered both through public agencies and through non-profit community development corporations. Whatever the level of expenditure on public works—and, we hope, also on public service—the goal should be to employ a substantial number of high-risk youth.

Employing Youth in High Technology

High risk inner city youth and persons who are getting off of welfare must not be left out of the employment that is generated by military conversion to high technologies in domestic sectors to close the investment gap. There already are partial models for how this can work. If high-risk young people are channeled into university education through "I Have A Dream" and related programs, their chances of employment in high tech industries are improved. But even if their education ends with a high school equivalency degree, we need a national policy that plans on their job involvement in high tech operations and the industries that serve them. For example, in France, in the city of Lille, there is a training center for computer maintenance by high-risk and disproportionately minority-foreign-born youths who have no previous work experience. The program is based on a contract with a corporation that deals in computer maintenance and computer networking services.

Replacing Fool's Gold with Responsibility

The contemporary dialogue on the legacy of the Kerner Commission is being framed with words like children, investment, replication, reinvention, bonding, leadership, responsibility and sacrifice.

These words need to replace many of the words used over the 1980s and early 1990s. The latter were sold as fool's gold, in our view, to try to distract the public from the federal government's decision to disinvest and to allow economic conditions to deteriorate for the middle class and the poor. In particular, fool's gold was sold in the form of supply side economics, enterprise zones, volunteerism, self-sufficiency, partnerships and empowerment.

These latter terms do have their place. Enterprise zones could contribute, eventually, to well-resourced multiple solutions. Most successful initiatives need and use volunteers; Head Start is a good example. We need to replicate the principles of ventures like Delancey Street which are financially independent. Linking remedial education, training and placement, as in Job Corps, is a partnership we need. Sufficient investments will give to disadvantaged more power. The concepts only become fool's gold when they are pro-offered [*sic*] as panaceas. That is what happened over the 1980s.

Levels of Investment to Fulfill the Kerner Commission

The Kerner Commission asked the nation "to mount programs on a scale equal to the dimension of the problem." For the initiatives in this report, our estimate is that mounting to scale means $15B more in annual appropriations for each of ten years to implement the recommendations for investing in children and youth. This covers funding Head Start preschool at levels that come close to three years for all eligible three, four and five year olds (and some two year olds), creating the national Corporation for Youth Investment, overhauling job training and placement and starting to bring expenditures back to pre-1980 levels, refocusing anti-drug initiatives to prevention and treatment, and implementing promising inner city school reforms—including refinement of the Elementary and Secondary Act of 1965, implementation of the recommendations from the several Carnegie reports, replication of the Comer plan, replication of programs like "I Have A Dream" if evaluations show them to be successful, and continued innovation in vocational and apprenticeship programs like Project Prepare and Project ProTech. The prime federal funding agencies for these ventures are Labor, HHS, Education and Justice.

The interrelated need is for $15B more per year in annual budget appropriations for each of ten years, at a minimum, to implement the recommendations for reconstructing the inner cities and for closing the investment and productivity gaps. The bulk of this funding is for employing the poor, welfare recipients and high-risk youth in the urban reconstruction. The work will expand housing and rehabilitation delivered by non-profits as well as by those for-profits, like TELESIS, which can integrate multiple solution youth development into economic development. Our budget here also covers repair of the urban infrastructure that employs inner city residents, creation of community development banks in the inner city owned by people who live there, expansion of tenant management in public housing, employment of those new community and problem-oriented police who live in the inner city neighborhoods where they patrol, and pursuit of those high tech investments linked to military conversion that generate jobs for high-risk youth and welfare populations in the inner city. The prime federal agencies are Labor, HUD, Transportation, Commerce, Justice—and a new, independent National Development Bank.

It is *this* level of investment—a minimum total of $150B in appropriations for children and youth and a minimum total of $150B in appropriations for coordinated housing, infrastructure and high tech investment—over a decade at least, and not the $1.2B, one year response by the federal government after the 1992 Los Angeles riot, that begins to address the Kerner Commission's "scale equal to the dimension of the problem."

Sources of Investment Funding

As structural reforms at existing expenditure levels are enacted to improve the present federal job training and job placement program and the present low income housing delivery system, we also can begin to secure new funds—first by eliminating or retargeting other existing programs. For example we can save nearly $5B per year by increasing demand side drug prevention and treatment to seventy percent of the anti-drug budget, reducing prison spending and eliminating ineffective programs, like "weed and seed." We also can redirect at least $500M in HHS, Labor, HUD and Justice discretionary and demonstration monies into replicating what already works.

However, most of the increased funding should be based on reductions in the military budget, reductions in the budget of the Agency for International Development, and taxes on the very rich. We support, as well, higher taxes on tobacco and alcohol—and a gasoline tax as long as lower income groups receive tax credits, so they do not end up paying.

The Timing of a Reform Scenario

What kind of scenario for financing investments in children, youth and the inner city makes sense, given many competing budgetary demands and the priority on the economy and deficit?

Over the 1990s, debt reduction will be a priority, but we also envision public works spending as an economic stimulus, and this may be where some of the reform proposed here can begin. We need to insure that significant numbers of high risk youth are placed in such employment and that community-based non-profit organizations implement as much as possible. We anticipate some progress toward these goals during the first two years of our scenario.

It also should be attractive politically to move fairly swiftly on reform of Chapter 1 of the Elementary and Secondary Education Act, reform of the Job Training Partnership Act, and the delivery of housing and economic development via nonprofit organizations and creative for-profit organizations. This will be especially true if such reform initially can be negotiated without increased federal spending. At the same time, we anticipate at least some progress on shifting drug spending from thirty percent demand side to seventy percent demand side, on discontinuing unsuccessful domestic programs, and on shifting some federal domestic discretionary money from demonstrations and experiments into replicating what already has been demonstrated to work. The net result could be as much as $5B in funds freed up—to begin expansion of Head Start to all eligible children, expansion of Comer-type inner city school reform, expansion of reformed job training and placement, creation of a Corporation for Youth Investment and expansion of drug prevention and treatment. It is within the realm of political feasibility in our view to achieve many of these goals by the end of the third year of the scenario.

Over the first four years, we anticipate significantly reduced military spending, increased taxes on the rich and an increase in gasoline taxes. This is likely to be used to reduce the debt and to finance infrastructure investment and conversion to high tech industries. But we recommend at least some of these revenues also be used to help expand Head Start and reform job training and placement. Our scenario then envisions increased funding for the package advocated here, so that by the fifth and sixth years of reform, the full $15B per year in new investment in children and youth and the full $15B per year in new investment in inner city reconstruction can be sustained while deficit reduction can proceed and a strong military still can be demonstrated.

Once we are up to $15B per year in new appropriations for child and youth investment and $15B per year in new appropriations for housing, community development, community banking, infrastructure development and high tech development that employs high risk youth and other truly disadvantaged, along with supportive services like community policing, that level of investment should be sustained for at least ten years.

This means that there will be an incremental process through which we work toward the $15B per year child and youth investment and $15B per year in inner city investment levels. Such a process is necessary because it is unreasonable economically and politically to expect all the new funds at once. It also is desirable because incremental increases allow for better managed growth and more orderly administrative expansion of capacity in the public and private (especially non-profit) sectors.

Hence, implementation of the scenario may take in the neighborhood of fifteen to sixteen years—almost a full inner city generation—depending on how quickly we reach the proposed levels of new investment, which then are sustained.

Political Feasibility

Public opinion suggests that our plan is politically feasible. For example, in 1992, right after the Los Angeles riots, the *New York Times* and CBS asked, in a nationwide poll: "Are we spending too much money, too little money or about the right amount of money on problems of the big cities, on improving the conditions of Blacks, and on the poor?" Sixty percent of the respondents said that too little was being spent on problems of the big cities, sixty-one percent said too little was being spent on improving the condition of African-Americans and sixty-four percent said too little was being spent on problems of the poor. The pollers also asked, "To reduce racial tension and prevent riots, would more jobs and job training help a lot, help a little or make not much difference?" Seventy-eight percent of the respondents said that more jobs and job training would help a lot.

Leadership

America found the money to fight the Persian Gulf War, and it found the hundreds of billions of dollars needed to bail out the failed, deregulated savings and loan industry. America can find the money for a true strategy of child investment, youth investment and community reconstruction if there is the right leadership at the very top. We now have that leadership.

Beyond finding the money over the long run for successful and promising programs, we ask that the White House reinvent and reorganize the present cost-ineffective bureaucracy of federal government initiatives for children, youth and the inner city. Only comprehensive, holistic, multiple solutions work. But federal legislation and bureaucracy is categorical, fragmented, narrow, inflexible—and doesn't allow for local, neighborhood-based "one stop shopping" for coordinated services, as is more common, for example, in France. We call for a White House summit, and a follow-up implementing task force, firmly led and controlled by the White House, on Replicating What Works.

Reversing the Betrayal of American Democracy

If we are to reverse the betrayal of the American democracy, we need even more than wise national leaders. In the words of William Greider, in *Who Will Tell the People,* "Rehabilitating democracy will require citizens to devote themselves first to challenging the status quo, disrupting the existing contours of power and opening the way to renewal." Common people must engage their surrounding reality and "question the conflict between with what they are told and what they see and experience."

In America, this means old fashioned grassroots political lobbying to gain full funding for preschool modeled after the French experience and job training modeled in part after the German experience. It means massive voter registration of the poor, following some of the lessons of Canada. It means tight controls on special interest group lobbyists in Washington, the people who walk around in thousand dollar suits and alligator shoes. It means public financing of political campaigns, elimination of contribution loopholes and far shorter campaigns that limit both the use of money and the use of television, as is the case in the United Kingdom.

A great many Americans hold Congress in contempt. Campaign finance reform is not just the best way to control lobbyists. It also is the best way to make Congress more honest. Citizen groups and the Executive Branch cannot allow Congress, and especially the majority leadership of Congress, to postpone the campaign finance reform proposed by Common Cause. In addition, legislators need to be educated on how multiple solutions work best and how legislation is fragmented, uncomprehensive and short term. Congressional appropriation set asides and earmarks should be validated by the Congressional Budget Office and the Office of Technology Assessment on the basis of scientific evaluations proving their success. . . . [W]e need uniform federal term limits on Members of Congress.

A Deeper Sense of Responsibility

As John Gardiner has warned, we must be prepared for sacrifice. Over the 1980s and longer, we consumed too much and saved too little. Quick fixes have substituted for public responsibility. The one trillion dollar debt is a tax on our children. Americans now must have the intelligence, willingness, courage and strength needed in face of hard realities. They must, for example, be willing to pay more taxes—even if most of those taxes are on the rich. They must acknowledge the need for long run solutions and have the patience to implement what works over time. They must, to paraphrase Vaclav Havel, rediscover within themselves a deeper sense of responsibility toward the world.

The Dream Deferred

Our most serious challenges to date have been external. Serious external dangers remain, but the graver threats to America today are internal. The greatness and durability of most civilizations has been finally determined by how they have responded to these challenges from within. Ours will be no exception and so, in the concluding words of the Kerner Commission, it is time "to end the destruction and the violence, not only in the streets of the ghetto but in the lives of the people."

With leadership both from the top as well as the grassroots, we can face those challenges and end that destruction. We no longer need to defer the American dream to substantial portions of the American population.

"What happens to a dream deferred?" asked the honored African American poet, Langston Hughes:

> Does it dry up
> Like a raisin in the sun?
> Or fester like a sore—
> and then run?
> Does it stink like rotten meat?
> Or crust and sugar over
> Like a syrupy sweet?
> Maybe it just sags
> Like a heavy load.
> Or does it explode?

March

UN TRUTH COMMISSION REPORT ON VIOLENCE IN EL SALVADOR

March 15, 1993

A little more than a year after a peace treaty had been signed in El Salvador, bringing a formal end to the twelve-year civil war that had ravaged the country and claimed at least 75,000 lives, a March 15 United Nations report revealed that systematic violence had been carried out by the El Salvadoran armed forces during the 1980s. The 250-page report of the UN Truth Commission, entitled From Madness to Hope: The 12-Year War in El Salvador, *concluded that senior Salvadoran military officers had played a major role in orchestrating the murder of thousands of civilians—including the massacre of 700 men, women, and children during a single episode in 1981.* (El Salvador peace treaty, background on civil war, establishment of UN commission, Historic Documents of 1992, p. 23)

Background of the Investigation

The Truth Commission was established at the behest of the parties to the 1992 peace agreement—the government of President Alfredo Cristiani and the guerrilla leadership of the Farabundo Marti National Liberation Front (FMLN). The three-member panel was comprised of former Colombian president Belisario Betancur, former Venezuelan foreign minister Reinaldo Figueredo, and Professor Thomas Buerganthal of the George Washington University Law School. Receiving confidential testimony from 2,000 sources over a six-month period, the commission documented what it determined were the worst human rights abuses by all sides, examining 18,000 cases in all.

Although it was not assigned to look into what U.S. officials knew about the atrocities, such questions became unavoidable given the alliance existing at the time between the Reagan and Bush administrations and the ruling Republican National Alliance (ARENA) in El Salvador. Moreover, many of the cases examined by the commission implicated

U.S. government-financed troops in killing U.S. citizens. For instance, the commission found that the murder of six Jesuit priests and their cook and her daughter in November 1989 had been ordered by several members of the Salvadoran army high command. (As a result, the defense minister, Gen. Rene Emilio Ponce, named in connection with the killings, submitted his resignation shortly before the UN report was made public.) Elements of the U.S.-trained Atlacatl battalion carried out the killings and then tried to leave evidence falsely implicating the FMLN, the report said.

The commission found that the 1981 massacre, which occurred at the hamlet of El Mozote, had also been carried out by the Atlacatl units. At the time, U.S. officials disputed news accounts of the massacre, claiming that it had never happened.

FMLN guerrillas were blamed by the commission for the murders of several U.S. servicemen, including four Marines who were gunned down at a San Salvador cafe in 1985.

U.S Role and Congressional Testimony

The day after the UN report was released, the three commission members summarized their findings before the House Foreign Affairs Western Hemisphere Subcommittee. While their report had cited hundreds of assassinations and other acts of violence committed by the FMLN, members of Congress zeroed in on the role of the United States in its support of the Salvadorian military, particularly in view of repeated requests by Congress in the 1980s to certify the country's record in improving human rights as a condition for receiving U.S. economic and military aid. With the Reagan and Bush administrations attesting to the progress being achieved in human rights and other areas, Congress had approved nearly $4 billion in aid to El Salvador during the 1980s.

"Those of us who participated in the debate on Central America many years ago feel outrage about your findings," Subcommittee Chairman Robert G. Torricelli, D-N.J., told members of the commission during the packed March 15 hearing. "It is now abundantly clear that Ronald Reagan made these certifications [that the Salvadorian government was improving its human rights record as a condition for military aid] not only in disregard of the truth but in defiance of it."

Former representative Michael D. Barnes, D-Md., who chaired the subcommittee from 1981 to 1987 and was a leading critic of Reagan's Central American policy, said, "Every suspicion we had has now been confirmed."

Findings and Recommendations

In its report, the UN panel said the purpose of the investigation was not to suggest a need for new prosecutions but to serve as an admonition that such crimes should not be repeated.

Stating that much of the violence had been deliberately planned and carried out by both sides, the commission concluded that about 85 percent of the abuses were attributed to the U.S.-supported Salvadorian army or the death squads, with the FMLN responsible for about 5 percent (resulting in the killing of at least 400 Salvadorans). Right-wing leader Roberto d'Aubuisson, the founder the ARENA party, was found guilty of ordering the murder of one of the country's most powerful leaders, Archbishop Oscar Romero, in March 1980 while he was saying mass.

The United States was also deeply implicated, having "tolerated, apparently with little attention," the management of death squads by Salvadorans in Miami. "The use of United States territory to carry out acts of terrorism abroad must be investigated and must never be repeated," the report concluded.

Among its recommendations, the commission called for a special inquiry into the death squads and for the dismissal of forty military officers who played a role in the violence. A number of current civilian leaders of the ruling ARENA party had been major supporters of the death squads. The panel also called for a restructuring of the country's judicial system and the resignation of all current members of the Supreme Court, saying that, as constituted, the system was "incapable of fairly assessing and carrying out punishment."

Reaction

President Cristiani, who had previously urged the commission to omit names from its report to avoid the possibility of renewing violence by "extremist elements," called for a general amnesty. "[I]f we really want reconciliation, we won't be doing any good by wasting time on the past," he said. In fact, shortly after the UN report was made public, right-wing political parties succeeded in pushing a general amnesty law through the National Assembly.

The former FMLN guerrillas who attended the congressional hearing embraced the commission's findings—including its recommendation that three top FMLN leaders be barred for a decade from public office—but offered no apologies for the killings of the servicemen. The commission had cited FMLN commander Joaquin Villalobos and other prominent guerrilla leaders as adopting "a policy of assassinating mayors they considered were from the opposition" during the years 1985 to 1988. Villalobos agreed to accept the recommendation that he be banned from public office.

The Clinton administration applauded the report. "Revealing the truth has to be a key element of an act of national reconciliation," said State Department spokesman Robert A. Boucher. "Some people have suggested that the Americans who trained the Salvadorean army were responsible for the killings," said a March 20 article in The Economist. *"That is unfair. The United States armed forces do not teach soldiers to kill priests or women and children. But in El Salvador the Americans failed to teach them not to—and then tried to cover up their failure."*

Following are excerpts from the report by the UN Commission on the Truth for El Salvador, released March 15, 1993, on widespread human rights violations in El Salvador during its twelve-year civil war:

I. Introduction

Between 1980 and 1991, the Republic of El Salvador in Central America was engulfed in a war which plunged Salvadorian society into violence, left it with thousands and thousands of people dead and exposed it to appalling crimes, until the day—16 January 1992—when the parties, reconciled, signed the Peace Agreement in the Castle of Chapultepec, Mexico, and brought back the light and the chance to re-emerge from madness to hope.

A. Institutions and Names

Violence was a fire which swept over the fields of El Salvador; it burst into villages, cut off roads and destroyed highways and bridges, energy sources and transmission lines; it reached the cities and entered families, sacred areas and educational centres; it struck at justice and filled the public administration with victims; and it singled out as an enemy anyone who was not on the list of friends. Violence turned everything to death and destruction, for such is the senselessness of that breach of the calm plenitude which accompanies the rule of law, the essential nature of violence being suddenly or gradually to alter the certainty which the law nurtures in human beings when this change does not take place through the normal mechanisms of the rule of law. The victims were Salvadorians and foreigners of all backgrounds and all social and economic classes, for in its blind cruelty violence leaves everyone equally defenceless.

When there came pause for thought, Salvadorians put their hands to their hearts and felt them pound with joy. No one was winning the war, everyone was losing it. Governments of friendly countries and organizations the world over that had looked on in anguish at the tragic events in that Central American country which, although small, was made great by the creativity of its people—all contributed their ideas to the process of reflection. A visionary, Javier Pérez de Cuéllar, then Secretary-General of the United Nations, heeded the unanimous outcry and answered it. The Presidents of Columbia, Mexico, Spain and Venezuela supported him. The Chapultepec Agreement expressed the support of the new Secretary-General, Mr. Boutros Boutros-Ghali, for the search for reconciliation.

B. The Creative Consequences

On the long road of the peace negotiations, the need to reach agreement on a Commission on the Truth arose from the Parties' recognition that the communism which had encouraged one side had collapsed, and perhaps also from the disillusionment of the Power which had encouraged the other. It emerged as a link in the chain of reflection and agreement and was motivated, ultimately, by the impact of events on Salvadorian society, which now faced the urgent task of confronting the issue of the widespread, institutionalized impunity which had struck at its very heart; under the protection of State bodies but outside the law, repeated human rights violations had been committed by members of the armed forces; these same rights had also been violated by members of the guerrilla forces.

In response to this situation, the negotiators agreed that such repugnant acts should be referred to a Commission on the Truth, which was the name they agreed to give it from the outset. Unlike the Ad Hoc Commission, so named because there was no agreement on what to call the body created to purify the armed forces, the Commission on the Truth was so named because its very purpose and function were to seek, find and publicize the truth about the acts of violence committed by both sides during the war....

C. The Mandate

Furthermore, by virtue of the scope which the negotiators gave to the agreements, it was understood that the Commission on the Truth would have to examine systematic atrocities both individually and collectively, since the flagrant human rights violations which had shocked Salvadorian society and the international community had been carried out not only by members of the armed forces but also by members of the insurgent forces.

The peace agreements were unambiguous when, in article 2, they defined the mandate and scope of the Commission as follows: "The Commission shall have the task of investigating serious acts of violence that have occurred since 1980 and whose impact on society urgently demands that the public should know the truth". Article 5 of the Chapultepec Peace Agreement gives the Commission the task of clarifying and putting an end to any indication of impunity on the part of officers of the armed forces and gives this explanation: "acts of this nature, regardless of the sector to which their perpetrators belong, must be the object of exemplary action by the law courts so that the punishment prescribed by law is meted out to those found responsible"....

D. "Open-Door" Policy

From the outset of their work, which began on 13 July 1992 when they were entrusted with their task by the Secretary-General of the United Nations, the Commissioners could perceive the skill of those who had negotiated the agreements in the breadth of the mandate and authority given to the Commission. They realized that the Secretary-General, upon learning from competent Salvadorian judges of the numerous acts of violence and atrocities of 12 years of war, had not been wrong in seeking to preserve the Commission's credibility by looking beyond considerations of sovereignty and entrusting this task to three scholars from other countries, in contrast to what had been done in Argentina and Chile after the military dictatorships there had ended. The Commissioners also saw a glimmer of hope dawn in the hearts of the Salvadorian people when it became clear that the truth would soon be revealed, not through bias or pressure but in its entirety and with complete impartiality, a fact which helped to restore the faith of people at all levels that justice would be effective and fitting. Accordingly, in their first meeting with the media upon arriving in El Salvador, the Commissioners stated that they would not let themselves be pressured or impressed: they were after the objective truth and the hard facts.

The Commissioners and the group of professionals who collaborated with them in the investigations succeeded in overcoming obstacles and limitations that made it difficult to establish what had really happened, starting with the brief period of time—six months—afforded them under the Chapultepec Agreement. Given the magnitude of their task, this time-frame, which seemed to stretch into Kafkaesque infinity when they embarked upon their task, ultimately seemed meagre and barely sufficient to allow them to complete their work satisfactorily.

The Commission maintained an "open-door" policy for hearing testimony and a "closed-door" policy for preserving confidentiality. Its findings illustrate the horrors of a war in which madness prevailed, and confirm beyond the shadow of doubt that the incidents denounced, recorded and substantiated in this report actually took place. Whenever the Commission decided that its investigation of a specific case had yielded sufficient evidence, the matter was recorded in detail, with mention of the guilty parties. When it was determined that no further progress could be made for the time being, the corresponding documentation that was not subject to secrecy was delivered to the courts or else kept confidential until new information enabled it to be reactivated....

E. A Convulsion of Violence

The warped psychology engendered by the conflict led to a convulsion of violence. The civilian population in disputed or guerrilla-controlled areas was automatically assumed to be the enemy, as at El Mozote and the Sumpul river. The opposing side behaved likewise, as when mayors were executed, the killings justified as acts of war because the victims had obstructed the delivery of supplies to combatants, or when defenceless pleasure-seekers became military targets, as in the case of the United States marines in the Zona Rosa of San Salvador. Meanwhile, the doctrine of national salvation and the principle of "he who is not for me is against me" were cited to ignore the neutrality, passivity and defencelessness of journalists and church workers, who served the community in various ways.

Such behavior also led to the clandestine refinement of the death squads: the bullet which struck Monsignor Romero in the chest while he was celebrating mass on 24 March 1980 in a San Salvador church is a brutal symbol of the nightmare the country experienced during the war. And the murder of the six Jesuit priests 10 years later was the final outburst of the delirium that had infected the armed forces and the innermost recesses of certain government circles. The bullet in the portrait of Monsignor Romero, mute witness to this latest crime, repeats the nightmare image of those days. . . .

I. Foundation for the Truth

The mass of reports, testimony, newspaper and magazine articles and books published in Spanish and other languages that was accumulated prompted the establishment within the Commission on the Truth itself of a centre for documentation on the different forms of violence in El Salvador. The public information relating to the war (books, pamphlets, research carried out by Salvadorian and international bodies); testimony from 2,000 primary sources referring to more than 7,000 victims; information from secondary sources relating to more than 20,000 victims; information from official bodies in the United States and other countries; information provided by government bodies and FMLN; an abundant photographic and videotape record of the conflict and even of the Commission's own activities; all of this material constitutes an invaluable resource—a part of El Salvador's heritage because (despite the painful reality it records) [it is] a part of the country's contemporary history—for historians and analysts of this most distressing period and for those who wish to study this painful reality in order to reinforce the effort to spread the message "never again".

IV. Cases and Patterns of Violence

A. General Overview of Cases and Patterns of Violence

The Commission on the Truth registered more than 22,000 complaints of serious acts of violence that occurred in El Salvador between January 1980 and July 1991. Over 7,000 were received directly at the Commission's offices in various locations. The remainder were received through governmental and non-governmental institutions.

Over 60 per cent of all complaints concerned extrajudicial executions, over 25 per cent concerned enforced disappearances, and over 20 per cent included complaints of torture.

Those giving testimony attributed almost 85 per cent of cases to agents of the State, paramilitary groups allied to them, and the death squads.

Armed forces personnel were accused in almost 60 per cent of complaints, members of the security forces in approximately 25 per cent, members of military escorts and civil defence units in approximately 20 per cent, and members of the death squads in more than 10 per cent of cases. The complaints registered accused FMLN in approximately 5 per cent of cases.

Despite their large number, these complaints do not cover every act of violence. The Commission was able to receive only a significant sample in its three months of gathering testimony.

This also does not mean that each act occurred as described in the testimony. The Commission investigated certain specific cases in particular circumstances, as well as overall patterns of violence. Some 30 of the cases dealt with in the report are illustrative of patterns of violence, in other words, involve systematic practices attested to by thousands of complainants.

Both the specific cases and the patterns of violence show that, during the 1980s, the country experienced an unusually high level of political violence. All Salvadorians without exception, albeit to differing degrees, suffered from this violence....

1. General Conclusions

The causes and conditions which generated the large number of serious acts of violence in El Salvador derive from very complex circumstances. The country's history and its deeply rooted relations of injustice cannot be attributed simply to one sector of the population or one group of persons. This or that Government institution, certain historical traditions, even the ideological struggle between East and West which went on until only recently, and of which El Salvador was a victim and an episode, are mere components. All these factors help to explain the complex situation in El Salvador during the 12-year period which concerns us. The Commission was not called upon to deal with all these factors, nor could it do so. Instead, it focused on certain considerations which prompted it to formulate its basic recommendations in such a way that this situation might be fully understood.

The lack of human rights guarantees in El Salvador and the fact that a society has operated outside the principles of a State subject to the rule of law imposes a serious responsibility on the Salvadorian State itself, rather than on one or other of its Governments. The political, legislative and institutional mechanisms required to ensure the existence of a society subject to the rule of law existed in theory, at least in part, but the reality was not what it should have been, perhaps as a consequence of excessive pragmatism. With the passage of time, the military establishment and, more specifically, some elements within the armed forces, having embarked upon a course from which they found it difficult to extricate themselves, ended up totally controlling the civilian authorities, frequently in collusion with some influential civilians.

None of the three branches of Government—judicial, legislative or executive—was capable of restraining the military's overwhelming control of society. The judiciary was weakened as it fell victim to intimidation and the foundations were laid for its corruption; since it had never enjoyed genuine institutional independence from the legislative and executive branches, its ineffectiveness steadily increased until it became, through its inaction or its appalling submissiveness, a factor which contributed to the tragedy suffered by the country. The various, frequently opportunistic, alliances which political leaders (legislators as well as members of the executive branch) forged with the military establishment and with members of the judiciary had the effect of further weakening civilian control over the military, police and security forces, all of which formed part of the military establishment.

The wide network of illegal armed groups, known as "death squads", which operated both within and outside the institutional framework with complete impunity, spread terror throughout Salvadorian society. They originated basically as a civilian operation, designed, financed and controlled by civilians. The core of serving officers, whose role was originally limited to that of mere executants and executioners, gradually seized control of the death squads for personal gain or to promote certain ideological or political objectives. Thus, within the military establishment and in contradiction with its real purpose and mandate, impunity *vis-à-vis* the civilian authorities became the rule. The institution as a whole was a hostage to specific groups of officers, which ... abused their power and their relations with certain civilian circles and intimidated fellow officers who were reluctant to join in to collaborate with their corrupt and illegal practices.

The internal armed conflict between opposing forces grew in intensity and magnitude. The inevitable outcome was acts of violence, some of which were brought before the Commission with anxiety and anticipation. The more bloody the conflict became, and the more widespread, the greater the power of the military hierarchy and of those who commanded armed insurgent groups. The outcome of that vicious circle was a situation in which certain elements of society found themselves immune from any governmental or political restraints and thus forged for themselves the most abject impunity. It was they who wielded the real power of the State, expressed in the most primitive terms, while the executive, legislative and judicial branches were unable to play any real role as branches of government. The sad fact is that they were transformed, in practice, into mere facades with marginal governmental authority.

How else can the *modus operandi* of the death squads be understood? The disappearance of large numbers of people, the assassination attempts on important Government officials, church leaders and judges, and the fact that the perpetrators of these atrocities were only rarely brought to trial. What is ironic is that the web of corruption, timidity and weakness within the judiciary and its investigative bodies greatly impeded the effective functioning of the judicial system even where crimes attributed to FMLN were involved....

I. Recommendations Inferred Directly from the Results of the Investigation

The Commission makes the following recommendations which must be carried out without delay:

A. Dismissal from the Armed Forces

The findings on the cases investigated by the Commission on the Truth also give the names of civilian officials in the civil service and the judiciary. These officials, acting in their professional capacity, covered up serious acts of violence or failed to discharge their responsibilities in the investigation of such acts. For these persons, the Commission recommends that they be dismissed from the civil service or judicial posts they currently occupy. For those who no longer occupy such posts, the Commission recommends application of the measure described in paragraph C below.

B. Dismissal from the Civil Service

The findings on the cases investigated by the Commission on the Truth also give the names of civilian officials in the civil service and the judiciary. These officials, acting in their professional capacity, covered up serious acts of violence or failed to discharge their responsibilities in the investigation of such acts. For these persons, the Commission recommends that they be dismissed from the civil service or judicial posts they currently occupy. For those who no longer occupy such posts, the Commission recommends application of the measure described in paragraph C below.

C. Disqualification from Holding Public Office

Under no circumstances would it be advisable to allow persons who committed acts of violence such as those which the Commission has investigated to participate in the running of the State. The Commission therefore believes that the persons referred to in the preceding paragraphs, as well as any others equally implicated in the perpetration of the acts of violence described in this report, including the civilians and members of the FMLN Command named in the findings on individual cases, should be disqualified from holding any public post or office for a period of not less than 10 years, and should be disqualified permanently from any activity related to public security or national defence. While the Commission does not have the power to apply such a provision directly, it does have the power to recommend to the National Commission for the Consolidation of Peace (COPAZ) that it prepare a preliminary legislative draft on this issue, offering proper guarantees in accordance with Salvadorian law, and that it submit such draft to the Legislative Assembly for early approval. It also has the power to recommend to the bodies authorized to make appointments to public office that they refrain from appointing the persons referred to above.

D. Judicial Reform

All aspects of the agreed judicial reform must be put into practice. Even if this reform must be complemented by additional measures, some of which will be the subject of other recommendations by the Commission, the agreements reached on this issue during the peace process must be complied with immediately and in full. Two specific aspects should be noted:

(a) Reform of the Supreme Court of Justice

The constitutional reform approved as part of the peace process provided a new procedure for the election of judges to the Supreme Court of Justice, the body which heads the judicial branch. Those innovations cannot be put into effect until the current judges' terms expire, with the result that the Court continues to consist of persons elected in accordance with the rules that applied before the constitutional reform and the peace agreements. Given the tremendous responsibility which the judiciary bears for the impunity with which serious acts of violence such as those described in this report occurred, there is not justification for further postponing the appointment of a new Supreme Court of Justice, whose current members should make way for the immediate implementation of the constitutional reform by resigning from their posts.

(b) National Council of the Judiciary

The peace agreements provided for the establishment of a National Council of the Judiciary independent from the organs of State and from political parties (Mexico Agreements: "Political agreements elaborating on the constitutional reform", A (b); Chapultepec Peace Agreement, chap. III (1) (A)). However, the National Council of the Judiciary Act, adopted in December 1992 by the Legislative Assembly, contains provisions which, in practice, leave the dismissal of some members of that Council to the discretion of the Supreme Court of Justice. The Commission recommends that this system be changed and that it be possible to dismiss members of the Council only for precise legal causes, to be weighed by the Legislative Assembly which, being the body constitutionally authorized to appoint such members, should, logically, also be the one to decide on their dismissal.

E. Judges

The Career Judicial Service Act, the amendment of which, the Commission understands, is under discussion for the date on which this report will be submitted, should establish that only those judges who, according to a rigorous evaluation made by the national council of the Judiciary, have demonstrated judicial aptitude, efficiency and concern for human rights and offer every guarantee of independence, judicial discretion, honesty and impartiality in their actions, may remain in the career judicial service.

F. Penalties

One of the direct consequences of the clarification of the serious acts which the Commission has investigated should, under normal circumstances, be the punishment which those responsible for such acts deserve.

However, in view of current conditions in the country and the situation of the administration of justice, the Commission is facing insurmountable difficulties which it will describe below.

It is not within the Commission's powers to directly impose penalties on those responsible: it does not have judicial functions and cannot therefore decide to impose a particular penalty on a person. That is a function which, by its nature, properly belongs to the courts, a question which raises serious problems for the Commission. Accordingly, the problem and possible solutions to it cannot be discussed in isolation from the current situation in the country.

One painfully clear aspect of that situation is the glaring inability of the judicial system either to investigate crimes or to enforce the law, especially when it comes to crimes committed with the direct or indirect support of State institutions. It was because these shortcomings were so apparent that the Government and FMLN agreed to create an instrument such as the Commission on the Truth to perform tasks which should normally be undertaken by the bodies responsible for the administration of justice. Had the judiciary functioned satisfactorily, not only would the acts which the Commission has had to investigate have been cleared up at the proper time, but the corresponding penalties would have been imposed. The inability of the courts to apply the law to acts of violence committed under the direct or indirect cover of the public authorities is part and parcel of the situation in which those acts took place and is inseparable from them. This is a conclusion which emerges clearly from most of the cases of this kind examined in this report.

We must ask ourselves, therefore, whether the judiciary is capable, all things being equal, of fulfilling the requirements of justice. If we take a detached view of the situation, this question cannot be answered in the affirmative. The structure of the judiciary is still substantially the same as it was when the acts described in this report took place. The reforms of the judicial system agreed on during the peace process have been implemented to only a limited extent, so that they have yet to have a significant impact which translates into a transformation of the administration of justice. What is more, the judiciary is still run by people whose omissions were part of the situation which must now be overcome, and there is nothing to indicate that their customary practices will change in the near future.

These considerations confront the Commission with a serious dilemma. The question is not whether the guilty should be punished, but whether justice can be done. Public morality demands that those responsible for the crimes described here be punished. However, El Salvador has no system for the administration of justice which meets the minimum requirements of objectivity and impartiality so that justice can be rendered reliably. This is a part of the country's current reality and overcoming it urgently should be a primary objective for Salvadorian society....

SUPREME COURT ON USE OF LEGISLATIVE INTENT

March 31, 1993

The Supreme Court is sometimes asked to determine if a law's meaning is exactly what Congress intended it to be. If the Court finds that it is not, the justices typically try to discern "legislative intent" by examining statements made in congressional debate and in reports from the House and Senate committees that studied and acted on the particular legislation.

Such a case decided March 31 touched off a debate in and beyond the Court over the validity of "legislative intent." As he had said on other occasions, Justice Antonin Scalia declared that it was nonsensical, even improper, for the judicial system to try to make such a judgment. He argued that the courts must consider nothing but the words of the law. "We are governed by laws, not the intentions of legislators," he wrote.

A bill's legislative history, Scalia contended, could be read selectively to produce whatever result a court might desire. Legislative history "is not merely a waste of research time and ink," he wrote, "it is a false and disruptive lesson in the law. . . ."

The case at hand, Conroy v. Aniskoff, *turned on the meaning of a provision in the 1940 Soldiers' and Sailors' Civil Relief Act and subsequent amendments. Relying on that law, Army officer Thomas F. Conroy in 1987 sued the town of Danforth, Maine, to recover a parcel of land the town seized from him because of his unpaid taxes in the previous three years.*

Conroy argued that his land should not have been seized because the law protected all military personnel from such losses. A state district court rejected his claim, as did the Supreme Judicial Court of Maine, saying that the intent of Congress was to protect only those who could show that their military service created a hardship sufficient to excuse tax deliquency.

Scalia on the Attack

Justice John Paul Stevens, writing for the Court, rejected those arguments. The provision, he wrote, "is unambiguous, unequivocal, and unlimited." To him it was clearly stated and to be accepted as law. There was no disagreement among the justices on that point; the other eight agreed with the ruling. But when Stevens went on to review the law's legislative history in support of his ruling, Scalia objected—emphatically and at length. His written opinion ran to eleven pages, four more than Stevens's.

Scalia said that by pursuing the legislative history of an "unambiguous [and] unequivocal" law, the Court suggested to lawyers that "the oracles of legislative history... must always be consulted," thus condemning "litigants (who, unlike us, must pay for it out of their own pockets) to subsidize historical research by lawyers." As if to prove the "illegitimacy" of legislative history, Scalia sought to show that excerpts of law could be interpreted to uphold the decisions of the Maine courts. But that did not matter, he said: "The language of the statute is entirely clear, and if that is not what Congress meant then Congress has made a mistake and Congress will have to correct it."

Debate in the Legal Community

Stevens answered Scalia only in a footnote. A jurisprudence that confines a court's inquiry only to "the law as it is passed" and that is wholly unconcerned about the intentions of legislators, Stevens wrote, "would enforce an unambiguous statutory text even if it produces manifestly unintended and profoundly unwise consequences."

In an earlier case in which Scalia had raised his argument, Justice David H. Souter took the opposing view, quoting former Justice Felix Frankfurter, who sat on the Court from 1939-1962, as saying, "A statute, like other living organisms, derives significance and sustenance from its environment.... The meaning of such a statute cannot be gained by confining inquiry within its four corners. Only the historic process... can reveal true meaning."

Only Justice Clarence Thomas gave support to Scalia's position in Conroy; *he declined to endorse Stevens's footnote. However, Kenneth S. Geller, a former deputy solicitor general, was quoted in the* Washington Post *as saying that Scalia had "sensitized" the legal community to the drawbacks of some legislative history. Robert W. Kastenmeier, chairman of a national commission on impeachment, said Scalia's theories had stimulated thinking but had not taken root.*

Following are excerpts from the decision of Justice John Paul Stevens, writing for the Supreme Court in the case of Conroy v. Aniskoff, *March 31, 1993, and from a separate opinion by Justice Antonin Scalia:*

No. 91-1353

Thomas F. Conroy, Petitioner v. Walter Aniskoff, Jr., et. al.	On writ of certiorari to the Supreme Judicial Court of Maine

[March 31, 1993]

JUSTICE STEVENS delivered the opinion of the Court.

The Soldiers' and Sailors' Civil Relief Act of 1940... suspends various civil liabilities of persons in military service. At issue in this case is the provision in § 525 that the "period of military service shall not be included in computing any period ... provided by any law for the redemption of real property sold or forfeited to enforce any obligation, tax, or assessment." The question presented is whether a member of the Armed Services must show that his military service prejudiced his ability to redeem title to property before he can qualify for the statutory suspension of time.

I

Petitioner is an officer in the United States Army. He was on active duty continuously from 1966 until the time of trial. In 1973 he purchased a parcel of vacant land in the town of Danforth, Maine. He paid taxes on the property for 10 years, but failed to pay the 1984, 1985, and 1986 local real estate taxes. In 1986, following the Maine statutory procedures that authorize it to acquire tax-delinquent real estate, the town sold the property.

In 1987 petitioner brought suit in the Maine District Court against the town and the two purchasers. He claimed that § 525 of the Act tolled the redemption period while he was in military service, and federal law therefore prevented the town from acquiring good title to the property even though the State's statutory procedures had been followed. The trial court rejected the claim. In an unreported opinion, it noted that some courts had construed § 525 literally, but it elected to follow a line of decisions that refused to toll the redemption period unless the taxpayer could show that "military service resulted in hardship excusing timely legal action." It agreed with those courts that it would be "absurd and illogical" to toll limitations periods for career service personnel who had not been "handicapped by their military status." The Supreme Judicial Court of Maine affirmed by an equally divided court. We granted certiorari to resolve the conflict in the interpretation of § 525.

II

The statutory command in § 525 is unambiguous, unequivocal, and unlimited. It states that the period of military service "shall not be included" in the computation of "any period now or hereafter provided by any law for the redemption of real property ...." Respondents do not dispute the plain meaning of this text. Rather, they argue that when § 525 is read in the context of the entire statute, it implicitly conditions its protection on a demonstration of hardship or prejudice resulting from military service. They make three points in support of this argument: that the history of the Act reveals an intent to provide protection only to those whose lives have been temporarily disrupted by military service; that other provisions of the Act are expressly conditioned on a showing of prejudice; and that a literal interpretation produces illogical and absurd results. Neither separately nor in combination do these points justify a departure from the unambiguous statutory text.

Respondents correctly describe the immediate cause for the statute's enactment in 1940, the year before our entry into World War II. Congress stated its purpose to "expedite the national defense under the emergent conditions which are threatening the peace and security of the United States. . . ." That purpose undoubtedly contemplated the special hardship that military duty imposed on those suddenly drafted into service by the national emergency. Neither that emergency, nor a particular legislative interest in easing sudden transfers from civilian to military status, however, justifies the conclusion that Congress did not intend all members of the Armed Forces, including career personnel, to receive the Act's protections. Indeed, because Congress extended the life of the Act indefinitely in 1948, well after the end of World War II, the complete legislative history confirms a congressional intent to protect all military personnel on active duty, just as the statutory language provides.

Respondents also correctly remind us to "follow the cardinal rule that a statute is to be read as a whole, see *Massachusetts v. Morash,* (1989), since the meaning of statutory language, plain or not, depends on context." *King v. St. Vincent's Hospital,* (1991). But as in *King,* the context of this statute actually supports the conclusion that Congress meant what § 525 says. Several provisions of the statute condition the protection they offer on a showing that military service adversely affected the ability to assert or protect a legal right. To choose one of many examples, § 532(2) authorizes a stay of enforcement of secured obligations unless "the ability of the defendant to comply with the terms of the obligation is not materially affected by reason of his military service." The comprehensive character of the entire statute indicates that Congress included a prejudice requirement whenever it considered it appropriate to do so, and that its omission of any such requirement in § 525 was deliberate.

Finally, both the history of this carefully reticulated statute, and our history of interpreting it, refute any argument that a literal construction of § 525 is so absurd or illogical that Congress could not have intended it. In many respects the 1940 Act was a re-enactment of World War I legislation that had, in turn, been modeled after legislation that several States adopted during the Civil War. See *Boone v. Lightner,* (1943). The Court had emphasized the comprehensive character and carefully segregated arrangement of the various provisions of the World War I statute in *Ebert v. Poston,* (1925), and it had considered the consequences of requiring a showing of prejudice when it construed the World War II statute in *Boone, supra.* Since we presume that Congress was familiar with those cases, we also assume that Congress considered the decision in Ebert to interpret and apply each provision of the Act separately when it temporarily re-established the law as a whole in 1940, and then considered *Boone*'s analysis of a prejudice requirement when it permanently extended the Act in 1948.

Legislative history confirms that assumption. Since the enactment of the 1918 Act, Congress has expressed its understanding that absolute exemptions might save time or money for service members only at the cost of injuring their own credit, their family's credit, and the domestic economy; it presumably required a showing of prejudice only when it seemed necessary to confer on the service member a genuine benefit. By distinguishing sharply between the two types of protections, Congress unquestionably contemplated the ways that either type of protection would affect both military debtors and their civilian creditors.

The long and consistent history and the structure of this legislation therefore lead us to conclude that—just as the language of § 525 suggests—Congress made a deliberate policy judgment placing a higher value on firmly protecting the service member's redemption fights than on occasionally burdening the tax collection process. Given the limited number of situations in which this precisely structured statute offers such absolute protection, we cannot say that Congress would have found our straightforward interpretation and application of its words either absurd or illogical. If the consequences of that interpretation had been—or prove to be—as unjust as respondents contend, we are confident that Congress would have corrected the injustice—or will do so in the future.

The judgment of the Supreme Judicial Court of Maine is reversed.

It is so ordered.

JUSTICE SCALIA, concurring in the judgment.

The Court begins its analysis with the observation: "The statutory command in § 525 is unambiguous, unequivocal, and unlimited." *Ante,* at 3. In my view, discussion of that point is where the remainder of the analysis should have ended. Instead, however, the Court feels compelled to demonstrate that its holding is consonant with legislative history, including some dating back to 1917—*a full quarter century* before the provision at issue was enacted. That is not merely a waste of research time and ink; it is a false and disruptive lesson in the law. It says to the bar that even an "unambiguous [and] unequivocal" statute can never be dispositive; that, presumably under penalty of malpractice liability, the oracles of legislative history, far into the dimmy past, must always be consulted. This undermines the clarity of law, and condemns litigants (who, unlike us, must pay for it out of their own pockets) to subsidizing historical research by lawyers.

The greatest defect of legislative history is its illegitimacy. We are governed by laws, not by the intentions of legislators. As the Court said in 1844: "The law as it passed is the will of the majority of both houses, and *the only mode in which that will is spoken is in the act itself ....*" *Aldridge v. Williams,* (emphasis added). But not the least of the defects of legislative history is its indeterminacy. If one were to search for an interpretive technique that, *on the whole,* was more likely to confuse than to clarify, one could hardly find a more promising candidate than legislative history. And the present case nicely proves that point.

Judge Harold Leventhal used to describe the use of legislative history as the equivalent of entering a crowded cocktail party and looking over the heads of the guests for one's friends. If I may pursue that metaphor: The legislative history of § 205 of the Soldiers' and Sailors' Civil Relief Act contains a variety of diverse personages, a selected few of whom—its "friends"—the Court has introduced to us in support of its result. But there are many other faces in the crowd, most of which, I think, are set against today's result.

I will limit my exposition of the legislative history to the enactment of four statutes:

1. The Soldiers' and Sailors' Civil Relief Act of 1918 (1918 Act), 40 Stat. 440;
2. The Soldiers' and Sailors' Civil Relief Act of 1940 (1940 Act or Act), 54 Stat. 1178;
3. The Soldiers' and Sailors' Civil Relief Act Amendments of 1942 (1942 Amendments), 56 Stat. 769;
4. The Selective Service Act of 1948, 62 Stat. 604.

That, of course, cannot be said to be the "*complete* legislative history" relevant to this provision.... One of the problems with legislative history is that it is inherently open-ended. In this case, for example, one could go back further in time to examine the Civil War-era relief Acts, many of which are in fact set forth in an appendix to the House Report on the 1918 Act.... Or one could extend the search abroad and consider the various foreign statutes that were mentioned in that same House Report.... Those additional statutes might be of questionable relevance, but then so too are the 1918 Act and the 1940 Act, neither of which contained a provision governing redemption periods. Nevertheless, I will limit my legislative history inquiry to those four statutes for the simple reason that that is the scope chosen by the Court.

The 1918 Act appears to have been the first comprehensive national soldiers' relief Act... The legislative history reveals that Congress intended that it serve the same vital purpose—providing "protection against suit to men in military service"—as various state statutes had served during the Civil War... Congress intended, however, that the 1918 Act should differ from the Civil War statutes "in two material respects." The first was that, being a national statute, it would produce a disposition "uniform throughout the Nation." But it is the second difference which has particular relevance to the Court's ruling today:

> "The next material difference between this law and the various State laws is this, and in this I think you will find the chief excellence of the bill which we propose: Instead of the bill we are now considering being arbitrary, inelastic, inflexible, the discretion as to dealing out even-handed justice between the creditor and the soldier, taking into consideration the fact that the soldier has been called to his country's cause, rests largely, and in some cases entirely, in the breast of the judge who tries the case."

This comment cannot be dismissed as the passing remark of an insignificant Member, since the speaker was the Chairman of the House Judiciary Committee, the committee that reported the bill to the House floor. Moreover, his remarks merely echoed the House Report, which barely a page into its text stated: "We cannot point out too soon, or too emphatically, that the bill is not an inflexible stay of all claims against persons in military service." Congress intended to depart from the "arbitrary and rigid protection" that had been provided under the Civil War-era stay laws, *ibid.*, which could give protection to men "who can and should pay their obligations in full," *id.*, at 3. It is clear, therefore, that in the 1918 Act Congress intended to create flexible rules that would permit denial of protection to members of the military who could show no hardship.

The 1918 Act expired by its own terms six months after the end of the First World War.... The 1940 Act was adopted as the Nation prepared for its coming participation in the Second World War. Both the House and Senate Reports described it as being, "in substance, identical with the [1918 Act]." Moreover, in *Boone v. Lightner*, (1943), we acknowledged that the 1940 Act was "a substantial reenactment" of the 1918 Act, and looked to the legislative history of the 1918 Act for indications of congressional intent with respect to the 1940 Act. Relying on that legislative history, we found that "the very heart of the policy of the Act" was to provide "judicial discretion ... instead of rigid and undiscriminating suspension of civil proceedings."

Although the Court never mentions this fact, it is clear that under the 1918 and 1940 Acts a redemption period would not be tolled during the period of military service. In both enactments, § 205 governed only statutes of limitations and did not mention redemption periods.

Moreover, in *Ebert v. Poston*, (1925), this Court held that neither § 205 nor § 302, which provides protection from foreclosures, conferred on a court any power to extend a statutory redemption period. Congress overturned the rule of *Ebert* in the 1942 Amendments, a central part of the legislative history that the Court curiously fails to discuss. Section 5 of those amendments rewrote § 205 of the Act to place it in its current form, which directly addresses the redemption periods. The crucial question in the present case (if one believes in legislative history) is whether Congress intended this amendment to be consistent with the "heart of the policy of the Act"—conferring judicial discretion—or rather intended it to confer an unqualified right to extend the period of redemption. Both the House and Senate Reports state that, under the amended § 205, "[t]he running of the statutory period during which real property may be redeemed after sale to enforce any obligation, tax, or assessment is *likewise* tolled during the part of such period which occurs after enactment of the [1942 Amendments]." The Reports also state that "[a]lthough the tolling of such periods is now within the spirit of the law, it has not been held to be within the letter thereof" (citing *Ebert*). These statements surely indicate an intention to provide a tolling period for redemptions similar to that already provided for statutes of limitations—which, on the basis of the legislative history I have described, can be considered discretionary rather than rigid. The existence of discretionary authority to suspend the tolling is also suggested by the House floor debates. Responding to questions, Representative Sparkman (who submitted the Report on behalf of the House Committee on Military Affairs) agreed that, while the bill "pertains to all persons in the armed forces," a man "serving in the armed forces for more money than he got in civil life ... is not entitled to any of the benefits of the provisions of this bill." In response to that last comment, another representative inquired further whether "[t]his is to take care of the men who are handicapped because of their military service." Representative Sparkman answered affirmatively. He confirmed that Congress did not intend to abandon the discretionary nature of the scheme: "With reference to all these matters we have tried to make the law flexible by lodging discretion within the courts to do or not to do as justice and equity may require." And finally, at a later point in the debates, Representative Brooks made clear that the Act was intended to remedy the prejudice resulting from compelled military service: "We feel that the normal obligations of the man contracted prior to service induction should be suspended as far as practicable during this tour of duty, and that the soldier should be protected from default in his obligations due to his inability to pay caused by reduction in income due to service."

The final component of the legislative history that I shall treat is the extension of the 1940 Act in the Selective Service Act of 1948, 62 Stat. 604. The Court misconstrues Congress's intent in this enactment in two respects. First, it asserts that "because Congress extended the life of the Act indefinitely in 1948, well after the end of World War II, the complete legislative history confirms a congressional intent to protect all military personnel on active duty, just as the statutory language provides." It is true enough that the War was over; but the draft was not. The extension of the 1940 Act was contained in the *Selective Service Act of 1948,* which *required* military service from citizens. And it would appear to have been contemplated that the "life of the Act" would be extended not "indefinitely," as the Court says, ante, at 4, but for the duration of the draft. The legislative history states that Congress intended to extend the provisions of the 1940 Act "to persons serving in the armed forces *pursuant to this act.*" Career members of the military such as petitioner would not have been serving "pursuant to" the Selective Service Act, since they were expressly excepted from its service requirement. In this focus upon draftees, the legislative history of the 1948 extension merely replicates that of the 1940 Act and the 1942 Amendments. The former was enacted on the heels of the Selective Training and Service Act of 1940... and was introduced on the Senate floor with the explanation that it would provide "relief ... to those who are to be *inducted* into the military service for training under [the Selective Training and Service Act of 1940]." In the debate on the 1942 Amendments, Representative Sparkman noted that "hundreds of thousands, and even millions, have been called" into military service since the enactment of the 1940 Act, and admonished his colleagues to "keep uppermost in your mind at all times the fact that the primary purpose of this legislation is to give relief to the boy that is called into service." In other words, the legislative history of the 1948 extension, like that of the Act itself and of the 1942 Amendments, suggests an intent to protect those who were *prejudiced* by military service, as many who were drafted would be.

The Court also errs in mistaking the probable effect of Congress's presumed awareness of our earlier opinions in *Ebert* and *Boone.* In *Boone,* we stated that the Act "is always to be liberally construed to protect those who have been *obliged* to drop their own affairs and take up the burdens of the nation," but that discretion was vested in the courts to insure that the immunities of the Act are not put to "unworthy use," since "the very heart of the policy of the Act" was to provide "judicial discretion ... instead of rigid and undiscriminating suspension of civil proceedings...."Awareness of *Boone* would likely have caused Congress to assume that the courts would *vindicate* "the very heart of the policy of the Act" by requiring a showing of prejudice. The Court argues, however, that Congress would *also* have been aware that *Ebert* recognized the "carefully segregated arrangement of the various provisions" of the Act. It is already an extension of the normal convention to assume that Congress was aware of the precise reasoning (as opposed to the holding) of earlier judicial opinions; but it goes much further to assume that Congress not only knew, but expected the courts would continue to follow, the reasoning of a case (*Ebert*) whose holding Congress had repudiated six years earlier. In any event, the Court seeks to use *Ebert* only to establish that Congress was aware that this Court was aware of the "carefully segregated arrangement" of the Act. That adds little, if anything, to direct reliance upon the plain language of the statute.

After reading the above described legislative history, one might well conclude that the result reached by the Court today, though faithful to law, betrays the congressional intent. Many have done so. Indeed, as far as I am aware, *every court* that has chosen to interpret § 205 in light of its legislative history rather than on the basis of its plain text has found that Congress did not intend § 205 to apply to career members of the military who cannot show prejudice or hardship. The only scholarly commentary I am aware of addressing this issue concludes: "An examination of the legislative history of the Act shows that the prevailing interpretation of section 205 [*i.e.,* the Court's interpretation] is not consistent with congressional intent." Finally, even the Government itself, which successfully urged in this case the position we have adopted, until recently believed, on the basis of legislative history, the contrary....

I confess that I have not personally investigated the entire legislative history—or even that portion of it which relates to the four statutes listed above. The excerpts I have examined and quoted were unearthed by a hapless law clerk to whom I assigned the task. The other Justices have, in the aggregate, many more law clerks than I, and it is quite possible that if they all were unleashed upon this enterprise they would discover, in the legislative materials dating back to 1917 *or earlier,* many faces friendly to the Court's holding. Whether they would or not makes no difference to me—and evidently makes no difference to the Court, which gives lipservice to legislative history but does not trouble to set forth and discuss the foregoing material that others found so persuasive. In my view, that is as it should be, except for the lipservice. The language of the statute is entirely clear, and if that is not what Congress meant then Congress has made a mistake and Congress will have to correct it. We should not pretend to care about legislative intent (as opposed to the meaning of the law), lest we impose upon the practicing bar and their clients obligations that we do not ourselves take seriously.

April

GAO REPORTS ON THREATS TO SAFE DRINKING WATER

April 9 and 14, 1993

A lack of federal funding made it impossible for states to properly protect public water supplies, according to a pair of reports released in April by the U.S. General Accounting Office (GAO). The reports came in the same year that two major American cities faced water crises.

In the spring, more than 400,000 Milwaukee residents became ill after a microorganism called cryptosporidium infected the city's water supply. The parasite was also blamed by federal health officials for speeding the deaths of forty people who were already sick. The only warning of a problem was cloudiness in the water. Such cloudiness occurs when the concentration of suspended particles becomes too great, clogging treatment plant filters and allowing harmful microorganisms to seep through.

In December, cloudiness like that found in Milwaukee was discovered in water at the treatment plant that served Washington, D.C., and many of its northern Virginia suburbs. There was no immediate evidence that cryptosporidium infected the water, but federal officials took no chances. The U.S. Environmental Protection Agency (EPA) advised the nearly 1 million people living in the affected area to boil their drinking water while tests were conducted on water from the Dalecarlia treatment plant, which was operated by the Army Corps of Engineers. Within hours after the advisory was issued, anxious residents had stripped grocery store shelves of virtually every drop of bottled water in the region. Subsequent tests found no cryptosporidium in the Dalecarlia water, and the advisory to boil water was lifted three days after it was issued. Later investigations blamed human error for the cloudy water.

People made uneasy by the Milwaukee and Washington crises could take little comfort from the two GAO reports. The first, titled "Drinking Water: Key Quality Assurance Program Is Flawed and Underfunded," found that states were not properly inspecting public water supplies. Such inspections, formally known as sanitary surveys, are critical in preventing problems in the nation's 198,000 public water systems, according to the GAO. In a report two years earlier, the GAO had called the surveys "one of the most effective tools that states can use to help ensure compliance and correct problems before they become serious."

Water System Inspections

The GAO found four major flaws with the sanitary surveys: the federal government did not give states enough money to conduct them properly; the U.S. Environmental Protection Agency had not established minimum requirements for the surveys; many of the surveys were conducted haphazardly; and, when problems were identified, often they were not corrected. These flaws were particularly serious, the GAO said, because sanitary surveys it examined revealed recurring problems with water systems' equipment and management, particularly among the smaller systems. About 80 percent of the surveys found problems, and 60 percent of those problems had been identified in prior surveys. State officials interviewed by the GAO reported that they had only enough money to fix problems that were actually hurting water quality; problems that could affect water quality in the future often went uncorrected.

Despite strong agreement about the importance of sanitary surveys, states varied widely in how often they conducted the inspections, the GAO said. States conducted the surveys anywhere from quarterly to once every ten years. Nearly half the states had reduced the frequency of inspections since 1988 because of financial constraints, the GAO reported.

The GAO noted the importance of ensuring that public water supplies are safe. It said that while some contaminants found in drinking water cause only relatively mild health problems, others have been linked to cancer, birth defects, and other serious health problems. The GAO also noted that its criticism of sanitary surveys was nothing new. In June 1990 it issued a report saying that many states had cut back on the surveys because of financial problems.

The GAO laid much of the blame for the continuing problem on the EPA. Under the Safe Drinking Water Act of 1974, the EPA gave states the primary responsibility for enforcing drinking water requirements, but did not provide enough money or direction for the states to do the job properly. The lack of proper sanitary surveys was only one part of a "crisis" affecting the overall drinking water program, the GAO said.

In addition to providing the funds necessary to conduct inspections, the GAO recommended that the EPA work with states to create standards for conducting and documenting surveys, help ensure that surveyors know how to react when problems are found, and help states develop procedures for correcting problems found during the surveys.

Threatened Well Water

The second GAO report, "Drinking Water: Stronger Efforts Needed to Protect Areas Around Public Wells From Contamination," said a lack of federal funds also hampered efforts to prevent contamination of drinking water drawn from underground wells. More than half of the nation's population depends upon water drawn from such wells.

In 1986, amendments to the Safe Drinking Water Act of 1974 created a program called Wellhead Protection (WHP). The aim was to have states develop plans for protecting areas around wells from contamination. However, no money was ever appropriated to pay for the program. In addition, although the legislation required states to develop WHP programs, it did not provide for any enforcement by the EPA. The result was not surprising: more than three years after the statutory deadline for developing WHP programs, only twenty-six states had complied, and, of these, none had a program that met all of the EPA's requirements. Of the remaining states, twenty-one were working on programs and three were ignoring the law.

While the lack of federal funds harmed the WHP effort, the GAO found another barrier in local opposition to state-imposed land use controls needed to protect wells. Both EPA and state officials agreed that some sort of land use control was crucial to protecting wells, yet not a single state had yet exerted its authority to impose such measures. The GAO said that public education about the necessity of preventing well contamination could overcome the opposition.

Environmentalists warned that the Milwaukee and Washington crises were only one indication of the need for tougher drinking water laws, and predicted further problems in the future. "Until they really do a full audit of the whole system, I can foresee something like this happening again," said Erik Olson of the Natural Resources Defense Council in an interview with the Washington Post. *"There are a lot of layers of this onion yet to be peeled away."*

Following are the executive summaries from two reports by the U.S. General Accounting Office: "Drinking Water: Key Quality Assurance Program Is Flawed," released April 9, 1993; and "Drinking Water: Stronger Efforts Needed to Protect Areas Around Public Wells From Contamination," released April 14, 1993:

APRIL 9 REPORT

Executive Summary

Purpose

Most Americans rely on public water systems to deliver high-quality water that meets federal and state standards. One key means of ensuring the quality of drinking water is a periodic inspection, or sanitary survey, of public water systems. GAO reported in July 1992 that sanitary surveys are "one of the most effective tools that states can use to help ensure compliance and correct problems before they become serious."

Concerned that financial problems may be leading many states to cut back on sanitary survey programs, the Chairman, Subcommittee on Health and the Environment, House Committee on Energy and Commerce, asked GAO to examine these programs. Among the issues GAO reviewed are (1) whether sanitary surveys are comprehensive enough to determine if public water systems are capable of providing good-quality drinking water and (2) what the results of surveys reveal about the operations and condition of water systems nationwide. GAO also provides observations on how the funding problems affecting [EPA's] overall drinking water program have affected states' ability to conduct sanitary surveys.

Background

The Safe Drinking Water Act of 1974 required EPA to establish drinking water standards and monitoring requirements to ensure that public water systems deliver safe drinking water to consumers. States that adopted regulations as stringent as EPA's and met certain other conditions (including adopting sanitary survey programs) could, with the agency's approval, administer their own drinking water programs. EPA has granted such authority ("primacy") to all states but Wyoming.

While EPA has not established minimum requirements for sanitary surveys, the agency's guidance recommends that they cover all components of a water system—including its sources of water, facilities, and equipment—as well as its operations and maintenance. EPA also recommends that surveys be performed at least every 3 years.

Results in Brief

On the basis of a nationwide questionnaire and a review of 200 sanitary surveys conducted in four states (Illinois, Montana, New Hampshire, and Tennessee), GAO found that sanitary surveys are often deficient in how they are conducted, documented, and/or interpreted. Specifically, 45 states omit one or more of the key elements of surveys, such as inspections of the water distribution system or reviews of water system operators' qualifications. Additionally, some states do not require documentation of the inspection of items or of the surveys' results, and results are sometimes interpreted inconsistently by surveyors.

Many of the 200 sanitary surveys revealed recurring problems with water systems' equipment and management, particularly among small systems. States' questionnaire responses confirmed that problems associated with the soundness of systems' infrastructures are largely found among smaller systems. GAO's detailed review of the four states' sanitary surveys also showed that, regardless of systems' size, deficiencies previously disclosed frequently went uncorrected.

The gap between the needs and available resources of state drinking water programs, estimated in the hundreds of millions of dollars annually, has severely affected states' capabilities to conduct sanitary surveys. The problem is compounded by the lack of any minimum requirements on how surveys are to be conducted and documented. State drinking water officials explained to GAO that in the absence of such requirements, it makes more sense to emphasize other activities that are subject to greater oversight by EPA than to emphasize sanitary surveys. The result, however, has been that a key benefit of surveys—identifying and correcting problems before they become larger problems affecting water quality—has often not been realized. GAO believes that while the problems discussed in this report are correctable, effective action will depend on resolving the drinking water program's acute funding shortage.

Principal Findings

Comprehensiveness of Survey Programs Is Inconsistent

GAO's review disclosed problems in the scope of many sanitary surveys, their documentation, and the reporting and interpretation of their results. Forty-five states reported that in conducting the surveys, they do not evaluate one or more of the 14 major components and operations that EPA recommends be evaluated. While some of the components and operations cited in EPA's guidance do not necessarily apply to all water systems, many states do not evaluate water distribution systems, operators' qualifications, or other key aspects of systems' design and operations that EPA believes should be reviewed during virtually every survey.

Documentation of surveys' results is needed so that state officials can assess the surveys' adequacy and inspectors can follow up on the problems detected. However, many of the documents GAO reviewed in Illinois, New Hampshire, and Tennessee contained incomplete entries or nondescriptive language, making it difficult to assess what the inspectors found. Documentation was particularly incomplete in Montana, which does not require detailed reports of surveys' results: County inspectors' reports frequently consisted of a simple statement such as, "The system looks OK." Importantly, only 30 percent of Montana's surveys disclosed deficiencies, while 97 percent of the surveys in the other three states—where documentation was more complete—disclosed deficiencies. GAO believes this disparity raises questions about the accuracy and completeness of Montana's documentation and about the reliability of the conclusions of the inspectors' final reports.

GAO also found variation in how surveyors interpret surveys' results. For example, in New Hampshire, surveyors at two different water systems reported that storage tank vents needed screens to protect the water from contamination, but only one of the surveyors rated the deficiency as "significant." The difference in the ratings is important because, according to a New Hampshire drinking water official, significant deficiencies are followed up on to ensure corrections are made while other deficiencies are not. Concerned about such inconsistencies, New Hampshire recently developed criteria to guide surveyors on what actions to take when specific types of deficiencies are detected.

Some Water Systems in Poor Condition

The most frequent deficiency cited in states' responses to GAO's questionnaire was inadequate cross-connection programs to ensure that potable water is not mixed with contaminated water. States reported that these programs are inadequate for about 20 percent of the large water systems and 50 percent of the small systems. Other problems often cited involved (1) deficiencies in equipment maintenance and records, (2) shortfalls in water systems' general management and operations, and (3) inadequate protection of water sources.

The 200 surveys GAO examined revealed that efforts to ensure that deficiencies are corrected have often been limited. About 80 percent of the surveys disclosed deficiencies; 60 percent of these surveys cited deficiencies that had already been identified in previous surveys. Citing resource constraints, state officials told GAO that they can only follow up on the most important deficiencies—ones actually affecting water quality—to ensure that corrective actions are taken. New Hampshire officials added that until recently, the state focused on performing surveys (an activity EPA monitors), not on ensuring that disclosed deficiencies were corrected (an activity EPA does not monitor).

Funding a Key Barrier to Correcting Problems

GAO believes that the problems identified in this report are serious but correctable. Correcting the problems, however, will require addressing the extreme shortage in funding affecting the drinking water program as a whole. As GAO's July 1992 report explained, EPA recently adopted a strategy formally acknowledging that at least in the near term, states will be unable to fulfill all of their responsibilities. The strategy therefore sets priorities in the drinking water program to ensure that it can adequately pursue the activities deemed most important in protecting public health. One effect of EPA's strategy was to downplay sanitary surveys.

GAO's July 1992 report took issue with the assertion that all key activities would still receive sufficient attention and asked that the Congress consider modifying EPA's budget request to a funding level more consistent with the agency's own risk-based determination that the program deserves high priority. The report specifically cited the lower priority given sanitary surveys and pointed out that sanitary surveys "traditionally formed the backbone of state drinking water programs."

Recommendations

To improve the quality and consistency of state sanitary survey programs, GAO recommends, among other things, that the Administrator, EPA, (1) work with states to establish minimum requirements as to how surveys should be conducted and documented; (2) assist states in developing criteria to guide surveyors as to the appropriate actions to be taken when specific types of deficiencies are detected; and (3) help states develop procedures to ensure that deficiencies are corrected. GAO recognizes, however, that progress on some of these matters will depend on the resolution of the severe funding problem affecting the drinking water program as a whole.

APRIL 14 REPORT

Executive Summary

Purpose

Over 50 percent of the nation's population relies on groundwater as its primary source of drinking water. However, in recent years, groundwater has been threatened or contaminated by harmful pollutants discharged by various sources into areas surrounding drinking water wells, often referred to as wellhead protection (WHP) areas. As a result, some communities have had to close their drinking water wells permanently or pay tens of millions of dollars in cleanup costs.

Concerned about the Environmental Protection Agency's (EPA) and states' progress in implementing the program intended to prevent the contamination of WHP areas, the Chairman, Environment, Energy, and Natural Resources Subcommittee, House Committee on Government Operations, asked GAO to examine (1) the barriers hindering the development and implementation of states' WHP programs and (2) the options available to deal with these barriers.

Background

The 1986 amendments to the Safe Drinking Water Act established the WHP Program to protect surface and subsurface areas surrounding public drinking water wells from contaminants that may adversely affect human health. The amendments required states to develop and submit their WHP programs to EPA by June 19, 1989. At a minimum, each program was required to specify the roles and duties of state and local governments and public water systems, define each WHP area, identify within each WHP area all potential sources of contamination, describe management approaches to be used to protect water supplies, include contingency plans for alternate water supplies, and include requirements for considering potential sources of contamination when siting new wells. Although authorized, funds have not been appropriated under the 1986 amendments for states' WHP programs.

Although the amendments required each state to have a WHP program, they did not give EPA the authority to develop a program for nonparticipating states or to impose sanctions against them. Rather, EPA's role primarily involves issuing technical guidance to assist states with their

WHP programs and approving or disapproving the programs. The responsibilities of local governments depend largely on the specific requirements of their state's program.

In a broader context, EPA adopted a groundwater protection strategy in July 1991 that may have implications for the WHP Program. This strategy (1) emphasizes preventing contamination (as does the WHP Program) as the most effective way to protect drinking water and avoid substantial cleanup costs and (2) encourages each state to integrate all federal, state, and local efforts to protect groundwater—including the state's WHP program—into a "comprehensive state groundwater protection program." EPA issued guidance in January 1993 to assist states in developing their comprehensive programs.

Results in Brief

Several barriers hinder states' efforts to develop and implement WHP programs, including (1) opposition at the local level against states' enactment of land-use controls and (2) a general lack of public awareness about the vulnerability of drinking water to contamination and about the need to protect wellhead areas. However, EPA and state officials identified a severe shortage of funds as the underlying cause of these barriers and the primary problem affecting states' WHP programs. This shortage also contributes to the lower priority accorded the WHP programs, even though the programs' objective is fully consistent with EPA's stated policy of emphasizing the prevention, rather than the remediation, of groundwater contamination.

One option to alleviate the funding barrier is for states to integrate their WHP programs with their comprehensive programs. According to EPA and state officials, the comprehensive programs will encourage states to set priorities across all groundwater-related programs. The officials maintain that integrating WHP into this process could lead to increased priority, funding, and managerial attention for WHP programs in many states. This integration, however, is only a partial solution at best, particularly in light of the overall scarcity of funding available for groundwater protection activities. Accordingly, GAO believes that a further enhancement would be for EPA and the Congress to reassess the absence of federal appropriations for WHP programs, in light of their preventive orientation and focus on protecting precious drinking water supplies.

Principal Findings

Barriers Hindering WHP Programs

Over 3 years after the June 1989 statutory deadline for submitting WHP programs to EPA, only 26 states have approved programs. Moreover, according to EPA regional officials, none of these states has completed all of the key elements expected of an approvable program, as defined by the Safe Drinking Water Act; in particular, no state has completed the task of defining all of its WHP areas. Of the remaining 24 states, 21 are developing programs and 3 have no plans to do so.

Among the barriers hindering states' development and implementation of WHP programs is local opposition against states' efforts to control, at the local level, land uses that often cause contamination. Although most of the EPA and state officials GAO interviewed generally agreed that some form of land-use controls is needed to prevent contamination in wellhead areas, none of the five states contacted has exerted its authority to institute such measures. EPA and state officials said that states do not exert such authority because they view controlling land uses as a controversial issue that should be addressed by local governments.

GAO found that one effective way to alleviate the reluctance to institute local land-use controls, and similar regulatory controls, is to increase public awareness about the risks contaminated groundwater may pose to drinking water supplies. For example, in the 1980s, officials in Florida's Dade and Broward counties undertook extensive outreach efforts to educate the general public and elected officials about the need to control land uses to protect drinking water supplies, and subsequently, both counties enacted stringent land-use controls that prohibit locating new industrial facilities in wellhead areas.

EPA officials noted that such outreach efforts are crucial because the public is much more willing to support controversial land-use decisions and preventive programs, such as WHP programs, if it understands the adverse health and economic consequences associated with contaminated drinking water. Nevertheless, EPA and state officials unanimously acknowledged that efforts to educate state and local politicians and the general public about the consequences of groundwater contamination are limited because of severe funding constraints.

Similarly, technical data on the risk or extent of groundwater contamination are also needed to delineate WHP areas and identify sources of contamination. However, a paucity of such data exists in most states. According to the EPA and state officials interviewed, states often lack the technical staffing, expertise, and resources needed to develop essential data about the characteristics of aquifers, the flow of the groundwater, and reactions of chemicals and other contaminants detected in the groundwater.

Options for Dealing With the Funding Problem

As a result of severe funding constraints, WHP programs are generally given lower priority than other programs mandated and funded by law, although WHP programs are directly associated with protecting the health of the nation's drinking water. According to nearly all of the EPA and state officials interviewed, integrating WHP programs with states' comprehensive groundwater protection programs would help the WHP programs compete with other programs for the limited groundwater protection funds available to the states. EPA headquarters officials explained that WHP areas are, by definition, high-priority areas because they involve drinking water supplies vulnerable to contamination. The agency issued guidance in January 1993 encouraging such integration.

Nevertheless, this integration alone will not completely resolve the funding problem. For one thing, some of the programs and activities included in states' comprehensive programs, such as conducting water system inspections, have been underfunded. Rather, GAO believes that a practical response to the funding problem—and one that is wholly consistent with EPA's policies and recent GAO reports emphasizing preventing pollution and setting risk-based priorities—is for EPA and the Congress to consider whether the budgetary priority given the WHP Program is consistent with the program's overall purposes of (1) preventing contamination rather than cleaning it up after it occurs and (2) protecting drinking water supplies from contamination.

Recommendations

GAO recommends that the Administrator, EPA, (1) work with states to determine minimum funding levels needed to implement their WHP programs and then (2) work with the cognizant congressional committees during the fiscal year 1994 budget process to identify the minimum funding levels needed to implement the program nationwide.

REPORT ON HEALTH CARE COSTS AND FAMILY FINANCES

April 13, 1994

As the nation waited for the Clinton administration to put forth its proposals for comprehensive health care reform, much of the debate centered on the high costs of care and the high number of Americans—estimated at 38.5 million in 1992—who were not covered by either private or public health insurance. Another important, "but too often neglected," consideration, according to a Washington, D.C., think tank, is the way that the costs of health care are distributed among the nation's families. "The $752 billion spent on health care in 1991 was the equivalent of $7,860 for each of the 96 million households in the country, or over half the annual income of more than 24 percent of all households," the Economic Policy Institute (EPI) said in a report released April 13. "When dealing with amounts of this magnitude, for services, which for the most part, are nondiscretionary and essential to well-being, how the costs are distributed among families and individuals is of major importance," the report said.

The three authors of the report, EPI economists Edith Rasell, Jared Bernstein, and Kainan Tang, looked at recently released government data on the three categories of health expenditures in 1987—insurance premiums, out-of-pocket costs, and programs financed through the tax system, such as Medicare, Medicaid, and the public health service. They found that premiums and out-of-pocket costs were regressively distributed; that is, low- and middle-income families paid a greater share of their income on these items than did high-income families.

Out-of-Pocket Spending and the Poor

Low-income families (those with annual income under $10,955) paid, on average, 8.5 percent of their income on out-of-pocket purchases of health care cost, including deductibles on insurance, all forms of cost-sharing such as co-payments, and services not covered by insurance such *as prescription drugs. In comparison, those with the highest income, (annual income above $92,912) spent 1 percent of their income on such purchases. Out-of-pocket costs were even more of a burden for people aged sixty-five and older. Forty-one percent of all spending on health care for this category was out of pocket, compared with just 21 percent in out-of-pocket spending for nonelderly families. Low-income elderly families paid nearly 13 percent of their income for out-of-pocket health care expenses, compared with 6 percent for nonelderly families.*

Although few of the poor bought private health insurance, those that did spent an average of 7.9 percent on premiums, compared with the highest-income families, who spent 2 percent of their income on premiums. According to the report, 55 percent of all health spending in 1987 went for premiums and out-of-pocket costs.

Public health programs were, for the most part, progressive, in that higher-income families paid a greater share of their income for these programs than did low-income families. Low-income families paid 4.1 percent of their income on programs financed through the tax system, while the highest-income families paid an average of 7.3 percent of their income.

"The regressive distribution of health care spending is of particular concern since families cannot escape consumption of health care," the three economists wrote. The cost distribution can have two adverse consequences. "First, the more regressive the cost distribution, the greater is the possibility that health care expenditures will leave low-income families with too little income for other necessities. Second, to the extent that the costs of the system prevent low-income persons from receiving the level of health care they require, society as a whole becomes worse off."

Improving the Equity of the System

Acknowledging that for the foreseeable future, health care would continue to be funded through out-of-pocket spending, insurance premiums, and the tax system, the authors of the report argued that equity could be improved by making the distribution within each funding source more progressive. Equity also could be improved by relying less on out-of-pocket spending and premiums and by increasing the amount of health care that is financed through the least regressive taxes.

The Clinton administration's proposal, formally introduced in Congress on October 27, would provide health insurance coverage for all Americans. That coverage would be financed through a combination of new revenues and savings in existing programs such as Medicare and Medicaid. Employers would be required to pay for 80 percent of their employees' health insurance premiums, and employees would pay the balance. Under that provision low-income workers would still pay a larger proportion of their income for health insurance than would high-income workers. But the president also proposed that the government provide subsidies to low-income workers, which could make the system less regressive. (Clinton Health Care Reform Package, p. 781)

The EPI is a nonprofit, nonpartisan think tank founded in 1986. Funding for the study was provided by the Henry J. Kaiser Family foundation, the Robert Wood Johnson Foundation, and the David and Lucile Packard Foundation Center for the Future of Children.

Following are excerpts from "The Impact of Health Care Financing on Family Budgets," a report issued by the Economic Policy Institute, April 13, 1993, on the varying effects of health care costs on family budgets:

Introduction

The problem of high expenditures for health care is well known. In 1992, 14 percent of national income, a total of $840 billion, was used to purchase medical care. What is not well known is who bears the burden of these high expenditures. A quick look at the statistics shows that federal and state governments, businesses, and insurance companies are major funding sources. However these are just intermediate sources of funds. Ultimately, individuals and families pay all health care costs through some combination of three financing streams: out-of-pocket spending; insurance premiums; or federal, state, and local government taxes. Even insurance premiums paid by employers are, for the most part, offset by reductions in wages and salaries. Thus, high expenditures for health care, while causing problems for business and government, ultimately are borne by and have their greatest impact on the budgets of families and individuals.

The $752 billion spent on health care in 1991 was the equivalent of approximately $7,860 for each of the 96 million households in the country, or over half the annual income of more than 24 percent of all households (U.S. Bureau of the Census 1992). When dealing with amounts of this magnitude, for services which, for the most part, are nondiscretionary and essential to well-being, how the costs are distributed among families and individuals is of major importance. This information is particularly relevant for policymakers at a time when major changes in health care financing are under consideration.

Using data from the 1987 National Medical Expenditure Survey, the "gold standard" for health expenditure information, and statistics from the Consumer Expenditure Survey and the Internal Revenue Service's Individual Tax Model, this study examines the distribution of health care spending among families by income level. We find that health expenditures—including out-of-pocket spending, premium purchases, and the share of taxes which ultimately purchase health care—are regressively distributed. In addition, these three financing streams have quite different distributional consequences. More progressive health care financing requires a shift toward increased reliance on taxes and a reduction in the share of expenditures financed through out-of-pocket spending and premiums. In particular, we find:

- Low-income families pay over twice the share of income for health care as do high-income families;
- Out-of-pocket spending is particularly regressive with low-income families' expenditures, as a share of income, nearly nine times the level of those of high-income families;
- As a share of income, expenditures for premiums by low-income families are nearly four times the level of high-income families, even though many of the poor do not purchase health insurance;
- If everyone purchased health insurance, premium costs as a share of income for low-income families would be five times the level for high-income families;
- Tax-financed health care spending is the only portion of the health care financing system which is progressive, and even some components of tax financing are regressive; and,
- Compared to the nonelderly, the elderly pay a larger share of income for health care and face a more regressive distribution of spending.

The regressive distribution of health care spending is of particular concern since families cannot escape consumption of health care. Therefore, they are subject to the regressivity of the system which potentially can lead to two adverse outcomes. First, the more regressive the cost distribution, the greater is the possibility that health care expenditures will leave low-income families with too little income for other necessities. Second, to the extent that the costs of the system prevent low-income persons from receiving the level of health care they require, society as a whole becomes worse off. There can be negative effects from cost-induced underconsumption of health care.

This study is the first part of a larger project which will examine the distributional effects of various health-financing reform proposals. This first stage estimates and analyzes the distribution of health care spending by families in 1987. Although describing conditions that existed six years ago, the analysis is important because it is based on the 1987 National Medical Expenditure Survey (NMES). The data from this survey are only now being released. NMES is by far the best source of information on family health expenditures, and for this reason we have chosen to report the distribution of spending for 1987....

This study focuses on families' spending for health care, not the level of benefits received from the expenditure. For nearly every family, benefits and spending diverge because of the tax financing of and the subsidies provided to health care. The purpose of this analysis is to determine the existing distribution of health costs against which proposed changes in financing can be measured.

Data and Methodology

We examine health care spending by single and multiple person families. To determine the distribution of spending across society, all families are assigned to one of ten groups (deciles) of equal size, with the one-tenth of families with the highest incomes in the first group, the one-tenth of families with the next highest incomes in the second group, and so on to the tenth group which contains the one-tenth of families with the lowest incomes. Incomes in the highest decile vary widely, from a "low" of $72,153 to a high of millions of dollars. For this reason, we separate the highest income decile into two parts: the five percent of families with the highest incomes (above $92,912) and the next highest five percent with family incomes of $72,153 to $92,912. Together, these two groups comprise the tenth decile.

This examination rests upon calculations of shares of income used to purchase health care. This measure is subject to error, particularly for the lowest income families in the tenth decile whose expenditures may exceed incomes. Placing too much reliance on data from the tenth decile may be misleading. For this reason, our determinations of distributional regressivity or progressivity will compare the ninth, not the tenth, decile with the top five percent of families. For ease of expression, we will call the families in the ninth decile "low-income families" even though families in the tenth decile have even lower incomes.

This study examines income prior to taxes, transfers, and receipt of benefits from public programs. The definition of income used throughout this report includes, in addition to money income, employer contributions to health insurance, the employer-share of payroll and unemployment insurance taxes, and corporate taxes.

The Distribution of Family Health Care Expenditures

Table 1 shows the distribution of expenditures from the three main health care funding sources: out-of-pocket spending, premiums, and taxes. Total health expenditures in dollars and as a share of income for families in each decile are shown in column 4. The table shows that the average family expenditure for health care in 1987 was $4,370, or about 15 percent of family income. However there was a wide range of spending among families at different income levels. Low-income families spent, on average, $1,756, or 20.5 percent of their income for the year. The top five percent of families spent an average of $13,234, or 10.2 percent of income. The next wealthiest five percent paid $8,754 or 10.8 percent of income. Thus, as a share of income, the burden on low-income families was two times the burden on high-income families. . . .

In comparison to the regressive burden of health care spending [is] the progressive distribution of 1992 federal taxes. . . . Families in the lowest income quintile pay on average 8.7 percent of income in taxes while families in the highest income decile average 27.5 percent. In this progres-

Table 1 Family Expenditures for Health Care, 1987 (By Family Income Decile)

Family Income Decile (Income Range)	Out of Pocket (1)		Total Premiums[1] (2)		Public Sector[2] (3)		Total Expenditures (4)	
	Dollars	Percent of Income	Dollars	Percent of Income	Dollars	Percent of Income	Dollars	Percent of Income
1a Top 5% (Above $92,912)	$1,222	1.0%	$2,362	2.0%	$9,650	7.3%	$13,234	10.2%
1b ($72,153-92,912)	1,056	1.3	2,302	2.8	5,396	6.6	8,754	10.8
2 ($52,558-72,152)	1,033	1.7	2,149	3.5	3,807	6.2	6,989	11.4
3 ($41,968-52,557)	857	1.8	2,002	4.3	2,743	5.8	5,602	12.0
4 ($33,700-41,967)	917	2.5	1,864	5.0	2,046	5.4	4,827	12.9
5 ($26,799-33,699)	768	2.6	1,590	5.3	1,547	5.1	3,905	12.9
6 ($21,098-26,798)	767	3.2	1,461	6.1	1,158	4.9	3,386	14.2
7 ($15,998-21,097)	739	4.0	1,187	6.4	828	4.4	2,755	14.9
8 ($10,956-15,997)	721	5.4	883	6.5	542	4.0	2,146	15.9
9 ($6,240-10,955)	728	8.5	680	7.9	348	4.1	1,756	20.5
10 Lowest 10% (Below $6,240)	432	11.6	314	8.6	214	6.8	960	26.9
Average, All Families	$ 814	4.2%	$1,459	5.6%	$2,097	5.4%	$4,370	15.1%
Ratio (9/1a)[3]	8.5		4.0		0.6		2.0	
Sum of Funding Type as a Percent of Total Expenditures	24%		31%		45%		100%	

Notes: [1] All premium expenditures, including Medicare, minus tax savings.
[2] Tax revenues spent on health care plus tax expenditures.
[3] The ratio of low-income families (ninth decile) to the top five percent.

sive distribution, as incomes rise and the ability to pay increases, taxes also rise as a share of income. The distribution of health care spending is just the opposite. As incomes rise, the share of income paid for health care falls.

This analysis of the cost burden ignores one of the other major problems of our current health care system—the uninsured and underinsured. Not only are financial costs high, but in addition, too many people cannot even afford to purchase the care they need. In 1987, there were 30.7 million people without any health insurance, or 14.4 percent of the population. . . . There are people at every income level who are uninsured, but the problem is particularly acute for those with low incomes. . . . In low-income families in the tenth decile, 33.9 percent of people were uninsured. Only 29.3 percent had private insurance, including 13.4 percent with employer coverage. Almost half, or 46.7 percent had Medicaid, Medicare, or other public insurance. The number of people with insurance and the percent of the insured covered by private policies rise with income until, among families with the highest incomes, 94.6 percent had private insurance. Insurance status has important implications for health expenditures.

Out-of-Pocket Spending

Table 1 also shows the expenditure distribution within each of the three health care funding sources. The major cause of the regressive distribution of total expenditures was out-of-pocket spending, shown in column 1. Out-of-pocket spending includes deductibles, all forms of cost sharing such as copayments and coinsurance, and expenditures for services not covered by insurance which might include prescription drugs or mental health care. For people without insurance or for those who are inadequately insured, out-of-pocket costs can be large, provided families have sufficient funds to purchase health care services. In addition, for those with insurance which requires cost sharing, out-of-pocket spending rises with the use of services. A seriously ill person covered by insurance with stiff cost-sharing requirements can face enormous out-of-pocket expenses. Health care expenses have become one of the leading causes of personal bankruptcy.

Column 1 in Table 1 shows that low-income families spent 8.5 percent of income, on average, on out-of-pocket health care purchases compared to 1 percent for those with the highest income. Thus, the burden on low-income families was nearly nine times the burden on high-income families. This regressive distribution existed despite the inherent limits on out-of-pocket spending by the poor due to their low incomes. Any increase in out-of-pocket spending requirements, without careful safeguards to protect the poor and the near poor, will worsen the regressivity of this distribution.

Insurance Premiums

The distribution of expenditures for insurance premiums was also very regressive in 1987. . . . Low-income families spent, on average, 4.1 percent of income, although few of the poor purchase private insurance. The highest income (top five percent) of families spent less than one percent of income on direct and employee purchases of premiums.

... Not unexpectedly, we find that for middle- and upper-income families, employer-sponsored insurance accounts for the largest share of health care spending after taxes. As a share of income, spending on employer-sponsored insurance rose from the tenth through the sixth deciles, then declined. There are two major reasons for this pattern. Many people who are poor or lower-middle class do not receive health insurance on the job, therefore as a group their expenditures of this type are low. As incomes rise, workers are more likely to receive health insurance on the job, and the policies offered are more comprehensive and thus more expensive, so average costs for the decile rise. Further, although the costs of policies vary with the comprehensiveness of the coverage, the variation in premiums between the least and most comprehensive policies is much smaller than the variation in income across society. Thus, expenditures as a share of income decline across the higher income deciles.

These data include families with and without health insurance. Thus, they understate the burden for families who do have private insurance since families without insurance (and those with Medicaid) make no premium payments. They also overstate the burden for those without insurance. Later, we show the distribution restricted to families with private insurance.

There is ongoing debate over who actually pays for premiums obtained through employers. In this study we adopt the predominant view and assume that all employer payments for premiums are completely offset by lower wages to workers. This view rests on the following logic. Since health insurance is received as a fringe benefit of employment, it is a part of the total compensation workers receive. If employers did not purchase insurance, the entire amount of money they would have spent would instead be received by workers as higher money wages. Therefore, workers—through their lower wages—are bearing the entire cost of premiums. However, others argue that the cost of health insurance is not completely offset by lower wages and that part of the cost is borne by employers, or passed on to consumers through higher prices. In the future we will consider this alternative hypothesis.

In any case, employees do receive some relief from the costs of their premiums. Health insurance received as compensation for employment is a form of income, but unlike income received as wages, federal law exempts from taxes income received in the form of health insurance coverage.

For example, consider a worker with a tax rate of 25 percent who receives $4,000 in money income. The worker would pay $1,000 in taxes and take home $3,000. If, instead of cash income, the employee received compensation in the form of a $4,000 health insurance policy, no taxes would be assessed. The worker would be exchanging $3,000 in (after-tax) income for a $4,000 health insurance policy. The health insurance is actually costing the worker just $3,000 since this is the amount of income he is giving up in exchange for the policy. This $1,000 difference is a tax savings to the worker, essentially a federal subsidy to facilitate the purchase of health insurance. But the $1,000 not paid in taxes by the worker is a tax expenditure that requires all taxpayers to pay more taxes as an offset. In addition to favorable income tax treatment, health insurance is also exempt from payroll taxes—a further increase in both tax savings to workers and tax expenditures.

All workers who receive health insurance as part of their compensation receive a tax savings, and the size of this subsidy rises with the cost of the insurance and with the worker's marginal tax rate. Thus, tax savings disproportionately accrue to those with higher incomes, higher marginal tax rates, and more expensive insurance. The higher taxes which result from the tax expenditure are distributed among all tax payers in proportion to their federal tax burden, with those with higher incomes paying a greater share. . . .

The tax savings received by families who obtain health insurance on the job . . . also [favor] higher income families. Families with the lowest incomes received essentially no subsidy, while those with the highest income received a subsidy that is greater than $1,000, although this constituted only about one percent of their income.

The net cost of employer-paid health insurance is . . . the difference between what employers (actually workers) paid for health insurance minus the workers' tax savings. For the reasons mentioned, the distribution of the net cost was more regressive than was the distribution of all employer expenditures. In 1987, employers spent approximately $130 billion for health insurance, or about 27 percent of the national health care total. . . . (This does not include the employer share of health insurance payroll taxes, workers compensation, or health services provided at the workplace. These amounted to another $37 billion or 8 percent of national health spending.) However, the tax savings received by workers were approximately $40 billion, or eight percent of total spending. Thus the share of national health care expenditures paid for by employers through health insurance premiums, net of the tax expenditure, was 19 percent of the national total. The share of total health spending financed through the public sector was about 45 percent when tax expenditures are included.

The two parts of the Medicare program have separate funding sources. The first and larger component, absorbing slightly more than 60 percent of all Medicare dollars, is hospital insurance and is funded primarily through the payroll tax. . . . The second part of the Medicare program (Part B) pays for doctors' and outpatient services. This is funded through premiums paid by the elderly and the disabled, through required deductibles and coinsurance paid by enrollees, and through general federal revenues. In 1987, premiums accounted for slightly less than one-quarter of Part B program costs. . . .

The distribution of Medicare premiums [was] somewhat regressive, but [costs] were a small share of income, even for families with the lowest incomes. However, if the Part B program were completely funded through premiums, this would raise the level of premium expenditures by a factor of approximately four, exacerbating the regressivity of the distribution.

Total spending on premiums ... includes spending for premiums for individual nongroup policies and Medicare as well as employer and employee spending, net of tax savings. The distribution was regressive with low-income families spending a share of income approximately four times that of high-income families.

Premiums for Nonelderly Families with Private Insurance

... [M]ost health reforms propose to cover everyone with premium-financed insurance purchased either through the workplace (by employers and employees) or through a public plan.... Low-income families spent 9.4 percent of income on premiums, while those with high incomes spent just 1.9 percent, about one-fifth as much.

Requiring all families (or their employers) to purchase health insurance premiums locks in place a regressive distribution of health care funding unless large subsidies are available to low-income families (which some reforms do include). The regressive distribution occurs because premium costs for low-income families are not very different than those for families with high incomes. So, as a share of income, there is a much greater burden on families in the lower deciles. As long as the variation in premium costs among families is less than the variation in income, the distribution of premiums will be regressive.

The Public Sector and Health Care Spending

In 1987, approximately 45 percent of all health care spending flowed through the tax systems of federal, state, and local governments. Tax dollars pay for most of Medicare and Medicaid; public health programs; research and construction; health care for veterans, military personnel and their dependents; and special services such as maternal and child health programs. This money is raised through all the ways in which taxes are collected, including personal and corporate income taxes at the federal and state levels, sales and excise taxes, and others. To fully calculate the health cost burden on families, this study includes health care purchased through the tax system. After estimating the various tax liabilities of families, those portions of their taxes which go to purchase health care are calculated and the distribution of these costs is determined.

Most of the money spent by governments for health care is raised as part of their general revenues. The major exception is the payroll tax earmarked for Medicare....

The total distribution was progressive, with low-income families paying 4.1 percent of income while the highest income families averaged 7.3 percent. For the most part, this parallels the distribution of the national tax burden. Tax-financed spending is the only component of the health-financing system that is progressive.

Federal Income Taxes

In 1987, personal and corporate federal income taxes provided 56 percent of total federal revenues. Both of these taxes are progressively distributed with the wealthy paying a larger share of income than the poor. . . . Health care spending through federal taxes is also progressively distributed. . . . In 1987, low-income families paid 0.6 percent of income while the highest income families paid 3.2 percent of income.

Federal Tax Expenditures

As mentioned above, federal law exempts employer-paid health insurance from income and payroll taxes. This means that recipients of employer-sponsored insurance receive subsidies to help purchase their insurance. However, to offset these tax expenditures, additional taxes must be raised. . . . Like federal income taxes, the distribution of tax expenditures was progressive. However, . . . both the lowest and the highest income families paid more in additional taxes than they received in tax savings. For the five percent of families with the highest incomes, net taxes equaled $1,368 or nearly one percent of income. However, low-income families also had a net tax liability that averaged $16 or 0.2 percent of income. Over the broad middle range of the income distribution, (deciles 2 through 8), on average families had a net savings.

In addition to being a burden on the lowest income families, the tax exclusion is troublesome for another reason. . . . [S]ince all taxpayers bore the added taxes, the tax savings went to families with employer-sponsored health insurance only, within each decile there was a transfer from taxpayer families without employer-sponsored insurance to those that did have this benefit. If a family that did not receive health insurance through an employer purchased a nongroup policy, it would not receive the tax savings. The subsidy for employer-sponsored health insurance is paid by taxpayers without such insurance, whatever their income level, and by the highest and lowest income families.

The tax exclusion for employer payments for health insurance enables families at all income levels to afford health insurance. But, it provides no help to families who do not receive employer-sponsored insurance, while increasing their taxes. However, eliminating the tax exclusion is not the answer. We need increased tax financing of health care and health insurance, not less. But, we must distribute the tax benefits and the tax burdens more equitably.

State and Local Taxes

State and local revenues for health care are raised primarily through income and sales taxes. . . . Because states raise more revenue through regressive sales and excise taxes than through progressive income taxes, low-income families paid a larger share of income in state taxes than did families with high incomes, although the differences were not great.

Payroll Taxes

The hospital component of the Medicare program is funded through two sources. The elderly pay deductibles and coinsurance when they receive Medicare services. These expenditures are included in out-of-pocket costs as shown in Table 1. The majority of funding, however, comes from the health insurance portion of the payroll tax. In addition, a portion of the social security component of the payroll tax buys health care.... Both low- and high-income families paid an average of about one percent of income for health care through the payroll tax. The share of income paid rose from the bottom through the middle of the income distribution, then declined. Overall, the incidence in 1987 was fairly flat.

Payroll tax liabilities are driven by two factors. First, the tax falls only on labor money income (wages and salaries) and not on other types of income such as dividends, interest, fringe benefits, or rents. Therefore, as the share of income received from nonlabor sources rises, as is the case as we move up the income ladder, a smaller and smaller share of total income is subject to the tax. Thus, payroll tax liabilities as a share of income will decline. Second, the amount of labor income subject to the tax is capped, further contributing to regressivity. In 1987, earnings above $43,800 were not subject to the payroll tax. However, since 1987, the cap has been raised and in 1992 stood at $130,200 for the health insurance portion and at $55,500 for the social security component of the payroll tax. This further flattens the distribution and makes it more progressive.

The Distribution of Spending Among Funding Sources

Thus far, the discussion has focused on the distribution of spending among family income deciles within each of the three types of health care funding: out-of-pocket, premiums, and taxes. But the distribution of total health care spending depends upon two factors. One is the distribution across deciles within any single funding source. But since each type of funding has a different incidence, the second factor is the funding mix, an equally important determinant of the final expenditure distribution. For example, if out-of-pocket spending were reduced by $20 billion and replaced by an equivalent increase in public funding, and if the incidence within these funding sources were maintained, then regressivity would be reduced.

In 1987, approximately 24 percent of all health care was financed through out-of-pocket spending.... Another 31 percent was paid for through premiums, including payments by individuals for nongroup policies, and employee and employer contributions to employer-sponsored insurance minus tax savings. This total also includes the $23 billion in premiums paid by federal, state, and local governments in their role as employer and $6 billion in Medicare Part B premiums. Forty-five percent of health care ($207 billion) was purchased through the public sector. If Medicare and public employee premiums are added to this total, the public sector paid for 51 percent of health care in 1987. An additional $14 billion was raised through nonpatient revenues such as donations.

The ratio showing the regressivity or progressivity of each type of spending is also shown in Table 1. The regressivity of the total expenditure distribution would be lessened by either reducing out-of-pocket expenditures, with a low-income to high income family incidence ratio of 8.6, or by reducing reliance on premiums, which have an incidence ratio of 4.

Expenditures of Elderly and Nonelderly Families

There are major differences in the funding of health care for people under and over age 65. Nearly everyone age 65 and above has Medicare coverage; there are few uninsured in this age group. As we have seen, the costs of Medicare are spread among all adults, not just the elderly. However, seniors do pay deductibles and coinsurance when they use services, and most also purchase supplemental Medicare insurance which covers doctors and outpatient services. In addition, many seniors purchase private "Medigap" insurance policies to cover some of their cost-sharing obligations and additional services.

The spending requirements for people under 65 years old are very different. Most receive insurance coverage through their employer. Some policies provide first dollar coverage that requires no contribution from the patient, while others have large cost-sharing requirements. Some cover a broad package of benefits, while people with more limited policies may have to pay for some services entirely out of pocket. People without insurance (numbering nearly 31 million in 1987) must forego care, pay out of pocket, or receive charity care.

These differences in insurance, cost sharing, and access to care have large effects on the distribution of costs among the elderly and the nonelderly. In addition, seniors use more medical services than do the under-65. However, many of these costs are covered by taxes paid by the elderly and nonelderly alike.

... In 1987, the average elderly family paid $3,707 for health care while the average nonelderly family paid $4,529. But because incomes of the elderly were generally lower than those of the nonelderly, seniors, on average, paid a larger share of income for health care than did the under 65, 20.5 percent compared to 13.8 percent, respectively.

The distribution of the burden across the income spectrum is worse for the elderly than for the nonelderly. Low-income elderly families paid 27.4 percent of their income for health care, a share which was nearly three times the 9.7 percent paid by high-income families. Among the nonelderly, low-income families paid 16.1 percent of income, while the highest income families paid slightly more than 10 percent. Compared to the nonelderly, seniors paid a larger share of income for health care and faced a more regressive distribution of the costs. Seniors paid much more out of pocket than did the nonelderly. The average elderly family's out-of-pocket expenditure was $1,239, compared to $712 for the nonelderly. Elderly low-income families made out-of-pocket expenditures which, as a share of income, were over eight times those made by high-income elderly. The ratio for the nonelderly was 6.6. Seniors also faced a more regressive distribution of premium costs. While the elderly paid, on average, slightly less through premiums than the nonelderly, $1,407 compared to $1,471, the distribution of premium costs was more regressive for the elderly.

... Nonelderly families made 49 percent of their health care purchases through the public sector. Premiums accounted for 31 percent, and just 21 percent of health care was purchased out of pocket. The picture for elderly families is quite different. Their lower incomes and lower consumption levels meant lower taxes. Just 25 percent of expenditures by the elderly occurred through the public sector. Premiums accounted for 34 percent, similar to the nonelderly. But fully 41 percent of spending was done out of pocket, and out-of-pocket spending for the elderly was even more regressive than for the nonelderly.

Conclusion

The U.S. spends a huge sum of money for health care, all of it ultimately paid by families. Costs are high, and the distribution of this spending is very regressive. In 1987, low-income families spent over 20 percent of income for health care, while families with the highest incomes paid about 10 percent. Low-income families paid over twice the share of income for health care as did high-income families.

Out-of-pocket spending was the most regressive type of financing with low-income families paying a share of income which was over eight times the share paid by those with high incomes. This occurred even though spending by the poor was limited by their low incomes. Premium expenditures were also regressively distributed with low-income families paying a share of income nearly four times the level paid by high-income families. But this picture was complicated by the uninsured, who spent nothing on premiums, thereby making the distribution less regressive than it would have been if everyone had insurance. Among only those families that did have insurance, the share of income spent on premiums by the poor was nearly five times the share paid by the wealthy.

Overall, health care spending financed through taxes is progressive. However, taxes at the state level are regressive, since the states raise more revenue through regressive sales and excise taxes than through more progressive income taxes. At the federal level, income taxes are progressive. The incidence of payroll taxes in 1987 was nearly flat.

As a share of income, health costs for the elderly were higher than for the nonelderly. Seniors also faced a more regressive distribution of spending. In large part this was due to large, out-of-pocket expenditures which accounted for 41 percent of all health care spending by the elderly, compared to 21 percent for the nonelderly.

There are many possible goals of health care financing. This analysis has focused on equity. Some would argue that other goals such as cost containment or severing the link with employment should also receive high priority. For the foreseeable future, health care will continue to be funded through all of the sources examined here: out-of-pocket spending, premiums, and taxes. Within this mix of financing, there must be balance between competing goals. However, we argue that equity in health care financing has been a neglected consideration. In the current evaluations of health-financing proposals, concern with equity should be central.

Equity can be improved by making the distribution within each funding source less regressive. There are numerous policies which could begin to move us in this direction. Some possibilities include lower limits on cost-sharing obligations, or subsidies for all premium purchases, not just those by employers. Equity can also be enhanced by changing the mix of funding—by reducing out-of-pocket spending and premiums, and by raising the portion of health care financed through the least regressive taxes.

In this paper, we have quantified what is all too well known by Americans struggling to pay for health care. The current financing system is highly regressive, and this is particularly true for out-of-pocket spending and premiums, which together account for 55 percent of all health care expenditures. As potential solutions to the health care crisis are considered, improving equity in the distribution of health care spending should be an important goal.

DOMESTIC VIOLENCE STUDY

April 19, 1993

Fourteen percent of American women say their husbands or boyfriends have beaten them, according to a study released by the San Francisco-based Family Violence Prevention Fund. It is not known how this rate compares to past rates because no similar studies have been conducted.

The study was released at a hearing of the House Subcommittee on Health and the Environment, which was considering a proposal by President Bill Clinton to give the federal Centers for Disease Control $10 million for a national domestic violence prevention program. It was based on a national survey of 1,900 people conducted by EDK Associates, a New York public opinion research firm.

Domestic violence is "a staggering social problem that affects every sector of American life," said Esta Soler, executive director of the Family Violence Prevention Fund, in testimony before the subcommittee. The FBI estimates that every fifteen seconds a woman is beaten by her husband or boyfriend, Soler said. In addition, one of every three women seeking emergency medical treatment does so because of a domestic assault. "More women are seriously injured by beatings than by car accidents, muggings, and rape combined," Soler said. "Domestic violence fills emergency rooms and morgues, contributes to juvenile delinquency, and destroys families, yet the issue is virtually absent from public discourse."

Thirty-four percent of those surveyed said they had witnessed domestic violence. By comparison, 19 percent said they had witnessed a robbery or mugging. Seven percent of the men and women said they had seen their mother or stepmother being assaulted.

Nearly 90 percent of those surveyed agreed that domestic violence is a serious problem, and 81 percent said something should be done to stop it. Yet few knew how to do so. Asked what could be done to stop abuse, respondents gave the following answers: "do not know" (26 percent);

"more counseling" (22 percent); "teach kids in school" (15 percent); "stronger laws" (9 percent); "women should become less emotionally and economically dependent on men" (7 percent); "change society" (6 percent); "more arrests" (5 percent); and "reduce violence in media/change TV" (4 percent).

A Pattern of Violence

The vast majority of both men and women believed that some people become violent because when they were children, they were beaten or witnessed violence in their homes. This perception matches findings of researchers, said Dr. Mark Rosenberg, a psychiatrist and senior official at the National Center for Injury Prevention and Control, which is part of the federal Centers for Disease Control. "Boys who witness violence in the home have an increased chance of growing up to be perpetrators of violence when they create their own family," he said in an interview with the Associated Press, "and girls who witness repeated violence in the home have an increased likelihood of growing up and becoming victims of their spouse."

With the study's release, the Family Violence Prevention Fund launched a multi-year national public education and media campaign. Using the theme "There's no excuse for domestic violence," the campaign was designed to reduce the incidence of domestic violence by reshaping public attitudes about battering. "Like with drunk driving," Soler said, "it is time for the American public and our nation's leaders to recognize that domestic violence has become a public health crisis, and that it can no longer be approached as a private matter."

Increased Awareness of Domestic Violence

The study was released amid growing attention to domestic violence at both the national and state levels. At the 1992 Democratic National Convention, presidential nominee Bill Clinton spoke about having an abusive stepfather. During her confirmation hearings to become secretary of Health and Human Services, Donna Shalala said preventing domestic violence was one of her priorities. Attorney General Janet Reno established a strong record of prosecuting perpetrators of domestic violence while she was a prosecutor in Florida.

At the state level, the Massachusetts legislature passed an anti-stalking bill as Gov. William F. Weld declared a "crisis of wife-battering." The bill established a minimum one-year jail term for anyone convicted of threatening or following a partner in violation of a restraining order. It also created a statewide computer network to help judges and police track restraining orders. In March, Gov. Lawton Chiles of Florida commuted the thirty-year prison sentence of a woman who killed her husband after he repeatedly assaulted her. The woman became the first released from prison under a new state program that reviews cases of women who kill or injure people who have abused them. More than two dozen other states were creating similar programs, according to the Family Violence Prevention Fund.

The fund's domestic violence study also reinforced other reports that documented widespread violence against American women. In 1992 the National Women's Study found that one of every eight women had been raped at least once. It said that 683,000 American women were raped in 1990, a figure five times higher than the Justice Department's National Crime Survey estimate of 130,000 attempted and completed rapes. (Report on Rape in America, Historic Documents of 1992, p. 385)

Following are excerpts from "Men Beating Women: Ending Domestic Violence," a report released April 19, 1993, by the Family Violence Prevention Fund:

Domestic violence is a staggering social problem with far-reaching consequences in every sector of American life. The Federal Bureau of Investigation estimates that every 15 seconds a woman is beaten by her husband or boyfriend. More women are injured or killed by being beaten than in car accidents, muggings and rapes combined. Juvenile delinquents are four times more likely to come from homes in which their fathers beat their mothers.

In the course of the past two decades the movement to end domestic violence has succeeded in raising public consciousness about male violence toward women. The movement has exposed the violence and made it clear that women don't ask for it. However, domestic violence incidents are still seen as isolated events. The blame is placed on the failures of individual men. To some extent it is still a "private problem."

The Family Violence Prevention Fund has launched the "There's No Excuse" National Domestic Violence Media Campaign to significantly reduce the incidence of violence against women in intimate relationships and to promote women's right to safety in the home by changing the attitudes of the American public and increasing their involvement in the issue.

Before launching this campaign, The Family Violence Prevention Fund set out to answer a variety of questions to help determine the current shape of public understanding of domestic violence. The objectives of the research were to assess how receptive or resistant people are to talking about domestic violence, to determine how much they already know and the perceived seriousness of the problem and to determine what people are willing to do to help end violence against women....

Violence as Part of Everyday Life

Our personal lives are not free from violence or fear of physical harm from the people we love. Americans acknowledge a pervasive amount of violence in private relationships.

Getting people to talk about domestic violence was seen as a major obstacle to conducting both the focus groups and survey research. Experts believed that people would refuse to open up in the groups or stay on the phone once they understood the topic.

We were wrong. One of the most striking findings of this research is that Americans across all race and ethnic backgrounds are both ready and willing to discuss this issue. People in the focus groups and on the phone discussed domestic violence as a real problem that they have seen in their own lives. And they want it to end.

We Hurt the Ones We Love

Shoving, pushing and throwing objects are not a rare occurrence when a man and a woman have a fight, according to this research. The public is not willing to draw a line where women are always good and men are always bad. When it comes to fighting, both men and women shove, push and throw objects during the course of an argument. But, as the level of physical violence escalates, both men and women acknowledge that men harm women more than women harm men. One in two women believes that battering is not an uncommon experience in women's relationships with men.

When it comes to physical blows: men beat women. And men *do* beat women—44% of Americans report that when a man and a woman have a fight he could wind up hitting her. Some people say he does it often (19%), but more likely it happens sometimes (25%). Given the extreme nature of this behavior, the noteworthy point is that less than half say it rarely happens (43%).

Men also physically restrain or push women. Six out of 10 Americans believe that when a man and a woman have a fight there is a good chance he will grab and shove her to make his point (57%—24% often and 33% sometimes). A woman is less likely to get this physical with him (40%—11% often and 29% sometimes). This is not to say that women never express rage or anger. She is more likely to throw something at him (55%—26% often and 29% sometimes) than he is at her (39%—13% often and 26% sometimes).

Moreover, abusive behavior isn't only physical. Men and women are often nasty to one another. Almost half say that he often says nasty things to hurt her (48% say often and only 11% say this rarely happens). She also says nasty things to hurt him (44% say often and 13% say rarely).

It Happens to Us

Public recognition of the seriousness of domestic abuse reflects the violence people acknowledge in their own lives. The majority of Americans have witnessed potentially violent circumstances (57%). *More people have directly witnessed an incidence of domestic violence (34%) than muggings and robberies combined (19%).*

One out of three American men and women have stared domestic violence in the face. Fourteen (14%) percent of American women acknowledge having been violently abused by a husband or boyfriend. Almost half of these are women who acknowledge having been abused. While domestic violence is not completely limited to men beating women—two out of 10 men report having witnessed a woman beating up on her husband or boyfriend—most Americans identify the case of men beating women as a very serious problem.

The survey results corroborate the surprising prevalence of experience with domestic violence found in the focus groups. Given that the people attending these groups were not selected on the basis of their exposure to incidents of violence nor were they told that the subject matter was domestic violence, the number of people who volunteered personal stories was quite striking. . . .

CLINTON ON DEADLY ATTACK ON ARMED CULT COMPOUND

April 20, 1993

For fifty-one suspenseful days an armed commune of religious cultists defied all U.S. government attempts to coax or force them safely out of their fortified compound near Waco, Texas. Their defiance began and ended in tragedy, starting with a raid on the compound February 28 by federal agents in a futile attempt to arrest cult leader David Koresh for illegal possession of firearms and explosives. The raid turned into a shootout in which four agents and at least two cult members died. Koresh asserted that six of his members, including a two-year-old child, had been killed and that he suffered wounds. Whatever the actual toll, the outcome of the botched mission was a long standoff. It ended April 19 in a raging fire that swept the compound, leaving behind the charred remains of seventy-two of its inhabitants. The fire broke out as FBI agents in armored combat vehicles crashed the compound walls and pumped tear gas inside. But authorities at the scene and investigative reports said that the defenders, not the attackers, set the fires—in what they said was an apparent mass suicide pact. The use of tear gas had been intended to flush out the barricaded defenders and force them into the open for easy capture without further bloodshed.

Miscalculation by government officials marked both the beginning and end of the confrontation with this band of zealots who claimed divine guidance and apparently chose death over surrender. In the aftermath came questions directed at decision making on the scene and in Washington, including the roles of Attorney General Janet Reno and President Bill Clinton, who felt compelled to hold a televised news conference April 20 to defend himself, Reno, and the FBI. The questions provoked congressional and internal inquiries by the FBI and the the U.S. Bureau of Alcohol, Tobacco and Firearms (ATF), which staged the February 28 raid. (ATF and FBI reports, p. 819)

The first fatal surprise was sprung in the February 28 raid. Apparently forewarned, gunmen in the compound ambushed and repelled the raiding party. It retreated, negotiated a cease-fire to recover the four slain agents, called in reinforcements, and took up positions encircling the compound. The FBI was put in charge of federal operations the next day and began round-the-clock negotiations with Koresh by telephone.

Koresh at times seemed conciliatory and at other times said he wanted to die a martyr. One one occasion he promised to surrender if Texas radio stations would broadcast a rambling fifty-eight-minute sermon he had recorded. He did not keep his end of the bargain. Bob Ricks, the senior FBI agent at the scene, said he learned that Koresh planned to strap grenades to his body and explode them as he appeared before television cameras to surrender. But Koresh never ventured out of the compound. As the siege wore on, he repeatedly scorned all outside pleas.

Koresh's Absolute Control

The cult had settled near Waco in the early 1980s and gradually developed an enclosed cluster of buildings they called Camp Carmel (later Ranch Apocalypse). All called themselves Branch Davidians, taking the name of a sect that had split from the Seventh-Day Adventist church in the 1930s. Although expelled from the church, Koresh continued to recruit from its membership both in the United States and abroad.

Revered as a messiah by his followers, Koresh appeared to exert total control over their lives—even holding the allegiance of men whose wives he took as his own. He asserted sexual rights to all women in his flock, as based on his interpretation of scripture. Twenty-one children, together with twelve adults, were permitted to leave during the long siege. Bruce D. Perry, a psychiatrist whose medical team interviewed nineteen of them, described the world they inhabited as a "misguided paramilitary community." Children were disciplined severely, according to a report the team issued May 3, and they feared Koresh as an all-powerful father, but many felt affection for him. Dr. Perry said some of the girls had lesions on their buttocks, indicating that they had been beaten, but at a news conference the following day he stopped short of corroborating statements by Clinton and Reno that the children had been abused physically and sexually. He said none of the children he examined had been sexually molested.

Members of the community lived almost entirely among themselves, and few ventured far from their seventy-seven-acre farm. When they did, according to police authorities, it was often to engage in a profitable trade in illegal weapons; some automatic weapons barred from the U.S. market were assembled at the compound from imported parts for undercover sales.

Nine people escaped the April 21 inferno by fleeing the burning compound. The others remained behind to face certain death—whether of their own choice or from coercion. Autopsies revealed that about two dozen of the victims, including Koresh, had suffered gunshot wounds. But it could not be determined if they had shot themselves and others to avoid the pain of immolation, or in derangement, or possibly to to prevent last-minute doubters from fleeing.

Clinton Defends Attack

In his April 20 news conference, President Clinton defended the attack on the Waco compound, although it ended in "a horrible human tragedy." He said Reno informed him of the plan, and, after asking some questions, "I told the attorney general to do what she thought was right, and I stand by that decision." In that sense, Clinton said he accepted responsibility for the decision to attack.

He made clear, however, that he blamed the disastrous outcome on Koresh, whom he called "irrational, dangerous, and probably insane." The president said the FBI had made "every reasonable effort to bring this perilous situation to an end without bloodshed" and further delay would likely increase the danger to those in the compound. He specifically said that children still there were being abused and forced to live in unsanitary and unsafe conditions.

Reno in the Spotlight

The president said he was "bewildered" that his silence the previous day was interpreted in the press as an attempt to let Reno take the heat. The attorney general had then told news reporters, "I made the decision [to attack]. I'm accountable. The buck stops here." Appearing that night on the "Larry King Live" program on Cable News Network, she said the assault "was based on what we knew then.... Obviously, if I thought the chances were great of a mass suicide, I would never have approved the plan."

In day-long testimony before the House Judiciary Committee April 28, Reno strongly defended the government's actions. Saying he would not try to "rationalize the deaths of two dozen children," Rep. John Conyers, Jr., D-Mich., told Reno she did the right thing by offering to resign—which Clinton refused. She angrily responded: "I feel more strongly about [the death of the children] than you will ever know. But I am not going to walk away from a compound where ATF agents had been killed."

An ABC News poll made public April 21 indicated that the public strongly supported the attack. Some 72 percent said it was the right thing to do; 95 percent blamed Koresh for the outcome; and 78 percent believed it was inevitable that the standoff would have resulted in violence.

> *Following are excerpts from a news conference in the White House Rose Garden, April 20, in which President Bill Clinton discussed the fire that killed scores of Branch Davidian religious cultists as their compound came under an FBI-directed tear-gas attack:*

PRESIDENT CLINTON: ... On February the 28th, four federal agents were killed in the line of duty trying to enforce the law against the Branch Davidian compound, which had illegally stockpiled weaponry and ammunition and placed innocent children at risk. Because the BATF [Bureau of Alcohol, Tobacco and Firearms] operation had failed to meet its objective, a 51-day standoff ensued. The Federal Bureau of Investigation then made every reasonable effort to bring this perilous situation to an end without bloodshed and further loss of life.

The bureau's efforts were ultimately unavailing because the individual with whom they were dealing, David Koresh, was dangerous, irrational and probably insane. He engaged in numerous activities which violated both federal law and common standards of decency. He was, moreover, responsible for the deaths and injuries which occurred during the action against the compound in February. Given his inclination toward violence, and in an effort to protect his young hostages, no provocative actions were taken for more than seven weeks by federal agents against the compound.

This weekend, I was briefed by Attorney General [Janet] Reno on an operation prepared by the FBI designed to increase pressure on Koresh and persuade those in the compound to surrender peacefully.

The plan included a decision to withhold the use of ammunition, even in the face of fire, and instead to use tear gas that would not cause permanent harm to health, but would, it was hoped, force the people in the compound to come outside and to surrender.

I was informed of the plan to end the siege. I discussed it with Attorney General Reno. I asked the questions I thought it was appropriate for me to ask. I then told her to do what she thought was right, and I take full responsibility for the implementation of the decision.

Yesterday's action ended in a horrible human tragedy. Mr. Koresh's response to the demands for his surrender by federal agents was to destroy himself and murder the children who were his captives as well as all the other people who were there who did not survive.

He killed those he controlled, and he bears ultimate responsibility for the carnage that ensued.

Now we must review the past with an eye toward the future. I have directed the United States departments of Justice and Treasury to undertake a vigorous and thorough investigation to uncover what happened and why, and whether anything could have been done differently.

I have told the departments to involve independent professional law enforcement officials in the investigation.

I expect to receive analysis and answers in whatever time is required to complete the review.

Finally, I have directed the departments to cooperate fully with all congressional inquiries so that we can continue to be fully accountable to the American people.

I want to express my appreciation to the attorney general, to the Justice Department, and to the federal agents on the front lines who did the best job they could under deeply difficult circumstances.

Again, I want to say as I did on yesterday: I am very sorry for the loss of life which occurred at the beginning and at the end of this tragedy in Waco. I hope very much that others who will be tempted to join cults and become involved with people like David Koresh will be deterred by the horrible scenes they have seen over the last seven weeks, and I hope very much that the difficult situations which federal agents confronted there, and which they will be doubtless required to confront in other contexts in the future will be somewhat better handled and better understood because of what has been learned now. . . .

[Call From Reno]

Q: Could you describe what Janet Reno told you in your 15-minute conversation you had with her on Sunday . . . about the nature of the operation and how much detail you knew about it?

P: I was told by the attorney general that the FBI strongly felt that the time had come to take another step in trying to dislodge the people in the compound. And she described generally what the operation would be, that they wanted to go in and use tear gas which had been tested, not to cause permanent damage to adults or to children, but which would make it very difficult for people to stay inside the building.

And it was hoped that the tear gas would permit them to come outside.

I was further told that under no circumstances would our people fire any shots at them even if fired upon. They were going to shoot the tear gas from armored vehicles which would protect them, and there would be no exchange of fire. In fact, as you know, an awful lot of shots were fired by the cult members at the federal officials. There were no shots coming back from the government side.

I asked a number of questions. The first question I asked is, why now? We have waited seven weeks — why now?

The reasons I was given were the following. No. 1, that there was a limit to how long the federal authorities could maintain, with their limited resources, the quality and intensity of coverage by experts there. They might be needed in other parts of the country.

No. 2, that the people who had reviewed this had never seen a case quite like this one before, and they were convinced that no progress had been made recently and no progress was going to be made through the normal means of getting Koresh and the other cult members to come out.

No. 3, that the danger of their doing something to themselves or to others was likely to increase, not decrease with the passage of time.

And No. 4, that they had reason to believe that the children who were still inside the compound were being abused significantly as well as being forced to live in unsanitary and unsafe conditions.

So for those reasons they wanted to move at that time.

The second question I asked the attorney general is whether they had given consideration to all the things that could go wrong and evaluated them against what might happen that was good. She said that the FBI personnel on the scene and those working with them were convinced that the chances of bad things happening would only increase with the passage of time.

The third question I asked was, has the military been consulted? As soon as the initial tragedy came to light in Waco, that's the first thing I asked to be done because it was obvious that this was not a typical law enforcement situation. Military people were then brought in, helped to analyze the situation and some of the problems that were presented by it.

So I asked if the military had been consulted. The attorney general said that they had and that they were in basic agreement that there was only one minor tactical difference of opinion between the FBI and the military, something that both sides thought was not of overwhelming significance.

Having asked those questions and gotten those answers, I said that if she thought it was the right thing to do that she should proceed and that I would support it, and I stand by that today.

Q: Can you address the widespread perception reported widely — television, radio and newspapers — that you were trying somehow to distance yourself from —

P: No, I'm bewildered by it. The only reason I made no public statement yesterday . . . is that I had nothing to add to what was being said and I literally did not know until rather late in the day whether anybody was still alive, other than those who had been actually seen and taken to the hospital or taken into custody. It was purely and simply a question of waiting for events to unfold.

I can't account for why people speculated one way or the other but I talked to the attorney general on the day before the action took place, I talked to her yesterday, I called her again late last night, after she appeared on the "Larry King Show", and I talked to her again this morning.

A president — it's not possible for a president to distance himself from things that happen when the federal government is in control. I will say this, however. I was frankly — surprised would be a mild word — to say that anyone that would suggest that the attorney general should resign because some religious fanatics murdered themselves.

I regret what happened. But it is not possible in this life to control the behavior of others in every circumstance. These people killed four federal officials in the line of duty. They were heavily armed. They fired on federal officials yesterday repeatedly, and they were never fired back on. We did everything we could to avoid the loss of life. They made the decision to immolate themselves — and I regret it terribly, and I feel awful about the children. But in the end, the last comment I had from Janet Reno — and I talked to her on Sunday — I said, now, I want you to tell me once more why you believe, not why they believe, why you believe we should move now rather than wait some more. And she said it's because of the children; they have evidence that those children are still being abused and that they are in increasingly unsafe conditions and that they don't think it will get any easier with time, with the passage of time — I have to take their word for that.

So that is where I think things stand.

[Support for FBI]

Q: Can we assume, then, that you don't think this was mishandled in view of the outcome, that you didn't run out of patience, and if you had it to do over again would you really decide that way?

P: I think what you can assume is just exactly what I announced today. The FBI has done a lot of things right for this country over a long period of time. You know, this is the same FBI that found the people that bombed the World Trade Center in lickety-split record time. We want an inquiry to analyze the steps along the way. Is there something else we should have known? Is there some other question they should have asked? Is there some other question I should have asked? Can I say for sure that we could have done nothing else to make the outcome different? I don't know that. That's why I want the inquiry, and that's why I would like to make sure we have some independent law enforcement people, not political people — but totally non-political outside experts who can bring to bear the best evidence we have.

There is unfortunately a rise in this sort of fanaticism all across the world, and we may have to confront it again. And I want to know whether there is anything else we can do, particularly when there are children involved. But I do think it is important to recognize that the wrongdoers in this case were the people who killed others and then killed themselves.

Q: Were there any other options presented to you for resolving this situation at any point from February 28th until yesterday?

P: . . . The FBI and the other authorities there pursued any number of other options all along the way, and a lot of them early on seemed to be working. Some of the children got out, some of the other people left. There was — at one point there seemed to be some lines of communication opening up between Koresh and the authorities, and then he would say things and not do them, and things just began to spin downward. Whether there were other — in terms of what happened yesterday, the conversation I had with the attorney general did not involve other options except whether we should take more time with the present strategy we were pursuing. Because they said they wanted to do this, because they thought this was the best way to get people out of the compound quickly before they could kill themselves — that's what they thought.

[Congressional Investigations]

Q: Sen. Arlen Specter [R-Pa.] is asking for a congressional hearing once the situation calms itself. Are you in agreement to that?

P: Well, that's up to the Congress. They can do whatever they want. But I think it's very important that the Treasury and Justice departments launch this investigation and bring in some outside experts, and as I said in my statement, if any congressional committees want to look into it, we will fully cooperate. There is nothing to hide here. This was probably the most well-covered operation of its kind in the history of the country.

Q: Sir, there are two questions I want to ask you. First is, I think that they knew very well that the children did not have gas masks while the adults did. So the children had no chance because this gas was very — she said it was not lethal, but it was very dangerous to the children and they could not have survived without gas masks.

And on February the 28th, let's go back — did those people have a right to practice their religion?

P: They were not just practicing their religion. They were — the Treasury Department believed that they had violated federal laws, any number of them.... I can't answer the question about the gas masks except to tell you that the whole purpose of using the tear gas was that it had been tested, they were convinced that it wouldn't kill either a child or an adult, but it would force anybody who breathed it to run outside.... [The FBI] also knew that there was an underground compound, a bus buried underground where the children could be sent. And I think they were hoping very much that if the children were not released immediately outside, that the humane thing would be done and that the children would be sent someplace where they could be protected.

In terms of the gas masks themselves, I learned yesterday — I did not ask this ... question before, that the gas was supposed to stay active in the compound longer than the gas masks themselves were to work, so that it was thought that even if they all had gas masks, that eventually the gas would force them out in a non-violent, non-shooting circumstance.

Q: Mr. President, could you tell us whether or not you ever asked Janet Reno about the possibility of a mass suicide? And when you learned about the actual fire and the explosion, what went through your mind during those horrendous moments?

P: What I asked Janet Reno is if they had considered all the worse things that could happen. And she said — and of course, the whole issue of suicide had been raised in the public. You know ... that had been debated anyway. And she said that the people who were most knowledgeable about these kinds of issues concluded that there was no greater risk of that now than there would be tomorrow or the next day or the day after that or at any time in the future.

That was the judgment they made. Whether they were right or wrong, of course, we will never know.

What happened when I saw the fire, when I saw the building burning, I was sick; I felt terrible. And my immediate concern was whether the children had gotten out and whether they were escaping or whether they were inside trying to burn themselves up. That's the first thing I wanted to know.

Q: Mr. President, why are you still saying it was Janet Reno's decision? Isn't it, in the end, your decision?

P: Well, what I'm saying is that I didn't have a four- or five-hour detailed briefing from the FBI. I didn't go over every strategic part of it. It is the decision for which I take responsibility. I'm the president of the United States and I signed off on the general decision and giving her the authority to make the last call. When I talked to her on Sunday, some time had elapsed. She might have made a decision to change her mind. I said if you decide to go forward with this tomorrow, I will support you, and I do support her.

She is not ultimately responsible to the American people. I am. But I think she has conducted her duties in an appropriate fashion and she has dealt with this situation I think as well as she could have.

CONVICTION OF GOVERNOR ON ETHICS LAW VIOLATION

April 22, 1993

Guy Hunt, Alabama's first Republican governor in this century, was convicted April 22 of illegally diverting money for his personal use from a nonprofit fund set up to finance his 1987 inauguration ceremonies. The felony conviction required him, by state law, to surrender his office. Jim Folsom, Jr., the Democratic lieutenant governor and forty-three-year-old son of a prominent former governor, James E. "Big Jim" Folsom, promptly succeeded Hunt. Folsom took the oath of office as governor less than five hours after a jury in Montgomery, the capital, found Hunt guilty of violating a state ethics law. Hunt thus became the fourth governor in U.S. history to be convicted of a felony while in office and the first since Gov. Marvin Mandel of Maryland in 1977.

On May 7 Judge Randall Thomas sentenced Hunt to pay $211,000 in fines and restitution and perform 1,000 hours of community service. Hunt's lawyers meanwhile had asked the Alabama Court of Criminal Appeals to overturn the conviction. Hunt conceivably could have been restored to the governorship if the appeals court so ruled before the end of his regular, and second, term in January 1995.

Hunt, a farmer-salesman-preacher with a high school education, was virtually unknown politically when he entered the 1986 gubernatorial race at age fifty-two. That year the usually dominant Democratic party was so bitterly split that its primary election winner was removed from the November ballot by court order. Hunt drew strong support from white conservatives in rural areas and won an unexpected victory. He was narrowly reelected in 1990.

Questions About Hunt's Funds

For nearly two years, the governor's use of public funds had been openly questioned. In addition, Hunt was accused of using a state airplane on preaching trips to Primitive Baptist churches throughout the South, where he received and kept donations as "love offerings." The allegations led to a grand jury investigation that resulted, in December 1992, in indictments charging him and three campaign aides with violating the ethics law and a dozen related laws on theft and conspiracy.

Facing trial separately and first, Hunt entered a plea of not guilty on January 20. He accused the prosecutor, Attorney General Jimmy Evans, a Democrat, of carrying out a politically motivated vendetta against him. Hunt maintained that he had run the state governnment honestly and openly. The prosecution contended that the governor siphoned $200,000 from his inaugural fund for his personal uses. Defense attorneys argued that he used the funds to repay himself for money he advanced to his own political campaigns. Moreover, they argued that Alabama ethics laws did not clearly specify proper use of excess campaign funds and that the way Hunt had used his funds was a common practice in Alabama.

Prospect for Ethics Law Reform

Nevertheless, over strong defense protests, Judge Thomas instructed the jurors to consider unlawful "any use of excess campaign funds for direct personal use." In closing arguments, defense attorney George Beck asked the jurors not to make the governor a scapegoat for the ills of government, while Evans urged them to "send a message" to all politicians by finding Hunt guilty. The jury took only slightly more than two hours to do so.

Many Alabamians perceived that the state's ethics and campaign-finance laws were on trial before the court of public opinion. A number of leading citizens demanded that the state legislature in 1994 undertake measures to eliminate such ethics-law ambiguities as the trial highlighted. David Martin, a political science professor at the University of Alabama, said, "The importance of the trial is not so much that Governor Hunt as an individual was on trial, but that this may well define more ethical campaign standards for Alabama in the future." At the trial's conclusion, the prosecutor-attorney general issued a statement saying the public as well as the law would hold all politicians to a high degree of accountability.

> *Following is a statement issued by Attorney General Jimmy Evans of Alabama, April 22, 1993, upon Gov. Guy Hunt's conviction and removal from office that day on a violation of ethics law:*

The people of Alabama owe this jury a debt of gratitude for having the courage to return a fair and just verdict against a powerful political figure.

This jury has stood by the honored principle that no one is above the law, no one is below the law, and we make no apology for requiring all people to obey the law.

This case has cast a bright light on the practices of political fundraising. I hope it will cause all politicians to be mindful of how funds should properly be spent, and that the public as well as the law will hold them to a high degree of accountability.

It is time for Alabama to move forward, our faith restored in the responsibility and integrity of our government.

DEDICATION OF HOLOCAUST MUSEUM

April 22, 1993

After a highly controversial start, an American museum dedicated to the memory of World War II Holocaust victims was officially opened by President Bill Clinton April 22. In his remarks before President Chaim Herzog of Israel and Nobel laureate Elie Wiesel, among others in the audience, Clinton spoke of the need "to memorialize the past and steel ourselves for the challenges of tomorrow." He stated that a principal objective of the museum was to "bind one of the darkest lessons in history to the hopeful soul of America."

Wiesel, who won a Nobel prize for his novel Night, *which depicted his memories as a Holocaust survivor, also spoke at the site, saying that "to forget would mean to kill the victims a second time. We could not prevent their first death; we must not allow them to be killed again." Wiesel also used the opportunity to admonish nations to take steps to halt "ethnic cleansing" among Serbs, Croatians, and Muslims in the former Yugoslavia. "Mr. President, this bloodshed must be stopped. It will not stop unless we stop it."*

Wiesel's statement may have been particularly intended for Croatian president Franjo Tudjman, whose presence at the ceremony had been hotly contested by Wiesel and others as a result of anti-Semitic statements that Tudjman allegedly had included in a book he had written.

Controversy Surrounding the Holocaust Museum

From its conception the museum faced opposition from several sources. Whether such a museum belonged in the United States capital seemed to be the major point of controversy and contention. The fact that its proposed initial location was on the Capitol Mall—beside monuments to Jefferson, Lincoln, and Washington—caused further consternation. Among others, literary critic Alfred Kazin said he was "not happy about having a building on the Mall. I belong to a generation that says a building cannot express this idea. . . . I don't think the Holocaust is part of American culture." Clinton's answer was to restate the purpose of the museum. "It is . . . for those of us who were not there at all, to learn the lessons, to deepen our memories . . . and to transmit these lessons from generation to generation." The museum, he said, was "a place of deep sadness and a sanctuary of bright hope."

Shortly before the museum opened, its director, Jeshajahu Weinberg, told an interviewer, "We would not have built this museum had we not thought that this event carries moral lessons that are relevant to Americans and non-Americans today and tomorrow. To me . . . the biggest moral problem in the Holocaust is the millions who didn't murder but who knew what was happening and didn't prevent the murder. Similar questions are raised today: Look at Bosnia or . . . at the U.S. action in Somalia. If you see someone being mugged in the street, do you intervene?"

Building the Museum

The idea for a memorial to commemorate the Holocaust was conceived in 1977 by President Jimmy Carter's administration in part to regain support lost from the American Jewish community after the administration endorsed the idea of a Palestinian homeland. In 1978 Carter announced the formation of a thirty-four-member commission to lay the groundwork for a museum and named Wiesel to serve as its head. On October 7, 1980, legislation establishing the Holocaust Museum cleared Congress. After the original idea of remodeling existing buildings to create the museum was abandoned on grounds of structural instability, the commission began work on designing a building that would be suited to its contents. In 1986 Wiesel resigned as chairman of the commission, apparently so that a new chairman could be chosen whose experience included more solid background in management and administration.

Philanthropist Harvey M. "Bud" Meyerhoff was selected to replace Wiesel. The commission raised $168 million, $140 million coming from some 100,000 private donors of many religions and races and $6 million from Meyerhoff's personal donations. Federal funds provided $21.27 million for fiscal year 1993. James L. Freed was selected as the architect, and, as plans for the museum—to be located just off the Mall—were approved, the commission dispatched staff members worldwide to begin collecting memorabilia. As opening day approached, speakers for the ceremony were selected. President Herzog refused to attend unless he was invited to speak; the White House subsequently extended the invitation, which Herzog accepted.

In addition to Herzog, leaders of a dozen foreign states attended the dedication ceremony, including the presidents of Slovenia and Bosnia. Germany was represented by Vice Chancellor Klaus Kinkel and several members of the German Bundestag (Parliament). German chancellor Helmut Kohl was not present, but he had toured the museum privately a month before it opened. In May Germany's president Richard von Weizsaecker praised the museum saying, "Germans will really have to accept it and understand its importance."

Approximately 10,000 spectators braved the chilly, wet, and windy day to attend the ceremony, at which Clinton, Meyerhoff, and Wiesel kindled an eternal commemorative flame.

Touring the Museum: A Unique, Emotional Experience

The politicking and struggles that surrounded the museum's construction end at the museum's front door. There, the visitor enters a veritable tour of the Holocaust itself, from descriptions of the political upheavals that led to the persecution of Jews in Germany and elsewhere to the eventual enactment of Hitler's "Final Solution." The museum is both foreboding and factory-like, reflecting the industrial efficiency and mechanization of the concentration camps. Steel elevators take visitors up to the fourth floor, from which they symbolically descend floor by floor to ground level. On entering, each visitor receives an "identity card" that contains a photograph and brief description of an actual victim; computer stations at each floor allow the visitor to punch in the card to update the victim's fate. Staircases become narrower as they end; piping and steel rods are visible throughout, giving visitors the sense that they are being "herded" through the museum in much the same way that prisoners in Auschwitz and other prison camps were rounded up.

The fourth floor, commemorating the years 1933-1939, displays a computer used to record and track Jews, a list of towns later destroyed in the Holocaust, and early Nazi propaganda and films. The third floor covers 1940-1944 and includes an exhibit on Anne Frank (the celebrated young Jewish author of a diary recovered from her years in hiding in Amsterdam), a room full of shoes taken from concentration camp prisoners, and an actual gate from Auschwitz. The second floor covers the years 1944-1945, the years of discovery and liberation; it includes a Danish fishing boat used to transport Jews away from German forces, a collection of children's drawings relating to the Holocaust, and a wall commemorating men and women who rescued Jews from the Nazis. The first floor serves as the entrance/lobby of the building. The Tower of Faces, an atrium extending from the third floor to the roof of the fourth, displays the pictures and family photos of the residents of a town in Lithuania that was obliterated during the Holocaust.

At various points throughout the museum, exit points are provided for visitors who find that, for example, going through a cattle car used to deport prisoners to the camps, or walking through a reconstruction of the gas chambers is too unsettling. On the other hand, a special installation entitled "Remember the Children: Daniel's Story," aimed at children between the ages of eight and twelve years old, allows them to read excerpts from the imaginary boy's diary, touch his toys, and follow the footsteps of his ordeal. In addition to the exhibits, the museum contains classrooms and auditoriums for human rights issues discussions and presentations.

Tracing Holocaust Victims

More than a year before the Holocaust Museum opened its doors, the American Red Cross and the National Archives announced a joint project involving documents recovered from Nazi forced labor and concentration camps. The documents, which have been stored in thousands of boxes at the U.S. Archives facility in Suitland, Maryland, contain between 300,000 and 500,000 names of victims. These names are being incorporated into the global files of the International Tracing Service so that family members can learn their fate. In 1989 the former Soviet Union released the names of 400,000 Holocaust victims.

Following is the text of President Clinton's speech dedicating the U.S. Holocaust Memorial Museum, April 22, 1993:

Thank you very much, Mr. Vice President and Mrs. Gore, President and Mrs. Herzog, the distinguished leaders of nations from around the world who have come here to be with us today, the leaders of our Congress and the citizens of America and especially to Mr. Meyerhoff and all of those who worked so hard to make this day possible. And even more to those who have spoken already on this program, whose lives and words bear eloquent witness to why we have come here today.

It is my purpose, on behalf of the United States, to commemorate this magnificent museum. Meeting as we do among memorials, within the site of the memorial to Thomas Jefferson, the author of our freedom, near where Abraham Lincoln is seated, who gave his life so that our nation might extend its mandate of freedom to all who live within our borders, we gather near the place where the legendary and recently departed Marian Anderson sang songs of freedom and where Martin Luther King summoned us all to dream and work together.

Here on the town square of our national life, on this 50th anniversary of the Warsaw uprising, at Eisenhower Plaza on Raoul Wallenberg Place, we dedicate the United States Holocaust Museum and so bind one of the darkest lessons in history to the hopeful soul of America.

(Applause.)

As we have seen already today, this museum is not for the dead alone, nor even for the survivors who have been so beautifully represented. It is, perhaps most of all, for those of us who were not there at all, to learn the lessons, to deepen our memories and our humanity and to transmit these lessons from generation to generation.

The Holocaust, to be sure, transformed the entire 20th century, sweeping aside the Enlightenment hope that evil somehow could be permanently banished from the face of the earth, demonstrating there is no war to end all war, that the struggle against the basest tendencies of our nature must continue forever and ever.

The Holocaust began when the most civilized country of its day unleashed unprecedented acts of cruelty and hatred, abetted by perversions of science, philosophy and law. A culture which produced Goëthe, Schiller and Beethoven then brought forth Hitler and Himmler, the merciless hordes who themselves were educated as others who were educated stood by and did nothing. Millions died for who they were, how they worshipped, what they believed and who they loved.

But one people, the Jews, were immutably marked for total destruction. They, who were among their nation's most patriotic citizens, whose extinction served no military purpose nor offered any political gain, they who threatened no one, were slaughtered by an efficient unrelenting bureaucracy dedicated solely to a radical evil with a curious antiseptic title, the Final Solution.

The Holocaust reminds us forever that knowledge divorced from values can only serve to deepen the human nightmare, that a head without a heart is not humanity.

For those of us here today representing the nations of the West, we must live forever with this knowledge. Even as our fragmentary awareness of crimes grew into indisputable facts, far too little was done. Before the war even started, doors to liberty were shut, and even after the United States and the allies attacked Germany, rail lines to the camps within miles of militarily significant targets were left undisturbed.

Still there were, as has been noted, many deeds of singular courage and resistance. The Danes and the Bulgarians, men like Emmanuel Ringelbaum, who died after preserving in metal milk cans the history of the Warsaw ghetto, Janusz Korczak, who stayed with children until their last breaths at Treblinka, and Raoul Wallenberg, who perhaps rescued as many as 100,000 Hungarian Jews, and those known and those never to be known who manned the thin line of righteousness, who risked and lost their lives to save others, accruing no advantage to themselves, but nobly serving the larger cause of humanity.

As the war ended, these rescuers were joined by our military forces who, alongside the allied armies, played the decisive role in bringing the Holocaust to an end. Overcoming the shock of discovery, they walked survivors from those dark, dark places into the sweet sunlight of redemption, soldiers and survivors being forever joined in history and humanity.

This place is their place, too, for them, as for us, to memorialize the past and steel ourselves for the challenges of tomorrow.

We must all now frankly admit that there will come a time in the not too distant future when the Holocaust will pass from living reality and shared experience to memory and to history. To preserve this shared history of anguish, to keep it vivid and real so that evil can be combatted and contained, we are here to consecrate this memorial and contemplate its meaning for us.

For more than any other event, the Holocaust gave rise to the universal declaration of human rights, the charter of our common humanity. And it contributed, indeed made certain the long overdue creation of the nation of Israel.

(Applause.)

Now, with the demise of communism and the rise of democracy out of the ashes of former communist states, with the end of the Cold War, we must not only rejoice in so much that is good in the world but recognize that not all in this new world is good. We learn again and again that the world is yet to run its course of animosity and violence. Ethnic cleansing in the former Yugoslavia is but the most brutal and blatant and ever-present manifestation of what we see also with the oppression of the Kurds in Iraq, the abusive treatment of the Bahai in Iran, the endless race-based violence in South Africa, and in many other places, we are reminded again and again how fragile are the safeguards of civilization.

So do the depraved and insensate bands now loose in the modern world. Look at the liars and the propagandists among us, the skinheads and the Liberty Lobby here at home, the Afrikaners Resistance Movement in South Africa, the Radical Party of Serbia, the Russian Black Shirts. With them, we must all compete for the interpretation and the preservation of history, of what we know and how we should behave.

The evil represented in this museum is incontestable, but as we are its witness, so must we remain its adversary in the world in which we live. So we must stop the fabricators of history and the bullies, as well. Left unchallenged, they would still prey upon the powerless, and we must not permit that to happen again.

To build bulwarks against this kind of evil, we know there is but one path to take. It is the direction opposite that which produced the Holocaust. It is that which recognizes that among all our differences we still cannot ever separate ourselves one from another.

We must find in our diversity our common humanity. We must reaffirm that common humanity, even in the darkest and deepest of our own disagreements. Sure, there is new hope in this world.

The emergence of new vibrant democratic states, many of whose leaders are here today, offers a shield against the inhumanity we remember. And it is particularly appropriate that this museum is here in this magnificent city, an enduring tribute to democracy.

It is a constant reminder of our duty to build and nurture the institutions of public tranquillity.... It occurs to me that some may be reluctant to come inside these doors because the photographs and remembrance of the past impart more pain than they can bear. I understand that. I walked through the museum on Monday night and spent more than two hours. But I think that our obligations to history and posterity alike should beckon us all inside these doors.

It is a journey that I hope every American who comes to Washington will take, a journey I hope all the visitors to this city from abroad will make.

I believe that this museum will touch the life of everyone who enters and leave everyone forever changed—a place of deep sadness and a sanctuary of bright hope, an ally of education against ignorance, of humility against arrogance, an investment in a secure future against whatever insanity lurks ahead.

If this museum can mobilize morality, then those who have perished will thereby gain a measure of immortality.

I know this is a difficult today for those we call survivors. Those of us born after the war cannot yet fully comprehend their sorrow or pain. But if our expressions are inadequate to this moment, at least may I share these words inscribed in the Book of Wisdom: "The souls of the righteous are in the hands of God, and no torment shall touch them. In the eyes of fools they seem to die, their passing away was thought to be an affliction and their going forth from us utter destruction. But they are in peace."

On this day of triumphant reunion and celebration, I hope those who have survived have found their peace. Our task, with God's blessing upon our souls and the memories of the fallen in our hearts and minds, is to the ceaseless struggle to preserve human rights and dignity. We are now strengthened and will be forever strengthened by remembrance. I pray that we shall prevail.

(Applause).

DEFENSE DEPARTMENT REPORT ON TAILHOOK

April 23, 1993

At least ninety people were assaulted at Tailhook 91, a conference attended by thousands of United States Navy and Marine Corps fliers in 1991, according to an investigation by the Defense Department's inspector general. Nearly all the attacks were sexual assaults on women, many of whom were navy officers.

In a blistering report complete with at least one X-rated photograph, the inspector general said many fliers considered the annual Las Vegas conference a "free fire zone" where drunkenness and sexual misconduct were officially condoned. Their attitudes arose from "a long-term failure of leadership in naval aviation," the report said. For years, senior Navy officers knew Tailhook included heavy drinking, strippers, sexual assaults, indecent exposure, and other improper behavior. Yet Navy officers—many of whom attended the convention—did nothing to stop the behavior. In addition, the Navy continued spending thousands of dollars each year to send aviators to the conference, the report stated.

The Navy's culture also contributed to Tailhook, the report said. "Many officers likened Tailhook to an overseas deployment, explaining that naval officers traditionally live a spartan existence while on board ship and then party while on liberty in foreign ports," it said. "Officers said such activities as adultery, drunkenness and indecent exposure which occur overseas are not to be discussed or otherwise revealed once the ship returns to home port."

A Three-Day Conference for Fliers

The Tailhook Association was a private group for present and past Navy and Marine Corps fliers. Its conference included educational sessions, but the inspector general found that most military people skipped them and simply partied for three days. After the scandal became public in the fall of 1991, the Navy broke off its official relationship with the Tailhook Association.

In addition, the Naval Investigative Service and the Navy's inspector general began separate investigations into Tailhook 91. Both, however, were widely viewed as attempts to cover up what happened and to protect senior officials. At the request of Navy Secretary H. Lawrence Garrett III, the Pentagon's inspector general opened his own probe of the two investigations and of what happened at Tailhook. In June 1992 Garrett became the first senior Navy official forced to resign because of the scandal. Three months later, the Pentagon inspector general released a report that sharply criticized the Navy's Tailhook investigations. (Pentagon Report on Tailhook Convention, Historic Documents of 1992, p. 879)

The new report detailed the results of the Defense Department's inspector general's investigation into the actual events at Tailhook. It accused 117 officers of indecent assault, indecent exposure, conduct unbecoming an officer, or failure to act in a proper leadership capacity. In addition, it said fifty-one officers lied to naval investigators. The report also noted that the investigation was continuing, and said additional officers might be implicated. The inspector general's office sent all its evidence to Navy and Justice Department officials for disciplinary action or criminal prosecution.

The report rejected claims by some Navy aviators that only a small percentage of those attending Tailhook did anything improper. "Although there were approximately 4,000 naval officers at Tailhook 91, and significant evidence of serious misconduct involving 117 officers has been developed, the number of individuals involved in all types of misconduct or other inappropriate behavior was more widespread than those figures would suggest," it said.

"Repeated and Deliberate" Efforts to Obstruct the Investigation

The report praised senior Navy officials for their cooperation in the investigation. However, it said that "repeated and deliberate" efforts by lower-level officers to obstruct the investigation made it impossible to identify some who should be charged. "Collective 'stonewalling' significantly increased the difficulty of the investigation," the report said. Some witnesses who reportedly took photographs at Tailhook told investigators they had misplaced or destroyed the pictures until they received a subpoena. Usually, the "lost" photographs then suddenly appeared.

The ten-month investigation, which cost millions of dollars, found that many of the sexual assaults occurred on the convention hotel's third floor. There, drunken aviators formed a "gauntlet" and grabbed the breasts and buttocks of women who walked by to get to squadron hospitality suites. In some cases, aviators ripped off women's clothes. The inspector general reported great difficulty, however, in identifying those who assaulted women. "Of the many officers and civilian Tailhook attendees who admitted witnessing the gauntlet, only a few witnesses stated they were able to identify anyone else who was in the hallway at the time they witnessed the gauntlet in operation," the report said. It found such claims "incredible."

The inspector general reported that besides committing sexual assaults, aviators hired strippers and prostitutes, showed pornographic movies, engaged in sex in public, exposed their sexual organs, shaved the legs and pubic hair of women, bit women's buttocks, vandalized property, were drunk in public, and engaged in fistfights.

By mid-August 1993 the Navy had resolved about half of the cases arising from Tailhook. Most of the officers received light penalties, with many getting fines and letters of reprimand or less serious letters of caution or counseling. However, three officers were scheduled for court-martial, and four others faced possible court-martial, according to USA Today. *Officers convicted in courts-martial could face dismissal from the Navy or prison. Although many of the penalties were light, some experts predicted that all officers implicated in Tailhook would have their Navy careers shortened.*

> *Following is an excerpt from "Tailhook 91—Part 2, Events at the 35th Annual Tailhook Symposium," prepared by the inspector general of the Department of Defense and released April 23, 1993:*

Officer Attitudes and Leadership Issues

Officer Attitudes

A discussion of the attitudes of the officers in attendance is central to an understanding of the misconduct at Tailhook 91. Until this point, we have focused on "what" happened with little discussion or commentary as to "why" events at the convention degenerated to a point where indecent assaults, indecent exposure and excessive alcohol consumption became commonplace.

Navy and Marine Corps aviation officers are well educated, physically fit, technically proficient and well trained. Many are Naval Academy graduates or alumni of other top colleges and universities and certainly have the education and background to recognize societal issues such as sexual harassment. Yet some of these individuals acted with disregard toward individual rights and failed by a wide margin to conduct themselves as officers and gentlemen in the Armed Forces of the United States.

Although there were approximately 4,000 naval officers at Tailhook 91, and significant evidence of serious misconduct involving 117 officers has been developed, the number of individuals involved in all types of misconduct or other inappropriate behavior was more widespread than these figures would suggest. Furthermore, several hundred other officers were aware of the misconduct and chose to ignore it. We believe that many of these officers deliberately lied or sought to mislead our investigators in an effort to protect themselves or their fellow officers. On the other hand, there were hundreds of other officers who, when questioned, gave full and truthful accounts of their actions and observations while at Tailhook 91. Similarly, there were several hundred officers who spent their time at Tailhook 91 attending symposium events, visiting tourist sites and otherwise occupying themselves in places other than the third floor. Unfortunately, the reputations of those officers, who are guilty of no wrongdoing, have been tarnished by the actions of their fellow officers.

Officers who engaged in misconduct gave a variety of reasons for their behavior at Tailhook 91. Perhaps the most common rationale was that such behavior was "expected" of junior officers and that Tailhook was comprised of "traditions" built on various lore. Another reason given by many attendees was that their behavior was somehow justified or at least excusable, because they were "returning heroes," from Desert Storm. Many attendees, especially younger officers, viewed Tailhook as a means of celebrating the United States' victory over Iraqi forces. Numerous officers expressed their belief that Tailhook was a type of "free fire zone" where they could celebrate without regard to rank or ordinary decorum. As one Navy officer opined, "It was condoned early in some of the senior officers' careers. It was probably condoned back when Tailhook started ... And I imagine at one time, when this first—the thing started, they were the elite, they thought they could [do] anything they wanted in Naval aviation and not have to answer the questions we're answering today about it."

Many officers told us they believed they could act free of normal constraints because Tailhook was an accepted part of a culture in some ways separate from the main stream of the Armed Forces. They stated that the career progression for naval aviators is such that most do not bear the leadership responsibilities of commanding a unit until they approach the 10-year point in their careers. (Aviation officers do not follow the career progression of command of increasingly larger units from the outset of their Military Service. Unlike Army ground units, where the newest second lieutenant is trained to be a unit leader, aviators for the most part are viewed as unit members for the initial portion of their careers.)

Some senior officers blamed the younger officers for rowdy behavior and cited a "Top Gun" mentality. They expressed their belief that many young officers had been influenced by the image of naval aviators portrayed in the movie "Top Gun". The officers told us that the movie fueled misconceptions on the part of junior officers as to what was expected of them and also served to increase the general awareness of naval aviation and glorify naval pilots in the eyes of many young women.

One female Navy commander opined that the 1991 Tailhook convention was different in some ways from previous years, in part because of the recent Gulf War and the congressional inquiries regarding women in combat.

> The heightened emotions from the Gulf War were also enhanced with the forthcoming . . . downsizing of the military, so that you had people feeling very threatened for their job security and to more than just their jobs, their lifestyle. So you had people worried about what was coming down with the future. You had quite a bit of change. You had people that had been to the Gulf War. You had alcohol. You had a convention that had a lot of ingredients for any emotional whirlwind of controversy.

She went on to say that these potentially explosive ingredients combined at Tailhook 91, and resulted in ". . . an animosity in this Tailhook that existed that was telling the women that 'We don't have any respect for you now as humans.' " The animosity, in this officer's opinion, was focused on women:

> "This was the woman that was making you, you know, change your ways. This was the woman that was threatening your livelihood. This was the woman that was threatening your lifestyle. This was the woman that wanted to take your spot in that combat aircraft."

We found that all those factors were at play among the Tailhook 91 attendees. One rationale, that of the returning heroes, emphasizes that naval aviation is among the most dangerous and stressful occupations in the world. During Desert Storm, for example, the U.S. Navy suffered six fatalities, all of whom were aviation officers. We also found that the "live for today for tomorrow you may die" attitude expressed by many officers is a fact of life for many aviation officers. Over 30 officers died in the one-year period following Tailhook 91 as a result of military aviation related accidents. Others were found to have died in nonmilitary plane accidents, in vehicle crashes and, in at least one incident, by suicide. Although none of these factors justify the activities at Tailhook, they help illuminate the attitudes of many attendees.

Many officers likened Tailhook to an overseas deployment, explaining that naval officers traditionally live a spartan existence while on board ship and then party while on liberty in foreign ports. Dozens of officers cited excessive drinking, indecent exposure and visits to prostitutes as common activities while on liberty. That was acknowledged by virtually all interviewees, from junior officers through flag officers. The most frequently heard comment in that regard was "what happens overseas, stays overseas." Officers said that activities such as adultery, drunkenness and indecent exposure which occur overseas are not to be discussed or otherwise revealed once the ship returns to home port.

A similar attitude carried over to the annual Tailhook conventions. Countless officers told us it was common knowledge that "what happened at Tailhook stayed at Tailhook" and there were unwritten rules to enforce the policy. Frequently cited was the "no wives, no cameras" rule, which dated back to the earliest Tailhook reunions. Reportedly, few officers took their wives and only a small number of women attended. Witnesses told us that at earlier Tailhooks, many of the women in attendance were prostitutes. As years went by, however, women began to play a larger role as officers in naval aviation. Civilian women also began attending Tailhook conventions as a means of meeting naval pilots. The increase in the number of women attendees is supported by the fact that we were able to identify over 470 female attendees, many of whom were interviewed. Officers told us that the improper activity discussed in this report was nothing new but had merely come to light as a result of the influx of female attendees. The officers frequently opined that gauntlet participants could not or would not differentiate between the groupies and prostitutes who had been a part of Tailhook for many years, and other women who attended Tailhook 91.

Despite the "no cameras" policy, our investigation collected more than 800 photographs, some of which depict indecent exposure. It is interesting to note that approximately two-thirds of the photographs were provided to us by female civilians and that nearly half of the remaining pictures were furnished by female naval officers.

One disturbing aspect of the attitudes exhibited at Tailhook 91 was the blatant sexism displayed by some cfficers toward women. That attitude is best exemplified in a T-shirt worn by several male officers. The back of the shirt reads "WOMEN ARE PROPERTY," while the front reads "HE-MAN WOMEN HATER'S CLUB." The shirts, as well as demeaning posters and lapel pins, expressed an attitude held by some male attendees that women were at Tailhook to "serve" the male attendees and that women were not welcome within naval aviation.

During the course of our investigation, an incident involving sexual harassment came to our attention. One of the squadron hospitality suites provided the forum for an informal job interview between a Navy captain and a civilian female. The woman had applied for a GM-15 position within the captain's command. The captain was the hiring official for the position. Our investigation determined that the captain made numerous sexually oriented comments to the woman, questioned her sexual preferences and also directed her to stand up and turn around in front of him so as to enable him to view her buttocks. The incident was witnessed by other naval officers, as well as a civilian. Details of this matter have been referred under separate cover to Navy authorities.

The Failure of Leadership

One of the most difficult issues we sought to address was accountability, from a leadership standpoint, for the events at Tailhook 91. The various types of misconduct that took place in the third floor corridor and in the suites, if not tacitly approved, were nevertheless allowed to continue by the leadership of the naval aviation community and the Tailhook Association.

The military is a hierarchical organization, which requires and is supposed to ensure accountability at every level. As one moves up through the chain of command, the focus on accountability narrows to fewer individuals. At the highest levels of the command structure, accountability becomes less dependent on actual knowledge of the specific actions of subordinates. At some point, "the buck stops here" applies. In the case of Tailhook 91, the buck stops with the senior leaders of naval aviation.

Tailhook 91 is the culmination of a long-term failure of leadership in naval aviation. What happened at Tailhook 91 was destined to happen sooner or later in the "can you top this" atmosphere that appeared to increase with each succeeding convention. Senior aviation leadership seemed to ignore the deteriorating standards of behavior and failed to deal with the increasing disorderly, improper and promiscuous behavior.

Throughout our investigation, officers told us that Tailhook 91 was not significantly different from earlier conventions with respect to outrageous behavior. Most of the officers we spoke to said that excesses seen at Tailhook 91 such as excessive consumption of alcohol, strippers, indecent exposure and other inappropriate behavior were accepted by senior officers simply because those things had gone on for years. Indeed, heavy drinking, the gauntlet and widespread promiscuity were part of the allure of Tailhook conventions to a significant number of the Navy and Marine Corps attendees.

In seeking to identify the measure of responsibility properly borne by senior officers, it would be unfair to focus solely on the senior officers who attended Tailhook 91. Some measure of responsibility is also borne by other senior officers, some still on active duty and others now retired who attended previous Tailhook conventions and permitted the excesses of the annual conventions to continue unchecked.

As we reported in Tailhook 91, Part 1, the nature of the misconduct at the annual conventions was well-known to senior aviation leaders. However, although aware of the activities and atmosphere, they were incapable of dealing with the increasingly indulgent behavior. The efforts taken to control their subordinates at Tailhook, through the years, were sometimes effective but only for limited periods. In our view, by September 1991, both individually and collectively, the senior leaders of naval aviation were unwilling to take the kinds of measures necessary to effectively end the types of misconduct that they had every reason to expect would occur at Tailhook 91.

Moreover, the misconduct at Tailhook 91 went far beyond the "treatment of women" issues for which the Navy had enacted new policies in the years preceding Tailhook 91. The Tailhook traditions (the gauntlet, ballwalking, leg shaving, mooning, streaking and lewd sexual conduct) so deviated from the standards of behavior the nation expects of its military officers that the repetition of this behavior year after year raises serious questions about the senior leadership of the Navy. We found a great disparity between espoused Navy policies regarding consumption of alcohol and treatment of women and the actual conduct of significant numbers of those officers at Tailhook 91.

We were repeatedly told that such behavior was widely condoned by Navy civilian and military leadership. Some senior officers themselves had participated in third floor improprieties in previous years when they were junior officers to the extent that certain offensive activities had become a matter of tradition. For example, we found that officers, including some field grade officers, engaged in improper conduct such as indecent exposure and physical contact with strippers.

In that regard, one Navy lieutenant told us, "... I don't think that anybody saw anything that they felt hadn't happened in the past. And so ... if it had been allowed to happen in the past, they'd just let it go. They felt there was no reason to stop anything that they hadn't (sic) seen before." Relatedly, a lieutenant commander stated: "And I think you have to say that aviators emulate those who preceded them, and that Tailhooks that preceded them have legends of their own, and young aviators are going to try to mimic those people who are in a position to teach them and train them."

Another junior officer, who admitted to participating in the gauntlet, told us "If I thought that going around and goosing a few girls on the breasts was going to create a national incident, do you think I would have done that?... We only did it because the party atmosphere seemed to promote that ... Admiral Dunleavy and the rest of his cronies who go to Hook every year, man, they must be wearing some blinders, because it has been happening every single year that I know of."

Senior officers, on the other hand, referred to their perception that the third floor was somehow the domain of the younger officers. Senior officers, including an admiral, told us there was a lack of respect exhibited toward older officers by some junior officers and noted their belief that they would have been powerless to act successfully in attempting to stop third floor improprieties.

An example of the lack of respect is illustrated in an anecdote related by a Navy lieutenant. He told us that on Saturday night at about 10:00 p.m. he and two other lieutenants were waiting in line to use a suite rest room. An admiral tried to cut in front of them. The lieutenant challenged the admiral who reminded the officers that he was an admiral (O-8). The lieutenant (O-3) objected to the admiral's attempt to pull rank and told the admiral that the three O-3s added up to an O-9 and the admiral should go to the back of the line.

Many factors contributed to a feeling of resentment by junior officers toward higher ranking officers. One aspect related to a perception that, despite their success in Desert Storm, junior officers would be adversely affected by the anticipated drawdown of troops. Yet another factor related to us was the squadron officers' use of their personal funds to pay for the suites, alcohol and entertainment. Flag officers and many of the Navy captains and Marine Corps colonels in attendance did not help fund the third floor activities. That fact, together with the lack of uniforms and absence of any official Navy participation with regard to squadron hospitality suites contributed to a perception held by many attendees that the party was a private one hosted by junior officers.

Numerous officers attributed the perception that they could act with impunity to the uniqueness of the naval aviation community. They explained that aviators are used to working in a rank-neutral environment, frequently addressing more senior officers by their pilot "call signs" rather than by their rank. The witnesses also noted that aviation officers are less rank conscious and, therefore, less intimidated by the presence of more senior officers.

The demarcation between junior and senior officers was further blurred by the abundance of alcohol and nearly everyone's dressing in T-shirts and shorts as opposed to Navy or Marine Corps uniforms. As told to us by one officer, "... the more you drink, the less noticeable any ranks would be, from looking upward and looking downward, you know."

Field Grade Officers

We interviewed 331 field grade officers who attended Tailhook 91. [This group consisted of 85 Navy captains, 7 Marine Corps colonels, 218 Navy commanders and 21 Marine Corps lieutenant colonels.]

A number of those officers were the commanders of squadrons that hosted suites at the convention. Others had responsibility over groups of squadrons represented at Tailhook 91 or had previously commanded or been members of those squadrons. The field grade officers typically had completed more than 12 years of service and many had more than 20 years of experience in naval aviation. A large portion of the field grade officers had attended prior Tailhook conventions.

As indicated throughout the report, there were isolated instances in which field grade officers sought to remedy or prevent acts of misconduct; while in other instances, field grade officers themselves engaged in misconduct.

With respect to the squadron commanders who attended Tailhook 91, we found similar patterns of behavior. Prior to Tailhook 91, the squadron commanders had received letters from the Tailhook Association president warning them about underage drinking and the "late night gang mentality" that had occurred at prior conventions.

Some squadron commanders enforced proper conduct within their suites. Others chose to ignore events in their suites under the premise that Tailhook 91 was a private function rather than an official Navy activity. Several commanders told us they had difficulty in ensuring proper decorum despite prohibitions they issued. In one instance, a commander closed his unit's suite because of damage done to the suite.

The commanders who sought to forestall improper conduct at Tailhook 91 nevertheless were unwilling or unable to take actions to determine those responsible for the misconduct that actually took place at Tailhook 91. We found no evidence that any commander initiated any inquiry or took any disciplinary measures in the month between the Las Vegas convention and the initiation of the NIS investigation into the assault on LT Coughlin. Further, even those commanders who later told us that their subordinates had violated their orders regarding operation of the hospitality suites did nothing to address the misconduct that they acknowledged to us.

The Flag Officers

We interviewed each of the 30 active duty admirals, 2 active duty Marine Corps generals and 3 Navy Reserve admirals who attended Tailhook 91. We believe a discussion of the activities of the flag officers at Tailhook 91 is necessary and relevant, as was the discussion of the participation of Secretary of the Navy H. Lawrence Garrett, III, which was included in Tailhook 91, Part 1, in order to provide the backdrop against which the misconduct of junior officers occurred, as well as to assess their accountability.

In interviewing the flag officers who attended Tailhook 91, we attempted to determine which of them had specific knowledge of any misconduct. For the most part, the flag officers participated in or attended the scheduled symposium activities such as seminars, sporting events and dinners. [A few of the flag officers did not attend the entire convention.] Of the 35 flag officers we interviewed, 28 told us that they visited the third floor on Friday or Saturday night, or both nights, shortly after the conclusion of the evening dinner. Most of the officers stated that they arrived on the third floor between 9:30 p.m. and 10:00 p.m. Some flag officers told us they remained only briefly while others stayed for up to several hours. According to their testimony, with one notable exception discussed at length below, none of the flag officers, including those who spent several hours on the third floor and adjoining patio, witnessed any nudity or indecent exposure (including ballwalking, streaking or mooning), nor any activity occurring during the gauntlet.

We interviewed VADM Richard M. Dunleavy, then the Assistant Chief of Naval Operations (Air Warfare) during the investigation. In his initial interview, VADM Dunleavy denied having observed both leg shaving and the gauntlet, even when confronted with information we had obtained alleging that he observed leg shaving at Tailhook 90, had made favorable comments about leg shaving to the officers engaged in the activity, and had observed it again at Tailhook 91.

When we interviewed VADM Dunleavy the next day, he acknowledged that he had encouraged leg shaving at Tailhook 91 based on his favorable impression of the activity during the previous year's convention. Further, he acknowledged knowing that strippers performed during Tailhook 91 and prior conventions. Most significantly, he acknowledged to us that he was aware of the existence of the gauntlet and observed the activity that occurred during the gauntlet at Tailhook 91.

VADM Dunleavy told us that after the 1990 convention, he learned that the term "gauntlet" was being used to identify a group of young aviators who gathered along the walls in the third floor hallway where they groped women who passed through the corridor. On Saturday night of the 1991 convention, he was on the third floor and became aware that the gauntlet was forming. He further told us that when he went into the third floor hallway, he saw that it was crowded and a commotion was occurring as the men "hooted and hollered." He stated he heard men yelling "Show us your tits!" but that he did not intervene because he believed he would not be heard above the commotion and because the activities "appeared to be in fun, rather than molestation." He stated that it was his impression at the time that no one was upset and he believed that "they [women] would not have gone down the hall if they did not like it."

We believe that VADM Dunleavy's attitude toward leg shaving—which was one of approval and encouragement—and, more significantly, toward the gauntlet—which was one of tolerance—represents a serious, individual failure to recognize the impropriety of these activities and to take action to stop them.

We find ourselves in a serious dilemma with respect to what the flag officers did not see. Although we obtained significant evidence that misconduct occurred at Tailhook 91 on a widespread basis, flag officers, according to their testimony, seemed to be relatively unaware of it. We are of the opinion that the majority of them are being truthful in stating their lack of knowledge with respect to specific acts of sexual misconduct. While we have reservations about the categorical denials of some of the flag officers that they were completely unaware of any specific misconduct, especially when viewed in light of their past experiences at prior Tailhook conventions, it would be unfair for us to question the credibility of any one of them in the absence of controverting evidence on this matter.

In addition to whatever specific knowledge any of the flag officers may have had, it is our opinion that there was general knowledge among the Navy's senior aviation leadership of the inappropriate behavior that had become commonplace on the third floor during annual Tailhook conventions. In part, we base this opinion on the fact that 33 of the 35 flag officers who attended Tailhook 91 had attended prior Tailhook conventions; that 2 of the flag officers were past Tailhook Association Presidents; and that all of the aviation flag officers were former squadron commanders. Further, concern was expressed by flag officers over the excesses at prior Tailhook conventions as early as 1985. Many of the junior officers we interviewed told us that knowledge of the type of misconduct which occurred at Tailhook 91 was widespread throughout the aviation community. Finally, we obtained eyewitness testimony that one former high-ranking Navy civilian official engaged in inappropriate activity with a stripper in front of junior officers at a prior Tailhook convention, indicating that, at least in one instance, a senior official was aware of and participated in the type of activities for which junior officers are now being criticized.

GAY/LESBIAN MARCH ON WASHINGTON

April 25, 1993

Thousands of homosexual men and women came to Washington to take part in a march April 25. Officially titled the "1993 March on Washington for Lesbian, Gay and Bi- Equal Rights and Liberation," its goals included passage of a civil rights bill encompassing homosexuals, more money for AIDS research, and the inclusion of gays in the education system and military.

Described as a "sea of marchers, rainbow flags, banners, signs, red ribbons and pink triangles," the march began at 8:30 a.m. at the Lincoln Memorial, where more than 1,000 people gathered for a nondenominational religious service. In addition to the major march, which passed the White House and ended at the Mall, there were countless other smaller, more specific, peripheral gatherings. One was a pre-march rally that addressed the special issues confronting African-American gays and lesbians, such as being alienated from the white homosexual population; participants emphasized "how difficult it has been . . . to be openly gay."

Speeches were brief, and a wide range of people were represented, ranging from politicians, such as Mayor David N. Dinkins of New York and Rep. Patricia Schroeder, D-Colo., to drag queens and members of religious groups. Barney Frank, D-Mass., one of two openly gay members of the U.S. House of Representatives, said that gays "would no longer submit to unequal treatment."

Clinton Response: Somewhat Disappointing

On April 16, at the White House, President Bill Clinton met with eight gay rights leaders, including those who organized the march. Until then, no president had invited gay leaders to the Oval Office. Those involved described the meeting as a positive experience that gave leaders hope that Clinton would become more involved in gay rights issues. Many were disappointed when, nine days later, the president did not attend the march. Instead, he sent a statement, read by Rep. Nancy Pelosi, D-Calif., in which Clinton said that he stood "with you in the struggle for equality for all Americans, including gay men and lesbians." Jesse Jackson, a leading civil rights activist, indirectly criticized Clinton's lack of involvement, telling the marchers, "People you voted for have fled the city."

Dispute Over Size of Demonstration

As has happened with other marches in Washington over the years, a controversy arose over the estimates of the numbers of participants. Organizers claimed that they reached their goal of 1 million, citing information obtained from the head of the D.C. government's Office of Emergency Preparedness. The U.S. Park Police, however, claimed that only 300,000 attended the march. This figure would still make the gay march a larger event than the 1963 civil rights March on Washington, to which it was compared, but the numbers would fall far short of the organizers' goal. The organizers charged that the Park Police tried to downsize the numbers because they wanted to diminish the importance of the rally or possibly because of political pressures. The Park Police claimed that they had superior measurement methods such as observing the crowd from helicopters, and that, while the march looked heavily attended from the ground, many bare patches could be seen from above.

The attendance figures were important to the organizers for several reasons. First, organizers hoped to inspire gays and lesbians to come out of the closet and go public with their sexual orientation. They also hoped that a large turnout would convince lawmakers that gays were a political force that no longer could be ignored. The dispute over the number of marchers paralleled the debate over the number of homosexuals in the U.S. population. Many gay leaders asserted that 10 percent of the overall population was gay, citing reports made by Alfred Kinsey in the 1940s. However, these reports have long been dismissed because of their flawed methodology. The Battelle Human Affairs Research Center reported that only 2.3 percent of American men had "even one homosexual experience" during their lives and that "less than half (1.1 percent) had been exclusively gay."

Opposition to gays was also evident. Throughout the day, many religious groups held small counterdemonstrations along the march route. Some of the counterdemonstrators chanted slogans such as "God hates fags," "fags burn in hell," and "fag equals AIDS." Those protesting any change in the ban against gays serving in the military carried signs reading "Protect Our Privates," "Armed Forces Forever Straight," and "No Sodomites In the Military."

Focus on Gay Rights in the Military

One of Clinton's campaign promises had been to lift the ban against gays serving in the military. The issue arose after the Navy discharged

Petty Officer Keith Meinhold, who revealed during a television interview that he was homosexual. He sued for reinstatement. On January 29, just after Clinton took office, a Los Angeles district judge granted Meinhold's request and barred the secretary of defense from discharging any person based on sexual orientation. But that action did not resolve the issue.

After heated debate, Congress wrote into law the military's ban on openly homosexual people serving. The military agreed to adopt the "don't ask, don't tell" policy, which meant that recruiters would no longer ask people about their sexual preferences and homosexuals were expected to keep their activities private. Neither side was satisfied with this compromise: the gay ban promoters viewed it as not tough enough, and gays maintained they should be allowed to serve in the military with no restrictions.

Later, on September 29, the Supreme Court lifted the district court order barring the military from discriminating against homosexuals, thus allowing the Pentagon to resume discharging gay soldiers and sailors. (Clinton Plan to Remove Military Homosexual Ban, p. 153)

Following are the texts of President Clinton's statement to participants in the gay rights march and the remarks of Torie Osborn, executive director of the Gay and Lesbian Task Force, both April 25, 1993, in Washington, D.C.:

CLINTON'S STATEMENT

Welcome to Washington, DC, your Nation's Capital.

During my campaign and since my election, I have said that America does not have a person to waste. Today I want you to know that I am still committed to that principle.

I stand with you in the struggle for equality for all Americans, including gay men and lesbians. In this great country, founded on the principle that all people are created equal, we must learn to put aside what divides us and focus on what we share. We all want the chance to excel in our work. We all want to be safe in our communities. We all want the support and acceptance of our friends and families.

Last November, the American people sent a message to make Government more accountable to all its citizens, regardless of race, class, gender, disability, or sexual orientation. I am proud of the strides we are making in that direction.

The Pentagon has stopped asking recruits about their sexual orientation, and I have asked the Secretary of Defense to determine how to implement an Executive order lifting the ban on gays and lesbians in the military by July 15.

My 1994 budget increases funding for AIDS research, and my economic plan will fully fund the Ryan White Act. Soon I will announce a new AIDS coordinator to implement the recommendations of the AIDS Commission reports.

I met 9 days ago with leaders of the gay and lesbian community in the Oval Office at the White House. I am told that this meeting marks the first time in history that the President of the United States has held such a meeting. In addition, members of my staff have been and will continue to be in regular communication with the gay and lesbian community.

I still believe every American who works hard and plays by the rules ought to be a part of the national community. Let us work together to make this vision real.

Thank you.

OSBORN'S SPEECH

My name is Torie Osborn. I'm here to talk about the future—our future—but to do that, I need to start with the past. Not so long ago, people actually believed that in order to have power in America, you had to be white. You had to be a man. And you had to be straight. All lies. In the sixties, the civil rights movement fought the lie that you had to be white.

The women's movement of the '70s revolutionized the very concept of power—and let us remember today that it was lesbian leadership that created that new vision.

And in 1969, those brave drag queens and working class dykes at Stonewall laid seige to that last lie—and catapulted us toward this moment—into this movement that proclaims our right to love and desire whom we choose.

By 1980 our movement was growing. We had begun to come out and we had begun to fight for our rights.

And then we began to die. At first, just a few, and then in terrifying numbers. Thousands, then tens of thousands, shunned by society, betrayed by America's leaders. At the beginning of the 1980's, we stood alone, outcasts, forsaken by family, lacking community. Frightened. Frustrated. Furious.

We were fighting for our very lives—and we began to link arms—around bedsides, in street demonstrations, in service organizations, before committees of Congress, and yes, at thousands of wakes, and funerals and memorial services that should have driven us insane—but only drove us closer together.

And, so the sorrow and the rage of AIDS propelled us out of the closets of fear and denial into the sunlight of community, and we came out in greater numbers than ever before—and each person who came out—every single one of you—added to the strength of this new community.

Well, my friends, if the '80's was the decade of coming out—the nineties will be the decade of coming home.

We're coming home, America—with our heads held high, not as strangers, but as the people we are—your daughters and sons. Your carpenters and teachers, captains of industry and captains in the Army—we're coming home.

We're coming home for Christmas and Hanukah and Kwanzaa, Easter and Passover, Ramadan and Solstice, Thanksgiving, and the Fourth of July. America, this brave community is coming home.

We're walking home. We're flying home, and we're going to drive home our powerful message: that in the midst of unrelenting hate and the agony of AIDS, we've had the power to move through anger to love and hope. And now we're bringing it home. We're coming home.

So, listen to us, America, you the divided country, a country with too little hope—just look at these faces, look at our diversity, look at our unity. America, if we could find hope and optimism, everyone can. America—we're coming home to help bring this country together. To make it whole, we're coming home.

We're coming home so everyone who isn't out can come out. I say to those still trapped in the prisons they call closets, we are here, waiting for you—a community of support—gay men and lesbians and bisexuals—and friends who are "straight but not narrow."

And come out you must. Your secrecy is killing you; it's killing us. We're coming home to lend you shoulders of support so you can tell your story without fear, so you can put your lover's picture on your desk at work, so you can finally find freedom in your lives. We're coming home.

We're coming home because the truth of who we are obliterates the lies of the religious right. Today, together, we say to those sexophobic, homophobic neopuritans—you have fair warning: We're coming home.

In order to survive, we built a community separate from the rest of society. But the ideal of America—a democracy that includes everyone—cannot be realized without us. So, we're coming in from the outside, to take our place at the table as equals, no more, no less. We're coming home.

And, America, do not be fooled by our loving spirit. Let no one doubt from this day forward our determination to take what is rightfully ours. We will drive that message home again and again and again. Are you listening, Pat Robertson and Pat Buchanan? Do you get the message, Sam Nunn? Yes, we're coming home to Army bases in Georgia and to living rooms in California and to community centers in Vermont and to farms in Kansas and to factory floors in Ohio. . . . America, are you listening? We are your family too, and we are everywhere—and we're finally coming home. We're coming home.

DEFENSE SECRETARY EASES BAN ON WOMEN IN COMBAT

April 28, 1993

Secretary of Defense Les Aspin announced April 28 that he would permit women to fly combat aircraft and asked Congress to repeal its ban on women serving aboard warships. He also ordered the armed services to reconsider the exclusion of women from other combat positions except those in front-line infantry and armored units. "The essence of the new policy is that the military services are to open up more specialties and assignments to women," Aspin said at a Pentagon news briefing. He was accompanied by the commanding generals of the Army, Navy, Air Force, and Marine Corps, who said they were prepared to carry out the directives despite prior opposition to combat flights by at least one service leader, Gen. Merrill A. McPeak, the Air Force chief of staff.

Following the 1991 Persian Gulf War, Congress repealed a law that restricted women fliers to noncombat missions. During the war, women pilots flew helicopters and airplanes on support and supply missions behind enemy lines and airlifted troops into enemy territory. According to Defense Department accounts, eleven women were killed during Operation Desert Storm, as the Gulf campaign was called. Five of them died from enemy action; the other six from accidents. In addition, two women soldiers, including a helicopter pilot, were captured and briefly held as prisoners of war. Of the 545,000 American military personnel sent to the Gulf region, about 40,000 were women. (Senate Debate on Women in Combat, Historic Documents of 1991, p. 491)

Follow-up to Congressional Action

Although it lifted the restriction, Congress did not compel the armed forces to assign women to combat flights. None had done so when Aspin ordered them to act. The previous November, a presidentially appointed study commission recommended that the only combat role appropriate for servicewomen was aboard Navy ships—except submarines and am-

phibious craft. That panel, the Presidential Commission on the Assignment of Women in the Armed Forces, was badly divided. Its advice, delivered to President George Bush two months before he left office, was not binding on him, Congress, or the military services. (Report on Women in Combat, Historic Documents of 1992, p. 1029)

But the report added to a growing debate over the role and treatment of women by the military services. Only months earlier there had been disclosures of sexual assaults on female officers at a naval aviators' convention. (Pentagon Report on Tailhook Convention, Historic Documents of 1992, p. 879)

Plans for Women Combat Pilots

"The steps we are taking today are historic," Aspin said at the news briefing. "The results of all this will be that the services will be able to call upon a much larger pool of talent to perform the vital tasks that [they] ... must perform.... Right now we're not able to do that." A number of female pilots in the Air Force, Army, and Navy were expected to transfer to combat squadrons. Many of them had lobbied for the right to do so. Gen. Gordon R. Sullivan, the Army chief of staff, said he expected that as many as one-third of the Army's 300 female pilots "will want to become attack pilots." Adm. Frank B. Kelso, the chief of naval operations, said some of the Navy's women pilots probably could "transition into [carrier-based] combat squadrons within a few months if the combat exclusion law is changed." Although women were now permitted to fly combat missions, those in the Navy presumably would have to do so from land bases. The law still prohibited women from serving on aircraft carriers and other combat warships.

The Marine Corps had no women fliers but its commandant, Gen. Carl E. Mundy, Jr., predicted that it soon would have. He said that henceforth all flight jobs would be filled without regard to sex. General McPeak said that although he opposed women in combat cockpits, he was "comfortable" with Aspin's decision and would abide by it. Besides, he quipped, "there's always a small chance that I was wrong." McPeak said seven women had already been chosen to become Air Force combat pilots and several others would be offered the same opportunity.

Muted Protests over the Plan

Aspin's plan appeared to cause less stir nationally than on some previous occasions when the women-in-combat question came into the spotlight. Some observers suggested that much of the attention, and heat, that would normally focus on that matter had been diverted by the issue of whether homosexuals should be permitted to serve in the military services, as President Bill Clinton advocated. (Clinton Plan to Remove Military Homosexual Ban, p. 153)

Even so, there were protests. Clarence A. Mark Hill, a retired rear admiral who had been chief of naval personnel, said: "The bottom line is, there's no way women can improve combat readiness, but they sure as hell can degrade it." Male combat fliers also appeared unreceptive to the idea of female colleagues. A poll conducted by the presidential commission in 1992 among male pilots in the Air Force, Navy, and Marine Corps indicated that 69 percent did not want women to fly combat aircraft. Even without the presence of female pilots, competition for combat flight positions had increased as defense cutbacks reduced the number available.

Linda Chavez, a former Reagan administration official, recalled in a Washington Post *article that another poll by the commission indicated 80 percent of the female noncommissioned officers and 71 percent of the other enlisted women would not volunteer for combat jobs. Chavez argued that if the armed forces became dependent on women serving in combat, the option of refusing combat duty might no longer be open to them. Several officials said they expected that the question of whether servicewomen could be denied any combat role—or all combat roles—would ultimately be decided by the Supreme Court.*

Following is the text of a memorandum from Secretary of Defense Les Aspin to Pentagon officials, dated April 28, 1992, directing that the armed forces open additional combat positions to servicewomen:

As we downsize the military to meet the conditions of the post-Cold War world, we must ensure that we have the most ready and effective force possible. In order to maintain readiness and effectiveness, we need to draw from the largest available talent pool and select the most qualified individual for each military job.

Throughout our nation's history, women have made important contributions to the readiness and effectiveness of our armed forces. Their contributions to the nation's defense have been restricted, however, by laws and regulations that have excluded them from a large number of important positions.

The military services, with the support of Congress, have made significant progress in recent years in assigning qualified women to an increasingly wide range of specialties and units. Two years ago, Congress repealed the law that prohibited women from being assigned to combat aircraft. It is now time to implement that mandate and address the remaining restrictions on the assignment of women.

Accordingly, I am directing the following actions, effective immediately.

A. The military services shall open up more specialties and assignments to women.
   1. The services shall permit women to compete for assignments in aircraft, including aircraft engaged in combat missions.

2. The Navy shall open as many additional ships to women as is practicable within current law. The Navy also shall develop a legislative proposal, which I will forward to Congress, to repeal the existing combat exclusion law and permit the assignment of women to ships that are engaged in combat missions.
3. The Army and the Marine Corps shall study opportunities for women to serve in additional assignments, including, but not limited to, field artillery and air defense artillery.
4. Exceptions to the general policy of opening assignments to women shall include units engaged in direct combat on the ground, assignments where physical requirements are prohibitive and assignments where the costs of appropriate berthing and privacy arrangements are prohibitive. The services may propose additional exceptions, together with the justification for such exceptions, as they deem appropriate.

B. An implementation committee shall be established to ensure that the policy on the assignment of women is applied consistently across the services, including the reserve components.
1. The committee shall be chaired by the Deputy Assistant Secretary for Military Manpower and Personnel Policy, and should include the Deputy Chiefs of Staff for Personnel for the Services and the Director of Manpower and Personnel of the Joint Staff.
2. Consistent with my emphasis on readiness and effectiveness, the committee shall review and make recommendations to me about the services' parental and family policies, pregnancy and deployability policies, and the appropriateness of the "Risk Rule."

The Service Secretaries and the chair of the implementation committee shall report their progress and plans to me in 30 days, and keep me apprised thereafter.

[signed]
Les Aspin

May

COMPLAINTS OVER THE RELEASE OF JUSTICE MARSHALL'S PAPERS

May 25 and 26, 1993

The public was afforded a revealing view of the Supreme Court's inner workings in papers left to the Library of Congress by the late Justice Thurgood Marshall. Upon his death in January 1993, the papers were quietly opened to researchers. Within five months, the Washington Post *began publishing a series of stories focusing on the deliberations in some major cases—all drawn from notes and memoranda Marshall retained during his long service on the Court, 1967-1991.* (Resignation of Justice Marshall from the Supreme Court, Historic Documents of 1991, p. 377)

For instance, in Webster v. Reproductive Health Services, *the 1989 case challenging the 1973* Roe v. Wade *decision legalizing abortion, Marshall's files show Chief Justice William H. Rehnquist's repeated attempts to obtain a majority for outright repeal but his ultimate failure to persuade Justice Sandra Day O'Connor, who held the critical fifth vote. All the while, Justice Harry A. Blackmun, the author of* Roe, *worked with equal fervor for support among his colleagues to preserve the law.*

Justices' Loss of Confidentiality

Public glimpses at the Court's internal debate tend to irk the sitting justices, who typically contend that only their final opinions have authority and that the loss of confidentiality might inhibit their exchange of ideas. This time was no exception. Rehnquist, saying he spoke for a majority of the active justices, accused the Library of Congress of using "bad judgment" in releasing Marshall's papers immediately after his death. In a letter to Librarian of Congress James H. Billington on May 25, two days after the newspaper series began, the chief justice said the Library first should have consulted the Supreme Court and the Marshall family.

The following day, Warren E. Burger, the former chief justice, called Billington's "decision to release the Marshall papers at this time ... an irresponsible and flagrant abuse" of discretionary authority. Marshall's widow, Cecelia, issued a statement through the family's attorney, William T. Coleman, saying: "My husband had great respect for the Court and its tradition of confidentiality. I am certain he never intended his papers to be released during the lifetime of the justices with whom he sat."

Several of the late justice's friends echoed that thought. The columnist Carl Rowan wrote that Marshall had refused to cooperate in Rowan's attempt to write his biography when Marshall realized that he was expected to comment on cases that had come before the Court, on which he was then still serving. Rowan added that Marshall was so indignant that he returned a much-needed advance payment he had initially accepted from the publisher.

Library Chief's Defense

Billington stood his ground. In a statement issued May 26 he said that the Library was carrying out instructions Marshall expressed verbally to him and two staff members, and in a written agreement he and Marshall signed in 1991. Billington said further that after reviewing the entire matter he remained confident that "we are carrying out his exact intentions in opening access to his papers after his death on January 24."

Access to the papers before Marshall's death was controlled exclusively by him; afterwards, according to the agreement, they "shall be made available to the public at the discretion of the Library." A separate section on use of the materials said it would "be limited to private study on the premises of the Library by researchers or scholars engaged in serious research."

In response to criticism that journalists should have been excluded, Billington said that under longstanding Library policy, the term "researchers" applied to adults working on specific research projects, "be they authors, journalists, or lawyers." Moreover, he said, Marshall was aware that journalists used Library manuscript collections and had expressed his approval.

Billington noted that the papers of former justice Harold H. Burton were opened, as requested, immediately after his death, and so were some of those left by Justice William O. Douglas. Justice Arthur J. Goldberg released his collection during his lifetime, but after leaving the Court. Billington said it was well known that journalists and scholars previously had access to documents of the Court and had written about its deliberations. "We are surprised to have the Library of Congress called upon to enforce a tradition of confidentiality which the Court itself has yet clearly to establish," he added.

Persuasion From the Grave?

Juan Williams, who was writing a book about Marshall, said in a Washington Post *article May 30 that Marshall wanted his papers released immediately as a means of "continuing his role as a Supreme Court justice who would not let his colleagues forget about the impact of discrimination and poverty as they deliberated on the laws of this land. The release of his papers is another reminder to the justices left behind that people are watching."*

The mastermind of the civil rights revolution, Marshall had fought for the underprivileged throughout his six-decade legal career. As a lawyer, he devised the litigation that abolished white-only primary elections, barred racial covenants in private housing, and outlawed racial segregation in public schools.

President John F. Kennedy appointed Marshall to the Second U.S. Circuit Court of Appeals, on which he served until 1965, when President Lyndon B. Johnson made him solicitor general. (The solicitor general represents the U.S. government before the Supreme Court.) Two years later Johnson nominated Marshall to the Court. Over the objection of southern senators, Marshall was confirmed, becoming the first black justice on the Supreme Court.

Toward the end of his twenty-four-year tenure, Marshall found himself most often among the dissenters; conservative majorities under Burger and Rehnquist weakened affirmative action rules and protection for criminal defendants. Marshall's later dissents often revealed an acute sense of frustration. He was never able to persuade the Court to outlaw death sentences, once they had been restored. In his final opinion, issued only hours before he announced his retirement on June 27, 1991, he bitterly assailed the majority's "assault on this Court's precedents." (Court on Murder Case Sentencing, Historic Documents of 1991, p. 381)

Following are a letter from Chief Justice William H. Rehnquist to Librarian of Congress James H. Billington on May 25, 1993, protesting the library's release of Justice Thurgood Marshall's papers, and Billington's reply issued the following day, together with a copy of the library's agreement with Marshall about its custody of his papers:

REHNQUIST LETTER

Dear Mr. Billington,

I speak for a majority of the active Justices of the Court when I say that we are both surprised and disappointed by the Library's decision to give unrestricted public access to Justice Thurgood Marshall's papers. It seems clear from the provisions of the "Instrument of Gift" which he executed, construing it least restrictively, that the matter was left to the discretion of the Library. So far as we know, the Library consulted with no one from this Court, and with no member of the Marshall family. Given the Court's long tradition of confidentiality in its deliberations, we believe this failure to consult reflects bad judgment on the part of the Library. Most members of the Court recognize that after the passage of a certain amount of time, our papers should be available for historical research. But to release Justice Marshall's papers dealing with deliberations which occurred as recently as two terms ago is something quite different. Unless there is some presently unknown basis for the Library's action, we think it is such that future donors of judicial papers will be inclined to look elsewhere for a repository.

Sincerely,
[signed: William H. Rehnquist]

BILLINGTON STATEMENT

We were surprised and distressed by the concerns voiced by the Marshall family, Chief Justice [William H.] Rehnquist, the Hon. William Coleman, and others over the opening of the papers of the late Thurgood Marshall....

I have met today with the Marshall family, the Chief Justice, and Mr. Coleman to discuss their concerns, review the Library's discussion and correspondence with Justice Marshall, and explain the Library's guiding philosophy on access to its collections.

We have conducted a thorough review of our internal documents and dealings with Justice Marshall. We remain confident that we are carrying out his exact intentions in opening access to his papers after his death on January 24.

In so doing, we have followed traditional library practice of strict adherence to the donor's explicit instructions. This has been our practice with collections left to the Library by all donors, including twelve other recent justices of the Supreme Court. To do otherwise is a breach of contract and a violation of the trust placed in the Library by the donor.

Requests in the wake of recent articles to impose additional restrictions on Justice Marshall's papers run counter both to this basic principle of custodianship and to Justice Marshall's expressed intentions to us.... Open access to the papers, as called for in Justice Marshall's instrument of gift, must be maintained.

Crucial to a free and democratic society is open access to information, limited only by formal secrecy classification and by specific restrictions laid down by the donors of papers.

In the case of Justice Marshall, following his death, the use of the papers "is limited to private study on the premises of the Library by researchers or scholars engaged in serious research."

One of the concerns that has been raised is that journalists ought not to be considered researchers. The term "researchers," under Library policy, has always referred to adults working on specific research projects, be they authors, journalists, or lawyers. Justice Marshall was aware that journalists used Library manuscript collections; indeed, during our meeting on his papers in October 1991, he mentioned with approval to me a particular book by a journalist on a fellow Supreme Court justice using his papers in the Library.

All who seek to use the Marshall papers—or any other open papers in the Library's manuscript collection—must register, present a photo I.D., state their names, addresses, institutional affiliations, and their research projects. Casual tourists and high school students are turned away. Undergraduates are normally encouraged to go elsewhere, although any adult may use the Library's general collections.

There has been some confusion over the "discretion" allowed to the Library under the terms of Justice Marshall's Instrument of Gift, signed October 24, 1991. As in the case of other collections, the "discretion" sought and obtained by the Library involved only the technical determination by our archival staff of when the papers were organized and ready for use. It is an abuse of such "discretion" to impose restrictions on access other than those proposed by the donor.

Under the Instrument, his papers were to be made available during his lifetime to researchers "only with my written permission." After his death, "the collection shall be made available to the public at the discretion of the Library."

Justice Marshall was quite clear in his meeting with me and other Library specialists earlier that month that he wanted his papers to be opened upon his death. . . .

Justice Marshall had ample opportunity to add restrictions if he so chose. In my letter of October 21 forwarding the Instrument of Gift to Justice Marshall for his signature, I wrote: "We will be happy to discuss any revisions you wish to propose." He proposed none. He signed the Instrument of Gift with no changes on October 24.

The restrictions placed by Supreme Court justices on access to their papers have varied with the individual. Justice Marshall is not the first Justice to ask that his papers be opened immediately following his death. Associate Justice [Harold H.] Burton gave unlimited access after his death. Associate Justice [William O.] Douglas permitted major portions of his papers to be made available immediately on his death. Associate Justice [Arthur J.] Goldberg allowed his papers to be open during his lifetime (but after he left the Court). Justice [Byron R.] White's Instrument of Gift allows access to individual researchers with his permission during his lifetime, then no access for ten years. Chief Justice [Earl] Warren allowed no access to his papers until 1985.

Some have argued that opening Justice Marshall's papers now threatens the privacy of Supreme Court deliberations. The Library does not hold itself above the law; it obeys Federal document classification edicts and follows the restrictions imposed by donors of papers. We have nothing but respect for the Court and its members. But we cannot serve as the Court's watchdog. In the recent past, as is well known, outside the Library of Congress, both journalists and scholars have gained access to Supreme Court documents and produced articles and books on its deliberations. We are surprised to have the Library of Congress called upon to enforce a tradition of confidentiality which the Court itself has yet clearly to establish....

We remain confident that we are complying with Justice Marshall's intentions regarding access to his papers. We are deeply concerned that the language of the Instrument of Gift may have been misunderstood by some. I have therefore directed Library staff to develop language for use in subsequent Instruments to reexamine access policies and ensure that future donors' intentions are not subject to any misinterpretation outside the Library....

INSTRUMENT OF GIFT

I, Thurgood Marshall (hereinafter: Donor), hereby give, grant, convey title in and set over to the United States of America for inclusion in the collections of the Library of Congress (hereinafter: Library), and for administration therein by the authorities thereof, a collection of my personal and professional papers, more particularly described on the attached schedule.

I hereby dedicate to the public all rights, including copyrights throughout the world, that I may possess in the Collection.

The papers constituting this gift shall be subject to the conditions hereinafter enumerated:

1. **Access.** With the exception that the entire Collection shall at all times be available to the staff of the Library for administrative purposes, access to the Collection during my lifetime is restricted to me and to others only with my written permission. Thereafter, the Collection shall be made available to the public at the discretion of the Library.
2. **Use.** Use of the materials constituting this gift shall be limited to private study on the premises of the Library by researchers or scholars engaged in serious research.
3. **Reproduction.** Persons granted access to the Collection may obtain single-copy reproductions of the unpublished writings contained therein.
4. **Additions.** Such other and related materials as the Donor may from time to time donate to the United States of America for inclusion in the collections of the Library shall be governed by the terms of this Instrument of Gift or such written amendments as may hereafter be agreed upon between the Donor and the Library.

5. **Disposal.** It is agreed that should any part of the Collection hereinabove described be found to include material which the Library deems inappropriate for permanent retention with the Collection or for transfer to other collections in the Library, the Library may dispose of those materials in accordance with its procedures for the disposition of materials not needed for the Library's collections.

In witness whereof, I have hereunto set my hand and seal this 24th day of October 1991, in the city of Washington, D.C.

[signed: Thurgood Marshall]

Accepted for the United States of America
[signed: James H. Billington]
The Librarian of Congress
November 8, 1991

CLINTON REMARKS AT VIETNAM WAR MEMORIAL

May 31, 1993

Facing a crowd that included jeering veterans of the Vietnam War, President Bill Clinton delivered a speech of reconciliation at the Vietnam Veterans Memorial in Washington on Memorial Day, May 31. The protesters denounced his opposition to the war and avoidance of military service. "To all of you who are shouting, I have heard you," he said. "I ask you now to hear me." Urging an end to the anger, Clinton asked his listeners to "continue to disagree, if we must, about the war, but let us not let it divide us as a people any longer. No one has come here today to disagree about the heroism of those whom we honor."

The president was joined on the dais by high-ranking military officers, by relatives of men and women who died in Vietnam, and by veterans of the war such as Jan Scruggs, who started the fund to build the memorial, and Lewis Puller, Jr., who lost both legs in battle. Gen. Colin L. Powell, chairman of the Joint Chiefs of Staff, introduced himself as "the senior Vietnam veteran on active duty" when he welcomed the president. Powell, near the end of his own speech, quoted from Abraham Lincoln's second inaugural address: "With malice toward none and charity for all, let us bind up the nation's wounds." Clinton added, "Lincoln speaks to us today across the years."

After the ceremony, Clinton and Scruggs walked alongside the black granite memorial inscribed with the names of some fifty-eight thousand war dead. The president touched the wall and took a rubbing of the name of a high school classmate, James Herbert Jeffries. In his speech, Clinton noted, "There's not a person in this crowd today who did not know someone on this wall. Four of my high school classmates are there."

Clinton's speech culminated a Memorial Day weekend devoted to addressing his problems with the military services and veterans groups. He spoke at ceremonies for the graduating class at the U.S. Military Academy at West Point, New York, met with veterans at the White

House, and laid a wreath on the Tomb of the Unknown Soldier at Arlington National Cemetery. At Arlington, he declared that before U.S. troops are sent to battle, "We will give them the clear mission, the means and support they need to win."

Among veterans and military personnel, opposition to Clinton began building during his presidential election campaign when it became known that as a graduate student he sought to avoid the draft. It was revealed that in 1969 he wrote in a letter to his ROTC commander, Col. Eugene Holmes, of "a war I opposed and despised with a depth of feeling I had reserved solely for racism in America before Vietnam." He added that he and others who opposed the war were in the position of "loving their country but loathing the military." After his election, Clinton faced further opposition from the military when his administration reduced the defense budget and sought to lift the ban on homosexuals in military service. (Clinton Plan to Remove Military Homosexual Ban, p. 153)

After the White House announced that the president would speak at the Vietnam Memorial in observance of Memorial Day, several Vietnam-veterans groups organized protests, including a postcard- and letter-writing campaign to persuade Clinton not to appear. When the president spoke that day, a group of veterans and their sympathizers in the audience turned their backs on him. Some displayed placards accusing him of cowardice.

Following is President Bill Clinton's address at the Vietnam Veterans Memorial in Washington, D.C., on May 31, 1993, Memorial Day, in which he asked Americans not to let disagreement over that war continue to divide the nation:

... To all of you who are shouting, I have heard you. I ask you now to hear me. I have heard you.

Some have suggested that it is wrong for me to be here with you today because I did not agree a quarter of a century ago with the decision made to send the young men and women to battle in Vietnam. Well, so much the better. Here we are celebrating America today. Just as war is freedom's cost, disagreement is freedom's privilege. And we honor it here today.

But I ask all of you to remember the words that have been said here today, and I ask you at this monument: Can any American be out of place? And can any commander in chief be in any other place but here on this day? I think not.

Many volumes have been written about this war and those complicated times, but the message of this memorial is quite simple. These men and women fought for freedom, brought honor to their communities, loved their country and died for it.

They were known to all of us. There's not a person in this crowd today who did not know someone on this wall. Four of my high school classmates are there, four who shared with me the joys and trials of childhood and did not live to see the threescore and 10 years the Scripture says we are entitled to.

Let us continue to disagree if we must about the war, but let [it not] divide us as a people any longer.

No one has come here today to disagree about the heroism of those whom we honor. But the only way we can really honor their memory is to resolve to live and serve today and tomorrow as best we can and to make America the best that she can be.

Surely that is what we owe to all those whose names are etched in this beautiful memorial.

As we all resolve to keep the finest military in the world, let us remember some of the lessons that all agree on. If the day should come when our servicemen and women must again go into combat, let us all resolve they will go with the training, the equipment, the support necessary to win—and, most important of all, with a clear mission to win.

Let us do what is necessary to regain control over our destiny as a people here at home, to strengthen our economy and to develop the capacities of all of our people, to rebuild our communities and our families where children are raised and character is developed. Let us keep the American dream alive.

Today let us also renew a pledge to the families whose names are not on this wall because their sons and daughters did not come home.

We will do all we can to give you not only the attention you have asked for but the answers you deserve.

Today I have ordered that by Veterans Day we will have declassified all United States government records related to POWs [prisoners of war] and MIAs [missing in action] from the Vietnam War—all those records except for a tiny fraction, which could still affect our national security or invade the privacy of their families.

As we allow the American public to have access to what our government knows, we will press harder to find out what other governments know.

We are pressing the Vietnamese to provide this accounting not only because it is the central outstanding issue in our relationship with Vietnam, but because it is a central commitment made by the American government to our people. And I intend to keep it.

You heard Gen. Powell quoting President Lincoln: "With malice toward none and charity for all, let us bind up the nation's wounds."

Lincoln speaks to us today across the years. Let us resolve to take from this haunting and beautiful memorial a renewed sense of our national unity and purpose, a deepened gratitude for the sacrifice of those whose names we touched and whose memories we revere—and a finer dedication to making America a better place for their children and for our children, too.

Thank you all for coming here today. God bless you, and God bless America.

June

REPORT ON SEXUAL HARASSMENT IN PUBLIC SCHOOLS

June 2, 1993

Four of every five public school students in grades eight through eleven have experienced some form of sexual harassment during their school hours, according to a survey released June 2 by the American Association of University Women (AAUW). Beginning as early as the elementary grades, a disturbingly high percentage of students reported experiencing some kind of unwanted overture having a sexual innuendo at some time during their years in public school. Girls reported more instances of sexual harassment than did boys—85 percent and 76 percent of respondents, respectively. Of those who said they had been sexually harassed, one-third said they had experienced the occurrence in the sixth grade or earlier.

Characterizing the findings as evidence of "a sexual harassment epidemic" in America's schools, Alice McKee, president of the AAUW Educational Foundation, warned, "Every day ... sexual harassment denies millions of children the educational environment they need to succeed."

Rising Concern About Sexual Misconduct

The AAUW study, entitled Hostile Hallways, *came at a time when public awareness of the many forms of alleged sexual harassment was becoming more acute, and legal action by the victims against the perpetrators was increasingly sought. News media throughout the country reported a rise in the number of legal or disciplinary actions brought against teachers, other school staff, and students themselves for having engaged in some form of sexual misconduct. Reports of harassment in the workplace by both females and males were rising, again with legal recourse being sought more frequently by males and females alike. The U.S. Navy had been plagued by numerous reports of sexual harassment, the most prominent of which occurred at a 1991 convention of the Navy fliers' Tailhook Association, when a large group of drunken male junior officers formed a "gauntlet" in a hotel hallway and assaulted women who tried to pass through.* (Defense Department report, p. 315; Tailhook case, Historic Documents of 1992, pp. 879, 1003)

Perhaps the best-known case of sexual harassment charges in recent years came in the fall of 1991 during Senate hearings on the nomination of Clarence Thomas to the position of associate justice on the Supreme Court, when Anita Hill—a law professor who had worked for Thomas—testified that he had sexually harassed her by making lewd comments. Although Thomas was confirmed by a close floor vote, the hearings spurred public concern about the sexual harassment issue. (Thomas confirmation, Historic Documents of 1991, p. 551)

Survey Findings

The AAUW commissioned the well-known polling firm of Louis Harris and Associates to conduct the survey as a follow-up to its 1992 study entitled How Schools Shortchange Girls. *Based on a synthesis of all the available research on girls in school, that report brought to light disturbing inequities in the way girls and boys were treated in school as well as the possibility that sexual harassment—involving both sexes—was on the rise.* (Report, Historic Documents of 1992, p. 141)

The sexual harassment survey, conducted in early 1993, asked a representative nationwide sample of 1,632 students of varied ethnicity in seventy-nine eighth- through twelfth-grade classrooms the following question: "During your whole school life, how often, if at all, has anyone (this includes students, teachers, other school employees, or anyone else) done the following things to you when you did not want them to?" *Students were instructed to answer only about their school-related experiences, such as those that occurred on the way to and from school, in classrooms and hallways, on school grounds during the school day, and on school trips. Among the items to which students were asked to respond were incidents that involved: making sexual comments, jokes, gestures, or looks; giving sexual pictures and messages; spreading sexual rumors; saying a student was gay or lesbian; spying while a student was dressing; "flashing"; touching, grabbing, or pinching; pulling at clothing or pulling it off or down; intentionally brushing against in a sexual way; forcing to kiss; and forcing to do something sexual other than kissing. The questionnaire emphasized to students that "Sexual harassment is ... not behaviors that you* like or want *(for example: wanted kissing, touching, or flirting)."*

The survey revealed a mixed situation: sexual harassment occurs with both girls and boys, but the frequency of its occurrence, nature, and impact on school life experiences differed significantly by sex. For example, the survey found that 39 percent of girls—compared with 8 percent of boys—who had been harassed were apprehensive about going to school. Girls also suffered a considerably greater loss of confidence in themselves than did boys as a result of such an incident, evidenced by their not wanting to talk as much in class.

Relating the sexual harassment survey to the organization's previous study, Anne Bryant, executive director of the AAUW Educational Foundation, noted, "In school, a girl doesn't get called on by her teacher, but she is the subject of catcalls; she doesn't hear stories about women of achievement, but she hears rumors about her sexual behavior. Sexual harassment takes a toll on all students, but the impact on girls is devastating."

Among the survey's other major findings were the following:

- *Harassment occurs out in the open—most frequently in the hallway or classroom—rather than in secluded corners.*
- *The majority of harassment in schools is student-on-student (59 percent of respondents admitted to being perpetrators), but 25 percent of harassed girls and 10 percent of harassed boys responded that they were harassed by teachers or other school employees.*
- *Only 7 percent of harassed students told a teacher about the incident; 23 percent told a parent or family member; and 23 percent told no one.*

Impact on School Policy, Teacher/Student Relations

"Ignoring sexual harassment in schools in effect condones it," said Sharon Schuster, president of AAUW. "More than half of the students surveyed didn't know if their school had a policy on sexual harassment. As parents, teachers, and administrators, we need to send a message that sexual harassment in school will not be tolerated and that classrooms and hallways in our schools must be a safe place to learn."

Others, however, cautioned that there was a "thin line" between harassment and normal child behavior. "We have to ask ourselves [about this distinction]," said Janet Parshall, special assistant to the president of the Concerned Women for America, which advocates family values. "If Johnny sticks his tongue out at Susie, has he now crossed the line?"

Leslie Wolfe, executive director of the Center for Women's Policy Studies, said, "We are in a transition era," where some still believe that "boys will be boys," while girls face "terrorizing behavior" like having to "run a gauntlet of obscene gestures" from male peers.

A number of teachers expressed apprehensions about the new awareness of sexual misconduct toward students, many of them saying that, for example, patting a child on the back for work well done or commenting on a child's nice appearance might be misconstrued as being something more than a friendly gesture.

Whatever might be the definition and parameters of sexual harassment in the nation's schools, however, most observers would agree with the conclusion of the report: "In the end, sexual harassment is everyone's problem. For when children's self-esteem and development are hampered, the repercussions echo throughout our society."

Following are excerpts from the report commissioned by the American Association of University Women Educational Foundation, entitled "Hostile Hallways: The AAUW Survey on Sexual Harassment in America's Schools," released June 2, 1993:

This survey, comprised of voices as well as numbers, shapes a picture that demands attention: sexual harassment in school—in hallways, classrooms, and beyond—is widespread, with both girls and boys being targeted by their peers as well as adults. Clearly, the process of getting an education is a large enough challenge for most students without the added challenge of contending with sexual harassment in school.

At the most basic, schools must have sexual harassment policies that are clearly communicated and routinely enforced. The mere fact that more than half the students surveyed (57%) do not know if their school has a policy on sexual harassment is disturbing.

As with past AAUW Educational Foundation research, we are confident that the results of this survey will become a focal point on the agendas of policy makers, educators, and others concerned with the education of America's children. Indeed, there is more work to be done, and the Foundation will continue to fund research, community action projects, and teachers. And the American Association of University Women, with more than 130,000 members nationwide, will continue its work in coalition with other groups and individuals to help ensure that the educational experiences of all public school students are positive and life-enriching.

While this survey establishes that sexual harassment in school is widespread, it also raises some important questions. Does adult sexual harassment have roots in school-based behavior? When behavior is shrugged off as permissible because it is widespread and "boys will be boys," are we unwittingly setting the stage for abusive behavior later on? Do students harass because they themselves are harassed?

The statements and statistics presented here add up to an undeniable mandate: parents, teachers, and administrators must acknowledge that sexual harassment in school is creating a hostile environment that compromises the education of America's children. Sexual harassment is clearly and measurably taking a toll on a significant percentage of students' educational, emotional, and behavioral lives. And although girls are experiencing more harassment—and suffering graver consequences—in the end, sexual harassment is everyone's problem. For when children's self-esteem and development are hampered, the repercussions echo throughout our society.

[The statistics in this survey, except where noted with an asterisk, refer to the 81% subgroup of students who report some experience of sexual harassment in school.]

Key Findings

Sexual harassment in school is widespread.

- Four in 5 students (81%) say they have experienced some form of sexual harassment during their school lives: 85% of girls and 76% of boys.
- One in 4 students (25%) have experienced 1 or more of the 14 surveyed types of sexual harassment in school and say they are targeted "often."
- More than half the students surveyed (58%) report that they have been targeted "often" or "occasionally."

There are notable gender and racial/ethnic gaps.

- Nearly 1 in 3 girls (31%) who have been harassed have experienced unwanted advances "often," compared with fewer than 1 in 5 boys (18%).
- Two in 3 girls (66%) who have been harassed report that they have been targeted "often" or "occasionally." This is true for fewer than 1 in 2 boys (49%).
- For girls, 87% of whites report having experienced sexual harassment, compared with 84% of African Americans and 82% of Hispanics.
- Among boys, African Americans (81%) have experienced sexual harassment, compared with whites (75%) and Hispanics (69%).

In grades 7, 8, and 9, many more girls than boys first experience sexual harassment in school.

- One in 3 students (32%) who have been harassed * first experience sexual harassment in grade 6 or earlier.
- Among girls who have been harassed, African Americans (42%) and Hispanics (40%) are more likely to first have experienced harassment in grade 6 or earlier—compared with whites (31%).
- For 6% of students who have been harassed, the first experience of sexual harassment took place before grade 3.
- Twice as many boys (36%) as girls (18%) are unable to recall the grade in which they were first harassed in school.

Sexual comments, jokes, looks, and gestures—as well as touching, grabbing, and/or pinching in a sexual way—are commonplace in school.

- Two in 3 of all students surveyed (66%) have been targets of the above forms of verbal/gestural abuse.
- 65% of all girls and 42% of all boys surveyed have experienced touching, grabbing, and/or pinching in a sexual way.

The third most common form of sexual harassment in school involves intentionally brushing up against someone in a sexual way—something girls experience far more often than boys.

- 57% of all girls surveyed have experienced this, in contrast to 36% of boys.
- Among all girls surveyed, African Americans (64%) have been the target of this physical form of harassment, compared with whites (58%) and Hispanics (49%).
- Among all boys surveyed, nearly half of African Americans (49%) experienced this behavior, compared with a third or less of whites (34%) and Hispanics (29%).

Students say they would be very upset if they were called gay or lesbian. Being called gay would be more upsetting to boys than actual physical abuse.

- 86% of all students say they would be very upset if they were called gay or lesbian—85% of boys and 87% of girls respond this way.
- For boys, this is the most disturbing form of unwanted behavior: 88% of Hispanic boys and 85% of both African American and white boys would be troubled by being called gay.
- 17% of students say they have been called lesbian or gay when they didn't want to be—10% of girls and 23% of boys.
- Of those boys who have been called gay, more than half (58%) say they have called someone else gay.

Experiences of student-to-student harassment outnumber all others, with notable gender and ethnic/racial gaps.

- Nearly 4 in 5 students (79%) who have been harassed have been targeted by peers: current or former students.
- Two in 3 (66%) of all boys and more than half (52%) of all girls say they have sexually harassed someone in the school setting.
- Similarly, of the 59% of students who admit to having perpetrated sexual harassment in school, 94% say they, themselves, have been harassed—98% of girl harassers and 92% of boy harassers.
- Among all girls surveyed: African Americans (63%) are more likely to have harassed than Hispanics and whites (50% for each group).
- Among all boys surveyed, roughly equal percentages of African Americans (67%) and whites (66%), compared with 56% of Hispanics, admit to having perpetrated such behavior.
- Half of those students (49%) who have harassed someone at school admit to having harassed a student of the opposite sex—43% of girls and 54% of boys say this. More than 1 in 10 (11%) admit to having harassed someone of the same sex as themselves—15% of boys and 5% of girls.
- Among girls who have been harassed: 81% report having been harassed by a male acting alone, 57% by a group of males.

- Among boys who have been harassed: 57% report having been harassed by a female acting alone.

Adult-to-student harassment is nonetheless considerable, with notable gender and ethnic/racial gaps.

- 18% of students who have been harassed cite adults as the perpetrators.
- One in 4 girls (25%) and 1 in 10 boys (10%) who have been harassed say they have been harassed by a school employee (such as a teacher, coach, bus driver, teacher's aide, security guard, principal, or counselor).
- Among girls, adult-student harassment is more commonly experienced by African Americans (33%) than whites (25%) and Hispanics (17%).

Harassing others is a routine part of school culture—more so for boys than for girls.

- Of those students who admit to having sexually harassed someone, 37% say "It's just part of school life/a lot of people do it/it's no big deal"—41% of boys and 31% of girls.
- Of the 25% of perpetrators who say "I thought the person liked it," 27% are boys and 23% are girls.

Public areas are the most common harassment sites—especially as reported by girls.

- Two in 3 students who have been harassed (66%) say they have been harassed in the hallway.
- More than half (55%) of those who have been harassed cite the classroom.
- Far more girls than boys have been harassed in the hallway (73% and 58%, respectively). The same holds true for the classroom: 65% of girls and 44% of boys report being harassed here.
- More than 2 in 5 harassed students (43%) have been targeted outside of school, on school grounds (other than the parking lot).
- More than one-third of students have been harassed in the school cafeteria, most notably white boys (37%), compared with African American boys (29%) and Hispanic boys (24%).
- More than 1 in 4 students (26%) have been harassed on school transportation (to and from school; on school trips). 38% of African American girls cite this, compared with 31% of white girls and 16% of Hispanic girls.

Students usually do not report incidents to adults. Boys are more likely than girls to tell no one.

- Fewer than 1 in 10 students who have been harassed (7%) say they have told a teacher, although girls are twice as likely to have done so as boys.

- Fewer than 1 in 4 students who have been harassed (23%) say they told a parent or other family member—roughly 1 in 3 girls (34%) and 1 in 10 boys (11%).
- 63% of harassed students say they told a friend—77% of girls and 49% of boys.
- 23% of harassed students say they told no one—27% of boys and 19% of girls.

Notably higher numbers of girls than boys say they have suffered as a result of sexual harassment in school; African American girls have suffered the most.

- Nearly 1 in 4 students (23%) who have been sexually harassed say that as a result they did not want to attend school: 33% of girls, compared with 12% of boys. The numbers are very similar for those who say they do not want to talk as much in class after having experienced harassment.
- Among harassed girls: 39% of African Americans did not want to attend school, in contrast with 33% of whites and 29% of Hispanics. Among harassed boys, the numbers are: 14% of whites, 9% of African Americans, and 8% of Hispanics.
- While half of all students who have been harassed (50%) state they have suffered embarrassment, nearly 2 in 3 girls (64%) report feeling this way, compared with roughly 1 in 3 (36%) boys.
- 37% of harassed students say that sexual harassment has caused them to feel self-conscious—1 in 2 girls (52%), compared with 1 in 5 boys (21%).
- Slightly less than one-third of harassed students (29%) report feeling less sure or less confident about themselves—43% of girls, compared with 14% of boys.
- Nearly half the students (48%) who were harassed say they were "very upset" or "somewhat upset" after having been harassed—an alarming 70% of girls respond this way. Twice as many boys (25%) as girls (13%) say they were not sure how they felt.
- One in 4 students (24%) of those harassed say the experience left them feeling afraid or scared—39% of girls and 8% of boys.
- Slightly more than 1 in 5 students who have been harassed (21%) say that harassment caused them to doubt whether they can have a happy romantic relationship—30% of girls, compared with 12% of boys. Higher percentages of African American girls respond this way (38%), compared with Hispanic girls (33%) and white girls (27%).
- Nearly 1 in 2 harassed students (49%) say they avoid the person(s) who harassed them, with 69% of girls responding this way.
- Slightly less than 1 in 4 students (23%) who have been harassed say they stay away from particular places in the school or outside on school grounds. 34% of girls report this—41% of African Americans, compared with 37% of Hispanics and 32% of whites.

Boys routinely experience harassment. Among African Americans, the incidence of harassment involving direct physical contact is alarming.

- 57% of boys who have been harassed have been targeted by a girl, 35% by a group of girls.
- 25% of boys who have been harassed have been targeted by another boy, 14% by a group of boys.
- 10% of harassed boys have been targeted by a teacher or other school employee.
- 24% of harassed boys, compared with 14% of harassed girls, have been targeted in the locker room.
- Boys who have been harassed (14%) are twice as likely as girls who have been harassed (7%) to be targeted in the rest room.
- Half of all African American boys surveyed (49%) have been intentionally brushed up against in a sexual way.*
- One in 5 African American boys surveyed (22%) have been forced to kiss someone; 19% have been forced to do something sexual other than kissing.

COURT ON USE OF SCHOOL BY RELIGIOUS GROUP

June 7, 1993

Displaying rare unanimity in deciding a church-state issue, the Supreme Court on June 7 said a local school board in New York had wrongly refused to permit after-hours public showings of church-sponsored films in school facilities to which other community groups were granted access. By a 9-0 vote the Court rejected the board's argument—an argument based on New York Department of Education directives and upheld by two lower federal courts—that opening public school facilities to a religious group would violate the First Amendment's separation of church and state. Justice Byron R. White, writing on behalf of the Court, disagreed with the lower courts, holding instead that the board's denial violated the constitutional guarantee of free speech, also set forth in the First Amendment. He said the denial could not legally be based on the film program's content, as the board's denial had been.

The case, Lamb's Chapel v. Center Moriches Union Free School District, *arose in 1990 in the the Long Island community of Center Moriches when an evangelical church known as Lamb's Chapel asked to use the school facilities. It proposed to invite the community to see a six-part film that advocated traditional family values "from a Christian perspective." When the district school board refused permission, the church and its pastor challenged the denial in federal district court.*

The trial court, noting that state rules said "school premises shall not be used by any group for religious purposes," upheld the school board. That judgment was affirmed by the U.S. Court of Appeals for the Second District (New York), which said the board had met a test previously invoked by the Supreme Court—that such exclusions from school property need only to be "reasonable and viewpoint neutral."

Justice White agreed that schools are not required to avail themselves of every type of public gathering, but he said access rules could not discriminate on the basis of the speaker's identity or viewpoint. "The principle that has emerged from our cases is that the First Amendment forbids the government to regulate speech in ways that favor some viewpoints or ideas at the expense of others," White wrote. In this case, he added, Lamb's Chapel had been denied permission "solely because the film dealt with the subject from a religious standpoint."

Dissent over Court's Reasoning

White rejected the argument that letting a religious group use school property amounted to a unconstitutional state endorsement of that group's beliefs. "The showing of this film would not have been during school hours, would not have been sponsored by the school, and would have been open to the public, not just to church members," he wrote. In those circumstances, he continued, the film showing would not have violated a three-part test the Court devised in the 1971 case of Lemon v. Kurtzman *to determine if government becomes too closely involved in religion. The test requires that the purpose is secular, does not have the primary or principal effect of advancing or inhibiting religion, and does not foster an excessive entanglement with religion.*

The Court's unanimity fell apart over White's application of the Lemon *test, which several of the conservative justices have criticized as an overly strict standard for separating church and state. Justices Antonin Scalia, joined by Clarence Thomas, and Anthony M. Kennedy wrote separate opinions agreeing with the decision but saying it could have been rendered without invoking the stringent test. Scalia declared that six of the sitting justices, including White, had at one time or another refused to support the test.*

Ruling Trends Since 1960s

During the 1960s and 1970s several Court decisions took a strict separatist approach to church-state questions. More recently, with an infusion of conservative justices, the Court had moved toward a more accommodationist position—but not entirely. In 1985, for instance, the Court ruled unconstitutional an Alabama law authorizing a one-minute period of silence in public schools "for mediation or voluntary prayer." However, a concurring opinion by Sandra Day O'Connor suggested that state laws calling for moments of silence without specific mention of prayer might "not necessarily manifest the same infirmity."

That year the Court prohibited public school teachers from giving remedial instruction to handicapped children in parochial schools, and in 1992 it forbade prayers at a public school graduation ceremony in Providence, Rhode Island. (Supreme Court on Prayer at Public School Graduation, Historic Documents of 1992, p. 553)

In contrast, the same day as the Lamb's Chapel *decision was issued, the Court let stand without comment an appeals court ruling that permitted prayer at a Texas school. Less than two weeks later, the Court in a 5-4 decision said the government could pay for a sign-language interpreter to accompany a deaf student at a parochial school.* (Court on aid to parochial school student, p. 399).

Following are excerpts from the Supreme Court's 9-0 decision June 7, 1993, in Lamb's Chapel v. Center Moriches Union Free School District, *declaring that a school board may not prevent a church group from using school facilities after hours because of the group's religious purpose, together with opinions concurring in the decision but disagreeing with the reasoning:*

No. 91-2024

Lamb's Chapel and John Steigerwald, Petitioners *v.* Center Moriches Union Free School District et al.	On writ of certiorari to the United States Court of Appeals for the Second Circuit

[June 7, 1993]

JUSTICE WHITE delivered the opinion of the Court.

Section 414 of the New York Education Law authorizes local school boards to adopt reasonable regulations for the use of school property for 10 specified purposes when the property is not in use for school purposes. Among the permitted uses is the holding of "social, civic and recreational meetings and entertainments, and other uses pertaining to the welfare of the community; but such meetings, entertainment and uses shall be non-exclusive and open to the general public." The list of permitted uses does not include meetings for religious purposes, and a New York appellate court in *Trietley v. Board of Ed. of Buffalo* (App. Div. 1978), ruled that local boards could not allow student bible clubs to meet on school property because "[r]eligious purposes are not included in the enumerated purposes for which a school may be used under section 414." . . .

Pursuant to § 414's empowerment of local school districts, the Board of Center Moriches Union Free School District (District) has issued rules and regulations with respect to the use of school property when not in use for school purposes. The rules allow only 2 of the 10 purposes authorized by § 414: social, civic, or recreational uses (Rule 10) and use by political organizations if secured in compliance with § 414 (Rule 8). Rule 7, however, consistent with the judicial interpretation of state law, provides that "[t]he school premises shall not be used by any group for religious purposes."

The issue in this case is whether, against this background of state law, it violates the Free Speech Clause of the First Amendment, made applicable to the States by the Fourteenth Amendment, to deny a church access to school premises to exhibit for public viewing and for assertedly religious purposes, a film dealing with family and child-rearing issues faced by parents today.

I

Petitioners (Church) are Lamb's Chapel, an evangelical church in the community of Center Moriches, and its pastor John Steigerwald. Twice the Church applied to the District for permission to use school facilities to show a six-part film series containing lectures by Doctor James Dobson. A brochure provided on request of the District identified Dr. Dobson as a licensed psychologist, former associate clinical professor of pediatrics at the University of Southern California, best-selling author, and radio commentator. The brochure stated that the film series would discuss Dr. Dobson's views on the undermining influences of the media that could only be counterbalanced by returning to traditional, Christian family values instilled at an early stage.... The District denied the first application, saying that "[t]his film does appear to be church related and therefore your request must be refused." The second application for permission to use school premises for showing the film, which described it as a "Family oriented movie—from the Christian perspective," was denied using identical language.

The Church brought suit in District Court, challenging the denial as a violation of the Freedom of Speech and Assembly Clauses, the Free Exercise Clause, and the Establishment Clause of the First Amendment, as well as the Equal Protection Clause of the Fourteenth Amendment.... The District Court granted summary judgment for respondents, rejecting all of the Church's claims. With respect to the free-speech claim under the First Amendment, the District Court characterized the District's facilities as a "limited public forum." The court noted that the enumerated purposes for which § 414 allowed access to school facilities did not include religious worship or instruction, that Rule 7 explicitly proscribes using school facilities for religious purposes, and that the Church had conceded that its showing of the film would be for religious purposes. The District Court stated that once a limited public forum is opened to a particular type of speech, selectively denying access to other activities of the same genre is forbidden. Noting that the District had not opened its facilities to organizations similar to Lamb's Chapel for religious purposes, the District Court held that the denial in this case was viewpoint neutral and, hence, not a violation of the Freedom of Speech Clause. The District Court also rejected the assertion by the Church that denying its application demonstrated a hostility to religion and advancement of nonreligion not justified under the Establishment of Religion Clause of the First Amendment.

The Court of Appeals affirmed the judgment of the District Court "in all respects." *Lamb's Chapel v. Center Moriches Union Free School Dist.* (CA2 1992)....

II

There is no question that the District, like the private owner of property, may legally preserve the property under its control for the use to which it is dedicated. *Cornelius v. NAACP Legal Defense and Ed. Fund, Inc.,* (1985); *Perry Ed. Assn. v. Perry Local Educators' Assn.* (1983).... It is also common ground that the District need not have permitted after-hours use of its property for any of the uses permitted by § 414 of the state education law. The District, however, did open its property for 2 of the 10 uses permitted by § 414. The Church argued below that because under Rule 10 of the rules issued by the District, school property could be used for "social, civic, and recreational" purposes, the District had opened its property for such a wide variety of communicative purposes that restrictions on communicative uses of the property were subject to the same constitutional limitations as restrictions in traditional public fora such as parks and sidewalks. Hence, its view was that subject-matter or speaker exclusions on District property were required to be justified by a compelling state interest and to be narrowly drawn to achieve that end. Both the District Court and the Court of Appeals rejected this submission, which is also presented to this Court. The argument has considerable force, for the District's property is heavily used by a wide variety of private organizations, including some that presented a "close question," which the Court of Appeals resolved in the District's favor, as to whether the District had in fact already opened its property for religious uses. We need not rule on this issue, however, for even if the courts below were correct in this respect—and we shall assume for present purposes that they were—the judgment below must be reversed.

With respect to public property that is not a designated public forum open for indiscriminate public use for communicative purposes, we have said that "[c]ontrol over access to a nonpublic forum can be based on subject matter and speaker identity so long as the distinctions drawn are reasonable in light of the purpose served by the forum and are viewpoint neutral." ... The Court of Appeals appeared to recognize that the total ban on using District property for religious purposes could survive First Amendment challenge only if excluding this category of speech was reasonable and viewpoint neutral. The court's conclusion in this case was that Rule 7 met this test. We cannot agree with this holding, for Rule 7 was unconstitutionally applied in this case.

The Court of Appeals thought that the application of Rule 7 in this case was viewpoint neutral because it had been and would be applied in the same way to all uses of school property for religious purposes. That all religions and all uses for religious purposes are treated alike under Rule 7, however, does not answer the critical question whether it discriminates on the basis of viewpoint to permit school property to be used for the presentation of all views about family issues and child-rearing except those dealing with the subject matter from a religious standpoint.

There is no suggestion from the courts below or from the District or the State that a lecture or film about child-rearing and family values would not be a use for social or civic purposes otherwise permitted by Rule 10. That subject matter is not one that the District has placed off limits to any and all speakers. Nor is there any indication in the record before us that the application to exhibit the particular film involved here was or would have been denied for any reason other than the fact that the presentation would have been from a religious perspective. In our view, denial on that basis was plainly invalid under our holding in *Cornelius* that

> "[a]lthough a speaker may be excluded from a nonpublic forum if he wishes to address a topic not encompassed within the purpose of the forum ... or if he is not a member of the class of speakers for whose special benefit the forum was created ... the government violates the First Amendment when it denies access to a speaker solely to suppress the point of view he espouses on an otherwise includable subject."

The film involved here no doubt dealt with a subject otherwise permissible under Rule 10, and its exhibition was denied solely because the film dealt with the subject from a religious standpoint. The principle that has emerged from our cases "is that the First Amendment forbids the government to regulate speech in ways that favor some viewpoints or ideas at the expense of others." *City Council of Los Angeles v. Taxpayers for Vincent* (1984). That principle applies in the circumstances of this case; as Judge Posner said for the Seventh Circuit Court of Appeals, to discriminate "against a particular point of view ... would ... flunk the test ... [of] *Cornelius,* provided that the defendants have no defense based on the establishment clause." *May v. Evansville-Vanderburgh School Corp.* (1986).

The District, as a respondent, would save its judgment below on the ground that to permit its property to be used for religious purposes would be an establishment of religion forbidden by the First Amendment. This Court suggested in *Widmar v. Vincent* (1981), that the interest of the State in avoiding an Establishment Clause violation "may be [a] compelling" one justifying an abridgment of free speech otherwise protected by the First Amendment; but the Court went on to hold that permitting use of University property for religious purposes under the open access policy involved there would not be incompatible with the Court's Establishment Clause cases.

We have no more trouble than did the *Widmar* Court in disposing of the claimed defense on the ground that the posited fears of an Establishment Clause violation are unfounded. The showing of this film would not have been during school hours, would not have been sponsored by the school, and would have been open to the public, not just to church members. The District property had repeatedly been used by a wide variety of private organizations. Under these circumstances, as in *Widmar,* there would have been no realistic danger that the community would think that the District was endorsing religion or any particular creed, and any benefit to religion or to the Church would have been no more than incidental. As in *Widmar,* permitting District property to be used to exhibit the film involved in this case would not have been an establishment of religion under the three-part test articulated in *Lemon v. Kurtzman* (1971): The challenged governmental action has a secular purpose, does not have the principal or primary effect of advancing or inhibiting religion, and does not foster an excessive entanglement with religion....

We note that the Attorney General for the State of New York, a respondent here, ... submits that the exclusion is justified because the purpose of the access rules is to promote the interests of the public in general rather than sectarian or other private interests. In light of the variety of the uses of District property that have been permitted under Rule 10, this approach has its difficulties. This is particularly so since Rule 10 states that District property may be used for social, civic, or recreational use "only if it can be nonexclusive and open to all residents of the school district that form a homogeneous group deemed relevant to the event." At least arguably, the Rule does not require that permitted uses need be open to the public at large. However that may be, this was not the basis of the judgment that we are reviewing. The Court of Appeals, as we understand it, ruled that because the District had the power to permit or exclude certain subject matters, it was entitled to deny use for any religious purpose, including the purpose in this case. The Attorney General also defends this as a permissible subject-matter exclusion rather than a denial based on viewpoint, a submission that we have already rejected....

For the reasons stated in this opinion, the judgment of the Court of Appeals is

Reversed.

JUSTICE KENNEDY, concurring in part and concurring in the judgment.

Given the issues presented as well as the apparent unanimity of our conclusion that this overt, viewpoint-based discrimination contradicts the Speech Clause of the First Amendment and that there has been no substantial showing of a potential Establishment Clause violation, I agree with JUSTICE SCALIA that the Court's citation of *Lemon v. Kurtzman* (1971) is unsettling and unnecessary. The same can be said of the Court's use of the phrase "endorsing religion," which, as I have indicated elsewhere, cannot suffice as a rule of decision consistent with our precedents and our traditions in this part of our jurisprudence....

JUSTICE SCALIA, with whom JUSTICE THOMAS joins, concurring in the judgment.

I join the Court's conclusion that the District's refusal to allow use of school facilities for petitioners' film viewing, while generally opening the schools for community activities, violates petitioners' First Amendment free-speech rights (as does N.Y. Educ. Law #414) to the extent it compelled the District's denial. I also agree with the Court that allowing Lamb's Chapel to use school facilities poses "no realistic danger" of a violation of the Establishment Clause, but I cannot accept most of its reasoning in this regard. The Court explains that the showing of petitioners' film on school property after school hours would not cause the community to "think that the District was endorsing religion or any particular creed," and further notes that access to school property would not violate the three-part test articulated in *Lemon v. Kurtzman* (1971).

As to the Court's invocation of the *Lemon* test: Like some ghoul in a late-night horror movie that repeatedly sits up in its grave and shuffles abroad, after being repeatedly killed and buried, *Lemon* stalks our Establishment Clause jurisprudence once again, frightening the little children and school attorneys of Center Moriches Union Free School District. Its most recent burial, only last Term, was, to be sure, not fully six-feet under: our decision in *Lee v. Weisman* (1992) conspicuously avoided using the supposed "test" but also declined the invitation to repudiate it. Over the years, however, no fewer than five of the currently sitting Justices have, in their own opinions, personally driven pencils through the creature's heart (the author of today's opinion repeatedly), and a sixth has joined an opinion doing so....

I cannot join for yet another reason: the Court's statement that the proposed use of the school's facilities is constitutional because (among other things) it would not signal endorsement of religion in general. What a strange notion, that a Constitution which itself gives "religion in general" preferential treatment (I refer to the Free Exercise Clause) forbids endorsement of religion in general. The Attorney General of New York not only agrees with that strange notion, he has an explanation for it: "Religious advocacy," he writes, "serves the community only in the eyes of its adherents and yields a benefit only to those who already believe." That was *not* the view of those who adopted our Constitution, who believed that the public virtues inculcated by religion are a public good. It suffices to point out that during the summer of 1789, when it was in the process of drafting the First Amendment, Congress enacted the famous Northwest Territory Ordinance of 1789, Article III of which provides, "Religion, morality, and knowledge, *being necessary to good government and the happiness of mankind,* schools and the means of education shall forever be encouraged." Unsurprisingly, then, indifference to "religion in general" is not what our cases, both old and recent, demand....

For the reasons given by the Court, I agree that the Free Speech Clause of the First Amendment forbids what respondents have done here. As for the asserted Establishment Clause justification, I would hold, simply and clearly, that giving Lamb's Chapel nondiscriminatory access to school facilities cannot violate that provision because it does not signify state or local embrace of a particular religious sect.

DISTRICT COURT ON ADMISSION OF HAITIANS

June 8, 1993

The long-simmering debate over the fate of Haitian refugees seeking political asylum in the United States took another turn June 8, when a U.S. district court ruled that the government should close down the detention camp for Haitians infected with the HIV virus, which can cause AIDS. In response, the Clinton administration announced the next day that it was releasing 158 Haitians who had been held for twenty months without legal representation at the American naval base in Guantánamo Bay, Cuba. The HIV-infected refugees were among the flood of forty thousand Haitians who had fled the country after September 1991, when the democratically elected president, Jean Bertrand Aristide, was overthrown and replaced by a harsh and repressive military dictatorship.

The 158 refugees, including 143 HIV-positive adults, two HIV-negative adults whose relatives had been infected, and thirteen minors who had not been tested, had "well-founded fears" of persecution if they returned to Haiti, according to officials of the U.S. Immigration and Naturalization Service (INS) who interviewed the detainees. However, the Bush and Clinton administrations, as well as Congress, argued that, although the Haitians qualified for political asylum, the government could bar their entry because they were infectious. That decision arose from 1990 legislation that would bar HIV-positive persons from entering the country unless the attorney general waived the ban.

During the 1992 presidential campaign, candidate Bill Clinton had pledged to close the detention camp, but after his election he continued the policy of his predecessor, President George Bush, to ban any HIV-infected refugees from entering the United States. Clinton signed the bill to uphold that law June 10. But the admininistration's policy came under increasing attack from protesters who demanded that Clinton close down what they called an "AIDS concentration camp" and lift the immigration ban. Numerous public health officials said it was unfair and unnecessary to treat HIV-infected people differently for immigration purposes because the disease was not spread by casual contact.

Background: Shifting U.S. Policy

A 1981 U.S.-Haitian agreement allowed the U.S. Coast Guard to board Haitian-flagged boats on the high seas to determine their destination; passengers were subject to return to Haiti if the Coast Guard found that a violation of U.S. or Haitian law had occurred. However, the agreement stated that the "United States does not intend to return to Haiti any Haitian migrants whom the United States authorities determine to qualify for refugee status." In the immediate aftermath of the 1991 coup, the United States temporarily suspended its repatriation program, pending a decision on procedures for handling the refugees, and housed the fleeing Haitians in makeshift facilities at Guantánamo. Shortly thereafter, the government decided that INS officers in the field would continue to have authority to determine which Haitians were "screened in" (eligible for U.S. asylum because there was a "credible fear of return" to Haiti) or "screened out" (deemed ineligible and therefore subject to repatriation).

On May 24, 1992, President George Bush had issued a controversial executive order halting the acceptance of Haitians seeking political asylum and authorizing the U.S. Coast Guard to begin repatriating boatloads of people attempting to escape Haiti's oppressive economic and political conditions. The order was reversed by a federal appeals court on July 29, which held that a 1980 law clearly stated that the United States "may not return aliens to their persecutors." The court granted an injunction preventing the Coast Guard from returning any Haitian "whose life or freedom would be threatened." The Justice Department promptly sought a reversal from the Supreme Court, which on August 1 allowed the Bush administration policy to remain in effect until it decided whether to rule on the policy's legality. (Bush and Court on Return of Haitian Refugees, Historic Documents of 1992, p. 453)

The Supreme Court ruled June 21, 1993, that the president indeed has the power to order the Coast Guard to intercept undocumented aliens on the high seas and return them to their home countries without conducting hearings to determine if they qualify for asylum. (Court on status of refugees, p. 413)

Congressional Concerns

In the interim, Congress had cleared legislation, signed by President Clinton, that further complicated the status of the Haitian refugees. In reauthorizing funding for the National Institutes of Health, Congress in May 1993 had adopted a provision that incorporated the administration's controversial position of establishing a permanent immigration ban on foreigners infected with HIV.

The AIDS immigration issue had been a principal point of contention during House and Senate negotiations on the final passage of the bill. The compromise, signed by the president June 10, included language that essentially wrote the status quo into the statute: it named HIV infection as of one of the public health concerns that would exclude foreigners from entering the country. Specific policy decisions, however, would be left to the discretion of the attorney general. Included in the ban were HIV-infected Haitians held at Guantánamo.

The HIV Camp and Court Ruling

After the presence of the HIV virus was discovered in a number of Haitian detainees, the government began to conduct AIDS testing for all screened-in refugees at Guantánamo, despite a longstanding U.S. policy that refugees would have medical tests only on their arrival in the United States. Those testing positive were required to undergo a second interview concerning their status; those that were screened-in were segregated in a separate camp surrounded by barbed wire.

The HIV detainees were repeatedly denied legal counsel. Although they had access to a clinic, military officials at Guantánamo requested that the refugees be evacuated because medical care was inadequate. Government spokespersons admitted that was the case, but there were no plans to send the refugees to the United States for treatment. Responding to these and other factors, a number of organizations (referred to by the district court as "Haitian Service Organizations") and individual Haitians brought suit against the government (including the attorney general, the INS acting commissioner, the secretary of state, the commandants of the U.S. Coast Guard, and the commander of the U.S. Naval Base at Guantánamo).

In their suit, the plaintiffs contended that the government had violated their First Amendment rights by denying legal access to the screened-in refugees, who were also denied Fifth Amendment due process rights. The plaintiffs also charged that the government violated the Administrative Procedure Act by "conducting unauthorized 'well-founded fear' interviews and that the Attorney General abused her discretion by denying parole for the screened-in Haitian plaintiffs." The court's ruling upheld the plaintiffs' arguments on all counts.

Describing conditions at the camp, Judge Sterling Johnson of the U.S. District Court in Brooklyn said the HIV-positive refugees had to "tie plastic garbage bags to the sides of the building to keep the rain out. They sleep on cots and hang sheets to create some semblance of privacy. They are guarded by the military and are not permitted to leave the camp, except under military escort. [They] have been subjected to predawn military sweeps as they sleep by as many as 400 soldiers dressed in full riot gear. They are confined like prisoners."

"Although the defendants [the U.S. government] euphemistically refer to its Guantánamo operation as a 'humanitarian camp,' the facts disclose that it is nothing more than an HIV prison camp presenting potential

public health risks to the Haitians held there," Johnson wrote in his fifty-three-page ruling. "The Haitians' plight is a tragedy of immense proportion, and their continued detainment is totally unacceptable to this court."

Reaction: Possible Appeal

"The [court] victory was long overdue for people who were suffering for more than 20 months," said Suzanne Shende of the Center for Constitutional Rights, one of the organizations representing the refugees. Shende said that "any appeal, if it happens, would be about future policy and future cases—not these 158."

However, White House spokesperson Dee Dee Myers said that the Justice Department would review the case and had not excluded the possibility of an appeal. She said a "resettlement task force" composed of representatives from the Justice Department's Community Relations Service, the Department of Health and Human Services, and private organizations that deal with refugees would help care for the refugees on their arrival in the United States.

Justice Department officials had concluded that "the best balance of the legal, practical, and humanitarian concerns was to comply with the order, and reserve our right to appeal," said Carl Stern, a department spokesman. "There are aspects of Judge Johnson's decision that we would find it difficult to live with in two regards," he said. First "would be the judge's very expansive view of the rights of aliens, who came into American hands purely out of our own humanitarian impulses to rescue them at sea. Second would be our concern about the judge's expansive view of the authority of courts to limit the Attorney General's exercise of her discretionary authority."

The first group of HIV-positive refugees (sixteen) were admitted into the United States June 9 under the attorney general's discretion, with the rest arriving throughout the week.

Following are excerpts from the June 8, 1993, ruling of the U.S. District Court for the Eastern District of New York, ordering that the U.S. government release Haitian refugees infected with the AIDS virus from a detention camp at the U.S. naval base at Guantánamo Bay, Cuba:

Statement of Facts

In 1981, the United States commenced the Alien Migration Interdiction Operation ("AMIO"), formerly known as the Haitian Migrant Interdiction Operation. A cooperative agreement between the United States and Haiti dated September 23, 1981 ("Haiti-U.S. Agreement") allows the United States Coast Guard ("Coast Guard") to board Haitian-flagged vessels on the high seas in order to inquire into the condition and destination of the vessel and the status of those on board. While the Agreement explicitly provides that the "United States does not intend to return to Haiti any Haitian migrants whom the United States authorities determine to qualify for refugee status," a vessel and its passengers were subject to return or repatriation to Haiti if the Coast Guard determined that a violation of United States or Haitian law had occurred. Between 1981 and 1991, the United States interdicted approximately 25,000 Haitians. The United States conducted refugee or asylum prescreening aboard Coast Guard cutters for interdicted Haitians as well as for interdicted nationals of 39 other countries including the Dominican Republic, the Bahamas, Pakistan, Iran, India, Colombia, and Chile during that period.

On September 30, 1991, Jean Bertrand Aristide ("Aristide"), the first democratically elected president in Haiti's history, was overthrown in a military coup. Fearing political persecution, thousands of Haitians fled the country by crossing the border into the Dominican Republic or taking to the high seas. Within a month of the coup, a large number of overcrowded, unseaworthy boats began departing from Haiti and the United States Coast Guard began interdicting an increasing number of such vessels in international waters.

Prior to interdicting a vessel, the Coast Guard inquired about the vessel's destination. Except when effecting a rescue at sea, the Coast Guard would not remove the passengers or master of a Haitian boat unless it was determined that the vessel was bound for the United States. However, the Coast Guard made no effort to determine the intended destination of each passenger on a particular vessel. If the Coast Guard believed that the vessel was headed for the United States, the Coast Guard interdicted all passengers, even if the passengers were willing to go to locations other than the United States. Because of their lack of seaworthiness, most of the interdicted Haitian vessels, if not all, would not have made it to the United States. In fact, some of the Haitian vessels landed in Cuba, Jamaica and the Bahamas. When the Coast Guard detained a Haitian vessel, it boarded the vessel and required all passengers to disembark. After all of the passengers had complied, the Coast Guard destroyed the Haitian vessel. Interdicted Haitians were thus given no option but to be detained on the Coast Guard cutter and to be taken to whatever location the Coast Guard elected.

Asylum Screening and Pre-Screening Procedures

Following the coup, the United States temporarily suspended its repatriation program while the Immigration and Naturalization Service ("INS") consulted with the United States Department of State ("State Department") on the procedures for handling the Haitian refugees. While the INS awaited a decision from Washington, the Coast Guard cutters with Haitian refugees aboard circled in international waters. For health and safety reasons, the cutters docked at Guantanamo Bay Naval Base, Cuba

("Guantanamo") on or about November 13, 1991 and the Haitians disembarked. A few days later, the decision making authority for determining whether interdicted Haitians were screened in or screened out was delegated back to INS officers in the field.

On November 22, 1991, the Office of the Deputy Commissioner of INS issued a memorandum stating that a "credible fear of return" standard was to be utilized in asylum pre-screening procedures. Under this "credible fear" standard, Haitians with only one or two "refugee-like" characteristics would be screened in, and thus determined to be eligible for political asylum. Interdicted Haitians with no "refugee-like" characteristics would be "screened out," and thus determined to be ineligible for political asylum and subject to repatriation. The "credible fear of return" standard was designed to be far more generous than the "well-founded fear of return" standard generally applied to asylum seekers.

As the number of interdicted Haitians rose, the INS transferred their interviewing operations from the Coast Guard cutters to Guantanamo. The interviews were conducted by highly trained members of the INS asylum corps which included INS officers, immigration lawyers, and human rights monitors. No attorneys representing the refugees were present during the "credible fear of return" interviews. Since October 1991, the INS screened in 10,500 Haitians found to have a "credible fear of return" and transported them to the United States to apply for asylum. An additional 25,000 interdictees were returned to Haiti by the Coast Guard after undergoing INS prescreening. A very small number were accepted by third countries.

Rescreening HIV+ Haitian Detainees

Soon after the INS began its Guantanamo operation, the United States began to seek third countries in which the Haitians could be relocated. The State Department pursued this with various countries in the region. Two countries, Belize and Honduras, offered to provide limited assistance, but prior to accepting the Haitians asked that they be tested for the HIV virus. The results of those tests disclosed the presence of the virus in a number of the Haitian detainees at Guantanamo leading the Government to conduct HIV testing for all screened-in Haitians. The Haitians are the only group of asylum seekers to be medically tested for HIV.

Prior to September 1991, all screened-in Haitian refugees were brought to the United States before receiving medical screening. As Gene McNary, then INS Commissioner, in a memorandum dated May 30, 1991, entitled "Asylum Pre-Screening of Interdicted Aliens and Asylum Seekers in INS Custody": "[i]nterdicted asylum seekers identified at sea for transfer to the United States will be properly inspected and medically screened *upon arrival* into the United States."

Then in a memorandum dated February 29, 1992, Grover Joseph Rees, INS General Counsel, stated a new INS policy requiring second or "well-founded fear" interviews of screened in persons who tested positive for the Human Immunodeficiency Virus ("HIV")....

By letter dated March 11, 1992, attorneys for the Haitian Service Organizations requested permission to communicate with the screened-in Haitians held on Guantanamo. The request was denied. The Screened In Plaintiffs detained on Guantanamo themselves repeatedly requested counsel. Their requests were also denied. The military did not oppose visits from counsel and when such visits have been permitted, the military has not found any disruption to the operation of the camp. Other groups, including the press, clergy, and non-U.S. contract workers (e.g., Cubans, Jamaicans and Filipinos) have been permitted access to Guantanamo. In the absence of attorneys, the Haitians have received legal advice from the military, INS, Community Relations Service representatives, ministers and even military doctors.

Notwithstanding the fact that attorneys are regularly present during nearly identical asylum interviews in the United States, the INS refused to permit the Screened In Plaintiffs to have counsel present at their "well-founded fear" interview. At trial, an INS official expressed the agency's concern with the presence of attorneys at asylum interviews saying that lawyers would only stress the positive element of an applicant's case and deemphasize the negative aspects. This Court finds that lawyers serve a necessary and useful purpose in representing an asylum seeker in connection with the well-founded fear of return interview. Their presence at these interviews is also clearly feasible. The Government's decision to deny Plaintiff Haitian Service Organizations access to Camp Bulkeley is based solely on the content of what they had to say and the viewpoint they would express.

The second interviews, like the first interviews, were conducted in the absence of attorneys. Of the HIV+ Screened In Plaintiffs who underwent the second interview, 115 Haitians were found to have a well-founded fear of return. A number of HIV+ Haitians who had been screened in were repatriated to Haiti after having failed the second interview or having declined to undergo the second interview. Haitians who received an adverse determination did not have the opportunity to appeal the decision.

Guantanamo Operation

. . . When the first group of Haitians arrived in November 1991, the existing facilities at Guantanamo were not sufficient to provide housing for all interdictees. A special Joint Task Force ("JTF") comprised of several branches of the Armed Services, was sent to Guantanamo to provide temporary humanitarian assistance to the Haitians including housing, food, and medical care from military physicians. In order to house the Haitians, the JTF evicted U.S. military personnel from the cinder block quarters at Camp Bulkeley on the eastern edge of the base. Tents were also erected at Camp Bulkeley to temporarily house the several thousand migrants who arrived at Guantanamo at the outset. When Camp Bulkeley's capacity proved inadequate, the JTF opened a new series of camps at the unused McCalla air field. These McCalla camps were all tent facilities except for the large hangar at the airfield....

In March 1992, after the prevalence of the HIV virus among the refugee population was ascertained, the JTF created a separate camp for them. Camp Bulkeley was chosen for that purpose. The then existing population of HIV negative Haitians at Camp Bulkeley remained until they were processed and departed Guantanamo. As "screened in" HIV+ Haitians were identified, they were transferred to Camp Bulkeley, eventually making it predominantly an HIV+ facility. The camp also contained HIV negative relatives of the HIV+ Haitians.

Today there are approximately 200 "screened in" HIV+ Haitians remaining at Guantanamo. They live in camps surrounded by razor barbed wire. They tie plastic garbage bags to the sides of the building to keep the rain out. They sleep on cots and hang sheets to create some semblance of privacy. They are guarded by the military and are not permitted to leave the camp, except under military escort. The Haitian detainees have been subjected to pre-dawn military sweeps as they sleep by as many as 400 soldiers dressed in full riot gear. They are confined like prisoners and are subject to detention in the brig without a hearing for camp rule infractions. Although the Haitian detainees have a chapel, weight room, bicycle repair shop, beauty parlor and other amenities at their disposal, none of these things are currently available to them, as they are now confined to Camp Alpha, a small section of Camp Bulkeley, or to the brig.

Medical Care at Guantanamo

... The two physicians [at the Haitian clinic] are assisted by a medical staff of four registered nurses, three independent duty corpsmen, a family practice nurse practitioner, 20 general duty corpsmen, and a preventive medicine technician whose duties include spraying standing water against insects, and rodent control. The clinic is a cinderblock, air conditioned building with four examining rooms, a large waiting area, a laboratory, and a pharmacy. The clinic, open generally from 7:30 a.m. to 4:00 p.m. daily, has 11 beds, but its capacity is expandable to about 55.

The Haitians do not need an appointment to come to the clinic, however, they may make appointments to see physicians as needed. The clinic is staffed 24 hours a day, seven days a week either by general duty corpsmen or physicians....

Despite the ability of military doctors and facilities to treat routine illnesses, the Government acknowledges that the medical facilities on the Guantanamo Naval Base are inadequate to provide medical care to those Haitians who have developed AIDS, particularly patients with T-cell counts of 200 or below or a percentage of 13 or less. The military doctors believe that the medical facilities on Guantanamo are inadequate to treat such AIDS patients.... The military doctors first raised these concerns at least as early as May, 1992. The military has requested that certain HIV+ Haitians be medically evacuated from Guantanamo because the military does not believe it can provide adequate medical care to those patients on Guantanamo. Certain of these requests have been denied by the INS on more than one occasion.

At trial the Government did not offer any evidence which would prove the facilities at Guantanamo to be adequate. In fact, defendants' counsel admitted that "the medical facilities at Guantanamo are not presently sufficient to provide treatment for such AIDS patients under the medical care standard applicable within the United States itself." But when asked whether the Government was "prepared to send those [patients] to the United States for treatment," Defendants' counsel responded, "The government does not intend at this point to do that." . . .

Although the defendants euphemistically refer to its Guantanamo operation as a "humanitarian camp," the facts disclose that it is nothing more than an HIV prison camp presenting potential public health risks to the Haitians held there. There is no dispute that because HIV+ individuals are immunosuppressed, they are more susceptible to a variety of infections, many of which can be transmitted from one person to the next. No major outbreak of infectious disease has occurred yet, but by segregating HIV+ individuals, the Government places the Haitian detainees at greater risk of contracting infections, including tuberculosis, measles and other life threatening diseases, than if they were permitted to live in the general population. . . .

In addition, the prison camp environment created by the Government is not conducive to an effective doctor-patient relationship. . . .

The seriously impaired doctor-patient relationship makes it more difficult for defendants to provide adequate medical care at the camp. Even if Defendants continue to provide medical services, many of the Haitian detainees will grow increasingly sick because they do not trust their diagnosis or the medication prescribed for them.

Conclusions of Law

[Parts I and II omitted]

III. Haitian Service Organizations' First Amendment Rights

Plaintiff Haitian Service Organizations' First Claim for Relief is that the Government has violated their First Amendment right by denying them and their attorneys access to the Screened In Plaintiffs for the purpose of counselling, advocacy and representation. . . .

The First Amendment says that "Congress shall make no Law . . . abridging the freedom of speech." U.S. Const. amend. 1. That provision applies on Guantanamo Bay Naval Base, which is under the complete control and jurisdiction of the United States government, and where the government exercises complete control over all means of delivering communications. . . . The Government has violated the Haitian Service Organization's First Amendment rights to free speech and to associate for the purpose of providing legal counsel by denying them equal access to the screened-in Haitians held on Guantanamo. Defendants have permitted press, clergy, politicians and other non-lawyers to meet with the Haitians and have permitted many others, including non-citizen contract workers, onto the base. In addition, the Haitians have received legal advice, which has often been erroneous, from the military, the INS, the Community Relations Service and even military doctors. The legal rights and options of Haitian detainees are discussed on Guantanamo, but only from the viewpoint of which the Government approves....

[T]he Haitian Service Organizations have been retained by the Screened In Plaintiffs and have asserted a right to speak with their clients, the screened-in Haitians. The lawyers here seek only to communicate, at their own expense, with clients who have specifically sought them out. The Court thus finds that the lawyers for the Haitian Service Organizations have been barred because of the viewpoint of the message they seek to convey to the Haitians, in violation of the First Amendment. Such Government discrimination against disfavored viewpoints strikes at the heart of the First Amendment....

IV. Due Process

Plaintiffs' Third Claim for Relief in the Amended Complaint states that the Government has violated the Screened In Plaintiffs' due process rights under the Fifth Amendment....

The Supreme Court has long held that aliens outside the United States are entitled to due process in civil suits in United States courts....

The United States government has already bound itself by treaty not to "impose penalties" on persons it has recognized as refugees who flee to the United States "directly from a territory where their life or freedom was threatened" on account of political persecution....

The Haitian detainees are imprisoned in squalid, prison-like camps surrounded by razor barbed wire. They are not free to wander about the base. Guarded by the military day and night, the Screened In Plaintiffs are subject to surprise pre-dawn military sweeps conducted by soldiers outfitted in full riot gear searching for missing detainees. Haitian detainees have been punished for rule infractions by being flexicuffed and sent to "administrative segregation camp" (Camp Alpha or Camp 7) or the brig. Such conditions cannot be tolerated when, as here, the detainees have a right to due process.

A. Access to Counsel During "Well-Founded" Interviews

The Screened In Plaintiffs have a protected liberty interest in not being wrongly repatriated to Haiti,... and to due process before defendants alter their screened in status....

... [T]he private interest of the Screened In Plaintiffs not to be returned to Haiti is of the highest order. Based on the INS's own findings, the screened-in Haitians have already been found to have at least a credible fear of return. This showing exceeds that of an unscreened asylum applicant in the United States whose interest in applying for asylum is constitutionally protected. . . .

B. Medical Care

Constitutional due process mandates both provision of adequate medical care to persons in official custody. . . . As persons in coercive, nonpunitive, and indefinite detention, the Haitian detainees on Guantanamo are constitutionally entitled to medically adequate conditions of confinement. . . .

The military's own doctors have made INS aware that Haitian detainees with T-cell counts of 200 or below or percentages of 13 or below should be medically evacuated to the United States because of a lack of facilities and specialists at Guantanamo. Despite this knowledge, Defendant INS has repeatedly failed to act on recommendations and deliberately ignored the medical advice of U.S. military doctors that all persons with T-cell count below 200 or percentages below 13 be transported to the United States for treatment. Such actions constitute deliberate indifference to the Haitians' medical needs in violation of their due process rights. . . .

[C omitted]

D. Indefinite Detention

As individuals held in custody by the United States, the Screened In Plaintiffs also have a liberty interest in not being arbitrarily or indefinitely detained. . . .

Here, the Screened In Plaintiffs' continued detention is the result of the Defendants' actions, not the aliens' own choices. The Government stopped processing the cases of these and other screened-in Haitians in June 1992, after the Second Circuit upheld this Court's injunction entitling the Haitians to be represented by counsel. One-hundred and fifteen Haitians at Guantanamo have met the well-founded fear standard in the second interviews and have remained in detention for almost two years. . . .

. . . [T]he detained Haitians are neither criminals nor national security risks. Some are pregnant mothers and others are children. Simply put, they are merely the unfortunate victims of a fatal disease. The Government has failed to demonstrate to this Court's satisfaction that the detainees' illness warrants the kind of indefinite detention usually reserved for spies and murderers. . . . Where detention no longer serves a legitimate purpose, the detainees must be released. The Haitian camp at Guantanamo is the only known refugee camp in the world composed entirely of HIV+ refugees. The Haitians' plight is a tragedy of immense proportion and their continued detainment is totally unacceptable to this Court. . . .

IV. Violations of Administrative Procedure Act

For their Fifth Claim for Relief, Plaintiffs allege that a) the Government violated the APA by conducting unauthorized "well-founded fear" interviews and b) the Attorney General abused her discretion by denying parole for the screened-in Haitian Plaintiffs....

Plaintiffs allege that the Attorney General's refusal to parole them from detention due to their HIV+ status constitutes an abuse of discretion. For the reason set forth below, the Court agrees and sets aside her denial of parole....

By effectively denying the plaintiffs release from detention, defendant Attorney General has abused her discretion.... Haitians remain in detention solely because they are Haitian and have tested HIV-positive. The Government has admitted that the ban on the admission of aliens with communciable diseases has not been strictly enforced against every person seeking entry. Each year many "non-immigrants" enter the United States, are legally entitled to remain for years, and are not subject to HIV testing. To date, the Government has only enforced the ban against Haitians....

The Attorney General has abused her discretion in failing to parole the HIV+ Haitian detainees on Guantanamo. Her decision to detain these Haitians deviates from established parole policy and is illegally based upon a statute which is selectively enforced against Haitian nationals and merely makes persons carrying the HIV virus excludable from "admission" or permanent residence. For foregoing reasons, the Court hereby sets aside the Attorney General's denial of parole....

Relief

For the reasons stated above,

1. The following class is hereby certified:
   (a) all Haitian citizens who have been or will be "screened in" who are, have been or will be detained on Guantanamo Bay Naval Base, or any other territory subject to United States jurisdiction, or on Coast Guard cutters, including those who have been or will be subject to post-screening processing (or who have resisted such processing) (hereinafter "Screened In Plaintiffs");
2. It is hereby,
   (a) DECLARED that the "Well-Founded Fear" Processing by Defendants set forth in the Rees Memorandum is in excess of Defendants' statutory authority, and
   (b) ORDERED that such "Well-Founded Fear" Processing be permanently enjoined, held unlawful and set aside pursuant to the Administrative Procedure Act: and
3. It is hereby further
   (a) DECLARED that defendant Attorney General's exercise of the statutory parole power under INA § 212(d)(5) to deny Screened In Plaintiffs parole out of detention constitutes an abuse of discretion; and
   (b) ORDERED that defendant Attorney General's exercise of the statutory parole power under INA § 212(d)(5) to deny Screened

In Plaintiffs parole out of detention be permanently enjoined, held unlawful and set aside pursuant to the Administrative Procedure Act; and

4. It is hereby further
   (a) DECLARED that the "Well-Founded Fear" Processing, Disciplinary Proceedings, Arbitrary and Indefinite Detention, Medical Care and Camp Conditions to which Screened In Plaintiffs are being subjected by Defendants denies those plaintiffs Due Process of Law; and
   (b) ORDERED that such "Well-Founded Fear" Processing, Disciplinary Proceedings, Arbitrary and Indefinite Detention, Medical Care and Camp Conditions be permanently enjoined pursuant to the Fifth Amendment of the United States Constitution; and that Screened In Plaintiffs be immediately released (to anywhere but Haiti) from such processing, proceedings, detention, medical care and camp conditions; and
5. It is hereby further
   (a) DECLARED that denying plaintiff Haitian Service Organizations immediate access to Guantanamo to communicate and associate with their detained Screened-In Plaintiff clients violates the First Amendment; and
   (b) ORDERED that Defendants are permanently enjoined from denying plaintiff Haitian Service Organizations immediate access at Guantanamo, on Coast Guard Cutters, or at any other place subject to U.S. jurisdiction to any member of the class of Screened In Plaintiffs (regardless of whether any such screened-in plaintiff has been furnished with an exact date and time for an interview), subject to reasonable time, place, and manner limitations for the purpose of providing class members legal counsel, advocacy, and representation; and
6. It is hereby finally
   (a) DECLARED that Plaintiffs are entitled to such other and further relief as the Court may deem just and proper, including reasonable attorneys' fees and costs, to be determined at a future hearing.

So ordered.

Sterling Johnson, Jr.
United States District Judge

Dated: Brooklyn, New York
June 8, 1993

COURT ON HATE CRIME SENTENCE

June 11, 1993

For the second time in two years, the Supreme Court ruled on the constitutionality of laws that specifically punish crimes committed out of hatred for the victims' race, religion, ethnic origin, or sexual orientation. On June 11 a unanimous Court in Wisconsin v. Mitchell *upheld a Wisconsin law the state invoked to lengthen the sentence for a racially motivated assault. A year earlier a divided Court, citing free-speech guarantees, struck down an ordinance enacted by St. Paul, Minnesota, to ban "fighting words" based on race, religion, or gender, and forbid the display of symbols, such as swastikas and burning crosses, likely to incite anger.* (Supreme Court on Hate-Crime Law, Historic Documents of 1992, p. 543)

In the 1992 case, R.A.V. v. City of St. Paul, *the Court held that in specifying types of "hate speech" for punishment, the ordinance violated the First Amendment by restricting speech on "disfavored subjects." That decision threw into question the legality of hundreds of state and local antibias laws and campus speech codes. The St. Paul decision left unanswered the question of whether it also undercut less direct laws imposing added penalties on persons guilty of committing hate crimes. Such laws were in effect in twenty-six states and the District of Columbia.*

In Wisconsin v. Mitchell, *that question was addressed directly. Wisconsin, joined by other states, the federal government and a coalition of civil rights groups, argued that the penalty-enhancement measure was based on conduct, not speech, and thus withstood the free-speech test. The Court agreed. Chief Justice William H. Rehnquist, writing for all nine justices, noted that a trial judge traditionally has been permitted to consider "a wide variety of factors" in sentencing a defendant, including the motive for the crime. Although judges cannot consider the "abstract beliefs" of defendants, he acknowledged, they can take racial bias or other prejudice into account when it is part of the motive.*

Turning to the free-speech issue, Rehnquist said the Wisconsin law "is aimed at conduct unprotected by the First Amendment." The Wisconsin lawmakers passed the law, the chief justice added, because they believed "bias-inspired conduct" causes great injury to individuals and society, and may provoke retaliation and incite community unrest. "The State's desire to redress these perceived harms provides an adequate explanation for its penalty-enhancement provisions over and above mere disagreement with offenders' belief or biases," Rehnquist continued.

Background

The Wisconsin case arose in 1989 when a white teenager walking along a street in Kenosha was attacked and badly beaten by a group of black youths who were angered by seeing Mississippi Burning, *a movie that portrayed white mistreatment of blacks during the civil rights struggle. Todd Mitchell, who instigated the attack, was tried and convicted of aggravated assault. The jury determined that Mitchell had selected the victim solely because of his race. The trial judge imposed the maximum two-year sentence for the offense and added two years under the hate-crime law.*

Mitchell challenged the conviction and sentence. The Wisconsin Court of Appeals rejected the challenge, but on further appeal the Wisconsin Supreme Court declared that the hate-crime law infringed on the First Amendment and was invalid. Citing the St. Paul case, the Wisconsin Supreme Court said the state's legislature "cannot criminalize bigoted thought with which it disagrees."

Separation of Conduct and Speech

The U.S. Supreme Court quickly called up the Wisconsin case in an apparent attempt to clarify the question of when a hate-crime law crosses the boundary between a permissible ban on misconduct and an impermissible ban on speech. Rehnquist denied defense assertions, adopted by the Wisconsin Supreme Court, that the law had a chilling effect on the right of free speech. The likelihood that someone would suppress "his bigoted beliefs" because they could be used against him later in a criminal trial was "too speculative" to support the contention that the law was unconstitutionally broad, Rehnquist wrote.

The Court spoke with one voice in upholding the Wisconsin law. None of the other justices wrote a separate opinion—seemingly to prevent confusion or uncertainty about the meaning of the decision. However, the Court largely ignored troublesome questions about how judges should conduct hate-crime trials. Rehnquist said only that evidence about a defendant's previous statements "is commonly admitted" in trials, "subject to evidentiary rules dealing with relevancy, reliability, and the like."

Following are excerpts from the Supreme Court opinion of June 11, 1993, written by Chief Justice William H. Rehn-

quist in the case Wisconsin v. Mitchell, *upholding a Wisconsin law permitting added punishment for perpetrators of so-called hate crimes:*

No. 92-515

Wisconsin, Petitioner *v.* Todd Mitchell	On writ of certiorari to the Supreme Court of Wisconsin

[June 11, 1993]

CHIEF JUSTICE REHNQUIST delivered the opinion of the Court.

Respondent Todd Mitchell's sentence for aggravated battery was enhanced because he intentionally selected his victim on account of the victim's race. The question presented in this case is whether this penalty enhancement is prohibited by the First and Fourteenth Amendments. We hold that it is not. . . .

. . . The [Wisconsin] Supreme Court held that the statute "violates the First Amendment directly by punishing what the legislature has deemed to be offensive thought." It rejected the State's contention "that the statute punishes only the 'conduct' of intentional selection of a victim." According to the court, "[t]he statute punishes the 'because of' aspect of the defendant's selection, the *reason* the defendant selected the victim, the *motive* behind the selection." ([E]mphasis in original). And under *R.A.V. v. St. Paul* (1992), "the Wisconsin legislature cannot criminalize bigoted thought with which it disagrees."

The [Wisconsin] Supreme Court also held that the penalty-enhancement statute was unconstitutionally overbroad. It reasoned that, in order to prove that a defendant intentionally selected his victim because of the victim's protected status, the State would often have to introduce evidence of the defendant's prior speech, such as racial epithets he may have uttered before the commission of the offense. This evidentiary use of protected speech, the court thought, would have a "chilling effect" on those who feared the possibility of prosecution for offenses subject to penalty enhancement. Finally, the court distinguished antidiscrimination laws, which have long been held constitutional, on the ground that the Wisconsin statute punishes the "subjective mental process" of selecting a victim because of his protected status, whereas antidiscrimination laws prohibit "objective acts of discrimination."

We granted certiorari because of the importance of the question presented and the existence of a conflict of authority among state high courts on the constitutionality of statutes similar to Wisconsin's penalty-enhancement provision. . . .

The State argues that the statute does not punish bigoted thought, as the Supreme Court of Wisconsin said, but instead punishes only conduct. While this argument is literally correct, it does not dispose of Mitchell's First Amendment challenge....

... [U]nder the Wisconsin statute the same criminal conduct may be more heavily punished if the victim is selected because of his race or other protected status than if no such motive obtained. Thus, although the statute punishes criminal conduct, it enhances the maximum penalty for conduct motivated by a discriminatory point of view more severely than the same conduct engaged in for some other reason or for no reason at all. Because the only reason for the enhancement is the defendant's discriminatory motive for selecting his victim, Mitchell argues (and the Wisconsin Supreme Court held) that the statute violates the First Amendment by punishing offenders' bigoted beliefs.

Traditionally, sentencing judges have considered a wide variety of factors in addition to evidence bearing on guilt in determining what sentence to impose on a convicted defendant.... The defendant's motive for committing the offense is one important factor.... Thus, in many States the commission of a murder, or other capital offense, for pecuniary gain is a separate aggravating circumstance under the capital-sentencing statute.

But it is equally true that a defendant's abstract beliefs, however obnoxious to most people, may not be taken into consideration by a sentencing judge. *Dawson v. Delaware* (1992). In *Dawson,* the State introduced evidence at a capital-sentencing hearing that the defendant was a member of a white supremacist prison gang. Because "the evidence proved nothing more than [the defendant's] abstract beliefs," we held that its admission violated the defendant's First Amendment rights. In so holding, however, we emphasized that "the Constitution does not erect a *per se* barrier to the admission of evidence concerning one's beliefs and associations at sentencing simply because those beliefs and associations are protected by the First Amendment." Thus, in *Barclay v. Florida* (1983) (plurality opinion), we allowed the sentencing judge to take into account the defendant's racial animus towards his victim. The evidence in that case showed that the defendant's membership in the Black Liberation Army and desire to provoke a "race war" were related to the murder of a white man for which he was convicted. Because "the elements of racial hatred in [the] murder" were relevant to several aggravating factors, we held that the trial judge permissibly took this evidence into account in sentencing the defendant to death.

Mitchell suggests that *Dawson* and *Barclay* are inapposite because they did not involve application of a penalty-enhancement provision. But in *Barclay* we held that it was permissible for the sentencing court to consider the defendant's racial animus in determining whether he should be sentenced to death, surely the most severe "enhancement" of all....

Mitchell argues that the Wisconsin penalty-enhancement statute is invalid because it punishes the defendant's discriminatory motive, or reason, for acting. But motive plays the same role under the Wisconsin statute as it does under federal and state antidiscrimination laws, which we have previously upheld against constitutional challenge....

Nothing in our decision last Term in *R.A.V.* compels a different result here. That case involved a First Amendment challenge to a municipal ordinance prohibiting the use of " 'fighting words' that insult, or provoke violence, 'on the basis of race, color, creed, religion or gender.' " Because the ordinance only proscribed a class of "fighting words" deemed particularly offensive by the city—*i.e.,* those "that contain ... messages of 'bias-motivated' hatred," we held that it violated the rule against content-based discrimination. But whereas the ordinance struck down in *R.A.V.* was explicitly directed at expression (*i.e.,* "speech" or "messages"), the statute in this case is aimed at conduct unprotected by the First Amendment.

Moreover, the Wisconsin statute singles out for enhancement bias-inspired conduct because this conduct is thought to inflict greater individual and societal harm. For example, according to the State and its *amici,* bias-motivated crimes are more likely to provoke retaliatory crimes, inflict distinct emotional harms on their victims, and incite community unrest. The State's desire to redress these perceived harms provides an adequate explanation for its penalty-enhancement provision over and above mere disagreement with offenders' beliefs or biases....

... Mitchell argues (and the Wisconsin Supreme Court agreed) that the statute is "overbroad" because evidence of the defendant's prior speech or associations may be used to prove that the defendant intentionally selected his victim on account of the victim's protected status. Consequently, the argument goes, the statute impermissibly chills free expression with respect to such matters by those concerned about the possibility of enhanced sentences if they should in the future commit a criminal offense covered by the statute. We find no merit in this contention.

...We must conjure up a vision of a Wisconsin citizen suppressing his unpopular bigoted opinions for fear that if he later commits an offense covered by the statute, these opinions will be offered at trial to establish that he selected his victim on account of the victim's protected status, thus qualifying him for penalty-enhancement.... This is simply too speculative a hypothesis to support Mitchell's overbreadth claim.

The First Amendment, moreover, does not prohibit the evidentiary use of speech to establish the elements of a crime or to prove motive or intent. Evidence of a defendant's previous declarations or statements is commonly admitted in criminal trials subject to evidentiary rules dealing with relevancy, reliability, and the like....

For the foregoing reasons, we hold that Mitchell's First Amendment rights were not violated by the application of the Wisconsin penalty-enhancement provision in sentencing him. The judgment of the Supreme Court of Wisconsin is therefore reversed, and the case is remanded for further proceedings not inconsistent with this opinion.

It is so ordered.

GINSBURG'S APPOINTMENT TO THE SUPREME COURT

June 14, 1993

After a protracted and closely watched search that involved the introduction and dismissal of several candidates, President Bill Clinton on June 14 nominated Ruth Bader Ginsburg to the Supreme Court. Replacing Justice Byron R. White, who was retiring at the end of the 1992-1993 term after thirty-one years on the Court, Ginsburg became the second woman to serve on the Court and the first Jew appointed since Abe Fortas. Her appointment was also the first by a Democratic president to the Court since 1967 when President Lyndon B. Johnson named Thurgood Marshall.

Regarding his criteria for the appointment, Clinton said in March that he was looking for a justice with "a fine mind, good judgment, wide experience in the law and the problems of real people, and someone with a big heart." In his remarks at Ginsburg's swearing-in ceremony August 10, he declared that the new justice had put her mark on "virtually every significant case brought before the Supreme Court in the decade of the seventies on behalf of women."

Ginsburg joined a Court on which Sandra Day O'Connor had served since 1981 as the first female justice. O'Connor was also the first of five justices (the others are Antonin Scalia, Anthony M. Kennedy, David H. Souter, and Clarence Thomas) placed on the Court by Presidents Ronald Reagan and George Bush, shifting its ideological leanings to the right. Although Ginsburg was noted in her legal career for her advocacy of women's rights, as a federal appellate court judge she had adopted a centrist approach which she was expected to follow on the Supreme Court.

Ginsburg, who taught at Rutgers University Law School and then at Columbia Law School, came to prominence as director of the Women's Rights Project of the American Civil Liberties Union during the 1970s. Between 1973 and 1976 she won five of six cases that she argued before the Supreme Court, establishing a legal basis under the Fourteenth Amendment for equal rights for women. In 1980 President Jimmy Carter placed her on the U.S. Court of Appeals for the District of Columbia.

From Immigrant Beginnings to Law School

Born Joan Ruth Bader March 15, 1933, Ginsburg grew up in a Brooklyn neighborhood populated by Jewish, Italian, and Irish immigrants. She showed her ability and ambition early under the encouragement of her mother, Celia, who had graduated from high school at fifteen but was denied a college education. Ruth Bader went to Cornell University as a scholarship student, dated Martin (Marty) Ginsburg, the son of a well-to-do department store executive, graduated first in her class of 1954, and married Ginsburg. They decided on careers in law. His freshman year at Harvard Law School was interrupted by the draft and while he was in military service the first of their two children was born.

After their return to Harvard, Ruth Bader Ginsburg also entered the law school, one of nine women in her class. She earned high grades and a place on the Law Review. *As her husband struggled with testicular cancer, she took notes in his classes and typed the papers he dictated. After his recovery he joined a New York law firm and Ruth Ginsburg transferred to Columbia where she also won a place on the* Law Review.

Rejection Despite Brilliance

Despite her accomplishments, Ruth Ginsburg could not get a job with any important Manhattan law firm or an interview for a Supreme Court clerkship. Of her rejections at that time, Ginsburg has written, "To be a woman, a Jew and mother to boot, that combination was a bit much."

Eventually, Ginsburg obtained a clerkship with a federal district judge and then accepted a Carnegie Foundation grant to study the Swedish legal system. She co-wrote two books on Swedish law and was awarded an honorary degree by the University of Lund. She also translated the Swedish Code of Criminal Procedure into English. Her teaching career began at Rutgers University Law School in 1963. In 1972 she moved to Columbia Law School, where she became the first tenured woman professor.

Rights Advocacy to Centrist Judge

Ginsburg's advocacy of women's rights when she was named to the court of appeals caused concern in the Senate during the confirmation process. She was able to convince influential Republican senators that she would be a moderate on the bench. She indeed was, voting more often than not with colleagues appointed by Republican presidents. In her rulings, Ginsburg frequently noted that she was "constrained" and "required" to adhere to precedents of law.

Although she strongly supported a woman's right to abortion, describing it during her Supreme Court nomination hearing as "something central to a woman's life, to her dignity," Ginsburg alarmed abortion-rights supporters when she criticized the scope of the Court's Roe v. Wade *decision, which legalized abortion in 1973. However, this view was consistent with her incremental approach to the law. When Ginsburg sought to enlarge the constitutional guarantee of equal protection to women, she chose cases representing ordinary people, many of them men, and nonthreatening issues. The net result was a series of landmark decisions. These decisions were not "activist," she said, because they "largely trailed and mirrored changing patterns in society."*

Clinton selected Ginsburg after several other potential nominees had been prominently mentioned in the press or, in some instances, by Clinton himself. One was Gov. Mario M. Cuomo of New York, who, after weeks of pondering, removed himself from consideration. So did Secretary of Education Richard W. Riley. Another cabinet member, Secretary of the Interior Bruce Babbitt, was reportedly under consideration, but environmental groups, wanting him to stay put, protested. After Babbitt, Clinton met with Stephen G. Breyer, a federal appeals court judge in Boston. When it was revealed that Breyer had not paid Social Security taxes for his household help, the president looked elsewhere and chose Ginsburg.

After hearings marked by bipartisan harmony, the Senate approved Ginsburg's nomination by a vote of 96 to 3. She was widely regarded as a "consensus" candidate who would support centrist positions, although she would likely veer closer to the liberal side than had Justice White, her predecessor. When she took the oath of office August 10, President Clinton declared that Justice Ginsburg "defied labels like liberal and conservative."

White, an appointee of President John F. Kennedy in 1962, was identified with the Court's conservative wing, although, as the Court's conservative bent became more pronounced during the Reagan and Bush presidencies, he sometimes assumed the role of a swing voter. Ginsburg's voting on the Court was expected to contrast most sharply with White's on issues concerning women's rights, including abortion. White had cast one of the two dissenting votes in the 1973 case legalizing abortion. In announcing Ginsburg's appointment, Clinton said White as had served the Court "with distinction, intelligence and honor, and he retires from public service with the deep gratitude of all the American people."

> *Following are excerpts from President Bill Clinton's announcement at a Rose Garden news conference, June 14, 1993, of his nomination of Ruth Bader Ginsburg for associate justice of the Supreme Court, replacing Byron R. White, who was retiring:*

PRESIDENT CLINTON: Please be seated. I wish you all a good afternoon, and I thank the members of the Congress and other interested Americans who are here. In just a few days, when the Supreme Court concludes its term, Justice Byron White will begin a new chapter in his long and productive life. He has served the court as he has lived, with distinction, intelligence and honor, and he retires from public service with the deep gratitude of all the American people.

Article 2, Section 2 of the United States Constitution empowers the president to select a nominee to fill a vacancy on the Supreme Court of the United States. This responsibility is one of the most significant duties assigned to the president by the Constitution.

A Supreme Court justice has life tenure, unlike the president, and along with his or her colleagues decides the most significant questions of our time, and shapes the continuing contours of our liberty.

I care a lot about this responsibility, not only because I am a lawyer, but because I used to teach constitutional law, and I served my state as attorney general. I know well how the Supreme Court affects the lives of all Americans, personally and deeply.

I know clearly that a Supreme Court justice should have the heart and spirit, the talent and discipline, the knowledge, common sense and wisdom to translate the hopes of the American people as presented in the cases before it into an enduring body of constitutional law, a constitutional law that will preserve our most cherished values that are enshrined in that Constitution and at the same time enable the American people to move forward.

That is what I promised the American people, just as when I ran for president, and I believe it is a promise that I am delivering on today.

After careful reflection I am proud to nominate for associate justice of the Supreme Court Judge Ruth Bader Ginsburg of the United States Court of Appeals for the District of Columbia.

I will send her name to the Senate to fill the vacancy created by Justice White's retirement. As I told Judge Ginsburg last night when I called to ask her to accept the nomination, I decided on her for three reasons:

First, in her years on the bench she has genuinely distinguished herself as one of our nation's best judges: progressive in outlook, wise in judgment, balanced and fair in her opinions.

Second, over the course of a lifetime, in her pioneering work on behalf of the women of this country, she has compiled a truly historic record of achievement in the finest traditions of American law and citizenship.

And finally, I believe that in the years ahead, she will be able to be a force for consensus-building on the Supreme Court just as she has been on the Court of Appeals, so that our judges can become an instrument of our common unity in the expression of their fidelity to the Constitution.

Judge Ginsburg received her undergraduate degree from Cornell. She attended both Harvard and Columbia law schools and served on the law reviews of both institutions, the first woman to have earned this distinction. She was a law clerk to a federal judge, a law professor at Rutgers and Columbia law schools; she argued six landmark cases in behalf of women before the United States Supreme Court and happily won five out of six.

For the past 13 years, she has served on the United States Court of Appeals for the District of Columbia, the second-highest court in our country, where her work has brought her national acclaim and on which she was able to amass a record that caused a national legal journal in 1991 to name her as one of the nation's leading centrist judges.

In the months and years ahead, the country will have the opportunity to get to know much more about Ruth Ginsburg's achievements, decency, humanity and fairness. People will find, as I have, that this nominee is a person of immense character. Quite simply, what's in her record speaks volumes about what is in her heart. Throughout her life, she has repeatedly stood for the individual, the person less well off, the outsider in society, and has given those people greater hope by telling them that they have a place in our legal system by giving them a sense that the Constitution and the laws protect all the American people, not simply the powerful.

Judge Ginsburg has also proven herself to be a healer, what attorneys call a moderate. Time and again, her moral imagination has cooled the fires of her colleagues' discord, ensuring that the right of jurists to dissent ennobles the law without entangling the court.

The announcement of this vacancy brought forth a unique outpouring of support from distinguished Americans on Judge Ginsburg's behalf. What caused that outpouring is the essential quality of the judge herself, her deep respect for others and her willingness to subvert self-interest to the interest of our people and their institutions.

In one of her own writings about what it is like to be a justice, Judge Ginsburg quotes Justice Louis Brandeis, who once said the Supreme Court is not a place for solo performers. If this is a time for consensus-building on the court, and I believe it is, Judge Ginsburg will be an able and effective architect of that effort.

It is important to me that Judge Ginsburg came to her reviews and attitudes by doing, not merely by reading and studying. Despite her enormous ability and academic achievements, she could not get a job with a law firm in the early 1960s because she was a woman and the mother of a small child.

Having experienced discrimination, she devoted the next 20 years of her career to fighting it and making this country a better place for our wives, our mothers, our sisters and our daughters. She herself argued and won many of the women's rights cases before the Supreme Court in the 1970s. Many admirers of her work say that she is to the women's movement what former Supreme Court Justice Thurgood Marshall was to the movement for the rights of African-Americans. I can think of no greater compliment to bestow on an American lawyer.

And she has done all of this and a lot of other things as well while raising a family with her husband, Marty, whom she married 39 years ago, as a very young woman.

Together they had two children, Jane and James, and they now have two grandchildren. Hers is a remarkable record of distinction and achievement, both professional and personal.

During the selection process, we reviewed the qualifications of more than 40 potential nominees. It was a long, exhaustive search, and during that time we identified several wonderful Americans, whom I think could be outstanding nominees to the Supreme Court in the future.

Among the best were the secretary of the Interior, Bruce Babbitt, whose strong legal background as Arizona's attorney general and recent work balancing the competing interests of environmentalists and others in the very difficult issues affecting the American West made him a highly qualified candidate for the court.

And I had the unusual experience, something unique to me, of being flooded with calls all across America from Babbitt admirers who pleaded with me not to put him on the Court and take him away from the Interior Department.

I also have carefully considered the chief judge of the 1st Circuit, Judge Stephen Breyer of Boston, a man whose character, confidence and legal scholarship impressed me very greatly.

I believe he has a very major role to play in public life. I believe he is superbly qualified to be on the Court, and I think either one of these candidates, as well as the handful of others whom I closely considered, may well find themselves in that position some day in the future.

Let me say, in closing, that Ruth Bader Ginsburg cannot be called a liberal or a conservative. She has proved herself too thoughtful for such labels. As she herself put it in one of her articles, and I quote: The greatest figures of the American judiciary have been independent-thinking individuals with open but not empty minds, individuals willing to listen and to learn. They have exhibited a readiness to re-examine their own premises, liberal or conservative, as thoroughly as those of others.

That I believe describes Judge Ginsburg, and those I too believe are the qualities of a great justice. If, as I believe, the measure of a person's values can best be measured by examining the life the person lives, then Judge Ginsburg's values are the very ones that represent the very best in America.

I am proud to nominate this path-breaking attorney, advocate and judge to be the 107th justice to the United States Supreme Court.

JUDGE GINSBURG: Mr. President, I am grateful beyond measure for the confidence you have placed in me, and I will strive, with all that I have, to live up to your expectations in making this appointment.

I appreciate, too, the special caring of Senator Daniel Patrick Moynihan [D-N.Y.], the more so because I do not actually know the senator. I was born and brought up in New York, the state Senator Moynihan represents, and he was the very first person to call with good wishes when President

Carter nominated me in 1980 to serve on the U.S. Court of Appeals for the District of Columbia Circuit. Senator Moynihan has offered the same encouragement on this occasion.

May I introduce at this happy moment three people very special to me: my husband, Martin D. Ginsburg; my son-in-law, George T. Spera Jr.; and my son, James Steven Ginsburg. . . .

The announcement the president just made is significant, I believe, because it contributes to the end of the days when women, at least half the talent pool in our society, appear in high places only as one-at-a-time performers.

Recall that when President Carter took office in 1976 no woman [had] ever served on the Supreme Court and only one woman, Shirley Hufstedler of California, then served at the next federal court level, the United States Courts of Appeals.

Today, Justice Sandra Day O'Connor graces the Supreme Court bench, and close to 25 women serve at the federal court of appeals level, too, as chief judges. I am confident that more will soon join them. That seems, to me, inevitable, given the change in law school enrollment.

My law school class, in the late 1950s, numbered over 500. That class included less than 10 women. As the president said, not a law firm in the entire city of New York bid for my employment as a lawyer when I earned my degree. Today, few law schools have female enrollment under 40 percent, and several have reached or passed the 50 percent market.

And thanks to Title VII, no entry doors are barred. My daughter, Jane, reminded me a few hours ago, in a good luck call from Australia, of a sign of the change we have had the good fortune to experience. In her high school yearbook, on her graduation in 1973, the listing for Jane Ginsburg under ambition was to see her mother appointed to the Supreme Court.

The next line read: If necessary, Jane will appoint her.

Jane is so pleased, Mr. President, that you did it instead, and her brother, James, is, too.

I expect to be asked in some detail about my views of the work of a good judge on a high court bench. This afternoon is not the moment for extended remarks on that subject, but I might state a few prime guides.

Chief Justice [William H.] Rehnquist offered one I keep in the front of my mind. A judge is bound to decide each case fairly in accord with the relevant facts and the applicable law, even when the decision is not, as he put it, what the home crowd wants.

Next, I know no better summary than the one Justice O'Connor recently provided, drawn from a paper by New York University Law School Professor Burt Neuborne. The remarks concerned the enduring influence of Justice Oliver Wendell Holmes.

They read: When a modern constitutional judge is confronted with a hard case, Holmes is at her side with three gentle reminders. First, intellectual honesty about the available policy choices; second, disciplined self-restraint in respecting the majority's policy choice; and third, principled commitment to defense of individual autonomy even in the face of majority action.

To that I can only say Amen.

I am indebted to so many for this extraordinary chance and challenge, to a revived women's movement in the 1970s that opened doors for people like me, to the civil rights movement of the 1960s from which the women's movement drew inspiration, to my teaching colleagues at Rutgers and Columbia, and for 13 years, my D.C. Circuit colleagues, who shaped and heightened my appreciation of the value of collegiality.

Most closely, I have been aided by my life's partner, Martin D. Ginsburg, who has been since our teenage years my best friend and biggest booster; by my mother-in-law, Evelyn Ginsburg, the most supportive parent a person could have; and by a daughter and son with the taste to appreciate that Daddy cooks ever so much better than Mommy—and so phased me out of the kitchen at a relatively early age.

Finally, I know Hillary Rodham Clinton has encouraged and supported the president's decision to utilize the skills and talents of all the people of the United States. I did not until today know Mrs. Clinton, but I hasten to add that I am not the first member of my family to stand close to her. There is another I love dearly to whom the first lady is already an old friend. My wonderful granddaughter Clara—witness this super, unposed photograph taken last October when Mrs. Clinton visited the nursery school in New York and led the little ones in the toothbrush song. . . . This small person, right in front, is Clara.

I have a last thank-you. It is to my mother, Celia Amster Bader, the bravest and strongest person I have known, who was taken from me much too soon. I pray that I may be all that she would have been, had she lived in an age when women could aspire and achieve, and daughters are cherished as much as sons.

I look forward to stimulating weeks this summer; and, if I am confirmed, to working at a neighboring court, to the best of my ability, for the advancement of the law in the service of society.

Thank you.

COURT ON PUBLIC AID FOR DEAF PAROCHIAL STUDENT

June 18, 1993

A sharply divided Supreme Court ruled June 18 that public funds could be used to pay a sign-language interpreter for a deaf student attending a Catholic high school. Chief Justice William H. Rehnquist, writing for the Court's five-member majority, rejected the reasoning of two lower federal courts that the payment would involve the government more deeply in religion than the Constitution permits.

Rehnquist said the student, not the school, would be the beneficiary of state support, and, therefore, state funding neither constituted a "direct subsidy" to the school nor violated the First Amendment's religion clause for the separation of church and state. Moreover, he said, it was not the state but the student's parents that initiated the request for an interpreter. "If a handicapped child chooses to enroll in a sectarian school, we hold that the Establishment Clause [of the First Amendment, prohibiting state establishment of religion] does not prevent the school district from furnishing him with a sign-language interpreter in order to facilitate his education." Justices Byron R. White, Antonin Scalia, Anthony M. Kennedy, and Clarence Thomas endorsed the opinion.

The case, Zobrest v. Catalina Foothills School District, *arose in Tucson, Arizona, when James Zobrest, a deaf student, prepared to enter Salpointe Catholic High School. During previous years in a public school, Zobrest was provided an interpreter at state expense. His parents asked the public school district to continue the service for James at Salpointe. Upon advice from the county attorney and Arizona attorney general, the school board refused.*

The Zobrests went to the U.S. district court in Arizona, arguing that a federal law known as the Individuals with Disabilities Education Act (IDEA) required the school district to comply with their request. They said the interpreter's role was purely mechanical and therefore would not result in impermissible government involvement with religion.

Their arguments were rejected first by the district court and then, in a split decision, by the U.S. Court of Appeals for the Ninth Circuit. The appeals court reasoned that by placing the interpreter, a public employee, in a church-run school, the government would create the appearance that it was a "joint sponsor" of the school's activities.

Dissent on Substance and Procedure

Justice Harry A. Blackmun, adopting the appeals court's position, declared that for the first time the Court "has authorized a public employee to participate directly in religious indoctrination." "[T]he interpreter's every gesture would be infused with religious significance," he wrote. Justice David H. Souter joined in Blackmun's dissenting opinion. Justice Sandra Day O'Connor, joined by Justice John Paul Stevens, also dissented but on technical grounds that the case should have been decided without considering issues of church and state.

All four dissenters agreed that the Court had improperly rushed to decide the constitutional issue. They said the Court should first have decided whether the federal law required the school district to pay the interpreter or, alternatively, whether the federal regulation implementing the law prohibited it. In reply, Rehnquist wrote that the Court could not avoid the constitutional issue because the two lower courts had focused solely on it.

The chief justice said that the interpreter service was "part of a general government program that distributes benefits neutrally to any child qualifying." Since the 1920s the Court has recognized a constitutional right for parents to send children to church-sponsored schools. But the Court also ruled on several subsequent occasions that the separation of church and state principle limits the assistance that government can provide those schools.

Court's Struggle to Draw Limits

The justices have struggled over the years to draw a clear line as to what aid is permitted. Blackmun, in his dissent, acknowledged that in some instances "distinctions are somewhat fine." The Court, for example, had approved tuition tax credits but not direct tuition reimbursements. It had approved textbook loans, but not reimbursement for field trips. Only thirteen days before handing down the Zobrest *decision, the present Court in a rare display of unanimity in a church-state case held that a church could use a public school after school hours to show a religious-oriented film to the public.* (Court on Use of School by Religious Group, p. 363)

Following are excerpts from the majority and dissenting opinions in the Supreme Court's ruling June 18, 1993, in the case Zobrest v. Catalina Foothills School District, *providing state funding for a sign-language interpreter to accompany a deaf student to a Catholic high school:*

No. 92-94

Larry Zobrest, et ux., et al., Petitioners *v.* Catalina Foothills School District	On writ of certiorari to the United States Court of Appeals for the Ninth Circuit

[June 18, 1993]

CHIEF JUSTICE REHNQUIST delivered the opinion of the Court.

... It is a familiar principle of our jurisprudence that federal courts will not pass on the constitutionality of an Act of Congress if a construction of the Act is fairly possible by which the constitutional question can be avoided....

Here ... only First Amendment questions were pressed in the Court of Appeals.... Respondent did not urge any statutory grounds for affirmance upon the Court of Appeals, and thus the Court of Appeals decided only the federal constitutional claims raised by petitioners. In the District Court, too, the parties chose to litigate the case on the federal constitutional issues alone.... Accordingly, the District Court's order granting respondent summary judgment addressed only the Establishment Clause question.

Given this posture of the case, we think the prudential rule of avoiding constitutional questions has no application.... We therefore turn to the merits of the constitutional claim.

We have never said that "religious institutions are disabled by the First Amendment from participating in publicly sponsored social welfare programs." *Bowen v. Kendrick* (1988). For if the Establishment Clause did bar religious groups from receiving general government benefits, then "a church could not be protected by the police and fire departments, or have its public sidewalk kept in repair." *Widmar v. Vincent* (1981). Given that a contrary rule would lead to such absurd results, we have consistently held that government programs that neutrally provide benefits to a broad class of citizens defined without reference to religion are not readily subject to an Establishment Clause challenge just because sectarian institutions may also receive an attenuated financial benefit. Nowhere have we stated this principle more clearly than in *Mueller v. Allen* (1983) and *Witters v. Washington Dept. of Services for Blind* (1986), two cases dealing specifically with government programs offering general educational assistance.

In *Mueller,* we rejected an Establishment Clause challenge to a Minnesota law allowing taxpayers to deduct certain educational expenses in computing their state income tax, even though the vast majority of those deductions (perhaps over 90%) went to parents whose children attended sectarian schools. Two factors, aside from States' traditionally broad taxing authority, informed our decision. We noted that the law "permits *all* parents—whether their children attend public school or private—to deduct their children's educational expenses." ... We also pointed out that under Minnesota's scheme, public funds become available to sectarian schools "only as a result of numerous private choices of individual parents of school-age children," thus distinguishing *Mueller* from our other cases involving "the direct transmission of assistance from the State to the schools themselves."

Witters was premised on virtually identical reasoning. In that case, we upheld against an Establishment Clause challenge the State of Washington's extension of vocational assistance, as part of a general state program, to a blind person studying at a private Christian college to become a pastor, missionary, or youth director. Looking at the statute as a whole, we observed that "[a]ny aid provided under Washington's program that ultimately flows to religious institutions does so only as a result of the genuinely independent and private choices of aid recipients." The program, we said, "creates no financial incentive for students to undertake sectarian education." We also remarked that, much like the law in *Mueller,* "Washington's program is 'made available generally without regard to the sectarian-nonsectarian, or public-nonpublic nature of the institution benefited.'" In light of these factors, we held that Washington's program—even as applied to a student who sought state assistance so that he could become a pastor—would not advance religion in a manner inconsistent with the Establishment Clause.

That same reasoning applies with equal force here. The service at issue in this case is part of a general government program that distributes benefits neutrally to any child qualifying as "handicapped" under the IDEA [Individuals with Disabilities Education Act], without regard to the "sectarian-nonsectarian, or public-nonpublic nature" of the school the child attends. By according parents freedom to select a school of their choice, the statute ensures that a government-paid interpreter will be present in a sectarian school only as a result of the private decision of individual parents. In other words, because the IDEA creates no financial incentive for parents to choose a sectarian school, an interpreter's presence there cannot be attributed to state decisionmaking. Viewed against the backdrop of *Mueller* and *Witters,* then, the Court of Appeals erred in its decision. When the government offers a neutral service on the premises of a sectarian school as part of a general program that "is in no way skewed towards religion," it follows under our prior decisions that provision of that service does not offend the Establishment Clause. Indeed, this is an even easier case than *Mueller* and *Witters* in the sense that, under the IDEA, no funds traceable to the government ever find their way into sectarian schools' coffers. The only indirect economic benefit a sectarian school might receive by client of the IDEA is the handicapped child's tuition—and that is, of course, assuming that the school makes a profit on each student; that, without an IDEA interpreter, the child would have gone to school elsewhere; and that the school, then, would have been unable to fill that child's spot.

Respondent contends, however, that this case differs from *Mueller* and *Witters*, in that petitioners seek to have a public employee physically present in a sectarian school to assist in James' religious education. In light of this distinction, respondent argues that this case more closely resembles *Meek v. Pittenger* (1975) and *School Dist. of Grand Rapids v. Ball* (1985). In *Meek*, we struck down a statute that, *inter alia*, provided "massive aid" to private schools—more than 75% of which were church related—through a direct loan of teaching material and equipment. The material and equipment covered by the statute included maps, charts, and tape recorders. According to respondent, if the government could not place a tape recorder in a sectarian school in *Meek*, then it surely cannot place an interpreter in Salpointe. The statute in *Meek* also authorized state-paid personnel to furnish "auxiliary services"—which included remedial and accelerated instruction and guidance counseling—on the premises of religious schools. We determined that this part of the statute offended the First Amendment as well. *Ball* similarly involved two public programs that provided services on private school premises; there, public employees taught classes to students in private school classrooms. We found that those programs likewise violated the Constitution. . . .

. . . [T]he task of a sign-language interpreter seems to us quite different from that of a teacher or guidance counselor. Notwithstanding the Court of Appeals' intimations to the contrary, the Establishment Clause lays down no absolute bar to the placing of a public employee in a sectarian school. Such a flat rule, smacking of antiquated notions of "taint," would indeed exalt form over substance. Nothing in this record suggests that a sign-language interpreter would do more than accurately interpret whatever material is presented to the class as a whole. In fact, ethical guidelines require interpreters to "transmit everything that is said in exactly the same way it was intended." James' parents have chosen of their own free will to place him in a pervasively sectarian environment. The sign-language interpreter they have requested will neither add to nor subtract from that environment, and hence the provision of such assistance is not barred by the Establishment Clause.

The IDEA creates a neutral government program dispensing aid not to schools but to individual handicapped children. If a handicapped child chooses to enroll in a sectarian school, we hold that the Establishment Clause does not prevent the school district from furnishing him with a sign-language interpreter there in order to facilitate his education. The judgment of the Court of Appeals is therefore

Reversed.

JUSTICE BLACKMUN, with whom JUSTICE SOUTER joins, . . . dissenting.

Today, the Court unnecessarily addresses an important constitutional issue, disregarding longstanding principles of constitutional adjudication.

In so doing, the Court holds that placement in a parochial school classroom of a public employee whose duty consists of relaying religious messages does not violate the Establishment Clause of the First Amendment. I disagree both with the Court's decision to reach this question and with its disposition on the merits. I therefore dissent.

I

... Respondent School District makes two arguments that could provide grounds for affirmance, rendering consideration of the constitutional question unnecessary. First, respondent maintains that the Individuals with Disabilities Education Act (IDEA) does not require it to furnish petitioner with an interpreter at any private school so long as special education services are made available at a public school. The United States endorses this interpretation of the statute, explaining that "the IDEA itself does not establish an individual entitlement to services for students placed in private schools at their parents' option." And several courts have reached the same conclusion.... Second, respondent contends that ... a regulation promulgated under the IDEA, which forbids the use of federal funds to pay for "[r]eligious worship, instruction, or proselytization," prohibits provision of a sign-language interpreter at a sectarian school. The United States asserts that this regulation does not preclude the relief petitioners seek, but at least one federal court has concluded otherwise. This Court could easily refrain from deciding the constitutional claim by vacating and remanding the case for consideration of the statutory and regulatory issues. Indeed, the majority's decision does not eliminate the need to resolve these remaining questions. For, regardless of the Court's views on the Establishment Clause, petitioners will not obtain what they seek if the federal statute does not require or the federal regulations prohibit provision of a sign-language interpreter in a sectarian school....

II

Despite my disagreement with the majority's decision to reach the constitutional question, its arguments on the merits deserve a response. Until now, the Court never has authorized a public employee to participate directly in religious indoctrination. Yet that is the consequence of today's decision....

At Salpointe ... governmental assistance to the educational function of the school necessarily entails governmental participation in the school's inculcation of religion.... In an environment so pervaded by discussions of the divine, the interpreter's every gesture would be infused with religious significance. Indeed, petitioners willingly concede this point: "That the interpreter conveys religious messages is a given in the case." By this concession, petitioners would seem to surrender their constitutional claim.

The majority attempts to elude the impact of the record by offering three reasons why this sort of aid to petitioners survives Establishment Clause scrutiny. First, the majority observes that provision of a sign-language interpreter occurs as "part of a general government program that distributes benefits neutrally to any child qualifying as 'handicapped' under the IDEA, without regard to the 'sectarian-nonsectarian, or public-nonpublic' nature of the school the child attends." Second, the majority finds significant the fact that aid is provided to pupils and their parents, rather than directly to sectarian schools. As a result, " '[a]ny aid ... that ultimately flows to religious institutions does so only as a result of the genuinely independent and private choices of aid recipients.' " And, finally, the majority opines that "the task of a sign-language interpreter seems to us quite different from that of a teacher or guidance counselor."

But the majority's arguments are unavailing. As to the first two, even a general welfare program may have specific applications that are constitutionally forbidden under the Establishment Clause. See *Bowen v. Kendrick* (1988) (holding that the Adolescent Family Life Act on its face did not violate the Establishment Clause, but remanding for examination of the constitutionality of particular applications). For example, a general program granting remedial assistance to disadvantaged schoolchildren attending public and private, secular and sectarian schools alike would clearly offend the Establishment Clause insofar as it authorized the provision of teachers.... Nor would the fact that teachers were furnished to pupils and their parents, rather than directly to sectarian schools, immunize such a program from Establishment Clause scrutiny.... The majority's decision must turn, then, upon the distinction between a teacher and a sign-language interpreter.

"Although Establishment Clause jurisprudence is characterized by few absolutes," at a minimum "the Clause does absolutely prohibit government-financed or government-sponsored indoctrination into the beliefs of a particular religious faith." ... In keeping with this restriction, our cases consistently have rejected the provision by government of any resource capable of advancing a school's religious mission. Although the Court generally has permitted the provision of "secular and nonideological services unrelated to the primary, religion-oriented educational function of the sectarian school," ... it has always proscribed the provision of benefits that afford even "the opportunity for the transmission of sectarian views." ...

Thus, the Court has upheld the use of public school buses to transport children to and from school, *Everson v. Board of Education* (1947), while striking down the employment of publicly funded buses for field trips controlled by parochial school teachers, *Wolman* [*v. Walter* (1977)]. Similarly, the Court has permitted the provision of secular textbooks whose content is immutable and can be ascertained in advance, *Board of Education v. Allen* (1968), while prohibiting the provision of any instructional materials or equipment that could be used to convey a religious message, such as slide projectors, tape recorders, record players, and the like, *Wolman*. State-paid speech and hearing therapists have been allowed to administer diagnostic testing on the premises of parochial schools,

Wolman, whereas state-paid remedial teachers and counselors have not been authorized to offer their services because of the risk that they may inculcate religious beliefs, *Meek* [*v. Pittenger* (1975)].

These distinctions perhaps are somewhat fine, but "'lines must be drawn."' ... And our cases make clear that government crosses the boundary when it furnishes the medium for communication of a religious message. If petitioners receive the relief they seek, it is beyond question that a state-employed sign-language interpreter would serve as the conduit for petitioner's religious education, thereby assisting Salpointe in its mission of religious indoctrination. But the Establishment Clause is violated when a sectarian school enlists "the machinery of the State to enforce a religious orthodoxy." *Lee v. Weisman* (1992).

Witters [*v. Washington Dept. of Services for Blind* (1986)] and *Mueller v. Allen* (1983) are not to the contrary. Those cases dealt with the payment of cash or a tax deduction, where governmental involvement ended with the disbursement of funds or lessening of tax. This case, on the other hand, involves ongoing, daily, and intimate governmental participation in the teaching and propagation of religious doctrine....

III

The Establishment Clause "rests upon the premise that both religion and government can best work to achieve their lofty aims if each is left free from the other within its respective sphere." *McCollum v. Board of Education* (1948). To this end, our cases have strived to "chart a course that preserve[s] the autonomy and freedom of religious bodies while avoiding any semblance of established religion." *Walz v. Tax Commission* (1970). I would not stray, as the Court does today, from the course set by nearly five decades of Establishment Clause jurisprudence. Accordingly, I dissent.

JUSTICE O'CONNOR, with whom JUSTICE STEVENS joins, dissenting.

I join Part I of JUSTICE BLACKMUN's dissent. In my view, the Court should vacate and remand this case for consideration of the various threshold problems, statutory and regulatory, that may moot the constitutional question urged upon us by the parties. "It is a fundamental rule of judicial restraint ... that this Court will not reach constitutional questions in advance of the necessity of deciding them." ... That "fundamental rule" suffices to dispose of the case before us, whatever the proper answer to the decidedly hypothetical issue addressed by the Court. I therefore refrain from addressing it myself....

POPE'S LETTER ON SEXUALLY ABUSIVE PRIESTS

June 21, 1993

In a letter to United States Catholic bishops, Pope John Paul II said he had appointed a committee to study how to deal with priests who sexually abuse children. In the June 11 letter, which the United States Catholic Conference released June 21, the pope said the committee included representatives of the Vatican and the U.S. National Conference of Bishops.

In public, American bishops applauded the pope's attention to the issue, which was causing major upheavals among the nation's 58 million Catholics. But Newsweek *reported that in private, American church officials were disappointed that the pope had rejected their pleas that he speed up procedures for defrocking priests who abused children. A* Newsweek *poll of American Catholics found that they, too, were upset about the church's leniency towards abusive priests. Nearly two-thirds said such priests should be defrocked.*

The issue continued to draw attention through a series of highly publicized cases. In June, Father David Holley was sentenced to 275 years in prison after he pleaded guilty to sexually assaulting eight boys in New Mexico. Late in the year, former priest James Porter went on trial in Massachusetts on forty-one charges of sexually molesting children three decades earlier. Before the trial, the church reportedly paid more than $5 million to settle civil claims arising from Porter's case. The Massachusetts trial was Porter's second. In December 1992 Porter, who left the church in 1974 and later married, was convicted in Minnesota of molesting a teenage babysitter.

The cases added fuel to charges that church officials routinely covered up for abusive priests. For years, church officials knew that both Holley and Porter were sexually abusing children. Both men—like many other abusive priests—were shuffled from parish to parish, with no warnings to their new congregations. Both also were sent to religious treatment centers where the "treatment" consisted largely of prayer and meditation. And both kept abusing children.

In another case, Thomas W. Smith, a sixty-eight-year-old priest at St. Stephen Church in Bradshaw, Maryland, committed suicide in the church rectory. Smith killed himself August 21, two days after being confronted with a letter from a lawyer alleging that Smith had abused a young boy in 1983. Less than two weeks after Smith's death, five other men told church officials that the priest, who spent two decades at St. Stephen, had molested them, too.

The Holley, Porter, and Smith cases were not unique, although the full extent of abuse among the nation's estimated 57,000 priests was unknown. Various experts estimated that between 1,700 and 2,500 priests had sexually abused children. Andrew Greeley, a Chicago priest and author, wrote in an article in the Jesuit magazine America *that up to 100,000 people in the United States may have been sexually abused by priests as children. The abuse was financially costly to the church. It was estimated that during the previous decade, Catholic dioceses and their insurers paid between $400 million and $500 million to settle hundreds of lawsuits filed by victims or their families.*

Catholic priests were not the only clergy who have sexually abused children. But Jeffrey Anderson, an attorney in St. Paul, Minnesota, who represented hundreds of victims, said most of them were abused by priests. "The severity of the problem in the Catholic Church is unique because it is a culture in which sexuality is repressed," he told Playboy. *Some experts argued that the church's rule requiring priests to remain celibate caused some to molest children. However, others said the celibacy rule had nothing to do with the problem. They said that other factors—the most important being whether the priest himself had been sexually abused as a child—caused some priests to molest children. Nonetheless, the celibacy issue arose again in July when the pope told a weekly audience of tourists and pilgrims that the celibacy rule would continue.*

Responses to the Problem

Despite what some perceived as inaction by the Vatican, many American church leaders started taking their own steps to fight the sexual abuse problem. In 1992 the Archdiocese of Chicago, the nation's second-largest Roman Catholic diocese, announced a series of measures to protect children against abuse. The most important included appointment of a nine-member board to investigate future charges of sexual abuse by priests, hiring of a full-time administrator and support staff to investigate complaints, and creation of a twenty-four-hour telephone hotline to report abuse. (Joseph Cardinal Bernardin on Sexual Abuse by Priests, Historic Documents of 1992, p. 507) *In 1993 New York's Cardinal John O'Connor announced the creation of a program to simplify investigations of abuse complaints. Cardinal Bernard Law of Boston ordered officials in his diocese to search personnel records for any evidence of abuse by priests. Seminaries started taking a harder look at those applying for admission. And in June, the National Conference of Bishops appointed a committee to determine how to handle abuse complaints.*

One of the biggest issues facing the committee was whether abusive priests should be defrocked. In the past, the church sent abusive priests to various treatment facilities and then usually allowed them to return to parish work. Yet many counselors who worked with sex abusers said the illness—like alcoholism or drug abuse—could be controlled on a day-to-day basis but never totally cured. Because of the lack of a cure, many church officials acknowledged that even if abusive priests received treatment and returned to duty, they should never again be allowed to work with children.

Following is the text of a letter written by Pope John Paul II to the Catholic bishops of the United States June 11, 1993, and released by the United States Catholic Conference June 21, 1993:

Venerable and Dear Brother Bishops of the United States:

"Woe to the world because of scandals!" (Mt 18:7).

During these last months I have become aware of how much you, the Pastors of the Church in the United States, together with all the faithful, are suffering because of certain cases of scandal given by members of the clergy. During the *ad Limina* visits many times the conversation has turned to this problem of how the sins of clerics have shocked the moral sensibilities of many and become an occasion of sin for others. The Gospel word "woe" has a special meaning, especially when Christ applies it to cases of scandal, and first of all *to the scandal "of the little ones"* (cf. Mt 18:6). How severe are Christ's words when he speaks of such scandal, how great must be that evil if "for him who gives scandal it would be better to have a great millstone hung around his neck and to be drowned in the depths of the sea" (cf. Mt 18:6).

The vast majority of Bishops and priests are devoted followers of Christ, ardent workers in his vineyard, and men who are deeply sensitive to the needs of their brothers and sisters. That is why I am deeply pained, like you, when it seems that the words of Christ can be applied to some ministers of the altar. Since Christ calls them his "friends" (cf. Jn 15:15), their sin—the sin of giving scandal to the innocent—must pain his heart indeed. Therefore, I fully share your sorrow and your concern, especially your concern for the victims so seriously hurt by these misdeeds.

Every sinner who follows the way of repentance, conversion and pardon can call on the mercy of God, and you in particular must encourage and assist those who stray to be reconciled and find peace of conscience. There is also the question of *the human means for responding to this evil.* The canonical penalties which are provided for certain offenses and which give a social expression of disapproval for the evil are fully justified. These help to maintain a clear distinction between good and evil, and contribute to moral behavior as well as to creating a proper awareness of the gravity of the evil involved. As you are aware, a joint Committee of experts from the Holy See and the Bishops' Conference has just been established to study how the universal canonical norms can best be applied to the particular situation of the United States.

I would also draw your attention to another aspect of the whole question. While acknowledging the right to due freedom of information, *one cannot acquiesce in treating moral evil as an occasion for sensationalism.* Public opinion often feeds on sensationalism and the mass media play a particular role therein. In fact, the search for sensationalism leads to the loss of something which is essential to the morality of society. Harm is done to the fundamental right of individuals not to be easily exposed to the ridicule of public opinion; even more, a distorted image of human life is created. Moreover, by making a moral offense the object of sensationalism, without reference to the dignity of human conscience, one acts in a direction which is in fact opposed to the pursuit of the moral good. There is already sufficient proof that the prevalence of violence and impropriety in the mass media has become a source of scandal. Evil can indeed be sensational, but the *sensationalism* surrounding it is always *dangerous for morality.*

Therefore, the words of Christ about scandal apply also to all those persons and institutions, often anonymous, that through sensationalism in various ways open the door to evil in the conscience and behavior of vast sectors of society, especially among the young who are particularly vulnerable. "Woe to the world because of scandals!" Woe to societies where scandal becomes an everyday event.

So then, Venerable Brothers, you are faced with two levels of serious responsibility: in relation to the clerics through whom scandal comes and their innocent victims, but also in relation to the whole of society systematically threatened by scandal and responsible for it. A great effort is needed to halt the trivializing of the great things of God and man.

I ask you to reflect together with the priests, who are your co-workers, and with the laity, and to respond with all the means at your disposal. Among these means, *the first and most important is prayer:* ardent, humble, confident prayer. This whole sad question must be placed in a context which is not exclusively human; it must be freed from being considered commonplace. Prayer makes us aware that everything—even evil—finds its principal and definitive *reference point in God.* In him every sinner can be raised up again. In this way sin will not become an unfortunate cause of sensationalism, but rather the occasion for an interior call, as Christ has said: "Repent" (Mt 4:17). "The Lord is near" (Phil 4:5).

Yes, dear Brothers, America needs much prayer—*lest it lose its soul.* We are one in this prayer, remembering the words of the Redeemer: "Watch and pray, that you may not enter into temptation" (Mk 14:38). Christ the Good Shepherd calls us to this attitude when he says, "Take courage, I have overcome the world" (Jn 16:33). United with you in the firm trust that our Savior is ever faithful in caring for his People and that he will not fail to give you the strength to fulfill your pastoral ministry, I commend the clergy, Religious and lay faithful of your Dioceses to the loving intercession of his Immaculate Mother Mary. With fraternal affection in Christ Jesus, I impart my Apostolic Blessing.

From the Vatican, June 11, 1993

COURT ON RETURN OF HAITIAN REFUGEES

June 21, 1993

The Supreme Court on June 21 upheld the president's authority to order U.S.-bound Haitians intercepted on the high seas and turned back to their homeland without a hearing to determine if they were political refugees who qualified for asylum. The "interdiction" policy, initiated by President George Bush and continued under President Bill Clinton, was invoked to stem a tide of Florida-bound Haitians fleeing a repressive military regime. After the overthrow in September 1991 of Haiti's first democratically elected president, Jean-Bertrand Aristide, many Haitians left in fear for their lives. They were joined by others who departed their impoverished country presumably for economic reasons.

Despite the risks of crossing six hundred miles of water in open boats that often were unfit and overcrowded, the human traffic from Haiti to American shores increased steadily. By some estimates, as many as 40,000 Haitians undertook the hazardous crossing in the months following Aristide's overthrow. Immigration officials were soon overwhelmed, as was a temporary screening station the United States set up at its Guantánamo Naval Base in Cuba.

In South Florida, where memories were still fresh from the Carter administration's unpopular 1980 boat lift of 125,000 Cuban refugees, there was alarm over the prospect of a new wave of "boat people." Bush administration officials estimated that between 200,000 and 500,000 Haitians might attempt to come to the United States if the gates were opened.

In what the White House described as a measure to protect Haitians from a perilous sea journey, Bush on May 23, 1992, ordered the Coast Guard to begin turning back the incoming boats before they reached American territorial waters. The government declared that it was not obligated to receive and screen would-be immigrants who never entered the United States.

A coalition of refugee interests challenged the government's action in the case, Sale v. Haitian Centers Council. *The council argued that interdiction violated the 1980 Refugee Act and a 1951 treaty on refugees the United States ratified in 1968. The treaty and the statute law barred the return of refugees to countries where their lives were endangered. The argument was accepted by the U.S. Court of Appeals in New York, which ruled July 29, 1992, that the law extended to international waters and American immigration officials thus must comply with its screening requirements.* (Bush and Court on Return of Haitian Refugees, Historic Documents of 1992, p. 453)

The appeals court issued an injunction to prevent the Coast Guard from returning any Haitian "whose life or freedom may be threatened." At the Justice Department's request, the Supreme Court lifted the injunction until it could decide on the legality of the practice. Clinton, in the 1992 election campaign, condemned the forced repatriation as cruel and illegal. But upon becoming president, he said the policy should be maintained to protect Haitians from death on the seas.

The Court's 8-1 decision, written by Justice John Paul Stevens, reversed the appellate court ruling. Stevens held that the law barring the return of political refugees did not apply beyond U.S. borders. Article 33 of the treaty (United Nations Convention Relating to the Status of Refugees), pledged not to return refugees to a place where they would face prosecution. The Refugee Act of 1980 amended the 1952 Immigration and Naturalization Act to conform with the treaty. The act stated that the attorney general "shall not deport or return any alien" to a country where "such alien's life would be threatened ... on account of race, religion, nationality, membership in a particular social group, or political opinion."

In a lone dissent, Justice Harry A. Blackmun contended that the treaty and refugee law plainly prohibited the return of "vulnerable refugees" such as the Haitians. He recalled that the treaty had been drawn up largely in response the experience of Jewish refugees in World War II. "The tragic consequences of the world's indifference at that time are well known," Blackmun added, drawing a parallel to the Haitians' situation.

Stevens conceded that interdiction might "violate the spirit" of Article 33, but he said "humanitarian intent" alone was not sufficient to "impose uncontemplated extraterritorial obligations on those who ratify [the treaty]." Article 33, he wrote, "cannot reasonably be read to say anything at all about a nation's actions toward aliens outside its own territory."

Even as the justices were deciding that question, the status of Haitian refugees was being complicated by other judicial action and by Congress. A federal district court in Brooklyn had heard complaints from Haitian groups that refugees with the AIDS-causing HIV virus had been held in a Guantánamo detention camp for up to twenty months and denied the right to legal counsel. On June 8 the presiding judge, Sterling Johnson, Jr., ordered the release of 158 infected Haitians. (District Court on Admission of Haitians, p. 371)

In holding them, the Bush and Clinton administrations both invoked a 1990 law barring HIV-infected immigrants unless the attorney general waived the ban. That ban, with the waiver proviso, was renewed in 1993 legislation but it, too, was expected to be subjected to a court challenge.

Following are excerpts from the Supreme Court's majority and dissenting opinions, issued June 21, 1993, in the case of Sale, Acting Commissioner, Immigration and Naturalization Service, v. Haitian Centers Council, Inc., *in which the Court ruled that U.S. authorities could intercept and turn back boatloads of would-be immigrants on the high seas:*

No. 92-344

Chris Sale, Acting Commissioner, Immigration and Naturalization Service, et al., Petitioners *v.* Haitian Centers Council, Inc., et al.	On writ of certiorari to the United States Court of Appeals for the Second Circuit

[June 21, 1993]

JUSTICE STEVENS delivered the opinion of the Court.

The President has directed the Coast Guard to intercept vessels illegally transporting passengers from Haiti to the United States and to return those passengers to Haiti without first determining whether they may qualify as refugees. The question presented in this case is whether such forced repatriation, "authorized to be undertaken only beyond the territorial sea of the United States," violates § 243(h)(1) of the Immigration and Nationality Act of 1952 (INA or Act). We hold that neither § 243(h) nor Article 33 of the United Nations Protocol Relating to the Status of Refugees applies to action taken by the Coast Guard on the high seas.

I

Aliens residing illegally in the United States are subject to deportation after a formal hearing. Aliens arriving at the border, or those who are temporarily paroled into the country, are subject to an exclusion hearing, the less formal process by which they, too, may eventually be removed from the United States. In either a deportation or exclusion proceeding the alien may seek asylum as a political refugee for whom removal to a particular country may threaten his life or freedom. Requests that the Attorney General grant asylum or withhold deportation to a particular country are typically, but not necessarily, advanced as parallel claims in either a deportation or an exclusion proceeding. When an alien proves that he is a "refugee," the Attorney General has discretion to grant him asylum pursuant to § 208 of the Act. If the proof shows that it is more likely than not that the alien's life or freedom would be threatened in a particular country because of his political or religious beliefs, under § 243(h) the Attorney General must not send him to that country. The INA offers these statutory protections only to aliens who reside in or have arrived at the border of the United States. For 12 years, in one form or another, the interdiction program challenged here has prevented Haitians such as respondents from reaching our shores and invoking those protections....

... Because so many interdicted Haitians could not be safely processed on Coast Guard cutters, the Department of Defense established temporary facilities at the United States Naval Base in Guantanamo, Cuba, to accommodate them during the screening process. Those temporary facilities, however, had a capacity of only about 12,500 persons. In the first three weeks of May 1992, the Coast Guard intercepted 127 vessels (many of which were considered unseaworthy, overcrowded, and unsafe); those vessels carried 10,497 undocumented aliens. On May 22, 1992, the United States Navy determined that no additional migrants could safely be accommodated at Guantanamo.

With both the facilities at Guantanamo and available Coast Guard cutters saturated, and with the number of Haitian emigrants in unseaworthy craft increasing (many had drowned as they attempted the trip to Florida), the Government could no longer both protect our borders and offer the Haitians even a modified screening process. It had to choose between allowing Haitians into the United States for the screening process or repatriating them without giving them any opportunity to establish their qualifications as refugees. In the judgment of the President's advisors, the first choice not only would have defeated the original purpose of the program (controlling illegal immigration), but also would have impeded diplomatic efforts to restore democratic government in Haiti and would have posed a life-threatening danger to thousands of persons embarking on long voyages in dangerous craft. The second choice would have advanced those policies but deprived the fleeing Haitians of any screening process at a time when a significant minority of them were being screened in.

On May 23, 1992, President Bush adopted the second choice. After assuming office, President Clinton decided not to modify that order; it remains in effect today. The wisdom of the policy choices made by Presidents Reagan, Bush, and Clinton is not a matter for our consideration. We must decide only whether Executive Order No. 12807, which reflects and implements those choices, is consistent with § 243(h) of the INA.

II

Respondents filed this lawsuit in the United States District Court for the Eastern District of New York on March 18, 1992—before the promulgation of Executive Order No. 12807. The plaintiffs include organizations that represent interdicted Haitians as well as Haitians who were then being detained at Guantanamo. They sued the Commissioner of the Immigration and Naturalization Service, the Attorney General, the Secretary of State, the Commandant of the Coast Guard, and the Commander of the Guantanamo Naval Base, complaining that the screening procedures provided on Coast Guard cutters and at Guantanamo did not adequately protect their statutory and treaty rights to apply for refugee status and avoid repatriation to Haiti.

They alleged that the September 1991 coup had "triggered a continuing widely publicized reign of terror in Haiti"; that over 1,500 Haitians were believed to "have been killed or subjected to violence and destruction of their property because of their political beliefs and affiliations"; and that thousands of Haitian refugees "have set out in small boats that are often overloaded, unseaworthy, lacking basic safety equipment, and operated by inexperienced persons, braving the hazards of a prolonged journey over high seas in search of safety and freedom."

In April, the District Court granted the plaintiffs a preliminary injunction requiring defendants to give Haitians on Guantanamo access to counsel for the screening process. We stayed that order on April 22, 1992, and, while the defendants' appeal from it was pending, the President issued the Executive Order now under attack. Plaintiffs then applied for a temporary restraining order to enjoin implementation of the Executive Order. They contended that it violated § 243(h) of the Act and Article 33 of the United Nations Protocol Relating to the Status of Refugees. The District Court denied the application because it concluded that § 243(h) is "unavailable as a source of relief for Haitian aliens in international waters," and that such a statutory provision was necessary because the Protocol's provisions are not "self-executing."

The Court of Appeals reversed.... The Court [of Appeals] found its conclusion mandated by both the broad definition of the term "alien" and the plain language of § 243(h), from which the 1980 amendment had removed the words "within the United States."...

Nor did the Court of Appeals accept the Government's reliance on Article 33 of the United Nations Convention Relating to the Status of Refugees. It recognized that the 1980 amendment to the INA had been intended to conform our statutory law to the provisions of the Convention, but it read Article 33.1's prohibition against return, like the statute's, "plainly" to cover "*all* refugees, regardless of location."... This reading was supported by the "object and purpose" not only of that Article but also of the Convention as a whole....

The Second Circuit's decision conflicted with the Eleventh Circuit's decision in *Haitian Refugee Center v. Baker* (1992), and with the opinion expressed by Judge Edwards in *Haitian Refugee Center v. Gracey* (1987). Because of the manifest importance of the issue, we granted certiorari (1992).

III

Both parties argue that the plain language of § 243(h)(1) is dispositive. It reads as follows:

> "The Attorney General shall not deport or return any alien (other than an alien described in section 1251(a)(4)(D) of this title) to a country if the Attorney General determines that such alien's life or freedom would be threatened in such country on account of race, religion, nationality, membership in a particular social group, or political opinion." 8 U.S.C. 1253(h)(1).

Respondents emphasize the words "any alien" and "return"; neither term is limited to aliens within the United States. Respondents also contend that the 1980 amendment deleting the words "within the United States" from the prior text of § 243(h) obviously gave the statute an extraterritorial effect. This change, they further argue, was required in order to conform the statute to the text of Article 33.1 of the Convention, which they find as unambiguous as the present statutory text.

Petitioners' response is that a fair reading of the INA as a whole demonstrates that § 243(h) does not apply to actions taken by the President or Coast Guard outside the United States; that the legislative history of the 1980 amendment supports their reading; and that both the text and the negotiating history of Article 33 of the Convention indicate that it was not intended to have any extraterritorial effect.

We shall first review the text and structure of the statute and its 1980 amendment, and then consider the text and negotiating history of the Convention.

A. The Text and Structure of the INA

Although § 243(h)(1) refers only to the Attorney General, the Court of Appeals found it "difficult to believe that the proscription of § 243(h)(l)—returning an alien to his persecutors—was forbidden if done by the attorney general but permitted if done by some other arm of the executive branch." Congress "understood" that the Attorney General is the "President's agent for dealing with immigration matters," and would intend any reference to her to restrict similar actions of any government official....

The reference to the Attorney General ... suggests that it applies only to the Attorney General's normal responsibilities under the INA. The most relevant of those responsibilities for our purposes are her conduct of the deportation and exclusion hearings in which requests for asylum or for withholding of deportation under § 243(h) are ordinarily advanced. Since there is no provision in the statute for the conduct of such proceedings outside the United States, and since Part V and other provisions of the INA obviously contemplate that such proceedings would be held in the country, we cannot reasonably construe § 243(h) to limit the Attorney General's actions in geographic areas where she has not been authorized to conduct such proceedings. Part V of the INA contains no reference to a possible extraterritorial application.

Even if Part V of the Act were not limited to strictly domestic procedures, the presumption that Acts of Congress do not ordinarily apply outside our borders would support an interpretation of § 243(h) as applying only within United States territory. . . .

Respondents' expansive interpretation of the word "return" raises another problem: it would make the word "deport" redundant. If "return" referred solely to the destination to which the alien is to be removed, it alone would have been sufficient to encompass aliens involved in both deportation and exclusion proceedings. And if Congress had meant to refer to all aliens who might be sent back to potential oppressors, regardless of their location, the word "deport" would have been unnecessary. By using both words, the statute implies an exclusively territorial application, in the context of both kinds of domestic immigration proceedings. The use of both words reflects the traditional division between the two kinds of aliens and the two kinds of hearings. We can reasonably conclude that Congress used the two words "deport or return" only to make § 243(h)'s protection available in both deportation and exclusion proceedings. Indeed, the history of the 1980 amendment confirms that conclusion.

B. The History of the Refugee Act of 1980

As enacted in 1952, § 243(h) authorized the Attorney General to withhold deportation of aliens "within the United States." Six years later we considered the question whether it applied to an alien who had been paroled into the country while her admissibility was being determined. We held that even though she was physically present within our borders, she was not "within the United States" as those words were used in § 243(h). *Leng May Ma v. Barber* (1958). . . . Under the INA, both then and now, those seeking "admission" and trying to avoid "exclusion" were already within our territory (or at its border), but the law treated them as though they had never entered the United States at all; they were within United States territory but not "within the United States." Those who had been admitted (or found their way in) but sought to avoid "expulsion" had the added benefit of "deportation proceedings"; they were both within United States territory *and* "within the United States." Although the phrase "within the United States" presumed the alien's actual presence in the United States, it had more to do with an alien's legal status than with his location.

The 1980 amendment erased the long-maintained distinction between deportable and excludable aliens for purposes of § 243(h). By adding the word "return" and removing the words "within the United States" from § 243(h), Congress extended the statute's protection to both types of aliens, but it did nothing to change the presumption that both types of aliens would continue to be found only within United States territory. The removal of the phrase "within the United States" cured the most obvious drawback of § 243(h): as interpreted in *Leng May Ma,* its protection was available only to aliens subject to deportation proceedings.

Of course, in addition to this most obvious purpose, it is possible that the 1980 amendment also removed any territorial limitation of the statute, and Congress might have intended a double-barreled result. That possibility, however, is not a substitute for the affirmative evidence of intended extraterritorial application that our cases require. Moreover, in our review of the history of the amendment, we have found no support whatsoever for that latter, alternative, purpose....

In sum, all available evidence about the meaning of § 243(h) ... leads unerringly to the conclusion that it applies in only one context: the domestic procedures by which the Attorney General determines whether deportable and excludable aliens may remain in the United States.

IV

... Like the text and the history of § 243(h), the text and negotiating history of Article 33 of the United Nations Convention are both completely silent with respect to the Article's possible application to actions taken by a country outside its own borders. Respondents argue that the Protocol's broad remedial goals require that a nation be prevented from repatriating refugees to their potential oppressors whether or not the refugees are within that nation's borders. In spite of the moral weight of that argument, both the text and negotiating history of Article 33 affirmatively indicate that it was not intended to have extraterritorial effect....

The drafters of the Convention and the parties to the Protocol—like the drafters of § 243(h)—may not have contemplated that any nation would gather fleeing refugees and return them to the one country they had desperately sought to escape; such actions may even violate the spirit of Article 33; but a treaty cannot impose uncontemplated extraterritorial obligations on those who ratify it through no more than its general humanitarian intent. Because the text of Article 33 cannot reasonably be read to say anything at all about a nation's actions toward aliens outside its own territory, it does not prohibit such actions....

V

Respondents contend that the dangers faced by Haitians who are unwillingly repatriated demonstrate that the judgment of the Court of Appeals fulfilled the central purpose of the Convention and the Refugee Act of 1980. While we must, of course, be guided by the high purpose of both the treaty and the statute, we are not persuaded that either one places any limit on the President's authority to repatriate aliens interdicted beyond the territorial seas of the United States.

It is perfectly clear that 8 U.S.C. § 1182(f) grants the President ample power to establish a naval blockade that would simply deny illegal Haitian migrants the ability to disembark on our shores. Whether the President's chosen method of preventing the "attempted mass migration" of thousands of Haitians ... poses a greater risk of harm to Haitians who might otherwise face a long and dangerous return voyage, is irrelevant to the scope of his authority to take action that neither the Convention nor the statute clearly prohibits. As we have already noted, Acts of Congress normally do not have extraterritorial application unless such an intent is clearly manifested. That presumption has special force when we are construing treaty and statutory provisions that may involve foreign and military affairs for which the President has unique responsibility. . . .

The judgment of the Court of Appeals is reversed.

It is so ordered.

JUSTICE BLACKMUN, dissenting.

When, in 1968, the United States acceded to the United Nations Protocol Relating to the Status of Refugees, it pledged not to "return *('refouler')* a refugee in any manner whatsoever" to a place where he would face political persecution. In 1980, Congress amended our immigration law to reflect the Protocol's directives. Refugee Act of 1980. . . . Today's majority nevertheless decides that the forced repatriation of the Haitian refugees is perfectly legal, because the word "return" does not mean return, because the opposite of "within the United States" is not outside the United States, and because the official charged with controlling immigration has no role in enforcing an order to control.

I believe that the duty of nonreturn expressed in both the Protocol and the statute is clear. The majority finds it "extraordinary" that Congress would have intended the ban on returning "any alien" to apply to aliens at sea. That Congress would have meant what it said is not remarkable. What is extraordinary in this case is that the Executive, in disregard of the law, would take to the seas to intercept fleeing refugees and force them back to their persecutors—and that the Court would strain to sanction that conduct. . . .

[I and II Omitted]

III

The Convention that the Refugee Act embodies was enacted largely in response to the experience of Jewish refugees in Europe during the period of World War II. The tragic consequences of the world's indifference at that time are well known. The resulting ban on *refoulement,* as broad as the humanitarian purpose that inspired it, is easily applicable here, the Court's protestations of impotence and regret notwithstanding.

The refugees attempting to escape from Haiti do not claim a right of admission to this country. They do not even argue that the Government has no right to intercept their boats. They demand only that the United States, land of refugees and guardian of freedom, cease forcibly driving them back to detention, abuse, and death. That is a modest plea, vindicated by the Treaty and the statute. We should not close our ears to it.

I dissent.

COURT ON JOB DISCRIMINATION

June 25, 1993

The Supreme Court on June 25 raised the burden of proof for anyone who claims job discrimination and seeks redress under the 1964 Civil Rights Act. The justices returned to a familiar and contentious topic, which in 1989 was the focus of a flurry of Court rulings that narrowed the legal remedies in bias cases arising from the workplace. Democrats in Congress accused the Court's conservative majority of misreading the law's intent and pushed for legislation to nullify the decisions. In 1991, after long and sometimes bitter debate, they succeeded in passing a compromise measure intended to weaken but not overturn the rulings. (Supreme Court Rulings on Civil Rights Laws, Historic Documents of 1989, p. 321)

St. Mary's Honor Center v. Hicks, *the case at hand, was decided by a five-member conservative majority, as were most of the previous cases. The makeup of the Court had changed in the intervening four years, but the numerical split remained. Two justices placed on the Court after 1989, both appointees of President George Bush, took opposite sides in* Hicks. *Clarence Thomas endorsed the majority view, and David H. Souter wrote the dissenting opinion.*

This case grew out of a lawsuit brought by Melvin Hicks, a corrections officer at St. Mary's Honor Center, a Missouri state correctional facility in St. Louis, accusing his supervisors of demoting and dismissing him as a corrections officer because he was a black man. His suit invoked Title VII of the 1964 act, under which individuals could seek to prove they were victims of discrimination in hiring, promotion, or firing because of their race, color, religion, sex, or national origin.

"A Crusade" To Fire Hicks

Hicks's supervisors denied his accusation, but the trial judge in federal district court rejected their explanations. The judge ruled that Hicks showed there was "a crusade" to fire him, but did not prove the crucial point that the dismissal was racially motivated. The Eighth U.S. Circuit Court of Appeals reviewed the finding and came to a different conclusion. It said Hicks was entitled to win the case once the judge rejected the prison officials' testimony as false. The Supreme Court, in its 5-4 ruling, then reversed the appeals court and returned the case for reconsideration.

The Burden-of-Proof Test

The Hicks *decision appeared to move away from a burden-of-proof test in Title VII cases that the Supreme Court had devised in 1973 in* McDonnell Douglas Corp. v. Green. *That Court, of a more liberal persuasion, decreed that once a plaintiff made a "prima facie" case of discrimination, the employer was given an opportunity to offer a legitimate, nondiscriminatory reason for his action. If the employer did so, the employee could try to discredit it. The trial judge would determine who prevailed.*

Writing the majority opinion in Hicks, *Justice Antonin Scalia said the appeals court "ignored our repeated admonition that the Title VII plaintiff at all times bears the ultimate burden of persuasion." Scalia added that an employer's dishonesty regarding the reasons for terminating an employee did not qualify as evidence of bias. "[W]e have no authority to impose liability upon an employer" unless direct evidence proved that the employer acted in a discriminatory manner. Scalia's opinion was endorsed by Chief Justice William H. Rehnquist and Justices Sandra Day O'Connor, Anthony M. Kennedy, and Clarence Thomas.*

In a vigorous dissent Souter said it was the Supreme Court, not the appeals court, that "departs from settled precedent." In its place, he added, the Court was "substituting a scheme of proof . . . that promises to be unfair and unworkable." Moreover, Souter said, the ruling would reward employers for lying. Souter was joined in dissent by Justices Byron R. White, Harry A. Blackmun, and John Paul Stevens.

Civil rights lawyers said the decision made job discrimination more difficult to prove because only rarely is it openly expressed in personnel decisions. However, the impact of the ruling may be lessened by a provision in the 1991 law permitting jury trials in Title VII cases. Presumably, jurors who do not believe an employer's argument may be inclined to rule for the plaintiff regardless of what is required by the courtroom rules of proof.

Following are excerpts from the Supreme Court's majority and dissenting opinions in the case of St. Mary's Honor Center v. Hicks, *issued June 25, 1993, declaring that whoever claims job discrimination is fully responsible for proving it:*

No. 92-602

St. Mary's Honor Center, et al., Petitioners v. Melvin Hicks	On Writ of Certiorari to the United States Court of Appeals for the Eighth Circuit

[June 25, 1993]

JUSTICE SCALIA delivered the opinion of the Court.

We granted certiorari to determine whether, in a suit against an employer alleging intentional racial discrimination in violation of § 703(a)(1) of Title VII of the Civil Rights Act of 1964, the trier of fact's rejection of the employer's asserted reasons for its actions mandates a finding for the plaintiff.

[I Omitted]

II

Section 703(a)(1) of Title VII of the Civil Rights Act of 1964 provides in relevant part:

> "It shall be an unlawful employment practice for an employer— "(1) ... to discharge any individual, or otherwise to discriminate against any individual with respect to his compensation, terms, conditions, or privileges of employment, because of such individual's race...." 42 U.S.C. § 2000e-2(a).

... [O]ur opinion in *McDonnell Douglas Corp. v. Green* (1973) established an allocation of the burden of production and an order for the presentation of proof in Title VII discriminatory-treatment cases. The plaintiff in such a case, we said, must first establish, by a preponderance of the evidence, a "prima facie" case of racial discrimination. *Burdine.* Petitioners do not challenge the District Court's finding that respondent satisfied the minimal requirements of such a prima facie case (set out in *McDonnell Douglas*) by proving (1) that he is black, (2) that he was qualified for the position of shift commander, (3) that he was demoted from that position and ultimately discharged, and (4) that the position remained open and was ultimately filled by a white man.

Under the *McDonnell Douglas* scheme, "[e]stablishment of the prima facie case in effect creates a presumption that the employer unlawfully discriminated against the employee." *Burdine.* To establish a "presumption" is to say that a finding of the predicate fact (here, the prima facie case) produces "a required conclusion in the absence of explanation" (here, the finding of unlawful discrimination). Thus, the *McDonnell Douglas* presumption places upon the defendant the burden of producing an explanation to rebut the prima facie case—*i.e.*, the burden of "producing evidence" that the adverse employment actions were taken "for a legitimate, nondiscriminatory reason." *Burdine.* "[T]he defendant must clearly set forth, through the introduction of admissible evidence," reasons for its actions which, *if believed by the trier of fact,* would support a finding that unlawful discrimination was not the cause of the employment action. It is important to note, however, that although the *McDonnell Douglas* presumption shifts the burden of *production* to the defendant, "[t]he ultimate burden of persuading the trier of fact that the defendant intentionally discriminated against the plaintiff remains at all times with the plaintiff." In this regard it operates like all presumptions, as described in Rule 301 of the Federal Rules of Evidence:

> "In all civil actions and proceedings not otherwise provided for by Act of Congress or by these rules, a presumption imposes on the party against whom it is directed the burden of going forward with evidence to rebut or meet the presumption, but does not shift to such party the burden of proof in the sense of the risk of nonpersuasion, which remains throughout the trial upon the party on whom it was originally cast."

Respondent does not challenge the District Court's finding that petitioners sustained their burden of production by introducing evidence of two legitimate, nondiscriminatory reasons for their actions: the severity and the accumulation of rules violations committed by respondent. Our cases make clear that at that point the shifted burden of production became irrelevant: "If the defendant carries this burden of production, the presumption raised by the prima facie case is rebutted," *Burdine,* and "drops from the case." The plaintiff then has "the full and fair opportunity to demonstrate," through presentation of his own case and through cross-examination of the defendant's witnesses, "that the proffered reason was not the true reason for the employment decision," and that race was. He retains that "ultimate burden of persuading the [trier of fact] that [he] has been the victim of intentional discrimination."

The District Court, acting as trier of fact in this bench trial, found that the reasons petitioners gave were not the real reasons for respondent's demotion and discharge. It found that respondent was the only supervisor disciplined for violations committed by his subordinates; that similar and even more serious violations committed by respondent's coworkers were either disregarded or treated more leniently; and that [supervisor John] Powell manufactured the final verbal confrontation in order to provoke respondent into threatening him. It nonetheless held that respondent had failed to carry his ultimate burden of proving that his race was the determining factor in petitioners' decision first to demote and then to dismiss him. In short, the District Court concluded that "although [respondent] has proven the existence of a crusade to terminate him, he has not proven that the crusade was racially rather than personally motivated."

The Court of Appeals set this determination aside on the ground that "[o]nce [respondent] proved all of [petitioners'] proffered reasons for the adverse employment actions to be pretextual, [respondent] was entitled to judgment as a matter of law." The Court of Appeals reasoned:

> "Because all of defendants' proffered reasons were discredited, defendants were in a position of having offered no legitimate reason for their actions. In other words, defendants were in no better position than if they had remained silent, offering no rebuttal to an established inference that they had unlawfully discriminated against plaintiff on the basis of his race."

That is not so. By producing *evidence* (whether ultimately persuasive or not) of nondiscriminatory reasons, petitioners sustained their burden of production, and thus placed themselves in a "better position than if they had remained silent." . . .

If . . . the defendant has succeeded in carrying its burden of production, the *McDonnell Douglas* framework—with its presumptions and burdens—is no longer relevant. To resurrect it later, after the trier of fact has determined that what was "produced" to meet the burden of production is not credible, flies in the face of our holding in [*Texas Dept. of Community Affairs v.] Burdine* [1981] that to rebut the presumption "[t]he defendant need not persuade the court that it was actually motivated by the proffered reasons." The presumption, having fulfilled its role of forcing the defendant to come forward with some response, simply drops out of the picture. The defendant's "production" (whatever its persuasive effect) having been made, the trier of fact proceeds to decide the ultimate question: whether plaintiff has proven "that the defendant intentionally discriminated against [him]" because of his race. The factfinder's disbelief of the reasons put forward by the defendant (particularly if disbelief is accompanied by a suspicion of mendacity) may, together with the elements of the prima facie case, suffice to show intentional discrimination. Thus, rejection of the defendant's proffered reasons, will *permit* the trier of fact to infer the ultimate fact of intentional discrimination, and the Court of Appeals was correct when it noted that, upon such rejection, "[n]o additional proof of discrimination is *required,*" (emphasis added). But the Court of Appeals' holding that rejection of the defendant's proffered reasons *compels* judgment for the plaintiff disregards the fundamental principle of Rule 301 that a presumption does not shift the burden of proof, and ignores our repeated admonition that the Title VII plaintiff at all times bears the "ultimate burden of persuasion." . . .

[III Omitted]

IV

We turn, finally, to the dire practical consequences that the respondents and the dissent claim our decision today will produce. What appears to trouble the dissent more than anything is that, in its view, our rule is adopted "for the benefit of employers who have been found to have given false evidence in a court of law," whom we "favo[r]" by "exempting them from responsibility for lies." As we shall explain, our rule in no way gives special favor to those employers whose evidence is disbelieved. But initially we must point out that there is no justification for assuming (as the dissent repeatedly does) that those employers whose evidence is disbelieved are perjurers and liars. . . . Even if these were typically cases in which an individual defendant's sworn assertion regarding a physical occurrence was pitted against an individual plaintiff's sworn assertion regarding the same physical occurrence, surely it would be imprudent to call the party whose assertion is (by a mere preponderance of the evidence) disbelieved, a perjurer and a liar. And in these Title VII cases, the defendant is ordinarily *not* an individual but a company, which must rely upon the statement of an employee—often a relatively low-level employee—as to the central fact; and that central fact is *not* a physical occurrence, but rather that employee's state of mind. To say that the company which in good faith introduces such testimony, or even the testifying employee himself, becomes a liar and a perjurer when the testimony is not believed, is nothing short of absurd.

Undoubtedly some employers (or at least their employees) will be lying. But even if we could readily identify these perjurers, what an extraordinary notion, that we "exempt them from responsibility for their lies" unless we enter Title VII judgments for the plaintiffs! Title VII is not a cause of action for perjury; we have other civil and criminal remedies for that. The dissent's notion of judgment-for-lying is seen to be not even a fair and evenhanded punishment for vice, when one realizes how strangely selective it is: the employer is free to lie to its heart's content about whether the plaintiff ever applied for a job, about how long he worked, how much he made—indeed, about anything and everything *except* the reason for the adverse employment action. And the plaintiff is permitted to lie about absolutely *everything* without losing a verdict he otherwise deserves. This is not a major, or even a sensible, blow against fibbery. . . .

Respondent contends that "[t]he litigation decision of the employer to place in controversy only . . . particular explanations eliminates from further consideration the alternative explanations that the employer chose not to advance." The employer should bear, he contends, "the responsibility for its choices and the risk that plaintiff will disprove any pretextual reasons *and therefore prevail.*" ([E]mphasis added.) It is the "therefore" that is problematic. Title VII does not award damages against employers who cannot prove a nondiscriminatory reason for adverse employment action, but only against employers who are proven to have taken adverse employment action by reason of (in the context of the present case) race. That the employer's proffered reason is unpersuasive, or even obviously contrived, does not necessarily establish that the plaintiff's proffered reason of race is correct. That remains a question for the factfinder to answer, subject, of course, to appellate review—which should be conducted on remand in this case under the "clearly erroneous" standard of Federal Rule of Civil Procedure 52(a). . . .

Finally, respondent argues that it "would be particularly ill-advised" for us to come forth with the holding we pronounce today "just as Congress has provided a right to jury trials in Title VII" cases. . . . We think quite the opposite is true. Clarity regarding the requisite elements of proof becomes all the more important when a jury must be instructed concerning them, and when detailed factual findings by the trial court will not be available upon review. . . .

The judgment of the Court of Appeals is reversed, and the case is remanded for further proceedings consistent with this opinion.

It is so ordered.

JUSTICE SOUTER, with whom JUSTICE WHITE, JUSTICE BLACKMUN, and JUSTICE STEVENS join, dissenting.

Twenty years ago, in *McDonnell Douglas Corp. v. Green* (1973), this Court unanimously prescribed a "sensible, orderly way to evaluate the evidence" in a Title VII disparate-treatment case, giving both plaintiff and defendant fair opportunities to litigate "in light of common experience as it bears on the critical question of discrimination." We have repeatedly reaffirmed and refined the *McDonnell Douglas* framework, most notably in *Texas Dept. of Community Affairs v. Burdine* (1981), another unanimous opinion. . . . But today, after two decades of stable law in this Court and only relatively recent disruption in some of the Circuits, the Court abandons this practical framework together with its central purpose, which is "to sharpen the inquiry into the elusive factual question of intentional discrimination." *Burdine.* Ignoring language to the contrary in both *McDonnell Douglas* and *Burdine,* the Court holds that, once a Title VII plaintiff succeeds in showing at trial that the defendant has come forward with pretextual reasons for its actions in response to a prima facie showing of discrimination, the factfinder still may proceed to roam the record, searching for some nondiscriminatory explanation that the defendant has not raised and that the plaintiff has had no fair opportunity to disprove. Because the majority departs from settled precedent in substituting a scheme of proof for disparate-treatment actions that promises to be unfair and unworkable, I respectfully dissent.

The *McDonnell Douglas* framework that the Court inexplicably casts aside today was summarized neatly in *Burdine:*

> "First, the plaintiff has the burden of proving by the preponderance of the evidence a prima facie case of discrimination. Second, if the plaintiff succeeds in proving the prima facie case, the burden shifts to the defendant to articulate some legitimate, nondiscriminatory reason for the employee's rejection. Third, should the defendant carry this burden, the plaintiff must then have an opportunity to prove by a preponderance of the evidence that the legitimate reasons offered by the defendant were not its true reasons, but were a pretext for discrimination."

We adopted this three-step process to implement, in an orderly fashion, "[t]he language of Title VII," which "makes plain the purpose of Congress to assure equality of employment opportunities and to eliminate those discriminatory practices and devices which have fostered racially stratified job environments to the disadvantage of minority citizens." Because "Title VII tolerates no racial discrimination, subtle or otherwise," we devised a framework that would allow both plaintiffs and the courts to deal effectively with employment discrimination revealed only through circumstantial evidence....

At the outset, under the *McDonnell Douglas* framework, a plaintiff alleging disparate treatment in the workplace in violation of Title VII must provide the basis for an inference of discrimination. In this case, as all agree, Melvin Hicks met this initial burden by proving by a preponderance of the evidence that he was black and therefore a member of a protected class; he was qualified to be a shift commander; he was demoted and then terminated; and his position remained available and was later filled by a qualified applicant. Hicks thus proved what we have called a "prima facie case" of discrimination, and it is important to note that in this context a prima facie case is indeed a proven case. Although, in other contexts, a prima facie case only requires production of enough evidence to raise an issue for the trier of fact, here it means that the plaintiff has actually established the elements of the prima facie case to the satisfaction of the factfinder by a preponderance of the evidence....

Under *McDonnell Douglas* and *Burdine,* however, proof of a prima facie case not only raises an inference of discrimination; in the absence of further evidence, it also creates a mandatory presumption in favor of the plaintiff. Although the employer bears no trial burden at all until the plaintiff proves his prima facie case, once the plaintiff does so the employer must either respond or lose....

The Court emphasizes that the employer's obligation at this stage is only a burden of production and that, if the employer meets the burden, the presumption entitling the plaintiff to judgment "drops from the case." This much is certainly true, but the obligation also serves an important function neglected by the majority, in requiring the employer "to frame the factual issue with sufficient clarity so that the plaintiff will have a full and fair opportunity to demonstrate pretext." The employer, in other words, has a "burden of production" that gives it the right to choose the scope of the factual issues to be resolved by the factfinder....

COURT ON SEIZURE OF CRIMINAL ASSETS

June 28, 1993

On the last day of its 1992-1993 term, the Supreme Court took another step in defining how far the government may go in seizing property belonging to criminals or suspects. In one case, Austin v. United States, *the Court held unanimously that the Eighth Amendment's prohibition of excessive fines applied to forfeitures arising from civil proceedings. In another case decided the same day, June 28,* Alexander v. United States, *the Court ruled 5-4 that the First Amendment offered no protection to a pornography dealer whose goods had been confiscated and destroyed. However, the justices unanimously agreed that assets the dealer forfeited might have represented an excessive fine.*

Austin *marked the first broad constitutional limit on the government's increasing use of forfeiture against offenders in drug-trafficking, racketeering, and money-laundering cases. At the urging of law-enforcement officials, several laws were enacted in the 1980s to make it easier for the government to seize money, goods, or property from criminal defendants or suspects. But defense attorneys and civil liberties groups protested that the laws were being used excessively, taking assets in disproportion to the offenses and punishing people who did not know they had received proceeds from criminal activity.*

The Court's ruling on civil forfeitures arose over the government's seizure of a mobile home, auto body shop, and cash belonging to Richard Austin of Sioux Falls, South Dakota, who was under indictment on state charges of selling cocaine to an undercover agent in June 1990. He ultimately pleaded guilty to one count and was sentenced to seven years in prison. In the meantime, federal authorities sought in U.S. district court an in rem *action, which technically is a lawsuit brought against the proceeds of a crime or property used in a crime, rather than against the person. The judge rejected Austin's argument that to permit the seizure of his home, business, and money—with a total value of about $42,700—*

would be to violate the Eighth Amendment. A three-judge panel of the Eighth U.S. Circuit Court of Appeals "reluctantly" upheld the ruling. "[It] does appear that the government is exacting too high a penalty in relation to the offense committed," the panel said. But it noted a 1974 Supreme Court decision, Calero-Toledo v. Pearson Yacht Leasing Co., *which said the guilt or innocence of the property's owner "is constitutionally irrelevant" when the government is proceeding against the property* in rem.

Government Arguments Rejected

After the Supreme Court agreed to review Austin, *the Justice Department argued that the Eighth Amendment applied only to criminal cases and not civil forfeiture actions. In addition, it said that drug forfeiture laws served a remedial purpose by removing the tools of the drug trade and compensating the government for the costs of dealing with crime. The Court unanimously rejected those arguments. Although the justices differed in their reasoning, all nine agreed that civil forfeitures were punishment to be treated as fines.*

Justice Harry A. Blackmun's opinion on behalf of the Court was joined by Justices Byron R. White, John Paul Stevens, Sandra Day O'Connor, and David H. Souter. Justice Anthony M. Kennedy wrote a concurring opinion that was joined by Chief Justice William H. Rehnquist and Justice Clarence Thomas. In his concurring opinion, Kennedy faulted Blackmun's historical review of the Eighth Amendment but not his conclusion. Justice Antonin Scalia issued a separate concurrence, differing in part with the two other written opinions. The Court left unanswered the question of what standard should be used to determine when forfeiture is excessive. Blackmun said the question initially should be left to the lower federal courts.

Property Destruction Upheld

The decision in Alexander v. United States *stemmed from the government's seizure of $25 million in assets from Ferris J. Alexander, Jr., who had been convicted on seventeen counts of obscenity and three counts of violating a federal racketeering law in his operation of thirteen adult bookstores and theaters in Minnesota. He was fined $100,000 and sentenced to six years in prison.*

In a counter action, Alexander charged that the government had violated his First Amendment rights by destroying thousands of his books that were not obscene. His argument was denied by Rehnquist, writing for the Court's majority, which included White, O'Connor, Scalia, and Thomas. Kennedy objected in a strongly worded dissent, joined by Blackmun and Stevens, that free-speech principles were being sacrificed. "What is at work in this case," Kennedy wrote, "is not the power to punish an individual for his past transgressions but the authority to suppress a particular class of disfavored speech." Souter essentially adopted the minority view in a separate dissent.

While rejecting the First Amendment argument, the Court sent the case back to the lower federal court to determine if the forfeiture constituted excessive punishment in light of the fine and prison term already imposed.

Following are excerpts from the majority, concurring, and dissenting opinions in the Supreme Court cases of Austin v. United States *and* Alexander v. United States, *decided June 28, 1993, in which the Court sought to define how far the government may go in seizing the property of criminals and suspects:*

No. 92-6073

Richard Lyle Austin, Petitioner *v.* United States	On writ of certiorari to the United States Court of Appeals for the Eighth Circuit

[June 28, 1993]

JUSTICE BLACKMUN delivered the opinion of the Court.

In this case, we are asked to decide whether the Excessive Fines Clause of the Eighth Amendment applies to forfeitures of property under 21 U.S.C. §§ 881(a)(4) and (a)(7). We hold that it does and therefore remand the case for consideration of the question whether the forfeiture at issue here was excessive.

[I Omitted]

II

Austin contends that the Eighth Amendment's Excessive Fines Clause applies to *in rem* civil forfeiture proceedings. We have had occasion to consider this Clause only once before. In *Browning-Ferris Industries v. Kelco Disposal, Inc.* (1989), we held that the Excessive Fines Clause does not limit the award of punitive damages to a private party in a civil suit when the government neither has prosecuted the action nor has any right to receive a share of the damages.... The Court concluded that both the Eighth Amendment and § 10 of the English Bill of Rights of 1689, from which it derives, were intended to prevent *the government* from abusing its power to punish and therefore "that the Excessive Fines Clause was intended to limit only those fines directly imposed by, and payable to, the government."

We found it unnecessary to decide in *Browning-Ferris* whether the Excessive Fines Clause applies only to criminal cases... [The government]

... suggests that the Eighth Amendment cannot apply to a civil proceeding unless that proceeding is so punitive that it must be considered criminal under *Kennedy v. Mendoza-Martinez* (1963) and *United States v. Ward* (1980). We disagree.

Some provisions of the Bill of Rights are expressly limited to criminal cases. The Fifth Amendment's Self-Incrimination Clause, for example, provides: "No person ... shall be compelled in any criminal case to be a witness against himself." The protections provided by the Sixth Amendment are explicitly confined to "criminal prosecutions." ... The text of the Eighth Amendment includes no similar limitation.

Nor does the history of the Eighth Amendment require such a limitation....

The purpose of the Eighth Amendment ... was to limit the government's power to punish.... The Cruel and Unusual Punishments Clause is self-evidently concerned with punishment. The Excessive Fines Clause limits the Government's power to extract payments, whether in cash or in kind, "as *punishment* for some offense." (Emphasis added.) "The notion of punishment, as we commonly understand it, cuts across the division between the civil and the criminal law." *United States v. Halper* (1989). "It is commonly understood that civil proceedings may advance punitive and remedial goals, and, conversely, that both punitive and remedial goals may be served by criminal penalties." See also *United States ex rel. Marcus v. Hess* (1943) (Frankfurter, J., concurring). Thus, the question is not, as the United States would have it, whether forfeiture under §§ 881(a)(4) and (a)(7) is civil or criminal, but rather whether it is punishment.

In considering this question, we are mindful of the fact that sanctions frequently serve more than one purpose. We need not exclude the possibility that a forfeiture serves remedial purposes to conclude that it is subject to the limitations of the Excessive Fines Clause. We, however, must determine that it can only be explained as serving in part to punish. We said in *Halper* that "a civil sanction that cannot fairly be said solely to serve a remedial purpose, but rather can only be explained as also serving either retributive or deterrent purposes, is punishment, as we have come to understand the term." We turn, then, to consider whether, at the time the Eighth Amendment was ratified, forfeiture was understood at least in part as punishment and whether forfeiture under §§ 881(a)(4) and (a)(7) should be so understood today.

III

[A Omitted]

B

... The First Congress passed laws subjecting ships and cargos involved in customs offenses to forfeiture. It does not follow from that fact, however, that the First Congress thought such forfeitures to be beyond the purview of the Eighth Amendment. Indeed, examination of those laws suggests that the First Congress viewed forfeiture as punishment. . . .

C

. . . The same understanding of forfeiture as punishment runs through our cases rejecting the "innocence" of the owner as a common-law defense to forfeiture. See, *e.g., Calero-Toledo [v. Pearson Yacht Leasing Co.,* 1974]; *Goldsmith-Grant Co. v. United States* (1921); *Dobbins's Distillery v. United States* (1878); *United States v. Brig Malek Adhe* (1844); *The Palmyra* (1827). In these cases, forfeiture has been justified on two theories—that the property itself is "guilty" of the offense, and that the owner may be held accountable for the wrongs of others to whom he entrusts his property. Both theories rest, at bottom, on the notion that the owner has been negligent in allowing his property to be misused and that he is properly punished for that negligence. . . .

. . . [E]ven though this Court has rejected the "innocence" of the owner as a common-law defense to forfeiture, it consistently has recognized that forfeiture serves, at least in part, to punish the owner. . . . We conclude, therefore, that forfeiture generally and statutory *in rem* forfeiture in particular historically have been understood, at least in part, as punishment.

IV

We turn next to consider whether forfeitures under 21 U.S.C. §§ 881(a)(4) and (a)(7) are properly considered punishment today. We find nothing in these provisions or their legislative history to contradict the historical understanding of forfeiture as punishment. Unlike traditional forfeiture statutes, §§ 881(a)(4) and (a)(7) expressly provide an "innocent owner" defense. . . . These exemptions serve to focus the provisions on the culpability of the owner in a way that makes them look more like punishment, not less. . . .

Furthermore, Congress has chosen to tie forfeiture directly to the commission of drug offenses. Thus, under § 881(a)(4), a conveyance is forfeitable if it is used or intended for use to facilitate the transportation of controlled substances, their raw materials, or the equipment used to manufacture or distribute them. Under § 881(a)(7), real property is forfeitable if it is used or intended for use to facilitate the commission of a drug-related crime punishable by more than one year's imprisonment.

The legislative history of § 881 confirms the punitive nature of these provisions. When it added subsection (a)(7) to § 881 in 1984, Congress recognized "that the traditional criminal sanctions of fine and imprisonment are inadequate to deter or punish the enormously profitable trade in dangerous drugs." It characterized the forfeiture of real property as "a powerful deterrent." . . .

The Government argues that §§ 881(a)(4) and (a)(7) are not punitive but, rather, should be considered remedial in two respects. First, they remove the "instruments" of the drug trade "thereby protecting the community from the threat of continued drug dealing." Second, the forfeited assets serve to compensate the Government for the expense of law enforcement activity and for its expenditure on societal problems such as urban blight, drug addiction, and other health concerns resulting from the drug trade.

In our view, neither argument withstands scrutiny. Concededly, we have recognized that the forfeiture of contraband itself may be characterized as remedial because it removes dangerous or illegal items from society. See *United States v. One Assortment of 89 Firearms* (1984). The Court, however, previously has rejected government's attempt to extend that reasoning to conveyances used to transport illegal liquor. See *One 1958 Plymouth Sedan v. Pennsylvania* (1965). In that case it noted: "There is nothing even remotely criminal in possessing an automobile." The same, without question, is true of the properties involved here, and the Government's attempt to characterize these properties as "instruments" of the drug trade must meet the same fate as Pennsylvania's effort to characterize the 1958 Plymouth Sedan as "contraband."

The Government's second argument about the remedial nature of this forfeiture is no more persuasive. We previously have upheld the forfeiture of goods involved in customs violations as "a reasonable form of liquidated damages." *One Lot Emerald Cut Stones v. United States* (1972). But the dramatic variations in the value of conveyances and real property forfeitable under §§ 881(a)(4) and (a)(7) undercut any similar argument with respect to those provisions. The Court made this very point in *Ward:* the "forfeiture of property ... [is] a penalty that ha[s] absolutely no correlation to any damages sustained by society or to the cost of enforcing the law."

Fundamentally, even assuming that §§ 881(a)(4) and (a)(7) serve some remedial purpose, the Government's argument must fail. "[A] civil sanction that cannot fairly be said *solely* to serve a remedial purpose, but rather can only be explained as also serving either retributive or deterrent purposes, is punishment, as we have come to understand the term." *Halper* (emphasis added)....

V

Austin asks that we establish a multifactor test for determining whether a forfeiture is constitutionally "excessive." We decline that invitation. Although the Court of Appeals opined "that the government is exacting too high a penalty in relation to the offense committed," it had no occasion to consider what factors should inform such a decision because it thought it was foreclosed from engaging in the inquiry. Prudence dictates that we allow the lower courts to consider that question in the first instance. See *Yee v. City of Escondido* (1992).

The judgment of the Court of Appeals is reversed and the case is remanded to that court for further proceedings consistent with this opinion.

It is so ordered.

JUSTICE SCALIA, concurring in part and concurring in the judgment.

We recently stated that, at the time the Eighth Amendment was drafted, the term "fine" was "understood to mean a payment to a sovereign as punishment for some offense." *Browning-Ferris Industries of Vermont, Inc. v. Kelco Disposal, Inc.* (1989). It seems to me that the Court's opinion obscures this clear statement, and needlessly attempts to derive from our sparse caselaw on the subject of *in rem* forfeiture the questionable proposition that the owner of property taken pursuant to such forfeiture is always blameworthy. . . .

I

. . . The theory of *in rem* forfeiture is said to be that the lawful property has committed an offense. . . .

However the theory may be expressed, it seems to me that this taking of lawful property must be considered, in whole or in part, see *United States v. Halper* (1989), punitive. Its purpose is not compensatory, to make someone whole for injury caused by unlawful use of the property. Punishment is being imposed, whether one quaintly considers its object to be the property itself, or more realistically regards its object to be the property's owner. . . .

The Court apparently believes, however, that only actual culpability of the affected property owner can establish that a forfeiture provision is punitive, and sets out to establish (in Part III) that such culpability exists in the case of *in rem* forfeitures. In my view, however, the caselaw is far more ambiguous than the Court acknowledges. We have never held that the Constitution requires negligence, or any other degree of culpability, to support such forfeitures. . . . Moreover, if some degree of personal culpability on the part of the property owner always exists for *in rem* forfeitures, then it is hard to understand why this Court has kept reserving the (therefore academic) question whether personal culpability is constitutionally required, as the Court does again today.

I would have reserved the question without engaging in the misleading discussion of culpability. . . .

II

That this forfeiture works as a fine raises the excessiveness issue, on which the Court remands. I agree that a remand is in order, but think it worth pointing out that on remand the excessiveness analysis must be different from that applicable to monetary fines and, perhaps, to *in personam* forfeitures. In the case of a monetary fine, the Eighth Amendment's origins in the English Bill of Rights, intended to limit the abusive penalties assessed against the king's opponents, see *Browning-Ferris*, demonstrate that the touchstone is value of the fine in relation to the offense. And in *Alexander v. United States* [1993], we indicated that the same is true for *in personam* forfeiture.

Here, however, the offense of which petitioner has been convicted is not relevant to the forfeiture. Section 881 requires only that the Government show probable cause that the subject property was used for the prohibited purpose. The burden then shifts to the property owner to show, by a preponderance of the evidence, that the use was made without his "knowledge, consent, or willful blindness," or that the property was not so used. Unlike monetary fines, statutory *in rem* forfeitures have traditionally been fixed, not by determining the appropriate value of the penalty in relation to the committed offense, but by determining what property has been "tainted" by unlawful use.... The question is not *how much* the confiscated property is worth, but *whether* the confiscated property has a close enough relationship to the offense.

... The relevant inquiry for an excessive forfeiture under § 881 is the relationship of the property to the offense: Was it close enough to render the property, under traditional standards, "guilty" and hence forfeitable?

I join the Court's opinion in part, and concur in the judgment.

JUSTICE KENNEDY, with whom THE CHIEF JUSTICE and JUSTICE THOMAS join, concurring in part and concurring in the judgment.

I am in substantial agreement with Part I of JUSTICE SCALIA's opinion concurring in part and concurring in the judgment. I share JUSTICE SCALIA's belief that Part III of the Court's opinion is quite unnecessary for the decision of the case, fails to support the Court's argument, and seems rather doubtful as well....

At some point, we may have to confront the constitutional question whether forfeiture is permitted when the owner has committed no wrong of any sort, intentional or negligent. That for me would raise a serious question. Though the history of forfeiture laws might not be determinative of that issue, it would have an important bearing on the outcome. I would reserve for that or some other necessary occasion the inquiry the Court undertakes here. Unlike JUSTICE SCALIA, I would also reserve the question whether *in rem* forfeitures always amount to an intended punishment of the owner of forfeited property.

With these observations, I concur in part and concur in the judgment.

No. 91-1526

Ferris J. Alexander, Sr., Petitioner
v.
United States

On writ of certiorari to the United States Court of Appeals for the Eighth Circuit

[June 28, 1993]

CHIEF JUSTICE REHNQUIST delivered the opinion of the Court.

After a full criminal trial, petitioner Ferris J. Alexander, owner of more than a dozen stores and theaters dealing in sexually explicit materials, was convicted on 17 obscenity counts and 3 counts of violating the Racketeer Influenced and Corrupt Organizations Act (RICO). The obscenity convictions, based on the jury's findings that four magazines and three videotapes sold at several of petitioner's stores were obscene, served as the predicates for his three RICO convictions. In addition to imposing a prison term and fine, the District Court ordered petitioner to forfeit ... certain assets that were directly related to his racketeering activity as punishment for his RICO violations. Petitioner argues that this forfeiture violated the First and Eighth Amendments to the Constitution. We reject petitioner's claims under the First Amendment but remand for reconsideration of his Eighth Amendment challenge....

Petitioner first contends that the forfeiture in this case, which effectively shut down his adult entertainment business, constituted an unconstitutional prior restraint on speech, rather than a permissible criminal punishment. According to petitioner, forfeiture of expressive materials and the assets of businesses engaged in expressive activity, when predicated solely upon previous obscenity violations, operates as a prior restraint because it prohibits future presumptively protected expression in retaliation for prior unprotected speech. Practically speaking, petitioner argues, the effect of the RICO forfeiture order here was no different from the injunction prohibiting the publication of expressive material found to be a prior restraint in *Near v. Minnesota ex rel. Olson.* (1931). As petitioner puts it, the forfeiture order imposed a complete *ban* on his future expression because of previous unprotected speech. We disagree. By lumping the forfeiture imposed in this case after a full criminal trial with an injunction enjoining future speech, petitioner stretches the term "prior restraint" well beyond the limits established by our cases. To accept petitioner's argument would virtually obliterate the distinction, solidly grounded in our cases, between prior restraints and subsequent punishments.

The term prior restraint is used "to describe administrative and judicial orders *forbidding* certain communications when issued in advance of the time that such communications are to occur."...

... [T]he RICO forfeiture order in this case does not *forbid* petitioner from engaging in any expressive activities in the future, nor does it require him to obtain prior approval for any expressive activities. It only deprives him of specific assets that were found to be related to his previous racketeering violations. Assuming, of course, that he has sufficient untainted assets to open new stores, restock his inventory, and hire staff, petitioner can go back into the adult entertainment business tomorrow, and sell as many sexually explicit magazines and videotapes as he likes, without any risk of being held in contempt for violating a court order....

Petitioner also argues that the forfeiture order in this case—considered atop his 6-year prison term and $100,000 fine—is disproportionate to the gravity of his offenses and therefore violates the Eighth Amendment, either as a "cruel and unusual punishment" or as an "excessive fine." The

Court of Appeals, though, failed to distinguish between these two components of petitioner's Eighth Amendment challenge. Instead, the court lumped the two together, disposing of them both with the general statement that the Eighth Amendment does not require any proportionality review of a sentence less than life imprisonment without the possibility of parole. But that statement has relevance only to the Eighth Amendment's prohibition against cruel and unusual punishments. Unlike the Cruel and Unusual Punishments Clause, which is concerned with matters such as the duration or conditions of confinement, "[t]he Excessive Fines Clause limits the Government's power to extract payments, whether in cash or in kind, as punishment for some offense." *Austin v. United States* (1993); accord, *Browning-Ferris Industries of Vermont, Inc. v. Kelco Disposal, Inc.* (1989) ("[A]t the time of the drafting and ratification of the [Eighth] Amendment, the word 'fine' was understood to mean a payment to a sovereign as punishment for some offense"). The *in personam* criminal forfeiture at issue here is clearly a form of monetary punishment no different, for Eighth Amendment purposes, from a traditional "fine." Accordingly, the forfeiture in this case should be analyzed under the Excessive Fines Clause.

Petitioner contends that forfeiture of his entire business was an "excessive" penalty for the Government to exact "[o]n the basis of a few materials the jury ultimately decided were obscene." It is somewhat misleading, we think, to characterize the racketeering crimes for which petitioner was convicted as involving just a few materials ultimately found to be obscene. Petitioner was convicted of creating and managing what the District Court described as "an enormous racketeering enterprise." It is in the light of the extensive criminal activities which petitioner apparently conducted through this racketeering enterprise over a substantial period of time that the question of whether or not the forfeiture was "excessive" must be considered. We think it preferable that this question be addressed by the Court of Appeals in the first instance.

For these reasons, we hold that RICO's forfeiture provisions, as applied in this case, did not violate the First Amendment, but that the Court of Appeals should have considered whether they resulted in an "excessive" penalty within the meaning of the Eighth Amendment's Excessive Fines Clause. Accordingly, we vacate the judgment of the Court of Appeals and remand the case for further proceedings consistent with this opinion.

It is so ordered.

JUSTICE KENNEDY, with whom JUSTICE BLACKMUN and JUSTICE STEVENS join, and with whom JUSTICE SOUTER joins as to Part II, dissenting.

The Court today embraces a rule that would find no affront to the First Amendment in the Government's destruction of a book and film business and its entire inventory of legitimate expression as punishment for a single past speech offense. Until now I had thought one could browse through any book or film store in the United States without fear that the proprietor had chosen each item to avoid risk to the whole inventory and indeed to the business itself. This ominous, onerous threat undermines free speech and press principles essential to our personal freedom.

Obscenity laws would not work unless an offender could be arrested and imprisoned despite the resulting chill on his own further speech. But, at least before today, we have understood state action directed at protected books or other expressive works themselves to raise distinct constitutional concerns. The Court's decision is a grave repudiation of First Amendment principles, and with respect I dissent.

I

A

... The fundamental defect in the majority's reasoning is a failure to recognize that the forfeiture here cannot be equated with traditional punishments such as fines and jail terms. Noting that petitioner does not challenge either the 6-year jail sentence or the $100,000 fine imposed against him as punishment for his RICO convictions, the majority ponders why RICO's forfeiture penalty should be any different. The answer is that RICO's forfeiture penalties are different from traditional punishments by Congress' own design as well as in their First Amendment consequences.

The federal Racketeer Influenced and Corrupt Organizations Act (RICO) statute was passed to eradicate the infiltration of legitimate business by organized crime. Earlier steps to combat organized crime were not successful, in large part because traditional penalties targeted individuals engaged in racketeering activity rather than the criminal enterprise itself. Punishing racketeers with fines and jail terms failed to break the cycle of racketeering activity because the criminal enterprises had the resources to replace convicted racketeers with new recruits. In passing RICO, Congress adopted a new approach aimed at the economic roots of organized crime....

Criminal liability under RICO is premised on the commission of a "pattern of racketeering activity," defined by the statute as engaging in two or more related predicate acts of racketeering within a 10-year period. A RICO conviction subjects the violator not only to traditional, though stringent, criminal fines and prison terms, but also mandatory forfeiture under § 1963. It is the mandatory forfeiture penalty that is at issue here.

While forfeiture remedies have been employed with increasing frequency in civil proceedings, forfeiture remedies and penalties are the subject of historic disfavor in our country. Although *in personam* forfeiture statutes were well grounded in the English common law ... *in personam* criminal forfeiture penalties like those authorized under § 1963 were unknown in the federal system until the enactment of RICO in 1970. Section 1963's forfeiture penalties are novel for their punitive character as well as for their unprecedented sweep. Civil *in rem* forfeiture is limited in application to contraband and articles put to unlawful use, or in its broadest reach, to proceeds traceable to unlawful activity.... Extending beyond contraband or its traceable proceeds, RICO mandates the forfeiture of property constituting the defendant's "interest in the racketeering enterprise" and property affording the violator a "source of influence" over the RICO enterprise. In a previous decision, we acknowledged the novelty of RICO's penalty scheme, stating that Congress passed RICO to provide "new weapons of unprecedented scope for an assault upon organized crime and its economic roots." *Russello v. United States* (1983).

As enacted in 1970, RICO targeted offenses then thought endemic to organized crime. When RICO was amended in 1984 to include obscenity as a predicate offense, there was no comment or debate in Congress on the First Amendment implications of the change. The consequence of adding a speech offense to a statutory scheme designed to curtail a different kind of criminal conduct went far beyond the imposition of severe penalties for obscenity offenses. The result was to render vulnerable to government destruction any business daring to deal in sexually explicit materials. The unrestrained power of the forfeiture weapon was not lost on the Executive Branch, which was quick to see in the amended statute the means and opportunity to move against certain types of disfavored speech. The Attorney General's Commission on Pornography soon advocated the use of RICO and similar state statutes to "substantially handicap" or "eliminate" pornography businesses. As these comments illustrate, the constitutional concerns raised by a penalty of this destructive capacity are distanced from the concerns raised by traditional methods of punishment.

The Court says that taken together, our decisions in *Fort Wayne Books* [*v. Indiana*, 1989] and *Arcara v. Cloud Books, Inc.* (1986) dispose of petitioner's First Amendment argument. But while instructive, neither case is dispositive. In *Fort Wayne Books* we considered a state law patterned on the federal RICO statute, and upheld its scheme of using obscenity offenses as the predicate acts resulting in fines and jail terms of great severity. We recognized that the fear of severe penalties may result in some self-censorship by cautious booksellers, but concluded that this is a necessary consequence of conventional obscenity prohibitions. In rejecting the argument that the fines and jail terms in *Fort Wayne Books* infringed upon First Amendment principles, we regarded the penalties as equivalent to a sentence enhancement for multiple obscenity violations, a remedy of accepted constitutional legitimacy. We did not consider in *Fort Wayne Books* the First Amendment implications of extensive penal forfeitures, including the official destruction of protected expression. Further, while *Fort Wayne Books* acknowledges that some degree of self-censorship may be unavoidable in obscenity regulation, the alarming element of the forfeiture scheme here is the pervasive danger of government censorship, an issue, I submit, the Court does not confront.

In *Arcara*, we upheld against First Amendment challenge a criminal law requiring the temporary closure of an adult book store as a penal sanction for acts of prostitution occurring on the premises. We did not subject the closure penalty to First Amendment scrutiny even though the collateral consequence of its imposition would be to affect interests of traditional First Amendment concern. We said that such scrutiny was not required when a criminal penalty followed conduct "manifest[ing] absolutely no element of protected expression." That the RICO prosecution of Alexander involved the targeting of a particular class of unlawful speech itself suffices to distinguish the instant case from *Arcara*. . . . [A] sanction requiring the temporary closure of a book store cannot be equated, as it is under the court's unfortunate analysis, with a forfeiture punishment mandating its permanent destruction.

B

The majority tries to occupy the high ground by assuming the role of the defender of the doctrine of prior restraint. It warns that we disparage the doctrine if we reason from it. But as an analysis of our prior restraint cases reveals, our application of the First Amendment has adjusted to meet new threats to speech. The First Amendment is a rule of substantive protection, not an artifice of categories. The admitted design and the overt purpose of the forfeiture in this case are to destroy an entire speech business and all its protected titles, thus depriving the public of access to lawful expression. This is restraint in more than theory. It is censorship all too real.

Relying on the distinction between prior restraints and subsequent punishments, the majority labels the forfeiture imposed here a punishment and dismisses any further debate over the constitutionality of the forfeiture penalty under the First Amendment. Our cases do recognize a distinction between prior restraints and subsequent punishments, but that distinction is neither so rigid nor so precise that it can bear the weight the Court places upon it to sustain the destruction of a speech business and its inventory as a punishment for past expression.

In its simple, most blatant form, a prior restraint is a law which requires submission of speech to an official who may grant or deny permission to utter or publish it based upon its contents. . . . In contrast are laws which punish speech or expression only after it has occurred and been found unlawful. . . . While each mechanism, once imposed, may abridge speech in a direct way by suppressing it, or in an indirect way by chilling its dissemination, we have interpreted the First Amendment as providing greater protection from prior restraints than from subsequent punishments. . . . In *Southeastern Promotions, Ltd. v. Conrad* [1975], we explained that "[b]ehind the distinction is a theory deeply etched in our law: a free society prefers to punish the few who abuse rights of speech *after* they break the law than to throttle them and all others beforehand.". . .

As our First Amendment law has developed, we have not confined the application of the prior restraint doctrine to its simpler forms, outright licensing or censorship before speech takes place. In considering governmental measures deviating from the classic form of a prior restraint yet posing many of the same dangers to First Amendment freedoms, we have extended prior restraint protection with some latitude, toward the end of declaring certain governmental actions to fall within the presumption of invalidity. This approach is evident in *Near v. Minnesota ex rel. Olson* (1931), the leading case in which we invoked the prior restraint doctrine to invalidate a state injunctive decree. In *Near* a Minnesota statute authorized judicial proceedings to abate as a nuisance a " 'malicious, scandalous and defamatory newspaper, magazine or other periodical.' " In a suit brought by the attorney for Hennepin County it was established that *Near* had published articles in various editions of *The Saturday Press* in violation of the statutory standard. Citing the instance of these past unlawful publications, the court enjoined any future violations of the state statute. In one sense the injunctive order, which paralleled the nuisance statute, did nothing more than announce the conditions under which some later punishment might be imposed, for one presumes that contempt could not be found until there was a further violation in contravention of the order. But in *Near* the publisher, because of past wrongs, was subjected to active state intervention for the control of future speech. We found that the scheme was a prior restraint because it embodied "the essence of censorship." This understanding is confirmed by our later decision in *Kingsley Books v. Brown* [1957], where we said that it had been enough to condemn the injunction in *Near* that Minnesota had "empowered its courts to enjoin the dissemination of future issues of a publication because its past issues had been found offensive."

Indeed, the Court has been consistent in adopting a speech-protective definition of prior restraint when the state attempts to attack future speech in retribution for a speaker's past transgressions. It is a flat misreading of our precedents to declare as the majority does that the definition of a prior restraint includes only those measures which impose a "legal impediment" on a speaker's ability to engage in future expressive activity. *Bantam Books, Inc. v. Sullivan* (1963) best illustrates the point. There a state commission did nothing more than warn book sellers that certain titles could be obscene, implying that criminal prosecutions could follow if their warnings were not heeded. The commission had no formal enforcement powers and failure to heed its warnings was not a criminal offense. Although the commission could impose no legal impediment on a speaker's ability to engage in future expressive activity, we held that scheme was an impermissible "system of prior administrative restraints." If mere warning against sale of certain materials was a prior restraint, I fail to see why the physical destruction of a speech enterprise and its protected inventory is not condemned by the same doctrinal principles.

One wonders what today's majority would have done if faced in *Near* with a novel argument to extend the traditional conception of the prior restraint doctrine. In view of the formalistic approach the Court advances today, the Court likely would have rejected Near's pleas on the theory that to accept his argument would be to "blur the line separating prior restraints from subsequent punishments to such a degree that it would be impossible to determine with any certainty whether a particular measure is a prior restraint or not." In so holding the Court would have ignored, as the Court does today, that the applicability of First Amendment analysis to a governmental action depends not alone upon the name by which the action is called, but upon its operation and effect on the suppression of speech....

Whatever one might label the RICO forfeiture provisions at issue in this case, be it effective, innovative, or draconian, § 1963 was not designed for sensitive and exacting application. What is happening here is simple: Books and films are condemned and destroyed not for their own content but for the content of their owner's prior speech. Our law does not permit the government to burden future speech for this sort of taint. Section 1963 requires trial courts to forfeit not only the unlawful items and any proceeds from their sale, but also the defendant's entire interest in the enterprise involved in the RICO violations and any assets affording the defendant a source of influence over the enterprise. A defendant's exposure to this massive penalty is grounded on the commission of just two or more related obscenity offenses committed within a 10-year period. Aptly described, RICO's forfeiture provisions "arm prosecutors not with scalpels to excise obscene portions of an adult bookstore's inventory but with sickles to mow down the entire undesired use."

What is at work in this case is not the power to punish an individual for his past transgressions but the authority to suppress a particular class of disfavored speech. The forfeiture provisions accomplish this in a direct way by seizing speech presumed to be protected along with the instruments of its dissemination, and in an indirect way by threatening all who engage in the business of distributing adult or sexually explicit materials with the same disabling measures.

In a society committed to freedom of thought, inquiry, and discussion without interference or guidance from the state, public confidence in the institutions devoted to the dissemination of written matter and films is essential. That confidence erodes if it is perceived that speakers and the press are vulnerable for all of their expression based on some errant expression in the past. Independence of speech and press can be just as compromised by the threat of official intervention as by the fact of it. Though perhaps not in the form of a classic prior restraint, the application of the forfeiture statute here bears its censorial cast....

The distinct concern raised by § 1963 forfeiture penalties is not a proportionality concern; all punishments are subject to analysis for proportionality and this concern should be addressed under the Eighth Amendment. Here, the question is whether, when imposed as punishment for violation of the federal obscenity laws, the operation of RICO's forfeiture provisions is an exercise of government censorship and control over protected speech as condemned in our prior restraint cases. In my view the effect is just that. For this reason I would invalidate those portions of the judgment which mandated the forfeiture of petitioner's business enterprise and inventory, as well as all property affording him a source of influence over that enterprise....

II

... Given the Court's principal holding, I can interpose no objection to remanding the case for further consideration under the Eighth Amendment. But it is unnecessary to reach the Eighth Amendment question. The Court's failure to reverse this flagrant violation of the right of free speech and expression is a deplorable abandonment of fundamental First Amendment principles. I dissent from the judgment and from the opinion of the Court.

NATIONAL COMMISSION ON AIDS FINAL REPORT

June 28, 1993

"AIDS: An Expanding Tragedy" was the fitting title of the final report by the National Commission on AIDS. Released June 28, the report summarized important statistics regarding the epidemic; suggested steps that should be taken to combat it; and called on the government and those involved with AIDS prevention, treatment, and research to step up their efforts. One indication of the growing awareness of the prevalence of the disease was that nearly 16,000 scientists, public health workers, activists, and journalists attended the Ninth International Conference on AIDS in Berlin in early June.

According to the commission's report, in the United States as of April 1993, a cumulative total of 289,320 AIDS cases and 179,748 deaths from AIDS had been reported to the Centers for Disease Control and Prevention (CDC). The report stated, "These awful numbers are in all likelihood lower than the actual toll, both because only about 80 percent of cases are officially reported to CDC and because many people have died of HIV-related disease that did not meet earlier definitions of AIDS." In January 1993 the CDC adopted an expanded categorization of AIDS-related disease, which had the effect of increasing the absolute numbers of AIDS cases.

One discouraging statistic the commission highlighted was the relatively high number of minorities contracting AIDS. The report said that "to date, nearly half of all AIDS cases have occurred among African Americans and Hispanics, although they make up only 21 percent of the overall population. This disproportionately high number is expected to increase in future years." During a briefing in January, commission member Don C. Des Jarlais, the director for research at the Chemical Dependency Institute of Beth Israel Medical Center in New York, pointed out that one-third of all AIDS cases were related to drug abuse, but that the figure was much higher among minorities. The report showed that among racial minorities the proportion of intravenous drug-related AIDS cases was four times that of whites. In response to these numbers, several commission members said that the ethnic nature of the disease in the United States needed to be emphasized "despite the risk that white people might start seeing AIDS as a minority disease that afflicted 'other' people and not themselves."

Predictions for the Future

The report predicted new HIV infection patterns for the coming years. These included increased risk for the younger generation of homosexual men, possibly because the previous generation that had contracted the disease were no longer alive to promote awareness. Noninjecting drug users—those abusing crack cocaine or alcohol— would also be at risk either from the exchange of sex for drugs or because of impaired judgment about their behavior. Finally, adolescents were at increased risk of contracting AIDS: "between 1991 and 1992, AIDS cases among people 13 to 19 years of age arising from heterosexual HIV transmission increased by 65 percent," according to commission findings.

Pointing to the skyrocketing number of adolescent AIDS cases, the commission warned that most Americans used few, if any, AIDS prevention methods when engaged in high-risk activities such as sexual intercourse. Seventy-five percent of graduating high school seniors "were sexually active, while studies of condom usage revealed mostly inconsistent or no use," the panel said. In addition, "25 percent of the [general] population were likely to have a sexually transmitted disease at some point," indicating that people who were engaging in activities that could increase the spread of sexually transmitted disease also were most likely engaging in activities that could give them AIDS. Furthermore, AIDS risk denial in the general population was evident. "Clearly, many individuals do not recognize or take action to reduce their vulnerability to infection and probably many parents mistakenly believe their children are not at risk," the commission stated.

It was this kind of ignorance the report sought to combat. The commission believed that prevention efforts were most important because "the very nature of HIV infection—in which the virus' genetic material is woven into the DNA of cells—makes true cure difficult to imagine, once infection has been established." The report stated, "It has become clear that, to be successful, HIV prevention efforts need to provide information, build skills to reduce risk, and provide easy access to the means to do so, for example, access to condoms and sterile injection equipment."

The panel concluded that cure or vaccine-oriented approaches should not be neglected for the sake of prevention. The commission said that because a vaccine was possible, it should be "pursued energetically and on a broad front." In addition, the report stated that "major benefits can be achieved in a synergistic, cost-effective manner through coordination and consolidation of HIV/AIDS-related programs with other health care and public health activities."

Suggestions for Slowing the Epidemic

Eight strategies were outlined for altering the future course of the AIDS epidemic: coordinated planning (between public and private sectors); comprehensive reform of the national health care system; human resources planning for underserved communities; a more effective drug policy; housing, rather than hospitalization, for people diagnosed as HIV-positive; educational efforts to increase understanding of HIV disease; adolescent health initiatives; and support for community-based organizations, providers, and volunteers.

Finally, two recommendations that the commission considered to be "central, vital, and critical to launching a more adequate national response to the central human crisis of our times" were that "leaders at all levels must speak out about AIDS to their constituencies" and that "we must develop a clear, well-articulated national plan for confronting AIDS."

Several months after it issued its report, many of the panel's recommendations continued to go unheeded, a fact that left many of its members frustrated about what they perceived to be prejudice and inertia on the part of the general public and the government in dealing with AIDS. Congress appropriated Clinton's full 1994 budget request of $1.8 billion for AIDS research and prevention programs in the National Institutes of Health and CDC—$272 million more than the previous year's funding.

Following are excerpts from the report of the National Commission on AIDS, released June 28, 1993:

The Future of the HIV/AIDS Epidemic

As the second decade of the HIV/AIDS pandemic progresses, it becomes increasingly clear that it will alter the course of many societies. It is worth a brief attempt to outline projections for the United States and the world to the year 2000.

As of April 1993, a cumulative total of 289,320 AIDS cases and 179,748 deaths from AIDS had been reported to the Centers for Disease Control and Prevention. In 1992, 47,106 newly diagnosed AIDS cases and 29,763 deaths were reported by year's end, but the number of deaths from AIDS in 1992 is expected to rise to around 50,000 as statistics are updated. These awful numbers are in all likelihood lower than the actual toll, both because only about 80 percent of cases are officially reported to CDC and because many people have died of HIV-related disease that did not meet earlier definitions of AIDS.

The number of persons meeting the 1987 criteria for AIDS diagnosis is anticipated to increase from 58,000 in 1991 to approximately 70,000 annually during the next two or three years. Due to longer survival after diagnosis, the numbers of people living with AIDS will increase as well—from 90,000 in January 1992 to 120,000 in January 1995. The number of new AIDS diagnoses among men who have sex with men and among injection drug users is projected to remain level during this period. However, AIDS diagnoses among persons whose infection is due to heterosexual transmission is likely to continue to increase. To date, nearly half of all AIDS cases have occurred among African Americans and Hispanics, although they make up only 21 percent of the overall population. This disproportionality is expected to increase in future years.

In January 1993, CDC adopted an expanded AIDS case definition that took into account severe immunosuppression per se and added recurrent bacterial pneumonias, pulmonary tuberculosis, and invasive cervical carcinoma in HIV seropositive people to the long list of AIDS-defining conditions. That change will increase the absolute numbers of AIDS cases reported in the next few years, particularly among drug users and women, compared with projections that used the 1987 definition. In the past, many people died with severe immunosuppression but without meeting criteria for AIDS diagnosis, so this change will increase the accuracy of the mortality toll.

AIDS diagnoses, of course, tell a story that is out of date, since it takes an average of 10 years between onset of infection and appearance of AIDS-defining disease manifestations. Present CDC estimates suggest that at least one million people are infected, so that during the remainder of the decade the annual number of new AIDS diagnoses will remain high, probably at between 40,000 and 80,000 per year. Indeed, even if there were no new instances of infection from now on, the nation would be severely challenged just to meet the care needs of those already infected. Yet new infections will continue unless we do far better at prevention, and of course their impact will extend beyond the year 2000.

Trends in U.S. HIV Incidence and Prevalence

As noted, the spread of AIDS among heterosexuals will account for all increasing percentages of new AIDS diagnoses in upcoming years, and thus care of women and children will present a more prominent need in the epidemic. With injection drug use and sexual transmission fueling that dynamic, births to infected mothers will result in more HIV-infected infants, and the death of infected mothers and fathers will result in growing numbers of "AIDS orphans." This has been the case already along the East Coast and is a dreadful problem in many countries around the world.

Some significant shifts are taking place in new HIV infection patterns compared with the pattern of AIDS to date. While HIV transmission among older men who have sex with men is sharply reduced from the early

1980s, transmission continues at high levels in younger gay men where a "generation gap" seems to have [led] to rejection of warnings from survivors of the first tragic decade. HIV transmission through injection drug use continues to pose a threat of "flash fire" spread of infection among drug users, through multiperson use of injection equipment, which can be followed by sexual transmission to their partners. Noninjecting drug use—especially of crack cocaine but also of alcohol—is a significant risk behavior for transmission, either from exchange of sex for drugs or impairment of behavioral decision making.

Expansion of the base of the epidemic, in large part through spread among heterosexuals, continues to gain ground, particularly among communities of color, women, and adolescents. AIDS cases in people exposed through heterosexual contact increased 17 percent in 1992. AIDS cases among women increased by 9 percent between 1991 and 1992, compared with 2.5 percent among men; and in some "snapshots" of HIV prevalence among adolescents, HIV infection had a one-to-one ratio of women to men, as it does throughout much of the world. The disproportionate representation of communities of color is at its most striking among women and children; while African American and Hispanic women make up 21 percent of all U.S. women, they constitute three-quarters of women diagnosed with AIDS. Among infants born with HIV infection due to drug use by their mothers or her sex partner, about 85 percent are African American or Hispanic.

Trends in HIV transmission among adolescents raise particular concerns. Between 1991 and 1992, AIDS cases among people 13 to 19 years of age arising from heterosexual HIV transmission increased by 65 percent; and increasing numbers of men and women in their twenties are developing AIDS, signifying infection in their teenage years. Among African American and Latino youth in the northeastern United States, 1 in 40 Job Corps applicants between 13 and 21 years of age was infected with HIV; and among teens aged 16 to 17 in the southeast, more females than males were infected.

The potential for spread of HIV is made clear by recent studies that estimated that 25 percent of the population were likely to have a sexually transmitted disease at some point in their lives. Furthermore, CDC has found that about 75 percent of graduating high school seniors were sexually active, while studies of condom usage revealed mostly inconsistent or no use. Adult risk of sexually transmitted diseases including HIV was illustrated by one recent survey that found that between 15 percent and 30 percent of a large survey sample reported unprotected sexual intercourse with multiple partners. Nevertheless, among the heterosexual population, disbelief and denial persist; in another recent study, condom use was less than 20 percent in risky sexual encounters. Clearly, many individuals do not recognize or take action to reduce their vulnerability to infection and probably many parents believe mistakenly that their children are not at risk.

HIV as an International Problem

The crisis faced in the United States has its counterpart in virtually every country in the world. Spread of HIV varied by a few years from one region to another, but by now there is no place free of the virus. The global number infected may double or triple by the year 2000. Denial has been a regular component of initial national response virtually everywhere, but many countries have overcome that first reaction and have mobilized in ways that need to be shared with others. The United States, by virtue of its early involvement, its biomedical research capacity, and the experience accumulated by many agencies and community groups in responding to the crisis, is in a position to be helpful; but we have also ignored some important lessons and thus are also in a position to learn from nations that have mobilized more effectively. All nations would benefit from a greater sharing of expertise and experience.

The international impact of HIV disease will expand dramatically in upcoming years, and with it will come the need and obligation to share progress in research, therapeutics, and vaccines as they develop. Notwithstanding its members' personal and collective concern for the situation abroad, our major task as a commission has been to focus on issues within the United States. It is our clear national obligation, however, to participate in a global response that is equitable, compassionate, and founded on a fundamental commitment to human rights.

Prospects for Prevention through Behavior Change

We must use the tools that are available now to confront the epidemic, especially since prospects for cure or vaccine are distant. Much success has been achieved in demonstrating the feasibility of preventing HIV transmission through interventions directed at reducing risky sexual or drug-injecting behavior. In general, successful research or pilot/demonstration projects have been targeted to particular groups (for example, older men who have sex with men, runaway street youth, early to mid adolescents, or injection drug users). These projects have enabled the identification of general principles and practices of intervention likely to predicate success.

It has become clear that, to be successful, HIV prevention efforts need to provide information, build skills to reduce risk, and provide easy access to the means to do so, for example, access to condoms and sterile injection equipment. They must also be culturally sensitive, reiterated, sustained over time, and complemented by broader efforts over the long haul, both to change behavioral norms within communities at risk and to empower individuals to change. It is also clear that those at highest risk *can* be reached and will change behavior in significant numbers if appropriate motivations are identified, explicit and targeted campaigns are developed, and natural and credible channels of communication are used. However, many more people need to be reached. The number of people at some degree of risk is large and the future patterns of the epidemic will make it more and more difficult to "target" them if we do not intensify efforts at prevention now....

Prospects for Therapy and Cure

The very nature of HIV infection—in which the virus' genetic material is woven into the DNA of cells—makes true cure difficult to imagine, once infection is established. The cells infected by HIV are important in their immune system and neurologic function, so destroying infected cells in order to get rid of the virus is not a realistic approach. Thus far the antiviral treatments available against HIV (AZT, ddI, and ddc) all work by inhibiting a viral enzyme necessary for replication; but while those drugs enhance well-being and delay onset of severe disease, their effect is finite and patients ultimately become refractory to them. In addition, HIV has shown the ability to develop resistance to the drugs themselves.

Potential new antiviral drugs and strategies are under development now, but most of them are still at the test tube stage, where their effectiveness and toxicity in patients cannot yet be gauged. Thus, while progress can be expected in the range of treatments available, truly curative therapies are unlikely in the foreseeable future and improvement in clinical strategies will be incremental....

Prospects for Prevention by Vaccine Prophylaxis

Evidence from animal model research over the past few years has suggested that a vaccine against HIV may be possible. While many legitimate possibilities are under investigation, there is not yet agreement among researchers as to the most promising approaches for a vaccine that would protect humans. Thus, the vaccine effort must be pursued energetically and on a broad front....

Altering the Future Course of the Epidemic: Neglected Strategies

There is much that could be done, even with present knowledge, that could soften the impact of the epidemic. Major benefits can be achieved in a synergistic, cost-effective manner through coordination and consolidation of HIV/AIDS-related programs with other health care and public health activities. For instance:

- *Coordinated planning.* The substantial benefits of information exchange and coordination of activities among federal, state, and local government agencies and the private sector (such as community-based organizations and workplace planners) unfortunately have not been achieved to date. It is in this context that the National Commission on AIDS has called for development of a national strategic plan; we continue to do so, since the quality of epidemic response, as well as inherent savings, could be significantly enhanced.
- *Comprehensive reform of the national health care system.* HIV disease (and other chronic diseases) should be carefully factored into

the design of health care reform proposals. Universal access to coverage for a continuum of comprehensive services including home care and long-term care, and support of case management approaches are key ingredients in such reform.

- *Human resources planning for underserved communities.* Overall health manpower needs should be assessed in light of the upcoming pressures of the epidemic. As noted, these are likely to be at their least adequate among populations at greatest need.
- *A more effective drug policy.* The crucial variable represented by substance use in determining the scope of the future epidemic must be grappled with realistically. An approach that emphasizes "harm reduction," for example, access to sterile injection equipment, is essential: this would not only prove more humane and effective in controlling drug use *per se* than the past "war on drugs," but would also yield dividends in reduced HIV and tuberculosis transmission. Resources should be shifted from interdiction and mandatory punishment toward drug treatment availability for all who seek it.
- *Housing, rather than hospitalization, for people with HIV.* More flexibility and attention by the Department of Housing and Urban Development regarding the housing needs of people living with HIV would diminish the problems associated with homelessness, which is a frequent consequence of illness and loss of income in poorly insured young adults. In particular, unnecessary hospitalizations can be substantially reduced by assuring stable housing arrangements appropriate for people with HIV disease.
- *Educational efforts to increase understanding of HIV disease.* Discrimination, stigmatization, or other callous and inappropriate responses to people living with HIV often arise out of unwarranted fear from lack of knowledge. Increased general awareness of basic facts can reduce such ignorant responses substantially and lay a foundation for preventive efforts. Public education should be redesigned and intensified with these goals in mind.
- *Adolescent health initiatives.* School-based health programs can provide a particularly effective resource for assuring access to basic health education and services for underserved adolescents. In addition to teaching about HIV and other STDs, information about teenage pregnancy, awareness of substance abuse hazards. nutritional knowledge, and other fundamental health skills can be conveyed in such a setting to teens whose home environments are deficient in such knowledge. Issues such as "safer sex" strategies must be dealt with in a manner acceptable to communities in which the programs are housed; but lack of access to such information can be life-threatening to youth at risk, and school-based health programs have yielded promising results to date.
- *Support for community-based organizations, providers, and volunteers.* The key role of community-based organizations in responding to

the complex needs of people living with HIV must be acknowledged and fostered. The history of response to the epidemic in the United States includes countless instances of community-based leadership and individual heroism without which the present picture would be much bleaker. The effectiveness of such organizations reflects their critical links with and trust from the community, whether the community is defined by ethnicity, geography, or sexual orientation. Of equal importance is the commitment of community workers—often volunteers. Such crucial functions must be sustained through enhanced mechanisms for funding, technical assistance, and recruitment of other organizations (especially religious groups or those in the workplace) not yet optimally involved.

Principles to Guide the Future Response to the Epidemic

While a series of clear and present steps are needed to initiate a more aggressive approach to the HIV epidemic, the Commission believes certain general principles can serve as a compass that can help guide the national response. Not all are AIDS specific.

1. Leadership is essential. Leadership in any context entails developing a vision of the response needed, establishing a plan to realize it, and accepting responsibility for its fulfillment. Leadership in the response to AIDS also provides the visible affirmation of the inclusion of people affected by HIV disease in the community.
2. Access to basic health care, including preventive, medical, and social services, should be a right for all. Our nation must find ways to finance that care for all.
3. The United States must have a vital and responsive public health system. This means rebuilding an adequately supported public health "infrastructure" with a sufficient number of trained personnel to carry out the primary public health functions of surveillance, assessment and analysis, and prevention. All levels—federal, state, and local—must have the necessary capacity to fulfill their designated roles.
4. The best science will yield the best public strategies. But the best science cannot flourish where it is blocked or constrained for ideological reasons or political convenience. Nor can it contribute properly where it is underfunded or its lessons are ignored in program design.
5. To the greatest extent possible, health care solutions (including those for HIV/AIDS) must avoid disease specificity. Solutions should offer a broad continuum of comprehensive services to those with problems of chronic relapsing disease. Strategies should recognize that the health of entire communities is often dependent upon the health of the least advantaged.
6. Partnerships are necessary. Collaboration between levels of government, with the business community, with the religious community,

with the voluntary not-for-profit sector, and with community-based organizations is essential to providing a coordinated response. A broad array of persons, including people with HIV disease, AIDS advocates, health professionals, and community representatives, must be included in formulating prevention, care, and research strategies.

7. The human face of AIDS should be ever before us. Respecting personal dignity and autonomy, respecting the need for confidentiality, reducing discrimination, and minimizing intrusiveness should all be touchstones in the development of HIV/AIDS policies and programs.

Recommendations

We will close with but two recommendations. They will not be unfamiliar to those who have followed our work, but we believe they are central, vital, and critical to launching a more adequate national response to the central human crisis of our times. The details of implementation are less important. Many are contained in our previous reports. But we need a new mind set, a new, less selfish national resolve. a new way of thinking about the epidemic that says this toll of human suffering and death is unacceptable to us. We need to acknowledge better the heroic contributions of those individuals and organizations who have been working so single-mindedly in the field of HIV and AIDS. Each of us must ask, "How can I be of help?"

Recommendation 1

Leaders at all levels must speak out about AIDS to their constituencies.

Our President must speak out clearly and forcibly about the nature, extent, and needs of the AIDS disaster. This has been our foremost recommendation since 1991. One AIDS activist group has as its symbol a pink triangle with the phrase, "silence=death." There is much to suggest that they are right. The appalling lack of frank discussion about the epidemic at all levels of national leadership fostered a woefully inadequate response, yielding death and suffering well in excess of what might have been. Silence has existed at too many levels of responsibility. Few governors, mayors, members of Congress, corporate executives, community or religious leaders, have stepped forward—perhaps taking their cue from previous Presidents. Consequently, the scale of the problem is seriously underestimated, and fear, prejudice, and misinformation abound. Leaders have both the capacity and the responsibility to coalesce their communities to find solutions.

We are vividly aware of the fact that addressing AIDS—and particularly issues that require discussing sexuality or drug use—is difficult for many to deal with comfortably. Further, some of the steps that will be required to address the epidemic better will be unpleasant or unpopular in the minds of many. But to confront difficult and sensitive issues is what true leadership means and requires. It would, in our judgment, make a profound difference in our national response to HIV disease if full and frank discussion of all its implications was initiated and encouraged by those in positions of responsibility at all levels.

Recommendation 2

We must develop a clear, well-articulated national plan for confronting AIDS.

Again, high on our list of recommendations, and that of the Presidential Commission preceding us, has been the development of a carefully crafted national strategic plan to address the issues of prevention, care, and research, required to deal with the HIV epidemic. To this end, we have suggested such a plan directly to the President in our report, *Mobilizing America's Response to AIDS.* We have spelled out the authority and resources necessary for the coordinating office required to deal with the numerous cabinet departments that must be involved in such planning. Along similar lines, we have pointed to the singular absence of a national prevention strategy worthy of the name. We have also indicated the need for more overall planning for HIV-related research, housed appropriately within the National Institutes of Health, and the desperate need for a compassionate continuum of care for those infected. The obvious reasons for having such overarching plans, still absent in the twelfth year of the epidemic, need little further comment, except perhaps that the underlying theme of the plans should be to address sexual and drug-use behavior from a public health perspective.

All of our other recommendations, past or present, follow logically from the above. There is a compelling need for a functioning public health system with the ability to conduct appropriate prevention programs, free from censorship, that would serve the special needs of gay men, of lesbians, of communities of color, of those who use drugs, of women, of children, and of adolescents. The need for better therapeutic agents, long-term care, housing, social support services, and their financing—all must be embodied in those plans. Our reports to date, and most particularly *America Living with AIDS,* spell out the particulars. Clearly our work is unfinished. Although the Commission has listened diligently, considered carefully, and kept the problem of AIDS before the public, most of our recommendations remain to be implemented. But it is time for AIDS to be swept into the mainstream of America's national agenda. To continue to treat HIV/AIDS as a marginal problem gravely threatens our nation's future. Without action on our nation's unfinished business on AIDS, we will have a continually expanding tragedy. We call on America to get on with the job. What should be done is not complicated. But it requires leadership, a plan, and the national resolve to implement it.

COURT ON CHALLENGES TO "RACIAL GERRYMANDERS"

June 28, 1993

On the last day of its term, June 28, the Supreme Court revealed the long-awaited result of its scrutiny of two North Carolina congressional districts drawn to create black voting majorities. The Court did not rule directly on whether they derived from unconstitutional "racial gerrymandering," as charged by a group of white North Carolinians in this case, Shaw v. Reno. *But by a bare 5-4 majority, the Court for the first time ruled that racially drawn districts invite legal challenges if they are "highly irregular" in shape and are created without "compelling" need.*

Both districts, the First and the Twelfth, were strangely configured. The shape of the First had been compared to a Rorschach ink-blot. The Twelfth cut diagonally across the state for 160 miles in snake-like fashion, enveloping black neighborhoods in four metropolitan areas, and narrowing in places to the width of an interstate highway.

Writing for the Court, Justice Sandra Day O'Connor said that while racial factors could not be excluded from the redistricting process, "in some exceptional cases" a reapportionment plan could become "so highly irregular that, on its face, it cannot rationally be understood as anything other than an effort 'to segregate . . . voters' on the basis of race." A district that ignores geographical and political boundaries to concentrate a particular race, she wrote, "bears an uncomfortable resemblance to political apartheid" and risks perpetuating "the very patterns of racial bloc voting that majority-minority districting is sometimes said to counteract."

Ruling's Potential Effect

Nationwide there were about fifty so-called majority-minority districts—those in which blacks, Hispanics, or other minority groups had attained a voting majority through redistricting. As in North Carolina, many were created in response to the 1965 Voting Rights Act, which applied federal oversight in several southern states and other areas where blacks often had been deprived of a political voice.

When North Carolina gained a twelfth congressional seat as a result of the 1990 census, the Democratic-controlled General Assembly devised a plan for a majority black population in one district. But the U.S. Justice Department, reviewing the plan under the Voting Rights Act's "preclearance" procedure, said the state should create two majority-black districts instead of one because about 20 percent of the population was African American. However, black voters were dispersed over much of the state, and fitting them into compact districts was difficult. Redistricting was further complicated by incumbent members of Congress who wanted to preserve areas of political strength.

The plan accomplished its purpose. For the first time in this century, two black North Carolinians, both Democrats, were elected to Congress: Eva Clayton from the First District and Melvin Watt from the Twelfth. But the redistricting drew protests from numerous North Carolinians. The Republican party and individual white voters brought lawsuits in federal district court to scuttle the plan.

A lawsuit filed by five voters in Durham County, from which part of the Twelfth District was carved, contended that the redistricting had set up a racially discriminatory voting process that deprived them of a constitutional right to vote in a "color-blind" election. The state, they said, illegally adopted a plan to concentrate black voting power without regard to any other consideration, and the Justice Department misconstrued the Voting Rights Act when it approved the plan. Attorney General Janet Reno was named a defendant.

A three-judge federal district court rejected the challenge in a split decision. When the Supreme Court agreed to review the case, the stakes were high. Civil rights advocates credited the reapportionment process with the election of thirteen of the African American members in Congress and six of the Hispanic members. They feared that a broad limitation on majority-minority districts would jeopardize those gains. Critics of the system argued that it had established a racial quota system in violation of white voters' rights.

Court's New "Strict Scrutiny" Test

The Court ruled that the lower court was correct in dismissing the claim against the federal government, for the state was responsible for drawing the new districts. As for the state, the lower court was told to reexamine the plan to see if it met a "strict scrutiny" test. This test, not previously used in reapportionment cases, would determine if the plan was narrowly tailored to serve a compelling government interest. The state argued that the plan was needed to comply with the Voting Rights Act and to erase the effects of past racial discrimination. O'Connor expressed doubt that either consideration would meet the new standard.

Supporting O'Connor's position were Justices Antonin Scalia, Anthony M. Kennedy, Clarence Thomas, and Chief Justice William H. Rehnquist. Justices Byron R. White, Harry A. Blackmun, John Paul Stevens, and David H. Souter opposed.

Dissenting Views

In the main dissenting opinion, White complained that the majority had never identified any harm that white voters had suffered because of the plan. He noted that white people accounted for 79 percent of the state's voting-age population, and they still had a majority in ten (83 percent) of the state's twelve congressional districts. "Though they might be dissatisfied with the prospect of casting a vote for a losing candidate," White wrote, "surely they cannot complain of discriminatory treatment."

Blackmun said it was "ironic" that the Court's ruling came after North Carolina had elected its first black members of Congress since Reconstruction. Stevens called it "perverse" to uphold redistricting plans drawn to provide adequate representation for other groups—he named rural voters, union members, Hasidic Jews, Polish Americans, and Republicans—but not for blacks. Souter, in a separate dissent, said the majority had "no justification" for adopting the strict scrutiny test. Instead, he said, the Court should have adhered to previous decisions that required proof of discriminatory intent and effect to invalidate a district plan based on racial considerations.

Following are excerpts from the Supreme Court's majority and dissenting opinions in Shaw v. Reno, *issued June 28, 1993, in which the Court decreed a "strict scrutiny" standard for determining the constitutionality of congressional districts drawn to ensure a majority of minorities:*

No. 92-357

Ruth O. Shaw, et al., Appellants v. Janet Reno, Attorney General, et al.	On appeal from the United States District Court for the Eastern District of North Carolina

[June 28, 1993]

JUSTICE O'CONNOR delivered the opinion of the Court.

This case involves two of the most complex and sensitive issues this Court has faced in recent years: the meaning of the constitutional "right" to vote, and the propriety of race-based state legislation designed to benefit members of historically disadvantaged racial minority groups. As a result of the 1990 census, North Carolina became entitled to a twelfth seat in the United States House of Representatives. The General Assembly enacted a reapportionment plan that included one majority-black congressional district. After the Attorney General of the United States objected to the plan pursuant to § 5 of the Voting Rights Act of 1965, the General Assembly passed new legislation creating a second majority-black district. Appellants allege that the revised plan, which contains district boundary lines of dramatically irregular shape, constitutes an unconstitutional racial gerrymander. The question before us is whether appellants have stated a cognizable claim.

I

The voting age population of North Carolina is approximately 78% white, 20% black, and 1% Native American; the remaining 1% is predominantly Asian. The black population is relatively dispersed; blacks constitute a majority of the general population in only 5 of the State's 100 counties. Geographically, the State divides into three regions: the eastern Coastal Plain, the central Piedmont Plateau, and the western mountains. The largest concentrations of black citizens live in the Coastal Plain, primarily in the northern part. The General Assembly's first redistricting plan contained one majority-black district centered in that area of the State.

Forty of North Carolina's one hundred counties are covered by § 5 of the Voting Rights Act of 1965, which prohibits a jurisdiction subject to its provisions from implementing changes in a "standard, practice, or procedure with respect to voting" without federal authorization. The jurisdiction must obtain either a judgment from the United States District Court for the District of Columbia declaring that the proposed change "does not have the purpose and will not have the effect of denying or abridging the right to vote on account of race or color" or administrative preclearance from the Attorney General. Because the General Assembly's reapportionment plan affected the covered counties, the parties agree that § 5 applied. The State chose to submit its plan to the Attorney General for preclearance.

The Attorney General, acting through the Assistant Attorney General for the Civil Rights Division, interposed a formal objection to the General Assembly's plan. The Attorney General specifically objected to the configuration of boundary lines drawn in the south-central to southeastern region of the State. In the Attorney General's view, the General Assembly could have created a second majority-minority district "to give effect to black and Native American voting strength in this area" by using boundary lines "no more irregular than [those] found elsewhere in the proposed plan," but failed to do so for "pretextual reasons."

Under § 5, the State remained free to seek a declaratory judgment from the District Court for the District of Columbia notwithstanding the Attorney General's objection. It did not do so. Instead, the General Assembly enacted a revised redistricting plan that included a second majority-black district. The General Assembly located the second district not in the south-central to southeastern part of the State, but in the north-central region along Interstate 85....

The first of the two majority-black districts contained in the revised plan, District 1, is somewhat hook shaped. Centered in the northeast portion of the State, it moves southward until it tapers to a narrow band; then, with finger-like extensions, it reaches far into the southernmost part of the State near the South Carolina border. District 1 has been compared to a "Rorschach ink-blot test," *Shaw v. Barr* (EDNC 1992) (Voorhees, C. J., concurring in part and dissenting in part) and a "bug splattered on a windshield."

The second majority-black district, District 12, is even more unusually shaped. It is approximately 160 miles long and, for much of its length, no wider than the I-85 corridor. It winds in snake-like fashion through tobacco country, financial centers, and manufacturing areas "until it gobbles in enough enclaves of black neighborhoods."... Northbound and southbound drivers on I-85 sometimes find themselves in separate districts in one county, only to "trade" districts when they enter the next county. Of the 10 counties through which District 12 passes, five are cut into three different districts; even towns are divided. At one point the district remains contiguous only because it intersects at a single point with two other districts before crossing over them....

The Attorney General did not object to the General Assembly's revised plan. But numerous North Carolinians did. The North Carolina Republican Party and individual voters brought suit in Federal District Court alleging that the plan constituted an unconstitutional political gerrymander under *Davis v. Bandemer* (1986). That claim was dismissed....

Shortly after the complaint in *Pope v. Blue* was filed, appellants instituted the present action in the United States District Court for the Eastern District of North Carolina. Appellants alleged not that the revised plan constituted a political gerrymander, nor that it violated the "one person, one vote" principle,... but that the State had created an unconstitutional *racial* gerrymander. Appellants are five residents of Durham County, North Carolina, all registered to vote in that county. Under the General Assembly's plan, two will vote for congressional representatives in District 12 and three will vote in neighboring District 2. Appellants sued the Governor of North Carolina, the Lieutenant Governor, the Secretary of State, the Speaker of the North Carolina House of Representatives, and members of the North Carolina State Board of Elections (state appellees), together with two federal officials, the Attorney General and the Assistant Attorney General for the Civil Rights Division (federal appellees).

Appellants contended that the General Assembly's revised reapportionment plan violated several provisions of the United States Constitution, including the Fourteenth Amendment. They alleged that the General Assembly deliberately "create[d] two Congressional Districts in which a majority of black voters was concentrated arbitrarily—without regard to any other considerations, such as compactness, contiguousness, geographical boundaries, or political subdivisions" with the purpose "to create Congressional Districts along racial lines" and to assure the election of two black representatives to Congress. Appellants sought declaratory and injunctive relief against the state appellees. They sought similar relief against the federal appellees, arguing, alternatively, that the federal appellees had misconstrued the Voting Rights Act or that the Act itself was unconstitutional.

The three-judge District Court granted the federal appellees' motion to dismiss. The court agreed unanimously that it lacked subject matter jurisdiction by reason of § 14(b) of the Voting Rights Act, which vests the District Court for the District of Columbia with exclusive jurisdiction to issue injunctions against the execution of the Act and to enjoin actions taken by federal officers pursuant thereto. Two judges also concluded that, to the extent appellants challenged the Attorney General's preclearance decisions, their claim was foreclosed by this Court's holding in *Morris v. Gressette* (1977).

By a 2-to-1 vote, the District Court also dismissed the complaint against the state appellees. The majority found no support for appellants' contentions that race-based districting is prohibited by Article I, § 4, or Article I, § 2, of the Constitution, or by the Privileges and Immunities Clause of the Fourteenth Amendment. It deemed appellants' claim under the Fifteenth Amendment essentially subsumed within their related claim under the Equal Protection Clause. That claim, the majority concluded, was barred by *United Jewish Organizations of Williamsburgh, Inc. v. Carey* (1977) *(UJO)*.

The majority first took judicial notice of a fact omitted from appellants' complaint: that appellants are white. It rejected the argument that race-conscious redistricting to benefit minority voters is *per se* unconstitutional. The majority also rejected appellants' claim that North Carolina's reapportionment plan was impermissible. The majority read *UJO* to stand for the proposition that a redistricting scheme violates white voters' rights only if it is "adopted with the purpose and effect of discriminating against white voters ... on account of their race." The purposes of favoring minority voters and complying with the Voting Rights Act are not discriminatory in the constitutional sense, the court reasoned, and majority-minority districts have an impermissibly discriminatory effect only when they unfairly dilute or cancel out white voting strength. Because the State's purpose here was to comply with the Voting Rights Act, and because the General Assembly's plan did not lead to proportional under-representation of white voters statewide, the majority concluded that appellants had failed to state an equal protection claim.

Chief Judge Voorhees agreed that race-conscious redistricting is not per se unconstitutional but dissented from the rest of the majority's equal protection analysis. He read JUSTICE WHITE's opinion in *UJO* to authorize race-based reapportionment only when the State employs traditional districting principles such as compactness and contiguity. North Carolina's failure to respect these principles, in Judge Voorhees' view, "augur[ed] a constitutionally suspect, and potentially unlawful, intent" sufficient to defeat the state appellees' motion to dismiss.

We noted probable jurisdiction.

II

A

"The right to vote freely for the candidate of one's choice is of the essence of a democratic society. . . ." *Reynolds v. Sims.* For much of our Nation's history, that right sadly has been denied to many because of race. The Fifteenth Amendment, ratified in 1870 after a bloody Civil War, promised unequivocally that "[t]he right of citizens of the United States to vote" no longer would be "denied or abridged . . . by any State on account of race, color, or previous condition of servitude."

But "[a] number of states . . . refused to take no for an answer and continued to circumvent the fifteenth amendment's prohibition through the use of both subtle and blunt instruments, perpetuating ugly patterns of pervasive racial discrimination." Ostensibly race-neutral devices such as literacy tests with "grandfather" clauses and "good character" provisos were devised to deprive black voters of the franchise. Another of the weapons in the States' arsenal was the racial gerrymander—"the deliberate and arbitrary distortion of district boundaries . . . for [racial] purposes." *Bandemer* (Powell, J., concurring in part and dissenting in part). In the 1870's, for example, opponents of Reconstruction in Mississippi "concentrated the bulk of the black population in a 'shoestring' Congressional district running the length of the Mississippi River, leaving five others with white majorities." Some 90 years later, Alabama redefined the boundaries of the city of Tuskegee "from a square to an uncouth twenty-eight-sided figure" in a manner that was alleged to exclude black voters, and only black voters, from the city limits. *Gomillion v. Lightfoot* (1960).

Alabama's exercise in geometry was but one example of the racial discrimination in voting that persisted in parts of this country nearly a century after ratification of the Fifteenth Amendment. In some States, registration of eligible black voters ran 50% behind that of whites. Congress enacted the Voting Rights Act of 1965 as a dramatic and severe response to the situation. The Act proved immediately successful in ensuring racial minorities access to the voting booth; by the early 1970's, the spread between black and white registration in several of the targeted Southern States had fallen to well below 10%

But it soon became apparent that guaranteeing equal access to the polls would not suffice to root out other racially discriminatory voting practices. Drawing on the "one person, one vote" principle, this Court recognized that "[t]he right to vote can be affected by a *dilution* of voting power as well as by an absolute prohibition on casting a ballot." *Allen v. State Board of Elections* (1969) (emphasis added). Where members of a racial minority group vote as a cohesive unit, practices such as multimember or at-large electoral systems can reduce or nullify minority voters' ability, as a group, "to elect the candidate of their choice." Accordingly, the Court held that such schemes violate the Fourteenth Amendment when they are adopted with a discriminatory purpose and have the effect of diluting minority voting strength. See, *e.g., Rogers v. Lodge* (1982); *White v. Regester* (1973). Congress, too, responded to the problem of vote dilution. In 1982, it amended § 2 of the Voting Rights Act to prohibit legislation that *results* in the dilution of a minority group's voting strength, regardless of the legislature's intent....

B

It is against this background that we confront the questions presented here. In our view, the District Court properly dismissed appellants' claims against the federal appellees. Our focus is on appellants' claim that the State engaged in unconstitutional racial gerrymandering. That argument strikes a powerful historical chord: It is unsettling how closely the North Carolina plan resembles the most egregious racial gerrymanders of the past.

An understanding of the nature of appellants' claim is critical to our resolution of the case. In their complaint, appellants did not claim that the General Assembly's reapportionment plan unconstitutionally "diluted" white voting strength. They did not even claim to be white. Rather, appellants' complaint alleged that the deliberate segregation of voters into separate districts on the basis of race violated their constitutional right to participate in a "color-blind" electoral process.

Despite their invocation of the ideal of a "color-blind" Constitution, ... appellants appear to concede that race-conscious redistricting is not always unconstitutional. That concession is wise: This Court never has held that race-conscious state decisionmaking is impermissible in *all* circumstances. What appellants object to is redistricting legislation that is so extremely irregular on its face that it rationally can be viewed only as an effort to segregate the races for purposes of voting, without regard for traditional districting principles and without sufficiently compelling justification. For the reasons that follow, we conclude that appellants have stated a claim upon which relief can be granted under the Equal Protection Clause.

III

A

The Equal Protection Clause provides that "[n]o State shall ... deny to any person within its jurisdiction the equal protection of the laws." Its central purpose is to prevent the States from purposefully discriminating between individuals on the basis of race. *Washington v. Davis* (1976). Laws that explicitly distinguish between individuals on racial grounds fall within the core of that prohibition.

No inquiry into legislative purpose is necessary when the racial classification appears on the face of the statute. . . . Express racial classifications are immediately suspect because, "[a]bsent searching judicial inquiry . . . , there is simply no way of determining what classifications are 'benign' or 'remedial' and what classifications are in fact motivated by illegitimate notions of racial inferiority or simple racial politics." *Richmond v. J. A. Croson Co.* (1989); see also *UJO* ("[A] purportedly preferential race assignment may in fact disguise a policy that perpetuates disadvantageous treatment of the plan's supposed beneficiaries").

Classifications of citizens solely on the basis of race "are by their very nature odious to a free people whose institutions are founded upon the doctrine of equality." . . . They threaten to stigmatize individuals by reason of their membership in a racial group and to incite racial hostility. . . . Accordingly, we have held that the Fourteenth Amendment requires state legislation that expressly distinguishes among citizens because of their race to be narrowly tailored to further a compelling governmental interest. See, *e.g., Wygant v. Jackson Bd. of Ed.* (1986).

These principles apply not only to legislation that contains explicit racial distinctions, but also to those "rare" statutes that, although race-neutral, are, on their face, "unexplainable on grounds other than race." *Arlington Heights v. Metropolitan Housing Development Corp.* (1977). . . .

B

Appellants contend that redistricting legislation that is so bizarre on its face that it is "unexplainable on grounds other than race" . . . demands the same close scrutiny that we give other state laws that classify citizens by race. Our voting rights precedents support that conclusion.

In *Guinn v. United States* (1915), the Court invalidated under the Fifteenth Amendment a statute that imposed a literacy requirement on voters but contained a "grandfather clause" applicable to individuals and their lineal descendants entitled to vote "on [or prior to] January 1, 1866." The determinative consideration for the Court was that the law, though ostensibly race-neutral, on its face "embod[ied] no exercise of judgment and rest[ed] upon no discernible reason" other than to circumvent the prohibitions of the Fifteenth Amendment. In other words, the statute was invalid because, on its face, it could not be explained on grounds other than race.

The Court applied the same reasoning to the "uncouth twenty-eight-sided" municipal boundary line at issue in *Gomillion*. Although the statute that redrew the city limits of Tuskegee was race-neutral on its face, plaintiffs alleged that its effect was impermissibly to remove from the city virtually all black voters and no white voters. The Court reasoned:

> "If these allegations upon a trial remained uncontradicted or unqualified, the conclusion would be irresistible, tantamount for all practical purposes to a mathematical demonstration, that the legislation is solely concerned with segregating white and colored voters by fencing Negro citizens out of town so as to deprive them of their pre-existing municipal vote."

The majority resolved the case under the Fifteenth Amendment. Justice Whittaker, however, concluded that the "unlawful segregation of races of citizens" into different voting districts was cognizable under the Equal Protection Clause. This Court's subsequent reliance on *Gomillion* in other Fourteenth Amendment cases suggests the correctness of Justice Whittaker's view.... *Gomillion* thus supports appellants' contention that district lines obviously drawn for the purpose of separating voters by race require careful scrutiny under the Equal Protection Clause regardless of the motivations underlying their adoption.

The Court extended the reasoning of *Gomillion* to congressional districting in *Wright v. Rockefeller* (1964). At issue in *Wright* were four districts contained in a New York apportionment statute. The plaintiffs alleged that the statute excluded nonwhites from one district and concentrated them in the other three. Every member of the Court assumed that the plaintiffs' allegation that the statute "segregate[d] eligible voters by race and place of origin" stated a constitutional claim. The Justices disagreed only as to whether the plaintiffs had carried their burden of proof at trial. The dissenters thought the unusual shape of the district lines could "be explained only in racial terms." The majority, however, accepted the District Court's finding that the plaintiffs had failed to establish that the districts were in fact drawn on racial lines....

Wright illustrates the difficulty of determining from the face of a single-member districting plan that it purposefully distinguishes between voters on the basis of race. A reapportionment statute typically does not classify persons at all; it classifies tracts of land, or addresses. Moreover, redistricting differs from other kinds of state decisionmaking in that the legislature always is *aware* of race when it draws district lines, just as it is aware of age, economic status, religious and political persuasion, and a variety of other demographic factors. That sort of race consciousness does not lead inevitably to impermissible race discrimination. As *Wright* demonstrates, when members of a racial group live together in one community, a reapportionment plan that concentrates members of the group in one district and excludes them from others may reflect wholly legitimate purposes. The district lines may be drawn, for example, to provide for compact districts of contiguous territory, or to maintain the integrity of political subdivisions. See *Reynolds* (recognizing these as legitimate state interests).

The difficulty of proof, of course, does not mean that a racial gerrymander, once established, should receive less scrutiny under the Equal Protection Clause than other state legislation classifying citizens by race. Moreover, it seems clear to us that proof sometimes will not be difficult at all. In some exceptional cases, a reapportionment plan may be so highly irregular that, on its face, it rationally cannot be understood as anything other than an effort to "segregat[e] ... voters" on the basis of race.... *Gomillion,* in which a tortured municipal boundary line was drawn to exclude black voters, was such a case. So, too, would be a case which a State concentrated a dispersed minority population in a single district by disregarding traditional districting principles such as compactness, contiguity, and respect for political subdivisions. We emphasize that these criteria are important not because they are constitutionally required—they are not ... —but because they are objective factors that may serve to defeat a claim that a district has been gerrymandered on racial lines....

Put differently, we believe that reapportionment is one area in which appearances do matter. A reapportionment plan that includes in one district individuals who belong to the same race, but who are otherwise widely separated by geographical and political boundaries, and who may have little in common with one another but the color of their skin, bears an uncomfortable resemblance to political apartheid. It reinforces the perception that members of the same racial group—regardless of their age, education, economic status, or the community in which they live—think alike, share the same political interests, and will prefer the same candidates at the polls. We have rejected such perceptions elsewhere as impermissible racial stereotypes.... By perpetuating such notions, a racial gerrymander may exacerbate the very patterns of racial bloc voting that majority-minority districting is sometimes said to counteract.

The message that such districting sends to elected representatives is equally pernicious. When a district obviously is created solely to effectuate the perceived common interests of one racial group, elected officials are more likely to believe that their primary obligation is to represent only the members of that group, rather than their constituency as a whole. This is altogether antithetical to our system of representative democracy....

For these reasons, we conclude that a plaintiff challenging a reapportionment statute under the Equal Protection Clause may state a claim by alleging that the legislation, though race-neutral on its face, rationally cannot be understood as anything other than an effort to separate voters into different districts on the basis of race, and that the separation lacks sufficient justification. It is unnecessary for us to decide whether or how a reapportionment plan that, on its face, can be explained in nonracial terms successfully could be challenged. Thus, we express no view as to whether "the intentional creation of majority-minority districts, without more" always gives rise to an equal protection claim. We hold only that, on the facts of this case, plaintiffs have stated a claim sufficient to defeat the state appellees' motion to dismiss.

C

The dissenters consider the circumstances of this case "functionally indistinguishable" from multimember districting and at-large voting systems, which are loosely described as "other varieties of gerrymandering." We have considered the constitutionality of these practices in other Fourteenth Amendment cases and have required plaintiffs to demonstrate that the challenged practice has the purpose and effect of diluting a racial group's voting strength.... At-large and multimember schemes, however, do not classify voters on the basis of race. Classifying citizens by race, as we have said, threatens special harms that are not present in our vote-dilution cases. It therefore warrants different analysis.

JUSTICE SOUTER apparently believes that racial gerrymandering is harmless unless it dilutes a racial group's voting strength. As we have explained, however, reapportionment legislation that cannot be understood as anything other than an effort to classify and separate voters by race injures voters in other ways. It reinforces racial stereotypes and threatens to undermine our system of representative democracy by signaling to elected officials that they represent a particular racial group rather than their constituency as a whole. JUSTICE SOUTER does not adequately explain why these harms are not cognizable under the Fourteenth Amendment.

The dissenters make two other arguments that cannot be reconciled with our precedents. First, they suggest that a racial gerrymander of the sort alleged here is functionally equivalent to gerrymanders for nonracial purposes, such as political gerrymanders. This Court has held political gerrymanders to be justiciable under the Equal Protection Clause. See *Davis v. Bandemer*. But nothing in our case law compels the conclusion that racial and political gerrymanders are subject to precisely the same constitutional scrutiny. In fact, our country's long and persistent history of racial discrimination in voting—as well as our Fourteenth Amendment jurisprudence, which always has reserved the strictest scrutiny for discrimination on the basis of race—would seem to compel the opposite conclusion.

Second, JUSTICE STEVENS argues that racial gerrymandering poses no constitutional difficulties when district lines are drawn to favor the minority, rather than the majority. We have made clear, however, that equal protection analysis "is not dependent on the race of those burdened or benefited by a particular classification." ... Indeed, racial classifications receive close scrutiny even when they may be said to burden or benefit the races equally....

Finally, nothing in the Court's highly fractured decision in *UJO* ... forecloses the claim we recognize today. *UJO* concerned New York's revision of a reapportionment plan to include additional majority-minority districts in response to the Attorney General's denial of administrative preclearance under § 5. In that regard, it closely resembles the present case. But the cases are critically different in another way. The plaintiffs in *UJO*—members of a Hasidic community split between two districts under New York's revised redistricting plan—did not allege that the plan, on its face, was so highly irregular that it rationally could be understood only as an effort to segregate voters by race. Indeed, the facts of the case would not have supported such a claim. Three Justices approved the New York statute, in part, precisely because it adhered to traditional districting principles. . . .

. . . *UJO*'s framework simply does not apply where, as here, a reapportionment plan is alleged to be so irrational on its face that it immediately offends principles of racial equality. *UJO* set forth a standard under which white voters can establish unconstitutional vote dilution. But it did not purport to overrule *Gomillion* or *Wright*. Nothing in the decision precludes white voters (or voters of any other race) from bringing the analytically distinct claim that a reapportionment plan rationally cannot be understood as anything other than an effort to segregate citizens into separate voting districts on the basis of race without sufficient justification. Because appellants here stated such a claim, the District Court erred in dismissing their complaint.

IV

JUSTICE SOUTER contends that exacting scrutiny of racial gerrymanders under the Fourteenth Amendment is inappropriate because reapportionment "nearly always require[s] some consideration of race for legitimate reasons." . . . JUSTICE SOUTER'S reasoning is flawed.

Earlier this Term, we unanimously reaffirmed that racial bloc voting and minority-group political cohesion never can be assumed, but specifically must be proved in each case in order to establish that a redistricting plan dilutes minority voting strength in violation of § 2. See *Growe v. Emison* (1993). That racial bloc voting or minority political cohesion may be found to exist in *some* cases, of course, is no reason to treat *all* racial gerrymanders differently from other kinds of racial classification. JUSTICE SOUTER apparently views racial gerrymandering of the type presented here as a special category of "benign" racial discrimination that should be subject to relaxed judicial review. As we have said, however, the very reason that the Equal Protection Clause demands strict scrutiny of all racial classifications is because without it, a court cannot determine whether or not the discrimination truly is "benign." Thus, if appellants' allegations of a racial gerrymander are not contradicted on remand, the District Court must determine whether the General Assembly's reapportionment plan satisfies strict scrutiny. We therefore consider what that level of scrutiny requires in the reapportionment context.

The state appellees suggest that a covered jurisdiction may have a compelling interest in creating majority-minority districts in order to comply with the Voting Rights Act. The States certainly have a very strong interest in complying with federal antidiscrimination laws that are constitutionally valid as interpreted and as applied. But in the context of a Fourteenth Amendment challenge, courts must bear in mind the difference between what the law permits, and what it requires.

For example, on remand North Carolina might claim that it adopted the revised plan in order to comply with the § 5 "nonretrogression" principle. Under that principle, a proposed voting change cannot be precleared if it will lead to "a retrogression in the position of racial minorities with respect to their effective exercise of the electoral franchise." *Beer v. United States* (1976). In *Beer,* we held that a reapportionment plan that created one majority-minority district where none existed before passed muster under § 5 because it improved the position of racial minorities....

Although the Court concluded that the redistricting scheme at issue in *Beer* was nonretrogressive, it did not hold that the plan, for that reason, was immune from constitutional challenge. The Court expressly declined to reach that question. Indeed, the Voting Rights Act and our case law make clear that a reapportionment plan that satisfies § 5 still may be enjoined as unconstitutional.... Thus, we do not read *Beer* or any of our other § 5 cases to give covered jurisdictions *carte blanche* to engage in racial gerrymandering in the name of nonretrogression. A reapportionment plan would not be narrowly tailored to the goal of avoiding retrogression if the State went beyond what was reasonably necessary to avoid retrogression....

Before us, the state appellees contend that the General Assembly's revised plan was necessary not to prevent retrogression, but to avoid dilution of black voting strength in violation of § 2, as construed in *Thornburg v. Gingles* (1986). In *Gingles* the Court considered a multimember redistricting plan for the North Carolina State Legislature. The Court held that members of a racial minority group claiming § 2 vote dilution through the use of multimember districts must prove three threshold conditions: that the minority group "is sufficiently large and geographically compact to constitute a majority in a single-member district," that the minority group is "politically cohesive," and that "the white majority votes sufficiently as a bloc to enable it ... usually to defeat the minority's preferred candidate." We have indicated that similar preconditions apply in challenges to single-member districts....

Appellants maintain that the General Assembly's revised plan could not have been required by § 2. They contend that the State's black population is too dispersed to support two geographically compact majority-black districts, as the bizarre shape of District 12 demonstrates, and that there is no evidence of black political cohesion. They also contend that recent black electoral successes demonstrate the willingness of white voters in North Carolina to vote for black candidates. Appellants point out that blacks currently hold the positions of State Auditor, Speaker of the North Carolina House of Representatives, and chair of the North Carolina State Board of Elections. They also point out that in 1990 a black candidate defeated a white opponent in the Democratic Party run-off for a United States Senate seat before being defeated narrowly by the Republican incumbent in the general election. Appellants further argue that if § 2 did require adoption of North Carolina's revised plan, § 2 is to that extent unconstitutional. These arguments were not developed below, and the issues remain open for consideration on remand.

The state appellees alternatively argue that the General Assembly's plan advanced a compelling interest entirely distinct from the Voting Rights Act. We previously have recognized a significant state interest in eradicating the effects of past racial discrimination. . . . But the State must have a " 'strong basis in evidence' for [concluding] that remedial action [is] necessary.' " . . .

The state appellees submit that two pieces of evidence gave the General Assembly a strong basis for believing that remedial action was warranted here: the Attorney General's imposition of the § 5 preclearance requirement on 40 North Carolina counties, and the *Gingles* District Court's findings of a long history of official racial discrimination in North Carolina's political system and of pervasive racial bloc voting. The state appellees assert that the deliberate creation of majority-minority districts is the most precise way—indeed the only effective way—to overcome the effects of racially polarized voting. This question also need not be decided at this stage of the litigation. We note, however, that only three Justices in *UJO* were prepared to say that States have a significant interest in minimizing the consequences of racial bloc voting apart from the requirements of the Voting Rights Act. And those three Justices specifically concluded that race-based districting, as a response to racially polarized voting, is constitutionally permissible only when the State "employ[s] sound districting principles," and only when the affected racial group's "residential patterns afford the opportunity of creating districts in which they will be in the majority."

V

Racial classifications of any sort pose the risk of lasting harm to our society. They reinforce the belief, held by too many for too much of our history, that individuals should be judged by the color of their skin. Racial classifications with respect to voting carry particular dangers. Racial gerrymandering, even for remedial purposes, may balkanize us into competing racial factions; it threatens to carry us further from the goal of a political system in which race no longer matters—a goal that the Fourteenth and Fifteenth Amendments embody, and to which the Nation continues to aspire. It is for these reasons that race-based districting by our state legislatures demands close judicial scrutiny.

In this case, the Attorney General suggested that North Carolina could have created a reasonably compact second majority-minority district in the south-central to southeastern part of the State. We express no view as to whether appellants successfully could have challenged such a district under the Fourteenth Amendment. We also do not decide whether appellants' complaint stated a claim under constitutional provisions other than the Fourteenth Amendment. Today we hold only that appellants have stated a claim under the Equal Protection Clause by alleging that the

North Carolina General Assembly adopted a reapportionment scheme so irrational on its face that it can be understood only as an effort to segregate voters into separate voting districts because of their race, and that the separation lacks sufficient justification. If the allegation of racial gerrymandering remains uncontradicted, the District Court further must determine whether the North Carolina plan is narrowly tailored to further a compelling governmental interest. Accordingly, we reverse the judgment of the District Court and remand the case for further proceedings consistent with this opinion.

It is so ordered.

JUSTICE WHITE, with whom JUSTICE BLACKMUN and JUSTICE STEVENS join, dissenting.

The facts of this case mirror those presented in *United Jewish Organizations of Williamsburgh, Inc. v. Carey* (1977) *(UJO),* where the Court rejected a claim that creation of a majority-minority district violated the Constitution, either as a *per se* matter or in light of the circumstances leading to the creation of such a district. Of particular relevance, five of the Justices reasoned that members of the white majority could not plausibly argue that their influence over the political process had been unfairly cancelled or that such had been the State's intent. Accordingly, they held that plaintiffs were not entitled to relief under the Constitution's Equal Protection Clause. On the same reasoning, I would affirm the district court's dismissal of appellants' claim in this instance.

The Court today chooses not to overrule, but rather to sidestep, *UJO*. It does so by glossing over the striking similarities, focusing on surface differences, most notably the (admittedly unusual) shape of the newly created district, and imagining an entirely new cause of action. Because the holding is limited to such anomalous circumstances, it perhaps will not substantially hamper a State's legitimate efforts to redistrict in favor of racial minorities. Nonetheless, the notion that North Carolina's plan, under which whites remain a voting majority in a disproportionate number of congressional districts, and pursuant to which the State has sent its first black representatives since Reconstruction to the United States Congress, might have violated appellants' constitutional rights is both a fiction and a departure from settled equal protection principles. Seeing no good reason to engage in either, I dissent.

I

A

The grounds for my disagreement with the majority are simply stated: Appellants have not presented a cognizable claim, because they have not alleged a cognizable injury. To date, we have held that only two types of state voting practices could give rise to a constitutional claim. The first involves direct and outright deprivation of the right to vote, for example by means of a poll tax or literacy test.... Plainly, this variety is not implicated by appellants' allegations and need not detain us further. The second type of unconstitutional practice is that which "affects the political strength of various groups,"... in violation of the Equal Protection Clause. As for this latter category, we have insisted that members of the political or racial group demonstrate that the challenged action have the intent and effect of unduly diminishing their influence on the political process. Although this severe burden has limited the number of successful suits, it was adopted for sound reasons.

The central explanation has to do with the nature of the redistricting process. As the majority recognizes, "redistricting differs from other kinds of state decisionmaking in that the legislature always is *aware* of race when it draws district lines, just as it is aware of age, economic status, religious and political persuasion, and a variety of other demographic factors." "Being aware," in this context, is shorthand for "taking into account," and it hardly can be doubted that legislators routinely engage in the business of making electoral predictions based on group characteristics—racial, ethnic, and the like.... Because extirpating such considerations from the redistricting process is unrealistic, the Court has not invalidated all plans that consciously use race, but rather has looked at their impact.

Redistricting plans also reflect group interests and inevitably are conceived with partisan aims in mind. To allow judicial interference whenever this occurs would be to invite constant and unmanageable intrusion. Moreover, a group's power to affect the political process does not automatically dissipate by virtue of an electoral loss. Accordingly, we have asked that an identifiable group demonstrate more than mere lack of success at the polls to make out a successful gerrymandering claim....

With these considerations in mind, we have limited such claims by insisting upon a showing that "the political processes ... were not equally open to participation by the group in question—that its members had less opportunity than did other residents in the district to participate in the political processes and to elect legislators of their choice." ... Indeed, as a brief survey of decisions illustrates, the Court's gerrymandering cases all carry this theme—that it is not mere suffering at the polls but discrimination in the polity with which the Constitution is concerned....

To distinguish a claim that alleges that the redistricting scheme has discriminatory intent and effect from one that does not has nothing to do with dividing racial classifications between the "benign" and the malicious—an enterprise which, as the majority notes, the Court has treated with skepticism. Rather, the issue is whether the classification based on race discriminates against *anyone* by denying equal access to the political process....

B

The most compelling evidence of the Court's position prior to this day, for it is most directly on point, is *UJO* (1977). The Court characterizes the decision as "highly fractured," but that should not detract attention from the rejection by a majority in UJO of the claim that the State's intentional creation of majority-minority districts transgressed constitutional norms. As stated above, five Justices were of the view that, absent any contention that the proposed plan was adopted with the intent, *or* had the effect, of unduly minimizing the white majority's voting strength, the Fourteenth Amendment was not implicated....

... As was the case in New York, a number of North Carolina's political subdivisions have interfered with black citizens' meaningful exercise of the franchise, and are therefore subject to §§ 4 and 5 of the Voting Rights Act. In other words, North Carolina was found by Congress to have " 'resorted to the extraordinary stratagem of contriving new rules of various kinds for the sole purpose of perpetuating voting discrimination in the face of adverse federal court decrees' " and therefore "would be likely to engage in 'similar maneuvers in the future in order to evade the remedies for voting discrimination contained in the Act itself.' " ...

Like New York, North Carolina failed to prove to the Attorney General's satisfaction that its proposed redistricting had neither the purpose nor the effect of abridging the right to vote on account of race or color. The Attorney General's interposition of a § 5 objection "properly is viewed" as "an administrative finding of discrimination" against a racial minority.... Finally, like New York, North Carolina reacted by modifying its plan and creating additional majority-minority districts.

In light of this background, it strains credulity to suggest that North Carolina's purpose in creating a second majority-minority district was to discriminate against members of the majority group by "impair[ing] or burden[ing their] opportunity ... to participate in the political process." The State has made no mystery of its intent, which was to respond to the Attorney General's objections by improving the minority group's prospects of electing a candidate of its choice. I doubt that this constitutes a discriminatory purpose as defined in the Court's equal protection cases—*i.e.*, an intent to aggravate "the unequal distribution of electoral power." But even assuming that it does, there is no question that appellants have not alleged the requisite discriminatory effects. Whites constitute roughly 76 percent of the total population and 79 percent of the voting age population in North Carolina. Yet, under the State's plan, they still constitute a voting majority in 10 (or 83 percent) of the 12 congressional districts. Though they might be dissatisfied at the prospect of casting a vote for a losing candidate—a lot shared by many, including a disproportionate number of minority voters—surely they cannot complain of discriminatory treatment.

II

The majority attempts to distinguish *UJO* by imagining a heretofore unknown type of constitutional claim. In its words, *"UJO* set forth a standard under which white voters can establish unconstitutional vote dilution.... Nothing in the decision precludes white voters (or voters of any other race) from bringing the analytically distinct claim that a reapportionment plan rationally cannot be understood as anything other than an effort to segregate citizens into separate voting districts on the basis of race without sufficent justification." There is no support for this distinction in *UJO,* and no authority in the cases relied on by the Court either. More importantly, the majority's submission does not withstand analysis. The logic of its theory appears to be that race-conscious redistricting that "segregates" by drawing odd-shaped lines is qualitatively different from race-conscious redistricting that affects groups in some other way. The distinction is without foundation.

A

The essence of the majority's argument is that *UJO* dealt with a claim of vote dilution—which required a specific showing of harm—and that cases such as *Gomillion v. Lightfoot* (1960), and *Wright v. Rockefeller* (1964), dealt with claims of racial segregation—which did not. I read these decisions quite differently. Petitioners' claim in *UJO* was that the State had "violated the Fourteenth and Fifteenth Amendments by *deliberately revising its reapportionment plan along racial lines.*" ([P]lurality opinion)(emphasis added). They also stated: " 'Our argument is ... that the history of the area demonstrates that there could be—and in fact was—*no reason other than race* to divide the community at this time.' " Nor was it ever in doubt that "the State deliberately used race in a purposeful manner." In other words, the "analytically distinct claim" the majority discovers today was in plain view and did not carry the day for petitioners. The fact that a demonstration of discriminatory effect was required in that case was not a function of the kind of claim that was made. It was a function of the type of injury upon which the Court insisted.

Gomillion is consistent with this view.... In *Gomillion,* ... the group that formed the majority at the state level purportedly set out to manipulate city boundaries in order to remove members of the minority, thereby denying them valuable municipal services. No analogous purpose or effect has been alleged in this case.

The only other case invoked by the majority is *Wright v. Rockefeller. Wright* involved a challenge to a legislative plan that created four districts. In the Seventeenth, Nineteenth, and Twentieth Districts, Whites constituted respectively 94.9%, 71.5%, and 72.5% of the population. 86.3% percent of the population in the Eighteenth District was classified as nonwhite or Puerto Rican.... The plaintiffs alleged that the plan was drawn with the intent to segregate voters on the basis of race, in violation of the Fourteenth and Fifteenth Amendments. The Court affirmed the District Court's dismissal of the complaint on the ground that plaintiffs had not met their burden of proving discriminatory intent. I fail to see how a decision based on a failure to establish discriminatory *intent* can support the inference that it is unnecessary to prove discriminatory *effect*.

Wright is relevant only to the extent that it illustrates a proposition with which I have no problem: That a complaint stating that a plan has carved out districts on the basis of race *can*, under certain circumstances, state a claim under the Fourteenth Amendment. To that end, however, there must be an allegation of discriminatory purpose and effect, for the constitutionality of a race-conscious redistricting plan depends on these twin elements. In *Wright*, for example, the facts might have supported the contention that the districts were intended to, and did in fact, shield the Seventeenth District from any minority influence and "pack" black and Puerto Rican voters in the Eighteenth, thereby invidiously minimizing their voting strength. In other words, the purposeful creation of a majority-minority district could have discriminatory effect if it is achieved by means of "packing"—*i.e.*, over-concentration of minority voters. In the present case, the facts could sustain no such allegation.

B

Lacking support in any of the Court's precedents, the majority's novel type of claim also makes no sense. As I understand the theory that is put forth, a redistricting plan that uses race to "segregate" voters by drawing "uncouth" lines is harmful in a way that a plan that uses race to distribute voters differently is not, for the former "bears an uncomfortable resemblance to political apartheid." The distinction is untenable.

Racial gerrymanders come in various shades: At-large voting schemes ...; the fragmentation of a minority group among various districts "so that it is a majority in none," ... otherwise known as "cracking" ... ; the "stacking" of "a large minority population concentration ... with a larger white population" ... ; and, finally, the "concentration of [minority voters] into districts where they constitute an excessive majority" ... also called "packing." In each instance, race is consciously utilized by the legislature for electoral purposes; in each instance, we have put the plaintiff challenging the district lines to the burden of demonstrating that the plan was meant to, and did in fact, exclude an identifiable racial group from participation in the political process.

Not so, apparently, when the districting "segregates" by drawing odd-shaped lines. In that case, we are told, such proof no longer is needed. Instead, it is the *State* that must rebut the allegation that race was taken into account, a fact that, together with the legislators' consideration of ethnic, religious, and other group characteristics, I had thought we practically took for granted. Part of the explanation for the majority's approach has to do, perhaps, with the emotions stirred by words such as "segregation" and "political apartheid." But their loose and imprecise use by today's majority has, I fear, led it astray. The consideration of race in "segregation" cases is no different than in other race-conscious districting; from the standpoint of the affected groups, moreover, the line-drawings all act in similar fashion. A plan that "segregates" being functionally indistinguishable from any of the other varieties of gerrymandering, we should be consistent in what we require from a claimant: Proof of discriminatory purpose and effect.

The other part of the majority's explanation of its holding is related to its simultaneous discomfort and fascination with irregularly shaped districts. Lack of compactness or contiguity, like uncouth district lines, certainly is a helpful indicator that some form of gerrymandering (racial or other) might have taken place and that "something may be amiss." ... Disregard for geographic divisions and compactness often goes hand in hand with partisan gerrymandering....

But while district irregularities may provide strong indicia of a potential gerrymander, they do no more than that. In particular, they have no bearing on whether the plan ultimately is found to violate the Constitution. Given two districts drawn on similar, race-based grounds, the one does not become more injurious than the other simply by virtue of being snake-like, at least so far as the Constitution is concerned and absent any evidence of differential racial impact. The majority's contrary view is perplexing in light of its concession that "compactness or attractiveness has never been held to constitute an independent federal constitutional requirement for state legislative districts." ... It is shortsighted as well, for a regularly shaped district can just as effectively effectuate racially discriminatory gerrymandering as an odd-shaped one. By focusing on looks rather than impact, the majority "immediately casts attention in the wrong direction—toward superficialities of shape and size, rather than toward the political realities of district composition."

Limited by its own terms to cases involving unusually-shaped districts, the Court's approach nonetheless will unnecessarily hinder to some extent a State's voluntary effort to ensure a modicum of minority representation. This will be true in areas where the minority population is geographically dispersed. It also will be true where the minority population is not scattered but, for reasons unrelated to race—for example incumbency protection—the State would rather not create the majority-minority district in its most "obvious" location. When, as is the case here, the creation of a majority-minority district does not unfairly minimize the voting power of any other group, the Constitution does not justify, much less mandate, such obstruction....

III

Although I disagree with the holding that appellants' claim is cognizable, the Court's discussion of the level of scrutiny it requires warrants a few comments. I have no doubt that a State's compliance with the Voting Rights Act clearly constitutes a compelling interest.... [T]he Attorney General objected to the State's plan on the ground that it failed to draw a second majority-minority district for what appeared to be pretextual reasons. Rather than challenge this conclusion, North Carolina chose to draw the second district. As *UJO* held, a State is entitled to take such action....

The Court, while seemingly agreeing with this position, warns that the State's redistricting effort must be "narrowly tailored" to further its interest in complying with the law. It is evident to me, however, that what North Carolina did was precisely tailored to meet the objection of the Attorney General to its prior plan. Hence, I see no need for a remand at all....

Furthermore, how it intends to manage this standard, I do not know. Is it more "narrowly tailored" to create an irregular majority-minority district as opposed to one that is compact but harms other State interests such as incumbency protection or the representation of rural interests? Of the following two options—creation of two minority influence districts or of a single majority-minority district—is one "narrowly tailored" and the other not? Once the Attorney General has found that a proposed redistricting change violates § 5's nonretrogression principle in that it will abridge a racial minority's right to vote, does "narrow tailoring" mean that the most the State can do is preserve the *status quo*? Or can it maintain that change, while attempting to enhance minority voting power in some other manner? This small sample only begins to scratch the surface of the problems raised by the majority's test. But it suffices to illustrate the unworkability of a standard that is divorced from any measure of constitutional harm. In that, State efforts to remedy minority vote dilution are wholly unlike what typically has been labeled "affirmative action." To the extent that no other racial group is injured, remedying a Voting Rights Act violation does not involve preferential treatment.... It involves, instead, an attempt to *equalize* treatment, and to provide minority voters with an effective voice in the political process. The Equal Protection Clause of the Constitution, surely, does not stand in the way.

IV

Since I do not agree that petitioners alleged an Equal Protection violation and because the Court of Appeals faithfully followed the Court's prior cases, I dissent and would affirm the judgment below.

JUSTICE BLACKMUN, dissenting.

I join JUSTICE WHITE's dissenting opinion.... I ... agree that the conscious use of race in redistricting does not violate the Equal Protection Clause unless the effect of the redistricting plan is to deny a particular group equal access to the political process or to minimize its voting strength unduly.... It is particularly ironic that the case in which today's majority chooses to abandon settled law and to recognize for the first time this "analytically distinct" constitutional claim is a challenge by white voters to the plan under which North Carolina has sent black representatives to Congress for the first time since Reconstruction. I dissent.

JUSTICE STEVENS, dissenting.

For the reasons stated by JUSTICE WHITE, the decision of the District Court should be affirmed....

... [W]e must ask whether otherwise permissible redistricting to benefit an underrepresented minority group becomes impermissible when the minority group is defined by its race. The Court today answers this question in the affirmative, and its answer is wrong. If it is permissible to draw boundaries to provide adequate representation for rural voters, for union members, for Hasidic Jews, for Polish Americans, or for Republicans, it necessarily follows that it is permissible to do the same thing for members of the very minority group whose history in the United States gave birth to the Equal Protection Clause. A contrary conclusion could only be described as perverse.

Accordingly, I respectfully dissent.

JUSTICE SOUTER, dissenting.

Today, the Court recognizes a new cause of action under which a State's electoral redistricting plan that includes a configuration "so bizarre" that it "rationally cannot be understood as anything other than an effort to separate voters into different districts on the basis of race [without] sufficient justification" will be subjected to strict scrutiny. In my view there is no justification for the Court's determination to depart from our prior decisions by carving out this narrow group of cases for strict scrutiny in place of the review customarily applied in cases dealing with discrimination in electoral districting on the basis of race....

CLINTON ON MIDWEST FLOODS

June 29, 1993

Unprecedented rains in the nation's heartland sent the waters of the Mississippi and Missouri rivers on a summer-long rampage of destruction. Previous flood records were shattered at cities and towns along both rivers and their tributaries.

According to federal officials' estimates in October, the floods caused more than $12 billion in property damage over an area equal to one-tenth the size of the forty-eight contiguous states. At least fifty people died from flood-related causes and more than 60,000 were made homeless.

Hundreds of businesses were destroyed or forced to close. Crop losses were put at about $7.8 billion. Roads and other transportation facilities were severely disrupted, including commercial barge, truck, and rail traffic. Numerous interstate highways were blocked by flood waters and every major east-west rail line in the Midwest was shut down at one time or another. Every bridge across the Mississippi along a 220-mile stretch was closed at some point during the summer.

While the financial losses to the region's economy were catastrophic, the disruption of daily life for hundreds of thousands of residents in the Midwest was impossible to quantify. Many people living near the rivers thought they had seen the worst of it in July only to experience subsequent crests. Parts of Iowa, Nebraska, Kansas, and Missouri were flooded anew in late August and September.

Major flooding affected parts of ten states. Hardest hit were Iowa and Missouri, but the storms caused extensive damage as well in North Dakota, South Dakota, Minnesota, Wisconsin, Illinois, Nebraska, Kansas, and, later, in Oklahoma. Rain fell somewhere in the Midwest for forty-six consecutive days. Between April and August, rainfall was 50 percent above normal in some states. In the St. Louis area, the Mississippi and Missouri rivers crested within a few days of each other, an occurrence hydrologists called "unprecedented."

Federal and state officials said they had never seen flooding on such a large scale. Unlike most disasters, such as hurricanes, which hit an area and then leave, the Great Flood of 1993 seemed to go forever. The Corps of Engineers, weather forecasters, and other officials were not prepared for the deluge. Previous flood models and computer projections were inadequate in forecasting the extent of the flooding. Estimates were repeatedly revised upward.

Levee System and the Weather

The floods were caused by a freak winter-type weather pattern that persisted throughout the summer. An unusually large, stationary Bermuda high off the eastern U.S. coast pumped hot, moist air from the Gulf of Mexico into the Mississippi Valley, where it collided with cool, dry air from Alaska. And the jet stream moved farther south than was usual in summer, pushing this cool air into the midsection of the United States. While the Midwest was being inundated with rain, the Plains states suffered unseasonably cool temperatures and the Southeast was abnormally hot and dry. Ironically, the same general area hit by the floods experienced a severe drought in 1988.

The severity of the floods was attributed to the system of levees built over many years to protect low-lying areas. The Midwest had the most extensive levee system in the world, stretching for 1,581 miles along the Mississippi and for 2,000 miles along its tributaries. "Levee anarchy" was the way a biologist with the Missouri Conservation Department described it. By concentrating the flood waters in narrow channels, levees did not allow the water to overflow onto flood plains, thus raising the water level in the river, increasing the flow, and making the resulting floods more extensive and destructive. Levees were breached at more than one thousand places on the Mississippi, Missouri, and Illinois rivers and their tributaries.

Suspense at St. Louis, Damage at Des Moines

On August 1 the Mississippi reached a record crest of 49.58 feet at St. Louis, breaking the old record of 43.2 feet set in 1973 (flood stage was 30 feet). The river was above flood stage for 121 days in 1993, including a record 78 consecutive days. The flooding caused the Corps of Engineers to close the locks between St. Louis and St. Paul, Minnesota, a distance of five hundred miles. This action disrupted barge traffic on the lower Mississippi.

The lower Mississippi did not flood, primarily because the river widens and deepens south of Cairo, Illinois. Moreover, the Ohio River, the major tributary south of St. Louis, did not reach flood stage.

Iowa governor Terry E. Branstad said the magnitude of the flood was "far beyond anything we've experienced in the history of the state." The worst hit major city was Des Moines, where the Des Moines and Raccoon rivers flooded parts of the business district and inundated the city's water treatment plant, cutting off water supplies and electricity to some 250,000 people for more than two weeks. All major roads into the city were closed, complicating the National Guard's task of supplying residents with fresh water.

Government Response

Officials of the Federal Emergency Management Agency (FEMA), who were sharply criticized in 1992 for their handling of emergency relief in the aftermath of Hurricane Andrew, were quick to assure flood victims that the agency would move rapidly this time. It was FEMA's first major test under its new director, James Lee Witt. (Hurricane Andrew, FEMA response, Historic Documents of 1992, p. 843)

Both President Bill Clinton and Vice President Al Gore visited some of the worst flooded areas, the president three times, assuring flood victims the government would do all it could to provide assistance. In May the president declared parts of southwestern Minnesota disaster areas. This later was revised to include the Minneapolis-St. Paul area after the Mississippi flooded in late June. After touring the Des Moines area July 14, Clinton proposed an emergency aid package for Iowa and the other flooded states. He asked Congress for $2.2 billion, but raised the amount twice as the situation worsened. By midsummer the Clinton administration had declared federal disasters in parts of ten states, and Congress eventually approved $5.7 billion in disaster relief.

As the flooding continued into the fall, large numbers of residents said they had had enough, declaring the river the victor over man's attempt to control the water. Individuals as well as whole towns asked Washington to buy out homes and communities in flood-prone areas. The government's willingness to consider such wholesale buyouts signaled a major change in policy. "For 50 years, national policy has been to dam, channelize, divert and levee rivers in order to avoid property losses," noted David Conrad of the National Wildlife Federation.

In a bizarre footnote to the summer's floods, a twenty-three-year-old man was charged in October with deliberately causing a levee to break July 16 in West Quincy, Missouri, flooding some 15,000 acres and knocking out the only usable bridge at the time across the upper Mississippi.

Following is the text of President Bill Clinton's June 29, 1993, statement on the Midwest floods:

I am very concerned about the flooding in the heartland of our country, and I've asked Agriculture Secretary Mike Espy to survey the region and see firsthand what the excessive rains have done to agriculture production there. I also have directed the Federal Emergency Management Agency to keep me fully informed of their activities on behalf of the affected States.

The Mississippi River is closed to navigation over a 500-mile stretch from the Twin Cities in Minnesota to St. Louis. Clearly, this is one of the most significant natural disasters midwestern residents, business owners, and agricultural producers have faced in a very long time. This region of the country is dependent upon agricultural production, and when agriculture faces a disaster like this one, everyone is adversely affected.

Tomorrow Secretary Espy will travel to Iowa, Wisconsin (weather permitting), Minnesota, and South Dakota to view the rain-related damage and talk face to face with farmers and area residents about the damage.

FEMA Director James Lee Witt reports that his Agency already has placed survey teams in the field where they are working with the State emergency operating centers. These teams are laying the groundwork necessary for Federal disaster assistance. We intend to speed the recovery of the affected communities and ensure disaster victims receive the help they need as rapidly as possible.

Upon his return, Secretary Espy will brief me on the condition of the area and make recommendations that will help our fellow citizens living in the region.

As you know, nine counties in southwestern Minnesota were declared disaster areas in late May. Last week, I granted Governor Arne Carlson's request to extend the incident period to allow for coverage for the torrential rains after May 19th through June.

Wisconsin has been hard hit. The break in the dam at Blackriver Falls has destroyed or damaged over 100 homes. Many of the town's residents have no flood insurance. Governor Tommy Thompson has already asked the National Guard to assist the evacuation of flood victims.

Iowa's Governor Branstad also is using the National Guard to assist flood victims in the eastern part of his State. He has told us that many homes and businesses have been flooded out, and thousands more are at risk if the levee breaks.

The Mississippi River continues to rise in Missouri, threatening towns still dealing with the ravages of the May floods. FEMA teams are in eastern Missouri, continuing to monitor the flooding of the Mississippi. Some areas have been evacuated, and preliminary damage assessment teams are in place for a formal assessment request, pending a call from Governor Mel Carnahan.

I commend the bravery and endurance of the many midwesterners facing torrents of rain and rivers that have not yet crested. We will work together to rebuild your communities as we work together to rebuild America.

NETWORK AGREEMENT ON PARENT ADVISORY ON TV VIOLENCE

June 30, 1993

Confronted with rising concern among parents, educators, members of Congress, and others, the major commercial television networks and the Motion Picture Association of America on June 30 agreed on a plan to warn TV audiences that a program about to be aired contained what the networks considered to be scenes of violence. The Advance Parental Advisory warning, to be given a two-year testing period, stated, "Due to some violent content, parental discretion advised."

"By empowering parents to make more informed viewing decisions for their children, we are reaffirming the proud network tradition of public interest combined with public responsibility," said CBS President Howard Stringer on release of the announcement. "[T]his is not just preferable to censorship; in the end, it is more likely to be effective in a democratic society."

In a June 30 letter to the network presidents, President Bill Clinton commended them "for this initial effort" to address the problem of television violence, noting that "children are exposed to far too many graphic pictures of murder and mayhem" on TV. Clinton urged the industry to continue efforts to limit the "excessive portrayal of violence," reminding it that "[i]n the past, the television industry has responded to public concerns and has dealt in a responsible manner with issues such as drug use, alcohol, and smoking." But Jack Valenti, president of the Motion Picture Association of America, warned that controlling depictions of violence was not as easy as warning about substance abuse. "When you get into the details—how you frame a scene, how you write the dialogue, what you show and what you leave to the imagination—it gets difficult."

Growing Concern About TV Violence

The impact of television violence had been the subject of numerous studies over the past four decades, most of which revealed a consistent correlation between "viewing violence and aggressive behavior," according to a report by the American Psychological Association (APA). The APA estimated that by the time a child had completed elementary school, he or she would have seen 8,000 murders and 100,000 acts of violence on the TV screen. A report by CQ Researcher *found that, in addition to exhibiting more aggressive behavior, many children were likely to become both more apprehensive about becoming victims of such violence and, at the same time, more callous about violence as a result of their television viewing.*

A poll of readers by USA Weekend *conducted in early June elicited one of the largest responses the magazine had received to its surveys. Of the 71,000 respondents, 95 percent were "very concerned" about television violence, 91 percent believed that TV was "significantly more violent" than it was five years ago, and 96 percent believed that television "glorifies violence."*

Of concern to the networks and some observers were issues of how to avoid censorship and how to monitor violence without making programs so dull that viewers would switch channels, particularly to cable TV—subscribed to by more than 60 percent of American viewers—which was not a party to the agreement. "We don't want to turn the vast wasteland into the dull wasteland," said Stringer. "It is the nature of violence and the absence of consequences that we are concerned about. We have, in effect, depersonalized violence. There is no grief, no remorse.... That's the kind that sends a message to children that it's okay."

Background

The issue of showing violence on television surfaced in Congress as early as 1961, when Sen. Thomas Dodd, D-Conn. (1959-1971), held hearings on the problem, which, according to a later account by a former NBC executive, revealed a deliberate decision on the part of some network executives to inject more sex and violence into some programs to make them more exciting. But apparently, the evidence—introduced in a closed-door hearing—was never made public.

Beginning in 1985 Sen. Paul Simon, D-Ill., spearheaded an attempt to renew congressional action on curtailing depictions of violence on television. After years of effort, the TV Violence Act of 1990 exempted the networks from antitrust laws for three years so they could develop a common policy on measures to deal with the issue. In December 1992 presidents of the major networks agreed on general "principles on the depiction of violence."

But that agreement apparently was not sufficient for a number of members of Congress. At a May 1993 hearing, Sen. Howard Metzenbaum, D-Ohio, warned the network executives that "if you just do nothing, and if you just tell us you're doing something while giving us the May [ratings] sweeps ... we're going to come down harder on you than you would like us to do."

In response, the executives hammered out the June advisory agreement after numerous meetings and conference calls and, according to press reports, at least fifteen revisions. Warren Littlefield of NBC's entertainment division said the networks also planned to address violence "proactively," airing programs that deal with violent acts' destructive consequences and demonstrating alternatives in an attempt to "deglamorize" violence. "We urge the entire entertainment industry to follow our lead," he added.

A "First Step," but Skepticism About Effect

"This is the dawning of a new era," said Rep. Edward Markey, D-Mass., as the new policy was unveiled. "For the last 40 years the debate has been whether violence on television affects antisocial behavior. Today we put an end to that debate."

A spokesperson for ABC said that the network had used viewer advisories for many years and felt they should be "tailored to the specific program to be truly effective." For example, an August 1993 airing of the film "Mississippi Burning" contained an advisory stating: "Tonight's film deals with the murder of three civil rights workers. As it contains scenes of violence and adult language, parental discretion is advised."

Nonetheless, the networks' action did not appear to satisfy a number of members of Congress, who introduced a number of bills and scheduled further hearings. Markey said the "next step" was to make widely available a "V-Chip" that would allow its owner to block out selected programs to prevent children from viewing them. Markey and Rep. Jack Fields, R-Texas, introduced legislation that would require every television sold in the United States to contain the V-Chip. The bill also proposed warning labels, inserted in television guides in advance of air dates, to alert viewers to programs containing violence. Another bill, sponsored by Sens. Ernest F. Hollings, D-S.C., and Daniel K. Inouye, D-Hawaii, would request the Federal Communications Commission (FCC) to limit violent programs to hours when children were less likely to be watching television. A measure sponsored by Rep. John Bryant, D-Texas, would require the Federal Communications Commission to establish regulations governing television violence, with fines for violations. In an August interview, Bryant was critical of the networks' efforts to date. "We moved mountains" to get an antitrust exemption for them to discuss violence, but "they did nothing about it until there were hearings on the matter. Their guidelines are more than ineffective," he said.

Simon said he had some misgivings about the proposed legislation; while not opposing the idea of the V-Chip, "my preference is for industry self-regulation and not for federal action." On August 2 he called on the industry to establish an independent office to monitor TV violence. He also said that most of the bills being considered have "as a major flaw that they do not deal with the cable question. And cable, I have to say up to this point, has been less responsive than the broadcast side of television."

James H. Rowe, a spokesman for NBC, said that while the network "applauds" Markey's concerns, it "agrees with Sen. Simon that voluntary steps and not legislative fiats are the way to go.... However well-intentioned, [Markey's] legislation would undoubtedly condemn any network program carrying an advisory, whether it was a historical drama on the Civil War ... or even a modern-day program on such vital issues as date rape and domestic violence."

Some observers noted that the warnings would not apply to cartoons, athletic events, and news and would not actually reduce the amount of televised violence that reached American homes. The decision to experiment with an advisory "doesn't necessarily demonstrate the [television] industry's newfound concern for violent programming," commented a July 1 editorial in The Washington Post. *"It demonstrates concern about government intervention.... [W]hat will these advisories ... actually accomplish? ... Some parents will use them to monitor their children's viewing habits.... Other viewers ... may use them to turn their sets on.... The labels may offer cover for more sensationalism and grisliness.... The unease over televised violence is spreading," the editorial concluded.*

The Attorney General's Testimony

In testimony before the Senate Commerce Committee October 20, Attorney General Janet Reno expressed her impatience with the entertainment industry's failure to address the problem of violence. "I think too often America has become numb to violence because it just drowns in it day in and day out," she said.

Reno urged the committee to set a January 1, 1994, deadline for the industry to take meaningful action. Otherwise, Reno warned, she would seek legislation compelling reforms. It was unclear if such legislation would pass constitutional muster.

Following is the text of the "Advance Parental Advisory Plan: A Four-Network Proposal for a Two-Year Test" on labeling programs that depicted violence, agreed to by ABC, CBS, Fox, and NBC television, released June 30, 1993:

ABC, CBS, FOX and NBC, in response to concern about depictions of violence in television programming from all sources—broadcast, cable and syndication—have joined together to adopt an Advance Parental Advisory plan to provide increased parental information regarding the violent content of entertainment program material. This new parental advisory plan is in addition to the ongoing commitment of each network to eliminate inappropriate depictions of violence on television.

This step is being taken under the auspices of the Simon-Glickman legislation which provides the television industry with an antitrust exemption to deal with the issue of violence.

The four broadcast networks hope that all members of the television production and distribution industry will endorse and implement the new Advance Parental Advisory plan.

The underlying principle of this initiative is to provide parents with adequate, timely information about depictions of violence that may be contained in specific television programs. While only a small fraction of the programming on the four networks involves any violent content, we believe that parental responsibility and decision-making is the best way to deal with instances of violent program content. Use of the Advance Parental Advisory will allow each parent or other supervising or responsible adult to make their own decision about family television viewing and, particularly, the appropriateness of having young children watch specific programs either alone or with an adult.

It is relevant and important to understand that we cannot allow broadcast television to become barren of dramatic excitement. We cannot participate in a process that, while well-intended, condemns advertiser-supported television to such bland fare that it would forsake a higher, more sophisticated level of dramatic conflict and realistic portrayal of the full range of the human condition. Somewhere in between lackluster drama, and the insertion of gratuitous violence, lies the tone of story-telling we seek: drama, suspense, the clash of opposite values—without an overlay of unnecessary violent content. We will strive to do that, hoping that the government will remain respectful of creativity and not intrude on the freedom of voices to be heard.

Following is the text of the Advance Parental Advisory for network entertainment programming, including series, theatrical movies, made-for-television movies, mini-series and specials:

> "Due to some violent content, parental discretion advised."

This basic advisory may be modified to provide further clarification in response to particular situations or to offer descriptive texts customized to specific programs.

Once the decision has been made to place an advisory on a program, all promotional material relating to that program, including press releases, on-air promos and print advertising will include the advisory.

While each network will decide on the appropriate use of the Advance Parental Advisory, the four networks have agreed on the following broad standards for its application:

1. An advisory will be used when, in the judgment of the network, the overall level of violence in a program, the graphic nature of the violent content, or the tone, message or mood of the program make it appropriate.
2. In considering the use of an advisory, the network will evaluate such factors as the context of the violent depiction, the composition of the intended audience and the time period of broadcast.

3. Advisories would be used selectively to highlight and single out for parents specific programs where the violent content is unexpected, graphic or pervasive. Subject to each network's program-by-program review, advisories would not necessarily be warranted for programs where there is only an isolated act of violence (e.g., a murder mystery) or for genres where violence is known to be present but is not graphically depicted (e.g., westerns or historical dramas). Each program will be evaluated on a case-by-case basis to assure that the advisory system highlights appropriate programs for parents.
4. When used by a network, the Advance Parental Advisory will precede a specific program and may reappear during the broadcast of the program, as appropriate.
5. The Advance Parental Advisory Plan will be introduced with the beginning of the 1993-94 television season in September, 1993, for movies, mini-series and specials. Series programs, which involve more difficult production and program review timetables, will be phased in during the 1993-94 season.
6. All other companies and organizations involved in the television production and distribution business will be informed of the new Advance Parental Advisory plan. Primary responsibility for the judgment to use an advisory on a particular program should be placed on the distributor of that program whether it be a broadcast network, cable network, syndicator or, in the case of locally-originated programming, a broadcast station or cable channel. The four networks will solicit support from all other segments of the television industry at the Aug. 2 industry-wide conference on violence to be held in Los Angeles.
7. At the end of two years, the networks will evaluate the use of the Advance Parental Advisory by the television industry and any proposed changes in the plan. Each network will determine at that time whether to continue its use of the Advance Parental Advisory, taking into account such factors as its adoption and usage by competing television distributors and reaction by viewers, advertisers, producers and affiliates.

July

CLINTON LOGGING DECISION

July 1, 1993

If the best indication of a true compromise is that it makes no one happy, the forest plan presented by President Bill Clinton July 1, was a success. Clinton tried to balance economic growth with environmental protection, but both loggers and environmentalists cried foul.

Logging interests said the plan would decimate communities that depended on the timber industry for their existence. This plan "amounts to economic and social destruction for the rural areas of the region," Mark Rey of the American Forest and Paper Association told USA Today. *Most environmentalists, on the other hand, said the plan contained huge loopholes that would allow extensive logging to continue in old-growth forests. "You can drive log trucks through those loopholes," Andy Kerr of the Oregon Natural Resources Council in Portland told the newspaper.*

The plan called for sharply reducing logging in old-growth forests in the Pacific Northwest. Old-growth forests are defined as forests that are at least two hundred years old. They are attractive to loggers because they have large, high-quality trees. In addition, second-growth forests on most private lands in the region are still fifteen to twenty years away from harvestable age. Nearly 90 percent of the region's old-growth forests have already been logged, leaving an estimated 8 million to 9 million acres. Most remaining old-growth forests are on federal land and are managed by the U.S. Forest Service.

Clinton's plan would protect about 75 percent of old-growth forests on federal lands. Timber companies could salvage dead trees and thin other trees in the protected areas. Environmentalists attacked this provision as a loophole, saying loggers would use it to destroy vast areas of forest. The Clinton plan called for about 1.2 billion board feet to be harvested from national forests annually, less than a quarter of the 5 billion board feet harvested annually in the mid-1980s.

The Clinton administration estimated the plan would cost about 6,000 jobs in the timber industry. To help ease the pain, the plan called for giving the Pacific Northwest about $1.5 billion in economic aid over the next five years. The money would go toward retraining workers and helping communities develop their economies.

Administration officials described the plan as an attempt to unify federal policy and eliminate the legal deadlock that had limited timber harvests in recent years. Previously, various federal agencies, environmentalists, and loggers had battled each other, and the dispute had ended up in federal court, which blocked most timber sales, leading to severe economic problems in the region.

The debate over how to protect the forests had begun in 1984, when the Forest Service adopted guidelines for managing the habitat of the northern spotted owl, which lives in old-growth forests. Starting in 1989, a series of injunctions issued by federal courts stopped nearly all timber sales in spotted owl habitats in Washington, Oregon, and northern California. The three states had an estimated 3,600 pairs of spotted owls. In July 1990 the Fish and Wildlife Service declared the owl a threatened species.

The spotted owl became a symbol, both in the struggle over old-growth forests and in efforts to gauge the health of ecosystems that included those forests. According to the Forest Service, the spotted owl's well-being was an indicator of the ecosystem's well-being. If the bird was in trouble, so was the ecosystem. But if the bird flourished, it showed that the ecosystem was healthy as well.

Too much logging threatened the ecosystem, not only wiping out the habitat for the spotted owl and other endangered creatures but also harming waterways and too rapidly depleting the supply of old-growth timber. Moreover, too much logging hurt other industries. For example, stream and river degradation caused by logging had helped reduce harvests for the region's salmon industry, which employed an estimated 60,000 people. The problem was that no one could agree on what constituted "too much."

Even before the spotted owl controversy began, the forest products industry had been losing jobs. Increased mechanization had reduced the amount of labor needed to produce lumber. In addition, large amounts of timber cut from private land in the Pacific Northwest were being exported to Japan, Korea, and China with little processing in the United States. Shipping unprocessed logs instead of finished lumber wiped out many sawmill jobs. In the two years before Clinton announced his plan, mechanization, court orders blocking timber sales, the export of raw logs, and other factors had cost an estimated 20,000 jobs in the Pacific Northwest's timber industry.

In an effort to encourage timber processing in the United States, Clinton's plan called for eliminating tax breaks for firms that exported logs. Federal law already barred export of raw logs from federal lands, and log exports from state-owned lands were severely restricted.

Clinton's plan was announced slightly more than a year after the Forest Service adopted a new policy aimed at sharply reducing clear-cutting in national forests. Forest Service officials said that the policy shift could reduce the controversial practice of clear-cutting by 70 percent, but would not significantly reduce the amount of timber harvested from federal lands. The new policy was designed to place greater emphasis on protecting wildlife habitat and keeping air and water clean. (Forest Service Order on Clear-Cutting and Spotted Owl, Historic Documents of 1992, p. 489)

Following is a transcript of remarks made by President Bill Clinton on July 1, 1993, at a press conference where he announced his forest policy:

Thank you very much. Ladies and gentlemen, this issue has been one which has bedeviled the people of the Pacific Northwest for some years now. It has been one that has particularly moved me for two reasons: First of all, because so many people in that part of the country brought their concerns to me in the campaign on all sides of this issue—the timber workers and companies, the environmentalists, the Native Americans, the people who live in those areas who just wanted to see the controversy so they could get on with their lives. And secondly, because I grew up in a place with a large timber industry and a vast amount of natural wilderness, including a large number of national forests. So I have a very close identity with all the forces at play in this great drama that has paralyzed the Pacific Northwest for too long.

We're announcing a plan today which we believe will strengthen the long-term economic and environmental health of the Pacific Northwest and northern California. The plan provides an innovative approach to forest management to protect the environment and to produce a predictable and sustainable level of timber sales. It offers a comprehensive, long-term plan for economic development. And it makes sure that federal agencies for a change will be working together for the good of all the people of the region.

The plan is a departure from the failed policies of the past, when as many as six different federal agencies took different positions on various interpretations of federal law and helped to create a situation in which, at length, no timber cutting at all could occur because of litigation, and still environmentalists believed that the long-term concerns of the environment were not being addressed.

The plan is more difficult than I had thought it would be in terms of the size of the timber cuts, in part because during this process the amount of timber actually in the forest and available for cutting was revised downward sharply, in no small measure because of years of overcutting, and in a way that provides an annual yield smaller than timber interests had wanted, and a plan without some of the protections that environmentalists had sought. I can only say that as with every other situation in life, we have to play the hand we were dealt. Had this crisis been dealt with years ago we might have a plan with a higher yield and with more environmentally protected areas. We are doing the best we can with the facts as they now exist in the Pacific Northwest.

I believe the plan is fair and balanced. I believe it will protect jobs and offer new job opportunities where they must be found. It will preserve the woodlands, the rivers, the streams that make the Northwest an attractive place to live and to visit. We believe in this case it is clear that the Pacific Northwest requires both a healthy economy and a healthy environment and that one cannot exist without the other.

I want to say a special word of thanks to the Vice President, to the Interior Secretary Bruce Babbitt, to Agriculture Secretary Mike Espy, to Labor Secretary Reich, Commerce Secretary Brown, Environmental Protection Administrator Browner, Environmental Policy Director Katie McGinty, and many others in our administration who work together to bring all the forces of the federal government into agreement not because they all agreed on every issue at every moment, but because they knew that we owed the people of the Pacific Northwest at least a unified federal position that would break the logjam of the past several years.

This shows that people can work together and make tough choices if they have the will and courage to do so. Too often in the past the issues which this plan addressed have simply wound up in court while the economy, the environment and the people suffered. These issues are clearly difficult and divisive; you will see that in the response to the position that our administration has taken. If they were easy they would have been answered long ago. The main virtue of our plan besides being fair and balanced, is that we attempt to answer the questions and let people get on with their lives.

We could not, we could not permit more years of the status quo to continue where everything was paralyzed in the courts. We reached out to hundreds of people, from lumber workers and fishermen to environmentalists, scientists, businesspeople, community leaders and Native American tribes. We've worked hard to balance all their interests and to understand their concerns. We know that our solutions will not make everybody happy. Indeed, they may not make anybody happy. But we do understand that we're all going to be better off if we act on the plan and end the deadlock and divisiveness.

We started bringing people together at the Forest Conference in April. In the words of Archbishop Thomas Murphy then, we began to find common ground for the common good. As people reasoned together in a conference room instead of confronting each other in a courtroom, they found at least that they shared common values: work and family, faith and a reverence for the majestic beauty of the natural environment God has bequeathed to that gifted part of our nation.

This plan meets the standards that I set as the conference concluded. It meets the need for year-round, high-wage, high-skilled jobs and a sustained, predictable level of economic activity in the forests. It protects the long-term health of the forests, our wildlife and our waterways. It is clearly scientifically sound, ecologically credible, and legally defensible.

By preserving the forests and setting predictable and sustainable levels of timber sales, it protects jobs not just in the short term, but for years to come.

We offer new assistance to workers and to families for job training and retraining where that will inevitably be needed as a result of the sustainable yield level set in the plan; new assistance to businesses and industries to expand and create new family wage jobs for local workers; new assistance to communities to build the infrastructure to support new and diverse sources of economic growth; and new initiatives to create jobs by investing in research and restoration in the forests themselves. And we end the subsidies for log exports that end up exporting American jobs.

This plan offers an innovative approach to conservation, protecting key watersheds and the most valuable of our old-growth forests. It protects key rivers and streams while saving the most important groves of ancient trees and providing habitat for salmon and other endangered species. And it establishes new adapted management areas to develop new ways to achieve economic and ecological goals, and to help communities to shape their own future.

Today I am signing a bill sponsored by Senator Patty Murray and Congresswoman Jolene Unsoeld of Washington and supported by the entire Northwest congressional delegation to restore the ban of export of raw logs from state-owned lands and other publicly owned lands. This act alone will save thousands of jobs in the Northwest, including over 6,000 in Washington State alone.

Today, Secretary Babbitt and Secretary Espy are going to the Northwest to talk to state and local officials about how to implement the plan and give to workers, companies and communities the help they need and deserve. And soon we will deliver an environmental impact statement based on the plan to the federal district court in Washington State. We will do all we can to resolve the legal actions that have halted timber sales, and we will continue to work with all those who share our commitment to achieve these goals and move the sales forward.

Together, we can build a better future for the families of the Northwest, for their children and for their children's children. We can preserve the jobs in the forest and we can preserve the forest. The time has come to act to end the logjam, to end the endless delay and bickering and to restore some genuine security and rootedness to the lives of the people who have for too long been torn from pillar to post in this important area of the United States.

I believe this plan will do that, and this administration is committed to implementing it.

Thank you very much. (Applause.)

INDEPENDENT COMMISSION REPORT ON MILITARY BASE CLOSINGS

July 1, 1993

It took President Clinton less than twenty-four hours to approve a potentially controversial list sent to him by an independent panel that recommended shutting down thirty-five major military bases and ninety-five smaller ones across the country and cutting back at twenty-seven major bases and eighteen minor facilities. The seven-member Defense Base Closure and Realignment Commission, which sent its final report to the White House on July 1, estimated that its recommendations would require a one-time expenditure of $7.4 billion, and would then save about $2.3 billion each year after 1999. While cities from San Francisco to Charleston were slated for base closings, some cities, like Norfolk, Va., and San Diego, would benefit from the move to consolidate U.S. armed forces at fewer bases.

In announcing that he had accepted the commission's list, Clinton also promised that he would take steps to reduce the economic pain of the closings. Among the measures he pledged to take were appointing a single federal coordinator to work with each affected community, offering grants averaging $1 million to help plan new uses for bases, speeding the cleanup of pollution that tainted many of the bases, and changing federal rules so that closed bases could be sold at a discount for new commercial uses that created jobs. "Compared to the past," he said, "we will respond more quickly, cut red tape more aggressively, and mobilize resources more assertively to help these communities, so that when they lose their bases they do not lose their future."

The commission's conclusions were based largely on recommendations made in March by Defense Secretary Les Aspin. But the commissioners spared five installations from Aspin's list, and they voted to drastically cut back operations at Homestead Air Force Base in Florida instead of closing it as Aspin had recommended. At the same time, the panel voted to close three major bases not on Aspin's list: Plattsburgh Air Force Base in New York, Agana Naval Air Station in Guam, and the Portsmouth Naval Electronics Systems Engineering Center in Virginia.

Following Clinton's approval, Congress had forty-five working days to block the base closings list from going into effect. But even some members representing districts standing to lose their bases acknowledged that such a congressional veto would not happen. Congress itself had designed the base-closing process—which permitted only an up-or-down vote on the entire package—in order to limit members' parochial instincts to defend local bases from elimination.

With timing that appeared aimed at underscoring the need for military belt-tightening, Aspin on July 1 announced plans to close or reduce ninety-two overseas bases. Those closures did not require congressional approval.

Difficult Decisions

When Congress established the commission in 1990, it had specified eight criteria that the Defense Department was required to use in recommending a base for closure. In trying to follow those standards, the Pentagon had constructed complex mathematical formulas to determine an array of influencing factors, such as the military value of a specified base and the cost that would be saved each year by closing it. After Aspin released the commission's proposed list on March 12, base offices launched a fierce lobbying campaign that deluged the panel with stacks of data intended to demonstrate that their local bases were more valuable or would cost too much to lose.

The commission faced some difficult decisions, wrestling with base requests and the Pentagon's calculations, which the law required the panel to accept unless it could prove evidence of "substantial deviation" from the Defense Department's conclusions. In the end, after months of hearings and careful weighing of the facts, the commission carefully fine-tuned the initial Pentagon recommendations. Compromises were made, influenced in part by the wide variety in numbers presented by various calculations concerning the military and socioeconomic value of certain bases.

In a letter to the president accompanying its report, the commission noted that it had "scrutinized thousands of pages of testimony and written documentation. We held 17 hearings across the United States, visited over 125 military activities, and met with hundreds of community representatives.... We recognize that closing a base creates economic hardship for communities that have offered our nation a priceless service by hosting a military facility. Nevertheless, continuing budget constraints mandated by Congress along with changing national security requirements compel the United States to reduce and realign its military." The panel went on to state that its conclusions reflected "the fiercely independent judgment" of its seven members—five men and two women of varying backgrounds and professions.

Commenting on his panel's decisions, commission chairman James Courter gave special praise to the "sea change" in the Navy that had led to far-reaching changes in its service plans. However, Courter—who was characterized by one reporter as making "succinct, persuasive arguments" and who "was in the majority in all but one of the commission's votes"—faulted the Pentagon's initial proposals for failing to cut overlapping services among the armed forces. "There was no knowledgeable, strong, experienced leadership in the Pentagon," he said. "There's nobody there to restrain the military leadership from doing what they think is best for their own service. . . . There was no cross-service analysis. They'll never get together unless they're forced to. Never. Never. They'll start a war first."

Following is the text of the executive summary of the report to the president, released July 1, 1993, by the Defense Base Closure and Realignment Commission, on its recommendations for closing and restructuring U.S. military bases:

Executive Summary

On November 5, 1990, President George Bush signed Public Law 101-510, which established the Defense Base Closure and Realignment Commission "to provide a fair process that will result in the timely closure and realignment of military installations inside the United States." Public Law 101-510 (Title XXIX, as amended) required the Secretary of Defense to submit a list of proposed military base closures and realignments to the Commission by March 15, 1995. The statute also required the Secretary of Defense to base all recommendations on a force-structure plan submitted to Congress with the Department's FY 1994 budget request and on selection criteria developed by the Secretary of Defense and approved by Congress.

Upon the Commission's receipt of the Secretary of Defense's recommendations, PL 101-510 required the Commission to hold public hearings to discuss the recommendations before it made any findings. To change any of the Secretary's recommendations the law required the Commission to find substantial deviation from the Secretary's force-structure plan and the final criteria approved by Congress.

The Commission's process was a model of open government. Its recommendations resulted from an independent review of the Secretary of Defense's recommendations, absent political or partisan influence. As part of its review and analysis process, the Commission solicited information from a wide variety of sources. Most important, communities were given a seat at the table. The Commission held investigative hearings, conducted over 125 fact-finding visits to activities at each major candidate installation, held 17 regional hearings nationwide to hear from affected communities, listened to hundreds of Members of Congress and responded to the hundreds of thousands of letters from concerned citizens from across the country. The Commission staff members maintained an active and ongoing dialogue with communities, and met throughout the process with community representatives at the Commission offices, during base visits, and during regional hearings.

The Commission also held seven investigative hearings in Washington, D.C., to question Military Department representatives directly responsible for the Secretary's recommendations. Several defense and base closure experts within the federal government, private sector, and academia provided an independent assessment of the base-closure process and the potential impacts of the Secretary of Defense's recommendations. All of the Commission's hearings and deliberations were held in public. Most were broadcast on national television.

Based on the Commission's review and analysis, alternatives and additions to the Secretary's list were considered and voted upon. On March 1993, and on May 21, 1993, the Commission voted to add a total of 73 installations for further consideration as alternatives and additions to the 165 bases recommended for closure or realignment by the Secretary of Defense.

Communities that contributed to our country's national security by hosting a military facility for many years should rest assured their pleas were heard, and did not go unnoticed. The Commission would also like to reassure communities there can be life after a base is closed. However, economic recovery is in large part dependent upon a concerted community effort to look towards the future. The same dedicated effort expended by communities over the last several months to save their bases should be redirected towards building and implementing a reuse plan that will revitalize the community and the economy.

The Department of Defense Office of Economic Adjustment (OEA) was established to help communities affected by base closures, as well as other defense program changes. The OEA's principal objective is to help the communities affected by base closures to maintain or restore economic stability. According to an OEA survey, approximately 158,000 new jobs were created between 1961 and 1992 to replace nearly 93,000 jobs lost as a result of base closures. The OEA has also been working with 47 communities located near bases recommended for closure by the 1988 and 1991 Commissions, and has provided $20 million in grants to help communities develop reuse plans.

The commissioners selected for the 1993 Defense Base Closure and Realignment Commission have diverse backgrounds in public service, business, and the military. In accordance with the base-closure statute, four commissioners were nominated in consultation with the Speaker of the U.S. House of Representatives and the U.S. Senate Majority Leader, and two commissioners with the advice of the House and Senate Minority Leaders. The remaining two nominations were made independently by the

President, who also designated one of the eight commissioners to serve as the Chairman.

The Commission staff included experts detailed from several government agencies, including the Department of Commerce, the Environmental Protection Agency, the Federal Aviation Administration, the General Accounting Office, the General Services Administration as well as the Department of Defense. Nine professional staff members were detailed by the General Accounting Office (GAO) to serve fulltime on the Commission's Review and Analysis staff. All detailees fully participated in all phases of the review and analysis effort; they verified data, visited candidate bases, participated in local hearings, and testified before the Commission at its public hearings.

Based on the Commission's review-and-analysis and deliberative processes, the Commission recommends to the President 130 bases be closed and 45 bases be realigned. These actions will result in FY 1994-99 net savings of approximately $3.8 billion after one-time costs of approximately $7.43 billion. The savings from these actions will total approximately $2.33 billion annually. The following list summarizes the closure and realignment recommendations of the 1993 Commission:

Department of the Army

Initial Entry Training/Branch School

(O) Fort McClellan, AL (major)

Commodity Oriented

(R) Fort Monmouth, NJ (major) (C) Vint Hill Farms, VA (major)

Depots

(R) Anniston Army Depot, AL (minor)
(O) Letterkenny Army Depot, PA (major)
(R) Red River Army Depot, TX (major)
(R) Tooele Army Depot, UT (major)

Command/Control

(R) Fort Belvoir, VA (major)

Professional Schools

(R) Presidio of Monterey Annex, CA (major)

Changes to Previously Approved BRAC 88/91 Recommendations

(R) Letterkenny Army Depot, PA (Systems Integration Management Activity - East remains at Letterkenny Army Depot, PA vice Rock Island, IL) (major)
(R) Presidio of San Francisco, CA (6th Army remains at the Presidio of San Francisco instead of moving to Fort Carson, CO) (major)

(R) Rock Island Arsenal, IL (AMCCOM remains at Rock Island, IL instead of moving to Redstone Arsenal, AL) (major)
(R) Pueblo Army Depot, CO (Redirects supply mission from Defense Distribution, Depot Tooele, UT, to new location within the Defense Distribution Depot System.) (minor)

Department of the Navy

Shipyards

(C) Charleston Naval Shipyard, SC (major)
(C) Mare Island Naval Shipyard, Vallejo, CA (major)

Operational Air Stations

(C) Marine Corps Air Station El Toro, CA (major)
(C) Naval Air Station Barbers Point, HI (major)
(C) Naval Air Station Cecil Field, FL (major)
(C) Naval Air Station Agana, GU (major)
(C) Naval Air Facility Midway Island (minor)

Training Air Stations

(R) Naval Air Station Memphis, TN (major)
(O) Naval Air Station Meridian, MS (major)

Reserve Air Stations

(C) Naval Air Facility Detroit, MI (major)
(C) Naval Air Facility Martinsburg, WV (minor)
(C) Naval Air Station Dallas, TX (major)
(C) Naval Air Station Glenview, IL (major)
(O) Naval Air Station South Weymouth, MA (major)
(R) Joint Armed Forces Aviation Facility Johnstown, PA (minor)

Naval Bases

(R) Naval Education and Training Center, Newport, RI (major)
(C) Naval Station Charleston, SC (major)
(C) Naval Station Mobile, AL (major)
(C) Naval Station Staten Island, NY (major)
(O) Naval Submarine Base, New London, CT (major)
(C) Naval Air Station Alameda, CA (major)
(C) Naval Station Treasure Island, San Francisco, CA (major)

Training Centers

(C) Naval Training Center Orlando, FL (major)
(C) Naval Training Center San Diego, CA (major)

Inventory Control

(O) Aviation Supply Office, Philadelphia, PA (major)

Depots

(C) Naval Aviation Depot Alameda, CA (major)
(C) Naval Aviation Depot Norfolk, VA (major)
(C) Naval Aviation Depot Pensacola, FL (major)

Naval Weapons Stations

(R) Naval Weapons Station Seal Beach, CA (minor)

Technical Centers (SPAWAR)

(C) Naval Air Warfare Center-Aircraft Division, Trenton, NJ (major)
(O) Naval Air Technical Services Facility, Philadelphia, PA (minor)
(C) Naval Civil Engineering Laboratory, Port Hueneme, CA (major)
(R) Naval Electronic Systems Engineering Center, St. Inigoes, MD (minor)
(C) Naval Electronic Security Systems Engineering Center, Washington DC (major)
(O) Naval Electronic Security Systems Engineering Center, Charleston, SC (major)
(C) Navy Radio Transmission Facility, Annapolis, MD (minor)
(C) Navy Radio Transmission Facility, Driver, VA (minor)
(C) Naval Electronic Systems Engineering Center, Portsmouth, VA (major)

Technical Centers (NAVSEA)

(R) Naval Surface Warfare Center-Dahlgren, White Oak Detachment, White Oak, MD (major)
(O) Naval Surface Warfare Center-Carderock, Annapolis Detachment, Annapolis, MD (major)
(R) Naval Surface Warfare Center-Port Huename, Virginia Beach Detachment, Virginia Beach, VA (major)
(R) Naval Undersea Warfare Center-Norfolk Detachment, Norfolk, VA (major)
(C) Planning, Estimating, Repair and Alterations (CV), Bremerton, WA (minor)
(C) Planning, Estimating, Repair and Alterations (Surface) Atlantic, Norfolk, VA (minor)
(C) Planning, Estimating, Repair and Alterations (Surface) Atlantic (HQ), Philadelphia, PA (minor)
(C) Planning, Estimating, Repair and Alterations (Surface) Pacific, San Francisco, CA (minor)
(C) Sea Automated Data Systems Activity, Indian Head, MD (minor)

(C) Submarine Maintenance, Engineering, Planning, and Procurement, Portsmouth, NH (minor)

Supply Centers

(O) Naval Supply Center Charleston, SC (major)
(O) Naval Supply Center Oakland, CA (major)
(C) Naval Supply Center Pensacola, FL (major)

Marine Corps Logistics Base

(R) Marine Corps Logistics Base Barstow, CA (minor)

National Capital Region (NCR) Activities

(R) Bureau of Navy Personnel, Arlington, VA (Including the Office of Military Manpower Management, Arlington, VA) (major)
(R) Naval Air Systems Command, Arlington, VA (major)
(R) Naval Facilities Engineering Command, Alexandria, VA (major)
(R) Naval Recruiting Command, Arlington, VA (major)
(R) Naval Sea Systems Command, Arlington, VA (major)
(R) Naval Supply Systems Command, Arlington, VA (Including Defense Printing Office, Alexandria, VA and Food Systems Office, Arlington, VA) (major)
(R) Security Group Command, Security Group Station, and Security-Group Detachment, Potomac, Washington, D.C. (major)
(R) Tactical Support Office, Arlington, VA (minor)

Other Bases

(O) 1st Marine Corps District, Garden City, NY (minor)
(C) Department of Defense Family Housing Office, Niagara Falls, NY (minor)
(C) Naval Facilities Engineering Command, Western Engineering Field Division, San Bruno, CA (minor)
(C) Public Works Center San Francisco, CA (major)

Reserve Activities

NAVAL RESERVE CENTERS AT:
(C) Gadsden, AL (minor)
(C) Montgomery, AL (minor)
(C) Fayetteville, AR (minor)
(C) Fort Smith, AR (minor)
(C) Pacific Grove, CA (minor)
(C) Macon, GA (minor)
(C) Terre Haute, IN (minor)
(C) Hutchinson, KS (minor)
(C) Monroe, LA (minor)
(C) New Bedford, MA (minor)

NAVAL RESERVE CENTERS AT:

(C) Pittsfield, MA (minor)
(C) Joplin, MO (minor)
(C) St. Joseph, MO (minor)
(C) Great Falls, MT (minor)
(C) Missoula, MT (minor)
(C) Atlantic City, NJ (minor)
(C) Perth Amboy, NJ (minor)
(C) Jamestown, NY (minor)
(C) Poughkeepsie, NY (minor)
(C) Altoona, PA (minor)
(C) Kingsport, TN (minor)
(C) Memphis, TN (minor)
(C) Ogden, UT (minor)
(C) Staunton, VA (minor)
(C) Parkersburg, WV (minor)
(C) Chicopee, MA (minor)
(C) Quincy, MA (minor)

NAVAL RESERVE FACILITIES AT:

(C) Alexandria, LA (minor)
(C) Midland, TX (minor)

NAVY/MARINE CORPS RESERVE CENTERS AT:

(C) Fort Wayne, IN (minor)
(C) Lawrence, MA (minor)
(O) Billings, MT (minor)
(C) Abilene, TX (minor)

READINESS COMMAND REGIONS AT:

(C) Olathe, KN (Region 18) (minor)
(C) Scotia, NY (Region 2) (minor)
(C) Ravenna, OH (Region 5) (minor)

HOSPITALS

(O) Naval Hospital Charleston, SC (major)
(C) Naval Hospital Oakland, CA (major)
(C) Naval Hospital Orlando, FL (major)

CHANGES TO PREVIOUSLY APPROVED
BRAC 88/91 RECOMMENDATIONS

(R) Hunters Point Annex to Naval Station Treasure Island, CA (Retain no facilities, dispose vice outlease all property) (minor)
(R) Marine Corps Air Station Tustin, CA (Substitute Naval Air Station Miramar for Marine Corps Air Station 29 Palms as one receiver of

Marine Corps Air Station Tustin's assets) (major)
(R) Naval Electronics Systems Engineering Center, San Diego, CA (Consolidate with Naval Electronics Systems Engineering Center, Vallejo, CA, into available Air Force space vice new construction) (major)
(R) Naval Mine Warfare Engineering Activity, Yorktown, VA (Realign to Panama City, FL vice Dam Neck, VA) (minor)
(R) Naval Weapons Evaluation Facility, Albuquerque, NM (Retain as a tenant of the Air Force) (minor)

Department of the Air Force

Large Aircraft

(R) Griffiss Air Force Base, NY (major)
(C) K.I. Sawyer Air Force Base, MI (major)
(R) March Air Force Base, CA (major)
(C) Plattsburgh Air Force Base, NY (major)
(O) McGuire Air Force Base, NJ (major)

Small Aircraft

(R) Homestead Air Force Base, FL (major)

Air Force Reserve

(C) O'Hare International Airport Air Force Reserve Station, Chicago, IL (major)

Other Air Force

(C) Gentile Air Force Station, OH (minor)

Air Force Depot

(C) Newark Air Force Base, OH (major)
(R) Ogden Air Force Logistics Center, Hill Air Force Base, UT (minor)

Changes to Previously Approved BRAC 88/91 Recommendations

(O) Bergstrom Air Force Base, TX (Requested redirect rejected) (minor)
(R) Carswell Air Force Base, TX (Fabrication function of the 436th Training Squadron redirected from Dyess AFB to Luke AFB, maintenance training function redirected from Dyess AFB to Hill AFB) (minor)
(R) Castle Air Force Base, CA (B-52 Combat Crew Training redirected from Fairchild AFB to Barksdale AFB and KC-135 Combat Crew Training from Fairchild AFB to Altus AFB) (major)
(R) Chanute Air Force Base, IL (Metals Technology and Aircraft Structural Maintenance training courses from Chanute AFB to Sheppard AFB redirected to NAS Memphis) (minor)
(R) MacDill Air Force Base, Florida (Airfield to be operated by the

Department of Commerce or another federal agency. Joint Communications Support Element stays at MacDill vice relocating to Charleston AFB.) (minor)

(R) Mather Air Force Base, CA (940th) Air Refueling Group redirected from McClellan AFB to Beale AFB) (minor)

(R) Rickenbacker Air National Guard Base, OH (Retain 121st Air Refueling Wing and the 160th Air Refueling Group in a cantonment area at Rickenbacker AGB instead of Wright-Patterson AFB. Rickenbacker AGB does not close.) (major)

Defense Logistics Agency

Inventory Control Points

(C) Defense Electronics Supply Center, Dayton, OH (major)
(O) Defense Industrial Supply Center, Philadelphia, PA (major)
(C) Defense Personnel Support Center, Philadelphia, PA (major)

Regional Headquarters

(R) Defense Contract Management District Midatlantic, Philadelphia, PA (minor)
(R) Defense Contract Management District Northcentral, Chicago, IL (minor)
(R) Defense Contract Management District West, El Segundo, CA (minor)

Defense Distribution Depots

(C) Defense Distribution Depot Oakland, CA (minor)
(C) Defense Distribution Depot Pensacola, FL (minor)
(O) Defense Distribution Depot Letterkenny, PA (minor)
(C) Defense Distribution Depot Charleston, SC (minor)
(C) Defense Distribution Depot Tooele, UT (minor)

Service/Support Activities

(O) Defense Logistics Support Center, Battle Creek, MI (major)
(O) Defense Reutilization and Marketing Service, Battle Creek, MI (major)
(C) Defense Logistics Agency Clothing Factory, Philadelphia, PA (major)

Data Center Consolidation

Navy Data Processing Centers

(C) Aviation Supply Office, Philadelphia, PA (minor)
(C) Bureau of Naval Personnel, Washington, DC (minor)
(C) Enlisted Personnel Management Center, New Orleans, LA (minor)
(C) Facilities Systems Office, Port Hueneme, CA (minor)
(C) Fleet Industrial Support Center, San Diego, CA (minor)
(C) Naval Air Station Brunswick, ME (minor)

(C) Naval Air Station Key West, FL (minor)
(C) Naval Air Station Mayport, FL (minor)
(C) Naval Air Station Oceana, VA (minor)
(C) Naval Air Station Whidbey Island, WA (minor)
(C) Naval Air Warfare Center, Aircraft Division, Patuxent River, MD (minor)
(C) Naval Air Warfare Center, Weapons Division, China Lake, CA (minor)
(C) Naval Air Warfare Center, Weapons Division, Point Mugu, CA (minor)
(C) Naval Command Control & Ocean Surveillance Center, San Diego, CA (minor)
(C) Naval Computer & Telecommunications Area Master Station, Atlantic, Norfolk, VA (minor)
(C) Naval Computer & Telecommunications Area Master Station, EASTPAC, Pearl Harbor, HI (minor)
(O) Naval Computer & Telecommunications Station, San Diego, CA (minor)
(C) Naval Computer & Telecommunications Station, Washington, DC (minor)
(C) Naval Computer & Telecommunications Station, New Orleans, LA (minor)
(C) Naval Computer & Telecommunications Station, Pensacola, FL (minor)
(C) Navy Regional Data Automation Center, San Francisco, CA (minor)
(C) Naval Supply Center, Charleston, SC (minor)
(C) Naval Supply Center, Norfolk, VA (minor)
(C) Naval Supply Center, Pearl Harbor, HI (minor)

Navy Data Processing Centers

(C) Naval Supply Center, Puget Sound, WA (minor)
(C) Navy Data Automation Facility, Corpus Christi, TX (minor)
(C) Navy Recruiting Command, Arlington, VA (minor)
(C) Trident Refit Facility, Bangor, WA (minor)
(C) Trident Refit Facility, Kings Bay, GA (minor)

Marine Corps Data Processing Centers

(C) Marine Corps Air Station Cherry Point, NC (minor)
(C) Marine Corps Air Station El Toro, CA (minor)
(C) Regional Automated Services Center, Camp Lejeune, NC (minor)
(C) Regional Automated Services Center, Camp Pendleton, CA (minor)

Air Force Data Processing Centers

(C) Air Force Military Personnel Center, Randolph AFB, TX (minor)
(C) Computer Service Center, San Antonio, TX (minor)
(C) 7th Communications Group, Pentagon, Arlington, VA (minor)

(O) Regional Processing Center, McClellan AFB, CA (minor)

Defense Logistics Agency Data Processing Centers

(C) Information Processing Center, Battle Creek, MI (minor)
(C) Information Processing Center, Ogden, UT (minor)
(C) Information Processing Center, Philadelphia, PA (minor)
(C) Information Processing Center, Richmond, VA (minor)

Defense Information Systems Agency (DISA) Data Processing Centers

(C) Defense Information Technology Service Organization, Columbus Annex Dayton, OH (minor)
(C) Defense Information Technology Service Organization, Indianapolis Information Processing Center, IN (minor)
(C) Defense Information Technology Service Organization, Kansas City Information Processing Center, MO (minor)
(C) Defense Information Technology Services Organization, Cleveland, OH (minor)

Legend

(C) = Installation recommended for closure
(R) = Installation recommended for realignment
(O) = Installation recommended to remain open

DECISION IN JESSICA DEBOER ADOPTION CASE

July 2, 1993

One of the most public and wrenching adoption disputes in recent years came to its legal close July 2 when the Michigan Supreme Court upheld an Iowa court order granting custody of a two-year-old girl to her biological parents, who are Iowa residents. The court said that under two relevant laws, the Uniform Child Custody Jurisdiction Act (UCCJA) and the federal Parental Kidnapping Protection Act (PKPA), Michigan tribunals did not have jurisdiction over the custody dispute, which had been brought in that state by residents Roberta and Jan DeBoer. They were seeking to adopt the little girl, whom they had named Jessica. Therefore, the orders of the Iowa courts granting custody to Cara Clausen and Daniel Schmidt, the child's biological parents, must be enforced.

The Michigan court decided two other related matters in the lengthy opinion: that the DeBoers lacked "standing," or the legal right, to bring the custody case under Michigan law and that a separate action brought on behalf of Jessica must be dismissed because it failed to state a legal claim for which relief could be granted. The court ordered the DeBoers to relinquish Jessica thirty-one days after the release of its opinion. She was returned to her birth parents August 2.

Five Michigan Supreme Court justices signed the decision: Chief Justice Michael Cavanagh and Justices James H. Brickley, Patricia J. Boyle, Dorothy C. Riley, Robert Griffin, and Conrad L. Mallett. Justice Charles Levin dissented.

"Nature versus Nurture"

The July 2 decision was the culmination of more than two years of legal maneuvering that prompted intense media coverage—Jessica was on the cover of Time *magazine—and debate around the country not only about the state of adoption laws but also about the rights of parents versus the "best interests" of the children and how those rights and interests should be defined and weighed in a conflict. Issues of social class were also swirling through this legal and emotional maelstrom because the prospective adoptive parents were thought to be able to give Jessica more material comforts than her biological parents, a factory worker and a trucker who were unmarried at the time of her birth. Cara Clausen, who later married Schmidt, had originally named a different man as her baby's father, and Daniel Schmidt had already fathered two other children that he had not helped to raise. In the shorthand of some analysts the dispute was about "nature versus nurture."*

There was no shortage of finger-pointing in the matter: many blamed the legal system, which, despite efforts at uniformity, was still a patchwork of state laws that foster litigation. Some states allow private adoptions, as this one was; others require adoptions to be done through agencies. Both couples were criticized—the DeBoers for pressing on too long after Cara Clausen changed her mind about allowing the adoption, and the Schmidts for seeking to disrupt the only home Jessica had known.

Background

Cara Clausen gave birth to a baby girl in Iowa February 8, 1991. She had just broken up with her boyfriend, Dan Schmidt, and had started going out with Scott Seefeldt, whose name she put on her baby's birth certificate. On February 10, Clausen signed a release of custody form, relinquishing her parental rights to the child and putting her up for adoption—twenty-four hours short of the seventy-two-hour waiting period. Seefeldt signed a similar form two days later.

Roberta DeBoer, known as "Robby," is unable to have children of her own, and she and her husband had been looking to adopt a child. Robby heard about Cara through a friend in Iowa and began negotiating to adopt the Clausen baby. On February 25 the DeBoers filed a petition for adoption in an Iowa juvenile court. A hearing was held the same day, and Clausen's and Seefeldt's parental rights were terminated and the DeBoers were granted custody of the child for the rest of the adoption proceeding. The DeBoers returned to Michigan with the baby girl.

Nine days later, on March 6, Cara Clausen changed her mind and filed a petition to revoke her release of custody. She had seen Schmidt at work and told him about the baby she had given up and had begun having second thoughts. In the affidavit that was part of the March petition, Clausen admitted she lied when she had named Seefeldt as the baby's father and said Schmidt was the real father. On March 12 Schmidt acknowledged paternity, and on March 27—twenty-six days after the DeBoers were given custody—he filed a petition to intervene in the adoption proceeding. It took six months before genetic tests determined that Schmidt was indeed the father. Because he had not signed away his rights, nor had the DeBoers proved that he abandoned the child, an Iowa district court determined December 27, 1991, that the adoption proceed-

ing the previous February was void. The DeBoers' petition to adopt the child was denied, and they were ordered to turn Jessica over to the Iowa couple.

Legal Tug-of-War

Rather than comply, the DeBoers decided to fight the decision, and a legal stay of the order allowed them to keep Jessica while the appeals proceeded. They contended that Dan Schmidt was not a fit parent, noting the two other children he had fathered but had not helped raise. At the same time Robby engaged in her own advocacy, writing letters to children's rights specialists and talking to reporters to make the couple's story public.

But the initial Iowa decision was upheld by that state's appellate courts, and in the meantime Cara and Dan had gotten married. The Iowa Supreme Court ordered the DeBoers to appear in a state district court on December 3, 1992, with the child, but they did not attend. The court nonetheless terminated the DeBoers' rights as temporary guardians and custodians of Jessica. But on the same day the DeBoers filed a petition in a Michigan circuit court asking the judge to take the case under the UCCJA and find a way to give the couple custody. The Washtenaw Circuit Court issued a temporary restraining order directing that the child remain in the DeBoers' custody.

On December 11 Schmidt sought to dissolve the order and to have the Iowa custody order enforced. The Washtenaw Circuit Court held a hearing on Schmidt's motion January 5, 1993, and, finding that it had authority to determine "the best interests of the child," the court denied Schmidt's request and directed that Jessica remain with the DeBoers.

On March 29, the Michigan Court of Appeals reversed the decision, concluding that the circuit court lacked jurisdiction under the uniform custody act and that under the relevant Michigan case, Bowie v. Arder, *the DeBoers were not appropriate parties to bring such a custody action.*

Two weeks later, on April 14, a lawyer appointed to represent Jessica filed a complaint for relief for the child asking that she be allowed to stay with the DeBoers. On April 22, the circuit judge ordered that she remain with the Michigan couple.

The Schmidts appealed the decision, setting the stage for the Michigan high court to rule on that court order and on the DeBoers' appeal of the order upholding the Iowa court decisions.

Dissenting Opinion

In his dissent, Justice Levin said that because Iowa was not the home state, it did not have jurisdiction under the federal PKPA. Levin stated that Michigan had no obligation to enforce Iowa's decree to transfer the child. Moreover, the focus of the PKPA was on the best interests of the child, and Michigan should hold a hearing to determine those interests. "If the danger confronting this child were physical injury," Levin wrote, "no one would question her right to invoke judicial process to protect herself against such injury. There is little difference, when viewed from the child's frame of reference, between a physical assault and a psychological assault.... It is only because this child cannot speak for herself that adults can avert their eyes from the pain that she will suffer."

Following are excerpts from the July 2, 1993, Michigan Supreme Court decision in In re Clausen (DeBoer v. Schmidt) *and* DeBoer v. DeBoer *upholding the orders of the Iowa courts granting custody of Jessica DeBoer to her biological parents, Cara and Daniel Schmidt, and dismissing a custody action brought on behalf of the child:*

No. 96-366 Nos. 96-441, 96-531, 96-532

In Re Baby Girl Clausen, Roberta and Jan DeBoer, Petitioners-Appellants, *v.* Daniel Schmidt, Respondent-Appellee.	Jessica DeBoer (a/k/a Baby Girl Classen), by her next friend, Peter Darrow, Plaintiff-Appellee, *v.* Roberta and Jan DeBoer, Defendants-Appellees, and Cara and Daniel Schmidt, Defendants-Appellants.

[July 2, 1993]

PER CURIAM

These two related cases arise out of a child custody dispute involving the competing claims of the child's natural parents (Cara and Daniel Schmidt) and the third-party custodians with whom the child now lives (Roberta and Jan DeBoer).

While we will deal at length with the various arguments marshalled in support of their claims, we sum up our analysis of the competing arguments by reference to the words of the United States Supreme Court: "No one would seriously dispute that a deeply loving and interdependent relationship with an adult and a child in his or her care may exist even in the absence of blood relationship." *Smith v. Organization of Foster Families* (1977). But there are limits to such claims. In the context of foster care, the Court has said:

> "[T]here are also important distinctions between the foster family and the natural family. First, unlike the earlier cases recognizing a right to family privacy, the State here seeks to interfere, not with a relationship having its origins entirely apart from the power of the State, but rather with a foster family which has its source in state law and contractual arrangements...

> "[T]he liberty interest in family privacy has its source, and its contours are ordinarily to be sought, not in state law, but in intrinsic human rights, as they have been understood in "this Nation's history and tradition." Here, however, whatever emotional ties may develop between foster parent and foster child have their origins in an arrangement in which the State has been a partner from the outset.
>
> * * *
>
> "A second consideration related to this is that ordinarily procedural protection may be afforded to a liberty interest of one person without derogating from the substantive liberty of another....
>
> "It is one thing to say that individuals may acquire a liberty interest against arbitrary governmental interference in the family-like associations into which they have freely entered, even in the absence of biological connection or state-law recognition of the relationship. It is quite another to say that one may acquire such an interest in the face of another's constitutionally recognized liberty interest that derives from blood relationship, state-law sanction, and basic human right—an interest the foster parent has recognized by contract from the outset."

Likewise, the DeBoers acquired temporary custody of this child, with whom they had no prior relationship, through the power of the state and must be taken to have known that their right to continue custody was contingent on the completion of the Iowa adoption. Within nine days of assuming physical custody and less than one month after the child's birth, the DeBoers learned of Cara Schmidt's claim that the waiver of rights procured by the attorney acting on behalf of the DeBoers was unlawful because she had not been afforded the seventy-two-hour waiting period required by Iowa law. Within two months of the child's birth, the DeBoers learned of Daniel Schmidt's claim of paternity when on March 27, 1991, he filed a petition to intervene in the DeBoers' adoption proceeding.

The State of Iowa has not arbitrarily interfered "in a family-like association freely entered." Rather, the Iowa courts have proceeded with the adoption action initiated by the DeBoers, and at the conclusion of that litigation ruled that there would be no adoption, preventing the creation of the family unit that was the objective of the adoption petition.

In Docket No. 96366, we affirm the judgment of the Court of Appeals for two independent reasons. First the Uniform Child Custody Jurisdiction Act (UCCJA) and the federal Parental Kidnapping Prevention Act (PKPA) deprive the Michigan courts of jurisdiction over this custody dispute and require the enforcement of the orders of the Iowa courts directing that the Schmidts have custody of the child. Second, the DeBoers lack standing to bring this custody action under our decision in *Bowie v. Arder* (1992).

In Docket Nos. 96441, 96531, and 96532 we vacate the orders of the Washtenaw Circuit Court and direct that the action be dismissed for failure to state a claim upon which relief may be granted. While a child has a constitutionally protected interest in family life, that interest is not independent of its parents in the absence of a showing that the parents are unfit. In this case, in the Iowa litigation the DeBoers were unable to prove that the child's father would not be a fit parent, and no claim has been made that her mother is unfit....

[Section I Omitted]

II

Interstate enforcement of child custody orders has long presented vexing problems. This arose principally from uncertainties about the applicability of the Full Faith and Credit Clause of the United States Constitution. Because custody decrees were generally regarded as subject to modification, states had traditionally felt free to modify another state's prior order.

The initial attempt to deal with these jurisdictional problems was the drafting of the Uniform Child Custody Jurisdiction Act, promulgated by the National Conference of Commissioners on Uniform State Laws in 1968. That uniform act has now been enacted, in some form, in all fifty states, the District of Columbia, and the U.S. Virgin Islands.... The act provides standards for determining whether a state may take jurisdiction of a child custody dispute, and sets forth the circumstances in which the courts of other states are prohibited from subsequently taking jurisdiction, are required to enforce custody decisions of the original state, and are permitted to modify such decisions.

Despite the widespread enactment of the UCCJA, variations in the versions adopted in some states, and differing interpretations, resulted in continuing uncertainty about the enforceability of custody decisions. In 1980, Congress responded by adopting the Parental Kidnapping Prevention Act. The PKPA "imposes a duty on the States to enforce a child custody determination entered by a court of a sister State if the determination is consistent with the provisions of the Act." *Thompson v. Thompson* (1988). The PKPA includes provisions similar to the UCCJA, and emphatically imposes the requirement that sister-state custody orders be given effect.

III

In its March 29, 1993, opinion, the Court of Appeals agreed with Daniel Schmidt that the Washtenaw Circuit Court lacked jurisdiction to modify the Iowa custody orders and was instead required to enforce them. It explained:

> ... "We find that the Washtenaw Circuit Court lacked jurisdiction to intervene in this case. The UCCJA has been enacted by every state, including Michigan. Its primary purpose is to avoid jurisdictional competition between states by establishing uniform rules for deciding when states have jurisdiction to make child custody determinations. Pursuant to § 656(1) of the UCCJA, Michigan is precluded from exercising jurisdiction if a matter concerning custody is pending in another state at the time the petition to modify is filed in this state. An adoption proceeding is included in the definition of a custody proceeding under the UCCJA....
>
> "The DeBoers filed their petition in Washtenaw Circuit Court on December 3, 1992. On that date the Iowa district court entered an order terminating the

> DeBoers' rights as temporary guardians and custodians of [the child], and scheduled a hearing for the DeBoers to show cause why they should not be held in contempt. Although the issues concerning the dismissal of the DeBoers' adoption petition and the right to physical custody of [the child] had been determined by the Iowa Supreme Court before December 3, 1992, further proceedings were scheduled in the case. Under § 656(1) of the UCCJA, the Washtenaw Circuit Court was precluded from intervening in this case, and was obligated to recognize and enforce the Iowa order of December 3, 1992.
>
> "We find that the DeBoers' contention that a Michigan court could modify the Iowa order because Iowa did not act substantially in conformity with the UCCJA by doing a 'best interests of the child' analysis is without merit. The Iowa court dismissed the adoption petition and granted custody of [the child] to Schmidt because he was the biological father of the child and because his parental rights had not been terminated. . . ."

IV

A

The DeBoers argue that the Iowa custody orders were subject to modification by Michigan courts because the Iowa proceedings were no longer "pending" under the UCCJA at the time the Washtenaw Circuit Court action was filed on December 3, 1992. They point to *Ford Motor Co. v. Jackson* (1973), for the proposition that an action is no longer pending once a final determination has been made on appeal. They maintain that when the Iowa Supreme Court affirmed the judgment awarding custody to the natural father on September 23, 1992, and thereafter denied the DeBoers' request for rehearing, that made the decree final, and therefore modifiable. The only remaining matters in Iowa were hearings to enforce the final order. They maintain that such enforcement proceedings do not involve custody issues, and thus the proceeding with regard to custody was no longer pending.

We reject the DeBoers' construction of the UCCJA. Enforcement of the Iowa decision is required by the PKPA, and therefore a detailed analysis of the UCCJA is not required.

The congressionally declared purpose of the PKPA is to deal with inconsistent and conflicting laws and practices by which courts determine their jurisdiction to decide disputes between persons claiming rights of custody. . . .

Congress also recognized that

> "among the results of those conditions and activities are the failure of the courts of such jurisdictions to give full faith and credit to the judicial proceedings of the other jurisdictions. . . and harm to the welfare of children and their parents and other custodians."

The suggestion that in this context the best interests purpose of the PKPA mandates a best interests analysis in Iowa, failing which the Iowa decision is not entitled to full faith and credit, would permit the forum state's view of the merits of the case to govern the assumption of jurisdiction to modify the foreign decree. It also suggests that Congress intended to impose the substantive best interests rule in all is in conflict with the directive of Congress that "[t]he appropriate authorities of every State shall enforce according to its terms, and shall not modify except as provided ... any child custody determination made consistently with the provisions of this section by a court of another State."

It has been aptly noted that the vulnerability of a custody decree to an out-of-state modification presented the greatest need of all for the reform effort of the PKPA. "In language that is subject to little or no misinterpretation the jurisdiction of the initial court continues to the exclusion of all others as long as that court has jurisdiction under the law of that state and the state remains the residence of the child or any contestant."

Certainty and stability are given priority under the PKPA, which gives the home state exclusive continuing jurisdiction. Thus, the PKPA expressly provides that if a custody determination is made consistently with its provisions, "[t]he appropriate authorities of every State *shall* enforce [it] according to its terms, and *shall not* modify" that custody decision. (Emphasis added). "A child custody determination ... is consistent with the provisions [of the PKPA] only if" the court making the determination had jurisdiction under its own laws, and the state was the "home state" of the child when the proceedings were commenced. At the time of commencement of both the termination and adoption proceedings, Iowa unquestionably had jurisdiction under its own laws and Iowa was unquestionably the home state of the child. Thus, the child custody determination made by the Iowa court was made consistently with the provisions of the PKPA.

Where the custody determination is made consistently with the provisions of the PKPA, the jurisdiction of the court that made the decision is exclusive and continuing as long as that state "remains the residence of the child or of any contestant," and it still has jurisdiction under its own laws. Unquestionably, Daniel Schmidt continues to reside in Iowa. Furthermore, Iowa law provides for continuing jurisdiction in custody matters, and the Iowa courts regarded themselves as continuing to have jurisdiction of the custody proceeding because they continued to issue orders in the case: the order of December 3, 1992, terminating the DeBoers' right to custody and appointing Daniel Schmidt as custodian, and the order of January 27, 1993, holding the DeBoers in contempt. Because the Iowa custody determination was made consistently with the terms of the PKPA, and because Iowa's jurisdiction continues, the Iowa court's order must be enforced.

The courts of this state may only modify Iowa's order if Iowa has declined to exercise its jurisdiction to modify it. Iowa has not declined to exercise its jurisdiction to modify its custody order; it has simply declined to order the relief sought by the DeBoers. Modification is not permitted on these facts: Iowa continues to have jurisdiction, it has not declined to exercise that jurisdiction, its jurisdiction is, therefore, exclusive, and Iowa's exclusive continuing jurisdiction precludes the courts of this state from exercising jurisdiction to modify the Iowa order....

B

The DeBoers argue that the Iowa judgment should not be enforced because the Iowa courts did not conduct a hearing into the best interests of the child in making the custody decision. They maintain that this undercuts the Iowa decision in two respects. First, they say this means that the Iowa decision was not in conformity with the UCCJA, and therefore not entitled to enforcement under that statute. Second, they believe that the Iowa proceeding was repugnant to Michigan public policy.

We reject the contention that the decision of the Iowa courts not to conduct a best interests of the child hearing in the circumstances of this case justifies the refusal "to enforce the Iowa judgments."

The UCCJA and the PKPA are procedural statutes. To be sure, they express the purpose of assuring that the state that is in the best position to make a proper determination regarding custody of the child be the one in which the action is brought, and that other states will follow the decision made there. That purpose has been achieved in this case. There can be no doubt that at the time the Iowa proceedings commenced in February 1991, that state was the appropriate one to take jurisdiction; it was in the best position to resolve the issues presented. As was conceded by counsel for the DeBoers during oral argument, the statutes do not provide that a best interests of the child standard is the substantive test by which all custody decisions are to be made. Each state, through legislation and the interpretative decisions of its courts, is free to fashion its own substantive law of family relationships within constitutional limitations.

Further, we do not find the Iowa proceedings to be so contrary to Michigan public policy as to require us to refuse to enforce the Iowa judgments. Before turning to Michigan public policy, however, a preliminary matter must be examined.

After passage of the PKPA, we are not free to refuse to enforce the Iowa judgment as being contrary to public policy.

That statute says:

> "The appropriate authorities of every State shall enforce according to the terms, and shall not modify except as provided in subsection (f) of this section, any child custody determination made consistently with the provisions of this section by a court of another State."

Subsection (f) does not provide a basis for declining to enforce the Iowa order. For the first time at oral argument, the DeBoers asserted that the order was not made consistently with the PKPA. As they contended regarding the UCCJA, they think an order is not made consistently with the statute if the best interests of the child test is not used. However, they point to no provision of the statute with which the Iowa courts did not comply, and they cite no authority for their interpretation of the PKPA.

Turning to the matter of Michigan public policy, while in many custody disputes Michigan does apply a best interests of the child test, there are circumstances in which we do not. For example, [section] 39 of the

Adoption Code has a pair of provisions regarding the termination of parental rights of putative fathers who seek custody of a child....

Similarly, in the case of limited guardianships, if the hearing establishes that the parent or parents have substantially complied with a limited guardianship placement plan, the court is required to terminate the guardianship without using the best interests test that is applied where there has not been such compliance. This is so even if the guardian could prevail on a best interests standard.

Finally, under Michigan law where a party has no legally cognizable claim to custody of a child, there is no right to a best interests hearing. E.g., *Ruppel v. Lesner* (1984); *Bowie v. Arder.*

We express no opinion about whether we would require a Michigan court to hold a best interests of the child hearing if we were faced with the circumstances presented to the Iowa courts. However, we cannot hold that the Iowa judgment is unenforceable under the UCCJA and PKPA because such a hearing was not held.

V

The Court of Appeals also concluded that the DeBoers lacked standing to claim custody of the child. The Court said:

> "We hold that the DeBoers lacked standing to bring this action in Washtenaw Circuit Court. The Iowa district court order of December 3, 1992, implemented the decision of the Iowa Supreme Court and stripped the DeBoers of any legal claim to custody of [the child]. The grant of temporary custody was rescinded. At that time, the DeBoers became third parties with respect to [the child], and no longer had a basis on which to claim a substantive right to custody. *Bowie* states that neither the Child Custody Act nor any other authority gives a third party who does not possess a substantive right to custody or is not a guardian, standing to create a custody dispute. A right to legal custody cannot be based on the fact that a child resides or has resided with the third party. We take the reference in Bowie to 'any other authority' to include the UCCJA.
>
> "... The Iowa Supreme Court decision, implemented by the Iowa district court's order of December 3, 1992, dismissed the DeBoers' petition to adopt [the child] and rescinded their status as temporary guardians and custodians. The DeBoers had no further legal rights to [the child]. The DeBoers have attempted to use the UCCJA and the Washtenaw Circuit Court to create anew a right that the Iowa courts had extinguished. The DeBoers initiated a custody dispute in this state. Pursuant to *Bowie,* they had no standing to do so. To disavow Bowie in this case would give an advantage to third parties in interstate custody disputes not enjoyed by third parties in intrastate disputes.
>
> "The DeBoers' reliance on *In re Danke* (1988) and *In re Weldon* (1976) (cases in which third parties with no legal right to custody were granted standing to bring a custody action), is misplaced. Both cases were decided before *Bowie.* The *Bowie* Court specifically stated that Weldor was overruled, and that a third party could not gain standing simply by filing a complaint and asserting that a change in custody would be in the best interests of the child. *Bowie."*

VI

The DeBoers advance a variety of arguments in support of their claim that they have standing to litigate regarding the custody of the child. First, they argue that the UCCJA grants them standing, pointing particularly to two of three jurisidictional provisions in § 653(1).

The DeBoers also argue that *Bowie v. Arder* does not deny them standing. To begin with, they think that *Bowie* let stand statements in the lower court decision to the effect that "once judicial intervention has already taken place, the court may award custody to third parties." Further, they see the only prohibition as being on the ability of a third party to *create* a custody dispute. In their view, judicial intervention in this dispute began over two years ago, and they did not create the dispute. The initial decree in Iowa resulted from Schmidt's creation of a custody dispute when he filed a petition for intervention on March 27, 1991. Their filing of the petition in Michigan was a response to and an effort to modify the Iowa custody decree dissolving their right to custody of the child.

Further, the DeBoers believe that *Bowie* is inapplicable because it is a case dealing with the Child Custody Act. This is a UCCJA action in which the Child Custody Act's provisions regarding best interests of the child are only incidentally involved. Even *Bowie* recognized that kind of incidental use of the Child Custody Act.

In addition *Bowie* said that a circuit court has the power to grant custody to "third parties according to the best interests of the child in an appropriate case (typically involving divorce)" and that "such an award of custody is based not on the third party's legal right to custody of the child, but on the court's determination of the child's best interests."

Finally, the DeBoers assert that despite *Bowie* they had a substantive right to custody because they had custody pursuant to the February 25, 1991, order of the Iowa district court.

In addition, the DeBoers maintain that there is a protected liberty interest in their relationship with the child, which gives them standing. They trace the recent history of constitutional protection of parental rights beginning with *Stanley v. Illinois* (1972) through *Quilloin v. Walcott* (1978), *Smith v. Organization of Foster Families* (1977), and *Lehr v. Robertson* (1983) to *Michael H v. Gerald D* (1989). From these cases, they extract the principles that it is the relationship between the parent and child that triggers significant constitutional protection and that the mere existence of a biological link is not determinative.

We reject these arguments. As the Court of Appeals noted, *Bowie* was not limited to Child Custody Act cases. The UCCJA is a procedural statute governing the jurisdiction of courts to entertain custody disputes. It is not enough that a person assert to be a "contestant," or "claim" a right to custody with respect to a child. If that were so, then any person could obtain standing by simply asserting a claim to custody, whether there was any legal basis for doing so or not. The Court of Appeals has correctly read our decision in *Bowie* as requiring the existence of some substantive right to custody of the child. We adhere to the holding of Bowie that a third party does not obtain such a substantive right by virtue of the child's having resided with the third party.

We also agree with the Court of Appeals rejection of the DeBoers' arguments regarding the "creation" of a dispute and that they only seek to modify the Iowa order. It is true that Bowie recognized the incidental application of the Child Custody Act standards in other kinds of actions—typically divorce cases. However, the problem with the DeBoers' reasoning is that there is no action that they are entitled to bring to which the Child Custody Act can be applied incidentally.

It may be that the Iowa district court's February 25, 1991, order appointing the DeBoers as custodians during the pendency of the Iowa adoption proceeding was sufficiently analogous to a Michigan guardianship (which would create standing) to have given them standing to prosecute a custody action during the effectiveness of that order. However, as the Court of Appeals said, when the temporary custody order was rescinded, they became third parties to the child and no longer had a basis on which to claim a substantive right of custody.

The United States Supreme Court cases on which the DeBoers rely do not establish that they have a federal constitutional right to seek custody of the child. None involved disputes between a natural parent or parents on one side and non parents on the other. While some of those cases place limits on the rights of natural parents, particularly unwed fathers, they involve litigation pitting one natural parent against the other, in which, almost of necessity, one natural parent must be denied rights that otherwise would have been protected. Sometimes a non parent in a sense "prevails" in such actions, but that has been in the context of adoption by a stepfather who is married to the child's natural mother or legitimization of the status of the natural mother's husband, who is not the biological father.

Several of the cases talk about an unwed father's rights as being dependent on the development of a relationship with the child. We read those decisions as providing the justification for denying the unwed father's rights, rather than as establishing that non parent custodians obtain such rights merely by having custody. Further, as the Iowa district court noted after reviewing these United States Supreme Court cases:

> "It is therefore now clearly established that an unwed father who has not had a custodial relationship with a child nevertheless has a constitutionally protected interest in establishing that relationship."

And, as the Iowa Supreme Court concluded:

> "We agree with the district court that abandonment was not established by clear and convincing evidence. In fact, virtually all of the evidence regarding Daniel's intent regarding this baby suggests just the opposite: Daniel did

everything he could reasonably do to assert his parental rights, beginning even before he actually knew that he was the father."

VII

In Docket Nos. 96441, 96531, and 96532, the next friend for the child argues that we should recognize the right of a minor child to bring a Child Custody Act action and obtain a best interests of the child hearing regarding her custody. Because of the interrelationship of this action to the DeBoers' application for leave to appeal in Docket No. 96366, we granted leave to appeal before decision by the Court of Appeals and directed the parties to brief the question whether the action should be dismissed for failure to state a claim upon which relief may be granted. Basically, the next friend advances three theories on which a child is entitled to bring such an action.

First, the next friend maintains that the Child Custody Act gives children the right to bring such actions.... The next friend asserts that there is nothing in the act that would deprive the child of the right to bring an action.

Second, the next friend maintains that the child has a due process liberty interest in her relationship with the DeBoers. Cases in other contexts are cited for the proposition that children are "persons" under the constitution and that constitutionally protected liberty interests run both to adults and minors.

The next friend reiterates the arguments made by the DeBoers that cases such as *Lehr v. Robertson* and *Smith v. Organization of Foster Families* establish that the liberty interest in family life arises out of relationships based on day-to-day contact and not on biological relationships.

Third, the next friend argues that the child is denied equal protection on two grounds. First, children are treated differently on the basis of whether they are in the custody of "psychological" parents rather than a biological parent. Second, the Child Custody Act grants some children residing with third-party custodians the right to a best interests hearing (those living with court-appointed guardians), but not others.

We do not believe that the Child Custody Act can be read as authorizing such an action. The act's consistent distinction between the "parties" and the "child" makes clear that the act is intended to resolve disputes among adults seeking custody of the child.

It is true that children, as well as their parents, have a due process liberty interest in their family life. However, in our view those interests are not independent of the child's parents. The Legislature has provided a right of parental custody and control of children:

> "Unless otherwise ordered by a court order, the parents of an unemancipated minor are equally entitled to the custody, control, services and earnings of the minor, but if 1 parent provides, to the exclusion of the other parent, for the maintenance and support of the minor, that parent has the paramount right to control the services and earnings of the minor."

The mutual rights of the parent and child come into conflict only when there is a showing of parental unfitness. As we have held in a series of cases, the natural parent's right to custody is not to be disturbed absent such a showing, sometimes despite the preferences of the child....

Nothing in the more recent United States Supreme Court decisions requires a different result. Indeed, several of its decisions emphasize the limitations on minors' rights to independently assert rights regarding their custody and care. *Michael H v. Gerald D; Parham v. JR* (1979).

In the Iowa proceedings, a challenge to Daniel Schmidt's fitness was vigorously prosecuted by the DeBoers, and they failed to prove that he was unfit. That determination is no longer challenged.

We also disagree with the next friend's assertion that the child's interests were not considered in Iowa. A guardian ad litem was appointed before Daniel Schmidt moved to intervene in the action. We have no reason to believe that the guardian ad litem's advice to the court was anything but a good-faith effort to advise regarding the interests of the child. While that proceeding did not use the "best interests of the child" standard that the next friend and the DeBoers prefer, there is no basis for requiring use of that standard.

With regard to the Equal Protection arguments, we reject the view that children residing with their parents are similarly situated to those residing with nonparents; as just explained, the relationship between natural parents and their children is fundamentally different than that between a child and nonparent custodians. Nor does the Child Custody Act's exception for guardians deny equal protection. Children living with guardians and those living with other third-party custodians are also not similarly situated. The safeguards in the guardianship statute provide protection against manipulative attempts to temporarily obtain possession and use that as the basis for a Child Custody Act action.

VIII

In Docket No. 96366, we affirm the judgment of the Court of Appeals, and in Docket Nos. 96441, 96531, and 96532, we remand the case to the Washtenaw Circuit Court with directions that the action be dismissed for failure to state claims upon which relief may be granted. The clerk is directed to issue the judgment orders forthwith.

... [T]he filing of a motion for rehearing will not stay enforcement of the judgments.

We direct the Washtenaw Circuit Court to enter an order enforcing the custody orders entered by the Iowa courts. In consultation with counsel for the Schmidts and the DeBoers, the circuit court shall promptly establish a plan for the transfer of custody, with the parties directed to cooperate in the transfer with the goal of easing the child's transition into the Schmidt home. The circuit court shall monitor and enforce the transfer process, employing all necessary resources of the court, and shall notify the clerk of this Court 21 days following the release of this opinion of the arrangements for transfer of custody. The actual transfer shall take place within 10 days thereafter.

To a perhaps unprecedented degree among the matters that reach this Court, these cases have been litigated through fervent emotional appeals, with counsel and the adult parties pleading that their only interests are to do what is best for the child, who is herself blameless for this protracted litigation and the grief that it has caused. However, the clearly applicable legal principles require that the Iowa judgment be enforced and that the child be placed in the custody of her natural parents. It is now time for the adults to move beyond saying that their only concern is the welfare of the child and to put those words into action by assuring that the transfer of custody is accomplished promptly with minimum disruption of the life of the child.

TRAVEL OFFICE PROBE, CLINTON ON FOSTER SUICIDE

July 2, July 21, and August 10, 1993

After suffering a number of difficulties—the embarrassment of having two nominees for attorney general forced to withdraw their names and the defeat of the economic stimulus package—the Clinton administration confronted two more significant setbacks halfway into its first year. A White House report released July 2 faulted the president's staff for its handling of an internal investigation of the White House travel office, which resulted in the firing of seven employees, five of whom were subsequently reinstated in other comparable government positions.

Less than three weeks later, on July 20, deputy White House counsel Vincent Foster, Jr., committed suicide. Foster was a close friend of both the president and Hillary Rodham Clinton, who had been a partner with Foster in the influential Rose law firm in Little Rock. Foster had played a role in the travel office affair, which resulted in an official White House reprimand of William Kennedy III, Foster's deputy.

Background of Travel Office Probe

The White House Office of Telegraph and Travel handled millions of dollars from news organizations to arrange White House press trips, although its employees were paid by the federal government. The office also arranged commercial travel for staff of the Executive Office, the president and vice president, members of the cabinet, visiting dignitaries, and guests of the president and vice president.

Administration officials undertook the probe expecting to receive praise for revealing what they considered to be mismanagement, lavish lifestyles, and corruption in the office. But when the administration announced May 19 that it was firing all seven employees and replacing them with three political appointees, Republicans seized on the issue to accuse the Clinton officials of cronyism and called for a congressional investigation of the administration's own probe, which critics dubbed

"Travelgate." They were joined by civil liberties groups who criticized the White House use of FBI agents to conduct an inquiry and warned that the FBI should not be used for political purposes. In response, the administration announced that it had rescinded the firing of five of the travel office staff members, placing them on paid leave instead, and would conduct an internal review of administration officials' actions.

Report Findings

The White House internal review was sharply critical of the Clinton administration's handling of its investigation of the travel office. In particular, the report singled out Kennedy, who had contacted the FBI about undertaking a criminal investigation, and David Watkins, director of the Office of Administration, who launched the original review of travel office operations and recommended firing all seven long-time employees, after the nongovernment auditing firm of KPMG Peat Marwick had been called in to conduct a review.

The White House report recommended that five of the employees who were not managers be reinstated in government jobs. While not recommending any disciplinary action against administration officials, the report found that the White House "erred in its handling of the incident in several respects" by:

- *"Not treating the Travel Office employees with more sensitivity;*
- *Not being sufficiently vigilant in guarding against even the appearance of pressure on the FBI;*
- *Permitting people with personal interests in the outcome to be involved in evaluating the Travel Office;*
- *... [N]ot being sufficiently sensitive to the appearance of favoritism toward friends;*
- *Not engaging in the kind of deliberate, careful planning that the reorganization of an Office like this warrants and requires."*

The report reaffirmed previous government policy—that White House contacts alleging possible criminal behavior should be handled through the Justice Department instead of directly by the FBI.

Stating that the travel office failed to follow many routine business and accounting practices, the report held the director and assistant director responsible for financial mismanagement. The review also urged reorganization of the travel office and establishment of new accounting procedures.

Foster Suicide

Foster's death came as a shock to those who knew him well. Characterized by friends as handsome, extremely intelligent, healthy, and devoted to his family, Foster had spent the morning of his death in routine meetings and then had a sandwich at his desk. At about 1 p.m., he left his office and eventually drove across the Potomac River to a Civil War memorial at a national park in Virginia, where he shot himself. Tipped off by an anonymous caller, U.S. Park Police discovered the body at about 6 p.m.

In the days before his suicide, Foster had begun efforts to hire a private lawyer to advise him regarding the travel office incident. "He was concerned there might be a congressional inquiry and he might need an attorney," said Foster's brother-in-law, Beryl F. Anthony, Jr., a Washington lobbyist and former representative from Arkansas. Anthony said Foster also expressed concern that several editorials in the Wall Street Journal *that had been critical of him had "tarnished his reputation."*

White House counsel Bernard Nussbaum said in an interview that Foster was concerned that a congressional investigation might be "politically driven," but he added, "Vince was not concerned that he did anything wrong in connection with the travel office." However, Foster's uneasiness about the affair was demonstrated by a torn-up handwritten note that was discovered in his briefcase after his death and released by the Justice Department. In the note, Foster wrote, "I did not knowingly violate any law or standard of conduct." He also contended that the FBI had "lied" in its report to Attorney General Janet Reno on its contacts with the White House counsel's office regarding the travel office.

Park Police investigators said that when they arrived at the White House after the suicide, they were denied permission to enter and search Foster's office. They said that at least four White House aides had entered Foster's office after his body was discovered and before the office was officially sealed by the Secret Service the following day.

Calling the death of his friend of forty-two years "an immense personal loss to me and to Hillary," Clinton told reporters July 21 that he had encouraged his staff "to remember that we're all people and that we have to pay maybe a little more attention to our friends and our families ... and try to remember that work can never be the only thing in life." Characterizing Foster as "normally the Rock of Gibraltar while other people were having trouble," the president said he "certainly" did not believe that Foster had felt guilt or blame for things that went wrong in the White House during the first six months of the Clinton administration.

> *Following are excerpts from the White House internal management review of decisions and events surrounding the dismissal of seven employees from the White House Travel Office, released July 2, 1993; the text of President Clinton's July 21 remarks following the suicide of Deputy White House Counsel Vincent Foster, Jr.; and the text of a note written by Foster that was found in his briefcase July 26 and released by the Justice Department August 10:*

TRAVEL OFFICE REVIEW

Discussion of Principal Issues

Travel Office Management

The review conducted by KPMG Peat Marwick uncovered serious financial mismanagement. Peat Marwick's findings were serious enough to warrant disciplinary action—including severance of the two employees who exercised financial control—quite apart from whether any employee of the Travel Office had engaged in criminal wrongdoing (a question beyond the scope of this review).

The key findings of the Peat Marwick review ... are:

- *Unaccounted for funds*—In the 17-month period studied, Peat Marwick found seven checks written to cash totalling $18,000 for which there was no record in the petty cash book. On Friday, May 14, Peat Marwick also found a $5,000 check written October 9, 1992 of which only $2,000 was entered in the petty cash book. The next day, [Billy] Dale [Director of the Travel Office] informed Peat Marwick that he had located $2,800 of the missing funds—in an envelope in his credenza. Peat Marwick asked for documentation of the unaccounted for funds, but the employees were unable to provide it.
- *Lack of accountability*—According to Peat Marwick, there were no adequate financial controls: (i) "no formal financial reporting process;" (ii) "no reconciliations of financial information other than ... bank statements;" (iii) "no documented system of checks and balances on transactions and accounting decisions within the office;" (iv) "no apparent oversight ... of financial activities or transactions of the office."
- *Billing by estimate*—The press corps was billed according to Dale's estimates of what the costs of a trip would be. If his estimate turned out to be too high or too low, he would increase or decrease his estimate of the next trip's expenses commensurately. There were no clear written records of his reconciliation process.
- *Poor cash management system*—The Office lacked a working system for keeping track of accounts receivable. For example, there was no general ledger or cash receipts/disbursements journal. There were no aging reports, no reports of outstanding accounts receivable, no apparent rebilling when receivables had remained outstanding for a given period of time. There was no segregation of authority between those who could sign and those who could endorse checks.
- *Lack of documentation*—The documentation for bills submitted to the press corps was either inadequate or nonexistent.
- *Lack of contractual support*—There was no written contract between the Travel Office and the primary domestic charter company it used (UltrAir or Airline of the Americas).

Treatment of the Travel Office Employees

While all White House Office employees serve at the pleasure of the President, the abrupt manner of dismissal of the Travel Office employees was unnecessary and insensitive. Although the Peat Marwick financial review provided ample justification to remove those with control over the Office's finances, the removal need not have been so abrupt. All of the employees should have had an opportunity to hear the reasons for their termination, especially the allegations of wrongdoing, and should have been afforded an opportunity to respond.

Moreover, the Peat Marwick report did not furnish sufficient cause for terminating the employees without financial authority. As a legal matter, the White House has the right to terminate an employee without cause. In this case, however, the White House asserted that the termination of all seven was for cause. Based on the information available, this assertion was inappropriate with respect to the employees who did not exercise financial authority.

Absent cause, a more humane approach was in order. For example, even if it were decided that the Travel Office would operate more efficiently with a reorganized, smaller staff, an effort could have been made to locate other federal employment for those who would be displaced.

The White House did take appropriate corrective action on May 25 by extending indefinitely the paid administrative leave status of the five employees with no financial authority. The White House, after consultation with the five employees, will place them on an interim basis in appropriate jobs in the Executive Office of the President or other agencies. No final decision on their status can be made until any other inquiries now underway have been completed.

The other major White House mistake in the treatment of the former Travel Office employees was in tarnishing their reputations. This resulted, as discussed above, from the inappropriate disclosure of an FBI investigation into potential wrongdoing in the Travel Office.

Contacts with the FBI

The White House contacts with the FBI regarding the Travel Office raise four distinct issues: (i) whether the initial direct contact between the White House and the Bureau was improper; (ii) whether the White House pressured the FBI into undertaking an investigation or otherwise sought to influence FBI officials; (iii) whether the White House erred in disclosing the existence of an FBI investigation; and (iv) whether the White House pressured the FBI to issue or alter a press statement.

Initial contact

Following the . . . May 12 meeting in Vince Foster's office, White House Counsel's office was faced with allegations of potential criminal activity and would have been remiss in not pursuing the matter. William Kennedy, the Associate White House Counsel in charge of security, was designated to identify a course of action. Kennedy had previously been in contact with the FBI on matters of internal White House security. He decided to call the FBI for guidance.

There were no internal policies at the White House, the Department of Justice or the FBI proscribing direct contact from the White House on a matter of this kind. With respect to the separate issue of the White House contacting the FBI directly about a pending investigation, there is a strict policy in force that such contact would be improper without initial approval by both White House Counsel and a top level Justice Department official. This reflects longstanding policies at the White House, Justice Department and FBI, and was reiterated by White House Counsel Bernard Nussbaum in policy guidance issued February 22 and March 8. . . .

There is no evidence that the White House tried to push the FBI to say anything inaccurate or inappropriate. In effect, the Bureau simply revised its written response to comport with what FBI spokespeople were already telling reporters. . . .

The Appearance of Favoritism

The White House took several actions that demonstrated insensitivity to the appearance of favoritism.

Hiring World Wide Travel on a no-bid basis—even as an interim, stop-gap measure—created the appearance of favoritism toward a local friend from the campaign. World Wide's president, Betta Carney, is a long-time acquaintance of [David] Watkins [Assistant to the President for Management and Administration]. Watkins' Little Rock advertising agency was a client of World Wide in the 1970s and World Wide was a client of Watkins' agency during that time period.

None of this implies any improper conduct by World Wide, which is a well-established, successful travel agency, twenty-third largest in the country. World Wide executives understood that they could secure White House business only through an open, competitive bidding process. But the impression of favoring a local supporter was impossible to dispel.

Bringing in Penny Sample, President of Air Advantage, to handle press charters on a no-bid, volunteer basis furthered the appearance that the White House was trying to help its friends. Sample was the Clinton-Gore campaign's charter broker. . . . This implies no improper conduct on Sample's part, but, again, created an appearance of favoritism.

The apparent placement of [Catherine] Cornelius, a distant cousin of the President, in the Travel Office after the dismissals fed the impression of favoritism. In fact, Cornelius' relation to the President did not play any role in the Travel Office incident. Very few people even knew of the family relationship.

White House Management

The White House made a number of management mistakes in handling the Travel Office.

Lax Procedures.

The responsibility for [Harry] Thomason's influence on the Travel Office incident must be attributed to White House management. Thomason should have avoided continued involvement in a matter in which his business partner and his friends in the charter business stood to benefit and in which there was an appearance of financial conflict of interest. But lax procedures allowed his continued participation in the process.

Thomason was advising the White House on the staging of presidential events, for which he was well qualified. He was given a pass like a White House staffer, affording him open passage throughout the White House complex. No one objected when he began looking into the affairs of the Travel Office, which clearly extended beyond what he was originally asked to do.

There should be better management control with respect to the mission that any non-White House staff person is brought in to carry out. Permitting Thomason—or any nonstaff person who comes in on special assignment—to work on problems outside the scope of his or her assignment is not a good practice.

Placing Cornelius in Travel Office.

Given Cornelius' personal interest in running the Travel Office, Watkins should not have placed her in the Office to make recommendations on how the Office should be structured.

Watkins compounded the problem when, in response to Thomason's complaints, he asked Cornelius to be alert to possible wrongdoing or corruption. Cornelius lacked the experience or preparation for this role. Nor was she given any guidance.

If in April, Watkins thought the allegations reported by Thomason should be looked at more seriously, he should have done so in a more professional manner.

Poor Planning.

There was no adequate plan in place to manage the Travel Office in the aftermath of the dismissals.

For example, no one in the decision-making chain spoke to the White House press and press advance staff members who worked closely with the Travel Office employees, knew the employees there, understood the services they provided and the degree to which they were relied upon by members of the travelling press and other considerations. None was contacted by Watkins.

The absence of a plan prompted the last-minute use of World Wide Travel and Penny Sample of Air Advantage, which fueled the charges of favoritism already discussed.

Overview.

The management problems in the handling of the Travel Office extended beyond the White House Office of Management and Administration. The Chief of Staff and the White House Counsel's Office had the opportunity to contain the momentum of the incident, but did not take adequate advantage of this opportunity.

The process should have been handled in a more careful, deliberate fashion. Before any decision was made, the Travel Office employees should have been interviewed and other White House staff who understood the operations of the Travel Office should have been consulted. If dismissals were deemed appropriate, a new structure should have been designed and readied for implementation before any action was taken. Throughout, the process should have treated the Travel Office employees with sensitivity and decency.

CLINTON'S REMARKS

The President. Good afternoon. I have just met with the White House staff to basically talk with them a little bit about the death of my friend of 42 years, Vince Foster. It is an immense personal loss to me and to Hillary and to many of his close friends here and a great loss to the White House and to the country.

As I tried to explain, especially to the young people on the staff, there is really no way to know why these things happen, and it is very important that his life not be judged simply by how it ended, because Vince Foster was a wonderful man in every way and because no one can know why things like this happen.

I also encouraged the staff to remember that we're all people and that we have to pay maybe a little more attention to our friends and our families and our coworkers and try to remember that work can never be the only thing in life and a little humility in the face of this is very, very important.

I also pointed out that we have to go on. We have the country's business to do. I am keeping my schedule today except for the public events. I'm keeping all my appointments, and I expect to resume my normal schedule tomorrow. And then, of course, when the funeral is held, Hillary and I will go home and be a part of that. But otherwise, we will go on with our schedule and keep doing our work.

Q. Mr. President, do you have any idea why he might have taken his life. There's no indication—

The President. No. I really don't. And frankly, none of us do. His closest friends sat around discussing it last night at some length. None of us do. For more years than most of us would like to admit, in times of difficulty he was normally the Rock of Gibraltar while other people were having trouble. No one could ever remember the reverse being the case. So I don't know that we'll ever know. But for me, it's just important that that not be the only measure of his life. He did too much good as a father, as a husband, as a friend, as a lawyer, as a citizen. And we'll just have to live with something else we can't understand, I think.

Q. There's some feeling that he might have felt the guilt or blame for things that went wrong in the White House during the first 6 months.

The President. I don't think so. I certainly don't think that can explain it, and I certainly don't think it's accurate.

Thank you.

FOSTER'S NOTE

I made mistakes from ignorance, inexperience and overwork.

I did not knowingly violate any law or standard of conduct.

No one in the White House, to my knowledge, violated any law or standard of conduct, including any action in the travel office. There was no intent to benefit any individual or specific group.

The FBI lied in their report to the AG [Attorney General Janet Reno].

The press is covering up the illegal benefits they received from the travel staff.

The GOP has lied and misrepresented its knowledge and role and covered up a prior investigation.

The Ushers Office plotted to have excessive costs incurred, taking advantage of Kaki and HRC [Little Rock interior designer Kaki Hockersmith and Hillary Rodham Clinton].

The public will never believe the innocence of the Clintons and their loyal staff.

The WSJ *[Wall Street Journal]* editors lie without consequence.

I was not meant for the job or the spotlight of public life in Washington. Here ruining people is considered sport.

TOKYO ECONOMIC SUMMIT

July 7-9, 1993

Participating in the first international conference of his presidency, President Bill Clinton joined six other leaders of the world's largest industrial democracies July 7-9 at the nineteenth annual Group of Seven (G-7) economic summit meeting. Although expectations for the meeting, held in Tokyo, had been low, the summit was widely viewed as a success. The G-7 leaders were praised for taking a major step toward liberalizing multilateral trade. The breakthrough on trade promised to revive the stalled Uruguay Round of trade negotiations.

In another significant move, the Group of Seven leaders, after meeting with Russian President Boris N. Yeltsin, announced an expanded $3-billion assistance package for Russia. Increased from $2 billion and including aid to newly privatized enterprises, the package had been strongly urged on the other summit leaders by President Clinton. Although Russia was not a member of the G-7, Yeltsin had also been invited to the previous economic summit, held in Munich, Germany, July 6-8, 1992. (Historic Documents of 1992, p. 637)

Taking advantage of the Tokyo setting, Clinton and Prime Minister Kiichi Miyazawa of Japan engaged in bilateral talks separate from the G-7 meeting. An announcement July 10, 1993, said the two leaders had agreed on a "framework" for reducing long-festering trade tensions between their countries.

Throughout their Japanese stay, Clinton and senior administration officials sought to tie the meeting's accomplishments to jobs for American workers. In that vein, Treasury Secretary Lloyd Bentsen told reporters that Clinton had "succeeded in making this economic summit a job summit." The president himself pressed for an international conference on global unemployment. His plan was endorsed by the other six leaders, and the conference was to be held in the United States.

Expectations versus Performance

In addition to Clinton and Miyazawa, G-7 leaders at the economic summit were Chancellor Helmut Kohl of Germany, President François Mitterrand of France, Prime Minister Kim Campbell of Canada, Prime Minister John Major of Great Britain, and Premier Carlo Azeglio Ciampi of Italy.

In the days before the summit, a spate of articles in the U.S. press expressed low expectations for the Tokyo meeting. An article in the July 12, 1993, issue of Business Week, *for example, bore the headline, "Summit of the Damned: The Not-So-Magnificent G-7 Leaders Are Limping into Tokyo."*

The articles pointed out that Campbell and Ciampi had only recently assumed office and that the host, Miyazawa, headed a caretaker government. (Miyazawa would resign on July 22, 1993, when the Liberal Democratic party was denied a majority in the lower house of the Japanese Diet.) Then, too, the popularity of Major and other leaders was at a low ebb in political polls in their respective countries. In fact, Campbell would lose her seat in Canada's parliamentary elections in the fall.

But the predictions were far too pessimistic. Writing in the Baltimore Sun *July 11, Gilbert A. Lewthwaite said the G-7 leaders, "[w]hile far from deserving reclassification as the 'Magnificent Seven,' could claim significant progress on a number of fronts." And the July 19 issue of* Newsweek *said Clinton "impressed his hosts, set the G-7 on a new course, and gained global stature."*

Breakthrough on Trade

Early in the summit, trade negotiators took a major step toward ensuring that the Uruguay Round of trade talks could be completed by their December 15, 1993, deadline. The breakthrough came July 7, when negotiators agreed to eliminate nine products, ranging from pharmaceuticals to liquor. President Clinton seized on the agreement to praise it as "good news for the world." The Uruguay Round of world trade talks—named for the country where they began seven years earlier—were being conducted in Geneva, Switzerland, under the auspices of the General Agreement on Tariffs and Trade (GATT). GATT itself was a multilateral treaty that in 1947 established rules for trade among about one hundred nations. (Houston economic summit, Historic Documents of 1990, p. 471; Munich economic summit, Historic Documents of 1992, p. 637) *The Uruguay Round had been stalled by contentious issues such as agricultural subsidies.*

Following the agreement, Sir Leon Brittan, trade negotiator for the European Community (EC), told reporters that the prospects for a "global GATT deal" had been "greatly brightened." An editorial in the July 8 Washington Post *said the Clinton administration "did a lot" to get the trade process "moving again." But the editorial added that "credit is shared" by all the governments meeting in Tokyo.*

Aid to Russia

The enlarged package of Russian assistance offered Yeltsin included $500 million in grants and technical assistance to formerly state-owned, recently privatized factories and other large enterprises. Under Secretary of State Lawrence Summers said in Tokyo that privatization was "the thing that makes the process of reform [in Russia] irreversible." Early in his presidency, Clinton had called supporting reform in Russia his number one foreign policy priority.

Reporting from Tokyo in the Los Angeles Times *July 9, Jack Nelson quoted a senior U.S. official as saying that Yeltsin arrived at the 1993 summit "less as a supplicant and more as a leader who had proved himself up to the Gargantuan task that still lies ahead."*

U.S.-Japan Accord

The bilateral agreement reached by Clinton and Miyazawa was announced July 10, a day after the close of the G-7 summit meeting. Providing a framework for further talks, the accord included a promise by the Japanese government to make reductions in its $130 billion global trade surplus as well as a pledge by the U.S. government to reduce its budget deficit.

President Clinton said the agreement could lead to "more jobs and opportunities for America's workers and businesses and new choices and lower prices for Japanese consumers." However, Clinton also said, "We should have no illusions. We announce today a framework to govern specific agreements yet to be negotiated."

War in Bosnia

In a political declaration, the G-7 leaders described the situation in the former Yugoslavia as "rapidly deteriorating" and reaffirmed their commitment to Bosnia's territorial integrity. But their statement was seen as weaker than a somewhat similar one issued at the 1992 economic summit in Munich. (Historic Documents of 1992, p. 637) *The G-7 participants also called for a strengthening of United Nations peace-keeping operations in the former Yugoslavia.*

In their economic communiqué, the G-7 participants failed to endorse a U.S. proposal to set a target of 3 percent for economic growth in all the Group of Seven countries. Both Germany and Japan feared inflationary pressures that might result if their economies were stimulated.

Following are excerpts from President Clinton's July 9 news conference, his July 10 news conference with Boris Yeltsin, and his July 10 remarks with Japanese Prime Minister Kiichi Miyazawa:

CLINTON'S NEWS CONFERENCE

The President. Good evening. The summit we have concluded today sends a message of hope to America and to the world. Some have called this a jobs summit, and they are right because the creation of new jobs in the United States and in all the other countries here present was at the center of all of our discussions.

All of us are mindful that we have a long way to go to restore real growth and opportunity to the global economy, but we have made a serious start. We reached an agreement here that can open manufacturing markets to American products and to all other products in ways that we have not seen in many years. Indeed, the agreement if finally concluded could bring the largest reduction in tariffs in world history.

While tough negotiations still remain, this world trade agreement captures the momentum that we have needed in these negotiations for a long time. We now can move toward completion of a broader trade agreement that could spur the creation of hundreds of thousands of jobs over the next decade in the United States and millions throughout the world.

We also agreed that the other industrialized nations will send their top education, labor, and economic ministers to Washington in the fall for a serious conference on the creation of jobs. All the advanced nations are having difficulty creating new jobs even when their economies are growing. This was a constant cause of concern in all of our conversations, and we are now going to make a serious effort to examine the problem from every angle and to try to come up with new and innovative solutions which can be helpful in the United States and throughout the G-7 countries. We have to figure out how to unlock the doors for people who are left behind in this new global economy.

I want to say a special word of appreciation that the other industrial nations expressed their support and praise for the United States' economic plan to reduce our deficit dramatically and invest in our future.

Ever since 1980, whenever these meetings have occurred, the statements issued at the end have either explicitly or implicitly criticized the United States for our budget deficit. This statement explicitly supports the United States for our effort to bring the deficit down and to bring growth and investment back into our economy.

Other nations clearly welcome our resolve. I might note that the fact that both Houses of Congress have passed the economic plan greatly strengthen [*sic*] my hand in the discussions and the negotiations which have taken place here this week.

This summit also held out fresh hope for other peoples of the world, especially those involved in democratic reform in Russia, led by President Yeltsin who joined us here today. The $3 billion program we announced here to help Russia move to a market system will not only bolster prospects for freedom there, it is a very solid investment for the United States. Funds to move state-owned industries to private hands to make the free enterprise system work, funds to make available operations for new enterprises, funds from the World Bank, and funds for credits for export, all these things will help Americans to do more business in Russia and will help Russia to succeed in a way that will continue the path charted by the end of the cold war, fewer nuclear weapons, fewer defense investments, more opportunities to invest in people and jobs and a peaceful future.

American leadership has been indispensable to growth and to freedom throughout this century. In partnership with others, we will now be able to continue to meet that responsibility in the years ahead. I have said before and I will say again, I came to this summit in the hope that we could get an agreement to open more markets to manufactured products, in the hope that we could get a strong program for Russian aid, in the hope that together we would demonstrate resolve to restore the ability of all of our countries to create jobs and opportunities for our people. I believe those objectives were achieved. And I am pleased at the first of these G-7 meetings which I was able to attend.

Helen [Helen Thomas, United Press International].

Q. Mr. President, a host of Presidents have tried to convince Japan that trade is a two-way street. What makes you think you can convince them? What is the chance of getting an agreement on trade talks? And what did you learn at the summit that you didn't know before?

The President. You ask a lot of questions. What did you say? You have a followup? [*Laughter*] No, Brit [Brit Hume, ABC News], you get the followup.

I think we do have a chance to get an agreement, and I think in part it is because we are coming to a common understanding that the serious imbalance in trade between our two nations cannot continue and that, in the end, it is not in the interest of either country.

I met this morning with several hundred members of the American Chamber of Commerce here in Tokyo, people who are selling their products and services in this country. They pointed out and illustrated to me once again why more sales of American products in the Japanese market would be good for both countries. When these people come here, they hire Japanese people. They create jobs here in Japan. But as the market has opened up, the price of products and services and their variety is dramatically expanded—the price is driven down; the variety and number of services and products are expanded. So the Japanese people will win if we can correct this imbalance. And of course, the American people will win. It will mean lots more jobs for our folks.

That's what I tried to say at Waseda University. I think that we are now coming to a common understanding that it is in the interest of both countries to change this policy. I think we're also coming to a common understanding that we have to try some new approaches, that Americans have had real increases in productivity and quality—we are now the high-quality, low-cost producer of many products and services—and that that alone is not going to be sufficient to change the market imbalance. And I think those two realizations give us a shot. And I'm hoping that we can move forward.

What did I learn that I didn't know when I got here? I learned a lot more about the other world leaders. I got to know them all better. I got to understand more about where they're coming from, what their countries' problems and opportunities are, and what we can achieve together. I'm, frankly, more optimistic about our potential for common action than I was before I came here.

I also feel much better about our long-term capacity to make some progress in our relationships with Japan. I was glad to be the first American President ever to address a university audience and to answer questions there. And I feel much more positively about that relationship than I did when I came here. And it is, perhaps, our most bilateral relationship. So that's very good.

Q: Mr. President, Boris Yeltsin said today that sooner or later Russia would make the G-7 a G-8. My question is why not sooner than later? What are the arguments against keeping Russia out of the G-7?

The President. Well, I don't want to make the argument against keeping Russia out of the G-7. I do believe that you will see him here every time we meet as long as he is President of Russia, which I think will be quite a while. And I think that's a very good thing.

I think that when the G-7 was organized, it was organized as a group of the world's most powerful economic interests and not just political interests. And I think that there will come a time when Russia will probably join this group when there is a consensus that that time has come.

To be fair to all the people who are here, there was really no serious discussion of that. But for the first time, President Yeltsin was invited to come next year before he ever even made a statement. That was part of the Chairman, Prime Minister Miyazawa's opening statement, to make sure he would know that he was going to be invited to come and participate in next year's meeting in Italy.

Q. Mr. President, you mentioned that further negotiation must be done toward a new world trade agreement. One of the major sticking points for a number of years has, of course, been the issue of agriculture subsidies and agriculture generally. I wondered what, if anything, you may have heard here from your counterparts from Europe and the EC and from Japan that renews your hope, if it does, that such a thing may be possible by December, as you've suggested.

The President. Well, if all the Europeans will adhere to the Blair House accords, I think there's a good chance we can have an agricultural agreement.

As you know, France has some problems with it and has expressed those. And it was an issue in the last election in France. But as I pointed out, the

United States cut our agricultural subsidies unilaterally and substantially in 1990, and we have proposed further reductions this year as part of the deficit reduction package. If we were to reopen the Blair House accord, our farmers would want us to go in the opposite direction on these issues from the direction that some of the European interests would take.

Because the European Community is made up of diverse nations, they have a mechanism within the Community to make adjustments among the countries if they adhere to an agreement like an agricultural agreement that affects some countries more adversely than others. So I'm still hopeful that as these negotiations resume—and they will resume in Geneva soon—that the Blair House accord will stand and that we'll be able to work out a balance of trade agreements that will enable it to stand.

If that happens, then much of what we need to do in agriculture will have been done. This market opening agreement, if it can be embraced by the other nations at the GATT, will be nailed down, and then we'll just have a few issues left to go. I remind you the majority of the issues have been resolved although some of the tough ones remain.

Q. Mr. President, a week ago before leaving for Asia, you said that North Korea was perhaps the scariest place in the world. And many analysts including Larry Eagleburger have said that North Korea already has the bomb; others believe that it is at least very close to having the bomb. Would you consider a preemptive strike? Would you rule that out? And what message do you want to send in your trip to South Korea about our military interests in the region and about the role of our American troops?

The President. Well, first of all, I don't answer hypothetical questions, especially as they relate to national security, for obvious reasons. But the message should be clear. Even as we move into and through the 6th year of defense cuts, we are not reducing our base presence in Japan; we are not reducing our base presence in Korea. We are strengthening our military presence in Asia and in the Pacific, and we reaffirm our security commitments to Korea and to all our other allies in this region. And we intend to press to see that the Non-Proliferation Treaty's regime is fully observed, including having the international observers there.

That is the position that the United States takes. And I think we have to adhere to it very firmly.

Q. So what should we do about North Korea, sir?

The President. Well, we don't—North Korea has not yet declined to comply. And we're going to have to—let us continue the negotiations. Until there is a rupture that seems final, I don't think we should talk about what would happen at that point.

Q. Sir, before the summit started it was noted widely that your own approval ratings, as unhappy as you may sometimes be with them, were higher than those of any other political leader here. Virtually all of these people are either on the way out or in some great difficulty at home. How did that diminish this summit? And having been to one now and seen how bureaucratic they can be, do you really think in these days of modern communications that these sorts of extravaganzas are necessary at all?

The President. Well, first of all, I think that it did not diminish the summit. In fact, there was more done here and there was more energy and more zip in it than I thought there would be. And I think part of it was, apparently this summit is less bureaucratic than its predecessors. We ended two of our meetings an hour early, which I liked awful well. And there was an amazing amount of open, free flow of honest exchange. It was very, very good.

I think that any time you have the major economies of the world in the doldrums, combined in some of these countries with a real impetus toward political reform and a felt need of the people to make their political systems work better, you can't expect to see high poll numbers. When people are having a tough time making ends meet, they don't tend to be very happy with their political leaders. So that is a given.

Notwithstanding that, this summit produced real substantive benefits for the people who sent these leaders here.

Now, there was a reaffirmation, a unanimous reaffirmation on the part of the heads of state in this meeting to make this process less bureaucratic, less expensive, and less cumbersome. And I think you will see an even more streamlined summit next year in Italy, one in which all the delegations are smaller and in which there is more flexibility. I hope that something was learned out of this summit, that if you focus on one or two objectives and really work at it and work at it, you can get something done....

Q. Mr. President, if I could follow up for a moment on your answer to Susan's [Susan Spencer, CBS News] question, I wonder, given that these things tend to be very scripted and set out ahead of time, was there any moment in this thing, any event that happened over the last few days that told you something that you didn't know, that presented things—in a new light that might give us some insight into how this process works?

The President. Well, first of all, there were moments that were not at all scripted. The first time we met everybody went around the table and sort of described the condition of the economy in each country and what the government was attempting to do about it. And that was somewhat scripted in the sense that everyone was told in advance we'd be asked to do that. After that, only the topics were basically scripted. Very few of us carried a lot of notes around. Very few people referred to them. We really talked about these issues.

I think the thing that impressed me the most—maybe it's just because what I'm most concerned about—was the high level of rather sophisticated knowledge that all these people had about the stagnation of their own economies when it comes to creating jobs. For example, it was pointed out that the French economy was actually, by every other measure, very, very strong in most years of the eighties and several years had a higher growth rate than the German economy. And they still never got their unemployment rate below 9.5 percent, even when they were just really chugging along. The Japanese economy which still enjoys quite a low unemployment rate, in part because of the structure of this economy, still is having quite a lot of difficulty creating jobs.

Most of these countries have very low population growth rates, rapidly aging population, and they're very worried that unless they can turn this situation around that 10 years from now they're going to have two people working for every person that's retired. And they're really quite concerned about it. I think the fact that they're all thinking about it and they all had a little bit different take on it, gave me some hope that we might be able to find some solutions.

Q. Did anyone offer solutions?

The President. Well, there were lots of different solutions offered. But one of the things—Helmut Kohl is a very wise man, I think, and one of the things he said that was interesting was that if we could come to grips with this in the same way we try to come to grips with the trade problems, for example, that if there are tough decisions to be made, it will be easier for each country who makes them if the people who live in each country are aware that this is a worldwide problem and that there have to be some new and different directions taken.

Q. Mr. President, your wife, Hillary Rodham Clinton, has caused quite a stir in Japan, and yet she's followed a very traditional wives' schedule here which, frankly, doesn't seem much like her. I wonder if she's been muzzled here perhaps to avoid offending Japanese sensibilities.

The President. No, she did what she wanted to do. She thought about it quite a lot, and I've been, frankly, impressed and gratified by the response that she's gotten from just the people in the street, especially the young working women as well as the students at the university the other day. And I think it's a real indication of the aspirations of younger Japanese people to see that everybody here has a chance to live up to their potential. I was really very pleased by it.

Q. You return home in a few days. You're going to be facing kind of a do-or-die situation with the budget bill which got you so much play here. How do you relate your accomplishments from this week to what faces you when you get back next week?

The President. Well, it certainly ought to strengthen the resolve of the Congress to carry through on this. There's no question that the other countries were very much encouraged by the determination of the United States to reduce its deficit, that they believe that's one of the things that has distorted the world economy for the last several years.

And likewise, there is no question that some of our job growth we're going to have to do on our own. So a lot of these investments, both the private and the public investments in the economic plan, to create jobs should be adopted.

So I am hoping that what happened this week will strengthen the resolve of the Congress to go ahead and pass the economic plan and to do it in short order so that we can go on to other things. We all, after all, have a lot of other things to do. We have to get the health care cost controls in and provide basic health care security to American families. We have to continue to deal with the transformation from a defense to a domestic economy and try to help people accommodate all those changes. We've got an enormous amount of work to do. We've got a crime bill we need to pass. We've got a lot of other things on the agenda. So we've got to get this economic plan passed....

Q. Mr. President, we were told that you came to this summit with growing concerns about the condition of former Soviet nuclear power plants that are deteriorating. Will you broach this personally with Yeltsin tomorrow? Is there another Chernobyl out there? In other words, how imminent of a crisis is this, and what's the West going to do about it?

The President. Actually, we talked about it today at some great length. And there were two issues raised. The first is, President Yeltsin thanked the West for the assistance which has already been given to try to help them make those plants either safer or decommission them. What he called the first generation of their nuclear plants, they're actually trying to decommission them all, just take them out of commission so they won't run the risk of another Chernobyl. He said they had virtually completed that task. And he talked a little bit about his plans for energy and for nuclear power specifically. And I think the conversation was quite reassuring to the others who were there. I say to the others because I had talked about it a little bit with him before.

The second thing that came up, which I was very impressed by, raised by President Mitterrand, was the question of whether the Russian plans for decommissioning these plants, as well as technical assistance to do it ought to be made available to other Republics of the former Soviet Union who had similar plants, and he agreed to do that. He said that if other Republics that had these kind of nuclear plants wanted the plans and wanted the technical assistance, he would be very happy to do it. And the rest of us said we'd be glad to support that. So that was the resolution that I thought quite good.

Q. Do you have any concern that the jobs summit may turn to looking like it's a union bashing event in that a lot of the work rules that are established in Europe that a lot of people think caused the problems are, in fact, union related?

The President. They could, but there's a serious factual problem, if that's the total slant on it, which is the experience of Germany before the East was integrated into it. That is, if you split out East Germany from West Germany and you look just at the unemployment rate in West Germany for the last year or two, you'll see that's the only country in Europe with an unemployment rate as low as ours. Ours is too high. And their is too high, but theirs is much lower than all the other European countries. And yet they have very high costs in terms of mandatory vacations, in terms of mandatory worker retraining, in terms of general education investment in workers, in terms of mandatory health care coverage. Although their health care is much less expensive than ours, all employers have to undertake it.

So it's a hard case to make in the case of Germany where they have rather high labor costs and manufacturing wage costs, higher than the United States on average, terrifically productive workers, and they have managed to keep their unemployment fairly low. Now, their overall unemployment is higher because of the very high unemployment in East Germany.

So we're going to have to be a little more sophisticated than that. I mean, there are some things that may add to unemployment or may prohibit job creation and some that aren't.

Q. Mr. President, you said in your political communique that stronger measures could be taken against Serbia to end the war in Bosnia, but you didn't say what those measures were, nor under what conditions they might be taken. Given your inability to bring the Europeans along on your efforts before in the fighting there regarding air strikes and lifting the arms embargo, why should we think that action will now be taken as a result of your communique?

The President. The discussions that I had at this meeting about Bosnia were almost all, not all but almost all, one-on-one with other leaders. And frankly, I counseled against raising hopes unnecessarily and focusing more on what we might do and saying less until we were prepared to do something.

I will say this: The one new statement that is in this policy that I am absolutely convinced that all the leaders of the other countries meant, that should have some impact on the situation, was the one proposed by Chancellor Kohl which says that essentially if Serbia and Croatia carve up Bosnia in the absence of an international peace agreement to which the Bosnian Government freely subscribes, that the rest of us have no intention of doing any business with either of them if that happens.

That would have a very serious detrimental economic consequence on both Croatia and Serbia. And it had never been said exactly like that before, particularly as it relates to Croatia. So I think that is the new part of this statement.

Q. Mr. President, the last time an American President was in this city the Japanese Prime Minister said he pitied the United States. It was a remark you cited often in the campaign. In your talks with the Prime Minister did you detect any change in that attitude, or did you think there's still pity for the United States?

The President. I did detect a change. But I have to tell you, I have tried very hard to move this dialog into a constructive frame of mind. When I spoke at Waseda University, I acknowledged that one of the reasons that there was such a big trade deficit with Japan in the 1980's was that we had such a huge Government deficit, we needed a lot of Japanese money to pay for our debt, to keep our interest rates down.

In other words, I tried to go beyond the rhetoric and finger-pointing of both sides. I also pointed out, however, that we have now had 10 years of high manufacturing productivity growth, that we really are the high quality, low cost producer of many goods and services, and that we have to recognize we have to have a new relationship.

I think we should focus on things that are positive for both of us and be very, very firm about the need to change. But I don't sense a lot of ridicule here. And as a matter of fact, what I was hoping was that the Japanese would not be too concerned about all the changes going on in this country. A lot of the political changes are without precedent in the postwar era, post-World-War-II era. But they are the inevitable part of growing in a democracy and changing. And I sense a real sense of anticipation and openness here that's perhaps a little greater than it has been in past years and pretty uniformly throughout the people that I met and talked with.

I must say a special word of appreciation to our host, Prime Minister Miyazawa, who, even though his party is facing elections, as you know, in just a few days, displayed a great vigor and willingness to discuss a lot of these issues and to try to bring them to closure, and clearly had to sign off on the market access agreement and had to make some changes to do so in his government's position. Thank you very much.

CLINTON'S NEWS CONFERENCE WITH YELTSIN

President Clinton. Good morning. I want to make just a couple of brief remarks and let President Yeltsin make a couple of remarks, and then we'll take a few questions.

Since I last met with President Yeltsin in Vancouver, the Russian people have voted in an historic referendum to continue their march toward democracy and toward a free market economy. They've taken bold steps to create a new constitution.

We have now obligated over two-thirds of the funds that we promised to contribute to Russia's march toward democracy and free markets at Vancouver. We are delivering the promised humanitarian food shipments. We have provided substantial support for Russia's efforts to privatize state-owned industries. Loans to create new Russian businesses and jobs will soon be on the way through our Russian-American Enterprise Fund. And just this week, the United States Export-Import Bank signed a \$2 billion oil and gas framework that will help to revitalize Russia's energy sector and provide for expanded sales of American equipment and services.

As I have said to the American people from the very beginning, an investment in Russia's future is good for the American people as well as good for the Russian people.

I want to mention a special project in particular that Hillary has been involved with. She discovered that Mrs. Yeltsin has a special interest in improving the dental health care of Russia's children, and she was able to arrange the delivery of surplus American military equipment for two dental clinics in Moscow. I very much appreciate Mrs. Yeltsin's efforts in this regard.

I've also been working, as all of you know, with the congressional leadership and members of both parties to pass a second round of Russian aid through the Congress, as well as to eliminate obsolete cold war restrictions that still impede our trade, scientific, and cultural contracts with Russia. I expect those will be successful also.

We discussed a lot of issues here today, but the bottom line is we believe we have a good partnership. We think it is working in the interests of the people of Russia and the people of the United States. And we intend to keep it going.

Mr. President.

President Yeltsin. Thank you.

After the Vancouver meeting, President Clinton and I have established a relationship over months that have been replete with significant work. It was President Clinton's purpose to ensure that Congress adopt the package of agreements that we had set. I, for my part, had to win the referendum and also ensure that we prepare ourselves for the adoption of our new constitution. And I think both parties, the two Presidents, have resolved these matters.

And today we had an opportunity of checking up on time limits, what has been accomplished since the Vancouver meeting, what has been failed in a sense, and it's like answering to the test that you have to undergo at school. And I think that, in a sense, well, I think that we managed to clear about 25 questions together. And this, of course, concerned bilateral relations and also international matters, starting with the Asian and the Pacific region, the Middle East, and also general problems or world problems that we share in connection with the military.

Now, I'd like to say that I'm happy with our meeting here. And I think that our partnership and our friendship is strengthening day by day, and this is indeed the guarantee of further developments and progress. . . .

Q. Were you able to persuade Mr. Yeltsin to cancel the sale of Russian missile technology to India and Libya? Did you discuss that, and where does that stand now?

President Clinton. We discussed the outstanding differences of opinion, and we agreed to continue the negotiations intensely and immediately. And I think you may have some sort of answer at least on the ongoing status of the negotiations next week.

Q. How do you evaluate the level of Russian and American relations in terms of dealing with problems? Are they at the level of mutual understanding or shall we say there is certain interaction, and how far are we getting in the relations between the two countries?

President Clinton. Is that for me or for President Yeltsin?

Q. Both.

President Clinton. I think we have forged a remarkable partnership. We have worked together on any number of issues including this G-7 summit we just completed, including our efforts to avoid the problems that would be created if North Korea were to withdraw from the nonproliferation regime, and a whole range of other issues.

I think it has been a remarkable partnership. Are there differences between our two countries and between our positions? Of course there are. Can we resolve every issue? Of course we can't. We represent two great countries that are now very much more alike than they have ever been in their histories but still have some differences. But I think the peoples of our nations should feel very good about the level of cooperation that we have and the deep bonds of partnership that we have formed.

President Yeltsin. I'd like to say that we do have a very good partnership, and I think that we're developing relations and more than that. Earlier, we used not to discuss matters of local conflicts within the Community of Independent States. But this time we have touched on matters concerning Georgia, the situation in Georgia, and we've also covered the Baltic States and a number of other aspects and issues. So indeed, we have started tackling specific issues. And so we have brought the oppositions closer, and there is a lot that is in parallel, so to speak.

Q. This is a question for both Presidents. Ukraine has said that it wants to be a nuclear power, and it does not want to give up its weapons. What do you think of that?

President Clinton. Well, there are different voices in Ukraine. Ukraine is also committed to join the NPT and to ratify START I and to go on to START II. We have a lot of outstanding negotiations with Ukraine. We are now trying to negotiate a comprehensive agreement for the disposition of highly enriched uranium in Ukraine and Kazakhstan, as well as in Russia. There are lots of things that we have going on.

And I can only tell you for my part that I hope that there will be a nonnuclear Ukraine, that the commitments the Government has made will be kept. And I hope the United States can be engaged with Ukraine in a positive way so that they will feel that it is very much in their interests to do that. And I think President Yeltsin feels the same way.

President Yeltsin. Yes, indeed, I agree with you. And we've agreed today to supplying certain ideas so that the concept of a trilateral agreement for Ukraine—let's say, Ukraine, U.S.A., and Russia.

Q. I heard—[*inaudible*]—yesterday that some 300 legislative acts in the United States discriminatory towards Russia would be lifted within 2 years or so. What can you say on that, and how soon Russia is going to get the most favorable nation status? Thank you.

President Clinton. First of all, I think that many of those acts discriminatory against Russia that date back to the cold war period will be removed from the books of Congress in this year. We have compiled quite a long list of them that we think cannot be justified anymore. And there is a strong base of support in both political parties in the United States Congress to remove those laws. So we will, as soon as I go home, we will begin to put in motion the process of removing many of those statutes.

As to the second question you mentioned, we are working also on the possibility of the graduation out of the Jackson-Vanik restrictions for Russia. And the President and I discussed a couple of items outstanding on that. And we made an agreement about how we would proceed with them. And I think if we can resolve them, you will see that moving forward as well.

Thank you very much.

Q. Are you going to have a meeting in Moscow?

President Clinton. It's possible. I hope so. We didn't set a definite date, but I accepted President Yeltsin's invitation.

Q. This year?

President Clinton. I hope it will be this year. That depends on what we do at home, you know. But I hope so.

CLINTON'S REMARKS WITH MIYAZAWA

Prime Minister Miyazawa. President Clinton and I were able to agree upon the establishment of the Japan-U.S. framework for a new economic partnership. This agreement comes at a time to coincide with the Tokyo summit, which symbolizes the cooperation and coordination between the G-7 partners in the international society in the post-cold-war era.

This framework is something that President Clinton and I agreed to establish in our bilateral summit meeting held in last April. President Clinton and I share the views that establishing such a new framework and stabilizing Japan-U.S. economic relations from the medium- to long-term perspective and managing our bilateral economic relationship constructively are extremely important not only to the enhancement of the national life of our two countries but also to the maintenance and strengthening of the free trading system of the world.

The negotiating teams of our two countries, based on those perspectives, the negotiating teams of both countries made serious negotiations both in Washington and Tokyo. And they made further negotiations on the occasion of President Clinton's visit, and subsequently, they have succeeded in reaching an agreement.

Let me share with you the gist of this framework in a few words. This framework aims at facilitating frank and broad exchange of views between our two countries, and aims at resolving the economic issues between our two countries based on the spirit of joint exercise between the two largest free market economies that are the United States and Japan, and also aims at advancing our cooperation on issues such as environment and technology which have significance. More concretely, under this framework we will operate on the principles of two-way dialog and limiting our consultations to matters within the scope and responsibility of government.

Under those principles, we will deal with the following: to Japan's efforts at reducing the current account surplus and the reduction of the American Federal budget deficit, in the macroeconomic area. In sectoral and structural area we will deal with government procurement and deregulation, et cetera. And on our common task for cooperation on global perspective, we will deal with issues such as environment and technology. And we will announce the achievements regarding these issues at our biannual bilateral summit meeting.

Furthermore, let me share with you that Japan intends to take measures on its own initiative to further expand its market access, to enhance its transparency, and promote deregulation, all along with our objective to achieve better quality of life. And I expect and hope that in the United States as well the U.S. Government will make progress in reducing the Federal budget deficit and in strengthening international competitiveness.

Through the efforts of our two governments, we would like to contribute to the strengthening of Japan-U.S. economic relations and also to contribute to the development of world economy in the future. Thank you, Mr. Clinton.

The President. Thank you. Thank you very much. Today's agreement is an important step toward a more balanced trade relationship between the United States and Japan, but it also benefits the world trading system.

For years we have had trade agreements that have failed to reduce our chronic trade deficits. Those agreements have not worked because they lacked a commitment to tangible results and they provided no way to measure success. This has caused resentment to build over time on both sides, threatening our vital friendship.

This framework agreement we are announcing today takes a different approach. As I said in my speech at Waseda University earlier this week, we are not interested in managed trade or trade by numbers but better results from better rules of trade. This framework launches us on that road.

As the Prime Minister said, we will negotiate a series of agreements under this framework, some to be completed within 6 months, the rest within a year, that will allow greater penetration of the Japanese marketplace in specific areas of the economy. And these new agreements will include specific timetables and objective criteria for measuring success. These results-oriented agreements can create bigger markets for key U.S. industries, including the automotive industry, computers, telecommunications, satellites, medical equipment, financial service, and insurance. If we are successful, we will create benefits for citizens in both the United States and Japan: more jobs and opportunities for America's workers and businesses, new choices and lower prices for Japanese consumers, and new jobs for Japanese citizens in business establishments located in Japan but owned by citizens of other countries.

Again, as the Prime Minister said, this framework also includes a basic bargain. We agree that the United States will significantly cut our budget deficit, which has clearly slowed the growth of the global economy. And we will continue our efforts to improve our competitive position, to be the high-quality, low-cost producer of more and more goods and services. In return, the Japanese agree to what the agree[ment] quotes as highly significant reductions in their trade surplus and increases in their imports of goods and services from the United States and other countries. In other words, both nations have made some tough choices.

We should have no illusions. We announced today a framework to govern specific agreements yet to be negotiated. Negotiating those agreements will surely be difficult. But now, at least, we have agreed what the outcome of these negotiations needs to be: tangible, measurable progress.

I have said for some time that the United States and Japan, the two largest economies of the world, must strengthen our friendship. Our political relationship is strong; our security relationship is firm. These trading disputes have been corrosive, and both of us are called upon to change. It is essential that we put this relationship on a footing of mutual respect and mutual responsibility. This framework is a good beginning.

As the Prime Minister said, many people worked very hard on these negotiations. And before I conclude my statement, I would like to express appreciation to people on both sides. I want to thank on the American side Mr. Bo Cutter, who was our lead negotiator and is the Deputy Director of the National Economic Council; Charlene Barshefsky, the Deputy U.S. Trade Representative; Roger Altman, the Deputy Secretary of the Treasury; and Joan Spero, the Under Secretary of State. They did an excellent job. They worked many long hours with their Japanese counterparts. I also want to thank the Japanese negotiating team, and I want to say a special word of appreciation to Prime Minister Miyazawa for his leadership here at the G-7 summit and his constant attention to these bilateral negotiations while they were going on. He has shown wisdom, determination, and genuine leadership.

Perhaps only I and a few others know how difficult these negotiations have been, how many late night discussions have been involved, how hard so many people have tried for our two countries to reach across the divide that has separated us on this issue. I do not believe that this day would have come to pass had it not been for Prime Minister Miyazawa, and I thank him in a very heartfelt way. I think he has done a great service today for the people of Japan, the people of the United States, and for the principle of a free world economy.

AMNESTY INTERNATIONAL REPORT ON HUMAN RIGHTS

July 8, 1993

Amnesty International charged in its annual report, released July 8, that 1992 was a year of "appalling human rights catastrophes" not only in the former Yugoslavia and Somalia but in dozens of other countries. Amnesty International surveyed 161 countries and determined that 110 still abuse human rights.

The carnage "was on a terrifying scale, with thousands of men, women and children tortured, killed or unaccounted for," the report said. Based on its investigations, Amnesty International charged that "scores of governments" let their police and soldiers "get away with beating, inflicting electric shocks or raping prisoners just to humiliate them or force them to sign false confessions." In addition the investigators reported gruesome torture that sometimes led to death and the disappearance of thousands of people who were "brutally murdered at the hands of security forces or government-linked 'death squads'—all because governments wanted to stamp out their opposition for good."

In all, Amnesty International charged that at least 45 governments were guilty of political killings involving state security forces or death squads. Prisoners were tortured or ill-treated in prisons, police stations, or secret detention centers in 110 countries. More than 500 prisoners in 48 countries died as a result of their mistreatment; 1,500 political prisoners were jailed without fair trial in 30 states; and another 950 people "disappeared" through abductions or unacknowledged detention in 27 countries.

"Horrifying Levels" of Abuse

The organization specifically cited Chad, China, Iraq, Liberia, Peru, and Sri Lanka as countries where human rights violations and abuses "continued at horrifying levels."

In Chad, for example, the report charged that several hundred people were executed without any legal proceedings in various parts of the country. "Some of those killed . . . were apparently executed because they refused to hand over their property to soldiers." In another incident, several dozen civilians were reported to have been executed because they failed to disclose the whereabouts of rebels loyal to the former vice president, Maldom Bada Abbas.

Among the atrocities in Peru were the deaths of at least nineteen university students in the city of Huancayo and the disappearance of another seven. All had allegedly been detained by security forces in or near the city. The attorney general appointed an ad hoc prosecutor to investigate the cases, but at year's end there was no resolution of the matter.

In China, according to the report, the death penalty continued to be used extensively: 1,891 death sentences were recorded and 1,079 executions took place. But the report said the true figures were believed to be much higher. The organization asserted that China and Iran accounted for 82 percent of all known executions.

The United States and countries in western Europe did not escape scrutiny. In the United States the report noted that thirty-one prisoners were executed in 1992, more than in any one year since excecutions resumed in 1977. (Amnesty International opposes the death penalty.) "Many of the executed prisoners had received inadequate legal representation at their trials," the report charged, because court-appointed lawyers had failed to present crucial mitigating evidence that could have prevented imposition of the death penalty.

Curt Goering, Amnesty International's acting director, noted in an interview with the Los Angeles Times *that Europe's record on human rights was deteriorating. "In the east, new democracies have been shown not to guarantee or protect fundamental human rights despite what these countries had earlier been through," he said. And in the West, racism and intolerance rose sharply in established democracies, evident in the attacks on foreigners in several countries, particularly Germany.*

The organization also contended that there were "glaring examples of double standards being applied" on human rights. For example, by the end of 1992 there still had been no serious attempt to address widespread torture, executions, or detentions in China. In South Africa, pressure to stop human rights violations eased when the political reform process began, even though black South Africans were "still being tortured in police cells and massacred in their townships."

World Community Fails

Amnesty International was unsparing in its criticism of the world community's response to the problems, contending that "politically motivated selectivity has continued to be the norm . . . and international treaty obligations have been cyncially ignored when convenient. In short," the report charged, "the response by governments to human rights crises in other countries has been marked by a conspicuous lack of political integrity."

What was strikingly apparent in 1992, the report said, was "the cumulative failure of nations to make the protection of human rights a genuine priority of government at home or abroad." When the international community remains silent, the report went on, "it provides a shield behind which governments believe they can order the secret police, the torturers and state assassins into action with impunity."

To help improve conditions, Amnesty International called on governments to provide better training for their police and military forces, diplomats, and other public servants. The group also said governments must make sure their citizens know about basic human rights and how to complain if those rights are violated. When violations occur, those involved should be subject to independent investigation "and brought to justice."

The goals may seem "unrealistic in the present world climate," but the report concluded that "we believe that if people around the world force their governments to take up these challenges, human rights can be defended honestly, vigorously and successfully."

> *Following are excerpts from Amnesty International's* Report 1993, *released July 8, 1993, and detailing human rights achievements and violations for 1992:*

Bosnia-Herzegovina

Ethnic tensions increased in Bosnia-Herzegovina with the break-up of the Socialist Federal Republic of Yugoslavia following declarations of independence by the Republics of Slovenia and Croatia in June 1991, and subsequent armed conflict, largely on Croatian territory. Bosnia-Herzegovina's Serbian communities sought to remain within a Yugoslav federation while its Muslim and Croatian communities demanded independence. At the beginning of March open conflict flared up when a referendum, supported by Muslim and Croatian communities but largely boycotted by Serbian communities, favoured independence for the republic. By mid-March serious fighting had broken out. On 7 April the European Community (EC) and the United States of America recognized Bosnia-Herzegovina's independence. The same day, Serbian political leaders proclaimed the independence of "the Serbian Republic of Bosnia-Herzegovina" (areas of the republic under Serbian control). Fighting spread rapidly throughout Bosnia-Herzegovina. In April the Republic of Bosnia-Herzegovina was accepted as a participatory state in the Conference on Security and Co-operation in Europe and in May it became a member of the United Nations (UN).

Numerous members of the Yugoslav National Army (JNA) of Bosnian origin, as well as JNA supplies and arms, remained in the republic after the official withdrawal of the JNA in May. By December, together with mobilized local Serbian reservists and Serbian irregulars, they had occupied some 70 per cent of the republic's territory. Local Croatian forces, aided by forces of the Croatian Army and Croatian irregulars from the Republic of Croatia, established control over much of Herzegovina, proclaimed as the "Croatian Community of Herceg-Bosna". This led to sporadic clashes with Bosnian government forces, although the two were supposedly allied. The area of the republic over which the Bosnian Government had effective control declined throughout the year.

Vast numbers of civilians fled their local communities to escape the conflict; many were deliberately intimidated by their opponents into leaving. This was particularly evident in areas under Serbian control, where many Muslims and Croats were rounded up and forcibly expelled. The scale of human rights abuses and the obstacles to collecting evidence made it difficult to substantiate allegations of atrocities. The difficulty was compounded by media reports in which all sides sought to minimize abuses committed by their own forces and maximize those of their opponents. While all parties to the conflict committed abuses, it was clear that the Serbian side was responsible for the majority of atrocities committed and that Muslims were the chief victims. In August the UN Commission on Human Rights appointed a Special Rapporteur to investigate the human rights situation in former Yugoslavia, and in particular in Bosnia-Herzegovina. At the end of August a joint UN-EC International Conference on the former Yugoslavia was established, which tried to achieve a cessation of hostilities in Bosnia-Herzegovina and to bring the parties together to negotiate a new constitutional arrangement for the country. In October the UN Security Council set up a Commission of Experts to investigate war crimes committed in former Yugoslavia.

There were many reported incidents in which civilians and unarmed or wounded combatants were deliberately and arbitrarily killed. The Yugoslav news agency Tanjug reported that 15 members of five Serb families had been massacred by Croatian troops on the night of 26 to 27 March in the village of Sijekovac near Bosanski Brod. A Muslim fighting with Croatian forces who claimed to have taken part in this massacre and others described in a statement video-recorded while he was held prisoner in Yugoslavia how he and other soldiers had killed over 30 elderly villagers in their homes and had abducted and raped young women.

On 16 May at least 83 Muslims, including men, women and children, were massacred in the village of Zaklopaca, near Vlasenica. According to eye-witnesses, the massacre was carried out by local uniformed Serbs who had previously surrounded the village. Some surviving eye-witnesses believed that as many as 105 people were killed.

In the town of Mostar on 13 June, according to the account of a surviving witness (a Muslim), Serbian forces rounded up some 150 people in his neighbourhood. After separating out the women, children and Serbs, they took the remaining men to the morgue at Sutina cemetery. While the witness was waiting to be questioned, he heard bursts of gunfire. After interrogation he and another prisoner were forced to carry the corpses of seven or eight men to a rubbish dump near the banks of the river Neretva. Their captors then fired on his companion; he himself escaped by throwing himself down an embankment. In August the police chief of the town of Mostar announced that 150 bodies had been found in mass graves, one of them in the Sutina quarter of town; a pathologist stated they had almost all been killed at close range....

Released Muslim prisoners stated that Serbs had deliberately and arbitrarily killed large numbers of prisoners, including civilians, detained in camps in Bosnia-Herzegovina. Not all these reports could be confirmed, but accounts from many former detainees agreed that in June and July prisoners were killed almost every night in Omarska camp. Many died after being clubbed to death by guards or by local Serbs who entered the camp at night. According to these accounts, on some nights as many as 30 men were killed. Detainees were also reportedly killed in other camps, including Keraterm, Manjaca and Trnopolje. There were also allegations that Serbian prisoners had been killed by their captors. Serbian sources alleged that at least five men held by Bosnian government forces in a place of detention near Konjic died as a result of beatings between mid-June and late July.

Thousands of non-combatants, the majority Muslims, were arbitrarily detained in connection with the conflict, in most cases solely because of their ethnic origin, sometimes as hostages for exchange. In May all parties agreed to give the International Committee of the Red Cross (ICRC) access to detention centres, but there continued to be unacknowledged places of detention, ranging from cellars in private houses to factories and school-halls. From September onwards considerable numbers of detainees were released, mostly under the supervision of the ICRC. Arbitrary detention was sometimes accompanied by forced expulsion, particularly in areas under Serbian control. For example, on 26 June local Serbs and irregulars from Serbia detained Muslim families in the village of Kozluk and forced them at gunpoint to board a convoy of lorries which took them to Loznica in Serbia. From there they were taken by train to the Hungarian border, where Serbian police issued them with passports before they crossed into Hungary.

Many detainees were tortured or ill-treated in detention centres, and conditions often amounted to cruel, inhuman or degrading treatment. In June large numbers of Muslim and Croat civilian men were detained by Serbian forces in the area of Bosanski Novi; witnesses believed that prominent and better-educated members of the local community had been targeted for detention and interrogation. Villagers from Blagaj were rounded up and transported en masse: women, children and men over 60 were subsequently expelled into Muslim controlled territory. Several hundred men were held in a football stadium at Mlakve, and individuals were held in Bosanski Novi town, in places such as the police station and a hotel. All witnesses reported that detainees were routinely beaten with truncheons and rifle butts. Former detainees often reported that prisoners were not only beaten, but were also deliberately humiliated and degraded in other ways. For example, prisoners detained by Serbian forces in Keraterm, a ceramics factory near Prijedor, in June and July, alleged that men were forced to perform sexual acts with each other. Almost all accounts indicated that prisoners were severely underfed in camps, and that in some cases, for instance at Omarska, Manjaca and Trnopolje, this amounted to near-starvation. Serbs held by Muslim forces similarly reported that they were subjected to regular beatings and other cruel, inhuman or degrading treatment. Among them was Milan Sobic, a Serbian journalist, who in July was reportedly severely beaten by Muslim irregulars and military police in Zenica. The available evidence indicated that all sides to the conflict raped female prisoners, including young girls, and in some cases kept selected women prisoners in conditions amounting to brothels for the use of the military and police, but the majority of victims were Muslim women held by local Serbian armed forces....

China

The police and security forces continued to exercise extensive powers of arbitrary arrest and detention. Political dissidents and others were detained for prolonged periods without trial or sentenced to lengthy terms of imprisonment for "crimes of counter-revolution". There was still no public inquiry into the killings of over 1,000 civilians by government forces in Beijing during the 1989 pro-democracy protests.

In August the government issued a "white paper" entitled *The Reform of Criminal Offenders in China,* but this failed to acknowledge or take into account the frequency of human rights violations in Chinese prisons and the need for urgent measures to remedy such violations. In September another government "white paper", *Tibet—Its Ownership and Human Rights Situation,* made clear that activities considered to be detrimental to "stability and unity" in Tibet—such as peaceful political demonstrations—would be "cracked down on relentlessly".

Hundreds of prisoners of conscience arrested in connection with the 1989 pro-democracy protests remained in prison; the fate of thousands of others remained unknown.... Many prisoners of conscience were serving prison sentences imposed after unfair trials; others were held without charge or trial.

Arrests of people suspected of involvement in political activities continued during the year. In June several dozen people were arrested in Beijing and elsewhere during a crackdown on pro-democracy activists. They included Chen Wei, a former student, and Wang Guoqi, a printer, both of whom had been arrested three times since 1989. Also detained were at least six members of the China Progressive Alliance, a newly formed non-violent political organization. The same month Wang Wanxin was arrested in Tiananmen Square, Beijing, for unfurling a banner commemorating the massacre of 4 June 1989. In July it was reported that he had been confined to a mental hospital and forcibly given drugs. Several other political activists were arrested in September. Two of them were released without charge a few weeks later, but the others were believed to be still detained at the end of the year.

Hundreds of people were arrested because of their religious activities or for their membership of ethnic or other groups. Some were released but others remained in detention without charge or trial. Early in the year at least 30 members of the "New Birth" Christian Church were arrested in Henan, Shanxi and Liaoning provinces: 20 of them were later sentenced administratively to three years' detention, known as "re-education through labour". In the same period some 160 other Christians were arrested in Henan, Jiangsu and Shanxi provinces. In September a further 160 Christians were reportedly arrested in Henan Province. In January it was reported that Pei Ronggui, a Trappist priest from Hebei Province, had been sentenced to five years' imprisonment: he was arrested in 1990 while administering the last rites to a dying man.

The same month Zhang Weiming, a Catholic intellectual from Baoding, Hebei Province, was sentenced administratively to two years of "re-education through labour" because of his religious activities. He had been held incommunicado in Baoding for over a year following his arrest in December 1990. He was moved to a labour camp in Shijiazhuang after being sentenced and released in November.

Some 60 Roman Catholic clergy and lay members remained held, including 76-year-old Bishop Yang Libo. However, several others were released. James Xie Shiguang, the 74-year-old bishop of Xiapu in Fujian Province, and two priests from Fujian who were arrested in July 1990 during a religious meeting, were freed in January. Among others reported released were Li Side, Roman Catholic bishop of Tianjin, and Liu Guangdong, bishop of Yixian in Hebei Province. All belong to the "underground" church which remains loyal to the Vatican.

Members of ethnic groups in the Autonomous Regions of Inner Mongolia and Xinjiang were arrested and accused of instigating "separatist activities". Others arrested in previous years remained in prison. In Inner Mongolia, those still held, apparently without charge or trial, included Huchin Togos, a teacher, and Wang Manglai, a linguist, both of whom had been arrested in May 1991 for founding two cultural organizations. In Xinjiang several political activists were reportedly detained in and around Kashgar at the beginning of the year. Scores of others who had been arrested in 1991 or before remained in prison throughout 1992. Kajikhumar Shabdan, a 62-year-old ethnic Kazakh writer and poet, was believed to be still serving a sentence of 12 years imprisonment. He was reported to have been arrested in 1988 with about 10 other people following peaceful demonstrations in Tacheng, northern Xinjiang. He had previously been arrested in 1958 and jailed for 18 years for allegedly "opposing socialism".

Arrests of Tibetan political activists continued. Over 200 political prisoners, including at least 100 prisoners of conscience, remained held in Tibet. They included Buddhist monks and nuns detained for peacefully advocating Tibetan independence, and lay Tibetans allegedly found in possession of Tibetan nationalist material. Some were serving prison terms imposed after unfair trials, others terms of "re-education through labour" imposed without formal charge or trial. Among the latter was Dawa Kyizom, a student, who was serving a three-year term imposed in October 1990 after she reportedly gave a Tibetan flag to a monk....

Trials continued to fall far short of international standards for fairness. Minimum standards for fair trial are not provided for in Chinese law, such as the right to have adequate time and facilities to prepare a defence, the right to be presumed innocent until proven guilty, and the right to call defence witnesses. In practice, the verdict and sentence are often decided by the authorities before trial. Other major obstacles to fair trial include extreme limitations on the role of defence lawyers and the use of torture to extract "confessions".

Prisoner of conscience Qi Lin, a journalist with the *Beijing Daily* newspaper, was tried in secret in Beijing and sentenced in April to four years' imprisonment on charges of "leaking state secrets". He was accused of telling a Taiwanese newspaper about political sanctions imposed on a member of China's National People's Congress. Qi Lin is diabetic and his health seriously deteriorated in prison. He was released on bail on medical grounds in June but his sentence remained in force....

Torture and ill-treatment of prisoners were common. The methods most frequently cited were severe beatings, shocks with electric batons and the use of shackles. Deprivation of sleep or food, exposure to extremes of cold or heat, and being forced to adopt exhausting postures were also reported to be common during interrogation....

Political prisoners in Lingyuan No. 2 Labour Reform Camp in Liaoning Province were repeatedly beaten and given electric shocks with high-voltage batons. As a result, several reportedly needed hospital treatment. However, despite international appeals on behalf of the victims, no investigation was known to have been initiated by the authorities and allegations of torture continued to be received. The victims included Liu Gang, who had been a student leader in Beijing during the 1989 protests.

Political prisoners reportedly tortured in Hunan Province included Yu Dongyue, Yu Zhijian and Lu Decheng, who were sentenced in 1989 to long prison terms after being convicted of defacing a portrait of Mao Zedong and distributing political leaflets. By early 1992 they had been held continuously in solitary confinement in extremely harsh conditions for more than two years in Hunan Provincial No. 3 Prison in Lingling....

Torture and ill-treatment of prisoners also reportedly continued in Tibet. Tane Jigme Sangpo, a primary teacher detained since 1983, and three others remained in solitary confinement: they had been put in solitary confinement in December 1991 after one of them shouted slogans supporting Tibetan independence. There were fears for the health of Tane Jigme Sangpo, who had spent a total of 25 years in prison since 1960. Information was received that Laba Dunzhu, a Tibetan political detainee, had died at the People's Hospital in Lhasa in November 1991 after being transferred there from Gutsa Detention Centre. He had been arrested in 1989 and was reportedly tortured in detention, suffering a ruptured spleen and other injuries.

Han Dongfang, a former prisoner of conscience and a prominent labour activist during the 1989 protests, was reportedly beaten, kicked and stunned with electric batons by court officials in May when he appeared before the Dongcheng District People's Court in Beijing on a matter related to his housing.

During the year the authorities revealed that 407 cases of "torture to extract confessions" had been investigated and prosecuted by the procuracy in 1991—a figure believed to represent only a fraction of actual cases.

Prison conditions were often harsh and many prisoners were reported to have fallen ill as a result. Prisoners faced prolonged periods in solitary confinement as punishment, often resulting in physical or psychological disorders. Medical care was frequently inadequate. Ren Wanding, a prisoner of conscience held in Beijing since 1989, was reported to be in danger of losing his sight and to have numerous other health problems. Li Guiren, an editor from Xi'an in Shaanxi Province held since 1989, became severely ill in prison in late 1991 but was still reportedly being denied adequate medical care in July. Several hunger-strikes were held by prisoners to protest against prison conditions, including one begun in August in Yang Qing Prison by Wang Juntao, a writer and political activist who had been sentenced to 13 years' imprisonment in 1991 for his involvement in the 1989 protests. . . .

The dramatic increase in the use of the death penalty which began in 1990 . . . continued, particularly during an anti-drug campaign in the first half of the year. At least 1,891 death sentences and 1,079 executions were recorded by Amnesty International, but the actual figures were believed to be far higher. Many of those executed were tried under legislation which allows for summary procedures. . . .

Iraq

. . . In December Iraq's Revolutionary Command Council issued a decree which forbids the arrest, interrogation and bringing to justice of law enforcement officials who kill or injure criminal suspects, security offenders or army deserters in the course of their duty. It was feared that the decree would give officials a free hand to adopt a "shoot-to-kill" policy against both criminal suspects and political opponents.

Kurdish opposition groups retained control of parts of the northern provinces of Duhok, Arbil, Sulaimaniya and Kirkuk following the withdrawal of Iraqi government forces and the imposition of an economic blockade by the Iraqi Government in October 1991. In January the Iraqi

Kurdistan Front (IKF), representing all the main Kurdish opposition groups, suspended negotiations with the government about greater autonomy for Kurds in Iraq. In May elections were held under the auspices of the IKF to elect a 105-member Kurdistan National Assembly for a three-year term, replacing the former (government-created) Legislative Assembly of the Autonomous Region of Kurdistan. The Patriotic Union of Kurdistan (PUK) and the Kurdistan Democratic Party (KDP) each received 50 seats, with five seats allocated to two Christian parties. In July a Council of Ministers for Iraqi Kurdistan was formed, which effectively administered IKF-held territory.

In March the IKF established a Special Court of the Revolution, which replaced the Revolutionary Court set up by the IKF in 1991. Both courts applied existing Iraqi legislation, namely the Penal Code and the Code of Criminal Procedure, but their proceedings fell far short of international standards and their decisions were not subject to appeal. In November the Kurdistan National Assembly abolished the Special Court and in December a Court of Cassation was set up, to sit in Arbil. In October and November the death penalty was introduced for two offences: premeditated murder of foreigners and using explosives to carry out acts of sabotage against the Kurdish people.

Several thousand Arab Shi'a Muslims were arrested by Iraqi government forces in southern Iraq. Most arrests were said to have begun after the imposition of the "air exclusion zone" in August and to have continued into December. Those detained were largely non-combatant civilians, including whole families, taken from their homes and public places and transferred to unknown destinations. In October random and widespread arrests of unarmed civilians were carried out in al-'Amara by the army and security forces as part of the officially-named "punitive campaign". Most were held at the 4th Army Corps' headquarters in al-'Amara city; many of them were reportedly held for short periods and tortured, and in some cases released only after making cash payments. Others were reported to have "disappeared" and there were fears that they were extrajudicially executed. The government publicly denied reports of a renewed crackdown on the Shi'a Muslim population, but in September President Saddam Hussein declared that attempts by saboteurs and infiltrators to "terrorize civilians and assassinate government officials" had been crushed.

Scores of military personnel, including army officers, were reportedly arrested during the year. At least 47 of them, arrested between May and July, were said to have been involved in military attacks against suspected Shi'a Muslim opponents in the southern marshes (al-Ahwar). Others were arrested after allegedly failing to comply with military orders. The fate and whereabouts of those detained remained unknown; among them were Brigadier Anwar Isma'il Hantush and Major Ghaffuri Ahmad Isma'il....

Thousands of government opponents arrested in previous years continued to be held throughout 1992, including prisoners of conscience. Among them were hundreds of Arabs and Kurds detained during the mass uprisings in April 1991, including at least 106 Shi'a Muslim religious scholars and students arrested in al-Najaf ... and at least 76 Kurds arrested in the Arbil region. The Kuwaiti Government said an estimated 870 Kuwaitis taken prisoner after the Iraqi invasion were still held in Iraq; the Iraqi Government continued to deny holding Kuwaiti detainees. Also still held was 'Aziz al-Sayyid Jassem, a Shi'a Muslim from al-Nasiriyya and former editor of the government magazine *Al-Ghad*. He was arrested in April 1991, apparently for his failure to write articles in support of the government following Iraq's invasion of Kuwait. Until January he was believed to be held in *Mudiriyyat al-Amn al'Amma* (General Security Directorate) in Baghdad, but thereafter his fate and whereabouts remained unknown.

Reports of torture and ill-treatment of detainees continued to be received. Two Shi'a Muslims released in June from al-Radwaniyya garrison, southwest of Baghdad, stated that they had been repeatedly beaten and subjected to electric shocks during their four months' detention. They also stated that a fellow detainee died from severe burns after being tied to a skewer and "roasted" over a flame. David Martin, a US national, and Joseph Ducat, a Filipino, stated upon their release in January that they had been thrown naked into a cell, forced to sleep on a concrete floor while blindfolded, and deprived of food and water for several days. They reported that detainees held with them, including Egyptians, Syrians and Iranians, had been beaten and subjected to electric shocks, and that they had heard the screams of others being tortured. Several Iraqi merchants and businessmen arrested in July were also reportedly tortured before being executed. In June and September further details were revealed of the torture of US and British military prisoners of war during the Gulf War. Torture methods reportedly used included severe beatings with truncheons and rubber hoses, electric shocks, prolonged isolation, mock executions, threats of dismemberment, and sexual abuse of a woman US army officer.

New information was received from documents obtained from areas under Kurdish control and other sources about some of the estimated 100,000 Kurds who "disappeared" in Iraqi government custody after being detained in 1988 during the "Anfal operations," ... including details of over 5,000 people who "disappeared" from Kalar in Sulaimaniya province. Further details were also received about 60 Shi'a Muslim Arabs who "disappeared" between 1979 and 1985, although their fate and whereabouts remained unknown.

Scores of executions were carried out during the year, although in many cases it was not possible to determine whether these were judicial or extrajudicial. The death penalty continued to be imposed for criminal offences, including rape and murder, but no overall figures for the year were available. On 26 July at least 42 merchants, traders and businessmen were executed in Baghdad: they had been accused of profiteering. They were among several hundred members of prominent Sunni and

Shi'a families who were detained that month in a wave of arrests. The government stated that those executed had been tried and convicted, but reports indicated that several were shot dead upon being apprehended. Among those executed was Salim 'Abd al-Hadi Hamra, former head of the Baghdad Chamber of Commerce. Unconfirmed reports suggested that 25 other merchants and traders may have been executed in September. Also in September Iraqi television broadcast details of the trials of seven Iraqis who were executed that month following their conviction for premeditated murder. In October there were unconfirmed reports of the execution of at least 30 military personnel following an alleged military coup attempt in July.

An unknown number of unarmed civilians were extrajudicially executed in the southern marshes region, where thousands of suspected government opponents and army deserters remained in hiding. In February President Hussein said that Shi'a Muslims who participated in the March 1991 uprising should be machine-gunned for treason. In April the government ordered villagers living in the marshes region to resettle in purpose-built camps outside the area. Between April and August, government forces, including the Republican Guards, launched repeated military attacks on the marshes region using helicopter gunships and fighter aircraft. The extent and persistence of the bombardment of civilian targets, which intensified in July, heightened fears that the government had adopted a policy of deliberately targeting non-combatant civilians. In one incident in May, 13 civilians, among them women and children, were reportedly killed after helicopter gunships attacked a wedding ceremony in the village of al-Agir in al-'Amara province. Scores of others were killed in similar attacks in the province in July and August. No aerial attacks were reported following the imposition of the "air exclusion zone". However, ground attacks intensified and were accompanied by widespread arrests and the torture or execution of detainees. Earlier, hundreds of Shi'a Muslim detainees arrested after the March 1991 uprising were reportedly extrajudicially executed at al-Radwaniyya garrison between March and June.

Information was received about extrajudicial executions perpetrated by government forces in northern Iraq in previous years. Several mass graves were found near Arbil, Sulaimaniya and other areas, each containing the remains of scores of Kurdish civilians and combatants who had "disappeared" in custody. One mass grave outside Arbil contained the remains of 107 Kurdish villagers killed in 1987: they were among a group of some 360 people who had survived chemical weapons attacks and were arrested after seeking medical treatment in Arbil's hospitals. They had been moved to an unknown location and in 1988 were reported to have been killed.... A Kurdish doctor who worked at the detention centre in Arbil where the victims had been held told Amnesty International that he had been prevented by Iraqi security personnel from providing them with medical treatment, and that they were left to die and then buried. He added that 15 men who survived had been shot dead and then buried with the others.

Human rights abuses were committed by Kurdish opposition groups and the Kurdish authorities in control of northern Iraq, including torture and execution. Several hundred people were held in detention centres and prisons in Arbil, Sulaimaniya, Duhok and other places under the jurisdiction of the EKF, Kurdish political parties and, after July, police and security personnel of the Kurdish Ministry of the Interior. Some were Iraqi Arabs accused of espionage, but the majority were Kurds arrested at various times since the 1991 uprising on charges including murder, robbery and security offences. Scores of those detained, including young people, were reported to have been tortured to extract "confessions" which were later used to convict them. Among them were 13 political detainees, four of them women, arrested during a demonstration in Arbil in August and charged with the murder of two members of Pesh Merga (armed Kurdish units). Other detainees were sentenced to death and executed by firing-squad, but it was not known how many prisoners in all were sentenced to death or executed. Scores of people were also reported to have "disappeared" during the year after being picked up by members of armed Kurdish groups or to have been killed for political reasons. However, in most cases there was insufficient information to identify the perpetrators. . . .

Peru

Internal armed conflict continued to afflict most of the country and large areas remained emergency zones under military control. Independent human rights defenders stated that they were unable to visit parts of the country for fear of attacks by the security forces or the PCP [Communist Party of Peru, also known as Shining Path]. An extensive pattern of human rights violations by the government's security forces was reported throughout the year. Widespread atrocities by the PCP were also reported and, on a significantly lesser scale, by a second armed opposition group, the *Movimiento Revolucionario Túpac Amaru* (MRTA), Túpac Amaru Revolutionary Movement. The PCP carried out deliberate and arbitrary executions of civilians; sabotaged public utilities, co-operatives and rural development projects; detonated powerful car bombs in urban centres; and threatened strike-breakers.

In January and February, in an attempt to strengthen civilian participation in counter-insurgency policies, Congress modified or repealed legislative decrees issued by the executive in 1991. However, on 5 April President Alberto Fujimori, with the full backing of the Armed Forces Joint Command, dissolved Congress, suspended constitutional rule, and set up an emergency government. The President also announced that the judiciary, Public Ministry, Congress and Constitution were to be comprehensively reformed. The judiciary and the Public Ministry were rendered inoperative for four weeks, during which complaints of human rights violations and *habeas corpus* petitions could not be filed. The dissolution of Congress meant that several commissions investigating human rights violations and political violence were forced to abandon their work.

From April President Fujimori and his Council of Ministers ruled the country by decree law. Decrees issued in April included the dismissal of the Attorney General, 13 Supreme Court judges and over 130 judges and prosecutors, and their replacement with appointees named by the executive.

Decrees issued in May and August widened the definition of "crimes of terrorism", accelerated judicial proceedings in such cases and lengthened prison sentences. The August decree defined the crime of treason and extended military jurisdiction to civilians accused of treason. The measures provided for secret trials. In July a decree penalizing "disappearances" was published, replacing a similar law issued in 1991 and repealed in May 1992.

In early May at least 39 PCP inmates and two policemen were killed during a police operation to regain control of two wings of the Castro Castro Prison in Lima, the capital. The authorities claimed the inmates died as a result of an armed confrontation or were deliberately killed by fellow inmates to prevent them from surrendering. PCP inmates subsequently claimed that at least 10 of the victims were killed after surrendering to the police.

Peter Cardenas, of the MRTA, and Victor Polay, its leader, were arrested in May and June respectively. In September PCP leader Abimael Guzmán and members of the organization's central committee were arrested and charged with treason; scores of other PCP activists were detained in the following months. President Fujimori stated repeatedly that he favoured the death penalty for those convicted of treason.

From mid-September the government refused the International Committee of the Red Cross (ICRC) access to all prisons.

In response to international pressure for a return to democratic rule, elections were held in November for an 80-member legislative Congress charged with reforming the Constitution. The party political alliance *Nueva Mayoria-Cambio 90,* New Majority-Change 90, backed by President Fujimori, achieved an outright majority. Three major opposition parties refused to participate in the elections.

Of the 178 people known to have "disappeared" after detention by the security forces, 139 remained unaccounted for, 22 were later found dead, 16 had their detention acknowledged or were released, and one said he had escaped. Among the "disappeared" were 10 peasants from the department of Junín, who were detained in February by a civil defence patrol acting with the support of the army. The victims, seven men and three boys from the Paccha community in the province of Huancayo, were reportedly beaten, tied up and taken away by the patrol.

Between April and July Amnesty International documented 23 "disappearances" and three extrajudicial executions in the department of San Martin, most of which were attributed to soldiers stationed at the Mariscal Cáceres military base in Tarapoto city.

Lecturer Hugo Muñoz Sánchez and nine students "disappeared" on 18 July after reportedly being detained by soldiers on the army-controlled campus of the Enrique Guzmán y Valle Education University on the outskirts of Lima. The authorities claimed to have investigated the case and concluded that the 10 victims had not been detained. However, their whereabouts remained unknown.

In May, five police officers were charged with "violating personal freedom and abuse of authority" in connection with the 1991 detention and transfer into army custody of three officials and a peasant from Chuschi, Ayacucho department.... However, the authorities failed to initiate proceedings against soldiers alleged to have been responsible for their subsequent "disappearance".

A judge decided in August to close the case against four police officers charged with abuse of authority in connection with the "disappearance" in 1990 of Ernesto Castillo Páez.... An appeal against the decision remained pending.

Scores of people were reported to have been extrajudicially executed by the security forces. On 8 February, five peasants were killed when police opened fire on some 200 unarmed peasants as they marched to a small police station in the district of Chavín, Huari province, Ancash department.

On 17 March, three members of the *Alianza Política Izquierda Unida* (UNIR), Political Alliance of the United Left, were reportedly extrajudicially executed by hanging in the presence of witnesses. According to reports, they were detained in the village of Para, Lucanas province, Ayacucho department, by hooded men in civilian clothing acting under the orders of the military stationed at the Chaviñas military base. The victims were apparently accused of "subversion" and ill-treated before being killed.

Between August and October at least 19 university students in the city of Huancayo, Junín department, were found dead in circumstances suggesting they had been extrajudicially executed. A further seven students were reported to have "disappeared" during this period. All had allegedly been detained by the security forces in or near the city. In October the Attorney General appointed an ad hoc prosecutor to investigate the "disappearances" and the circumstances and manner in which eight of the students had died.

With few exceptions, the courts failed to bring to justice those responsible for human rights violations. In February a civilian court contested the jurisdiction of the military justice system over the trial of soldiers accused of murdering 14 peasants from the community of Santa Bárbara, Huancavelica department, in 1991.... A decision on jurisdiction by the Supreme Court remained pending.

In March it was reported that a military tribunal had sentenced an officer to six years' imprisonment for the death of 30 of the 69 peasants killed in Accomarca, Ayacucho department, in 1985.... The officer was said to have been conditionally freed pending an appeal against conviction. In September a sergeant accused of the massacre of 18 peasants from San Pedro de Cachi, Ayacucho department, was reportedly absolved by the Supreme Council of Military Justice of responsibility for the killings.... In December the Army Command published a communique claiming that a document publicly circulated by former vice-president Máximo San Román was forged: the document stated that soldiers had carried out the massacre of 16 people in Lima in 1991.... However, *Sí*, a national magazine, subsequently published the testimony of an officer attached to the Army Intelligence Service confirming the army's involvement in the killings.

Torture and ill-treatment were frequently reported. In April, 15-year-old Olivia Pérez, who was seven months pregnant, was reportedly beaten by soldiers stationed at the Mariscal Cáceres military base in San Martín department. She subsequently lost her baby. In November members of the Lima Bar Association voted unanimously to condemn the "proven" police torture of a PCP leader and lawyer, Dr Martha Huatay, before her military trial on treason charges. Relatives and lawyers representing four active and retired army officers detained with 13 others following a coup attempt on 13 November against President Fujimori's emergency government claimed that the four had been tortured while in the custody of the army.

The systematic ill-treatment of hundreds of political detainees was reported from several prisons. In May, after the authorities regained control of two wings of the Castro Castro Prison, hundreds of men and women were transferred to other prisons and some 300 men kept in Castro Castro Prison. These and the transferred prisoners alleged that they were subsequently denied adequate clothing, food and medical attention. Those held in Castro Castro Prison also alleged that they were kept lying down in the prison yard for nearly two weeks and that many of them were severely beaten by armed guards on 22 May.

The procedures under which members of armed opposition groups were tried for treason by secret military tribunals fell short of international fair trial standards. Some 70 alleged PCP and MRTA activists, many of them leading members, were reported to have been sentenced to life imprisonment by such tribunals.

The authorities incarcerated two prisoners of conscience on false terrorism-related charges. In March Michael Soto Rodríguez, a medical student, was detained and charged with being a member of *Socorro Popular,* a welfare organization attached to the PCP. Amnesty International believes he was detained solely for giving medical attention to an alleged PCP member wounded in an armed confrontation with the police. In September Ayacucho-based journalist Magno Sosa was detained by the police and charged with having links to the PCP. Amnesty International believes Magno Sosa was detained for no other reason than his newspaper articles drawing attention to human rights violations by the security forces.... At least 16 other people were imprisoned during the year who appeared to be possible prisoners of conscience.

The PCP carried out scores of . . . executions of civilians. Many of those killed had been previously tortured. Among the unarmed civilians killed were members of local authorities, aid workers, community leaders, peasants and town dwellers. On 15 February María Elena Moyano, a deputy mayor, was gunned down by members of the PCP and her body dynamited in Villa El Salvador, a Lima shanty town. Men, women and children were killed by PCP car bomb attacks on civilian targets in Lima. For instance, 25 people were killed in separate attacks on the headquarters of a television station and a residential street in June and July respectively. On the night of 10 October a PCP unit attacked the community of Huayllao, Ayacucho department, and massacred 47 peasants, including 14 children aged four to 15. The community had reportedly established a civil defence patrol but was said to have been armed with no more than five shotguns. On 18 December Pedro Huillca, Secretary General of the *Confederación General de Trabajadores del Perú,* General Confederation of Workers of Peru, was shot dead in Lima. *El Diario,* a clandestine newspaper sympathetic to the PCP, claimed the PCP had carried out the killing. . . .

Sri Lanka

Armed conflict between government forces and the LTTE [Liberation Tigers of Tamil Eelam] continued in the northeast with heavy casualties reported on both sides. Control of much of the northeast remained uncertain: the government retained control of towns and most main roads, but fighting continued intermittently in rural areas. The Jaffna peninsula largely remained in LTTE hands, but government forces took over part of the peninsula and access was closed. Heightened tensions between the Tamil, Muslim and Sinhalese communities in the east were manifest in a series of communal attacks and counterattacks.

The government of President Ranasinghe Premadasa took steps to implement some of the Amnesty International recommendations for human rights safeguards which it had accepted in December 1991. . . . However, crucial procedural safeguards for the protection of prisoners had not been implemented by the end of the year and the state of emergency remained in force island-wide.

The mandate of the Presidential Commission of Inquiry into the Involuntary Removal of Persons was extended for one year, enabling it to investigate "disappearances" occurring from 11 January 1991 to 11 January 1993, and regional officers were appointed to transmit complaints of "disappearances" to the Commission. The Human Rights Task Force, established in 1991 to maintain a register of detainees and monitor their rights, opened several regional offices and established a 24-hour information service in the capital, Colombo. The United Nations (UN) Working Group on Enforced or Involuntary Disappearances visited Sri Lanka for the second time in October at the government's invitation.

Draft legislation to amend the fundamental rights chapter of the

Constitution, to create a new Human Rights Commission and to provide temporary death certificates to relatives of the "disappeared" as a basis for compensation payments, continued to be discussed. However, none of these proposals had been approved or implemented by the end of the year.

The LTTE committed numerous gross abuses of human rights, including the deliberate killing of hundreds of noncombatant Muslim and Sinhalese civilians, the arbitrary killing of civilians in bomb attacks on buses and trains, the torture and killing of prisoners, and abductions for ransom. The LTTE executed several prisoners accused of being informers.

Extrajudicial executions were committed in the northeast by military and ancillary forces, police and home guards. At Mandur, Batticaloa District, in April, a family of seven were among eight people killed by soldiers and members of the Tamil Eelam Liberation Organization (TELO), which operates alongside the army in the east. This followed the killing by the LTTE of two TELO members. The day after 10 senior army and navy officers had been killed by the LTTE on Kayts island in August, soldiers from Poonani camp killed 39 Tamil men, women and children at Mailanthanai, Batticaloa District, over 180 miles away, apparently in reprisal. At least 16 soldiers were remanded in custody following an identity parade, but they had not been charged by the end of the year. Following the extrajudicial execution of some 10 Tamil civilians by government soldiers at Velaveli, Batticaloa District, in October, the government said it would mount an inquiry, but no findings had been published by the end of the year.

In April, following an attack by the LTTE on Alanchipotana, a Muslim village in Polonnaruwa District, during which 54 Muslims were shot and stabbed to death, Muslim home guards retaliated by attacking Tamil villages, killing more than 80 Tamils. Police personnel did not attempt to prevent the reprisal attack. A committee of inquiry recommended a review of the home guard system—which had not been completed by the end of the year—and three home guards were charged with murder.

An inquiry into the reprisal killings of 67 civilians in June 1991 in Kokkadichcholai ... found that the deaths had not resulted from crossfire, as the military claimed, but from "deliberate retaliatory action" by the army. Twenty military personnel were tried by a military tribunal. None was found guilty of murder. The lieutenant in charge was convicted of failing to control his troops and disposing of bodies illegally at the site of the massacre; he was dismissed from the army. The 19 other military personnel were acquitted.

Scores of "disappearances" in military custody were reported from Batticaloa District, and three in Amparai District from the custody of the Special Task Force (STF), a police commando unit. After 25 young men had been detained by the army in the Kiran area, Batticaloa District, in January and February, 11 were released and the military denied that it had detained the remaining 14. Two of the 14 were later found to be in detention and two more were released, but 10 boys and young men—including 12-year-old Manikkam Siventhiran—were not accounted for.

"Disappearances" were also reported following detention by Muslim home guards in Batticaloa District. Home guards detained 13 Tamil men, women and children near Thiyavaddavan in April. One boy escaped; the other 12 prisoners "disappeared".

In the south, several imprisoned *Janatha Vimukthi Peramuna* (JVP), People's Liberation Front, suspects were said by the police to have been shot dead during escape attempts or to have committed suicide. Emergency Regulations do not require that full, independent investigations be held into deaths in custody.

In the south, human rights lawyers, witnesses to human rights violations, journalists and trade unionists received death threats which they believed were made by government forces. Some lawyers refused to accept cases against security force personnel for fear of retaliatory action. Journalists critical of government policy were intimidated and attacked, including Yoonus, a newspaper cartoonist, who was physically injured and repeatedly threatened by people he identified as associates of a senior government minister.

Torture and ill-treatment of political detainees appeared to be routine in military, STF and police custody in both the northeast and the south. Members of TELO and the People's Liberation Organization of Tamil Eelam (PLOTE), both ancillary forces operating alongside the army, were also said to have tortured prisoners in the east. In Badulla and Nuwara Eliya Districts, torture of Tamil prisoners of Indian origin was reported in both military and police custody. Methods of torture included electric shocks; pouring petrol into prisoners' nostrils and then placing a plastic bag over their heads; suspending prisoners by their thumbs and beating them; beating with barbed wire; repeatedly submerging prisoners' heads in water while they were suspended by their ankles; and rape of women. Criminal suspects were also tortured: for example, a gem miner suspected of theft was beaten on the soles of his feet, suspended by his thumbs and beaten with clubs by Lunugala police in September.

Prisoners were subjected to other forms of ill-treatment. For example, prisoners, including a 73-year-old man apparently detained in place of his son, were held in chains at Pioneer Road police camp in Batticaloa. Severe overcrowding was reported from the sixth floor of Police Headquarters in Colombo, where political detainees had been held for more than a year in the custody of the Crime Detection Bureau.

According to official figures, 4,456 people detained in the south in connection with the activities of the JVF since their arrest in 1989 or 1990 had been released by the end of September. However, over 4,800 suspected insurgents remained in detention without charge or trial, including some who had been held for over three years. Emergency Regulations empower the authorities to hold suspects indefinitely under administrative orders;

the PTA permits up to 18 months' administrative detention. In at least 120 cases, the Supreme Court awarded compensation to detainees who had been illegally detained.

According to official figures, in October 4,823 political detainees were being held under Emergency Regulations or the PTA: 1,523 in detention camps, 1,113 in prisons, 569 in police custody and 1,618 in rehabilitation camps, to which detainees deemed to have had minor connection with insurgent activity were referred. The number of prisoners held in army camps was not revealed. Of those held in prisons, 826 were said to be held in connection with the conflict in the northeast and 287 in connection with the southern JVF insurgency of 1988 to 1990. The majority of prisoners in detention and rehabilitation camps were Sinhalese.

In the south, hundreds of Tamil people were periodically rounded up in Colombo and screened for connections with the LTTE. These arrests were made by the police and by members of the Eelam People's Democratic Party (EPDP), an ancillary group which sometimes detained prisoners itself instead of handing them over to police custody. The EPDP has no known legal power to arrest and detain prisoners but has not been prevented from doing so by the authorities. Following the assassination by an LTTE suicide bomber of the Commander of the Navy in Colombo in November, over 3,000 Tamils were rounded up for questioning and hundreds were kept in detention. In Badulla and Nuwara Eliya Districts, dozens of Tamils of Indian origin were detained without trial on account of their alleged connections with the LTTE. Hundreds of Sinhalese people suspected of connections with the JVP were also arrested and detained in the south....

The LTTE also committed gross abuses of human rights. Among the thousands of prisoners believed to be held by the LTTE were police and military personnel, Tamils perceived as opponents by the LTTE, and Tamils and Muslims who were held as hostages for ransom. Some prisoners were reportedly tortured by the LTTE, which only rarely disclosed information about the whereabouts or fate of its political prisoners to their relatives. Those held for ransom included an 84-year-old Tamil man who was abducted by the LTTE in September, apparently because he had relatives living abroad who were presumed to be wealthy. In March, 12 of the 32 Muslim businessmen who had been held in Jaffna since 1990 were released, but the fate of the others was not known....

ADDRESS BY BENJAMIN CHAVIS, NEW DIRECTOR OF NAACP

July 11, 1993

In naming a new executive director April 9, the National Association for the Advancement of Colored People (NAACP) signaled a return to the activism that had marked its earlier years. After a year-long search, Dr. Benjamin F. Chavis, Jr., was chosen to direct America's oldest and largest civil rights organization. He succeeded Dr. Benjamin L. Hooks, who retired after fifteen years with the 500,000-member group, which during his tenure often was criticized by some in the black community as excessively cautious. William F. Gibson, chairman of the sixty-four-member executive board, which met in Atlanta to elect Chavis, said the new director fitted the NAACP's "new imagery."

Chavis, vowing to bring "new energy, new momentum, expanded vision, expanded mission" to the organization, then in its eighty-fifth year, quickly placed it—and himself—in the public spotlight. He gave television interviews, engaged in high-profile lobbying in Washington, called on President Bill Clinton, addressed a conference in Gabon aspiring to build cooperation between African leaders and black Americans, and took up temporary quarters in a rundown housing development in the Watts district of Los Angeles, hoping to be a peaceful influence on the black community as it awaited jury verdicts on police officers accused of beating a black man. (Verdicts in Los Angeles riot cases, p. 631)

Moreover, the new director promptly established an endowment fund aimed at ultimately raising $100 million to keep the NAACP from becoming "financially vulnerable" to outside influences. When the organization opened its annual convention in Indianapolis, July 11, he triumphantly announced that $2 million had been raised.

Blueprint for Change

In his convention address, Chavis spelled out more fully several of his plans for the organization. These included broadening its appeal to include Hispanics, Asian Americans, and American Indians; creating closer ties with Africa; setting up business enterprises to provide jobs for black Americans; and forging "a strategic alliance" with the Congressional Black Caucus, composed of the African-American members of Congress. He lavished praise on Rep. Kweisi Mfume, a Maryland Democrat who headed the caucus. Mfume also addressed the convention, as did Nelson Mandela, leader of the African National Congress then negotiating with the South African government for political control of that country. (Political settlement in South Africa, p. 1003)

However, not all of Chavis's early efforts went smoothly. His choice of assistants drew criticism from within the organization and from the outside. His deputy director, Chicago lawyer Lewis Myers, Jr. was general counsel to Louis Farrakhan and the Nation of Islam, whose anti-white and anti-Jewish remarks were condemned by many Americans as hatemongering. Don Rojas, the NAACP's new communications director, had been press secretary to Maurice Bishop, the leftist leader of Grenada, whose slaying in a 1983 coup led to the U.S. invasion of that Caribbean island.

In an apparent effort to assuage the fears of members who believed he was veering too far left, Chavis insisted that he sought a centrist position. Time *magazine quoted him on the eve of the convention as saying, "We're not here to rock the boat." Chavis likewise declined to criticize his predecessor, except obliquely, explaining that he and Hooks came from different generations and perhaps saw matters differently.*

Chavis's Activist Career

Chavis's civil rights activism dated from his youth in North Carolina. He and nine other young protesters, who were labeled the Wilmington Ten in press headlines, went to prison for their 1971 protest activities. He had served four and a half years when their conviction was overturned in 1980 by a federal judge who ruled that the police had coerced prosecution witnesses. Once freed, Chavis returned to college, taking a doctoral degree and becoming an ordained minister in the United Church of Christ.

At age forty-five, when selected by the NAACP, he was director of the church's Commission on Racial Justice, a vice chairman of the National Council of Churches, co-leader of the Southern Organizing Committee for Economic and Social Justice, president of the Angola Foundation, and chairman of the National Coalition for Peace in Angola. In addition, Chavis wrote a syndicated newspaper column and broadcast a weekly radio commentary on four networks. Upon Clinton's election, he served on the incoming administration's transition team.

Chavis's chief rival for the NAACP position was Jesse L. Jackson, a former colleague in many civil rights undertakings. Jackson withdrew two days before the executive board voted, saying he could not accept a rules change proposed by Gibson to reduce the executive director's authority.

Jackson's critics contended that he realized that he could not defeat Chavis, who had vigorously campaigned for the job. No action was taken on the proposal, and Chavis signed a three-year contract at a salary of $132,000 a year.

Following are excerpts from the opening address to the 1993 convention of the National Association for the Advancement of Colored People by its new executive director, Dr. Benjamin F. Chavis, Jr., delivered July 11, 1993, in Indianapolis:

... The NAACP is taking care of business in the name of the freedom struggle and we are proud of it on this night. So I just feel good tonight. The theme of our convention is "Passing the Torch—Preparing for a Better Tomorrow" and my remarks tonight will be focused on that theme.

For 84 years, the NAACP has stood the test of time as our nation's oldest and largest civil rights organization. The historical record confirms beyond the shadow of a doubt that the NAACP also has been one of the boldest, one of the most respected, one of the most aggressive, one of the most tenacious and one of the most feared organizations in the world.

Yet, the truth is we have also, on occasion, been one of the most misunderstood and maligned organizations, particularly by certain forces that are opposed to freedom....

Now sometimes when you use the language of the freedom movement, it makes some people who are opposed to freedom uncomfortable. So tonight, if I step on some toes forgive me.

The quest for freedom has been long. The NAACP has a unique place in the leadership of the struggle for justice, freedom and equality. We, therefore, affirm that we all stand on the shoulders of others. Thirty years ago in 1963 we all well remember that our state field secretary down in Mississippi was slain, was shot to death in the sight of his wife, in the sight of his children solely because he dared to mobilize, he dared to organize African Americans for the right to vote and yet, thirty years later, if the truth will be told, we still have to mobilize, we still have to organize to get the full right to vote, to get the full representation of our communities, of our constituencies.

The recent rulings by the Supreme Court seek to challenge whether or not we can have equal representation in the halls of Congress. I am so proud that on this day I can say without fear of contradiction we have the strongest Chairman of the Congressional Black Caucus in its whole history, Kweisi Mfume... Kweisi Mfume, we are proud of you. And we at the NAACP intend to forge a strategic alliance with the Congressional Black Caucus. When the Congressional Black Caucus takes a stand on Capitol Hill, we will take a stand on our hill and in 2,000 places throughout the United States of America.

It is about closing our ranks. We accept the torch and we intend to run the race. Not just to mark time, but we intend to run the race to win the race for the benefit of our people who have been denied too long, who have been denied equal justice too long, who have been denied racial justice too long, who have been denied economic justice too long, who have been denied full justice too long.

Now, I have to be careful because in tomorrow's *Time Magazine* even before I speak, they have already concluded that I am too radical for the NAACP. I got my membership card when I was twelve years old.... I thanked my mamma, I thanked my daddy for placing that card in my hands and for telling me one Sunday morning before we even had grace, they said, "son take this card, put it in your pocket, but also put it in your soul, put it in your life ... stand up ... don't bow down to injustice."...

And I want to tell you, for a mamma and a daddy to tell their child to stand up; "Lord Have Mercy" ... If we would tell our children to stand up in 1993, do away with drugs, stand up in 1993, do away with fratricidal killing, stand up in 1993, tell our children not only to join the NAACP, tell our children to participate in resurrecting the life, revitalizing the life of the NAACP. Because if you revitalize the life of the NAACP, we help to revitalize the life of the community where the NAACP has a residence....

... [F]rom the very moment of my election, there have been attempts ... this is a family meeting ... there have been attempts to divide me from the Chairman. I want to put it out so that everybody will hear it. There is a rigid solidarity between the Executive Director and the Chairman of the Board, there is no disunity and people say well, "How can you deal with a strong Chairman?" ... I want a strong Chairman, a strong Executive Director.... I want all of the Branch Presidents to be strong Branch Presidents, because as strong as you are, it enables our NAACP to be strong....

No national organization is any stronger than its local base. It you want to know where the strength of the NAACP is, go to our local branches. That's where the strength is ... and by the grace of God we are going to use all of our strength, we are going to use the interest from the Endowment over these many years into the future to strengthen our local base, to strengthen our outreach into the community, to strengthen our participation in the life of our beloved Association.

I have come a long way to get here, be patient with me. I wish I could really take the time to tell you how it feels to have chains around your ankles, to have somebody strip search you in the sight of your children, to have somebody put you in prison because you stand up for other people's children. But you know, through it all like Nelson Mandela said yesterday to us, the forces of oppression only endure or only last as long as those who are oppressed will tolerate ... and things in South Africa are changing, but they are changing because sisters and brothers in the ANC [African National Congress] and sisters and brothers in the anti-apartheid movement in South Africa have sacrificed much....

And you will see going through this, the 84th Annual Convention there is one theme among many themes and it is a necessity for us as we move toward the 21st century to tackle the problem of economic inequity, of economic inequality. . . .

And we at the NAACP understand that we are not a social service organization, we are a social change organization, but in trying to create and bring about social change, sometimes it is necessary to exhibit the kind of social change methodology in life at the community level that we want the government and the state and others to abide by. The Fair Share Agreement with Flagstar [Corporation] is an example, it is not the totality but just a small example, because over the next seven years we are going to put over one billion dollars of economic benefit directly into the hands of African Americans, where they will own the franchises, where they will be controlling the marketing, where they will receive economic benefit, but that does not mean that we will back off from our stance of being against discrimination.

What it does mean is that where there is a Denny's or Hardee's or whatever the name of the restaurant, we are not only going to demand that we be treated fairly, but we are going to demand that we have equal access to owning businesses in our community ... and this subject about enterprise zones needs to be expanded. Right now, enterprise zones in South Central and other parts of the country have not really served our needs.

We would rather have empowerment zones. Zones where we become economically empowered in the communities where we live, in the communities where we work, rather than for outside interests to come in and exploit our work forces and take the capital and apply it outside of our communities. We want the benefit of our labor, the benefit of our work to stay in our communities so that our communities will get the economic uplift and benefit from it. So economic development, community development is high on our agenda as we move toward the 21st century.

Now, I am very pleased to say that we have a national housing corporation and in a few weeks . . . in a few weeks the NAACP is going to announce a joint venture in the City of Baltimore that will derive over 600 units of housing for low income persons in the City of Baltimore through the work of our national housing corporation.

And does it mean that we are going into the housing business? It means that we will go into the business until we can find others to take it on right and show how it should be done. . . .

Secondly, when I talked about expanding the mission of the NAACP to other racial and ethnic communities, I was also talking about expanding the mission and the totality of the NAACP to the diversity that is within the African American community. . . .

Thirty years ago, a couple of months after the tragic assassination of Medgar Evers in Jackson, Mississippi, we assembled ourselves in Washington, D.C. for the historic March on Washington. It was the day that Martin

Luther King, Jr. made his famous "I Have A Dream" speech. A month after the March on Washington, in Birmingham, Alabama, a bomb was placed in the 16th Street Baptist Church and four of our little sisters in Sunday School were tragically murdered. And yet this is 1993, 30 years later and while we have been here in Indianapolis, we have also planned for the 30th Anniversary Memorial March on Washington.

Now my concept of having memorials is that we do something in the present that will signify and give dignity to our respect for what happened in the past. In other words, we are interested in doing something more than having a nostalgic replay of '63. What we want to have is to mobilize our constituencies, our branches, to come to Washington with a clear civil rights agenda, with a clear set of programs, public policy issues affecting every neighborhood, in every congressional district. Everyone knows why we are marching. See, marching is therapeutic, but the question is, after the march is over—what do we do?

Because if you were to have a commemorative account of all of the marches that we have had, all of the marches that we have participated in, we would have to admit that we have some homework to do. And so as we plan this march, and as the NAACP repositions itself to provide leadership for the 1993 March on Washington, we have said in clear terms that as we mobilize our troops, our forces, our constituencies, we are marching to demand justice, we are marching for jobs, we are marching for health care.

We are marching for an end to the kind of neglect of the urban centers that have gone on far too long. We are marching for our children. We are marching for ourselves. We are marching for the unborn generation....

You see, one of the things about being the oldest and the largest, it may make you think that we have got to relax. But being the oldest and the largest means that we have the most responsibility. It means that we have the most determination to mobilize our constituencies so that we can make a difference. So, when you see those banners and when you wear those buttons about marching on Washington is not just marching on Washington, it is marching on the State Houses, it's marching on the municipal houses, it's marching around our houses to straighten out the lives in our communities....

God Bless You. May God Keep You. May God Bless the NAACP. "Come Back Home to the NAACP". God Bless You.

RADIO TALK SHOW SURVEY

July 16, 1993

The voices that dominate the ever-growing talk radio shows are distorting and exaggerating public opinion. That was the conclusion of a report, "The Vocal Minority in American Politics," released July 16 by the Times Mirror Center for the People and the Press. In its principal finding, the report noted that "these new voices of public opinion can caricature discontent with American political institutions rather than genuinely reflect public disquiet."

The report was based on surveys from telephone interviews with members of the general public and with talk show hosts. A nationwide sample of 1,507 adults at least eighteen years old was chosen, and these individuals were contacted between May 18 and May 24. A sample of 112 talk show hosts was contacted shortly after, May 25-June 11.

The growth of talk radio shows over the past few years and the emergence of heavy hitters such as Rush Limbaugh, who parlayed his radio success into books and television, have made clear that these radio shows represent, as the report said, "the widest window on the world of politics and issues for the vocal minority." Indeed, the Times Mirror survey found that almost one-half of all Americans listen to talk radio on a relatively frequent basis, with one in six listening regularly.

Conservative Callers

Of particular importance to politicians was the additional finding that this vocal minority "sounds a conservative tone on many issues, and is much more critical of Bill Clinton and his policies than the average American." At the time of the survey, nationwide public opinion was fairly evenly divided about Clinton's overall job performance, with 43 percent disapproving and 39 percent approving. But among those who had called into talk radio, the disapproval registered was far greater than approval—53 percent to 38 percent.

The report noted further that "Republicans have louder voices than Democrats in almost all of the important venues of public expression." And it found that Republicans (26 percent) are twice as likely as Democrats (12 percent) to report regularly listening to talk radio. Overall, half of those who identified themselves as Republicans said they listened to talk radio either regularly or sometimes, while only 35 percent of those identified as Democrats did.

Even though Ross Perot's presidential campaign was born on the Larry King show, he was not more of a hero to activists than to the broader public, the report observed.

Noting the Limbaugh factor, some Democrats saw a link between Limbaugh and the demagogic radio personalities of the past, Father Charles Coughlin and Huey Long, who used the airwaves to rail against a host of perceived enemies.

The talk-show public is also "rabidly anti-congressional," far more critical of Congress than the public at large, the Times Mirror Center reported. Only 35 percent of this activist segment of the public had a favorable view of Congress, while 58 percent held an unfavorable view. Comparable numbers for the less vocal elements of the public were 52 percent favorable versus 36 percent unfavorable.

Some segments in the "vocal minority" also had less favorable opinions than the general public toward many institutions, including network TV news, daily newspapers, the United Nations, and the Supreme Court. But the differences were not nearly as large as the gaps in opinion about Congress.

In the current climate, said Rep. Bill Hefner, D-N.C., a former radio broadcaster, many of the talk shows "are nothing but negative attacks on institutions, especially government, at all levels. It's getting to the point where we're not able to govern."

Views Held by Talk Show Hosts

To determine whether the "vocal minority's" views on President Clinton reflected the influence of the talk show hosts who conduct the political debate, the Times Mirror group interviewed hosts in major markets. The results showed them to be extremely critical of the president at the time of the survey. Just 26 percent said they approved of Clinton's performance in the White House, and by a margin of 48 percent to 32 percent, the hosts said they expected Clinton to fail rather than succeed in achieving his most important legislative goals.

But despite the prominence of the conservative Limbaugh, Times Mirror surveyors found that the talk show hosts were more middle-of-the-road and politically independent than their audiences. The survey determined that a slight plurality of hosts leaned toward the Democratic party, and in fact those in the sample said they voted for Clinton over Bush and Ross Perot by a 39 percent to 23 percent and 18 percent margin, respectively.

In trying to determine why people listen to talk radio, the Times Mirror Center found that slightly more than one-third believe it is a good way to keep up on issues and current events. About 20 percent reported listening primarily to learn how different people feel about the issues of the day, and about 10 percent reported listening just to be entertained. Only 1 percent said that the main reason they listened was because they liked the host of a particular program.

Following are excerpts from the Times Mirror Center for the People and the Press report, "The Vocal Minority in American Politics," released July 16, 1993:

Talk Radio

The General Public

The Scope—Numbers of Listeners and Callers

Talk radio has become a staple in the diet of about one-in-six Americans. About 17 percent say they *regularly* listen to shows that "invite listeners to call in to discuss current events, public issues and politics." However, when added to another quarter of the public who say they *sometimes* listen to such shows, the power of talk radio becomes clearer, with about four-in-ten Americans listening on a relatively frequent basis. One-quarter of the public reported having listened to a radio talk show either the day they were interviewed for this study or on the previous day.

How Many Are Listening?

- 61% say they have *ever* listened
- 42% say they listen either "regularly" or "sometimes"
- 23% say they listened either "yesterday" or "today"
- 17% say they listen regularly

Far fewer Americans have actually tried to *participate* in talk radio by calling in to make their opinions heard. While 61% of the citizenry say they have listened to talk radio at some point, only 11% report having attempted to call into a radio program. Moreover, only half of this number (6%) reports having made it through to actually talk on the air to make their views known, and only half of this number (3%) reports having done so in the last year. As can be seen below, the Times Mirror survey estimates that *just one percent of Americans* have actually talked on the radio at any point in the last month or two.

How Many Are Calling and Talking

- 11% say they have tried to call in
- 6% say they have ever talked on the air

• 3% say they talked on the air in the past year
• 1% say they have talked on the air in the last month or two

The Shape—Who Listens to and Calls into Talk Radio

Who Listens

In one sense, the audience for talk radio looks very much like the nation as a whole. While not a perfect sampling of the American public, variations in its demographics—age, sex, race, education and income—are not terribly large. In another sense—in terms of its politics—those who listen to talk radio are considerably different from the nation as a whole. They are more likely to be Republican in their partisanship, and more likely to be conservative in their political outlook.

Looking at those who say they listen either "regularly" or "sometimes," there is a slight gender gap, with a greater proportion of men (45%) than women (38%) reporting this level of listening. There are few differences by either race or age, although a slightly higher number of those over 30 report listening regularly. There is a slightly larger socio-economic gap, with better educated individuals and wealthier households reporting more exposure to talk radio. These differences, however, are quite modest, ranging only about 9 percentage points from the lowest category in the groupings to the highest.

The largest group differences in listening to talk radio are clearly by political orientation. Republicans (26%) are twice as likely as Democrats (12%) to report regularly listening to talk radio. Overall, 50% of Republicans say they listen to talk radio either regularly or sometimes, compared to 35% of Democrats and 41% of Independents. The same pattern holds true with ideology. Conservatives (24%) are twice as likely to be regular listeners as are liberals (11%). Half of all conservatives say they listen either regularly or sometimes, compared to 36% of liberals and 40% of those in between.

Who Calls and Who Talks

Overall, 11% say they have tried to call into a radio talk show to register their opinion, with 6% saying they have successfully made it on the air. Interestingly, while there are no age, gender or racial differences in who listens to talk radio, there *are* differences in terms of who tries to call, *and* there is an additional filtering process in terms of who actually makes it onto the air. Men, for example, are far more likely to call than are women, by a margin of 14% to 7%, and are almost twice as likely to actually make their views known on the air, by a margin of 9% to 5%, as well. While non-whites (17%) are more likely than whites to call (11%), they are *equally* likely to make it on the air.

On the other hand, while there are modest differences in who *listens* according to education and age, those differences are largely muted in

Table 1 Listens to Talk Radio

	Regularly	Sometimes	Rarely	Never	*N*
Total	17	25	19	39	(1,507)
Sex					
Male	18	27	20	34	(760)
Female	15	23	18	44	(747)
Race					
White	17	24	19	39	(1,292)
Non-White	13	26	18	41	(210)
Age					
Under 30	12	28	20	39	(380)
30-49	17	25	20	37	(620)
50+	19	22	16	42	(490)
Education					
College Grad.	22	24	23	31	(499)
Other College	17	25	20	27	(434)
H.S. Grad.	14	25	17	43	(499)
<H.S. grad.	15	21	14	51	(122)
Family Income					
$50,000+	24	22	21	32	(339)
$30,000-$49,999.	17	27	17	38	(348)
$20,000-$29,999.	16	27	23	33	(295)
<$20,000.	13	24	16	46	(411)
Region					
East	17	20	14	49	(301)
Midwest	14	23	22	39	(408)
South	17	26	19	37	(550)
West	18	29	20	33	(248)
Party ID					
Republican	26	24	18	32	(434)
Democrat	12	23	19	44	(490)
Independent	14	27	20	38	(506)
Ideology					
Liberal	11	25	19	43	(203)
Conservative	24	25	20	30	(381)
In Between	15	25	19	41	(871)

terms of the proportion who call into the radio station and the number who actually speak on the air.

The partisan differences observed in who listens to talk radio *are*, however, also reflected in the make-up of callers and talkers. Republicans are more likely than Democrats both to call in, and to make it on the air; conservatives are also more likely than liberals both to call in and to actually give voice to their opinions over the airwaves. Thus there appears to be both a Republican and conservative *tone*, or bias, to the voice of public opinion one might hear listening to talk radio. Overall, 50% of Republicans say they have talked on the air, compared to just 3% of Democrats. The ratio of conservatives (9%) to liberals (4%) who say

Table 2 Calls to Talk Radio

	Ever Called	Ever Talked	*N*
Total	11	6	(1,507)
Sex			
Male	14	9	(760)
Female	7	5	(747)
Race			
White	11	6	(1292)
Non-White	17	7	(210)
Age			
Under 30	8	2	(380)
30-49	15	7	(620)
50+	10	6	(490)
Education			
College Grad.	11	7	(499)
Other College	14	6	(434)
H.S. Grad.	10	4	(499)
<H.S. grad.	11	7	(122)
Family Income			
$50,000+	12	8	(339)
$30,000-$49,999	13	7	(348)
$20,000-$29,999	13	7	(295)
<$20,000	10	3	(411)
Region			
East	11	6	(301)
Midwest	10	5	(408)
South	13	7	(550)
West	11	4	(248)
Party ID			
Republican	14	8	(434)
Democrat	9	3	(490)
Independent	12	6	(506)
Ideology			
Liberal	12	4	(203)
Conservative	16	9	(381)
In Between	10	5	(871)

they have been able to verbalize their opinions over the radio is also two-to-one.

Why People Listen

There is no single reason that stands out as the primary attraction of "talk radio." When asked to identify the "most important reason" why they listen to talk radio, just over one-third (36%) mention something having to do with it being a good way to keep up on issues and current events. One-in-five (21%) report listening primarily to learn how different people feel about issues of the day and to hear other viewpoints, with another 10% offering the related view that they mainly listen to talk radio because it serves as a forum for a discussion of public opinion. About one-in-ten each say they listen simply to be entertained. No other single reason was mentioned by more than 5% of respondents. *Surprisingly, just one percent volunteered the most important reason why they listened was because they liked the host of a particular program.*

The talk radio audience was also read a list of six reasons and asked to describe each as a "major," "minor," or "not a reason" why they listen to the *specific* radio program they listen to most often. Better than seven-in-ten of all listeners (and an even greater number of regular listeners and callers) give *surveillance* reasons—keeping up on issues of the day, and learning how different people feel about different issues—as major reasons why they listen to talk radio. Additionally, 58 percent give another informational-related reason: that talk radio is a good place to learn things that cannot be learned elsewhere.

Second, in addition to these primary reasons, there are a variety of other appeals of talk radio that are of lesser importance, but still significant. Some four-in-ten of all listeners, and half of regular listeners, cite the entertainment value of talk radio as a "major" reason why they listen. One-third also say they listen to use what they hear on talk radio in discussions of current events with other people.

Finally, the appeal of the host ranked at the *bottom* of the list as a primary appeal of talk radio. Just over one-quarter of all listeners, increasing to just under 40% of regular listeners and callers, say that the host of the show is a major reason why they listen to the *specific* talk radio program they listen to most often.

Talk listeners say they are eager to hear opposing viewpoints on an issue. By a two-to-one margin, more say they are more interested when they are listening to people with an *opposite* point of view (47%), than when they hear someone expressing a point of view similar to their own (22%).

The Ideology of Talk Radio

Both listeners and callers see talk radio as non-ideological, presenting a diversity of views rather than being dominated by either liberals or conservatives. Overall, just 16% feel that talk radio basically presents a liberal point of view, with an even smaller 11% saying that it is dominated by conservatives. Fully six-in-ten believe that talk radio presents a mixture of different views to its audience, with the remaining 13% saying that talk radio presents no particular point of view.

The Times Mirror Survey also finds a small amount of "reverse finger pointing," as people with strong ideologies or partisan views are more likely than others to think that talk radio over-represents people with views the opposite of themselves. For example:

- More conservatives feel that talk radio offers a liberal (27%) rather than conservative (12%) point of view. Among self-described liberals there is much greater balance, with slightly more saying that talk radio offers a liberal (18%) rather than conservative (14%) point of view.

- More Democrats feel that talk radio is dominated by a conservative viewpoint (14%) rather than a liberal one (8%); far more Republicans feel talk radio is liberal in its orientation (23%) than feel it offers a conservative point of view (8%).
- While those who voted for George Bush are far more likely to see talk radio as a liberal (24%) versus a conservative (7%) platform, the reverse is true among those having voted for Bill Clinton, with just 9% saying that talk radio is generally liberal and 18% feeling that it is conservative in its orientation. Ross Perot voters are in the middle, with 15% feeling that talk radio expresses a liberal point of view and 10% saying that a conservative ideology dominates the airwaves.

While the vast majority of listeners believe the "opinion" they hear on the radio represents a diverse set of views, they find talk show *hosts* more easy to classify in ideological terms. When asked to think about "most of the hosts on talk radio," 33% of listeners say the hosts are more liberal than they are, with 19% saying they find hosts to be more conservative than they are. Forty-two percent of the public either say that talk show hosts have roughly the same ideology as they do, or that there is a mixture of talk show hosts in terms of their beliefs and opinions.

While regular listeners and callers differ little from the larger audience of *all* listeners, there are predictable differences in perceptions of talk show hosts among those with clear partisan or ideological views. Among conservative listeners, 52% think hosts are more liberal than they are, while just 7% say that the hosts are more conservative. Liberals offer somewhat of a mirror image—30% say hosts are more conservative than they themselves are, although 20% say hosts are actually more liberal.

A large plurality of those voting for either Bush or Perot believe that talk show hosts are more liberal than they are. Slightly more Clinton voters find talk show hosts to be more conservative than they are (29%), than feel hosts are more liberal than they are (20%). While Democrats are evenly divided about whether talk show hosts are more liberal or conservative than they themselves are, far more among both Independents and Republicans believe talk radio show hosts are to the left of them on the ideological spectrum.

Talk Show Hosts

Who They Are

The Times Mirror Center interviewed 112 hosts of radio talk shows, including 66 from the top 25 markets in the country and 46 from smaller markets. An overview finds them to be well educated, affluent and largely independent politically.

In terms of political orientation, talk show hosts describe themselves as politically independent and ideologically moderate. Just 16%

Table 3 Partisan and Ideological Differences Between Hosts and Their Audiences (in percentages)

	Republican	Lean Republican	Democrat	Lean Democrat	No Affiliation
Public					
Listeners	42	13	26	10	9
Talkers	39	19	20	19	11
Hosts	16	22	17	27	18
	Conservative	Lean Conservative	Liberal	Lean Liberal	No Inclination
Public					
Listeners	36	31	9	13	11
Talkers	39	29	9	15	9
Hosts	21	25	22	21	10

identify themselves as Republicans, with a like number (17%) saying they are Democrats. But when the Independents were probed further a slight Democratic plurality was found with 44% of the hosts saying they were Democrats or leaned Democratic and 38% Republican or Republican leaners.

They also reject ideological labels, with 21% describing themselves as conservative, a like number describing themselves as liberal (22), and most (53%) saying they are in-between. When the "in betweens" were asked for their inclinations the division was a narrow 43% liberal or liberal-leaning vs. 46% conservative or conservative-leaning.

While appearing to be fairly independent, talk show hosts were no friend of George Bush in the last election, giving Bill Clinton more support than the public as a whole. Hosts favored Clinton over Bush by a margin of 39% to 23%, with 18% saying they voted for Ross Perot. As many as 8% say they voted for some other candidate, with the remaining 12% saying they did not vote. The survey finds however, that Clinton appears to have lost support among talk show hosts since becoming President. When asked how they would vote in a three way race, Clinton barely squeaks by Republican Senate leader Robert Dole by a margin of 33% to 31%, with additional support also going to Ross Perot (25%).

As would be expected, talk show hosts are extremely well educated. Only 15% have never attended college. Fully 60% report having a college degree, compared to just 21% of the general public. Almost one-quarter of hosts have gone on to graduate school. And, as would be expected, they are also extremely affluent: just one-quarter (27%) earn under $50,000, 33% make between $50,000 and $100,000, and 30% make in excess of $100,000. The remainder declined to disclose their income. By way of comparison 63% of hosts and 18% of the public have incomes of over $50,000.

Radio show hosts are also quite non-religious when compared to the public as a whole. Fully 30% say they have no religious affiliation, while 37% describe themselves as Protestant, 17% as Roman Catholic, and 10% as Jewish. The remainder express some other religious affiliation. In the large population, just 10% say they have no religious attachment, while 60% describe themselves as Protestants, 24% as Roman Catholics and 2% as Jews.

How Talk Show Hosts View Their Callers and Listeners

Most talk show hosts say that the people who call into their programs are representative of the larger public in their listening area. Just over half, 56%, feel their callers are representative, although a very sizeable minority, 38%, believes they are not. But when presented with a list of how callers might be different from others in their listening area, *almost all talk show hosts acknowledge some biases in the opinions of those who call.* Moreover, of the 12 possible ways in which callers might be different, on only one did a majority of talk show hosts say that their callers were in fact representative of others in the same media market.

In general talk show hosts describe their callers as being angry, anti-government, more critical of the President and Congress, and more conservative than are other people. A majority of hosts feel that "people who are angry" are over represented by those who call into their programs. Just 7% say these people are under represented, with 39% saying there is no difference between callers and the larger community they are drawn from.

Besides being more angry, talk radio callers are also unrepresentative in that they are more *critical* than others, according to the hosts. By a wide margin of 45% to 8% hosts say that people who dislike President Clinton are over represented on their shows, with 45% saying callers are representative of others' views of the President. The same pattern holds for Congress, although by a lesser margin. By 36% to only 5% hosts feel that negative opinions about Congress are *over* rather than *under* represented by their callers, although the majority believe that callers' views of Congress are representative of the larger public.

This more negative view of the President and the Congress goes beyond specific actors to the political system itself. Hosts characterize their callers as being unrepresentative of the general public in that they express a strong "anti-government" bias. The margin of being over to under represented is an extremely wide 45% to 8%.

In keeping with this anti-government philosophy, hosts acknowledge that callers are far more conservative in their political orientation than is the public as a whole. Half of all hosts interviewed say that conservatives are over represented by those who call into their programs. Just 19% say conservatives are under-represented. Liberals are said to be under-represented by roughly the same amount—50%.

This conservative tone of public opinion extends to a number of issues and groups. Large pluralities of talk show hosts feel that people who are pro-life are over-represented and people who are pro-choice are under-represented by those who call in. They further feel that feminists are under-represented by callers, but that those who are strongly moralistic or religious, and those who are hostile to gays and lesbians are over-represented by their callers.

While unrepresentative of the general public talk show hosts believe that callers are more representative of another important community—their *listeners*. Hosts describe their listeners as being more anti-government in orientation and more conservative in their ideology than others in their listening area. An extraordinary 71% of hosts describe their listeners as "more critical in their views of government and politics than others in their listening area." Just 4% say their listeners are less critical than others, with the remaining quarter saying their listeners are neither more or less critical than others. While a bare majority of hosts (51%) say their listeners are representative of the larger community, far more say there is a conservative bias to their audience (34%), than feel their listeners are more liberal than the public as a whole (13%).

How Talk Show Hosts View Themselves

Talk radio hosts take themselves seriously and see themselves as "players" in shaping and influencing public opinion. When asked whether they felt their job was mainly one of *informing* the public or *entertaining* them, 40% say it is primarily to inform; just 25% describe themselves mainly as entertainers. A large number (35%) volunteer that their job entails both.

Most (63%) feel they "often play an important role in shaping or influencing public opinion" in their community, and three-quarters say they are able to recall a case in the recent past when they or something that happened on their show had an impact on public policy or politics. Most of these recountings (40%) have to do with bringing a local issue to the forefront. Another 19% say they feel a local election was influenced by something that took place on their show, while another 15% believe they affected a matter of public policy by bringing what they believe to be public opinion to the attention of governmental decision makers. Approximately this same number, 14%, say they have had an impact on politics or policy through pointing out an instance of corruption in government.

How Talk Show Hosts View Political Issues and Prominent Politicians

Agenda. The samples of talk show hosts and the general public evaluated some 13 issues as "critical," "very important," or just "somewhat important." There are large differences on half of them. Talk show hosts are far *more* likely to be concerned about the quality of public education, the general shape of the economy and the federal budget deficit than are others.

Three-quarters of hosts, for example, feel improving the nation's education system is a critical issue facing the country, compared to half of those in the public. Hosts are about 19 percentage points more likely than the American public to feel economic conditions are of critical importance, and 15 percentage points more likely to see reducing the federal budget deficit as critically important.

Talk hosts are *less* likely to give a high priority to environmental protection, problems of the homeless and the controversy over abortion than are others. There was less than a 10 percentage point difference between talk hosts and the public on seven other issues asked about, including the importance of health care, the situation in Bosnia, and protecting American family values, among others.

Issue Positions. A comparison of talk show hosts and the American public across 8 controversial issues of the day shows a wide chasm on two: where the majority of both radio talk show listeners (63%) and others in the citizenry (53%) *oppose* allowing gays and lesbians to serve in the military, talk show hosts give strong support to this proposal by a margin of 63% in favor to 33% in opposition; where about 7-in-10 of those in the public *favor* a constitutional amendment to allow prayer in school, talk show hosts are decidedly against this idea, with just 39% in favor and 58% opposing.

On another two of the issues examined there are just modest differences between the hosts of radio call-in programs and others. While a majority of the public (60%) opposes changing the laws to make it more difficult for a woman to obtain an abortion, a larger number of hosts (83%) take this position. And while sizable majorities of all groups favor term limits for members of Congress, there is slightly more opposition (28%) among hosts than there is in the public (18%). There are even fewer differences between hosts, their listeners and the public as a whole on other important issues such as gun control, increasing taxes to reduce the deficit, and whether the U.S. should take a more active military role in Bosnia.

Political Evaluations. Despite their moderate views on issues, hosts of talk radio are far more critical than the public of the President, the Congress and Ross Perot.

At the time of the survey, a slight plurality of the public disapproved of how Bill Clinton was handling his job as President (39% approved, 43% disapproved). Among hosts, the gap was a much clearer disapproval margin of 26% to 62%. Whereas Clinton was *personally* popular with the American public, with favorable opinions outnumbering unfavorable ones by a comfortable 60% to 34%, a majority of talk radio hosts held an unfavorable view of the President (46% favorable, 53% unfavorable).

Talk hosts and the public displayed an even greater disparity in their

Table 4 Evaluations of Institutions and Political Figures

	Favorable	Unfavorable	No Opinion	*N*
Bill Clinton				
Talk Hosts	46	53	5=100	(112)
Regular Listeners	48	48	3=100	(277)
General Public	60	34	1=100	(1,507)
Robert Dole				
Talk Hosts	56	42	2=100	(112)
Regular Listeners	60	27	13=100	(277)
General Public	48	28	24=100	(1,507)
Ross Perot				
Talk Hosts	39	58	3=100	(112)
Regular Listeners	65	30	5=100	(277)
General Public	64	31	5=100	(1,507)
The Congress				
Talk Hosts	25	73	2=100	(112)
Regular Listeners	34	59	6=100	(277)
General Public	43	48	9=100	(1,507)
The United Nations				
Talk Hosts	62	34	4=100	(112)
Regular Listeners	68	20	12=100	(277)
General Public	73	17	10=100	(1,507)
Daily Papers				
Talk Hosts	54	42	4=100	(112)
Regular Listeners	78	18	4=100	(231)
General Public	81	13	6=100	(1,235)
Network TV News				
Talk Hosts	54	42	4=100	(112)
Regular Listeners	76	22	4=100	(231)
General Public	81	15	4=100	(1,235)
The Supreme Court				
Talk Hosts	86	12	2=100	(112)
Regular Listeners	72	18	10=100	(277)
General Public	73	18	9=100	(1,507)
The Church				
Talk Hosts	64	26	10=100	(112)
Regular Listeners	82	12	6=100	(277)
General Public	82	10	8=100	(1,507)

opinions of Ross Perot. At the time of the survey Perot was quite popular with the American public—twice as many held favorable (64%) as unfavorable (31%) opinions. The view of Perot held by talk show hosts, however, was decidedly negative with far more saying they had an unfavorable (58%) than favorable (39%) opinion of the Texas billionaire.

While the general public is mixed in its assessment of Congress (43% favorable, 48% unfavorable), talk show hosts are extremely critical, with just 25% holding a favorable impression of the institution and 73% offering an unflattering view.

The talk show hosts surveyed express more negative opinions than the general public of the UN, network TV news and the Church. On the other hand, talk show hosts were more positive than the public about the Supreme Court and daily newspapers.

Values. Talk show hosts are most different from the general public when it comes to matters of freedom of expression. For example, where one-third of the public feel school boards ought to have the right to fire homosexual teachers, just 11% of talk show hosts hold this same view. And, where more than half (52%) of the public believes that "books that contain dangerous ideas should be banned from public school libraries," fully 89% of talk show hosts *disagree* with this sentiment.

Relative to the general public, talk show hosts are also more likely to feel they are influential and that public officials pay heed to their opinions, that the United States should be involved in international affairs rather than solely paying attention to domestic concerns, and are also less likely to express strongly religious or moralistic views.

REPORT ON EXISTENCE OF GAY GENE

July 16, 1993

New evidence in the debate over whether people choose to be homosexual or are born that way was reported by scientists at the National Cancer Institute, part of the National Institutes of Health. In a study involving gay men, the scientists found evidence that many of them inherited genes that predisposed them to be homosexual.

The scientists did not find a "gay gene" that invariably causes homosexuality and that is present in all gay men. Instead, they found indications that one or more genes affect the sexual orientation of at least some gay men. It was still unknown how the gene worked, how many gay men had it, how many gay men the gene influenced, or how the gene affected women.

In fact, the scientists did not find the gene itself. What they found was the general area on the X chromosome where the gene is located. That area may contain several hundred genes, meaning there was far more work to do before the correct one could be identified. Earlier in 1993, scientists discovered the gene that causes Huntington's disease—more than a decade after it had been traced to the tip of a chromosome.

The scientists started their investigation by looking at the family trees of seventy-six homosexual men. They found that 13.5 percent of the brothers of the gay men also were homosexual, far higher than the 2 percent homosexual rate in the general population. This finding reinforced earlier studies that found that brothers of gay men had a higher rate of homosexuality than the general population.

The scientists then explored the family trees further, looking at relatives outside the immediate family. At that point they uncovered something new: the men had more gay relatives on the maternal side than on the paternal side of their families, which indicated that, at least in some cases, a tendency toward homosexuality was inherited from female members of the family. Based on that knowledge, the scientists zeroed in on the X chromosome, inherited by men from their mothers.

In the next phase of the study, the scientists took DNA samples from forty pairs of homosexual brothers. They examined the X chromosomes to see if the brothers shared "gene markers," bits of DNA inside the chromosome whose placement can be precisely mapped. Thirty-three of the forty pairs of brothers had the same five genetic markers near one part of their X chromosomes, which suggests that the gene lies somewhere near the genetic markers.

The fact that seven pairs of brothers did not share the genetic markers indicates the gene is not the only factor inclining some men toward homosexuality, said Dean Hamer, head of the NCI research team, in an interview with the Washington Post. *Hamer said other genes, environmental factors, or life experiences also may contribute to homosexuality.*

Gay-rights groups generally praised the study. "We find the study very relevant, and what's most relevant is that it's one more piece of evidence that sexual orientation is not chosen," Gregory King, spokesman for the Human Rights Campaign Fund, told the Washington Post. *However, some expressed fears that once the gene was found, a genetic test could be developed to identify and discriminate against homosexuals.*

In reporting their study in the journal Science, *the scientists noted concerns that genetic information could be used improperly. "We believe that it would be fundamentally unethical to use such information to try to assess or alter a person's current or future sexual orientation, either heterosexual or homosexual, or other normal attributes of human behavior," they wrote.*

Hamer and others noted that the study still needed to be replicated to ensure its accuracy. Demonstrating a link between genes and behavior is notoriously difficult. Other researchers previously have tied genes to manic-depressive illness, schizophrenia, and alcoholism, but in all three cases have had to withdraw their claims after the studies were proven wrong. However, experts interviewed by the Post *who were familiar with Hamer's work said they believed it would hold up. "It's an excellent study," said Elliott Gershon, a behavioral geneticist at the National Institute of Mental Health. "As always, it needs to be replicated and if it is, it's a major breakthrough. This will be the first time we have a gene that relates to a normal human function—sexual orientation—in people who are mentally intact."*

Following is the article "A Linkage Between DNA Markers on the X Chromosome and Male Sexual Orientation," published in Science, *July 16, 1993:*

The role of genetics in male sexual orientation was investigated by pedigree and linkage analyses on 114 families of homosexual men. Increased rates of same-sex orientation were found in the maternal uncles and male cousins of these subjects, but not in their fathers or paternal relatives, suggesting the possibility of sex-linked transmission in a portion of the population. DNA linkage analysis of a selected group of 40 families in which there were two gay brothers and no indication of nonmaternal transmission revealed a correlation between homosexual orientation and the inheritance of polymorphic markers on the X chromosome in approximately 64 percent of the sib-pairs tested. The linkage to markers on Xq28, the subtelomeric region of the long arm of the sex chromosome, had a multipoint lod score of 4.0 ($P = 10^{-5}$), indicating a statistical confidence level of more than 99 percent that at least one subtype of male sexual orientation is genetically influenced.

Human sexual orientation is variable. Although most people exhibit a heterosexual preference for members of the opposite sex, a significant minority display a homosexual orientation. This naturally occurring variation presents an opportunity to explore the mechanisms underlying human sexual development and differentiation.

The role of genetics in sexual orientation has been previously approached by twin, adoption, and nuclear family studies. From the rates of homosexuality observed in the monozygotic and dizygotic twins, ordinary siblings, and adoptive (adopted in) brothers and sisters of homosexual men and women, overall heritabilities of 31 to 74 percent for males and 27 to 76 percent for females were estimated. However, the precise extent of genetic loading is unclear because systematic data on relatives raised apart (adopted out) are not available and because the number and nature of the putative inherited factors are unknown. The observation that male homosexuals usually have more gay brothers than gay sisters, whereas lesbians have more gay sisters than gay brothers, suggests that the factors responsible for this familial aggregation are at least partially distinct in men compared to women.

Recent neuroanatomical studies have revealed differences between heterosexual and homosexual men in the structure of three regions of the brain; namely, the third interstitial nucleus of the anterior hypothalamus, the anterior commissure, and the suprachiasmatic nucleus. The role of gonadal steroids in the sexual differentiation of the mammalian brain is well established, but thus far the role of hormonal variations in normal human sexual development is unknown. Nonbiological sources of variation in human sexual expression have been under consideration in diverse disciplines including psychiatry, psychology, religion, history, and anthropology.

The goal of our work was to determine whether or not male sexual orientation is genetically influenced. We used the standard techniques of modern human genetics, namely pedigree analysis and family DNA linkage studies. Recent advances in human genome analysis, in particular the development of chromosomal genetic maps that are densely populated with highly polymorphic markers, make it feasible to apply such methods to complex traits, such as sexual orientation, even if these traits are influenced by multiple genes or environmental or experiential factors, or some combination of these. Our data indicate a statistically significant correlation between the inheritance of genetic markers on chromosomal region Xq28 and sexual orientation in a selected group of homosexual males.

Characteristics of Study Participants

The subjects studied were self-acknowledged homosexual men and their relatives over age 18. The initial sample for pedigree analysis consisted of 76 index subjects who were recruited through the outpatient HIV clinic at the National Institutes of Health Clinical Center, the Whitman-Walker Clinic in Washington, D.C., and local homophile organizations. One or more relatives from 26 of these families also participated in the project (total $n = 122$). The sample for the sib-pair pedigree study consisted of 38 pairs of homosexual brothers, together with their parents or other relatives when available, who were recruited through advertisements in local and national homophile publications. Two additional families who were originally in the randomly ascertained pool were added to this group for the DNA linkage study (total $n = 114$). Subjects signed an Informed Consent, approved by the NCI Clinical Review Subpanel, prior to donating blood and completing an interview or questionnaire covering childhood gender identification, childhood and adolescent sexual development, adult sexual behavior, the Kinsey scales, handedness, alcohol and substance use, mental health history, medical genetics screen, HIV status, and demographics. The participants were white non-Hispanic (92 percent), African American (4 percent), Hispanic (3 percent), and Asian (1 percent) and had an average educational level of 15.5 ± 2.4 (mean $\pm$ SD) years and an average age of 36 ± 9 (mean $\pm$ SD) years.

Sexual orientation was assessed by the Kinsey scales, which range from 0 for exclusive heterosexuality to 6 for exclusive homosexuality. Subjects rated themselves on four aspects of their sexuality: self-identification, attraction, fantasy, and behavior. Of the homosexual subjects, >90 percent self-identified as either Kinsey 5 or 6 whereas >90 percent of their nonhomosexual male relatives self-identified as either 0 or 1. The sexual attraction and fantasy scales gave even greater dispersions between the groups, with ≥ 95 percent of the participants either less than Kinsey 2 or more than Kinsey 4. Only the sexual behavior scale gave a small overlap between the two groups largely because of adolescent and early adult experiences. Therefore, for our study, it was appropriate to treat sexual orientation as a dimorphic rather than as a continuously variable trait. Similar bimodal distributions of Kinsey scores in males have been reported by others.

The age of phenotypic expression of homosexuality was assessed by asking the subjects at what age they were first attracted to another male, when they acknowledged their sexual orientation to themselves, and when they acknowledged their orientation to others. Most of the subjects experienced their first same-sex attraction by age 10, which was prior to the average age of puberty at 12 years. Self-acknowledgement occurred over a broad range of ages between 5 and 30 years, with the greatest increase occurring between years 11 and 19. The mean age for public acknowledgement was 21 years, which is similar to the average age for "coming out" reported by others. Since the average age of our subjects was 36 ± 9 years, we did not correct for age-dependent phenotypic expression in subsequent analyses.

Pedigree Analysis

Traits that are genetically influenced aggregate in families and, in the case of dominant or sex-linked inheritance, are transmitted from one generation to the next. Family histories were collected from 114 homosexual male probands who were asked to rate their fathers, sons, brothers, uncles, and male cousins as either definitely homosexual (Kinsey 5 or 6, acknowledged to the proband or another family member) or not definitely known to be homosexual (heterosexual, bisexual, or unclear). The reliability of the probands' assessment of their family members' sexual orientation was estimated by conducting interviews with 99 relatives of the index subjects. All (69/69) of the relatives identified as definitely homosexual verified the initial assessment, as did most (27/30) of the relatives considered to be nonhomosexual; the only possible discrepancies were one individual who considered himself to be asexual and two subjects who declined to answer all of the interview questions. Hence describing individuals as either homosexual or nonhomosexual, while undoubtedly overly simplistic, appears to represent a reliable categorization of the population under study.

On the basis of a separate study in which the uncles and male cousins of lesbians were interviewed, we estimated that the population prevalence of male homosexuality is 2 percent (14/717). Although this rate is lower than the popularly accepted figures of 4 to 10 percent for male homosexuality, probably due to the more stringent definition applied here, it was considered more accurate for this analysis since the sampling, interview format, and definition of homosexual orientation were identical to those used in the male study. Similarly low rates for the population incidence of homosexuality have been reported when recent sexual behavior was used as the criterion.

The pedigree analysis for the male relatives of the 76 randomly ascertained homosexual male probands indicated that the highest rate of homosexual orientation was in brothers, who had a 13.5 percent chance of being gay, representing a significant 6.7-fold increase over the estimated background rate of 2 percent ($P < 0.001$). Among more distant relatives, only two groups had significantly higher rates of homosexual orientation than the population incidence, namely maternal uncles and the sons of maternal aunts. Both of these maternally related classes of relatives had rates of $\approx$ 7.5 percent, which were significantly higher than the background rate ($P < 0.01$). By contrast, fathers and all other types of paternally related relatives had rates that were lower or not significantly different from the background. Background rates of homosexuality were also observed in the female relatives of the homosexual male probands (except for sisters, who had a 5.4 percent rate versus a 1 percent background rate) and in the male relatives of lesbian probands (except brothers, who had a 4.7 percent rate).

Although the observed rates of homosexual orientation in the maternally derived uncles and male cousins of gay men were higher than in female and paternally related male relatives, they were lower than would be expected for a simple Mendelian trait. Furthermore, there was a substantial number of families in which lesbians or paternally related gay men were present. This could be explained if some instances of homosexuality were male-limited and maternally inherited whereas others were either sporadic, not sex-limited, or not maternally transmitted. To test this, we recruited 38 families in which there were two homosexual brothers, no more than one lesbian relative, and no indication of direct father-to-son transmission of homosexuality (that is, neither the father nor son of a proband was gay). We hypothesized that this selected population of families would be enriched for the putative maternally transmitted genetic factor and therefore display further increases in the rates of homosexuality in maternally derived uncles and male cousins. Indeed, the rates of homosexuality in the relatives of these selected sib-pair probands were increased from 7.3 to 10.3 percent for maternal uncles and from 7.7 to 12.9 percent for the sons of maternal aunts. By contrast, the rates of homosexuality in the other types of male relatives were unchanged or decreased compared to the initial study. The differences between the random and sib-pair populations were not significantly different ($P > 0.1$); however, the differences between all maternal relatives as compared to all nonmaternal relatives were significant within both the randomly ascertained group ($P < 0.05$) and the sib-pair group ($P < 0.001$)....

These results demonstrate increased rates of homosexual orientation not only in the brothers of gay men, as has been previously reported, but also in maternal uncles and the sons of maternal aunts. Because uncles and cousins share inherited information with the index subjects, but are raised in different households by different parents, this observation favored an interpretation based on genetics rather than the rearing environment and suggested that linkage studies might be fruitful.

X Chromosome Linkage

One explanation for the maternal transmission of a male-limited trait is X chromosome linkage. Since males receive their single X chromosome exclusively from their mothers, any trait that is influenced by an X-linked gene will be preferentially passed through the mother's side of the family.

DNA linkage analysis provides the means to distinguish X-linked inheritance from competing hypotheses such as maternal effects, imprinting, decreased reproductive rates of expressing males, or differential knowledge concerning maternal versus paternal family members. If the X chromosome contains a gene that increases the probability of an individual's being homosexual, then genetically related gay men should share X chromosome markers close to that gene. If no such gene exists, then no statistically significant correlations between sexual orientation and X chromosome markers will be observed.

We performed the linkage analysis on [a] selected population of families ... in which there were two homosexual brothers. This sib-pair experimental design has several theoretical and practical benefits: (i) it is nonparametric and independent of gene penetrance and frequency; (ii) it is capable of detecting a single linked locus even if additional genes or environmental conditions are required to express the trait; (iii) it is more powerful to study siblings than more distant relatives for traits displaying limited familiality; (iv) "false negatives" (individuals who have or will have a homosexual orientation but choose to identify themselves as heterosexual) are irrelevant to the analysis because they are not studied; (v) "false positives" (individuals who have a heterosexual orientation but choose to identify themselves as homosexual) are expected to be rare; (vi) the sib-pair method is more stable to errors in genotyping and to mistakes or alterations in phenotype than are large pedigree methods; and (vii) it was more practical to obtain the cooperation of nuclear sib-pair families than of multigenerational families.

The sample for the linkage analysis consisted of 40 pairs of homosexual brothers (38 from the sib-pair pedigree study and 2 from the random sample) together with their mothers or other siblings if available. DNA was prepared from all available members of these families and typed for a series of 22 markers that span the X chromosome. Each sib-pair was scored as either concordant-by-descent (D) if the mother was known to be heterozygous and both sons inherited the same allele, concordant-by-state (S) if the mother was unavailable and both sons shared the same allele, discordant (−) if the two sons carried different alleles, or noninformative (n) if the mother was homozygous for the marker. For families in which DNA from the mother was not available, the data for the concordant-by-state pairs were corrected for the possibility that the mother was homozygous for the marker by taking into account the population frequency of the allele coinherited by the two sons. Using a likelihood ratio test, we then calculated for each locus the probability (z_1) of the brothers sharing the marker by-descent and the statistical significance (P) of deviations from the value of $z_1 = 1/2$ expected under the null hypothesis of no linkage.

The X chromosome markers used for linkage analysis were simple sequence repeats, variable number of tandem repeats, and restriction fragment length polymorphisms, all of which were detected by the polymerase chain reaction (PCR). Heterozygosities, which were determined by analyzing 62 to 150 independent X chromosomes from the sib-pair and related populations, ranged from 0.35 to 0.87.... Despite the presence of shadow bands [in the genotype determinations], the individual alleles were readily distinguishable, and concordant and discordant sib-pairs could be clearly differentiated. As expected for this X-specific marker, the alleles inherited by the sons were derived exclusively from the mother. By contrast, the marker DXYS154, which lies on the tip of Xq in a region of subtelomeric homology and genetic exchange between the X and Y chromosomes, displayed alleles contributed by both the father and the mother. As expected for this tightly sex-linked marker, almost all of the male siblings inherited the same Y chromosome allele from their fathers; therefore, only the contribution from the maternal X chromosome was considered in the analysis of this locus.

The linkage analysis included a statistical analysis of the pair-by-pair data and multipoint mapping analysis of the X chromosome. The main outcome was the detection of linkage between homosexual orientation and markers in the distal portion of Xq28....

Evaluation of the data by multipoint mapping with the LINKMAP routine of the computer program LINKAGE 5.1 supported the linkage between homosexual orientation and distal Xq28. The model used for analysis was an X-linked, male-specific gene with a mutation rate of 0. The population frequency of the homosexuality-associated allele was assumed to be 0.02, and penetrances were set at 0 for all females, 0 for males lacking the trait-associated allele, and 0.5 for males having the trait-associated allele; heterosexual brothers were not included in the analysis. The peak multipoint lod score was 3.96 to 4.02, depending on whether compressed or full allele information was used; because the lod score is the logarithm to the base 10 of the odds ratio, this corresponds to an odds ratio of ≈10,000:1. The apparent location of the peak was 8 cM distal of DXYS154. However, this is likely to be an overestimate due to the well-known phenomenon of biased recombination fraction estimation in the case of complex traits where the analysis model differs from the true model. Therefore, the data were reanalyzed under two alternative models. When the frequency of the trait-associated allele was increased from 0.02 to 0.1, as suggested by Risch and Giuffra, the peak lod score decreased to 3.9 and the distance from DXYS154 decreased to 5 cM. When the penetrance of the non-trait-associated allele was increased from 0 to 0.05, giving a substantial level of phenocopies, the peak lod score of 3.9 fell directly over DXYS154, and the lod scores throughout distal Xq28 were greater than 3.5. Given that DXYS154 lies within 1 Mb of the telomere, these latter models probably yield more accurate estimates of the locus position. More precise mapping will require more distal markers, a larger number of families, and additional information concerning the trait parameters.

There was no significant evidence for linkage between sexual orientation and loci lying outside of Xq28. Most of the markers on the remainder of the long arm, and all of the markers on the short arm, gave values of z_1 that were statistically indistinguishable from the null hypothesis ($P > 0.05$). Although there was a moderate excess of concordant pairs at the markers DXS456, DXS297, and DXS548 ($0.002 \leq P \leq 0.02$), it is unlikely that these loci play a significant role in sexual orientation because they were adjacent to markers that gave negative results. Furthermore, multipoint mapping gave lod score less than -2 throughout the region between the KAL locus at Xp22.3 and the DXS994 locus at Xq26 and around the fragile X locus at Xq27.3. However, a much larger sample would be required to stringently eliminate these regions from playing a role in sexual development in a small proportion of families.

Contribution of Genetics to Male Sexual Orientation

The proof for the involvement of genes in a human behavioral trait must ultimately consist of the chromosomal mapping of the loci and isolation of the relevant DNA sequences. Such molecular studies are essential to separate the role of inheritance from environmental, experiential, social, and cultural factors. DNA linkage studies of families in which the trait appears to be genetically segregating represent the first step in this approach.

We have now produced evidence that one form of male homosexuality is preferentially transmitted through the maternal side and is genetically linked to chromosomal region Xq28. In a selected population of families in which there were two homosexual brothers and no transmission through fathers or to females, 33 of 40 sib-pairs had coinherited genetic information in this subtelomeric region. Observing such an association by chance alone has a type I error rate of approximately 0.001 percent for a single tested region of the genome (haplotype $P = 1.2 \times 10^{-5}$), and therefore an error rate of less than 0.03 percent for a collection of 22 independent markers ($P = 22 \times 1.2 \times 10^{-5} = 0.0003$). Similarly, multipoint linkage mapping gave a peak lod score of 4.0, which is associated with an overall type I error level of 0.5 percent, even for a complete genome search. Thus, both forms of analysis indicate that the linkage results are statistically significant at a confidence level of >99 percent. As with all linkage studies, replication and confirmation of our results are essential. The observed excess coinheritance of Xq28 markers by homosexual brothers is not due to segregation distortion because normal, Mendelian segregation has been demonstrated for many different Xq28-linked traits and polymorphic markers. Rather, it appears that Xq28 contains a gene that contributes to homosexual orientation in males.

There were seven pairs of brothers who did not coinherit all of the Xq28 markers. Such discordant pairs could arise because of homozygosity of the mother at the sexual orientation-related locus, recombination between the locus and a marker gene, genetic heterogeneity, or nongenetic sources of variation in sexual orientation. We estimate that the last two categories comprise approximately 36 percent of the sib-pair population. At present, we can say nothing about the fraction of all instances of male homosexuality that are related or unrelated to the Xq28 candidate locus because of the selection for genetically loaded families that is imposed by linkage methods. We also have no information about the role, or lack thereof, of the Xq28 region in multiplex families containing multiple gay men or lesbians (or both), nor about the presence or absence of the homosexuality-associated allele in brothers or other male relatives who identify as heterosexual. Given the overall complexity of human sexuality, it is not surprising that a single genetic locus does not account for all of the observed variability. Sib-pairs that are discordant at Xq28 should provide a useful resource for identifying additional genes or environmental, experiential, or cultural factors (or some combination of these) that influence the development of male sexual orientation.

Our experiments suggest that a locus (or loci) related to sexual orientation lies within approximately 4 million base pairs of DNA on the tip of the long arm of the X chromosome. Although this represents less than 0.2 percent of the human genome, it is large enough to contain several hundred genes. The fine mapping and eventual isolation of this locus will require either large numbers of sib-pairs, more extended families, or the complete DNA sequence of the region. Once a specific gene has been identified, we can find out where and when it is expressed and how it ultimately contributes to the development of both homosexual and heterosexual orientation. The Xq28 region is characterized by a high density of genetic loci and contains both repeated DNA sequences and a pseudoautosomal region of homology and genetic exchange between the X and Y chromosomes. Recombination between tandemly repeated sequences, or between active and inactive loci on the X and Y chromosomes, could generate DNA sequence variants at a high rate and thereby account for the genetic transmission of a trait that may reduce reproduction.

The subjects for our linkage study were males who self-identified as predominantly or exclusively homosexual within the context of modern American society; such studies could be broadened to include individuals who identify as bisexual or ambisexual. The role of the Xq28 candidate locus, and of other chromosomal regions, in female sexual orientation remains to be tested. Although nuclear family studies suggest that the overall heritability of sexual orientation is similar in men and women, their pedigree segregation patterns appear to be distinct.

Our work represents an early application of molecular linkage methods to a normal variation in human behavior. As the human genome project proceeds, it is likely that many such correlations will be discovered. We believe that it would be fundamentally unethical to use such information to try to assess or alter a person's current or future sexual orientation, either heterosexual or homosexual, or other normal attributes of human behavior. Rather, scientists, educators, policy-makers, and the public should work together to ensure that such research is used to benefit all members of society.

REMOVAL OF FBI DIRECTOR, NOMINATION OF SUCCESSOR

July 19, 20, 1993

William S. Sessions was removed as director of the Federal Bureau of Investigation (FBI) on July 19, five months after the results of a probe into allegations of professional impropriety were released. President Bill Clinton terminated Sessions's employment after he was informed by Attorney General Janet Reno that the director could "no longer effectively lead the bureau and law enforcement community." Sessions was the first director in the FBI's seventy-year history to be fired.

Hours after announcing that he was firing Sessions, Clinton nominated federal judge Louis J. Freeh as the next FBI director.

A Plethora Of Charges

Sessions had been the subject of an intensive investigation by the Office of Professional Responsibility (OPR), a branch of the Justice Department under the auspices of William P. Barr, who served as attorney general in the Bush administration. The investigation, as outlined in a report issued by the OPR January 19, focused on Sessions's alleged use of FBI funds for personal, not professional, purposes. The OPR alleged that Sessions used almost $10,000 in FBI funds to buy a fence for his house that did not enhance, and actually detracted from, the director's security. The OPR further alleged that Sessions had made excessive and improper use of bureau cars and limousines by allowing his wife and other guests to ride with him and that he had failed to report the benefit of his limousine service as taxable income. Perhaps more serious, the OPR found that Sessions was approved for a substantial mortgage loan that OPR investigators claimed had been granted on the basis of his high-ranking position rather than any normally acceptable qualification. Additionally, the report found that Sessions failed to cooperate with the inquiry into the charges. All of these actions were generally deemed improper by the FBI and the Justice Department. Barr *censured Sessions before the report was released, saying that it revealed "a pattern of your taking advantage of the government" that the OPR had found unacceptable.*

Rebuttal and Support

Sessions, however, was quick to rebut the OPR's findings. "As a lawyer, judge, and government servant, I have lived a life of respect for the law," Sessions said soon after the report was made public. "I believe that I have conducted myself in accordance with the law and with uncompromised ethical standards. I have done so as director, and through this proceeding. I will continue to do so."

Sessions's supporters were equally vocal in their praise for the director, citing a long list of reforms he had initiated at the bureau, including updated fingerprinting and genetic testing techniques. Cited as well were his efforts to expand the role of minority groups in the FBI, efforts generally regarded as a major advancement for the bureau. Rep. Don Edwards, D-Calif., chairman of the House Judiciary Subcommittee on Civil and Constitutional Rights, called the report "sort of a Pearl Harbor, a sneak attack," and said, "It's not the way the highest law enforcement officer [Barr] should act, to hit and run." Others who defended Sessions included Sen. Orrin Hatch, R-Utah, who termed Sessions "a very fine person." Supporters began to voice suspicion that the report was the result of a probe Sessions had launched into what some considered to be the Justice Department's questionable actions in investigating the role of the Atlanta branch of the Italian BNL (Banca Nazioinale del Lavaro) loan of billions to Iraq. The OPR report was issued just two days after Sessions announced the Justice Department/BNL investigation.

Mounting Accusations, but Praise for Freeh

While the controversy swirled around the director—who defended his record and repeatedly said he would not step down—additional accusations surfaced against him, generally centering on the role of his wife, Alice, in the alleged improprieties. The OPR report stated that FBI vehicles had been used so that Alice Sessions could shop, pick up firewood, and get her nails done. FBI planes were diverted to pick up Mrs. Sessions, and security guards were bumped off those planes so she could accompany her husband, the report found. Additionally, Mrs. Sessions was found to have been present at official FBI meetings without sanction, including the meeting in which the fence issue was disputed. Further, Sessions's stance was weakened somewhat by the firing of his executive assistant, Sarah W. Munford, for misconduct.

Throughout the months following the report's release, Attorney General Janet Reno, top FBI officials, and others urged Sessions to resign, saying that a defensive stance by the director could damage both the bureau and the fledgling Clinton administration. Sessions, however, refused to resign midway through his ten-year term as a "matter of principle," stating that the charges against him were "simply not true" and that the OPR "knew that there was no impropriety, but sought to create the impression that there was." He defended building the controversial fence, saying that it had been "approved through proper channels," and he said that he "did not authorize and would not permit" his wife to use FBI transport for errands.

Although Sessions feared that his removal would set a precedent that would make the position of FBI director increasingly subject to politics, he refused to resign even when Attorney General Reno advised him that his replacement was imminent. On July 19, President Clinton informed Sessions by phone and letter that his position as director had been terminated and that Deputy FBI Director Floyd Clark would serve as acting director until a replacement was nominated.

The next day, appearing before reporters in the White House Rose Garden with the vice president, attorney general, and former FBI director William Webster, the president announced his nomination of Freeh, praising him as "experienced, energetic and independent. He will be both good and tough—good for the FBI and tough on criminals." Freeh had been appointed to the federal bench in 1991 by President George Bush after serving almost ten years as a federal prosecutor specializing in organized crime cases. The nomination brought widespread approval from both parties. Senate Judiciary chairman Joseph R. Biden, D-Del., said Freeh appeared "ideally suited to continuing the strong, effective, and independent tradition of the FBI." Sen. Alfonse M. D'Amato, R-N.Y., who had recommended Freeh for the judgeship, said, "He's fearless, indefatigable.... The president couldn't have picked better."

Following are the texts of President Clinton's July 19, 1993, announcement that he had dismissed William S. Sessions as director of the FBI, and the July 20 statement nominating federal judge Louis J. Freeh to succeed him:

DISMISSAL OF SESSIONS

Good afternoon. In recent months, serious questions have been raised about the conduct and the leadership of the Director of the FBI William Sessions. Among other matters, the Department's Office of Professional Responsibility has issued a report on certain conduct by the Director. I asked the Attorney General, Janet Reno, to assess the Director's tenure and the proper response to the turmoil now in the Bureau. After a thorough review by the Attorney General of Mr. Sessions' leadership of the FBI, she has reported to me in no uncertain terms that he can no longer effectively lead the Bureau and law enforcement community.

I had hoped very much that this matter could be resolved within the Justice Department. The Attorney General met with Judge Sessions over the weekend and asked him to resign, but he refused. In accord with the recommendation of the Attorney General, with which I fully agree, I called Director Sessions a few moments ago and informed him that I was dismissing him, effective immediately, as the Director of the FBI.

We cannot have a leadership vacuum at an agency as important to the United States as the FBI. It is time that this difficult chapter in the Agency's history is brought to a close. The FBI is the nation's premier investigative and enforcement agency. Law-abiding citizens rely on the FBI to handle a wide array of complex and sensitive matters, to protect our shores against terrorism, our neighborhoods against the scourge of drugs and guns, our public life against white-collar crime, corruption, and crimes of violence. The Agency's brilliant detective work in the wake of the World Trade Center bombing has shown even in a time of difficulty the men and women on the street and in the labs have continued to give their country their best. With a change in management in the FBI, we can now give the crime fighters the leadership they deserve.

Tomorrow, I expect to make an announcement about my nominee to be the next Director of the FBI. In the meanwhile, the Attorney General and I have asked Floyd Clark to serve as Acting Director of the Bureau....

NOMINATION OF FREEH

Good morning. Please sit down. Mr. Vice President. Attorney General Reno. The Acting FBI Director Floyd Clark. Former Director of the FBI, Judge William Webster, we're delighted to have you here. Senator D'Amato. Judge Robert Bonner, the DEA Administrator. The representatives of all the law enforcement agencies who are here and friends and family of the nominee to be the next director of the FBI.

The Federal Bureau of Investigation is the federal government's cutting edge in the fight against crime. Its agents are the best-trained in the world. Its sophisticated technology enable law enforcement agents to catch criminals with a fragment of a fingerprint.

As we saw only recently in the remarkably swift arrest in the World Trade Center bombing, the Agency continues its preeminent place in the law enforcement world. The Agency itself must clearly adapt to new times. It must continue the progress of opening its ranks to minorities and to women that began in recent years. It must work cooperatively with other agencies in the United States and in international partnerships against crime with police forces of other nations.

Yesterday I announced my intention to appoint a new director of the FBI. Today I am pleased to nominate a law enforcement legend to be the director of the FBI, Judge Louis Freeh. Judge Freeh knows the FBI. He is a highly decorated former agent and supervisor. He has investigated and prosecuted some of the most notorious and complex crimes of our time. He is experienced, energetic and independent. He will be both good and tough—good for the FBI and tough on criminals.

It can truly be said that Louis Freeh is the best possible person to head the FBI as it faces new challenges and a new century. He has spent his career in the federal justice system. After working his way through law school, he became an FBI agent. He knows the agency as only an agent can, working the dangerous streets. He helped lead the waterfront investigations that led to the criminal convictions of 125 people, including leading organized crime figures.

From the FBI Judge Freeh became a federal prosecutor in New York City. He prosecuted and won convictions against the leaders of what was then the largest heroin importation case in our history, the legendary "Pizza Connection" case. The trial lasted over a year. Among other defendants, Judge Freeh sent the head of the Sicilian mafia to jail. Observers were dazzled. He was called, and I quote, "one of the government's toughest investigators. A ramrod straight and ferocious crusader against the mob. An investigative genius."

Three years ago, as Judge Freeh neared the end of his work as a prosecutor, the Department of Justice selected him to head a special task force in one of the most notorious and difficult criminal cases of our day. A mysterious bomber was at work in the South mailing parcels that killed Federal Judge Robert Vance near Birmingham, Alabama and civil rights leader Robbie Robinson in Savannah, Georgia.

Many predicted that the case would never be solved. But led by Louis Freeh, the task force tracked down the bomber and Freeh himself prosecuted the case and obtained convictions. The bomber is now serving seven life terms in prison. In recognition of his service to the law, President Bush appointed Louis Freeh to the federal bench. Now Judge Freeh has agreed to leave that lifetime post to serve his nation once again in a difficult new job. There are few jobs in our government that are more important.

Our federal law enforcement agencies face an ever changing array of threats. Drugs continue to ravage our young people and our streets. Law-abiding citizens can be caught in the crossfire between gangs today equipped like armies. White collar swindlers practice inventive forms of what Al Capone once called "the legitimate rackets." And our nation, so long immune from the terrorism that has plagued the world, now faces that threat, too.

With Attorney General Janet Reno, Drug Policy Coordinator Lee Brown, and now, we hope, FBI Director Louis Freeh, our administration has a street-smart front line against crime. These law enforcers did not learn about crime in theory books, they learned about it on the streets and in the courtroom. And they have learned the best lessons of state and local enforcers. With all of their hard-won experience, this crime-fighting team can work hard every day to protect the American people's right to safety in their homes and in their communities.

I must tell you that I am very proud and very grateful that Judge Freeh was willing to leave his lifetime appointment on the federal bench for the somewhat less secure work that the rest of us find in the Executive Branch. (Laughter.) I hope the American people will be grateful as well, and I look forward to his speedy confirmation.

Judge Freeh. (Applause.)

JUDGE FREEH: Thank you very much. Thank you, Mr. President, for your kind and, indeed, your humbling words. And thank you for the honor of this nomination. I also want to thank Attorney General Reno for her support and confidence.

I'd like to introduce to you my wonderful wife, Marilyn, sitting in the front row; and our four sons, Justin, Brendan, Sean and Connor. They can all stand up, except Conner, who can't walk yet.

Do you want to stand up, guys? (Applause.)

Thank you. They've never been better behaved. (Laughter.) I was born in Jersey City, and from about the age of my eldest son, I wanted to be an FBI agent. It was my first job after law school at age 25. The FBI is the greatest organization for law enforcement ever created by a democratic society. The brave men and women who serve in its ranks exemplify all of our country's police professionals dedicated to ensuring both safety and liberty.

If confirmed by the Senate, I pledge my total commitment to a Federal Bureau of Investigation whose only beacon is the rule of law, whose sole task is protecting all of our people from crime and violence.

The FBI's duties include virtually every important aspect of the crimes that take such a dreadful toll in American life. They include: violent street crimes, drug trafficking, civil rights violations, organized crime and racketeering, public corruption, fraud, health care abuses, white collar crime, environmental crimes and crimes against our domestic and national security.

Our country must be made safe again—in cities, towns, villages and countryside. Safety is particularly important for our children and young people who all too often are now trapped in virtual war zones controlled by vicious criminals. The issue is stark: Do we allow criminals to destroy our Constitution and our freedoms, or do we as a people committed to the rule of law, take effective steps to preserve our most basic civil rights to be protected against harm, to be free from fear, and to enjoy the full measure of liberty and opportunity in this great nation?

Anyone doubting the need for an efficient FBI need only read the front page or watch the evening news. What most Americans once thought impossible has now occurred here: a terrorist bomb that killed, maimed and spread terror in our nation's largest city. We now live in a global village in terms of law enforcement. When my friend and colleague, Italy's Judge Giovanni Falcone, and his wife were assassinated in 1992 outside Palermo, it was an attack against the cooperative efforts of the FBI and the Italian police and judges to combat international narco terrorism.

The Department of Justice has spearheaded these international police and judicial assistance operations, which are critical to our success and which must continued.

The FBI must not only catch those who have committed crimes, it must be an important step ahead of criminals as often as possible to prevent crime from being committed. It also has the unique ability in a democratic society to exculpate the innocent.

To do all these things takes expert and dedicated personnel, state-of-the-art technology, and the support of the American people. It also takes the greatest possible cooperation with state and local enforcement agencies.

I had the privilege of working investigations and prosecutions which represent the long and dedicated efforts of thousands of federal, state, local and foreign law enforcement officers. Both the pizza case and the mail bombing case required the careful coordination of scores of separate investigative agencies, police forces, prosecutors and governments—all working together toward common professional goals.

The harmonious and cooperative efforts of the policemen and women who solve these difficult cases without the occurrence of a single leak throughout years of intensive investigations were in the highest tradition of great law enforcement. In our country's rich traditions, we must make certain that the best of the past is surely the prologue of the challenges we face today and in the future.

Before going on the Supreme Court, Attorney General Harlan Fiske Stone set into motion in the 1920s reforms that eventually led to the outstanding FBI of today, an FBI which has been strengthened by Judge Sessions's efforts to diversify its excellent work force. These important efforts should be continued and strengthened. At its bedrock, the FBI must stand for absolute integrity, be free of all political influence, be free of any racial or other bias, and work solely in the public interest.

Without exception, the FBI must be responsible to the Attorney General, the President and the Congress. Most importantly, the FBI must be responsible to the American people. Thank you and God bless you. (Applause.)

ISRAELI COURT DECISION TO ACQUIT DEMJANJUK

July 29 and August 18, 1993

The Israeli Supreme Court voted unanimously July 29 to overturn John Demjanjuk's 1988 conviction for war crimes committed at the Treblinka concentration camp in Poland. Four years earlier Demjanjuk had been convicted of being "Ivan the Terrible," the notoriously sadistic gas chamber operator of Treblinka. Even though Demjanjuk was acquitted of that particular set of crimes, many questions remained regarding his activities during World War II. Also of concern was the message that his acquittal might send to other Nazi war criminals and the public.

The story of Demjanjuk's identification, capture, conviction, and later retrial spanned more than four decades, starting shortly after the end of the war. Demjanjuk applied for permission to emigrate to the United States in 1950, claiming that he was a farmer in Poland. Two years later he entered the United States and settled in Cleveland. In 1977 the Justice Department, alleging that Demjanjuk had hidden his past as a Nazi SS guard, began measures to revoke his citizenship, an effort that succeeded in 1981. Five years later, in 1986, Secretary of State George P. Shultz signed a warrant allowing Israel to extradite Demjanjuk to be tried for war crimes. An Israeli court convicted Demjanjuk in 1988 and sentenced him to hang. Demjanjuk appealed and the Israeli Supreme Court overturned the conviction, citing insufficient evidence to prove that Demjanjuk was indeed Ivan the Terrible. Amid much controversy, Demjanjuk returned to Ohio, where he secluded himself from protesters who marched outside his house.

A Question of Identity

The basic issue to be resolved during Demjanjuk's trial was his identity: Was he Ivan the Terrible, as the prosecution and some camp survivors claimed? More than 800,000 Jews were slaughtered at Treblinka, a place described by its commandant as Dante's Inferno. Ivan was notorious for his stupefying cruelty. For example, he was said to have forced a prisoner to lie silently while he used a wood drill on his buttocks.

The Ukrainian-born Demjanjuk claimed to have been captured and held in several different concentration camps including Rovno in what is now Ukraine until 1945, when he joined the German-funded Russian Liberation Army, where he served for the remainder of the war. The prosecution agreed with the first part of that statement but argued that, like many others held in Rovno, Demjanjuk elected to work for the Germans. The prosecution argued that he was taken to the Trawniki unit, where he was trained to become a member of the Wachmanner group. According to some accounts, this group was established for one purpose—"to study and to teach" its members how to annihilate and bring about the "final solution" of the "Jewish problem." The evidence for Demjanjuk's participation was a card issued to the Wachmanner group correctly listing his date of birth, his father's name, hair color, and scar on his back. The card did not indicate that he ever served at Treblinka, where Ivan served, but it did list his service at the Polish death camp, Sobibor, where more than 250,000 Jews were killed. The court also found convincing evidence that Demjanjuk was a guard at both the Regensburg and Flossenburg death camps in Germany.

Five survivors of Treblinka positively identified Demjanjuk as the person they knew as Ivan the Terrible. In addition, his known involvement at Sobibor made it likely that he had indeed served at Treblinka. However, considerable evidence suggested that another individual, not John Demjanjuk, was the gas chamber operator.

Israeli lawyers gained access to thirty-seven depositions given to the Soviet KGB in the 1940s and 1950s by former Treblinka guards who identified the gas chamber operator as Ivan Marchenko, whose whereabouts and fate remained unknown. The guards also claimed that Ivan had scars on his neck, which Demjanjuk did not have. Two guards stated that Ivan's last name was Marchenko, not Demjanjuk, and they were unable to identify Demjanjuk from photographs. The Justice Department also had a list from Poland of 43 of the estimated 100 Ukrainians who had served as Treblinka guards, which listed Marchenko's name, but not Demjanjuk's. Another survivor referred to Ivan as black-haired. Marchenko had black hair, but Demjanjuk's hair was blond. None of this evidence had been available for Demjanjuk's first trial, but it surfaced with the ending of the cold war and the beginning of increased U.S.-Soviet cooperation. In addition, the judges were reluctant to rely on photo identifications by the Treblinka survivors who had not seen Ivan for more than thirty years.

The question of Demjanjuk's identity was muddled further by U.S. government actions. There was possible Justice Department prosecutorial misconduct during the ten years following the discovery that Demjanjuk had lied on his entry papers. The department had evidence that pointed to Marchenko as the real Ivan. Federal appeals court judges claimed that it was an "undisputed fact that the Department had in its possession prior to the extradition proceeding statements and documents indicating that John Demjanjuk was not 'Ivan the Terrible,' but that another Ukrainian guard at Treblinka, Ivan Marchenko, was the operator of the gas chambers." Demjanjuk's family contended that, had the Justice Department released the evidence pointing to Marchenko, Demjanjuk never would have been extradited.

However, the government's lawyers argued that "Demjanjuk's service as an SS guard at any one of these [death] camps was sufficient to render him ineligible for immigration." In papers discarded by the Justice Department, Demjanjuk's son-in-law, Ed Nishnic, found an account of an interview with one of Ivan's coworkers, which clearly showed that the witness was unable to identify photographs of Demjanjuk until they were displayed in a manner that singled him out. Demjanjuk's supporters claimed that the Justice Department suppressed evidence, and in November a three-judge panel rebuked the Justice Department for what the court said was its "win at any cost" attitude.

Israeli High Court Decision

Demjanjuk's prosecutors contended that it was enough that he worked in a Nazi camp where Jews were exterminated to uphold his conviction for genocide. But Justice Aharon Barak told the prosecutor, "Unless you have proof beyond a reasonable doubt that Demjanjuk was at Treblinka, there is no point in proceeding." Demjanjuk's lawyer, Yoram Sheftel, argued that because Demjanjuk was specifically extradited and convicted for being Ivan the Terrible, allegations about his presence in other camps were irrelevant. The prosecutor, Michael Shaked, argued that "The death camp Wachmann is the direct servant of Satan. He is there to kill Jews throughout the time that he is there. Sobibor and Treblinka are one and the same, both morally and legally. Sobibor and Treblinka will always be the same crime, one that the Jewish people and all of humanity have yet to recover from." Nevertheless, the conviction was overturned "because of doubt of the terrible charges attributed to 'Ivan the Terrible' of Treblinka."

The reversal of the guilty verdict provoked concern among observers who raised questions such as why Demjanjuk was not retried for his service as a Wachmann guard, or on Sobibor-related charges, and why he was allowed to return to the United States after his service as a Nazi death camp guard was unearthed. Rabbi Marvin Hier, founder of the Simon Wiesenthal Institute, which searches for Nazi criminals, said that he feared the acquittal "will discredit survivor testimony." Many Holocaust survivors expressed anger and shock at the Supreme Court's decision, particularly in view of the fact that the Israeli justices agreed that Demjanjuk participated in the extermination of millions of Jews. Others worried that the decision might provide fuel for revisionist claims that the Holocaust never occurred.

As of the end of 1993, the Justice Department was continuing efforts to strip Demjanjuk of his U.S. citizenship.

Following are the unofficial summary of the decision of Israel's Supreme Court to acquit John Demjanjuk on charges of being Ivan the Terrible, July 29, 1993, and the conclusion of the verdict handed down by the court August 18, 1993:

UNOFFICIAL SUMMARY OF DECISION

On August 18, 1993 the Supreme Court of Israel sitting as the High Court of Justice gave its decision on 10 petitions brought by survivors of the Holocaust and others demanding that John (Ivan) Demjanjuk should be brought to trial on charges of war-crimes at Sobibor and other concentration camps. These petitions follow the decision of the Supreme Court to acquit Demjanjuk, by reason of doubt, of the brutal offenses attributed to Ivan the Terrible of Treblinka.

The court of three judges dismissed the petitions.

JUSTICE SHLOMO LEVIN considered in detail the reasons set out in the opinion of the Attorney-General which argued against bringing Demjanjuk to trial. This opinion was based on four arguments:

1. That a further trial would infringe the rule of 'double jeopardy' in that Demjanjuk would be standing trial for offenses in respect of which he had already been tried and acquitted.
2. That the Supreme Court, in acquitting Demjanjuk of charges attributed to Ivan the Terrible of Treblinka, had stated that it did not think it reasonable to commence new proceedings against him, in view of the seriousness of the offenses with which he had originally been charged and the nature and circumstances of the alternative charges.
3. That on the basis of the evidence available, it was unlikely that Demjanjuk would be convicted of the alternative charges, and that risking a further acquittal was not in the public interest.
4. That Demjanjuk was extradited from the United States specifically to stand trial for offenses attributed to Ivan the Terrible of Treblinka, and not for other alternative charges.

Justice Levin noted that under Israeli law, it was established that authority in criminal matters is vested with the Attorney-General, who is authorized to bring charges in any case where there is sufficient evidence, unless he believes that there is no public interest in bringing the case. He further noted that the Attorney-General has a wide discretion in making such a decision and that the Court should only intervene when the decision is so untenable as to be totally unreasonable.

Justice Levin went on to consider the arguments put forward by the Attorney-General. He found that it was not unreasonable to consider that bringing charges against Demjanjuk might infringe the 'double jeopardy' rule. Similarly, it was not unreasonable to estimate that chances of convicting Demjanjuk were small, particularly in view of the fact that none of the survivors of the Sobibor camp had identified him. Justice Levin also held that, although the opinion of the Supreme Court as regards further proceedings only related to the case before it, the Attorney-General could not be criticized for giving weight to the Court's comments in this regard.

Justice Levin considered a number of other arguments raised by the petitioners, among them that a failure to bring Demjanjuk to trial would effectively broadcast a message that the time when Nazi war criminals could be brought to trial has passed. This, he said, was not so. The obligation to bring Nazis and collaborators to trial remains binding on every state, when there is evidence to substantiate the charges.

JUSTICE GAVRIEL BACH noted the difficulties involved in releasing a defendant who may be guilty of the barbaric and bestial offenses committed by the Nazis.

Justice Bach stated that he differed from his colleagues in that he did not attach any significant weight to some of the arguments put forward by the Attorney-General. Among these was the argument that the decision of the Supreme Court acquitting Demjanjuk of the crimes attributed to Ivan the Terrible contained a direction, express or implied, not to institute further proceedings against him. The relevant portion of the court's decision, stated Justice Bach, related only to the specific question whether the case should be referred back to the District Court. A case should be referred back to a lower court when new evidence which may cast light on the charge in question is presented to the court. This was not the situation before the Supreme Court; the question was whether the defendant should be convicted of offenses at Sobibor and Trawniki, charges substantially different from those in the indictment before the Court. For this reason, stated Justice Bach, the court was unable to refer the case back to the lower court. It was not the Court's intention, however, to instruct the prosecutorial system on the issue of whether to bring additional charges.

As regards the argument that Demjanjuk had been extradited specifically to stand trial for offenses attributed to Ivan the Terrible of Treblinka, Justice Bach found that this also was not persuasive. Even if the consent of the United States authorities was required in order to bring further charges, such consent could be requested. If the request was refused, no charges need be filed and the defendant could be deported.

Accordingly, if the decision of the Attorney-General had been based on these considerations alone, Justice Bach stated that there would have been grounds to intervene in the decision.

However, a number of other arguments put forward in favor of the decision were not unreasonable. Among these was the possibility that the 'double jeopardy' rule would be infringed. The Attorney-General's concern in this regard was supported by the fact that Demjanjuk's presence in the Sobibor camp had been mentioned in the indictment and in other documents submitted as evidence in the original trial and in the appeal. Moreover, the prosecution had argued in the appeal that the Court could convict Demjanjuk of offenses committed at Sobibor since these had been proved before the Court, and the defendant had had an opportunity to defend himself against these charges. Similarly, the presence of Demjanjuk at Trawniki had also been considered by the Court.

Justice Bach also considered the argument that bringing further charges would not serve the public interest, since evidentiary difficulties raised the likelihood of a further acquittal. He did not feel that this consideration was unreasonable. Accordingly, Justice Bach concurred in dismissing the petitions. He emphasized, however, that this should in no way be taken to imply that war criminals can no longer be brought to trial. The Israeli legislator placed no statute of limitations on offenses committed by Nazis and their collaborators, and in many cases no evidentiary difficulties in proving the identity and activities of the defendant arise. Nazis and collaborators should continue to be found and brought to trial, as long as they live.

JUSTICE MISHAEL CHESHIN noted the grave responsibility that rests on the Court when deciding whether to intervene in an administrative decision. He also noted the inadequacy of the legal system, which is designed to deal with behavioral norms, when confronted with the scale of the atrocities committed by the Nazis.

Justice Cheshin then considered the decision of the Supreme Court not to convict Demjanjuk of the charges other than those relating to offenses committed at Treblinka. In this decision he saw more than a hint to conclude the proceedings against Demjanjuk. He concurred with Justice Levin in finding that the Attorney-General was entitled to take guidance from the comments of the court, even though strictly they related only to the proceedings actually before the Court.

Justice Cheshin stated that he saw no room to intervene in the decision of the Attorney-General, and that he concurred with the view and reasoning of Justice Levin.

CONCLUSION OF THE PROCEEDINGS

More than seven years ago, Ivan Demjanjuk, the appellant, was extradited from the United States to Israel. He was lawfully extradited; there existed *prima facie* evidence upon which to base the extradition decision. Before the Courts in Israel, the District Court and before us, evidence was brought that the appellant was a member of the group of *Wachmanner*, the product of the Trawniki unit, which was established for one purpose—in order "to study and to teach" its members how to exterminate, annihilate, destroy and bring about the "final solution" of the "Jewish problem". Further evidence was brought that when the appellant obtained the Trawniki certificate, he was posted to Sobibor, one of the three Extermination Camps established by the German government of the Third Reich, according to the plan of *Aktion Reinhard.* It was also found that he served as a guard of the *S.S.* at the Concentration Camps of Flossenbuerg and Regensbuerg.

The main issue of the indictment sheet filed against the appellant was his identification as Ivan the Terrible, an operator of the gas chambers in the Extermination Camp in Treblinka. A substantial number of survivors of the Treblinka inferno identified the appellant as Ivan the Terrible, one of the chief murderers and tormentors of the Jews who were brought to Treblinka on their way to suffocation in the gas chambers. He was therefore convicted in the District Court. Before us, after the hearing of the appeal ended, there were submitted statements of various *Wachmanner,* which spoke of someone else as Ivan the Terrible of Treblinka. We do not know how these statements came into the world and who gave birth to them; but we admitted them by the most lenient application of the law and procedure. And when they came before us, doubt began to gnaw away at our judicial conscience; perhaps the appellant was not Ivan the Terrible of Treblinka. By virtue of this gnawing—whose nature we knew, but not the meaning—we restrained ourselves from convicting the appellant of the horrors of Treblinka.

Wachmann Ivan Demjanjuk has been acquitted by us, because of doubt, of the terrible charges attributed to Ivan the Terrible of Treblinka. This was the proper course for judges who cannot examine the heart and the mind, but have only what their eyes see and read. The matter is closed—but not complete. The complete truth is not the prerogative of the human judge.

Given today, the 11th of the month of Av, 5753 (the 29th of July, 1993).

Meir Shamgar
President

Menachem Elon
Deputy President

Aharon Barak
Justice

Eliezer Goldberg
Justice

Yaakov Maltz
Justice

CENTERS FOR DISEASE CONTROL ON SEDENTARY LIFESTYLE

July 30, 1993

Nearly 60 percent of Americans are too sedentary for their own good, and of these, almost 30 percent report no leisure time activity at all. These findings were the result of a survey conducted by the Centers for Disease Control (CDC) in 1991 and published July 30, 1993, in a report entitled "Prevalence of Sedentary Lifestyle—Behavioral Risk Factor Surveillance System, United States, 1991."

In an exhaustive study, the CDC asked a representative sample of 90,000 Americans to rate themselves according to the frequency, duration, and intensity of activities on the following scale: (1) no physical activity; (2) irregular activity only; (3) regular but not intensive activity; and (4) regular and intensive activity. For the CDC's purposes, respondents who answered "no or irregular activity only" are sedentary.

The CDC then correlated its findings by sex, race, age, and income. In the thirty-five to fifty-four age group, women were found to be more active than men, but the opposite was true in those over fifty-five. Likewise, the higher the income, the greater the physical activity. Race also played a role—with nonwhites exercising less than whites.

Risks of Sedentary Lifestyle

A number serious of health problems are associated with being sedentary, according an article in the May-June 1993 Journal of Physical Education, Recreation and Dance (JPERD). *A sedentary lifestyle contributes to low back pain, osteoporosis, and poor posture, and is the "single greatest risk to cardiovascular health." A study by CDC researchers published in the* Journal of the American Medical Association *in 1990 blamed sedentary behavior for 23 percent of deaths from stroke, heart disease, diabetes, chronic obstructive pulmonary disease, lung cancer, breast cancer, cervical cancer, colorectal cancer, and chronic liver disease.*

Disturbed by the serious health implications of its study, the CDC joined with the American College of Sports Medicine to devise a "concise public health message" promoting physical activity. Their recommendation was that all U.S. residents age eighteen and older participate in moderate physical activity for thirty minutes or more almost every day.

Benefits of Exercise

The JPERD *defined physical fitness as the "ability to handle normal physical demands of life, engage in a variety of leisure activities, and still be able to function effectively in emergency situations." Fitness relates to "aerobic endurance, body composition, flexibility, muscular strength, and muscular endurance."*

Preliminary research findings at Columbia University's School of Public Health suggested that women who exercise throughout their pregnancies have bigger babies than sedentary women.

Significant health benefits can accrue with even moderate changes in physical activity. Exercise does not have to be painful. "We made a mistake by insisting that exercise must be sustained by aerobic activity," said Steven Blair, former president of the American College of Sports Medicine. "Walking up stairs, gardening, raking leaves, or walking" are acceptable, according to Russell R. Pate, president of the American College of Sports Medicine. It is "not necessary to be an athlete to benefit from physical exercise," the CDC stated.

The JPERD *made some suggestions with regard to getting people started. Learning "warm-up, exercise techniques, and training guidelines" may help some individuals, while others can benefit from knowing about positive and enjoyable ways to exercise. Someone "who had to run laps as punishment in physical education classes" may not want to take up running.*

The JPERD *also noted that exercising increases the desire to exercise even more, and that people who feel and look better often enjoy greater confidence and energy.*

Children and Exercise

Contrary to widespread opinion, children have not become couch potatoes. Researchers at Arizona State University found that scores for 1957, 1965, 1975, and 1985 for children taking the test for the President's Council on Physical Fitness and Sports had not changed much. A study conducted by Michigan State University's Institute for the Study of Youth Sports showed that the best of today's young athletes outscore their 1960s counterparts. The Institute's director, Dr. Vern Seefeldt, suggested that as children's sports have become more intense and competitive, "the best athletes are even better today because they're active earlier."

However, less gifted children may be denied opportunities to engage in sports, a trend that discouraged physical fitness. Seefeldt noted that when kids played video games, they were competing against themselves. "They don't have to worry about being scorned by teammates, parents or coaches."

Following is the text of the Centers for Disease Control study, entitled "Prevalence of Sedentary Lifestyle—Behavioral Risk Factor Surveillance System, United States, 1991," released July 30, 1993:

Despite increasing evidence of the health benefits of physical activity, the United States remains predominantly a sedentary society. In 1990, nearly 60% of the U.S. adult population reported little or no leisure-time physical activity. Persons who engage in no physical activity are at higher risk for death from coronary heart disease than are persons who exercise regularly. To estimate the prevalence of sedentary lifestyle and identify groups characterized by a high prevalence of physical inactivity, CDC analyzed data on leisure-time physical activity from the 1991 Behavioral Risk Factor Surveillance System (BRFSS). This report summarized the results of the survey.

Data were available for 87,433 respondents aged ≥18 years in 47 states and the District of Columbia that participated in the BRFSS, a population-based, random-digit-dialed telephone survey. Respondents were asked about the frequency, duration, and intensity of activities and were scored and categorized as having 1) no physical activity, 2) irregular activity only, 3) regular but not intensive activity (less than 50% of predicted maximal cardiorespiratory capacity, based on age), or 4) regular and intensive activity. Persons with no or irregular leisure-time activity were defined as having a sedentary lifestyle. Data were weighted and aggregated, and composite estimates and standard errors for selected groups were calculated using SESUDAAN [standard errors program for computing of standardized rates from sample survey data]. Prevalence of sedentary lifestyle and 95% confidence intervals were estimated by sex, race, and age. Because of limitations in sample sizes, race-specific prevalences could be estimated only for non-Hispanic whites and other races combined.

Overall, 58.1% of respondents were classified as sedentary; 29.8% reported no leisure-time activity. The crude prevalence did not differ by sex (57.7% for men and 58.5% for women). The prevalence of sedentary lifestyle was higher for other races (63.7%) than for non-Hispanic whites (56.7%), particularly for women of other races (64.9%).

The prevalence of sedentary lifestyle increased steadily with age. For younger respondents (aged 18-34 years) the prevalence was 54.6%; for persons aged 35-54 years, 58.9%; and for older respondents (aged ≥55 years), 61.9%. Prevalence did not differ by sex for the youngest age group

(55.0% for men and 54.2% for women); however, for the 35-54 year age group, men (60.9%) were more sedentary than women (56.9%), and for the older age group, women (64.9%) were more sedentary than men (59.1%).

The prevalence of sedentary lifestyle was inversely related to income (i.e., prevalence was highest [65.0%] for the lowest income category [<$15,000] and lowest [48.3%] for persons in the highest income category [>$50,000]). Prevalence also was inversely related to education and was 71.9% among persons with less than a 12th-grade education, compared with 50.1% among persons with a college education.

Editorial Note: The findings in this report underscore the need for most persons in the United States to increase physical activity. A national health objective for the year 2000 is to reduce to 15% the proportion of persons aged ≥6 years who engage in no leisure-time physical activity.

The measurement of physical activity based on the BRFSS is subject to at least two limitations. First, the BRFSS findings reflect self-reported data and cannot be validated. Second, no equivalent estimates are available for occupational activity, which may be substantially higher in low-income and low-education groups; therefore, estimates restricted to leisure-time activities may overestimate the prevalence of sedentary lifestyle in these populations.

The increased prevalence of sedentary lifestyle among racial/ethnic minorities may be attributable to disparities in education and income, which were not adjusted for in this analysis. This pattern may reflect differences in availability of leisure time, access to facilities, or other barriers to increased physical activity.

Because of the high prevalence of sedentary lifestyle in the United States, CDC and the American College of Sports Medicine (ACSM) recently convened experts on physical activity and health to examine the science base supporting the health benefits of moderate physical activity and to develop a concise public health message for physical activity promotion. CDC and ACSM recommend that all U.S. residents aged ≥18 years participate in moderate physical activity for 30 minutes or more on most days. Participation in such activity at least 5 days per week is a suggested goal. Achievement of this goal will require intensified efforts by health-care providers and others to increase public awareness of the health benefits of an active lifestyle and to establish environments in which persons can be more physically active.

August

SENTENCING OF OFFICERS CONVICTED IN KING CASE

August 4, 1993

Los Angeles police officers Stacey C. Koon and Laurence M. Powell were sentenced to thirty months in prison for their roles in the beating of Rodney King two and a half years earlier. U.S. District Court judge John G. Davies handed down the sentences on August 4, ending a chapter in a story that had begun more than two years earlier when a man named George Holliday pointed his new video camera toward the scene unfolding below his balcony in the early morning hours of March 3, 1991.

Holliday's videotape quickly came to symbolize all that was wrong—and all that could go wrong—in the nation's cities. For many, it represented the racism, economic hardship, police brutality, and injustice in Los Angeles' South Central area, in particular, as well as the wider LA community and the nation. It turned its participants' names into household words and became the primary evidence in two trials. The defendants' state trial ended in acquittal April 29, 1992, and the verdict touched off massive civil disorder in Los Angeles. (Bush and King on L.A. Riots; Report on Police Response, Historic Documents of 1992, p. 407)

During the second trial, on federal offenses, Holliday's videotape was referred to in intervals of one second of time. In his sentencing memorandum, Judge Davies described, second-by-second, the actions that had occurred, in order to make clear the background, the sentencing guidelines, and mitigating circumstances of the case.

Background

In the early morning hours of March 3, 1991, King and his friends had been drinking Old English 800, a malt beer, for several hours when King drove onto the freeway. Spotted by a highway patrol officer, King's car was clocked at approximately 100 miles per hour.

King stopped the car after an eight-mile chase. By then, the highway patrol had been joined by a school district vehicle, and a police helicopter hovered overhead. Soon Holliday, awakened by the noise, began documenting the event that became known as the "Rodney King beating." What the world saw was several police officers relentlessly beating an unarmed, prone man in apparent gratuitous violence.

Shock, revulsion, and anger accompanied the widespread dissemination of Holliday's videotape. The incident also prompted charges of racism, as it became clear that King, an African American, was beaten by white police officers. President George Bush called the beating "sickening," and for many the videotape represented a open-and-shut case against the four policemen charged with beating King.

During the state trial, California prosecutors relied mainly on the video as the key to their case. The strategy backfired. Defense witnesses convinced the jury that the officers acted within police guidelines. The jury acquitted the officers of almost all the charges. The verdict stunned many, and in the South Central part of Los Angeles, a riot began that lasted nearly six days, killed more than fifty people, and destroyed thousands of businesses.

Federal Charges and a New Trial

Within an hour of the verdict, President Bush ordered the Justice Department to direct its own independent criminal investigation. Bush said, "Civil rights leaders and just plain citizens fearful of, and sometimes victimized by, police brutality were deeply hurt [by the acquittal].... For fourteen months they waited patiently, hopefully. They waited for the system to work. And when the verdict came in, they felt betrayed."

The federal case was tried in the U.S. District Court for the Central District of California. Prosecutors in the federal case did something the state had not done: they called Rodney King as a witness. Jurors later said that although King admitted lying and contradicted himself, he was an effective witness. His humanity came through and in that context, the beating he suffered at the hands of the defendants became more poignant. Prosecutors introduced evidence proving that King sustained fifteen broken facial bones because of Powell's baton blows.

Another difference between the two trials was that Powell did not testify in his own defense in the federal trial. In the earlier trial, Powell had testified that he feared for his life when King charged him and that he believed that King was on the strength-enhancing drug PCP because he threw officers off his back when they tried to handcuff him. Dan Caplis, a criminal attorney who monitored the federal trial, claimed Powell's decision not to take the stand was "fatal." According to Caplis, "Juries give the benefit of the doubt to police, but when the evidence is stacked against them, they expect officers to take the stand and tell their story."

On April 17, 1993, almost exactly a year after the earlier acquittals and subsequent riot, Koon and Powell were found guilty. The two other officers involved, Theodore J. Briseno and Timothy E. Wind, were acquitted. Afterward, Briseno's attorney, Harland W. Braun, offered what may have been the real reason for the outcome. With the threat of riots following another acquittal, Braun asked, "Is it better that two innocent people get convicted or that fifty people die tommorow? I don't know."

Jurors interviewed after the trial said the videotape was crucial to their decision. One noted that the videotape portrayed King's attempt to cooperate with the police: "He's trying to put out his hands behind his back and they're just not letting him." Deliberations became so emotional that at one point one juror sought medical help. A fellow juror was quoted as saying, "On the news, I understood later they said one of the jurors got sick. No, he couldn't take it in there."

Sentencing

Koon and Powell were sentenced to thirty months in prison, far less than the five- to seven-year sentences called for in the federal guidelines judges are supposed to follow. Citing several factors, Judge Davies outlined the reasons for his departure from the guidelines. The two officers had endured punishment outside of any enforced by his court, Davies contended. "The extraordinary notoriety and national media coverage of this case, coupled with the defendants' status as police officers, make Koon and Powell unusually susceptible to prison abuse. Moreover, Koon and Powell will be subjected to multiple adversarial proceedings and stripped of their positions and tenure by the LAPD [Los Angeles Police Department]," Davies wrote. He also noted that although the state and federal governments each have dual sovereignty, "a federal conviction following a state acquittal based on the same underlying conduct ... raises a specter of unfairness."

However, Davies said that Rodney King himself was the primary reason for giving Koon and Powell a lesser sentence. The officers' conduct began as a "legal use of force against a resistant suspect and subsequently crossed the line to unlawfulness, all in a matter of seconds...." According to Davies, before second 1:07:28, the actions of Powell—and Koon as the officer in charge—were mitigated by King, who "engaged in illegal conduct prior to and during his arrest."

King resisted arrest, tried to escape custody, and charged at Powell. He had not been searched. Therefore, the officers' perception of King as dangerous was reasonable. Davies noted, "From the time of that first baton blow until [second] 1:07:28 ... Mr. King persisted in his failure to obey the police. Defendants Koon and Powell repeatedly ordered Mr. King to assume the felony-prone position to avoid further confrontation."

Davies continued by noting second 1:07:28. The "Court recognizes that by the time the defendants' conduct crossed the line to unlawfulness, Mr. King was no longer resisting arrest.... Nevertheless, the incident would not have escalated to this point, indeed it would not have occurred at all, but for Mr. King's initial misconduct," he said.

The Healing Process

People throughout Los Angeles and the nation expressed a collective sigh of relief. Civil rights leaders and followers assembled at the First African Methodist Episcopal Church in South Central Los Angeles, where the rioting had been the worst a year before, cheered when they heard the verdict. On the street, motorists honked their horns as community activists waved peace signs. It had been a long year.

Many had hoped for a stiffer sentence, noting what appeared to be a double standard of justice. One South Central resident said he was pleased by the verdicts, but added, "If that was one of us doing one of them, we'd have got life." Yet just hearing the word "guilty" twice was enough to make Manuel Lozano, the manager of neighborhood produce market, happy. "I think people should feel good about the verdict," he said.

> *Following are excerpts from the memorandum issued August 4, 1993, by Judge John G. Davies, sentencing two Los Angeles police officers, Stacey C. Koon and Laurence M. Powell, for federal offenses related to the beating of Rodney King:*

Introduction

Four Los Angeles Police Officers, Stacey C. Koon, Laurence M. Powell, Timothy E. Wind, and Theodore J. Briseno, were indicted by the United States in a Two-Count Indictment filed August 4, 1992. The Indictment charges in Count One that defendants Laurence M. Powell, Timothy E. Wind, and Theodore J. Briseno violated Title 18, United States Code, Section 2, and Title 18, United States Code, Section 242, and aided and abetted each other. The Government charges that while acting under color of the laws of the state of California, said officers willfully struck with batons, kicked, and stomped Rodney Glen King, resulting in bodily injury to him and, thereby, willfully deprived him of the right preserved and protected by the Constitution of the United States not to be deprived of liberty without due process of law, including the right to be secure in his person and free from the intentional use of unreasonable force by one making an arrest under color of law. The aiding and abetting count was stated in Count One of the Indictment, but at trial was treated as a separate count and was submitted to the jury as such.

Count Two of the Indictment alleges violation of Title 18, United States Code, Section 242, and is directed against Stacey C. Koon alone. He is charged with willfully permitting the other officers in his presence, and under his supervision, to unlawfully strike with batons, kick, and stomp Rodney Glen King and with the willful failure to prevent the unlawful assault by said officers, all in violation of the right preserved and protected by the Constitution of the United States not to be deprived of liberty without due process of law, including the right to be kept free from harm while in official custody.

The case was tried to a jury commencing February 25, 1993. The jury reached its verdicts on April 16, 1993, and the verdicts were handed up on April 17, 1993.

By said verdicts the jury found that none of the defendants was guilty of aiding and abetting, that Officer Briseno was not guilty of the charges alleged in Count One and was acquitted, that Officer Wind was not guilty of the charges alleged in Count One and was acquitted, that Officer Powell was guilty of the charges other than aiding and abetting alleged in Count One, and that Sergeant Koon was guilty of the charges alleged in Count Two.

The matter is now before this Court for the sentencing of Lawrence M. Powell and Stacey C. Koon. The Court has reviewed, read, and considered the presentence reports, the addenda thereto, the position papers and sentencing memoranda filed by the defendants and by the Government. The Court has reviewed and considered a multitude of letters relating to the trial of the case and sentencing, and letters written in support of the defendants. The Court has also considered the United States Sentencing Commission *Guidelines Manual,* effective November 1, 1992, and the arguments of counsel. Based thereon, the Court makes its findings as follows and sentences the defendants as follows.

Findings of Fact

The details of the arrest of Rodney Glen King in the early morning hours of March 3, 1991, on Osborne Street near Hanson Dam, Los Angeles, were disclosed at trial. Multiple motions were made before trial in an effort to resolve the many legal problems that emerged, and witnesses testified and evidence was taken between February 25, 1993, and April 6, 1993. The Government presented its case in great detail. It is hard to imagine that the Government overlooked any fact. However, because the verdicts were general and no special findings were made by the jury, certain factual conclusions and findings remain undetermined. For the purposes of sentencing it falls to the Court to make those findings.

The essential facts proved at trial were as follows:

During the early evening hours of March 2, 1991, Rodney Glen King met with two friends and sat in his wife's Hyundai automobile in Altadena, a suburb of Los Angeles, drinking a malt beer beverage, Old English 800, packaged in 40-ounce bottles. Mr. King consumed at least two bottles. His friends also drank Old English 800. Although it is not clear precisely how much they each consumed, it is certain that Mr. King consumed more than

80 ounces. Mr. King and his friends drank in the parked automobile for a number of hours. Late in the evening, they left Altadena in the Hyundai. Mr. King drove. Their intended destination is not clear. Mr. King testified that it was Hanson Dam, but his friend Bryant Allen testified that the three companions left Altadena to "look for women."

Mr. King was intoxicated. He drove the Hyundai from Altadena to the 210 Freeway, then west from Pasadena towards the city of San Fernando. While westbound, in the vicinity of La Tuna Canyon Road, CHP [California Highway Patrol] Officer Melanie Singer and Officer Tim Singer, her husband and training officer, observed the Hyundai speeding westbound on the freeway behind the CHP cruiser. Officer Melanie Singer was driving. The CHP vehicle exited and re-entered the freeway at Sunland Boulevard, and with red lights and siren activated followed the Hyundai, which was by then about one mile west of the CHP vehicle. Officer Melanie Singer estimated the speed of the Hyundai west of Wheatland Avenue as being in excess of 100 m.p.h.

Mr. King left the freeway at Paxton Avenue and commenced traveling on surface streets, followed by the Singers' CHP unit. Officer Melanie Singer called for back up. The CHP dispatcher alerted LAPD by radio call. The call was heard by patrol officers of the Los Angeles Unified School District in a unit nearby which joined the chase. In addition, Officers Powell and Wind in an LAPD unit responded to the call. During the pursuit, the CHP officers attempted to communicate with Mr. King as he drove on the surface streets, and ordered him to pull over. He failed to do so. Mr. King testified that he did not pull over because he was afraid of returning to prison. Mr. King continued on the route chosen by him, at times stopping for red lights, at times proceeding through red lights. The CHP vehicle and the school district vehicle followed the Hyundai at varying speeds. They were joined by Officers Powell and Wind's vehicle. After the Hyundai left the freeway, the pursuit was always at moderate to slow speeds. The three police vehicles followed the Hyundai for a number of miles on surface streets to the point where it stopped at an entrance to the Hanson Dam recreation area on Osborne Street. In all, the CHP unit followed the Hyundai for approximately eight miles before the pursuit ended.

The CHP vehicle, the school district vehicle, and Officer Powell's vehicle came to rest in the immediate vicinity of the Hyundai. The occupants of the Hyundai were ordered out of the vehicle by Officers Singer. The two passengers exited the Hyundai and followed instructions of the police officers. Mr. King was slow to move from the driver's seat but ultimately did and was repeatedly ordered to lie on the ground. He emerged from the Hyundai smiling. This was the scene when Sergeant Koon arrived. Officers Briseno and Rolando Solano arrived in their unit moments after Sergeant Koon.

Mr. King did what appeared to be a dance step, and then waved at an LAPD helicopter overhead. Officer Melanie Singer ordered Mr. King to move away from the Hyundai and to place his hands where she could see them, and then again ordered him to the ground. When she did so, he grabbed his buttocks. Officer Singer pointed her service revolver at him. Mr. King did not lie prone but moved around on his hands and knees.

Sergeant Koon took command and ordered Officer Melanie Singer to holster her service revolver. The LAPD officers then commenced the arrest process. Mr. King was a large muscular man and a felony suspect. Sergeant Koon testified that he thought Mr. King may have been recently imprisoned because Mr. King appeared to have engaged in the bodybuilding common among prison inmates. The officers ordered Mr. King to lie in the felony-prone position. He refused to do so. Officers Powell, Wind, Briseno, and Solano jointly attempted to place Mr. King in a felony-prone position. He resisted and became combative, forcing the officers to retreat. The subsequent events were captured by Mr. George Holliday on videotape. . . .

The tape does not capture the entire sequence. It records the events commencing with a view of Mr. King on the ground, surrounded by officers. The Holliday videotape became the focus of a good deal of testimony at trial and was analyzed in thorough detail by expert and other witnesses called by each side. The Court has reviewed the tape for the purpose of sentencing. Although the videotape creates a vivid impression of a violent encounter, careful analysis shows that it is sometimes an ambiguous record of the crucial events. A meaningful understanding of the events it depicts required the explanation of witnesses who are experts in law enforcement. At trial the Government and defendants agreed that much of the officers' conduct was justified and legal, yet vigorously disputed whether and when their behavior became illegal.

The principal question for sentencing not answered by the verdicts is, when did the offenses committed by Officer Powell and by Sergeant Koon occur? The answer to this question determines the extent to which these defendants are liable for Mr. King's injuries. Injury is an element of the offenses with which Officer Powell and Sergeant Koon were charged, and is relevant to the determination of their sentences under the Sentencing Guidelines.

Answering this question requires a two-tiered inquiry. The offenses the jury found to have been committed occurred when Officer Powell used excessive force and formed the intent to deprive Mr. King of his civil rights, and when Sergeant Koon intended to refrain from preventing the officers under his control from using excessive force which deprived Mr. King of his constitutional rights. Sergeant Koon's criminal liability is not derivative from Officer Powell's liability. Sergeant Koon's conviction rests entirely upon the wrongfulness of his own conduct, that is, his willful refusal to prevent illegal use of force in his presence. Thus, the Court must make separate determinations concerning Officer Powell's and Sergeant Koon's illegal behavior.

(1) Officer Powell

The videotape displays a continuum of events involving behavior that was initially legal and which became criminal. The initial task for the Court, for the purposes of sentencing, is to determine when Officer Powell's behavior became illegal. Did it become illegal only once and then continue to be illegal for a period of time, or was it at times legal and at times illegal? The Court finds that Officer Powell crossed the line between legal behavior and illegal behavior once.

Although the videotape is reliable evidence of the physical events that unfolded in the course of Mr. King's arrest, it provides less direct evidence concerning two factors central to Officer Powell's illegal behavior. To determine that at any given point Officer Powell's behaviors crossed the line into illegality, the Court must find that Officer Powell used objectively unreasonable force, and that he intended to use excessive force. The standard for objectively unreasonable force is supplied by the Supreme Court in *Graham* v. *Connor*, which held that "the 'reasonableness' of a particular use of force must be judged from the perspective of a reasonable officer on the scene, rather than with the 20/20 vision of hindsight." The Graham Court cautioned that "[t]he calculus of reasonableness must embody allowance for the fact that police officers are often forced to make split-second judgments—in circumstances that are tense, uncertain, and rapidly evolving—about the amount of force that is necessary in a particular situation." Accordingly, in evaluating the videotape, the Court must take into account the totality of the circumstances, including facts not displayed on the tape. Mr. King had not been searched. Mr. King did not respond to the electrical charge of Sergeant Koon's taser. Sergeant Koon testified that he observed Mr. King sweating profusely. At least during the initial stages of the arrest process, Sergeant Koon may reasonably have suspected that Mr. King was under the influence of PCP because of Mr. King's erratic and recalcitrant behavior.

The initial image on the Holliday videotape is of Mr. King on the ground surrounded by officers. For a brief period, he appears to have been motionless. Mr. King testified that during that moment he decided to try to escape through a gap between the Hyundai and a police vehicle into the Hanson Dam recreation area. He then rapidly rose to his hands and knees, and to his feet. He turned, outstretched his arms forward, and charged towards Officer Powell. Officer Powell took a step and struck Mr. King on the right side of his face and head with the side-handle baton. Mr. King fell to the ground. As Mr. King continued to attempt to rise, he was struck by Officer Powell and then by Officer Wind.

Officer Powell struck Mr. King repeatedly on the lower extremities from the 35th second of the tape to the 51st second of the tape. Officer Powell also delivered a blow to Mr. King's upper torso. Mr. King moved throughout this period, posing an apparent threat. He was ordered to assume the felony-prone position, but failed to respond to these commands. At 55 seconds into the tape, Officer Powell struck Mr. King on the chest or upper abdomen. He rolled over from a position with his abdomen on the ground to a position on his back. Mr. King's right hand moved in a downward direction across his chest and abdomen. Officer Powell struck Mr. King's chest or upper abdomen while Mr. King's hand was moving. After this blow, ... the application of force was suspended. The officers observed Mr. King roll over once more onto his abdomen. They watched him for 10 seconds.

In frames 1:03 and 1:04, Officer Powell reached for and briefly handled his cuffs, which were dangling from his right, back trousers pocket. This movement is evidence that Officer Powell perceived Mr. King to be no longer a threat and ready for cuffing.

At 1:05:20, Officer Briseno used his left foot to kick or stomp Mr. King in the upper thoracic area. Mr. King's body writhed in response. His feet rose, his head rose, and he raised his upper torso on his elbows. These movements by Mr. King were reflexive and nonvoluntary. He posed no threat.

Officer Powell struck Mr. King with his baton at 1:07:28 and thereafter struck him another 5 or 6 times. Officer Wind struck Mr. King 4 times with his baton, and kicked him in the upper thoracic or cervical area six times. Mr. King suffered this series of blows until approximately 1:26. At 1:30:13, Officer Powell handed his cuffs to Officer Briseno, and officers surrounded Mr. King. Mr. King was cuffed at 1:42. The procedure continued to 2:05, by which time Mr. King was tied.

As explained below, the Court finds that Officer Powell's offense conduct commenced when he struck King at 1:07:28 ... and continued to 1:26:00. He crossed the line between legal and illegal behavior at this time. No force used by Officer Powell prior to the blow memorialized on the videotape at 1:07:28 rose to the level of criminal deprivation of Mr. King's rights. Some of it was beyond the standards and practice of the LAPD. However, none of this conduct constitutes a violation of 18 U.S.C. § 242.

To determine the extent to which Mr. King's injuries resulted from Officer Powell's illegal behavior, it is necessary to determine when they occurred and whether they were the product of illegal force. These injuries fall into three broad categories: (1) fractures of facial bones and lacerations to the right forehead and facial area, (2) fracture of the distal fibula in the right leg, and (3) body bruises, contusions, and abrasions. The Court's inquiry is whether any of these injuries occurred prior to 1:07:28.

The Facial Fractures and Forehead Laceration. The most contested issue at trial relating to injuries was whether Mr. King's facial fractures and forehead laceration were the result of a baton blow, or blows, by Officer Powell, or the result of his face coming into contact with the ground surface. The Court finds that these facial injuries were caused by Officer Powell and that they occurred in the earliest sequence on the videotape when Mr. King, attempting to escape, charged toward Officer Powell. . . .

At trial the government presented evidence that this blow to the head was outside LAPD use-of-force policy guidelines if Officer Powell intended to strike Mr. King's head. However, the Court cannot find that this blow was objectively unreasonable in the totality of circumstances or that Officer Powell acted with an illegal intent. In view of Mr. King's sudden approach and Officer Powell's legitimate interest in stopping the hard-charging Mr. King, Officer Powell may have directed a blow at Mr. King that inadvertently struck his head. Telling evidence that the head blow was unintentional is provided by the fact that Officer Powell never clearly applied force to Mr. King's head again, although he had ample opportunity to do so. Accordingly, Officer Powell is not criminally liable for Mr. King's head and facial injuries.

The Leg Fracture. Mr. King sustained a fracture of the fibula in the right leg. This fracture was in the lower portion of the leg, and the Government argues that it was the result of a blow administered by Officer Powell at approximately 43 seconds into the videotape. The Court agrees it is clear that at that point Officer Powell struck Mr. King with the baton in the area of the right ankle, and that this blow caused Mr. King's fracture.

However, blows to leg joints are within the policy guidelines of the Los Angeles Police Department if necessary to forestall a threat. Preceding the relevant moments the situation had evolved rapidly. Mr. King had tried to rise, and as Officer Powell delivered the blows to the legs, Mr. King continued to move and resist repeated attempts to place him into the felony-prone position. It is unclear that a reasonable officer at the scene would not have delivered at least some of these blows. Moreover, in view of the rapidly shifting nature of the situation, the Court cannot find that Officer Powell intended to use excessive force. Accordingly, although Officer Powell's blow may have been tortious, he is not criminally liable for the fracture of the fibula.

Body Bruises and Contusions. ... At 55 seconds into the tape, Officer Powell struck Mr. King on the chest or upper abdomen as Mr. King's body moved and Mr. King's right hand reached downward across his chest in the direction of the waistline of his pants. At trial Sergeant Mark Conta testified that this was a flagrant violation of the LAPD's use-of-force policy guidelines. However, Mr. King had not been searched, and a reasonable officer at the scene may have judged that Mr. King was reaching for a weapon. Moreover, it is unlikely that Officer Powell intended to use excessive force. The situation forced him to react swiftly to Mr. King's hand movement, and it was not unreasonable for Officer Powell to block the hand movement with his baton. Under the circumstances this blow was not objectively unreasonable. The chest blow did not produce chargeable injury under 18 U.S.C. § 242.

Officer Powell's conduct clearly crossed the line into illegality at 1:07:28 when he struck Mr. King despite his perception that Mr. King was no longer a threat. Officer Powell is liable for the bodily injury he inflicted. He is not liable for bodily injury inflicted by Officer Wind during this period. The precise injuries caused by Powell were not demonstrated at trial. Mr. King undoubtedly sustained contusions as a result of the six blows by Powell. But the nature and extent thereof are unknown. It is impossible to distinguish between the injury inflicted by Wind and that inflicted by Powell. However, the injuries for which Powell is liable are limited to contusions, perhaps abrasions, but no fractures. For the reasons cited above, the Court finds that Officer Powell's behavior did not violate 18 U.S.C. § 242 prior to this moment. Thus, Officer Powell is not criminally liable for injuries sustained before this moment.

(2) Sergeant Koon

The remaining task is to determine when Sergeant Koon's behavior became criminal. The Ninth Circuit has stated that "a police sergeant who stands by and watches while officers under his command use excessive force and refuses to order them to stop may thereby 'subject' the victim to the loss of his or her right to be kept free from harm while in official custody or detention." The police sergeant must recognize that the force is excessive and that there are reasonable steps within his power that he could take to prevent the use of force. Finally, the police sergeant must deliberately or willfully refrain from preventing the excessive force.

The court in *Reese* does not squarely address whether the unlawfully excessive force must stem from criminal conduct by officers under the police sergeant's control. Nonetheless, the court's reasoning in *Reese,* as well as authority from other circuits, implies that a police sergeant is liable for permitting harm from excessive force, even when the supervised officers' conduct does not rise to the level of criminal activity, provided that the conduct is a constitutional tort. Accordingly, to determine the extent of Sergeant Koon's criminal liability, it is necessary to assess whether he failed to prevent tortious or criminal excessive force applied by Officers Powell, Wind, and Briseno.

Three facts simplify this inquiry. First, Officer Briseno's use of force against Mr. King was limited to a single stomp or kick at 1:05.20. Because Sergeant Koon could not have anticipated Officer Briseno's sudden movement, he is not criminally liable for failing to prevent this kick or stomp.

Second, prior to 1:07.28, Officer Wind delivered several blows to Mr. King in response to Mr. King's attempt to flee and his repeated efforts to rise from the ground. Because Mr. King posed a continuing threat, the Court cannot find that a reasonable officer would not have delivered these blows, or that Sergeant Koon had the requisite criminal intent in permitting them.

Third, the Court has found that prior to 1:07.28, Officer Powell's conduct did not violate 18 U.S.C. § 242.

For these reasons, the Court's inquiry concerning Sergeant Koon is limited to Officer Powell's potentially tortious use of force prior to 1:07.28, and Officers Powell and Wind's use of force after 1:07.28.

The Facial Injuries. Because the Court has found that these injuries were caused by Officer Powell's lawful application of force, Sergeant Koon is not criminally liable for permitting the blow or blows that caused these injuries.

The Leg Fracture.... The Court has found that Officer Powell lacked the requisite criminal intent to use excessive force when he delivered the blow that caused Mr. King's leg fracture. The same reasons compel the Court to find that Sergeant Koon lacked the requisite criminal intent to permit the use of excessive force....

Body Bruises and Contusions. Because Officer Powell's blow to Mr. King's chest or upper abdomen was a sudden response to Mr. King's hand movement, Sergeant Koon had no reasonable opportunity to anticipate or prevent it, and cannot be charged with injuries stemming from it.

By contrast, Sergeant Koon is liable for permitting Officers Powell and Wind's conduct after 1:07.28. At this point, Officer Powell's conduct crossed the line into criminal illegality. Moreover, because Mr. King posed no threat, Officer Wind's baton blows and leg kicks were objectively unreasonable. Sergeant Koon could have seen that Mr. King's movements in response to Officer Briseno's kick or stomp were involuntary, and he had a reasonable opportunity to halt Officers Powell and Wind's use of force. Sergeant Koon is liable for his failure to order the cuffing of Mr. King during the 10 seconds immediately prior to the kick by Officer Briseno, and for permitting the application of force by Officers Powell and Wind thereafter. Accordingly, bruises and contusions incurred during this period are chargeable to Sergeant Koon.

Summary

Neither Officer Powell nor Sergeant Koon is liable for Mr. King's serious bodily injuries, namely, his facial injuries and leg fracture. Both officers are liable to differing degrees for Mr. King's bruises and abrasions sustained after 1:07:28. Because neither officer violated 18 U.S.C. S 242 prior to this moment, neither is liable for injuries sustained by Mr. King before the event recorded at 1:07.28 of the videotape, and the Court so finds.

For purposes of calculating Mr. Powell's base offense level, the Court considers his relevant conduct to be the blows he administered after 1:07:28. Mr. Koon, on the other hand, was convicted of an offense of omission, and is liable for failing to stop Powell's and Wind's excessive use of force when he could have and should have. The excessive force used by Powell and Wind with Koon's permission constitutes "relevant conduct" for purposes of calculating Koon's base offense level....

Based on the defendants' "relevant conduct," the appropriate underlying offense for each is assault. The corresponding offense level, however, depends on whether Powell committed and Koon permitted an aggravated or a minor assault.

1. Aggravated vs. Minor Assault

The government takes the position that the underlying criminal conduct constitutes an aggravated assault....

Discussion

Calculation of Offense Level Under the Sentencing Guidelines

Both defendants Stacey C. Koon and Laurence M. Powell were convicted of violations of 18 U.S.C. § 242. Section 2H1.4 of the Guidelines addresses the calculation of a base offense level for this offense....

Where the Guidelines specify more than one base level offense, the Court's determination of which to apply is to be based on the defendant's "relevant conduct" ... "Relevant conduct" includes:

> all acts and omissions committed, aided, abetted, counseled, commanded, induced, procured, or willfully caused by the defendant....

The Court agrees.

An aggravated assault, within the meaning of the Guidelines, is a "felonious assault that involved (a) a dangerous weapon with intent to do bodily harm (*i.e.*, not merely to frighten), or (b) serious bodily injury, or (c) an intent to commit the felony.

In this case, the assault committed by Powell and permitted by Koon is a felony. Pursuant to 18 U.S.C. § 3559, an offense is a Class C felony if the maximum term of imprisonment authorized is at least ten years, but less than twenty years. Ten years is the maximum term of imprisonment authorized for a violation of 18 U. S. C. § 242 when bodily injury results.

Additionally, the felonious assault in this case involved a dangerous weapon. The term "dangerous weapon," as used in the Guidelines, means an "instrument capable of inflicting death or serious bodily injury." Where an object that appears to be a dangerous weapon is "brandished, displayed, or possessed, the object is to be treated as a dangerous weapon for purposes of sentencing. The side-handle baton which Powell used and Koon permitted to be used against Mr. King is certainly capable of inflicting death or serious bodily injury. On this point, there is consensus among the government, the Probation Officer, the applicable case law, and Mr. Powell's own expert witness....

Further, the evidence presented at trial and the verdicts clearly demonstrate that defendant Powell used the side-handle baton, and defendant Koon permitted its use, with the intent to harm Mr. King....

Because the relevant conduct attributable to both defendants Koon and Powell constitutes a felonious assault involving a dangerous weapon with intent to do bodily harm, the appropriate underlying offense is aggravated assault. Pursuant to Guidelines Section 2A2.2, the base offense level for aggravated assault is 15....

2. Specific Offense Characteristics Under Aggravated Assault Guideline

... It is certain that Mr. King sustained extensive and "serious" bodily injury at some point during the course of the March 3, 1991 use of force. Substantial evidence was presented at trial that Mr. King suffered numerous facial fractures, contusions and lacerations, and a fracture of the fibula in his right leg. Mr. King's injuries required medical intervention, including numerous sutures to close lacerations of his face and scalp, reconstructive surgery to repair his facial fractures, and a cast to set his fractured leg.

However, in reviewing the continuum of events that were initially legal and later became criminal, the Court has found Mr. Powell's use of force to be lawful until 1:07:28, after Briseno's kick. Mr. Koon's conduct was also lawful until 1:07:28. For purposes of sentencing, the Court considers only those injuries sustained by Mr. King after Koon and Powell crossed the line between legal and illegal conduct at 1:07:28. Because the Court finds that Mr. King's head injuries and facial fractures, as well as the fibula fracture, occurred prior to Briseno's kick at 1:05:20, these serious bodily injuries do not warrant an upward adjustment to the aggravated assault offense level.

In addition to the facial fractures, head injuries, fibula fracture, and some contusions, all of which were lawfully inflicted, Mr. King sustained contusions on his arms, legs, chest, shoulders, and back. It is hard to imagine that the six or more illegal baton blows delivered by Powell between 1 minute 7 and 1 minute 26 on the tape did not cause some of these contusions. The points at which Powell's illegal blows contacted Mr. King's body, insofar as those points can be determined from the evidence, include the arms, shoulders and back, corresponding to the locations of the contusions. Mr. King's contusions were obvious, as established, by the testimony and photographic evidence at trial. Common experience proves that such extensive bruising is painful and may warrant medical attention. In sum, Mr. King sustained some bodily injury, as that term is used in the Guidelines, as a result of unlawful baton blows inflicted by defendant Powell and permitted by defendant Koon....

B. Adjustments to the Offense Level

Chapter Three of the Guidelines provides for certain adjustments to the Chapter Two offense level based on the victim's characteristics and the defendant's role in the offense, obstruction of justice, and acceptance of responsibility. None of the Chapter Three adjustments are applicable here.

Mr. King was neither unusually vulnerable nor a government official. Mr. King was not physically restrained during the course of the offense. Therefore, none of the victim-related adjustments apply.

Nor does Mr. Koon's role in the offense warrant an adjustment of the offense level....

Pursuant to Guidelines Section 3C1.1, a 2-level increase applies where a defendant "willfully obstructed or impeded, or attempted to obstruct or impede, the administration of justice during the investigation, prosecution, or sentencing of the instant offense." The Commentary to Section 3C1.1 is explicit that the enhancement applies where a defendant commits perjury.

Mr. Koon testified at trial and denied having acted with the unlawful intent to refrain from protecting Mr. King from an unreasonable use of force. The government contends that the enhancement for obstruction of justice applies here, reasoning that the jury's verdict against Koon necessarily constitutes a finding that Koon testified falsely. The Court disagrees.

A witness testifying under oath commits perjury if he "gives false testimony concerning a material matter with the willful intent to provide false testimony." A defendant who chooses to testify at trial and makes false statements in his own defense may be subject to an enhancement for obstruction of justice. However, not every accused who testifies at trial and is convicted will incur an enhanced sentence under Section 3C1.1 for committing perjury. An accused may give inaccurate testimony due to confusion, mistake, or memory loss. In determining whether to apply Section 3C1.1 to alleged false testimony or statements by a defendant, the testimony or statements are to be "evaluated in a light most favorable to the defendant."

Although Mr. Koon's belief that he acted lawfully is mistaken, as indicated by the jury's verdict, the Court finds that Koon's testimony reflects a personal belief which, at the time of trial, he held in earnest. Mr. Koon did not wilfully intend to provide false testimony. That the jury chose to disbelieve Koon's testimony, or found it insufficient to prove lack of intent, does not establish that Koon committed perjury.

An enhancement for obstruction of justice is inappropriate. . . .

D. Downward Departure

The Court must impose a sentence sufficient, but not greater than necessary, to comply with the purposes set forth at 18 U.S.C. § 3553(a)(2). Ordinarily, it must select a sentence from within the Guideline range. However, the Sentencing Commission expressly recognized the inherent difficulties in prescribing "a single set of guidelines that encompasses the vast range of human conduct relevant to a sentencing decision." Thus, the Guidelines are intended to carve out a "heartland" of typical cases. When presented with an atypical case, to which a particular Guideline linguistically applies, but where the underlying conduct significantly differs from the norm, the Court may consider whether a departure is warranted.

Departure from the Guidelines and sentencing outside the prescribed range is unusual. The Commission adopted the departure policy based, in part, on the belief that courts would not invoke it very often. Departure is permissible only where the Court finds "an aggravating or mitigating circumstance of a kind, or to a degree, not adequately taken into consideration by the Sentencing Commission in formulating the guidelines that should result in a sentence different from that described."

A number of specific factors, including race, sex, national origin, creed, religion, and socio-economic status, may never be considered as "aggravating or mitigating circumstances" warranting a departure. With those specific exceptions, however, the Commission did not intend to limit the kinds of factors which may constitute grounds for departure in an atypical case.

The present case is atypical in several respects. First, Mr. King's wrongful conduct contributed significantly to provoking the offense behavior. Consequently, though the offense of which defendants Koon and Powell were convicted falls within the language of the Guidelines, Koon's and Powell's underlying conduct falls outside the range of more typical offenses for which the Guidelines were designed.

Second, defendants Koon and Powell have already sustained, and will continue to incur, punishment in addition to the sentence imposed by this Court. The extraordinary notoriety and national media coverage of this case, coupled with the defendants' status as police officers, make Koon and Powell unusually susceptible to prison abuse. Moreover, Koon and Powell will be subjected to multiple adversarial proceedings and stripped of their positions and tenure by the LAPD.

Third, while the offense of conviction involves a serious assault, there is no evidence, and the government does not argue, that Koon and Powell are dangerous or likely to commit crimes in the future.

Fourth, defendants Koon and Powell were indicted for their respective roles in beating Mr. King only after a state court jury acquitted them of charges based on the same underlying conduct. Under these circumstances, the successive state and federal prosecutions, though legal, raise a specter of unfairness.

Of these four factors, only Mr. King's wrongful conduct independently warrants a sentence reduction. Standing alone, none of the other enumerated factors clearly justifies a departure from the Guidelines. However, the Court's decision whether to depart "require[s] the evaluation of a complex of factors." As the Ninth Circuit observed in *Cook*:

> No single factor may be enough to point to the wise course of decision. But a wise person will not look on each particular factor abstractly and alone. Rather, it will be how the particular pieces fit together, converge, and influence each other that will lead to the correct decision.

The Court finds that the second, third and fourth factors, taken together, justify a reduced sentence. Each of the first and second factors, as well as the third and fourth factors in combination, constitute "mitigating circumstances," not adequately considered by the Commission in formulating the Guidelines. Based on these unique circumstances, a sentence outside the prescribed Guideline range is appropriate for both defendants Koon and Powell.

i. King's Wrongful Conduct

In reducing Mr. Koon's and Mr. Powell's sentence below the prescribed Guidelines range, the Court finds, and considers as a mitigating circumstance, that Mr. King's wrongful conduct contributed significantly to provoking the offense behavior. . . .

The evidence at trial supports a finding that Mr. King engaged in illegal conduct prior to and during his arrest. Mr. King was admittedly intoxicated while driving. He exceeded the speed limit at times. Mr. King failed to stop his vehicle, even after he belatedly perceived the flashing police lights and sirens. Perhaps due to his intoxication, Mr. King was slow to comply with police orders to exit his car. In any event, he failed to remain prone on the ground as the police ordered him to do. Rather, Mr. King resisted Officers Briseno, Solano, Powell, and Wind. He attempted to escape from police custody. In doing so, Mr. King, a still unsearched felony suspect, ran in the direction of Mr. Powell. He intended to escape into the unlit recreation area. At this point, the officers' use of the baton commenced. The initial provocation for the subsequent course of events was Mr. King's wrongful conduct.

Significantly, defendants Koon and Powell, along with the other LAPD, CHP, and School District officers at the scene of Mr. King's arrest, were present only by happenstance. Had Mr. King pulled over, and not caused the CHP officers to pursue him for up to eight miles, Koon, Powell and the other LAPD officers would not have been summoned. Messrs. Koon and Powell did not seek out a victim; rather, their very presence at the scene was a consequence of Mr. King's wrongful conduct.

At 6' 3" and approximately 225 lbs., Mr. King was appreciably larger than both Koon and Powell. Mr. King's reputation for violence was unknown to the officers, but he was a felony suspect. Mr. King resisted and evaded arrest, persistently failed to comply with police commands, and had not been searched for weapons. As such, the defendants' early perception of Mr. King as dangerous was reasonable. . . .

From the time of that first baton blow until 1:07:28, when the defendant's conduct crossed the line to illegality, Mr. King persisted in his failure to obey the police. Defendants Koon and Powell repeatedly ordered Mr. King to assume the felony-prone position to avoid further confrontation.

While Mr. King's wrongdoing precipitated the initial, lawful use of force, and thereby substantially contributed to the offense conduct, Mr. King's provocative behavior eventually subsided. The Court recognizes that by the time the defendants' conduct crossed the line to unlawfulness, Mr. King was no longer resisting arrest. He posed no objective threat, and the defendants had no reasonable perception of danger. Nevertheless, the incident would not have escalated to this point, indeed it would not have occurred at all, but for Mr. King's initial misconduct.

Because the defendants were convicted of violation of 18 U.S.C. § 242,

Guideline Section 2H4.1 for interference with civil rights under color of law, and Guideline Section 2A2.2 for aggravated assault linguistically apply. However, Mr. King's wrongdoing and the substantial role it played in bringing about the defendants' unlawful conduct remove this case from the "heartland" of offenses contemplated by the aggravated assault Guideline.

Messrs. Koon and Powell were convicted of conduct which began as a legal use of force against a resistant suspect and subsequently crossed the line to unlawfulness, all in a matter of seconds, during the course of a dynamic arrest situation....

... Police officers are always armed with "dangerous weapons" and may legitimately employ those weapons to administer reasonable force. Where an officer's initial use of force is provoked and lawful, the line between a legal arrest and an unlawful deprivation of civil rights within the aggravated assault Guideline is relatively thin. The stringent aggravated assault Guideline, along with its upward adjustments for use of a deadly weapon and bodily injury, contemplates a range of offenses involving deliberate and unprovoked assaultive conduct. The Guidelines do not adequately account for the differences between such "heartland" offenses and the case at hand....

ii. Additional Punishment

A legitimate mitigating circumstance arises where a defendant is subject to punishment in addition to the court imposed sentence. The courts have recognized two categories of "additional punishment" as valid bases for downward departure: (1) the defendant's extreme vulnerability to prison abuse; and (2) the defendant's exposure to additional adversarial proceedings as a result of his conviction. Both categories are applicable to each defendant Koon and Powell.

(a). Extreme Vulnerability to Abuse in Prison. Where the severity of any imposed sentence is increased due to the defendant's "extreme vulnerability" to prison abuse, a downward departure may be considered....

... From a purely physical standpoint, defendants Koon and Powell are not unusually vulnerable to prison abuse. However, the widespread publicity and emotional outrage which have surrounded this case from the outset, in addition to the defendants' status as police officers, lead the Court to find that Koon and Powell are particularly likely to be targets of abuse during their incarceration. While the Commission did consider the vulnerability of prisoners to physical assault in formulating the Guidelines, the circumstances of this case are extraordinary and were not adequately contemplated....

The Court would certainly hesitate to grant a departure based solely on Koon's and Powell's vulnerability to abuse. The few cases that support "extreme vulnerability" as a factor for departure are limited to consideration of a defendant's physical characteristics, and are therefore distinguishable. Moreover, while the Second Circuit has expressly upheld a prisoner's extreme vulnerability as a proper ground for departure, the Ninth Circuit has not ruled on the issue. Finally, as the government notes, many police officers are now, and have been, safely incarcerated in the federal prison system.

However, the Court considers the defendants' vulnerability to prison abuse, not by itself, but in combination with other factors, including another source of additional punishment recognized by the Ninth Circuit: multiple adversarial proceedings. As such, the unusual likelihood that Koon and Powell will be fearful of or actually subjected to physical harm while incarcerated, and the resultant increased severity of any sentence imposed, are legitimate factors in the Court's decision to depart downward.

(b). Additional Adversarial Proceedings. In *Aguilar*, the Ninth Circuit recognized that defendants may incur "additional punishment" warranting a downward departure where, as a result of their conviction, they are subjected to further public, quasi-judicial proceedings and the burdensome consequences that flow therefrom. . . .

Defendants Koon and Powell will be subjected to a multiplicity of adversarial proceedings. The LAPD Board of Rights will charge Koon and Powell with a felony conviction and, in a quasi-judicial proceeding, will strip them of their positions and tenure. Koon and Powell will be disqualified from other law enforcement careers. In combination, the additional proceedings, the loss of employment and tenure, prospective disqualification from the field of law enforcement, and the anguish and disgrace these deprivations entail, will constitute substantial punishment in addition to any court imposed sentence. In short, because Koon and Powell are police officers, certain unique burdens flow from their convictions.

Additional punishment will be visited upon defendants Koon and Powell as a result of their vulnerability to prison abuse and the adversarial proceedings and related consequences they will suffer as police officers. Such additional punishment constitutes a mitigating circumstance not adequately considered by the Guidelines.

iii. Absence of Need to Protect the Public

In determining the sentence to be imposed, the Court must consider both the need to reflect the seriousness of the offense, and the need to afford adequate deterrence to criminal conduct. In this case, defendants Koon and Powell abused their positions of public trust. The offenses of which they were convicted are serious, and the Guidelines emphasize the "compelling public interest in deterring and adequately punishing" such conduct.

However, the sentence imposed must also take into account the need to protect the public from further criminal activity by defendants Koon and Powell. The Court finds, and the government does not dispute, that neither Koon nor Powell are violent, dangerous, or likely to engage in future criminal conduct. There is no reason to impose a sentence that reflects a need to protect the public from these defendants....

iv. Successive State and Federal Prosecutions

In the California state court case, *People* v. *Powell. et al.*, Messrs. Koon and Powell were tried by a jury and acquitted of criminal charges for their respective roles in the March 3, 1991 beating of Mr. King. The same underlying conduct gives rise to the convictions on which the Court must now sentence Koon and Powell. As the Court has repeatedly stated, both in its pretrial orders and on the record at trial, the federal prosecution of Messrs. Koon, Powell, Wind and Briseno did not place those defendants in double jeopardy. Under the doctrine of "dual sovereignty," the state and federal governments are free to prosecute violations of their respective laws. Successive state and federal prosecutions for the same act do not violate the Fifth Amendment.

Nevertheless, a federal conviction following a state acquittal based on the same underlying conduct does create an unusual circumstance, and significantly burdens the defendants. The state of California vigorously prosecuted Koon and Powell, and lost. Many disagreed with the outcome, but there has been no showing that a clear miscarriage of justice occurred. While the federal government has certainly not transgressed the defendants' constitutional rights, its indictment of Koon and Powell after verdicts of acquittal by a state court Jury raises a specter of unfairness.

In sum, the Court finds that the combined extraordinary circumstances of this case give rise to "mitigating circumstances" that warrant a departure from the Guidelines range....

The Court's decision to depart from the Guidelines in this case is the result of a considered effort to assess the unusual circumstances of the underlying conduct, with the aim of fashioning fair and appropriate sentences for Mr. Koon and Mr. Powell as individuals.

v. Extent of the Departure

The Court finds that the convergence of extraordinary factors in this case warrants a downward departure of 8 levels, resulting in a final offense level of 19. The downward departure is appropriate for each defendant, Koon and Powell.

The Court does not have limitless discretion in determining an appropriate departure, but is guided by the judgments of Congress and the Sentencing Commission....

... [T]he final offense level for each defendant after downward departure is 19. An offense level of 19 with a Criminal History Category I results in a prescribed Guideline sentencing range of 30 to 37 months.

E. Appropriate Sentence Within Guideline Range

Having departed downward to offense level 19, the sentences defendants Koon and Powell at the low end of the prescribed Guideline range to a term of 30 months. In reaching this decision, the Court has considered the Pre-Sentence Reports and numerous letters written on behalf of both defendants Koon and Powell. Based on their strong family and community ties and distinguished records of public service, the Court sentences each defendants at the low end of the prescribed Guidelines range to a term of 30 months. . . .

G. Restitution, Fines, and Costs of Confinement

Restitution

The Court, when sentencing a defendant convicted of an offense under Title 18, may order in addition to any other penalty authorized by law that the defendant make restitution to any victim of the offense.

In determining whether to impose an order of restitution, the Court must consider the amount of loss sustained by the victim as a result of the offense, the financial resources of the defendant, the financial needs and earning ability of the defendant and his dependents, and such other factors as it deems appropriate. . . .

Restitution is claimed in the amount of $189,494.31 for both Mr. Koon and Mr. Powell. Said claim is unsubstantiated and is best left for the pending civil action. Moreover, neither defendant is able, or is likely to become able to pay restitution. An order to pay restitution would place an undue burden on Mr. Koon's dependents. For these reasons, restitution will not be ordered. . . .

The Clerk is ordered to prepare judgment and commitment orders consistent with the Court's findings and orders expressed herein, and with such other orders the Court may articulate during the sentencing hearing.

It is so ordered.

HEALTH CARE FOR WOMEN

August 12, 1993

Deficiencies in medical research about women and women's health care received increasing attention in 1993, with the publication of several articles pointing to the disparity in the amount and quality of medical care and research directed toward males and females in the United States. A special report appearing in the highly regarded New England Journal of Medicine *August 12 focused on the issue of providing preventive services for women and concluded that women were likely to receive more comprehensive services if they saw a female, rather than male, physician, particularly if the physician was an internist or family practitioner.*

"There is a growing and substantial body of evidence that for a long time women's health issues have not received enough attention," said Dr. Nicole Lurie, primary author of the Journal *article. "Previously we've talked about deficiencies on a national level—in terms of not enough research on women's health. Now we are saying it's also a problem on a very basic clinical level—that patients are not getting what they need."*

Background

A new way of thinking about women's health surfaced in 1973 with publication of the Boston Women's Health Collective's best-selling study, Our Bodies, Ourselves. *The book offered practical information on women's health and sexuality and challenged women to take responsibility for their own health. But it was years before women's political power brought about any action. In 1989 the Congressional Caucus for Women's Issues released a report that criticized the lack of research on women at the National Institutes of Health and insisted on change.*

The debate on the state of women's health care focused on a number of issues, including the lack of drugs tested on women, the little-known or -understood differences in disease epidemiology between the sexes, the nature of menopause and aging in women, and the divisions and fragmentation in the medical services and specialties offered to men and women.

In an attempt to remedy the relative lack of pharmaceutical testing on women, the National Institutes of Health established the Office of Research on Women's Health in 1990. Its specific mandate was to "guarantee the inclusion of women in clinical trials of new treatment strategies, to encourage women to enter medical research and to spur research into diseases or conditions that are exclusive to women."

Differences Between the Sexes

It has been observed that men and women react in significantly different ways to drugs administered to control depression and heart disease. Depression, a prevalent mental illness that is diagnosed more often in women than in men, is commonly treated with antidepressive medication, but its effects on women have not been well studied. "Probably part of the reason for this is a lot of the randomized trials for antidepressants were done with the intent of getting [Food and Drug Administration] approval for the compound, and frequently women were excluded from those studies," said Ellen Frank, a professor of psychiatry at the University of Pittsburgh School of Medicine and director of the Depression Prevention Clinic at the Western Psychiatric Institute and Clinic. Heart disease is another area that is not well understood in women. The effects of clot-dissolving drugs, one of the common treatments for heart disease, have not even been studied in women, although there are indications that women may be receiving doses that are too high for them—a fact that could explain why they are more likely than men to experience bleeding problems.

Another gap in knowledge was pointed out by Dr. Frank, who raised "the question of whether a woman's body used medication in a different manner at different points in the menstrual cycle. It may be [that] the idea of giving [a] drug at the same dose all month long is perfectly reasonable for men and completely unreasonable for women."

Disparities between the sexes in the prevalence of diseases are also little understood. Recent studies pointed to data showing that women were experiencing the highest proportional increase of AIDS occurring in any group and that the disease was the leading cause of death among women between the ages of fifteen and forty-nine in several American cities. In addition to depression, women were more likely to have addictive disorders than men, a difference that required further research.

The average woman will spend one-third of her life in menopause, yet "[t]he fundamental biologic processes involved in menopause, as well as the full range of its consequences, are largely unknown at this point," according to a recent research agenda of the Office of Research on Women's Health. "Research on the middle years of a woman's life must be a high priority." For example, a question of importance to many women is whether to take hormone replacement therapy (HRT) when they reach menopause. Some researchers point to its effects on protecting women from osteoporosis and heart disease, while others maintain that it may increase the risk of uterine and breast cancer. Little information is available to answer these and other related questions because no controlled study has been conducted to document the effects on women randomly assigned to take HRT or a placebo.

A Specialty in Women's Medicine?

Concerns about health care for women also focused on the question of whether a specialty area should be created to address female health, or whether all medical practitioners should be required to be well versed in women's medicine. That issue was debated during a 1992 conference at the Center for Research on Women and Gender at the University of Illinois at Chicago and was the subject of several articles in medical journals. Women's health care is more fragmented than men's; while men make a single visit to a physician for exams that cover all aspects of preventive care, it is common for women to have to visit a generalist, a gynecologist, and more specific doctors such as urologists and breast cancer specialists to receive equivalent care.

Dr. Vicki Hufnagle, an obstetrician-gynecologist at Thompson Memorial Hospital in Burbank, California, said in an interview in the New York Times *(October 13, 1993) that she believed health care should be specialized. To that end, she was working to establish a women's hospital with specialists in women's medicine. Some physicians argued, however, that such specialization in the treatment of women would isolate women's health concerns and let other medical specialties "off the hook" in their responsibilities to improve care and research of women's health problems.*

> *Following are excerpts from "Preventive Care for Women: Does the Sex of the Physician Matter?" by Dr. Nicole Lurie and colleagues, published in the August 12, 1993,* New England Journal of Medicine:

The growing consensus among the public and the scientific community that women's health issues have been neglected has kindled unprecedented interest in the quality and quantity of health care that women receive. In response, Congress and others have increased their emphasis on ensuring women's access to appropriate medical care, including preventive services. Rates of screening for breast and cervical cancer are considered important markers of access to and quality of health care by both government and private-sector agencies.

Many factors affect women's cancer-screening rates, among them the sociodemographic characteristics of the target population; knowledge, attitudes, and beliefs about disease, screening, and the efficacy of treatment; patients' compliance with recommendations: and structural factors, such as health insurance coverage. The most common reason women give for not undergoing screening for breast and cervical cancer, however, is that it was not offered or recommended by their physicians. In order to improve screening rates, it is critical to understand further what characteristics of physicians may be associated with low rates of preventive services offered to and accepted by women.

There is reason to suspect that the sex of the physician may be an important factor. Although Link and Zabar found no difference in the rates of breast, rectal, and genitourinary examinations performed by male and female residents in a teaching setting, three other studies have found that the sex of the physician influences the provision of preventive care. Hall et al. studied practices in teaching hospitals and affiliated neighborhood clinics and concluded that female staff physicians were more likely to meet a standard of appropriateness for breast examinations and Pap smears than were male staff physicians, whereas female residents were less likely than male residents to treat and follow up urinary tract infections in children appropriately.

Although the sex of the physician is easy to determine, studying its correlation with the provision of health services is complicated by a variety of possible confounding relations. For example, female physicians are generally younger than their male counterparts, and thus there may have been more emphasis on preventive care in their training. Older physicians are more likely to care for older women, who may have different attitudes about cancer screening than younger women. Because previous studies have not controlled for the age of the patient and the physician, they have not adjusted for the potential effects of these factors. In this study, we examined differences in the use of screening mammograms and Pap smears between female and male physicians caring for women enrolled in a large Midwestern health plan....

This study documents differences between female and male physicians in the rate of cancer-screening tests among their women patients; the differences are particularly striking among physicians in internal medicine and family practice. In obstetrics and gynecology, in contrast, there were significant differences between the sexes in only one age group (those 38 to 42 years old), and these physicians had screening rates that were consistently higher than those for internists and family practitioners. We also found that the lowest rates for both Pap smears and mammograms were in the youngest group of internists and family practitioners (those less than 38 years old).

These low screening rates for young physicians are particularly disturbing when one considers the increased attention to preventive care in the medical school and residency curriculum over the past decade. The data suggest that improving cancer-screening rates through better education of physicians about preventive care may be difficult. Moreover, the low screening rates for all groups of internists and family practitioners, regardless of sex, suggest that administrative changes are needed to increase screening. Prototypes for such interventions have been described elsewhere and include reminders to patients and physicians or office-based systems that bypass the physician and rely on nurses or other medical staff to offer a targeted service.

The fact that screening rates differ according to the sex of the physician raises some interesting issues. Many patients report a preference for a physician of the same sex; this is particularly true for female patients and in clinical situations requiring rectal and genital examinations. This preference is reflected in the unequal sex distribution of patients between male and female physicians, with more women choosing female physicians. Women patients also report greater satisfaction with female physicians than with male physicians. Women patients who choose female physicians may also pay more attention to preventive care, or they may differ from other patients in other factors—such as socioeconomic status or attitudes toward preventive care—that might predispose them to seek screening. Thus, though we know that all the women in this sample were insured and had coverage for mammograms and Pap smears, we do not know whether there were systematic differences in characteristics—other than age—between the patients of male physicians and those of female physicians. If self-selection was partially responsible for the findings, however, these data should serve to increase awareness of the special challenge male physicians face in ensuring that their women patients obtain preventive care.

The sex of the physician may correlate with other behavior and characteristics of physicians that affect screening. Women physicians may be more likely to offer screening tests, or they may exercise greater diligence in repeatedly offering screening or may communicate the risk of cancer more effectively to their patients. Women patients may also be more likely to follow through in obtaining tests suggested by women physicians because they are more comfortable discussing issues of concern with female physicians or being examined by them.

Female physicians may be more comfortable than male physicians in discussing or performing breast examinations or Pap smears. In particular, young male physicians may be uncomfortable examining women's reproductive organs or discussing issues related to sexuality and therefore uncomfortable offering cancer-screening tests. This discomfort may lessen as physicians mature with age and gain practice experience, and it may explain why screening rates among older physicians are higher than those among younger physicians. It is also possible that male physicians may be concerned about accusations of sexual harassment and may thus be less likely to obtain Pap smears or perform the clinical breast examinations that should accompany mammograms.

We found far fewer differences between female and male physicians in obstetrics-gynecology. The relatively consistent rate of cancer screening may result from the unique focus of obstetrician-gynecologists on women's health, from fewer differences in the interpretation or use of guidelines in the field, or from the fact that obstetrician-gynecologists feel more comfortable in caring for female patients.

Finally, these data suggest that certain aspects of the care rendered by women physicians may be more effective than the care provided by male physicians, at least for women patients. If so, it will be beneficial to identify the factors responsible for the differences, particularly if they can be incorporated into the practice of all physicians, regardless of sex.

POPE IN DENVER

August 12-15, 1993

In a historic visit to Denver, Pope John Paul II met with President Bill Clinton and then addressed hundreds of thousands of young people during several events sponsored by the Catholic church's World Youth Day. His first speech attracted at least 170,000 young people (some estimates put the number at 186,000), who came from across the United States and throughout the world. Repeatedly during his visit, the pope delivered the same message: the church remained adamantly opposed to contraception, abortion, divorce, ordaining women as priests, and other controversial reform proposals. But an equally important theme was the need to revitalize the church among young people.

Before arriving in Denver, the pope had visited Jamaica—where he asked for universal pardon for the African slave trade—and Mexico in an attempt to reach out to that country's Indians, many of whom had become alienated from the Catholic church. (Pope's refusal to celebrate Columbus Day mass at a controversial lighthouse in the Dominican Republic, Historic Documents of 1992, p. 897)

World Youth Day: A Catholic "Woodstock"

The tradition of "youth days" began in 1985, when Pope John Paul II called on every Roman Catholic diocese to sponsor an annual event for the church's young people. Beginning in 1987, the pope himself led an international youth event, which was held every other year thereafter. World Youth Days have been celebrated in Argentina, Spain, and Portugal.

The Denver event attracted throngs of young people, who, some observers noted, expressed enthusiasm as eagerly as had participants at the famous 1969 rock concert in Woodstock, N.Y.—but without the beer cans, marijuana, and raucousness that had made Woodstock notorious. Reporters and observers characterized the youth who attended the Denver gathering as invariably polite.

Some church leaders attending the rally expressed concern about polls indicating that many of the nation's Catholic youth did not consider themselves bound by certain church doctrines, such as opposition to birth control and extramarital sex. Although some young people at the event expressed doubts about some of the church's teachings, the overwhelming sentiment appeared to be one of "keeping your family values," in the words of one eighteen-year-old.

Arrival and Meeting with Clinton

Arriving in Denver August 12 in a driving rain, the pope called on political and church dignitaries and young people gathered at the airport welcoming ceremony to "defend life. All the great causes that are yours today will have meaning only to the extent that you guarantee the right to life and protect the human person," the pontiff said.

Although he did not mention abortion directly, the pope said, "The ultimate test of your greatness is the way you treat every human being, but especially the weakest and most defenseless ones."

The pope had a busy schedule. Shortly after his arrival, he met with President Clinton, whose position in support of freedom of choice on the abortion issue was strongly opposed by the Catholic church. Later, the pope said that "at the heart of the church's message and action in the world" were "the inalienable dignity of every human being and the rights which flow from that dignity—in the first place, the right to life and the defense of life."

Clinton, who said the subject of abortion had not come up, said the two had discussed a "wide range" of global issues. The meeting had "laid the basis for a productive and constructive relationship in the future" because the two shared a common belief "in work and family and the importance of pursuing policies that support them," as well as a "commitment to correcting the social problems," the president said. Raymond W. Flynn, the U.S. ambassador to the Vatican, said the crisis in Bosnia was "probably the most significant issue they discussed" and that Clinton had expressed "his commitment and his support for full diplomatic relations between the Vatican and Israel." (Israel-Vatican relations, p. 1033)

Other Events

After meeting with Clinton, the pope was flown to Mile High Stadium in Allenspark outside Denver, where he was met by about 90,000 cheering World Youth Day participants. Delivering greetings in fifteen languages, the pope's central theme—spoken in English—was that young people should share what they had learned in Denver on returning home.

The following morning, the pope celebrated mass for U.S. bishops at the Cathedral of the Immaculate Conception. In his homily, he noted that young people were "thirsty" for spiritual guidance and admonished that "we bishops and priests have a great responsibility" to them. "The church of the third millennium needs to be firmly planted in the heart of the new generation," he warned.

After the mass, the pope departed for a spiritual mountain retreat at a church-run conference center called Camp St. Malo, after a seventh century Celtic missionary who lived in what is now France. The pope then returned to Mile High Stadium, where he walked the Stations of the Cross in the evening.

The next day, the pope celebrated mass with World Youth Day delegates at the Cathedral of the Immaculate Conception, where he warned that "many Catholics are in danger of losing their faith" and called on youth to launch a "new evangelization" to spread the word. Later, the pope was greeted by the Archdiocese of Denver and other dignitaries, among them Clinton, at the Denver McNichols Sports Arena. Speaking before an audience of about 18,000, the pontiff called on Catholics to obey the church's teaching, especially in matters of contraception and abortion. But in remarks that went beyond defending traditional church teachings, the pope condemned child sexual abuse scandals by priests (revelations of such abuse had been growing alarmingly), saying that "every human means must be used" to respond to "the sins of some ministers of the alter." The pontiff also lamented widespread U.S. urban violence. (Pope's Letter on Sexually Abusive Priests, p. 407)

In the early evening, the pope flew to Cherry Creek State Park, fourteen miles away (the rally's participants had begun the pilgrimage there earlier in the day)—where he held an evening vigil.

On the last day of his visit, the pope said mass at the park before an estimated 375,000 people—many of whom had camped overnight in chilly temperatures. Again, he called on Catholic young people to combat "a culture of death," warning that "the family especially is under attack. And the sacred character of human life denied." Capping his visit, the pope said, "Young people, Christ needs you to enlighten the world and show it the 'path to life.'"

> *Following are excerpts from remarks by Pope John Paul II during his visit to Denver to celebrate World Youth Day August 12-15: remarks on arrival at the Stapleton International Airport, August 12; address to youth at Denver's Mile High Stadium, August 12; homily to bishops, August 13; homily to World Youth Day delegates, August 14; remarks to Colorado Catholics and dignitaries at the McNichols Sports Arena, August 14; and homily at Cherry Creek State Park, August 15:*

REMARKS AT STAPLETON INTERNATIONAL AIRPORT

I greatly appreciate your generous words of welcome. The World Youth Day being celebrated this year in Denver gives me the opportunity to meet you, and through you to express once again to the American people my sentiments of deep esteem and friendship. I thank you and Mrs. Clinton for your kind gesture in coming here personally to welcome me....

There is a special joy in coming to America for the celebration of this World Youth Day. A nation which is itself still young according to historical standards is hosting young people gathered from all over the world for a serious reflection on the theme of life: the human life which is God's marvelous gift to each one of us and the transcendent life which Jesus Christ our savior offers to those who believe in his name.

I come to Denver to listen to the young people gathered here, to experience their inexhaustible quest for life. Each successive World Youth Day has been a confirmation of young people's openness to the meaning of life as a gift received, a gift to which they are eager to respond by striving for a better world for themselves and their fellow human beings. I believe that we would correctly interpret their deepest aspirations by saying that what they ask is that society—especially the leaders of nations and all who control the destinies of peoples—accept them as true partners in the construction of a more humane, more just, more compassionate world. They ask to be able to contribute their specific ideas and energies to this task.

The well-being of the world's children and young people must be of immense concern to all who have public responsibilities. In my pastoral visits to the church in every part of the world I have been deeply moved by the almost universal conditions of difficulty in which young people grow up and live. Too many sufferings are visited upon them by natural calamities, famines, epidemics, by economic and political crises, by the atrocities of wars. And where material conditions are at least adequate, other obstacles arise, not the least of which is the breakdown of family values, and stability. In developed countries, a serious moral crisis is already affecting the lives of many young people, leaving them adrift, often without hope, and conditioned to look only for instant gratification. Yet everywhere there are young men and women deeply concerned about the world around them, ready to give the best of themselves in service to others and particularly sensitive to life's transcendent meaning.

But how do we help them? Only by instilling a high moral vision can a society ensure that its young people are given the possibility to mature as free and intelligent human beings, endowed with a robust sense of responsibility to the common good, capable of working with others to create a community and a nation with a strong moral fiber....

America has a strong tradition of respect for the individual, for human dignity and human rights. I gladly acknowledged this during my previous visit to the United States in 1987, and I would like to repeat today the hope I expressed on that occasion:

"America, you are beautiful and blessed in so many ways.... But your best beauty and your richest blessing is found in the human person: in each man, woman and child, in every immigrant, in every native-born son and daughter.... The ultimate test of your greatness is the way you treat every human being, but especially the weakest and most defenseless ones. The best traditions of your land presume respect for those who cannot defend themselves. If you want equal justice for all, and true freedom and lasting peace, then, America, defend life! All the great causes that are yours today will have meaning only to the extent that you guarantee the right to life and protect the human person."

Mr. President, my reference to the moral truths which sustain the life of the nation is not without relevance to the privileged position which the United States holds in the international community. In the face of tensions and conflicts that too many peoples have endured for so long—I am thinking in particular of the Middle East region and some African countries—and in the new situation emerging from the events of 1989—especially in view of the tragic conflicts now going on in the Balkans and in the Caucasus—the international community ought to establish more effective structures for maintaining justice and peace....

ADDRESS AT STADIUM

...Tomorrow, Friday, is meant to be a day of solidarity and penance. As a gesture of love toward our less-fortunate brothers and sisters we are all asked to make a sacrifice at tomorrow's midday meal and to give what we save for St. Joseph's Hospital of Kitovu in Uganda, where many AIDS patients are being cared for with great love and attention. That region has been drastically affected by this dreaded disease and thousands of children have been left orphans as a result of it. Our gesture is a small sign of our love, an invitation to society not to neglect those who are suffering, especially when that suffering, which Jesus takes to himself, can only be alleviated by the close, personal, caring presence of others.

Jesus has called each one of you to Denver for a purpose! You must live these days in such a way that when the time comes to return home, each one of you will have a clearer idea of what Christ expects of you. Each one must have the courage to go and spread the good news among the people of the last part of the 20th century, in particular among young people of your own age who will take the church and society into the next century....

With great joy I look forward to our next meeting.

Hasta la vista!

HOMILY TO BISHOPS

... From the altar of the cathedral of Denver I warmly greet each one of you who are taking part in the World Youth Day. You are here, just as I am, out of fidelity to our specific ministry in the church. We are here to be with the young pilgrims during these days in which we are witnesses of the grace of the Holy Spirit at work in so many generous young hearts.

In a sense we, the pastors, have been called here by the young people themselves. Their response to the World Youth Day clearly indicates that they have perceived something of what the eternal Father reveals to the "little ones." They are thirsty to know more, to penetrate more deeply into the mystery of Christ and the church. They know that the Father can open that door to them, just as he revealed the heart of the mystery to Peter at Caesarea Philippi.

In this interior advancement of grace, we bishops and priests have a great responsibility. Are we always ready to help the young people discover the transcendent elements of the Christian life? From our words and actions do they conclude that the church is indeed a mystery of communion with the blessed Trinity, and not just a human institution with temporal aims? Through our ministry, the young people present here need to be able to discover, above all, that they are temples of God and that the Spirit of God dwells in them (cf. 1 Cor. 3:16).

These are the days in which the light of the Gospel must shine before them with a particular brilliance.

For they are the church of today and tomorrow—the church that rises on the rock of divine truth, on the rock of the apostolic faith. The church of the third millennium needs to be firmly planted in the heart of the new generation of the sons and daughters of the living God....

HOMILY TO DELEGATES

... In a sense, the International Youth Forum represents the nucleus of the World Youth Day. Not only are you praying and reflecting on the theme of the life in abundance which Christ came to give, but you are comparing experiences of the apostolate in different parts of the world in order to learn from one another and to be confirmed in the Christian leadership which you are called to exercise among your contemporaries. Only a great love of Christ and of the church will sustain you in the apostolate awaiting you when you return home.

As leaders in the field of the youth apostolate, your task will be to help your parishes, dioceses, associations and movements to be truly open to the personal, social and spiritual needs of young people. You will have to find ways of involving young people in projects and activities of formation, spirituality and service, giving them responsibility for themselves and their work, and taking care to avoid isolating them and their apostolate from the rest of the ecclesial community. Young people need to be able to see the practical relevance of their efforts to meet the real needs of people, especially the poor and neglected. They should also be able to see that their apostolate belongs fully to the church's mission in the world.

Have no fear! Denver, like the previous World Youth Days, is a time of grace: a great gathering of young people, all speaking different languages but all united in proclaiming the mystery of Christ and the new life he gives. This is especially evident in the catecheses being given each day in various languages. In prayer and song, so many different tongues ring out in praise of God. All this makes Denver a reflection of what happened in Jerusalem at Pentecost (cf. Acts 2:1-4). Out of all the diversity of the young people gathered here—diversity of origin, race and language—the Spirit of truth will create the deep and abiding unity of commitment to the new evangelization, in which the defense of human life, the promotion of human rights and the fostering of a civilization of love are urgent tasks. . . .

We know that Christ never abandons his church. At a time like this, when many are confused regarding the fundamental truths and values on which to build their lives and seek their eternal salvation, when many Catholics are in danger of losing their faith—the pearl of great price—when there are not enough priests, not enough religious sisters and brothers to give support and guidance, not enough contemplative [religions] to keep before people's eyes the sense of the absolute supremacy of God, we must be convinced that Christ is knocking at many hearts, looking for young people like you to send into the vineyard, where an abundant harvest is ready. . . .

Christ is asking the young people of the World Youth Day: "Whom shall I send?"

And, with fervor, let each one respond: "Here am I! Send me."

Do not forget the needs of your homelands! Heed the cry of the poor and the oppressed in the countries and continents from which you come! Be convinced that the Gospel is the only path of genuine liberation and salvation for the world's peoples: "Your salvation, O Lord, is for all the peoples."

Everyone who, in response to Christ's invitation, comes to Denver to take part in the World Youth Day must hear his words: "Go . . . and proclaim the good news."

Let us earnestly pray the Lord of the harvest that the youth of the world will not hesitate to reply: "Here am I! Send me!. . . . Send us!" Amen.

REMARKS TO COLORADO CATHOLICS

The church in the United States is vital and dynamic, rich in "faith and love and holiness" (1 Tm. 2:15). By far the vast majority of her bishops, priests, religious and laity are dedicated followers of Christ and generous servants of the Gospel message of love. Nevertheless, at a time when all institutions are suspect, the church herself has not escaped reproach. I have already written to the bishops of the United States about the pain of the suffering and scandal caused by the sins of some ministers of the altar. Sad situations such as these invite us anew to look at the mystery of the church with the eyes of faith. While every human means for responding to this evil must be implemented, we cannot forget that the first and most important means is prayer: ardent, humble, confident prayer. America needs much prayer—lest it lose its soul.

On many issues, especially with regard to moral questions, "the teaching of the church in our day is placed in a social and cultural context which renders it more difficult to understand and yet more urgent and irreplaceable for promoting the true good of men and women." Nowhere is this more evident than in questions relating to the transmission of human life and to the inalienable right to life of the unborn.

Twenty-five years ago Pope Paul VI published the encyclical *Humanae Vitae.* Your bishops recently issued a statement to mark this anniversary. They call everyone "to listen to the wisdom of *Humanae Vitae* and to make the church's teaching the foundation for a renewed understanding of marriage and family life". The church calls married couples to responsible parenthood by acting as "ministers"—and not "arbiters"—of God's saving plan. Since the publication of *Humanae Vitae,* significant steps have been taken to promote natural family planning among those who wish to live their conjugal love according to the fullness of its truth. Yet more efforts must be made to educate the consciences of married couples in this form of conjugal chastity, which is grounded on "dialogue, reciprocal respect, shared responsibility and self-control." I appeal especially to young people to rediscover the wealth of wisdom, the integrity of conscience and the deep interior joy which flow from respect for human sexuality understood as a great gift from God and lived according to the truth of the body's nuptial meaning.

Likewise, building an authentic civilization of love must include a massive effort to educate consciences in the moral truths which sustain respect for life in the face of every threat against it. In her vigorous concern for human rights and justice, the Catholic Church is unambiguously committed to protecting and cherishing every human life, including the life of the unborn. As sent by Christ to serve the weak, downtrodden and defenseless, the church must speak on behalf of those most in need of protection. It is a source of comfort that this position is shared by people of many faiths. Those who respect life must accompany their teaching about the value of every human life with concrete and effective acts of solidarity to people in difficult situations. Without charity, the struggle to defend life would be lacking the essential ingredient of the Christian ethic; as St. Paul writes: "Do not be overcome by evil, but overcome evil with good" (Rom. 12:21).

Archbishop Stafford has told me of the deep concern of many Americans about urban violence as a negative sign of the times that needs to be read in light of the Gospel. Violence is always a failure to respect God's image and likeness in our neighbor, in every human person, without exception. Violence in any form is a denial of human dignity. The question which must be asked is, Who is responsible? Individuals have a responsibility for what is happening. Families have a responsibility. Society has a heavy responsibility. Everybody must be willing to accept their part of this responsibility, including the media which in part [need] to become more aware of the effect they can have on their audiences.

And when the question is asked, What is to be done? everybody must be committed to fostering a profound sense of the value of life and dignity of the human person. The whole of society must work to change the structural conditions which lead people, especially the young, to the lack of vision, the loss of esteem for themselves and for others which lead to violence. But since the root of violence is in the human heart, society will be condemned to go on causing it, feeding it and even, to an extent, glorifying it, unless it reaffirms the moral and religious truths which alone are an effective barrier to lawlessness and violence, because these truths alone are capable of enlightening and strengthening conscience. Ultimately, it is the victory of grace over sin that leads to fraternal harmony and reconciliation.

Brothers and sisters in Christ, I urge you to renew your trust in the richness of the Father's mercy, in the incarnation and redemption accomplished by his beloved Son, in the Holy Spirit's vivifying presence in your hearts. This immense mystery of love is made present to us through holy church's sacraments, teaching and solidarity with pilgrim humanity. The church, through your bishops and other ministers, in your parishes, associations and movements, needs your love and your active support in defending the inviolable right to life and the integrity of the family, in promoting Christian principles in private and public life, in serving the poor and the weak, and in overcoming all manner of evil with good....

HOMILY AT STATE PARK

...With my heart full of praise for the Queen of Heaven, the sign of hope and source of comfort on our pilgrimage of faith to "the heavenly Jerusalem", I greet all of you who are present at this solemn liturgy. It is a pleasure for me to see so many priests, religious and lay faithful from Denver, from the state of Colorado, from all parts of the United States and from so many countries of the world, who have joined the young people of the World Youth Day to honor the definitive victory of grace in Mary, the mother of the Redeemer.

The eighth World Youth Day is a celebration of life. This gathering has been the occasion of a serious reflection on the words of Jesus Christ: "I came that they may have life, and have it abundantly". Young people from every corner of the world, in ardent prayer you have opened your hearts to the truth of Christ's promise of new life. Through the sacraments, especially penance and the eucharist, and by means of the unity and friendship created among so many, you have had a real and transforming experience of the new life which only Christ can give. You, young pilgrims, have also shown that you understand that Christ's gift of life is not for you alone. You have become more conscious of your vocation and mission in the church and in the world. For me, our meeting has been a deep and moving experience of your faith in Christ, and I make my own the words of St. Paul: "I have great confidence in you, I have great pride in you; I am filled with encouragement, I am overflowing with joy."

These are not words of empty praise. I am confident that you have grasped the scale of the challenge that lies before you and that you will have the wisdom and courage to meet that challenge. So much depends on you.

This marvelous world—so loved by the Father that he sent his only Son for its salvation—is the theater of a never-ending battle being waged for our dignity and identity as free, spiritual beings. This struggle parallels the apocalyptic combat described in the first reading of this Mass. Death battles against life: A "culture of death" seeks to impose itself on our desire to live and live to the full. There are those who reject the light of life, preferring "the fruitless works of darkness." Their harvest is injustice, discrimination, exploitation, deceit, violence. In every age, a measure of their apparent success is the death of the innocents. In our own century, as at no other time in history, the "culture of death" has assumed a social and institutional form of legality to justify the most horrible crimes against humanity: genocide, "final solutions, ... ethnic cleansings" and the massive "taking of lives of human beings even before they are born or before they reach the natural point of death"....

The family especially is under attack. And the sacred character of human life denied. Naturally, the weakest members of society are the most at risk: the unborn children, the sick, the handicapped, the old, the poor and unemployed, the immigrant and refugee, the South of the world!

Young pilgrims, Christ needs you to enlighten the world and to show it the "path to life." The challenge is to make the church's yes to life concrete and effective. The struggle will be long, and it needs each one of you. Place your intelligence, your talents, your enthusiasm, your compassion and your fortitude at the service of life!

Have no fear. The outcome of the battle for life is already decided, even though the struggle goes on against great odds and with much suffering....

Christ—the head—has already conquered sin and death. Christ in his body—the pilgrim people of God—continually suffers the onslaught of the Evil One and all the evil which sinful humanity is capable of.

At this stage of history, the liberating message of the Gospel of life has been put into your hands. And the mission of proclaiming it to the ends of the earth is now passing to your generation. Like the great apostle Paul, you too must feel the full urgency of the task: "Woe to me if I do not evangelize." Woe to you if you do not succeed in defending life. The church needs your energies, your enthusiasm, your youthful ideals, in order to make the Gospel of life penetrate the fabric of society, transforming people's hearts and the structures of society in order to create a civilization of true justice and love. Now more than ever, in a world that is often without light and without the courage of noble ideals, people need the fresh, vital spirituality of the Gospel.

Do not be afraid to go out on the streets and into public places like the first apostles, who preached Christ and the good news of salvation in the squares of cities, towns and villages. This is no time to be ashamed of the Gospel. It is the time to preach it from the rooftops. Do not be afraid to break out of comfortable and routine modes of living in order to take up the challenge of making Christ known in the modern "metropolis." It is you who must "go out into the byroads" and invite everyone you meet to the banquet which God has prepared for his people. The Gospel must not be kept hidden because of fear or indifference. It was never meant to be hidden away in private. It has to be put on a stand so that people may see its light and give praise to our heavenly Father. . . .

The world at the approach of a new millennium, for which the whole church is preparing, is like a field ready for the harvest. Christ needs laborers ready to work in his vineyard. May you, the Catholic young people of the world, not fail him. In your hands, carry the cross of Christ. On your lips, the words of life. In your hearts, the saving grace of the Lord. . . .

RACIAL DIFFERENCES IN HEART ATTACK INCIDENCE AND CARE

August 26, 1993

Two studies published August 26 in the New England Journal of Medicine *demonstrated striking differences between blacks and whites in the incidence and treatment of heart disease. One study, conducted in Chicago, found that black Americans were more likely to suffer cardiac arrest and were less likely to survive than whites. The other study showed that blacks with cardiovascular disease who were admitted to Veterans Hospitals received less aggressive care than did white patients. In an accompanying editorial, the* Journal *declared that "health care is no exception" to the "racial disparities [that] persist in all areas of American society."*

The Chicago study, entitled "The CPR Chicago Project," gathered data on out-of-hospital heart attacks in the city in 1987 and 1988. The study collected information on 6,451 men and women; approximately 50 percent were white and 45 percent black. The study found that black men and women in all age groups had higher rates of cardiac arrest than did their white counterparts. Blacks were also more likely to suffer faulty heart rhythms and, when they did, were less likely to be admitted to a hospital.

Both black and white victims of cardiac arrest had low survival rates, but chances of survival were higher for the whites (2.6 percent) than for the blacks (0.8 percent). Among those who were still alive when they reached a hospital, white patients were twice as likely to survive. The study found no significant differences in the response time of ambulance crews, but it did note—and could not explain why—that among whites someone was more likely to observe the heart attack and call for help.

Blacks' Need for More Comprehensive Health Care

The Chicago study was supported by the American Heart Association of Metropolitan Chicago and the Section of Emergency Medicine at the University of Chicago, in cooperation with the city police and fire departments and forty-six hospitals. The authors of the study, Dr. Lance Becker and colleagues, wrote that since cardiac arrest was often a late manifestation of long-standing cardiovascular disease, blacks particularly were in need of comprehensive health care services.

Noting a greater prevalence of fatal heart attacks in the black community, the study expressed the hope that "this information may provide additional motivation for reducing risk factors amenable to change (such as hypertension, diet, smoking, and control of diabetes)." Failure to reduce these risk factors, it said, "may be the critical weak link in the chain of survival."

Racial Disparity in VA Care

The other study, conducted by the Pittsburgh Department of Veterans Affairs Medical Center, surveyed the treatment of 428,300 men admitted to Veterans Hospitals for cardiovascular disease over a five-year period. The study determined that white patients were far more likely to undergo major coronary procedures than were blacks. Whites had bypass-graft surgery more than twice as often as black patients, and were 50 percent more likely to undergo angioplasty, a procedure that uses a balloon to open clogged arteries.

In its editorial, the Journal *noted that discrepancies in treatment at veterans hospitals were not due to financial considerations because physicians were salaried and the treatment was free. Little difference was detected between black and white patients in the use of surgical procedures that were relatively commonplace. Differences did become apparent when doctors were free to exercise more discretion.*

"These findings lead to the inescapable conclusion that race influences decisions about medical treatment," the editorial said. It added that the decisions might not reflect overt racism but, rather, "subtle racial biases that can permeate reasoning and communication with patients and other physicians." Citing other studies in the past decade that indicated racial differences in the use of medical procedures, the editorial concluded that "many physicians do not communicate effectively with black patients about their options for treatment . . . Whether this deficit reflects racism or not, the result is the same."

> *Following are excerpts from the study "Racial Differences in the Incidence of Cardiac Arrest and Subsequent Survival," published in the* New England Journal of Medicine, *August 26, 1993:*

Differences between blacks and whites have been reported for the prevalence of many cardiovascular diseases, such as hypertension, renal failure, and stroke. In the case of cardiac arrest, however, there is a paucity of data and conflicting results. In an article on minorities and cardiovascular diseases, the American Heart Association reported that as compared with whites, blacks have more hypertension-related morbidity, a higher mortality rate from stroke, more frequent left ventricular hypertrophy by electrocardiographic criteria, and strikingly more end-stage renal disease. On the basis of these data one might suspect that the risk of cardiac arrest also differs between blacks and whites, but no analysis of cardiac arrest was presented....

... Studies from Nashville, New Orleans, and South Carolina all report higher rates of cardiac arrest in blacks than in whites. A recent retrospective, multivariate analysis found no significant racial differences The study was inconclusive, however, in that it contained relatively small numbers of blacks, provided no information on the population served by the emergency medical services (EMS) system or the incidence of cardiac arrest, and reported an unusually high rate of ventricular fibrillation.

Risk factors for survival after cardiac arrest have been identified, including age, initial cardiac rhythm, whether there were witnesses to the cardiac arrest, whether cardiopulmonary resuscitation (CPR) was initiated by a bystander, time to treatment, location and, in one study, socioeconomic status. However, race has not been identified as an important risk factor. This may be due to the small numbers of nonwhite patients in previous studies.

The CPR Chicago Project was created to gather data on out-of-hospital cardiac arrests in Chicago. We have previously reported a high incidence of cardiac arrest in Chicago and a low overall survival as compared with other studies. This report examines racial differences in the incidence of cardiac arrest and of survival after cardiac arrest and assesses whether these differences persist after previously recognized risk factors are taken into account....

Results

The study population comprised 6451 patients, of which 3207 (50 percent) were white, 2910 (45 percent) were black, and 334 (5 percent) were from other races; 3664 (57 percent) were men, and 2787 (43 percent) were women. There were 114 survivors (2 percent), 439 patients who were admitted but died in the hospital (7 percent), and 5898 patients who were pronounced dead in emergency departments (91 percent). Overall, 2972 of the arrests were witnessed (46 percent), 1381 patients received CPR from a bystander (21 percent), and 1394 were noted to have ventricular fibrillation or ventricular tachycardia as the initial cardiac rhythm (22 percent). The mean age was 67.4 years. Women, on average, were five years older than men. The annual incidence of cardiac arrest for persons over the age of 17 was 167 per 100,000.

Incidence

In all age groups, both black men and black women had higher rates of cardiac arrest than their white counterparts. In each racial group, men had higher incidence rates than women. The relative risks indicate that the incidence was higher among blacks than among whites. This difference in relative risk ranged from 239 percent in the youngest age group to 128 percent in the oldest age group.

Survival Rates

The overall survival rate for blacks was 0.8 percent (24 of 2910), and for whites it was 2.6 percent (84 of 3207). The higher survival rate for whites was similar among men and women. The chances of admission to the hospital were likewise lower for blacks (183 of 2910, or 6.3 percent) than for whites (336 of 3207, or 10.5 percent). In the subgroup of patients admitted to the hospital, 13 percent of the black patients (24 of 183) survived to discharge, as compared with 25 percent of the white patients (84 of 336).

A significantly lower survival rate for blacks was also seen among patients with ventricular fibrillation or ventricular tachycardia and patients with intervals of less than six minutes from the 911 call to the arrival of the ambulance. Even with short intervals before a response and an initial rhythm of ventricular fibrillation or ventricular tachycardia, the survival rate for blacks was lower than that for whites. Similarly lower survival was observed for black patients with arrests witnessed by a paramedic.

Frequency of Witnessed Cardiac Arrest and Bystander CPR

Cardiac arrests were witnessed at a significantly higher rate among whites than among blacks (49 percent vs. 42 percent). There was no difference between whites and blacks in the rate of paramedic-witnessed cardiac arrest. Whites were more likely to receive CPR from a bystander than blacks (25 percent vs. 18 percent).

Discussion

In our analysis of racial differences in cardiac arrest, there were two major findings. First, the incidence of cardiac arrest was significantly higher among blacks in every age group than among whites. Second, the survival rate after an out-of-hospital cardiac arrest among blacks was only 31 percent of that among whites. Even among patients admitted to the hospital, survival for blacks was 52 percent of that for whites....

These results may be viewed from another perspective. Although we report survival rates, it would be equally valid to report mortality rates. Given our data, the mortality from cardiac arrest for whites would be 97 percent, whereas for blacks it would be 99 percent. This perspective highlights the fact that in Chicago nearly every victim of cardiac arrest dies, and only a slight (2 percent) difference separates whites from blacks. Part of the reason for this low overall survival rate is that we included patients who would not be considered for resuscitation in some other studies of CPR.

The quality of EMS services does not appear to explain the lower survival rates among blacks. In the distribution of intervals from the 911 call to the arrival of the ambulance, our data reveal a small shift toward shorter intervals for whites than for blacks. However, the difference in the mean time interval was only 18 seconds, which could account for only a fraction of the difference in survival. Given the overall low survival rates and long intervals until defibrillation, the speed with which EMS services reach both blacks and whites needs improvement.

The American Heart Association emphasizes that successful treatment for cardiac arrest depends on community-wide emergency cardiac care (a "chain of survival"); responsibility does not lie with the EMS system alone. . . .

The first link, early access, refers to the critical events of witnessing the arrest, calling 911, dispatching the ambulance, driving the ambulance, and reaching the patient's side. There are important intervals we could not measure. For example, the interval from the patient's collapse to the 911 call is currently unmeasured in all studies. It is unclear why blacks had more unwitnessed cardiac arrests. . . .

The second link, early CPR, has been shown repeatedly to be associated with improved survival. Our findings reveal a significant difference between blacks and whites in the rate at which bystanders initiate CPR. New initiatives in education about CPR could be effective in increasing the rate of bystander-initiated CPR in blacks.

The third link, early defibrillation, is the most important for patients in cardiac arrest. Our analysis suggests no racial differences. . . .

Our study is primarily descriptive and raises many unanswered questions about the factors responsible for racial differences in survival. Race may be a marker for other coexisting factors, such as environment, genetics, or reduced access to health care. If reliable data on socioeconomic status were available, one might be able to separate the effect of this variable from that of race. . . .

. . . If problems in the chain of survival are particular to the black community, they should be identified. Primary care providers and black patients should be aware that blacks are at significantly higher risk for cardiac arrest and death than are whites. This information may provide additional motivation for reducing cardiovascular risk factors amendable to change (such as hypertension, diet, smoking, and control of diabetes). Failure may be the critical weak link in the chain of survival.

THIRTIETH ANNIVERSARY OF THE MARCH ON WASHINGTON

August 28, 1993

Thirty years after 250,000 Americans blanketed the Mall and heard Dr. Martin Luther King, Jr., deliver his "I have a dream" speech, 75,000 Americans convened again in Washington, D.C. to commemorate that historic turning point in the civil rights movement. Coming from across the nation and representing all ages, races, and walks of life, the participants repeated the parade route of 1963, ending at the Lincoln Memorial. There they heard dozens of speakers, including King's widow, Coretta Scott King, proclaim that although much had been accomplished, much more needed to be done to provide all Americans with equal opportunity.

The two-day celebration for jobs, justice, and peace began August 27 with a "People's University" on the Mall, and culminated the next day in the march, speeches at the Lincoln Memorial, and an evening "I Remember" concert at the John F. Kennedy Center for the Performing Arts.

On both days, participants braved temperatures that soared above ninety degrees, causing people to begin to leave midway through the August 28 Lincoln Memorial program.

Activities Preceding the March

The People's University was the principal event occurring before the march, in a day that was also filled with numerous rallies, protests, and news conferences. Meeting with young activists, leaders from the 1963 march held a teleconference from the Lincoln Memorial to discuss their experience and the future prospects of civil rights marches.

The People's University programs reflected the diverse reasons and interests that people had in coming to the event. March organizers had hoped that such diversity in topics would engender a broader camaraderie and build coalitions among the various interest and age groups. Large white tents set up near the Mall housed sixteen workshops on topics that included "Jobs and Justice," "Housing, Homelessness and Foreign Policy," "Racism, Classism & the Criminal Justice System," and "Violence in the United States." According to observers and participants alike, reaction to the discussions ranged from enthusiasm to boredom. Some expressed disappointment that they had not heard much about issues that were particularly pressing for them. Said a sixteen-year-old from Garden City Park, N.Y., "These workshops have nothing to do with the problems we are dealing with today.... I'm worried about drugs. I'm worried about black-on-black crime, black-on Puerto Rican crime.... I wanted to hear what they are going to do for us."

"The workshops were intended to take issues of concern and turn them into tangible things to do," said Hilary Shelton, coordinator of the People's University. "It was a substantive day, packed with issues." Organizers estimated that, overall, about 1,000 people participated at some time during the day, but they expressed regret that so many buses carrying young people from out of town arrived too late for them to participate.

The August 28 Rally

Participants came to Washington to voice their hopes for many things, including better jobs, an end to violence, housing for the homeless, women's rights, religious freedom, equality for the disabled, and protection of workers' rights. Labor unions were represented in large numbers, protesting what they considered to be the potential loss of U.S. jobs resulting from ratification of the North American Free Trade Agreement, which at that point was still uncertain. (Clinton Remarks on House Passage of NAFTA, p. 953)

The nature of the turnout contrasted with the 1963 march, which had the primary purpose of furthering civil rights for blacks. The thirteen speakers in 1963 had focused on civil rights issues; the fifty speakers at the 1993 rally represented more than five hundred groups. Many young people, however, said they had come to learn more about the 1963 march that they had heard so much about from their parents and to be able to relate their own 1993 experience to their children.

"There are many who said that no one would come out today to march, but we are so pleased to see that you have come out to raise your voices for jobs, justice, and peace," said Benjamin F. Chavis, executive director of the NAACP. Chavis was one of several speakers criticizing the absence of President Bill Clinton, who was vacationing on Martha's Vineyard and sent Attorney General Janet Reno to represent him. The president issued a statement saying that Americans must "rededicate ourselves to vigorous enforcement of the civil rights laws, to eradicating discrimination of every kind, and to opposing intolerance in all its forms." Also addressing those who predicted a low turnout, Joseph E. Lowery, president of the Southern Christian Leadership Conference, said, "The dream busters

were foiled. The dream busters were wrong." Participants had "come from north, south, east, and west," he said.

"We march to challenge despair and raise up hope," said Jesse L. Jackson, founder of the Rainbow Coalition. "We march to demand justice.... We've come a long way, but justice is still not colorblind.... Through it all, don't let them break your spirit. Keep hope alive!"

"Dr. King's spirit is here with us," said Coretta Scott King. "When Martin Luther King, Jr., stood on these steps thirty years ago today, he challenged good people across the nation to rise up and fulfill his dream.... There is still too much racism, there is still too much poverty, there is still too much hunger and there is still too much homelessness."

"Today we return in unity, to raise one voice against hate, against greed and persecution," said AFL-CIO president Lane Kirkland. "We want a trade policy that will uplift human standards rather then destroy them."

One of the highlights of the program occurred when Rosa Parks—whose refusal to give up her seat to a white man launched the Montgomery, Alabama, bus boycott—came to the podium. As she did so, the crowd rose to give her a standing ovation. "Everyone ... keep this in mind," Parks said. "In order to have a good, strong future for tomorrow, we have to take care of our seniors and respect our peers and train and [prepare] our children, and we cannot start too early."

Following are excerpts from August 28, 1993, remarks delivered at the March on Washington for Jobs, Justice, and Peace by Benjamin F. Chavis, Jr., president of the NAACP; and by Jesse Jackson, president of the Rainbow Coalition; and the statement by President Clinton on the thirtieth anniversary of the 1963 March on Washington:

CHAVIS'S SPEECH

Fellow Freedom Marchers, Fellow Justice Seekers, Sisters and Brothers:

Once again we have come to this historic and sacred place to serve notice to the national and to the international community that the civil rights movement in the United States is alive, well, expanding, building and growing throughout the nation.

There are many who said that no one would come out today to march, but we are so pleased to see that you have come out to raise your voices for jobs, justice and peace and we are going to continue to raise our voices for jobs, justice and peace until we get jobs, until we get justice and until we have peace in our communities.

Now we understand that President Clinton is in Martha's Vineyard. We believe that the President should take a vacation. There's nothing wrong with that, but we want President Clinton to know that most of the marchers here today, voted for you and so Mr. President when you come back from your vacation, there is another vineyard in the hood . . . in the neighborhoods across this nation that need jobs, justice and peace.

Mr. President, we want you to hear us. We want jobs, justice and peace. To the Supreme Court that has gone mad with bad decisions, we want you to hear us. But more important than a message to the government, we come today to send a message to ourselves, to send a message to our children, to send a message to future generations. . . .

Now, particularly to the young people who have gathered here, this is a sacred moment as we pass the torch to you and as you receive the torch, we must struggle against all of the various forms of injustice; racial injustice, economic injustice, environmental injustice, healthcare injustice; all of the forms of injustice.

Some of us have become too single issued in our focus. You will only come out when your injustice issue is mentioned, but Martin Luther King, Jr., taught us from the Birmingham jail that an injustice anywhere is a threat to justice everywhere and so we must come together, we must keep this new coalition of conscience together and keep moving forward. . . .

We must envision building a mass-based, multi-racial, multi-cultural, multi-lingual, activist, grass roots, freedom-fighting movement; a human rights and civil rights struggle from the grass roots that move up to impact our nation.

Thirty years ago they were bombing black churches, they were shooting our leaders, they were jailing our activists and, yes 30 years have passed but they are still bombing offices of the NAACP. They are still beating us unjustly as in Los Angeles or shooting us unjustly as in Detroit. We know that we must have jobs, justice and peace and we want it now, not tomorrow, we want it now.

Why do we march and what do we want? The time has come for us to take the next step in our continuing struggle for freedom. From protest to politics, we must now move on to view economics as a civil rights priority. We want more than just fair treatment, we want a fair share of the economy.

So much of the deprivation and degredation that exist in our communities is a direct result of not only racial and social discrimination, it is a direct result of economic inequality, of economic inequities that are institutionalized in our societies.

During the remaining years of this last decade of the 20th century, we shall pursue the course to obtain economic justice. Economic democracy is defined as equal participation, not only in the political economy of a democratic society but also the equal participation in the economic infrastructure, development and expansion as well as the provision of equal access to the accumulation of wealth in this society. In other words we must now move to desegregate Wall Street and the Corporate Suites.

Please keep your marching shoes on after this great march and rally. We are going back to our communities fired up with a new determination and spirit to fight injustice, from getting rid of toxic waste in Columbia, Mississippi to getting rid of police brutality in Los Angeles, California; from challenging racist violence by skin heads in Tacoma, Washington to challenging racial discrimination against federal workers right here in Washington, DC.

We have got to keep on marching with gang leaders and I am glad that many of them are standing here on the podium with me today, gang leaders and gang members from Chicago, Minneapolis, Cleveland and Kansas City. What better way to end gang violence than to get the gang members themselves to participate in ending gang violence. So we have got to keep on marching for freedom. . . .

But we must not just march for justice here in the United States, we must also march with our sisters and brothers in Haiti and welcome the return of President Ariste. [*sic*] We must march with our sisters and brothers in the Republic of Angola who are still caught in a life and death struggle against the terrorism of Jonas Savimbi.

And yes there is a great day coming. We are going to march with Nelson Mandela and the ANC in South Africa as they issue in the final dismantling of apartheid. So whether it is in Africa or the Caribbean or whether it is in our own communities across this land, we will continue to march and to all of the young people who are here, we love you, we embrace you, we need you.

We need you to carry the torch high, we need you to help rejuvenate our organizations. We have proved on this day that we can mobilize, now we must prove from this day that we can organize, that we can challenge all of the vestiges of racism, all of the vestiges of economic exploitation and we need young people to help us win more victories for the freedom movement and so we march on. . . .

JACKSON'S SPEECH

To the faithful remnant who have kept the Covenant and returned thirty years later to the spot where our forefathers and foremothers sighed and to a new generation of freedom fighters—welcome.

We gather today—ardent messengers of an urgent petition, crying out with our very bodies for jobs, for justice, for equal opportunity and equal protection. Many despair. The day is hot. The road is long. The mountain too steep. The people too tired. The powerful too distant. But do not despair. We have come a long way.

When we came there thirty years ago, we had no right to vote. We could not stop along the road and find room in an inn for sleep or to relieve our bodies. In every valley at every stop, there was a prevailing terrorism against blacks and browns sanctioned by the government. In every valley, there were Bull Conners to avoid, Klan to fear.

But we did not stop. We won our civil rights. We won the right to vote.

We helped lift a people from segregation, and a nation from shame. We have come a long way. But we can't stop now.

Thirty years ago, we came seeking jobs and justice. We sought to redeem a check that had bounced, Dr. King told us, marked "insufficient funds." We urged America to honor the sacred obligation to all Americans. Sorry, we were told, "there was a Cold War to fight." The Soviet bear was in the woods. The conservative Congress would not help. A young President could not help.

But Dr. King did not stop. With the younger generation fired up with a passion for justice and a will to suffer and sacrifice for an authentic new world order, young America changed the course of the world with human rights as its centerpiece.

Now thirty years later, there are more poor people, more working poor people than thirty years ago. The ghettos and barrios of our cities are more abandoned and more endangered than thirty years ago. Jobs have gone. Drugs and guns have spread. Hope is down; violence is up.

We come down this road again. The need is there. The opportunity is clear. The Soviet bear is gone. A new administration promised a Covenant to rebuild America, to put people back to work.

Once again, the check has bounced. Insufficient funds they say. The deficit must be addressed. The military must police the world. A conservative Congress will not help. A young President cannot deliver.

So just as thirty years ago—the march was a beginning, not an end, so this march is a beginning, too. We cannot sit on our hands when so many of our brothers and sisters are forced to their knees. And so we march.

We march to challenge despair, and raise up hope. We march to challenge the moral and ethical collapse that engulfs our society. Our young lost to despair, to drugs and guns, to a culture that puts a price on everything and a value on nothing. This is not a racial or an urban problem only—it is as true in the suburbs as the city, among the affluent young as among the poor, among white as well as black and brown. We need a moral movement to help regenerate hope, to renew the will to live, the desire to struggle.

We must end the killing. The fruits of despair. If death has merely changed its name from rope to dope, from genocide to fratricide to homicide; that's retrogression. Brothers and sisters, we must go forward by hope and life, not backward by fear and death. We must reclaim, project and secure our youth. And so we march.

We march to demand a program to rebuild America, to save our children, to put people back to work. Fulfill the Covenant. Put people first. No more broken promises. And so we march.

We march to demand justice. We've come a long way. But, today, justice is still not color blind. Black males are arrested and jailed at four times the rate of white. There are four times as many young black males in US jails than in South African prisons. More black men in jail than in college. Black, brown and poor people receive more time for less crime than those who are affluent or white. 46,000 cases of police brutality reported to the Justice Department since 1986. Fewer than 200 prosecuted. Injustice abounds, so we march. Too often, it seems the more things change the more they stay the same.

In an attempt to gain the conscience and attention of the nation, I left jail, thirty years ago, to come here fighting for public accomodations. This week along with other citizens of the nation's capital, we had to face jail again while urging the President to honor his Covenant and the Congress to be as committed to democracy here at home as it is in the world.

We march to demand the right to vote. DC remains the last colony. Its citizens pay more taxes than forty-eight states. It has more residents than five states. Its citizens pay taxes in dollars that are green. Its soldiers shed blood that is red. But we are taxed and serve without the right to vote largely because our skin color is black. We demand DC statehood.

We march to reverse the assault on equal protection and equal opportunity laws. Attempts to turn back the clock abound. A conservative Supreme Court has challenged reapportionments that gave long excluded minorities some measure of representation. And yet today, neither a Democratic Congress nor a Democratic President has spoken clearly on the continuing wounds caused by racism and the need for affirmative action if this nation is to remain one. Indifference and cynical posturing abounds. And, so we march.

We march for jobs, for an economic plan that puts people first. For a trade accord with Mexico that lifts their workers up, not an investor's treaty like NAFTA that will drag our workers down, and drain our jobs South.

For a single payer national health care plan that makes health care a right for everyone; not a plan that sacrifices care for some to protect profits for a few. In order to achieve these ends, politics as we know it is not working for us. Too often, we're rounding up votes to empower people to humiliate us and be indifferent to our legitimate interest. We must see more clearly from this mountain than we saw from the valley.

We must unleash the strength of our freedom struggle in new political forms. Our legitimate needs and interests are beyond the reach and boundaries of concern for both parties. But, the waters of justice must not be dammed up and become stagnant while urban Americans and family farmers perish in valleys of neglect. The levee is breaking. We must unleash the flood gates, waters of deep passion yearning to break free roll over the rocks of broken Covenants and deceit. We must become free political agents bound only by principles not limited by party. There were 12 million African-Americans alone who voted for change and legal protection, yet we do not have an Attorney General for Civil Rights that we can call on to fight our cause.

Through it all, don't let them break your spirit. Though the tide of fascist racism is on the rise, though the arrogant forces of indifference expand jails, underfund our schools, and warehouse our youths as they languish unemployed and unskilled with broken dreams. Don't let them break your spirit. KEEP HOPE ALIVE! Though the media stereotypes us as less worthy, less intelligent, less hardworking, less universal, less patriotic, and more violent. Don't let them break your spirit. KEEP HOPE ALIVE!

Though the plant gates are closing and jobs are shifting to cheap labor markets subsidized by our own government. Though the White House and the Congress offer a crime bill to contain the people rather than an economic stimulus plan to develop the people. Don't let them break your spirit. KEEP HOPE ALIVE! It's tough but thirty years ago, it was tougher. The sun was hotter and there was no shade. The winters were colder and there was no place of warm refuge. When torrential rains poured, we were trapped in the lowlands. Yet, we did not let it break our spirits. We must be caring not callous, loving not rejecting, putting character over color, ethics over ethnicity. We must trust in God's word.

Let's go forward back to our towns and hamlets to build new structures for freedom, new vehicles for hope in our quest to redeem the soul of America and make our world more secure. From Angola to Alabama, New York to Nigeria, Birmingham to Brazil, let the world know that we will stand fast and never surrender.

Hear this Biblical admonition and promise: If my people were called by my name, will humble themselves and pray, and seek my face and turn from their wicked ways, God will forgive their sins and they will hear from heaven. Then, God will heal their land.

KEEP HOPE ALIVE!!!

CLINTON'S STATEMENT

On this day 30 years ago, almost a quarter million Americans gathered in the shadow of the Lincoln Memorial to ask our Nation to uphold its founding ideals of equal justice and equal opportunity for all.

As he looked at the crowd, Martin Luther King, Jr., must have been inspired by what he saw: people of every color, united in mutual respect and common purpose, representing America as it was meant to be and as it must be. In the words of A. Philip Randolph, whose vision of a multiracial movement for social justice inspired this historic demonstration, those who marched on August 28, 1963, were "the advance guard of a massive moral revolution for jobs and freedom."

Three decades later, we remember how far we have come on freedom's trail, and we rededicate ourselves to completing the journey. As a son of the South, I have seen in my own lifetime how racism held all of us down and how the civil rights movement set all of us free. We must never forget the hard-earned lesson that America can only move forward when we move forward together.

That is why we rededicate ourselves to rigorous enforcement of the civil rights laws, to eradicating discrimination of every kind, and to opposing intolerance in all its forms. And we firmly believe that, as such visionary leaders as Martin Luther King, A. Philip Randolph, and Bayard Rustin understood three decades ago, jobs and freedom are inextricably linked. Human dignity demands that each of us have the opportunity to use our God-given abilities, to support ourselves and our families, and to produce something of value for our fellow men and women.

In everything we do, we are guided by that vision of economic empowerment. That is why we have struggled to lift the working poor out of poverty. That is why we have struggled to expand the opportunities for education, training, and national service. That is why we have struggled to bring new jobs, new opportunities, and new hope to communities all across this country, from our smallest towns to our oldest cities. That is why we will spare no effort to provide every family in America with health care they can count on, health care that's always there. And as we pursue the timeless goals of opportunity for all and responsibility for all, let us follow the example of those who marched 30 years ago and work together, regardless of race or region or religion or party.

As we honor the past and build the future, let us listen again to the words of Martin Luther King, Jr., "Now is the time to make real the promises of democracy . . . now is the time to make justice a reality for all God's children." Together, we can make that dream a reality. Together, we can make the country we love everything it was meant to be.

September

REPORT ON CHINESE FOOD AND NUTRITION

September 1, 1993

Chinese restaurants reported a 25 percent drop in business in late 1993 following the release of a report by the Center for Science in the Public Interest (CSPI) documenting the nutritional content of Chinese restaurant fare. Answering the howls of protest from restaurateurs and patrons, the CSPI pointed out that its researchers were not picking on Chinese food; they planned to release similar reports on Italian and Mexican restaurant food.

"Chinese Food: A Wok on the Wild Side," written by Jayne Hurley and Stephen Schmidt, appeared in the center's Nutrition Action Newsletter. The CSPI analyzed the nutritional content of fifteen popular dishes from twenty Chinese restaurants in Washington, D.C., Chicago, and San Francisco. Reduced to their specific levels of fat, saturated fat, calories, sodium, and cholesterol, old favorites such as Kung Pao Chicken and Sweet and Sour Pork became less and less appetizing.

You Are What You Eat

According to the CSPI, an average Chinese restaurant entree "contains more sodium than you should eat in an entire day. It also has 70 percent of a day's fat, 80 percent of a day's cholesterol, and almost half a day's saturated fat."

Some dishes are healthier than others. Ranked according to percentage of calories from fat, the worst offenders include egg rolls, with 52 percent; Moo Shu Pork, with 47 percent; and Kung Pao Chicken, with 42 percent. Szechuan Shrimp, on the other hand, came in with only 18 percent of its calories from fat—but contained a day's worth of cholesterol.

High sodium content was another serious offender. Stir-Fried Vegetables had one of the lowest sodium rankings of the dishes checked, yet it contained over 2,100 mg—the maximum recommendation for a day. And House Lo Mein, the highest, had an astounding 3,460 mg.

However, the CSPI discovered that the level of saturated fat in Chinese restaurant food was lower than in the majority of American dishes. Moo Shu Pork was the exception, with 10 percent of its calories coming from saturated fats.

"But I Like Chinese Food!"

The good news was that just as the CSPI was scaring the public with its exhaustive analysis of Chinese food, it was also sharing insights into how to reduce the caloric, sodium, and fat content of any dish. By following the CSPI's guidelines, Chinese food lovers could actually turn the dietary odds in their favor.

The most important recommendation was simply to match a cup of rice for every cup of entree. This technique alone would significantly improve the healthfulness of even Sweet and Sour Pork, which had the highest calorie and fat ranking of all the dishes tested.

Other options included the "forklift," removing the entree from its sauce and adding it to the bowl of rice. As the CSPI advised, "Leave behind the sauce, excess egg and nuts, and anything else you'd rather not eat." CSPI also recommended ordering steamed vegetables to go along with the entree and removing the fried batter from dishes such as Sweet and Sour Pork.

Why the Fuss?

Michael Jacobson, executive director of the CSPI, once appeared on television with a hammer and chisel whacking away at a fifty-pound block of vegetable shortening. His target was the fast food industry, which had replaced beef tallow with vegetable shortening. Their efforts were not enough, Jacobson said; the level of saturated fat was still too high.

Jacobson had used flamboyant tactics since the founding of the CSPI in 1971, when healthy foods such as yogurt and whole wheat breads were hardly in the vocabulary of many Americans, much less taking up shelf space at the local supermarket. The CSPI's public relations tactics—outrageous zealotry to detractors, necessary enlightenment to others—has played a role in raising the health consciousness of many Americans. At a time when more and more of Americans' food dollars are spent in restaurants, the data provided by the CSPI may be regarded as unpleasant but necessary.

Following is the text of "Chinese Food: A Wok on the Wild Side," released September 1, 1993, by the Center for Science in the Public Interest:

An order of House Lo Mein with as much salt as a whole Pizza Hut Cheese Pizza? An order of Kung Pao Chicken with almost as much fat as four Quarter Pounders? An order of Moo Shu Pork with more than twice the cholesterol of an Egg McMuffin?

According to a recent report by the Food Marketing Institute and *Prevention Magazine*, 52 percent of all Americans say that Chinese food is "more healthful" than their usual diet.

If only they knew.

The Great Stir-Off

No one's ever looked—really looked—at just how good (or bad) Chinese food is. So we recently decided to find out. We bought dinner-size take-out portions of 15 popular dishes from 20 mid-priced Chinese restaurants in Washington, D.C., Chicago, and San Francisco. Then we shipped them to an independent lab to be analyzed for calories, fat, saturated fat, and sodium. Cholesterol we estimated by weighing the ingredients in each dish.

Soup and egg roll aside, what we found would make your chopsticks splinter.

- Fat ranged from a respectable 19 grams (Szechuan Shrimp or Stir-Fried Vegetables) to an outrageous 76 grams (Kung Pao Chicken). That's more than you should eat in an entire day, and more than 40 percent of calories. (Most experts recommend a 30-percent limit. We say 20 percent.)
- Other than Sweet and Sour Pork, the lowest-sodium dinner (Stir-Fried Vegetables) had over 2,100 mg—about your quota for a day. The highest-sodium plate (House Lo Mein) clocked in at an incredible 3,460 mg.
- On the plus side, the saturated fat was lower than you'll find in most American food. Only once (Moo Shu Pork) did it hit the ten percent of calories that most experts recommend. About half the dishes were even below our seven-percent limit. But many contained at least a day's worth of cholesterol. Good old Moo Shu Pork had a two-day supply.

With numbers like those, it's a good thing it's easy to turn almost any dish into a healthy one. It's simple, convenient, and cheap. It's spelled R-I-C-E, and it's the first of our "Three Steps to Healthy Chinese."

Step 1. One Cup Entree, One Cup Rice. The more rice you pile on, the more portions you create, and the less fat and sodium each one has. That's more like the healthy Chinese diet you think you're getting down at your local Hard Wok Cafe.

For example, one of the nastiest dishes is Kung Pao Chicken. A dinner portion without the rice averaged 1,275 calories, 75 grams of fat (13 of them saturated), and more than 2,600 mg of sodium. That's about a day's worth of fat and sodium crammed into one entree.

But if you add one cup of rice to every cup of Kung Pao and then divide it into two-cup portions (split it with friends, take some to work . . . you get the idea), each will have about 653 calories, 23 grams of fat (four of them saturated), and 791 mg of sodium. That's still not great, but it's much better....

Step 2. Say "Steamed Veggies." What makes real Chinese food healthy is not just the rice, but the vegetables. American Chinese focuses on the chicken and meat. So order a portion of steamed veggies and add it to your entree. You'll have more than enough sauce to make it flavorful. And if you're only ordering one dish, at least make it a vegetable-rich one like Chicken Chow Mein or Shrimp with Garlic Sauce.

Step 3. Do the "Forklift." It's how the Chinese eat. Use your fork (or chopsticks) to lift the food out of the sauce and on to your big (if you followed Step 1) bowl of rice. Leave behind the sauce, excess egg and nuts, and anything else you'd rather not eat. Then eat from your rice bowl.

Behind the Bamboo Curtain

So here are our 15 dishes. We've ranked them from worst (highest percent of calories from fat) to best (lowest percent).

We analyzed them without rice, then added nutrition information for 1 1/3 cups of steamed rice to each (except the House Fried Rice, House Lo Mein, Egg Roll, and Hot and Sour Soup). That's how much rice came with the average take-out order in Washington and Chicago. In San Francisco rice was *a la carte.*

The percent of calories from fat and the grams of fat in each dish are in parentheses following the name.

1. Egg Roll (52%-11g fat). No surprise here. Most of the fat comes from the fried wonton wrapper that surrounds the smidgen of vegetables and pork or shrimp. The one nice thing about an egg roll is that it's not likely to have any cholesterol-laden egg.

Make it Better: *Sop up some grease. Roll it in a napkin.*

2. Moo Shu Pork (47%-64g fat). *(Pork, stir-fried with vegetables and egg and served with thin pancakes.)*

There's no reason for Moo Shu to be this fatty. After all, it averages three times more vegetables than pork. So why the 64 grams (15 teaspoons) of fat? And why a higher percent of calories from saturated fat than any other dish? Blame it on the oil in which all those veggies are stir-fried. While you're at it, you can blame all the cholesterol on the eggs—an average of two per order.

Make it Better: *Order Moo Shu Vegetable, no egg. Mix it with rice before you wrap it in the pancake.*

3. Kung Pao Chicken (42%-76g fat). *(Diced chicken, stir-fried with peanuts.)*

Nuts. That's the only way to explain how a chicken dish could end up with 76 grams of fat. The average Kung Pao contained almost a quarter-pound (3/4 cup) of peanuts. Two restaurants in Washington dumped on more than a half pound each. That's 118 grams of fat (almost two days' worth), not to mention 1,400 calories. Ugh.

Make it Better: *Ask for two or three tablespoons of nuts, max.*

4. Sweet and Sour Pork (39%-71g fat). *(Batter-dipped pork, deep-fried then stir-fried with pineapple.)* This was the only entree to average less than 1,000 mg of sodium. (Heck. It was the only one under 2,000 mg!) That's probably because it's loaded with sugar. Vegetables were sparse, averaging about a half cup.

Make it Better: *Most of the fat's in the breading. So take it off.*

5. Beef with Broccoli (35%-46g fat). *(Sliced beef, stir-fried with broccoli.)*

They averaged more than a half pound of beef (one Chicago restaurant gave us a pound). The dish also was one of the four members of the "3,000 Club" (milligrams of sodium, that is).

Make it Better: *Ask for less beef and more broccoli.*

6. General Tso's Chicken (33%-59g fat). *(Flour-coated chicken, stir-fried.)*

Don't expect miracles. The chef's got little more than chicken, oil, and (in some cases) batter to work with. Oh yeah. Salt, too. This dish's 3,000 + milligrams top your 2,400-mg daily limit in one chickeny swoop.

Make it Better: *If the chicken is batter-fried, peel it.*

7. Orange Crispy Beef (33%-66g fat). *(Flour-coated beef, stir-fried.)*

Expect a lot of meat (three-quarters of a pound, on average) and very few veggies (a half-cup). Only one restaurant (in San Francisco) served as much vegetables as beef. All told, you get more than a day's sodium, a day's fat and cholesterol, and a half-day's sat fat.

Make it Better: *If the beef is batter-fried, peel it.*

8. Hot and Sour Soup (32%-4g fat). *(Pork, tofu, and egg in broth.)*

If only you could remove the egg. That's where half your daily cholesterol allowance is. But most restaurants prepare their soups ahead of time. You won't be able to remove the 1,100 mg of sodium per cup, either. Or the MSG that's in soups—and most everything else on Chinese restaurant menus.

"Unless the menu says that the restaurant doesn't use MSG," explains Barbara Tropp, who owns the China Moon Cafe in San Francisco, "you're almost certainly going to get it in your food, no matter what the waiter says." That's because MSG is used in the sauces and stocks that are prepared ahead of time, she says.

Make it Better: *You can't.*

9. House Lo-Mein (31%-36g fat). *(Chicken, shrimp, beef, and pork, stir-fried with soft noodles.)*

Seventy percent noodles and ten percent vegetables mean low in saturated fat. And most of the meat is chicken. Too bad this was the saltiest dish we found.

Make it Better: *Order Vegetable Lo Mein. Mix it with rice.*

10. House Fried Rice (30%-50g fat). You probably don't think cholesterol when you think Fried Rice. But only Moo Shu Pork had more. When we picked apart the food, we saw why: an average of one egg per order.

Make it Better: *Never order Fried Rice to go under your entree. If it's your main dish, ask for Vegetable Fried Rice with no egg, and mix it with steamed rice.*

11. Chicken Chow Mein (28%-32g fat). *(Chicken with Chinese vegetables.)*

Fifty-five percent veggies and 30 percent chicken. That's our kind of dish . . . as long as you stay away from the fried noodles we were served in Washington and Chicago, (We didn't include them in our analyses. Ditto for the lo mein noodles we were served in San Francisco.)

Make it Better: *Ax the fried noodles.*

12. Hunan Tofu (27%-28g fat). *(Tofu, stir-fried in hot sauce.)*

The sauce only accounts for about a third of the dish's fat. The rest comes from its pound of tofu. Veggies? Pretty scarce. At least it has no cholesterol and not too much sat fat.

13. Shrimp with Garlic Sauce (25%-27g fat). *(Shrimp, stir-fried with vegetables.)*

Only four percent of calories from saturated fat (wow!), but more than a day's worth of cholesterol in each order (oof!). Most restaurants gave us six ounces of shrimp, though one in Chicago piled on almost a pound. That would sock you with close to 900 mg of cholesterol—three days' worth.

Make it Better: *Try scallops instead.*

14. Stir-Fried Vegetables (22%p-19g fat).

Vegetables and sauce. You won't get much lower in saturated fat. And you sure can't beat zero cholesterol. You're not likely to do better than its 2,150 mg of sodium, either.

Make it Better: *Try them steamed (or braised in broth). Sprinkle lightly with soy sauce. But go easy; every teaspoon costs you 350 mg of sodium.*

15. Szechuan Shrimp (18%-19g fat). *(Shrimp, stir-fried in hot sauce.)* Except for the day's worth of cholesterol, this was the best entree. It was lowest in saturated fat, tied for lowest in fat, and close to lowest in calories.

That's if you get it without peanuts. Most of the restaurants served it that way, but one in Chicago piled on almost a half pound. (We didn't include any nuts in our analysis.) Also, three San Francisco restaurants breaded and deep-fried the shrimp. (We didn't analyze those, either.)

Make it Better: *Make sure it's nut-less and not breaded and deep-fried. Try scallops instead.*

PENTAGON REVIEW OF NATIONAL SECURITY NEEDS

September 1, 1993

Defense Secretary Les Aspin on September 1 released the results of a six-month review of U.S. national security needs in the post-Cold War era. The future likelihood of major regional wars was the driving force behind much of the review's analysis and conclusions. Labeled "The Bottom-Up Review," the review process was headed by John Deutch, Undersecretary of Defense for Acquisition, with help from Joint Chiefs of Staff Chairman Colin L. Powell, who headed a similar review by the Bush administration. The Clinton administration's review was developed by senior officials in the offices of the defense secretary and the joint chiefs and by strategists of the four military services.

The Bottom-Up Review formed part of a comprehensive Clinton administration reevaluation of the military establishment. As a candidate for president, Bill Clinton had vowed to "restructure our military forces for a new era." The review examined the Bush administration's projected defense budgets for fiscal years 1995-99, the ongoing military base closure and realignment process, the Pentagon's weapons procurement methods, the nation's strategic nuclear programs and defenses, and potential financial savings for the military as suggested in Vice President Al Gore's National Performance Review recommendations. (National Performance Review, p. 717)

The post-Cold War strategy plan marked Aspin's last major initiative as defense secretary. He announced his resignation Dec. 15 after a tumultuous year in office. In October Aspin was indirectly blamed in the death of 18 U.S. service personnel in Somalia after he denied a request for tanks and armored vehicles by U.S. commanders directing the peacekeeping effort. President Clinton replaced Aspin in February 1994 with Deputy Defense Secretary William Perry. Clinton's first choice, Retired Admiral Bobby Ray Inman, abruptly withdrew as the nominee because of what he called "vitriolic attack" by a handful of newspaper columnists that he portrayed as "modern McCarthyism."

The Clinton defense strategy review reached conclusions similar to the Bush administration's review, "Base Force," on fundamental issues, differing primarily on the cost of implementing the post-Cold War strategy. Some military analysts charged that the Clinton administration's five-year Pentagon budget, which was $104 billion below Bush's projections, could not pay for the defense strategy outlined in the Bottom-Up Review. But Aspin maintained that a gradual reduction in U.S. armed forces could be achieved and that "our national security requirements" could still be met at the same time.

Besides formulating defense strategy, the review made decisions on the size and shape of U.S. armed forces, weapons and equipment research, procurement and modernization, methods for retaining a viable industrial base for America's defense-unique industries, and other aspects of maintaining a strong national defense.

New Dangers to National Security

The Bottom-Up Review named one key goal for America's future defense strategy: the ability to win two major, nearly simultaneous, regional wars and still maintain enough reserves to carry out limited peacekeeping operations. U.S. defense experts contended that it is necessary to meet this goal so that potential aggressors will not feel that they can attack other countries without retribution from an overburdened United States. With the breakup of the Soviet Union and the demise of the Warsaw Pact, Pentagon planners focused especially on the adequacy of a future U.S. response to new aggression in the Persian Gulf by Iraq or Iran and in East Asia by communist North Korea. The U.S. commitment to South Korea remained "undiminished," the administration stressed.

One goal of the defense study was to build a national consensus on the U.S. role in keeping international peace. While Americans in the past had been aware of the Soviet threat, policy makers needed to explain why it was in the U.S. national interest to intervene militarily to prevent or stop regional conflicts in other countries. "It is difficult to predict precisely what threats we will confront 10 to 20 years from now.... [I]n this dynamic and unpredictable post-Cold War world we must maintain military capabilities that are flexible and sufficient to cope with unforeseen threats," the review warned.

The review grouped potential post-Cold War dangers into four categories: (1) the nuclear threat represented by the proliferation of nuclear weapons in various states of the former Soviet Union and the potential for terrorist organizations acquiring such arms; (2) heightened major regional conflicts, particularly in Eastern Europe, the Middle East, and East Asia; (3) dangers to democratic reform, especially in the former Soviet bloc and the developing world; and (4) economic instability in the

U.S. that would threaten the nation's industrial base and technological edge in weapons development.

Smaller, More Mobile Armed Forces

The U.S. military of the future would be smaller and more mobile, and would carry weapons of greater devastation and accuracy. The Bottom-Up Review recommended reducing the size of the armed forces from a current level of 1.6 million service personnel to 1.4 million. The Marine Corps would be cut to 174,000 from 197,000. (The Bush plan had proposed an even larger cut—to 159,000.) U.S. troops in Europe would be reduced to 100,000 from 315,000, while U.S. forces in East Asia would remain at about 98,000 because of the continuing threat from North Korea. Another 20,000 troops would remain in the Middle East region.

To ensure the ability to successfully fight two nearly simultaneous wars, military planners estimated the United States would need ten active Army divisions and fifteen trained and mobile Army and National Guard brigades. The Navy would need eleven aircraft carrier battle groups and one reserve carrier used mainly for training; the Marine Corps, five active brigades and one reserve division; and the Air Force, thirteen active fighter wings and seven reserve fighter wings. The continuing need for large armed forces also was important, defense officials said, to project America's military presence abroad as evidence of the nation's commitment to deter regional aggression.

To provide the mobility needed for quick response, Pentagon planners called for five major initiatives: expand U.S. airlift capability by finding a replacement for the aging C-141 transport fleet; position a heavy armored army brigade on ships that could be deployed either in the Persian Gulf region or near the Korean peninsula; increase U.S. sealift capacity by building specially designed ships; improve the readiness of the Ready Reserve Force (RRF0); and improve the flow of personnel and military equipment from U.S. bases to overseas transit points. In addition, U.S. early warning (AWACS) and satellite communications (MILSTAR) systems would have to be upgraded.

Certain weapons systems and equipment would have to be modernized, while research and development would continue on others. The Strategic Defense initiative ("Star Wars") would be renamed the Ballistic Missile Defense program and would focus on the short-range missile threat. Some weapons and military equipment already under development would be cancelled, including a new Navy attack plane and a multi-role fighter for the Air Force. Other expensive weapons programs would go forward, including the F-22, an Air Force advanced tactical fighter, and the B1 and B2 bombers—which the Pentagon said eventually would comprise a fleet of 100.

The review did not address future nuclear strategy in detail because a separate study on that topic was underway. It did, however, point out that "significant uncertanties" existed in the aftermath of the breakup of the Soviet Union, and that these uncertainties affected U.S. nuclear weapons policy. U.S. policy must be an effective deterrent while at the same time remaining within the START I and START II Treaty limits, the review stated, and it must allow for additional nuclear capability in the event of a reversal, or threat of a reversal, of current international nuclear nonproliferation agreements. Although the United States had removed more than 3,500 nuclear warheads from ballistic missile systems slated for elimination under the treaties, "in light of current uncertainties we must take a measured approach to further reductions," the review concluded.

Following is the text of "Force Structure Excerpts, Bottom-Up Review," released September 1, 1993, by Les Aspin, secretary of defense:

National Security in the Post-Cold War World

Introduction

The Cold War is behind us. The Soviet Union is no longer. The threat that drove our defense decisionmaking for four and a half decades—that determined our strategy and tactics, our doctrine, the size and shape of our forces, the design of our weapons, and the size of our defense budgets—is gone.

Now that the Cold War is over, the questions we face in the Department of Defense are: How do we structure the armed forces of the United States for the future? How much defense is enough in the post-Cold War era?

Several important events over the past four years underscore the revolutionary nature of recent changes in the international security environment and shed light on this new era and on America's future defense and security requirements.

- In 1989, the fall of the Berlin Wall and the collapse of communism throughout Eastern Europe precipitated a strategic shift away from containment of the Soviet empire.
- In 1990, Iraq's brutal invasion of Kuwait signaled a new class of regional dangers facing America—dangers spurred not by a global, empire-building ideological power, but by rogue leaders set on regional domination through military aggression while simultaneously pursuing nuclear, biological, and chemical weapons capabilities. The world's response to Saddam's invasion also demonstrated the potential in the new era for broad-based, collective military action to thwart such tyrants.
- In 1991, the failed Soviet coup demonstrated the Russian people's desire for democratic change and hastened the collapse of the Soviet Union as a national entity and military foe.

In the aftermath of such epochal events, it has become clear that the framework that guided our security policy during the Cold War is inadequate for the future. We must determine the characteristics of this new era, develop a new strategy, and restructure our armed forces and defense programs accordingly. We cannot, as we did for the past several decades, premise this year's forces, programs, and budgets on incremental shifts from last year's efforts. We must rebuild our defense strategy, forces, and defense programs and budgets from the bottom up.

The purpose of the Bottom-Up Review is to define the strategy, force structure, modernization programs, industrial base, and infrastructure needed to meet new dangers and seize new opportunities.

An Era of New Dangers

Most striking in the transition from the Cold War is the shift in the nature of the dangers to our interests. . . .

The new dangers fall into four broad categories:

- **Dangers posed by nuclear weapons and other weapons of mass destruction**, including dangers associated with the proliferation of nuclear, biological, and chemical weapons as well as those associated with the large stocks of these weapons that remain in the former Soviet Union.
- **Regional dangers**, posed primarily by the threat of large-scale aggression by major regional powers with interests antithetical to our own, but also by the potential for smaller, often internal, conflicts based on ethnic or religious animosities, state-sponsored terrorism, and subversion of friendly governments.
- **Dangers to democracy and reform,** in the former Soviet Union, Eastern Europe, and elsewhere.
- **Economic dangers** to our national security, which could result if we fail to build a strong, competitive, and growing economy.

Our armed forces are central to combating the first two dangers and can play a significant role in meeting the second two. Our predictions and conclusions about the nature and characteristics of these dangers will help mold our strategy and size and shape our future military forces.

An Era of New Opportunities

During the Cold War, few entertained realistic aspirations for a markedly safer, freer world. Our strategy of containment was, perforce, defensive in nature, designed primarily to hold the Soviet Union and China in check. Today, there is promise that we can replace the East-West confrontation of the Cold War with an era in which the community of nations, guided by a common commitment to democratic principles, free-market economics, and the rule of law, can be significantly enlarged.

. . . [B]eyond new dangers, there are new opportunities: realistic aspirations that, if we dedicate ourselves to pursue worthy goals, we can reach a world of greater safety, freedom, and prosperity. Our armed forces can contribute to this objective. In brief, we see new opportunities to:

- Expand and adapt our existing security partnerships and alliances and build a larger community of democratic nations.
- Promote new regional security arrangements and alliances to improve deterrence and reduce the potential for aggression by hostile regional powers.
- Implement the dramatic reductions in the strategic nuclear arsenals of the United States and the former Soviet Union achieved in the START I and II treaties.
- Protect and advance our security with fewer resources, freeing excess resources to be invested in other areas vital to our prosperity.

Objectives and Methodology of the Bottom-Up Review

We undertook the Bottom-Up Review to select the right strategy, force structure, modernization programs, and supporting industrial base and infrastructure to provide for America's defense in the post-Cold War era.

[We used a step-by-step process] to develop key assumptions, broad principles, and general objectives and translate them into a specific plan for our strategy, forces, and defense resources.

These steps included:

1. Assessing the post-Cold War era, and particularly the new dangers, opportunities, and uncertainties it presents.
2. Devising a U.S. defense strategy to protect and advance our interests in this new period.
3. Constructing building blocks of forces to implement this strategy.
4. Combining these force building blocks to produce options for our overall force structure.
5. Complementing the force structure with weapons acquisition programs to modernize our forces, defense foundations to sustain them, and policy initiatives to address new dangers and take advantage of new opportunities.

With the Bottom-Up Review now complete, we will utilize its results to build a multi-year plan for America's future security, detailing the forces, programs, and defense budgets the United States needs to protect and advance its interests in the post-Cold War period.

The Bottom-Up Review represented a close collaboration between the civilian and military sectors of the Department of Defense. Task forces were established—including representatives from the Office of the Secretary of Defense, the Joint Staff, the unified and specified commands, each of the armed services, and, where appropriate, other defense agencies—to review the major issues entailed in planning defense strategy, forces, modernization programs, and other defense foundations. Numerous studies helped to formulate the key issues for decisionmakers and provided the analytical underpinning for our review.

We offer this plan for public consideration as a means of forming a new national consensus on America's strategic role in global affairs, the military instruments needed to fulfill that role, and the level of resources necessary to provide those instruments.

Building Future Capabilities: Guiding Principles

Certain other underlying principles guided our effort during the Bottom-Up Review. In his inaugural address, President Clinton pledged to keep America's military the best trained, best equipped, best prepared fighting force in the world. To fulfill that pledge, we must keep it the focus of our effort throughout the planning, programming, and budgeting process.

First, we must **keep our forces ready to fight**. We have already witnessed the challenges posed by the new dangers in operations like Just Cause (Panama), Desert Storm (Iraq), and Restore Hope (Somalia). Each of these was a "come as you are" campaign with little time to prepare our forces for the challenges they met.

The new dangers thus demand that we keep our forces ready to fight as a top priority in allocating scarce defense resources. We must adequately fund operations and maintenance accounts, maintain sufficient stocks of spare parts, keep our forces well-trained and equipped, and take the other steps essential to preserving readiness.

A key element of maintaining forces ready to fight is to **maintain the quality of our people**, so that they remain the best fighting force in the world. This means keeping our personnel highly motivated by treating them fairly and maintaining their quality of life. It also means continuing to recruit talented young men and women, expanding career opportunities for all service personnel, and putting in place programs to ease the transition to civilian life for many of our troops as we bring down the size of our forces.

We must also **maintain the technological superiority** of our weapons and equipment. Operation Desert Storm demonstrated that we produce the best weapons and military equipment in the world. This technological edge helps us to achieve victory more swiftly and with fewer casualties. We must design a balanced modernization program that will safeguard this edge and the necessary supporting industrial base without buying more weapons than we need or can afford.

Forces to Implement Our Defense Strategy

Major Regional Conflicts

During the Cold War, our military planning was dominated by the need to confront numerically superior Soviet forces in Europe, the Far East, and Southwest Asia. Now, our focus is on the need to project power into regions important to our interests and to defeat potentially hostile regional powers, such as North Korea and Iraq. Although these powers are unlikely to threaten the United States directly, these countries and others like them have shown that they are willing and able to field forces sufficient to threaten important U.S. interests, friends, and allies. Operation Desert Storm was a powerful demonstration of the need to counter such regional aggression.

Potential regional aggressors are expected to be capable of fielding military forces in the following ranges:

- 400,000-750,000 total personnel under arms
- 2,000-4,000 tanks
- 3,000-5,000 armored fighting vehicles
- 2,000-3,000 artillery pieces
- 500-1,000 combat aircraft
- 100-200 naval vessels, primarily patrol craft armed with surface-to-surface missiles, and up to 50 submarines
- 100-1,000 Scud-class ballistic missiles, some possibly with nuclear, chemical, or biological warheads.

Military forces of this size can threaten regions important to the United States because allied or friendly states are often unable to match the power of such a potentially aggressive neighbor. Hence, we must prepare our forces to assist those of our friends and allies in deterring, and ultimately, defeating aggression, should it occur.

Scenarios as Planning Tools. Every war that the United States has fought has been different from the last, and different from what defense planners had envisioned. For example, the majority of the bases and facilities used by the United States and its coalition partners in Operation Desert Storm were built in the 1980s, when we envisioned a Soviet invasion through Iran to be the principal threat to the Gulf region. In planning forces capable of fighting and winning major regional conflicts (MRCs), we must avoid preparing for past wars. History suggests that we most often deter the conflicts that we plan for and actually fight the ones we do not anticipate.

For planning and assessment purposes, we have selected two illustrative scenarios that are both plausible and that posit demands characteristic of those that could be posed by conflicts with a wide range of regional powers. While a number of scenarios were examined, the two that we focused on most closely in the Bottom-Up Review envisioned aggression by a remilitarized Iraq against Kuwait and Saudi Arabia, and by North Korea against the Republic of Korea.

Neither of these scenarios should be regarded as a prediction of future conflicts, but each provides a useful representation of the challenge presented by a well-armed regional power initiating aggression thousands of miles from the United States. As such, the scenarios serve as yardsticks against which to assess, in gross terms, the capabilities of U.S. forces....

In each scenario, we examined the performance of projected U.S. forces in relation to many critical parameters, including warning time, the threat, terrain, weather, duration of hostilities, and combat intensity. Overall, these scenarios were representative of likely ranges of these critical parameters.

Both scenarios assumed a similar enemy operation: an armor-heavy, combined-arms offensive against the outnumbered forces of a neighboring state. U.S. forces, most of which were not present in the region when hostilities commenced, had to deploy to the region quickly, supplement indigenous forces, halt the invasion, and defeat the aggressor.

Such a short-notice scenario, in which only a modest number of U.S. forces are in a region at the commencement of hostilities, is both highly stressing and plausible. History shows that we frequently fail to anticipate the location and timing of aggression, even large-scale attacks against our interests. In such cases, it may also not be possible, prior to an attack, to reach a political consensus on the proper U.S. response or to convince our allies to grant U.S. forces access to facilities in their countries.

We also expect that the United States will often be fighting as the leader of a coalition, with allies providing some support and combat forces. As was the case in Desert Storm, the need to defend common interests should prompt our allies in many cases to contribute capable forces to the war effort. However, our forces must be sized and structured to preserve the flexibility and the capability to act unilaterally, should we choose to do so.

The Four Phases of U.S. Combat Operations

Our first priority in preparing for regional conflicts is to prevent them from ever occurring. This is the purpose of our overseas presence forces and operations, joint exercises, and other military capabilities—to deter potential regional aggressors from even contemplating an attack. Should deterrence fail and conflict occur, it is envisioned that combat operations would unfold in four main phases:

Phase 1: Halt the invasion. The highest priority in defending against a large-scale attack will most often be to minimize the territory and critical facilities that the invader can capture. Should important strategic assets fall to the invader, it might attempt to use them as bargaining chips. In addition, stopping the invasion quickly may be key to ensuring that the threatened ally can continue its crucial role in the collective effort to defeat the aggressor. Further, the more territory the enemy captures, the greater the price to take it back: The number of forces required for the counteroffensive to repel an invasion can increase, with correspondingly greater casualties, depending on the progress the enemy makes. In the event of a short-warning attack, more U.S. forces would need to deploy rapidly to the theater and enter the battle as quickly as possible.

Phase 2: Build up U.S. combat power in the theater while reducing the enemy's. Once the enemy attack had been stopped and the front stabilized, U.S. and allied efforts would focus on continuing to build up combat forces and logistics support in the theater while reducing the enemy's capacity to fight. Land, air, maritime, and special operations forces from the United States and coalition countries would continue to arrive. These forces would seek to ensure that the enemy did not regain the initiative on the ground, and they would mount sustained attacks to reduce the enemy's military capabilities in preparation for the combined-arms counteroffensive.

Phase 3: Decisively defeat the enemy. In the third phase, U.S. and allied forces would seek to mount a large-scale, air-land counteroffensive to defeat the enemy decisively by attacking his centers of gravity, retaking territory he had occupied, destroying his warmaking capabilities, and successfully achieving other operational or strategic objectives.

Phase 4: Provide for post-war stability. Although a majority of U.S. and coalition forces would begin returning to their home bases, some forces might be called upon to remain in the theater after the enemy had been defeated to ensure that the conditions that resulted in conflict did not recur. These forces could help repatriate prisoners, occupy and administer some or all of the enemy's territory, or to ensure compliance with the provisions of war-termination or cease-fire agreements.

Forces for Combat Operations

Described below are the types of forces that are needed to conduct joint combat operations in all four phases of an MRC.

Forces for Phase 1. Primary responsibility for the initial defense of their territory rests, of course, with our allies. As forces of the besieged country move to blunt an attack, U.S. forces already in the theater would move rapidly to provide assistance. However, as already mentioned, we are drawing down our overseas presence in response to the end of the Cold War. Thus, the bulk of our forces, even during the early stages of conflict, would have to come from the United States. This places a premium on rapidly deployable yet highly lethal forces to blunt an attack.

The major tasks to be performed in this phase and beyond are:

- Help allied forces establish a viable defense that halts enemy ground forces before they can achieve critical objectives.
- Delay, disrupt, and destroy enemy ground forces and damage the roads along which they are moving, in order to halt the attack. U.S. attacks would be mounted by a combination of land- and sea-based strike aircraft, heavy bombers, long-range tactical missiles, ground maneuver forces with anti-armor capabilities, and special operations forces.
- Protect friendly forces and rear-area assets from attack by aircraft or cruise and ballistic missiles, using land- and sea-based aircraft, ground- and sea-based surface-to-air missiles, and special operations forces.
- Establish air superiority and suppress enemy air defenses as needed,

including those in rear areas and those accompanying invading ground forces, using land- and sea-based strike and jamming aircraft as well as surface-to-surface missiles, such as the Army Tactical Missile System (ATACMS).

- Destroy high-value targets, such as weapons of mass destruction, and degrade the enemy's ability to prosecute military operations through attacks focused on his central command, control, and communications facilities. For such attacks, we would rely heavily on long-range bombers, land- and sea-based strike aircraft, cruise missiles, and special operations forces.
- Establish maritime superiority, using naval task forces with mine countermeasure ships, in order to ensure access to ports and sea lines of communication, and as a precondition for amphibious assaults.

Forces for Phase 2. Many of the same forces employed in Phase 1 would be used in the second phase to perform similar tasks—grinding down the enemy's military potential while additional U.S. and other coalition combat power is brought into the region. As more land- and sea-based air forces arrived, emphasis would shift from halting the invasion to isolating enemy ground forces and destroying them, destroying enemy air and naval forces, destroying stocks of supplies, and broadening attacks on military-related targets in the enemy's rear area. These attacks could be supplemented with direct and indirect missile and artillery fire from ground, air, and sea forces.

Meanwhile, other U.S. forces, including heavy ground forces, would begin arriving in the theater to help maintain the defensive line established at the end of Phase I and to begin preparations for the counteroffensive.

Forces for Phase 3. The centerpiece of Phase 3 would be the U.S. and allied counteroffensive, aimed at engaging, enveloping, and destroying or capturing enemy ground forces occupying friendly territory. Major tasks within the counteroffensive include:

- Breaching tactical and protective minefields.
- Maneuvering to envelop or flank and destroy enemy forces, including armored vehicles in dug-in positions.
- Conducting or threatening an amphibious invasion.
- Dislodging and defeating infantry fighting from dug-in positions; defeating light infantry in urban terrain.
- Destroying enemy artillery.
- Locating and destroying mobile enemy reserves.

Combat power in this phase would include highly mobile armored, mechanized, and air assault forces, supported by the full complement of air power, special operations forces, and land- and sea-based fire support. Amphibious forces would provide additional operational flexibility to the theater commander.

Forces for Phase 4. Finally, a smaller complement of joint forces would remain in the theater once the enemy had been defeated. These forces might include a carrier battle group, one to two wings of fighters, a division or less of ground forces, and special operations units.

Supporting Capabilities

The foregoing list of forces for the various phases of combat operations included only combat force elements. Several types of support capabilities would play essential roles throughout all phases.

Airlift. Adequate airlift capacity is needed to bring in forces and material required for the first weeks of an operation. In Operation Desert Shield/Desert Storm, the United States delivered to the Gulf region, on average, more than 2,400 tons of material per day by airlift. We anticipate that at least the same level of lift capacity will be needed to support high-intensity military operations in the opening phase of a future MRC and to help sustain operations thereafter.

Prepositioning. Prepositioning heavy combat equipment and supplies, both ashore and afloat, can greatly reduce both the time required to deploy forces to distant regions and the number of airlift sorties devoted to moving such supplies. Initiatives now underway will accelerate the arrival of the Army's heavy forces in distant theaters.

Sealift. In any major regional conflict, most combat equipment and supplies would be transported by sea. While airlift and prepositioning provide the most rapid response for deterrence and initial defense, the deployment of significant heavy ground and air forces, their support equipment, and sustainment must come by sea.

Battlefield Surveillance; Command, Control, and Communications. Accurate information on the location and disposition of enemy forces is a prerequisite for effective military operations. Hence, our planning envisions the early deployment of reconnaissance and command and control aircraft and ground-based assets to enable our forces to see the enemy and to pass information quickly through all echelons of our forces. Total U.S. intelligence and surveillance capability will be less than it was during the Cold War, but it will be better able to provide timely information to battlefield commanders. Advanced systems, such as the Joint Surveillance and Target Attack Radar System (JSTARS), the upgraded Airborne Warning and Control System (AWACS), and the MILSTAR satellite communications system, will ensure that U.S. forces have a decisive advantage in tactical intelligence and communications.

Advanced Munitions. As U.S. operations in the Gulf War demonstrated, advanced precision-guided munitions can dramatically increase the effectiveness of U.S. forces. Precision-guided munitions already in the U.S. inventory (for example, laser-guided bombs) as well as new types of munitions still under development are needed to ensure that U.S. forces can operate successfully in future MRCs and other types of conflicts. New "smart" and "brilliant" munitions under development hold promise of dramatically improving the capabilities of U.S. air, ground, and maritime forces to destroy enemy armored vehicles and halt invading ground forces, as well as destroy fixed targets at longer ranges, reducing exposure to enemy air defenses.

Aerial Refueling. Large numbers of aerial refueling aircraft would be needed to support many components of a U.S. theater campaign. Fighter aircraft deploying over long distances require aerial refueling. Airlifters can also carry more cargo longer distances if enroute aerial refueling is available. Aerial surveillance and control platforms, such as AWACS and JSTARS, also need airborne refueling in order to achieve maximum mission effectiveness.

The MRC Building Block

In planning future force structure and allocating resources, we established forces levels and support which should enable us to win one MRC across a wide range of likely conflicts. Our detailed analyses of future MRCs, coupled with military judgment of the outcomes, suggest that the following forces will be adequate to execute the strategy outlined above for a single MRC:

4-5 Army divisions
4-5 Marine Expeditionary Brigades
10 Air Force fighter wings
100 Air Force heavy bombers
4-5 Navy aircraft carrier battle groups
Special operations forces

These forces constitute a prudent building block for force planning purposes. In the event of an actual regional conflict, our response would depend on the nature and scale of the aggression and circumstances elsewhere in the world. If the initial defense fails to halt the invasion quickly, or if circumstances in other parts of the world permit, U.S. decisionmakers may decide to commit more forces than those listed (for example, two additional Army divisions). These added forces would help either to achieve the needed advantage over the enemy, to mount the decisive counteroffensive, or accomplish more ambitious war objectives, such as the complete destruction of the enemy's warmaking potential. But our analysis also led us to the conclusion that enhancements to our military forces, focused on ensuring our ability to conduct a successful initial defense, would both reduce our overall ground force requirements and increase the responsiveness and effectiveness of our power projection forces.

Fighting Two MRCs

In this context, we decided early in the Bottom-Up review that the United States must field forces sufficient to fight and win two nearly simultaneous major regional conflicts. This is prudent for two reasons:

- First, we need to avoid a situation in which the United States in effect makes simultaneous wars more likely by leaving an opening for potential aggressors to attack their neighbors, should our engagement in a war in one region leave little or no force available to respond effectively to defend our interests in another.
- Second, fielding forces sufficient to win two wars nearly simultaneously provides a hedge against the possibility that a future adversary—or coalition of adversaries—might one day confront us with a larger-than-expected threat. In short, it is difficult to predict precisely what threats we will confront ten to twenty years from now. In this dynamic and unpredictable post-Cold War world we must maintain military capabilities that are flexible and sufficient to cope with unforeseen threats.

For the bulk of our ground, naval, and air forces, fielding forces sufficient to provide this capability involves duplicating the MRC building block described above. However, in planning our overall force structure, we must recognize two other factors. First, we must have sufficient strategic lift to deploy forces when and where we need them. Second, certain specialized high-leverage units or unique assets might be "dual tasked," that is, used in both MRCs.

For example, certain advanced aircraft—such as B-2s, F-117s, JSTARs, AWACS, and EF-111s—that we have purchased in limited numbers because of their expense would probably be dual-tasked.

Force Enhancements to Support Our Strategy

As previously mentioned, we have already undertaken or are planning a series of enhancements to our forces to improve their capability, flexibility, and lethality. These enhancements are especially geared toward buttressing our ability to conduct a successful initial defense in any major regional conflict.

... [T]hese enhancements include improving: (1) strategic mobility through more prepositioning and enhancements to airlift and sealift; (2) the strike capabilities of aircraft carriers; (3) the lethality of Army firepower; and (4) the ability of long-range bombers to deliver conventional smart munitions.

Strategic Mobility. Our plans call for substantial enhancements to our strategic mobility—most of which were first identified in the 1991 Mobility Requirements Study (MRS). First, we will either continue the program to purchase and deploy the C-17 airlifter or purchase other airlifters to replace our aging C-141 transport aircraft. Development of the C-17 has been troubled from the start and we will continue to monitor the program's progress closely, but significant, modern, flexible airlift capacity is essential to our defense strategy. A decision on the C-17 will be made after a thorough review by the Defense Acquisition Board is completed over the next several weeks. Second, we plan to keep an Army brigade set of heavy armor afloat on ships deployed abroad that could be sent either to the

Persian Gulf or to Northeast Asia on short notice. Other prepositioning initiatives would accelerate the arrival of Army heavy units in Southwest Asia and Korea. Third, we will increase the capacity of our surge sealift fleet to transport forces and equipment rapidly from the United States to distant regions by purchasing additional roll-on/roll-off ships. Fourth, we will improve the readiness and responsiveness of the Ready Reserve Force (RRF) through a variety of enhancements. Finally, we will fund various efforts to improve the "fort-to-port" flow of personnel, equipment, and supplies in the United States.

Naval Strike Aircraft. The Navy is examining a number of innovative ways to improve the firepower aboard its aircraft carriers. First, the Navy will improve its strike potential by providing a precision ground-attack capability to many of its F-14 aircraft. It will also acquire stocks of new "brilliant" antiarmor weapons for delivery by attack aircraft. Finally, the Navy plans to develop the capability to fly additional squadrons of F/A-18s to forward-deployed aircraft carriers that would be the first to arrive in response to a regional contingency. These additional aircraft would increase the power of the carriers during the critical early stages of a conflict.

Army Firepower. The Army is developing new, smart submunitions that can be delivered by ATACMS, the Multiple-Launch Rocket System (MLRS), the TriService Standoff Attack Missile (TSSAM) now under development, and by standard tube artillery. In addition, the Longbow fire control radar system will increase the effectiveness and survivability of the AH-64 Apache attack helicopter. We are also examining more prepositioning of ATACMS and MLRS and having Apaches self-deploy from their overseas bases so that all would be available in the early stages of a conflict.

Air Force Long-Range Bombers and Munitions. The Air Force enhancements will be in two areas, bombers and munitions. First, we plan to modify the Air Force's B-1 and B-2 long-range, heavy bombers to improve their ability to deliver "smart" conventional munitions against attacking enemy forces and fixed targets. Second, we will develop all-weather munitions. For example, the Air Force is developing a guidance package for a tactical munitions dispenser filled with anti-armor submunitions that can be used in all types of weather. These programs will dramatically increase our capacity to attack and destroy critical targets in the crucial opening days of a short-warning conflict.

In addition, two other force enhancements are important to improving our ability to respond to the demanding requirement of two nearly simultaneous MRCs:

Reserve Component Forces. We have undertaken several initiatives to improve the readiness and flexibility of Army National Guard combat units and other Reserve Component forces in order to make them more readily available for MRCs and other tasks. For example, one important role for combat elements of the Army National Guard is to provide forces to supplement active divisions, should more ground combat power be needed to deter or fight a second MRC. In the future, Army National Guard combat units will be better trained, more capable, and more ready. If mobilized early during a conflict, brigade-sized units could provide extra security and flexibility if a second conflict arose while the first was still going on. In addition, the Navy plans to increase the capability and effectiveness of its Navy/Marine Corps Reserve Air Wing through the introduction of a reserve/training aircraft carrier.

Allied Military Capabilities. We will continue to help our allies in key regions improve their own defense capabilities. For example, we are assisting South Korea in its efforts to modernize its armed forces and take on greater responsibility for its own defense—including conclusion of an agreement to co-produce F-16 aircraft.

In Southwest Asia, we are continuing to improve our defense ties with our friends and allies in the region through defense cooperation agreements, more frequent joint and combined exercises, equipment propositioning, frequent force deployments, and security assistance. We are also providing modern weapons, such as the MIA2 tank to Kuwait and the Patriot system to Kuwait and Saudi Arabia, to improve the self-defense capabilities of our friends and allies in the Gulf region.

Peace Enforcement and Intervention Operations

The second set of operations for which we must shape and size our forces includes peace enforcement and intervention. The types, numbers, and sophistication of weapons in the hands of potential adversaries in such operations can vary widely, with enforcement type operations being the most demanding. For planning purposes, we assume that the threat we would face would include a mix of regular and irregular forces possessing mostly light weapons, supplemented by moderately sophisticated systems, such as antitank and antiship guided missiles, surface-to-air missiles, land and sea mines, T-54 and T-72-class tanks, armored personnel carriers, and towed artillery and mortars. Adversary forces might also possess a limited number of mostly older combat aircraft (e.g., MiG-21s, 23s), a few smaller surface ships (e.g., patrol craft), and perhaps a few submarines.

In most cases, U.S. involvement in peace enforcement operations would be as part of a multinational effort under the auspices of the United Nations or another international body. U.S. and coalition forces would have several key objectives in a peace enforcement or intervention operation, each of which would require certain types of combat forces to achieve:

- Forced entry into defended airfields, ports, and other facilities and seizing and holding these facilities.
- Controlling the movement of troops and supplies across borders and within the target country, including enforcing a blockade or quarantine of maritime commerce.
- Establishing and defending zones in which civilians are protected from external attacks.

- Securing protected zones from internal threats, such as snipers, terrorist attacks, and sabotage.
- Preparing to turn over responsibility for security to peacekeeping units and/or a reconstituted administrative authority.

The prudent level of forces that should be planned for a major intervention or peace enforcement operation is:

1 air assault or airborne division
1 light infantry division
1 Marine Expeditionary Brigade
1-2 carrier battle groups
1-2 composite wings of Air Force aircraft
Special operations forces
Civil affairs units
Airlift and sealift forces
Combat support and service support units
50,000 total combat and support personnel.

These capabilities can be provided largely by the same collection of general purpose forces needed for the MRCs, so long as those forces had the appropriate training needed for peacekeeping or peace enforcement. This means that the United States would have to forgo the option of conducting sizable peace enforcement or intervention operations at the same time it was fighting two MRCs.

Overseas Presence

The final set of requirements that we use to size general purpose forces are those related to sustaining the overseas presence of U.S. military forces. U.S. forces deployed abroad protect and advance our interests and perform a wide range of functions that contribute to our security.

The Bottom-Up Review reached a number of conclusions on the future size and shape of our overseas presence.

In **Europe,** we will continue to provide leadership in a reinvigorated NATO, which has been the bedrock of European security for over four decades. We plan to retain about 100,000 troops there—a commitment that will allow the United States to continue to play a leading role in the NATO alliance and provide a robust capability for multinational training and crisis response. This force will include about two and one-third wings of Air Force fighters and substantial elements of two Army divisions, along with a corps headquarters and other supporting elements. Equipment for bringing these in-place divisions to full strength will remain prepositioned in Europe, along with the equipment of one additional division that would deploy to the region in the event of conflict.

U.S. Army forces will participate in two multinational corps with German forces. Theft training will focus on missions involving rapid deployment to conflicts outside of central Europe and "nontraditional" operations, such as peace enforcement, in addition to their long-standing mission of stabilization of central Europe. These missions might lead, over time, to changes in the equipment and configuration of Army units stationed in Europe. The Air Force will continue to provide unique theater intelligence, lift, and all-weather precision-strike capabilities critical to U.S. and NATO missions. In addition, U.S. Navy ships and submarines will continue to patrol the Mediterranean Sea and other waters surrounding Europe.

In **Northeast Asia,** we also plan to retain close to 100,000 troops. As recently announced by President Clinton, our commitment to South Korea's security remains undiminished, as demonstrated by the one U.S. Army division consisting of two brigades and one wing of U.S. Air Force combat aircraft we have stationed there. In light of the continuing threat of aggression from North Korea, we have frozen our troop levels in South Korea and are modernizing South Korean and American forces on the peninsula. We are also exploring the possibility of prepositioning more military equipment in South Korea to increase our crisis-response capability. While plans call for the eventual withdrawal of one of our two Army brigades from South Korea, President Clinton recently reiterated that our troops will stay in South Korea as long as its people want and need us there.

On Okinawa, we will continue to station a Marine Expeditionary Force and an Army special forces battalion. In Japan, we have homeported the aircraft carrier *Independence,* the amphibious assault ship *Bellau Wood,* and their support ships. We will also retain approximately one and one-half wings of Air Force combat aircraft in Japan and Okinawa, and the Navy's Seventh Fleet will continue to routinely patrol the western Pacific.

In **Southwest Asia,** local sensitivities to a large-scale Western military presence on land necessitate heavier reliance on periodic deployments of forces, rather than routine stationing of forces on the ground. The Navy's Middle East Force of four to six ships, which has been continuously on patrol in the Persian Gulf since 1945, will remain. In addition, we plan to have a brigade-sized set of equipment in Kuwait to be used by rotating deployments of U.S. forces that will train and exercise there with their Kuwaiti counterparts. We are also exploring options to preposition a second brigade set elsewhere on the Arabian peninsula.

These forces have been supplemented temporarily by several squadrons of land-based combat aircraft that have remained in the Gulf region since Operation Desert Storm and, along with other coalition aircraft, are now helping to enforce U.N. resolutions toward Iraq.

Another significant element of our military posture in Southwest Asia is the equipment prepositioned on ships that are normally anchored at Diego Garcia. In addition to a brigade-sized set of equipment for the Marine Corps, we have seven afloat prepositioning ships supporting Army, Air Force, and Navy forces.

In **Africa,** we will continue important formal and informal access agreements to key facilities and ports which allow our forces to transit or stop on the African continent. We will also deploy forces to Africa, as in recent operations like Sharp Edge (Liberia) and Restore Hope (Somalia), when our interests are threatened or our assistance is needed and requested. Today, more than 4,000 U.S. troops remain deployed in Somalia as part of the U.N. force seeking to provide humanitarian assistance to that country.

In **Latin America,** our armed forces will help to promote and expand recent trends toward democracy in many countries. They will also continue to work in concert with the armed forces and police of Latin American countries to combat drug traffickers. The United States will also retain a military presence in Panama, acting as Panama's partner in operating and defending the Canal during the transition to full Panamanian control of the canal in 1999.

Naval Presence. Sizing our naval forces for two nearly simultaneous MRCs provides a fairly large and robust force structure that can easily support other, smaller regional operations. However, our overseas presence needs can impose requirements for naval forces, especially aircraft carriers, that exceed those needed to win two MRCs. The flexibility of our carriers, and their ability to operate effectively with relative independence from shore bases, makes them well suited to overseas presence operations, especially in areas such as the Persian Gulf, where our land-based military infrastructure is relatively underdeveloped. For these reasons, the force of carriers, amphibious ships, and other surface combatants in the Clinton-Aspin defense plan was sized based on the exigencies of overseas presence, as well as the MRCs.

U.S. Navy and Marine forces play important roles in our approach to overseas presence in these three regions, as well as others. In recent years, we have sought to deploy a sizable U.S. naval presence—generally, a carrier battle group accompanied by an amphibious ready group—more or less continuously in the waters off Southwest Asia, Northeast Asia, and Europe (most often, in the Mediterranean Sea). However, in order to avoid serious morale and retention problems that can arise when our forces are asked to remain deployed for excessively long periods, we will experience some gaps in carrier presence in these areas in the future.

In order to avoid degradation in our regional security posture, we have identified a number of ways to fill these gaps and to supplement our posture even when carriers are present. For example, in some circumstances, we may find it possible to center naval expeditionary forces around large-deck amphibious assault ships carrying AV-8B attack jets and Cobra attack helicopters, as well as a 2,000-man Marine Expeditionary Unit. Another force might consist of a Tomahawk sea-launched cruise missile-equipped Aegis cruiser, a guided missile destroyer, attack submarines, and P-3 land-based maritime patrol aircraft.

In addition to these "maritime" approaches to sustaining overseas presence, a new concept is being developed that envisions using tailored joint forces to conduct overseas presence operations. These "Adaptive Joint Force Packages" could contain a mix of air, land, special operations, and maritime forces tailored to meet a theater commander's needs. These forces, plus designated backup units in the United States, would train jointly to provide the specific capabilities needed on station and on call during any particular period. Like maritime task forces, these joint force packages will also be capable of participating in combined military exercises with allied and friendly forces.

Together, these approaches will give us a variety of ways to manage our overseas presence profile, balancing carrier availability with the deployment of other types of units. Given this flexible approach to providing forces for overseas presence, we can meet the needs of our strategy with a fleet of eleven active aircraft carriers and one reserve/training carrier.

Strategic Nuclear Forces

The changing security environment presents us with significant uncertainties and challenges in planning our strategic nuclear force structure. In light of the dissolution of the Warsaw Pact, the break-up of the Soviet Union, the conclusion of the START I and II treaties, and our improving relationship with Russia, the threat of massive nuclear attack on the United States is lower than at any time in many years.

However, a number of issues affecting our future strategic nuclear posture must still be addressed. Tens of thousands of nuclear weapons continue to be deployed on Russian territory and on the territory of three other former Soviet republics. Even under START II, Russia will retain a sizable residual nuclear arsenal. And, despite promising trends, the future political situation in Russia remains highly uncertain.

In addition, many obstacles must be overcome before the ratification of START II, foremost of which are Ukranian ratification of START I and Ukraine's and Kazakhstan's accession to the Nuclear Nonproliferation Treaty as nonnuclear-weapon states—a condition required by Russia prior to implementing START I. Moreover, even if these obstacles can be overcome, implementation of the reductions mandated in START I and II will not be completed for almost 10 years. Thus, while the United States has already removed more than 3,500 warheads from ballistic missile systems slated for elimination under START I (some 90 percent of the total required), in light of current uncertainties, we must take a measured approach to further reductions.

Two principal guidelines shape our future requirements for strategic nuclear forces: to provide an effective deterrent while remaining within START I/II limits, and to allow for additional forces to be reconstituted, in the event of a threatening reversal of events.

The Bottom-Up Review did not address nuclear force structure in detail. As a follow-up to the Bottom-Up review, a comprehensive study of U.S. nuclear forces is being conducted. For planning purposes, we are evolving toward a future strategic nuclear force that by 2003 will include:

- 18 Trident submarines equipped with C-4 and D-5 missiles.
- 500 Minuteman III missiles, each carrying a single warhead.
- Up to 94 B-52H bombers equipped with air-launched cruise missiles and 20 B-2 bombers.

Conclusion

At the conclusion of its comprehensive assessment of future U.S. defense needs, the Bottom-Up Review determined that the reduced force structure . . . which will be reached by about the end of the decade, can carry out our strategy and meet our national security requirements.

This force structure meets our requirements for overseas presence in peacetime and a wide range of smaller-scale operations. It will also give the United States the capability to meet the most stressing situation we may face—the requirement to fight and win two major regional conflicts occurring nearly simultaneously.

In addition, this force structure provides sufficient capabilities for strategic deterrence and defense. It also provides sufficient forces, primarily Reserve Component, to be held in strategic reserve and utilized if and when needed. For example, they could deploy to one or both MRCs, if operations do not go as we had planned. Alternatively, these forces could be used to "backfill" for overseas presence forces redeployed to an MRC. Finally, this force structure also meets an important new criterion for our forces—flexibility to deal with the uncertain nature of the new dangers.

VICE PRESIDENT GORE'S REPORT ON "REINVENTING" GOVERNMENT

September 7, 1993

After six months of intensive study, the National Performance Review (NPR) panel, headed by Vice President Al Gore, released a 167-page report on measures to overhaul the federal government. The initiative for the undertaking to "reinvent" government came from President Bill Clinton, who on March 3 announced that he was appointing Gore to lead the review panel. The results of what was often referred to as the "Gore report" were made public September 7. The report put forward 384 recommendations to streamline government that, if adopted, would slash the federal budget by $108 billion over the next five years by reducing government waste, eliminating unnecessary bureaucracy, and improving services. The NPR projected that $36.4 billion could be saved by consolidating or closing agencies, $40.4 billion by eliminating 252,000 jobs (12 percent of the federal payroll), $22.5 billion by streamlining procurement procedures, $5.4 billion by modernizing information technology, and $3.3 billion by reducing reporting requirements.

The recommendations of the NPR panel—which relied primarily on input from federal employees—drew heavily on successful corporate experiences, based on the premise that government could emulate techniques that had worked in the private sphere.

Clinton strongly endorsed the report's proposals and pledged a personal commitment to act on them. "Make no mistake about this," he said in remarks upon release of the study. "This is one report that will not gather dust in a warehouse."

Many Recommendations, Few Details

The report, entitled "From Red Tape to Results: Creating a Government that Works Better and Costs Less," outlined actions that the president could take by executive order, but many of the more far-reaching measures would require congressional approval. Although the recommendations were numerous, the report contained few specifics about how the goals might be accomplished.

Following are the NPR's major recommendations in each of the report's four chapters.

"Cutting Red Tape"

- *Institute two-year, instead of annual, budgets and appropriations and limit congressional power to "earmark" funds for special purposes*
- *Allow agencies to carry over unspent funds at the end of a fiscal year*
- *Decentralize job candidate recruiting, simplify the job classification system, and reduce the time required to fire employees*
- *Update procurement procedures*
- *Review regulations and cut them by half*

"Putting Customers First"

- *Require agencies to provide best-in-the-business, competitive customer service*
- *Eliminate the Government Printing Office's monopoly over government publications and the General Service Administration's monopoly over real estate*
- *Establish a governmentwide cost accounting system that would provide a method for identifying the true unit cost of all government activities*
- *Restructure the air traffic control system into a government-owned corporation, funded by user fees and overseen by a board "that represents the system's customers"*

"Empowering Employees"

- *Decentralize agency decision making*
- *Designate a chief operating officer in each department to implement all proposals*
- *Upgrade computer technology*
- *Establish a labor-management partnership*
- *Provide quality management "basic training" for all employees*

"Cutting Back to Basics"

- *Give the president greater authority to cut items from the budget ("line item veto")*
- *Close or consolidate federal civilian facilities, including closing 1,200 Agriculture Department field offices; cutting Department of Housing and Urban Development regional offices and 1,500 staff; consolidating Energy Department labs, production, and testing; reducing Army Corps of Engineers regional offices from eleven to six; consolidating Small Business Administration services and reducing field offices;*

cutting in half U.S. Agency for International Development overseas missions; reducing U.S. Information Agency overseas libraries
- *Eliminate forty-one Education Department grants*
- *Consolidate training programs for the unemployed*
- *Allow agencies to set user fees and use that revenue*

One of the report's most controversial proposals was to reduce the number of federal workers by 252,000—more than double the 100,000 reduction ordered by the administration earlier in the year. If carried out, the Civil Service would fall below 2 million for the first time since 1966.

The two-year budget proposal and limits on congressional earmarking practices were also controversial. Although many on Capitol Hill supported the idea of going to a biennial budget—agreeing that the current process was clumsy and time-consuming—there was likely to be strong resistance to encroaching on congressional appropriations powers to earmark funds. The idea of a two-year budget cycle was warmly supported by members of the bipartisan Joint Committee on the Organization of Congress, as well as numerous congressional leaders on both sides of the aisle. But critics charged that it would entail more work than envisaged and might reduce congressional oversight. They also said it would be extremely difficult to come up with a two-year budget that would not have to be revised numerous times to respond to changing circumstances, particularly emergencies.

Generally Positive, but Skeptical, Reaction

A number of spokesmen from the private sector questioned whether the administration's reliance on management theories, such as "downsizing" or "re-engineering," to achieve efficiency in government was realistic. "You can use all the buzzwords you want, but if there isn't a crisis, if there isn't a competitor stealing your market share . . . it's not going to happen," said Alan Webber, president of Fast Track, *a magazine targeted at growing businesses. "The U.S. isn't just a conglomerate," said Philip Lader, deputy director of the Office of Management and Budget, who was a member of the NPR. "It's a conglomerate of conglomerates."*

Skeptics also noted that many of the report's recommendations were similar to those made by past reform commissions that were at first enthusiastically received but ultimately failed in the light of political realities.

Although the NPR plan drew general approval from congressional Republicans and Democrats alike, a number of members predicted that, when it came to actual legislation, many aspects of the plan would incur strong opposition, especially from powerful congressional leaders. "We all know that the toughest thing in Washington are the turf wars," warned Sen. William V. Roth, Jr., R-Del. "No committee likes their authority cut back."

Leaders of the three largest federal employee unions were quick to praise the NPR's proposal that they should be given a greater voice in major personnel decisions. On the other hand, organizations representing federal supervisors disagreed sharply with the report's recommendation that the administration should "pare down" the number of white-collar bureaucrats who run "systems of overcontrol and micromanagement."

A November analysis by the Congressional Budget Office showed that the NPR's projections would fall far short in actual savings. However, a 279-page report by the General Accounting Office (GAO), released December 3, fully agreed with 116 proposals and generally agreed with 146 of the 384 recommendations. (The Gore panel had used GAO publications and research as a basis for much of its review.) The GAO said it could not assess 121 of the NPR recommendations because it lacked sufficient information about them. Although they noted in their report that the NPR "emphasized many of the basic themes that we have stressed for years," the GAO analysts also expressed concern about the recommendation to reduce the federal workforce by 252,000 over the next five years. "Across-the-board reductions that do not recognize the differing capabilities of agencies to absorb such cuts could significantly exacerbate existing gaps in agencies' abilities to meet their missions," the GAO warned.

John Conyers, Jr., D-Mich., chairman of the House Government Operations Committee, also questioned the wisdom of such a drastic staff reduction. "Hearing after hearing before the committee has shown the fallout of understaffed programs," he said.

"Eliminating 250,000 jobs . . . won't necessarily achieve the $108 billion in savings the NPR projects, nor will it necessarily assure that the government works any better," said Bruce Moyer, executive director of the Federal Managers Association, whose members the NPR had targeted for a large share of the personnel cuts.

"While we certainly agree with some of the program cuts Mr. Gore suggests, there is a danger that the report will encourage the mistaken view that a better-managed government could produce easy budget cuts," said a September 8 editorial in the Washington Post. *"As the Gore budget cuts are scrutinized, it will be clear that such reductions, even if worthy, aren't easy."*

A Lengthy Process Foreseen

Members of the cabinet immediately began moving to implement some of the recommendations, if they had not already done so. However, Attorney General Janet Reno was noncommittal on a proposal to fold the Drug Enforcement Administration into the FBI. Others, such as Secretary of Agriculture Mike Espy, enthusiastically endorsed the NPR's proposed overhaul, saying it outlined "long overdue" savings. Espy estimated that the proposed closing of Agriculture field offices would *result in the elimination of 7,500 jobs and save $2.3 billion in salaries and overhead between 1994 and 1999.*

Congressional leaders predicted that consideration of the proposals would move at the regular legislative pace in 1994. Because the proposals were so numerous and disparate and their means of implementation generally were unspecific, it was highly unlikely that the administration would develop an overall "grand strategy" or propose one piece of legislation to cover the entire package.

Following are the preface and introduction from the Report of the National Performance Review on consolidating and reorganizing the federal government, released September 7, and excerpts from President Clinton's remarks announcing the report:

EXCERPTS FROM THE NATIONAL PERFORMANCE REVIEW

The National Performance Review is about change—historic change—in the way the government works. The Clinton administration believes it is time for a new customer service contract with the American people, a new guarantee of effective, efficient, and responsive government. As our title makes clear, the National Performance Review is about moving from red tape to results to create a government that works better and costs less.

These are our twin missions: to make government work better and cost less. The President has already addressed the federal deficit with the largest deficit reduction package in history. The National Performance Review can reduce the deficit further, but it is not just about cutting spending. It is also about closing the trust deficit: proving to the American people that their tax dollars will be treated with respect for the hard work that earned them. We are taking action to put America's house in order.

The National Performance Review began on March 3, 1993, when President Clinton announced a 6-month review of the federal government and asked me to lead the effort. We organized a team of experienced federal employees from all corners of the government—a marked change from past efforts, which relied on outsiders.

We turned to the people who know government best—who know what works, what doesn't, and how things ought to be changed. We organized these people into a series of teams, to examine both agencies and cross-cutting systems, such as budgeting, procurement, and personnel. The President also asked all cabinet members to create Reinvention Teams to lead transformations at their departments, and Reinvention Laboratories, to begin experimenting with new ways of doing business. Thousands of federal employees joined these two efforts.

But the National Performance Review did not stop there. From the beginning, I wanted to hear from as many Americans as possible. I spoke with federal employees at every major agency and at federal centers across the country—seeking their ideas, their input, and their inspiration. I visited programs that work: a Miami school that also serves as a community center, a Minnesota pilot program that provides benefits more efficiently by using technology and debit cards, a Chicago neighborhood that has put community policing to work, a U.S. Air Force base that has made quality management a way of life.

We also heard from citizens all across America, in more than 30,000 letters and phone calls. We sought the views of hundreds of different organizations, large and small. We learned from the experience of state and local leaders who have restructured their organizations. And we listened to business leaders who have used innovative management practices to turn their companies around.

At a national conference in Tennessee, we brought together experts to explore how best to apply the principles of reinventing government to improving family services. In Philadelphia Independence Square, where our government was born, we gathered for a day-long "Reinventing Government Summit" with the best minds from business, government, and the academic community.

This report is the first product of our efforts. It describes roughly 100 of our most important actions and recommendations, while hundreds more are listed in the appendices at the end of this report. In the coming months, we will publish additional information providing more detail on those recommendations.

This report represents the beginning of what will be—what *must* be—an ongoing commitment to change. It includes actions that will be taken now, by directive of the President; actions that will be taken by the cabinet secretaries and agency heads; and recommendations for congressional action.

The National Performance Review focused primarily on *how* government should work, not on *what* it should do. Our job was to improve performance in areas where policymakers had already decided government should play a role.

We examined every cabinet department and 10 agencies. At two departments, Defense and Health and Human Services, our work paralleled other large-scale reviews already under way. Defense had launched a Bottom-Up Review to meet the President's 1994-1997 spending reduction target. In addition, comprehensive health and welfare reform task forces had been established to make large-scale changes in significant parts of Health and Human Services. Nevertheless, we made additional recommendations regarding both these departments and passed other findings on to the relevant task force for review.

The National Performance Review recommendations, if enacted, would produce savings of $108 billion over 5 years. $36.4 billion of these savings come from specific changes proposed in the agencies and departments of the government.

We also expect that the reinventions we propose will allow us to reduce the size of the civilian, non-postal workforce by 12 percent over the next 5 years. This will bring the federal workforce below two million employees for the first time since 1966. This reduction in the workforce will total 252,000 positions—152,000 over and above the 100,000 already promised by President Clinton.

Most of the personnel reductions will be concentrated in the structures of overcontrol and micromanagement that now bind the federal government: supervisors, headquarters staffs, personnel specialists, budget analysts, procurement specialists, accountants, and auditors. These central control structures not only stifle the creativity of line managers and workers, they consume billions per year in salary, benefits, and administrative costs. Additional personnel cuts will result as each agency reengineers its basic work processes to achieve higher productivity at lower costs—eliminating unnecessary layers of management and nonessential staff.

We will accomplish as much of this as possible through attrition, early retirement, and a time-limited program of cash incentives to leave federal service. If an employee whose job is eliminated cannot take early retirement and elects not to take a cash incentive to leave government service, we will help that employee find another job offer through out-placement assistance.

In addition to savings from the agencies and savings in personnel we expect that systematic reform of the procurement process should reduce the cost of everything the government buys. Our antiquated procurement system costs the government in two ways: first, we pay for all the bureaucracy we have created to buy things, and second, manufacturers build the price of dealing with this bureaucracy into the prices they charge us. If we reform the procurement system, we should be able to save $22 billion over 5 years.

As everyone knows, the computer revolution allows us to do things faster and more cheaply than we ever have before. Savings due to consolidation and modernization of the information infrastructure amount to $5.4 billion over 5 years.

Finally, by simplifying paperwork and reducing administrative costs, we expect to save $3.3 billion over 5 years in the cost of administering grant programs to state and local governments.

Many of the spending cuts we propose can be done by simplifying the internal organization of our departments and agencies. Others will require legislation. We recognize that there is broad support in Congress for both spending cuts and government reforms, and we look forward to working with Congress to pass this package of recommendations. As President Clinton said when he announced the National Performance Review:

> This performance review is not about politics. Programs passed by both Democratic presidents and Republican presidents, voted on by members of Congress of both parties, and supported by the American people at the time,

> are being undermined by an inefficient and outdated bureaucracy, and by our huge debt. For too long the basic functioning of the government has gone unexamined. We want to make improving the way government does business a permanent part of how government works, regardless of which party is in power.

We have not a moment to lose. President Kennedy once told a story about a French general who asked his gardener to plant a tree. "Oh, this tree grows slowly," the gardener said. "It won't mature for a hundred years."

"Then there's no time to lose," the general answered. "Plant it this afternoon."

Al Gore
Vice President of the United States

Introduction

Public confidence in the federal government has never been lower. The average American believes we waste 48 cents of every tax dollar. Five of every six want "fundamental change" in Washington. Only 20 percent of Americans trust the federal government to do the right thing most of the time—down from 76 percent 30 years ago.

We all know why. Washington's failures are large and obvious. For a decade, the deficit has run out of control. The national debt now exceeds $4 trillion—$16,600 for every man, woman, and child in America.

But the deficit is only the tip of the iceberg. Below the surface, Americans believe, lies enormous unseen waste. The Defense Department owns more than $40 billion in unnecessary supplies. The Internal Revenue Service struggles to collect billions in unpaid bills. A century after industry replaced farming as America's principal business, the Agriculture Department still operates more than 12,000 field service offices, an average of nearly 4 for every county in the nation—rural, urban, or suburban. The federal government seems unable to abandon the obsolete. It knows how to add, but not to subtract.

And yet, waste is not the only problem. The federal government is not simply broke; it is broken. Ineffective regulation of the financial industry brought us the savings and loan debacle. Ineffective education and training programs jeopardize our competitive edge. Ineffective welfare and housing programs undermine our families and cities.

We spend $25 billion a year on welfare, $27 billion on food stamps, and $13 billion on public housing—yet more Americans fall into poverty every year. We spend $12 billion a year waging war on drugs—yet see few signs of victory. We fund 150 different employment and training programs—yet the average American has no idea where to get job training, and the skills of our workforce fall further behind those of our competitors.

It is almost as if federal programs were *designed* not to work. In truth, few are "designed" at all; the legislative process simply churns them out, one after another, year after year. It's little wonder that when asked if "government always manages to mess things up," two-thirds of Americans say "yes."

To borrow the words of a recent Brookings Institution book, we suffer not only a budget deficit but a performance deficit. Indeed, public opinion experts argue that we are suffering the deepest crisis of faith in government in our lifetimes. In past crises, Watergate or the Vietnam War, for example, Americans doubted their leaders on moral or ideological grounds. They felt their government was deceiving them or failing to represent their values. Today's crisis is different: people simply feel that government doesn't work.

In Washington, debate rarely focuses on the performance deficit. Our leaders spend most of their time debating policy issues. But if the vehicle designed to carry out policy is broken, new policies won't take us anywhere. If the car won't run, it hardly matters where we point it; we won't get there. Today, the central issue we face is not what government does, but how it works.

We have spent too much money for programs that don't work. It's time to make our government work for the people, learn to do more with less, and treat taxpayers like customers.

President Clinton created the National Performance Review to do just that. In this report we make hundreds of recommendations for actions that, if implemented, will revolutionize the way the federal government does business. They will reduce waste, eliminate unneeded bureaucracy, improve service to taxpayers, and create a leaner but more productive government. As noted in the preface, they can save $108 billion over 5 years if those which will be enacted by the President and his cabinet are added to those we propose for enactment by Congress. Some of these proposals can be enacted by the President and his cabinet, others will require legislative action. We are going to fight for these changes. We are determined to create a government that works better and costs less.

A Cure Worse Than The Disease

Government is not alone in its troubles. As the Industrial Era has given way to the Information Age, institutions—both public and private—have come face to face with obsolescence. The past decade has witnessed profound restructuring: In the 1980s, major American corporations reinvented themselves; in the 1990s, governments are struggling to do the same.

In recent years, our national leaders responded to the growing crisis with traditional medicine. They blamed the bureaucrats. They railed against "fraud, waste, and abuse." And they slapped ever more controls on the bureaucracy to prevent it.

But the cure has become indistinguishable from the disease. The problem is not lazy or incompetent people; it is red tape and regulation so suffocating that they stifle every ounce of creativity. No one would offer a drowning man a drink of water. And yet, for more than a decade, we have added red tape to a system already strangling in it.

The federal government is filled with good people trapped in bad systems: budget systems, personnel systems, procurement systems, financial management systems, information systems. When we blame the people and impose more controls, we make the systems worse. Over the past 15 years, for example, Congress has created within each agency an independent office of the inspector general. The idea was to root out fraud, waste, and abuse. The inspectors general have certainly uncovered important problems. But as we learned in conversation after conversation, they have so intimidated federal employees that many are now afraid to deviate even slightly from standard operating procedure.

Yet innovation, by its nature, requires deviation. Unfortunately, faced with so many controls, many employees have simply given up. They do everything by the book whether it makes sense or not. They fill out forms that should never have been created, follow rules that should never have been imposed, and prepare reports that serve no purpose—and are often never even read. In the name of controlling waste, we have created paralyzing inefficiency. It's time we found a way to get rid of waste and encourage efficiency.

The Root Problem: Industrial-Era Bureaucracies in an Information Age

Is government inherently incompetent? Absolutely not. Are federal agencies filled with incompetent people? No. The problem is much deeper: Washington is filled with organizations designed for an environment that no longer exists—bureaucracies so big and wasteful they can no longer serve the American people.

From the 1930s through the 1960s, we built large, top-down, centralized bureaucracies to do the public's business. They were patterned after the corporate structures of the age: hierarchical bureaucracies in which tasks were broken into simple parts, each the responsibility of a different layer of employees, each defined by specific rules and regulations. With their rigid preoccupation with standard operating procedure, their vertical chains of command, and their standardized services, these bureaucracies were steady—but slow and cumbersome. And in today's world of rapid change, lightning-quick information technologies, tough global competition, and demanding customers, large, top-down bureaucracies—public or private—don't work very well. Saturn isn't run the way General Motors was. Intel isn't run the way IBM was.

Many federal organizations are also monopolies, with few incentives to innovate or improve. Employees have virtual lifetime tenure, regardless of their performance. Success offers few rewards; failure, few penalties. And customers are captive; they can't walk away from the air traffic control system or the Internal Revenue Service and sign up with a competitor. Worse, most federal monopolies receive their money without any direct input from their customers. Consequently, they try a lot harder to please

Congressional appropriations subcommittees than the people they are meant to serve. Taxpayers pay more than they should and get poorer service.

Politics intensifies the problem. In Washington's highly politicized world, the greatest risk is not that a program will perform poorly, but that a scandal will erupt. Scandals are front-page news, while routine failure is ignored. Hence control system after control system is piled up to minimize the risk of scandal. The budget system, the personnel rules, the procurement process, the inspectors general all are designed to prevent the tiniest misstep. We assume that we can't trust employees to make decisions, so we spell out in precise detail how they must do virtually everything, then audit them to ensure that they have obeyed every rule.

The slightest deviation prompts new regulations and even more audits. Before long, simple procedures are too complex for employees to navigate, so we hire more budget analysts, more personnel experts, and more procurement officers to make things work. By then, the process involves so much red tape that the smallest action takes far longer and costs far more than it should. Simple travel arrangements require endless forms and numerous signatures. Straightforward purchases take months; larger ones take years. Routine printing jobs take a dozen approvals.

This emphasis on process steals resources from the real job: serving the customer. Indeed, the federal government spends billions of dollars paying people who control, check up on, or investigate others—supervisors, headquarters staffs, budget officers, personnel officers, procurement officers, and staffs of the General Accounting Office (GAO) and the inspectors general. Not all this money is wasted, of course. But the real waste is no doubt larger, because the endless regulations and layers of control consume every employee's time. Who pays? The taxpayer.

Consider but one example, shared with Vice President Gore at a meeting of federal employees in Atlanta. After federal marshals seize drug dealers' homes, they are allowed to sell them and use the money to help finance the war on drugs. To sell the houses, they must keep them presentable, which includes keeping the lawns mowed.

In Atlanta, the employee explained, most organizations would hire neighborhood teenagers to mow a lawn for $10. But procurement regulations require the U.S. Marshals Service to bid out all work competitively, and neighborhood teenagers don't compete for contracts. So the federal government pays $40 a lawn to professional landscape firms. Regulations designed to save money waste it, because they take decisions out of the hands of those responsible for doing the work. And taxpayers lose $30 for every lawn mowed.

What would happen if the marshals used their common sense and hired neighborhood teenagers? Someone would notice—perhaps the Washington office, perhaps the inspector general's office, perhaps even the GAO. An investigation might well follow hindering a career or damaging a reputation.

In this way, federal employees quickly learn that common sense is risky—and creativity is downright dangerous. They learn that the goal is not to produce results, please customers, or save taxpayers' money, but to avoid mistakes. Those who dare to innovate do so quietly.

This is perhaps the saddest lesson learned by those who worked on the National Performance Review: Yes, innovators exist within the federal government, but many work hard to keep their innovations quiet. By its nature, innovation requires a departure from standard operating procedure. In the federal government, such departures invite repercussions.

The result is a culture of fear and resignation. To survive, employees keep a low profile. They decide that the safest answer in any given situation is a firm "maybe." They follow the rules, pass the buck, and keep their heads down. They develop what one employee, speaking with Vice President Gore at a Department of Veterans Affairs meeting, called "a government attitude."

The Solution: Creating Entrepreneurial Organizations

How do we solve these problems? It won't be easy. We know all about government's problems, but little about solutions. The National Performance Review began by compiling a comprehensive list of problems. We had the GAO's 28-volume report on federal management problems, published last fall. We had GAO's *High-Risk Series,* a 17-volume series of pamphlets on troubled programs and agencies. We had the House Government Operations Committee's report on federal mismanagement, called *Managing the Federal Government: A Decade of Decline.* And we had 83 notebooks summarizing just the tables of contents of reports published by the inspectors general, the Congressional Budget Office, the agencies, and think tanks.

Unfortunately, few of these studies helped us design solutions. Few of the investigating bodies had studied success stories—organizations that had solved their problems. And without studying success, it is hard to devise real solutions. For years, the federal government has studied failure, and for years, failure has endured. Six of every ten major agencies have programs on the Office of Management and Budget's "high-risk" list, meaning they carry a significant risk of runaway spending or fraud.

The National Performance Review approached its task differently. Not only did we look for potential savings and efficiencies, we searched for success. We looked for organizations that produced results, satisfied customers, and increased productivity. We looked for organizations that constantly learned, innovated, and improved. We looked for effective, entrepreneurial public organizations. And we found them: in local government, in state government, in other countries—and right here in our federal government.

At the Air Combat Command, for example, we found units that had doubled their productivity in 5 years. Why? Because the command measured performance everywhere; squadrons and bases competed proudly for the best maintenance, flight, and safety records; and top management had empowered employees to strip away red tape and redesign work processes. A supply system that had once required 243 entries by 22 people on 13 forms to get one spare part into an F-15 had been radically simplified and decentralized. Teams of employees were saving millions of dollars by moving supply operations to the front line, developing their own flight schedules, and repairing parts that were once discarded.

At the Internal Revenue Service, we found tax return centers competing for the best productivity records. Performance on key customer service criteria—such as the accuracy of answers provided to taxpayers—had improved dramatically. Utah's Ogden Service Center, to cite but one example, had more than 50 "productivity improvement teams" simplifying forms and reengineering work processes. Not only had employees saved more than $11 million, they had won the 1992 Presidential Award for Quality.

At the Forest Service, we found a pilot project in the 22-state Eastern Region that had increased productivity by 15 percent in just 2 years. The region had simplified its budget systems, eliminated layers of middle management, pared central headquarters staff by a fifth, and empowered front-line employees to make their own decisions. At the Mark Twain National Forest, for instance, the time needed to grant a grazing permit had shrunk from 30 days to a few hours—because employees could grant permits themselves rather than process them through headquarters.

We discovered that several other governments were also reinventing themselves, from Australia to Great Britain, Singapore to Sweden, the Netherlands to New Zealand. Throughout the developed world, the needs of information-age societies were colliding with the limits of industrial-era government. Regardless of party, regardless of ideology, these governments were responding. In Great Britain, conservatives led the way. In New Zealand, the Labor Party revolutionized government. In Australia and Sweden, both conservative and liberal parties embraced fundamental change.

In the United States, we found the same phenomenon at the state and local levels. The movement to reinvent government is as bipartisan as it is widespread. It is driven not by political ideology, but by absolute necessity. Governors, mayors, and legislators of both parties have reached the same conclusion: Government is broken, and it is time to fix it.

Where we found success, we found many common characteristics. Early on, we articulated these in a one-page statement of our commitment. In organizing this report, we have boiled these characteristics down to four key principles.

1. Cutting Red Tape

Effective, entrepreneurial governments cast aside red tape, shifting from systems in which people are accountable for following rules to systems in which they are accountable for achieving results. They streamline their budget, personnel, and procurement systems—liberating organizations to pursue their missions. They reorient their control systems to prevent problems rather than simply punish those who make mistakes. They strip away unnecessary layers of regulation that stifle innovation. And they deregulate organizations that depend upon them for funding, such as lower levels of government.

2. Putting Customers First

Effective, entrepreneurial governments insist on customer satisfaction. They listen carefully to their customers—using surveys, focus groups, and the like. They restructure their basic operations to meet customers' needs. And they use market dynamics such as competition and customer choice to create incentives that drive their employees to put customers first.

By "customer," we do not mean "citizen." A citizen can participate in democratic decisionmaking; a customer receives benefits from a specific service. All Americans are citizens. Most are also customers: of the U.S. Postal Service, the Social Security Administration, the Department of Veterans Affairs, the National Park Service, and scores of other federal organizations.

In a democracy, citizens and customers both matter. But when they vote, citizens seldom have much chance to influence the behavior of public institutions that directly affect their lives: schools, hospitals, farm service agencies, social security offices. It is a sad irony: citizens own their government, but private businesses they do not own work much harder to cater to their needs.

3. Empowering Employees to Get Results

Effective, entrepreneurial governments transform their cultures by decentralizing authority. They empower those who work on the front lines to make more of their own decisions and solve more of their own problems. They embrace labor management cooperation, provide training and other tools employees need to be effective, and humanize the workplace. While stripping away layers and empowering front-line employees, they hold organizations accountable for producing results.

4. Cutting Back to Basics:
Producing Better Government for Less

Effective, entrepreneurial governments constantly find ways to make government work better and cost less—reengineering how they do their work and reexamining programs and processes. They abandon the obsolete, eliminate duplication, and end special interest privileges. They invest in greater productivity, through loan funds and long-term capital investments. And they embrace advanced technologies to cut costs.

These are the bedrock principles on which the reinvention of the federal bureaucracy must build and the principles around which we have organized our actions. They fit together much like the pieces of a puzzle: if one is missing, the others lose their power. To create organizations that deliver value to American taxpayers, we must embrace all four.

Our approach goes far beyond fixing specific problems in specific agencies. Piecemeal efforts have been under way for years, but they have not delivered what Americans demand. The failure in Washington is embedded in the very systems by which we organize the federal bureaucracy. In recent years, Congress has taken the lead in reinventing these systems. In 1990, it passed the Chief Financial Officers Act, designed to overhaul financial management systems; in July 1993, it passed the Government Performance and Results Act, which will introduce performance measurement throughout the federal government. With Congress's leadership, we hope to reinvent government's other basic systems, such as budget, personnel, information, and procurement.

Our approach has much in common with other management philosophies, such as quality management and business process reengineering. But these management disciplines were developed for the private sector, where conditions are quite different. In business, red tape may be bad, but it is not the suffocating presence it is in government. In business, market incentives already exist; no one need invent them. Powerful incentives are always at work, forcing organizations to do more with less. Indeed, businesses that fail to increase their productivity—or that tie themselves up in red tape—shrink or die. Hence, private sector management doctrines tend to overlook some central problems of government: its monopolies, its lack of a bottom line, its obsession with process rather than results. Consequently, our approach goes beyond private sector methods. It is aimed at the heart and soul of government.

The National Performance Review also shares certain goals with past efforts to cut costs in government. But our mission goes beyond cost-cutting. Our goal is not simply to weed the federal garden; it is to create a regimen that will *keep* the garden free of weeds. It is not simply to trim *pieces* of government, but to reinvent the way government does everything. It is not simply to produce a more efficient government, but to create a more *effective* one. After all, Americans don't want a government that fails more efficiently. They want a government that *works.*

To deliver what the people want, we need not jettison the traditional values that underlie democratic governance—values such as equal opportunity, justice, diversity, and democracy. We hold these values dear. We seek to transform bureaucracies precisely *because* they have failed to nurture these values. We believe that those who resist change for fear of jeopardizing our democratic values doom us to a government that continues—through its failures—to subvert those very values.

Our Commitment: A Long-Term Investment in Change

This is not the first time Americans have felt compelled to reinvent their government. In 1776, our founding fathers rejected the old model of a central power issuing edicts for all to abide. In its place, they created a government that broadly distributed power. Their vision of democracy, which gave citizens a voice in managing the United States, was untried and untested in 1776. It required a tremendous leap of faith. But it worked.

Later generations extended this experiment in democracy to those not yet enfranchised. As the 20th century dawned, a generation of "Progressives" such as Teddy Roosevelt and Woodrow Wilson invented the modern bureaucratic state, designed to meet the needs of a new industrial society. Franklin Roosevelt brought it to full flower. Indeed, Roosevelt's 1937 announcement of his Committee on Administrative Management sounds as if it were written only yesterday:

> The time has come to set our house in order. The administrative management of the government needs overhauling. The executive structure of the government is sadly out of date.... If we have faith in our republican form of government... we must devote ourselves energetically and courageously to the task of making that government efficient.

Through the ages, public management has tended to follow the prevailing paradigm of private management. The 1930s were no exception. Roosevelt's committee—and the two Hoover commissions that followed—recommended a structure patterned largely after those of corporate America in the 1930s. In a sense, they brought to government the GM model of organization.

By the 1980s, even GM recognized that this model no longer worked. When it created Saturn, its first new division in 67 years, GM embraced a very different model. It picked its best and brightest and asked them to create a more entrepreneurial organization, with fewer layers, fewer rules, and employees empowered to do whatever was necessary to satisfy the customer. Faced with the very real threat of bankruptcy, major American corporations have revolutionized the way they do business.

Confronted with our twin budget and performance deficits—which so undermine public trust in government—President Clinton intends to do the same thing. He did not staff the Performance Review primarily with outside consultants or corporate experts, as past presidents have. Instead, he chose federal employees to take the lead. They consulted with experts from state government, local government, and the private sector. But as Vice President Gore said over and over at his meetings with federal employees: "The people who work closest to the problem know the most about how to solve the problem."

Nor did the effort stop with the men and women who staffed the Performance Review. President Clinton asked every cabinet member to create a Reinvention Team to redesign his or her department, and Reinvention Laboratories to begin experimenting immediately. Since April, people all across our government have been working full time to reinvent the federal bureaucracy.

The process is not easy, nor will it be quick. There are changes we can make immediately, but even if all of our recommendations are enacted, we will have only begun to reinvent the federal government. Our efforts are but a down payment—the first installment of a long-term investment in change. Every expert with whom we talked reminded us that change takes time. In a large corporation, transformation takes 6 to 8 years at best. In the federal government, which has more than 7 times as many employees as America's largest corporation, it will undoubtedly take longer to bring about the historic changes we propose.

Along the way, we will make mistakes. Some reforms will succeed beyond our wildest dreams; others will not. As in any experimental process, we will need to monitor results and correct as we go. But we must not confuse mistakes with failure. As Tom Peters and Robert Waterman wrote in *In Search of Excellence,* any organization that is not making mistakes is not trying hard enough. Babe Ruth, the Sultan of Swat, struck out 1,330 times.

With this report, then, we begin a decade-long process of reinvention. We hope this process will involve not only the thousands of federal employees now at work on Reinvention Teams and in Reinvention Labs, but millions more who are not yet engaged. We hope it will transform the habits, culture, and performance of all federal organizations.

Some may say that the risk is too large; that we should not attempt it because we are bound to make mistakes; that it cannot be done. But we have no choice. Our government is in trouble. It has lost its sense of mission; it has lost its ethic of public service; and, most importantly, it has lost the faith of the American people.

In times such as these, the most dangerous course is to do nothing. We must have the courage to risk change.

CLINTON'S REMARKS

The President. Mr. Vice President and members of the Cabinet, distinguished guests, Mrs. Gore, Senator Gore [*sic*], thank you for coming. To all of you from the Federal Government and from the private sector who worked on this report and all of you who care about seeing it implemented, I think we all owe an enormous debt of gratitude to the Vice President for the difficult and thorough work which has been done and for the outstanding product which has been produced. My gratitude is great also to the staff of the National Performance Review and to the employees of the Federal Government and the people in the private sector who helped us to do this and to the Cabinet members who have supported it.

I will say I had the opportunity to read this report in draft over the weekend. I read it very carefully. I read some sections of it more than once. And if the report is any indication of where we're going, then the future looks bright indeed, because this is an oxymoron; this is a Government report that's fun to read. [*Laughter*] It's well written. It's interesting. It's compelling, and it is hopeful.

I ran for President because I wanted to get America on the move and I wanted to pull our country together. And it became quickly apparent to me in the campaign that the feelings I had developed not only as a citizen but as a Governor over the previous 12 years were widely shared by others. It's hard for the National Government to take a leadership role, even a partnership role, in bringing America together and putting America on the move when people have no confidence in the operations of the Government, when they don't believe they get good value for the dollars they give to the Government in taxes, when they don't believe that they're being treated like customers, when they don't really feel that they are the bosses in this great democratic enterprise.

And so, 6 months ago, I asked the Vice President to embark on a risky adventure, to see if we could make the Government work better and cost less, to serve our people better, and to, as important as anything else, rebuild the confidence of the American people in this great public enterprise. Our Founders clearly understood that every generation would have to reinvent the Government, and they knew that long before the Government was nearly as big or cumbersome or bureaucratic or far-reaching as it is today. Thomas Jefferson said, laws and institutions must go hand in hand with the progress of [the] human mind as that becomes more developed, more enlightened, as new discoveries are made and new truths discovered and manners and opinions change. With the change of circumstances, institutions must advance also to keep pace with the time.

That is what the Vice President and this group tried to do, to listen and to learn from people who best understand how to make Government work better. This report reflects the practical experiences of Federal employees whose best efforts have too often been smothered in red tape, business people who have streamlined their own companies, State and local officials who are reinventing government at the grassroots, and concerned citizens who deserve and demand more value for their tax dollars. To meet the challenges of the global economy and to better use new technology, our most successful companies have been through this process, many of them starting more than a decade ago: eliminating unnecessary layers of management, empowering frontline workers, becoming more responsive to their customers, and seeking constantly to improve the products they make, the services they provide, and the people they employ. Meanwhile, I have seen too little of this happen nationally. I do want to say that there are many reasons for this. Government, as we all know, has too often a monopoly on the money of the American people and on those who have to be its customers. Government also does not have the pressure from time to time to change that the private sector does, so that what we have today, as the Vice President said, is a lot of good people trapped in bad systems. We still have a Government that's largely organized on a top-down, bureaucratic, industrial model when we're in an information age. And very often, it is just Federal Government. And we intend to make a beginning on that.

There's no reason that we can't have a post office where you always get served within 5 minutes of the time you walk up to the counter; why you can't have an IRS that always gives you the right answer and takes your phone call; why you can't have a Government that pays no more for a hammer or a pair of pliers, or more importantly, for a personal computer than you'd pay at a local commercial outlet.

The Vice President and I are going to work with the Cabinet to find ways to make the Government more responsive and to implement this report. We're going to rely on the innovations of our leaders in the Cabinet. . . .

In the weeks ahead, we have other challenges to face from reforming our health care system to provide security for every family, to opening new markets for our products and services abroad so that we can start creating jobs again. But to accomplish any of these goals, we have to revolutionize the Government itself so that the American people trust the decisions that are made and trust us to do the work that Government has to do. The entire agenda of change depends upon our ability to change the way we do our own business with the people's money. That is the only way we can restore the faith of our citizens. An effective Government can offer people opportunities they need to take greater responsibilities for their own lives and to rebuild their families, their communities, and our beloved country.

We ask the support of Americans from every walk of life, from every party, from every region. The Government is broken, and we intend to fix it. But we can't do it unless we all understand that this isn't a Democratic goal or a Republican goal. This is an American imperative, and we all need to be a part of it.

REPORT ON ADULT LITERACY

September 8, 1993

Nearly half of all adult Americans are "functionally illiterate" when it comes to handling daily transactions and holding a decent job, according to the results of the National Adult Literacy Survey released September 8 by the National Center for Education Statistics (NCES) in a 150-page report entitled "Adult Literacy in America." The $14 million survey—the most comprehensive ever of adult literacy in the United States—did not seek to measure intelligence. Rather, its purpose was to assess whether adults had the reading skills necessary to participate effectively in the workplace and civic activities such as voting.

Based on a broad definition of literacy to mean adults' ability "to use printed and written information to function in society," the test results indicated that between 40 million and 44 million Americans functioned at the lowest of five levels on a five-hundred-point scale. They were unable to calculate the total of a purchase, locate an intersection on a street map, and enter basic information on a document form. An additional 40 million of the nation's 191 million adults scored in the second lowest level, still below what was required to perform a moderately demanding job. They could not answer questions about basic facts in a newspaper article or write a paragraph summarizing information on a chart about schools. According to survey results, 61 million Americans functioned with middle-level skills, while 40 million performed at the highest literacy level. Only 20 percent of survey participants could determine the correct change using prices in a menu, and only 4 percent could use a calculator to figure the total cost of carpet to cover a room.

Perhaps most unsettling was the fact that, when asked if they read well or very well, 71 percent of those in the lowest level said they did. According to many educators, this misperception was a principal impediment to getting adults to read more and obtain further education and retraining.

Background and Survey Findings

While recent government-funded studies had focused on the literacy of young adults, the National Adult Literacy Survey was the first to provide accurate and detailed information on the skills of the adult population as a whole—information that previously had been unavailable. The last comprehensive government-sponsored survey of adult literacy—conducted in 1975—had estimated the number of functionally illiterate Americans at between 23 million and 27 million.

In 1988 Congress passed legislation instructing the Department of Education to undertake a new national adult literacy survey. The study was conducted by the Educational Testing Service (ETS) in Princeton, New Jersey, which also administers the Scholastic Aptitude Test (SAT) for college admissions as well as other standardized tests. During 1992 ETS staff interviewed a representative sample of more than 26,000 Americans above the age of fifteen, including 1,100 inmates from eighty federal and state prisons. Participants in the survey completed questions that focused on problems they were likely to encounter in their daily lives, such as reading a bus schedule and calculating the length of a trip, writing a letter about a billing error, making out a bank deposit slip, and understanding instructions for prospective jurors. The fifty-minute survey was divided into three types of questions: reading comprehension, filling out documents, and answering questions requiring simple arithmetic.

Among the principal reasons for the low scores, according to ETS researchers, were lack of education and the increasing number of adults whose primary language was not English. Of those adults in the lowest skill rank, about 25 percent were born in another country; another 25 percent reported a physical, mental, or health disability; and 50 percent were high school dropouts. The researchers found that participants with higher incomes—those with a median weekly salary of $620 to $680—did better on the test—compared with the lowest scorers, who earned a median weekly income of $230 to $245. Whites outscored blacks and Hispanics in all three literacy categories. Nearly 60 percent of Hispanic adults who scored in the lowest level were born outside the United States.

A "Wake-up Call"

"The results are very sobering and they indicate the need for a much greater effort than has been expended until now," said Madeleine M. Kunin, deputy secretary of education in the Office of Educational Research and Improvement, the department's statistical branch. "The overall education level of Americans has increased in terms of schooling and even in fundamental literacy. But the demands of the workplace simultaneously have vastly increased. We simply are not keeping pace with the kinds of skills required in today's economy."

"This is clearly disappointing in terms of where we are and where we want to be as a society," said Irwin Kirsch of the ETS, who directed the

study. "It is not a singular problem and points to a complexity of literacy problems and challenges we face as a nation as we move into the next century."

"This should be a wake-up call for all Americans to consider going back to school and getting a tune-up," said Secretary of Education Richard W. Riley. "It paints a picture of a society in which the vast majority of Americans do not know that they do not have the skills they need to earn a living in our increasingly technological society and international marketplace." Riley called the results "shocking." He said that schools must improve, businesses must increase their workplace training efforts, and parents should "slow down their lives to give their children's education more attention."

Riley and others noted that, traditionally, community colleges, churches, and service organizations have been the principal suppliers of adult literacy programs, but their efforts have been underfunded and uncoordinated. Increasingly, business has taken the lead in the move to improve adult literacy by offering job retraining programs and joining with local community colleges to bring professors to the workplace to teach advanced skills. It has been estimated that poor literacy costs businesses between $25 billion and $30 billion a year in lost productivity, errors, and accidents.

"I am not shocked. This reaffirms what we have known," said Keith Poston, a spokesman for the National Alliance of Business. Poston said it was not unusual for employers to "reject three out of four applicants because they cannot read or write well enough to hold entry-level jobs."

In releasing the study, the NCES emphasized that schools alone could not strengthen the literacy skills of present and future employees and of the population as a whole. Rather, a broad-based response, involving businesses, government, community groups, and schools, was essential. "What these data show is that literacy has become a currency in our society," said Kirsch. "It is not equally distributed and we need to find new and better ways to address the . . . challenge that we face."

> *Following is the executive summary of the report by the National Center for Education Statistics on "Adult Literacy in America," released September 8, 1993:*

This report provides a first look at the results of the National Adult Literacy Survey, a project funded by the U.S. Department of Education and administered by Educational Testing Service, in collaboration with Westat, Inc. It provides the most detailed portrait that has ever been available on the condition of literacy in this nation—and on the unrealized potential of its citizens.

Many past studies of adult literacy have tried to count the number of "illiterates" in this nation, thereby treating literacy as a condition that individuals either do or do not have. We believe that such efforts are inherently arbitrary and misleading. They are also damaging, in that they fail to acknowledge both the complexity of the literacy problem and the range of solutions needed to address it.

The National Adult Literacy Survey (NALS) is based on a different definition of literacy, and therefore follows a different approach to measuring it. The aim of this survey is to profile the English literacy of adults in the United States based on their performance across a wide array of tasks that reflect the types of materials and demands they encounter in their daily lives.

To gather the information on adults' literacy skills, trained staff interviewed nearly 13,600 individuals aged 16 and older during the first eight months of 1992. These participants had been randomly selected to represent the adult population in the country as a whole. In addition, about 1,000 adults were surveyed in each of 12 states that chose to participate in a special study designed to provide state-level results that are comparable to the national data. Finally, some 1,100 inmates from 80 federal and state prisons were interviewed to gather information on the proficiencies of the prison population. In total, over 26,000 adults were surveyed.

Each survey participant was asked to spend approximately an hour responding to a series of diverse literacy tasks as well as questions about his or her demographic characteristics, educational background, reading practices, and other areas related to literacy. Based on their responses to the survey tasks, adults received proficiency scores along three scales which reflect varying degrees of skill in prose, document, and quantitative literacy. The scales are powerful tools which make it possible to explore the proportions of adults in various subpopulations of interest who demonstrated successive levels of performance.

This report describes the types and levels of literacy skills demonstrated by adults in this country and analyzes the variation in skills across major subgroups in the population. It also explores connections between literacy skills and social and economic variables such as voting, economic status, weeks worked, and earnings. Some of the major findings are highlighted here.

The Literacy Skills of America's Adults

- Twenty-one to 23 percent—or some 40 to 44 million of the 191 million adults in this country—demonstrated skills in the lowest level of prose, document, and quantitative proficiencies (Level 1). Though all adults in this level displayed limited skills, their characteristics are diverse. Many adults in this level performed simple, routine tasks involving brief and uncomplicated texts and documents. For example, they were able to total an entry on a deposit slip, locate the time or place of a meeting on a form, and identify a piece of specific information in a brief news article. Others were unable to perform these types of tasks, and some had such limited skills that they were unable to respond to much of the survey.

- Many factors help to explain why so many adults demonstrated English literacy skills in the lowest proficiency level defined (Level 1). Twenty-five percent of the respondents who performed in this level were immigrants who may have been just learning to speak English. Nearly two-thirds of those in Level 1 (62 percent) had terminated their education before completing high school. A third were age 65 or older, and 26 percent had physical, mental, or health conditions that kept them from participating fully in work, school, housework, or other activities. Nineteen percent of the respondents in Level 1 reported having visual difficulties that affect their ability to read print.
- Some 25 to 28 percent of the respondents, representing about 50 million adults nationwide, demonstrated skills in the next higher level of proficiency (Level 2) on each of the literacy scales. While their skills were more varied than those of individuals performing in Level 1, their repertoire was still quite limited. They were generally able to locate information in text, to make low-level inferences using printed materials, and to integrate easily identifiable pieces of information. Further, they demonstrated the ability to perform quantitative tasks that involve a single operation where the numbers are either stated or can be easily found in text. For example, adults in this level were able to calculate the total cost of a purchase or determine the difference in price between two items. They could also locate a particular intersection on a street map and enter background information on a simple form.
- Individuals in Levels 1 and 2 were much less likely to respond correctly to the more challenging literacy tasks in the assessment—those requiring higher level reading and problem-solving skills. In particular, they were apt to experience considerable difficulty in performing tasks that required them to integrate or synthesize information from complex or lengthy texts or to perform quantitative tasks that involved two or more sequential operations and in which the individual had to set up the problem.
- The approximately 90 million adults who performed in Levels 1 and 2 did not necessarily perceive themselves as being "at risk." Across the literacy scales, 66 to 75 percent of the adults in the lowest level and 93 to 97 percent in the second lowest level described themselves as being able to read or write English "well" or "very well." Moreover, only 14 to 25 percent of the adults in Level 1 and 4 to 12 percent in Level 2 said they get a lot of help from family members or friends with everyday prose, document, and quantitative literacy tasks. It is therefore possible that their skills, while limited, allow them to meet some or most of their personal and occupational literacy needs.
- Nearly one-third of the survey participants, or about 61 million adults nationwide, demonstrated performance in Level 3 on each of the

literacy scales. Respondents performing in this level on the prose and document scales were able to integrate information from relatively long or dense text or from documents. Those in the third level on the quantitative scale were able to determine the appropriate arithmetic operation based on information contained in the directive, and to identify the quantities needed to perform that operation.

- Eighteen to 21 percent of the respondents, or 34 to 40 million adults, performed in the two highest levels of prose, document, and quantitative literacy (Levels 4 and 5). These adults demonstrated proficiencies associated with the most challenging tasks in this assessment, many of which involved long and complex documents and text passages.
- The literacy proficiencies of young adults assessed in 1992 were somewhat lower, on average, than the proficiencies of young adults who participated in a 1985 literacy survey. NALS participants aged 21 to 25 had average prose, document, and quantitative scores that were 11 to 14 points lower than the scores of 21- to 25-year-olds assessed in 1985. Although other factors may also be involved, these performance discrepancies are probably due in large part to changes in the demographic composition of the population—in particular, the dramatic increase in the percentages of young Hispanic adults, many of whom were born in other countries and are learning English as a second language.
- Adults with relatively few years of education were more likely to perform in the lower literacy levels than those who completed high school or received some type of postsecondary education. For example, on each of the three literacy scales, some 75 to 80 percent of adults with 0 to 8 years of education are in Level 1, while fewer than 1 percent are in Levels 4 and 5. In contrast, among adults with a high school diploma, 16 to 20 percent are in the lowest level on each scale, while 10 to 13 percent are in the two highest levels. Only 4 percent of adults with four year college degrees are in Level 1; 44 to 50 percent are in the two highest levels.
- Older adults were more likely than middle-aged and younger adults to demonstrate limited literacy skills. For example, adults over the age of 65 have average literacy scores that range from 56 to 61 points (or more than one level) below those of adults 40 to 54 years of age. Adults aged 55 to 64 scored, on average, between middle-aged adults and those 65 years and older. These differences can be explained in part by the fact that older adults tend to have completed fewer years of schooling than adults in the younger age groups.
- Black, American Indian/Alaskan Native, Hispanic, and Asian/Pacific Islander adults were more likely than White adults to perform in the lowest two literacy levels. These performance differences are affected by many factors. For example, with the exception of Asian/Pacific Islander adults, individuals in these groups tended to have completed

fewer years of schooling in this country than had White individuals. Further, many adults of Asian/Pacific Islander and Hispanic origin were born in other countries and were likely to have learned English as a second language.

- Of all the racial/ethnic groups, Hispanic adults reported the fewest years of schooling in this country (just over 10 years, on average). The average years of schooling attained by Black adults and American Indian/Alaskan Native adults were similar, at 11.6 and 11.7 years, respectively. These groups had completed more years of schooling than Hispanic adults had, on average, but more than a year less than either White adults or those of Asian/Pacific Islander origin.
- With one exception, for each racial or ethnic group, individuals born in the United States outperformed those born abroad. The exception occurs among Black adults, where there was essentially no difference (only 3 to 7 points). Among White and Asian/Pacific Islander adults, the average differences between native-born and foreign-born individuals range from 26 to 41 points across the literacy scales. Among Hispanic adults, the differences range from 40 to 94 points in favor of the native born.
- Twelve percent of the respondents reported having a physical, mental, or other health condition that kept them from participating fully in work or other activities. These individuals were far more likely than adults in the population as a whole to demonstrate performance in the range for Levels 1 and 2. Among those who said they had vision problems, 54 percent were in Level 1 on the prose scale and another 26 percent were in Level 2.
- Men demonstrated the same average prose proficiencies as women, but their document and quantitative proficiencies were somewhat higher. Adults in the Midwest and West had higher average proficiencies than those residing in either the Northeast or South.
- Adults in prison were far more likely than those in the population as a whole to perform in the lowest two literacy levels. These incarcerated adults tended to be younger, less well educated, and to be from minority backgrounds.

Literacy and Social and Economic Characteristics

- Individuals demonstrating higher levels of literacy were more likely to be employed, work more weeks in a year, and earn higher wages than individuals demonstrating lower proficiencies. For example, while adults in Level 1 on each scale reported working an average of only 18 to 19 weeks in the year prior to the survey, those in the three highest levels reported working about twice as many weeks—between 34 and 44. Moreover, across the scales, individuals in the lowest level reported median weekly earnings of about $230 to $245, compared with about $350 for individuals performing in Level 3 and $620 to $680 for those in Level 5.

- Adults in the lowest level on each of the literacy scales (17 to 19 percent) were far more likely than those in the two highest levels (4 percent) to report receiving food stamps. In contrast, only 23 to 27 percent of the respondents who performed in Level 1 said they received interest from a savings or bank account, compared with 70 to 85 percent in Levels 4 or 5.
- Nearly half (41 to 44 percent) of all adults in the lowest level on each literacy scale were living in poverty, compared with only 4 to 8 percent of those in the two highest proficiency levels.
- On all three literacy scales, adults in the higher levels were more likely than those in the lower levels to report voting in a recent state or national election. Slightly more than half (55 to 58 percent) of the adults in Level 1 who were eligible to vote said they voted in the past five years, compared with about 80 percent of those who performed in Level 4 and nearly 90 percent of those in Level 5.

Reflections on the Results

In reflecting on the results of the National Adult Literacy Survey, many readers will undoubtedly seek an answer to a fundamental question: Are the literacy skills of America's adults adequate? That is, are the distributions of prose, document, and quantitative proficiency observed in this survey adequate to ensure individual opportunities for all adults, to increase worker productivity, or to strengthen America's competitiveness around the world?

Because it is impossible to say precisely what literacy skills are essential for individuals to succeed in this or any other society, the results of the National Adult Literacy Survey provide no firm answers to such questions. As the authors examined the survey data and deliberated on the results with members of the advisory committees, however, several observations and concerns emerged.

Perhaps the most salient finding of this survey is that such large percentages of adults performed in the lowest levels (Levels 1 and 2) of prose, document, and quantitative literacy. In and of itself, this may not indicate a serious problem. After all, the majority of adults who demonstrated limited skills described themselves as reading or writing English well, and relatively few said they get a lot of assistance from others in performing everyday literacy tasks. Perhaps these individuals are able to meet most of the literacy demands they encounter currently at work, at home, and in their communities.

Yet, some argue that lower literacy skills mean a lower quality of life and more limited employment opportunities. As noted in a recent report from the American Society for Training and Development, "The association between skills and opportunity for individual Americans is powerful and growing .... Individuals with poor skills do not have much to bargain with; they are condemned to low earnings and limited choices."

The data from this survey appear to support such views. On each of the literacy scales, adults whose proficiencies were within the two lowest levels were far less likely than their more literate peers to be employed full-time, to earn high wages, and to vote. Moreover, they were far more likely to receive food stamps, to be in poverty, and to rely on nonprint sources (such as radio and television) for information about current events, public affairs, and government.

Literacy is not the only factor that contributes to how we live our lives, however. Some adults who displayed limited skills reported working in professional or managerial jobs, earning high wages, and participating in various aspects of our society, for example, while others who demonstrated high levels of proficiency reported being unemployed or out of the labor force. Thus, having advanced literacy skills does not necessarily guarantee individual opportunities.

Still, literacy can be thought of as a currency in this society. Just as adults with little money have difficulty meeting their basic needs, those with limited literacy skills are likely to find it more challenging to pursue their goals—whether these involve job advancement, consumer decisionmaking, citizenship, or other aspects of their lives. Even if adults who performed in the lowest literacy levels are not experiencing difficulties at present, they may be at risk as the nation's economy and social fabric continue to change.

Beyond these personal consequences, what implications are there for society when so many individuals display limited skills? The answer to this question is elusive. Still, it seems apparent that a nation in which large numbers of citizens display limited literacy skills has fewer resources with which to meet its goals and objectives, whether these are social, political, civic, or economic.

If large percentages of adults had to do little more than be able to sign their name on a form or locate a single fact in a newspaper or table, then the levels of literacy seen in this survey might not warrant concern. We live in a nation, however, where both the volume and variety of written information are growing and where increasing numbers of citizens are expected to be able to read, understand, and use these materials.

Historians remind us that during the last 200 years, our nation's literacy skills have increased dramatically in response to new requirements and expanded opportunities for social and economic growth. Today we are a better educated and more literate society than at any time in our history. Yet, there have also been periods of imbalance—times when demands seemed to surpass levels of attainment.

In recent years, our society has grown more technologically advanced and the roles of formal institutions have expanded. As this has occurred, many have argued that there is a greater need for all individuals to become more literate and for a larger proportion to develop advanced skills. Growing numbers of individuals are expected to be able to attend to multiple features of information in lengthy and sometimes complex displays, to compare and contrast information, to integrate information from various parts of a text or document, to generate ideas and information based on what they read, and to apply arithmetic operations sequentially to solve a problem.

The results from this and other surveys, however, indicate that many adults do not demonstrate these levels of proficiency. Further, the continuing process of demographic, social, and economic change within this country could lead to a more divided society along both racial and socioeconomic lines.

Already there is evidence of a widening division. According to the report *America's Choice: High Skills or Low Wages!*, over the past 15 years the gap in earnings between professionals and clerical workers has grown from 47 to 86 percent while the gap between white collar workers and skilled tradespeople has risen from 2 to 37 percent. At the same time, earnings for college educated males 24 to 34 years of age have increased by 10 percent while earnings for those with high school diplomas have declined by 9 percent. Moreover, the poverty rate for Black families is nearly three times that for White families. One child in five is born into poverty, and for minority populations, this rate approaches one in two.

In 1990, then-President Bush and the nation's governors, including then-Governor Clinton, adopted the goal that all of America's adults be literate by the year 2000. The responsibility for meeting this objective must, in the end, be shared among individuals, groups, and organizations throughout our society. Programs that serve adult learners cannot be expected to solve the literacy problem alone, and neither can the schools. Other institutions—ranging from the largest and most complex government agency, to large and small businesses, to the family—all have a role to play in ensuring that adults who need or wish to improve their literacy skills have the opportunity to do so. It is also important that individuals themselves come to realize the value of literacy in their lives and to recognize the benefits associated with having better skills. Only then will more adults in this nation develop the literacy resources they need to function in society, to achieve their goals, and to develop their knowledge and potential.

ISRAELI-PALESTINIAN PEACE ACCORD

September 13, 1993

Israel and the Palestine Liberation Organization (PLO) September 13 ended three decades of mutual hostility by approving a "Declaration of Principles" that promised limited self-government for Palestinians living in the Gaza Strip and the West Bank town of Jericho and committed both sides to resolve their differences by peaceful means.

In a ceremony on the south lawn of the White House in Washington, D.C., hosted by President Bill Clinton, the peace accord formally ending the virtual state of war between Jews and Palestinians was signed by Israeli foreign minister Shimon Peres and PLO foreign affairs spokesman Mahmoud Abbas. Also signing the pact as cosponsors of the Middle East peace process were Secretary of State Warren M. Christopher and Russian foreign minister Andrei Kozyrov.

A Symbolic Handshake

Of equal or perhaps even greater significance was the psychological breakthrough represented by PLO chairman Yasir Arafat and Israeli prime minister Yitzhak Rabin, who, standing on the same platform as witnesses to the signing, sealed the agreement with a handshake. Rabin, the former army commander and hero of the 1967 Six-Day War, said: "Let me say to you, the Palestinians, we are destined to live together on the same soil in the same land.... We who have fought against you, the Palestinians, we say to you today in a loud and clear voice: 'Enough of blood and tears! Enough!'" Arafat, the head of an organization that had the avowed purpose of destroying Israel, replied: "My people are hoping that this agreement ... marks the beginning of the end of a chapter of pain and suffering which has lasted throughout this century ... [and that] it will usher in an age of peace, coexistence and equal rights."

President Clinton commended the leaders on both sides for having the courage to turn away from the hatreds of the past and take risks for a peaceful future. Also at the signing ceremony were Norwegian foreign minister Johan Joergen Holst, whose government rescued the talks in 1992 when negotiations foundered, and Jimmy Carter and George Bush, the U.S. presidents who had done the most to promote peace in the Middle East.

Both domestic and international events influenced the timing of the decision of Israel and the PLO to seek an accommodation. The end of the cold war and the Persian Gulf War left the PLO with little room to maneuver. And the intifada, the Palestinian armed resistance to Israeli rule in the occupied territories, spurred both sides to make a deal. The Israelis had grown weary of the incessant armed strife, while Arafat found himself losing influence to a new generation of militant Islamic leaders. In the end, leaders on both sides came to the realization that neither could destroy the other.

Details of Accord

The peace accord was a declaration of principles, a starting point for living "in peaceful coexistence and mutual dignity and security" rather than a specific blueprint of how peace and limited self-rule were to be achieved. It fell far short of giving the Palestinans full sovereignty in an independent state. Even in Gaza and Jericho, Israel would maintain a still-to-be-determined security presence. The agreement was left deliberately vague as negotiators on both sides realized the detailed decisions necessary to implement the accord would require hard compromises and concessions.

Besides the promise of local autonomy in the two areas, the agreement called for an elected Palestinian council with some legislative functions for governing Gaza and Jericho. Palestinians would gain authority over municipal functions such as police, communications, taxation, tourism, civic administration, health, and welfare. Israel would retain control over external affairs and responsibility for protecting Jewish settlements. It was assumed that the settlers, particularly in Gaza, eventually would have to decide whether to remain under a Palestinian government or relocate in Israel. Israel agreed to a troop withdrawal plan beginning December 13, 1993, a date that soon proved too optimistic. After five years, the final status of the remainder of the occupied West Bank would be determined. Also put off until later was the emotional issue of East Jerusalem, which both Israelis and Palestinians claimed as their political and religious capital.

Economically and financially, the Palestinians would remain largely dependent on Israel for years to come. The infrastructure in the occupied lands, such as roads, ports, water supplies, and communications, would necessarily remain closely linked with Israel.

In the months that followed the signing, reaching agreement on the details was to prove exceedingly difficult. The immediate points of disagreement centered on the size of the Jericho enclave from which

Israel would withdraw, the extent of the Israeli military presence that would remain, control over the border crossings into the autonomous area, unhindered Palestinian access to Jordan across the Allenby Bridge near Jericho, the fate of Jewish settlements in the West Bank and Gaza, the right of Palestinian refugees to return to their former homes, the release by Israel of thousands of Palestinian prisoners, and the ultimate size and power of an independent Palestinian state.

Secret Talks

The peace talks between Israelis and Palestinians, initiated by the Bush administration in 1991, appeared to be hopelessly stalled until Norway in 1992 offered its services as mediator much as President Jimmy Carter had done in 1978 in helping to broker the Camp David peace settlement between Israel and Egypt. This time, negotiations were held in secret, unknown even to negotiators conducting the official talks in Washington. Rabin and Peres agreed to drop their refusal to talk directly with the PLO. (The Israeli Knesset subsequently abolished a law that barred direct talks with the PLO.) (Camp David Accords, Historic Documents of 1978, p. 605)

Rabin, elected prime minister in July 1992, had vowed to resolve the Palestinian issue. He proposed a limited automony plan that was similar to that endorsed by Egyptian president Anwar al-Sadat and Israeli prime minister Menachem Begin in 1979. Violent attacks on settlers and soldiers made a pullout from Gaza an appealing idea in Israel, and Rabin announced his government's support for a "Gaza first" policy. The Palestinians, however, insisted on linking any autonomy proposal to the West Bank, and Israel eventually agreed to add the West Bank town of Jericho to the interim self-rule accord, although the size of the Jericho entity was left for later negotiation.

Secret talks continued throughout the spring and summer of 1993, undeterred by rising terrorist attacks and the temporary closing of the occupied territories. By August 20 final agreement had been reached on the main provisions of the peace plan. In all, some fourteen secret meetings were held in Norway, beginning in January 1993. (Rabin's election, autonomy plan, Historic Documents of 1992, p. 655)

Approval of the peace accord was preceded—and made possible—by an exchange of letters between Arafat and Rabin in which Israel and the PLO recognized each other's legitimacy. Arafat's letter also said the PLO acknowledged Israel's right "to exist in peace and security," renounced the use of terrorism, and pledged to discipline supporters who continued to commit acts of violence.

In a separate letter to Norway's foreign minister, Arafat called on the Palestinians in the occupied territories to end their five-year-old uprising. An end to the intifada and formal PLO recognition were Israeli prerequisites to an agreement. Tel Aviv also insisted that the PLO officially abolish provisions in its covenant denying Israel's right to exist. Arafat reassured Israel such provisions were now "inoperative." The Palestinian National Council subsequently voted to eliminate the provisions.

Although the agreement represented a great achievement and held out at least the hope for an eventual regional settlement, many Israelis and Palestinians backing the accord remained skeptical that a genuine peace could be achieved. Terrorist attacks, shootings, retaliatory strikes, and arrests remained daily occurrences in Gaza and the West Bank after the signing, a sober reminder that implementing the declaration would be excruciatingly difficult. Already, offshoots of the PLO, such as Hamas, had established a rejectionist alliance dedicated to Arafat's removal and even vowed to fight the proposed Palestinian police force if necessary. Palestinian attacks and retaliations by settlers escalated during the fall, threatening to delay the deadline for beginning the Israeli withdrawal from Gaza and Jericho. For the accord to have any chance of success, it was important to be able to show concrete results quickly.

Implications Beyond Israel's Borders

The peace settlement had repercussions outside the occupied territories as well. Once Israel and the PLO recognized each other and pledged to work for a permanent peace settlement, the Arab world lost its common enemy. Ever since it declared independence in 1948, Israel had provided Arab rulers and rival politicians with a unifying target against which to mobilize their followers. Without a common rallying force, age-old rivalries from the Mediterranean to the Persian Gulf threatened to surface. Arab states—Saudi Arabia, for example—now would have to reassess their stance toward Israel. For Iraq and Iran, the peace agreement wiped out a major tenet of their foreign policy. In the near term at least, the accord was likely to increase their political and economic isolation. While the peace accord vindicated Egypt for its groundbreaking accommodation with Israel in 1979, it eliminated the special diplomatic role Cairo had played between Arabs and Jews and diminished Egypt's importance to the United States.

At the same time, the peace accord provided a momentum for further steps toward regional peace. The day after the signing, Israel and Jordan initialed in Washington an "Agenda for Peace" for achieving a "just, lasting and comprehensive peace." The two nations had been technically at war since 1967, and the agenda set the foundation for talks on a peace treaty and diplomatic recognition. And, although the outcome was far less certain, the new era also opened up the possibility of an eventual settlement between Israel and its other neighbors, Syria and Lebanon.

Following are the text of the "Declaration of Principles on Interim Self-Government Arrangements" signed by Foreign Minister Shimon Peres and PLO foreign affairs spokesman

Mahmoud Abbas, in Washington, D.C., September, 13, 1993; and the text of remarks at the signing ceremony by President Bill Clinton, Peres, Abbas, Prime Minister Yitzhak Rabin, and Chairman Yasir Arafat:

DECLARATION OF PRINCIPLES ON INTERIM SELF-GOVERNMENT ARRANGEMENTS

The Government of the State of Israel and the P.L.O. team (in the Jordanian-Palestinian delegation to the Middle East Peace Conference) (the "Palestinian Delegation"), representing the Palestinian people, agree that it is time to put an end to decades of confrontation and conflict, recognize their mutual legitimate and political rights, and strive to live in peaceful coexistence and mutual dignity and security and achieve a just, lasting and comprehensive peace settlement and historic reconciliation through the agreed political process. Accordingly, the two sides agree to the following principles:

Article I

Aim of the Negotiations

The aim of the Israeli-Palestinian negotiations within the current Middle East peace process is, among other things, to establish a Palestinian Interim Self-Government Authority, the elected Council (the "Council"), for the Palestinian people in the West Bank and the Gaza Strip, for a transitional period not exceeding five years, leading to a permanent settlement based on Security Council Resolutions 242 and 338.

It is understood that the interim arrangements are an integral part of the whole peace process and that the negotiations on the permanent status will lead to the implementation of Security Council Resolutions 242 and 338.

Article II

Framework for the Interim Period

The agreed framework for the interim period is set forth in this Declaration of Principles.

Article III

Elections

1. In order that the Palestinian people in the West Bank and Gaza Strip may govern themselves according to democratic principles, direct, free and general political elections will be held for the Council under

agreed supervision and international observation, while the Palestinian police will ensure public order.

2. An agreement will be concluded on the exact mode and conditions of the elections in accordance with the protocol attached as Annex I, with the goal of holding the elections not later than nine months after the entry into force of this Declaration of Principles.
3. These elections will constitute a significant interim preparatory step toward the realization of the legitimate rights of the Palestinian people and their just requirements.

Article IV

Jurisdiction

Jurisdiction of the Council will cover West Bank and Gaza Strip territory, except for issues that will be negotiated in the permanent status negotiations. The two sides view the West Bank and the Gaza Strip as a single territorial unit, whose integrity will be preserved during the interim period.

Article V

Transitional Period and Permanent Status Negotiations

1. The five-year transitional period will begin upon the withdrawal from the Gaza Strip and Jericho area.
2. Permanent status negotiations will commence as soon as possible, but not later than the beginning of the third year of the interim period, between the Government of Israel and the Palestinian people representatives.
3. It is understood that these negotiations shall cover remaining issues, including: Jerusalem, refugees, settlements, security arrangements, borders, relations and cooperation with other neighbors, and other issues of common interest.
4. The two parties agree that the outcome of the permanent status negotiations should not be prejudiced or preempted by agreements reached for the interim period.

Article VI

Preparatory Transfer of Powers and Responsibilities

1. Upon the entry into force of this Declaration of Principles and the withdrawal from the Gaza Strip and the Jericho area, a transfer of authority from the Israeli military government and its Civil Administration to the authorised Palestinians for this task, as detailed herein, will commence. This transfer of authority will be of a preparatory nature until the inauguration of the Council.
2. Immediately after the entry into force of this Declaration of Princi-

ples and the withdrawal from the Gaza Strip and Jericho area, with the view to promoting economic development in the West Bank and Gaza Strip, authority will be transferred to the Palestinians on the following spheres: education and culture, health, social welfare, direct taxation, and tourism. The Palestinian side will commence in building the Palestinian police force, as agreed upon. Pending the inauguration of the Council, the two parties may negotiate the transfer of additional powers and responsibilities, as agreed upon.

Article VII

Interim Agreement

1. The Israeli and Palestinian delegations will negotiate an agreement on the interim period (the "Interim Agreement").
2. The Interim Agreement shall specify, among other things, the structure of the Council, the number of its members, and the transfer of powers and responsibilities from the Israeli military government and its Civil Administration to the Council. The Interim Agreement shall also specify the Council's executive authority, legislative authority in accordance with Article IX below, and the independent Palestinian judicial organs.
3. The Interim Agreement shall include arrangements, to be implemented upon the inauguration of the Council, for the assumption by the Council of all of the powers and responsibilities transferred previously in accordance with Article VI above.
4. In order to enable the Council to promote economic growth, upon its inauguration, the Council will establish, among other things, a Palestinian Electricity Authority, a Gaza Sea Port Authority, a Palestinian Development Bank, a Palestinian Export Promotion Board, a Palestinian Environmental Authority, a Palestinian Land Authority and a Palestinian Water Administration Authority, and any other Authorities agreed upon, in accordance with the Interim Agreement that will specify their powers and responsibilities.
5. After the inauguration of the Council, the Civil Administration will be dissolved, and the Israeli military government will be withdrawn.

Article VIII

Public Order and Security

In order to guarantee public order and internal security for the Palestinians of the West Bank and the Gaza Strip, the Council will establish a strong police force, while Israel will continue to carry the responsibility for defending against external threats, as well as the responsibility for overall security of Israelis for the purpose of safeguarding their internal security and public order.

Article IX

Laws and Military Orders

1. The Council will be empowered to legislate, in accordance with the Interim Agreement, within all authorities transferred to it.
2. Both parties will review jointly laws and military orders presently in force in remaining spheres.

Article X

Joint Israeli-Palestinian Liaison Committee

In order to provide for a smooth implementation of this Declaration of Principles and any subsequent agreements pertaining to the interim period, upon the entry into force of this Declaration of Principles, a Joint Israeli-Palestinian Liaison Committee will be established in order to deal with issues requiring coordination, other issues of common interest, and disputes.

Article XI

Israeli-Palestinian Cooperation in Economic Fields

Recognizing the mutual benefit of cooperation in promoting the development of the West Bank, the Gaza Strip and Israel, upon the entry into force of this Declaration of Principles, an Israeli-Palestinian Economic Cooperation Committee will be established in order to develop and implement in a cooperative manner the programs identified in the protocols attached as Annex III and Annex IV.

Article XII

Liaison and Cooperation with Jordan and Egypt

The two parties will invite the Governments of Jordan and Egypt to participate in establishing further liaison and cooperation arrangements between the Government of Israel and the Palestinian representatives, on the one hand, and the Governments of Jordan and Egypt, on the other hand, to promote cooperation between them. These arrangements will include the constitution of a Continuing Committee that will decide by agreement on the modalities of admission of persons displaced from the West Bank and Gaza Strip in 1967, together with necessary measures to prevent disruption and disorder. Other matters of common concern will be dealt with by this Committee.

Article XIII

Redeployment of Israeli Forces

1. After the entry into force of this Declaration of Principles, and not later than the eve of elections for the Council, a redeployment of Israeli military forces in the West Bank and the Gaza Strip will take place, in addition to withdrawal of Israeli forces carried out in accordance with Article XIV.
2. In redeploying its military forces, Israel will be guided by the principle that its military forces should be redeployed outside populated areas.
3. Further redeployments to specified locations will be gradually implemented commensurate with the assumption of responsibility for public order and internal security by the Palestinian police force pursuant to Article VIII above.

Article XIV

Israeli Withdrawal from the Gaza Strip and Jericho Area

Israel will withdraw from the Gaza Strip and Jericho area, as detailed in the protocol attached as Annex II.

Article XV

Resolution of Disputes

1. Disputes arising out of the application or interpretation of this Declaration of Principles, or any subsequent agreements pertaining to the interim period, shall be resolved by negotiations through the Joint Liaison Committee to be established pursuant to Article X above.
2. Disputes which cannot be settled by negotiations may be resolved by a mechanism of conciliation to be agreed upon by the parties.
3. The parties may agree to submit to arbitration disputes relating to the interim period, which cannot be settled through conciliation. To this end, upon the agreement of both parties, the parties will establish an Arbitration Committee.

Article XVI

Israeli-Palestinian Cooperation Concerning Regional Programs

Both parties view the multilateral working groups as an appropriate instrument for promoting a "Marshall Plan," the regional programs and other programs, including special programs for the West Bank and Gaza Strip, as indicated in the protocol attached as Annex IV.

Article XVII

Miscellaneous Provisions

1. This Declaration of Principles will enter into force one month after its signing.
2. All protocols annexed to this Declaration of Principles and Agreed Minutes pertaining thereto shall be regarded as an integral part hereof.

DONE at Washington, D.C., this thirteenth day of September, 1993.

Annex I

Protocol on the Mode and Conditions of Elections

1. Palestinians of Jerusalem who live there will have the right to participate in the election process, according to an agreement between the two sides.
2. In addition, the election agreement should cover, among other things, the following issues:
   a. the system of elections;
   b. the mode of the agreed supervision and international observation and their personal composition; and
   c. rules and regulations regarding election campaign, including agreed arrangements for the organizing of mass media, and the possibility of licensing a broadcasting and TV station.
3. The future status of displaced Palestinians who were registered on 4th June 1967 will not be prejudiced because they are unable to participate in the election process due to practical reasons.

Annex II

Protocol on Withdrawal of Israeli Forces from the Gaza Strip and Jericho Area

1. The two sides will conclude and sign within two months from the date of entry into force of this Declaration of Principles, an agreement on the withdrawal of Israeli military forces from the Gaza Strip and Jericho area. This agreement will include comprehensive arrangements to apply in the Gaza Strip and the Jericho area subsequent to the Israeli withdrawal.
2. Israel will implement an accelerated and scheduled withdrawal of Israeli military forces from the Gaza Strip and Jericho area, beginning immediately with the signing of the agreement on the Gaza Strip and Jericho area and to be completed within a period not exceeding four months after the signing of this agreement.
3. The above agreement will include, among other things:
   a. Arrangements for a smooth and peaceful transfer of authority from

the Israeli military government and its Civil Administration to the Palestinian representatives.

b. Structure, powers and responsibilities of the Palestinian authority in these areas, except: external security, settlements, Israelis, foreign relations, and other mutually agreed matters.
c. Arrangements for the assumption of internal security and public order by the Palestinian police force consisting of police officers recruited locally and from abroad (holding Jordanian passports and Palestinian documents issued by Egypt). Those who will participate in the Palestinian police force coming from abroad should be trained as police and police officers.
d. A temporary international or foreign presence, as agreed upon.
e. Establishment of a joint Palestinian-Israeli Coordination and Cooperation Committee for mutual security purposes.
f. An economic development and stabilization program, including the establishment of an Emergency Fund, to encourage foreign investment, and financial and economic support. Both sides will coordinate and cooperate jointly and unilaterally with regional and international parties to support these aims.
g. Arrangements for a safe passage for persons and transportation between the Gaza Strip and Jericho area.

4. The above agreement will include arrangements for coordination between both parties regarding passages:
   a. Gaza-Egypt; and
   b. Jericho-Jordan.
5. The offices responsible for carrying out the powers and responsibilities of the Palestinian authority under this Annex II and Article VI of the Declaration of Principles will be located in the Gaza Strip and in the Jericho area pending the inauguration of the Council.
6. Other than these agreed arrangements, the status of the Gaza Strip and Jericho area will continue to be an integral part of the West Bank and Gaza Strip, and will not be changed in the interim period.

Annex III

Protocol on Israeli-Palestinian Cooperation in Economic and Development Programs

The two sides agree to establish an Israeli-Palestinian Continuing Committee for Economic Cooperation, focusing, among other things, on the following:

1. Cooperation in the field of water, including a Water Development Program prepared by experts from both sides, which will also specify the mode of cooperation in the management of water resources in the West Bank and Gaza Strip, and will include proposals for studies and plans on water rights of each party, as well as on the equitable

utilization of joint water resources for implementation in and beyond the interim period.

2. Cooperation in the field of electricity, including an Electricity Development Program, which will specify the mode of cooperation for the production, maintenance, purchase and sale of electricity resources.
3. Cooperation in the field of energy, including an Energy Development Program, which will provide for the exploitation of oil and gas for industrial purposes, particularly in the Gaza Strip and in the Negev, and will encourage further joint exploitation of other energy resources. This Program may also provide for the construction of a Petrochemical industrial complex in the Gaza Strip and the construction of oil and gas pipelines.
4. Cooperation in the field of finance, including a Financial Development and Action Program for the encouragement of international investment in the West Bank and the Gaza Strip, and in Israel, as well as the establishment of a Palestinian Development Bank.
5. Cooperation in the field of transport and communications, including a Program, which will define guidelines for the establishment of a Gaza Sea Port Area, and will provide for the establishing of transport and communications lines to and from the West Bank and the Gaza Strip to Israel and to other countries. In addition, this Program will provide for carrying out the necessary construction of roads, railways, communications lines, etc.
6. Cooperation in the field of trade, including studies, and Trade Promotion Programs, which will encourage local, regional and interregional trade, as well as a feasibility study of creating free trade zones in the Gaza Strip and in Israel, mutual access to these zones, and cooperation in other areas related to trade and commerce.
7. Cooperation in the field of industry, including Industrial Development Programs, which will provide for the establishment of joint Israeli-Palestinian Industrial Research and Development Centers, will promote Palestinian-Israeli joint ventures, and provide guidelines for cooperation in the textile, food, pharmaceutical, electronics, diamonds, computer and science-based industries.
8. A program for cooperation in, and regulation of, labor relations and cooperation in social welfare issues.
9. A Human Resources Development and Cooperation Plan, providing for joint Israeli-Palestinian workshops and seminars, and for the establishment of joint vocational training centers, research institutes and data banks.
10. An Environmental Protection Plan, providing for joint and/or coordinated measures in this sphere.
11. A program for developing coordination and cooperation in the field of communication and media.
12. Any other programs of mutual interest.

Annex IV

Protocol on Israeli-Palestinian Cooperation Concerning Regional Development Programs

1. The two sides will cooperate in the context of the multilateral peace efforts in promoting a Development Program for the region, including the West Bank and the Gaza Strip, to be initiated by the G-7. The parties will request the G-7 to seek the participation in this program of other interested states, such as members of the Organization for Economic Cooperation and Development, regional Arab states and institutions, as well as members of the private sector.
2. The Development Program will consist of two elements:
a) an Economic Development Program for the West Bank and the Gaza Strip.
b) a Regional Economic Development Program.
A. The Economic Development Program for the West Bank and the Gaza Strip will consist of the following elements:
(1) A Social Rehabilitation Program, including a Housing and Construction Program.
(2) A Small and Medium Business Development Plan.
(3) An Infrastructure Development Program (water, electricity, transportation and communications, etc.).
(4) A Human Resources Plan.
(5) Other programs.
B. The Regional Economic Development Program may consist of the following elements:
(1) The establishment of a Middle East Development Fund, as a first step, and a Middle East Development Bank, as a second step.
(2) The development of a joint Israeli-Palestinian-Jordanian Plan for coordinated exploitation of the Dead Sea area.
(3) The Mediterranean Sea (Gaza)-Dead Sea Canal.
(4) Regional Desalinization and other water development projects.
(5) A regional plan for agricultural development, including a coordinated regional effort for the prevention of desertification.
(6) Interconnection of electricity grids.
(7) Regional cooperation for the transfer, distribution and industrial exploitation of gas, oil and other energy resources.
(8) A Regional Tourism, Transportation and Telecommunications Development Plan.
(9) Regional cooperation in other spheres.
3. The two sides will encourage the multilateral working groups, and will coordinate towards their success. The two parties will encourage intersessional activities, as well as pre-feasibility and feasibility studies, within the various multilateral working groups.

Agreed Minutes to the Declaration of Principles on Interim Self-Government Arrangements

A. General Understandings and Agreements

Any powers and responsibilities transferred to the Palestinians pursuant to the Declaration of Principles prior to the inauguration of the Council will be subject to the same principles pertaining to Article IV, as set out in these Agreed Minutes below.

B. Specific Understandings and Agreements

Article IV

It is understood that:

1. Jurisdiction of the Council will cover West Bank and Gaza Strip territory, except for issues that will be negotiated in the permanent status negotiations: Jerusalem, settlements, military locations, and Israelis.
2. The Council's jurisdiction will apply with regard to the agreed powers, responsibilities, spheres and authorities transferred to it.

Article VI(2)

It is agreed that the transfer of authority will be as follows:

(1) The Palestinian side will inform the Israeli side of the names of the authorised Palestinians who will assume the powers, authorities and responsibilities that will be transferred to the Palestinians according to the Declaration of Principles in the following fields: education and culture, health, social welfare, direct taxation, tourism, and any other authorities agreed upon.

(2) It is understood that the rights and obligations of these offices will not be affected.

(3) Each of the spheres described above will continue to enjoy existing budgetary allocations in accordance with arrangements to be mutually agreed upon. These arrangements also will provide for the necessary adjustments required in order to take into account the taxes collected by the direct taxation office.

(4) Upon the execution of the Declaration of Principles, the Israeli and Palestinian delegations will immediately commence negotiations on a detailed plan for the transfer of authority on the above offices in accordance with the above understandings.

Article VII(2)

The Interim Agreement will also include arrangements for coordination and cooperation.

Article VII(5)

The withdrawal of the military government will not prevent Israel from exercising the powers and responsibilities not transferred to the Council.

Article VIII
It is understood that the Interim Agreement will include arrangements for cooperation and coordination between the two parties in this regard. It is also agreed that the transfer of powers and responsibilities to the Palestinian police will be accomplished in a phased manner, as agreed in the Interim Agreement.

Article X
It is agreed that, upon the entry into force of the Declaration of Principles, the Israeli and Palestinian delegations will exchange the names of the individuals designated by them as members of the Joint Israeli-Palestinian Liaison Committee. It is further agreed that each side will have an equal number of members in the Joint Committee. The Joint Committee will reach decisions by agreement. The Joint Committee may add other technicians and experts, as necessary. The Joint Committee will decide on the frequency and place or places of its meetings.

Annex II
It is understood that, subsequent to the Israeli withdrawal, Israel will continue to be responsible for external security, and for internal security and public order of settlements and Israelis. Israeli military forces and civilians may continue to use roads freely within the Gaza Strip and the Jericho area.

DONE at Washington, D.C., this thirteenth day of September, 1993.

CLINTON'S REMARKS

Prime Minister Rabin, Chairman Arafat, Foreign Minister Peres, Mr. Abbas, President Carter, President Bush, distinguished guests. On behalf of the United States and Russia, co-sponsors of the Middle East peace process, welcome to this great occasion of history and hope. Today we bear witness to an extraordinary act in one of history's defining dramas—a drama that began in a time of our ancestors when the word went forth from a sliver of land between the River Jordan and the Mediterranean Sea. That hallowed piece of earth, that land of light and revelation, is the home to the memories and dreams of Jews, Muslims and Christians throughout the world.

As we all know, devotion to that land has also been the source of conflict and bloodshed for too long. Throughout this century bitterness between the Palestinian and Jewish people has robbed the entire region of its resources, its potential and too many of its sons and daughters. The land has been so drenched in warfare and hatred, the conflicting claims of history etched so deeply in the souls of the combatants there, that many believe the past would always have the upper hand. Then, 14 years ago, the past began to give way when, at this place and upon this desk, three men of great vision signed their names to the Camp David accords. Today we honor the memories of Menachem Begin and Anwar Sadat. And we salute the wise leadership of President Jimmy Carter.

Then, as now, we heard from those who said that conflict would come again soon, but the peace between Egypt and Israel has endured. Just so this bold new venture today, this brave gamble that the future can be better than the past, must endure.

Two years ago in Madrid another President took a major step on the road to peace by bringing Israel and all her neighbors together to launch direct negotiations, and today we also express our deep thanks for the skillful leadership of President George Bush.

Ever since Harry Truman first recognized Israel, every American President, Democrat and Republican, has worked for peace between Israel and her neighbors. Now the efforts of all who have labored before us bring us to this moment—a moment when we dare to pledge what for so long seemed difficult even to imagine: that the security of the Israeli people will be reconciled with the hopes of the Palestinian people, and there will be more security and more hope for all.

Today the leadership of Israel and the Palestine Liberation Organization will sign a declaration of principles on interim Palestinian self-government. It charts a course toward reconciliation, between two peoples who have both known the bitterness of exile. Now both pledge to put old sorrows and antagonisms behind them and to work for a shared future shaped by the values of the Torah, the Koran and the Bible. Let us salute also today the Government of Norway, for its remarkable role in nurturing this agreement.

But above all, let us today pay tribute to the leaders who had the courage to lead their people toward peace, away from the scars of battle, the wounds and the losses of the past, toward a brighter tomorrow. The world today thanks Prime Minister Rabin, Foreign Minister Peres and Chairman Arafat.

That tenacity and vision has given us the promise of a new beginning. What these leaders have done now must be done by others. Their achievement must be a catalyst for progress in all aspects of the peace process. And those of us who support them must be there to help in all aspects, for the peace must render the people who make it more secure. A peace of the brave is within our reach. Throughout the Middle East there is a great yearning for the quiet miracle of a normal life. We know a difficult road lies ahead. Every peace has its enemies, those who still prefer the easy habits of hatred to the hard labors of reconciliation, but Prime

Minister Rabin has reminded us that you do not have to make peace with your friends, and the Koran teaches that if the enemy inclines toward peace, do thou also incline toward peace.

Therefore, let us resolve that this new mutual recognition will be a continuing process in which the parties transform the very way they see and understand each other. Let the skeptics of this peace recall what once existed among these people. There was a time when the traffic of ideas and commerce and pilgrims flowed uninterrupted among the cities of the fertile crescent. In Spain, in the Middle East, Muslims and Jews once worked together to write brilliant chapters in the history of literature and science. All this can come to pass again.

Mr. Prime Minister, Mr. Chairman, I pledge the active support of the United States of America to the difficult work that lies ahead.

The United States is committed to insuring that the people who are affected by this agreement will be made more secure by it and to leading the world in marshaling the resources necessary to implement the difficult details that will make real the principles to which you commit yourselves today. Together let us imagine what can be accomplished if all the energy and ability the Israelis and the Palestinians have invested into your struggle can now be channeled into cultivating the land and freshening the waters; into ending the boycotts and creating new industry; into building a land as bountiful and peaceful as it is holy. Above all, let us dedicate ourselves today to your region's next generation. In this entire assembly, no one is more important than the group of Israeli and Arab children who are seated here with us today.

Mr. Prime Minister, Mr. Chairman, this day belongs to you. And because of what you have done, tomorrow belongs to them. We must not leave them prey to the politics of extremism and despair, to those who would derail this process because they cannot overcome the fears and hatreds of the past. We must not betray their future.

For too long the young of the Middle East have been caught in a web of hatred not of their own making. For too long they have been taught from the chronicles of war; now we give them the chance to know the season of peace. For them we must realize the prophecy of Isaiah, that the cry of violence shall no more be heard in your land, nor wrack nor ruin within your borders. The children of Abraham, the descendants of Isaac and Ishmael, have embarked together on a bold journey. Together today with all our hearts and all our souls, we bid them Shalom. Salaam. Peace.

PERES'S REMARKS

Mr. President, your excellencies, ladies and gentlemen: Mr. President, I would like to thank you and the great American people for peace and support. Indeed I would like to thank all those who have made this day possible. What we are doing today is more than signing an agreement; it is a revolution. Yesterday a dream, today a commitment.

The Israeli and the Palestinian peoples who fought each other for almost a century have agreed to move decisively on the path of dialogue, understanding and cooperation. We live in an ancient land and as our land is small, so must our reconciliation be great. As our wars have been long, so must our healing be swift. Deep gaps call for lofty breezes. I want to tell the Palestinian delegation that we are sincere, that we mean business. We do not seek to shape your lives or determine your destiny. Let all of us turn from bullets to ballots, from guns to shovels. We shall pray with you. We shall offer you our help in making Gaza prosper and Jericho blossom again.

As we have promised, we shall negotiate with you a permanent settlement and with all our neighbors a comprehensive peace, peace for all. We shall support the agreement with an economic structure. We shall convert the bitter triangle of Jordanians, Palestinians and Israelis into a triangle of political triumph and economic prosperity.

We shall lower our barriers and widen our roads so goods and guests will be able to move freely all about the places holy and other places. This should be another Genesis. We have to build a new commonwealth on our old soil: a Middle East of the people and a Middle East for their children. For their sake we must put an end to the waste of arms races and invest our resources in education.

Ladies and gentlemen, two parallel tragedies have unfolded. Let us become a civic community. Let us bid once and for all farewell to wars, to tricks, to human misery, let us bid farewell to enmity and may there be no more victims on either side.

Let us build a Middle East of hope where today's food is produced and tomorrow's prosperity is guaranteed, a region with a common market, a Near East with a long-range agenda. We owe it to our own soldiers, to the memories of the victims of the Holocaust. Our hearts today grieve for the lost lives of young and innocent people yesterday in our own country. Let their memory be our foundation we are establishing today, a memory of peace on fresh and old tombs.

Suffering is first of all human. We also feel for the innocent loss of Palestinian lives. We begin a new day. The day may be long and the challenges enormous. Our calendar must meet an intensive schedule.

Mr. President, historically you are presiding over a most promising day in the very long history of our region, or our people. I thank all of you ladies and gentlemen, and let's pray together. Let's add hope to determination as all of us since Abraham believe in freedom, in peace, in the blessing of our great land and great spirit.

[Speaking in Hebrew]. From the eternal city of Jerusalem, from this green, promising lawn of the White House, let's say together in the language of our Bible: "Peace, peace to him that is far off and to him that is near," sayeth the Lord, "and I will hear."

Thank you.

ABBAS'S REMARKS

Mr. President, ladies and gentlemen: In these historic moments with feelings of joy that are mixed with a maximum sense of responsibility regarding events that are affecting our entire region, I greet you and I greet this distinguished gathering. I hope that this meeting in Washington will prove to be the onset of a positive and constructive change that will serve the interests of the Palestinian and Israeli peoples.

We have come to this point because we believe that peaceful coexistence and cooperation are the only means for reaching understanding and for realizing the hopes of the Palestinians and the Israelis. The agreement we will sign reflects the decision we made in the Palestine Liberation Organization to turn a new page in our relationship with Israel.

We know quite well that this is merely the beginning of a journey that is surrounded by numerous dangers and difficulties and yet our mutual determination to overcome everything that stands in the way of the cause for peace, our common belief that peace is the only means to security and stability and our mutual aspiration for a secure peace characterized by cooperation—all this will enable us to overcome all obstacles with the support of the international community. And here I would like to mention, in particular, the United States Government, which will shoulder the responsibility of continuing to play an effective and distinct role in the next stage so that this great achievement may be completed.

In this regard, it is important to me to affirm that we are looking forward with a great deal of hope and optimism to a date that is two years from today, when negotiations over the final status of our country are set to begin. We will then settle the remaining fundamental issues, especially those of Jerusalem, the refugees and the settlements. At that time, we will be laying the last brick in the edifice of peace whose foundation has been established today.

Economic development is the principal challenge facing the Palestinian people after years of struggle during which our national infrastructure and institutions were overburdened and drained. We are looking to the world for its support and encouragement in our struggle for growth and development, which begins today.

I thank the Government of the United States of America and the Government of the Russian Federation for the part they played and for their efforts and their sponsorship of the peace process. I also appreciate the role played by the Government of Norway in bringing about this agreement. And I look forward to seeing positive results soon on the remaining Arab-Israeli tracks so we can proceed together with our Arab brothers on this comprehensive quest for peace.

Thank you.

RABIN'S REMARKS

President of the United States, your excellencies, ladies and gentlemen: This signing of the Israeli-Palestinian declaration of principle here today—it's not so easy—neither for myself as a soldier in Israel's war nor for the people of Israel, not to the Jewish people in the diaspora, who are watching us now with great hope mixed with apprehension. It is certainly not easy for the families of the victims of the war's violence, terror, whose pain will never heal, for the many thousands who defended our lives in their own and have even sacrificed their lives for our own. For them this ceremony has come too late.

Today on the eve of an opportunity, opportunity for peace and perhaps end of violence and war, we remember each and every one of them with everlasting love. We have come from Jerusalem, the ancient and eternal capital of the Jewish people. We have come from an anguished and grieving land. We have come from a people, a home, a family that has not known a single year, not a single month, in which mothers have not wept for their sons. We have come to try and put an end to the hostilities so that our children, our children's children, will no longer experience the painful cost of war: violence and terror. We have come to secure their lives and to ease the soul and the painful memories of the past—to hope and pray for peace.

Let me say to you, the Palestinians, we are destined to live together on the same soil in the same land. We, the soldiers who have returned from battles stained with blood; we who have seen our relatives and friends killed before our eyes; we who have attended their funerals and cannot look in the eyes of their parents; we who have come from a land where parents bury their children; we who have fought against you, the Palestinians—we say to you today, in a loud and clear voice: enough of blood and tears. Enough.

We have no desire for revenge. We harbor no hatred towards you. We, like you, are people—people who want to build a home. To plant a tree. To love—live side by side with you. In dignity. In empathy. As human beings. As free men. We are today giving peace a chance—and saying to you and saying again to you: enough. Let us pray that a day will come when we all will say farewell to the arms. We wish to open a new chapter in the sad book of our lives together—a chapter of mutual recognition, of good neighborliness, of mutual respect, of understanding. We hope to embark on a new era in the history of the Middle East. Today here in Washington at the White House, we will begin a new reckoning in the relations between peoples, between parents tired of war, between children who will not know war.

President of the United States, ladies and gentlemen, our inner strength, our high moral values, have been the right for thousands of years, from the book of the books. In one of which, we read: To everything there is a season and a time to every purpose under heaven: a time to be born and a time to die, a time to kill and a time to heal, a time to weep and a time to laugh, a time to love and a time to hate, a time of war and a time of peace. Ladies and gentlemen, the time for peace has come.

In two days the Jewish people will celebrate the beginning of a new year. I believe, I hope, I pray that the new year will bring a message of redemption for all peoples—a good year for you, for all of you; a good year for Israelis and Palestinians; a good year for all the peoples of the Middle East; a good year for our American friends who so want peace and are helping to achieve it.

For Presidents and members of previous Administrations, especially for you, President Clinton, and your staff, for all citizens of the world, may peace come to all your homes. In the Jewish tradition it is customary to conclude our prayers with the word Amen. With your permission, men of peace, I shall conclude with the words taken from the prayer recited by Jews daily, and whoever of you who volunteer, I would ask the entire audience to join me in saying Amen. [Speaking in Hebrew]. May He who brings peace to His universe bring peace to us and to all Israel. Amen.

ARAFAT'S REMARKS

In the name of God the most merciful, the compassionate. Mr. President, ladies and gentlemen: I would like to express our tremendous appreciation to President Clinton and to his Administration for sponsoring this historic event, which the entire world has been waiting for. Mr. President, I am taking this opportunity to assure you and to assure the great American people that we share your values for freedom, justice, and human rights—values for which my people have been striving.

My people are hoping that this agreement, which we are signing today, marks the beginning of the end of a chapter of pain and suffering which has lasted throughout this century. My people are hoping that this agreement which we are signing today will usher in an age of peace, coexistence and equal rights. We are relying on your role, Mr. President, and on the role of all the countries which believe that without peace in the Middle East, peace in the world will not be complete.

Enforcing the agreements and moving toward the final settlement, after two years to implement all aspects of U.N. resolutions 242 and 338 in all of their aspects, and resolve all the issues of Jerusalem, the settlements, the refugees and the boundaries, will be a Palestinian and an Israeli responsibility. It is also the responsibility of the international community in its entirety to help the parties overcome the tremendous difficulties which are still standing in the way of reaching a final and comprehensive settlement.

Now, as we stand on the threshold of this new historic era, let me address the people of Israel and their leaders, with whom we are meeting today for the first time. And let me assure them that the difficult decision we reached together was one that required great and exceptional courage.

We will need more courage and determination to continue the course of building coexistence and peace between us. This is possible. And it will happen with mutual determination and with the effort that will be made with all parties on all the tracks to establish the foundations of a just and comprehensive peace. Our people do not consider that exercising the right to self-determination could violate the rights of their neighbors or infringe on their security. Rather, putting an end to their feelings of being wronged and of having suffered an historic injustice is the strongest guarantee to achieve coexistence and openness between our two peoples and future generations.

Our two peoples are awaiting today this historic hope. And they want to give peace a real chance.

Such a shift will give us an opportunity to embark upon the process of economic, social and cultural growth and development. And we hope that international participation in that process will be as extensive as it can be. This shift will also provide an opportunity for all forms of cooperation on a broad scale and in all fields.

I thank you, Mr. President. We hope that our meeting will be a new beginning for fruitful and effective relations between the American people and the Palestinian people.

I wish to thank the Russian Federation and President Boris Yeltsin. Our thanks also go to Secretary [of State Warren] Christopher and Foreign Minister [Andrei V.] Kozyrev [of Russia] to the Government of Norway and to the Foreign Minister of Norway, for the positive part they played in bringing about this major achievement.

I extend greetings to all the Arab leaders, our brothers, and to all the world leaders who contributed to this achievement.

Ladies and gentlemen, the battle for peace is the most difficult battle of our lives. It deserves our utmost efforts because the land of peace, the land of peace yearns for a just and comprehensive peace.

[Speaking in English] Mr. President, thank you. Thank you. Thank you.

CLINTON'S CLOSING REMARKS

We have been granted the great privilege of witnessing this victory for peace. Just as the Jewish people this week celebrate the dawn of a new year, let us all go from this place to celebrate the dawn of a new era, not only for the Middle East but for the entire world.

The sound we heard today, once again as in ancient Jericho, was of trumpets toppling walls, the walls of anger and suspicion between Israeli and Palestinian, between Arab and Jew. This time, praise God, the trumpets herald not the destruction of that city but its new beginning.

Now let each of us here today return to our portion of that effort, uplifted by the spirit of the moment, refreshed in our hopes and guided by the wisdom of the Almighty, who has brought us to this joyous day. Go in peace. Go as peacemakers.

YELTSIN ON CRISES IN RUSSIA

September 22, October 4, and October 6, 1993

It had been widely predicted, but the showdown was much more dramatic than many had expected, yet slower in coming than some had foreseen. After months of political gridlock and growing struggle between Russian president Boris Yeltsin and strident conservative parliamentary foes of his efforts to initiate political and economic reform, Yeltsin on September 21 issued a dramatic decree, dissolving the Congress of People's Deputies (the Russian legislature) and calling for new parliamentary elections on December 12. In announcing the move over national television the next day, Yeltsin—who in 1991 had won a five-year term as Russia's first popularly elected president—acknowledged that he was violating the existing communist-era constitution, but contended that the April 25 referendum, in which 58 percent of voters expressed their confidence in his rule, had "supreme judicial power." "The security of Russia and her peoples is more precious than formal compliance with contradictory regulations created by the legislature," he said. By parliament's "fruitless, senseless, and destructive struggle," the nation was becoming paralyzed, he concluded. (End of Soviet Union, election of Yeltsin, Historic Documents of 1991, p. 785)

The rebel legislators responded to the decree at midnight by voting to depose Yeltsin. They declared his conservative rival, Vice President Aleksandr V. Rutskoi, acting president. Anti-Yeltsin factions, comprised of hard-line communists and ultra-nationalists, set up barricades in and around the parliament building (known as the White House), while the Constitutional Court declared Yeltsin's decree unconstitutional. Leaders of the Russian army pledged "strict neutrality" in the confrontation.

Escalating Crisis

The Kremlin's reaction to the legislators' defiance was to cut off telephone lines to the parliament building. At the same time, Yeltsin pledged to hold presidential elections on June 12, 1994, two years before his term was to expire. Rebels in Congress responded two days later by voting to hold simultaneous parliamentary and presidential elections in March 1994. Rejecting that countermove, Yeltsin ordered a cut-off of electricity and hot water to the parliament building and continued to step up pressure on the recalcitrant legislators, stopping short of using armed force. However, as the impasse continued, he ordered the Interior Ministry on September 28 to seal off the Russian White House with concertina wire, trucks, and thousands of troops. The government ordered the anti-Yeltsin defendants to surrender their arms, warning that they would face "serious consequences" if they failed to do so. Clashes between police officers and anti-Yeltsin demonstrators began to escalate in the streets of Moscow, as gunmen attacked a number of government buildings and police officers using night sticks fought several hundred protesters trying to break through the government's cordon of the parliament. On October 1 opposition legislators rejected an agreement to surrender, and the next day widespread street violence broke out, as Rutskoi issued an appeal for "everyone [to] rise up for the struggle against the dictatorship."

The crisis reached the boiling point October 3, when several thousand antigovernment demonstrators convened in October Square. Responding to calls by Viktor Anpilov, leader of the militant Communist Working Moscow movement, the protesters began moving to the parliament building three miles away, easily overwhelming thin lines of police officers along the route. Reaching the White House, the demonstrators broke through the government cordon. The Kremlin's initial response was a surprising and disconcerting silence; Yeltsin was away at his dacha (summer home) at the time. However, later that afternoon, the Russian president returned to Moscow and declared a state of emergency, outlawing all public meetings and demonstrations. But crowds continued to gather, waving Soviet and nationalist flags exuberantly.

Meanwhile, the government began drawing up plans to storm the parliament, with the attack set for 7 a.m. October 4. After the government issued appeals to those inside the building to surrender ("This is your last chance, and the only possibility to save Russia and her citizens"), dozens of tanks and armored personnel carriers loyal to Yeltsin opened fire and special antiterrorist troops under Yeltsin's direct control stormed the building. The president went on national television to vow that "the armed fascist putsch in Moscow will be crushed."

Fighting continued throughout the morning, with tank fire from the military setting the White House ablaze. As one reporter described it, "The area shook and thudded like a city at war as round after round was fired toward the massive parliament building and bursts of machine-gun fire resounded back."

The parliamentary rebels and their allies in the barricaded building finally asked for a cease-fire, which was called around noon, and began leaving the building. However, shooting by isolated gunmen and snipers continued into the afternoon, with several people killed or wounded. When all the fighting was over, more than 150 people were dead and hundreds more wounded.

The stand-off between hard-liners and more reform-bent politicians recalled the events of August 1991, when those opposed to economic reform attempted to overthrow Yeltsin's predecessor, President Mikhail S. Gorbachev. Gorbachev was slow to respond, but the popular Yeltsin set aside the rivalry that had developed between them to demand that Gorbachev be returned to power. Although the coup failed, Gorbachev quickly resigned from the communist party and announced a restructuring of the Soviet Union into a commonwealth of independent states. By the end of the year, however, the arrangement had disintegrated and Gorbachev resigned, leaving Yeltsin as the dominant political leader of the Russian Federation. (Failure of Soviet coup attempt, Historic Documents of 1991, p. 515)

Remembering the events of 1991, some criticized Yeltsin's hesitation to act more decisively and immediately after dissolving parliament. Indeed, in subsequent interviews before the October 4 crackdown, Yeltsin sympathizers said they were certain that he had lost the battle by waiting too long to take more forcible action against his opponents.

Censorship Invoked

Immediately after the parliamentary uprising, Yeltsin outlawed the most vociferous opposition in the news media and fringe political parties; ousted political opponents in the central government, the courts, and the nation's outlying regions; disbanded regional legislatures; and restricted debate on the draft of a new constitution. On October 8, he banned the militant Communist Party of the Russian Federation, as well as the nationalist People's Party of Free Russia, bringing to ten the number of suspended political parties and organizations, as well as thirteen newspapers. Even Yeltsin supporters were critical of the move. A group of reform-minded journalists held a news conference September 29 to condemn the "strict censorship."

Despite the crackdown, Pravda, *which had been the official newspaper during the communist era, resumed publication November 2 in defiance of the decree, displaying the Orders of Lenin on its masthead. "Let it be clear to everyone, we are not changing our conviction," the newspaper said in a letter to readers entitled, "We Return."*

In the weeks following the uprising, Yeltsin reinstated most of the major political parties and newspapers and said that the communist party would be allowed to participate in the December elections.

Western Support for Yeltsin

Although a number of his supporters both within and outside Russia questioned what they considered undemocratic actions in the name of democracy, most expressed the view that Yeltsin had no other choice but to act as he did. President Bill Clinton responded to Yeltsin's decision to dissolve the parliament by immediately telephoning him to ask for assurances that he would act in a way "that ensures peace, stability, and an open political process." After receiving Yeltsin's pledge that elections for a new legislature would be "held on a democratic and free basis," Clinton issued a statement strongly endorsing Yeltsin's move as "ultimately consistent with the democratic and reform course that he has charted. . . . There is no question that President Yeltsin acted in response to a constitutional crisis that had reached critical impasse and paralyzed the political system. . . . I support him fully." Other Western nations joined Clinton in supporting Yeltsin, among them British prime minister John Major, who said Yeltsin had "made it clear that he is taking exceptional steps in exceptional circumstances."

Similar endorsements were repeated by Clinton and other Western leaders after the events of October 3 and 4. British, French, German, and other North Atlantic Treaty Organization (NATO) leaders were quick to voice their firm backing of the Russian president, who "deserves the support of all democrats inside and outside Russia," in the words of Prime Minister Major.

Aftermath of the New "Russian Revolution"

On November 6 Yeltsin stated that, rather than holding presidential elections in June 1994, he would serve out his full term, which was due to expire in 1996. Speaking to newspaper editors, the sixty-two-year-old president, whose health had been a matter of speculation for some time, indicated that he would not seek reelection. "Everybody knows how many blows of fate I have already suffered. It is too much for one man," he said. A week later, however, Yeltsin changed his mind. In an interview with Izvestia, *Yeltsin said his decree calling for elections June 12, 1994, was in effect "unless I cancel it."*

Also in early November, Yeltsin revealed the details of a new constitution that would significantly expand the powers of the presidency at the expense of parliament while at the same time providing guarantees of private property, civil, and human rights, as well as the right to strike. The sixty-six-page document would replace the communist-era constitution adopted in 1977 under Leonid Brezhnev, which had been amended numerous times and all but ignored. (Historic Documents of 1977, p. 747)

On October 15 Yeltsin had announced that adoption of the constitution would be decided by a nationwide "yes-or-no-vote" referendum scheduled for December 12, the same day as voters were scheduled to elect the legislature, the first open and freely contested elections in the nation's history. According to reporters, the president had told an ally, Yuri Luzhkov, the mayor of Moscow, that he was determined not to repeat the mistakes of 1991 when, after surviving the coup attempt, many Soviet-era institutions had been allowed to survive.

"The [proposed] constitution establishes a dependable barrier to confrontation" between the presidential, judicial, and legislative branches of government, Yeltsin said in his statement. "It steers power toward consensus [and] cooperation." The new document, framed largely by the Russian president himself, would give a two-chambered Federal Assembly the power to register a vote of no confidence in the president; it also outlined procedures, although complicated and cumbersome, for giving the Assembly power to initiate impeachment action against the president. However, the president could dissolve the parliament if it rejected his choice for prime minister three times or if it delivered a no-confidence vote in the government twice in three months. A two-thirds, rather than simple, majority would be required to override a presidential veto. After 1996, when Yeltsin said he would step down, presidents would serve a maximum of two four-year terms.

Critics in Russia expressed reservations about the new document. "On December 12, a constitution will be approved in a referendum containing a gentlemen's set of rights, liberties, and democratic institutions," said Vitaly Tretyakov, chief editor of Nezavisimaya Gazeta. *"But it will be a constitution for the president in general and for President Yeltsin in particular."*

In his speech unveiling the constitution, Yeltsin said, "Skeptics say a majority of people won't be able to make sense of this constitution, that its text is too complicated.... But I'm sure people have already figured out the main principles of this constitution ... that the human being is the supreme value, not a class or nation."

Following are excerpts from President Boris Yeltsin's September 22 televised announcement of his decision to dissolve parliament and hold elections for a new legislature in December; his October 4 announcement that the government was mobilizing forces against the rebels in the parliament building; and excerpts from his October 6 address explaining the decision to storm the building:

SEPTEMBER 22 ADDRESS

Esteemed Citizens,

The only way to overcome the paralysis of state power in the Russian Federation is its crucial renovation on the basis of principles of people's power and constitutionality.

The current constitution does not allow to do it, the current constitution does not offer a procedure to adopt a new fundamental law to provide for a worthy way out from the statehood crisis.

Being the guarantor of security of our state, I must suggest a way out from the deadend and break the destructive and vicious circle.

The highest body of the legislative power will be a federal assembly of the Russian federation, a two-chamber parliament operating on a professional basis. Elections have been scheduled for December 11-12, 1993. I point out that it is not early elections of the congress and the parliament, but an absolutely different highest body of the legislative power in Russia.

Any actions aimed at disrupting the elections will be regarded as illegal. Those who take such actions will be brought to justice in accordance with Russia's criminal code. The Russian parliament should consist of people who will not engage in political games at the expense of the people, but primarily will enact laws so necessary in Russia.

More competent, more democratic and more cultured people should come to the Russian parliament. I believe that there are such people in Russia and that we shall find them and elect them.

I seek no advantages in transformations of the federal power and make no exceptions for myself, the president of the Russian federation. I come out for early presidential elections to be held some time after the federal assembly begins to work.

Taking into account numerous appeals addressed to me by subjects of the Russian federation, groups of deputies, participants of the constitutional assembly, political parties, movements and representatives of the public, I have done the following:

Entrusted with power received at nationwide elections in 1991 and confidence, confirmed by Russian citizens in the April 1993 referendum, I have decreed amendments and addenda to the existing constitution. They mainly concern federal bodies of the legislative and executive power, their relationship on the basis of the separation of powers.

Only you voters must decide who will fill the supreme state post of Russia for the next term.

In accordance with the presidential decree which has already been signed, the exercise of the legislative, administrative and controlling powers vested in the congress of people's deputies and the supreme soviet of the Russian federation are terminated as of today, no more sessions of the congress shall be convened. The powers of the people's deputies of the Russian federation are voided. Naturally, their labor rights will be fully guaranteed. They are entitled to return to the enterprises or offices where they worked prior to their election as deputies of Russia, and fill their former posts. At the same time, every one of them has the right to be nominated candidate to run in the elections to the federal assembly.

The authority of the local bodies of power remains intact. In this connection I appeal to local leaders: use the entire legal potential to ensure public order. I want to note that the constitution in the Russian federation, legislation of the Russian federation and the subjects of the Russian federation continue to be in full force apart from the changes and additions introduced by the presidential decree. The rights and freedoms of the citizens of the Russian federation laid down in the constitution and the law are guarantees.

I appeal to the leaders and peoples of foreign states, to our friends abroad—there are lots of them around the world—your support is important and valuable for Russia. In the most crucial moments of the most difficult changes in this country, you were with us. I call on you to once again understand the complexity of the situation in this country and the measures to which I, the president of the Russian federation, had to resort because they are the only way to defend democracy and freedom in Russia, to defend reform of Russia's admittedly weak market. These measures are necessary in order to protect Russia and the whole world against catastrophic effects of the disintegration of Russian statehood, against the triumph of anarchy in a country with a huge nuclear arsenal. I have no other objectives.

Esteemed Countrymen,

A moment has come when by pooling our efforts we can and must put an end to the deep crisis of Russian statehood. I count on your understanding and support, I count on your good sense and the sense of civic duty. We still have a chance to help Russia. I believe that we shall use this chance for the sake of peace and quiet in our country, for the sake of driving away this exhaustive struggle from which we have long since tried.

By pooling our efforts, let us save Russia for ourselves, our children and grandchildren. Thank you.

OCTOBER 4 ADDRESS

Dear Compatriots,

I am addressing you at a very difficult moment.

In the capital of Russia shots are being fired and blood is being spilled. Militants brought in from all over the country, instigated by the leadership of the White House, are causing death and destruction.

I know that for many of you this was a sleepless night. I know that you understood everything.

This alarming and tragic night taught us many lessons. We did not get ready for war. We hoped that it would be possible to reach understanding and preserve peace in the capital.

Those who acted against the peaceful city and unleashed bloody massacre are criminals. But theirs is not only crime committed by separate thugs and ruffians. Everything that has happened and is happening in Moscow is a pre-planned armed mutiny. It is organized by communist revenge-seekers, fascist chieftains, some former deputies and representatives of soviets (councils).

While holding sham negotiations they accumulated forces, brought together bandit groups of mercenaries inured to killings and arbitrariness.

A negligible bunch of politicking individuals has tried to impose its will on the entire country at gun-point. Means with which they wanted to rule Russia now stand exposed to the whole world. These means include cynical lies and bribery. They include rocks, sharpened metal rods, automatic rifles and machine-guns.

Those who are waving red flags have again plunged Russia in a bloodbath.

They hoped that their action would come unexpectedly, that their insolence and unparalleled ruthlessness will sow fear and confusion.

They hoped that the military would stay away looking calmly on unarmed Muscovites being dealt with and a bloody dictatorship re-installed in the country.

They hoped that Russian citizens would believe their lies. They hoped for a prompt victory.

They have miscalculated, and the people will condemn the criminals.

They and those on whose order they acted cannot be forgiven. For they have raised their hands against civilians, Moscow, Russia, children, women and old men.

The armed revolt is doomed to failure. To restore order, calm and peace, troops are arriving in Moscow.

Their goal is to liberate and unblock the installations held by the criminal elements, as well as to disarm the illegal armed formations.

I beg you, dear Muscovites, to support the moral of Russian soldiers and officers. They are our people's army and military and today their only task is to defend our children, mothers and fathers, to stop and render harmless program-makers and murderers.

Moscow, Russia [is] looking to you for courage and decisive action.

The organizations which took part in mass rioting and other illegal activities are herewith banned on the entire territory of Russia.

The central bank has been ordered to stop immediately all transactions with the accounts of these associations.

The procurator-general's office has been ordered to institute without delay criminal proceedings and begin the investigation into the organization of mass rioting.

The decree providing for these and other measures was signed last night and is being translated into life.

I am appealing to all political forces of Russia. For the sake of those whose lives have been cut short, for the sake of those whose innocent blood has been spilled already—I ask you to forget what seemed important yesterday—about internal strife.

All those who cherish peace and quiet, honor and dignity of our country, all those who oppose war must be together.

I am appealing to the leaders of Russia's regions, republics, territories, regions and autonomies.

Has not enough blood been spilled to sort things out and for all of us to take—at least—a firm and principled stand for the sake of Russia's integrity?

I am appealing to the citizens of Russia. The armed fascist-communist rebellion in Moscow will be suppressed the soonest possible.

For this the Russian state has sufficient strength.

I think it is my duty to appeal to the Muscovites.

Our numbers have been depleted over the past day and night. Innocent peaceful civilians have fallen victims to bandits. Let us bow our heads to the fallen.

Responding to the call of the heart, many of you spent this past night in the centre of Moscow, at the far and close approaches to the Kremlin. Tens of thousands of people risked their lives. Your will power, your civic courage and the power of your spirit have proved the most effective weapon.

I bow my head low to you.

OCTOBER 6 ADDRESS

Esteemed citizens of Russia,

On October 3 and 4, Russia experienced a great tragedy. Gangs of murderers and destroyers swept the streets of our capital. They broke into state offices, they humiliated people whom they took hostage. They captured city buses and trucks. The militants had a great amount of weapons, ammunition and military equipment. The lives of peaceful civilians were in mortal danger.

What happened in Moscow last Sunday was not a sporadic outburst. All that deserved another name—an armed mutiny, planned and prepared by the leaders of the former supreme soviet and the former vice-president, the leaders of some parties and public organisations.

Among them were the National Salvation Front, including its arm Labour Russia, some communist parties and groups, the Nazi-style Russian national unity and some others. Nazis and communists merged in this damnable cause. The swastika join the sickle and hammer.

Some former people's deputies were among the organizers and active parliaments of the mutiny. They had long since begun essential, criminal activity. They used their deputy immunity as a shield from behind which to incite violence, stimulate mass unrest, organize mass-scale bloody rioting and unleash civil war. . . .

The bloodletting events of that night compelled (US) to bring in regular army units into Moscow. The difficult decision was made to storm the supreme soviet building, which had turned into the stronghold of terrorism with a great amount of weapons and ammunition and the most important factor of unleashing civil war in Russia.

The actions of the militants were coordinated from the House of Soviets (parliament building), illegal armed groups were formed inside it. Calls to storm the mayor's office building, the outstanding (television broadcasting centre) and the Kremlin came from the House of Soviets.

But the White House (parliament) building also became a symbol of perfidy and betrayal. All preparations for the mutiny were carried out while sham negotiations were being conducted. The noble intentions of the Russian orthodox church to help settle the crisis were trampled.

I must also speak about one other thing. There would have been fewer casualties, if the militants and snipers held up in the House of Soviets had not targeted peaceful civilians, if they had been ordered to lay down arms when resistance became senseless.

The smoldering source of civil war in Russia has been extinguished. But my heart is heavy because we had to pay an immense price. I feel bitter because some people are already fussing on the cold ashes seeking petty political gains, seeking to save the reputations of those who covered themselves with disgrace during that night. May God be their judge.

We must draw most serious conclusions, learn lessons in order to avert any recurrence of the same.

Why did we put up with the organizations in Russia which acted legally not only calling for violence but also preparing it. They were not duly rebuffed by either the prosecutors or by the law-enforcement agencies....

Straight after the abolition of the supreme soviet and the announcement of the date of the elections to the parliament a total brainwashing of the regime began. A new enemy of the executive was created—the so called council of the subjects of the federation. It is now difficult to say whether there was more political ignorance and naivety or cool calculation behind this move. For it is clear that every step in this direction was a strike at the state, at Russia's unity and integrity.

Each step of this sort enhanced the aggressiveness and insolence of those who opted for violence and aggressiveness.

I think that the constitutional court has to take much of the blame for what has come to pass. This agency has long since abandoned its most important principle—the court's independence from political time-serving.

It has long since turned into a persecutor of the executive and connived with the legislative power.

The court appeared to overlook how endless amendments violated the Russian constitution. Overlook the glaring contradictions in the constitution which were deliberately enhanced by the congress.

I want to say a few words in particular about the soviets (councils).

There are people's deputies in each of them who favor reforms, but despite this, the stance of most of them after September 21 practically implied that they prejudiciously justified any actions of the former supreme soviet. More, they were being provoked and pushed towards violence with all sorts of hints at support. I have no doubt that should the mutineers have won, most of the soviets (councils) would have voiced support for them.

I announce with full responsibility: most bodies of Soviet power are directly responsible for the extreme aggravation of the situation in Moscow. The system of soviets showed full disregard for the security of the state and its citizens and thus put a full stop to its own political life....

They failed to split the country, to split the army and the state.

But the problems exposed by the mutiny are extremely serious. We need a normal democratic constitution as we need air to breathe. We need a united Russia. Playing at regional isolation is contrary to the interests and will of the majority of the country's population. We need full reform of the army and security agencies.

We need to consistently carry on economic transformations and support for all efforts the government makes in this direction.

In order to restore law and order, restore peace and eventually purge Moscow of the militants, the state of emergency was introduced in the capital for one week. Depending on the circumstances, its term may be cut short or prolonged somewhat.

Most Muscovities and citizens of Russia understand and back the need for this tough measure.

Along with this, some tough measures stipulated in the law on the state of emergency are superfluous in the present situation. The lifting of preliminary censorship in the media has already been ordered.

But I would like to warn (people). If you think that the situation is completely back to normal, you are making a big mistake. Passions have not yet abated. Any careless, irresponsible word can enflame them again. I am appealing to the sense of civic responsibility of journalists.

Dear Russians, the most fearful things are now past. But in order to make peace and quiet inviolable in our country, we must pool efforts in strengthening our state, strengthening democracy, elections to the federal assembly—and, I believe, new local bodies of representative power—will take place on December 12.

All politicians, parties and movements who have not smeared themselves with direct involvement in the mutiny are guaranteed equal opportunities.

In the past few days we came to understand the immense cost of political indifference. It is unable to save anyone or secure personal safety. Can one sleep quietly when one's house is being set on fire?

I am calling on you, dear compatriots, to take an active part in the elections and vote for the worthiest, most competent, clever and intelligent people. Those who are unable to betray.

Dear Compatriots,

The nightmare of the black days is over. Do not say that someone has won and someone lost. At this moment, these are inappropriate, blasphemous words. We have all been scorched by the deadly breath of fratricide.

People have died, our compatriots. They cannot be brought back. Grief and suffering have entered many families.

No matter how different outlooks may be, all of them are children of Russia, this is our common tragedy, our common grief, great grief.

Let us remember this insanity in order to never let it recur.

CLINTON'S HEALTH CARE PLAN

September 22 and October 21, 1993

Addressing a joint session of Congress September 22, President Bill Clinton launched a far-reaching plan for reforming the country's health care system. In its scope, the plan was the most ambitious domestic reform proposed by any president in decades. It was certain to dominate all of Clinton's domestic initiatives in his first term.

The Clinton administration task force that developed the proposal over a period of eight months was headed by Hillary Rodham Clinton, the president's wife. The first lady also vigorously promoted the complex plan before congressional committees and in numerous speeches across the country.

The 1,364-page health care reform bill that the administration presented to Congress had two goals: first, to establish universal health insurance coverage and, second, to control rapidly advancing health care costs. The plan was designed to bring the 39 million Americans lacking health insurance into the system by extending job-based coverage. It was also aimed at containing medical costs by establishing about two hundred regional health alliances to serve as brokers between consumers and their health care providers.

By the end of the year, a number of competing health care reform bills had been introduced into Congress by members with diverse political backgrounds. Critics of the president's plan focused on its huge management and regulatory implications. Still, most observers believed that, although the legislative warfare would be fierce, a health care reform measure would be enacted in 1994.

The first lady said that the Clinton proposal was "negotiable." But she insisted that alternative plans that failed to guarantee universal coverage and a comprehensive set of health services would not meet that fundamental test. In an October 21 speech in Chicago, she stated, "Every single American deserves to have health insurance at an affordable cost to himself and his family."

Background

Among the world's industrialized countries, only the United States lacks a system of national health insurance. Germany established a comprehensive health insurance system in 1883, and it survived two world wars. President Clinton called the U.S. situation a "national disgrace."

The earliest push in the United States for national health insurance came in President Franklin D. Roosevelt's first term. Appointed by Roosevelt, the same Committee on Economic Security that recommended Social Security also proposed health insurance for all Americans. The Social Security program was enacted in 1935, but compulsory health insurance was defeated by the opposition of the American Medical Association. In 1943 Sen. Robert F. Wagner, D-N.Y., Sen. James E. Murray, D-Mont., and Rep. John Dingell, Sr., D-Mich., introduced a bill calling for a national health insurance system financed by a payroll tax. Once again, the plan was defeated by the opposition of organized medicine.

President Lyndon B. Johnson in 1965 signed into law the Medicare program for the elderly and the Medicaid program, the state-federal health insurance system for the poor. It represented the last successful effort by the federal government to expand guaranteed health coverage.

In 1992 health care became an issue in the presidential election campaign. President George Bush presented his health care reform plan, which relied on vouchers, tax incentives, insurance reform, and less red tape. Democrats backed several plans including a single-payer proposal and an employer mandate known as "play or pay."

Impetus for Reform

In recent years, spending on health care had gone up nearly 10 percent annually, far outstripping the general rate of inflation. But the escalation of costs was only one reason why basic change had become urgent for many Americans. The steady increase in the number of Americans without insurance included many children. Moreover, the proportion of workers who obtained insurance through their jobs was falling as employers cut back coverage. Statistics showed that 85 percent of the uninsured were workers and their dependents. In addition, the drive for reform was fueled by the still larger number of Americans who had insurance but feared losing it.

Americans spent about $832 billion on health care in 1992, amounting to about 14 percent of the gross domestic product. Many Americans agreed that the risks and fears could be eased only by the establishment of a strong government role.

Clinton's Speech

In his September 22 speech Clinton spelled out his prescription for an ailing health care system. "We must fix this system," he said, "and it has to begin with congressional action."

He also told his audience that with his plan, "If you lose your job, or switch jobs, you're covered. If you leave your job to start a small business, you're covered. If you're an early retiree, you're covered."

Writing in the September 25 issue of the CQ Weekly Report, *Allison J. Rubin and Janet Hook said that during the hour the president spoke, "members of Congress shared a sense of optimism and common purpose." And Rep. Ron Wyden, D-Ore., was quoted in the press as saying of the speech, "He created a sense that change is inevitable; people have been very skeptical."*

First Lady's Role

In the course of pressing for the Clinton health care reform plan, Hillary Clinton appeared as a witness at hearings conducted by three House committees, Ways and Means, Energy and Commerce, and Education and Labor; and two Senate committees, Finance and Labor and Human Relations. She was lauded for her work with the task force and as an advocate of the administration's plan. Her testimony before the Ways and Means Committee was lavishly praised by its chairman, Rep. Dan Rostenkowski, D-Ill. Roskenkowski told her, "I'm tempted to applaud you. . . . You were marvelous."

A more cautionary note was struck by Sen. Daniel Patrick Moynihan, D-N.Y., chairman of the Senate Finance Committee. Moynihan reminded the first lady that "over the last quarter century, we have all been wrong" in predicting the true cost of entitlement programs.

Regional Health Alliances

At the core of Clinton's plan would be the creation of about two hundred regional health alliances. In effect, the alliances would serve as large health insurance purchasing cooperatives. All employers, except those with more than five thousand workers, would be required to buy insurance for their employees from these alliances. Employers would be required to pay 80 percent and the workers 20 percent of the premium cost. Large corporations, those with more than five thousand workers, could buy insurance directly from health plans, in a sense acting as "alliances" themselves.

The rationale underlying the health alliances was that a large collection of consumers would be far more effective in obtaining the lowest price for health care than an individual or small business acting alone. Describing the alliances, Ira Magaziner, the Clinton administration's senior health policy adviser, explained the administration's position, saying, "We view them as a kind of brokering agent. We don't want them to be regulatory bodies."

Employer Mandates

Another major aspect of the plan involved the way payments for private insurance would be financed. Under the plan, 80 percent of workers' insurance premiums would be paid by employers. (This provision became known as the "employer mandate.") The regressive nature of the plan would be softened by the federal government's subsidizing the payments of small businesses and low-income workers.

In the months following the introduction of Clinton's massive measure, the regional health alliances and the employer mandate became the most hotly debated parts of the entire plan. The alliances particularly were criticized for representing a new layer of bureaucracy. For example, Rep. Jim McDermott, D-Wash., a supporter of a single-payer system, under which the government would directly pay for health insurance, said of the alliances, "You are looking at the beginning of a monstrous and potentially powerful agency."

Spokesmen for the administration countered that even if the alliances did constitute "bureaucracy," it would be just "one bureaucracy replacing thousands of inefficient bureaucracies" that, they said, characterized the current situation.

Paying for the Plan

The president's plan would meet the cost of bringing 39 million Americans into the health insurance system by increasing taxes on tobacco, imposing a tax on large corporations choosing to insure themselves, and reducing the growth in the cost of Medicare and Medicaid. Over five years, the growth in Medicare would be reduced by $124 billion and the growth in Medicaid by $114 billion.

Administration officials said that while the massive plan would cost the government an extra $350 billion over the first five years, the financing method and cost constraints would, in six years, reduce the budget deficit by $59 billion.

Other Provisions

While the debate over the Clinton measure rapidly focused on the regional health alliances and on the employer mandate, a number of other provisions also promised profound economic changes. For example, in a major regulatory move, the federal government would impose a limit on how much health insurance premiums could rise each year. The architects of the plan saw the move as suppressing rising health care costs throughout the entire system.

A new National Health Board would be established to regulate a standard health care benefits package, and the Department of Health and Human Services would be called on to oversee the entire system. The plan would provide, for the first time, a prescription drug benefit for Medicare beneficiaries.

Finally, under the health plan proposed by Clinton, the federal government would stop insurance companies from denying insurance coverage to the elderly and to people with health problems.

Following are the text of President Bill Clinton's address to a joint session of Congress on September 22 and the text of First Lady Hillary Clinton's October 21 remarks at a health care briefing in Chicago, Illinois:

PRESIDENT CLINTON'S SPEECH

...My fellow Americans, tonight we come together to write a new chapter in the American story. Our forebears enshrined the American dream: life, liberty, the pursuit of happiness. Every generation of Americans has worked to strengthen that legacy to make our country a place of freedom and opportunity, a place where people who work hard can rise to their full potential, a place where their children can have a better future.

From the settling of the frontier to the landing on the Moon, ours has been a continuous story of challenges defined, obstacles overcome, new horizons secured. That is what makes America what it is and Americans what we are.

Now we are in a time of profound change and opportunity. The end of the cold war, the information age, the global economy have brought us both opportunity and hope and strife and uncertainty. Our purpose in this dynamic age must be to make change our friend and not our enemy. To achieve that goal we must face all our challenges with confidence, with faith and with discipline, whether we are reducing the deficit, creating tomorrow's jobs and training our people to fill them, converting from a high-tech defense to a high-tech domestic economy, expanding trade, reinventing government, making our streets safer, or rewarding work over idleness. All these challenges require us to change.

If Americans are to have the courage to change in a difficult time, we must first be secure in our most basic needs. Tonight I want to talk to you about the most critical thing we can do to build that security.

This health care system of ours is badly broken, and it is time to fix it.

Despite the dedication of literally millions of talented health care professionals, our health care is too uncertain and too expensive, too bureaucratic and too wasteful. It has too much fraud and too much greed. At long last, after decades of false starts, we must make this our most urgent priority, giving every American health security, health care that can never be taken away, health care that is always there. That is what we must do.

On this journey, as on all others of true consequences, there will be rough spots in the road and honest disagreements about how we should proceed. After all, this is a complicated issue. But every successful journey is guided by fixed stars, and if we can agree on some basic values and principles, we will reach this destination and we will reach it together.

So tonight I want to talk to you about the principles that I believe must embody our efforts to reform America's health care system: security, simplicity, savings, choice, quality, and responsibility.

When I launched our Nation on this journey to reform the health care system, I knew we needed a talented navigator, someone with a rigorous mind, a steady compass, a caring heart. Luckily for me and for our Nation, I did not have to look very far.

[*At this point, the Chamber applauded Hillary Clinton, and she acknowledged them.*]

Over the last 8 months, Hillary and those working with her have talked to literally thousands of Americans to understand the strengths and the frailties of this system of ours. They met with over 1,100 health care organizations. They talked with doctors and nurses, pharmacists and drug company representatives, hospital administrators, insurance company executives and small and large businesses. They spoke with self-employed people. They talked with people who had insurance and people who did not. They talked with union members, and older Americans, and advocates for our children. The First Lady also consulted, as all of you know, extensively with governmental leaders in both parties, in the States of our Nation, and especially here on Capitol Hill.

Hillary and the task force received and read over 700,000 letters from ordinary citizens. What they wrote and the bravery with which they told their stories is really what calls us all here tonight. Every one of us knows someone who has worked hard and played by the rules and still been hurt by this system that just does not work for too many people, but I would like to tell you about just one.

Kerry Kennedy owns a small furniture store that employs seven people in Titusville, Florida. Like most small business owners, he has poured his heart and soul, his sweat and blood into that business for years. But over the last several years, again like most small business owners, he has seen his health care premiums skyrocket, even in years when no claims were made. And last year he painfully discovered he could no longer afford to provide coverage for all his workers because his insurance company told him that two of his workers had become high risks because of their advanced age. The problem was that those two people were his mother and father, the people who founded the business and still work in the store.

This story speaks for millions of others. And from them we have learned a powerful truth: We have to preserve and strengthen what is right with the health care system, but we have got to fix what is wrong with it.

Now, we all know what is right. We are blessed with the best health care professionals on Earth, the finest health care institutions, the best medical research, the most sophisticated technology. My mother is a nurse. I grew up around hospitals. Doctors and nurses were the first professional people I ever knew and learned to look up to. They are what is right with this health care system. But we also know that we can no longer afford to continue to ignore what is wrong.

Millions of Americans are just a pink slip away from losing their health insurance, and one serious illness away from losing all their savings. Millions more are locked into the jobs they have now just because they or someone in their family has once been sick and they have what is called a preexisting condition.

And on any given day over 37 million Americans, most of them working people and their little children, have no health insurance at all.

And in spite of all this, our medical bills are growing at over twice the rate of inflation, and the United States spends over a third more of its income on health care than any other nation on Earth. And the gap is growing, causing many of our companies in global competition severe disadvantage. There is no excuse for this kind of system. We know other people have done better. We know people in our own country are doing better. We have no excuse. My fellow Americans, we must fix this system, and it has to begin with congressional action.

I believe as strongly as I can say that we can reform the costliest and most wasteful system on the face of the Earth without enacting new broad-based taxes. I believe it because of the conversations I have had with thousands of health care professionals around the country, with people who are outside this city but are inside experts on the way this system works and wastes money.

The proposal that I describe tonight borrows many of the principles and ideas that have been embraced in plans introduced by both Republicans and Democrats in this Congress. For the first time in this century, leaders of both political parties have joined together around the principle of providing universal, comprehensive health care. It is a magic moment, and we must seize it.

I want to say to all of you I have been deeply moved by the spirit of this debate, by the openness of all people to new ideas and argument and information. The American people will be proud to know that earlier this week when a health care university was held for Members of Congress, just to try to give everybody the same amount of information, over 320 Republicans and Democrats signed up and showed up for two days just to learn the basic facts of the complicated problem before us.

Both sides are willing to say, "We have listened to the people. We know the cost of going forward with this system is far greater than the cost of change." Both sides, I think, understand the literal ethical imperative of doing something about the system we have now. Rising above these difficulties and our past differences to solve this problem will go a long way toward defining who we are and who we intend to be as a people in this difficult and challenging era. I believe we all understand that. And so tonight let me ask all of you, every Member of the House, every Member of the Senate, each Republican and each Democrat, let us keep this spirit and let us keep this commitment until this job is done. We owe it to the American people. [*Applause*]

Thank you. Thank you very much.

Now, if I might, I would like to review the six principles I mentioned earlier and describe how we think we can best fulfill those principles.

First and most important, security. This principle speaks to the human misery, to the costs, to the anxiety we hear about every day, all of us, when people talk about their problems with the present system. Security means that those who do not now have health care coverage will have it, and for those who have it, it will never be taken away. We must achieve that security as soon as possible.

Under our plan every American will receive a health care security card that will guarantee a comprehensive package of benefits over the course of an entire lifetime, roughly comparable to the benefit packages offered by most Fortune 500 companies. This health care security card will offer this package of benefits in a way that can never be taken away. So let us agree on this, whatever else we disagree on: Before this Congress finishes its work next year, you will pass and I will sign legislation to guarantee this security to every citizen of this country. With this card, if you lose your job or you switch jobs, you are covered. If you leave your job to start a small business, you are covered. If you are an early retiree, you are covered. If someone in your family has unfortunately had an illness that qualifies as a preexisting condition, you are still covered. If you get sick or a member of your family gets sick, even if it is a life-threatening illness, you are covered. And if an insurance company tries to drop you for any reason, you will still be covered because that will be illegal. This card will give comprehensive coverage. It will cover people for hospital care, doctor visits, emergency and lab services, diagnostic services like Pap smears and mammograms and cholesterol tests, substance abuse, and mental health treatment.

And equally important, for both health care and economic reasons, this program for the first time will provide a broad range of preventive services, including regular check-ups and well-baby visits. It is just common sense. We know, any family doctor will tell you, that people will stay healthier and long-term costs to the health system will be lower if we have comprehensive preventive services. You know how all of our mothers told us that an ounce of prevention was worth a pound of cure? Our mothers were right. And it is a lesson, like so many lessons from our mothers, that we have waited too long to live by. It is time to start doing it.

Health care security must also apply to older Americans. This is something I imagine all of us in this room feel very deeply about. The first thing I want to say about that is that we must retain the Medicare program. It works to provide that kind of security. But this time, and for the first time, I believe Medicare should provide coverage for the cost of prescription drugs.

Yes, it will cost some more in the beginning. But again, any physician who deals with the elderly will tell you that there are thousands of elderly people in every State who are not poor enough to be on Medicaid but just above that line and on Medicare, who desperately need medicine, who make decisions every week between medicine and food. Any doctor who deals with the elderly will tell you that there are many elderly people who don't get medicine, who get sicker and sicker and eventually go to the doctor, and wind up spending more money and draining more money from the health care system than they would if they had regular treatment in the way that only adequate medicine can provide.

I also believe that, over time, we should phase in long-term care for the disabled and the elderly on a comprehensive basis. As we proceed with this health care reform, we cannot forget that the most rapidly growing percentage of Americans are those over 80. We cannot break faith with them. We have to do better by them.

The second principle is simplicity. Our health care system must be simpler for the patients and simpler for those who actually deliver health care: our doctors, our nurses, our other medical professionals. Today we have more than 1,500 insurers with hundreds and hundreds of different forms. No other nation has a system like this. These forms are time-consuming for health care providers, they are expensive for health care consumers, they are exasperating for anyone who has ever tried to sit down around a table and wade through them and figure them out. The medical industry is literally drowning in paperwork. In recent years the number of administrators in our hospitals has grown by four times the rate that the number of doctors has grown. A hospital ought to be a house of healing, not a monument to paperwork and bureaucracy.

Just a few days ago, the Vice President and I had the honor of visiting the Children's Hospital here in Washington, where they do wonderful, often miraculous things for very sick children. A nurse named Debbie Feinberg told us that she is in the cancer and bone marrow unit, and the other day a little boy asked her just to stay at his side during his chemotherapy. And she had to walk away from that child because she had been instructed to go to yet another class to learn how to fill out another form for something that didn't have a lick to do with the health care of the children she was helping. That is wrong, and we can stop it, and we ought to do it.

We met a very compelling doctor named Lillian Beard who said that she did not get into her profession to spend hours and hours, some doctors up to 25 hours a week, just filling out forms. She told us she became a doctor to keep children well and to help save those who got sick. We can relieve people like her of this burden. We learned, the Vice President and I did, that in the Washington Children's Hospital alone, the administrators told us that they spend $2 million a year, in one hospital, filling out forms that have nothing whatever to do with keeping up with the treatment of the patients.

And the doctors there applauded when I was told and I related to them that they spend so much time filling out paperwork that, if they only had to fill out those paperwork requirements necessary to monitor the health of the children, each doctor on that one hospital staff, 200 of them, could see another 500 children a year. That is 10,000 children a year. I think we can save money in this system if we simplify it. And we can make the doctors and the nurses and the people that have given their lives to help us all be healthier a whole lot happier, too, on their jobs.

Under our proposal there would be one standard insurance form, not hundreds of them. We will simplify also, and we must, the Government's rules and regulations because they are a big part of this problem. This is one of those cases where the physician should heal thyself. We have to reinvent the way we relate to the health care system along with reinventing Government. A doctor should not have to check with a bureaucrat in an office thousands of miles away before ordering a simple blood test; that is not right, and we can change it. And doctors, nurses, and consumers should not have to worry about the fine print. If we have this one simple form, there will not be any fine print. People will know what it means.

The third principle is savings. Reform must produce savings in this health care system; it has to. We are spending over 14 percent of our income on health care; Canada is at 10; nobody else is over 9. We are competing with all these people for the future. And the other major countries, they cover everybody, and they cover them with services as generous as the best company policies here in this country.

Rampant medical inflation is eating away at our wages, our savings, our investment capital, our ability to create new jobs in the private sector and this public Treasury. You know the budget we just adopted had steep cuts in defense, a 5-year freeze on the discretionary spending so critical to reeducating America, and investing in jobs and helping us to convert from a defense to a domestic economy. But we passed a budget which has Medicaid increases of between 16 and 11 percent a year over the next 5 years and Medicare increases of between 11 and 9 percent in an environment where we assume inflation will be at 4 percent or less. We cannot continue to do this. Our competitiveness, our whole economy, the integrity of the way the Government works, and ultimately our living standards depend upon our ability to achieve savings without harming the quality of health care.

Unless we do this, our workers will lose $655 in income each year by the end of the decade. Small businesses will continue to face skyrocketing premiums, and a full third of small businesses now covering their employees say they will be forced to drop their insurance. Large corporations will bear bigger disadvantages in global competition, and health care costs will devour more and more and more of our budget. Pretty soon all of you, or the people who succeed you, will be showing up here and writing out checks for health care and interest on the debt and worrying about whether we have got enough defense, and that will be it, unless we have the courage to achieve the savings that are plainly there before us. Every State and local government will continue to cut back on everything from education to law enforcement to pay more and more for the same health care.

These rising costs are a special nightmare for our small businesses, the engine of our entrepreneurship and our job creation in America today. Health care premiums for small businesses are 35 percent higher than those of large corporations today, and they will keep rising at double-digit rates unless we act.

So how will we achieve these savings? Rather than looking at price controls or looking away as the price spiral continues, rather than using the heavy hand of Government to try to control what is happening or continuing to ignore what is happening, we believe there is a third way to achieve these savings: First, to give groups of consumers and small businesses the same market bargaining power that large corporations and large groups of public employees now have. We want to let market forces enable plans to compete. We want to force these plans to compete on the basis of price and quality, not simply to allow them to continue making money by turning people away who are sick or old or performing mountains of unnecessary procedures. But we also believe we should back this system up with limits on how much plans can raise their premiums year in and year out, forcing people again to continue to pay more for the same health care without regard to inflation or the rising population needs.

We want to create what has been missing in this system for too long and what every successful nation who has dealt with this problem has already had to do: to have a combination of private market forces and a sound public policy that will support that competition but limit the rate at which prices can exceed the rate of inflation and population growth if the competition does not work, especially in the early going.

The second thing I want to say is that, unless everybody is covered—and this is a very important thing—unless everybody is covered, we will never be able to fully put the brakes on health care inflation. Why is that? Because when people do not have any health insurance, they still get health care; but they get it when it is too late, when it is too expensive, often from the most expensive place of all: the emergency room. Usually by the time they show up, their illnesses are more severe and their mortality rates are much higher in our hospitals than those who have insurance. So they cost us more. And what else happens? Since they get the care but they do not pay, who does pay? All the rest of us. We pay in higher hospital bills and higher insurance premiums. This cost shifting is a major problem.

The third thing we can do to save money is simply by simplifying the system, what we have already discussed. Freeing the health care providers from these costly and unnecessary paperwork and administrative decisions will save tens of billions of dollars. We spend twice as much as any other major country does on paperwork. We spend at least a dime on the dollar more than any other major country. That is a stunning statistic, and it is something that every Republican and every Democrat ought to be able to say: "We agree that we are going to squeeze this out; we cannot tolerate this. This has nothing to do with keeping people well or helping them when they are sick." We should invest the money in something else.

We also have to crack down on fraud and abuse in the system. That drains billions of dollars a year. It is a very large figure, according to every health care expert I have ever spoken with. I believe we can achieve large savings, and that large savings can be used to cover the unemployed, uninsured, and will be used for people who realize those savings in the private sector to increase their ability to invest and grow, to hire new workers or to give their workers pay raises, many of them for the first time in years.

Now, nobody has to take my word for this; you can ask Dr. Koop. He is up here with us tonight, and I thank him for being here. Since he left his distinguished tenure as our Surgeon General, he has spent an enormous amount of time studying our health care system, how it operates, what is right and wrong with it. He says we could [save] $200 billion every year, more than 20 percent of the total budget, without sacrificing the high quality of American medicine.

Ask the public employees in California, who have held their own premiums down by adopting the same strategy that I want every American to be able to adopt, bargaining within the limits of a strict budget. Ask Xerox, which saved an estimated thousand dollars per worker on their health insurance premium. Ask the staff of the Mayo Clinic, who we all agree provides some of the finest health care in the world. They are holding their cost increases to less than half the national average. Ask the people of Hawaii, the only State that covers virtually all of their citizens and have still been able to keep costs below the national average.

People may disagree over the best way to fix this system. We may all disagree about how quickly we can do what, the thing that we have to do; but we cannot disagree that we can find tens of billions of dollars in savings in what is clearly the most costly and the most bureaucratic system in the entire world. And we have to do something about that, and we have to do it now.

The fourth principle is choice. Americans believe they ought to be able to choose their own health care plans and keep their own doctors. And I think all of us agree. Under any plan we pass, they ought to have that right. But today under our broken health care system, in spite of the rhetoric of choice, the fact is that that power is slipping away from more and more Americans.

Of course it is usually the employer, not the employee, who makes the initial choice of what health care plan the employee will be in. And if your employer offers only one plan, as nearly three-quarters of small- and medium-size firms do today, you are stuck with that plan and the doctors that it covers.

We propose to give every American a choice among high quality plans. You can stay with your current doctor, join a network of doctors and hospitals, or join a health maintenance organization. If you do not like your plan, every year you will have the chance to choose a new one. The choice will be left to the American citizen, the worker, not the boss, and certainly not some Government bureaucrat.

We also believe that doctors should have a choice as to what plans they practice in; otherwise citizens may have their own choices limited. We want to end the discrimination that is now growing against doctors and to permit them to practice in several different plans. Choice is important for doctors, and it is absolutely critical for our consumers. We have got to have it in whatever plan we pass.

The fifth principle is quality. If we reform everything else in health care but fail to preserve and enhance the high quality of our medical care, we will have taken a step backward, not forward. Quality is something that we simply can't leave to chance. When you board an airplane, you feel better knowing that the plane had to meet the standards designed to protect your safety, and we can not ask any less of our health care system.

Our proposal will create report cards on health plans, so that consumers can choose the highest quality health care providers and reward them with their business. At the same time, our plan will track quality indicators so that doctors can make better and smarter choices of the kind of care they provide. We have evidence that more efficient delivery of health care doesn't decrease quality. In fact, it may enhance it.

Let me just give you one example of one commonly performed procedure, the coronary bypass operation. Pennsylvania discovered that patients who were charged $21,000 for this surgery received as good or better care as patients who were charged $84,000 for the same procedure in the same State. High prices simply don't always equal good quality. Our plan will guarantee that high quality information is available in even the most remote areas of this country, so that we can have high quality service, linking rural doctors, for example, with hospitals, with high-technology urban medical centers. And our plan will ensure the quality of continuing progress on a whole range of issues by speeding research on effective prevention and treatment measures for cancer, for AIDS, for Alzheimer's, for heart disease, and for other chronic diseases. We have to safeguard the finest medical research establishment in the entire world, and we will do that with this plan. Indeed, we will even make it better.

The sixth and final principle is responsibility. We need to restore a sense that we are all in this together and that we all have a responsibility to be a part of the solution. Responsibility has to start with those who profit from the current system. Responsibility means insurance companies should no longer be allowed to cast people aside when they get sick. It should apply to laboratories that submit fraudulent bills, to lawyers who abuse malpractice claims, to doctors who order unnecessary procedures. It means drug companies should no longer charge three times more for prescription drugs made in America here in the United States than they charge for the same drugs overseas.

In short, responsibility should apply to anybody who abuses this system and drives up the cost for honest, hard-working citizens, and undermines confidence in the honest, gifted health care providers we have. Responsibility also means changing some behaviors in this country that drive up our costs like crazy, and without charging them we will never have the system we ought to have. We will never.

Let me just mention a few, and start with the most important. The outrageous costs of violence in this country stem in large measure from the fact that this is the only country in the world where teenagers can walk the streets at random with semiautomatic weapons and be better armed than the police. Let us not kid ourselves. It is not that simple. We also have higher rates of AIDS, of smoking and excessive drinking, of teen pregnancy, of low birth weight babies, and we have the third worst immunization rate of any nation in the Western Hemisphere. We have to change our ways if we ever really want to be healthy as a people and have an affordable health care system, and no one can deny that.

But let me say this, and I hope every American will listen, because this is not an easy thing to hear. Responsibility in our health care system is not just about them. It is about you. It is about me. It is about each of us. Too many of us have not taken responsibility for our own health care and for our own relations to the health care system. Many of us who have had fully paid health care plans have used the system whether we needed it or not, without thinking what the costs were. Many people who use this system do not pay a penny for their care, even though they can afford to. I think those who do not have any health insurance should be responsible for paying a portion of their new coverage. There cannot be any something for nothing, and we have to demonstrate that to people. This is not a free system. Even small contributions, as small as a $10 copayment when you visit a doctor, illustrate that this is something of value. There is a cost to it. It is not free.

And I want to tell you that I believe that all of us should have insurance. Why should the rest of us pick up the tab when a guy who does not think he needs insurance or says he cannot afford it gets in an accident, winds up in an emergency room, gets good care, and everybody else pays? Why should the small business people who are struggling to keep afloat and take care of their employees have to pay to maintain this wonderful health care infrastructure for those who refuse to do anything? If we are going to produce a better health care system for every one of us, every one of us is going to have to do our part. There cannot be any such thing as a free ride. We have to pay for it. We have to pay for it.

Tonight I want to say plainly how I think we should do that. Most of the money would come, under my way of thinking, as it does today, from premiums paid by employers and individuals. That is the way it happens today. But under this health care security plan, every employer and every individual will be asked to contribute something to help here.

This concept was first conveyed to the Congress about 20 years ago by President Nixon, and today a lot of people agree with the concept of shared responsibility between employers and employees, and that the best thing to do is to ask every employer and every employee to share that. The Chamber of Commerce has said that, and they are not in the business of hurting small business. The American Medical Association has said that.

Some call it an employer mandate, but I think it is the fairest way to achieve responsibility in the health care system, and it is the easiest for ordinary Americans to understand, because it builds on what we already have and what already works for so many Americans. It is the reform that is not only easiest to understand but easiest to implement in a way that is fair to small business, because we can give a discount to help struggling small businesses meet the cost of covering their employees. We should require the least bureaucracy or disruption and create the cooperation we need to make the system cost-conscious even as we expand coverage, and we should do it in a way that does not cripple small businesses and low-wage workers.

Every employer should provide coverage, just as three-quarters do now. Those who pay are picking up the tab for those who do not today. I do not think that is right. To finance the rest of reform, we can achieve new savings, as I have outlined, in both the Federal Government and the private sector through better decisionmaking and increased competition. And we will impose new taxes on tobacco. I do not think that should be the only source of revenues. I believe we should also ask for a modest contribution from big employers who opt out of the system, to make up for that those who are in the system pay for medical research, for health education centers, for all of the subsidies to small business, for all of the things that everyone else is contributing to. But between those two things, we believe we can pay for this package of benefits and universal coverage and a subsidy program that will help small business.

These sources can cover the cost of the proposal that I have described tonight. We subjected the numbers in our proposal to the scrutiny of not only all the major agencies in Government. I know a lot of people don't trust them, but it would be interesting for the American people to know that this was the first time that the financial experts on health care in all the different Government agencies had ever been required to sit in a room together and agree on numbers. It had never happened before. But obviously that is not enough, so then we gave these numbers to actuaries from major accounting firms and major Fortune 500 companies who have no stake in this, other than to see that our efforts succeed. So I believe our numbers are good and achievable.

Now what does this mean to an individual American citizen? Some will be asked to pay more. If you are an employer and you are not insuring your workers at all, you will have to pay more. But if you are a small business with fewer than 50 employees, you will get a subsidy. If you are a firm that provides only very limited coverage, you may have to pay more, but some firms will pay the same or less for more coverage.

If you are a young single person in your twenties, and you are already insured, your rates may go up somewhat because you are going to go into a big pool with middle-aged people and older people, and we want to enable people to keep that insurance even when someone in their family gets sick. But I think that is fair, because when the young get older they will benefit from it, first; and, second, even those who pay a little more today will benefit four, five, six, seven years from now by our bringing health care costs closer to inflation.

Over the long run we can all win, but some will have to pay more in the short run. Nevertheless, the vast majority of the Americans watching this tonight will pay the same or less for health care coverage that will be the same or better than the coverage they have tonight. That is the simple reality.

If you currently get your health insurance through your job, you still will. And for the first time, everybody will get to choose from among at least three plans to belong to. If you are a small business owner who wants to provide health insurance to your family and your employees but you cannot afford it because the system is stacked against you, this plan will give you a discount that will finally make insurance affordable. If you are already providing insurance, your rates may well drop because we will help you as a small business person join thousands of others to get the same benefits big corporations get at the same price they get those benefits. If you are self-employed, you will pay less, and you will get to deduct from your taxes 100 percent of your health care premiums. If you are a large employer, your health care costs will not go up as fast, so that you will have more money to put into higher wages, and new jobs, and to put into the work of being competitive in this tough global economy.

Now, these, my fellow Americans, are the principles on which I think we should base our efforts: security, simplicity, savings, choice, quality, and responsibility. These are guiding stars that we should follow on our journey toward health care reform.

Over the coming months you will be bombarded with information from all kinds of sources. There will be some who will stoutly disagree with what I have proposed, and with all other plans in the Congress for that matter. And some of the arguments will be genuinely sincere and enlightening; others may simply be scare tactics by those who are motivated by the self-interests they have in the waste the system now generates, because that waste is providing jobs, incomes, and money for some people. I ask you only to think of this when you hear all these arguments: Ask yourself whether the cost of staying on this same course is not greater than the cost of change. And ask yourself when you hear the arguments whether the arguments are in your interests or someone else's. This is something we have got to try to do together.

I want also to say to the Representatives in Congress, you have a special duty to look beyond these arguments. I ask you instead to look into the eyes of the sick child who needs care; to think of the face of the woman who has been told not only that her condition is malignant, but not covered by her insurance; to look at the bottom lines of the businesses driven to bankruptcy by health care costs; to look at the "for sale" signs in front of the homes of families who have lost everything because of their health care costs.

I ask you to remember the kind of people I have met for the last year and a half: the elderly couple in New Hampshire that broke down and cried because of their shame at having an empty refrigerator to pay for their drugs; a woman who lost a $50,000 job that she used to support her six children because her youngest child was so ill that she could not keep health insurance and the only way to get care for the child was to get public assistance; a young couple that had a sick child and could only get insurance from one of the parents' employers that was a nonprofit corporation with 20 employees, and so they had to face the question of whether to let this poor person with the sick child go or raise the premiums of every employee in the firm by $200. And on and on and on.

I know we have differences of opinion, but we are here tonight in a spirit that is animated by the problems of those people and by the sure knowledge that, if we can look into our hearts, we will not be able to say that the greatest Nation in the history of the world is powerless to confront this crisis.

Our history and our heritage tell us that we can meet this challenge. Everything about America's past tells us we will do it. So I say to you, "Let us write that new chapter in the American story. Let us guarantee every American comprehensive health benefits that can never be taken away."

You know, in spite of all the work we have done together and all the progress we have made, there are still a lot of people who say it would be an outright miracle if we passed health care reform. But, my fellow Americans, in a time of change you have to have miracles; and miracles do happen. I mean, just a few days ago we saw a simple handshake shatter decades of deadlock in the Middle East. We have seen the walls crumble in Berlin and South Africa. We see the ongoing brave struggle of the people of Russia to seize freedom and democracy.

And now it is our turn to strike a blow for freedom in this country, the freedom of Americans to live without fear that their own Nation's health care system will not be there for them when they need it. It is hard to believe that there was once a time in this century when that kind of fear gripped old age, when retirement was nearly synonymous with poverty, and older Americans died in the street. That is unthinkable today because over a half a century ago Americans had the courage to change, to create a Social Security system that ensures that no Americans will be forgotten in their later years.

Forty years from now our grandchildren will also find it unthinkable that there was a time in this country when hard-working families lost their homes, their savings, their businesses, lost everything simply because their children got sick or because they had to change jobs. Our grandchildren will find such things unthinkable tomorrow if we have the courage to change today.

This is our chance. This is our journey. And when our work is done, we will know that we have answered the call of history and met the challenge of our time.

Thank you very much and God bless America.

HILLARY CLINTON'S SPEECH

... What I would like to do is briefly review for you what we are attempting to accomplish with health care reform. And then I would like the opportunity to answer questions. And I think we have arranged to have a microphone that can travel around and try to get to people and have a chance to take some questions.

Because I hope that your presence here this afternoon signals your commitment to be part of what will be the most important domestic discussion that we've had in our country for a very long time.

We have to resolve the crises in health care that [are] not only making human costs unbearable but are putting the kind of strains on our economic systems at the city, the state, the national level that we cannot go on. In order to do that, all of us have to be part of the solution.

Now, when the President spoke before Congress, he outlined six principles that we want to hold firm to as we go forward in this discussion. As I mention each of those and give you an example, I want you to try to think how they will affect your personal health care future, because each of us has a stake in the outcome of this debate.

The first principle and the most important one is security. And when I say health security, I'm not talking just about people who don't have insurance. Although in this State, like every other State, there are millions who do not. I am talking about all of us who are currently insured as well, because every month in America, 2.25 million Americans lose their health insurance.

Now, maybe they only lose it for a week or maybe for a month, but sometimes they don't get it back. Sometimes that layoff or that job loss happens at just the wrong time. Sometimes when they have lost the insurance, it is just at that most tragic moment that the accident occurs or the illness is discovered. And then they have something called a "preexisting condition," so they are either not insurable again or insurable only at a very high cost.

So the health security debate is about all of us, because I don't think there is any person in this beautiful atrium who can honestly say to themselves, "Next year, I will absolutely have the health insurance I have now at the price that I now pay for it." That's not the way our current system operates.

At the end of this health care reform discussion, the bill that is passed by the Congress and signed by the President must provide universal coverage for every American. (Applause)

Every single American deserves to have health insurance at an affordable cost to himself and his family. (Applause)

So the first question I will ask you to ask yourselves and others, when someone comes forward with a plan, ask: Will this plan cover every American, no matter who that person is, where or whether that person works, and whether that person has a preexisting condition or other kind of problem?

If the answer is no, then that cannot be an acceptable alternative plan.

The second part of health security is to have a comprehensive package of benefits for every American. It will not mean very much if we say everybody has health insurance but that health insurance doesn't buy very much for you.

There are some who will come forward in the next months and say, "Well, you know, all we should really do is just make sure everybody has some kind of catastrophic health insurance, or we should make sure that everybody has some kind of health insurance but it has a deductible of about $3,000. That's what we should do."

I don't agree with that. I think every American who is insured should have access to outpatient care, to hospitalization, to mental health benefits, and to preventive health care. And that's the kind of package of benefits that the President has proposed. (Applause)

Because, you know, it's very easy for some people to say, "Well, why should we pay for preventive health care?"

The reason we pay for preventive health care is to save money in the long run. There are too many people who, because their insurance doesn't cover physical exams, doesn't cover Pap smears or mammograms, doesn't cover well-child exams, doesn't cover preventive care, they postpone going to the doctor until they are really sick. And then when they go, it costs them and us more than we should have to pay.

Under the President's proposal, preventive care is stressed. And much of the preventive care will be free, because it is so important that people take advantage of it. We want people to go to their doctor early so that they can have their problems taken care of. We don't want them to continue to stay away until they get really sick and show up at the emergency room.

So the second question is: When someone comes forward with an alternative plan, ask them what the benefits are.

Now, there are some plans that will come forward and say, "We want to pass health care reform, but we don't want to set the benefits yet. We want to do that later. We want to have some board set the benefits."

Now, I can understand the attitude of some of those who have proposed that, because it's difficult to set benefits and to determine what is in and what is out and how much we can afford to pay for.

But as a person, as a citizen, I'm a little reluctant to say we would pass health care reform and not know what the benefits are. I think we need to know what the benefits are, and the President's plan clearly lays out those benefits.

So when you are evaluating what is going to be proposed, make sure you know what the benefits are. And if you have a particular concern or particular experience, be sure you ask the hard questions about how a certain condition or problem would be taken care of.

And I want to mention one other specific point about this. There are many people who have said, "The President should not include mental health benefits in the benefits package."

Anyone who has studied our health care system knows mental health is a serious problem that we have not addressed adequately in this country. (Applause)

We have got to start taking care of the mental health problems that confront us. (Applause)

So the President has included that.

The second principle, after security, is we have to simplify this system. We have to make it easier for you to use it, for doctors and hospitals and nurses to be involved in it.

And anytime someone says, "You know, what the President has proposed sure does sound complicated," I always ask, "Well, could you explain for me how our present health care system works?"

I want all of you just to take a little time—maybe later tonight—sit down, and try to explain how this system we currently have works, how you get or don't get insurance, how you pay for it, what is covered, what the fine print says; who actually reimburses, under what formula, or how much you get when you go to the doctor or the hospital; and how many people get left out.

Under the President's plan, we want to move toward eliminating the thousands of forms that take up too much time for people right now. We want to have a single claims form. We want to take doctors and nurses and quit treating them like accountants and bookkeepers, and put them back to the business of taking care of patients on a daily basis. (Applause)

Anyone who has any acquaintance with a doctor or a nurse, if you talk to them for about a minute and a half, you're going to start hearing complaints about our present system and the paperwork that is demanded of them. We can do better at what we are doing. And if we do, we will save money, and we will provide better care.

So the next question to ask about any alternative is: Does this begin to cut down the paperwork? Does this move toward a single-form approach? Does this eliminate a lot of the bureaucracy we are currently living with?

The third big principle is savings. How much money can we save from our current system?

And, you know, there would be a lot of debate about this. But again, spend time talking to nurses, people who work with patients, hospital administrators and workers, physicians whom you know, people who work in nursing homes.

You will learn very quickly what I have learned, that everybody knows that we can save money in the system that we have. It should not be any surprise to conclude that, because in the system we have, we spend more money than any other country by far, and we don't even insure everybody, and we don't insure them with comprehensive benefits and preventive health care.

So you have to ask: Couldn't we do better with the money that we have?

One of the reasons the President did not want to have a big tax increase, as some have advocated, for health care reform is because until we figure out to use the money we currently have more efficiently, why would we add more to it? Let's try to figure out how to get the savings we know are in the system.

Dr. Everett Koop, the former Surgeon General, has said on several occasions, in his opinion, there is more than $200 billion of unnecessary costs in the system. And if you compare costs in one city to costs in another city, as I have done, you will discover that, without any difference in quality, some people in our country are paying a whole lot more for the same health care than others. We need to squeeze out the waste, the fraud, the abuse which still exists in this system and get it to run more efficiently.

So ask anybody who comes forward with a plan, "Are you going to take on the insurance companies? Are you going to take on those who defraud the system? Are you going to try to weed out the waste and abuse?"

Because if the answer is no or a weak yes, that's not the kind of system we need. We need to get the savings out of the system so that it can be more efficient so more people can be taken better care of than they are now.

The next principle is choice. Are we going to be able to choose our health plans and our doctors?

And the answer is absolutely yes. And in fact for most Americans who are insured as they are now, we are losing choice as I stand here today.

How many of you who are currently insured have seen, in the last several years, your employers tell you who you can go to for your health care, which plans you have to join?

Choice is already being decreased in the current system in an effort to fight control of costs.

In the new system that the President has proposed, your employer will not make the choice of your health plan. You will make the choice of your health plan. Every year you will decide what health plan you intend to belong to. And if you don't like the one you're in, you can switch out of that.

And in every region of the country, you will be entitled to have access to what is called a fee-for-service network in which every doctor belongs, so you can always go to the doctors you choose to go to. And there will be different ways of delivering health care services. So choice is important.

But when you think about choice as a principle, compare it to what is happening today, and recognize that if we do nothing, more and more of us will lose the choice to determine who takes care of us when we are sick.

If we go with the President's plan, that choice will always belong to us. It will not belong to our employers. It will not belong to insurance companies. It will not belong to the government. That is the best way to insure choice for all of us in the future. (Applause)

The difference is quality, because if we do all of this reform and we don't enhance quality, we will not have succeeded. But one of the ways we're going to enhance quality in the future is by giving this choice to you as a consumer and giving you better information than you have now.

Every year when you sign up for your health plan, you will get information about the plans, and there will be report cards. How well has that plan done in the past year?

You know, most of us—we don't buy health care the way we buy a car. We don't know as much about health care. We leave that to experts. We have to become better-informed consumers so we can make good judgments for ourselves.

And we're going to have to invest in research and quality outcomes so that we know what are the better ways to take care of ourselves, and we can make judgments as to how well we are being taken care of when it comes time to sign up for a health plan.

So in the President's plan, there are specific investments in medical schools that will be at the forefront of helping us to find quality, of insuring that these report cards are put together so we get good information.

So again, when alternatives come forward, ask yourself: Does this alternative plan give me the same assurance that quality will be taken care of as the President's plan, and how does it attempt to do it?

Because in most instances, the way that the President's plan has been constructed will put more money into research, which is one of the surest ways of increasing quality and give all of us the power to make decisions about what really is quality when it comes to making choices about our health care plans.

And the final point is responsibility. And by "responsibility" we mean a lot of things. We mean each of us should take more responsibility for our own health, because ultimately we are the only ones who can make that difference.

It also means that the system has to be responsibly financed. Right now the way health care financing works is like this. Those of us who are privately insured, we pay a premium that is increased every year, not just because of whatever happens to us or the people we work with, but because of all the people who get taken care of who cannot pay because they don't have any insurance.

So, you know, when somebody shows up at the emergency room here in Chicago or anywhere else, they will eventually be taken care of. But if they are uninsured, when they leave the hospital and they have not been able to pay for that cost, the hospital has to get it from somewhere, so they get it from two sources.

They get it from those of us who pay insurance premiums by increasing our premiums, and they get it from tax money, which we all pay, which goes to pay the hospital, because it couldn't get money from people who got taken care of.

There are a lot of folks who cannot afford to be insured in today's current system. There are others who choose not to be. There are large groups of young people in their 20s, for example, who don't think they will ever get sick and often, in those ages, think they're immortal. So they don't want to have insurance. And so they, too, don't pay on a regular basis to be insured, but when sick or in an accident, show up in the same place the rest of us do.

Now, the way to solve this is to get everybody paying something. If everybody pays something, those of us who have borne the biggest burden through our employers or on our own will be paying less, because there will be more people in the system.

Now, there are three ways to do that. One is to have a big tax increase and have what's called a single-payer system, like Canada does. You put in your tax money, and the government runs the system.

Another way to do it is to make your requirement for paying for insurance what is called an individual mandate, like auto insurance, where you have to go out and buy your own.

The third way, which is the way the President has chosen, is to build on what already works in our country. And what works for most insured people is the employer-employee system, where the employers and the employees contribute. But not everybody does it, so we have to require that everybody does it.

But in order to avoid an undue financial burden on those who don't do it, we need to have discounts for small businesses, and we need to have supporting payments for low-wage workers.

But if we get everybody into the system—and that's where most of the new money will come from. It won't come from a tax. It's not pie in the sky or fantasy. It comes from individuals who are currently uninsured, businesses which do not currently insure or do not insure adequately making their contributions, so that everybody is paying their fair share, and there are no more free rides.

And if everybody pays and if we protect small business and we protect low-wage workers, we can actually lower the costs of most companies that currently insure and most individuals who currently insure. In order to achieve that, we will cap the amount of money that businesses and individuals have to pay for health insurance.

Now, there are many other detailed features of this, and we might get some questions about it. But ultimately, the decision will be all of ours, and we will have to give direction to our Members of Congress. But this is an historic opportunity.

We know what will happen if we do nothing. If we do nothing, you will continue to have rising premium costs. We will continue to see more people lose their insurance. We will continue to see hospitals put under incredible financial stress. Doctors will be drowning in more paperwork. Nurses will be spending more than the 50 percent of their time that many of them do now filling out forms that have nothing to do with patient care.

If we change, we will spend less in the long run on health care. We will provide security for every American. And more than that, we will have shown that we can take on a serious challenge as a country and come up with a good, positive solution to it.

So if I were betting, I would bet on the American people, and I would bet on health care reform. And I just want to do everything I can, as a person in this country who cares about our future together, to make that happen.

Thank you all very much. (Applause)

CLINTON ADDRESS TO THE UNITED NATIONS

September 27, 1993

President Bill Clinton made his first address to the United Nations General Assembly September 27, pledging a continued U.S. commitment to the world organization but also calling for a hard look at the UN's global activities and internal operations. His speech came at a time when UN forces were trying to control the fractious armed conflict in Somalia and provide humanitarian aid in the carnage of Bosnia. These events, along with UN participation in other hot spots around the world, were prompting debate over the organization's mission and capabilities.

As if to underscore the new post-communist, post-cold war era, Clinton noted that he was the first American president born after the founding of the UN. The opening of the General Assembly, the president said, "offers us an opportunity to take stock of where we are, as common shareholders in the progress of humankind and in the preservation of our planet."

Threats to World Stability

Two "powerful tendencies working from opposite directions" threatened stability and peace among nations, Clinton went on. The first consisted of economic and technological forces that fuel "a welcome explosion of entrepreneurship and political liberalization. But they also threaten to destroy the insularity and independence of national economies, he said, "quickening the pace of change and making many of our people feel more insecure." The second, the president said, was an internal matter within nations—the "resurgent aspirations of ethnic and religious groups challenging governments on terms that traditional nation states cannot easily accommodate."

These challenges required leaders to "find new ways to work together more effectively in pursuit of national interests and to think anew about whether our institutions of national cooperation are adequate to this moment," Clinton said. Added to that task is the need for leaders to educate their citizens about each nation's role in the larger world. "Domestic renewal is an overdue tonic," the president said. "But isolationism and protectionism are still poison. We must inspire our people to look beyond their immediate fears toward a broader horizon."

Clinton called specifically for a new effort to stop the proliferation of weapons of mass destruction of all types. He said the United States would press for an international agreement that would ban production of plutonium and highly enriched uranium, materials used in manufacturing nuclear weapons. He also called on nations to fight the spread of biological and chemical weapons.

The U.S. Role

Despite the end of the cold war, the United States would not retreat from its world obligations, Clinton said. "The United States intends to remain engaged and to lead. We cannot solve every problem, but we must and will serve as a fulcrum for change and a pivot point for peace." The overriding purpose of nations, he added, "must be to expand and strengthen the world's community of market-based democracies."

The United States would not lead "some crusade to force our way of life and doing things on others or to replicate our institutions," Clinton said, "but we know clearly throughout the world, from Poland to Eritrea, from Guatemala to South Korea, there is an enormous yearning among people who wish to be masters of their own economic and political lives. Where it matters the most and where we can make the greatest difference," Clinton said, "we will, therefore, patiently and firmly align ourselves with that yearning."

UN Peacekeepers

Turning to the difficult issue of peacekeeping, Clinton praised the UN efforts, countering critics by pointing out the recent success in Cambodia, "when the UN's operations have helped turn the killing fields into fertile soil through reconciliation." The United States has supported peacekeeping missions not because it wants to "subcontract American foreign policy, but to strengthen our security, protect our interests and to share among nations the costs and effort of pursuing peace."

But Clinton bluntly pointed out that UN peacekeeping activities were not able to keep pace with "rising responsibilities and challenges." Six years earlier there nearly ten thousand peacekeepers around the world; now, he said, the UN has some eighty thousand individuals deployed in seventeen operations on four continents. The time has come for harder analysis of requests for peacekeeping, Clinton said, and the United States has led the way in asking tough questions about proposals for new missions. "The United Nations simply cannot become engaged in every one of the world's conflicts," Clinton asserted. "If the American people are to say yes to UN peacekeeping, the United Nations must know when to say no."

The president added that the United States supported creation of a "genuine UN peacekeeping headquarters" with adequate staff, access to timely intelligence, a logistics unit that can be deployed quickly and an operations center with global communications. He announced that the United States would soon be current in paying its peacekeeping bills—it owes $400 million—but added that he also wanted to work to reduce the U.S. assessment for these missions, an assessment system unchanged since 1973. In 1993 the United States was paying about 30 percent of the peacekeeping bill. U.S. officials wanted the figure reduced to 25 percent because the United States percentage of the economic pie is not as great as it once was. Clinton said the U.S. rate should be reduced to reflect the rise of other nations "that now can bear more of the financial burden."

Clinton's Change of Tone

Clinton's remarks sounded a different tone from that struck during the 1992 presidential campaign, when he called for a larger UN peacekeeping role. As president, Clinton has taken criticism from Congress and other quarters about the difficulties of UN missions, and he had encountered resistance to committing U.S. troops to any peacekeeping operation in Bosnia.

The president concluded his remarks by telling the General Assembly that history had granted them a moment of opportunity, "when old dangers and old walls are crumbling; future generations will judge us, every one of us, above all, by what we make of this magic moment."

"Let us resolve that we will dream larger, that we will work harder so that they can conclude that we did not merely turn walls to rubble, but instead laid the foundation for great things to come."

Following is the text of President Bill Clinton's September 27, 1993, address to the United Nations General Assembly:

Thank you very much. Mr. President, let me first congratulate you on your election as president of this General Assembly.

Mr. Secretary-General, distinguished delegates and guests, it is a great honor for me to address you and to stand in this great chamber which symbolizes so much of the 20th century—its darkest crises and its brightest aspirations.

I come before you as the first American president born after the founding of the United Nations. Like most of the people in the world today, I was not even alive during the convulsive World War that convinced humankind of the need for this organization, nor during the San Francisco Conference [on International Organization] that led to its birth. Yet I have followed the work of the United Nations throughout my life, with admiration for its accomplishments, with sadness for its failures, and conviction that through common effort our generation can take the bold steps needed to redeem the mission entrusted to the United Nations 48 years ago.

I pledge to you that my nation remains committed to helping make the United Nations' vision a reality. The start of this General Assembly offers us an opportunity to take stock of where we are, as common shareholders in the progress of humankind and in the preservation of our planet.

It is clear that we live at a turning point in human history. Immense and promising changes seem to wash over us every day. The Cold War is over. The world is no longer divided into two armed and angry camps. Dozens of new democracies have been born.

It is a moment of miracles. We see Nelson Mandela stand side by side with President [F. W.] De Klerk, proclaiming a date for South Africa's first non-racial election. We see Russia's first popularly elected president, Boris [N.] Yeltsin, leading his nation on its bold democratic journey. We have seen decades of deadlock shattered in the Middle East, as the prime minister of Israel [Yitzhak Rabin] and the chairman of the Palestine Liberation Organization [Yasir Arafat] reached past enmity and suspicion to shake each other's hands and exhilarate the entire world with the hope of peace.

We have begun to see the doomsday weapons of nuclear annihilation dismantled and destroyed. Thirty-two years ago, President [John F.] Kennedy warned this chamber that humanity lived under a nuclear sword of Damocles that hung by the slenderest of threads. Now the United States is working with Russia, Ukraine, Belarus and others to take that sword down, to lock it away in a secure vault where we hope and pray it will remain forever.

It is a new era in this hall as well. The superpower standoff that for so long stymied the United Nations' work almost from its first day has now yielded to a new promise of practical cooperation. Yet today we must all admit that there are two powerful tendencies working from opposite directions to challenge the authority of nation-states everywhere and to undermine the authority of nation-states to work together.

From beyond nations, economic and technological forces all over the globe are compelling the world toward integration. These forces are fueling a welcome explosion of entrepreneurship and political liberalization. But they also threaten to destroy the insularity and independence of national economies, quickening the pace of change and making many of our people feel more insecure.

At the same time, from within nations, the resurgent aspirations of ethnic and religious groups challenge governments on terms that traditional nation-states cannot easily accommodate.

These twin forces lie at the heart of the challenges not only to our national government, but also to all our international institutions. They require all of us in this room to find new ways to work together more effectively in pursuit of our national interests and to think anew about whether our institutions of international cooperation are adequate to this moment.

Thus, as we marvel at this era's promise of new peace, we must also recognize that serious threats remain. Bloody ethnic, religious and civil wars rage from Angola to the Caucasus to Kashmir. As weapons of mass destruction fall into more hands, even small conflicts can threaten to take on murderous proportions. Hunger and disease continue to take a tragic toll, especially among the world's children. The malignant neglect of our global environment threatens our children's health and their very security.

The repression of conscience continues in too many nations. And terrorism, which has taken so many innocent lives, assumes a horrifying immediacy for us here when militant fanatics bombed the World Trade Center and planned to attack even this very hall of peace.

Let me assure you, whether the fathers of those crimes, or the mass murderers who bombed Pan Am Flight 103, my government is determined to see that such terrorists are brought to justice.

As this moment of panoramic change, of vast opportunities and troubling threats, we must all ask ourselves what we can do and what we should do as a community of nations. We must once again dare to dream of what might be, for our dreams may be within our reach. For that to happen, we must all be willing to honestly confront the challenges of the broader world. That has never been easy.

When this organization was founded 48 years ago, the world's nations stood devastated by war or exhausted by its expense. There was little appetite for cooperative efforts among nations. Most people simply wanted to get on with their lives. But a far-sighted generation of leaders from the United States and elsewhere rallied the world. Their efforts built the institutions of postwar security and prosperity.

We are at a similar moment today. The momentum of the Cold War no longer propels us in our daily actions. And with daunting economic and political pressures upon almost every nation represented in this room, many of us are turning to focus greater attention and energy on our domestic needs and problems. And we must. But putting each of our economic houses in order cannot mean that we shut our windows to the world. The pursuit of self-renewal in many of the world's largest and most powerful economies—in Europe, in Japan, in North America—is absolutely crucial because unless the great industrial nations can recapture their robust economic growth, the global economy will languish.

Yet, the industrial nations also need growth elsewhere in order to lift their own. Indeed, prosperity in each of our nations and regions also depends upon active and responsible engagement in a host of shared concerns.

For example, a thriving and democratic Russia not only makes the world safer, it also can help to expand the world's economy. A strong GATT [General Agreement on Tariffs and Trade] agreement will create millions of jobs worldwide. Peace in the Middle East, buttressed as it should be by the repeal of outdated U.N. resolutions, can help to unleash that region's great economic potential and calm a perpetual source of tension in global affairs. And the growing economic power of China, coupled with greater political openness, could bring enormous benefits to all of Asia and to the rest of the world.

We must help our publics to understand this distinction: Domestic renewal is an overdue tonic. But isolationism and protectionism are still poison. We must inspire our people to look beyond their immediate fears toward a broader horizon.

Let me start by being clear about where the United States stands. The United States occupies a unique position in world affairs today. We recognize that, and we welcome it. Yet, with the Cold War over, I know many people ask whether the United States plans to retreat or remain active in the world, and if active, to what end. Many people are asking that in our own country as well. Let me answer that question as clearly and plainly as I can.

The United States intends to remain engaged and to lead. We cannot solve every problem, but we must and will serve as a fulcrum for change and a pivot point for peace.

In a new era of peril and opportunity, our overriding purpose must be to expand and strengthen the world's community of market-based democracies. During the Cold War we sought to contain a threat to survival of free institutions. Now we seek to enlarge the circle of nations that live under those free institutions.

For our dream is of a day when the opinions and energies of every person in the world will be given full expression, in a world of thriving democracies that cooperate with each other and live in peace.

With this statement, I do not mean to announce some crusade to force our way of life and doing things on others, or to replicate our institutions, but we now know clearly that throughout the world, from Poland to Eritrea, from Guatemala to South Korea, there is an enormous yearning among people who wish to be the masters of their own economic and political lives. Where it matters most and where we can make the greatest difference, we will, therefore, patiently and firmly align ourselves with that yearning.

Today, there are still those who claim that democracy is simply not applicable to many cultures and that its recent expansion is an aberration, an accident, in history that will soon fade away. But I agree with President [Franklin D.] Roosevelt, who once said, "The democratic aspiration is no mere recent phase of human history. It is human history."

We will work to strengthen the free market democracies, by revitalizing our economy here at home, by opening world trade through the GATT, the North American Free Trade Agreement and other accords, and by updating our shared institutions, asking with you and answering the hard questions about whether they are adequate to the present challenges.

We will support the consolidation of market democracy where it is taking new root, as in the states of the former Soviet Union and all over

Latin America. And we seek to foster the practices of good government that distribute the benefits of democracy and economic growth fairly to all people.

We will work to reduce the threat from regimes that are hostile to democracies and to support liberalization of non-democratic states when they are willing to live in peace with the rest of us.

As a country that has over 150 different racial, ethnic and religious groups within our borders, our policy is and must be rooted in a profound respect for all the world's religions and cultures. But we must oppose everywhere extremism that produces terrorism and hate.

And we must pursue our humanitarian goal of reducing suffering, fostering sustainable development, and improving the health and living conditions, particularly for our world's children.

On efforts from export control to trade agreements to peacekeeping, we will often work in partnership with others and through multilateral institutions, such as the United Nations. It is in our national interest to do so. But we must not hesitate to act unilaterally when there is a threat to our core interests or to those of our allies.

The United States believes that an expanded community of market democracies not only serves our own security interests, it also advances the goals enshrined in this body's charter and its Universal Declaration of Human Rights. For broadly based prosperity is clearly the strongest form of preventive diplomacy. And the habits of democracy are the habits of peace.

Democracy is rooted in compromise, not conquest. It rewards tolerance, not hatred. Democracies rarely wage war on one another. They make more reliable partners in trade, in diplomacy and in the stewardship of our global environment. And democracies with the rule of law and respect for political, religious and cultural minorities are more responsive to their own people and to the protection of human rights.

But as we work toward this vision we must confront the storm clouds that may overwhelm our work and darken the march toward freedom. If we do not stem the proliferation of the world's deadliest weapons, no democracy can feel secure. If we do not strengthen the capacity to resolve conflict among and within nations, those conflicts will smother the birth of free institutions, threaten the development of entire regions and continue to take innocent lives.

If we do not nurture our people and our planet through sustainable development, we will deepen conflict and waste the very wonders that make our efforts worth doing.

Let me talk more about what I believe we must do in each of these three categories: non-proliferation, conflict resolution and sustainable development.

One of our most urgent priorities must be attacking the proliferation of weapons of mass destruction, whether they are nuclear, chemical or biological, and the ballistic missiles that can rain them down on populations hundreds of miles away.

We know this is not an idle problem. All of us are still haunted by the pictures of Kurdish women and children cut down by poison gas. We saw Scud missiles dropped during the gulf war that would have been far graver in their consequence if they had carried nuclear weapons. And we know that many nations still believe it is in their interest to develop weapons of mass destruction or to sell them or the necessary technologies to others for financial gain.

More than a score of nations likely possess such weapons, and their number threatens to grow. These weapons destabilize entire regions. They could turn a local conflict into a global human and environmental catastrophe. We simply have got to find ways to control these weapons and to reduce the number of states that possess them by supporting and strengthening the IAEA [International Atomic Energy Agency] and by taking other necessary measures.

I have made non-proliferation one of our nation's highest priorities. We intend to weave it more deeply into the fabric of all of our relationships with the world's nations and institutions. We seek to build a world of increasing pressures for non-proliferation but increasingly open trade and technology for those states that live by accepted international rules.

Today, let me describe several new policies that our government will pursue to stem proliferation. We will pursue new steps to control the materials for nuclear weapons. Growing global stockpiles of plutonium and highly enriched uranium are raising the danger of nuclear terrorism for all nations. We will press for an international agreement that would ban production of these materials for weapons forever.

As we reduce our nuclear stockpiles, the United States has also begun negotiations toward a comprehensive ban on nuclear testing. This summer I declared that to facilitate these negotiations, our nation would suspend our testing if all other nuclear states would do the same. Today, in the face of disturbing signs, I renew my call on the nuclear states to abide by that moratorium as we negotiate to stop nuclear testing for all time.

I am also proposing new efforts to fight the proliferation of biological and chemical weapons. Today, only a handful of nations has ratified the Chemical Weapons Convention. I call on all nations, including my own, to ratify this accord quickly so that it may enter into force by Jan. 13, 1995.

We will also seek to strengthen the Biological Weapons Convention by making every nation's biological activities and facilities open to more international students. I am proposing as well new steps to thwart the proliferation of ballistic missiles. Recently, working with Russia, Argentina, Hungary and South Africa, we have made significant progress toward that goal. Now, we will seek to strengthen the principles of the Missile Technology Control Regime by transforming it from an agreement on technology transfer among just 23 nations to a set of rules that can command universal adherence.

We will also reform our own system of export controls in the United States to reflect the realities of the post-Cold War world, where we seek to enlist the support of our former adversaries in the battle against proliferation.

At the same time that we stop deadly technologies from falling into the wrong hands, we will work with our partners to remove outdated controls that unfairly burden legitimate commerce and unduly restrain growth and opportunity all over the world.

As we work to keep the world's most destructive weapons out of conflict, we must also strengthen the international community's ability to address those conflicts themselves. For as we all now know so painfully, the end of the Cold War did not bring us to the millennium of peace. And, indeed, it simply removed the lid from many cauldrons of ethnic, religious and territorial animosity.

The philosopher Isaiah Berlin has said that a wounded nationalism is like a bent twig forced down so severely that when released it lashes back with fury.

The world today is thick with both bent and recoiling twigs of wounded communal identities.

This scourge of bitter conflict has placed high demands on United Nations peacekeeping forces. Frequently the blue helmets have worked wonders. In Namibia, El Salvador, the Golan Heights and elsewhere, U.N. peacekeepers have helped to stop the fighting, restore civil authority and enable free elections.

In Bosnia, U.N. peacekeepers, against the danger and frustration of that continuing tragedy, [have] maintained a valiant humanitarian effort. And if the parties of that conflict take the hard steps needed to make a real peace, the international community including the United States must be ready to help in its effective implementation.

In Somalia, the United States and the United Nations have worked together to achieve a stunning humanitarian rescue, saving literally hundreds of thousands of lives and restoring the conditions of security for almost the entire country.

U.N. peacekeepers from over two dozen nations remain in Somalia today. And some, including brave Americans, have lost their lives to ensure that we complete our mission and to ensure that anarchy and starvation do not return just as quickly as they were abolished.

Many still criticize U.N. peacekeeping, but those who do should talk to the people of Cambodia, where the U.N.'s operations have helped to turn the killing fields into fertile soil through reconciliation. Last May's elections in Cambodia marked a proud accomplishment for that war-weary nation and for the United Nations. And I am pleased to announce that the United States has recognized Cambodia's new government.

U.N. peacekeeping holds the promise to resolve many of this era's conflicts. The reason we have supported such missions is not, as some critics in the United States have charged, to subcontract American foreign policy, but to strengthen our security, protect our interests, and to share among nations the costs and effort of pursuing peace.

Peacekeeping cannot be a substitute for our own national defense efforts, but it can strongly supplement them.

Today, there is wide recognition that the U.N. peacekeeping ability has not kept pace with the rising responsibilities and challenges. Just six years ago, about 10,000 U.N. peacekeepers were stationed around the world. Today, the United Nations has some 80,000 deployed in 17 operations on four continents.

Yet, until recently, if a peacekeeping commander called in from across the globe when it was nighttime here in New York, there was no one in the peacekeeping office even to answer the call. When lives are on the line, you cannot let the reach of the United Nations exceed its grasp.

As the secretary-general and others have argued, if U.N. peacekeeping is to be a sound security investment for our nation and for other U.N. members, it must adapt to new times. Together we must prepare U.N. peacekeeping for the 21st century. We need to begin by bringing the rigors of military and political analysis to every U.N. peace mission.

In recent weeks in the Security Council, our nation has begun asking harder questions about proposals for new peacekeeping missions: Is there a real threat to international peace? Does the proposed mission have clear objectives? Can an end point be identified for those who will be asked to participate? How much will the mission cost?

From now on, the United Nations should address these and other hard questions for every proposed mission before we vote and before the mission begins.

The United Nations simply cannot become engaged in every one of the world's conflicts. If the American people are to say yes to U.N. peacekeeping, the United Nations must know when to say no. The United Nations must also have the technical means to run a modern world-class peacekeeping operation.

We support the creation of a genuine U.N. peacekeeping headquarters with a planning staff, with access to timely intelligence, with a logistics unit that can be deployed on a moment's notice, and a modern operations center with global communications.

And the United Nations' operations must not only be adequately funded, but also fairly funded. Within the next few weeks, the United States will be current in our peacekeeping bills. I have worked hard with the Congress to get this done.

I believe the United States should lead the way in being timely in its payments, and I will work to continue to see that we pay our bills in full. But I am also committed to work with the United Nations to reduce our nation's assessment for these missions.

The assessment system has not been changed since 1973. And everyone in our country knows that our percentage of the world's economic pie is not as great as it was then. Therefore, I believe our rates should be reduced to reflect the rise of other nations that can now bear more of the financial burden. That will make it easier for me as president to make sure we pay in a timely and full fashion.

Changes in the United Nations' peacekeeping operations must be part of an even broader program of United Nations reform. I say that again not to criticize the United Nations, but to help to improve it. As our Ambassador Madeleine K. Albright has suggested, the United States has always played a twin role to the United Nations—first friend and first critic.

Today corporations all around the world are finding ways to move from the Industrial Age to the Information Age, improving service, reducing bureaucracy and cutting costs.

Here in the United States, our Vice President Al Gore and I have launched an effort to literally reinvent how our government operates. We see this going on in other governments around the world. Now the time has come to reinvent the way the United Nations operates as well.

I applaud the initial steps the secretary general [Boutros Boutros-Ghali] has taken to reduce and to reform the United Nations bureaucracy. Now, we must all do even more to root out waste.

Before this General Assembly is over, let us establish a strong mandate for an office of inspector general so that it can attain a reputation for toughness, for integrity, for effectiveness. Let us build new confidence among our people that the United Nations is changing with the needs of our times.

Ultimately, the key for reforming the United Nations, as in reforming our own government, is to remember why we are here and whom we serve.

It is wise to recall that the first words of the U.N. Charter are not "We, the governments," but, "We, the people of the United Nations." That means in every country the teachers, the workers, the farmers, the professionals, the fathers, the mothers, the children, from the most remote village in the world to the largest metropolis—they are why we gather in this great hall. It is their futures that are at risk when we act or fail to act. It is they who ultimately pay our bills.

As we dream new dreams in this age when miracles now seem possible, let us focus on the lives of those people and especially on the children who will inherit this world. Let us work with a new urgency and imagine what kind of world we could create for them in the coming generations.

Let us work with new energy to protect the world's people from torture and repression. As Secretary of State [Warren M.] Christopher stressed at the recent Vienna Conference, human rights are not something conditional, founded by culture, but rather something universal granted by God.

This General Assembly should create, at long last, a high commissioner for human rights. I hope you will do it soon and with vigor and energy and conviction.

Let us also work far more ambitiously to fulfill our obligations as custodians of this planet, not only to improve the quality of life for our citizens and the quality of our air and water and the Earth itself, but also because the roots of conflict are so often entangled with the roots of environmental neglect and the calamity of famine and disease.

During the course of our campaign in the United States last year, Vice President Gore and I promised the American people major changes in our nation's policy toward the global environment. Those were promises to keep, and today the United States is doing so.

Today we are working with other nations to build on the promising work of the United Nations' Commission on Sustainable Development. We are working to make sure that all nations meet their commitments under the Global Climate Convention. We are seeking to complete negotiations on an accord to prevent the world's deserts from further expansion. And we seek to strengthen the World Health Organization's efforts to combat the plague of AIDS, which is not only killing millions, but also exhausting the resources of nations that can least afford it.

Let us make a new commitment to the world's children. It is tragic enough that 1.5 million children died as a result of wars over the past decade. But it is far more unforgivable that in that same period, 40 million children died from diseases completely preventable with simple vaccines or medicine. Every day—this day, as we meet here—over 30,000 of the world's children will die of malnutrition and disease.

Our UNICEF director, Jim Grant, has reminded me that each of those children had a name and a nationality, a family, a personality and a potential. We are compelled to do better by the world's children. Just as our own nation has launched new reforms to ensure that every child has adequate health care, we must do more to get basic vaccines and other treatment for curable diseases to children all over the world. It's the best investment we'll ever make.

We can find new ways to ensure that every child grows up with clean drinkable water, that most precious commodity of life itself. And the United Nations can work even harder to ensure that each child has at least a full primary education—and I mean that opportunity for girls as well as boys.

And to ensure a healthier and more abundant world, we simply must slow the world's explosive growth in population. We cannot afford to see the human race doubled by the middle of the next century.

Our nation has, at last, renewed its commitment to work with the United Nations to expand the availability of the world's family planning education and services. We must ensure that there is a place at the table for every one of our world's children. And we can do it.

At the birth of this organization 48 years ago, another time of both victory and danger, a generation of gifted leaders from many nations stepped forward to organize the world's efforts on behalf of security and prosperity.

One American leader during that period said this: "It is time we steered by the stars rather than by the light of each passing ship." His generation picked peace, human dignity and freedom. Those are good stars; they should remain the highest in our own firmament.

Now history has granted to us a moment of even greater opportunity, when old dangers and old walls are crumbling; future generations will judge us, every one of us, above all, by what we make of this magic moment.

Let us resolve that we will dream larger, that we will work harder so that they can conclude that we did not merely turn walls to rubble, but instead laid the foundation for great things to come.

Let us ensure that the tide of freedom and democracy is not pushed back by the fierce winds of ethnic hatred. Let us ensure that the world's most dangerous weapons are safely reduced and denied to dangerous hands. Let us ensure that the world we pass to our children is healthier, safer and more abundant than the one we inhabit today.

I believe—I know—that together we can extend this moment of miracles into an age of great work and new wonders. Thank you very much.

FEDERAL INQUIRIES INTO WACO DISASTER

September 30 and October 8, 1993

Two government reports issued only a few days apart in Washington differed widely as to whether federal law enforcement officials mishandled a fifty-one-day siege of an armed cult compound near Waco, Texas, occupied by a fanatical religious group known as the Branch Davidians. The standoff ended April 19 in a fire that swept the compound after the FBI sprayed tear gas to flush out and capture the occupants. Seventy-five bodies were found in the charred ruins—victims of what the FBI described as a mass suicide. They had died from burns and smoke inhalation, and in some cases from gunshot wounds they apparently inflicted upon themselves and each other. The government inquiries were ordered at that time by President Bill Clinton. (Clinton Defends Deadly Attack on Armed Waco Cult Compound, p. 293)

The first report, released September 30 by the Treasury Department, faulted its agency, the U.S. Bureau of Alcohol, Tobacco, and Firearms, for bad planning and decision making in an initial raid on the compound February 28 to arrest cult leader David Koresh for illegal possession of weapons and explosives. The cultists, who had learned of the raid, ambushed the arresting party and killed four ATF agents. Two to six cultists were fatally wounded in the exchange of gunfire.

The second report, issued in three parts by the Justice Department on October 8, exonerated Attorney General Janet Reno and the FBI of any mistakes in their handling of the situation. The day after the ATF raid, the FBI was called in. It took charge of the siege, undertook futile negotiations with Koresh, and staged the April 19 attack with Reno's concurrence. The report was supervised by Deputy Attorney General Philip B. Heymann, who wrote an accompanying set of recommendations entitled "Lessons of Waco." A separate evaluation section was written by Edward S. G. Dennis, Jr., a Justice Department official in the Bush administration. His mild tone in evaluating roles of the department and the FBI stood in stark contrast to the scathing treatment the ATF received in another report, and drew criticism in Congress and the press as too inadequate.

"Tragically Wrong" Decisions

The Treasury report was supervised by Assistant Secretary Ronald K. Noble, who was aided by three "independent reviewers"—Edwin O. Guthman, a journalism professor, former newspaper editor, and former aide to Attorney General Robert F. Kennedy; Henry S. Ruth, Jr., a former Justice Department attorney and chief Watergate prosecutor; and Willie Williams, chief of the Los Angeles Police Department.

The report pointed out that the February 28 planners became aware shortly before the raid began that Koresh knew it was coming. The decision to proceed was "tragically wrong, not just in retrospect, but because of what the decision-makers knew at the time," the report said. The agency lacked the experience to undertake the raid, it continued, and had not fully explored the possibility of arresting Koresh outside the compound.

Moreover, "numerous officials were less than truthful" with their superiors and investigating authorities. The report charged that tactical coordinator Charles Sarabyn and supervising agent Phillip Chojnacki had altered evidence, revising their original written plan for the raid and passing it off as the original, in an attempt to justify their decision.

The report faulted ATF Director Stephen Higgins for relying on the deceitful accounts and thus misleading others. Treasury Secretary Lloyd Bentsen said September 30 he had accepted Higgins's resignation. Bentsen also placed five other ATF officials on administrative leave. Two of the five, associate director Dan Harnett and duputy associate director Dan Conroy, resigned October 2 over disagreements with the report.

According to the report, a local television news cameraman had unwittingly alerted the Branch Davidians about the impending raid. James Peeler of Waco station KWTX had been tipped off by an ATF-retained ambulance company that the raid was imminent. Unable to find the compound, he asked a local postal carrier, David Jones, for directions. Unaware the carrier was a Branch Davidian, Peeler explained his reason for inquiring. Jones promptly informed Koresh. Robert Rodriguez, an undercover agent who was with Koresh, slipped out and warned his supervisors that the secret was out.

The report said Peeler should not be made a scapegoat. ATF agents, it said, should have done a better job of keeping Peeler and other news reporters from the compound area at that time. It also cleared the daily Waco Tribune-Herald *of allegations that the newspaper's investigation of the cult impeded the ATF's own investigation. The ATF was unable to persuade the paper to postpone publication of articles about illegal activity in the compound.*

Conflict Over Reasons for Attack

In the Justice Department report, Dennis said allegations that the FBI had set the compound fire were "utterly false." At a news conference the day the report was released, Dennis said Koresh "choreographed his own death and the deaths of most of his followers." As for the possibility that a tear gas attack might have provoked the cultists to take their own lives, the report cited conflicting advice the FBI received from psychologists and other experts. In the hours after the fire, Reno told reporters that the FBI and its experts had informed her there was little chance of mass suicide at the compound. In a news conference on October 8, Reno said, "I don't think there were any misleading statements about suicide.... We made the best judgment we could."

The attorney general had said in April that her decision to go ahead with the tear gas plan was influenced by FBI reports that babies were "being beaten" inside the compound during the standoff. However, a lengthy factual chronology accompanying the report said there was no evidence of child abuse in the compound during that time. "I now understand that nobody in the bureau told me that [child abuse] was ongoing," she said at the news conference. "We were briefed, and I misunderstood."

Reno had said that another factor for going ahead with the plan was that the FBI hostage rescue team was suffering fatigue and was without adequate replacements. In other matters, the report described disputes between hostage negotiators who sought to win Koresh's trust and agents who opted for "aggressive" psychological tactics to frighten or dishearten the cultists.

Following are excerpts from the Treasury Department report on the "Bureau of Alcohol, Tobacco, and Firearms Investigation of Vernon Wayne Howell, also known as David Koresh," issued September 30, 1993; and the Justice Department's "Report to the Deputy Attorney General on the Events at Waco, Texas"; "Evaluation of the Handling of the Branch Davidian Stand-off in Waco, Texas"; and "Lessons of Waco: Proposed Changes in Federal Law Enforcement"; all issued October 8, 1993:

TREASURY DEPARTMENT REPORT

The Propriety of Investigating Koresh and Other Cult Members

.... Since ATF's repulsed effort to search the Branch Davidian Compound, some members of the public and the media have questioned the propriety of ATF's decision to initiate an investigation of Koresh and his followers. Questions have been raised as to whether the cult members were justifiably suspected of violating any applicable federal laws. Others have conceded that Koresh was violating the law but have suggested that the violations should have been ignored....

These criticisms are not supported by the evidence. A review of the investigation makes it clear that the ATF inquiry into the activities of Koresh and his followers was consistent with the agency's congressional mandate to enforce federal laws regulating the possession and manufacture of automatic weapons and explosive devices. Indeed, ATF would have been remiss if it had permitted considerations of religious freedom to insulate the Branch Davidians from such an investigation.

At the outset, it should be emphasized that ATF focused on the Branch Davidians only after it was asked to do so by local law enforcement authorities who had been scrutinizing the conduct of cult members....

While some have suggested that ATF targeted Koresh because of his religious beliefs and life-style, the Review has found no evidence of any such motivation. Indeed, ATF recognized early the delicacy of an investigation of such an unorthodox community ... thus ensuring greater supervisory scrutiny of a case that was perceived at the outset to have the potential for raising thorny religious issues as well as difficult safety issues, particularly regarding the women and children living at the Compound.

Whatever controversy there might be about the types of weapons American citizens should be permitted to maintain, federal laws draw a definite line at fully automatic guns and explosive devices such as grenades, which are thought to be more suited for battlefield use than any other purpose. That a private individual has access to a single unlawful machine gun must be cause for federal concern. Where a group is found to be stockpiling many such weapons and to be developing the capability to manufacture many more, ATF must pursue the case. And while the group's religious beliefs should not be cause for targeting it, neither should the beliefs insulate the group from federal scrutiny....

The Compound became a rural fortress, often patrolled by armed guards, in which Koresh's word or the word that Koresh purported to extrapolate from the Scriptures was the only law. And the accounts by former cult members, including an abused child, that Koresh was sexually abusing minors made it clear that Koresh believed he was beyond society's laws. Were Koresh to decide to turn his weapons on society, he would have devotees to follow him, and they would be equipped with weapons that could inflict serious damage.

In the wake of the tragic consequences of the ATF raid on February 28, 1993, and the evidence discovered at the Compound after it burned down on April 19, 1993, it is no longer necessary to speculate on the threat that Koresh and his followers posed....

The Decision to Use Force When Executing the Warrants

The threshold issue presented to ATF was whether any force would be needed to execute the arrest warrant for Koresh and the search warrant for the Compound. Some have suggested that, having obtained such warrants, ATF should simply have asked Koresh to surrender himself and his weapons or asked him for free passage into the Compound so that ATF could conduct a search for unlawful firearms and explosives. . . .

The Review finds no basis for these criticisms and believes that the decision not to rely on Koresh's goodwill was entirely appropriate and rested on valid considerations. . . .

Based on information developed during the course of [the] investigation—which showed Koresh's propensity toward violence, his use of armed guards, and his control of a massive arsenal of automatic and semiautomatic weapons—the ATF planners reasonably concluded that a polite request to search the Compound without readiness to use force would have been foolhardy and irresponsible. . . .

Having understandably decided not to rely solely on Koresh's voluntary compliance with the warrants, ATF tactical planners initially focused their attention on arresting Koresh while he was away from the Compound, either by luring him off or by waiting until he had left it on his own accord. Koresh's followers, the planners believed, had become so accustomed to relying on his leadership and guidance that they would be far less likely to resist ATF in any organized way if Koresh could be removed from the scene. . . . That effort . . . was abandoned prematurely, without adequate exploration of its feasibility. . . .

A Siege With Koresh Present on the Compound

ATF still had to decide how it would execute the search warrant at the Compound. Initially, the tactical planners considered the siege option. In this scenario, agents would first ask those inside the Compound to honor the warrant. If access were denied, ATF would immediately establish a perimeter around the Compound and seal off its inhabitants until they relented and permitted the search to proceed. . . .

The planners ultimately rejected the siege option mainly because . . . several former cult members noted the distinct danger that Koresh would respond to a siege by leading his followers in a mass suicide. Even if no suicides occurred, the costs of a siege would be high. . . . [T]he Branch Davidians, former cult members believed, could withstand a long and arduous standoff. The planners were also concerned that siege would give Koresh and his followers time to destroy evidence of their violations of federal firearms and explosives laws. Several tactical planners expressed concern that Koresh would outlast the patience of the American public and that they might be directed to raid the Compound after a lengthy stalemate. They feared that such a raid, against a prepared and fortified foe, would be far more dangerous than a surprise raid.

The chief attraction of a raid scenario was that it offered the possibility of catching Koresh and his followers by surprise and avoided the risk of a protracted and costly standoff. The element of surprise seemed quite achievable to the planners, based on their flawed understanding of the daily routine in the Compound. . . . The operation was far more vulnerable than its planners . . . ever realized. And this vulnerability was increased by the failure of the planning process to produce a common understanding among the planners of what the operation's key assumptions were, and of the importance of surprise to the mission's success. . . .

No Meaningful Contingency Planning

The same confidence that led ATF raid planners to discard intelligence inconsistent with the assumptions central to their plan might also have led them to do little to prepare for the possibility that conditions would not be right on raid day. . . . That failure also meant that when ATF agents encountered heavy gunfire upon their arrival at the Compound, most had little choice but to proceed with their mission, at great cost. . . .

If the tactical planners had given sufficient thought to the level of firepower that Koresh and his followers could bring to bear on agents massed in front of the Compound, they might have done more to ensure that the raid would not go forward without the advantage of surprise. . . . They also would have prepared some scheme to help agents withdraw from their vulnerable positions if they became pinned down by hostile fire. One method of extracting the agents might have been to send in Bradley Fighting Vehicles, which could have been positioned a short distance from the Compound, concealed on flatbed trucks. In any event, a reserve force of agents could have been deployed nearby. To the extent that these precautions would have taxed or exceeded ATF's resources, the agency might have reached out for assistance from other law enforcement authorities. . . .

Having failed to prepare for an ambush, the planners also failed to prepare for a stand-off. Given their fears that Koresh might lead his followers in a mass suicide if surrounded by agents, it is unfortunate that the planners did not heed Deputy Tactical Coordinator James Cavanaugh's repeated requests that ATF have a contingency plan to negotiate with those inside the Compound. The raid commanders did not even arrange to have the telephone number for the Compound on the day of the raid. . . .

The absence of any contingency planning cannot be attributed entirely to the planners' confidence that conditions would be favorable and that ATF's advantage of surprise would be decisive. It also reflected the planners' lack of experience in orchestrating operations of this magnitude. Only Buford had been involved in the planning of an enforcement action of comparable size. . . .

Command and Control Flaws in the Raid Plan

Other deficiencies in the planning effort that likely contributed to the pressures felt by the raid commanders on February 28 rest with the command and control structure established for the operation and with the selection, placement, and use of command personnel. Overall command of an operation of this magnitude must be placed in the hands of commanders who have access to the information on which decisions to proceed or abort must be based, who have an understanding of that information, and who have a perspective from which they can make measured judgments on how to proceed. Furthermore, because ATF's raid commanders placed themselves in locations where calm deliberation was difficult and because they lacked appropriate intelligence support, the likelihood that these commanders would make the right decisions on raid day was reduced. . . .

The planning failures in the Waco raid stemmed in large part from an assumption on the part of ATF's leadership and those given specific planning responsibilities that an operation involving more than 100 agents against an extremely well-armed group of hostile cult members was just like any other enforcement action, only bigger. . . .

Media Impact

The media's interest in covering suspected criminal conduct and official responses to it will frequently be at odds with law enforcement's desire to have the advantage of surprise in its activities. However, the two sides generally accommodate each other partly out of necessity and partly out of each side's respect for the mission of the other. No such accommodation was reached at Waco. During their parallel investigations, both ATF and the media missed opportunities to take actions that might have averted the tragedy of February 28. . . .

ATF's Efforts to Delay the Publication of the "Sinful Messiah" Series

Early in ATF's investigation of alleged criminal activity at the Branch Davidian Compound, Special Agent Davy Aguilera learned that the [Waco] Tribune-Herald also was investigating Koresh. The two investigations continued on their separate courses for some time, with ATF trying to conceal the extent of its interest in the Branch Davidians. When Anguilera learned that former cult member Marc Breault was providing information to Mark England, a Tribune-Herald reporter, Aguilera asked Breault to stop speaking to the newspaper; it appears that Breault complied with this request. By January 1993, however, ATF's tactical planners began to fear that the Tribune-Herald's publication of its series about Koresh would interfere with, or at least complicate, the agency's plans to execute warrants at the Compound. It was thus on February 1 that Chuck Sarabyn and Earl Dunagan met with Barbara Elmore, the Tribune-Herald's managing editor, at the U.S. Attorney's office in Waco, and asked her to delay publication . . . until ATF could complete its operation. In the course of this meeting with Elmore, and subsequent meetings with Tribune-Herald personnel, Sarabyn, Dunagan, and, later, Phillip Chojnacki, disclosed not only ATF's intent to take action against the Compound, but also the anticipated date of that action.

Nothing in the agency's formal guidelines at the time barred this kind of media contact or even addressed it. The question remains, however, whether ATF exercised good judgment in initiating contact with the Tribune-Herald. Informed opinion differs on this point. Indeed, one of the tactical experts consulted by the Review wrote that ATF's efforts to obtain press cooperation violated basic principles of operational security. On balance, though, the Review believes that ATF made a reasonable judgment call in deciding to contact the Tribune-Herald....

ATF agents arrived in Waco and simply asked newspaper representatives to give up something of tremendous value to the paper—the opportunity to expose a local problem with independent, in-depth coverage. Were the paper to delay its series until after a raid had exposed the Compound's activities, the story would lose its exclusivity and its profitability. In exchange, the agents offered the paper security advice, advice that any law enforcement agency would give freely if asked and a chance to watch raid training at Fort Hood, an event with minimal news value.

Had Chojnacki entrusted the press negotiations to those in ATF with more experience in media relations, an arrangement that would have been more suitable to ATF and the Tribune-Herald might have been made.... And even if those responsible for press relations at ATF could not present better arguments to convince the Tribune-Herald to delay publication, they may have recognized the benefits of seeking assistance from local law enforcement officials in these negotiations, officials with whom the newspaper had a working relationship....

If an ATF representative with more media relations experience and no critical role to play in the coming raid had been responsible for ATF's negotiations with the Tribune Herald, ATF might have pressed its case beyond the February 24 meeting, perhaps with executives at Cox Enterprises [the newspaper's parent company]. Chojnacki, however, was understandably preoccupied with his responsibilities as overall raid commander. When his presentation at that meeting failed, Chojnacki decided not to negotiate further with the newspaper....

Media Activity Raid Day

By daybreak February 28, Tribune-Herald reporter Tommy Witherspoon's informant had alerted him to the timing of the raid. Tribune-Herald executives had seen helicopters landing at the Texas State Technical College air field and had interpreted them correctly as a sign that an ATF raid was imminent. AMT ambulance dispatcher Darlene Helmstetter disclosed details about a pending law enforcement operation to her friend Dan Mullony, a cameraman at KWTX.

... KWTX and the Tribune-Herald decided to send a total of 11 of their personnel ... to the Compound vicinity to cover the raid. The reporters arrived at the scene early and travelled up and down the roads around the Compound as they prepared to cover the story. One of their number,

KWTX cameraman [James] Peeler, became lost, and, in asking for directions, unwittingly tipped a cult member that a raid was imminent. Another group of reporters went to a house directly across from the Compound and asked for permission to watch ATF's enforcement action, without taking any precautions to ensure that these neighbors would not in turn alert Koresh to the impending raid. Many media personnel used cellular phones—unsecure communication devices whose signals are capable of easy, although illegal, interception.

The foregoing actions, which were taken by representatives of news organizations aware that Koresh and his followers were suspected of stockpiling weapons and manufacturing illegal firearms and explosives, belie the claim recently made by the Society of Professional Journalists' Waco Task Force that both KWTX and the Tribune-Herald "took precautions to prevent any alerting of the Davidians." The extent of those precautions consisted only in using unmarked vehicles in the Compound's vicinity.

The Society of Professional Journalists' Waco Task Force makes another claim that bears mention here. According to its report, the Task Force "found no concrete evidence validating the accusations that journalists from the newspaper or the television station tipped off the Branch Davidians as to what was happening." In contrast to this claim, James Peeler has admitted to the Review that he told someone later identified as David Jones that a law enforcement action would soon take place at the Compound. It is undisputed that Jones took this information and alerted Koresh. But however tragic the results of his carelessness may have been, Peeler should not be made the scapegoat for the fact that Koresh learned of the raid. Given the extent of other obvious media activity in the area, had Koresh not learned of the raid from Peeler, he might just as easily have been placed on guard by that other activity.

The prospect of substantial media activity in the area, and the dangers such activity could pose to the raid, should have been clear to ATF's raid commanders. . . .

Had ATF attempted to monitor media movements in the area, it might have prevented KWTX cameraman Peeler from ever speaking to cult member David Jones. At the very least, ATF would have recognized the significance of Jones racing to the Compound after his conversation with Peeler. . . .

Media activity in the vicinity of the Compound was not the immediate cause of the casualties suffered by ATF agents on February 28. These were inflicted by Koresh and his followers, and could have been avoided had ATF's raid commanders called off the operation once they recognized that they had lost the advantage of surprise. But the media's conduct posed a substantial danger not only to the security of ATF's operation but also to the lives of agents and civilians alike. While it is not the purpose of this report to suggest what the media might do to minimize such dangers in the future, the media should further examine its conduct on February 28.

ATF Post-raid Dissemination of Misleading Information

Following a tragedy of this magnitude, it was inevitable that the law enforcement community, the Executive Branch, Congress and concerned private citizens would demand an accounting of these events.

In the wake of the tragedy on February 28, the raid commanders, who made the decision to proceed with the raid despite the clear evidence that Koresh had been forewarned, and their superiors in the ATF hierarchy endeavored to answer the call for explanations. But critical aspects of the information that they provided—to superiors, to investigators, and to the public—were misleading or plain wrong. It was not that they lacked access to the relevant facts. Rather, raid commanders Chojnacki and [Charles] Sarabyn appear to have engaged in a concerted effort to conceal their errors in judgment. And ATF's management, perhaps out of a misplaced desire to protect the agency from criticism, offered accounts based on Chojnacki and Sarabyn's statements, disregarding clear evidence that those statements were false....

ATF's top management appropriately set about to determine whether surprise had been lost, and how. They established a "shooting review" team, and that team systematically looked for answers. Even before a complete picture of the Waco tragedy had emerged, however, Associate Director for Law Enforcement Daniel Hartnett and Deputy Associate Director for Law Enforcement Edward Daniel Conroy, together with Intelligence Division Chief David Troy—who became ATF's principal spokesman about the incident—soon began to make false or misleading public statements about the raid. Moreover, Director Stephen Higgins, relying on their reports from Waco, unknowingly made similar misstatements. To some extent, these misstatements were the product of inaccurate, untruthful or misleading information from Sarabyn and Chojnacki about what they had learned from [undercover agent Robert] Rodriguez before deciding to go forward with the raid. In making his initial public statements, Hartnett appears to have consciously avoided confronting the truth and, at the very least, displayed a serious lack of judgment.

As top ATF officials began to receive additional information from line agents and other sources indicating that the raid commanders had proceeded with full knowledge that they had lost the element of surprise, those officials must have realized, had they not already known, that their earlier public statements were either misleading or flatly false. Yet they stuck to their original story, thereby misleading the public and undermining the integrity of their agency....

In addition to making misleading statements to their superiors and investigators about the basis for their decision to proceed with the raid, Chojnacki and Sarabyn altered documentary evidence, misleading those probing their operational judgments....

After the failed raid, authorities began to ask ATF officials for the raid plan. The Texas Rangers were the first to ask ATF's Houston Office for the raid plan. When Support Coordinator Darrell Dyer was told of the request, he realized that the written plan had never been put in a satisfactory form. He advised Chojnacki and Sarabyn, and the three decided to revise the plan to make it more thorough and complete. Nowhere on the new version of the plan they crafted was there any indication that this was not the original document, or any identification of what had been added.... Indeed, when the Review asked ATF for all documents relating to ATF's investigation of the Branch Davidians, initially only the altered raid plan was received, without any indication that it was anything other than a document prepared prior to the raid.... At no time did any ATF official inform the Review that the plan submitted was not the original raid plan.

The alterations indicate not an attempt to create a plan that existed in the minds of the tactical planners and raid commanders on February 28. Rather, they suggest a selfserving effort to clarify the assumptions on which the planners had relied and enhance the reader's sense of their professionalism....

The readiness of Chojnacki, Sarabyn, and Dyer to revise an official document that would likely be of great significance in any official inquiry into the raid without making clear what they had done is extremely troubling and itself reflects a lack of judgment. This conduct, however, does not necessarily reveal an intent to deceive. And, in the case of Dyer, there does not appear to have been any such intent. The behavior of Chojnacki and Sarabyn when the alteration was investigated does not lead to the same conclusion....

JUSTICE DEPARTMENT REPORT

The Role of Experts During the Standoff

...During the Waco standoff the FBI utilized the Behavioral Sciences Unit [at the FBI Academy, Quantico, Virginia] for advice in dealing with Koresh and his followers. In addition to utilizing its in-house resources, the FBI also solicited and received input from various outside experts in many fields....

The FBI received this input both orally and in writing, and in each case ensured that the appropriate officials at FBI headquarters and on scene at Waco were made aware of the input. The FBI and the Attorney General also received input from various military and medical experts in connection with the planning for the April 19 tear gas plan.

The FBI also received unsolicited advice and offers of assistance from many individuals; not surprisingly, this input was rarely used.... Throughout the Waco standoff, the FBI meticulously kept track of all unsolicited offers of assistance, and followed up on those that seemed to promise any reasonable chance of producing helpful information. There were certain areas of activity in which the FBI did not seek outside help. For example, the FBI did not request assistance from any outside law enforcement agencies in performing any of its tactical operations, it did not request assistance with negotiations, since the FBI's best negotiators were assigned to Waco throughout the 51-day standoff, and it did not consult with outside experts regarding the decision to play loud music and Tibetan Monk chants over the loudspeakers to irritate those inside the compound.

Ultimately, the most useful information came from those experts (both inside and outside the FBI) from whom the FBI solicited information. These experts supplied a wide range of information about Koresh's state of mind and behavior, and provided input on some of the most important issues the FBI faced. For example, many of the experts agreed that the possibility of mass suicide existed, but no consensus emerged about the likelihood of suicide. Significantly, all the experts agreed that Koresh would not leave the compound voluntarily. On other issues, however, the expert opinions were not consistent. For example, some of the experts believed that Koresh was psychotic, while others believed he was not. The FBI considered all the information it received and made the best judgment it could considering how such information could best be used to further the FBI's goals of achieving a peaceful end to the standoff with no loss of life....

FBI Behavioral Scientists

... Later in the standoff, the Behavioral Sciences Unit prepared a short memorandum commenting on Koresh's personality as observed through the negotiation process. The Behavioral Sciences Unit noted that Koresh had displayed a variety of personality traits throughout the negotiations, ranging from friendly to angry, cooperative to confrontational, compliant to defiant, upbeat to morose, and pragmatic to delusional. The negotiation team reported its "growing concern" that, despite his statements to the contrary, Koresh might be planning a mass suicide similar to Jonestown. Nevertheless, the BSU concluded that Koresh exhibited traits of an anti-social personality, including: (1) exhibits low levels of stress in situations and under conditions others would find extremely stressful; (2) generally acts only in self-interest; (3) rarely has close, meaningful relationships; (4) statistically shows a low suicide rate; (5) more likely to arrange a "suicide by cop" situation than to commit suicide; (6) rarely accepts blame for anything negative; and (7) displays rapid flashes of anger.

In hindsight, [Quantico investigative analyst] Smerick regards Koresh as a con man who manipulated people and used religion to obtain sex and power. He does not know whether Koresh actually believed that he was the Messiah or "the Lamb," but he does think that Koresh may have started to believe the sermons that he had been preaching to his followers for the past several years. Finally, Smerick does not think the FBI should have consulted more or different theologians during the standoff. Smerick thinks such consultations would have been useless because in Koresh's theology only Koresh was capable of interpreting the Seven Seals and the Bible. Smerick noted that even if the Pope had come to Waco, Koresh would have said that God told Koresh that only Koresh was able to interpret the scriptures.

The other FBI "in-house" experts felt that the FBI on-scene commanders used tactical methods that undermined the negotiations and the credibility of the FBI negotiators. Some of the experts felt that the aggressive tactical moves played into Koresh's hands and strengthened Koresh's credibility among his followers, given that Koresh had been prophesizing all along that the government was preparing for the final confrontation. The in-house experts also believe that it was a mistake for the commanders to have "punished" the Davidians by cutting off power (March 12) or clearing out the Davidians' vehicles (March 21) in response to positive acts that the Davidians had taken (allowing people inside to leave).

Finally, the Tibetan Monk chants and other irritating sounds broadcast into the compound were played against the recommendation of some of the FBI's "in-house" experts.

Religious/Theological Experts

Smerick's feelings notwithstanding, the FBI did use religious experts and theologians to a limited extent during the standoff with the Branch Davidians. The FBI received unsolicited contact from a number of persons claiming religious/Biblical expertise, but most of those contacts resulted in little useful information. The FBI also contacted several religious experts for background information about the Branch Davidians and the Seventh Day Adventists. . . .

The FBI consulted more frequently with Dr. Glenn Hilburn [dean of the Baylor University religion department] throughout the standoff than any other theologian. Dr. Hilburn made his entire staff of 23 available to the FBI, and he and his staff had frequent contact with the negotiators and the commanders. Baylor University has one of the largest "cult" reference and research facilities in the country. It also had the advantage of being located nearby in Waco.

Dr. Hilburn provided information on the Book of Revelations, the Seven Seals, and other Biblical matters. The FBI relied heavily on Dr. Hilburn early on in the negotiations, when it engaged Koresh in long discussions about the Bible as a negotiating tactic . . .

Attitudes of Koresh and Others in the Compound

Religion/Devotion to Koresh

The Branch Davidians' religion emphasized the apocalyptic nature of Koresh's preachings. They believed Koresh was the "Lamb" through whom God communicated to them. They also believed the end of the world was near, that the world would end in a cataclysmic confrontation between themselves and the government, and that they would thereafter be resurrected. The February 28 ATF raid only reinforced the truth of Koresh's prophetic pronouncements in the minds of his followers.

The key to Koresh's hold on his followers was his ability to recite lengthy portions of the Bible from memory, and to "harmonize" disparate, seemingly unrelated scriptures by showing how they "tied together." This ability, combined with Koresh's charismatic/mercurial personality and the low self-esteem of his followers, created an environment in which Koresh was elevated to near God-like status.

Koresh exercised great control over the lives of his followers. He told them what to eat, where to work, where to sleep, and what to think.

Koresh's charismatic hold permitted him to take extraordinary liberties with his followers. Koresh preached that as the "Lamb of God" only his "seed" was pure, meaning that only he could have sex with the over-puberty aged girls and women in the compound, and that none of the men could have sex. Koresh even convinced Schneider to give up his wife, Judy, to Koresh for sexual purposes. Koresh would humiliate Steve Schneider by talking about his sexual experiences with Judy in front of all the Davidians at their Bible study sessions. But Schneider believed in Koresh to the end.

Intention to Stay Inside the Compound

Probably the most important observation that can be made about the Waco standoff is that after all is said and done, after all the analysis, investigations, hearings, and so forth, nothing would have changed the outcome because the people who remained inside had no intention of leaving.

The March 9 videotape [that Koresh made for broadcast] provides compelling evidence of the desire of Koresh's followers to stay inside with him. Other evidence supporting this conclusion comes from the many telephone conversations the negotiators had with persons inside the compound. Approximately 50 of those people told the negotiators they did not want to leave.

In addition, Koresh repeatedly lied to the negotiators about whether he would come out. On March 2, of course, he promised to come out with his followers "immediately" upon the broadcasting of his 58 minute audio tape over the radio. After the tape was broadcast Koresh reneged on his promise, saying God had told him to wait. On March 19 Koresh promised to come out "in the next few days." Later that day Koresh said "it could be as early as tomorrow evening . . . that's a promise, a guarantee." Several days later Koresh promised to come out after Passover. Once Passover came and went, with the Davidians still inside, Koresh promised that he would leave as soon as he finished writing a manuscript regarding the Seven Seals.

Law Enforcement/Government

In Koresh's theology, the government, particularly the federal law enforcement agencies, were the "Assyrians" or the "Babylonians" who were bent on destroying the true believers, the Branch Davidians. Koresh had predicted to his followers well before the February 28 ATF raid that law enforcement agents planned to kill him and his followers. Koresh planned for the predicted apocalyptic showdown with the government by massively arming himself and his followers beginning in early 1992 and continuing through early 1993. Koresh was fascinated with guns. Former compound members have described the shooting practice, the conversion of semi-automatic weapons to fully automatic, the sewing of specially designed vests with pockets for extra ammunition clips, and the early morning para-military drills for the males in the compound.

Koresh and his followers demonstrated the level of their hatred for the ATF by ambushing the agents who arrived on February 28 with a valid search and arrest warrant. The ATF raid reinforced Koresh's status as a prophet among his followers, because they viewed it as consistent with Koresh's earlier predictions of confrontation. Following the raid Koresh continued to preach that the standoff with the FBI was a continuation of the cataclysmic battle between the Davidians and the federal government.

Koresh's hatred of the government did not always seem apparent. The tapes of the negotiations between Koresh and the FBI contain many lighthearted moments, and many hours of calm, peaceful conversations between Koresh and the negotiators. Koresh even proclaimed his admiration for law enforcement during some of the conversations. However, Koresh also made many threats during the conversations, including threats to start "World War III," threats to blow the FBI's armored vehicles into the air, and threats to shoot FBI agents if they tried anything "silly."

Death and Suicide

No one could have predicted with certainty that Koresh and his followers would commit suicide. There were many pieces of evidence suggesting both that Koresh was not suicidal and that he was suicidal. While so much of Koresh's preaching and the Davidians' religious beliefs revolved around notions of mass destruction, apocalyptic confrontations, and the like, it was very difficult during the standoff for the FBI to reach any particular conclusion regarding the possibility of suicide. . . .

Child Abuse

One of the issues that received some attention in Congress and the media in the aftermath of the standoff involved allegations of prior and ongoing child physical and sexual abuse inside the compound, and the extent to which those allegations affected the Attorney General's decision to authorize the tear gas action. This inquiry has determined that:

Evidence suggested that Koresh had engaged in child physical and sexual abuse over a long period of time prior to the ATF shootout on February 28. This evidence was insufficient to establish probable cause to indict or proof beyond a reasonable doubt to convict, but it was sufficient to be relevant to the decisionmaking process involving the proposed tear gas plan....

There was no direct evidence indicating that Koresh engaged in any physical or sexual abuse of children during the standoff. Given that Koresh had been shot and wounded on February 28, he probably lacked the physical ability to continue his abuse. However, there was evidence that sanitary conditions inside the compound, primitive to begin with, had worsened considerably during the standoff. It was unhealthy at best, and potentially life-threatening at worst, for children to continue to be forced to live in such an environment.

The FBI did not exaggerate the child abuse issue when it presented the tear gas option to the Attorney General. The FBI did not try to "sell" the tear gas plan to the Attorney General as a way to save the children. While one of the FBI representatives made one misstatement indicating that Koresh was continuing to beat children during the standoff, that misstatement did not materially influence the Attorney General's decision. Indeed, the FBI included virtually no mention of child abuse in its initial briefing book for the Attorney General. In the final briefing book, prepared on the weekend before April 19, the FBI included the historical evidence of child abuse and in no way indicated that it had any evidence of continuing abuse....

Planning and Decision-Making

The CS Gas-Insertion Plan

... [I]t was apparent that permitting the standoff to continue would neither lead to the peaceful surrender of Koresh, nor eliminate the risk to the safety of the innocent children in the compound, the public at large, and the government agents at the scene. Accordingly, the strategy continued to be aimed at restricting the options of those inside the compound and reducing their level of comfort.

The FBI hoped to make the Davidians' environment sufficiently unpleasant that their only choices would be to come out or resume negotiating in good faith.

... [T]he FBI proposed beginning to restrict access to certain parts of the compound by the use of CS gas. The plan was to introduce the liquid CS into the compound in stages. Initially, only one small part of the compound was to be affected. The goal of this restrained "response" was to allow the insiders ready access to other exits or unaffected portions of the compound, while at the same time minimizing the risk of panic. Medical support was to be available, and the FBI planned to use loudspeakers and large signs to guide people out of the compound. The FBI hoped thereby to indicate that the action was neither an assault nor a modification of the rules of engagement. Except for two controlled exit routes, concertina wire had been strung around the compound to diminish the possibility that people would escape. Those people leaving the compound would be guided to safety by the loudspeakers down a single path to a large Red Cross flag. A joint law-enforcement contingent would be in place to surround the compound and ensure the safety of those who came out.

In the event that everyone did not leave the compound after the initial introduction of gas, or that good faith negotiations intended to resolve the conflict were not resumed, gas would be introduced in other wings of the compound. Eventually, walls would be torn down to increase the exposure of those remaining inside. The FBI's intention was to develop the "response" gradually and only to the degree needed to accomplish the evacuation of the compound. . . .

Week of April 12, 1993

On April 12, 1993, the FBI presented the tear gas plan to the Attorney General for her approval. Over the next several days the Attorney General and senior Justice Department and FBI officials discussed, debated and dissected every aspect of the plan. Before even discussing the merits of the plan the Attorney General repeatedly asked why it is was necessary to do anything to change the status quo: "Why now, why not wait," she asked.

After becoming convinced that some action was needed, the Attorney General vigorously questioned every aspect of the proposed plan, and the FBI provided her the answers to all her questions. Ultimately, she approved the plan on the night of Saturday, April 17, 1993. . . .

April 12 Meetings

. . . [March 12] was the first time that the Attorney General was briefed on the proposal to use gas. She asked how the gas might affect pregnant women and children. Hubbell suggested that they consult with the military about the effects of the gas.

The Attorney General also asked whether the Branch Davidians might injure themselves, as well as the need to resolve the standoff by Wednesday, April 14, the date the FBI proposed for executing the plan. . . . Although the FBI gave no reasons for the urgency, its representatives stated that Koresh and the other Branch Davidians did not appear to be coming out. Instead, due to the supply of food and water in the compound, it looked like they were going to stay for an extended period of time. FBI personnel giving the briefing felt that the pressure on the Davidians had to be increased to move the negotiations forward. The Attorney General asked additional questions, but made no decision to act at the time. . . .

April 14 Meetings

Once the Attorney General was convinced that the gas was non-lethal and would not cause permanent harm to children, pregnant women and others, she turned her attention to the HRT [Hostage Rescue Team]....

The FBI asserted that law enforcement on the scene in Waco could not safely maintain the security perimeter indefinitely. There was a vast open area surrounding the compound, and it was impossible safely to keep people from wandering in and out. Moreover, the Branch Davidian compound itself was a heavily armed camp, with dangerous people inside who had already killed four law enforcement agents. The situation was difficult to control, and the area was difficult to defend. In the FBI's view, there were extraordinary public safety issues. Containment of the Branch Davidians in the building with walls or wire appeared infeasible, and posse comitatus proscriptions prevented the use of a military force to secure the area. Some experts had raised the distinct possibility that Koresh might actually mount an offensive attack against the perimeter security, with Branch Davidians using children as shields. This would have required the best trained forces available to the FBI. Finally, the FBI expressed its concern about the possible incursions of fringe groups intent on coming to Koresh's aid....

April 18 Meetings

On April 18, Reno discussed the plan with the President. She told him that she had considered every possibility and had approved the use of tear gas.... Reno considered the President to have been fully briefed....

The Attorney General's Retrospective

The Attorney General believes she was adequately informed and that the FBI was forthcoming. She was impressed with the quality and timeliness of responses to her questions or to her requests for additional information.... The FBI did not try to "railroad" her. Instead, they were respectful and seemed genuinely appreciative of the hard questions she posed....

JUSTICE DEPARTMENT EVALUATION

After reviewing the stand-off at Waco, including the progress of the negotiations and the conception, approval and implementation of the tear gas plan on April 19, 1993, this Report concludes as follows. The fire on April 19, 1993 was deliberately set by persons inside the compound and was not started by the FBI's tear gas insertion operations. It is not certain, however, whether a substantial number of the persons who died in the compound on April 19 remained inside voluntarily, were being held in the compound against their will or were shot in order to prevent their escape from the fire. Preliminary medical reports are that a substantial number of individuals had died of gunshot wounds. Among those shot were young children. [David] Koresh's body was found with a gunshot wound to the forehead. The

FBI did not fire on the compound during the tear gas operation, although shots were fired at the FBI from the compound. The FBI did not fire on the compound at any time during the fifty-one day stand-off.

The evidence forecasting David Koresh's intention to orchestrate a mass suicide was contradictory. Koresh and his followers repeatedly assured the negotiators that they did not intend to commit suicide. On several occasions agents were told that suicide was against the Davidians' religious beliefs. However, one released member said there was a suicide plan. Other released members denied there was a suicide plan. In any event, the risk of suicide was taken into account during the negotiations and in the development of the gas plan.

The FBI developed a coherent negotiating strategy to talk the Davidians out. However, the negotiators had strong objections to pressure tactics they felt were counterproductive. The use of pressure tactics immediately after Koresh sent out Davidians from the compound may have undermined the negotiators' credibility and blunted their efforts to gain the Davidians' trust and to discredit Koresh in the eyes of his followers. Nevertheless, tactical actions designed to increase the safety margin for agents were appropriately given priority over negotiating considerations. I conclude that the events of April 19 were the result of David Koresh's determined efforts to choreograph his own death and the deaths of his followers in a confrontation with federal authorities to fulfill Koresh's apocalyptic prophesy. The deaths of Koresh, his followers and their children on April 19th were not the result of a flaw in the gas plan or the negotiation strategy.

The FBI used many qualified experts, including its own FBI behavioral experts to evaluate Koresh. Their assessments were thorough and many proved quite accurate.

The Attorney General was adequately briefed on the tear gassing plan, was fully informed of the options, and was given a realistic appraisal of the risks. All reasonable alternatives were considered and the decision to insert CS [tear] gas was a reasonable one. I conclude that an indefinite siege was not a realistic option. According to the plan, gas would be inserted in stages and the FBI would wait 48 hours for it to have an effect. As the plan was being implemented, the tanks were ordered to enlarge openings in the compound to provide escape routes for the Davidians.

The FBI did anticipate that a fire might occur at the compound. Fire fighting equipment was not kept close to the scene because the heavy weaponry used by Koresh and his followers presented unacceptable risks to fire fighters. In any event, the independent arson experts concluded that the fire spread so quickly in the poorly constructed compound that even prompt fire fighting efforts would have been ineffective.

The FBI exhibited extraordinary restraint and handled the crisis with great professionalism. . . .

JUSTICE DEPARTMENT'S PROPOSED CHANGES

Recommendations

An Overview

. . . When faced with complex hostage/barricade incidents, law enforcement must respond with four critical elements and an organization that provides additional support functions. The critical elements are (1) a well-equipped and highly skilled tactical team to contain the suspects and bring the incident to a close, using, if necessary, appropriate force; (2) trained and experienced negotiators, supported by pertinent research on successful techniques in similar situations, who can attempt to achieve a peaceful resolution; (3) behavioral science experts who can advise the tacticians and the negotiators about the suspects and assist them in developing strategies; and (4) a command structure that integrates the other elements and develops a coherent overall strategy. . . .

The Responsibility of the FBI

. . . The United States government should have one such structure available to serve wherever a major threat of the sort I have described calls for federal law enforcement. With its Hostage Rescue Team, Critical Incident Negotiation Team, Behavioral Science Unit, other relevant components and large number of personnel, the FBI, according to the experts, is the obvious choice. . . .

The Size and Location of the Hostage Rescue Team

Our experts agree that the FBI Hostage Rescue Team is as good as any in the world, a remarkable compliment. But they also agree that it is, at fifty persons, too small to deal with the variety of situations that may arise. I will propose to the Director of the FBI and the Attorney General that the size of the team be doubled, a figure within the range of acceptability according to most of our experts.

. . . We intend that most FBI SWAT [Special Weapons and Tactics] teams include one former HRT [Hostage Rescue team] member who can bring to bear that unit's specialized experience and training. The FBI and SWAT teams from the various federal law enforcement agencies should be able to maintain the situation until the arrival of the rescue/negotiation force which can at any time be in the air within a very reasonable period.

. . . [W]e should also promote research to develop non-lethal technology to expand the number of options available to subdue suspects.

Negotiations Capacity

. . . If the FBI is given the responsibility for dealing with these events, it must supplement its present, largely dispersed negotiating capacity with an increased central component at Quantico.

... [T]he negotiators should be familiar with the capacities of the HRT operations, and the HRT should be familiar with the strategies of the negotiating team. What is necessary in many circumstances is a highly coordinated effort using both sets of capacities....

Behavioral Science Capacity

... Several of our experts suggested that David Koresh and his Branch Davidian followers believed that the unfolding events were part of a script that had been foretold in the Bible as interpreted by David Koresh. These experts suggested that relating the combined negotiation/assault tactics to that script would have been helpful....

Federal law enforcement cannot and should not collect and study the writings of groups characterized only by views very different from the mainstream in the United States. This would be an undertaking far more dangerous to civil liberties and far more unstructured in its reach than collecting information, under traditional carefully written Attorney General guidelines, about violent organizations. What the experts suggest is that our training of law enforcement agents include material designed to alert agents to the potential importance of differences in views among Americans on such subjects as religion and political ideology. Those who provide this training should themselves become expert in the range and diversity of beliefs held by Americans—including the more unconventional beliefs—and should be available for advice when events like this occur.

As to particular groups, like the Branch Davidians, we should consult with academic scholars for detailed information that may be useful to negotiators or others.... For this, federal law enforcement must, our experts urge, begin to make contact with a wide range of experts in the social sciences—from religion to sociology to psychiatry—so that we can very promptly enlist their assistance when needed.

Crisis Management

... We need field managers with the training, experience, and leadership qualities to orchestrate rescue and negotiation efforts in light of social science knowledge. That means that the FBI, if it is to be in charge of this national responsibility, will have to depart from its strong tradition of placing responsibility in the hands of the Special Agent in Charge ("SAC") of the local division.

The FBI has plans underway to select fifteen of its most senior field commanders to receive special training with the Hostage Rescue Team and with negotiators and to learn to call upon the social science capacity that we will be building. On any major occasion three or four of these specially chosen SACs will be called into action so that fatigue is not a factor in their operations any more than it will be in the operations of the newly expanded Hostage Rescue Team.

The local SAC will continue to play a highly central role as deputy to the field commander, responsible for coordinating relations with the variety of local authorities, state and federal, who continue to have significant responsibilities. The SAC should also assume responsibility for whatever criminal investigation is behind the confrontation....

To the extent that time allows, the major policy decisions recommended by the field commander should be reviewed by the Director of the FBI and the Attorney General or their immediate deputies. The structure for this phase of the operation is generally well in place. An Assistant Director of the FBI should have the full-time responsibility in Washington....

...Officials of the Department of Justice should be included in crisis planning exercises so that the entire chain of command will be prepared for emergencies.

The Responsibility of Other Federal Law Enforcement Agencies

Finally, while it is important to define a category of tactical situations in which the FBI should take control, other agencies will and should continue to conduct operations that may on occasion develop into hostage/barricade situations....

The Department of the Treasury's Federal Law Enforcement Training Center has a "First Response Training Program" that teaches law enforcement officers the basics of handling a hostage/barricade situation, including setting up a command post, establishing an inner and outer perimeter, engaging in preliminary negotiations, and dealing with the media. Basic training of this sort should be provided to all federal agencies....

An orderly transition from ATF responsibility to FBI responsibility took place at Waco. This important transition stage could be facilitated by efforts to have SWAT teams from other agencies participate in training exercises with the HRT and the FBI negotiators....

I am confident that when this structure is fully implemented, we will have substantially improved our ability to deal successfully with complex hostage/barricade situations with a reduced risk of losing innocent lives.

October

POPE'S ENCYCLICAL ON MORAL THEOLOGY

October 5, 1993

In response to what he perceived as increasing threats to the Roman Catholic church's moral authority, Pope John Paul II on October 5 released the tenth encyclical of his papacy, entitled Veritatis Splendor *(The Splendor of Truth). In this doctrinal treatise of more than 40,000 words, addressed specifically to the bishops of the church as teachers and guardians of sound doctrine, the pontiff focused on holy scripture as the foundation of moral theology. John Paul informed the bishops, "It seems necessary to reflect on the whole of the church's moral teachings, with the precise goal of recalling certain fundamental truths of Catholic doctrine which . . . risk being distorted or denied." He warned, "It is no longer a matter of limited and occasional dissent, but of an overall and systematic calling into question of traditional moral doctrine."*

The pope concentrated on abstract moral theory, discussing such concepts as freedom, conscience, and moral relativism. He reaffirmed the church's proscription against "intrinsically evil" acts, including abortion and contraceptive practices. At one stage of the document's six-year-preparation, press reports indicated that it would focus on a list of sexual sins and declare the church's teaching on birth control infallible. Neither theme was developed in the final document.

An apparently earlier draft, leaked to the press in mid-1993, included a section on infallibility but did not break new ground. That section did not appear in the encyclical's final form. Portions of the final document had also been leaked to the press days before its official release. The leaks, coupled with an obviously long drafting process, indicated dissension within the Catholic hierarchy. Cardinal Joseph Ratzinger, head of the Vatican Congregation for the Doctrine of the Faith, told a Vatican news conference that consultations included theologians from every continent representing "varied orientations" and contributed to a long delay in publication.

Traditional Teachings Reaffirmed

Veritatis Splendor *began by asserting a biblical basis for Christian moral theology. Promoting faith and the moral life "is the task entrusted by Jesus to the apostles, a task which continues in the ministry of their successors," the pope wrote. Through the mandate from Jesus and "the help of the Holy Spirit," he added, quoting Catholic canon law, "the church has the right always and everywhere to proclaim moral principles, even in respect to the social order, and to make judgments about any human matter insofar as this is required by fundamental human rights or the salvation of souls."*

While denying the intention of imposing any particular theological or philosophical system, the encyclical maintained that "the magisterium [church's teaching authority] has the duty to state that some trends of theological thinking and certain philosophical affirmations are incompatible with revealed truth." The pope declared that God, not the individual, was the arbiter in decisions about good and evil.

Faith-Morality Separation Criticized

Behavioral sciences, while they have "rightly drawn attention to many kinds of ... conditioning which influence the exercise of human freedom," have contributed to a view that questions or denies "the very reality of human freedom," the document continued, declaring that although man is free "his freedom is not unlimited." He is called to accept "the moral law given by God," under which the church has declared certain acts "intrinsically evil." They remain so, the pope asserted, despite good intentions or mitigating circumstances. Quoting the Second Vatican Council and Pope Paul VI, he said that intrinsically evil acts included those "hostile to life itself," such as homicide, genocide, abortion, euthanasia, voluntary suicide, and contraceptive practices; "whatever violates the integrity of the human person"; or whatever "is offensive to human dignity."

The pope emphasized "the urgent need of the church herself to develop an intense pastoral effort" to help mankind rediscover the "essential bond between truth, the good and freedom." He warned against the tendency of present-day culture to separate freedom from truth, and faith from morality. The faith-morality separation, he declared, "represents one of the most acute pastoral concerns of the church" in a society in which "many ... people think and live as if God did not exist."

Charges of Stifling Debate

John Paul declared that theologians must not dissent from "the teachings of the church's pastors" and must respect the "right of the faithful to receive Catholic doctrine in its purity and integrity." Finally, he called on the bishops to exercise their pastoral duty "to be vigilant that the word of God is faithfully taught." Dissension arose, nevertheless.

Critics included the Rev. Charles Curran, a priest and moral theologian whom the Vatican had censured for his teaching at the Catholic University of America. Curran was quoted in the Washington Post *as saying that moral theologians would find the pope's messages very threatening.*

Colman McCarthy, a columnist for the newspaper and a prominent Catholic commentator, praised the pope for having "the courage to take a stand." But he was troubled by the "irrelevance of the stand." The pope, McCarthy wrote, "is silent about what he and the Vatican propose to do about the tens of millions of unwanted births that will result if his orders against contraception are followed and secular society has to pick up the tab for the immense social costs of overpopulation."

Catholic officials in Rome and the United States sought to counter the impression that the encyclical was meant to stifle debate. The Rev. Augustine DiNoia, head of the office on theological doctrine for the National Conference of Catholic Bishops, said in Washington, D.C., "The encyclical is meant to invite a dialogue between theologians and bishops."

> *Following are excerpts from the papal encyclical* Veritatis Splendor *(The Splendor of Truth) of John Paul II, released by the Vatican October 5, 1993, and provided in English translation by the Catholic News Service in Washington, D.C., in which the pope reaffirmed a traditional Catholic basis for moral theology:*

... At all times, but particularly in the last two centuries, the popes, whether individually or together with the college of bishops, have developed and proposed a moral teaching regarding the many different spheres of human life. In Christ's name and with his authority they have exhorted, passed judgment and explained....

Today, however, it seems necessary to reflect on the whole of the church's moral teaching, with the precise goal of recalling certain fundamental truths of Catholic doctrine which, in the present circumstances, risk being distorted or denied.... It is no longer a matter of limited and occasional dissent, but of an overall and systematic calling into question of traditional moral doctrine on the basis of certain anthropological and ethical presuppositions.... Certain of the church's moral teachings are found simply unacceptable; and the magisterium itself is considered capable of intervening in matters of morality only in order to "exhort consciences" and to "propose values," in the light of which each individual will independently make his or her decisions and life choices.

In particular, note should be taken of the lack of harmony between the traditional response of the church and certain theological positions encountered even in seminaries and in faculties of theology with regard to questions of the greatest importance for the church and for the life of faith of Christians as well as for the life of society itself.... Commandments of God, which are written on the human heart and are part of the covenant, really have the capacity to clarify the daily decisions of individuals and entire societies? It is possible to obey God and thus love God and neighbor without respecting these commandments in all circumstances? Also, an opinion is frequently heard which questions the intrinsic and unbreakable bond between faith and morality, as if membership in the church and her internal unity were to be decided on the basis of faith alone, while in the sphere of morality a pluralism of opinions and of kinds of behavior could be tolerated, these being left to the judgment of the individual subjective conscience or to the diversity of social and cultural contexts.

Given these circumstances ... I came to the decision ... to write an encyclical with the aim of treating "more fully and more deeply the issues regarding the very foundations of moral theology," foundations which are being undermined by certain present-day tendencies.

[Chapter 1 Omitted]

Chapter 2

... The church's moral reflection, always conducted in the light of Christ, the "good teacher," has also developed in the specific form of the theological science called *moral theology* a science which accepts and examines divine revelation while at the same time responding to the demands of human reason....

The Second Vatican Council invited scholars to take "special care for the renewal of moral theology," in such a way that "its scientific presentation, increasingly based on the teaching of Scripture, will cast light on the exalted vocation of the faithful in Christ and on their obligation to bear fruit in charity for the life of the world."...

The work of many theologians who found support in the council's encouragement has already borne fruit in interesting and helpful reflections about the truths of faith to be believed and applied in life.... The church, and particularly the bishops, to whom Jesus Christ primarily entrusted the ministry of teaching, are deeply appreciative of this work and encourage theologians to continue their efforts....

At the same time, however, within the context of the theological debates which followed the council there have developed certain interpretations of Christian morality which are not consistent with "sound teaching". Certainly the church's magisterium does not intend to impose upon the faithful any particular theological system, still less a philosophical one. Nevertheless, in order to "reverently preserve and faithfully expound" the word of God, the magisterium has the duty to state that some trends of theological thinking and certain philosophical affirmations are incompatible with revealed truth....

The human issues most frequently debated and differently resolved in contemporary moral reflection are all closely related, albeit in various ways, to a crucial issue: human freedom....

This heightened sense of the dignity of the human person and of his or her uniqueness, and of the respect due to the journey of conscience, certainly represents one of the positive achievements of modern culture. This perception, authentic as it is, has been expressed in a number of more or less adequate ways, some of which, however, diverge from the truth about man as a creature and the image of God, and thus need to be corrected and purified in the light of faith.

Certain currents of modern thought have gone so far as to exalt freedom to such an extent that it becomes an absolute, which would then be the source of values.... Such an outlook is quite congenial to an individualist ethic, wherein each individual is faced with his own truth, different from the truth of others. Taken to its extreme consequences, this individualism leads to a denial of the very idea of human nature....

Side by side with its exaltation of freedom yet oddly in contrast with it, modern culture radically questions the very existence of this freedom. A number of disciplines, grouped under the name of the "behavioral sciences," have rightly drawn attention to the many kinds of psychological and social conditioning which influence the exercise of human freedom. Knowledge of these conditionings and the study they have received represent important achievements which have found application in various areas, for example, in pedagogy or the administration of justice. But some people, going beyond the conclusions which can be legitimately drawn from these observations, have come to question or even deny the very reality of human freedom....

Although each individual has a right to be respected in his own journey in search of the truth, there exists a prior moral obligation, and a grave one at that, to seek the truth and to adhere to it once it is known....

Revelation teaches that the power to decide what is good and what is evil does not belong to man, but to God alone. The man is certainly free, inasmuch as he can understand and accept God's commands.... But his freedom is not unlimited: It must halt before the "tree of the knowledge of good and evil," for it is called to accept the moral law given by God. In fact, human freedom finds its authentic and complete fulfillment precisely in the acceptance of that law....

The modern concern for the claims of autonomy has not failed to exercise an influence also in the sphere of Catholic moral theology....

In their desire, however, to keep the moral life in a Christian context, certain moral theologians have introduced a sharp distinction, contrary to Catholic doctrine, between an ethical order, which would be human in origin and of value for this world alone, and an order of salvation for which only certain intentions and interior attitudes regarding God and neighbor would be significant. This has then led to an actual denial that there exists, in divine revelation, a specific and determined moral content, universally valid and permanent....

No one can fail to see that such an interpretation of the autonomy of human reason involves positions incompatible with Catholic teaching....

Man's genuine moral autonomy in no way means the rejection but rather the acceptance of the moral law, of God's command: "The Lord God gave this command to the man" (Gn. 2:16). Human freedom and God's law meet and are called to intersect, in the sense of man's free obedience to God and of God's completely gratuitous benevolence toward man....

Jesus' call to "come, follow me" marks the greatest possible exaltation of human freedom, yet at the same time it witnesses to the truth and to the obligation of acts of faith and of decisions which can be described as involving a fundamental option....

To separate the fundamental option from concrete kinds of behavior means to contradict the substantial integrity or personal unity of the moral agent in his body and in his soul....

Judgments about morality cannot be made without taking into consideration whether or not the deliberate choice of a specific kind of behavior is in conformity with the dignity and integral vocation of the human person.... Once the moral species of an action prohibited by a universal rule is concretely recognized, the only morally good act is that of obeying the moral law and of refraining from the action which it forbids....

As the Catechism of the Catholic Church teaches, "there are certain specific kinds of behavior that are always wrong to choose, because choosing them involves a disorder of the will, that is, a moral evil...."

Reason attests that there are objects of the human act which are by their nature "incapable of being ordered" to God because they radically contradict the good of the person made in his image. These are acts which, in the church's moral tradition, have been termed "intrinsically evil" *(intrinsece malum):* They are such always and per se, in other words, on account of their very object and quite apart from the ulterior intentions of the one acting and the circumstances. Consequently, without in the least denying the influence on morality exercised by circumstances and especially by intentions, the church teaches that "there exist acts which per se and in themselves, independently of circumstances, are always seriously wrong by reason of their object." The Second Vatican Council itself, in discussing the respect due to the human person, gives a number of examples of such acts:

"Whatever is hostile to life itself, such as any kind of homicide, genocide, abortion, euthanasia and voluntary suicide; whatever violates the integrity of the human person, such as mutilation, physical and mental torture and attempts to coerce the spirit; whatever is offensive to human dignity such as subhuman living conditions, arbitrary imprisonment, deportation, slavery, prostitution and trafficking in women and children; degrading conditions of work which treat laborers as mere instruments of profit, and not as free responsible persons: All these and the like are a disgrace, and so long as they infect human civilization they contaminate those who inflict them more than those who suffer injustice, and they are a negation of the honor due to the Creator."

With regard to intrinsically evil acts and in reference to contraceptive practices whereby the conjugal act is intentionally rendered infertile, Pope Paul VI teaches:

"Though it is true that sometimes it is lawful to tolerate a lesser moral evil in order to avoid a greater evil or in order to promote a greater good, it is never lawful even for the gravest reasons to do evil that good may come of it—in other words, to intend directly something which of its very nature contradicts the moral order and which must therefore be judged unworthy of man, even though the intention is to protect or promote the welfare of an individual, of a family or of society in general."

If acts are intrinsically evil, a good intention or particular circumstances can diminish their evil, but they cannot remove it....

Consequently, circumstances or intentions can never transform an act intrinsically evil by virtue of its object into an act "subjectively" good or defensible as a choice....

Chapter 3

Moral Good for the Life of The Church and of the World

According to Christian faith and the church's teaching, "only the freedom which submits to the truth leads the human person to his true good." The good of the person is to be in the truth and to do the truth.

A comparison between the church's teaching and today's social and cultural situation immediately makes clear the urgent need for the church herself to develop an intense pastoral effort precisely with regard to this fundamental question.

"This essential bond between truth, the good and freedom has been largely lost sight of by present-day culture. As a result, helping man to rediscover it represents nowadays one of the specific requirements of the church's mission, for the salvation of the world.... "

The attempt to set freedom in opposition to truth, and indeed to separate them radically, is the consequence, manifestation and consummation of another more serious and destructive dichotomy, that which separates faith from morality.

This separation represents one of the most acute pastoral concerns of the church amid today's growing secularism, wherein many, indeed too many, people think and live "as if God did not exist." We are speaking of a mentality which affects, often in a profound, extensive and all-embracing way, even the attitudes and behavior of Christians, whose faith is weakened and loses its character as a new and original criterion for thinking and acting in personal, family and social life. In a widely de-Christianized culture, the criteria employed by believers themselves in making judgments and decisions often appear extraneous or even contrary to those of the Gospel....

Faced with the many difficulties which fidelity to the moral order can demand even in the most ordinary circumstances, the Christian is called, with the grace of God invoked in prayer, to a sometimes heroic commitment.

Even in the most difficult situations man must respect the norm of morality so that he can be obedient to God's holy commandment and consistent with his own dignity as a person....

De-Christianization, which weighs heavily upon entire peoples and communities once rich in faith and Christian life, involves not only the loss of faith or in any event its becoming irrelevant for everyday life, but also, and of necessity, a decline or obscuring of the moral sense. This comes about both as a result of a loss of awareness of the originality of Gospel morality and as a result of an eclipse of fundamental principles and ethical values themselves. Today's widespread tendencies toward subjectivism, utilitarianism and relativism appear not merely as pragmatic attitudes or patterns of behavior, but rather as approaches having a basis in theory and claiming full cultural and social legitimacy....

The service which moral theologians are called to provide at the present time is of the utmost importance, not only for the church's life and mission, but also for human society and culture....

While exchanges and conflicts of opinion may constitute normal expressions of public life in a representative democracy, moral teaching certainly cannot depend simply upon respect for a process: Indeed, it is in no way established by following the rules and deliberative procedures typical of democracy.... Opposition to the teaching of the church's pastors cannot be seen as a legitimate expression either of Christian freedom or of the diversity of the Spirit's gifts. When this happens, the church's pastors have the duty to act in conformity with their apostolic mission, insisting that the right of the faithful to receive Catholic doctrine in its purity and integrity must always be respected....

Each of us knows how important is the teaching which represents the central theme of this encyclical and which is today being restated with the authority of the successor of Peter. Each of us can see the seriousness of what is involved, not only for individuals but also for the whole of society, with the reaffirmation of the universality and immutability of the moral commandments, particularly those which prohibit always and without exception intrinsically evil acts.... My brothers in the episcopate, it is part of our pastoral ministry to see to it that this moral teaching is faithfully handed down and to have recourse to appropriate measures to ensure that the faithful are guarded from every doctrine and theory contrary to it....

At the end of these considerations, let us entrust ourselves, the sufferings and the joys of our life, the moral life of believers and people of good will, and the research of moralists, to Mary, mother of God and mother of mercy....

OTA REPORT ON TUBERCULOSIS

October 7, 1993

Although widely characterized as a disease of "yesteryear" that many perceived as all but eradicated, a 150-page congressional Office of Technology Assessment (OTA) report, released October 7, 1993, found that the incidence of tuberculosis (TB) had increased 20 percent since 1985 and was reaching epidemic proportions in some urban areas of the United States.

In response to rising concern about the rapid escalation of TB cases, the OTA was requested to undertake the study by three congressional committees: the House Committee on Energy and Commerce Subcommittee on Health and the Environment, the House Committee on Government Operations' Subcommittee on Human Resources and Intergovernmental Relations, and the Senate Committee on Labor and Human Resources. The OTA team was assisted in its efforts by a group of public health leaders from academia, industry, government, and public interest groups, who met in a workshop in March 1993.

"In some communities, the problem is extremely serious, compounding other social ills, including AIDS, homelessness, drug abuse, and poverty," said OTA Director Roger C. Herdman in a foreword to the report. "Particularly disturbing is the emergence of multidrug-resistant tuberculosis (MDR-TB). MDR-TB has been directly linked to inappropriate and incomplete treatment, which in turn has been linked, in part, to a lack of resources to ensure the proper delivery of tuberculosis services."

The report faulted the federal government for failing to provide sufficient health service and research funds to stem the alarming rise in the incidence of tuberculosis. Over the past seven years, the number of new cases exceeded by about 52,000 the number that had been projected historically before 1985.

Until that year, cases of TB had been declining; however, 1985 saw the beginning of a steady annual increase, from 22,000 cases to 27,000 in

1992. According to Dr. Michael Gluck, who led the OTA study team, the rise in the number of TB cases was showing no abatement. "All three of the last administrations, on a bipartisan basis, have ignored the warnings of public health experts," said Rep. Henry A. Waxman, D-Calif., chairman of the House Subcommittee on Health and the Environment, at a bipartisan news conference on release of the OTA report. "If there were such a thing as public health malpractice, all three administrations [Reagan, Bush, and Clinton] would be guilty."

The Nature of TB and Its Demographics

In 1882 the German scientist Robert Koch identified a species of bacteria, Mycobacterium tuberculosis, as the cause of TB. The disease has two general states: tuberculosis infection ("latent TB") and active tuberculosis. Only about 10 percent of people with the infection ever develop active TB. Tuberculosis is caused by bacteria that can be transmitted through the air when an infected person sneezes or coughs. The infection can be cured through the use of antibiotics, but a cure takes at least six months of steady treatment.

Because the bacteria is transmitted most easily in crowded conditions, tuberculosis affects the poor and homeless more than other groups. According to OTA researchers, the most populous states recorded the largest number of people with TB. In 1991 more than half of all individuals with TB in the United States came from California, New York, Texas, Florida, and Illinois. Urban areas with more than 250,000 residents accounted for 18 percent of the nation's overall population but 43 percent of new TB cases that year.

For example, the increase in TB cases in New York State was considerably higher than the national average. During the 1970s and early 1980s the rate was about 2,000 a year; by 1992, 4,574 cases were reported (3,811 of them in New York City)—or 50.3 cases per 100,000 people, five times the national average. Between one-quarter and one-third of the cases involved those infected with the more virulent MDR-TB strain. The highest per capita TB rate in the country in 1991 was in Atlanta, with 76.4 per 100,000.

In 1991, 71 percent of new TB cases occurred in racial and ethnic minority populations, the OTA reported. In New York City's Central Harlem, the rate was 169.2 per 100,000 in 1989. Among minorities in particular, the incidence of TB was proportionately higher among younger adults and children. Immigrants, prisoners, drug users, migrant workers, and the homeless had particularly high TB rates, as did AIDS-infected people.

Indeed, eradicating tuberculosis was a worldwide problem. According to some researchers, left unchecked, TB would claim 30 million lives over the next decade—considerably more than deaths from AIDS, malaria, and other infectious diseases. Early in 1993, the World Health Organization asked the United States to join in a modest international effort to combat the spread of TB in the developing world, calling TB "the world's most neglected health crisis."

"TB is also on the move across Europe," noted an editorial in the December 29, 1993, Washington Post. *"That's because people are on the move everywhere, across borders and oceans. The TB emergency is global. The difference is that most industrialized nations have the capacity to eradicate the disease."*

OTA Recommendations and Observations

The OTA's principal recommendation was to fund considerably more than had been requested by the White House for a TB control program, as suggested by the Centers for Disease Control (CDC). In particular, the report cited the need for increased funding for research on and prevention of MDR-TB, which is more resistent to antibiotics and more difficult and expensive to treat than the regular TB strain. In 1989 the CDC had proposed a National Action Plan to Combat MDR-TB. Although the Department of Health and Human Services supported the proposal, the White House cut the funding from its budget each year. In 1993 the CDC estimated that Congress would need to increase its budget for TB control by $380 million for fiscal 1994 to implement fully the CDC's responsibilities under the MDR-TB Action Plan. That amount was $330 million more than was requested in President Clinton's fiscal 1994 budget.

In addition to recommending funding of about $484 million for a TB control program, as suggested by the CDC, the OTA study team also called for strengthening the capability of state and local health departments to treat people with the disease.

The OTA researchers "found a lack of systematic research on the effectiveness or cost-effectiveness of individual interventions to control TB infection in hospitals or to ensure that patients in different communities or treatment settings complete anti-TB therapy. In addition, little effort in health services and health economics research has been devoted to understanding variation in the use of hospitalization and costs of treating TB, especially during the disease's acute, infectious period." They concluded that "better health services and economic research results could help policymakers target TB control efforts more efficiently."

Following are excerpts from the "Summary and Policy Options" chapter of the report by the congressional Office of Technology Assessment, entitled "The Continuing Challenge of Tuberculosis," and released October 7, 1993:

Tuberculosis (TB) is a contagious disease that has killed millions of people worldwide over the centuries. The lack of a reliable cure prior to this century and TB's perceived randomness made it a common theme in literature and a metaphor for larger social and political ills. Today, TB continues to be a public health threat in the United States. After decreasing in the country as a whole for many decades, rates of TB disease are again on the rise. In some communities, particularly among economically disadvantaged groups, TB rates have consistently remained high.

Recent trends in the incidence of TB have been linked, in part, to decreases in public health investment over the last two decades. Other factors associated with the resurgence of TB include the human immunodeficiency virus (HIV) epidemic, foreign birth, substance abuse, poverty, and homelessness. An important complication is the emergence of TB strains resistant to the most commonly used anti-TB drugs.

Unchecked, these recent trends in TB represent a serious threat to communities already saddled with poor health, poverty, and other social problems. Furthermore, this disease could become an additional major burden to the Nation's health care system.

Unlike the TB of past centuries, however, today's TB is amenable to human intervention. We know how it is spread. We know how to cure it, and we know how to prevent it. Although the primary governmental responsibility for controlling TB in the United States falls to State and local authorities, the Federal Government has had, and continues to have, a substantial role in eliminating this disease. This report synthesizes scientific understanding of TB in the United States in 1993 and considers the Federal role in its control....

Tuberculosis, Health Care Reform, and Public Health Investments

As policymakers focus on health care reform, the analysis in this report indicates that TB will not disappear with improved access and better cost control of health care services alone. Even with universal access to medical services, a change in the organization and financing of health care will not, in and of itself, eliminate the need for Federal funding and coordination of the infrastructure to conduct education, surveillance, screening, diagnosis, research, and even treatment.

Furthermore, TB control is an exercise in vigilance. With an estimated one-third of the world's population infected with TB and the relative mobility of people in and out of the United States through immigration and tourism, the complete eradication of tuberculosis from this country is unlikely in the foreseeable future. In addition, people infected with the organism that causes TB now may progress to active disease many years in the future, after the current epidemic is brought under control. Nevertheless, TB control measures can lower disease rates and minimize the public health threat posed by the disease. Achieving such a goal will require a properly targeted and sustained effort. Once this goal is achieved, continued investment to identify, treat, and prevent TB will be necessary to maintain low disease rates. The current resurgence in TB is evidence that this last lesson was not learned in the past. Even in the last year, the

Centers for Disease Control and Prevention (CDC) noted its own failure to implement recent TB control recommendations, due largely to a lack of resources. . . .

What Is the Risk of TB Infection?

People with TB are contagious when they expel airborne particles containing viable tubercle bacilli through, for example, coughing, singing, speaking, or sneezing. The likelihood of infection depends mainly on the:

- Probability of coming into contact with someone with contagious, active TB;
- Closeness or intimacy of the contact;
- Duration of the contact;
- Number of viable bacilli present in the air;
- Susceptibility of the uninfected case; and
- Environmental conditions (e.g., volume of airspace, ventilation with outside air, relative humidity, presence of sunlight).

Health care workers (HCWs) are at increased risk of infection, particularly if they perform cough-inducing medical procedures on patients with active pulmonary TB and if they work in environments with inadequate infection control measures.

Casual contact with an infectious person—i.e. with active, untreated TB—in a public place such as a movie theater or subway is unlikely to lead to infection, although the risk is not zero. Although infection occurs at a specific point in time when an infectious particle is inhaled, the longer the exposure, the greater the likelihood an infectious particle will be inhaled. Hence, exposure to an infectious person over a period of months is usually necessary for transmission to occur.

In general, less than 30 percent of household members become infected while living with an infectious person, but the risk is highly variable. Under extraordinary circumstances (when the concentration of airborne infectious particles is unusually high), exposures as brief as 2 hours have reportedly led to infection.

Adequate anti-microbial or anti-tuberculosis treatment can reduce the infectiousness of drug-susceptible TB within days. Although the exact amount of time needed to eliminate the infection completely varies by patient, it is about 6 months or longer. While there is no evidence that drug-resistant TB is more contagious than drug susceptible TB, delays in diagnosis and treatment allow patients to remain infectious for a longer period of time, thus increasing chances of infecting others.

Trends in the Incidence of Active TB

Between 1953, when the Public Health Service (PHS) first implemented a national reporting system for active TB cases, and 1984, the number of annually reported cases declined 74 percent from 84,304 (53 per 100,000 population) to 22,255 (9.4 per 100,000). Beginning in 1985, this decline slowed and then reversed. The number of new cases reported in 1992 was 26,673 (10.5 per 100,000), a 20 percent increase over 1985.

The Changing Demographics of TB

Over the years, TB has gradually shifted from a disease broadly distributed over the whole population to one that is more narrowly concentrated among certain portions of the population. Although the rapid increase in the overall number of new cases suggests a potential threat to the population as a whole, the current concentrations of the disease offer TB-control experts and policymakers a guide in targeting resources for controlling TB. Groups with particularly high rates of TB can be described according to geography, race, ethnicity, and factors causally related to the disease.

Heavy Concentrations in Certain Parts of the Country

The most populous States have the largest number of cases. In 1991, over half of all TB cases came from California, New York, Texas, Florida, and Illinois. Urban areas with populations over 250,000 contained 18 percent of the country's population but 43 percent of its new TB cases in that year. The number of new TB cases per 100,000 of the population in the South has always been above the national average, although New York, Hawaii, and California have the highest rates. Among cities, Atlanta (76.4 per 100,000), Newark (71.8 per 100,000), New York (50.3 per 100,000), Miami (48.5 per 100,000), and San Francisco (46.0 per 100,000) had the highest case rates during 1991.

Accounting for 14 percent of the total number of new TB cases reported in the United States during 1991 and with a TB case rate five times the national average, New York City alone has a significant, concentrated portion of the Nation's entire TB problem. In one part of the city, Central Harlem, the case rate was 169.2 per 100,000 in 1989 and has never dipped below 52 during the 40 years that data have been kept.

Heavy Concentrations Among Minorities and the Young

Within a given geographic area, certain demographic groups are more likely than others to produce new cases of TB. In 1991, 71 percent of new cases occurred in racial and ethnic minorities. Hispanic Americans, Black Americans, and Americans of Asian or Pacific Island origin showed relatively large increases in TB during the 1985-91 period. Although the risk of TB in adults increased with age, this pattern was not consistent across different racial and ethnic groups. Among white, non-Hispanic Americans, most TB cases occurred among elderly people, while among Black and Hispanic Americans, the bulk occurred in the 25 to 44 year-old age group.

Rates of increase have been disproportionately high among children; this trend is also concentrated among racial and ethnic minorities, who accounted for 86 percent of all childhood cases in 1991. Childhood cases of TB are strong evidence of recent transmission of the disease, suggesting contact with other infectious individuals in the community and possibly more, undetected cases of infection. High rates of TB among immigrants and increases in TB among parents in the 25 to 44 age group may account for the observed increases among children. Furthermore, children infected now could suffer active disease years in the future.

High Rates Among Immigrants, Prisoners, Drug Users, Migrant Workers, and Homeless People

Being born outside the United States, being homeless, being a substance abuser, being incarcerated, or being a migrant worker is a risk factor for tuberculous infection. In addition, being coinfected with HIV increases one's risk of progressing from infection to active disease. The overlap among these groups reinforces the concentration of TB within the United States population and the particular risk for members of these groups.

Given the high prevalence of TB infection in many other parts of the world, a large percentage of new TB cases in the United States occurs among individuals born elsewhere (27 percent in 1991). Among homeless populations, several studies have found latent TB infection to be as high as 50 percent. Impaired immunity due to poor overall health, substance abuse, or HIV infection may cause homeless people with tuberculous infection to progress to active disease. In addition, homeless shelters can generate new transmissions, due to crowding and poor ventilation. Twenty percent of newly diagnosed TB cases in New York City in 1991 were homeless.

Substance-abusing populations overlap with other groups at high risk of TB, especially with homeless and HIV-infected people.

The prevalence of TB in prisons is related to the close living quarters, poor ventilation, and other risk factors that inmates may possess. In some States, epidemiologists have estimated that TB may be as much as 6 to 11 times more prevalent among prisoners than among the general population. Prison populations comprise other groups at high risk of TB—drug users, HIV-infected people, and individuals homeless prior to incarceration. Persons with active TB in prisons cannot only spread the disease among other prisoners, but they also place at-risk prison staff and family or friends with whom they have close contact upon their release.

Among migrant workers, lack of access to health services and lack of adequate working and housing conditions are believed to contribute to the heightened risk of TB as noted among some limited recent studies. Many members of this group are also poor, minorities, foreign born, or former homeless shelter residents.

People With HIV Have High TB Rates

HIV is the pathogen that causes acquired immunodeficiency syndrome (AIDS). Because HIV-related immunosuppression impairs the body's ability to fight a tuberculous infection, individuals infected with both tubercle bacilli and HIV are estimated to have a risk of as high as 8 percent per year of progressing rapidly to active TB disease, compared with a 10 percent lifetime risk for HIV-negative individuals.

Epidemiologic evidence has consistently shown a higher prevalence of TB among individuals with AIDS compared with the general population, even after adjustment for age, race, and sex. In addition, more than one-half of deaths with TB in individuals 20 to 49 years old appear to occur in people who also have AIDS.

Multidrug-Resistant Tuberculosis

When a patient takes TB medication erratically or when an inadequate combination of drugs is prescribed, active, infectious TB can recur in a form resistant to one or more of the drugs used in the original treatment. Cases of MDR-TB are far more difficult and costly to treat than drug-sensitive TB, and can be fatal despite the best available treatment. CDC began regularly collecting drug susceptibility data on each reported case of TB in 1993, a practice done periodically with surveys prior to 1986.

Preliminary data from a 1991 CDC survey indicate that drug resistant TB cases have been reported in all regions of the country, but are most heavily concentrated in a few States. Cases resistant to at least one drug were found in 36 States and to two or more drugs in 13 States. Of the cases found to be resistant to the two most commonly used drugs, isoniazid (INH) and rifampin (RIF), over half were in New York City. In a separate study, 33 percent of the 466 TB cases reported in New York City during April 1991 were resistant to one or more drugs, and 19 percent were resistant to both INH and RIF.

Since 1990, there have been at least 9 outbreaks of MDR-TB among 297 individuals in prisons and hospitals. Most of these people were HIV infected. As many as 89 percent of those with MDR-TB (including 6 health care workers and 1 prison guard) have died from their TB. Delayed or inadequate infection control measures, premature discontinuation of patient isolation, delayed reporting of drug resistance, and lack of isolation facilities were major factors in the spread of MDR-TB in these institutions....

Policy Options for Congress

Through its analysis, OTA has identified 11 options for congressional consideration. Each option has the underlying goal of improving TB control capabilities in the United States. They fall into three categories that affect:

- The public health infrastructure for combating TB;
- The research, development, and availability of technologies for combating TB; and

- The financial security and financial access to health care services for persons with, or at risk of TB.

The focus of this discussion is on potential actions of the Federal Government in providing leadership and resources for the Nation's TB control activities, rather than on potential actions of the State, local, and private authorities that carry out many of the programs to fight this disease. A fuller discussion of these options and their potential implications follows.

Options That Affect the Public Health Intrastucture for Combating TB

Option 1. *Fully fund the public health activities identified in the CDC's 1992 National Action Plan to Combat Multidrug-Resistant Tuberculosis.*

CDC estimates that full implementation of all activities in its 1992 National Action Plan to combat MDR-TB for which it would be responsible would require appropriations of $380 million during the first year over and above the $105 million appropriated in fiscal year 1993. This estimate includes $62 million in R&D expenditures, with the remainder allocated toward various forms of public health activities. Although CDC currently has no estimates of amounts that would be required for subsequent years, the $380 million increase would include some one-year-only spending as well as some spending that would be continued subsequently. No estimates currently exist of the cost of fully implementing activities in the National Action Plan that are the responsibility of other Federal agencies.

OTA found that CDC and other TB experts agreed on the need for increased Federal involvement and resources. However, some of the options that follow in this section highlight major policy questions that would need answers to fully implement the CDC plan. In addition, because CDC has given only rough indicators of priority among all of the actions it recommends, Congress and other policymakers cannot evaluate in detail how CDC and other Federal agencies would propose to allocate funding increases if Congress appropriated less than the amount required for full implementation.

Immediate full funding of the plan may not be more effective or more efficient than a more incremental phase-in. On the one hand, such a dramatic increase in funding would alert the country to the threat of TB to affected communities and the value the ... Government places on TB control.

On the other hand, the public health and research system may not be able to absorb such a large influx of cash as efficiently as it could if the increases came more gradually. In the course of OTA's analysis, public health officials pointed out the highly regulated and slow process some State and local governments face in hiring qualified individuals to administer TB therapy and to perform other public health functions. Additional Federal grants would not immediately increase the supply of qualified public health workers or speed up local governmental hiring processes.

Also, this report highlights the lack of information about the relative effectiveness of individual infection control procedures. Without first developing better experimental data on these technologies, some money devoted to retrofitting hospital rooms and other facilities to serve active TB patients would probably be spent inefficiently or unnecessarily. In an era of limited Federal resources and many competing public health needs, policymakers may wish to weigh the value for spending some TB control dollars better in the future against the value of providing maximum resources for TB now.

Option 2. *Establish a mechanism for direct Federal intervention in cities and other jurisdictions with extraordinarily high levels of active TB, MDR-TB, or HIV and TB coinfection.*

Support for this option would rest on the assumption that TB can pose a significant enough threat in some communities that State and local authorities alone are unable to respond quickly and sufficiently, even with Federal financial support. One TB expert suggested to OTA that the magnitude of drug resistance, HIV dual infection, substance abuse, homelessness, and incomplete TB treatment is great enough in New York City to warrant the formation of a Federal task force to supply personnel and expertise from elsewhere on a short-term, emergency basis. Such a plan would extend the technical expertise that CDC routinely provides to State and local health authorities. Federal personnel would help provide TB treatment, find cases of TB in facilities that public health officials suspect to harbor the disease, and perform other TB services needed in the community.

This option raises several questions. First, by what criteria would the Federal Government decide to intervene? Given that most legal authority to protect the public health has been traditionally vested in State and local governments, any Federal intervention would almost certainly, at a minimum, require a request from the relevant local governments. Second, Federal officials would need to develop epidemiologic or other criteria for judging that TB has reached levels high enough to justify this Federal action. These criteria would need to be measurable and perhaps flexible. Inclusion of TB and HIV coinfection rates or numbers of foreign-born residents, if measurable, could make this option available for communities with low rates of existing TB but the potential for high rates in the future. The emphasis of Federal intervention in these communities may be on screening high-risk groups and preventive treatment, rather than on providing resources for treating active disease.

Decisionmakers would also want to question whether Federal Government intervention would actually be more effective than the local governments and private organizations acting alone. As noted, the ability to bring in Federal personnel may offer a significant advantage for State and local governments that face limitations in hiring, although the Federal Government may also face hiring restrictions. Reassignment of professionals from the Commissioned Public Health Service Corps would mean these individuals would be unable to continue to fulfill their current responsibilities.

The cost of hiring additional Federal personnel on a short-term basis would depend on the number hired, their qualifications, the duration of their employment, and perhaps whether they currently reside in the targeted community or must relocate. Another possibility would be to make voluntary service on such task forces one means of paying back government loans for health professional education and training as was done in greater numbers during the 1970s and 1980s under the National Health Service Corps. There is also precedent for providing special visas for qualified foreign medical personnel to fill positions in underserved areas.

Option 3. *Require universal directly observed treatment (DOT) through legislation, regulation, or as a condition of receiving Federal TB control funds.*

The American Lung Association recently recommended DOT for all persons with active TB. In contrast, CDC has recommended that DOT be considered for active cases.

Supporters of universal DOT point to the practical difficulty of predicting *a priori* which patients will complete treatment without supervision. These supporters argue that human nature should lead health professionals to expect that patients will forget to take medication without reminders. Universal DOT proponents also argue that some health authorities may be more likely to assume that homeless individuals, drug users, and people without access to regular health care would be less likely than other TB patients to complete therapy. These groups may be subjected to more restrictive treatment measures without a strong medical or public health rationale. Requiring universal DOT helps insure that all TB patients are treated in an equitable manner.

Opponents of requiring universal DOT point out that despite the difficulties in predicting who is unlikely to complete treatment, between 1976 and 1990, over 80 percent of persons with active TB in the United States completed treatment without DOT. One estimate for New York City suggests that DOT costs may fall between $2,000 and $3,000 per person excluding the cost of drugs. Opponents argue that universal DOT is a wasteful use of limited resources and needlessly intrusive for most patients.

In addition, Federal policymakers would need to define exactly what State and local governments would have to do to conform to the Federal requirement. DOT can take many different forms and degrees of restrictiveness, require varying intensities of resources, and be combined with a variety of complementary programs such as incentives or inducements to complete therapy.

... [T]here are more options available to policymakers than just requiring DOT for everybody or trying to predict *a priori* which TB patients will not complete therapy. One alternative, used in some communities, is to monitor all patients' therapy, but allow their behaviors to be indicators of the need for more intensive supervision of therapy. Only when patients do not show up for medical appointments or give other evidence that they might not complete therapy would public health officials require patients to be observed taking their medications. Although this alternative to universal DOT requires that public health authorities have the resources to track down missing patients quickly, a potentially difficult and labor-intensive task, particularly for homeless or other difficult-to-locate patients, it may be less expensive and as effective in some communities.

Option 4. *Require periodic TB skin testing, active case finding (by chest x-ray) and preventive treatment in Federal hospitals, prisons, and other facilities.*

Epidemiological evidence indicates that hospitals, prisons, and other facilities housing people in congregate settings may be appropriate targets for TB prevention because institutions house many individuals at high risk of progressing to active disease. Identifying infected residents and workers at high risk of developing active TB, as well as those who already have active TB, offers an opportunity to prevent the potential spread of the disease to others with whom the active cases have close contact. Immigrants, currently screened for active disease for legal entry into the United States, are another high-risk group that the Federal Government may wish to consider for screening and preventive treatment if found to have tuberculous infection.

Positive skin tests would help identify candidates for preventive treatment, although health officials would have to consider the problem of false negative among immunocompromised individuals with tuberculous infection. In addition, officials would need to consider the best way to use chest x-ray technology in order to identify active disease.

By requiring screening and preventive treatment programs in its own facilities, the Federal Government would be setting a standard that could encourage State and local authorities to adopt voluntarily for their own congregate institutions. However, there are some potential drawbacks to a Federal policy. The Federal agencies charged with administering each type of institution may not correctly identify groups at high enough risk of active disease to warrant screening and follow-up preventive treatment.

For example, many patients admitted to Veterans Administration or other Federal hospitals for short periods of time may be at very low risk of developing active TB if infected. In addition, nonfederal institutions attempting to follow the Federal Government's lead might also establish screening programs where they are likely to yield little benefit. Workplace screening in low-risk settings such as a factory are unlikely to have much effect on the spread of much TB. Analysis in this report suggests that research into the most cost-effective ways of running screening and preventive treatment programs may not be available to guide the implementation of this option.

Funding for screening and prevention in Federal institutions would presumably come from the budgets of the agencies charged with administering them as do most current TB control efforts. The Department of Veterans Affairs (U.S. DVA) currently pays for TB control in its own hospitals, the Bureau of Prisons in Federal prisons, and so on. This decentralized administration of Federal facilities raises the further problem of ensuring compliance with a screening and prevention requirement. Current Bureau of Prisons policy already requires chest x-rays for new inmates and tuberculin skin testing every 2 years, but no data are available on the extent to which such testing is actually carried out. Adoption of screening requirements would require mechanisms to ensure they are carried out as well as sufficient resources to ensure appropriate diagnostic followup and treatment; this includes not just money, but trained personnel as well.

Option 5. *Directly purchase anti-TB drugs and distribute them to State and local authorities.*

The rationale behind universal TB drug purchase is that the Federal Government, acting as a single, large-volume buyer, should get the needed pharmaceuticals at a lower cost than can individual States or local health departments. The same considerations could apply to universal purchase of PPD skin testing kits.

The Federal Government already purchases some childhood vaccines under contract at prices substantially below retail. The CDC's recent survey of trends in anti-TB drug prices revealed that the price paid for the same form and dose of a drug can vary greatly from State to State. In addition, if the Federal Government were to take on the function of paying for all TB drugs, State and local governments could use the money that would have gone to pharmaceutical purchase for other purposes.

CDC currently has the statutory authority to take on this activity; it requires only the appropriations to do so. CDC estimates that in 1993, the cost of purchasing all anti-TB drugs used at the State and local levels would total $80 million. This figure is included in the CDC's estimates of fully implementing its National Action Plan for the elimination of TB.

However, this amount of money would cover only the cost of the drugs themselves and does not include the cost of administering the drug purchase program or distributing the pharmaceuticals. CDC currently has no estimates of the costs of these functions. It is also not clear whether the Federal Government would take on the function of distributing the drugs to the States or whether that function would continue to be done by the drug suppliers. U.S. DVA currently purchases drugs in bulk for use in its own hospitals, but does so with a highly centralized distribution system, thus minimizing the distribution costs borne by the pharmaceutical suppliers. The willingness of suppliers to give discounts for bulk purchasing may be partially dependent on whether the Federal Government took on responsibility for distributing the drugs since the suppliers' costs would be lower.

CDC has not indicated the assumptions that went into its $80 million estimate. Not only is it not clear what prices the government would expect to pay for each pharmaceutical, but also CDC has not shown how improved case finding might increase drug costs in subsequent years or how decreases in TB rates would ultimately decrease funds necessary to purchase drugs.

The final price negotiated for these drugs could also depend on the number of manufacturers for a drug. Some of the more expensive drugs are still covered by patents and hence only have one manufacturer. When manufacturers do not face competition, they may not see an incentive to give significant discounts in order to sell their products. In other cases, there may be only one manufacturer of a drug or its active ingredient even though it is no longer covered by a patent. These manufacturers may also be reluctant to give significant discounts. Finally, the pharmaceutical industry has suggested that centralized purchase would provide an added disincentive for firms to invest in research to develop new drugs as discussed in option 8 below.

Option 5a. *Directly purchase anti-TB drugs with State and local authorities reimbursing the Federal Government.*

This option would be identical to Option 5 except that the Federal Government would not bear the $80 million estimated to be necessary for the purchase of the pharmaceuticals themselves. Instead, State and local governments would continue to pay for drugs, but would reap any cost savings the Federal Government can realize by purchasing on their behalf. Such cost savings might not be spread evenly among the States. The CDC survey indicates that some States, presumably those purchasing large quantities of drugs, already receive a discount through negotiated contracts with drug suppliers. These States would likely benefit less per unit of drug purchased than would areas of the country paying higher retail prices for their TB drugs.

Option 6. *Increase support for international TB control activities.*

The American Lung Association, among others, advocates greater support of the World Health Organization's TB programs, greater CDC provision of its technical staff to international organizations, and selected nations, more support for TB research in developing countries through NIH, and greater involvement of AID in tuberculosis control as well as in bilateral programs with other countries and through WHO.... [T]he Federal Government supports each of these activities to a certain extent, although the vast bulk of current and expected TB spending is targeted to the United States.

If Congress decided to increase TB control efforts in less developed countries, it could decide to do so purely on humanitarian grounds. However, even if Congress sought only to protect this nation's health, controlling TB abroad could lower TB incidence of the disease here given the mobility of foreign born people to the United States. Research oriented toward developing countries could also have benefits at home; for example, a fast, definitive diagnostic test designed for developing countries that do not have easy access to sophisticated clinical laboratories could be of great use in many urban and rural areas of the United States as well.

A potential danger of increasing United States support of TB efforts abroad is that it might divert resources from domestic TB control activities. The Federal Government has already laid out an ambitious domestic agenda to control TB for which there may not be sufficient funds to fully implement in the short-run. If money for expanded TB control efforts outside the United States would come from appropriations that would otherwise go to domestic public health and research activities, Congress may need to weigh the value of supporting efforts abroad against the impact that money would have on the health of people with TB at home.

Options That Affect the Research, Development, and Availability of Technologies for Combating TB

Option 7. *Make a concerted effort to develop health services research relevant to the fight against tuberculosis and to disseminate research results to policymakers and health professionals.*

Several areas of this report suggest that better health services and economic research results could help policymakers target TB control efforts more efficiently. Through legislation or through direction of U.S. DHHS, relevant agencies such as the CDC, AHCPR, HCFA, NIH, and HRSA could publicize TB health services research as a priority in various types of extramural funding programs. Several of these agencies have said they intend to expand their efforts in this area. Two sample questions suggested by OTA's analysis that might be answered by health services and health economics research are:

- What are the effectiveness and cost-effectiveness of various forms of DOT and how do these measures vary among different parts of the country and different groups of patients?
- What sources of income do TB patients have and what impact do government benefits have on the identification, treatment, and control of TB such as through SSI, Aid to Families with Dependent Children, housing programs, and food stamps?

This option could include efforts to disseminate to policymakers and health professionals the results of both health services and clinic research to improve the delivery of health services and to ensure appropriate clinical treatment for TB.

One drawback of this such research is that it could draw resources away from direct TB control. Data on the effectiveness and cost-effectiveness of treatment strategies such as DOT are best gained through randomized clinical trials, which are expensive. In addition, the size of such studies increases as one wants to learn more about differences in effectiveness among different sociodemographic groups or according to other ways that differentiate TB patients. Policymakers would also want to consider health services research already being undertaken by State and local governments and private groups such as foundations to assess its quality and to avoid duplication.

CDC's estimates of funds necessary to implement its responsibilities under the 1992 National Action Plan include funds for the health services and health economics it hopes to carry out. Estimates of funds needed for new health sources research that other Federal agencies would support are not available.

Option 8. *Fully fund basic and clinical TB research as outlined in the CDC's 1992 National Action Plan to Combat Multidrug-Resistant Tuberculosis and NIH's 1993 Tuberculosis Research Opportunities.*

CDC estimates that its research under the 1992 National Action Plan would cost $62 million in the first year above fiscal year 1993 spending. NIH estimates that new TB research would cost $102 million over several years. These research activities include not only basic research on the TB organism and its behavior in the human body, but also clinical investigations of new forms of prophylaxis, diagnosis, and treatment; the experimental study of environmental infection control technologies; and relevant human behavioral research.

On the rate of funding increases, the same considerations for policymakers described under Option 1 apply here. The ability of the scientific infrastructure to absorb funding for certain types of TB research include a limited number of researchers and clinicians trained to perform work in this area and a limited number of biomedical laboratories with sufficient containment facilities to prevent accidental infection of laboratory staff and others. On the other hand, some researchers have suggested that increases in funding will naturally lead to an increased capacity to do research.

As with Option 1, clarification of funding priorities for R&D activities would help Congress and other policymakers understand better the implications of partial or phased-in funding of the CDC National Action Plan. NIH has provided detailed priorities for research projects in its plan. In addition, analysis in this report suggests several areas of relatively high priority: development of faster and definitive diagnostic and drug susceptibility testing techniques, development of new anti-tuberculosis drugs, and the development of easier-to-use dosage forms of the treatments, such as combinations of commonly used drugs and slowly released, implantable formulations, and new research to bolster our understanding of the TB bacilli and its manifestations in the human body.

The area of drug development raises a few additional issues for the Federal Government. The FDA indicates that some drug companies have been reluctant to develop a drug for both TB and non-TB uses for fear that many physicians would reserve the drug for TB treatment only rather than using it for more common infections. The companies fear that these implicit restrictions of the drugs' use would limit the revenue they generate and their ability to recoup the manufacturers' initial R&D costs. In addition, the pharmaceutical industry is concerned about disincentives to engage in research should the Federal Government attempt to force discounts for TB drugs as discussed in Option 5.

This situation suggests that there are important constraints other than funding and resources in making new therapies available. Congress, executive branch agencies, and groups outside of government may wish to examine new ways to encourage drug industry participation in TB drug development beyond those that the FDA has already tried. New ideas could run the gamut of measures, from focusing public attention on the need for new treatments, to clarifying the applicability of orphan drug subsidies to this area, and to offering new, more direct financial incentives.

Option 9. *Support the creation of additional regional "centers of excellence" for TB treatment and research.*

Several centers that specialize in the treatment of drug-susceptible and more complicated cases of TB already exist. One TB expert has suggested establishing a total of 6 to 12 centers funded at a cost of about $5 million each per year. In addition to treating difficult cases and training TB clinicians and researchers who would pursue future work on this disease, these centers would provide an opportunity to study and disseminate new technologies for the diagnosis and treatment of TB. Not only would researchers be able to study the technologies under relatively controlled conditions, but also the centers could train clinicians and technicians in their use.

The main question for policymakers is whether establishing additional centers is the most efficient public policy to treat difficult patients, train TB professionals, and bring together TB research interests. Even if it were an efficient approach to TB care, research, and training, it is not clear whether 6 to 12 centers (or any other suggested number) are commensurate with the threat posed by TB. It is also not clear how sick patients would be before they would have to be transferred to the centers for treatment. Policymakers would want to consider the number of patients in need of such specialized services in determining how many centers the country needs. The existence of such centers might encourage their use for some patients that could be treated in institutions closer to their homes. Furthermore, once the current epidemic is brought under control, the country might not need as many such centers.

Policymakers may want to understand better whether there would be cost or other advantages to treating patients in centers instead of other institutions. They may also want to consider whether existing institutions could be modified for less than the cost of establishing a new center to conduct biomedical TB research. Similarly, it might be possible to train clinicians and other professionals sufficiently in existing institutions for less money.

Another issue that would need to be examined is how centers would be reimbursed for the care of patients from a separate jurisdiction if the cost of such care would usually be borne by the health department or Medicaid program where the patient currently usually lives. The centers would also require trained personnel who may only be available in sufficient numbers over time.

Options That Affect the Financial Security and Financial Access to Housing and Health Care Services for Persons with or at Risk of TB

Option 10. *Expand the Federal Government's definition of disability to include active TB as a disabling condition for the purposes of Supplemental Security Income and Disability Insurance benefits.*

Underlying this proposal is the observation that many people with active TB are in precarious financial situations. Their poverty may interfere with their ability to receive treatment and to prevent transmission of the disease to others. Many TB patients are homeless. For disabled individuals without other sources of income, SSI provides a very basic subsistence and categorical eligibility for Medicaid health insurance. In the case of substance abusers, many residential treatment programs have been successful in receiving SSI to cover some of the costs of those patients in treatment [that] may last more than a year.

... [M]ost individuals with TB alone are not considered disabled because their condition does not prevent them from working for a year or longer. Changing this rule in order to make active TB patients eligible for SSI would require congressional legislation to amend the Social Security Act. In passing such legislation, Congress would also need to decide whether this exception applies only to the SSI program or whether it would also apply to the DI program as well since both currently rely on the same definition and processes for determining disability.

A new law would establish a significant exception to one of the most basic tenets of current disability policy. A major drawback of this option is that it would use a disability program to provide financial benefits to a group of people who are not disabled according to the way Congress has defined disability over the history of the SSI and DI programs. In adopting this option, Congress could be opening a Pandora's box of requests to use disability programs as a means of providing income to other groups of individuals who are not currently considered disabled.

A proposal to revise the SSA's disability definition to include TB may reflect two other problems perceived by proponents of this option: 1) a perceived lack of coordination of all public benefits for which TB patients may currently be eligible, and 2) a lack of resources to provide housing for many TB patients in some areas of the country.

To the extent these two perceived problems are real, the Federal Government, along with State and local authorities, may wish to consider other options for coordination of relevant Federal benefits for each case of active TB and directly to consider other ways the Federal Government could help alleviate TB patients' need for housing....

One alternative action for policymakers that would not require a change in statute would be to educate patients and their caregivers to make sure

TB patients currently eligible for SSI already because of HIV, substance abuse, or protracted TB treatment actually apply for the program.

Option 11. *Provide states with the option to expand categorical Medicaid coverage to persons without other forms of health insurance who have tuberculous infection or active TB.*

Over the years, Congress has expanded categorical Medicaid eligibility, especially for certain groups of women and children. Congress offers States the option of extending eligibility to all persons with tuberculous infection or active disease with the usual mix of Federal and State funds. The added cost of this option to State or Federal Medicaid budgets is uncertain. For the State government, the cost largely depends on the prevalence of TB in the State. For the Federal Government, it depends on how many and which States decide to adopt the option. In addition, to the extent that patients with TB have other medical problems but were not previously covered by Medicaid, the costs of expanding Medicaid eligibility would be more than just those costs associated with TB care.

This option would transfer some share of the burden for TB services from public health department budgets to the Medicaid program at both the Federal and State levels. The option would also reinforce the trend toward the "privatization" of TB services shifting the focus of TB control from public health activities to individual, reimbursable health services. Another impact of this option would be to add to the administrative costs of State Medicaid programs in processing applications for eligibility and claims reimbursement. Finally, as noted in chapter 6, financial access is not the only factor in ensuring that patients receive and complete treatment; expanding Medicaid eligibility does not guarantee that there will be enough trained professionals to provide and supervise appropriate therapy.

Option 11a. *Limit the option of expanding categorical Medicaid eligibility to those with active disease only.*

Although limiting Medicaid coverage to active disease cases only would reduce the cost of this option, it would also exclude from Medicaid reimbursement any diagnostic services and preventive therapy for people with tuberculous infection (unless the infected patients were eligible for Medicaid through some other provision in the Medicaid statutes).

Option 11b. *Limit categorical Medicaid eligibility to TB-related services only.*

This option would also save money by limiting the reimbursement to services related to TB only. Under this option, Congress could cover all people with tuberculous infection or limit coverage to those with active TB only. This option has the disadvantage of excluding treatments for other conditions the individual may have, such as HIV. Treatment for these other conditions not only affects the individual's overall health, but can affect his or her ability to recover from TB itself. However, some portion of patients with both TB and other conditions like HIV would qualify for full Medicaid eligibility through other provisions in the Medicaid statutes.

STUDY OF GUNS IN THE HOME

October 7, 1993

Keeping a gun at home nearly triples the chance that someone will be killed on the premises, according to a study published October 7 in the New England Journal of Medicine. *The study also concluded that the victim is far more likely to be a member of the household than an intruder, stating that "[d]espite the widespread belief that guns are effective for protection, our results suggest that they actually pose a substantial threat to the members of the household."*

"The study is the first to link the immediate availability of a gun with the increased risk of homicide," said Dr. Arthur L. Kellermann, who led the research team that conducted the study. Kellerman, associate professor of emergency medicine and public health at Emory University in Atlanta, was joined in the research by health-care professionals at the Universities of Tennessee and Washington and Case Western Reserve University.

The researchers studied 420 killings in or immediately outside of homes in Shelby County (Memphis), Tennessee; King County (Seattle), Washington; and Cuyahoga County (Cleveland), Ohio. The deaths occurred between August 23, 1987, and August 23, 1992, in Shelby and King counties, and between January 1, 1990, and August 23, 1992, in Cuyahoga County. Together, these killings accounted for nearly one-fourth of all the homicides in these areas during those periods.

In the at-home killings, nearly half of the victims died of gunshot wounds, mainly from handguns. Relatives or persons known to the victims accounted for three-fourths of the deaths. Only 3.6 percent died at the hands of strangers. About two-thirds of the victims were men, and about half of all the deaths occurred in the context of a quarrel or romantic triangle. Some 30 percent of the killings occurred during robberies, rapes, burglaries, drug deals, and other felonies.

Medical Community's Involvement

The study marked another step by the medical community into the fight for gun control. The federal Centers for Disease Control and Prevention, which financed the study, reported that firearms had accounted for 90 percent of the increase in homicides among young Americans since the mid-1980s. It found that more teenagers in the U.S. died from firearms than all biological diseases combined. In 1992, gunfire displaced traffic fatalities as the leading killer of young adults in Louisiana and Texas.

Aside from the gunfire, the Center reported 240,000 nonfatal gunshot injuries in 1989, the last year for which full statistics were available. Gunshot wounds cost $14 billion a year to treat, according to an estimate by Frederick P. Rivera, director of the Harborview Injury Prevention and Research Center in Seattle. Dr. George D. Lundberg, editor of the Journal of the American Medical Association (JAMA), *was quoted as saying that, for emergency room personnel, "It's like working in a war zone."*

Medical Journals for Gun Control

In an editorial published a year earlier in JAMA, *Lundberg and former U.S. Surgeon General C. Everett Koop declared violence a "public health emergency" and called for a national system of gun registration and licensing to help control it. The June 10, 1992, journal was devoted entirely to violence as a health issue.* (Report on Gun Violence, Historic Documents of 1992, p. 493)

Similarly, the Kellermann report in the New England Journal of Medicine *was accompanied by an editorial, signed by editor Dr. Jerome P. Kassirer, advocating substantive national gun control laws. He specifically endorsed the "Brady bill," then before Congress, as a small step in the right direction. The bill, passed later in the year, imposed a waiting period on gun purchases to give police time to screen would-be buyers.* (Passage of Brady bill, p. 965)

National Rifle Association Objections

The National Rifle Association, the principal foe of gun control, denounced the Kellermann study as "flawed," saying that it ignored nonfatal protection provided by guns in the home. The previous year, after JAMA *had editorialized for gun control, the NRA had suggested that doctors had no place commenting on gun deaths. "Statistics show that 93,000 accidental deaths are caused by the medical profession annually," a spokesman said. "It would make more sense for these doctors to look at their own house first."*

Following are excerpts from "Gun Ownership as a Risk for Homicide in the Home" from the October 7, 1993, issue of the New England Journal of Medicine, *by Arthur L.*

Kellermann and others, reporting their study of gun deaths showing that guns in the home create greater risk than protection to the occupants:

Homicide claims the lives of approximately 24,000 Americans each year, making it the 11th leading cause of death among all age groups, the 2nd leading cause of death among all people 15 to 24 years old, and the leading cause of death among male African Americans 15 to 34 years old. Homicide rates declined in the United States during the early 1980s but rebounded thereafter. One category of homicide that is particularly threatening to our sense of safety is homicide in the home.

Unfortunately, the influence of individual and household characteristics on the risk of homicide in the home is poorly understood. Illicit-drug use, alcoholism, and domestic violence are widely believed to increase the risk of homicide, but the relative importance of these factors is unknown. Frequently cited options to improve home security include the installation of electronic security systems, burglar bars, and reinforced security doors. The effectiveness of these protective measures is unclear, however.

Many people also keep firearms (particularly handguns) in the home for personal protection. One recent survey determined that handgun owners are twice as likely as owners of long guns to report "protection from crime" as their single most important reason for keeping a gun in the home. It is possible, however, that the risks of keeping a firearm in the home may outweigh the potential benefits.

To clarify these issues, we conducted a population-based case-control study to determine the strength of the association between a variety of potential risk factors and the incidence of homicide in the home.

Methods

Identification of Cases

Shelby County, Tennessee; King County, Washington; and Cuyahoga County, Ohio, are the most populous counties in their respective states. The population of King County is predominantly white and enjoys a relatively high standard of living. In contrast, 44 percent of the population of Shelby County and 25 percent of the population of Cuyahoga County are African American. Fifteen percent of the households in Shelby County and 11 percent in Cuyahoga County live below the poverty level, as compared with 5 percent in King County.

All homicides involving residents of King County or Shelby County that occurred between August 23, 1987, and August 23, 1992, and all homicides involving residents of Cuyahoga County that occurred between January 1, 1990, and August 23, 1992, were reviewed to identify those that took place in the home of the victim. Any death ruled a homicide was included, regardless of the method used. Assault-related injuries that were not immediately fatal were included if death followed within three months. Cases of homicide involving children 12 years of age or younger were excluded at the request of the medical examiners....

Selection of Case Subjects and Recruitment of Case Proxies

...Reports made at the scene were collected to ensure that study criteria were met. In King County, the medical examiner's staff conducted all investigations of the homicide scene. In Shelby County and Cuyahoga County, police detectives conducted these investigations. In addition to recording the details of the incident for law enforcement purposes, investigators obtained the names of persons close to the victim who might provide us with an interview at a later date, thereby serving as proxies for the victim. These lists were supplemented with names obtained from newspaper accounts, obituaries, and calls to funeral homes.

Approximately three weeks after a victim's death, each proxy was sent a signed letter outlining the nature of the project. A $10 incentive was offered, and a follow-up telephone call was made a few days later to arrange a time and place for an interview. At the time of this meeting, informed consent was obtained....

Results

Study Population

There were 1860 homicides in the three counties during the study period. Four hundred forty-four (23.9 percent) took place in the home of the victim. After we excluded the younger victim in 19 double deaths, 2 homicides that were not reported to project staff, and 3 late changes to a death certificate, 420 cases (94.6 percent) were available for study.

Reports on the Scene

Most of the homicides occurred inside the victim's home. Eleven percent occurred outside the home but within the immediate property lines. Two hundred sixty-five victims (63.1 percent) were men; 36.9 percent were women. A majority of the homicides (50.9 percent) occurred in the context of a quarrel or a romantic triangle. An additional 4.5 percent of the victims were killed by a family member or an intimate acquaintance as part of a murder-suicide. Thirty-two homicides (7.6 percent) were related to drug dealing, and 92 homicides (21.9 percent) occurred during the commission of another felony, such as a robbery, rape, or burglary. No motive other than homicide could be established in 56 cases (13.3 percent).

The great majority of the victims (76.7 percent) were killed by a relative or someone known to them. Homicides by a stranger accounted for only 15 cases (3.6 percent). The identity of the offender could not be established in 73 cases (17.4 percent). The remaining cases involved other offenders or police acting in the line of duty.

Two hundred nine victims (49.8 percent) died from gunshot wounds. A knife or some other sharp instrument was used to kill 111 victims (26.4 percent). The remaining victims were either bludgeoned (11.7 percent), strangled (6.4 percent), or killed by other means (5.7 percent).

Evidence of forced entry was noted in 59 cases (14.0 percent). Eighteen of these involved an unidentified intruder; six involved strangers. Two involved the police. The rest involved a spouse, family member, or some other person known to the victim.

Attempted resistance was reported in 184 cases (43.8 percent). In 21 of these (5.0 percent) the victim unsuccessfully attempted to use a gun in self-defense. In 56.2 percent of the cases no specific signs of resistance were noted. Fifteen victims (3.6 percent) were killed under legally excusable circumstances. Four were shot by police acting in the line of duty. The rest were killed by another member of the household or a private citizen acting in self-defense. . . .

Discussion

Although firearms are often kept in homes for personal protection, this study shows that the practice is counterproductive. Our data indicate that keeping a gun in the home is independently associated with an increase in the risk of homicide in the home. The use of illicit drugs and a history of physical fights in the home are also important risk factors. Efforts to increase home security have largely focused on preventing unwanted entry, but the greatest threat to the lives of household members appears to come from within.

We restricted our study to homicides that occurred in the home of the victim, because these events can be most plausibly linked to specific individual and household characteristics. If, for example, the ready availability of a gun increases the risk of homicide, this effect should be most noticeable in the immediate environment where the gun is kept. Although our case definition excluded the rare instances in which a nonresident intruder was killed by a homeowner, our methodology was capable of demonstrating significant protective effects of gun ownership as readily as any evidence of increased risk. . . .

Large amounts of money are spent each year on home-security systems, locks, and other measures intended to improve home security. Unfortunately, our results suggest that these efforts have little effect on the risk of homicide in the home. This finding should come as no surprise, since most homicides in the home involve disputes between family members, intimate acquaintances, friends, or others who have ready access to the home. It is important to realize, however, that these data offer no insight into the effectiveness of home-security measures against other household crimes such as burglary, robbery, or sexual assault. In a 1983 poll, Seattle homeowners feared "having someone break into your home while you are gone" most and "having someone break into your home while you are at home" 4th on a list of 16 crimes. Although homicide is the most serious of crimes, it occurs far less frequently than other types of household crime. Measures that make a home more difficult to enter are probably more effective against these crimes.

Despite the widely held belief that guns are effective for protection, our results suggest that they actually pose a substantial threat to members of the household. People who keep guns in their homes appear to be at greater risk of homicide in the home than people who do not. Most of this risk is due to a substantially greater risk of homicide at the hands of a family member or intimate acquaintance. We did not find evidence of a protective effect of keeping a gun in the home, even in the small subgroup of cases that involved forced entry....

A gun kept in the home is far more likely to be involved in the death of a member of the household than it is to be used to kill in self-defense. Previous case-control research has demonstrated a strong association between the ownership of firearms and suicide in the home. Also, unintentional shooting deaths can occur when children play with loaded guns they have found at home. In the light of these observations and our present findings, people should be strongly discouraged from keeping guns in their homes....

STATEMENTS ON AWARDING OF NOBEL PEACE PRIZE

October 15, 1993

Two former enemies were awarded the Nobel Peace Prize October 15 for their efforts to end the policy of apartheid (strict racial segregation) in South Africa and to begin the arduous process of establishing a nonracial democracy in the bitterly divided nation. The internationally prestigious $825,000 prize went to black African National Congress (ANC) leader Nelson Mandela and white South African president Frederik W. de Klerk for their attempts, beginning in 1990, to negotiate an end to racial segregation and pave the way for the formation of a new government based on a new constitution that granted universal suffrage to the people of the nation.

It was an interesting coincidence that the peace prize to the two South Africans was awarded slightly more than a month after a peace accord was reached by Israel and the Palestine Liberation Organization (PLO), designed to end three decades of enmity and signed by former archenemies PLO Chairman Yasir Arafat and Israeli Prime Minister Yizhak Rabin on September 9. (Israeli-Palestinian Peace Accord, p. 747)

Delicate Peace Process

In announcing its decision in Oslo, the Norwegian Nobel Committee said the two leaders had displayed "personal integrity and great political courage" in negotiating an agreement to allow the black majority to participate in a future democratic constitutional government, with elections scheduled for April 1994. "South Africa has been the symbol of racially conditioned suppression. Mandela's and de Klerk's constructive policy of peace and reconciliation also points the way to the peaceful resolution of similar deep-rooted conflicts elsewhere in the world," the committee said. In receiving the peace award (official ceremonies were held at the Stockholm Concert Hall December 10), de Klerk and Mandela joined two of their compatriots: Zulu chief Albert Luthuli, who won in

1960 for leading the ANC in nonviolent protest against racist laws; and Anglican Archbishop Desmond Tutu, who won in 1984 for his impassioned speeches against apartheid. (Tutu Nobel prize, Historic Documents of 1984, p. 1027)

Mandela and de Klerk, whose relationship had been correct but never close or warm, accepted the award in separate appearances before reporters with what a New York Times *reporter described as "the strained grace that has become characteristic of their complex relationship as leaders of mistrustful camps who now depend on each other to complete their work." Indeed, despite the two leaders' efforts, an estimated ten thousand to twelve thousand people—most of them blacks—had died in continuing political violence since early 1990. The two leaders, who would face each other as rivals in the forthcoming elections, blamed one another for the situation.*

Implicitly recognizing that much still needed to be accomplished on the road to instituting a democracy, the Nobel Committee's announcement seemed to honor the process they had begun as much as the two leaders themselves. "These are not saints," said Francis Sejersted, chairman of the committee. "They are politicians in a complicated reality and it is the total picture that was decisive."

The seventy-five-year-old Mandela called the honor a "deeply humbling experience," while fifty-seven-year-old de Klerk said he was "basically a modest man, and I was embarrassed in a certain sense of the word." Asked about his relationship with de Klerk, Mandela responded, "We have no alternative but to work together to bring about a new democratic South Africa."

Even as Mandela met with reporters at ANC headquarters, crowds of black demonstrators swarmed the streets of Johannesburg to celebrate the death sentence handed down by a white judge against two white men convicted of murdering Chris Hani, a popular black communist leader. (The executions were suspended, pending election of a new government.)

Two Widely Divergent Paths to Leadership

The only son of a sheepherding tribal chief, Mandela was born in the Transkei region of South Africa in 1918. After receiving a law degree and trying a stint as an amateur boxer, he joined the ANC in 1944, rising to head its youth league in 1951. In 1952 Mandela established South Africa's first black law firm and was put in charge of the ANC's civil disobedience drive. The ANC was outlawed after the bloody suppression of black protesters in the township of Sharpsville in 1960; Mandela then went underground to help form an armed ANC wing that conducted a campaign of sabotage and limited guerrilla insurgency. He was sentenced to life in prison in 1964 and, after twenty-seven years, was released by de Klerk in 1990, receiving a hero's welcome, even though the government had banned the appearance of his picture in the media and forbidden anyone to speak to him during his years in jail.

Also a lawyer, de Klerk was born in Johannesburg in 1936 into a family of pro-apartheid politicians. After attending Afrikaner schools, he entered Parliament in 1972, where he was widely regarded as an antireform, "orthodox" conservative. After the intractable conservative President P. W. Botha suffered a stroke in 1989, de Klerk (who had been elected leader of the National party) became acting president and then president. In that position, he was initially considered to be a pragmatic but unimaginative compromise choice. Gradually, however, de Klerk's perception of South Africa's political, economic, and social future began to modify as international conditions changed; worldwide sanctions took their toll in isolating the nation economically, politically, morally, and financially, and the South African economy began to unravel. The result was that de Klerk persuaded Parliament to recognize the ANC and to release Mandela, an event that captured media attention worldwide. Thereafter, de Klerk launched an effort to persuade Parliament to repeal apartheid laws, culminating in his 1992 announcement of plans for a new constitution providing for black majority rule, while simultaneously giving assurances to the 15 percent white minority that its property, living standards, and culture would remain largely intact. According to his brother, de Klerk's political evolution was not dramatic but "was built, rather, on pragmatism . . . [he] has slowly outgrown apartheid."

The government and black political leaders reached agreement November 18 on the new constitution, which is designed to eliminate institutionalized racism. It was expected that Mandela would become the nation's first majority president. After the election, the ten black homelands created under apartheid will cease to exist, but nine new regions, each with its own constitution, will be formed.

Mixed, but Hopeful, Reactions and Outlook

"The committee has conferred an equivalence on the two men that is not entirely just," said an October 18 New York Times *editorial. "Mr. Mandela and the millions of black victims for whom he speaks have long earned the support and admiration of the world. Mr. de Klerk, while he possesses a vision lacked by his predecessors, had to be pushed down the road to justice and national unity. . . . The December prize ceremonies in Oslo will give the new laureates a chance to focus world attention on positive changes in South Africa. To that extent the prize will surely be as useful as it is deserved."*

"[Mandela and de Klerk] are, most assuredly, an odd couple, the man held captive for more than two decades of his life and whose name could not be publicly uttered without fear of penalty in his own country and the man who came out of the ranks of those who imprisoned him," commented an editorial in the October 18 Washington Post. *"But together in a protracted and not always friendly dialogue they have transformed the politics of South Africa. . . . They both deserved a prize and their country . . . deserves the kind of support they are jointly seeking." "Had another*

white leader come to power instead of de Klerk, one could easily see the apartheid regime holding out another five, ten years," observed political scientist Robert Schrire. "And with a different black leader, someone without Mandela's self-confidence and stature, you could see the ANC feeling pressed to make demands that no negotiating partner could possibly meet."

"De Klerk wins his share of the prize as an individual, one who inspired difficult and dramatic change from a position of power and privilege," wrote columnist Jim Hoagland in the October 18 Washington Post. *"Mandela wins his through the suffering and forbearance of an entire people, who lost a generation to apartheid in the way Mandela lost most of his adult years in prison. Mandela's personal odyssey—carrying him from nonviolent protest to armed struggle to imprisonment and now to electoral politics—mirrors a people's journey as few lives ever have."*

President Clinton called the joint award an "inspired choice" and urged South Africans "who have withdrawn from the common political process to rethink their positions and contribute their efforts to complete the great work undertaken by Presidents Mandela and de Klerk."

In an interview with a Norwegian radio station, Archbishop Tutu said he was "thrilled" about the award. "They have worked together to bring about an end to one of the most horrible tragedies of modern times, apartheid," he said.

Many obstacles continued to confront South Africa's peace process, however. Principal among them was strident opposition from both the Zulu-based Inkatha Freedom party and the hard-line white Conservative party, as well as the difficulties facing both leaders in keeping their fragile coalitions together.

> *Following are the texts of remarks on the award of the Nobel Peace Prize to South Africa's Nelson R. Mandela, president of the African National Congress; and President Frederik W. de Klerk, October 15, 1993. They include the statements of Norwegian foreign minister Johan Joergen Holst; the Norwegian Nobel Committee; President Clinton; President de Klerk; and President Mandela:*

HOLST'S STATEMENT

"It is with great pleasure and satisfaction that I received the news that the Nobel Committee has decided to award the 1993 Nobel Peace Prize to Nelson Mandela and President F. W. de Klerk," says Foreign Minister Johan Joergen Holst. "They are following in the footsteps of Albert Luthuli and Desmond Tutu. The Peace Prize has been awarded to two men who, together, have managed to bring to an end the inhuman, degrading policy of apartheid in South Africa. Each of them has, in his own way, contributed to the decisive breakthrough we have witnessed in the struggle for human dignity and equality," Holst continues. "Black and white must stand together to build a new South Africa. Many are fighting to obstruct necessary and peaceful change. This year's Peace Laureates have, independently and together, been instrumental in creating the basis for a new, free and peaceful South Africa. We are looking forward to democratic elections in South Africa in April next year."

NOBEL COMMITTEE'S STATEMENT

The Norwegian Nobel Committee has decided to award the Nobel Peace Prize for 1993 to Nelson Mandela and Frederik Willem de Klerk for their work for the peaceful termination of the apartheid regime, and for laying the foundations for a new democratic South Africa.

From their different points of departure, Mandela and de Klerk have reached agreement on the principles for the transition to a new political order based on the tenet of one man-one vote. By looking ahead to South African reconciliation instead of back at the deep wounds of the past, they have shown personal integrity and great political courage.

Ethnic disparities cause the bitterest conflicts. South Africa has been the symbol of racially conditioned suppression. Mandela's and de Klerk's constructive policy of peace and reconciliation also points the way to the peaceful resolution of similar deep-rooted conflicts elsewhere in the world.

The previous Nobel Laureates Albert Luthuli and Desmond Tutu made important contributions to progress towards racial equality in South Africa. Mandela and de Klerk have taken the process a major step further. The Nobel Peace Prize for 1993 is awarded in recognition of their efforts and as a pledge of support for the forces of good, in the hope that the advance towards equality and democracy will reach its goal in the very near future.

CLINTON'S STATEMENT

The Nobel Committee has made an inspired choice in selecting ANC President Nelson Mandela and State President F. W. de Klerk to share the 1993 Nobel Peace Prize. These two farsighted and courageous leaders have overcome a legacy of racial distrust to reach agreement on a framework which has set South Africa on the path of peaceful reconciliation and non-racial democracy. It is entirely fitting that, having worked so closely together for progress, they should share the most prestigious international recognition for their success in setting in motion the transition to a new political order in South Africa.

In selecting these two great leaders, the Nobel Committee has also chosen to honor the many other South Africans who have struggled for so long to achieve racial harmony and justice. It is a testament to the great strides for progress they have made and an endorsement of their hope for a free and democratic South Africa.

It is sadly ironic that just as Presidents de Klerk and Mandela receive the recognition they and their associates so richly deserve, others hesitate to join them in the creation of a new, fully democratic South Africa. Still others are committed to violence which could destroy their current and future achievements. I urge those who have withdrawn from the common political process to re-think their positions and contribute their efforts to complete the great work undertaken by Presidents Mandela and de Klerk.

The American people join me in offering their deepest congratulations to these two great statesmen and all the people of South Africa. I am certain that with similar courage and dedication they can face the challenges and tasks ahead. The many Americans from all walks of life who supported the struggle to end apartheid will be at the side of South Africans as they build a non-racial democracy.

DE KLERK'S STATEMENT

I am deeply honoured by the decision of the Nobel Committee to award the 1993 Nobel Peace Prize to two South Africans. The Prize gives further international recognition to the process which South African leaders—and the South African people—began more than three years ago.

The challenge which confronted us then—and which continues to confront us now—was whether we would be able to bridge decades of bitterness, suspicion and fear and establish the foundations for a new society which would provide security and the prospect of a better life for all our people.

Since then we have made great progress. Through patient and often difficult negotiations we have set the date for our first national election and have reached agreement on the establishment of a Transitional Executive Council, which will help to prepare the country for that election. We have also made substantial progress toward agreements on a transition constitution, a Charter of Fundamental Rights and constitutional principles in terms of which the final constitution will be drafted.

It would have been difficult to imagine such progress four years ago. The credit for this must go to all South Africans who have committed themselves to the process of peaceful negotiations. However, we dare not be complacent. There are still far too many leaders who have not yet committed themselves fully to the negotiation process. There are still too many people and parties who continue to use the rhetoric of racial hatred, armed struggle and war. There are still far too many South Africans who continue to suffer the effects of mindless and brutal violence.

I trust that the awarding of this prize to two South Africans will motivate all South Africans to rededicate themselves to the peaceful resolution of our problems and that it will inspire us all to work for a new and better society.

MANDELA'S STATEMENT

Today's announcement that I have been named to receive this most prestigious award for peace was a deeply humbling experience. The Nobel Peace Prize is amongst the highest accolades that can be bestowed on any human being. To be chosen from amongst the millions of deserving men and women throughout the world is a singular honour to which grave responsibilities are attached.

This is the third occasion since the end of the Second World War that our country has been so recognised. I would like to use this occasion to pay tribute to those other great South Africans who have been past recipients of the Peace Prize: Chief Albert J. Luthuli—an outstanding leader of our people and past President of the African National Congress; and that great son of our country who fought so selflessly against the evils of racism during the darkest days of apartheid repression, Archbishop Desmond Mpilo Tutu.

That South Africa has once again been given the Nobel Peace Prize is a tribute to all South Africans. It is an expression of the profound confidence the international community has vested in us that we can collectively address the enormous problems our country faces without recourse to violence and coercion. This is a prize won in the first instance by all those who have, over the decades, struggled so steadfastly for democracy and peace, in the teeth of ruthless and brutal repression. This coveted honour is a challenge to us all as co-equal compatriots to so conduct ourselves that those who seek to foster racial and ethnic hatred and war are isolated and cauterized. In the world that values justice, democracy and peace for all humankind there is no place for such politics.

I am keenly aware that the Nobel Peace Prize imposes an even greater obligation on me personally to strive even harder, in the interests of all South Africans, for peace, justice and democracy.

But this is a burden I hope to share with my co-recipient, State President F. W. de Klerk. I extend my heartfelt congratulations to him for this illustrious award and express the hope that we can jointly work towards a future in which the children of South Africa can grow up with the right to a life full of opportunities in a country that recognises, defends and protects the human worth of each and every individual.

There is very little we can give to reciprocate the esteem showered upon us by the world community today. What we can do is to ensure that this negotiation process is successfully concluded, that the agreements reached are adhered to by us all, so that the first democratic elections take place on the 27th of April 1994, as scheduled. The people of South Africa have waited too long for a government elected by all the people. We must not and we dare not fail them. A democratic government, so elected, can and will address the terrible legacy of apartheid and allow every man, woman and child to walk tall, free and proud in the country of their birth.

I dedicate this award to all the courageous people of my country, black and white, who have suffered and endured so much, and pledge that in whatever time remains to me I will spare no effort to bring peace, freedom and justice for all to South Africa.

ECOLOGICAL RESTORATION OF THE TALLGRASS PRAIRIE

October 18, 1993

Three hundred bison were released October 18 onto five thousand acres of unobstructed tallgrass prairie near Pawhuska, Oklahoma; they were the first of the planned eighteen hundred bison that eventually will roam the Tallgrass Prairie Preserve. The effort represented years of work by conservationists who are seeking to restore the tallgrass prairie, North America's rarest major biome, to its former splendor. The undertaking was part of an initiative by The Nature Company, a private conservation group, entitled "Last Great Places: An Alliance for People and the Environment," which targeted for conservation seventy-five at-risk ecosystems in the Western hemisphere. It was the first-ever attempt to recreate and maintain the tallgrass environment.

A Dependent Ecosystem

The plains bison, or buffalo as it is popularly known, was itself the recipient of conservation efforts in the mid-1900s. After reaching numbers of 60 million-plus in the years before European settlement in America, bison were by 1900 on the verge of extinction. Estimates of their total head count at that time range from 300 to 1,000. With help from ecologists and conservationsists, however, the number of bison grew in the twentieth century to between 130,000 and 150,000, making the bison an endangered species no longer. On October 18 the New York Times *noted, "Now conservationists hope to cast it in yet another new role: the buffalo as an ecological restorationist."*

The existence and survival of the tallgrass prairie, ecologists believed, depended upon two factors: grazing bison and intermittent fires. Before European settlement in the New World, tallgrass prairie covered over 220,000 square miles in central North America, stretching north-south from Canada to Texas and east-west from Nebraska to the Great Lakes. Each year, parts of the prairie burned; in the summer, lightning often ignited dry grass, and at other times the Osage Indians set prairie fires to block enemy advances. The Native Americans also had another purpose for setting fires: they attracted game. Because prairie plants need deep roots to reach water, they are nearly impossible to destroy completely; when the top layer of a plant is killed, as in a fire, the roots survive and new growth occurs rapidly. Game, especially bison, fed on this lush new grass and moved to other areas when it was gone, leaving behind flammable dead grass and plants ready for the next fire. William K. Stevens of the New York Times *explained, "As the vegetation returned, plant species reappeared in a specific order of succession, with different species combinations characterizing each stage. Myriad patches were in different stages of succession at any given time, creating a sort of ecological crazy-quilt. This ... is what gave the prairie its biological richness and diversity."*

Salvaging the Prairie

Agriculture and development, as well as the hunting of bison, gradually eradicated most of the tallgrass prairie from the central United States; less than 10 percent survives today. Until The Nature Conservancy acquired Barnard Ranch, on which the Tallgrass Prairie Preserve is located, no suitable tracts of land were available to conservationists trying to restore the prairie. While controlled burning was instituted on some small prairie reserves in past years, Stevens pointed out that there had not been an unrestricted area "large enough for the system to function naturally and unfettered."

The Tallgrass Prairie Preserve, comprising 36,000 acres, is one of the largest areas of tallgrass in the United States. Bought by the Nature Conservancy in 1989, the land was a pasture that had supported a cattle ranch. Most importantly, it had never been plowed; thus, original prairie plants had survived and grown there. In the spring of 1993 controlled burning was commenced on 26,000 acres at the preserve, and that summer the prairie bloomed with more than 500 species of grasses and wildflowers. The 300 bison released October 18 are expected to eat approximately 25 percent of the preserve's vegetation each year.

"A Conservation Success Story"

The celebration that accompanied the release of the bison onto the prairie included a black-tie-and-blue-jeans dinner, a Western swing band concert, and speeches made to the crowd of one thousand that viewed the release. In addition, retired Army general Norman Schwarzkopf, a member of the conservancy's board of governors, was honored at an Osage Indian ceremony.

Speakers at the release focused on the cooperative aspect of the bison-prairie project, noting that environmentalists, Native Americans, businesspeople, and ranchers, as well as local citizens, came together to achieve a common goal. Calling the bison release a "conservation success story," John Sawhill, president of The Nature Conservancy, emphasized the importance of this cooperation, stating, "The central idea . . . is to protect large landscapes while meeting the needs of the people who live and work there. To do so means forging long-term partnerships . . . all in the name of establishing alliances *between people and their environments. The two are inextricably linked."*

Following are speeches by John Sawhill, president of The Nature Conservancy; Joe Williams, chairman of The Nature Conservancy's Board of Governors; and retired Army general Norman Schwarzkopf on the occasion of the release of three hundred bison onto the Tallgrass Prairie Preserve in Oklahoma, October 18:

SAWHILL'S REMARKS

Good morning. This is a very exciting day for us at the Conservancy. With the release of the bison onto the Tallgrass Prairie Preserve in a few hours, we celebrate a conservation success story.

Bison—that quintessentially American animal remembered in song, place names, and legend—were once hunted into near extinction. The majority of the tallgrass prairie—that most fertile swath of grassland boasting lush vegetation and abundant wildlife—was plowed under years ago. Today, we celebrate the endurance of both the bison and the tallgrass prairie, which together here form a living piece of our country's rich natural heritage.

We are also celebrating an important moment in the Conservancy's most ambitious undertaking to date: an initiative called "Last Great Places: An Alliance for People and the Environment." This program is targeting some 75 sites throughout the Western Hemisphere and the Pacific that, with effort, can still be saved as functioning ecosystems.

The central idea behind the program is to protect large landscapes while meeting the needs of the people who live and work there. To do so means forging long-term partnerships with diverse interests, all in the name of establishing *alliances* between people and their environments. The two are inextricably linked.

The Tallgrass Prairie Preserve is a "last great place."

We began assembling this preserve in 1989 because we saw an opportunity to restore a functioning tallgrass ecosystem. We were very fortunate in being able to acquire the Barnard Ranch, which had maintained its tallgrass in superb condition for nearly 80 years. We also recognized opportunities to work with diverse constituents to demonstrate that conservation and economic activities need not be at odds.

Since then, we have focused on developing partnerships here in northeastern Oklahoma. With thanks due in large part to dedicated, energized leaders across the state—many of whom serve on Conservancy boards—we have been able to establish the preserve and secure most of the funding required to manage it now and in the years ahead. We have been working to build cooperative relationships with community, state, and business leaders; with independent oil producers, who lease and operate the working wells on the preserve; with members of the Osage Tribe, which owns the mineral rights in the county; with neighboring cattle ranchers, who still graze their herds on parts of the preserve and on adjacent lands; and, perhaps most importantly, with the people of Osage County, Pawhuska, and the surrounding communities.

If support for the preserve's existence can be judged from the enthusiastic donations that have poured in from across the county and state, then I'd have to say that many Oklahomans are behind us in this endeavor. Their goodwill toward the preserve is evident in financial gifts; in contributions of goods and services; and in donations of thousands of volunteer hours. Fourteen miles of fence was constructed from steel pipe donated by several oil field drillers, producers, and suppliers; the bison herd and bison-working equipment were given to us by Kenneth and Diana Adams, of Ken-Ada Ranches in Bartlesville. Volunteers helped us conduct controlled burns on the preserve and dig holes for fencing, and more than 75 volunteers have put on this event for you today.

The goodwill we have received in Oklahoma has been immeasurable.

But while this has been a victory for Oklahoma, I want to stress that it is also a victory for the country. The Tallgrass Prairie Preserve can light the way for conservation efforts across America, showing other communities how to balance the needs of nature with those of people....

Today, the release of bison onto the prairie is a linchpin in our efforts to restore this expanse of prairie to its former grandeur. In the days ahead, we look forward to continuing to build our partnerships that will make the preserve an integral part of Oklahoma's economy and cultural history.

WILLIAMS'S REMARKS

... We're here today to commemorate a landmark in American history: the restoration of a lost landscape—the tallgrass prairie.

Shaped by the interplay of climate, fire, and bison, the tallgrass prairie once rolled down from Canada to Texas on the eastern edges of the Great Plains. It covered some 142 million acres of the North American heartland.

Over the past century, the tallgrass prairie has all but disappeared. This heartland was transformed into the breadbasket of a growing nation. Across the expanse of the plains today can be found a patchwork of towns, farms, ranches, and major cities. But only bits and pieces of the tallgrass prairie remain nationally.

Here in northeastern Oklahoma, the 36,000-acre Tallgrass Prairie Preserve represents one of the largest intact fragments of tallgrass in the country—and it lies at the southern end of the greatest stretch of tallgrass remaining in North America. We are fortunate that the ranchers in Osage County have taken such good care of the prairie they own, and we are particularly fortunate that the Barnard Family, whose ranch is the core of the Tallgrass Prairie Preserve, maintained the tallgrass in such wonderful condition.

Today marks an exciting achievement in conservation history. With the release of 300 head of bison onto the prairie, the Conservancy is taking a major step toward recreating a fully functioning prairie ecosystem. Bison are a key management tool for the prairie. Their grazing and wallowing habits historically were crucial to the grasslands.

For the people of Oklahoma, today also symbolizes a major victory in our state's history. We are reclaiming a living part of our heritage. Once pushed to the edge of extinction, the bison are making a welcome comeback on the preserve. As an Oklahoman, I am proud of what we've been able to accomplish together in establishing the preserve.

The Tallgrass Prairie Preserve stands at the apex of what conservationists can accomplish when working with business and other private interests to protect both ecological and economic needs. Here in Osage County, we're working with oil and gas producers, ranchers, and building relationships within the Osage Tribe to create and manage this preserve for the long term. Cattle continue to graze parts of the preserve and the surrounding lands; working derricks continue to pump oil and gas.

And we hope that the preserve will ultimately provide a stimulus to the local economy. Last year, more than 15,000 visitors came to see the preserve—one of the largest tourism draws in Osage County. This number is bound to grow in the coming years, with bison roaming the land.

This preserve stands as evidence that land can be protected in private hands, without public assistance. The prairie has been a private initiative that has garnered nearly $12 million in private funds to support our work here.

We are dedicated to making this preserve a success over the long term and a showcase of partnerships that can achieve conservation and economic goals—for the Conservancy, for Oklahoma, and for the country.

SCHWARZKOPF'S REMARKS

I'm thrilled to be here today to join with the Conservancy and the people of Oklahoma in celebrating the bison release on this magnificent preserve.

Restoring an ecosystem to its former health and grandeur is no small task. Many factors have to come together to make this possible, and to make the prairie a distinctively tallgrass one. Ecologists have learned that bison are one of these key factors. Returning them to the landscape in such massive numbers as the Conservancy proposes is a heroic effort. I salute them and all the people who have been involved in this project.

After I retired from the Army, I decided to join The Nature Conservancy's Board of Governors, to fulfill my lifelong desire to help conserve our beautiful, varied natural world. The Conservancy was a logical vehicle through which to do this.

I agree with the organization's non-confrontational, non-political approach, and with its willingness to work with all sectors of society in meeting conservation objectives. The Conservancy realizes that people, too, are part of the landscape, and it wants to see human communities flourishing alongside vibrant natural communities.

When I decided to join the board, I was particularly intrigued by the Conservancy's bold efforts to conserve nature while addressing the needs of people. In a world so racked by resource-use conflicts, it seems critical to me that the conservation movement search for solutions that help people lead productive economic lives while maintaining the integrity of their environment.

At places like the Tallgrass Prairie Preserve, the Conservancy aims to do just that. Here, the Conservancy wants to recreate a thriving expanse of tallgrass prairie while encouraging people to live harmoniously within the ecosystem. By working closely with the Pawhuska community, I believe the Conservancy and its many partners can find ways to manage the land and Oklahoma's abundant natural resources sustainably, and for the long term.

For instance, I find it especially heartening to learn that more and more people are visiting the preserve. They're coming to enjoy this beautiful landscape and the friendly town of Pawhuska. These visitors are bringing revenue into the area, and that's just one way in which the preserve is becoming an asset to the area, I'm glad to learn. In the years ahead, I feel confident that the partnerships forged out here on the prairie will bear more fruit, to the benefit of both people and nature.

This morning, I was paid a great honor. In a ceremony whose roots are ancient, I was made an honorary Osage Chief. I was given the name Eagle Chief by Mr. Ed Red Eagle, the official name-giver of his clan, the Tsi-zho Wa-shta-ke.

It was a very moving moment in my life, to be embraced by the Osage Tribe and brought into their age-old traditions. I was struck with the full force of their reverence for the Earth and the cosmos, manifest in the clan's life symbol—the golden eagle—and in the ceremony's rich symbolism. Their respect for nature is immutable.

To the tribe's ancestors, the world was not polarized into those who exploit the land and waters and those who do not. Theirs was a world in which an abiding reverence for the gifts and powers of this Earth held sway.

The America of today doesn't much resemble the America of centuries past. Yet our modern society would do well to take a lesson from the practices and customs of ancient cultures. History is a powerful teacher. From our past, we can glean lessons about living harmoniously with nature, and about coming together in alliances for change.

I'm convinced that we, the American people, can solve any problem and meet any challenge when we make up our minds to do so—and when we all work together. My faith in this nation of ours is great. I know we can build successful alliances for change.

The Tallgrass Prairie Preserve stands as a crowning achievement of what we—conservationists and businessmen alike—can do when we come together as partners. All of us should revel in the knowledge that our great-great-grandchildren will have a chance to experience a living piece of our past out here on the tallgrass prairie.

FANFARE FOR BICENTENNIAL OF THE NATION'S CAPITOL

October 23, 1993

Two hundred years after George Washington laid the cornerstone of the U.S. Capitol, President Bill Clinton and other dignitaries gathered on the building's lower west terrace on October 23 to commemorate the event and extoll what historian David McCullough, master of ceremonies, called "the best known, most important, and most revered structure in our nation."

On that site two centuries earlier, Alexander Hamilton proclaimed, "Here, the people govern." And more than a century ago, after a Civil War visit to Washington, Nathaniel Hawthorne wrote that "the center and heart of America is the Capitol." Although those remarks in praise of the Capitol were not recalled at the ceremony, many others were. The president, vice president, various leaders of Congress, and Justice Harry A. Blackmun of the Supreme Court told of the Capitol's history and significance, and the nation's official poet laureate, Rita Dove, recited her new poem "written for the glory of this day."

George Mitchell, the Senate Democratic leader, recalled that when the Capitol's cornerstone was set in place by George Washington, there were but fifteen states with five million people, and the government was seated in Philadelphia awaiting a move, seven years later, to the still-raw landscape of the newly created District of Columbia.

Restoring the Statue of Freedom

The cornerstone laying occurred September 18, 1793, but no one at the bicentennial event voiced any concern that the 1993 ceremony was not itself being held on September 18. It had to wait until the Statue of Freedom had been placed back on its pedestal atop the Capitol dome. After one hundred thirty years on that perch, the statue was eased down by helicopter on May 9 so workers could repair the effects of corrosion and restore its original color.

The statue, weighing seven and a half tons and reaching upward nineteen and a half feet, is a woman robed as an ancient Roman and crowned with a helmet depicting an eagle's head and feathers. She clutches a sheathed sword in one hand and a laurel of victory in the other. The statue was sculpted in an Italian studio by an American, Thomas Crawford, and cast in bronze by slaves under the direction of artist Clark Mills in Maryland. In 1863, during the Civil War, the statue was hoisted in sections above the Capitol, becoming the highest standing object in Washington. It was affixed to the present dome, which was nearing completion. Abraham Lincoln insisted that work on the Capitol continue in wartime as "a sign we intend the Union shall go on."

Phases of Capitol Construction

The Capitol was built in stages, first one wing, then another, finally the central section, and over it the dome. The winning design was by submitted in 1792 by William Thornton, who was awarded $500 and a nearby vacant lot for his design. Following Pierre Charles L'Enfant's grand plan for the yet-unbuilt city of Washington, he placed the Capitol on Jenkins Heights, now Capitol Hill. Since Thornton was a physician and painter by trade, others were chosen to carry out the design. In quick succession, two architects were found wanting. Then in 1803 Thomas Jefferson appointed an English architect, Benjamin Henry Latrobe, to be surveyor of public buildings and placed him in charge of finishing the Capitol.

When Congress met for the first time in Washington, in 1800, only one wing of the Capitol was ready. It housed the Senate and House of Representatives, the Supreme Court, and the Library of Congress. The other wing was completed in 1807, but construction and design problems arose at once, requiring nearly three years of remodeling. Both wings were burned by the British in the War of 1812, forcing Congress to take up quarters until 1919 in a nearby brick building, on land where the Supreme Court now stands. By then Charles Bulfinch of Boston had replaced Latrobe as architect. Under his direction, work on the original Capitol was finished in 1829.

Still, the Capitol's problems were not over. The House and Senate chambers had poor heating, ventilation, and acoustics. And by mid-century they were becoming overcrowded. Both wings were enlarged during the 1850s, relieving the old problems but creating a new one: the enlarged building dwarfed the old dome. A bigger dome, which remains today, was completed in 1865.

Still other alterations were made in the 20th century, most notably an extension of the east front in 1958-62. As that work drew to a close, a heated argument arose over whether to restore or rebuild and extend the deteriorating west front. By 1983 the advocates of restoration had won out. That work was completed in 1987—the last work of consequence until the Statue of Freedom was removed, cleaned, and restored.

Following are excerpts from remarks made at the U.S. Capitol's bicentennial ceremony, October 23, 1993, by historian David McCullough, Senate Democratic leader George Mitchell, Senate Republican leader Bob Dole, Senate Pro Tempore Robert C. Byrd, Vice President Al Gore, Supreme Court Justice Harry A. Blackmun, U.S. Poet Laureate Rita Dove, Rep. Robert H. Michel, Rep. Charlie Rose, House Speaker Thomas S. Foley, and President Bill Clinton:

David McCullough: Mr. President. Ladies and gentlemen. My name is David McCullough. On this magnificent morning, at this historic place, here at latitude 38 degrees, 53 minutes north; longitude 77 degrees west, on a hill above the Potomac, we are gathered to celebrate the bicentennial of the best known, most important, and most revered structure in our nation. The United States Capitol.

We are Americans. And for us, this is a proud day. For this great building holds a place in our hearts and in our way of life like no other. It is a shrine on a hill, and it is the national stage upon which are enacted the difficult tasks and continuing drama of representative government. The bedrock of our faith in the land of the free.

. . . And at the summit of the Dome, now there in sunshine, the emblem of freedom is again in her place. Older by a generation than the Statue of Liberty, she has stood on high since the year 1863. Since the autumn of Abraham Lincoln's Gettysburg Address. She has weathered civil war. World war. She has seen the deaths of presidents. The Great Depression. The sky turned dark by prairie dust blown from half a continent away. She has been pelted by sleet and snow, and struck by lightning. And, she has seen triumphant times. Good times. Lots of good times. Never has she looked better than today, October 23, 1993.

All newly, thoroughly refurbished. Ready for another two hundred years, or more. And never—ever—has our Capitol looked better than today. Not ever before in all of its days.

Ladies and gentlemen, a hundred years ago in this very place the nation celebrated the Capitol's first century. The President of the United States, leaders of Congress, and justices of the Supreme Court addressed another vast audience. On this equally festive occasion a century later, we will now hear from the successors of those leaders who represented our government's three branches. . . .

Senator George Mitchell: Mr. President. Mr. Vice President. Friends. Much has changed in the two hundred years since the cornerstone of this Capitol was laid. Then there were 5 million Americans, 15 states, with 30 senators, and 106 representatives. Now, of course, there are 250 million Americans, 50 states, 100 senators, 435 members of the House. But more striking than the change is that so much is the same.

In 1793 the government faced a serious national debt. In 1993 it still does. In 1793 umbrella makers in Philadelphia petitioned Congress for protection against imported French umbrellas. We still get such petitions.

But the most important thing that hasn't changed is the American commitment to liberty. The crowning achievement of the early American government was the Bill of Rights, the first ten amendments to the Constitution. They remain today, as they have been for two centuries, the most concise and eloquent statement ever written by human beings of the fundamental rights of free men and women against the power of government.

The Bill of Rights is the defining act of American history. The Constitution was ratified, and this nation was launched on the bedrock principle of individual liberty. That is, as expressed in the Bill of Rights, both uniquely American and universal in its reach. It is that spirit which we celebrate today.

This building, the United States Capitol, is the preeminent physical symbol of freedom in the world. But more important even than this great structure is the spirit which led to its construction and which inhabits it today. We are fortunate and very proud to be Americans. Citizens of the most free, the most open, the most just society in all of history. That is our benefit. With that benefit comes the responsibility to act so that two hundred years from today Americans and people all over the world will still admire this building. And Americans will still live in freedom protected by an unchanged and an unchangeable Bill of Rights. On this brilliant day it's obvious that God is smiling on America. May it always be so. . . .

Senator Bob Dole: Mr. President. Mr. Vice President. My colleagues. Distinguished guests. We gather this morning on the grounds of the third Capitol of the United States. When the First Congress convened in 1789 it met in New York City, occupying the former city hall. That location was only temporary, however, as the recently ratified Constitution provided for the establishment of a permanent capital city. A location for that city was selected in 1790 when Congress passed the Residence Act directing by the year 1800 that the government should occupy a new Federal district along the Potomac River.

While the new capital city was under construction, Congress moved from New York to Philadelphia where they carried on the task of building a democracy. At the same time, hundreds of workmen were building a new Federal city on the Potomac. In his plan for the city, Pierre Charles L'Enfant placed the Capitol on the crest of what was then known as Jenkins Hill, a site that he described as a "pedestal waiting for a monument."

On September 18, 1793, a large and boisterous crowd gathered here to watch an elaborate Masonic ceremony highlighted by placing the Capitol cornerstone by President George Washington. As many of you know, my colleague Senator Strom Thurmond who was here on that day [laughter] refuses to reveal just exactly where the cornerstone is.

The *Alexandria Gazette* reported that the ceremony concluded with fifteen salutes from the artillery, and then "the whole company retired to an extensive booth where an ox of five hundred pounds was barbecued." History will note this is the first time—but certainly not the last—that someone's ox was gored in the United States Capitol. [Laughter]....

Senator Robert C. Byrd: Mr. President. Mr. Speaker. Mr. Justice Blackmun. My fellow Americans. The United States Capitol building is a visible symbol of America's link to ancient Rome. Of all that made Rome great, nothing was more basic than Rome's noble attachment to a mixed constitution of checks and balances and separation of powers that lifted her from the lowest beginnings to that radiant summit of splendor and magnificence that has never ceased to attract the admiration and the wonder of the world.

But when that devotion to a mixed constitution was lost, the short sword of the Roman legions and the wooden galleys that plied the Adriatic could no longer save her, and the ancient empress of the classical world sank into a hopeless impotence and eventual obscurity as a military power and territorial empire.

Two hundred years ago, our Forefathers laid the cornerstone for this building, within which is domiciled the branch of government that springs directly from the people and from whom it derives its constant renewal, and which, only a few years before, had been set in place by the Framers of the Constitution, the cornerstone of this republic.

As we today commemorate with pride the cornerstone-laying of this temple that houses the "people's branch," let us renew afresh our fealty to the American constitutional system, the foundation upon which this republic rests. We received it from our fathers. Let us as surely hand it on to our sons and daughters and their children who will stand in our place a hundred years from now—a system of government under a mixed constitution that raised this American republic to a summit more glorious than ancient Rome ever saw....

Vice President Al Gore: Thank you, Senator Byrd. Mr. President. Distinguished members of the Congress. Ladies and gentlemen. Of all the symbols of our republic, none moves our hearts the way this Capitol building moves our hearts. We have heard about the history of this structure, and I would like to add only a brief description of some small moments in the recent history of this structure.

As President of the Senate, I still have the privilege—sometimes—of greeting visitors who are seeing this structure for the first time. And for the past seventeen years, I've had the privilege of sometimes greeting school children who come from all over the United States to stand in front of this building and look up at the Capitol Dome. It has never ceased to stir me, white against the sky with the Statue of Freedom at the top. The reaction of those children who still come—almost every day—to see this site is testament to the living history of this building.

It was startling these last few months to look up and see scaffolding there. And it's wonderful to see the Statue of Freedom back this morning. Our country is very different now than that first day when she was hoisted into place in 1863, but it is a comfortable feeling to see this old friend back securely in place ready to look out over Washington for another 130 years and more. A reminder to all of us that as we look ahead to the future we must never forget the legacy of our past....

Justice Harry A. Blackmun: Mr. Chairman. Mr. President. Mr. Vice President. Distinguished participants. Ladies and gentlemen. Your Supreme Court of the United States has very substantial roots in this building. Although the Judiciary is one of three branches of our government, for the first 145 years of its existence the court had no home of its own. In a building sense, during that period of almost a century and a half, it distinctly was an orphan.

The Court first convened in February 1790, at the Royal Exchange in New York City, then the seat of government. But the following year, the seat was in Philadelphia, and the court assembled there. First, at Independence Hall, and then, at the City Hall. It arrived in Washington in 1801, and, until 1809, sat in various, small, and rather inadequate rooms in the Capitol building. This building.

Somewhat more acceptable quarters outside the building were found for the 1809 term. But the Court returned here in 1810. It then was allowed to use the original Senate Chamber when the Senate moved upstairs to larger quarters. And that chamber, now beautifully restored and available for visiting, was its courtroom for fifty years except for the period of unpleasantness during the War of 1812, when the building was burned by the British with official court papers used as tinder. It is in that room here in this building that Chief Justice Marshall and Chief Justice Taney successively presided. And it is there that Daniel Webster argued the Dartmouth College case, and the Dred Scott case was argued and announced.

Once again, however, in December 1860, the Court followed the Senate and inherited its chamber upstairs when that body moved into the Capitol's North Wing it presently occupies. The Court used the second Senate chamber for seventy-five years, from 1860 to 1935, when it moved into its present building. I think one may say—fairly—that the Court's own edifice came into being primarily due to the influence of Chief Justice William Howard Taft, who had been President of these United States.

The site on which today's Supreme Court stands has its historical interest, too, related to this building. It is there that the so-called Brick Capitol stood. The Brick Capitol was used by Congress from 1815 to 1819, while this one was being repaired. And it is there that Henry Clay presided as Speaker of the House. And it is there that Chief Justice Marshall administered the oath of office to President James Monroe in 1817. And on that site was located the capitol prison during the War Between the States. Incarcerated there were Belle Boyd, the noted confederate; and Captain

Henry Wirz of the Confederacy's own Andersonville prison.

Thus, despite the physical separation of the court's present building from the Capitol building, the Court has deep roots here in this building. It feels that it has been a distinct part of the edifice. It knows that long was this building its original home, and it is honored to participate in this celebration today.

The Statue of Freedom is again in place. And, again, it faces east. Does she look over to the Court as the symbol of the judiciary with the expectation and the challenge that its decisions be wise and neutral and correct? I like to think so. And I also like to think that the judiciary always will maintain its proper role in the government of this country which, despite its warts and despite its defects, we all so dearly love.

The Statue of Freedom is on its pedestal and rightly demands the best from all of us. May we fulfill that very precious promise. . . .

David McCullough: President Clinton has designated the month of October as National Arts and Humanities Month. In that spirit, we present our next speaker, reading from her specially prepared poem, *Lady Freedom Among Us,* the Poet Laureate of the United States, Rita Dove.

Rita Dove: . . . I offer this poem written for the glory of this day.

Lady Freedom Among Us

Don't lower your eyes
Or stare straight ahead to where
You think you ought to be going
Don't mutter *oh no*
Not another one
Get a job fly a kite
Go bury a bone

With her oldfashioned sandals
With her leaden skirts
With her stained cheeks and whiskers and heaped up trinkets
She has risen among us in blunt reproach
She has fitted her hair under a hand-me-down cap
And spruced it up with feathers and stars
Slung over one shoulder she bears
The rainbowed layers of charity and murmurs
All of you even the least of you

Don't cross to the other side of the square
Don't think *another item to fit on a tourist's agenda*
Consider her drenched gaze her shining brow
She who has brought mercy back into the streets
And will not retire politely to the potter's field

Having assumed the thick skin of this town
Its gritted exhaust its sunscorch and blear
She rests in her weathered plumage
Bigboned resolute

Don't think you can ever forget her
Don't even try
She's not going to budge

No choice but to grant her space
Crown her with sky
For she is one of the many
and she is each of us

Representative Robert H. Michel: Mr. President. Mr. Vice President. Mr. Speaker. My colleagues and fellow Americans. It's a very great honor for all of us to be part of this historic ceremony. I'd like to devote my brief remarks this morning to the cornerstone of 1851, which began the enlargement of the Capitol Building.

The enlargement was necessary because, as has been mentioned by the distinguished Majority Leader, between 1793 and 1850, the number of states in the Union had more than doubled; and as the nation grew, so did the Congress.

It was evident that the Capitol building would have to be enlarged, and a plan for the North and South Wings was devised.

And so, on the Fourth of July, 1851, with church bells ringing and artillery salutes from various spots in the city, the cornerstone ceremony took place.

The principal address on that occasion was given by the great orator, Daniel Webster.

He spoke brilliantly for two solid hours. This was, of course, before the age of the thirty-second sound bite; and, thank heaven, none of our participants today has been prone to emulate Webster.

Webster deposited in the cornerstone a sheet of paper on which he wrote to posterity the following: "... the Union of the United States of America stands firm, that their Constitution still exists unimpaired ... growing every day stronger and stronger in the affections of the great body of the American people, and attracting more and more the admiration of the world..."

It seems to me that the 1851 cornerstone says something very wonderful about our country.

We Americans have never seen permanence and change as contradictory terms but, rather, as complimentary parts of our national vision.

The new addition to the Capitol Building in 1851 certainly changed this building. But in doing so, it helped to keep it a permanent part of our national life.

We Americans retain the permanent things in our national life only when we are willing to strengthen them through change.

And, in Webster's words, "growing stronger and stronger every day."

This is the great paradox—and the great blessing—of American freedom and progress.

The 1851 cornerstone symbolizes that blessing, and I am glad we can all honor it here today.

Representative Charlie Rose: Mr. President. Mr. Vice President. Mr. Speaker. Mr. Justice Blackmun. Distinguished colleagues of the Senate and the House: It was less than two weeks after President Lincoln's Gettysburg Address, with its emphasis on binding up the nation's wounds and moving forward in brotherhood and unity, that the Statue of Freedom was first elevated to her place of inspiration atop the Capitol Dome.

Today, as our nation embarks on a new journey of regeneration and healing, it is fitting that the statue is restored, refreshed, and reconsecrated. This symbolic ceremony comes at a time when the American people, our President, and our Congress are dedicated to the renewal of our beloved United States.

The crest of an eagle's head crowning the Statue is an ancient symbol of human aspiration toward universal good, of being reborn, through enlightenment, with higher awareness. Let this statue inspire our efforts.

When he left this country and returned to France at the end of our Revolution, General Lafayette said, "Freedom has found a home, and it is in this country of the United States."

Thomas Jefferson envisioned this capitol two hundred years ago, when it was dedicated, as a living shrine of democracy. It would demonstrate the principles of self-government to all humanity and inspire emulation throughout the world.

The Statue we honor today, a feminine figure, suggests the female role of healing; her sword depicting the defense of our values. There is no woman speaker on our program today; but the statue herself speaks louder than words.

The Holy Bible refers to a city on the hill. As we regard this statue towering above our Capitol Building, briefly recall that we are enjoined to let our light shine forth before all that they may see our good works. Standing on her own two feet, as Americans strive to do, the statue suggests that we move with individualism and autonomy to build together a better American community for the future, a society based upon reconciliation, on sharing, caring, and love for one another.

As we look above, we gather strength and courage from our past, as the spirit of freedom guides us toward a future that fulfills the dreams of those who dedicated this Capitol Building 200 years ago.

Welcome home, Lady Freedom. It's good to have you back on the dome and in our hearts. Thank you.

Speaker Tom Foley: Thank you, Mr. McCullough. Two centuries ago the first president of the United States, George Washington, came to this site to lay the cornerstone of the Capitol. We are deeply honored that the forty-second president of the United States has returned to help us celebrate.

And to you, Mr. President, and to the Vice President, and to the Joint Congressional leadership, and to Justice Blackmun, and the Architect of the Capitol, and to all the architects, workers, and engineers, and to the wonderful crew of the helicopter and all who placed Freedom back on her perch today, and to Rita Dove, and to all the citizens who contributed by the purchase of their commemorative coins to the elevation of Freedom today, we thank you for coming to make this a celebration of America. This Capitol, this majestic architectural metaphor for the growth of a nation, adorned by the Statue of Freedom, is a symbol of an extraordinary experiment in representative democracy, and a beacon to people around the world who seek equal rights, justice, and freedom.

Today, the 103rd Congress meets here, and I have the honor to be the forty-ninth Speaker of the House. But, in November of 1800, Theodore Sedgwick of Massachusetts, the seventh Speaker, came with representatives from the sixteen United States to a wilderness town of woodland, swamp, and half-finished buildings to convene the Sixth Congress in the new Capitol where masons were still working on the first sections of the building.

As I stand here and look westward, I can see what Speaker Sedgwick could only imagine—a vista of the two hundred years of democracy—the monuments and museums that trace the political and cultural history of this nation stretched out before us. When Speaker Sedgwick looked westward in 1800, he could see only the plans of Pierre L'Enfant beginning to take shape from the forest, and the White House in the distance.

When he convened the Sixth Congress, only one wing of the original Capitol was finished, but its majesty and all that it represents were already set in stone. American democracy was in its infancy. This building was in progress, and both have sometimes gracefully, and sometimes not so gracefully, adjusted to the changing tides of history. The Capitol has survived war and destruction. It has survived restoration, reconstruction, and redesign. It is, in fact, an amalgamation of many buildings, fashioned from many materials—from limestone to cast iron, sandstone to steel, marble, and brick.

In so many ways the Capitol, with the Statue of Freedom on its dome, symbolizes not just who we are as a people, but what we are as a nation: a diverse people unified under one lasting principle that today we have raised above everything else: "Freedom."

Under the watchful eye of Freedom, in this temple of democracy, echo the voices of history—voices that rose to the challenges of war and peace, slavery and freedom, and for the preservation of the Union itself—voices of courage, dedication, sacrifice, and honor that shaped this Nation.

Speaker Theodore Sedgwick could never have imagined today's vision from Capitol Hill—the National Gallery, the Museum of American History, the Lincoln Memorial, the Air and Space Museum. And, above all, the Capitol itself, the importance of which was most dramatically felt in 1865 when delegations representing the governments of the United States and the Confederacy met on shipboard at Hampton Roads to discuss the end of the Civil War.

At that historic moment, the first thing former Senator Hunter of Virginia, who represented the Confederacy, said to Secretary of State William Seward was, "How is the Capitol? Is it finished?"

Like democracy this Capitol will never be finished. It is a work in progress—a moving picture of a dynamic government. In the new book, *The United States Capitol,* by Fred and Suzy Maroon, published this year to commemorate the bicentennial, is this quote:

"Over the course of its two hundred year history the United States Capitol has grown, sometimes fitfully and sometimes gracefully, from being the mere symbol of an idea to being a cherished monument that embodies the nation's rich remembrance of the past, and high hopes for the future. In that respect, it is timeless." . . .

President Bill Clinton: Thank you. Thank you, Mr. Speaker. Mr. Vice President. Distinguished leaders of the House and Senate. Mr. Justice Blackmun. My fellow Americans.

We come here today to celebrate the two-hundredth birthday of this great building, the cornerstone of our republic. We come here to watch our Capitol made whole 130 years after the beautiful Statue of Freedom was first raised above this Capitol.

This is a moment of unity in this great city of ours so often known for its conflicts. In this moment, we all agree, we know in our minds and feel in our hearts the words that Thomas Jefferson spoke in the first inaugural address ever given on these grounds. He said that people of little faith were doubtful about America's future, but he believed our government was the world's best hope.

What was that hope? The hope that still endures that in this country every man and woman without regard to race or region or station in life would have the freedom to live up to the fullest of his or her God-given potential; the hope that every citizen would get from government not a guarantee but the promise of an opportunity; to do one's best; to have an equal chance; for the most humble and the most well born, to do what God meant for them to be able to do.

That hope was almost dashed in the great Civil War—when the Statue of Freedom was raised. Many people questioned whether Abraham Lincoln should permit this work to go on. But he said during the war, when so many thought our country would come to an end that, if people see the Capitol going on, it is a sign we intend the Union to go on.

In 1865 Abraham Lincoln gave the first inaugural address ever given under the Statue of Freedom. And he said,

"With malice toward none, with charity for all, with firmness in right as God gives us to see the right, let us strive on to finish the work we are in."

And in that, the greatest of all presidential inaugural addresses, Abraham Lincoln gave us our charge for today. For the work of keeping the hope of America alive never finishes.

It is not enough for us to be mere stewards of our inheritance. We must always be the architects of its renewal. The Capitol is here after two-hundred years, this beautiful Statue of Freedom can be raised, renewed after 130 years, because our forbearers never stopped thinking about tomorrow.

We require the freedom to preserve what is best and the freedom to change, the freedom to explore, the freedom to build, the freedom to grow. My fellow Americans, I tell you that perhaps the biggest of our problems today is that too many of our people no longer believe the future can be better than the past. And too many others, most of them young, have no connection to the future whatever because the present is so chaotic. But the future, the future, has a claim on all of us.

We have, because of our birthright as Americans, a moral obligation to face the day's challenges and to make tomorrow better than today. All we really owe to this great country after 200 years is to make sure that 200 years from now this building will still be here and our grandchildren many generations in the future will be here to celebrate it anew.

PRESIDENTIAL PANEL REPORT ON BREAST CANCER

October 27, 1993

Of the nearly two million women diagnosed with breast cancer, the disease will prove fatal for 460,000 during the 1990s, according to a report released October 27 by a presidential panel appointed to make recommendations on how the disease could be better detected and treated. The report was the result of a fifteen-month study, during which the twenty-member Special Commission on Breast Cancer (a group within the President's Cancer Panel of the National Institutes of Health's National Cancer Institute) received testimony from more than 190 experts on topics that included research in basic science, epidemiology, treatment and prevention, detection and early diagnosis, rehabilitation, and quality of life. To make any meaningful inroads in combatting the disease—the incidence of which increased by 53 percent between 1950 and 1989—the commission estimated that at least $500 million would be needed annually for research.

The commission released its findings soon after a rally sponsored by the 70,000-member grassroots organization, the National Breast Cancer Coalition, which was founded in 1991. Members of the group met with President Bill Clinton and Hillary Rodham Clinton, and the president pledged to draw up a "national action plan" for preventing, diagnosing, and treating the disease.

Growing Awareness and Activism

Breast cancer is one of the most rapidly growing diseases in the nation and the leading cause of death among women between the ages of thirty-two and fifty-two. According to a widely cited statistic, it strikes one of every nine women in the United States. However, that figure is adjusted for factors such as age, race, and geographical region. For example, the disease strikes 434 in 100,000 women ages seventy to seventy-four, compared with 27 per 100,000 women ages thirty to thirty-four. The mortality rate is 10 percent higher for blacks overall and for women who live in the Northeast.

Breast cancer has received more government funds than any other kind of malignancy, including lung cancer, which kills more women overall each year than does breast cancer. While the causes of other kinds of cancer are better understood, researchers are uncertain about what factors—genetic, environmental, or dietary, among others— predispose a woman to develop breast cancer. Moreover, between 70 percent and 80 percent of women who acquire the disease have no known risk factors, such as having a relative with breast cancer, having early onset of menstruation, having late menopause, or giving birth late in life.

Awareness of breast cancer was highlighted in the 1970s, when well-known women, such as Betty Ford in 1974, revealed that they had the disease. Congress became more sensitive to breast cancer as a political issue related to heightened awareness of women's concerns in general in 1988, when female legislators lobbied, although unsuccessfully, for coverage of mammography under Medicare. The breast cancer movement also took inspiration from the AIDS activism of the 1980s and 1990s. In 1992 a coalition of advocacy groups organized a "Breast Cancer Awareness Month," delivering a petition with 800,000 signatures to Washington.

Recommendations: Controversy over Mammograms

Among its recommendations, the panel urged that treatment alternatives to the often painful and debilitating radiation and chemotherapy regimes be developed to improve the quality of life for breast cancer patients. In addition, the panel recommended a greater role for industry in developing new products for diagnosis, prevention, and treatment; improved education and information dissemination for patients, the public, and health care professionals; reforms in health care delivery and the role of the payers; greater focus on the contribution of patient advocacy and volunteer organizations; and formulation of public policy and legislation. The group devoted a separate section to highlighting special issues confronting minority and underserved women, saying, "Diversity within these groups in culture, tradition, language, education, and other factors associated with breast cancer risk and access to optimal care must be considered in developing culturally sensitive programs." The group called for greater access to breast cancer education and outreach services for these women.

The group also suggested that official standards for mammography examinations (breast X-rays) be established. Clinton had proclaimed October 19 as National Mammography Day, despite controversy over using the X-ray tests to detect early stages of breast cancer in younger women. In December 1993 the National Cancer Institute reversed its previous recommendation that women in their forties have routine periodic mammograms. That decision was challenged by the American Cancer Society, breast-cancer activists, and some members of Congress.

To buttress their arguments, mammogram advocates pointed to an article in Cancer *by Thomas Jefferson University Breast Imaging Center researchers, indicating that such tests would be beneficial. "Our experience indicates that high-quality mammography is able to detect substantial numbers of early breast cancers among women aged 40 to 49 years," said Stephen Feig, coauthor of the study. The researchers found that women without invasive cancers could be treated without either radiation or mastectomy, if the tumor was detected early by mammogram.*

More Funds Needed?

According to the panel's report, the National Cancer Institute more than doubled its funding for breast cancer research between 1991 and 1993. In addition, Congress appropriated $210 million to the Department of Defense for a five-year research program. Nonetheless, panel members noted that lack of funds impeded efforts to pursue promising research in genetics, molecular biology, and other fields, including analyzing the impact of taking hormonal supplements such as estrogen in a woman's later years.

"There are two things we don't know about breast cancer," said Nancy A. Brinker, founder of the Susan G. Korman Breast Cancer Foundation in Dallas, Texas, who served on the president's panel. "We don't know the cause, and we don't know the cure. Until we make such a commitment, we're not going to get either one."

However, "people say that [additional research] money will save lives, but that's not necessarily true," commented Ann Flood, a sociologist at Dartmouth Medical School. "It's not like we are close to brand-new information that would benefit from such funds."

> *Following are excerpts from the report released October 27, 1993, by the President's Cancer Panel Special Commission on Breast Cancer, entitled "Breast Cancer: A National Strategy—A Report to the Nation":*

Introduction

Over the last decade, patients and their families have directed increasing national attention to breast cancer. Their input has stimulated breast cancer research, focusing on the need for prevention and cure. During the 1970s and 1980s, breast cancer incidence rose by 21 percent among women of all ages in the United States, and increased by 49 percent among women 65 and older. Even among women least likely to experience breast cancer—those under 50—incidence rose by 13 percent. National Cancer Institute funding for breast cancer has increased from $92.7 million in 1991 to

$196.6 million in 1993. In addition, Congress appropriated $210 million to the Department of Defense in Fiscal Year 1993 for a multi-year breast cancer research program. There is wide public demand for even greater levels of funding of a national breast cancer program and an outcry for effective prevention and cure.

In response to a request from the Vice President of the United States to the Chairman of the President's Cancer Panel, the President's Cancer Panel Special Commission on Breast Cancer was appointed by the Director of the National Cancer Institute in 1992. Its 19 members held 11 meetings over 14 months, hearing testimony from more than 190 scientists, clinicians, patient advocates, and experts in all aspects of breast cancer. This report contains the findings and recommendations of the Commission based on this comprehensive review.

Breast cancer is a large and growing public health problem in the United States. All women are at considerable risk for developing breast cancer during most of their lives. It is estimated that during the 1990s nearly 2 million women in the United States will be diagnosed with the disease and that 460,000 women will die of it. Between 1950 and 1989, the incidence of breast cancer increased by 53 percent. Expanded use of screening mammography explains part of the recent rise in incidence, but the causes of the long-term increase are largely not known. The increasing magnitude of this problem has understandably resulted in considerable anxiety in the population, particularly among young women and especially regarding future generations of females.

Specific points about breast cancer should be recognized. The incidence of breast cancer rises continuously as women age: At age 30-34, the rate is 27 per 100,000; at 40-44, it is 127 per 100,000; at 50-54, it is 222 per 100,000; at 60-64, it is 343 per 100,000; and at 70-74, it is 434 per 100,000 women. Also, the natural history of the disease is prolonged. The time from the inception of breast cancer to its detection using current methods is estimated to be at least several years. The time following initial diagnosis and treatment to the development of recurrence and death is measured in years. Furthermore, there is no time period beyond which recurrence and death may not occur. If a cure is defined as elimination of any chance of recurrence and metastases, it is not correct at present to describe a "cure" of the disease. Nevertheless, most patients diagnosed with breast cancer live out the remainder of their lives without recurrence. As reported by the National Cancer Institute's Surveillance, Epidemiology, and End Results program, women diagnosed with early-stage breast cancer have a 5-year survival rate of 93 percent, in contrast to 70 percent and 17 percent for those diagnosed with regional and distant metastases, respectively. Finally, the clinical course of breast cancer varies greatly among patients, suggesting that there is heterogeneity in the factors that affect both the occurrence and the natural history of the disease.

Breast cancer is now believed to result from a series of alterations (mutations) in the genes of the breast cells. Some such genetic changes may be inherited, but most are not. These alterations can result in an increased likelihood of additional genetic changes (genomic instability), uncontrolled cell growth (proliferation), invasion into adjacent tissues, and spread to other sites in the body (metastases). The causes of these genetic alterations are largely unknown. Ovarian hormones (estrogen and progesterone) clearly play an important role in the development of breast cancer. It appears likely that influences beginning very early in life and continuing throughout adulthood are important. At this time, there are no proven methods of preventing breast cancer.

Some improvements in breast cancer diagnosis and treatment have occurred over the past few decades. A major advance has been achieved through screening with mammography and clinical breast examination. Screening mammography can detect many cancers before they are clinically evident and can lead to a breast cancer mortality reduction of about 25 percent. However, the mortality benefit from mammography has been unequivocally demonstrated only in women aged 50-69. Possibly due to limitations in study design and implementation, the data for women aged 40-49 are inconclusive, and there is a paucity of information regarding the effectiveness of screening women aged 70 and older, despite their high risk.

Breast-conserving treatment (consisting of excision of the cancer—commonly referred to as "lumpectomy" combined with breast irradiation) results in survival rates equivalent to those following mastectomy and provides important quality-of-life gains for many patients. In addition, new surgical techniques facilitate breast reconstruction in patients treated with mastectomy. Drug treatment, such as chemotherapy and Tamoxifen, given at the time of local therapy can decrease breast cancer mortality. While these improvements are important, the survival benefit of about 26 percent is relatively modest given the magnitude of the problem, and is achieved at a substantial cost in toxicity. Most current therapies (surgery, radiation therapy, and chemotherapy) are toxic to normal tissues and organs and thus frequently impact negatively on quality-of-life. Moreover, although the last decade has brought refinements in the available treatment modalities, no major treatment advances have been introduced, and the mortality rate has remained constant.

Even these modest improvements are not uniformly provided for all women. For many women, optimal early detection, diagnosis, and treatment measures are unavailable for financial reasons—they are unable to pay and have inadequate or no health insurance. These women represent a large and growing percentage of the population. Access is a particular problem for women who are low income, minority, young, old, and living in rural areas. The inequities of this situation have become painfully manifest. Even well-insured women with adequate resources often do not receive the best of care, indicating the presence of significant non-financial barriers to optimal health services delivery.

The past decade has seen a major increase in understanding of the basic biological processes underlying both normal cell division and growth and the biology and genetics of cancer. This knowledge is beginning to be applied to breast cancer. Many excellent investigators have been supported in a broad spectrum of breast cancer research by the National Cancer Institute, the American Cancer Society, and other federal agencies and private organizations. This and other basic biomedical and cancer research have increased our understanding of many aspects of breast cancer and led to some promising new approaches for patients. However, more detailed information is needed about the biology and action of hormones on the normal breast, the genetic changes that lead to breast cancer, biologic factors that cause these genetic changes, and the means by which breast cancer cells grow and spread. It is reasonable to hope that this information will lead to new, more specific methods of earlier detection and diagnosis, treatment, and prevention.

In Fiscal Year 1993, the Department of Defense received an appropriation of $210 million to spend over 2 years on a breast cancer research program. The Commission notes the effort being made by the Army to ensure that this money is well spent, including an Institute of Medicine study commissioned by the Department of Defense to recommend funding priorities. The Institute of Medicine advised that most of the money be spent on investigator-initiated research projects, with some funds allocated to training, recruitment, and infrastructure enhancement.

There is a widespread sense of urgency that more can and should be done to address the problem of breast cancer in this country. This report provides our findings and recommendations. The Commission concludes that more and sustained resources are required to address breast cancer problems effectively. Specific areas and approaches that we believe are most likely to result in meaningful progress are emphasized. Our recommendation for support of breast cancer research at a level of no less than $500 million per year is congruent with the funding level recommended in the Fiscal Year 1995 NCI bypass budget.

Breast Cancer Etiology and Prevention

Findings

• The ultimate goal of breast cancer research is prevention. To develop effective prevention strategies, basic and epidemiologic research must first identify risk factors that can be modified. Prevention studies can then determine the most useful approaches to reducing breast cancer risk by modifying such factors. Prevention trials can evaluate the relative effectiveness of modifying several risk factors and determine the impact of changing single risk factors.

• Today, the most promising areas of research for understanding breast cancer causes and developing optimal prevention methods include: genetics, hormones, diet, physical activity, environmental risk factors, premalignant and tumor markers, and, for secondary prevention, understanding the metastatic process.

Genetics and Tumor Markers

• There is both molecular and epidemiologic evidence that genetic changes are involved in the development of breast cancer, as has been observed for all cancers. Mutations in normal genes, loss of tumor suppressor genes, and altered expression of cellular proto-oncogenes may all be involved in converting a normal breast cell to a malignant one. Additional genetic changes altering expression of proteins on the tumor cell surface can increase or decrease tumor aggressiveness or metastasis. Knowledge of these genes and the proteins they encode potentially may be used to facilitate early detection and diagnosis and to identify high-risk women for prevention trials.

Hormones

• Being a woman is the major risk factor for breast cancer. Women develop breast cancer not only because they have breasts, but also because they have ovaries. Sex hormones, particularly the steroids made by the ovaries, have a central role in breast cancer. They increase the circulating level of two key ovarian hormones, estradiol and progesterone, and modify the levels of other hormones and locally acting growth factors. These changes alter the hormonal environment in the breast, increasing breast cancer risk.

• Other proxy indicators of hormonal activity support the concept that an altered hormonal environment is a major influence on breast cancer risk. Early age at menarche, late age at menopause, obesity in postmenopausal women, nulliparity, and older age at first full-term pregnancy are each associated with increases in risk.

• The effects of steroid hormone contraceptives and hormone replacement therapy have been studied extensively, but the findings have not been totally consistent. However, with each of these hormonal treatments, some elevation in breast cancer risks [is] noted for specific subgroups of women or in relation to particular characteristics of the hormonal regimen.

Diet

• Five-fold international differences in breast cancer incidence rates and major changes in rates among migrating populations indicate that nonheritable factors play a major role in disease development. Correlations between dietary factors and breast cancer incidence rates internationally, as well as animal studies, suggest that nutritional factors strongly influence development of breast cancer. At this time, no dietary change has been proven to reduce breast cancer risk in humans.

- Alcohol: A modest positive association between alcohol consumption and breast cancer risk has been shown in many case-control and cohort studies.
- Vitamin A and precursors (carotenoids): Animal studies show reduced mammary carcinogenesis from high doses of vitamin A and related

synthetic compounds; human case-control and cohort studies suggest a modest protective effect of pre-formed vitamin A and carotenoids.

- Total energy intake: In animal models, restricting total energy intake profoundly and consistently reduces mammary carcinogenesis. Human epidemiologic data are consistent with an important effect of childhood and adolescent energy balance (caloric intake and energy expenditure) as rates of breast cancer are associated with height.
- Plant constituents: In several studies, women with higher vegetable intake experienced lower rates of breast cancer. Epidemiologic evidence does not generally support a major role for dietary fiber in breast cancer prevention, although this was suggested in some laboratory studies.
- Dietary fat: In some animal models, high-fat diets increase mammary tumors; polyunsaturated fats appear to have the strongest influence. Some human case-control studies show an association between fat intake and breast cancer risk, but little or no association has been shown in all recent, large, prospective studies, which are less subject to methodologic biases. Protective effects of very low fat intake or alterations in dietary fat early in life cannot be excluded by available data.
- Vitamin D: Women in latitudes with low sunlight exposure, and presumably lower vitamin D levels, appear to have higher breast cancer incidence rates, but more direct evidence for a protective effect of vitamin D is lacking.
- Little is known about the influence of dietary factors on breast cancer prognosis.

Physical Activity

A few studies have suggested that breast cancer risk is lower among female athletes and among women who have engaged in moderate physical activity.

Environment

• There have been few studies of environmental or occupational exposures as etiologic agents for breast cancer. Most conducted to date were severely flawed methodologically or based on small samples. Research on the effects of exposures to environmental and occupational agents must include assessment of known breast cancer risk factors.

• For none of the 30 known human chemical carcinogens is the human breast the primary site for the initiation of cancer. Exposure to high doses of ionizing radiation, such as that experienced by female atomic bomb survivors in Japan and women who had multiple fluoroscopic examinations for tuberculosis, is known to increase the risk of female breast cancer. Whether non-ionizing radiation from electromagnetic fields increases breast cancer risk is currently being studied....

Screening and Early Detection and the Development of New Technologies for Detection and Diagnosis

Findings

• While prevention is the ultimate goal, earlier detection increases the likelihood of reducing mortality and should have a high research priority.

• Mammography in conjunction with breast physical examination has been shown to reduce mortality from breast cancer in women ages 50-69. Data regarding the benefit from mammography screening in women ages 40-49 are inconclusive, possibly due to limitations in study design or implementation.

• The technology of film-screen mammography has improved greatly over the past decade, but its sensitivity and specificity are still not adequate to detect all breast cancers at an early stage, especially in premenopausal women.

• Screening mammography is underutilized, especially by women aged 60 and older, who are most at risk. Racial and ethnic minorities and low-income women are also less likely to get mammograms.

• Failure of health care providers to recommend mammography is a major cause of poor utilization.

• The Mammography Quality Standards Act, designed to ensure high-quality mammography facilities across the country, was passed in 1992, but has not yet been implemented. The Food and Drug Administration is responsible for implementing this law, but instead is expending its efforts modifying it.

• Ultrasonography has limited use for breast cancer detection. Newer imaging modalities such as positron emission tomography and magnetic resonance imaging are still under development and should be used only in the context of well-designed studies.

Recommendations

Practice and Outreach

• Immediately implement the Mammography Quality Standards Act to ensure that all women receive mammography of acceptable quality, and remove overlapping and conflicting standards. Current multiple certifications required at federal and state levels and from private organizations impose an excessive burden on mammography facilities, waste tax dollars, and increase costs.

• Promote utilization of screening mammography and clinical breast examination for groups of women who are currently being screened at disproportionately low rates (e.g., older women, rural women, women of lower socioeconomic status, and specific racial and ethnic populations, especially African American, Native American, Latino, and Asian women). This will require gathering additional information on barriers to screening and the information needs of these groups, and using existing information to develop effective educational materials and programs. Special attention should be given to conveying the message that increasing age is the major risk factor for developing breast cancer. These efforts should recognize the diversity of needs among and within specific groups and the necessity to develop materials, services, and interventions that address these specific needs.

• Educate and encourage physicians to recommend screening mammography actively.

• Provide screening and appropriate followup services for women, regardless of financial status or extent of insurance coverage.

• Help women assure their own breast health by providing financial and psychological support, enabling them to take responsibility for following recommended breast cancer screening guidelines and practicing breast self-examination.

Screening Research

• Conduct further studies to determine the mortality benefit of screening in women ages 40-49 and in women ages 70 and older, the optimal periodicity of screening in relation to age, and the relative utility of mammography and clinical breast examination. Investigators should first assess whether case-control studies could answer some of these questions as a less costly and more rapid approach than randomized controlled trials. Such studies should use state-of-the-art mammography and must be well designed and well executed. Consideration should be given to providing support for the ongoing trial in the United Kingdom to resolve questions related to screening women in their 40s.

• Develop a system designed to provide information about the practice of breast cancer screening in the United States.

• Assess the effects of co-morbid medical illnesses on breast cancer screening outcomes in women in different age groups.

• Determine the full range of breast cancer screening roles that nurses and physician extenders can play.

New Technologies Research

• Develop better technologies for detection and diagnosis. Such technology should detect breast cancer at its earliest stages, be highly sensitive and specific, noninvasive, and effective for women of all ages.

• Study the feasibility of earlier detection using computer-assisted mammography interpretation and techniques using digitization of mammographic images. Continue research into improving ultrasonography.

• Determine the comparative efficacy of stereotactic fine-needle and core biopsy and ultrasound-guided fine-needle and core biopsy with the goal of reducing the need for excisional biopsy.

Improving the Outcome for Breast Cancer Patients: Treatment and Quality-of-Life Effects

Findings

• Despite some recent improvements in treatment, many thousands of women diagnosed with breast cancer die of the disease. No currently available treatment can be defined as curative.

• Since current treatments result in modest improvements in survival, assessing the effects of treatment on quality of life is important to inform patients adequately about treatment options. Quality-of-life issues include functional status, psychological well-being, social (work and home) functioning, sexuality and fertility, and spiritual well-being. Quality of life is influenced by personal factors (e.g., developmental stage and social support), clinical factors (e.g., stage of disease and type of treatment), and demographic factors (e.g., ethnicity and geographic location). The effects of treatment on long-term quality of life are not adequately known at this time.

• Adjustment to breast cancer is an ongoing process. While some patients do well following diagnosis and treatment, many experience adjustment difficulties in succeeding years. Fear is an overriding issue for women who have had a diagnosis of breast cancer.

Treatment recommendations are best made in a clinical setting that includes experts in the various disciplines. Patients should be empowered to participate actively in making treatment decisions.

Recommendations

Treatment

• Exploit advances in molecular biology to find a cure for breast cancer. In particular, new and more specific therapeutic strategies should be developed, including: therapy directed at tumor growth factors or growth factor receptors; inhibitors of angiogenesis and metastases; gene therapy; and immunologic therapy, including vaccines. Innovative research should be encouraged.

• Identify cell surface factors associated with the ability of tumors to invade and metastasize; develop strategies to modulate the expression of such factors. Explain the predilection of metastatic cells to home to some but not other target organs.

• Improve current treatment strategies to make them more effective—identify mechanisms of resistance to hormonal and chemotherapy, develop ways to avoid or overcome resistance, evaluate dose intensification of chemotherapy in primary and metastatic breast cancer, evaluate preoperative chemotherapy effectiveness, and optimize the long-term results of breast-conserving treatment and breast reconstructive surgery.

• Determine prognostic and predictive factors (or markers) for systemic therapy in order to select patients who are likely to benefit....

• Continue drug development research to discover new, more active agents.

• Ensure adequate funding for clinical investigations of new treatments and provide positive inducements for physicians and patients to participate in studies of promising new approaches. In particular, continue support of single institution pilot studies and of cooperative group randomized clinical trials.

• Define the natural history of ductal carcinoma in situ and other proliferative breast lesions, including factors strongly associated with progression to invasive breast cancer.

Quality-of-Life

• Evaluate the frequency, severity, and persistence of adverse physical changes caused by treatment and develop strategies to deal with these changes. In particular, evaluate treatment effects on fertility in premenopausal patients, and on sexual function in women of all ages. Strategies to treat menopausal symptoms and arm edema, as well as improved breast implants or other methods of reconstruction, must be developed.

• Include quality-of-life measures in clinical trials of new treatment and prevention regimens and approaches.

• Develop guidelines for psychosocial evaluation and support over time of women diagnosed with breast cancer and those at risk for the disease; develop and test effective interventions to improve psychosocial adjustment. Specifically, studies should involve patients of all ages, women at high risk for developing breast cancer, and patients with recurrent disease. Research also should include the effects of diagnosis and treatment on patients' families and social functioning.

• Develop better strategies for supportive care of end-stage breast cancer patients and ensure availability of these services to patients and their families.

Conduct clinical trials to provide information on the effects on survival and quality of survival of systemic hormonal contraceptives, pregnancy, and hormone replacement therapy at menopause in breast cancer survivors, including women in whom treatment of premenopausal breast cancer induced premature menopause.

Infrastructure, Education, and Training

Findings

• Breast cancer research requires resources such as repositories, registries, and specialized research centers which must operate for many years. It is difficult to obtain stable, long-term funding to establish and maintain such resources outside an hypothesis-driven research proposal.

• Advances in understanding the biology and genetics of breast cancer are not likely to be immediately applicable to improved prevention and treatment methods. A new generation of trained, basic, translational and clinical investigators is needed to ensure that the knowledge gained from basic research leads to human benefit, specifically the prevention and cure of breast cancer.

• It is essential to ensure that clinical studies of prevention, detection, diagnosis, and treatment include women of diverse ethnic and sociocultural backgrounds. Culturally acceptable study design and recruitment of women from varied ethnic and racial groups are facilitated by the participation of investigators sensitive to sociocultural issues and who also come from diverse backgrounds.

Recommendations

• The preponderance of research funding should be directed to investigator-initiated inquiry. A major emphasis should be placed on supporting innovative and imaginative research.

• Expand or create specialized research resources: breast cancer SPOREs (Specialized Programs of Research Excellence), the National Cancer Institute's Surveillance, Epidemiology, and End Results program, and other high-quality cancer registries capable of providing data to monitor long-term trends in breast cancer, relevant animal models and cell lines, and repositories for biological specimens.

• Develop an information-sharing network for breast cancer researchers.

• Fund training grants specifically targeted to the next generation of investigators in all aspects of breast cancer research.

• Train investigators in translational research and in clinical trials to facilitate the development of improved prevention, detection, and treatment strategies.

• Emphasize during research training the role of ethnic and sociocultural diversity in risk of breast cancer, as well as the need to develop acceptable and sensitive strategies for research on prevention, early detection, diagnosis, and treatment for diverse population groups.

• Train future clinical investigators in both translational and clinical trials research. These investigators need broad training in the biology, genetics, and clinical manifestations of breast cancer, and in epidemiology and biostatistics.

• Utilize tumor boards in institutions that treat breast cancer to ensure optimal care through proper and timely input from various cancer specialists and to help train young physicians.

• Ensure that oncologists (medical, surgical, radiation, and nursing) receive interdisciplinary training to improve the quality of breast cancer care.

• Train clinicians of diverse ethnic heritage in breast cancer care.

• Promote continuing education programs for all professional and technical personnel dealing with breast cancer patients to ensure that advances in care are translated to practice.

• Ensure that medical school, residency, and fellowship training programs and training for advanced nursing practice include education on the need for regular breast examinations, including mammography and clinical breast examination, and on the performance of a thorough clinical examination of the breast.

• Encourage health care providers to educate patients about breast cancer, including treatment and rehabilitation options.

Public Communication

Findings

• Information appropriate for and appealing to the mass media and information necessary for public education differs substantially. A fundamental principle of communicating with the public about breast cancer issues is to distinguish between information that is newsworthy and that which is needed for educational purposes. News media professionals (generally consider it their responsibility to report news accurately, but not to serve as public educators. Therefore, channels other than the media are required for education.

• There is a discrepancy between the media attention given to breast cancer and its importance as a public health problem. While the media do give some attention to breast cancer, more resources could be expended by the media to present breast cancer-related issues to the public.... It is clear that news media respond to activism. The more assertive breast cancer advocacy groups are, the more attention breast cancer will receive from the press.

• A significant segment of the U.S. population has a low level of literacy. It is essential to present educational materials and media messages in diverse formats so that all target audiences are reached. In some situations, it may be best to present both news and education via audio and visual channels (radio and television).

Recommendations

• Support a national work group on low literacy and cancer information and education.

• Make publicly funded public information and educational materials understandable to individuals at all literacy levels.

• Encourage breast cancer scientists, clinicians, and advocates to collaborate to determine the most effective methods for presenting clear messages to the public which neither understate nor overstate specific issues or overall progress in breast cancer research and care.

• Emphasize coordination of public information efforts between components of the National Institutes of Health and with other federal agencies, such as the Centers for Disease Control and Prevention.

• Work with news media to promote accurate, responsible, and adequate coverage of breast cancer issues.

Patient Advocacy

Findings

• Breast cancer is a public health problem involving multiple constituencies. It must be a high priority for all concerned with the health of women. Improving breast cancer research, prevention, detection, and treatment is a shared responsibility of consumers, health care providers, biotechnology and pharmaceutical industries, health educators and researchers, public health agencies, legislators, third party payors, the National Cancer Institute, and other government agencies.

• Over the past decade, patients and their families have promoted breast cancer as a national priority and have focused attention on the need for a cure and for prevention.

• Service, patient support, and advocacy organizations exist for women, including underserved and minority women, at local, state, regional, and national levels. These organizations are valuable resources for many women and are influential in shaping public policy. Voluntary organizations fund and operate breast cancer screening programs, often targeted to underserved and minority women, and provide outreach and support to women during and following treatment for breast cancer. Some fund breast cancer research. Patient organizations provide psychosocial support; advocate for individual patients within the health care system and with payors; urge specific research emphases; and work at local, state, and national levels for policies and legislation on many breast cancer issues. Unfortunately, many minority and low income women do not feel that most existing organizations represent them, although there are some exceptions. Improved communication between patient advocacy groups and voluntary and government organizations would be beneficial to all.

• Breast cancer advocates want more participation in decision-making concerned with research and the optimal use of breast cancer research funding.

Recommendations

• Encourage patient advocates and voluntary organizations to work cooperatively to achieve legislation that provides funding, research, treatment, education, and support for women with breast cancer.

• Support voluntary and advocacy organizations' work to ensure access to care for all women and fund community-based programs to bring breast cancer information, education, and interventions to affected groups where they live and work.

• Ensure that health care reform implementation in each state reflects breast cancer issues specific to that population and geographic area.

• Educate physicians about the medical and psychosocial aspects of breast cancer and women's needs for screening, diagnosis, treatment, and continuing care. Physicians must include the woman as a partner in arriving at a diagnosis and choosing the most suitable care.

• Integrate breast cancer advocates into decision-making regarding the optimal use of breast cancer research funding.

• Encourage efforts by patient advocate organizations and other voluntary and educational groups to ensure that women are fully informed and educated about their own breast health, including adopting healthy lifestyles, practicing monthly breast self-examination, following recommended guidelines for early detection, and obtaining immediate diagnostic and treatment services when an abnormality is observed.

Public Policy

Findings

National and State Legislation

• Recent breast cancer research funding increases have provided a large infusion of support for this area of biomedical investigation and raised the priority level of breast cancer within biomedical research. However, increased National Cancer Institute support for research on breast and other specific cancers without the addition of sufficient funds has required redirection of resources from other areas of cancer research. A sustained level of increased funding should include additions to the budget to strengthen breast cancer research specifically, and cancer research generally.

• In addition to federal legislation pertaining to aspects of breast cancer detection and treatment, states have enacted laws to provide quality assurance for mammography, ensure that treatment options are presented to women diagnosed with breast cancer, mandate payment for some off-label uses of chemotherapeutic drugs, and improve access to mammography by requiring insurance companies and Medicaid programs to cover breast cancer screening.

• Impending health care reform is projected to improve access to breast cancer screening, education, treatment, and supportive care. The main principles expected to govern these reforms include security in health care coverage, eliminating exclusions for pre-existing conditions; provider of quality of care and accountability; cost controls; and comprehensiveness of care....

Recommendations

National Legislation

• New funds should be appropriated to support the President's Cancer Panel Special Commission on Breast Cancer's recommended program at a level no less than $500 million per year until breast cancer prevention and cure are achieved. This research effort should be under the leadership of the National Cancer Institute.

State Legislation

• Support state legislation to provide quality assurance for mammography and insurance coverage for screening, diagnostic tests, treatment, and patient care costs of clinical trials.

Special Issues for Minority and Underserved Women

Findings

• Minority and underserved women are heterogeneous, encompassing diverse ethnic groups (e.g., Native Americans, African Americans, Latinas, and Asian Americans); rural women; women with low literacy; women with inadequate health care, health insurance, or financial resources; women with disabilities from other illnesses or injuries; and women 65 and older, who often do not receive breast cancer screening or obtain state of-the-art treatment.

• Diversity must be a key word in breast cancer research, prevention, diagnosis, treatment, and supportive and continuing care. No subgroup of women is homogenous: white women in the United States are considered as a single, homogeneous entity, yet they have diverse demographic, socioeconomic, and ethnic backgrounds which influence their risk of breast cancer and their potential for access to the full range of appropriate care from prevention and early detection to rehabilitation. Similarly, other ethnic groups, such as Latino, African American, and Asian women are treated as if they all were similar. Diversity within these groups in culture, tradition, language, education, and other factors associated with breast cancer risk and access to optimal care must be considered in developing culturally sensitive programs.

• Access to breast cancer education, early detection, treatment, and rehabilitation is often restricted among women having one or more of the characteristics described above. Breast cancer research rarely includes women from many of these populations and fails to encompass their issues in developing strategies for optimal care.

Recommendations

• Where scientifically appropriate, structure clinical trials to reflect the racial and ethnic population diversity.

• Build partnerships with underserved communities to encourage their involvement and self-advocacy in health care. Hospitals, clinics, health departments, and other providers should be encouraged to assist the underserved in navigating the health care system. Such strategies will increase early detection and reduce costly use of emergency rooms.

• Precede design of outreach and research projects in minority populations with consultation and interaction with community leaders where the project will take place. Provide adequate funding for long-term efforts.

• Conduct behavioral/social research on culturally sensitive approaches to current and future primary prevention strategies and ways to increase access to and utilization of early detection techniques and state-of-the-art treatment.

- Reduce geographic barriers to optimal education, early detection, treatment, and rehabilitation, particularly in rural areas.
- Investigate the psychosocial impact of breast cancer on women and their families and differences related to diversity by ethnicity, urban/suburban/rural residence, and socioeconomic status.
- Conduct studies to determine risk factor prevalence across diverse ethnic, socioeconomic, and cultural (e.g., urban/suburban/rural) populations.
- Make available breast cancer incidence and mortality data for all major ethnic groups: African American, Latino, Native American, Chinese, Japanese, Native Hawaiian, etc. The U.S. Census Bureau should provide intercensal population estimates for these groups. The National Cancer Institute's Surveillance, Epidemiology, and End Results program should provide the incidence data, while the mortality information should be provided by the National Center for Health Statistics.
- Target public information and media channels for providing breast cancer education to specific ethnic communities by: focusing on their media outlets, emphasizing radio advertisements and print media, and developing diverse programming that takes into account differences within an ethnic group in acculturation, literacy, language, and traditional cultural practices and beliefs.
- Remove linguistic and cultural barriers to screening, treatment, and rehabilitation.

STATEMENTS ON BRITISH-IRISH EFFORTS TO FIND PEACE

October 29 and November 29, 1993

Seeking to end decades of bloodshed in Northern Ireland, the British and Irish governments stepped up negotiations in 1993 over that strife-torn country. On October 29 the British and Irish prime ministers issued a statement promising that "new doors could open" toward peace if the Irish Republican Army (IRA) ended its campaign of violence to drive the British out of the country and reunite it with Ireland.

Four weeks later, on November 29, the British government issued an extraordinary statement conceding that there had been secret talks between emissaries of Prime Minister John Major and the IRA, despite Major's denials of such meetings. The statement, made by Sir Patrick Mayhew, secretary of state for Northern Ireland, said that for "some years" there was a "means of communication by which messages could be conveyed indirectly, between the [British] Government and the IRA leadership." He said that such a link could have functioned only in secrecy.

Responding to the anger of those who opposed any contacts with the IRA, British officials said they had a duty to take risks to seek an end to the conflict, which has cost more than three thousand lives. Reaction was so strong in the House of Commons that one member who opposed any dealings with the IRA was ejected for breaching parliamentary etiquette; he accused government officials of lying about its activities.

Background of Conflict

The conflict between England and Ireland began centuries earlier, with Ireland's conquest by Henry VIII and Britain's subsequent attempt to increase the Protestant population there. James I, who followed Elizabeth I to the throne, seized land in Ulster and gave it to English and Scottish settlers, the ancestors of the Protestants living there today.

Efforts by the Irish to gain independence from Great Britain culminated in passage of a home rule bill in 1914. When the bill was not implemented, a rebellion broke out and was harshly put down by British soldiers. In 1919 seventy-three Irish members of the British Parliament declared that Ireland was an independent country. Fearing that Protestants would come under attack, the Parliament in 1920 passed the Government of Ireland Act, dividing Ireland into two countries—one consisting of six counties of Ulster and the other made up of the remaining three counties of Ulster and twenty-three southern counties. The six Ulster counties, with their Protestant majority, accepted the act and formed the state of Northern Ireland. But Catholics in southern Ireland rejected it and began fighting for complete independence and reunification.

Rebels, primarily the Irish Republican Army, attacked British army installations and government buildings, prompting harsh reprisals by the British. Finally in 1921 Great Britain and the rebels agreed to a treaty allowing southern Ireland to become a self-governing country of the British Commonwealth called the Irish Free State.

But this step failed to satisfy everyone. One group wanted complete independence from Great Britain and a union with Northern Ireland. The other supported the treaty, leading to a year-long civil war that ended in 1923. The Irish Free State outlawed the IRA, but some Irish people continued to belong to the organization and conducted periodic guerrilla warfare against the British.

Over the years the Catholic minority in Northern Ireland complained that Protestants violated their civil rights, discriminating against them in jobs, housing, and other areas. On October 15, 1968, the newly formed Northern Ireland Civil Rights Association planned a march in Londonderry to demand reform. When the government tried to stop the march, riots broke out. Some reforms were enacted in the aftermath, but riots broke out again the next year. British troops were sent to Northern Ireland but were unable to prevent further rioting. The IRA and other militant groups carried out bombing and other terrorist acts, and, in the face of continuing violence, Britain in 1972 took over direct rule of the country. Violence continued over the next fifteen years despite efforts to find a social and political solution acceptable to Catholics and Protestants.

The October 29 Statement

The joint statement issued by Major and Irish Prime Minister Albert Reynolds reaffirmed that the "situation in Northern Ireland should never be changed by violence or the threat of violence." They called on "all those claiming a serious interest in advancing the cause of peace" to "renounce for good the use, or support for violence."

The wording of the statement appeared to provide a place in the negotiations for Sinn Fein, the political wing of the IRA, if the bombing and random killings ceased. The statement referred to an initiative undertaken by John Hume, a British Parliament member, and Gerry Adams, president of Sinn Finn, but, while it praised Hume's efforts, it did not mention Adams. Nor did the prime ministers endorse the Hume/Adams effort, saying that "any initiative can only be taken by the two Governments."

The November 29 Statement

The statement released by Sir Patrick Mayhew offered the government's version of secret talks between British officials and IRA spokesmen. It said that in February the government received a message from the IRA offering "an unannounced cease-fire in order to hold a dialogue leading to peace." The IRA said it could not make the offer public "as it will lead to confusion," nor could it offer a public renunciation of violence, "but it would be given privately as long as we were sure that we were not being tricked."

Mayhew said the government responded to the message in March, reiterating its view that the violence must stop. The message also said that the government "has no desire to inhibit or impede legitimate constitutional expression of any political opinion, or any input into the political process, and wants to see included in this process all main parties which have sufficiently shown they genuinely do not espouse violence." The statement said the government sought "an agreed accommodation, not an imposed settlement, arrived at through an inclusive process in which the parties are free agents."

The IRA responded in May, but not with the "unequivocal assurance of a genuine end to violence," the statement said. There was no more substantive contact with the IRA until November 2, when the organization sent a new message complaining that "we can't even have a dialogue to work out how a total end to all the violence can come about."

The British responded a few days later, repeating that if the IRA offered "an unequivocal assurance that violence has indeed been brought to a permanent end . . . we will make clear publicly our commitment to enter exploratory dialogue with you." Mayhew concluded the statement by saying, "It lies therefore with the IRA and with them alone, to end their inhuman crimes. It is for them and those who support and justify them to explain why they have wickedly failed to do that. . . . The key to peace is in the hands of the IRA."

The IRA angrily denied the British version of events, accusing the government of "duplicity" and contending that it was the British who requested a suspension of violence.

The day after Mayhew's statement, Prime Minister Major went to the House of Commons to defend his actions, asserting that his government had "acted properly and done its duty" in taking part in the secret talks.

Following are the October 29, 1993, joint statement by the British and Irish prime ministers on Northern Ireland and the November 29, 1993, statement by Sir Patrick Mayhew, the secretary of state for Northern Ireland, on messages between the IRA leadership and the British government:

OCTOBER 29 STATEMENT

The Prime Minister and the Taoiseach [Irish Prime Minister] discussed a range of matters of common interest, with particular focus on Northern Ireland.

They condemned the recent terrorist outrages as murderous and premeditated acts which could serve no other end than to deepen the bloodshed in Northern Ireland, and they expressed their deep sympathy to the innocent victims, children, women and men who had been injured or bereaved.

The Prime Minister and Taoiseach called for restraint from all members of the Community in Northern Ireland, expressed their support for the security forces in their fight against all forms of terrorism, and noted the recent successes of cross-border security cooperation.

They utterly repudiated the use of violence for political ends. Their two Governments were resolute in their determination to ensure that those who adopted or supported such methods should never succeed.

The Taoiseach gave the Prime Minister an account of the outcome of the Hume/Adams dialogue, in the light of the Irish Government's own assessment of these and other related matters. They acknowledged John Hume's courageous and imaginative efforts. The Prime Minister and Taoiseach agreed that any initiative can only be taken by the two Governments, and that there could be no question of their adopting or endorsing the report of the dialogue which was recently given to the Taoiseach and which had not been passed on to the British Government. They agreed that the two Governments must continue to work together in their own terms on a framework for peace, stability and reconciliation, consistent with their international obligations and their wider responsibilities to both communities.

Against this background the Prime Minister and the Taoiseach reaffirmed that:

- The situation in Northern Ireland should never be changed by violence or the threat of violence.
- Any political settlement must depend on consent freely given in the absence of force or intimidation.
- Negotiations on a political settlement could only take place between democratic Governments and parties committed exclusively to constitutional methods and consequently there can be no talks or negotia-

tions between their Governments and those who use, threaten or support violence for political ends.

- There could be no secret agreements or understandings between Governments and organisations supporting violence as a price for its cessation.
- All those claiming a serious interest in advancing the cause of peace in Ireland should renounce for good the use [of], or support for, violence.
- If and when such a renunciation of violence had been made and sufficiently demonstrated, new doors could open, and both Governments would wish to respond imaginatively to the new situation which would arise.

The Prime Minister and the Taoiseach renewed their support for the objectives of the talks process involving political dialogue between the two Governments and the main constitutional parties in Northern Ireland. They regard that process as vital and its objectives as valid and achievable. They urged the Northern Ireland parties to intensify their efforts to find a basis for new talks. The Taoiseach and the Prime Minister agreed that the two Governments will continue their discussions to provide a framework to carry the process forward.

NOVEMBER 29 STATEMENT

With permission, Madam Speaker, I will make a statement about messages between the IRA leadership and the Government.

There has for some years been a means of communication by which messages could be conveyed indirectly, between the Government and the IRA leadership. Clearly such a chain could only function if its secrecy was respected on both sides.

At the end of February this year a message was received from the IRA leadership. It said:

> The conflict is over but we need your advice on how to bring it to a close. We wish to have an unannounced ceasefire in order to hold dialogue leading to peace. We cannot announce such a move as it will lead to confusion for the volunteers because the press will misinterpret it as a surrender. We cannot meet Secretary of State's public renunciation of violence, but it would be given privately as long as we were sure that we were not being tricked.

That message came from Martin McGuinness. Madam Speaker, I have placed in the Library and the Vote Office all consequent messages which HMG has received and despatched.

The Government had a duty to respond to that message. I will read to the House the substantive response which, after an intermediate exchange, we despatched on 19 March. The text published yesterday was no more than instructions as to how this was to be transmitted. The message was in these terms:

1. The importance of what has been said, the wish to take it seriously, and the influence of events on the ground, have been acknowledged. All of those involved share a responsibility to work to end the conflict. No one has a monopoly of suffering. There is a need for a healing process.
2. It is essential that there should be no deception on either side, and also that no deception should, through any misunderstanding, be seen where it is not intended. It is also essential that both sides have a clear and realistic understanding of what it is possible to achieve, so that neither side can in the future claim that it has been tricked.
3. The position of the British Government on dealing with those who espouse violence is clearly understood. This is why the envisaged sequence of events is important. We note that what is being sought at this stage is advice, and that any dialogue would follow an unannounced halt to violent activity. We confirm that if violence had genuinely been brought to an end, whether or not that fact had been announced, then dialogue could take place.
4. It must be understood, though, that once a halt to activity became public, the British Government would have to acknowledge and defend its entry into dialogue. It would do so by pointing out that its agreement to exploratory dialogue about the possibility of an inclusive process had been given because—and only because—it had received a private assurance that organised violence had been brought to an end.
5. The British Government has made clear that:
   - no political objective which is advocated by constitutional means alone could properly be excluded from discussion in the talks process
   - the commitment to return as much responsibility as possible to local politicians should be seen within a wider framework of stable relationships to be worked out with all concerned
   - new political arrangements would be designed to ensure that no legitimate group was excluded from eligibility to share in the exercise of this responsibility
   - in the event of a genuine and established ending of violence, the whole range of responses to it would inevitably be looked at afresh.
6. The British Government has no desire to inhibit or impede legitimate constitutional expression of any political opinion, or any input to the political process, and wants to see included in this process all main parties which have sufficiently shown they genuinely do not espouse violence. It has no blueprint. It wants an agreed accommodation, not an imposed settlement, arrived at through an inclusive process in which the parties are free agents.
7. The British Government does not have, and will not adopt, any prior objective of 'ending of partition'. The British Government cannot

enter a talks process, or expect others to do so, with the purpose of achieving a predetermined outcome, whether the 'ending of partition' or anything else. It has accepted that the eventual outcome of such a process could be a united Ireland, but only on the basis of the consent of the people of Northern Ireland. Should this be the eventual outcome of a peaceful democratic process, the British Government would bring forward legislation to implement the will of the people here. But unless the people of Northern Ireland come to express such a view, the British Government will continue to uphold the union, seeking to ensure the good governance of Northern Ireland, in the interests of all its people, within the totality of relationships in these islands.

8. Evidence on the ground that any group had ceased violent activity would induce resulting reduction of security force activity. Were violence to end, the British Government's overall response in terms of security force activity on the ground would still have to take account of the overall threat. The threat posed by Republican and Loyalist groups which remained active would have to continue to be countered.
9. It is important to establish whether this provides a basis for the way forward. We are ready to answer specific questions or to give further explanation.

It is clear that this message was consistent with our declared policy: namely that if such people wanted to enter into talks or negotiations with the Government they first had genuinely to end violence. Not just temporarily, but for good. If they did, and showed sufficiently that they meant it, we would not want, for our part, to continue to exclude them from political talks. That remains our policy.

The IRA sent a reply on 10 May which did not constitute the unequivocal assurance of a genuine end to violence on which we had insisted. Clearly a temporary ceasefire would not do.

Substantive contact was resumed on 2 November. The IRA sent the following message:

> 'This problem cannot be solved by the Reynolds Spring situation, although they're part of it. You appear to have rejected the Hume Adams situation though they too are part of it.
>
> Every day all the main players are looking for singular solutions. It can't be solved singularly. We offered the 10 May. You've rejected it. Now we can't even have dialogue to work out how a total end to all violence can come about. We believe that the country could be at the point of no return. In plain language please tell us as a matter of urgency when you will open dialogue in the event of a total end to hostilities. We believe that if all the documents involved are put on the table—including your 9 paragrapher and our 10 May that we have the basis of an understanding.'

Our reply was despatched on 5 November:

1. Your message of 2 November is taken as being of the greatest importance and significance. The answer to the specific question you raise is given in paragraph 4 below.
2. We hold to what was said jointly and in public by the Prime Minister and the Taoiseach in Brussels on 29 October. A copy of the Statement is annexed. There can be no departure from what is said there and in particular its statement that there could be no secret agreements or understandings between Governments and organisations supporting violence as a price for its cessation and its call on them to renounce for good the use of, or support for, violence. There can also be no departure from the constitutional guarantee that Northern Ireland's status as part of the United Kingdom will not change without the consent of a majority of its people.
3. It is the public and consistent position of the British Government that any dialogue could only follow a permanent end to violent activity.
4. You ask about the sequence of events in the event of a total end to hostilities. If, as you have offered, you were to give us an unequivocal assurance that violence has indeed been brought to a permanent end, and that accordingly Sinn Fein is now committed to political progress by peaceful and democratic means alone, we will make clear publicly our commitment to enter exploratory dialogue with you. Our public statement will make clear that, provided your private assurance is promptly confirmed publicly after our public statement and that events on the ground are fully consistent with this, a first meeting for exploratory dialogue will take place within a week of Parliament's return in January.
5. Exploratory dialogue will have the following purposes:
   - (i) to explore the basis upon which Sinn Fein would come to be admitted to an inclusive political talks process to which the British Government is committed but without anticipating the negotiations within that process
   - (ii) to exchange views on how Sinn Fein would be able over a period to play the same part as the current constitutional parties in the public life of Northern Ireland
   - (iii) to examine the practical consequences of the ending of violence.

[6. Deleted]

7. If, in advance of our public statement, any public statement is made on your behalf which appears to us inconsistent with this basis for proceeding it would not be possible for us then to proceed.
8. If we receive the necessary assurance, which you have offered, that violence has been brought to an end, we shall assume that you are assenting to the basis for proceeding explained in this note and its attachment.

The House will appreciate from what I have read out, and from the other messages when they have time to study them, that our main objective has been to reinforce and spell out in private our publicly stated positions.

It is for the IRA and their supporters to explain why they have failed to deliver the promised ending of violence. They should do so at once. Murder in Northern Ireland is no more tolerable than murder anywhere else in the United Kingdom. We must never lose sight of the fact that it is the terrorists who must answer for the deaths, destruction and misery of the last 25 years.

It lies therefore with the IRA, and with them alone, to end their inhuman crimes. It is for them and those who support and justify them to explain why they have wickedly failed to do that.

I promise the House and the people of Northern Ireland that, for our part, we shall not cease our efforts to bring violence to a permanent end. As my right Hon. Friend told the House on 18 November, if we do not succeed on this occasion we shall keep exploring again and again the opportunities for peace. Peace, properly attained, is a prize worth risks.

If a genuine end to violence is promised, the way would still be open for Sinn Fein to enter the political arena after a sufficient interval to demonstrate that they mean it. Our message of 5 November again spelt that out.

The key to peace is in the hands of the IRA.

November

COURT ON RESTRICTING USE OF AUDIOTAPES

November 1, 1993

The Supreme Court decided November 1 to reverse its position on the public use of audiotapes of oral arguments from Supreme Court cases. The Court lifted some copying restrictions on the tapes; the restrictions had been imposed in August when a professor prepared tapes to be published commercially with a companion book about the Court.

Since 1969, the Court had sent audiotapes to the National Archives for safekeeping. Use of the tapes was restricted initially to federal government personnel pursuing official duties and to the general public for "scholarly and legal research." The tapes could be copied only under limited circumstances and were not for commercial use.

Specific Restrictions on Professor

In August the Court asked the Archives to tighten restrictions on Peter Irons, a political science professor at the University of California at San Diego, after he published a tape-and-book set of oral arguments from twenty-three significant cases. The narrated series covered lawyers' presentations before the Court and the Justices' give-and-take in such famous cases as Roe v. Wade, *which made abortion legal;* Gideon v. Wainwright, *which required lawyers to be provided for poor criminal defendants; and* Regents of the University of California v. Bakke, *which upheld "race-conscious" admissions programs. The project sold well and was a critical success. The* Los Angeles Times *called the collection "an intellectual treasure trove," and the* American Bar Association Journal *praised it as "a front row seat in America's most powerful courtroom."*

However, the Court, which cherishes secrecy and tradition, believed that Irons had reneged on a statement he signed promising to use the tapes only for his private work. As a result, Alfred Wong, the Court's marshal, informed the Archives on August 31 that Irons would have to get specific permission from the marshal's office before duplicating any tapes in the future. Wong said in his letter to Acting Archivist Trudy H. Peterson that "in light of his willingness to violate the agreements he signed, future requests for copying audiotapes by Mr. Irons or by any project with which he is associated, should be considered a request for 'commercial use or broadcast.'" Irons was the only person required to get such permission to use the tapes.

The professor reacted angrily to the Court's restrictions, asserting to one newspaper reporter that the action was "an obvious attempt to stop me from continuing the work I'm doing.... There are serious questions about the legality of this effort to prevent a scholar from making public records more widely available." He said he felt singled out "for punishment without trial" and contended that the limit on commercial use of the tapes violated the First Amendment. Irons added that he was considering filing a lawsuit over the matter—in effect, taking the Court to court.

Reversal of Decision

Within two months, the Court changed its mind. On November 1 it announced that the tapes would be available to the public on a generally unrestricted basis, although tapes from a case would not be available until several months after an argument actually took place.

In a letter to the archivist, Wong noted that although use and copying restrictions had been "relaxed" in the last few years, "some restrictions have remained in place. The Court has now examined those restrictions and has determined that they no longer serve the purposes of the Court."

Not suprisingly, Irons was pleased with the outcome, saying, "I think it's great. I think it's long overdue."

Following is Alfred Wong's November 1, 1993, letter to acting Archivist of the United States Trudy Peterson, and the new agreement concerning the tapes between the Supreme Court and the National Archives:

WONG'S LETTER

Dear Ms. Peterson:

As you know, beginning in 1969 the Supreme Court arranged for audiotapes of oral arguments to be transferred to the Archives for safekeeping and access by scholars and the public. Initially, restrictions were placed on access to the tapes. Use was restricted to federal government personnel in connection with official duties and to the general public for "scholarly and legal research" only. Copying of the tapes was permitted only in limited circumstances.

Although use and copying restrictions were relaxed somewhat over the years, some restrictions have remained in place. The Court has now examined those restrictions and has determined that they no longer serve the purposes of the Court. I am authorized to inform you that the Court has decided to make the audiotapes available to the public on a generally unrestricted basis.

Doing so will require modification of the Court's agreement with the Archives governing access to the audiotapes and the transcripts of oral arguments. A proposed modification to this agreement is attached for your signature and return to me. If, however, you have any questions, please do not hesitate to call.

Very truly yours,

Alfred Wong
Marshal

ARCHIVES AGREEMENT

The restrictions governing access to the audiotapes and transcripts of oral arguments heard in the Supreme Court of the United States (the "Supreme Court") that are deposited in the National Archives (the "Archives"), including all past and future accretions of similar materials, are revised as follows:

(a) *Deposit of Audiotapes and Transcripts.*
From time to time, the Supreme Court may deposit with the Archives, and the Archives will accept for deposit, audiotapes and transcripts.

(b) *Use of Audiotapes and Transcripts on the Archives' Premises.*
From the date of its deposit with the Archives, the Archives may make available to members of the public any audiotape or transcript for listening or review on the Archives premises.

(c) *Copying of Audiotapes.*
The Archives shall furnish copies of any audiotape to the Court or to any Justice of the Supreme Court, at any time upon request. The Archives may also furnish a copy of any audiotape or transcript to any person upon terms and conditions it believes are appropriate.

The signatures of the officials below indicate acceptance by the parties of the terms of this Agreement.

Marshal of the Court Nov. 1, 1993

Archivist of the United States

COURT ON SEXUAL HARASSMENT

November 9, 1993

The Supreme Court November 9 spoke swiftly and with unanimity on the issue of sexual harassment, ruling in a brief opinion that workers did not have to show psychological harm or an inability to do their jobs to win a lawsuit. The decision, only the second in seven years to address sexual harassment, was generally hailed by groups representing workers, particularly women, who have brought the lion's share of harassment cases.

Justice Sandra Day O'Connor wrote the opinion for the Court. She rejected a standard that several lower courts had adopted requiring a plaintiff to show "severe psychological injury" as a result of a hostile work environment. Psychological harm may be one factor that courts can weigh in a harassment case, O'Connor wrote, but federal law protections "come into play before the harassing conduct leads to a nervous breakdown."

The decision was handed down just twenty-seven days after the oral argument in the case, virtually a record for Supreme Court deliberations. It involved Teresa Harris, who sued her former employer, Forklift Systems, Inc., and came against a backdrop of increasing awareness of sexual harassment not only in the workplace, the situation in this dispute, but in other arenas, particularly education. Allegations of sexual harassment in elementary and secondary schools and on college campuses were reported in the media and studied with increasing frequency. (Report on Sexual Harassment in Public Schools, p. 353)

It took Teresa Harris six years before the Court ruled in her favor, but the opinion did not award her an immediate victory. Rather, the justices instructed a federal appeals court to reconsider the case in light of the standards set out in the decision.

An "Abusive" Work Environment

Harris had worked as a rental manager for Forklift from April 1985 until October 1987. She finally quit because of frequent taunts and unwanted sexual innuendoes thrown her way by Charles Hardy, Forklift's president. In the presence of other employees, Hardy had said to Harris on several occasions, "You're a woman, what do you know" and "we need a man as the rental agent." On at least one occasion he called her a "dumb ass woman." In front other workers, Hardy once suggested that he and Harris "go to the Holiday Inn to negotiate [Harris's] raise." Occasionally, Hardy asked Harris and other female employees to get coins from his front pants pocket.

In mid-August 1987, Harris complained to Hardy about his conduct. He expressed surprise that she was offended, claimed he was only joking, apologized, and promised to stop. Although Harris had considered quitting, she decided to stay after her conversation with Hardy. But within weeks, he returned to his old conduct. While Harris was arranging a deal with a Forklift customer, Hardy asked her in front of other employees, "What did you do, promise the guy ... some [sex] Saturday night?"

On October 1, Harris collected her paycheck and quit. She also filed a lawsuit, charging that Hardy and Forklift had created an abusive work environment for her because of her gender in violation of federal law. A federal district judge in Tennessee called Harris's lawsuit "a close case" but decided that Hardy's conduct, offensive as it may be, did not create the requisite abusive environment.

The judge added that Hardy's comments "offended [Harris] and would offend the reasonable woman" but did not find that they were "so severe as to be expected to seriously affect [Harris's] psychological well-being." A federal appeals court affirmed the decision.

In her opinion, O'Connor noted that there was a difference among the appellate courts about whether such psychological injury or other kind of injury was required to prove sexual harassment. The high court took the case, she said, to resolve these differences.

A "Middle Path"

O'Connor described the Court's standard in the Harris case as a "middle path" between upholding lawsuits for "any conduct that is merely offensive and requiring the conduct to cause a tangible psychological injury." She said that "a discriminatorily abusive work environment, even one that does not seriously affect employees' psychological well-being, can and often will detract from employees' job performance, discourage employees from remaining on the job or keep them from advancing their careers." As long as the environment "would reasonably be perceived, and is perceived as hostile or abusive," she wrote, "there is no need for it also to be psychologically injurious."

To determine whether such an environment exists, O'Connor added, a court must look at "all the circumstances. These may include the frequency of the discriminatory conduct; its severity, whether it is physically threatening or humiliating, or a mere offensive utterance; and whether it interferes with an employee's work performance."

Justice Ruth Bader Ginsburg, who joined the Court in October, wrote a brief concurring opinion, as did Justice Antonin Scalia. Ginsburg, in her first opinion as a justice, suggested that discrimination based on sex should be taken as seriously by the court as discrimination based on race. In a footnote, Ginsburg, who had argued several sex discrimination cases before the Supreme Court in the 1970s, wrote that "it remains an open question" whether the justices should consider classifications based on sex "inherently suspect" as they do for race.

In his concurrence, Scalia said he was concerned that the decision did not present a "very clear standard" for judging harassment. But "be that as it may," he wrote, "I know of no alternative to the course the Court has taken today."

The opinion drew praise from lawyers representing women not only for its content but for the speed with which it was announced and the unanimity. Kathryn Abrams, a law professor at Cornell University, observed that by acting as it did the Court "clearly intended to send a message to the lower courts, to employers and to the American public that the legal system will take women's claims of sexual harassment seriously."

And Shelley Mandell, a Los Angeles attorney whose firm specializes in harassment cases, predicted that the case would be good for lawyers. "The defense lawyers are happy because now employers are worried, and the plaintiffs' lawyers are happy because companies are going to settle."

> *Following are excerpts from the Supreme Court's opinion in* Harris v. Forklift Systems, Inc., *decided November 9, 1993, in which the Court ruled that a worker did not have to show psychological harm to prove harassment by an employer, and concurring opinions by Justices Antonin Scalia and Ruth Bader Ginsburg:*

No. 92-1168

Teresa Harris, Petitioner *v.* Forklift Systems, Inc.	On writ of certiorari to the United States Court of Appeals for the Sixth Circuit

[November 9, 1993]

JUSTICE O'CONNOR delivered the opinion of the Court.

In this case we consider the definition of a discriminatory "abusive work environment" (also known as a "hostile work environment") under Title VII of the Civil Rights Act of 1964.

I

Teresa Harris worked as a manager at Forklift Systems, Inc., an equipment rental company, from April 1985 until October 1987. Charles Hardy was Forklift's president.

The Magistrate found that, throughout Harris's time at Forklift, Hardy often insulted her because of her gender and often made her the target of unwanted sexual innuendos....

Harris then sued Forklift, claiming that Hardy's conduct had created an abusive work environment for her because of her gender. The United States District Court for the Middle District of Tennessee, adopting the report and recommendation of the Magistrate, found this to be "a close case," but held that Hardy's conduct did not create an abusive environment. The court found that some of Hardy's comments "offended [Harris], and would offend the reasonable woman," but that they were not

> "so severe as to be expected to seriously affect [Harris'] psychological well-being. A reasonable woman manager under like circumstances would have been offended by Hardy, but his conduct would not have risen to the level of interfering with that person's work performance."
>
> "Neither do I believe that [Harris] was subjectively so offended that she suffered injury.... Although Hardy may at times have genuinely offended [Harris], I do not believe that he created a working environment so poisoned as to be intimidating or abusive to [Harris]."

In focusing on the employee's psychological well-being, the District Court was following Circuit precedent.... The United States Court of Appeals for the Sixth Circuit affirmed in a brief unpublished decision.

We granted certiorari (1993) to resolve a conflict among the Circuits on whether conduct, to be actionable as "abusive work environment" harassment (no *quid pro quo* harassment issue is present here), must "seriously affect [an employee's] psychological well being" or lead the plaintiff to "suffe[r] injury."

II

Title VII of the Civil Rights Act of 1964 makes it "an unlawful employment practice for an employer ... to discriminate against any individual with respect to his compensation, terms, conditions, or privileges of employment, because of such individual's race, color, religion, sex, or national origin." As we made clear in *Meritor Savings Bank* v. *Vinson* (1986), this language "is not limited to 'economic' or 'tangible' discrimination. The phrase 'terms, conditions, or privileges of employment' evinces a congressional intent 'to strike at the entire spectrum of disparate treatment of men and women' in employment," which includes requiring people to work in a discriminatorily hostile or abusive environment.... When the workplace is permeated with "discriminatory intimidation, ridicule, and insult" that is "sufficiently severe or pervasive to alter the conditions of the victim's employment and create an abusive working environment," Title VII is violated.

This standard, which we reaffirm today, takes a middle path between making actionable any conduct that is merely offensive and requiring the conduct to cause a tangible psychological injury. As we pointed out in Meritor, "mere utterance of an ... epithet which engenders offensive feelings in an employee" does not sufficiently affect the conditions of employment to implicate Title VII. Conduct that is not severe or pervasive enough to create an objectively hostile or abusive work environment—an environment that a reasonable person would find hostile or abusive—is beyond Title VII's purview. Likewise, if the victim does not subjectively perceive the environment to be abusive, the conduct has not actually altered the conditions of the victim's employment, and there is no Title VII violation.

But Title VII comes into play before the harassing conduct leads to a nervous breakdown. A discriminatorily abusive work environment, even one that does not seriously affect employees' psychological well-being, can and often will detract from employees' job performance, discourage employees from remaining on the job, or keep them from advancing in their careers. Moreover, even without regard to these tangible effects, the very fact that the discriminatory conduct was so severe or pervasive that it created a work environment abusive to employees because of their race, gender, religion, or national origin offends Title VII's broad rule of workplace equality. The appalling conduct alleged in *Meritor,* and the reference in that case to environments " 'so heavily polluted with discrimination as to destroy completely the emotional and psychological stability of minority group workers' " merely present some especially egregious examples of harassment. They do not mark the boundary of what is actionable.

We therefore believe the District Court erred in relying on whether the conduct "seriously affect[ed] plaintiff's psychological well-being" or led her to "suffe[r] injury." Such an inquiry may needlessly focus the factfinder's attention on concrete psychological harm, an element Title VII does not require. Certainly Title VII bars conduct that would seriously affect a reasonable person's psychological well-being, but the statute is not limited to such conduct. So long as the environment would reasonably be perceived, and is perceived, as hostile or abusive, *Meritor,* there is no need for it also to be psychologically injurious.

This is not, and by its nature cannot be, a mathematically precise test. We need not answer today all the potential questions it raises, nor specifically address the EEOC's new regulations on this subject. But we can say that whether an environment is "hostile" or "abusive" can be determined only by looking at all the circumstances. These may include the frequency of the discriminatory conduct; its severity; whether it is physically threatening or humiliating, or a mere offensive utterance; and whether it unreasonably interferes with an employee's work performance. The effect on the employee's psychological well-being is, of course, relevant to determining whether the plaintiff actually found the environment abusive. But while psychological harm, like any other relevant factor, may be taken into account, no single factor is required.

III

Forklift, while conceding that a requirement that the conduct seriously affect psychological well-being is unfounded, argues that the District Court nonetheless correctly applied the *Meritor* standard. We disagree. Though the District Court did conclude that the work environment was not "intimidating or abusive to [Harris]," it did so only after finding that the conduct was not "so severe as to be expected to seriously affect plaintiff's psychological well-being" and that Harris was not "subjectively so offended that she suffered injury." The District Court's application of these incorrect standards may well have influenced its ultimate conclusion, especially given that the court found this to be a "close case."

We therefore reverse the judgment of the Court of Appeals, and remand the case for further proceedings consistent with this opinion.

So ordered.

JUSTICE SCALIA, concurring.

Meritor Savings Bank v. *Vinson* (1986) held that Title VII prohibits sexual harassment that takes the form of a hostile work environment. The Court stated that sexual harassment is actionable if it is "sufficiently severe or pervasive 'to alter the conditions of [the victim's] employment and create an abusive work environment.'" Today's opinion elaborates that the challenged conduct must be severe or pervasive enough "to create an objectively hostile or abusive work environment—an environment that a reasonable person would find hostile or abusive."

"Abusive" (or "hostile," which in this context I take to mean the same thing) does not seem to me a very clear standard—and I do not think clarity is at all increased by adding the adverb "objectively" or by appealing to a "reasonable person's" notion of what the vague word means. Today's opinion does list a number of factors that contribute to abusiveness, but since it neither says how much of each is necessary (an impossible task) nor identifies any single factor as determinative, it thereby adds little certitude. As a practical matter, today's holding lets virtually unguided juries decide whether sex-related conduct engaged in (or permitted by) an employer is egregious enough to warrant an award of damages. One might say that what constitutes "negligence" (a traditional jury question) is not much more clear and certain than what constitutes "abusiveness." Perhaps so. But the class of plaintiffs seeking to recover for negligence is limited to those who have suffered harm, whereas under this statute "abusiveness" is to be the test of whether legal harm has been suffered, opening more expansive vistas of litigation.

Be that as it may, I know of no alternative to the course the Court today has taken. One of the factors mentioned in the Court's nonexhaustive list—whether the conduct unreasonably interferes with an employee's work performance—would, if it were made an absolute test, provide greater guidance to juries and employers. But I see no basis for such a limitation in the language of the statute. Accepting *Meritor*'s interpretation of the term "conditions of employment" as the law, the test is not whether work has been impaired, but whether working conditions have been discriminatorily altered. I know of no test more faithful to the inherently vague, statutory language than the one the Court today adopts. For these reasons, I join the opinion of the Court.

JUSTICE GINSBURG, concurring.

Today the Court reaffirms the holding of *Meritor Savings Bank* v. *Vinson* (1986): "[A] plaintiff may establish a violation of Title VII by proving that discrimination based on sex has created a hostile or abusive work environment." The critical issue, Title VII's text indicates, is whether members of one sex are exposed to disadvantageous terms or conditions of employment to which members of the other sex are not exposed. . . . As the Equal Employment Opportunity Commission emphasized, . . . the adjudicator's inquiry should center, dominantly, on whether the discriminatory conduct has unreasonably interfered with the plaintiff's work performance. To show such interference, "the plaintiff need not prove that his or her tangible productivity has declined as a result of the harassment." *Davis* v. *Monsanto Chemical Co.* (CA6 1988). It suffices to prove that a reasonable person subjected to the discriminatory conduct would find, as the plaintiff did, that the harassment so altered working conditions as to "ma[k]e it more difficult to do the job." *Davis* concerned race-based discrimination, but that difference does not alter the analysis; except in the rare case in which a bonafide occupational qualification is shown, see *Automobile Workers* v. *Johnson Controls, Inc.* (1991). Title VII declares discriminatory practices based on race, gender, religion, or national origin equally unlawful.

The Court's opinion, which I join, seems to me in harmony with the view expressed in this concurring statement.

PUERTO RICAN PLEBISCITE ON FUTURE STATUS

November 14 and December 9, 1993

By a close margin of slightly more than two percentage points, in a plebiscite held November 14 Puerto Ricans rejected the path toward becoming the fifty-first state and chose instead to retain their status as a U.S. commonwealth. Another 4.4 percent opted for independence, with fewer than 1 percent returning blank ballots. About 1.7 million Puerto Ricans—nearly 74 percent of eligible voters—went to the polls. The plurality decision meant that, for the foreseeable future, America's largest and oldest colony would remain a U.S. territory. But the referendum's results also indicated that a majority of voters were dissatisfied with the existing U.S.-Puerto Rican relationship.

The vote could be considered a defeat for Gov. Pedro Rossello, leader of the New Progressive Party (NPP). Established in 1967, the NPP had lobbied vigorously for statehood. By 1993 the party had surged to the majority, holding 20 of the 28 seats in the insular Senate, 36 of the 53 seats in the House of Representatives, and 54 of the 78 mayoralties. Despite the voters' rejection of statehood status, however, Rossello noted to President Bill Clinton in a November 17 letter that the margin of defeat was considerably less than the 21 percent differential with territorial status posted in the previous referendum, held in 1967.

From Territory to Commonwealth

The five-month-long, flag-waving, political-style campaign preceding the referendum was an emotional one for the residents of an island with more than a half-century of close ties with the United States. Discovered by Columbus in 1493, Puerto Rico was ceded by Spain to the United States in 1898 at the conclusion of the Spanish-American War. Two years after the island received status as an unincorporated territory in 1900, Puerto Rico's resident commissioner was admitted to the floor of the U.S. House of Representatives and, in 1904, was accorded privileges of a nonvoting delegate. (A nonvoting delegate may serve on committees and participate in debate, but not vote on the floor of the House.) In 1917 island residents were granted U.S. citizenship, and in 1947 Congress enacted legislation giving them the right to elect their own governor. A 1952 law made Puerto Rico a commonwealth—associated with the United States but retaining autonomy in internal affairs.

The results of a plebiscite initiated by the island government in 1967 showed that 60.5 percent of those voting preferred to retain the commonwealth arrangement, as endorsed by the Popular Democratic Party (PDP), while almost 39 percent of voters for the newly formed NPP joined its call for statehood. The Puerto Rican Independence Party (PIP) boycotted the elections.

Two years later, leaders of the three parties petitioned the U.S. president and Congress to allow a new referendum on the island's status. The Senate Energy and Natural Resources Committee, with principal jurisdiction over Puerto Rican affairs, approved a bill authorizing a plebiscite, and the full House followed suit soon after. However, the bill became snagged in the Senate, due in part to the perceived fiscal ramifications of a vote on Puerto Rico's status, as well as partisan considerations of what the results of a referendum could produce. Senate Republicans were apprehensive that full Puerto Rican representation in Congress would be overwhelmingly Democratic; skeptics of possible statehood in both parties said that it might open the doors to increasingly vocal calls for statehood for the District of Columbia, which many in Congress opposed. The demise of the referendum legislation was viewed as a victory for Rafael Hernandez Colón, leader of the pro-commonwealth PDP and Puerto Rico's governor at the time. But in November 1992 the statehood NPP swept to power, and its leader, Rossello, pledged to shepherd an economic revival and a referendum on the island's "status issue."

Speaking at a September 16 Congressional Hispanic Caucus Institute Gala, less than a month before the 1993 plebiscite, President Clinton said, "I am excited about the upcoming referendum in Puerto Rico. Whatever they're for, I'm for."

Party Positions and Options

Founded in 1938, the PDP, which won 48.7 percent of the popular vote in the 1988 gubernatorial contest, endorsed the existing commonwealth status and was widely identified with the U.S. Democratic party. In support of its position, the PDP cited the benefits of guaranteed U.S. citizenship; fiscal and cultural autonomy; and common markets, currency, and defense with the United States. Advocating an "enhanced" commonwealth relationship, the PDP supported greater authority to negotiate independent foreign trade agreements, airline landing rights, and import restrictions, as well as to decide on "inappropriate" federal laws and regulations (such as snow removal mandates), language spoken in federal courts, and federal appointments in the island.

The NPP—with close ideological inclinations to the U.S. Republican party, although it included a large portion of Democrats—supported statehood because it would afford Puerto Ricans parity in federal programs and full voting representation in Congress. Based on its 3.6 million residents, Puerto Rico would have at least six House members, as well as two senators. It would guarantee a permanent union with the United States and U.S. citizenship, while maintaining Spanish as a language equal to English. Although federal income and excise taxes would be collected and tax breaks for U.S. companies that located on the island would be gradually eliminated, Puerto Ricans would be phased in to full participation in all federal benefit and entitlement programs.

The PIP—which avoided association with mainland parties—held one insular Senate seat, one House seat, and no mayoral or gubernatorial positions in 1993. It advocated sovereignty for the island, based on a constitution that would provide for a democratic government, protection of human rights, and affirmation of Puerto Rican nationality and heritage. It would lobby for treaties with the United States to guarantee U.S. citizenship for those who sought it, free access to U.S. markets, investment tax incentives, and federal aid equivalent to the current amount.

Commonwealth Versus Statehood

Cultural factors were among the reasons cited by some Puerto Rican voters for their choice of commonwealth status. "I don't want to be able to speak Spanish only in my home," said Elsa Tio, a poet. "I want Spanish to remain the language of creativity and power in Puerto Rico."

Other commonwealth advocates cited special tax incentives that encouraged U.S. companies to locate in Puerto Rico and emphasized that Puerto Ricans were exempt from federal income taxes (although they were subject to heavy local and island taxes) but were eligible for U.S. welfare assistance. The result, they argued, was to elevate an island that had once been characterized as "the poorhouse of the Caribbean" to the wealthiest in the region. "Why change a good thing?" queried Yvonne Alejandro, an executive at a Pepsi Cola plant on the island.

Those supporting statehood, on the other hand, said that it would give them more leverage in Washington—particularly in having voting members of Congress—and would promote economic stability and tourism. They also warned that Congress could, at any time, revoke Puerto Ricans' welfare benefits and U.S. citizenship if the island remained a commonwealth.

Among the mainland advocates of statehood were Sen. Paul Simon, D-Ill., and Rep. Austin J. Murphy, D-Pa., who had expressed the hope that a vote in its favor might send a message to Congress to enact legislation establishing the fifty-first state. Simon said, "I have long believed that Puerto Ricans . . . deserve first class U.S. citizenship and I expect the plebiscite to set into motion Congressional action to make that happen." Former presidents Gerald R. Ford, Ronald Reagan, and George Bush also endorsed advertisements favoring statehood that preceded the 1993 vote. "The people have spoken and I must obey," said Rossello after the referendum. However, he said he would continue to press for statehood status.

"The vote reflected deep discontent with the status quo, which has relegated Puerto Ricans to second-class citizenship," said Sen. Charles Rodriguez, majority leader of the Puerto Rican Senate. Summarizing the aftermath of the referendum, the Washington Post *editorialized November 18, "For years the principal issue in Puerto Rican politics has been the so-called status question. Is the island better off in the constitutional halfway house it currently occupies as a 'commonwealth,' or should it try to become a state? . . . The lesson may be to leave status alone for a while and work on the island's other problems. Status aside, what should U.S. policy be toward Puerto Rico, and how well do present policies fulfill the federal obligation?"*

Following are the texts of a November 17, 1993, letter to President Clinton from Gov. Pedro Rossello of Puerto Rico explaining the outcome of the November 14 referendum in which the island's voters elected to retain commonwealth status, and the English translation of the December 9 affidavit by the Puerto Rican Electoral Commission certifying the returns of the plebiscite:

ROSSELLO'S LETTER TO CLINTON

Dear Mr. President:

While awaiting receipt of the Puerto Rico State Elections Commission certification that must accompany my formal report to the Federal Government on the outcome of the Puerto Rico plebiscite of November 14, 1993, I take this opportunity to inform you that the people of Puerto Rico have yet to reach a final decision with respect to political status.

. . . [T]he Puerto Rican electorate endorsed neither U.S. statehood nor independence . . . either of which would permanently resolve our perennial status dilemma.

It had been 26 years since Puerto Ricans previously expressed themselves at the polls on the fundamental issue of our island's destiny. In seeking the governorship last year, I promised to offer our people another such opportunity—for most of our electorate, the first such opportunity.

On the November 14, 1993 plebiscite ballot, two of the three proposed alternatives postulated the continuation of Puerto Rico's status as a community of American citizens. Together, those alternatives attracted 95% of the total vote.

Accordingly, the plebiscite *did* have the effect of overwhelmingly reaffirming our people's loyalty to the United States.

Moreover, the equality option—U.S. statehood—attracted 46% of the vote: a noteworthy increase over the 39% support received by statehood in the plebiscite of 1967 ... an increase that erased a 21% differential with the territorial status.

In contrast to that, retention of the territorial status quo was endorsed by only a 48% plurality ... a figure that reflects dramatic erosion in this formula's popularity during the 41 years since adoption of the "commonwealth" constitution:

- In 1952, "commonwealth" garnered 82% of the vote, in a constitutional referendum;
- Fifteen years later, pitted against statehood and independence in our only previous plebiscite, "commonwealth" obtained a convincing 60% majority;
- Today, that majority is gone—on November 14, 1993, with the participation of 1.7 million voters (74% of an almost universally-registered adult population), support for "commonwealth" dwindled to 48%.

No one disputes the accuracy of this trend: allegations of error and fraud in the November 14 plebiscite were nonexistent; on the contrary, observers and journalists—from around the world—effusively praised the integrity and efficiency with which the balloting and vote-counting were conducted.

To Summarize:

- The Government of Puerto Rico has kept faith with the mandate of the Puerto Rican people; we have sponsored an indisputably fair and comprehensive test of sentiment on the political status issue.
- Although our voters manifested a disinclination to perpetuate the territorial relationship denominated "commonwealth," they likewise fell short of achieving a consensus on the desirability of statehood.

However, I am confident that the question of our destiny as a people will be addressed again in the not too distant future ... and that the Federal Government will not be confronted with another quarter-century of inaction on the profoundly significant matter of self-determination for our island's 3.6-million U.S. citizens.

For now, on behalf of all Puerto Ricans, I thank you for your interest in our island's current and future well-being ... and in our aggressive ongoing efforts to enhance Puerto Rico's role as an asset to our nation.

Sincerely,

Pedro Rosselló
Governor of Puerto Rico

CERTIFICATION

Upon concluding the General Scrutiny of Votes ordered by Article 6008 of the Electoral Law of Puerto Rico and in conformance with Article 27 of the Enabling Act of the Plebiscite on Puerto Rico's Political Status Law Number 22 of the Fourth of July of 1993, we hereby certify that the following official results of the Plebiscite held on the 14th day of November of 1993:

Results Islandwide

	Votes	Percentage
Commonwealth	$26,326	48.6
Statehood	788,296	46.3
Independence	75,620	4.4
* Other Votes	10,748	0.6

* Null: 6,549 *Blank Ballots: 4,199
Total ballots counted: 1,700,990 of 2,312,913 for 73.5%
Polls counted: 6,563 of 6,569 for 100.0%
BE REGISTERED AND NOTIFIED: In San Juan, Puerto Rico, on December 3, 1993

/signature/
Juan R. Melecio
Presidente

/signature/	/signature/	/signature/
Carlos Camals Mora	Josè Ariel Nazario	Manuel Rodriguez Orellana
NPP Electoral Commissioner	PDP Electoral Commissioner	PIP Electoral Commissioner

I HEREBY CERTIFY: That on the same date I have sent a copy of this certification to the Honorable Governor and to the Honorable Secretary of State of the Commonwealth of Puerto Rico.

In San Juan, Puerto Rico on December 9, 1993

Nestor J. Colón Berlingeri
Clerk

NOTE: Of the total of 8,825 cases of persons who voted and were added manually, it was determined that 3,854 did not have the right to vote in the Plebiscite, but for this statistical report they appear as null ballots. Therefore, the net result of null ballots is 2,695 and the net of participating electors with the right to vote was 1,697,136. However, this statistical fraction does not affect significantly the percentages indicated in this report.

CLINTON REMARKS ON HOUSE PASSAGE OF NAFTA

November 17, 1993

Overcoming opposition from organized labor and 1992 independent presidential candidate Ross Perot, as well as from protectionist sentiment in Congress, President Bill Clinton in November 1993 won congressional approval of the North American Free Trade Agreement (NAFTA). The landmark agreement, which went into effect January 1, 1994, linked the United States with Canada and Mexico in a free trade area with a population of 370 million and a gross national product of $6 trillion.

The crucial vote took place in the U.S. House of Representatives the evening of November 17. By working the phones and making deals, Clinton locked up his victory in the last few weeks leading up to the House vote. Previously, anti-NAFTA forces had built up their strength, and, when it came, the clash between supporters and opponents of the trade agreement was particularly bitter.

NAFTA supporters, including most of the country's elites, argued that reducing or eliminating trade and investment barriers with Mexico would have mostly positive consequences for the United States. Opponents, especially concentrated in the heavily industrialized Northeast and Midwest, insisted that NAFTA would put American jobs at risk because of competition from lower-wage Mexican workers. Environmental groups contended that Mexico's failure to enforce environmental laws would result in even worse conditions than presently existed in Mexico, especially along the U.S.-Mexico border.

To win his legislative triumph, Clinton constructed a centrist coalition in the House that included more Republicans than Democrats. The legislative strategy represented a striking difference with that leading to the approval of the Omnibus Budget Reconciliation Act, Clinton's other substantial legislative victory in 1993, which cleared Congress August 5 and 6 without a single Republican vote.

The U.S. Senate, where support for NAFTA was never in doubt, endorsed the trade agreement by a vote of 61-38 August 20, 1993.

Speaking immediately after the dramatic House vote, which came at 10:30 p.m., President Clinton called the action "a defining moment for our nation." He also said, "At a time when many of our people are hurting from the strains of this tough global economy, we chose to compete, not retreat."

Background

NAFTA had its origins in the extensive modernization of Mexico's economy since the early 1980s. Two Mexican presidents, Miguel de la Madrid and Carlos Salinas de Gortari, strove to transform their nation's economy from one of Latin America's most controlled to one of the region's most open.

As recounted by David S. Cloud in the November 20 Congressional Quarterly Weekly Report, *Salinas in the spring of 1990 proposed that the United States join Mexico in negotiating a free trade agreement. At first cool toward Salinas's plan, President George Bush changed his mind, and negotiations began in September 1990.*

Opposition to implementation of the agreement sprang up when Bush sought an extension by Congress of the so-called fast-track rules. Extension of the rules was essential to prevent legislative amendments to deals negotiated by the president.

Committing large resources to the fight against the fast track, the AFL-CIO was joined in opposition by conservation groups such as Greenpeace, Friends of the Earth, and the Sierra Club. Still, the Bush administration won the fast-track struggle, negotiations with Mexico and Canada were concluded, and Mexico, the United States, and Canada agreed to the accord on August 12, 1992. (Historic Documents of 1992, pp. 759-769)

As a presidential candidate, Clinton endorsed NAFTA, but he also insisted that supplemental or "side" agreements were needed to ensure enforcement of labor and environmental laws. Successful in negotiating these agreements, Clinton signed them September 14. At the signing ceremonies, President Clinton said that NAFTA "will create jobs, thanks to trade with our neighbors." But neither organized labor nor environmental groups pulled back from their fierce opposition.

Provisions

The North American Free Trade Agreement was designed to eliminate, over fifteen years, tariffs on roughly nine thousand categories of customs goods. When NAFTA took effect on January 1, 1994, the volume of U.S. exports entering Mexico duty-free increased to 50 percent from 20 percent. At the same time, more than 60 percent of Mexican products entered the United States duty-free.

Under the agreement, each country pledged to treat all North American investors equally. Mexico promised to end special requirements previously imposed on U.S. companies operating in that country. In addition, all limits on the ownership of banks, insurance companies, and brokerage houses were to be removed by the year 2000.

NAFTA contained rules designed to prevent goods produced either completely or in large part outside North America from being exported duty-free among the three countries. Specifically, automobiles, footwear, and chemicals had to contain at least half, and in some cases more than 60 percent, North American content to move duty-free across borders.

The trade agreement obligated the three countries to work toward common standards to protect the food supply and the environment. Also, the United States and Mexico pledged to pay to clean up environmental problems along the U.S.-Mexico border. In part, the cleanup would be financed by a new North American Development Bank.

Debate in the Nation

The controversy over implementation of NAFTA began to build with the passage by Congress of the fast-track legislation, and it burgeoned with the signing, on August 12, 1992, of the accord by leaders of the three countries. (Bush remarks on NAFTA signing, Historic Documents of 1992, p. 759)

No trade agreement in memory had aroused such impassioned responses by Americans. Across the country, supporters and opponents formed unlikely coalitions. Ross Perot was linked in opposition with Pat Buchanan, a conservative Republican who was a candidate for his party's nomination in 1992, and with Ralph Nader, a liberal consumer advocate. Organized labor and a number of militant conservation groups, usually at loggerheads, also were joined in opposition. But farmers in the Midwest favored the accord, while growers in Florida, California, and North Dakota opposed it.

Perot and his organization, United We Stand, comprised a major force in the battle until November 9, when Perot and Vice President Al Gore debated the accord on "Larry King Live," a talk show televised nationwide on Cable News Network. The program was seen by Americans in an estimated 11.2 million homes. By a large margin, viewers thought Gore "won" the debate, and Perot's influence rapidly waned.

During the discussion, Perot repeated his argument that NAFTA would lead to substantial job losses in the United States and would worsen environmental conditions in Mexico. Gore asserted that, on the contrary, economic growth would be fueled in the United States by a vast increase in exports to Mexico and that a prosperous Mexico would boost economic growth in the United States and Canada.

Debate in the House

The acrimonious division over NAFTA in the country as a whole was mirrored in the U.S. House of Representatives, where some old loyalties were suspended and unexpected alliances were formed. Although the vote was a comfortable 234-200 in favor of NAFTA, the outcome was by no means certain from the start.

Only two weeks before the vote, Washington Post *columnist David Broder wrote that the odds were "against approval." Broder went on, "but now that he has joined the battle, Clinton may still have a chance to win."*

The Democratic House leadership was split over NAFTA in a highly unusual way. Rep. Richard A. Gephardt, D-Mo., the majority leader, and David E. Bonior, D-Mich., the Democratic whip, fought against the accord. Thus they were in opposition not only to the president by also to Speaker Thomas S. Foley, D-Wash., who supported the agreement. On the other hand, Rep. Newt Gingrich, R-Ga., the Republican whip, with a reputation for fierce partisanship, vigorously rounded up Republican votes for approval.

The victory, observers said, belonged to President Clinton. An editorial in the Baltimore Evening Sun *November 18 said that President Clinton's "victory in the House last night . . . wrote a new chapter in the 'comeback kid' saga that has marked his political career."*

Following are remarks by President Bill Clinton on House Passage of the North American Free Trade Agreement and a brief exchange with reporters, November 17, 1993:

The President. Thank you very much. Just a few minutes ago the House of Representatives voted to approve the North American Free Trade Agreement. NAFTA will expand our exports, create new jobs, and help us reassert America's leadership in the global economy. This agreement is in the deep self-interest of the United States. It will help make working Americans, the world's most productive workers, winners in the world economy.

I want to thank the lawmakers of both parties who gave their support to NAFTA. Many of them, as everyone knows, showed real courage in voting their consciences and what they knew to be in the best interest for their Nation. I want to thank all the citizens who worked so hard for this, the business leaders, especially the small business leaders, the spokespersons for the NAFTA fight, including Lee Iacocca who's here with us tonight.

I want to say a special word of thanks to the members of the Cabinet who labored so hard and long, especially Mickey Kantor, our Trade Ambassador, for his tireless effort on the side agreements and to lobby this through, and the Secretary of the Treasury, who is a native of south Texas and who understands so clearly why this is in our interests. And I want to say a special word of thanks to Vice President Gore for bringing home the message to the American people in his superb debate performance.

Tonight's vote is a defining moment for our Nation. At a time when many of our people are hurting from the strains of this tough global economy, we chose to compete, not to retreat, to lead a new world economy, to lead as America has done so often in the past. The debate over NAFTA has been contentious. Men and women of good will raised strong arguments for and against this agreement. But every participant in this debate wanted the same things: more jobs, more security, more opportunity for every American. And so do I.

I thank those who worked with us. . . . I also thank the passionate defenders of the working people who oppose NAFTA for exercising their right to speak out. And they were right to speak out against economic conditions which have produced too few jobs and stagnant incomes, as well as inadequate strategies for retraining our workers and investing in our people and our places that need them. They fought hard, and they have my respect.

But in an economy where competition is global and change is the only constant, we simply cannot advance the security of American workers by building walls of protection around our economy or by pretending that global competition isn't there. Our only choice is to take this new world head on, to compete, and to win. That's why it's so important that we pass NAFTA, and I hope the Senate will complete the process in the next few days.

By eliminating Mexico's tariffs and restrictive rules we'll be able to export more cars, more computers, and other products and keep more American workers on the job here at home. NAFTA will raise environmental and labor standards in Mexico. And I want to ask tonight labor and management to work together with our administration to ensure that the labor and environmental provisions of NAFTA are honored. We must make sure that this pact works to America's advantage.

NAFTA is a big step, but just the first step in our effort to expand trade and spark an economic revival here and around the world. One legitimate point that the opponents of NAFTA made is that we will do even better in the global economy if we have a training system and a retraining system and a job placement system for our workers worthy of the challenges they face. We simply must guarantee our workers the training and education they need to compete in the global marketplace. And I call on the coalition that passed NAFTA to help me early next year present to the Congress and pass a world-class reemployment system that will give our working people the security of knowing that they'll be able always to get the training they need as economic conditions change.

We must also provide our citizens with other things . . . with increased investment in people and places and jobs. And we must continue the fight to lower foreign trade barriers which slow economic growth here in the United States and around the world.

Tomorrow I go to Seattle to meet with the leaders of 15 Asian Pacific economies. I will ask them to work toward more open markets for our products. When I return, I'll reach out to the other market-oriented democracies of Latin America, to ask them to join in this great American pact that I believe offers so much hope to our future. And next month we will urge our European and Asian competitors to complete work on the worldwide trade agreement that can literally create hundreds of thousands of jobs here in the United States as we open markets all across the globe.

We've faced choices before like the one we faced tonight, whether to turn inward or turn outward. After World War I, the United States turned inward and built walls of protection around our economy. The result was a depression and ultimately another world war. After the Second World War, we made a very different choice. We turned outward. We built a system of expanded trade and collective security. We rebuilt the economies of our former foes and . . . created the great American middle class.

Tonight, with the cold war over, our Nation is facing that choice again. And tonight I am proud to say, we have not flinched. Tonight the leaders of both parties found common ground in supporting the common good. We voted for the future tonight. We once again showed our strength. We once again showed our self-confidence, even in this difficult time. Our people are winners. And I believe we showed tonight we are ready together to compete and win and to shape the world of the 21st century. Thank you very much.

Q. Mr. President, how are you going to make up with the Democratic leaders who fought this trade agreement so vociferously?

The President. Well, I thought what they all said tonight was a very good signal. At the end of that debate I was deeply moved by the efforts that people on both sides of the issue made to reach out to each other and to say that we have to make this work now, we have to go forward now, we have to build our economy. And I think you will see that happening—I think you will see a greater sense of unity and commitment to have the kind of job training programs we need, to have the kind of investment strategies we need to keep forcing these trade barriers down abroad.

And I must say, too, I hope we'll see in the future some more of this bipartisan effort to build economic security for Americans, because a lot of our national security in the future is going to be involved with rebuilding our economic strength from the grassroots up. And that's a very hopeful part of this debate.

Q. What about the relationship with organized labor, sir?

The President. Well, one of the things I learned, again, in this fight is that they have an enormous amount of energy and ability to organize and channel the passions and feelings of their workers. You know, when you think about it, we had the White House, the leaders of both parties, an enormous amount of support, and we had to come from a long way back to win this fight because of the work they did largely. And what I want to do is to ask them to join me now, as I said tonight, in making sure that the labor and environmental agreements are honored, in going on to the health care battle, in going on to other economic battles, and in making sure we give our working people the kind of education and training programs they need to compete in this different and very competitive global economy. Thank you.

THIRTIETH ANNIVERSARY OF KENNEDY ASSASSINATION

November 22, 1993

Thousands of people commemorated the thirtieth anniversary of the assassination of former president John F. Kennedy on November 22. At Kennedy's grave in Arlington National Cemetery, where an eternal flame burns in his memory, tourists laid flowers and knelt in prayer. In Dallas, Texas, onlookers watched as Dealey Plaza, where Kennedy was shot, was designated a historic landmark.

Visitors to Kennedy's grave just outside Washington, D.C., included his only surviving brother, Sen. Edward M. Kennedy, and his nephew, Rep. Joseph P. Kennedy II. With their wives they laid white roses at the foot of the tombstone and then lingered for several minutes alone. Other family members did not visit the grave, saying that they preferred to celebrate Kennedy's birthday on May 29 instead of remembering his death.

Other visitors to Arlington Cemetery represented a cross-section of America. The Washington Post *described the crowd as extremely varied: "[There were] a Dominican nun; men in blue caps with the names of naval ships on them in gold. . . ; an older Japanese woman; high school kids in tiny glasses and huge Doc Martens shoes; tentative, arrogant college boys. . . ; old guys in earmuffs; old gals wearing drugstore sunglasses. . . ." Some were too young to remember the assassination; others had not even been born at the time. Still, they came along with older generations to commemorate the Kennedy mystique and the legendary sense of hopefulness attached to the era known as "Camelot."* Washington Post *reporter Henry Allen explained, "[W]e create the Kennedy we want. . . . What's important is what he stood for, what he promised, what he was rather than what he did and what he inspired. And it was the sense of something lost."*

In Texas, the Dallas County Historical Foundation held a dedication ceremony at Dealey Plaza. Speakers, including Nellie Connally, widow of former Texas governor John B. Connally, paid homage to Kennedy's life and recalled the tragic day when Kennedy was shot and Connally seriously injured while they travelled together in a presidential motorcade. Texas senator Kay Bailey Hutchison said, "[The] event . . . changed all of us who were alive at that time, and it changed the country that those who were not yet born would enter." U.S. District Judge Barefoot Sanders, who was the U.S. attorney in Dallas at the time of the assassination, told the crowd of several thousand people that Kennedy's legacy was that he "symbolized what could be, the belief that problems can be solved, and a hope for a brighter tomorrow."

The Conspiracy Theories

The plot behind the Kennedy assassination has been a source of controversy ever since that fateful day in 1963 when the president and Connally were shot by Lee Harvey Oswald from an open window on the sixth floor of the Texas School Book Depository. Oswald was apprehended and then gunned down by Jack Ruby while in police custody. The world has long speculated whether the same bullet could have struck both Kennedy and Connally nearly simultaneously. According to the August 30, 1993, issue of U.S. News & World Report, *the single bullet question has been "the central issue raised by the physical evidence."*

The obvious question raised by the single bullet theory was whether Lee Harvey Oswald acted alone or whether he was part of a conspiracy. The Warren Commission, appointed by President Lyndon Johnson to investigate the assassination, determined that Oswald was not involved in any type of plot and that he was the only person involved in the assassination. However, numerous conspiracy theories surfaced, most focusing on Oswald's connections with the governments of Cuba and the Soviet Union, where he lived from 1959 to 1962. Other conspiracy theories implicated the Central Intelligence Agency (CIA) and the U.S. government and speculated about the involvement of organized crime.

For people on both sides of the conspiracy theory, the anniversary of the assassination provided ample opportunity for voicing opinions and again stirring up the controversy. The anniversary caused a media and publishing frenzy, with magazines featuring JFK on their covers, television stations showing specials on the Kennedy clan, and newspapers like the New York Times *and the* Washington Post *running retrospectives on Kennedy's life.*

Release of Assassination Information

Conspiracy theorists and researchers alike were thrilled when previously classified documents relating to the assassination were released into the public domain on August 23, 1993. Under the JFK Assassination Records Collection Act of 1992, the U.S. government was required to disclose nearly all files pertaining to the assassination. The 800,000 pages of material included documents from many government organizations, including the CIA, FBI, State Department, Defense Department, the

Warren Commission, and the House Select Committee on Assassinations.

The documents contained endless, albeit fascinating, examples of leads that went nowhere, as well as pertinent information valuable to researchers looking for answers. One 500-page report, like many of the documents, offered new and complicated insights: the 1979 House Select Committee on Assassinations report refuted the Warren Commission's findings and questioned the validity of the one-gunman theory. However, despite the onslaught of new information containing countless pieces of the puzzle, according to G. Robert Blakey, chief counsel to the House committee, "Nothing is going to settle this controversy."

Following are the texts of speeches given by Sen. Kay Bailey Hutchison, U.S. District Judge Barefoot Sanders, Assistant Secretary of the Department of the Interior Robert Armstrong, and Nellie Connally on November 22, 1993, at the Dallas County Historical Foundation Dealey Plaza dedication:

HUTCHISON'S REMARKS

Thirty years ago today an event occurred which changed the course of American history. The Kennedy assassination brought about a sea of change in American politics and American society.

Today we gather to celebrate the memory of John Fitzgerald Kennedy, not just the anniversary of his death. Arthur Schlesinger once said, "Above all John Kennedy gave the world for an imperishable moment the vision of a leader who greatly understood the terror and the hope, the diversity and the possibility of life on this planet, and to make people look beyond nation and race to the future of humanity." The restoration of the Schoolbook Depository at Dealey Plaza is a poignant reminder of an event that changed all of us who were alive at the time, and it changed the country that those who were not yet born would enter. Sometimes the spirit of the American people is best shown when we endure tragedy. We come together. We rebuild. We look to the future and we vow to make it better. I am proud that the people of Dallas are making this place of this historic event a tribute to the life of this president, his dedication, and his successes. It is an honor for me as an American, as a United States Senator, as a resident of Dallas, to be with you today to commemorate this occasion. Thank you very much.

SANDERS'S REMARKS

Thank you, Judge Jackson, and to you and your distinguished guests here on the platform, and particularly to the members of the Dallas County Historical Foundation. I wish to say I am honored to be asked to substitute for my good friend Congressman Bryant, who serves this area with such energy and distinction. I am complimented to have the opportunity to play a part in this program.

As has already been pointed out, thirty years ago today President and Mrs. John F. Kennedy came to Dallas. Those of us who were in that fateful cavalcade which proceeded from the airport to downtown Dallas will recall that November 22, 1963 was a day very much like today—pleasant, much sunshine and good cheer. And as the cavalcade came down the street which we face here today, we will also recall the huge crowd which gave such an enthusiastic welcome to President and Mrs. Kennedy and to Governor and Mrs. Connally. And then suddenly here in this plaza, just a few yards from where we now stand for our ceremony, the president was shot to death.

Today we meet to dedicate this plaza, in the place of the Kennedy assassination as a national historic landmark. As we remember his tragic death as a sadness and frustration which is impossible to describe. We also remember and celebrate the challenges which he brought to all of us when he lived. President Kennedy once said that a nation reveals itself not by the men it produces but by the men it honors. Today and every November 22 we reveal ourselves as a nation by honoring John Fitzgerald Kennedy. His brief administration introduced us to new avenues for creativity and discovery and for equality and compassion. We remember John Kennedy's ringing eloquence calling upon our best instincts and our greatest talents. We remember him for his style, grace, wit and charm, and his ability to laugh at himself. And we remember John Kennedy most of all because of the inspiration and hope which he brought to us at his inauguration and left as his legacy, "Ask not what your country can do for you, rather, what you can do for your country," an urging which sometimes seems to be observed more nowadays in the breach than in the observance.

It has been said that John F. Kennedy did not solve the problems of war and peace. But he created the conviction that they could be solved. He did not end the problems of racial discrimination, the problems of poverty in the world, the problems of governments, but he inspired the hope that they could be solved. The nation was captivated by John F. Kennedy thirty years ago and it is today because he symbolized what could be the belief that problems can be solved and a hope for a brighter tomorrow. That is President Kennedy's legacy to us, and it is that legacy which we honor and remember today as we dedicate this plaza.

Thank you.

ARMSTRONG'S REMARKS

Thank you very much, Your Honor.... Secretary Babbitt has asked me to express his thanks to each of you for the community's effort to bring this about, and to make this one of the truly fine national monuments not just in Texas but in the United States of America. And so I carry his thanks to you. This happened only a month ago. He worked hard to get it to happen so that we could have this event on the anniversary day.

We suppose that all of us remember exactly where they were when they heard about what happened in this plaza. I happen to remember even before then that I was invited to the inauguration and I stood on a very cold day in a corner of the Capitol and looked down as Jack Kennedy said to each of us something that struck home with many, many people. It changed our perception about what we were about, and that was to ask what we could do for our country. And I think millions of Americans took him at his word, as I did. Subsequently I ran for public office. I was sworn in in a special election at ten o'clock on the twenty-second of November 1963 in Austin, Texas, in the House chamber, and two hours later Jack Kennedy rode into this plaza. I, like Jack Valenti said, refused to believe it. My mind could not grasp this fact, but it was important for us to know that it happened and it was important for us to deal with it. And as the Constitution provided for succession, and as the people began to realize we were going to have a new president and all of the tragedy of that day washed over us we realized that, again as Jack said, the light flickered but it didn't go out because the Constitution provided the ability for a nation to go forward even in the face of this kind of tragedy.

So we gather today to make a national monument out of this plaza with a lot of people who have done much to make it happen, and they should be thanked and appreciated for what they have done. Everyone will come here with varying things on their minds. They will pass here with various thoughts. But let me tell you what my thought will be. I will be thinking of the end as much as I will think of the beginning. I will think of the invitation that Jack Kennedy issued to me and millions of Americans to become a part of this nation and to do what we could for our country, and I will thank him for that invitation and I will thank him for lighting the way.

CONNALLY'S REMARKS

Thirty years ago fate brought me here as an unwilling player in the most unforgettable tragic drama of our time. Now, three decades later, we are gathered not to look back with grief but to look forward with hope. Many of us share our own indelible memories of that awful hour, but today we recognize the lasting place this site will ever have in our nation's history.

On behalf of the property owners it is my honor to unveil this replica of the plaque which officially designates the Dealey Plaza Historic Landmark. It is hereby dedicated to the future generations of Americans with the hope that the legacy of John F. Kennedy will inspire them to reach for greatness in their own lives, and the hope that all young people who hear this message will dedicate their lives to preserving our nation's heritage.

Thank you.

CLINTON ON SIGNING OF BRADY BILL

November 30, 1993

After a seven-year fight pitting gun control advocates against the powerful National Rifle Association (NRA), Congress passed legislation known as the "Brady bill," which President Bill Clinton signed into law November 30. The legislation imposed a waiting period of five business days for the purchase of a handgun so that law enforcement officials would be able to check the backgrounds of prospective buyers for criminal records. The waiting period would be dropped after five years when a nationwide, computerized system should be in place to do the background checks.

The legislation was named for former White House press secretary James Brady, who was permanently disabled in the 1981 assassination attempt on President Ronald Reagan. The bill, which was first thought to be dead for the year, was revived at the end of the session amid a growing public clamor about violent crime. It cleared its final hurdle in the Senate November 24 just before members left for the Thanksgiving-Christmas recess.

The measure was the most stringent gun control bill passed by Congress since the 1968 ban on mail-order rifle sales. In addition to the waiting-period requirement, the new law provided states with more than $200 million to upgrade their computerized records on criminals.

President Clinton signed the bill into law at an emotional White House ceremony with Brady and his wife, Sarah, a leading gun control proponent, in attendance along with two hundred guests. Among them were police officers who had worked hard for the bill, other gun control advocates, members of Congress who had engineered passage of the legislation, and relatives of victims killed by handguns.

Countering the NRA

Previous versions of the Brady bill had made progress in Congress in years past, but the NRA and its legislative allies always had mustered enough clout to block passage. An example of the NRA's muscle was apparent when Clinton pointedly thanked former representative Beryl Anthony, D-Ark., for his support. The president noted that Anthony had lost a tough reelection in 1992 "and part of the reason was that he voted for the Brady bill. And the NRA came after him in an unusual election."

Ten years after he was shot, Reagan endorsed the bill. Speaking at George Washington University Hospital, where he had been treated for his injuries, Reagan said, "[M]y position on the right to bear arms is well known. But I want you to know something else ... I support the Brady Bill and I urge the Congress to enact it without further delay." (Reagan on Gun Control, Historic Documents of 1991, p. 185)

In contrast, Clinton had long championed the legislation, saying during the 1992 presidential campaign and after he was elected that if Congress would send him the Brady bill, he would sign it. Vice President Al Gore and Attorney General Janet Reno were also staunch supporters, and in her remarks at the ceremony Sarah Brady said that "to have an administration, an Attorney General, a Vice President, and a President who we knew would sign this bill is of the utmost importance."

In earlier legislative battles and all through 1993, the NRA and its allies contended that the Brady bill would do little good, was an infringement on the rights of law-abiding gun owners, and was the first step to more draconian gun control laws. But those arguments were not strong enough to counter the rising tide of concern over gun crimes. "Americans are finally fed up with violence that cuts down another citizen with gunfire every twenty minutes," Clinton told the White House gathering.

One government study found that in 1992 bullets killed more black males between the ages of fifteen and nineteen than any other cause of death in the United States. Also in 1992 former surgeon general C. Everett Koop signed an editorial in the New England Journal of Medicine *that declared violence in America a "public health emergency." Koop's stance represented a change of heart from his days in office when he contended that gun violence was not a health issue.* (Report on Gun Violence, Historic Documents of 1992, p. 493)

Melanie Musick, whose husband had been slain with a handgun, was a guest at the signing ceremony. She sought to rebut one of the NRA's arguments with her personal experience. Her husband was shot April 24, 1990, by a man who had just been released from a mental institution. A waiting period in Atlanta deterred him from getting a gun in the city, but he went to a neighboring county and easily bought the gun that he used in the killing. Musick said the Brady bill, with its nationwide coverage, would have saved her husband's life.

In his remarks Clinton cited a news report that about fifty thousand individuals had been denied the right to buy a handgun in just four states since 1989. "Don't let anybody tell you that this won't work," he said.

But the limits of a waiting period's effectiveness were tragically demonstrated just five weeks after the president signed the Brady bill. A gunman, who had purchased a semiautomatic handgun in California and waited the state's required fifteen days for a background check, went on a shooting spree aboard a New York commuter train. He killed five people and wounded eighteen. The suspect, Colin Ferguson, was from the New York area, but had gone to California and stayed just long enough to make the gun purchase. He had no criminal record, but authorities failed to learn that he was not a California resident. Federal law requires that a gun buyer be a resident of the state of purchase.

A First Step

At the signing Clinton described enactment of the bill as just a first step, calling for Congress to pass a ban on assault weapons—echoed a month later by FBI head Louis J. Freeh—and to bar handgun ownership for minors. The president said he was also mindful of the concerns of sportsmen and hunters, noting that he had grown up amidst guns. They are "a part of the culture of a big part of America," he said, but quickly added that the Brady bill and other gun control proposals have nothing to do with law abiding sports or hunting activities. What has happened, the president said, is that "we have taken this important part of the life of millions of Americans and turned it into an instrument of maintaining madness. It is crazy."

Less than a month after the Brady bill became law, Wal-Mart, the nation's largest retailer, announced it would discontinue selling handguns over the counter by February 1, 1994. Wal-Mart joined a number of large department stores that already had discontinued handgun sales. The store said it would continue to offer handguns to customers through its catalogue.

A Wal-Mart spokesman said that customers were making clear "they're uncomfortable in a store with handguns on-site. The country is changing, and customers feel differently this year from last."

Following are excerpts of President Bill Clinton's remarks November 30, 1993, during the signing ceremony for the Brady bill:

. . . Everything that has been—that should be said about this has already been said by people whose lives are more profoundly imbued with this issue than mine. But there are some things I think we need to think about that we learned from this endeavor as we look ahead to what still needs to be done.

Since Jim and Sarah began this crusade, more than 150,000 Americans—men, women, teenagers, children, even infants have been killed with handguns. And many more have been wounded. One hundred and fifty thousand people from all walks of life who should have been here to share Christmas with us. This couple saw through a fight that really never should have had to occur; because still, when people are confronted with issues of clear common sense and overwhelming evidence, too often we are prevented from doing what we know we ought to do by our collective fears, whatever they may be.

The Brady Bill has finally become law, in a fundamental sense not because of any of us, but because grass roots America changed its mind and demanded that this Congress not leave here without doing something about this. And all the rest of us, even Jim and Sarah, did was to somehow light that spark that swept across the people of this country and proved once again that democracy can work. America won this battle. Americans are finally fed up with violence that cuts down another citizen with gunfire every 20 minutes.

And we know that this bill will make a difference. As Sarah said, the *Washington Post* pointed out that about 50,000 people have been denied the right to buy a handgun in just four states since 1989. Don't let anybody tell you that this won't work. I got a friend back home who sold a gun years ago to a guy who had escaped from a mental hospital that he hadn't seen in 10 years. And he pulled out that old form from the 1968 act, and said, have you ever been convicted of a crime? Have you ever been in a mental hospital? The guy said, no, no—and put the form back in the drawer. And 12 hours later six people were dead and my friend is not over it to this day. Don't tell me this bill will not make a difference. That is not true. (Applause.) It is not true.

But we all know there is more to be done. The crime bill not only has 100,000 new police officers who, properly trained and deployed, will lower the crime rate by preventing crime, not just by catching criminals. It also has a ban on several assault weapons, long overdue—(applause); a ban on handgun ownership and restrictions on possession of handguns by minors, the beginning of reform of our federal firearms licensing systems, and an effort to make our schools safer. This is a good beginning. And there will be more to be done after that.

But I ask you to think about what this means and what we can all do to keep this going. We cannot stop here. I'm so proud of what others are doing; I'm proud of the work that Reverend Jesse Jackson has been doing, going back now to the streets and talking to the kids and telling them to stop shooting each other and cutting each other up, and to turn away from violence. I'm proud of people like David Plaza, not so well-known, a former gang member who has turned his life around and now coordinates a program called Gang Alternative Programs in Norwalk, California, telling gang members they have to take personal responsibility for their actions and turn away from violence. Reverend William Moore, who organized parents and educators and other clergy in North Philadelphia to provide safety corridors for kids going to and from school. One hundred and sixty thousand children stay home every day because they're scared to go to school in this country. And all the police officers on the street who have restored confidence in their neighborhoods, becoming involved in ways that often are way beyond the call of duty; people like Officer Anthony Fuedo of Boston, who took a tough section of East Boston and transformed it from a neighborhood full of fear to one which elderly people now feel safe sitting on benches again.

We can do this, but only if we do it together. And I ask you to think about this. I come from a state where half the folks have hunting and fishing licenses. I can still remember the first day when I was a little boy out in the country putting a can on top of a fencepost and shooting a .22 at it. I can still remember the first time I pulled a trigger on a .410 shotgun because I was too little to hold a .12 gauge. I can remember these things.

This is part of the culture of a big part of America. But people have taken that culture. We just started deer season—I live in a place where we still close schools and plants on the first day of deer season—nobody is going to show up anyway. (Laughter.) We just started deer season at home and a lot of other places. We have taken this important part of the life of millions of Americans and turned it into an instrument of maintaining madness. It is crazy.

Would I let anybody change that life in America? Not on your life. Has that got anything to do with the Brady Bill or assault weapons, or whether the police have to go out on the street confronting teenagers who are better armed than they are? Of course not.

This is the beginning of something truly wonderful in this country if we have learned to separate out all this stuff we've been hearing all these years; trying to make the American people afraid that somehow their quality of life is going to be undermined by doing stuff that people of common sense and goodwill would clearly want to do. And every law enforcement official in American telling us to do it.

So, I plead with all of you today, when you leave here to be reinvigorated by this; to be exhilarated by the triumph of Jim and Sarah Brady and all these other folks who didn't let their personal losses defeat them but instead used it to come out here and push us to do better.

And each of you in turn, take your opportunity not to let people ever again in this country use a legitimate part of our American heritage in ways that blinds us to our obligation to the present and the future. If we have broken that, then there is nothing we cannot do. And when I go and sign this bill in a minute, it will be step one in taking our streets back, taking our children back, reclaiming our families and our future. Thank you. (Applause.)

(The bill is signed.) (Applause.)

December

ARMY'S FIRST MUSLIM CHAPLAIN

December 3, 1993

For the first time in U.S. military history, a religious leader who was neither Christian nor Jewish joined the ranks of the 3,150 active-duty chaplains representing 243 religious denominations in the armed forces. Abdul-Rasheed Muhammad, an imam of the Church of Islam, was sworn in as an Army chaplain, and simultaneously appointed to the rank of captain, at a Pentagon ceremony attended by family, friends, and reporters. Muhammad, who was raised as a Baptist but converted to Islam as a young man, became the first Muslim named to serve as a spiritual leader for the rapidly increasing numbers of Muslims in the Army.

The result of ten years of negotiations between military officials and representatives of the U.S. Islamic community, the event was hailed by both military and Islamic leaders as a symbol of increasing respect for diverse religious beliefs in the armed forces. "This is very historic," said Col. Herman Keizer, Jr., an Army chaplain and executive director of the Armed Forces Chaplain Board, noting that American Buddhists were also seeking a candidate to serve as their first chaplain.

The process of appointing a Muslim chaplain was not easy. A Muslim organization had to be found to vouch for the candidate's credentials, a step complicated by the fact that the Islamic religion is not organized on a hierarchical structure. The American Muslim Council, based in Washington, D.C., was finally selected to certify the candidate. Then, letters soliciting nominees were sent to mosques throughout the country. The final selection was Muhammad, who had served in the Army from 1982 to 1985 as a behavioral science specialist at Fort Lee in Virginia, where he sometimes presided over Friday prayer services.

Muhammad's Background

Born Myron Maxwell in Buffalo, New York, Muhammad was the tenth of eleven children. Although he attended the Baptist church, he was never baptized and, as a teenager, began to question why the congregation was black "but symbols were not African American. I wasn't comfortable with it," he told a reporter in an interview published in the December 24, 1993, New York Times. *"It didn't sit right with my nature."*

Muhammad said he began listening to recordings of speeches by Malcolm X, and, after taking a course in religion as an anthropology major at the State University of New York at Brockport in 1973, decided that "Islam was the right way for me personally." In 1974 he joined the Lost-Found Nation of Islam, a group which advocated racial separatism and black nationalism. But he said he was uneasy about some of the platforms of the black Muslim movement and, as a consequence, joined with those who repudiated black nationalism and embraced the more traditional practices of Islam which were espoused by Imam W. Deen Mohammed.

In 1978 Captain Muhammad became an assistant imam—an official qualified both to advise other Muslims and preside over religious ceremonies.

Rising Number of Muslims in Army

The number of Muslims in the military was difficult to estimate. According to Pentagon spokesman Lt. Col. Doug Hart, twenty-five hundred individuals in the military identified themselves as Muslims, with more than half of them in the Army. But because recruits were not required to list their religion, Hart said, there could be many more. According to a group called the Muslim Military Members, the number could be as high as 10,000.

There was little doubt, however, that the ranks of Muslims in the military had swelled rapidly in recent years, particularly in the Army and in the aftermath of exposure to Islam during the 1991 Persian Gulf War. According to news reports, as many as five thousand U.S. troops had converted to Islam, spurred by tent-side programs sponsored by the Saudi government.

Nonetheless, many enlisted Muslims said they had encountered discrimination and harassment when their religious beliefs came in conflict with military regulations. For example, some officers were reluctant to allow practicing Muslims to attend required congregational prayers at midday each Friday. Others refused permission for enlisted Muslim women to wear the traditional hijaab *head covering. The military's field rations, known as MREs (meals ready to eat), often contained pork, which Muslims are forbidden to eat. However, Marine Gunnery Sgt. Archie Barnes, executive director of the Muslim Military Members, said that many in the military had tried to accommodate Islamic religious practices—for example, limiting physical exercise for Muslims during the month of Ramadan, when Muslims fast from dawn to sunset.*

"We Can't Wait"

The appointment of Captain Muhammad as chaplain was hailed as a step toward acceptance of Islam as a major religious tradition, reflective of the growing numbers of Muslims in the United States. According to Mustafa Malik, research director of the American Muslim Council, there were more than 5 million Muslims in the United States, 42 percent of them black.

"We've come from the extreme of being antigovernment to having a representative in the military," said Fajri Ansart, imam of the mosque in which Captain Muhammad served. Muhammad also told an interviewer that he believed his appointment represented a step toward wider acceptance of Islam as a major religion. "Muslims can now feel themselves becoming a little more mainstream," he said, noting that he perceived his role as "not to change the Army. It is to educate the Army."

"We can't wait," said Abdul Rashid Abdullah, who was raised a Roman Catholic and joined the Islamic faith in college. "The chaplains who are there don't know enough about Islam to service the soldiers. And sometimes the soldiers are new to Islam; they are gung-ho, and they need guidance."

Following is the text of the U.S. Army news release of December 3, 1993, announcing the swearing in of the Army's first Muslim chaplain:

Mr. Abdul-Rasheed Muhammad was sworn into the U.S. Army as the first Islamic Chaplain in Army history at the Pentagon, Washington, D.C. at 10 a.m. today.

Mr. Muhammad will start the Army Chaplain Officer Basic Course in January 1994 at Fort Monmouth, N.J. and will be stationed at Fort Bragg, N.C. upon completion of his course in April 1994.

Mr. Muhammad has three years of previous enlisted experience in the Army as a supply specialist from November 1982 to November 1985. He has a bachelor's of science degree from New York State University at Brockport, N.Y. in Anthropology, a master's of science degree from San Diego State University in Counseling Education and a Master's degree in Social Work from the University of Michigan.

Mr. Muhammad currently works at the Albion Correctional Facility for Women and the Orleans Correctional Facility for Men as a chaplain and is looking forward to his first assignment in the Army as a chaplain.

NOBEL PRIZE FOR LITERATURE

December 7, 1993

Toni Morrison became the first African American to win the Nobel Prize in literature, as well as only the eighth woman in history to receive the honor. She delivered her Nobel lecture December 7 in the Grand Hall of the Swedish Academy in Stockholm, receiving two standing ovations as she spoke. Along with the other Nobel winners of 1993, she was also honored at a formal banquet at the city hall.

Born Chloe Anthony Wofford in Lorain, Ohio, in 1931, the setting for her first novel, The Bluest Eye, *Morrison was one of four children in a working-class family. She graduated Harvard University in 1953, received her M.A. in American literature from Cornell University, and taught at Texas Southern, Howard, and Yale Universities. Since 1989 Morrison has held a chair in the humanities at Princeton; she has worked outside the ivory tower as well, as a critic and as a lecturer on African-American literature. She began writing fiction early in her career, at the time when she worked as an editor at Random House. She resigned that job to become a full-time writer.*

The author of six novels and several essays, Morrison was described by the academy as "a literary artist of the first rank. She delves into the language itself, a language she wants to liberate from the fetters of race. And she addresses us with the lustre of poetry." The prize committee lauded Morrison's work as a whole, saying, "Her oeuvre is unusually finely wrought and cohesive, yet at the same time rich in variation. One can delight in her unique narrative technique, varying from book to book and developed independently.... The lasting impression is ... sympathy, humanity, of the kind which is always based on profound humour."

*Although Morrison was selected for the prize because of the quality of the entire body of her work, the prize committee singled out three of her novels—*Song of Solomon, Beloved, *and* Jazz*—as ones deserving special praise. In* Song of Solomon, *published in 1977, protagonist Milkman Dead* *searches for self-meaning in his past, finding insight through his southern ancestor Solomon, whom he knows only through childhood songs.* Beloved, *published in 1987, is a "combination of realistic notation and folklore," telling the story of Sethe, a woman who kills her child so that she will not become a slave. In 1992 Morrison published* Jazz, *a novel written so that its structure imitates the form and nature of the music of its title. The prize committee noted that "[t]he book's first lines provide a synopsis, and in reading the novel one becomes aware of a narrator who varies, embellishes and intensifies. The result is a richly complex, sensuously conveyed image of the events, the characters and moods."*

Reactions to the Award

Morrison's initial reaction upon learning of the prize was one of disbelief; she had not yet received official word when a colleague heard the news on television and notified her. Later, Morrison responded with obvious enthusiasm. In an interview published in the Washington Post *on October 8, she said, "I feel good about this, really good. Part of the pleasure is the fact that it was wholly unexpected.... It's not a narrow, personal, subjective delight. I feel it on a very large scale." She went on to refer to other African-American writers, explaining that the prize "feels expanded somehow, like a very large honor, because one can share it with more people than one's neighborhood or one's family. I feel like it's shared among us."*

Other American authors expressed their pleasure at Morrison's award. Alice Walker, winner of the Pulitzer Prize and the American Book Award for The Color Purple, *commented of Morrison, "No one writes more beautifully.... She has consistently explored issues of true complexity and terror and love in the lives of African Americans. Harsh criticism has not dissuaded her. Prizes have not trapped her. She is a writer who well deserves this honor."*

The criticism that Walker mentioned refers to a small number of writers and critics who have argued that Morrison's Nobel Prize, and her Pulitzer Prize of 1988, were granted on the basis of political correctness rather than on the literary merit of her work. When Beloved *was published, it was favored for the National Book Award, but was upset by Larry Heinemann's* Paco's Story; *forty-eight African-American writers protested the award by issuing a statement to the* New York Times, *pointing out that Morrison had never won the National Book Award or the Pulitzer. Morrison then went on to garner the 1988 Pulitzer for* Beloved, *fueling the controversy. The matter continued to irk some writers: Charles Johnson, whose novel* Middle Passage *won the 1990 National Book Award, said of the 1993 Nobel Prize that Morrison "has been the beneficiary of goodwill." However, author John Williams, who was pleased by Morrison's selection, put some of the criticism in perspective when he noted that it often seemed to run along gender lines: "Quite a number of African-American males feel that some of*

Toni's work portrays males negatively. But people never need a reason to trash anyone."

A Call to Preserve Language

Morrison's Nobel lecture centered on the tale of a wise blind woman, visited by children who intend to play a prank by having her guess whether the bird in their hands is alive or dead. The woman's answer—"I don't know ... but what I do know is that it is in your hands"—is, according to Morrison, an assigning of responsibility. She explains that "[t]he blind woman shifts attention away from assertions of power to the instrument through which that power is exercised."

By describing the woman as a "practiced writer" and the bird as language, Morrison then developed the intricate argument that the use of language, as well as the actual existence of language itself, is the entity that creates a society and that enables expression by giving voice to ideas. It is an essential tool, she warned, that must not be lost, or even conveniently disregarded, in modern times: "She [the writer] is convinced that when language dies, out of carelessness, disuse, and absence of esteem ... not only she herself, but all users and makers are accountable for its demise. In her country children have bitten their tongues off and use bullets instead to iterate the voice of speechlessness, ... of language adults have abandoned altogether as a device for grappling with meaning, providing guidance, or expressing love." In addition to violence, Morrison continues, the absence of appropriate expression leads to oppression: "[T]ongue-suicide is not only the choice of children. It is common among the infantile heads of state and power merchants whose evacuated language leaves them with no access to what is left of their human instincts for they speak only to those who obey, or in order to force obedience." The responsibility assigned to the children by the blind woman in the parable, Morrison implied, is the responsibility that must be accepted by all people today; to refuse the use of language as a mediator is to lose our power of peaceful expression.

Morrison explored this theme by analyzing the types of language that exert control through their daily influence on society. Criticizing the intolerant and slow-to-change language of both institutions and individuals, she stated, "Whether it is obscuring state language or the faux-language of mindless media; whether it is the proud but calcified language of the academy or the commodity driven language of science; whether it is the malign language of law-without-ethics, or language designed for the estrangement of minorities, hiding its racist plunder in its literary cheek—it must be rejected, altered and exposed...."

Morrison ended her lecture with a positive stance: if people work together, the mutual expression of ideas through language can bridge the chasm that lies between different beliefs or ideologies. The key, Morrison noted, is sharing and the desire to understand; it is only when the children want to learn from the blind woman, rather than deceive her, that true communication can occur. They say to her, "Passion is never enough; neither is skill. But try.... You, old woman, blessed with blindness, can speak the language that tells us what only language can: how to see without pictures. Language alone protects us from the scariness of things with no names."

Following is the text of Toni Morrison's Nobel lecture, delivered in Stockholm, Sweden, December 7, 1993:

"Once upon a time there was an old woman. Blind but wise." Or was it an old man? A guru, perhaps. Or a griot soothing restless children. I have heard this story, or one exactly like it, in the lore of several cultures.

"Once upon a time there was an old woman. Blind. Wise."

In the version I know the woman is the daughter of slaves, black, American, and lives alone in a small house outside of town. Her reputation for wisdom is without peer and without question. Among her people she is both the law and its transgression. The honor she is paid and the awe in which she is held reach beyond her neighborhood to places far away; to the city where the intelligence of rural prophets is the source of much amusement.

One day the woman is visited by some young people who seem to be bent on disproving her clairvoyance and showing her up for the fraud they believe she is. Their plan is simple: they enter her house and ask the one question the answer to which rides solely on her difference from them, a difference they regard as a profound disability: her blindness. They stand before her, and one of them says, "Old woman, I hold in my hand a bird. Tell me whether it is living or dead."

She does not answer, and the question is repeated. "Is the bird I am holding living or dead?"

Still she doesn't answer. She is blind and cannot see her visitors, let alone what is in their hands. She does not know their color, gender or homeland. She only knows their motive.

The old woman's silence is so long, the young people have trouble holding their laughter.

Finally she speaks and her voice is soft but stern. "I don't know," she says. "I don't know whether the bird you are holding is dead or alive, but what I do know is that it is in your hands. It is in your hands."

Her answer can be taken to mean: if it is dead, you have either found it that way or you have killed it. If it is alive, you can still kill it. Whether it is to stay alive, it is your decision. Whatever the case, it is your responsibility.

For parading their power and her helplessness, the young visitors are reprimanded, told they are responsible not only for the act of mockery but also for the small bundle of life sacrificed to achieve its aims. The blind woman shifts attention away from assertions of power to the instrument through which that power is exercised.

Speculation on what (other than its own frail body) that bird-in-the-hand might signify has always been attractive to me, but especially so now, thinking as I have been, about the work I do that has brought me to this company. So I choose to read the bird as language and the woman as a practiced writer. She is worried about how the language she dreams in, given to her at birth, is handled, put into service, even withheld from her for certain nefarious purposes. Being a writer she thinks of language partly as a system, partly as a living thing over which one has control, but mostly as agency—as an act with consequences. So the question the children put to her: "Is it living or dead?" is not unreal because she thinks of language as susceptible to death, erasure; certainly imperiled and salvageable only by an effort of the will. She believes that if the bird in the hands of her visitors is dead the custodians are responsible for the corpse. For her a dead language is not only one no longer spoken or written, it is unyielding language content to admire its own paralysis. Like statist language, censored and censoring. Ruthless in its policing duties, it has no desire or purpose other than maintaining the free range of its own narcotic narcissism, its own exclusivity and dominance. However, moribund, it is not without effect for it actively thwarts the intellect, stalls conscience, suppresses human potential. Unreceptive to interrogation, it cannot form or tolerate new ideas, shape other thoughts, tell another story, fill baffling silences. Official language smitheryed to sanction ignorance and preserve privilege is a suit of armor, polished to shocking glitter, a husk from which the knight departed long ago. Yet there it is: dumb, predatory, sentimental. Exciting reverence in schoolchildren, providing shelter for despots, summoning false memories of stability, harmony among the public.

She is convinced that when language dies, out of carelessness, disuse, and absence of esteem, indifference or killed by fiat, not only she herself, but all users and makers are accountable for its demise. In her country children have bitten their tongues off and use bullets instead to iterate the voice of speechlessness, of disabled and disabling language, of language adults have abandoned altogether as a device for grappling with meaning, providing guidance, or expressing love. But she knows tongue-suicide is not only the choice of children. It is common among the infantile heads of state and power merchants whose evacuated language leaves them with no access to what is left of their human instincts for they speak only to those who obey, or in order to force obedience.

The systematic looting of language can be recognized by the tendency of its users to forgo its nuanced, complex, mid-wifery properties for menace and subjugation. Oppressive language does more than represent violence; it is violence; does more than represent the limits of knowledge; it limits knowledge. Whether it is obscuring state language or the faux-language of mindless media; whether it is the proud but calcified language of the academy or the commodity driven language of science; whether it is the malign language of law-without-ethics, or language designed for the estrangement of minorities, hiding its racist plunder in its literary cheek—

it must be rejected, altered and exposed. It is the language that drinks blood, laps vulnerabilities, tucks its fascist boots under crinolines of respectability and patriotism as it moves relentlessly toward the bottom line and the bottomed-out mind. Sexist language, racist language, theistic language—all are typical of the policing languages of mastery, and cannot, do not permit new knowledge or encourage the mutual exchange of ideas.

The old woman is keenly aware that no intellectual mercenary, nor insatiable dictator, no paid-for politician or demagogue; no counterfeit journalist would be persuaded by her thoughts. There is and will be rousing language to keep citizens armed and arming; slaughtered and slaughtering in the malls, courthouses, post offices, playgrounds, bedrooms and boulevards; stirring, memorializing language to mask the pity and waste of needless death. There will be more diplomatic language to countenance rape, torture, assassination. There is and will be more seductive, mutant language designed to throttle women, to pack their throats like pate-producing geese with their own unsayable, transgressive words; there will be more of the language of surveillance disguised as research; of politics and history calculated to render the suffering of millions mute; language glamorized to thrill the dissatisfied and bereft into assaulting their neighbors; arrogant pseudoempirical language crafted to lock creative people into cages of inferiority and hopelessness.

Underneath the eloquence, the glamour, the scholarly associations, however, stirring or seductive, the heart of such language is languishing, or perhaps not beating at all—if the bird is already dead.

She has thought about what could have been the intellectual history of any discipline if it had not insisted upon, or been forced into, the waste of time and life that rationalizations for and representations of dominance required—lethal discourses of exclusion blocking access to cognition for both the excluder and the excluded.

The conventional wisdom of the Tower of Babel story is that the collapse was a misfortune. That it was the distraction, or the weight of many languages that precipitated the tower's failed architecture. That one monolithic language would have expedited the building and heaven would have been reached. Whose heaven, she wonders? And what kind? Perhaps the achievement of Paradise was premature, a little hasty if no one could take the time to understand other languages, other views, other narratives. Had they, the heaven they imagined might have been found at their feet. Complicated, demanding yes, but a view of heaven as life; not heaven as postlife.

She would not want to leave her young visitors with the impression that language should be forced to stay alive merely to be. The vitality of language lies in its ability to limn the actual, imagined, and possible lives of its speakers, readers, writers. Although its poise is sometimes in displacing experience it is not a substitute for it. It arcs toward the place where meaning may lie. When a President of the United States thought about the graveyard his country had become, and said "The world will little note nor long remember what we say here. But it will never forget what they did here." His simple words are exhilarating in their life-sustaining properties because they refused to encapsulate the reality of 600,000 dead men in a cataclysmic race war. Refusing to monumentalize, disdaining the "final word," the precise "summing up," acknowledging their "poor power to add or detract," his words signal deference to the uncapturability of the life it mourns. It is the deference that moves her, that recognition that language can never live up to life once and for all. Nor should it. Language can never "pin down" slavery, genocide, war. Nor should it yearn for the arrogance to be able to do so. Its force, its felicity is in its reach toward the ineffable.

Be it grand or slender, burrowing, blasting, or refusing to sanctify; whether it laughs out loud or is a cry without an alphabet, the choice word, the chosen silence, unmolested language surges toward knowledge, not its destruction. But who does not know of literature banned because it is interrogative; discredited because it is critical; erased because alternative? And how many are outraged by the thought of a self-ravaged tongue?

Word-work is sublime, she thinks, because it is generative; it makes meaning that secures our difference, our human difference—the way in which we are like no other life.

We die. That may be the meaning of life. But we do language. That may be the measure of our lives.

"Once upon a time, . . ." visitors ask an old woman a question. Who are they, these children? What did they make of that encounter? What did they hear in those final words: 'The bird is in your hands?" A sentence that gestures toward possibility or one that drops a latch? Perhaps what the children heard was "It's not my problem. I am old, female, black, blind. What wisdom I have now is in knowing I can not help you. The future of language is yours."

They stand there. Suppose nothing was in their hands? Suppose the visit was only a ruse, a trick to get to be spoken to, taken seriously as they have not been before? A chance to interrupt, to violate the adult world, its miasma of discourse about them, for them, but never to them? Urgent questions are at stake, including the one they have asked: "Is the bird we hold living or dead?" Perhaps the question meant: "Could someone tell us what is life? What is death?" No trick at all; no silliness. A straightforward question worthy of the attention of a wise one. An old one. And if the old and wise who have lived life and faced death cannot describe either, who can?

But she does not; she keeps her secret; her good opinion of herself; her gnomic pronouncements; her art without commitment. She keeps her distance, enforces it and retreats into the singularity of isolation, in sophisticated, privileged space.

Nothing, no word follows her declarations of transfer. That silence is deep, deeper than the meaning available in the words she has spoken. It shivers, this silence, and the children, annoyed, fill it with language invented on the spot.

"Is there no speech," they ask her, "no words you can give us that help us break through your dossier of failures? Through the education you have just given us that is no education at all because we are paying close attention to what you have done as well as to what you have said? To the barrier you have erected between generosity and wisdom?

"We have no bird in our hands, living or dead. We have only you and our important question. Is the nothing in our hands something you could not bear to contemplate, to even guess? Don't you remember being young when language was magic without meaning? When what you could say, could not mean? When the invisible was what imagination strove to see? When questions and demands for answers burned so brightly you trembled with fury at not knowing?

"Do we have to begin consciousness with a battle heroines and heroes like you have already fought and lost leaving us with nothing in our hands except what you have imagined is there? Your answer is artful, but its artiness embarrasses us and ought to embarrass you. Your answer is indecent in its self-congratulation. A made-for-television script that makes no sense if there is nothing in our hands.

"Why didn't you reach out, touch us with your soft fingers, delay the sound bite, the lesson, until you knew who we were? Did you so despise our trick, our modus operandi you could not see that we were baffled about how to get your attention? We are young. Unripe. We have heard all our short lives that we have to be responsible. What could that possibly mean in the catastrophe this world has become; where, as a poet said, "nothing needs to be exposed since it is already barefaced." Our inheritance is an affront. You want us to have your old, blank eyes and see only cruelty and mediocrity. Do you think we are stupid enough to perjure ourselves again and again with the fiction of nationhood? How dare you talk to us of duty when we stand waist deep in the toxin of your past?

"You trivialize us and trivialize the bird that is not in our hands. Is there no context for our lives? No song, no literature, no poem full of vitamins, no history connected to experience that you can pass along to help us start strong? You are an adult. The old one, the wise one. Stop thinking about saving your face. Think of our lives and tell us your particularized world. Make up a story. Narrative is radical, creating us at the very moment it is being created. We will not blame you if your reach exceeds your grasp; if love so ignites your words they go down in flames and nothing is left but their scald. Or if, with the reticence of a surgeon's hands, your words suture only the places where blood might flow. We know you can never do it properly—once and for all. Passion is never enough; neither is skill. But try. For our sake and yours forget your name in the street; tell us what the world has been to you in the dark places and in the light. Don't tell us what to believe, what to fear. Show us belief's wide skirt and the stitch that unravels fear's caul. You, old woman, blessed with blindness, can speak the language that tells us what only language can: how to see without pictures. Language alone protects us from the scariness of things with no names. Language alone is meditation.

"Tell us what it is to be a woman so that we may know what it is to be a man. What moves at the margin. What it is to have no home on this place. To be set adrift from the one you knew. What it is to live at the edge of towns that cannot bear your company.

"Tell us about ships turned away from shorelines at Easter, placenta in a field. Tell us about a wagonload of slaves, how they sang so softly their breath was indistinguishable from the falling snow. How they knew from the hunch of the nearest shoulder that the next stop would be their last. How, with hands prayered in their sex they thought of heat, then suns. Lifting their faces, as though it was there for the taking. Turning as though there for the taking. They stop at an inn. The driver and his mate go in with the lamp leaving them humming in the dark. The horse's void steams into the snow beneath its hooves and its hiss and melt is the envy of the freezing slaves.

"The inn door opens: a girl and a boy step away from its light. They climb into the wagon bed. The boy will have a gun in three years, but now he carries a lamp and a jug of warm cider. They pass it from mouth to mouth. The girl offers bread, pieces of meat and something more: a glance into the eyes of the one she serves. One helping for each man, two for each woman. And a look. They look back. The next stop will be their last. But not this one. This one is warmed."

It's quiet again when the children finish speaking, until the woman breaks into the silence.

"Finally," she says, "I trust you now. I trust you with the bird that is not in your hands because you have truly caught it. Look. How lovely it is, this thing we have done—together."

O'LEARY PRESS CONFERENCE ON RADIATION TESTS ON CITIZENS

December 7, 1993

Revelations that the U.S. government had conducted radiation tests on unsuspecting citizens during the cold war era sent waves of shock and indignation across the country. In one of several statements following the disclosure, Department of Energy (DOE) secretary Hazel R. O'Leary on December 7 said she was "appalled, shocked, and deeply saddened" and pledged to undertake a thorough investigation. In her press conference, O'Leary also disclosed that the government had conducted 204 secret underground nuclear tests between 1963 and 1990.

O'Leary directed the DOE (formerly the Atomic Energy Commission) to determine how many radiation experiments had been conducted, to find participants and their survivors, and to investigate the propriety of the research. She also directed the department to declassify millions of documents, including many related to the radiation experiments, and other involved government departments said they would follow suit. As part of the effort, the department set up a toll-free hotline, which was immediately swamped by hundreds of callers. "We've had an unbelievable response to the hotline," said Peter Brush, the department's principal deputy assistant secretary for environment, safety, and health. "It's a much greater volume than we anticipated."

On December 28 O'Leary publicly recommended financial compensation for radiation experiment victims; the next day, several thousand callers telephoned the hotline, according to a department spokesperson.

Growing Revelations About Experiments

Concern over the government's radiation experiments on humans was sparked in November, when the Albuquerque Tribune *published a series of articles on an experiment in which eighteen patients were injected with plutonium. In December the paper reported on a research experiment conducted in Memphis in 1953-1954 in which seven newborn boys, six of them black, were injected with radioactive iron. On December 26 the* Boston Globe *reported that nineteen mentally retarded teen-age boys at a state school in Massachusetts had been exposed to radioactive iron and calcium in their breakfast cereal. The experiments, conducted from 1946 to 1956 by researchers at Harvard University and Massachusetts Institute of Technology (supported by the Atomic Energy Commission), were intended to further scientific understanding of nutrition and metabolism. Consent forms mailed to parents failed to mention that radioactive elements would be used.*

In late December the National Aeronautics and Space Administration announced it was beginning an investigation into a 1964 agreement with the Atomic Energy Commission to conduct human medical research aimed at understanding the risks astronauts might face from exposure to radiation in space. NASA and the commission sponsored research in Oak Ridge, Tennessee, in which radioactive cobalt and cesium were implanted in the walls of a special laboratory. About two hundred patients from civilian hospitals were placed in the room and exposed to what one official called "virtually a sea of radiation."

On January 10, 1994, the Department of Veterans Affairs released documents showing that the government had carried out human radiation experiments at thirty-three VA hospitals during the Cold War (in November 1993, the VA had acknowledged that military patients in fourteen facilities had participated in radiation tests). As a result of the disclosure, Veterans Affairs secretary Jesse Brown ordered all VA hospitals to search for records pertaining to radiation experiments. In another case, reported in January 1994, Navy researchers gave radium treatments to thousands of military personnel in the 1940s and 1950s.

By early 1994 it had become apparent that the experiments were considerably more widespread than originally believed and were conducted not only by the Atomic Energy Commission, the VA, and NASA, but also by the Defense Department, among other agencies. Moreover, contrary to previous assumptions, the tests were carried out not only in the 1940s and 1950s but for years afterward. For example, in 1973 federal scientists exposed prisoners in Oregon and Washington State to increased doses of radiation in order to help determine the risks faced in high-radiation environments. By the end of 1993 and early 1994, government officials were estimating that at least one thousand people had been involved in a variety of radiation experiments, many receiving exposure to potentially threatening doses; some officials forecast that the numbers could go much higher.

Previous Warnings

A 1950 memorandum published in the New York Times *in December 1993 revealed that the U.S. government official who directed radiation experiments had been advised that the research could provoke public criticism. The memorandum, to Dr. Shields Warren, a top official of the*

Atomic Energy Commission, from Dr. Joseph G. Hamilton, a leading radiation biologist who worked for the agency, warned that the tests might be compared to Nazi experiments on concentration camp inmates. The memorandum had been declassified in the early 1970s.

In fact, one of the issues involved in the radiation testing was whether any of the experiments violated the 1947 Nuremberg Code, established after the Nazi war crime trials, which required full, informed, and voluntary consent for all experiments involving human subjects. "We want to make sure the [radiation research] was consistent with whatever ethical guidelines existed at the time," said Brush. "Certainly some of the stuff I've read leads one to question whether it could have been consistent with any established ethics of the time."

The 1993-1994 disclosures of radiation experiments vindicated a 1986 report commissioned by Rep. Edward J. Markey, D-Mass., entitled "American Nuclear Guinea Pigs: Three Decades of Radioactive Experiments on U.S. Citizens." Markey said officials had conducted "repugnant" and "bizarre" experiments on terminally ill patients, prison inmates, and hundreds of other Americans who "might not have retained their full facilities for informed consent." But the report received little attention at the time. Throughout the two-year investigation, Markey said, Reagan administration officials repeatedly attempted to block access to necessary records. "It was an era that sanctified the nuclear arms race," he said. "Except for my subcommittee, there wasn't much going on in officialdom that could echo the criticism I was making."

Testing Continues, Along with Investigations

In testimony before the Senate Governmental Affairs Committee January 25, 1994, O'Leary said the DOE was continuing to conduct more than two hundred radiation-related experiments involving humans, but she asserted that the tests—which involved low-level tracer doses—did not violate ethical standards. She pledged to provide Congress with a full report on the tests. Governmental Affairs Chairman John Glenn, D-Ohio, also called for a report on whether any experiments in which human consent might be questionable were currently being conducted. O'Leary said President Bill Clinton planned to issue a directive to all federal agencies to halt any such experiments. "Only by 'coming clean' on the details of these experiments and separating Cold War habits of secrecy from proper ethics in scientific and medical research will we eventually reduce the bitterness and suspicion which has surrounded the debate on the health effects of radiation," O'Leary said.

In January 1994 the White House announced formation of an interdepartmental advisory task force charged with determining the extent of federal radiation experiments and whether the victims should receive compensation. The group included the secretaries of energy, defense, health and human services, and veterans affairs; the directors of the CIA and Office of Management and Budget; and experts in medicine, science, and ethics.

O'Leary stepped up her crusade on behalf of radiation experiment victims in travels throughout the country to meet with potential victims. Her efforts received considerable praise; but some warned about the need for caution. Several well-known scientists said that the public should not overlook the positive value of some of the experiments and that in many cases the dosages had negligible effects on human health. Physicist Edward Teller, a pioneer in work on the hydrogen bomb, called the surge of new radiation victims "exaggerated." Critics also warned that O'Leary's strong stand in favor of compensation might open the door to a flood of lawsuits against the government. Others questioned why radiation experiment victims should be singled out for potential compensation when other victims of radioactive fallout from open air atomic bomb testing were not. White House communications director Mark Gearan said it was "premature" to state that radiation test victims would be compensated but that President Clinton believed "if Americans are deemed to have been wronged," some recompense should be given.

Following are excerpts from a December 7, 1993, news conference by Department of Energy Secretary Hazel R. O'Leary on steps the department was taking in the aftermath of disclosures of widespread radiation experiments on U.S. citizens during the Cold War era:

SECRETARY O'LEARY: First of all, thank you so much for being here this morning....

We are starting with a simple piece to say that the Cold War is over. Somebody who had a lot spiffier sense of humor than I did late last week decided that maybe we would talk about "coming clean." Later you will decide if we meet that mark.

I guess those who have dealt with the Department over time would know the history, but let me weave it just a bit.

One really must go back to 1942 or 1943 and certainly to the early days of the Atomic Energy Commission. Remember where we were. We were in a struggle for survival as a nation and national security was at the heart of everything that happened in the Department of Energy.

The work to produce that atomic bomb was thought to be the core to ending World War II. All that came after was to keep the nuclear deterrent in place and to be certain to stay technologically ahead and superior. That was what drove the Department of Energy. We were shrouded and clouded in an atmosphere of secrecy. I would even take it a step further. I would call it repression.

As we have looked at what has happened since the falling of the Berlin Wall, many have known and quite a few people working in the Department of Energy, in what was called the Classification Office, also knew it. In August of 1992 they produced a study that moved through the hierarchy of the Department of Energy and came to the conclusion that we now share as a Department entirely that there is much information that can be declassified.

I guess the point to be made is people have looked for the dramatic information, because when you throw up a stack of papers, they are just papers: what's the big deal here? Let me talk to you about the big deal.

The big deal is that we are declassifying the largest amount of information in the history of the Department of Energy. Perhaps most importantly, since I'm aware of the fact there have been other announcements of such magnitude or drama, we are also putting behind it the systems, the technology and the people to get that declassification work done. We'll talk more about that later.

What has led us here? The stuff I've talked about. Overhauling our Cold War policies. Anybody who watched the press yesterday and the beginnings of the discussion between President Clinton and President Yeltsin and those representing our government to talk about even aiming our capability to deliver nuclear weapons away from Russia pretty much tells us where we are in this overhauling of our Cold War policies and even the way we view former combatants or people with whom we had no allegiance or felt no confidence in. We are responding clearly to our stakeholders. I want to point out to you who those stakeholders are. It's hard to start at the right hierarchy, but let me start here.

Those who have been interested for years in denuclearization and those who are interested really in issues involving nonproliferation as well, ensuring that while we are releasing information we are not putting other information in the hands of people from terrorist states who could design a very crude bomb and do damage. That really is a threat that we look at today, but certainly not "the old enemies."

Other stakeholders would clearly be citizens living nearby our nuclear production sites; those who have been involved in the issue of health studies and health effects, our workers, environmentalists, and historians who have been interested in studying the legacy of the Cold War to understand what we can teach each other in terms of science and ethics and morality and governance.

Finally, the changing world also forces us to take a bite out of the bureaucracy, to focus not just on ensuring that you can get in here sooner, but also that we are not now classifying new information. As we wade through the three miles of paper that we must wade through to get this job done we will begin to serve people better.

I thought it was important to point out to you who is impacted by decisions we've made and are acting on today.

I've been taught to always talk about the benefits. So let's do that.

I've already talked about the fact that those of us who are interested in nonproliferation need this information. Why?

First of all, the United States, if it is to lead the march, as our President started this summer, on the effort toward nonproliferation. The United States from its stand as leader in determining and letting the world know what it's able and wanting to release in terms of information to inform the dialogue and to also embrace and deal first hand with issues involving transparency. You've got to be certain that stockpiles being reduced are reduced and the material is where we say it is and it's being managed correctly. By releasing information today and further in June and through the year and in the coming years, I think we will be able to posture ourselves in that leadership position that our President took earlier this summer.

Another benefit. We've got to expose the impact of the Cold War both in terms of its environmental health and safety impacts and also impacts on, if you will, the psyche of the nation. I know that's a strong piece to say.

One of the benefits from openness will be to build public trust. If we in the Department of Energy or any of the other agencies in the Department who have responsibility for these details are to really enter into informed dialogue with the public, there has got to be some trust around that informing, and that only happens when we release information that is necessary for the dialogue.

Finally, as we know more about what is at the sites we can improve the work conditions and the safety of our employees who work there, and that we already know is one of our major vulnerabilities. So the more we know, the more we share, the better we are in a position to do that.

Today you are really here to focus on the first installment. So let me just get right to it in a hurry.

Some of you have been through the press clips. I have been clearly told today and I knew it last month and the month before and I've described it as just having the foot in the tub. This is the beginning and doesn't meet everybody's or anyone's need completely, but we think this is where we need to start.

First of all, information on nuclear testing. We have revealed the fact that fully 20 percent of the tests done were not informed tests. At the time, you must understand, the reason the Department of Energy was not releasing that information was so as to prevent the Russians from being aware and monitoring. The startling fact is that so many, 20 percent of our tests, were unannounced....

Our view was it was time to end the mystery on the nuclear tests and we'll put the facts up. I've told you what the benchmark was. There were 925 total nuclear tests. There were some 204 which were secret. What I am learning from people who were in the community is that that is a shock because, quite frankly, people thought there were 50 percent fewer. The fact that this is now known lets the public assess clearly the impact both to health and safety and again puts us honestly out front as a nation willing to share and hoping that the other nuclear nations will do the same....

There is one final piece that I want to discuss today, and that is the human radiation experiments that have been ongoing. Several questions have been asked of me by some of you and your colleagues in the past week about the experimentations that were played in the press over the last half month and which were very much being discussed in the press back in 1986. We know a little more than you know, but I'm telling you that we are not in a position today to share more.

Let's start first with where we were. What I discovered when some of my colleagues here shared the information with me as the press was beginning to review it once again is that the plutonium experiments involved some 18 people. Some of the names of those individuals have been released. It was my desire today to release the names of the other individuals who were involved in this experimentation. I would like to tell you that what I've been told about these experiments and what I think I know in that process with respect to these 18 citizens of our country leaves me appalled, shocked and deeply saddened.

What I have read about the informed consent that the individuals had before they were subjected to these experiments leads me to understand, on the facts as have been presented, that certainly by standards of today it is apparent that informed consent could not have taken place. . . .

Where we are now is attempting to carefully identify the unnamed individuals who were subjected to those experiments and to now inform their families of what we know and to get from the families an agreement or a nonagreement that we should share those names. First of all, the Privacy Act requires that I do so, and ethics certainly would dictate that as well. So I have no names to release today.

However, I will share with you more details of what we now have come to understand. Approximately 800 human experiments were conducted during the time in question. Nothing that our Administration owns, but I think we owe a great deal of correcting both the public perception and informing about what has occurred. . . .

QUESTION: If you could just tell us a little bit more about what you mean by those experiments?

MS. TARA O'TOOLE (of the DOE): There have clearly been a lot of unique experiments by the Department of Energy and its predecessor agencies. We have not baselined that. We are trying to do that. These experiments were conducted by laboratories and universities and hospitals all over the country. It hasn't been inventoried. One of the things we are trying to figure out is how we get our arms around that and proceed.

SECRETARY O'LEARY: Thanks, Tara.

QUESTION: I was also struck by your description of those 18 experiments. Could you just explain basically what you think took place? . . .

SECRETARY O'LEARY: I can tell you what I know. I hate ever to say what I think because I'll eat it later and a legion of people will be angry with me because I have not spoken carefully.

Let me talk about what I do know. What I do know is what I have been told and what I've read in summary fashion, which is there was an attempt to try and understand the impact of plutonium exposure on people so that folks could understand how much exposure was appropriate for a worker. A clear set of problems. We know today normally how you do that. You very rarely do it using human beings as your research subject.

The other fact I believe I know from summary information is that there was very little follow-up done on those 18 people involved....

QUESTION: Two questions. What is your overall reaction or just gut feeling about the way the Department of Energy has been conducting its business in terms of experimentation and environmental messes? Do you feel this has all been a necessary evil, or are you sort of shocked at what has been going on?

Number two, do you feel that the release of all of this information is going to open the Department up to all kinds of lawsuits from victims?

SECRETARY O'LEARY: What do I feel? What do I think, looking back? This is a very difficult piece, because I have attempted to be very balanced and nonsensational in this.

On the health experiments, I have to tell you that my immediate reaction was that I was appalled and shocked. It just gave me an ache in my gut and my heart....

QUESTION: On the experiments issue, the 800, are you saying there were 800 individuals that were exposed to experiments or there were 800 individuals separate from the 18? And what kind of experiments were those? Did they also involve plutonium?

SECRETARY O'LEARY: I don't know.... The one point I was making early on is I know the 18 are a part of the 800, but beyond that, with respect to the other experiments conducted, I don't know yet.... That's the thing we've got to now begin to unravel....

MS. O'TOOLE: There was a congressional report [Markey report] released in 1986, I believe, that detailed some 800 separate experiments. That is not numbers of people. I think it was around 600 people chronicled in that congressional report. That had involved human experimentation with radiation. Some of these experiments were perfectly legitimate, scientifically valid, and clearly were in accord with the Nuremberg Code of informed consent, and so on and so forth, and involved attempts to use radiation for medical therapeutic purposes.

It is not clear to me that that is the whole universe of human experimentation that DOE and its predecessor agencies were involved in. Some of the human experiments were of a somewhat informal variety such as those that are now being called the plutonium experiments and may be buried in this mile-high stack of documents that we haven't really delved into in detail.

The plutonium experiments, as far as I know now, were somewhat isolated. The plutonium experiments' purpose was to track the metabolism of plutonium in the human body. Not really to figure out the adverse effects the plutonium might have, but to figure out how fast and in what way humans excreted plutonium as an aid to informing then the AEC on how to control worker doses of plutonium or exposures to plutonium....

There are all manner of experiments, some of which are fairly disturbing, chronicled in that congressional report. Some, as I said, are perfectly legitimate and we are trying to figure out what the total universe of human experimentation might be and where it is. None of this data resides in the Department of Energy headquarters building. It's in laboratories, it's in hospitals, and so on and so forth. It is going to be subject, we expect, at least in part to medical confidentiality rules, Privacy Act rules, and so on and so forth. And we are going to try and find out as much about it as we can and let you know....

amount the plutonium might have, [illegible] to figure out how [illegible] and [illegible] what way humans excrete plutonium as an aid to interpreting then the AEC on how to control work [illegible] doses of plutonium or exposures to plutonium. There are a small number of experiments, some of which were fairly disturbing, chronicled in that congressional report. Some, as I said, are perfectly legitimate and we are trying to figure out what the total universe of human experimentation might be and where it is. Some of this data resides in the Department of Energy headquarters building, it's in laboratories, it's in notebooks, and so on and so forth. It's supposed to be subject [illegible] tees in part to medical [illegible] Privacy Act rules, and [illegible] [illegible]. And we're trying to [illegible] find out as much about it as [illegible] and let you know.

CLINTON LETTER TO CONGRESS ON RENEWAL OF TRADE AGREEMENT

December 15, 1993

After a marathon negotiating session, trade delegates representing the 117 member nations that were parties to the General Agreement on Tariffs and Trade (GATT) hammered out a far-reaching pact that, when implemented, would be the largest expansion of international trading rules enacted to date. After seven years of crisis-filled talks, participants agreed to bring agriculture, financial services, patents, and other intellectual property under the purview of GATT trading regulations and to eliminate border taxes on thousands of products.

In sending his message of approval to Congress on December 15, President Bill Clinton said that the measure—which would sharply reduce trade barriers such as tariffs, import quotas, and export subsidies— would produce expanded trade and "add as much as $100 billion to $200 billion per year to our economy once it is fully phased in" while creating "hundreds of thousands of good-paying American jobs." For the United States, the pact was expected to lead to increased exports of agricultural products and greater copyright and patent protections for high-tech industries, such as computers and semiconductors. But some, including textile and drug manufacturers, might suffer setbacks.

Major Features

The so-called Uruguay Round of negotiations to revise GATT began in September 1986 in Punta del Este, Uruguay. The resulting agreement, concluded in Geneva, was the seventh renegotiation of GATT, which was created as a voluntary agreement at the end of World War II and governs most world trade. The new 550-page agreement, which must be approved by Congress and the governments of the 116 other participants in the negotiations, was originally slated to be concluded in 1990. Completion of the talks, however, was stalled by several thorny issues, among them a major dispute between the United States and Europe over farm subsi-

dies. However, acting on a congressionally imposed December 15 deadline, U.S. trade negotiators and the rest of the participants hammered out an accord at the last minute.

In general, the agreement would reduce worldwide tariffs by more than one-third, cut agriculture subsidies, and phase out quotas on textile imports. At the same time, the pact would preserve the right of the United States to retaliate using U.S. laws designed to block imports "dumped" on domestic markets at unfairly low prices.

Major features of the changes in existing trade policies included the following:

Tariffs: Tariffs would be cut on approximately 85 percent of world trade and eliminated or significantly reduced on a broad range of products.

Agriculture: Trade in farm commodities would be covered under GATT for the first time. Governments would have to reduce the amount spent on agriculture subsidies by an average of 36 percent; the total volume of agricultural products exported with the help of subsidies would have to be reduced by 21 percent.

Textiles: The Multi-Fiber Arrangement, under which industrial nations had imposed quotas on textile imports from developing countries for more than thirty years, would be phased out over ten years, with protection afforded the U.S. textile industry.

Anti-dumping: The United States and Europe would preserve existing authority to use domestic anti-dumping laws to impose fines or countervailing duties against countries that exported goods at prices below costs. Disputes arising on dumping matters would be settled under a new, binding multilateral dispute-settlement mechanism.

Other provisions included applying GATT rules to the world market in services, valued at almost $1 trillion annually, although U.S. negotiators failed to win multilateral agreements to open markets in specific service sectors, such as shipping, banking, and insurance. GATT rules would also be extended to protect intellectual property—such as computer programs, semiconductor chip designs, films, books, and music—from piracy. However, a major disappointment for the movie and television industry was the U.S. failure to break a European quota system that limited foreign programming, one of America's most lucrative areas of export.

Finally, the agreement would replace the existing GATT structure with a World Trade Organization, a permanent body with greater authority to force member nations to comply with the Uruguay Round decisions.

Need for Congressional Action

The GATT agreement was submitted one month after Clinton won a hard-fought victory to secure congressional passage of the North American Free Trade Agreement (NAFTA). The administration would return to Congress in 1994 for what many observers predicted would be rela-

tively easy—at least compared with the NAFTA battle—approval of the GATT pact. (NAFTA approval, p. 953)

Under "fast-track" procedures governing congressional action on trade agreements, Clinton was required to sign the agreement by April 15, 1994. Then, after an unspecified period to consult with Capitol Hill on an implementing bill, he must submit it to Congress, where neither the agreement nor the implementing legislation could be amended. "I don't see a lot of controversy in this. It's not going to be an election issue," said Rep. Robert T. Matsui, D-Calif., a leader in the NAFTA fight. "There's not a lot of passion for it, but there's not a lot of reasons to vote it down. To vote it down would be catastrophic."

Some observers predicted that the biggest battle during the drafting of implementing legislation would concern provisions that preserved U.S. anti-dumping laws. Although the language was aimed at protecting steel and other domestic industries from unfairly priced imports, free traders expressed apprehension that an overly broad anti-dumping provision could allow foreign countries to restrict U.S. exports.

"In the end, confronted with a firm deadline after seven years of quarreling, the trade negotiators in Geneva arrived at an agreement," said the Washington Post *in a December 16 editorial. "It will not turn out to be ideal.... There are a number of disappointments. But a lot has been accomplished ... and there's a high probability that ... there will be a strong case to enact it into American law when Congress takes it up [in 1994]."*

Following is the text of the letter sent by President Clinton to congressional leaders on December 15, 1993, submitting the agreements reached by participants in the General Agreement on Tariffs and Trade, which provided for the largest expansion of world trading rules in history:

Dear Mr. Speaker:

I believe that we have created a unique opportunity to build an international trading system that will ensure the orderly and equitable expansion of world trade and contribute to the prosperity of the United States in coming generations. After seven long years the conclusion of the Uruguay Round of multilateral trade negotiations is at hand. The Round will result in the largest, most comprehensive set of trade agreements in history. With the conclusion of the Round, we will have successfully achieved the objectives that Congress set for the United States in the negotiations.

In accordance with section 1103(a)(1) of the Omnibus Trade and Competitiveness Act of 1988, as amended ("Act"), I am pleased to notify the House of Representatives and the Senate of my intent to enter into the trade agreements resulting from the Uruguay Round of multilateral trade negotiations under the auspices of the General Agreement on Tariffs and Trade. These agreements are listed and identified below and are more fully described in an attachment to this letter.

The United States can and must compete in the global economy. In many areas of economic activity we are already world leaders and we are taking measures at home to strengthen further our ability to compete. In section 1101 of the Act the Congress set as the first overall U.S. negotiating objectives for the Uruguay Round more open, equitable and reciprocal market access. I am particularly pleased to advise you that the Uruguay Round results will provide an unprecedented level of new *market access* opportunities for U.S. goods and services exports. In the attachment to this letter is a summary description of the agreements on market access for goods and services that we have achieved in the Round. Of special note are the number of areas where we and our major trading partners have each agreed to reduce tariffs on goods to zero. The schedules of commitments reflecting market access in services cover a wide range of service sectors that are of great interest to our exporting community.

The *Agreement on Agriculture* will achieve, as Congress directed, more open and fair conditions of trade in agricultural commodities by establishing specific commitments to reduce foreign export subsidies, tariffs and non-tariff barriers and internal supports.

The *Agreement on Textiles and Clothing* provides for trade in textiles and apparel to be fully integrated into the GATT for the first time. As a result, trade in textiles will be subject to the same disciplines as other sectors. This transition will take place gradually over an extended period. At the same time, the agreement provides an improved safeguards mechanism. It also requires apparel exporting countries to lower specific tariff and non-tariff barriers, providing new market opportunities for U.S. exporters of textile and apparel goods. The agreement contributes to the achievement of the U.S. negotiating objectives of expanding the coverage of the GATT while getting developing countries to provide reciprocal benefits.

In fulfillment of the second overall U.S. negotiating objective, the reduction or elimination of barriers and other trade-distorting policies and practices, the Uruguay Round package includes a number of agreements to reduce or eliminate non-tariff barriers to trade. These agreements, which are described in the attachment, address *Safeguards, Antidumping, Subsidies and Countervailing Measures, Trade-Related Investment Measures, Import Licensing Procedures, Customs Valuation, Preshipment Inspection, Rules of Origin, Technical Barriers to Trade,* and *Sanitary and Phytosanitary Measures.* The agreements strengthen existing GATT rules and, for the first time in the GATT, discipline non-tariff barriers in the areas of investment, rules of origin and preshipment inspection. The agreements preserve the ability of the United States to impose measures necessary to protect the health and safety of our citizens and our environment and to enforce vigorously our laws on unfair trade practices.

The *Agreement on Government Procurement* will provide new opportunities for U.S. exporters as a result of the decision to expand the coverage of the agreement to government procurement of services and construction; we will, however, only extend the full benefits of the agreement to those countries that provide satisfactory coverage of their own procurement. Negotiations on improvements in the *Agreement on Trade in Civil Aircraft* and on a *Multilateral Steel Agreement* are continuing. These agreements should provide for more effective disciplines and reduce or eliminate trade-distorting policies and practices in two industries of importance to our economy. I will fully consult with the Congress throughout these negotiations, and plan to enter into these agreements if the negotiations produce results that are acceptable to the United States.

As a result of the *Agreement on Trade Related Intellectual Property Rights (TRIPS)* and the *General Agreement on Trade in Services (GATS),* we will now have for the first time internationally agreed rules covering areas of trade of enormous importance to the United States. These agreements represent a major step forward in establishing a more effective system of international trading disciplines and procedures. GATS contains legally enforceable provisions dealing with both cross-border trade and investment in services and sectoral annexes on financial services, labor movement, telecommunications and aviation services. More than 50 countries have submitted schedules of commitments on market access for services. The TRIPS agreement provides for the establishment of standards for the protection of a full range of intellectual property rights and for the enforcement of those standards both internationally and at the border.

The Uruguay Round has produced a number of other agreements that will create a more effective system of international trading disciplines and procedures.

The *Understanding on Rules and Procedures Governing the Settlement of Disputes* will provide for a more effective and expeditious dispute resolution mechanism and procedures which will enable better enforcement of United States rights. Congress identified the establishment of such a system as the first principal U.S. trade negotiating objective for the Round. The procedures complement U.S. laws for dealing with foreign unfair trade practices such as section 301 of the Trade Act of 1974.

The *Agreement Establishing the World Trade Organization [WTO]* will facilitate the implementation of the trade agreements reached in the Uruguay Round by bringing them under one institutional umbrella, requiring full participation of all countries in the new trading system and providing a permanent forum to address new issues facing the international trading system. The WTO text recognizes the importance of protecting the environment while expanding world trade; negotiators have also agreed to develop a work program on trade and the environment and will recommend an appropriate institutional structure to carry out this work program. Creation of the WTO will contribute to the achievement of the second principal U.S. negotiating objective of improving the operation of the GATT and multilateral trade agreements.

The U.S. objective of improving the operation of the GATT is also furthered by a number of understandings, decisions and declarations regarding the GATT and its operations. The *Trade Policy Review Mechanism* will enhance surveillance of members' trade policies. The *Understandings Concerning Interpretation of Specific Articles of the General Agreement on Tariffs and Trade 1994 (GATT 1994)* concern the Interpretation of Articles II:l(b), XVII, XXIV, XXVIII and XXXV, and Balance-of-Payments Provisions. There is also an *Understanding in Respect of Waivers of Obligations Under the General Agreement on Tariffs and Trade 1994.*

The *Ministerial Decisions and Declarations* state the views and objectives of Uruguay Round participants on a number of issues relating to the operation of the global trading system, provide for the continuation of the improvements to the dispute settlement system that became effective in 1989 and deal with other matters concerning the dispute settlement system. The Ministerial Decisions and Declarations that are now proposed for adoption are described in the attachment. At this time, implementing legislation does not appear to be necessary for these instruments.

I will continue to consult closely with the Congress as we conclude the Round. There are a few areas of significance that we were unable to resolve at this time. In order to ensure more open, equitable and reciprocal market access, in certain agreements we have made U.S. obligations contingent on receiving satisfactory commitments from other countries, and we will continue to work to ensure that the best possible agreement for the United States is achieved. I will not enter into any agreement unless I am satisfied that U.S. interests are protected. With regard to entertainment issues, we were unable to overcome our differences with our major trading partners, and we agreed to disagree. We will continue to negotiate, however, and until we reach a satisfactory agreement, we think we can best advance the interests of our entertainment industry by reserving all our legal rights to respond to policies that discriminate in these areas.

In accordance with the procedures in the Act, the United States will not enter into the agreements outlined above until April 15, 1994. After the agreements have been signed, they will be submitted for Congressional approval, together with whatever legislation and administrative actions may be necessary or appropriate to implement the agreements in the United States. The agreements will not take effect with respect to the United States, and will have no domestic legal force, until the Congress has approved them and enacted any appropriate implementing legislation.

Sincerely,
William J. Clinton

SOUTH AFRICAN CONSTITUTION

December 22, 1993

A major step on the road from apartheid to democracy in South Africa was taken on December 22, when the nation's parliament ratified a new interim constitution that would provide power-sharing between the nation's minority white and overwhelmingly majority black populations.

Ratification came a little over two months after South African president F. W. de Klerk, who is white, and Nelson Mandela, leader of the African National Congress (ANC), were awarded the Nobel Peace Prize for their efforts to bring an end to racial strife in South Africa. The movement away from apartheid had begun in 1990, when de Klerk freed Mandela, the nation's leading political prisoner, and inaugurated a series of measures designed to dismantle major racial segregation laws. De Klerk won a significant victory on March 18, 1992, when a solid majority of the nation's whites voted in favor of negotiating a new constitution. (Nobel Peace Prize, p. 000; background and constitutional referendum, Historic Documents of 1992, p. 283)

After stop-and-start talks, negotiators reached agreement on the document in the early morning hours of November 18. "We are at the beginning of a new era," declared Mandela, who was almost certain to become the country's first black president after elections scheduled for April 27—the first in which all races would participate. De Klerk said the new, interim constitution fulfilled his vision of a country "where freedom, peace, and justice could walk hand in hand."

"No force can now stop or even delay our emancipation from the pain and the shame of our racist past," said Ismail Mohamed, the Indian judge who presided over the constitutional negotiations. (Mohamed was the only nonwhite judge in a country where whites constituted less than 15 percent of the population.) Three weeks later, the nation marked another milestone: on December 7 black South Africans began exercising power at the national level for the first time as members of the newly

created Transitional Executive Council. The council, comprised of representatives from the nineteen parties to the constitutional negotiations, was to oversee government policy leading up to the election of a new, nonracial parliament in April 1994.

Constitution's Major Provisions

The agreement on the interim constitution, providing for a five-year "national unity" government and a bill of rights aimed at protecting minority rights, came after an often contentious, three-year process. Negotiators struggled to find accommodations that would satisfy the country's disenfranchised black population and simultaneously reassure the whites who had ruled South Africa since its creation as an independent nation in 1910.

Opening with a preamble proclaiming the need to "create a new order" that ensures "equality between men and women of all races," the 220-page interim charter covers subjects ranging from the structure of the new government and individual rights to official languages and pensions for former officeholders and anti-apartheid figures.

The interim constitution's principal chapters provided for the following:

Fundamental Rights. *Includes broad provisions for individual rights, including freedom of speech and press; freedom of religion and conscience; political rights; right of privacy, including limits on search and seizure; right to travel; right to "fair labor practices," including the right to strike; property rights; right to counsel in legal proceedings. Prohibits torture and cruel, inhuman, or degrading punishment. Permits temporary state of emergency when declared by two-thirds vote of National Assembly; permits detention without trial with restrictions.*

Parliament. *Establishes a four-hundred-member National Assembly popularly elected from national and regional party lists on basis of proportional representation; a ninety-member Senate, elected by each of nine provincial legislatures. Bills to be passed by a simple majority of each house or a majority of the total number of members of both houses.*

President/Deputy Presidents. *Establishes the position of executive president to be elected by the National Assembly; executive deputy presidents to be designated by second largest party or any party that obtains eighty or more seats in National Assembly. President to have broad executive powers.*

Cabinet. *Calls for a multiparty cabinet of about twenty-seven members composed according to proportional representation of those parties that obtain 5 percent or more of the vote in the election; various portfolios to be designated by the president.*

Judiciary. *Provides existing court structure to remain largely intact, with addition of an eleven-member Constitutional Court to have final jurisdiction on interpretation, protection, and enforcement of constitution at all levels of government; members of Constitutional Court to be* *appointed by the president for nonrenewable seven-year terms from list designed by new Judicial Service Commission.*

Provinces. *Creates nine provinces with legislatures, premiers, and multiparty executive councils; provincial legislatures to have concurrent power with national government over many areas, including police, primary and secondary education, housing, health, and welfare.*

Constitutional Assembly. *Calls on the National Assembly and Senate sitting together as Constitutional Assembly to draft final constitution within two years; approval of final constitution requires two-thirds majority or 60 percent of voters in referendum. National unity government to function until next election, to be held April 27, 1999.*

Some observers were critical of the numerous compromises contained in the arrangement. "The future government will be so constrained by the political compromises that have been arrived at that the government of national unity is going to be translated into a government of political paralysis," said Eugene Nyati, an independent political analyst in Johannesburg. Other observers, however, said they believed there were advantages to the forced coalition formula. "They still have to rule in a coalition," said Pauline Baker, an expert on South Africa at the Aspen Institute in Washington, D.C. "You don't get a winner-take-all mentality."

Outlook: Continued Violence, Political Uncertainties

Despite the undoubted accomplishments, South Africa still faced political dangers between ratification of the constitution and the April 1994 elections. Most troublesome was the threat of violence from a holdout alliance of conservative whites, the black Inkatha Freedom party of Zulu chief Mangosuthu Buthelezei, and leaders of black "homelands" being abolished under the new constitution.

"There's an enormous amount of violence in South African society that will inhibit the easy run-up to elections and make dangerous the development of democracy," said Robert Rotberg, a Harvard University professor of African politics. Indeed, the country's traditions of violence and intolerance, the limited education of many of the newly enfranchised black voters, and the disaffection of white right-wingers and some black political leaders made a truly free election unlikely.

In their remarks after parliament's approval of the new constitution, Mandela and de Klerk both acknowledged the threat of violence. De Klerk promised that the government would use force to prevent the holdout groups from disrupting the elections. For his part, Mandela issued a statement urging "all South Africans, regardless of race, creed or gender, [to] take hands and work together to bring an end to the terrible violence that is tearing our country apart."

The new government that emerged after the April 1994 elections would confront an agenda of pressing social, economic, and political issues that would strain the most stable of democracies. "It's inevitably going to face severe difficulties," said Steven Friedman, director of the Center of Policy Studies in Johannesburg, the nation's largest city and financial center. Despite the acknowledged risks, however, most observers in and out of South Africa expressed optimism about the future. "My vote will bring an end to the humiliation and injustices of apartheid which we have suffered for decades," wrote Reuters correspondent Rich Mkhondo, a black South African. "[O]ur hopes are high."

Following are excerpts from the Constitution of the Republic of South Africa, approved by the parliament December 22, 1993, establishing a new coalition government, providing guarantees of freedoms, and allowing the nation's black majority to vote for the first time:

Preamble

In humble submission to Almighty God,

We, the people of South Africa declare that—

WHEREAS there is a need to create a new order in which all South Africans will be entitled to a common South African citizenship in a sovereign and democratic constitutional state in which there is equality between men and women and people of all races so that all citizens shall be able to enjoy and exercise their fundamental rights and freedoms;

AND WHEREAS in order to secure the achievement of this goal, elected representatives of all the people of South Africa should be mandated to adopt a new Constitution in accordance with a solemn pact recorded as Constitutional Principles;

AND WHEREAS it is necessary for such purposes that provision should be made for the promotion of national unity and the restructuring and continued governance of South Africa while an elected Constitutional Assembly draws up a final Constitution;

NOW THEREFORE the following provisions are adopted as the Constitution of the Republic of South Africa:

Chapter 1

Constituent and Formal Provisions

Republic of South Africa

1. (1) The Republic of South Africa shall be one, sovereign state....

Supremacy of the Constitution

4. (1) This Constitution shall be the supreme law of the Republic and any law or act inconsistent with its provisions shall, unless

otherwise provided expressly or by necessary implication in this Constitution, be of no force and effect to the extent of the inconsistency.

(2) This Constitution shall bind all legislative, executive and judicial organs of state at all levels of government.

Chapter 2

Citizenship and Franchise

Citizenship

5. (1) There shall be a South African citizenship.

(2) South African citizenship and the acquisition, loss and restoration of South African citizenship shall, subject to section 20 read with section 33(1), be regulated by an Act of Parliament.

(3) Every person who is a South African citizen shall, subject to this Constitution, be entitled to enjoy all rights, privileges and benefits of South African citizenship, and shall be subject to all duties, obligations and responsibilities of South African citizenship as are accorded or imposed upon him or her in terms of this Constitution or an Act of Parliament.

The Franchise

6. Every person who is—

(a) (i) a South African citizen; or

(ii) not such a citizen but who in terms of an Act of Parliament has been accorded the right to exercise the franchise;

(b) of or over the age of 18 years; and

(c) not subject to any disqualifications as may be prescribed by law, shall be entitled to vote in elections of the National Assembly, a provincial legislature or a local government and in referenda or plebiscites contemplated in this Constitution, in accordance with and subject to the laws. . . .

Chapter 3

Fundamental Rights

Application

7. (1) This Chapter shall bind all legislative and executive organs of state at all levels of government. . . .

Equality

8. (1) Every person shall have the right to equality before the law and to equal protection of the law.

(2) No person shall be unfairly discriminated against, directly or indirectly, and, without derogating from the generality of this provision, on one or more of the following grounds in particular: race, gender, sex, ethnic or social origin, colour, sexual orientation, age, disability, religion, conscience, belief, culture or language.

(3) (a) This section shall not preclude measures designed to achieve the adequate protection and advancement of persons or groups or categories of persons disadvantaged by unfair discrimination, in order to enable their full and equal enjoyment of all rights and freedoms.

(b) Every person or community dispossessed of rights in land before the commencement of this Constitution under any law which would have been inconsistent with subsection (2) had that subsection been in operation at the time of the dispossession, shall be entitled to claim restitution of such rights subject to and in accordance with sections 121, 122 and 123.

(4) *Prima facie* proof of discrimination on any of the grounds specified in subsection (2) shall be presumed to be sufficient proof of unfair discrimination as contemplated in that subsection, until the contrary is established.

Life

9. Every person shall have the right to life.

Human Dignity

10. Every person shall have the right to respect for and protection of his or her dignity.

Freedom and Security of the Person

11. (1) Every person shall have the right to freedom and security of the person, which shall include the right not to be detained without trial.

(2) No person shall be subject to torture of any kind, whether physical, mental or emotional, nor shall any person be subject to cruel, inhuman or degrading treatment or punishment.

Servitude and Forced Labour

12. No person shall be subject to servitude or forced labour.

Privacy

13. Every person shall have the right to his or her personal privacy, which shall include the right not to be subject to searches of his or her person, home or property, the seizure of private possessions or the violation of private communications.

Religion, Belief and Opinion

14. (1) Every person shall have the right to freedom of conscience, religion, thought, belief and opinion, which shall include academic freedom in institutions of higher learning....

Freedom of Expression

15. (1) Every person shall have the right to freedom of speech and expression, which shall include freedom of the press and other media, and the freedom of artistic creativity and scientific research.
(2) All media financed by or under the control of the state shall be regulated in a manner which ensures impartiality and the expression of a diversity of opinion.

Assembly, Demonstration and Petition

16. Every person shall have the right to assemble and demonstrate with others peacefully and unarmed, and to present petitions.

Freedom of Association

17. Every person shall have the right to freedom of association.

Freedom of Movement

18. Every person shall have the right to freedom of movement anywhere within the national territory.

Residence

19. Every person shall have the right freely to choose his or her place of residence anywhere in the national territory.

Citizens' Rights

20. Every citizen shall have the right to enter, remain in and leave the Republic, and no citizen shall without justification be deprived of his or her citizenship.

Political Rights

21. (1) Every citizen shall have the right—
(a) to form, to participate in the activities of and to recruit members for a political party;
(b) to campaign for a political party or cause; and
(c) freely to make political choices.
(2) Every citizen shall have the right to vote, to do so in secret and to stand for election to public office.

Access to Court

22. Every person shall have the right to have justiciable disputes settled

by a court of law or, where appropriate, another independent and impartial forum.

Access to Information

23. Every person shall have the right of access to all information held by the state or any of its organs at any level of government in so far as such information is required for the exercise or protection of any of his or her rights.

Administrative Justice

24. Every person shall have the right to—
    (a) lawful administrative action where any of his or her rights or interests is affected or threatened;
    (b) procedurally fair administrative action where any of his or her rights or legitimate expectations is affected or threatened;
    (c) be furnished with reasons in writing for administrative action which affects any of his or her rights or interests unless the reasons for such action have been made public; and
    (d) administrative action which is justifiable in relation to the reasons given for it where any of his or her rights is affected or threatened.

Detained, Arrested and Accused Persons

25. (1) Every person who is detained . . . shall have the right—
    (a) to be informed promptly in a language which he or she understands of the reason for his or her detention;
    (b) to be detained under conditions consonant with human dignity, which shall include at least the provision of adequate nutrition, reading material and medical treatment at state expense;
    (c) to consult with a legal practitioner of his or her choice, to be informed of this right promptly and, where substantial injustice would otherwise result, to be provided with the services of a legal practitioner by the state;
    (d) to be given the opportunity to communicate with, and to be visited by, his or her spouse or partner, next-of-kin, religious counsellor and a medical practitioner of his or her choice; and
    (e) to challenge the lawfulness of his or her detention in person before a court of law and to be released if such detention is unlawful.

    (2) Every person arrested for the alleged commission of an offence shall, in addition to the rights which he or she has as a detained person, have the right—

(a) promptly to be informed, in a language which he or she understands, that he or she has the right to remain silent and to be warned of the consequences of making any statement;
(b) as soon as it is reasonably possible, but not later than 48 hours after the arrest or, if the said period of 48 hours expires outside ordinary court hours or on a day which is not a court day, the first court day after such expiry, to be brought before an ordinary court of law and to be charged or to be informed of the reason for his or her further detention, failing which he or she shall be entitled to be released;
(c) not to be compelled to make a confession or admission which could be used in evidence against him or her; and
(d) to be released from detention with or without bail, unless the interests of justice require otherwise.

(3) Every accused person shall have the right to a fair trial, which shall include the right—
(a) to a public trial before an ordinary court of law within a reasonable time after having been charged;
(b) to be informed with sufficient particularity of the charge;
(c) to be presumed innocent and to remain silent during plea proceedings or trial and not to testify during trial;
(d) to adduce and challenge evidence, and not to be a compellable witness against himself or herself;
(e) to be represented by a legal practitioner of his or her choice or, where substantial injustice would otherwise result, to be provided with legal representation at state expense, and to be informed of these rights;
(f) not to be convicted of an offence in respect of any act or omission which was not an offence at the time it was committed, and not to be sentenced to a more severe punishment than that which was applicable when the offence was committed;
(g) not to be tried again for any offence of which he or she has previously been convicted or acquitted;
(h) to have recourse by way of appeal or review to a higher court than the court of first instance;
(i) to be tried in a language which he or she understands or, failing this, to have the proceedings interpreted to him or her; and
(j) to be sentenced within a reasonable time after conviction.

Economic Activity

26. (1) Every person shall have the right freely to engage in economic activity and to pursue a livelihood anywhere in the national territory.

(2) Subsection (l) shall not preclude measures designed to promote the protection or the improvement of the quality of life, economic growth, human development, social justice, basic conditions of employment, fair labour practices or equal opportunity for all, provided such measures are justifiable in an open and democratic society based on freedom and equality.

Labour Relations

27. (1) Every person shall have the right to fair labour practices.

(2) Workers shall have the right to form and join trade unions, and employers shall have the right to form and join employers' organisations.

(3) Workers and employers shall have the right to organise and bargain collectively.

(4) Workers shall have the right to strike for the purpose of collective bargaining.

(5) Employers' recourse to the lock-out for the purpose of collective bargaining shall not be impaired, subject to section 33(l).

Property

28. (1) Every person shall have the right to acquire and hold rights in property and, to the extent that the nature of the rights permits, to dispose of such rights.

(2) No deprivation of any rights in property shall be permitted otherwise than in accordance with a law.

(3) Where any rights in property are expropriated pursuant to a law referred to in subsection (2), such expropriation shall be permissible for public purposes only and shall be subject to the payment of agreed compensation or, failing agreement, to the payment of such compensation and within such period as may be determined by a court of law as just and equitable, taking into account all relevant factors, including, in the case of the determination of compensation, the use to which the property is being put, the history of its acquisition, its market value, the value of the investments in it by those affected and the interests of those affected.

Environment

29. Every person shall have the right to an environment which is not detrimental to his or her health or well-being....

Children

30. (1) Every child shall have the right—

(a) to a name and nationality from birth;

(b) to parental care;

(c) to security, basic nutrition and basic health and social services;
(d) not to be subject to neglect or abuse; and
(e) not to be subject to exploitative labour practices nor to be required or permitted to perform work which is hazardous or harmful to his or her education, health or well-being....

Language and Culture

31. Every person shall have the right to use the language and to participate in the cultural life of his or her choice.

Education

32. Every person shall have the right—
    (a) to basic education and to equal access to educational institutions;
    (b) to instruction in the language of his or her choice where this is reasonably practicable; and
    (c) to establish, where practicable, educational institutions based on a common culture, language or religion, provided that there shall be no discrimination on the ground of race.

Limitation

33. (1) The rights entrenched in this Chapter may be limited by law of general application, provided that such limitation—
    (a) shall be permissible only to the extent that it is—
        (i) reasonable; and
        (ii) justifiable in an open and democratic society based on freedom and equality; and
    (b) shall not negate the essential content of the right in question....

State of Emergency and Suspension

34. (1) A state of emergency shall be proclaimed prospectively under an Act of Parliament, and shall be declared only where the security of the Republic is threatened by war, invasion, general insurrection or disorder or at a time of national disaster, and if the declaration of a state of emergency is necessary to restore peace or order.

(2) The declaration of a state of emergency and any action taken, including any regulation enacted, in consequence thereof, shall be of force for a period of not more than 21 days, unless it is extended for a period of not longer than three months or consecutive periods of not longer than three months at a time, by resolution of the National Assembly adopted by a majority of at least two-thirds of all its members.

(3) Any superior court shall be competent to enquire into the

validity of a declaration of a state of emergency, any extension thereof, and any action taken, including any regulation enacted, under such declaration.

(4) The rights entrenched in this Chapter may be suspended only in consequence of the declaration of a state of emergency, and only to the extent necessary to restore peace or order....

Chapter 4

Parliament

Constitution of Parliament

36. Parliament shall consist of the National Assembly and the Senate.

Legislative Authority of Republic

37. The legislative authority of the Republic shall, subject to this Constitution, vest in Parliament, which shall have the power to make laws for the Republic in accordance with this Constitution.

Duration of Parliament

38. (1) Parliament as constituted in terms of the first election under this Constitution shall ... continue for five years as from the date of the first sitting of the National Assembly under this Constitution....

Elections

39. (1) Upon a dissolution of Parliament ... the President shall by proclamation in the *Gazette*—

(a) call an election of the National Assembly, which election shall take place within 90 days after the dissolution of Parliament on a date or dates specified in the proclamation; and

(b) request parties represented in the provincial legislatures to nominate persons as senators for the respective provinces....

The National Assembly

Composition of National Assembly

40. (1) The National Assembly shall consist of 400 members elected in accordance with the system of proportional representation of voters....

(2) A person nominated as a candidate for election to the National Assembly on a regional list contemplated in Schedule 2 shall at the time of the nomination be ordinarily resident in the province in respect of which that regional list applies.

Speaker and Deputy Speaker of National Assembly

41. (1) At its first sitting after it has been convened . . . and after the election of the President, the National Assembly, with the Chief Justice or a judge of the Supreme Court designated by him or her acting as the chairperson, shall elect one of its members to be the Speaker, and shall thereafter elect another of its members to be the Deputy Speaker. . . .

(7) The Speaker, the Deputy Speaker or any other member of the National Assembly designated for that purpose in terms of the rules and orders, shall preside over sittings of the National Assembly.

(8) While presiding at a sitting of the National Assembly, the Speaker, Deputy Speaker or other member presiding shall not have a deliberative vote, but shall have and exercise a casting vote in the case of an equality of votes.

(9) The Speaker or Deputy Speaker shall vacate his or her office if he or she ceases to be a member of the National Assembly, and may be removed from office by resolution of the National Assembly, and may resign by lodging his or her resignation in writing with the Secretary to Parliament.

(10) If the office of Speaker or Deputy Speaker becomes vacant, the National Assembly, under the chairpersonship of the Chief Justice or a judge . . . shall elect a member to fill the vacancy: Provided that the Speaker shall in such event preside at the election of the Deputy Speaker.

Qualification for Membership of National Assembly

42. (1) No person shall become or remain a member of the National Assembly unless he or she is a South African citizen and is and remains qualified . . . to vote in an election of the National Assembly, or he or she—

(a) at the time of the first election of the National Assembly held under this Constitution is serving a sentence of imprisonment of more than 12 months without the option of a fine;

(b) at any time after the promulgation of this Constitution is convicted of an offence in the Republic, or outside the Republic if the conduct constituting such offence would have constituted an offence in the Republic, and for which he or she has been sentenced to imprisonment of more than 12 months without the option of a fine, unless he or she has received a pardon;

(c) is an unrehabilitated insolvent;

(d) is of unsound mind and has been so declared by a competent court; or

(e) holds any office of profit under the Republic. . . .

The Senate

Composition of Senate

48. (1) The Senate shall be composed of 10 senators for each province, nominated by the parties represented in a provincial legislature within 10 days of—
    (a) the first sitting of such legislature after an election of the legislature; or
    (b) an election of the National Assembly held in pursuance of a dissolution of Parliament.
(2) Each party represented in a provincial legislature shall be entitled to nominate a senator or senators for the relevant province in accordance with the principle of proportional representation. . . .
(3) A member of a provincial legislature or local government nominated as a senator in terms of this section, shall vacate his or her seat in the provincial legislature or local government upon his or her acceptance of such nomination.

President and Deputy President of Senate

49. (1) At its first sitting after it has been convened . . . and before proceeding to dispatch any other business, the Senate, with the Chief Justice or a judge of the Supreme Court designated by him or her acting as the chairperson, shall elect one of its members to be the President of the Senate, and shall thereafter elect another of its members to be the Deputy President of the Senate. . . .
(3) The President of the Senate shall be vested with all the powers and functions assigned to him or her by this Constitution, an Act of Parliament and the rules and orders. . . .
(7) The President or Deputy President of the Senate or any other senator designated for that purpose in terms of the rules and orders shall preside over sittings of the Senate.
(8) While presiding at a sitting of the Senate, the President or Deputy President of the Senate or other senator presiding shall not have a deliberative vote, but shall have and exercise a casting vote in the case of an equality of votes.
(9) The President or Deputy President of the Senate shall vacate his or her office if he or she ceases to be a senator, and may be removed from office by resolution of the Senate, and may resign by lodging his or her resignation in writing with the Secretary to Parliament. . . .

Qualification for Membership of Senate

50. No person shall be qualified to become or remain a senator unless he

or she is or remains qualified to become a member of the National Assembly. . . .

The National Assembly and the Senate

Powers, Privileges and Immunities of Parliament and Benefits of Members

55. (1) Parliament shall have full power to control, regulate and dispose of its internal affairs, and shall have all such other powers, privileges and immunities as may, subject to this Constitution, be prescribed by an Act of Parliament.

(2) Subject to the rules and orders there shall be freedom of speech and debate in or before Parliament and any committee thereof, and such freedom shall not be impeached or questioned in any court.

(3) A member of Parliament shall not be liable to any civil or criminal proceedings, arrest, imprisonment or damages by reason of anything which he or she has said, produced or submitted in or before or to Parliament or any committee thereof or by reason of anything which may have been revealed as a result of what he or she has said, produced or submitted in or before or to Parliament or any committee thereof. . . .

Ordinary Bills

59. (1) An ordinary Bill may be introduced in either the National Assembly or the Senate and shall for its passing by Parliament, . . . be required to be adopted by each House.

(2) An ordinary Bill passed by one House and rejected by the other shall be referred to a joint committee consisting of members of both Houses and of all the parties represented in Parliament and willing to participate in the joint committee, to consider and report on any proposed amendments to the Bill, whereafter the Bill shall be referred to a joint sitting of both Houses, at which it may be passed with or without amendment by a majority of the total number of members of both Houses.

(3) All Bills, except the new constitutional text . . . shall for the purposes of this Constitution be considered to be ordinary Bills.

Finance Bills

60. (1) Bills appropriating revenue or moneys or imposing taxation shall be introduced in the National Assembly only. . . .

Bills Affecting Certain Provincial Matters

61. Bills affecting the boundaries or the exercise or performance of the powers and functions of the provinces shall be deemed not to be passed by Parliament unless passed separately by both Houses and,

in the case of a Bill affecting the boundaries or the exercise or performance of the powers or functions of a particular province or provinces only, unless also approved by a majority of the senators of the province or provinces in question in the Senate.

Bills Amending Constitution

62. ... [A] Bill amending this Constitution shall, for its passing by Parliament, be required to be adopted at a joint sitting of the National Assembly and the Senate by a majority of at least two-thirds of the total number of members of both Houses....

Requisite Majorities

63. Save where otherwise required in this Constitution, all questions before the National Assembly or the Senate or before the National Assembly and the Senate in a joint sitting, shall be determined by a majority of votes cast....

Chapter 5

The Adoption of the New Constitution

Constitution-Making Body

68. (1) The National Assembly and the Senate, sitting jointly of this Chapter, shall be the Constitutional Assembly.
(2) The Constitutional Assembly shall draft and adopt a new constitutional text in accordance with this Chapter.
(3) (a) The first sitting of the Constitutional Assembly shall be convened by the President of the Senate not later than seven days as from the first sitting of the Senate under this Constitution.
(b) Any subsequent sittings of the Constitutional Assembly shall be convened by the Chairperson of the Constitutional Assembly after consultation with the Speaker and the President of the Senate....

Adoption of New Constitutional Text

73. (1) The Constitutional Assembly shall pass the new constitutional text within two years as from the date of the first sitting of the National Assembly under this Constitution.
(2) For the passing of the new constitutional text by the Constitutional Assembly, a majority of at least two-thirds of all the members of the Constitutional Assembly shall be required: Provided that provisions of such text relating to the boundaries, powers and functions of provinces shall not be considered passed by the Constitutional Assembly unless approved also by a majority of two-thirds of all the members of the Senate....

(6) A text approved . . . shall, after it has been certified by the Constitutional Court, . . . be referred by the President for a decision by the electorate by way of a national referendum.
(7) The question put before the electorate in the referendum shall be the acceptance or rejection of the text approved. . . .
(8) The text presented to the electorate in the referendum shall, if approved by a majority of at least 60 per cent of the votes cast in the referendum . . . become the Constitution of the Republic of South Africa.
(9) If the relevant text is not approved in the referendum . . . or if a new constitutional text is not passed in terms of this Chapter within the period of two years . . . the President shall dissolve Parliament by proclamation in the *Gazette* within 14 days after the referendum or the expiry of the said period, whereupon an election . . . shall be held.
(10) The Constitutional Assembly as constituted after such an election shall pass the new constitutional text within a period of one year as from the date of its first sitting after such election. . . .

Chapter 6

The National Executive

Executive Authority of the Republic

75. The executive authority of the Republic with regard to all matters failing within the legislative competence of Parliament shall vest in the President, who shall exercise and perform his or her powers and functions subject to and in accordance with this Constitution.

Head of State

76. The President shall be the Head of State.

Election of President

77. (1) (a) The National Assembly shall at its first sitting after it has been convened . . . elect one of its members as the President.
(b) The National Assembly and the Senate shall thereafter, as often as it again becomes necessary to elect a President, elect at a joint sitting one of the members of the National Assembly as the President. . . .

Tenure of Office of President

80. (1) The President . . . shall . . . hold office—
(a) for the period terminating on a date five years as from the date of the first sitting of the National Assembly under this Constitution; or

(b) if Parliament is dissolved during such period, for the period until a President has been elected ... after such dissolution and has assumed office....

Responsibilities of President

81. (1) The President shall be responsible for the observance of the provisions of this Constitution by the executive and shall as head of state defend and uphold the Constitution as the supreme law of the land.

(2) The President shall with dignity provide executive leadership in the interest of national unity in accordance with this Constitution and the law of the Republic.

(3) The President shall not hold any other public office and shall not perform remunerative work outside the duties of his or her office.

Powers and Functions of President

82. (1) The President shall be competent to exercise and perform the following powers and functions, namely—

(a) to assent to, sign and promulgate Bills duly passed by Parliament;

(b) in the event of a procedural shortcoming in the legislative process, to refer a Bill passed by Parliament back for further consideration by Parliament;

(c) to convene meetings of the Cabinet;

(d) to refer disputes of a constitutional nature between parties represented in Parliament or between organs of state at any level of government to the Constitutional Court or other appropriate institution, commission or body for resolution;

(e) to confer honours;

(f) to appoint, accredit, receive, and recognise ambassadors, plenipotentiaries, diplomatic representatives and other diplomatic officers, consuls and consular officers;

(g) to appoint commissions of enquiry;

(h) to make such appointments as may be necessary under powers conferred upon him or her by this Constitution or any other law;

(i) to negotiate and sign international agreements;

(j) to proclaim referenda and plebiscites in terms of this Constitution or an Act of Parliament; and

(k) to pardon or reprieve offenders, either unconditionally or subject to such conditions as he or she may deem fit, and to remit any fines, penalties or forfeitures.

(2) The President shall consult the Executive Deputy Presidents—

(a) in the development and execution of the policies of the national government;

(b) in all matters relating to the management of the Cabinet and the performance of Cabinet business;
(c) in the assignment and allocation of functions contemplated in section 84(5) to an Executive Deputy President;
(d) regarding appointments under subsection (1)(f); and
(e) before exercising any of the competences referred to in subsection (1)(g) to (k).

(3) The President shall exercise and perform all powers and functions assigned to him or her by this Constitution or any other law, except those specified in subsections (1) and (2) or where otherwise expressly or by implication provided in this Constitution, in consultation with the Cabinet: Provided that the Cabinet may delegate its consultation function in terms of this subsection, with reference to any particular power or function of the President, to any Minister or Ministers.

(4) (a) The President shall be the Commander-in-Chief of the National Defence Force.
(b) The President may—
(i) with the approval of Parliament, declare a state of national defence;
(ii) employ the National Defence Force in accordance with and subject to sections 227 and 228; and
(iii) confer upon members of the National Defence Force permanent commissions and cancel such commissions.

Confirmation of Executive Acts of President

83. (1) Decisions of the President taken in terms of section 82 shall be expressed in writing under his or her signature.
(2) Any instrument signed by the President in the exercise or performance of a power or function referred to in section 82(3) shall be countersigned by a Minister.
(3) The signature of the President on any instrument shall be confirmed by the seal of the Republic.

Executive Deputy Presidents

84. (1) Every party holding at least 80 seats in the National Assembly shall be entitled to designate an Executive Deputy President from among the members of the National Assembly.
(2) Should no party or only one party hold 80 or more seats in the National Assembly, the party holding the largest number of seats and the party holding the second largest number of seats shall each be entitled to designate one Executive Deputy President from among the members of the National Assembly.
(3) On being designated as such, an Executive Deputy President may elect to vacate or not to vacate his or her seat in the National Assembly.

(4) Section 81 shall apply *mutatis mutandis* to an Executive Deputy President.

(5) An Executive Deputy President may exercise the powers and shall perform the functions vested in the office of Executive Deputy President by this Constitution or assigned to him or her by the President.

(6) An Executive Deputy President shall, before formally assuming office, make and subscribe an oath or solemn affirmation in the terms set out in Schedule 3 before the Chief Justice or a judge of the Supreme Court designated by the Chief Justice for this purpose.

Tenure of Office of Executive Deputy Presidents and Filling of Vacancies

85. (1) An Executive Deputy President shall . . . hold office (a) for the period terminating on a date five years as from the date of the first sitting of the National Assembly under this Constitution, unless he or she is before the expiry of such period replaced as Executive Deputy President by the party which designated him or her; or (b) if Parliament is dissolved during such period, for the period until a President has been elected after such dissolution and has assumed office. . . .

Removal from Office of President or Executive Deputy President

87. The President or an Executive Deputy President shall cease to hold office on a resolution adopted at a joint sitting of the National Assembly and the Senate by a majority of at least two-thirds of the total number of members of the Houses and impeaching the President or such Executive Deputy President on the ground of a serious violation of this Constitution or the other laws of the Republic, or of misconduct or inability rendering him or her unfit to exercise and perform his or her powers and functions. . . .

Cabinet

88. (1) The Cabinet shall consist of the President, the Executive Deputy Presidents and not more than 27 Ministers appointed by the President in accordance with this section.

(2) A party holding at least 20 seats in the National Assembly and which has decided to participate in the government of national unity, shall be entitled to be allocated one or more of the Cabinet portfolios in proportion to the number of seats held by it in the National Assembly relative to the number of seats held by the leaders of the other participating parties. . . .

(4) The President shall after consultation with the Executive Deputy Presidents and the leaders of the participating parties—

(a) determine the specific portfolios to be allocated to the respective participating parties in accordance with the number of portfolios allocated to them. . . ;

(b) appoint in respect of each such portfolio a member of Parliament who is a member of the party to which that portfolio was allocated . . . as the Minister responsible for that portfolio. . . ;

Accountability of Ministers and Cabinet

92. (1) A Minister shall be accountable individually both to the President and to Parliament for the administration of the portfolio entrusted to him or her, and all members of the Cabinet shall correspondingly be accountable collectively for the performance of the functions of the national government and for its policies. . . .

Votes of No Confidence

93. (1) If Parliament passes a vote of no confidence in the Cabinet, including the President, the President shall, unless he or she resigns, dissolve Parliament and call an election. . . .

(2) If Parliament passes a vote of no confidence in the President, but not in the other members of the Cabinet, the President shall resign.

(3) If Parliament passes a vote of no confidence in the Cabinet, excluding the President, the President may—

(a) resign;

(b) reconstitute the Cabinet in accordance . . . ; or

(c) dissolve Parliament and call an election. . . .

(4) The President shall where required, or where he or she elects, to do so in terms of this section, dissolve Parliament by proclamation in the *Gazette* within 14 days of the relevant vote of no confidence. . . .

Chapter 7

The Judicial Authority and the Administration of Justice

Judicial Authority

96. (1) The judicial authority of the Republic shall vest in the courts established by this Constitution and any other law.

(2) The judiciary shall be independent, impartial and subject only to this Constitution and the law.

(3) No person and no organ of state shall interfere with judicial officers in the performance of their functions.

Appointment of Chief Justice and President of Constitutional Court

97. (1) There shall be a Chief Justice of the Supreme Court of South Africa, who shall . . . be appointed by the President in consultation with the Cabinet and after consultation with the Judicial Service Commission.

(2) (a) There shall be a President of the Constitutional Court who shall . . . be appointed by the President in consultation with the Cabinet and after consultation with the Chief Justice.

(b) Unless the new constitutional text provides otherwise, the President of the Constitutional Court shall hold office for a non-renewable period of seven years.

Constitutional Court and Its Jurisdiction

98. (1) There shall be a Constitutional Court consisting of a President and 10 other judges. . . .

(2) The Constitutional Court shall have jurisdiction in the Republic as the court of final instance over all matters relating to the interpretation, protection and enforcement of the provisions of this Constitution. . . .

(4) A decision of the Constitutional Court shall bind all persons and all legislative, executive and judicial organs of state.

(5) In the event of the Constitutional Court finding that any law or any provision thereof is inconsistent with this Constitution, it shall declare such law or provision invalid to the extent of its inconsistency: Provided that the Constitutional Court may, in the interests of justice and good government, require Parliament or any other competent authority, within a period specified by the Court, to correct the defect in the law or provision, which shall then remain in force pending correction or the expiry of the period so specified. . . .

Composition of Constitutional Court and Appointment of Judges of Constitutional Court

99. (1) Unless the new constitutional text provides otherwise, the judges of the Constitutional Court shall be appointed by the President for a non-renewable period of seven years.

(2) No person shall be qualified to be appointed President or a judge of the Constitutional Court unless he or she—

(a) is a South African citizen; and

(b) is a fit and proper person to be a judge of the Constitutional Court; and

(c) (i) is a judge of the Supreme Court or is qualified to be admitted as an advocate or attorney and has, for a cumulative period of at least 10 years after having so qualified, practised as an advocate or an attorney or lectured in law at a university; or

(ii) is a person who, by reason of his or her training and experience, has expertise in the field of constitutional law relevant to the application of this Constitution and the law of the Republic.

(3) Four judges of the Constitutional Court shall be appointed from among the judges of the Supreme Court by the President in consultation with the Cabinet and with the Chief Justice.

(4) ... [S]ix judges of the Constitutional Court shall be appointed by the President in consultation with the Cabinet and after consultation with the President of the Constitutional Court....

(5) ... [A]n appointment or appointments under section 97(2) or subsection (4) or (7) of this section shall only be made from the recommendations of the Judicial Service Commission, and with due regard to its reasons for such recommendations, of not more than three nominees in excess of the number of persons required to be appointed....

Supreme Court

101. (1) There shall be a Supreme Court of South Africa, which shall consist of an Appellate Division and such provincial and local divisions, and with such areas of jurisdiction, as may be prescribed by law.

(2) Subject to this Constitution, the Supreme Court shall have the jurisdiction, including the inherent jurisdiction, vested in the Supreme Court immediately before the commencement of this Constitution, and any further jurisdiction conferred upon it by this Constitution or by any law.

(3) Subject to this Constitution, a provincial or local division of the Supreme Court shall, within its area of jurisdiction, have jurisdiction in respect of the following additional matters, namely—

(a) any alleged violation or threatened violation of any fundamental right entrenched in Chapter 3;

(b) any dispute over the constitutionality of any executive or administrative act or conduct or threatened executive or administrative act or conduct of any organ of state;

(c) any inquiry into the constitutionality of any law applicable within its area of jurisdiction, other than an Act of Parliament, irrespective of whether such law was passed or made before or after the commencement of this Constitution;

(d) any dispute of a constitutional nature between local governments or between a local and a provincial government;

(e) any dispute over the constitutionality of a Bill before a provincial legislature...;

(f) the determination of questions whether any matter falls within its jurisdiction; and

(g) the determination of any other matters as may be entrusted to it by an Act of Parliament.

(4) For the purposes of exercising its jurisdiction . . . a provincial or local division of the Supreme Court shall have the powers of the Constitutional Court ... relating to the interpretation, protection and enforcement of this Constitution.

(5) The Appellate Division shall have no jurisdiction to adjudicate any matter within the jurisdiction of the Constitutional Court. . . .

Appointment, Removal from Office and Remuneration of Judges

104. (1) Judges of the Supreme Court shall be fit and proper persons appointed by the President acting on the advice of the Judicial Service Commission. . . .

(4) A judge may only be removed from office by the President on the grounds of misbehaviour, incapacity or incompetence established by the Judicial Service Commission and upon receipt of an address from both the National Assembly and the Senate praying for such removal.

(5) A judge who is the subject of an investigation by the Judicial Service Commission ... may be suspended by the President pending such investigation.

Judicial Service Commission

105. (1) There shall be a Judicial Service Commission, which shall, subject to subsection (3), consist of—

(a) the Chief Justice, who shall preside at meetings of the Commission;

(b) the President of the Constitutional Court;

(c) one Judge President designated by the Judges President;

(d) the Minister responsible for the administration of justice or his or her nominee;

(e) two practising advocates designated by the advocates' profession;

(f) two practising attorneys designated by the attorneys' profession;

(g) one professor of law designated by the deans of all the law faculties at South African universities;

(h) four senators designated *en bloc* by the Senate by resolution adopted by a majority of at least two-thirds of all its members;

(i) four persons, two of whom shall be practising attorneys or advocates, who shall be designated by the President in consultation with the Cabinet;

(j) on the occasion of the consideration of matters specifically relating to a provincial division of the Supreme Court, the Judge President of the relevant division and the Premier of the relevant province.

(2) The functions of the Judicial Service Commission shall be—

(a) to make recommendations regarding the appointment, removal from office, term of office and tenure of judges of the Supreme Court...;

(b) to make recommendations regarding the removal from office of judges of the Constitutional Court...; and

(c) to advise the national and provincial governments on all matters relating to the judiciary and the administration of justice....

Chapter 8

The Public Protector, Human Rights Commission, Commission on Gender Issues and Restitution of Land Rights

The Public Protector

Establishment and Appointment

110. (1) There shall be a Public Protector for the Republic.

(2) The President shall, whenever it becomes necessary, appoint as the Public Protector a person—

(a) nominated by a joint committee of the Houses of Parliament composed of one member of each party represented in Parliament and willing to serve on the committee; and

(b) approved by the National Assembly and the Senate by a resolution adopted by a majority of at least 75 per cent of the members present and voting at a joint meeting;...

(3) The first appointment of a person as the Public Protector after the commencement of this Constitution shall be made within 60 days of the first sitting of the Senate under this Constitution.

(4) The Public Protector shall be a South African citizen who is a fit and proper person to hold such office, and who—

(a) is a Judge of the Supreme Court of South Africa; or

(b) is qualified to be admitted as an advocate and has, for a cumulative period of at least 10 years after having so qualified—

(i) practised as an advocate or an attorney; or

(ii) lectured in law at a university; or

(c) has specialised knowledge of or experience for a period of at least 10 years in the administration of justice, public administration or public finance.

(5) Unless the new constitutional text provides otherwise, the Public Protector shall hold office for a period of seven years....

Independence and Impartiality

111. (1) The Public Protector shall be independent and impartial....

Powers and Functions

112. (1) The Public Protector shall, in addition to any powers and functions assigned to him or her by any law, be competent—
(a) to investigate, on his or her own initiative or on receipt of a complaint, any alleged—
(i) maladministration in connection with the affairs of government at any level;
(ii) abuse or unjustifiable exercise of power or unfair, capricious, discourteous or other improper conduct or undue delay by a person performing a public function;
(iii) improper or dishonest act, or omission or corruption, with respect to public money;
(iv) improper or unlawful enrichment, or receipt of any improper advantage, or promise of such enrichment or advantage, by a person as a result of an act or omission in the public administration or in connection with the affairs of government at any level or of a person performing a public function; or
(v) act or omission by a person in the employ of government at any level, or a person performing a public function, which results in unlawful or improper prejudice to any other persons;...

(2) Nothing in subsection (1) shall be construed as empowering the Public Protector to investigate the performance of judicial functions by any court of law....

Human Rights Commission

Establishment and Appointments

115. (1) There shall be a Human Rights Commission, which shall consist of a chairperson and 10 members who are fit and proper persons, South African citizens and broadly representative of the South African community.

(2) The members of the Commission shall be appointed as provided in subsection (3) and vacancies in the Commission shall be filled accordingly.

(3) The President shall, whenever it becomes necessary, appoint as a member of the Commission a person—
(a) nominated by a joint committee of the Houses of Parliament composed of one member of each party represented

in Parliament and willing to participate in the committee; and

(b) approved by the National Assembly and the Senate by a resolution adopted by a majority of at least 75 per cent of the members present and voting at a joint meeting:

Provided that if any nomination is not approved as required in paragraph (b), the joint committee shall nominate another person.

(4) The first members of the Commission after the commencement of this Constitution, shall be appointed within 60 days of the first sitting of the Senate under this Constitution.

(5) A Chairperson and a Deputy Chairperson of the Commission shall as often as it becomes necessary be elected by the members of the Commission from among their number.

Powers and Functions

116. (1) The Commission shall, in addition to any powers and functions assigned to it by law, be competent and be obliged to—

(a) promote the observance of, respect for and the protection of fundamental rights;

(b) develop an awareness of fundamental rights among all people of the Republic;

(c) make recommendations to organs of state at all levels of government where it considers such action advisable for the adoption of progressive measures for the promotion of fundamental rights within the framework of the law and this Constitution, as well as appropriate measures for the further observance of such rights;

(d) undertake such studies for report on or relating to fundamental rights as it considers advisable in the performance of its functions; and

(e) request any organ of state to supply it with information on any legislative or executive measures adopted by it relating to fundamental rights.

(2) If the Commission is of the opinion that any proposed legislation might be contrary to Chapter 3 or to norms of international human rights law which form part of South African law or to other relevant norms of international law, it shall immediately report that fact to the relevant legislature.

(3) The Commission shall be competent to investigate on its own initiative or on receipt of a complaint any alleged violation of fundamental rights, and if, after due investigation, the Commission is of the opinion that there is substance in any complaint made to it, it shall, in so far as it is able to do so, assist the complainant and other persons adversely affected thereby, to secure redress, and where it is necessary for that

purpose to do so, it may arrange for or provide financial assistance to enable proceedings to be taken to a court ... or may direct a complainant to an appropriate forum....

Reports

118. The Commission shall report to the President at least once every year on its activities, and the President shall cause such report to be tabled promptly in the National Assembly and the Senate.

Commission on Gender Equality

Establishment

119. (1) There shall be a Commission on Gender Equality, which shall consist of a chairperson and such number of members as may be determined by an Act of Parliament.

(2) The Commission shall consist of persons who are fit and proper for appointment, South African citizens and broadly representative of the South African community.

(3) The object of the Commission shall be to promote gender equality and to advise and to make recommendations to Parliament or any other legislature with regard to any laws or proposed legislation which affects gender equality and the status of women....

Chapter 9

Provincial Government

Establishment of Provinces

124. (1) The following provinces are hereby established, which shall for the purposes of this Constitution be recognised as the provinces of the Republic:

(a) Eastern Cape;
(b) Eastern Transvaal;
(c) Natal;
(d) Northern Cape;
(e) Northern Transvaal;
(f) North-West;
(g) Orange Free State;
(h) Pretoria-Witwatersrand-Vereeniging; and
(i) Western Cape....

(10) The President shall by proclamation in the *Gazette* amend Schedule I to give effect to the result of a referendum referred to in subsection (5) or (6) or to an agreement referred to in subsection (8).

Provincial Legislative Authority

Provincial Legislature

125. (1) There shall be a legislature for each province.

(2) The legislative authority of a province shall, subject to this Constitution, vest in the provincial legislature, which shall have the power to make laws for the province in accordance with this Constitution.

(3) Laws made by a provincial legislature shall, subject to any exceptions as may be provided for by an Act of Parliament, be applicable only within the territory of the province.

Legislative Competence of Provinces

126. (1) A provincial legislature shall ... have concurrent competence with Parliament to make laws for the province with regard to all matters which fall within the functional areas specified....

(2) The legislative competence referred to in subsection (1), shall include the competence to make laws which are reasonably necessary for or incidental to the effective exercise of such legislative competence.

(3) An Act of Parliament which deals with a matter referred to in subsection (1) or (2) shall prevail over a provincial law inconsistent therewith, only to the extent that—

(a) it deals with a matter that cannot be regulated effectively by provincial legislation;

(b) it deals with a matter that, to be performed effectively, requires to be regulated or co-ordinated by uniform norms or standards that apply generally throughout the Republic;

(c) it is necessary to set minimum standards across the nation for the rendering of public services;

(d) it is necessary for the determination of national economic policies, the maintenance of economic unity, the protection of the environment, the promotion of inter-provincial commerce, the protection of the common market in respect of the mobility of goods, services, capital or labour, or the maintenance of national security; or

(e) the provincial law materially prejudices the economic, health or security interests of another province or the country as a whole.

(4) An Act of Parliament shall prevail over a provincial law, as provided for in subsection (3), only if it applies uniformly in all parts of the Republic.

(5) An Act of Parliament and a provincial law shall be construed as being consistent with each other, unless ... they are, expressly or by necessary implication, inconsistent with each other.

(6) A provincial legislature may recommend to Parliament the passing of any law relating to any matter in respect of which such legislature is not competent to make laws or in respect of which an Act of Parliament prevails over a provincial law in terms of subsection (3).

Composition of Provincial Legislatures

127. (1) A provincial legislature shall consist of not fewer than 30 and not more than 100 members elected in accordance with the system of proportional representation of voters....

Duration and Dissolution of Provincial Legislatures

128. (1) A provincial legislature as constituted in terms of an election of such legislature under this Constitution shall ... continue for five years as from the date of such election at the expiry of which it shall be dissolved....

Chapter 14

South African Police Service

Establishment

214. (1) There shall be established and regulated by an Act of Parliament a South African Police Service, which shall be structured at both national and provincial levels and shall function under the direction of the national government as well as the various provincial governments.

(2) The Act of Parliament referred to in subsection (1) shall—

(a) ... provide for the appointment of a Commissioner of the South African Police Service (hereinafter in this Chapter called the "National Commissioner") and a Commissioner for each province (hereinafter in this Chapter called a "Provincial Commissioner");

(b) provide for the establishment and maintenance of uniform standards of policing at all levels....

Powers and Functions

215. The powers and functions of the Service shall be—

(a) the prevention of crime;
(b) the investigation of any offence or alleged offence;
(c) the maintenance of law and order; and
(d) the preservation of the internal security of the Republic.

VATICAN, ISRAEL ACCORD ON DIPLOMATIC RELATIONS

December 30, 1993

After eighteen months of arduous negotiations, representatives of the Vatican and Israel December 30 took a major step to end hundreds of years of enmity when they signed a fifteen-point agreement intended to lead to the establishment of full diplomatic relations. In a low-key ceremony at the Foreign Ministry in Jerusalem, representatives of the Holy See and Israel set the stage for an exchange of ambassadors and the possibility of a 1994 visit to the Holy Land by Pope John Paul II, which would be his first. The exchange of ambassadors would depend on ratification of the accord by the Vatican and Israel's parliament; in the meantime, "personal representatives" would be appointed by both sides.

Long Process to End Mutual Distrust

Efforts to improve ties between the Vatican and Israel had a more than thirty-year history, spurred by attempts on the part of Catholic leaders to repudiate theological condemnation of Judaism and explicitly reject antisemitism. Pope John XXIII (1958-1963) ordered words offensive to Jews eliminated from the church's Good Friday liturgy. In 1965 the Second Vatican Council issued "Nostra Aetate" (In Our Time), which stated that the crucifixion of Jesus "cannot be blamed on all the Jews then living, without distinction, nor upon the Jews of today." In 1986 John Paul II became the first pope to visit a synagogue (in Rome), where he called Jews "our beloved elder brothers" and condemned antisemitism. The following year the pope added further impetus to the effort to improve relations by stating that the Vatican saw no theological objections to recognizing Israel.

The road to the agreement was thorny. A major stumbling block was what many Jews perceived as the Vatican's reluctance to take more decisive action in opposing the World War II Holocaust that killed 6 million Jews, a charge the Vatican denied, and its subsequent silence on condemning the Holocaust. Reflecting a view held by many, Israeli's Ashkenazi chief rabbi Yisrael Lau said, "The silence of the Vatican during the terrible time of World War II must be learned in future generations so that it won't happen again."

Although it had not questioned Israel's right to exist after the nation gained independence in 1948, the Vatican had held off on formal recognition, citing the fact that Israel did not have internationally recognized borders; the lack of guarantees on the status of Jerusalem as a city holy to Jews, Christians, and Muslims; and lack of adequate Israeli protection for Catholics and their institutions in matters of free speech and taxation. The Vatican had also expressed concern about the treatment of Palestinians in the occupied territories and apprehension that establishing relations with Israel could jeopardize the position of Catholics in Arab countries.

A major turning point came in 1991 with the beginning of U.S.-sponsored Middle East peace negotiations. The Vatican, which previously had moved closer to the Palestine Liberation Organization (PLO) and Arab governments, began to reassess its policy as the PLO's leader Yasser Arafat began to soften his own anti-Israel position—culminating in the September 13, 1993, Israel-PLO agreement on the Gaza Strip and Jericho. (Israeli-Palestinian Peace Accord, p. 747)

Terms of the Agreement

In formally recognizing Israel, the Vatican stipulated that it reserved the right to speak out on moral issues but pledged not to become involved in temporal conflicts such as "disputed territories and unsettled borders." The two sides agreed to "combat all forms of antisemitism, racism, and religious intolerance." The agreement also contained guarantees of freedom of worship and the church's right to run its schools, hospitals, and other agencies in the Holy Land—although its tax status had yet to be resolved. (A commission was to be appointed to work out legal and fiscal details within two years.)

The agreement did not fully resolve the issue of the future status of Jerusalem, which Israel had insisted was its eternal capital. Although the Vatican abandoned its traditional position that Jerusalem should be granted international status, it continued to insist on guarantees of access to holy places. Like the majority of other nations, the Vatican said its embassy would not be in Jerusalem but in Jaffa, which had a large Arab-Israeli population.

Reaction: Agreement Generally Hailed

In the United States, Roman Catholic and Jewish leaders praised the accord. "We believe it is a positive and historic moment in the relationship between the Catholic Church and the Jewish people in this country," said Archbishop William H. Keeler of Baltimore at a December 30 news conference. Archbishop Keeler was the president of the National

Conference of Catholic Bishops. In a joint statement, the conference and the Synagogue Council of America hailed the pact as "a revolution in relations" between Catholics and Jews. Itamar Rabinovich, Israel's ambassador to the United States, said the agreement could contribute to progress on a Middle East peace. By normalizing relations with Israel, the Catholic church affirmed the message that "a sovereign Jewish state in the Middle East is a normal state of affairs," he said.

The Clinton administration also endorsed the accord, which would contribute "to the overall stability and peace process in the Middle East," according to Raymond Flynn, U.S. ambassador to the Vatican. A White House statement said that President Clinton "warmly welcomes" the agreement. "We congratulate both parties on this historic reconciliation." During his August meeting with Pope John Paul II in Denver, Clinton had expressed his support for establishing full diplomatic relations between the Vatican and Israel. (Pope in Denver, p. 659)

"Behind the agreement there are thousands of years of history, full of hatred, fear and ignorance, with a few islands of understanding," warned Deputy Foreign Minister Yosai Beilin, who signed the pact for Israel. "Behind the agreement there are very few years of light and many more years of darkness."

Said Beilin's Vatican counterpart, Monsignor Claudio Celli, "The Holy See is convinced that a dialogue and respectful cooperation between Catholics and Jews will now be given new impetus and energy both in Israel and throughout the world."

Following is the text of the December 30, 1993, agreement between the Vatican and Israel on measures leading to the establishment of full diplomatic relations:

Fundamental Agreement Between the Holy See and the State of Israel

Preamble

The Holy See and the State of Israel,

Mindful of the singular character and universal significance of the Holy Land;

Aware of the unique nature of the relationship between the Catholic Church and the Jewish people, and of the historic process of reconciliation and growth in mutual understanding and friendship between Catholics and Jews;

Having decided on 29 July 1992 to establish a 'Bilateral Permanent Working Commission', in order to study and define together issues of common interest, and in view of normalizing their relations;

Recognizing that the work of the aforementioned Commission has produced sufficient material for a first and Fundamental Agreement;

Realizing that such Agreement will provide a sound and lasting basis for the continued development of their present and future relations and for the furtherance of the Commission's task,

Agree upon the following Articles:

Article 1

1. The State of Israel, recalling its Declaration of Independence, affirms its continuing commitment to uphold and observe the human right to freedom of religion and conscience, as set forth in the Universal Declaration of Human Rights and in other international instruments to which it is a party.
2. The Holy See, recalling the Declaration on Religious Freedom of the Second Vatican Ecumenical Council, 'Dignitatis humanea', affirms the Catholic Church's commitment to uphold the human right to freedom of religion and conscience, as set forth in the Universal Declaration of Human Rights and in other international instruments to which it is a party. The Holy See wishes to affirm as well the Catholic Church's respect for other religions and their followers as solemnly stated by the Second Vatican Ecumenical Council in its Declaration on the Relation of the Church to Non-Christian Religions, 'Nostra aetate'.

Article 2

1. The Holy See and the State of Israel are committed to appropriate cooperation in combating all forms of antisemitism and all kinds of racism and of religious intolerance, and in promoting mutual understanding among nations, tolerance among communities and respect for human life and dignity.
2. The Holy See takes this occasion to reiterate its condemnation of hatred, persecution and all other manifestations of antisemitism directed against the Jewish people and individual Jews anywhere, at any time and by anyone. In particular, the Holy See deplores attacks on Jews and desecration of Jewish synagogues and cemeteries, acts which offend the memory of the victims of' the Holocaust, especially when they occur in the same places which witnessed it.

Article 3

1. The Holy See and the State of Israel recognize that both are free in the exercise of their respective rights and powers, and commit themselves to respect this principle in their mutual relations and in their cooperation for the good of the people.
2. The State of Israel recognizes the right of the Catholic Church to carry out its religious, moral, educational and charitable functions,

and to have its own institutions, and to train, appoint and deploy its own personnel in the said institutions or for the said functions to these ends. The Church recognizes the right of the State to carry out its functions, such as promoting and protecting the welfare and the safety of the people. Both the State and the Church recognize the need for dialogue and cooperation in such matters as by their nature call for it.

3. Concerning Catholic legal personality at canon law the Holy See and the State of Israel will negotiate on giving it full effect in Israeli law, following a report from a joint subcommission of experts.

Article 4

1. The State of Israel affirms its continuing commitment to maintain and respect the 'Status quo' in the Christian Holy Places to which it applies and the respective rights of the Christian communities thereunder. The Holy See affirms the Catholic Church's continuing commitment to respect the aforementioned 'Status quo' and the said rights.
2. The above shall apply notwithstanding an interpretation to the contrary of any Article in this Fundamental Agreement.
3. The State of Israel agrees with the Holy See on the obligation of continuing respect for and protection of the character proper to Catholic sacred places, such as churches, monasteries, convents, cemeteries and their like.
4. The State of Israel agrees with the Holy See on the continuing guarantee of the freedom of Catholic worship.

Article 5

1. The Holy See and the State of Israel recognize that both have an interest in favouring Christian pilgrimages to the Holy Land. Whenever the need for coordination arises, the proper agencies of the Church and of the State will consult and cooperate as required.
2. The State of Israel and the Holy See express the hope that such pilgrimages will provide an occasion for better understanding between the pilgrims and the people and religions in Israel.

Article 6

The Holy See and the State of Israel jointly reaffirm the right of the Catholic Church to establish, maintain and direct schools and institutes of study at all levels; this right being exercised in harmony with the rights of the State in the field of education.

Article 7

The Holy See and the State of Israel recognize a common interest in promoting and encouraging cultural exchanges between Catholic institutions worldwide, and educational, cultural and research institutions in

Israel, and in facilitating access to manuscripts, historical documents and similar source materials, in conformity with applicable laws and regulations.

Article 8

The State of Israel recognizes that the right of the Catholic Church to freedom of expression in the carrying out of its functions is exercised also through the Church's own communications media; this right being exercised in harmony with the rights of the State in the field of communications media.

Article 9

The Holy See and the State of Israel jointly reaffirm the right of the Catholic Church to carry out its charitable functions through its health care and social welfare institutions, this right being exercised in harmony with the rights of the State in this field.

Article 10

1. The Holy See and the State of Israel jointly reaffirm the right of the Catholic Church to property.
2. Without prejudice to rights relied upon by the Parties:
   (a) The Holy See and the State of Israel will negotiate in good faith a comprehensive agreement, containing solutions acceptable to both Parties, on unclear, unsettled, and disputed issues concerning property, economic and fiscal matters relating to the Catholic Church generally, or to specific Catholic Communities or institutions;
   (b) For the purpose of the said negotiations, the Permanent Bilateral Working Commission will appoint one or more bilateral subcommissions of experts to study the issues and make proposals.
   (c) The Parties intend to commence the aforementioned negotiations within three months of entry into force of the present Agreement, and aim to reach agreement within two years from the beginning of the negotiations.
   (d) During the period of these negotiations, actions incompatible with these commitments shall be avoided.

Article 11

1. The Holy See and the State of Israel declare their respective commitment to the promotion of the peaceful resolution of conflicts among States and nations, excluding violence and terror from international life.
2. The Holy See, while maintaining in every case the right to exercise its moral and spiritual teaching-office, deems it opportune to recall that, owing to its own character, it is solemnly committed to remaining a stranger to all merely temporal conflicts, which principle applies specifically to disputed territories and unsettled borders.

Article 12

The Holy See and the State of Israel will continue to negotiate in good faith in pursuance of the Agenda agreed upon in Jerusalem, on 15 July 1992, and confirmed at the Vatican, on 29 July 1992; likewise on issues arising from Articles of the present Agreement, as well as on other issues bilaterally agreed upon as objects of negotiation.

Article 13

1. In this Agreement the Parties use these terms in the following sense:
   (a) The Catholic Church and the Church—including, inter alia, its Communities and institutions;
   (b) Communities of the Catholic Church—meaning the Catholic religious entities considered by the Holy See as Churches sui juris and by the State of Israel as Recognized Religious Communities;
   (c) The State of Israel and the State—including, inter alia, its authorities established by law.
2. Notwithstanding the validity of this Agreement as between the Parties, and without detracting from the generality of any applicable rule of law with reference to treaties, the Parties agree that this Agreement does not prejudice rights and obligations arising from existing treaties between either Party and a State or States, which are known and in fact available to both Parties at the time of the signature of this Agreement.

Article 14

1. Upon signature of the present Fundamental Agreement and in preparation for the establishment of full diplomatic relations, the Holy See and the State of Israel exchange Special Representatives, whose rank and privileges are specified in an Additional Protocol.
2. Following the entry into force and immediately upon the beginning of the implementation of the present Fundamental Agreement, the Holy See and the State of Israel will establish full diplomatic relations at the level of Apostolic Nunciature, on the part of the Holy See, and Embassy, on the part of the State of Israel.

Article 15

This Agreement shall enter into force on the date of the latter notification of ratification by a Party.

Done in two original copies in the English and Hebrew languages, both texts being equally authentic. In case of divergency, the English text shall prevail.

Signed in Jerusalem, this thirtieth day of the month of December, in the year 1993, which corresponds to the sixteenth day of the month of Tevet, in the year 5754.

Additional Protocol

1. In relation to Art. 14 (1) of the Fundamental Agreement, signed by the Holy See and the State of Israel, the 'Special Representatives' shall have, respectively, the personal rank of Apostolic Nuncio and Ambassador.
2. These Special Representatives shall enjoy all the rights, privileges and immunities granted to Heads of Diplomatic Missions under international law and common usage, on the basis of reciprocity.
3. The Special Representative of the State of Israel to the Holy See, while residing in Italy, shall enjoy all the rights, privileges and immunities defined by Art. 12 of the Treaty of 1929 between the Holy See and Italy, regarding Envoys of Foreign Governments to the Holy See residing in Italy. The rights, privileges and immunities extended to the personnel of a Diplomatic Mission shall likewise be granted to the personnel of the Israeli Special Representative's Mission. According to an established custom, neither the Special Representative, nor the official members of his Mission, can at the same time be members of Israel's Diplomatic Mission to Italy.
4. The Special Representative of the Holy See to the State of Israel may at the same time exercise other representative functions of the Holy See and be accredited to other States. He and the personnel of his Mission shall enjoy all the rights, privileges and immunities granted by Israel to Diplomatic Agents and Missions.
5. The names, rank and functions of the Special Representatives will appear, in an appropriate way, in the official lists of Foreign Missions accredited to each Party.

Signed in Jerusalem, this thirtieth day of the month of December, in the year 1993, which corresponds to the sixteenth day of the month of Tevet, in the year 5754.

CUMULATIVE INDEX, 1989-1993

A

B

C

D

F

J

K

L

O

P

Q

R

T

U

V